Frommer's®

W9-CCB-084

POSTCARDS

FROM

CALIFORNIA

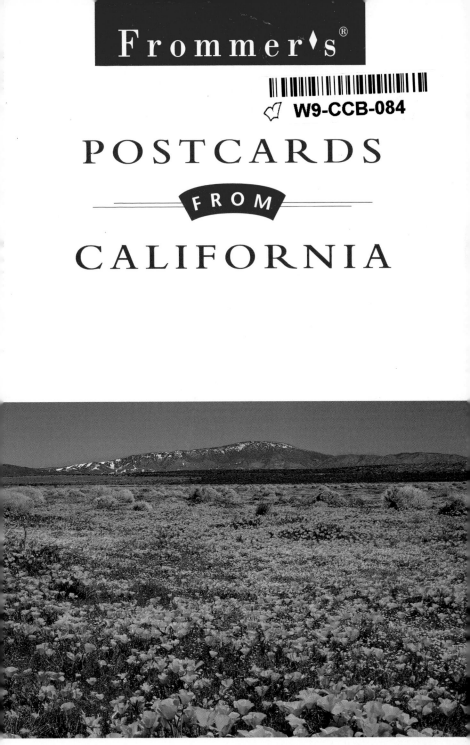

California's state flower, the poppy, carpets Antelope Valley, near Los Angeles. See "The Best of Natural California," in chapter 1. © Christopher Talbot Frank Photography

San Francisco and the Golden Gate Bridge. See chapter 4. © Jose Fuste Raga/The Stock Market

San Francisco's Lombard Street, known as the "crookedest street in the world." See chapter 4. © George Ranalli Photography

Napa Valley vineyards. See chapter 6. © *Catherine Karnow Photography*

Emerald Bay, one of Lake Tahoe's prettiest little inlets. See chapter 8. © *Robert Holmes Photography*

The Merced River, Yosemite National Park, in autumn. See chapter 9. © Christopher Talbot Frank Photography

Giant sequoias in Sequoia and Kings Canyon National Parks. See chapter 9. © George Ranalli Photography

Bridalveil Fall in Yosemite National Park. See chapter 9. © Christopher Talbot Frank Photography

The Santa Cruz Beach Boardwalk, the West Coast's only seaside amusement park. See chapter 11. © Matt Lindsay/Photophile

The Mission San Carlos Borromeo del Rio Carmelo, also known as the Carmel Mission, dates back to 1771. See chapter 11. © Dave G. Houser Photography

Sea otters can be spotted from the Sonoma Coast State Beaches (see chapter 7), Monterey Bay (chapter 11), and other points along the coast. © *Jeff Foott Photography*

Sea lion hangouts include San Francisco's Fisherman's Wharf (see chapter 4), Point Reyes (chapter 7), Monterey Bay (chapter 11), and Point Lobos State Reserve (chapter 11). © *Jeff Foott Photography*

Big Sur at dusk. See chapter 11. © David D. Keaton/The Stock Market

One of the lavish pools at Hearst Castle, the 165-room estate of William Randolph Hearst. See chapter 12. © Richard Cummins Photography

Elephant seals at Channel Islands National Park, home to the biggest seal and sea lion breeding colony in the United States. See chapter 12. © Jeff Foott Photography

Downtown Los Angeles from the steps of the Central Library. See chapter 13. © Richard Cummins Photography

In-line skaters at Venice Beach. See chapter 13. © Stephen Wilkes/The Image Bank

Surfer at Huntington Beach along the Orange Coast, site of the U.S. Open of Surfing each August. See chapter 14. © Sunstar/Instock

Fields of wind turbines en route to Palm Springs. See chapter 15 for details on a unique guided tour. © Richard Cummins Photography

The Palm Springs desert resorts are famous for their golf courses. See chapter 15. © Robert Holmes Photography

Joshua Tree National Park. See chapter 15. © *Photophile*

Death Valley National Park. See chapter 15. © George Ranalli Photography

After the spring rains, wildflowers flourish in Anza-Borrego Desert State Park. See chapter 16. © Christopher Talbot Frank Photography

The Coronado coast and the Hotel del Coronado, a National Historic Landmark. See chapter 16. © James Blank Photography

Shamu the killer whale at Sea World, San Diego. See chapter 10. © Richard Cummins Photography

Sand dunes in the Mojave National Preserve. See chapter 15. © Christopher Talbot Frank Photography

Frommer's® 2000

California

by Erika Lenkert, Matthew R. Poole &
Stephanie Avnet Yates

with Online Directory by Michael Shapiro

MACMILLAN • USA

ABOUT THE AUTHORS

Combining the only three things he's good at—eating, sleeping, and criticizing—**Matthew R. Poole** has written and co-authored more than 20 travel guides to California and Hawaii, including *Frommer's San Francisco* and *Frommer's Portable California Wine Country.* A native Northern Californian, he currently lives in San Francisco.

Native San Franciscan **Erika Lenkert** is a contributing writer with a monthly restaurant gossip column for *Los Angeles* magazine; has contributed to *InStyle, Travel & Leisure,* and *Bon Appetit;* and recently co-authored *Raw: The Uncook Book.* Her latest project is as a director of content for WineShopper.com.

A native of Los Angeles and an avid traveler, antiques hound, and pop-history enthusiast, **Stephanie Avnet Yates** used to work in the music business, but now prefers to hit the road exploring the Golden State. Stephanie has also written *Frommer's Los Angeles, Frommer's San Diego,* and the getaway guide *Wonderful Weekends from Los Angeles.*

MACMILLAN TRAVEL

Macmillan General Reference USA, Inc.
1633 Broadway
New York, NY 10019

Find us online at **www.frommers.com**

ISBN 0-02-863028-9
ISSN 1044-2146

Editors: Leslie Shen, Claudia Kirschhoch
Production Editor: Mark Enochs
Photo Editor: Richard Fox
Design by Michele Laseau
Staff Cartographers: John Decamillis, Roberta Stockwell
Additional cartography by Hans Andersson
Page Creation by Ellen Considine, Sean Monkhouse, Angel Perez, and Carl Pierce
Front Cover Photo: Yosemite National Park
Back Cover Photo: The California coast, near Carmel

SPECIAL SALES

Bulk purchases (10+ copies) of Frommer's and selected Macmillan travel guides are available to corporations, organizations, mail-order catalogs, institutions, and charities at special discounts and can be customized to suit individual needs. For more information, write to: Special Sales, Macmillan General Reference, 1633 Broadway, New York, NY 10019.

5 4 3 2 1

Contents

iii

5 The San Francisco Bay Area 130

6 The Wine Country 152

7 The Northern Coast 188

8 The Far North: Lake Tahoe, the Shasta Cascades & Lassen Volcanic National Park 229

9 The High Sierra: Yosemite, Mammoth Lakes & Sequoia/Kings Canyon 269

List of Maps

ACKNOWLEDGMENTS

Erika Lenkert would like to thank Cindy Sassman, for her invaluable country-meets-cosmopolitan perspective on the Central Coast, and Catherine Maxwell, for her inexhaustible search for the facts.

AN INVITATION TO THE READER

In researching this book, we discovered many wonderful places—hotels, restaurants, shops, and more. We're sure you'll find others. Please tell us about them, so we can share the information with your fellow travelers in upcoming editions. If you were disappointed with a recommendation, we'd love to know that, too. Please write to:

Frommer's California 2000
Macmillan Travel
1633 Broadway
New York, NY 10019

AN ADDITIONAL NOTE

Please be advised that travel information is subject to change at any time—and this is especially true of prices. We therefore suggest that you write or call ahead for confirmation when making your travel plans. The authors, editors, and publisher cannot be held responsible for the experiences of readers while traveling. Your safety is important to us, however, so we encourage you to stay alert and be aware of your surroundings. Keep a close eye on cameras, purses, and wallets, all favorite targets of thieves and pickpockets.

WHAT THE SYMBOLS MEAN

✪ Frommer's Favorites

Our favorite places and experiences—outstanding for quality, value, or both.

The following abbreviations are used for credit cards:

AE	American Express	EURO	Eurocard
CB	Carte Blanche	JCB	Japan Credit Bank
DC	Diners Club	MC	MasterCard
DISC	Discover	V	Visa
ER	EnRoute		

FIND FROMMER'S ONLINE

Arthur Frommer's Budget Travel Online (**www.frommers.com**) offers more than 6,000 pages of up-to-the-minute travel information—including the latest bargains and candid, personal articles updated daily by Arthur Frommer himself. No other Web site offers such comprehensive and timely coverage of the world of travel.

The Best of California

by Erika Lenkert, Matthew R. Poole & Stephanie Avnet Yates

In my early twenties, I took the requisite college student's pilgrimage to Europe, exploring its finer train stations and sleeping on the premier park benches from London to Istanbul. I was relatively anonymous—just another tanned and skinny, blond and blue-eyed American lugging around 60 pounds of backpack. That is, until I crossed over into the former Eastern Bloc.

The reaction was dramatic, almost palpable. Like Moses parting the sea, I would wander through the crowded streets of Prague and citizens would stop, stare, and sidestep as if a scarlet "A" were emblazoned across my chest. It wasn't until a man who spoke faltering English finally approached me that I discovered the reason for my newfound celebrity status.

"Eh, you. Where you from? No, no. Let me guess." He steps back, gives a cursory examination followed by pregnant pause. "Ah. I've got it! California! You're from California, no?" A gleam in his eyes as I tell him that, yes, he's quite correct. "Wonderful! Wonderful!" A dozen or so pilsners later with my loquacious new friend and it all becomes clear to me: To him, I truly am a celebrity—a rich, convertible-driving surfer who spends most his days lazing on the beach, fending off hordes of buxom blondes while I argue with my agent via my portable phone. The myth is complete. I *am* the Beach Boys. I *am* *Baywatch*. Status by association. The tentacles of Hollywood have done what no NATO pact could achieve—they've leapfrogged the staid issues of capitalism versus communism by offering a far more potent narcotic: the alluring mystique of sun-drenched California, of movie stars strolling down Sunset Boulevard, of beautiful women in tight shorts and bikini tops roller-skating along Venice Beach. It short, they've bought what we're selling.

Of course, the allure is understandable. It really is warm and sunny most days of the year, movie stars actually do abound in Los Angeles, and you can't swing a cat by its tail without hitting a roller-blading babe in Venice Beach. This part of the California mystique—however exaggerated it may be—truly does exist, and it's not hard to find.

But there's more—a lot more—to California that isn't scripted, sanitized, and squeezed through a cathode-ray tube to the world's millions of mesmerized masses. Beyond the glitter and glamour of Hollywood is an incredibly diverse state that, if it ever seceded from the Union, would be one of the most productive and powerful nations in the world. We've got it all: misty redwood forests, an incredibly verdant

Central Valley teeming with agriculture, the mighty Sierra Nevada Mountain Range, eerily fascinating deserts, a host of world-renowned cities, and, of course, hundreds of miles of stunning coastline.

And despite the endemic crime, pollution, traffic, and bowel-shaking earthquakes that California is famous for, we're still the golden child of the United States, America's spoiled rich kid whom everyone else either loves or loathes. (Neighboring Oregon, for example, sells lots of license-plate rims that proudly state, "I hate California.") But, truth be told, we really don't care what anyone thinks of us. Californians *know* they live in one of the most diverse and interesting places in the world, and we're proud of the state we call home.

Granted, there's no guarantee that you'll bump into Arnold Schwarzenegger or learn how to surf, but if you have a little time, a little money, and—most important—an adventurous spirit, then Erika, Stephanie, and I will help guide you through one of the most fulfilling vacations of your life. The three of us travel the world for a living, but we *choose* to live in California, simply because there's no other place on earth that has so much to offer.

—*Matthew R. Poole*

1 The Best of Natural California

- **Año Nuevo State Reserve:** Nature enthusiasts come from all over the world to this spot 22 miles north of Santa Cruz to view the elephant-seal colony. Pups are born from December through March, and molting follows between April and August. You can also spot sea lions in spring and summer, whales in winter and spring, plus more than 250 bird species. See chapter 5.
- **Point Reyes National Seashore:** This extraordinarily scenic stretch of coast and wetlands is one of the best bird-watching spots in California for shorebirds, songbirds, and waterfowl, as well as osprey and red-shouldered hawks. There's a rainbow-hued wildflower garden, too, and you might catch a glimpse of a whale from the Point Reyes Lighthouse. See chapter 7.
- **Sonoma Coast State Beaches:** Stretching about 10 miles from Bodega Bay to Jenner, these beaches attract more than 300 species of birds. From December through September, look for osprey. Seal pups can be spotted from March through June, and the gray whale from December through April. See chapter 7.
- **Redwood National and State Parks:** A wildlife enthusiast's dream. More than 300 bird species and 100 mammals can be seen, many of them year-round. Also watch (or watch out!) for black bears in summer. See chapter 7.
- **Yosemite National Park:** You're in for the ultimate treat at Yosemite. Nothing in the state—maybe even the world—compares to this vast wilderness playground and its miles of rivers, lakes, peaks, and valleys. With 3 out of 10 of the world's tallest waterfalls, the largest single granite monolith in the world, and some of the world's largest trees, Yosemite is one of the most fantastic natural places on the planet. You'll have a sweeping 180° view of it all from high atop Glacier Point, where a majestic High Sierra panorama unfolds at 3,200 feet. See chapter 9.
- **Elkhorn Slough** (Moss Landing): It's as close as you'll ever get to feeling like you're on a *National Geographic* adventure. Captain Gideon's 2-hour cruise takes you into the heart of the northern California shore's wildlife reserve, where you'll encounter dozens of otters and harbor seals and hundreds of bird species. See chapter 11.
- **The Big Sur Coast:** Rock-strewn beaches, towering cliffs, and redwood forests combine to form what may be the world's most dramatic coastal panorama. Our

favorite vantage point for taking it all in is Garrapata State Park, a 2,879-acre preserve that lords over 4 spectacular miles of coastline. See chapter 11.

- **Cachuma Lake:** Situated on mountainous and scenic Calif. 154, halfway between Solvang and Santa Barbara, is this stunning winter home to dozens of American bald eagles. Loons, white pelicans, and Canada geese are some of the other migratory birds that call this glassy lake home part of the year. See chapter 12.
- **Channel Islands National Park:** This is California in its most natural state. Paddle a kayak into sea caves; camp among indigenous island fox and seabirds; and swim, snorkel, or scuba-dive tide pools and kelp forests teeming with wildlife. The channel waters are prime for whale watching, and winter brings elephant-seal mating season, when you'll see them and their sea-lion cousins sunbathing on cove beaches. See chapter 12.
- **California Poppy Reserve** (Antelope Valley): California's state flower, the poppy, blooms between March and May, carpeting the hillsides in brilliant hues of red, orange, and gold. This reserve, in the high desert near Los Angeles, is one of the poppy's most consistent natural growing sites. The fields extend for miles around—many motorists pull to the side of the road to marvel at the breathtaking spectacle. For information and directions, call ☎ **805/724-1180.** For information on the annual **California Poppy Festival** (usually in April), call ☎ **805/723-6000.**
- **Joshua Tree National Park:** You'll find awesome rock formations, groves of flowering cacti and stately Joshua trees, ancient Native American petroglyphs, and shifting sand dunes in this desert wonderland—and a brilliant night sky, if you choose to camp here. See chapter 15.
- **Death Valley National Park:** Its inhospitable climate makes it the state's most unlikely tourist attraction—but the same conditions that thwarted settlers create some of the most dramatic landscapes you'll ever see. Mesmerizing rock formations, ever-changing dry lake beds, and often stifling heat provide the setting for relics of hardy 19th-century borax miners and (fool-) hardy dwellers from the 1930s. See chapter 15.
- **Torrey Pines State Reserve:** Poised on a majestic cliff overlooking the Pacific Ocean, this reserve is home to the rare torrey pine. Exhibits on the local ecology are housed in the visitor center, and numerous hiking trails fan out throughout the park. See chapter 16.
- **Anza-Borrego Desert State Park:** The largest state park in the lower 48 states attracts the most visitors during the spring wildflower season, when a kaleidoscopic carpet blankets the desert floor. Others come year-round to hike the more than 100 miles of designated trails. See chapter 16.

2 The Best Beaches

- **Drake's Beach:** A massive stretch of white sand at Point Reyes National Seashore, west of Inverness. Winds and choppy seas make it rough for swimmers, but sun worshippers can have their Marin County tan for the day. If the rangers say it's all right, beach driftwood can make a romantic campfire in the early evening. See chapter 7.
- **Sand Dollar Beach:** The best Big Sur beach lies beyond Pacific Valley—ideal for swimming and surfing, with a panoramic view of Cone Peak, one of the coast's highest mountains. See chapter 11.
- **Santa Barbara's East Beach:** This wide swath of clean white sand hosts beach umbrellas, sandcastle builders, and spirited volleyball games. A grassy, parklike

median keeps the happy beachgoers insulated from busy Cabrillo Boulevard. On Sundays, local artists display their wares beneath the elegant palm trees. See chapter 12.

- **Malibu's Legendary Beaches:** Zuma and Surfrider beaches served as inspiration for the 1960s surf music that embodies the Southern California beach experience. Surfrider, just up from Malibu Pier, is home to L.A.'s best waves. Zuma is loaded with amenities, including snack bars, rest rooms, and jungle gyms. In addition to some of the state's best sunbathing, you can walk in front of the Malibu Colony, a star-studded enclave of multimillion-dollar homes set on this seductively curvaceous stretch of coast. See chapter 13.

- **Hermosa City Beach:** This is one of L.A.'s top beaches for family outings. It's also popular with the volleyball set. It offers wide sands, a paved boardwalk ("The Strand") that's great for strolling and biking, and loads of amenities—including plenty of parking. See chapter 13.

- **La Jolla's Beaches:** Roughly translated, *La Jolla* means "the jewel," and the beaches of La Jolla's cliff-lined coast truly are gems. Each has a distinct personality: Surfers love Windansea's waves, Torrey Pines and La Jolla Shores are popular for swimming and sunbathing, and Black's Beach is San Diego's unofficial (and illegal) nude beach. See chapter 16.

- **Coronado Beach:** On the west side of Coronado extending to the Hotel del Coronado, this beautiful beach is uncrowded and great for watching the sunset. Marilyn Monroe romped in the surf here during the filming of *Some Like It Hot.* See chapter 16.

3 The Best Walks

- **Golden Gate Park:** Strolling this magnificent park lets you escape the bustle of San Francisco and takes you past an array of attractions, beginning with the 1878 Conservatory of Flowers, but also including museums, the Japanese Tea Garden, and even a 430-foot-high man-made island, Strawberry Hill. End your walk by renting a rowboat and taking it for a spin. See chapter 4.

- **Point Reyes National Seashore:** In Marin County, west of Inverness and a quarter mile north of Drake's Beach, Point Reyes Lighthouse, 6 miles to the west, will be your final goal. The scenery is among the most beautiful and enticing in the Golden State—especially the hike to Chimney Rock (follow the signs on your way to the lighthouse). See chapter 7.

- **Mendocino Headlands State Park:** Between Mendocino and the Pacific is one of the most scenic nature trails in the north. From December through March, the California gray whales pass by on their migration from the Arctic Ocean and Bering Sea to Baja California. Sunset vistas are worth the detour. See chapter 7.

- **Yosemite National Park:** Relatively short and easy hikes will take you to Yosemite Falls, the highest waterfall in North America and the fifth highest in the world (upper fall at 1,430 feet), or to Bridalveil Fall, a ragged 620-foot cascade that can be wind-tossed as much as 20 feet from side to side. A third option is the more strenuous 3½-mile Yosemite Falls Trail, which rises to a height of 2,700 feet for one of the most panoramic vistas in the West. See chapter 9.

- **The Beachfront Trails at Big Sur:** Take towering cliffs, rock-strewn beaches, and a backdrop of redwood forests, and you have one of the most dramatic stretches for coastline hiking in the world. Begin your adventure about 8 miles south of Point Lobos. See chapter 11.

- **Beverly Hills's "Golden Triangle":** Defined by Wilshire Boulevard, Crescent Drive, and Santa Monica Boulevard, this is a window-shopper's fantasyland of tony shops with picture-perfect displays and sky-high price tags. It even boasts a cluster of shops built to resemble an Italian plaza, with its own faux-cobblestone "streets." If Rodeo Drive tariffs are out of your reach, don't worry; there are plenty of down-to-earth shops and restaurants, plus an elegant Moorish-Mediterranean City Hall that's worth a look. See chapter 13.

- **The L.A. Conservancy's Guided Walking Tours of Downtown Los Angeles:** The conservancy conducts a dozen fascinating, information-packed tours of historic downtown L.A., seed of today's sprawling metropolis. The most popular is "Broadway Theaters," a loving look at movie palaces; other intriguing ones include "Marble Masterpieces," "Art Deco," "Mecca for Merchants," and tours of the landmark Biltmore Hotel and City Hall. See chapter 13.

- **Griffith Park:** This wooded enclave linking Hollywood with the San Fernando Valley has something for everyone. Be on the lookout for golf carts crossing near the picturesque Wilson and Harding golf courses, and for horseback riders from the nearby Equestrian Center. The L.A. Zoo and the Autry Museum lie at the northeast corner near I-5; the hills are loaded with hiking trails and picnic areas, and kids love the merry-go-round and pony rides. See chapter 13.

- **From Crystal Pier (in Pacific Beach) south to the jetty, and then north along the Bay Side to the Catamaran Hotel:** During the first part of this walk, you'll share the sidewalk with joggers, cyclists, and in-line skaters, and surfers will be testing their skills on the waves to your right. After you cross over to the Mission Bay side of Mission Boulevard, you'll experience the more subdued side of things: quiet water lapping onto white-sand beaches, and the local residents tending their gardens. A lovely way to spend the day in San Diego. See chapter 16.

4 The Best Golf Courses

- **Pebble Beach Golf Links:** The famous 17-Mile Drive is the site of 10 national championships and the winter telecast of the celebrity-laden AT&T Pebble Beach National Pro-Am. The raging nearby Pacific and a scenic backdrop of the Del Monte Forest justify astronomical greens fees. See chapter 11.

- **Spyglass Hill** (Pebble Beach): Five holes border the ocean, and the rest extend deep within Del Monte Forest. The holes here have been called "long and unforgiving" by golf magazines. Its slope rating of 143 makes it one of the toughest courses in California. See chapter 11.

- **Poppy Hills** (Pebble Beach): *Golf Digest* has called this Robert Trent Jones, Jr.–designed course "one of the world's top 20 courses." Also used for AT&T festivities, it cuts right through the pines of Del Monte Forest. One golf pro said the course is "long and tough on short hitters." It's maintained in state-of-the-art condition and, unlike some of its competitors, is rarely overcrowded. See chapter 11.

- **The Links at Spanish Bay:** Perched along the 17-Mile Drive, the Links were also designed by Robert Trent Jones, Jr., with a little help from Tom Watson and former USGA president Frank Tatum. Their aim was to simulate the experience of playing golf on true Scottish links. Its fescue grasses and natural fairways lead to rolls and unexpected bounces for your ball. Holes 14 through 18—taking you to the sea and back again through high dunes—call for some trick shot making, but make the whole experience worthwhile. See chapter 11.

- **Industry Hills Golf Club, Eisenhower Course** (Los Angeles): Designed by William Francis Bell in 1979, this course consistently ranks among *Golf Digest's* top 25 public courses. Often home to the U.S. Open qualifying rounds, the Eisenhower course has extra-large, undulating greens and the challenge of thick Kikuyu roughs. See chapter 13.
- **Westin Mission Hills Resort, Pete Dye Course** (Rancho Mirage): Since 1987, when course-architect Pete Dye sculpted this links-style, par-70 challenger, players have wrangled with the pot bunkers, hidden pin placements, and carries over water that are his classic trademarks. Rolling fairways and railroad ties also characterize Dye's 6,706-yard classic. The course takes full scenic advantage of the lavender hills all around. See chapter 15.
- **PGA West TPC Stadium Course** (La Quinta): The par-3 17th has a picturesque island green where Lee Trevino made Skins Game history with a spectacular hole-in-one. The rest of Pete Dye's 7,261-yard design is flat with huge bunkers, lots of water, and severe mounding throughout. The PGA West is part of the La Quinta Resort & Club, which received *Golf* magazine's 1994 Gold Medal Award for the total golf-resort experience. See chapter 15.
- **Torrey Pines Golf Course** (La Jolla): Two gorgeous 18-hole championship courses overlook the ocean and provide players with plenty of challenge. In February, the Buick Invitational Tournament is held here; the rest of the year, these popular municipal courses are open to everybody. See chapter 16.
- **Coronado Municipal Golf Course** (San Diego): This 18-hole, par-72 municipal course overlooking Glorietta Bay is located to the left of the Coronado Bay Bridge. It's the first thing you see when you arrive in Coronado—a fabulous welcome for duffers. See chapter 16.

5 The Best Offbeat Travel Experiences

- **Hot-Air Ballooning over Napa Valley:** It's all the rage, and for good reason: Northern California's temperate weather allows for ballooning year-round, and the valley is simply beautiful from up high. Flights are best right after sunrise, when the air is calm and cool. Hotels throughout the valley can arrange a trip aloft for you, or you can book one directly with **Bonaventura Balloon Company** (☎ 800/FLY-NAPA) or **Adventures Aloft** (☎ 800/944-4408). Sometimes there's a catered champagne brunch at the end of the adventure. See chapter 6.
- **Taking a Mud Bath in Calistoga:** In this town's famous volcanic-ash mud—mixed with mineral water—you can get buck naked and covered in gooey mud. At a dozen or so places you can immerse yourself in the mud, followed by a mineral-water shower and a whirlpool bath, and then a steam bath. It's perhaps the most relaxing experience in California. See chapter 6.
- **Panning for Gold in the Gold Country:** In the southern Gold Country, you can dig into living history and pan for gold. Several companies, including **Gold Prospecting Expeditions** (☎ 800/596-0009 or 209/984-4653) in Jamestown, offer dredging lessons and gold-panning tours. You'll quickly learn that this adventure is back-breaking labor. But who knows? You might get lucky and launch a new gold rush. See chapter 10.
- **Riding the Amtrak Rails Along the Southern California Coast:** Relive the golden age of train travel and see the natural beauty of California, avoiding the crowded highways at the same time. Spanish-style Union Station, a marble-floored Streamline Moderne masterpiece, is the Los Angeles hub. Trains run between L.A. and the romantic mission towns of San Juan Capistrano, San

Diego, Santa Barbara, and San Luis Obispo. The scenery includes lush valleys, windswept coastline, and the occasional urban stretch. Call Amtrak (☎ **800/ USA-RAIL**) for information. See chapter 12.

- **Discovering Downtown L.A.'s Public Art:** The wealth of public art on display in downtown Los Angeles is one of the city's best-kept secrets. Some works make political or social commentary (the black experience as represented by the life of former slave Biddy Mason in a multimedia exhibit between Broadway and Spring sts. just south of Third St.). Others are abstract and open to a variety of interpretations. Pershing Square, a formerly untended eyesore bounded by Fifth, Sixth, Olive, and Hill streets, has been reincarnated as a modern sculpture garden. See chapter 13.
- **Strolling Venice Beach:** All of humanity—for better and worse—is represented on a boardwalk framed by broad sands, swaying palms, and the sparkling blue Pacific. The day's carnival might include well-tanned bodybuilders, outrageous street performers, scantily clad beach bunnies (bimbos *and* himbos), roving gangs of teens, psychedelic-era hippies, and much more. Experiment with style at the cheap-sunglasses stalls, grab an exotic dog at Jody Maroni's Sausage Kingdom, and make your way to the Santa Monica pier to check out the historic photo gallery and carousel. See chapter 13.
- **Skydiving over Southern California:** Enjoy a bird's-eye view of the Southland. Local schools offer instruction at all levels (including tandem jumps for first-timers). At the **California City Skydive Center** (☎ 800/2-JUMP-HI) in the Mojave Desert, you can soar through the same skies as the space shuttle, which lands at nearby Edwards Air Force Base. Hemet and Perris are home to world-renowned schools—**Skydiving Adventures** at Hemet–Ryan Airport (☎ 800/ 526-9682) and the **Perris Valley Skydiving School** (☎ 800/832-8818)—as is Skylark Airport at Lake Elsinore, where you'll find **Jim Wallace Skydiving** (☎ 800/795-DIVE).
- **Going to the Movies, San Diego Style:** Imagine sitting on the deck of the world's oldest merchant ship, watching a film projected on the "screen-sail"; floating on a raft in a huge indoor pool while a movie is shown on the wall; watching a silent film accompanied by the San Diego Symphony; or sitting on the beach taking in a flick that's projected on a floating barge. Only in San Diego! See chapter 16.

6 The Best of Small-Town California

- **St. Helena:** A small town in the heart of the Napa Valley, St. Helena is known for its Main Street, which is lined with Victorian storefronts featuring intriguing wares. In a horse and buggy, Robert Louis Stevenson and his new bride, the cantankerous Fanny, made their way down this street. Come for the old-timey, tranquil mood and the wonderful food. See chapter 6.
- **Mendocino:** An artists' colony with a New England flavor, Mendocino served as the backdrop for *Murder, She Wrote*. Perched on the cliff tops above the Pacific Ocean, it's filled with small art galleries, general stores, weathered wooden houses, and elbow-to-elbow tourists. See chapter 7.
- **Nevada City:** The whole town is a national historic landmark and the best place to understand gold-rush fever. Settled in 1849, it offers fine dining and shopping and a stock of multigabled Victorian frame houses of the Old West. Relics of the cannibalistic Donner Party are on display at the 1861 Firehouse No. 1. See chapter 10.

- **Pacific Grove:** You can escape the Monterey crowds by heading just 2 miles west to Pacific Grove, which is known for its tranquil waterfront location and quiet, unspoiled air. Thousands of monarch butterflies flock here between October and March to make their winter home in Washington Park. See chapter 11.
- **Cambria:** Near Hearst Castle, Cambria benefits from a constant stream of visitors, who bring the right amount of sophistication to this picturesque coastal town. Moonstone Beach holds a string of seaside lodges; farther north are dozens of sunbathing elephant seals, while the village itself is filled with charming B&Bs, artists' studios and galleries, and friendly shops. See chapter 12.
- **Ojai:** When Hollywood needed a Shangri-La for the movie *Lost Horizon,* they drove north to idyllic Ojai Valley, an unspoiled hideaway of eucalyptus groves and small ranches warmly nestled among soft, green hills. Ojai is the amiable village at the valley's heart. It's a mecca for artists, free spirits, and weary city folk in need of a restful weekend in the country. See chapter 12.
- **Ventura:** This charming mission town is filled with colorful Victorians. It's also home to a pleasantly eclectic old Main Street lined with thrift and antiques shops, used-record stores, friendly diners, and even old-time saloons operating beneath broken-down, second-story hotels. Don't miss the historic mission on its landscaped plaza, and the deco-era Greek Revival San Buenaventura City Hall looming over the town, bedecked with smiling stone faces of the founding Franciscan friars. See chapter 12.
- **Avalon:** This crescent-shaped hamlet on idyllic Santa Catalina Island may welcome the summer influx of city-savvy tourists, but off-season visitors get to see a close-knit community that cherishes its isolation. Phone numbers are given in four digits here (the entire island shares a single exchange), and many residents rarely bother traveling to the mainland. There are very few cars, lots of cozy cafes and friendly pubs, a charming art-deco history, and the sparkling blue Pacific everywhere you look—you might not want to leave, either! See chapter 14.
- **Julian:** This old mining town in the Cuyamaca Mountains near San Diego is well known today for its wildflower fields, the fall apple harvest, and tasty flavored breads from Dudley's Bakery. There's plenty of pioneer history here, too, including a local-history museum, a circa-1888 schoolhouse, and mining demonstrations. A smattering of antiques shops, plenty of barbecue, and an old-fashioned soda fountain operating since 1886 round out the experience. See chapter 16.

7 The Best Family-Vacation Experiences

- **San Francisco:** The City by the Bay is filled with unexpected pleasures for every member of the family. Ride the cable cars that "climb halfway to the stars" and visit the Exploratorium, the California Academy of Sciences (which includes the Steinhart Aquarium), the zoo, the ships at the National Maritime Museum, Golden Gate Park, and much more. See chapter 4.
- **Lake Tahoe:** California's Disneyland of outdoor adventure, Lake Tahoe has loads of family-fun things to do. Skiing, snowboarding, hiking, tobogganing, swimming, fishing, boating, waterskiing, mountain biking—the list is nearly endless. Even the casinos cater to kids while mom and pop play the slots. See chapter 8.
- **Yosemite National Park:** Camping or staying in a cabin in Yosemite is a premier family attraction in California. Sites are scattered over 17 different campgrounds, and the rugged beauty of the Sierra Nevada surrounds you. During the day, the family calendar is packed with hiking, bicycling, white-water rafting, and even mountaineering to rugged, snowy peaks. See chapter 9.

- **Santa Cruz:** Surfing, sea kayaking, hiking, fishing, and great shopping, not to mention those fantastic beaches and the legendary amusement park on the boardwalk—this wonderfully funky bayside town has everything you need for the perfect family vacation. See chapter 11.
- **Monterey:** It's been called "Disneyland-by-the-Sea" due of its wealth of family-friendly activities, including those on Cannery Row and Fisherman's Wharf. Be sure to check out the state-of-the-art aquarium. See chapter 11.
- **Big Bear Lake:** Families flock year-round to this lake in the San Bernardino Mountains, and not just for the skiing. Horseback riding, miniature golf, water sports, and the Alpine Slide (kind of a snowless bobsled) are fun alternatives, and you can see and learn about native wildlife at the Moonridge Animal Park. The recently expanded village has a movie theater, arcade, and dozens of cutesy bear-themed businesses. The area's woodsy cabins are perfect for families. See chapter 14.
- **Disneyland:** The "Happiest Place on Earth" is family entertainment at its best. Whether you're wowed by Disney animation come alive, thrilled by the roller-coaster rides, or interested in the history and hidden secrets of this pop-culture icon, you won't walk away disappointed. Stay at the nearby Disneyland Hotel (connected directly to the park by monorail), a wild attraction unto itself, which offers appealing packages and, on most days, early entrance to the park. See chapter 14.
- **San Diego Zoo, Wild Animal Park, and Sea World:** San Diego boasts three of the world's best animal attractions. At the zoo, animals live in creatively designed habitats such as Tiger River and Hippo Beach. At the Wild Animal Park, 3,000 animals roam freely over 2,200 acres. And Sea World, with its ever-changing animal shows and exhibits, is an aquatic wonderland. See chapter 16.

8 The Best Architectural Landmarks

- **The Civic Center** (San Francisco): The creation of designers John Bakewell, Jr., and Arthur Brown, Jr., this is perhaps the most beautiful beaux-arts complex in America. See chapter 4.
- **The Painted Ladies** (San Francisco): The so-called Painted Ladies are the city's famous, ornately decorated Victorian homes. Check out the brilliant beauties around Alamo Square. Most of the extant 14,000 structures date from the second half of the 19th century. See chapter 4.
- **Winchester Mystery House** (San Jose): The heiress to the Winchester rifle fortune, Sarah Winchester, created one of the major "Believe It or Not?" curiosities of California, a 160-room Victorian mansion. It's been called the "world's strangest monument to a woman's fear." When a fortune-teller told her she wouldn't die if she continued to build onto her house, her mansion underwent construction day and night from 1884 to 1922. She did die eventually, and the hammers were silenced. See chapter 5.
- **The Carson House** (Eureka): A splendidly flamboyant Victorian—and one of the state's most photographed Queen Anne–style structures. It was built in 1885 by the Newsom brothers for William Carson, the local timber baron. Today, it's the headquarters of a men's club. See chapter 7.
- **Mission San Carlos Borromeo del Rio Carmelo** (Carmel): The second mission founded in California in 1770 by Father Junípero Serra (who is buried here) is perhaps the most beautiful. Its stone church and tower dome have been authentically restored, and a peaceful garden of California poppies adjoins the church.

Sights include an early kitchen and the founding father's spartan sleeping quarters. See chapter 11.

- **The Theme Building at Los Angeles International Airport:** The spacey *Jetsons*-style "Theme Building," which once loomed over underdeveloped LAX, still holds court in the center of the airport and unmistakably signals your arrival. Enjoy the view of arriving and departing jets from the building's observation deck or its groovy *Star Trek*–ish Encounter restaurant and bar, whose eerie purple neon floods the surrounding area after dark. See chapter 13.

- **Los Angeles's Central Library:** The city rallied to save the downtown library when an arson fire nearly destroyed it in 1986; the triumphant result has returned much of its original splendor. Working in the early 1920s, architect Bertram G. Goodhue employed the Egyptian motifs and materials popularized by the recent discovery of King Tut's tomb, combined with the more modern use of concrete block. See chapter 13.

- **Tail o' the Pup** (Los Angeles): At first glance, you might not think twice about this hot-dog–shaped bit of kitsch on West Hollywood's San Vicente Boulevard, just across from the Beverly Center. But locals adored this closet-sized wiener dispensary so much that when it was threatened by the developer's bulldozer, they spoke out en masse to save it. One of the few remaining examples of 1950s representational architecture, the "little dog that could" also serves up a great Baseball Special. See chapter 13.

- **The Gamble House** (Pasadena): The Smithsonian Institution calls this Pasadena landmark, built in 1908, "one of the most important houses in the United States." Architects Charles and Henry Greene created a masterpiece of the Japanese-influenced Arts and Crafts movement. Tours are conducted of the spectacular interior, designed by the Greenes down to the last piece of teak furniture and coordinating Tiffany lamp, and executed with impeccable craftsmanship. After you're done, stroll the immediate neighborhood to view several more Greene and Greene creations. See chapter 13.

- **Balboa Park** (San Diego): These Spanish/Mayan-style buildings were originally built as temporary structures for the Panama–California Exposition between 1915 and 1916. Set amidst the vast hilly terrain of one of the country's finest city parks, the ornately decorated and imposing facades have a special magic. Although some have been rebuilt over the years, many of the original buildings still remain, housing San Diego's finest museums. See chapter 16.

- **Hotel del Coronado** (Coronado): The "Hotel Del" stands in all its ornate Victorian red-tiled glory on some of the loveliest beach in Southern California. Built in 1888, it's one of the largest remaining wooden structures in the world. Even if you're not staying, stop by to take a detailed tour of the splendidly restored interiors, elegant grounds, and fascinating mini-museum of the hotel's spirited history. On your way to Coronado, you can't miss the soaring **Coronado Bay Bridge,** an architectural landmark in its own right. See chapter 16.

9 The Best Museums

- **The Exploratorium** (San Francisco): The hands-on, interactive Exploratorium boasts 650 exhibits that help to show how things work. You use all your senses and stretch them to a new dimension. Every exhibit is designed to be useful. See chapter 4.

- **The Oakland Museum:** This one might be dubbed the "Museum of California." The colorful people and history of the Golden State, and its sometimes overpowering art and culture, are all here. Everything from the region's first inhabitants to today's urban violence is depicted. See chapter 5.

- **California State Railroad Museum** (Sacramento): Old Sacramento's biggest attraction, the 100,000-square-foot museum was once the terminus of the Transcontinental and Sacramento Valley railways. The largest museum of its type in the United States, it displays 21 locomotives and railroad cars, among other attractions. One sleeping car simulates travel, with all the swaying and flashing lights of lonely towns passed in the night. See chapter 10.

- **J. Paul Getty Museum at the Getty Center** (Los Angeles): Since opening in 1997, the Getty has been deluged by visitors eager to see whether this ambitiously conceived (14 years and $1 billion in the making) complex fulfills its promise as new cultural cornerstone of L.A. Besides boasting a superb, international-class art collection, the center is a striking—and starkly futuristic—architectural landmark. From its picturesque vantage point, the Getty offers panoramic city views and perhaps even a glimpse into the next millennium. See chapter 13.

- **Autry Museum of Western Heritage** (Los Angeles): This one's a treat for both young and old. Relive California's historic cowboy past and see how the period has been depicted by Hollywood through the years, from Disney cartoon re-creations to founder Gene Autry's "singing cowboy" films to popular 1960s TV series. Highlights include a life-size woolly mammoth and a glimmering vault of ornate frontier firearms. See chapter 13.

- **Petersen Automotive Museum** (Los Angeles): This museum is a natural for Los Angeles, a city whose personality is so entwined with the popularity of the car. Impeccably restored vintage autos are displayed in life-size dioramas accurate to the last period detail (including an authentic 1930s–era service station). Upstairs galleries house movie-star and motion-picture vehicles, car-related artwork, and visiting exhibits. See chapter 13.

- **Museum of Contemporary Art** (San Diego): MCA is actually one museum with two locations: one in La Jolla, the other downtown. Perched on a seaside cliff, the La Jolla branch wins praise for outstanding views, site-specific outdoor sculpture, and the recent restoration of the museum's facade, a 1916 Irving Gill–designed home originally built for benefactor Ellen Browning Scripps. The permanent collection is known internationally, and focuses primarily on work produced since 1950. See chapter 16.

- **The Museums of Balboa Park** (San Diego): Located in a relaxed, verdant setting, these museums offer a unique variety of cultural experiences. Highlights include the Aerospace Historical Center, Museum of Man, Museum of Photographic Arts, Model Railroad Museum, Natural History Museum, and the lily pond and Botanical Building. Check in at the House of Hospitality for a map and "Passport to Balboa Park," a low-cost pass to a combination of the museums. See chapter 16.

10 The Best Luxury Hotels & Resorts

- **Ritz-Carlton San Francisco** (San Francisco; ☎ **800/241-3333**): Two short blocks from the top of Nob Hill, San Francisco's Ritz is world-renowned among discerning travelers for its superfluously accommodating staff, luxurious amenities, and top-rated restaurant. Another bonus is the most lavish brunch in town, served on Sundays in the Terrace Room or on the patio amidst blooming rose bushes. See chapter 4.

- **Auberge du Soleil** (Rutherford; ☎ 707/963-1211): The "Inn of the Sun," a Relais & Châteaux member in a 33-acre olive grove, stands above the vineyards of Napa Valley. This French country–style inn is the Wine Country's best resort. Each of the spacious villas is named after a region of France. It's very private, discreet, and romantic. See chapter 6.
- **Meadowood Resort** (St. Helena; ☎ 800/458-8080): A retreat of towering charm and style, this 256-acre Wine Country estate was inspired by New England's grand turn-of-the-century cottages. With its plethora of sports facilities and stress-relieving treatments, it attracts such clients as megabuck novelist Danielle Steel. See chapter 6.
- **The Estate by the Elderberries** (Oakhurst; ☎ 209/683-6860): Close to Yosemite, the Château Sureau and Erna's Elderberry House, established in 1984, evoke the best of Europe. Exquisite furnishings, individually decorated rooms, and a cuisine worthy of the stars make for a memorable lodging and dining experience at this gateway to the wilderness. See chapter 9.
- **Post Ranch Inn** (Big Sur; ☎ 800/527-2200): The freestanding, architecturally sophisticated cabins—which virtually hang over the cliffs of Big Sur—combined with first-rate amenities, hiking trails, spectacular views, a top-notch restaurant, and a celestial outdoor heated pool make this one of the most exclusive—and romantic—resorts we've ever visited. See chapter 11.
- **Ventana Big Sur Resort** (Big Sur; ☎ 800/628-6500): A luxurious wilderness resort on 243 mountainous oceanfront acres, this place is chic, tranquil, and hip—the pioneer sylvan retreat at Big Sur is a magnet for celebrities. Accommodations in one- and two-story buildings—each "worthy of the wild"— blend in with the dramatic Big Sur coastline. The cuisine is first-rate. See chapter 11.
- **Four Seasons Biltmore** (Santa Barbara; ☎ 800/332-3442): Open since 1927, the Biltmore has palm-studded formal gardens and a prime beachfront location along "America's Riviera." Meander through the elegant Spanish/Moorish arcades and walkways, all accented by exquisite Mexican tile, then play croquet on manicured lawns or relax at the Coral Casino Beach and Cabana Club. The rooms are the epitome of refined luxury, and the service couldn't be more friendly and accommodating. See chapter 12.
- **San Ysidro Ranch** (Santa Barbara area; ☎ 800/368-6788): It's expensive beyond belief, but if you can afford the price tag, you'll be staying at one of our favorite resorts in the state. Set on 540 acres with freestanding cottages, a stellar restaurant, and superfluous service, this is pastoral luxury at its finest. See chapter 12.
- **Hotel Bel-Air** (Los Angeles; ☎ 800/648-4097): Nestled in the foothills above UCLA, this is the choice of visiting European royalty, world leaders, and top celebrities. The graceful hotel was built in the 1920s, its grounds landscaped like a fairy-tale kingdom: Stone footbridges pass over koi-filled streams, flowering trees surround a swan-filled pond, and flagstone paths lead to richly traditional rooms. See chapter 13.
- **The Inn on Mt. Ada** (Santa Catalina Island; ☎ 800/608-7669): This former mansion of the wealthy Wrigley family is one of the most exclusive B&B experiences you'll ever have. With only six guest rooms, the hilltop inn's hefty rates include all your meals (and thoughtful snacks laid out each afternoon), plus the use of a golf cart to putter around this auto-eschewing island paradise. You'll feel like an honored guest at a friend's Mediterranean villa. See chapter 14.
- **Ritz-Carlton Laguna Niguel** (Dana Point; ☎ 800/241-3333): This jewel in the Ritz-Carlton chain is well known for its warmth, charm, picture-perfect

setting, and impeccable service. On dramatic cliffs overlooking 2 miles of prime beach, the Ritz is done in an easy yet elegant nautical/seashore decor, accented by well-chosen antiques and fine art. See chapter 14.

- **La Quinta Resort & Club** (La Quinta; ☎ **800/854-1271**): This luxury resort, set in a grove of palms at the base of the rocky Santa Rosa Mountains, is surrounded by some of the desert's best golf courses. Single-story, Spanish-style cottages are surrounded by a gardenlike setting and 24 "private" swimming pools. The tranquil lounge/library in the unaltered original hacienda hearkens back to the early days of the resort, when Clark Gable, Greta Garbo, and other luminaries regularly escaped to the seclusion of La Quinta's casitas. See chapter 15.

- **Loews Coronado Bay Resort** (Coronado; ☎ **800/23-LOEWS**): Occupying a private peninsula across the bay from downtown San Diego's skyline, this resort looks out over a luxurious private marina, with the Pacific only steps away. You'll find little excuse to leave this upscale playground, with swimming pools, tennis courts, and bike/skate/water-sport rentals at the ready. There's even an authentic Venetian gondola service with romantic cruises of nearby canals. See chapter 16.

- **La Valencia Hotel** (La Jolla; ☎ **800/451-0772**): Meticulously preserved to look just as it has since opening in 1926, this elegant Spanish/Moorish grande dame is still the choice of celebrities and the centerpiece of La Jolla's charming clifftop "village." The hotel's rich history and lavish good taste are reflected everywhere, and the ocean views are stupendous. See chapter 16.

11 The Best Moderately Priced Hotels & Inns

- **Hotel Bohème** (San Francisco; ☎ **415/433-9111**): The rooms may be small and lack extra amenities, but there's no better San Francisco experience than staying at the impeccably stylish Hotel Bohème, in the heart of North Beach. You need only step outside your door to find some of the city's best cafes, restaurants, and nightlife. See chapter 4.

- **Deer Run Bed & Breakfast** (St. Helena; ☎ **800/843-3408**): You may spend the day fighting the crowds at Napa's wineries, but stay here and you'll find respite in Deer Run's romantic rustic hideaway. The four accommodations are upscale cabin–like and are surrounded by nothing but nature. See chapter 6.

- **St. Orres** (Gualala; ☎ **707/884-3303**): Designed in a Russian style—complete with two Kremlinesque onion-domed towers—St. Orres offers secluded accommodations constructed from century-old timbers salvaged from a nearby mill. One of the most eye-catching inns on California's North Coast. See chapter 7.

- **Albion River Inn** (Albion; ☎ **800/479-7944**): Easily one of the best rooms-with-a-view on the California coast, the Albion River Inn is dripping with romance. Perched on a cliff overlooking the rugged shoreline, most of the luxuriously appointed rooms have Jacuzzi tubs for two, elevated to window level. Add champagne and you're guaranteed to have a night you won't soon forget. See chapter 7.

- **Olallieberry Inn** (Cambria; ☎ **888/927-3222**): Nestled in the charming town of Cambria, this 1873 Greek Revival house, furnished in a romantic floral-and-lace Victorian style, is a perfect base for exploring Hearst Castle. The gracious innkeepers have your comfort and convenience at heart, providing everything from directions to Moonstone Beach to restaurant recommendations—and a scrumptious breakfast in the morning, of course. See chapter 12.

- **Bath Street Inn** (Santa Barbara; ☎ **800/341-BATH**): This is one of the sweetest, most immaculate B&Bs in California. The inn makes special efforts to coddle guests and also has a wonderfully peaceful back deck shaded by an enormous wisteria. See chapter 12.

- L.A. is home to two upstart hangouts, catering to an MTV generation with more style than bucks: The **Standard** (☎ 323/650-9090) is a Warhol-hued party place combining 1970s chic, 1960s architecture, and jet-age modernity with touches like a barbershop/tattoo parlor in the lobby. Across town, the **Avalon** (☎ 800/ 535-4715) exudes a postwar Hollywood glamour accented with mid-century modern furnishings and a sophisticated 1950s aura inspired by the hotel's classic lines. Both offer top-of-the-line luxury amenities—at ultra-reasonable rates. See chapter 13.

- **Hollywood Roosevelt** (Los Angeles; ☎ 800/950-7667): This hotel, overlooking the Walk of Fame, is a legendary survivor from Hollywood's golden age. Centrally located for sightseeing, it offers terrific city views, one of the city's most elegant lobbies, and evening entertainment at the popular art-deco Cinegrill. The first Academy Awards ceremony was held here in 1929, and legends claim the hotel is haunted by the ghosts of Marilyn Monroe and Montgomery Clift. See chapter 13.

- **Casa Malibu** (Malibu; ☎ 800/831-0858): This beachfront motel will fool you from the front. Its cheesy 1970s entrance, right on noisy Pacific Coast Highway, belies the quiet, restful charm found within. Situated around the courtyard garden are 21 rooms, many with private decks above the Malibu sands. Rooftops and balconies are festooned with bougainvillea vines, creating an effect reminiscent of a Mexican seaside village. There's easy beach access, and one elegant suite that was Lana Turner's favorite. See chapter 13.

- **Sommerset Suites Hotel** (San Diego; ☎ 800/962-9665): This terrific bargain is also a good choice for those who find traditional hotels too impersonal; originally built as apartments, it sports a spacious, residential ambiance. The staff is friendly and helpful, and in the late afternoon they serve complimentary snacks, soda, beer, and wine in the cozy guest lounge. Most of the stylish Hillcrest neighborhood is within walking distance. See chapter 16.

- **Ocean Park Inn** (San Diego; ☎ 800/231-7735): This three-story standout, located right on Pacific Beach's lively beach path, has a level of sophistication uncommon for this casual, surfer-populated area. Beyond the hotel's sharply designed marble lobby are less-splendid (but completely comfortable) guest rooms with sunset views. See chapter 16.

12 The Best Alternative Accommodations

- **An Elegant Victorian Mansion** (Eureka; ☎ 707/444-3144): Yes, that's the name of this inn. Guests relive the golden age of Victoria in an authentic way here—right down to the music and entertainment. At this 1888 house, the butler greets you in morning dress. Stay in the Lily Langtry room, named after the actress and king's mistress who boarded here when she performed locally. See chapter 7.

- **KOA Kamping Kabins** (Point Arena; ☎ 800/562-4188): Once you see the adorable little log cabins at this KOA campground, you can't help but admit that, rich or poor, this is one cool way to spend the weekend on the coast. Rustic is the key word here: mattresses, a heater, and a light bulb are the standard amenities. All you need is some bedding (or a sleeping bag), cooking and eating utensils, and a bag of charcoal for the barbecue out on the front porch. See chapter 7.

- **Camping at Yosemite's Tuolumne Meadows** (☎ 800/436-7275): It's especially memorable in late spring, when the meadow is carpeted with wildflowers. At an elevation of 8,600 feet, this is the largest alpine meadow in the High Sierra and a gateway to the "high country." A large campground is operated here by park authorities, with a full-scale naturalist program. True adventurers should backpack into the wilderness. See chapter 9.

- *Delta King* **Riverboat** (Old Sacramento; ☎ 800/825-5464): This paddle wheeler is the only major floating hotel in California (with the exception of the *Queen Mary* at Long Beach). In the 1930s, it carried passengers between San Francisco and California's capital, but now it's permanently moored here, its former cabins turned into bedrooms and its old staterooms serving hungry diners. See chapter 10.

- **Oceanfront Camping at Big Sur:** Kirk Creek Campground, about 3 miles north of Pacific Valley, offers camping with dramatic ocean views and access to the beach. But there are dozens more—take your pick. See chapter 11.

- **Madonna Inn** (San Luis Obispo; ☎ 800/543-9666): You can't miss this Pepto Bismol–colored San Luis Obispo landmark when you're driving down U.S. 101. Every room of this family-run Bavarian-style chateau is unique, reflecting a love of old-world motifs, uncommon building materials, and the color pink. Try the rock-lined "Caveman" room, the frilly "Victorian" room, the atmospheric "Waterfall" room, or another of the 109 different theme rooms. This is a design genre all its own—and an experience not to be missed! See chapter 12.

- **The Venice Beach House** (Venice; ☎ 310/823-1966): This delightful B&B, in a sprawling 1911 bungalow just 2 blocks from the beach and boardwalk, is a great alternative to the standard cookie-cutter L.A. hotels. The guest rooms are furnished with antiques and period artwork. The wood-paneled living room, bright and airy alcove, cozy patio, and lush garden are captivating. And the nearby Venice Pier offers bicycle and roller-skate rentals—perfect for exploring this offbeat neighborhood. See chapter 13.

- **Two Bunch Palms Resort & Spa** (Desert Hot Springs; ☎ 800/472-4334): The spiritual sanctuary in Desert Hot Springs has been drawing weary city dwellers with its healing mineral springs since Chicago mobster Al Capone built this hideaway in the 1930s. Two Bunch Palms later became a playground for the movie community, but today it's a friendly and informal haven offering full spa services, quiet bungalows nestled among the palms, and trademark pools of steaming mineral water. See chapter 15.

- **Crystal Pier Hotel** (San Diego; ☎ 800/748-5894): Occupying a historic private pier that extends into the Pacific Ocean, this property affords guests the unusual experience of actually sleeping *over* the ocean in a darling cottage. Ideal for beach-loving families. See chapter 16.

13 The Best Restaurants

- **San Francisco's Finest:** We can't choose! It's practically sacrilege to even attempt to name the "top" San Francisco restaurant. But for a perfect combo of great food and atmosphere, we always count on **Boulevard** (☎ 415/543-6084), **La Folie** (☎ 415/776-5577), and **Fringale** (☎ 415/543-0573). See chapter 4.

- **Chez Panisse** (Berkeley; ☎ 510/548-5525): This is the culinary domain of Alice Waters, often called "the queen of California cuisine." Her food captivates the senses and the imagination. Although originally inspired by the Mediterranean, her kitchen has found its own style. Even Bill Clinton deserted the Big Mac for some Chez Panisse delights, such as grilled fish wrapped in fig leaves with red-wine sauce, and Seckel pears poached in red wine with burnt caramel. See chapter 5.

- **The French Laundry** (Yountville; ☎ **707/944-2380**): The best restaurant in the Wine Country also happens to be one of the top-ranked restaurants in the nation. Renowned chef/owner Thomas Keller, dubbed "Chef of the Nation" in 1997 by judges of the James Beard Award, offers a multicourse masterpiece that almost justifies the 6-month waiting list (though we offer some tips on how to skip the wait). See chapter 6.

- **Terra** (St. Helena; ☎ **707/963-8931**): One of the Napa Valley's premier dining rooms is the creation of Lissa Doumani and her Japanese husband, Hiro Sone. It's on every gastronome's tour of the Wine Country, a celebration of the region's bounty—sublime, flavorful, well crafted. The wine list is a tribute to the Golden State, emphasizing nearly unknown selections from the small estates. See chapter 6.

- **Pangaea** (Point Arena; ☎ **707/882-3001**): North Coast locals have been going nuts about chef/owner Shannon Hughes's wondrously fresh, inventive, and organically grown cuisine. Pork confit, served on a potato tart with homemade apricot chutney; Thai-style crab cakes served with a Thai green-curry coconut sauce; Niman-Schell burgers topped with organic cheese and greens, caramelized onions, and Thai chili sauce—it's all fantastic. Even the decor is a work of art. See chapter 7.

- **Erna's Elderberry House** (Oakhurst; ☎ **209/683-6800**): It's like a beacon shining across the culinary wasteland of the region around Yosemite. The six-course menu—which changes nightly—is an almost perfect blend of continental and Californian. The food is bountiful, and as fully satisfying as the elegant European ambiance. Fresh, fresh, fresh—and no natural flavor is cooked beyond recognition. Ingredients are deftly and skillfully handled to bring out their natural flavors. See chapter 9.

- **Stonehouse** (Santa Barbara area; ☎ **805/969-5046**): Sure, it's almost unheard of to spend $40 on a main course—but if money's no object and you're looking for a real culinary celebration, our vote goes to Stonehouse. Chef David Adjey's menu covers many areas of the globe; somehow each mouthwatering dish manages to remain true to its cultural origins, while still revealing his magical touch as well. See chapter 12.

- **The Ranch House** (Ojai; ☎ **805/646-2360**): This charming restaurant has been placing its emphasis on using the freshest vegetables, fruits, and herbs since it opened its doors in 1965, long before it became a national craze. If you stroll through the lush herb garden before your meal, you might later recognize the freshly snipped sprigs that will aromatically transform your simple meat, fish, or game dish into a work of art. See chapter 12.

- **Patina** (Los Angeles; ☎ **323/467-1108**): The flagship restaurant of superchef Joachim Splichal, who also conceived the (slightly) more affordable Pinot eateries, Patina's menu consistently wows otherwise jaded Angelenos, who keep coming back to this beautifully comfortable Cal-French dining room. Meticulously chosen seasonal menus are always fine-tuned to perfection, featuring partridge, pheasant, or other game in winter, and spotlighting exotic vegetables and tropical fish in summer. See chapter 13.

- **Röckenwagner** (Santa Monica; ☎ **310/399-6504**): L.A.'s gossipy tongues regularly wag about handsome chef Hans Röckenwagner, but he seems more concerned with maintaining the culinary perfection that propelled him from obscurity in funky Venice to this gallery-like space on Santa Monica's trendy Main Street. Although he trained in Europe, Röckenwagner co-opts ethnic dishes from around the world and elevates them to culinary works of multicultural art. Don't be surprised to find Scandinavian treats like spätzle, Knödel, and smoked salmon sharing space with Pacific Rim elements like mangoes, wasabi, and hoisin. See chapter 13.

- **Azzura Point** (Coronado; ☎ **619/424-4477**): Elevating hotel dining from simply expensive to sophisticated, memorable, inventive—and still expensive— chef James Boyce presides benevolently over Loews Coronado Bay's fine restaurant, offering Mediterranean-California cuisine and the added choice of exceptional five-course tasting menus. Also notable is the room's plush, dramatic decor and always-striking bay views. See chapter 16.
- **George's at the Cove** (La Jolla; ☎ **858/454-4244**): A beloved La Jolla tradition, George's wins consistent praise for impeccable service, gorgeous views of the cove, and outstanding California cuisine. In typical San Diego fashion, the menu showcases inventive seafood dishes; every selection, though, features diverse flavors from Asia, the Mediterranean, and the Middle East masterfully fused together. See chapter 16.

14 The Best Culinary Experiences

- **Dungeness Crab at San Francisco's Fisherman's Wharf:** Crabs, which are best consumed as soon as possible after being cooked, emerge right from boiling pots onto your plate. You crack the shells and pick the delectable meat out. Gastronomes treasure even the edible organs (crab butter) inside the carapace. See chapter 4.
- **A San Francisco Burrito:** No matter where we go in California, we just can't find a burrito as luscious as those served throughout San Francisco. The tortilla-wrapped meal takes on a gourmet dimension here: flavored tortillas; fresh-grilled meats, fish, and vegetables; three types of beans; a symphony of salsas; guacamole; and sour cream all tidily tucked in the perfect to-go feast. See chapter 4.
- **A Dim Sum Lunch, San Francisco Style:** Eating a dim sum lunch is like Christmas morning, only the continual stream of presents is edible, including the wrappers. Throughout the meal, waiters stop at your table and offer an exotic selection of appetizer-size Chinese dishes: from dumplings and pot stickers to salt-fried shrimp, shark-fin soup, and stuffed eggplant. No one this side of China does dim sum as well as San Francisco. Our favorite place to indulge is **Ton Kiang** (☎ **415/387-8273**). See chapter 4.
- **Gourmet Food Shopping in St. Helena:** This is gourmet grocery shopping at its finest. New York's **Dean & DeLuca** (☎ **707/967-9980**) opened its gastronomic warehouse in 1997 as a world's fair of foods, where everything is beautifully displayed and often painfully pricey. If you're into food, you've got to check this place out. Across the street is the **Oakville Grocery Co.** (☎ **707/944-8802**), which has a small-town vibe and crowds liable to send any claustrophobe into a rage. You'll find shelves crammed with perfect picnic provisions. See chapter 6.
- **A Decadent Meal in the Wine Country:** The Wine Country atmosphere sets a better stage for indulgent dining than anywhere else in the state. Add the best wines and some of the most talented chefs in the nation and you've got what we consider the ultimate dining experience. Deep-pocketed diners simply must reserve an evening at the **French Laundry** (St. Helena; ☎ 707/944-2380). **Pinot Blanc** (☎ 707/963-6191) and **Auberge du Soleil** (☎ 707/963-1211) are

two other expensive favorites. More moderately priced memories can be made at **Mustards Grill** (☎ 707/944-2424), **Oakville Grocery Café** (☎ 707/944-0111), and Tra Vigne's **Cantinetta** (☎ 707/963-8888). See chapter 6.

- **Tomales Bay Oysters: Johnson's Oyster Farm** (☎ **415/669-1149**) sells its farm-fresh oysters—by the dozen or the hundred—for a fraction of the price you'd pay at a restaurant. Our modus operandi is to 1) buy a couple dozen, 2) head for an empty campsite along the bay, 3) fire up the barbecue pit (don't forget the charcoal), 4) split and 'cue the little guys, 5) slather them in Johnson's special sauce, and then 6) slurp 'em down—yum. See chapter 7.

- **A Sunset Horseback Ride Through Griffith Park to a Mexican Feast:** This culinary/equine excursion departs Friday evenings from Beachwood Stables in the Hollywood Hills just before dusk, winding up in Burbank at the modest but tasty—especially coming off the trail!—Viva Restaurant. Tie up your steed outside and saunter in for a steaming plate of enchiladas accompanied by an ice-cold cerveza, just like the real *vaqueros* (cowboys). For information, call the Sunset Ranch at ☎ **323/464-9612.** See chapter 13.

- **Grand Central Market** (Los Angeles; ☎ **213/624-2378**): Fresh-produce stands, exotic spice and condiment vendors, butchers and fishmongers, and prepared-food counters create a noisy, fragrant, vaguely comforting atmosphere in this L.A. mainstay. The gem of the airy, cavernous complex is the fresh juice bar at the southwest corner. A market fixture for many years, it dispenses dozens of varieties from an elaborate system of wall spigots (just like an old-fashioned soda fountain), deftly blending unlikely but heavenly combinations. See chapter 13.

- **Sunday Champagne Brunch Aboard the** *Queen Mary* (Long Beach; ☎ **562/435-3511** or 562/432-6964): This elegant ocean liner was the largest, finest vessel when she was built in 1934, and the grandeur of those Atlantic-crossing days remains. A sumptuous buffet-style feast, accompanied by harp soloist and ice sculpture, is presented in the richly wood-furnished, first-class dining room. Walk off your overindulgence on the spectacular teak decks and through the art-deco interiors. See chapter 14.

- **A Date with the Coachella Valley:** Some 95% of the world's dates are farmed here in the desert. While the groves of date palms make evocative scenery, it's their savory fruit that draws visitors to the National Date Festival in Indio each February. Amid the Arabian Nights parade and dusty camel races, you can feast on an exotic array of plump Medjool, amber Deglet Noor, caramel-like Halawy, and buttery Empress. The rest of the year, date farms and markets throughout the valley sell dates from the season's harvest, as well as date milk shakes, sticky-date coconut rolls, and more. See chapter 15 and the "Calendar of Events" in chapter 2.

- **San Diego County Farmers Markets:** The bountiful harvest of San Diego County is sold on various days at moveable markets throughout the area. Finds are fresh local fruits, vegetables, and flowers, as well as specialty items such as raw apple cider (in the fall), macadamia nuts, and rhubarb pies. See chapter 16.

15 The Best Destinations for Serious Shoppers

- **San Francisco:** It's been called "a boutique town on the Bay." It's filled with hundreds of small and smart specialty shops, selling unusual clothes, books, antiques, jewelry, and gifts, much of it from the Pacific Rim. Of all the great stores in San Francisco, one must-stop is Gump's, on Post Street, between Grant Avenue and Kearny Street. Founded by German immigrants in 1865, the landmark store is known worldwide for its "treasures of Asia," including jade and pearls—plus the largest selection of fine crystal and china in the United States. See chapter 4.

- **Mendocino/Fort Bragg:** Mendocino is tailor-made for art-gallery hopping, antiquing, and wine tasting. And there's even better shopping just a short drive up the coast at Fort Bragg, especially along the 300 block of North Franklin Street, which is lined with antiques stores. See chapter 7.

- **Carmel:** Some 600 shops and boutiques are tucked into this serene little town. They sell virtually everything—fashions, housewares, art, imported goods, baskets, you name it. Seek out Carmel Plaza, a multilevel complex of boutiques and crafts shops, and especially the Barnyard, with its authentic early California barns, now converted into more than 60 shops, boutiques, and restaurants. See chapter 11.

- **Santa Monica:** The entire city is a shopper's paradise. In addition to the movie theater–laden Third Street Promenade and the more traditional multilevel Santa Monica Place, you can browse the shops—some funky, some down-to-earth—and trendy cafes of Main Street and the upscale stores of quaint Montana Avenue, or lose yourself in the expansive Fred Segal complex, where, in addition to a string of unusual boutiques, you'll find a fantastic ladies' milliner. See chapter 13.

- **L.A.'s West Third Street,** between La Cienega Boulevard and Fairfax Avenue: The Beverly Center? Bypass that unsightly behemoth and instead stroll in its shadow along West Third Street. You'll enjoy an eclectic mix of new- and vintage-clothing boutiques, intimate cafes, and specialty shops, interspersed with 1940s–era storefronts housing drapery makers, leather workers, stationery printers, and other craftspeople. The cluttered blocks around Orlando and Sweetzer avenues hold such treasures as the Chado Tea Room, the Traveler's Bookcase and Cook's Library specialty bookstores, Janice McCarty clothing designs, and Polkadots & Moonbeams boutique. See chapter 13.

- **South Coast Plaza** (Costa Mesa): This is the suburban shopping mall taken to its grandest extreme. With more "anchor stores" than several malls put together (including Nordstrom and Saks Fifth Avenue), South Coast Plaza is also home to a branch of Tiffany & Co., a Chanel boutique, a Versace salon, and a host of unusually highbrow shops. If your budget is in a more reasonable range, never fear—all the familiar stores are here, next to some unique Southern California specialties and a mind-boggling selection of restaurants. See chapter 14.

- **Laguna Beach:** Shopping is a primary pastime in this exquisite seaside artists' enclave; the village's streets are lined mainly with art galleries and stylish boutiques. Not all the art requires a hardy gold card, though—there are plenty of the affordable and unique local craft works you'll also see at the area's annual Festival of Arts and Sawdust Festival. See chapter 14 and the "Calendar of Events" in chapter 2.

- **Horton Plaza:** The Disneyland of shopping malls, this place is right in the heart of San Diego and covers 6½ city blocks. More than 140 specialty shops, a seven-screen cinema, three department stores, and a variety of sit-down and short-order restaurants sprawl over myriad levels. See chapter 16.

16 The Best of the Performing Arts

- **The San Francisco Opera:** This world-class company performs at the War Memorial Opera House, which is modeled after the Opéra Garnier in Paris. The opera season opens with a gala in September and runs through December. This was the first municipal opera in the United States, and its brilliant members have been acclaimed by critics throughout the world. See chapter 4.

- **The American Conservatory Theatre** (San Francisco): The ACT is one of the nation's leading regional theaters, dating from 1967. It's been called the American equivalent of the British National Theatre, the Berliner Ensemble, and the Comédie Française in Paris. Both classical and experimental works are brilliantly performed. See chapter 4.
- **Warehouse Repertory Theatre:** Living proof that poor, maligned ol' Fort Bragg is on the road to respect is its upstart new theatrical company. Determined to make Fort Bragg the Ashland of California, Warehouse Repertory Theatre is a cadre of highly talented professional actors from around the country. From Shakespeare to Shepard, artistic director Meg Patterson and her crew have brought top productions to the North Coast. See chapter 7.
- **The Monterey Jazz Festival:** When the third weekend of September rolls around, the Monterey Fairgrounds hosts this fabled classic, drawing jazz fans from around the world. The 3-day festival (which is usually sold out about a month in advance) is known for presenting the sweetest jazz west of the Mississippi. It even draws fans from that city of jazz, New Orleans. See chapters 2 and 11.
- **The Carmel Bach Festival:** For more than 50 years, Carmel has hosted an annual 3-week celebration honoring Johann Sebastian Bach and his contemporaries. It culminates in a candlelit concert in the chapel of the Carmel Mission. It starts in mid-July, and you must order tickets way in advance. See chapters 2 and 11.
- **The Hollywood Bowl:** This iconic outdoor amphitheater is the summer home of the Los Angeles Philharmonic, a stage for visiting virtuosos—including the occasional pop star—and the setting for several splendid fireworks shows throughout the summer. It's customary to feast on a gourmet picnic before the performance, either at your seat or on the grounds; at evening's end, the aisles are littered with empty wine bottles. Those lucky enough to obtain a box seat can set their own private table. See chapter 13.
- **The Viper Room:** Head to this West Hollywood closet for a glimpse of L.A.'s hippest scene. Owner Johnny Depp took this small but historic club space on the famous Sunset Strip and gave it an atmospheric art-deco vibe. He hangs out here regularly with all his trend-setting friends; visiting celebrities and musicians can be found mingling and listening to live bands every night of the week. After midnight or so, don't be surprised if big-name recording artists take the stage for an impromptu jam. See chapter 13.
- **The Groundling Theater** (Hollywood): Many Groundling alumni have hit the big time, graduating to *Saturday Night Live,* TV sitcoms, and motion pictures. The ensemble is best known for split-second improvisation and off-beat, irreverent original skits, all performed in their small, intimate theater on Melrose Avenue. You're bound to bust a gut here. See chapter 13.
- **Festival of the Arts and Pageant of the Masters** (Laguna Beach): These events draw enormous crowds to the Orange County coast every July and August. Begun in 1932 by a handful of area painters, the festival has grown to showcase hundreds of artists. In the evening, crowds marvel at the Pageant of the Masters' *tableaux vivants,* in which costumed townsfolk pose convincingly inside a giant frame and depict famous works of art, accompanied by music and narration. See chapters 2 and 14.
- **Old Globe Theatre:** This Tony Award–winning theater, fashioned after Shakespeare's original stage, produced the revival of *Damn Yankees,* and has billed such notable performers as John Goodman, Marsha Mason, Cliff Robertson, Jon Voight, and Christopher Walken. See chapter 16.

- **La Jolla Playhouse:** Winner of the 1993 Tony Award for Outstanding American Regional Theater, the LJ Playhouse stages six productions each year in its 400-seat Mandell Weiss Theater and 400-seat Mandell Weiss Forum on the campus of UCSD. This is where the Tony Award–winning production of *Tommy* was launched, and *Doogie Howser's* Neil Patrick Harris starred in the West Coast premier of the acclaimed musical *Rent.* See chapter 16.

2 Planning a Trip to California

by Stephanie Avnet Yates

In the pages that follow, we've compiled everything you need to know to handle the practical details of planning your trip in advance—from making campsite reservations to finding great deals on the Internet, plus a calendar of events and much more.

1 Visitor Information & Money

VISITOR INFORMATION

For information on the state as a whole, contact the **California Office of Tourism,** 801 K St., Suite 1600, Sacramento, CA 95812 (☎ 800/862-2543; www.gocalif.ca.gov), and ask for a free information packet. In addition, almost every city and town in the state has a dedicated tourist bureau or chamber of commerce that will be happy to send you information on its particular parcel. These are listed under the appropriate headings in the geographically organized chapters that follow.

Foreign travelers should also see chapter 3, "For Foreign Visitors," for entry requirements and other pertinent information.

INFORMATION ON CALIFORNIA'S PARKS   To find out more about California's national parks, contact the **Western Region Information Center,** National Park Service, Fort Mason, Building 201, San Francisco, CA 94123 (☎ 415/556-0560; www.nps.gov). Reservations can be made at national park campsites by calling ☎ 800/365-2267 (800/436-7275 for Yosemite) or logging on to **http://reservations.nps.gov.**

For information on state parks, contact the **Department of Parks and Recreation,** P.O. Box 942896, Sacramento, CA 94296-0001 (☎ 916/653-6995; http://cal-parks.ca.gov). Ten thousand campsites are on the department's reservation system, and can be booked up to 8 weeks in advance by calling **Park-Net** at ☎ **800/444-7275.** You can also get reservations information online at **www.park-net.com/usa/xca.**

For information on fishing and hunting licenses, contact the **California Department of Fish and Game,** License and Revenue Branch, 3211 S St., Sacramento, CA 95816 (☎ 916/227-2244).

MONEY

Wells Fargo Bank is linked with the Star, Plus, Cirrus, and Global-Access systems; it has hundreds of ATMs at branches and in-store

Plan Ahead for the Unexpected

Before you leave home, make photocopies—two sets—o...
ports for international travelers), credit cards (front and ...
itinerary confirmation. Leave one set at home where a ...
you if necessary, and carry one set with you separately f...
case of emergency, you'll have proof of your identity, eve...
and replace your credit cards, and a receipt for your plane trip home!

locations. To find the one nearest you, call ☎ **800/869-3557** or visit the Web site at **www.wellsfargo.com/findus**. Other statewide banks include Bank of America (which accepts Plus, Star, and Interlink cards) and First Interstate Bank (Cirrus). To locate other ATMs in the **Cirrus** system, call ☎ **800/424-7787** or search online at **www.mastercard.com**; to find a **Plus** ATM, call ☎ **800/843-7587** or visit **www.visa.com**. Be sure to check your bank's daily withdrawal limit before you depart.

2 When to Go

California's climate is so varied that it's impossible to generalize about the state as a whole.

San Francisco's temperate marine climate means relatively mild weather year-round. In summer, temperatures rarely top 70°F (pack sweaters, even in August), and the city's famous fog rolls in most mornings and evenings. In winter, the mercury seldom falls below freezing, and snow is almost unheard of. Because of San Francisco's fog, summer rarely sees more than a few hot days in a row. Head a few miles inland, though, and it's likely to be clear and hot.

The Central Coast shares San Francisco's climate, although it gets warmer as you get farther south. Seasonal changes are less pronounced south of San Luis Obispo, where temperatures remain relatively stable year-round. The North Coast is rainier and foggier; winters tend to be mild but wet.

Summers are refreshingly cool around Lake Tahoe and in the Shasta Cascades—a perfect climate for hiking, camping, and other outdoor activities and a popular escape for residents of California's sweltering deserts and valleys who are looking to beat the heat. Skiers flock to this area for terrific snowfall from late November to early April.

Southern California—including Los Angeles and San Diego—is usually much warmer than the Bay Area, and it gets significantly more sun. This is the place to hit the beach. Even in winter, daytime thermometer readings regularly reach into the 60s and warmer. Summers can be stifling inland, but southern California's coastal communities are always comfortable. The area's limited rainfall is generally seen between January and mid-April, and is rarely intense enough to be more than a slight inconvenience. It's possible to sunbathe throughout the year, but only die-hard enthusiasts and wet-suited surfers venture into the ocean in winter. The water is warmest in summer and fall, but even then, the Pacific is too chilly for many.

The deserts, including Palm Springs and the desert national parks, are sizzling hot in summer; temperatures regularly top 100°F. Winter is the time to visit the desert resorts (and remember, it gets surprisingly cold at night in the desert).

o's Average Temperatures (°F)

	Jan	Feb	Mar	Apr	May	June	July	Aug	Sept	Oct	Nov	Dec
High	56	59	60	61	63	64	64	65	69	68	63	57
Avg. Low	46	48	49	49	51	53	53	54	56	55	52	47

Los Angeles's Average Temperatures (°F)

	Jan	Feb	Mar	Apr	May	June	July	Aug	Sept	Oct	Nov	Dec
Avg. High	65	66	67	69	72	75	81	81	81	77	73	69
Avg. Low	46	48	49	52	54	57	60	60	59	55	51	49

California Calendar of Events

January

- ✪ **Tournament of Roses,** Pasadena. A spectacular parade down Colorado Boulevard, with lavish floats, music, and extraordinary equestrian entries, followed by the Rose Bowl Game. Call ☎ **626/449-4100** for details, or just stay home and watch it on TV (you'll have a better view). January 1.
- **Bob Hope Chrysler Classic,** Palm Springs Desert Resorts. 2000 marks the 41st year (and Bob's 97th birthday) of this weeklong PGA golf tournament, which raises money for charity and includes a celebrity-studded Pro-Am. For spectator information and tickets, call ☎ **888/MR-BHOPE** or 760/346-8184. January 17 to 23, 2000.

February

- **AT&T Pebble Beach National Pro-Am,** Pebble Beach. A PGA-sponsored tour where pros are teamed with celebrities to compete on three world-famous golf courses. Call ☎ **800/541-9091** or 831/649-1533. January 31 to February 6, 2000.
- ✪ **Chinese New Year Festival and Parade.** The largest Chinese New Year festival in the United States is in San Francisco. The celebration includes a Golden Dragon parade with lion dancing, marching bands, street fair, flower sale, and festive food. Call ☎ **415/982-3000** or 391-9680. In 2000, the New Year begins February 5; the parade will be February 19.

    L.A.'s celebration is colorful as well, with dragon dancers parading through the streets of downtown's Chinatown. Chinese opera and other events are scheduled. For this year's schedule, contact the Chinese Chamber of Commerce at ☎ **213/617-0396.**
- **National Date Festival,** Indio. Crowds gather to celebrate the Coachella Valley desert's most beloved cash crop with appropriately themed events like camel and ostrich races, the Blessing of the Date Garden, and festive Arabian Nights pageants. Plenty of date-sampling booths are set up, along with rides, food vendors, and other county-fair trappings. Call ☎ **800/811-3247** or 760/863-8247. Two weeks in February.
- **Mustard Festival,** Napa Valley. Celebrating the blossom of yellow-petaled mustard flowers, which coat the valley during February and March, the event was originally conceived to drum up interest in visiting during this once-slow season. The festival has evolved into 6 weeks worth of events ranging from a kick-off gourmet gala at the CIA Greystone to a wine auction, golf benefit, recipe and photography competitions, and plenty of food and wine celebrations. For information and a schedule of events, call ☎ **707/259-9020** or 707/938-1133, or visit online at **www.mustardfestival.com**. January 29 to March 25, 2000.

March

- **Return of the Swallows,** San Juan Capistrano. Each St. Joseph's Day (March 19), visitors flock to this charming village for the arrival of the mission's loyal flock of swallows that will nest and remain until October. The celebration includes a parade, dances, and special programs. Call ☎ 949/248-2048 for details. March 17 to 19, 2000.
- **Santa Barbara International Film Festival.** For 10 days each March, pretty Santa Barbara does its best impression of Cannes. There's a flurry of foreign- and independent-film premieres, personal appearances by noted actors and directors, and symposia on hot cinematic topics. For a rundown of events, call ☎ 805/963-0023. March 2 to 12, 2000.
- **Nabisco Dinah Shore,** Rancho Mirage. This 31-year-old LPGA golf tournament takes place near Palm Springs. After the celebrity Pro-Am early in the week, the best female pros get down to business. For further information, call ☎ 760/324-4546. Other special-interest events for women usually take place around the Dinah Shore, including the country's largest annual lesbian gathering. Last week of March.
- **Redwood Coast Dixieland Jazz Festival,** Eureka. Three days of jazz featuring 12 of the best Dixieland groups, including a variety of jam sessions. Call ☎ 707/445-3378. Late March.

April

- ✪ **San Francisco International Film Festival.** One of America's oldest film festivals, featuring more than 100 films and videos from more than 30 countries. Tickets are relatively inexpensive, and screenings are very accessible to the general public during 2 weeks early in the month. Call ☎ 415/931-FILM.
- **Toyota Grand Prix,** Long Beach. An exciting weekend of Indy-class auto racing and entertainment in and around downtown Long Beach, drawing world-class drivers from the United States and Europe. Contact the **Grand Prix Association** at ☎ 800/752-9524 or 562/981-2600. Mid-April.
- ✪ **Renaissance Pleasure Faire,** San Bernardino. One of America's largest Renaissance festivals, this annual happening is set in Glen Helen Regional Park in L.A.'s relatively remote countryside. Performers (and many attendees) dress in 16th-century costume and revel in this festive re-creation of a medieval English village. For ticket information, phone ☎ 800/52-FAIRE. Weekends from late April to Memorial Day.
- **Ramona Pageant,** Hemet. A unique outdoor play that portrays the lives of the Southern California Mission Indians. The play was adapted from Helen Hunt Jackson's 1884 novel *Ramona.* Call ☎ 909/658-3111 for details. Late April to early May.
- **Del Mar National Horse Show.** Horse-and-rider teams compete in national championships at the Del Mar Fairgrounds. Call ☎ 858/792-4288 or 858/755-1161 for more information. Late April to early May.

May

- ✪ **Cinco de Mayo.** A weeklong celebration of one of Mexico's most jubilant holidays takes place throughout the city of Los Angeles. The fiesta's carnival-like atmosphere is created by large crowds, live music, dances, and food. The main festivities are held in El Pueblo de Los Angeles State Historic Park, downtown, with other events around the city. Phone ☎ 213/485-6855 for information.

    There's also a Cinco de Mayo celebration in San Diego, featuring folkloric music, dance, food, and historical reenactments. Held in Old Town. Call ☎ 619/296-3161 or 619/220-5422 for more information.

⊙ **Calaveras County Fair and Jumping Frog Jubilee,** Angels Camp. The event inspired by Mark Twain's story "The Celebrated Jumping Frog of Calaveras County." Entrants from all over the world arrive with their frog participants. There's also a children's parade, livestock competition, rodeo, carnival, and fireworks. Call ☎ **209/736-2561.** Third weekend in May.

• **Bay to Breakers Foot Race,** Golden Gate Park, San Francisco. One of the city's most popular annual events, it's really more fun than run. Thousands of entrants show up dressed in their best Halloween-style costumes for the approximately 7½-mile run across the park. Call ☎ **415/777-7770.** Third Sunday of May.

• **Paso Robles Wine Festival.** What began as a small, neighborly gathering has grown into the largest outdoor wine tasting in California. The 3-day event features winery open houses and tastings, a golf tournament, 5K run and 10K bike ride, concerts, plus a carnival-like festival in downtown's City Park. For a schedule of events and fees, call ☎ **800/549-WINE.** Third weekend in May.

⊙ **Carnival,** San Francisco. The Mission District's largest annual event is a 2-day series of festivities that culminates with a parade on Mission Street over Memorial Day weekend. More than half a million spectators line the route, and the samba musicians and dancers continue to play on 14th Street, near Harrison, at the end of the march. Call the **Mission Economic and Cultural Association** at ☎ **415/826-1401.** Memorial Day weekend.

June

• **Playboy Jazz Festival,** Los Angeles. Bill Cosby is the traditional Master of Ceremonies, presiding over top artists at the Hollywood Bowl. Call ☎ **310/246-4000.** Mid-June.

• **Lesbian and Gay Freedom Day Parade.** It's celebrated all over the state, but San Francisco's party draws up to half a million participants. The parade's start and finish have been moved around in recent years to accommodate road construction, but traditionally it begins and ends at Civic Center Plaza, where hundreds of food, art, and information booths are set up around several sound stages. Call ☎ **415/864-3733** for information. Usually the third or last Sunday of June.

• **Ojai Music Festival.** This 3-day event has been drawing world-class classical and jazz personalities to the open-air Libbey Bowl since 1947. Past events have featured Igor Stravinsky, Aaron Copland, and the Juilliard String Quartet. Seats (and local lodgings) fill up quickly; call ☎ **805/646-2094** for more information. First half of June.

• **Mariachi USA Festival,** Los Angeles. A 2-day family-oriented celebration of Mexican culture and tradition at the Hollywood Bowl, where festival-goers pack their picnic baskets and enjoy music, ballet, folklorico, and related performances by special guests. Call ☎ **323/848-7717.** Late June.

July

• **Mammoth Lakes Jazz Jubilee.** A 4-day festival featuring 20 bands on 10 different stages, plus food, drink, and dancing—all under the pine trees and stars. Call ☎ **800/367-6572** or 760/934-2478. Second weekend in July.

⊙ **Festival of Arts and Pageant of the Masters,** Laguna Beach. A fantastic performance-art production in which live actors re-create famous Old Masters paintings. Other festivities include live music, crafts sales, art demonstrations and workshops, and the grass-roots Sawdust Festival across the street. Grounds admission is $3; pageant tickets range from $15 to $40. Call ☎ **800/487-FEST** or 949/494-1145, or check out **www.foapom.com.** July through August.

- **Gilroy Garlic Festival.** A gourmet food fair with more than 85 booths serving garlicky food from almost every ethnic background, plus close to 100 arts, crafts, and entertainment booths. Call ☎ 831/842-1625. Last full weekend in July.
- **Shakespeare at the Beach,** Lake Tahoe. A bewitching experience of the Bard at Sand Harbor on the shore beneath the stars. Call ☎ 702/832-1606. Three weeks in late July and August.
- **Beach Festival,** Huntington Beach. Two straight weeks of fun in the sun, featuring two surfing competitions—the U.S. Open of Surfing *and* the world-class Pro of Surfing—plus extreme-sports events like in-line skating, BMX biking, skateboarding, and more. Includes entertainment, food, tons of product booths and giveaways—and plenty of tanned, swimsuit-clad bodies of both sexes. Call US Surfing (☎ 949/366-4584) for more information. End of July.

August

- **Old Spanish Days Fiesta,** Santa Barbara. The city's biggest annual event, this 5-day festival features a grand parade with horse-drawn carriages, music and dance performances, *mercados* (marketplaces), and a rodeo. Call ☎ 805/962-8101. Early August.
- **Nisei Week Japanese Festival,** Los Angeles. This weeklong celebration of Japanese culture and heritage is held in Little Tokyo at the Japanese American Cultural and Community Center Plaza. Festivities include parades, food, music, arts, and crafts. Call ☎ 213/687-7193. Mid-August.
- **California State Fair,** Sacramento. At the California Exposition Grounds, a gala celebration with livestock, carnival food, exhibits, entertainment on 10 different stages, plus thoroughbred racing and a 1-mile monorail for panoramic views over the scope of it all. Call ☎ 916/263-FAIR. Late August to early September.

September

- **Sausalito Art Festival.** A juried exhibit of more than 180 artists. It's accompanied by music provided by Bay Area jazz, rock, and blues performers and international cuisine enhanced by wines from some 50 different Napa and Sonoma producers. Call ☎ 415/332-3555 for information. Labor Day weekend.
- ✪ **San Diego Street Scene.** The historic Gaslamp Quarter is transformed by this 3-day extravaganza featuring food, dance, international character, and live music on 12 separate stages. Saturday is set aside as an all-ages day; attendees must be 21 and over the other 2 days. Call ☎ 619/557-0505 for more information. First weekend after Labor Day.
- ✪ **Monterey Jazz Festival.** Top names in traditional and modern jazz. One of the oldest annual jazz festivals in the world. Call ☎ 800/307-3378 or 831/373-0244. Mid-September.
- **Los Angeles County Fair.** Horse racing, arts, agricultural displays, celebrity entertainment, and carnival rides are among the attractions of the largest county fair in the world, held at the Los Angeles County Fair and Exposition Center, in Pomona. Call ☎ 909/623-3111 for information. Usually all month.
- **Danish Days,** Solvang. Since 1936 this 3-day event has been celebrating old-world customs and pageantry with a parade, gymnastics exhibitions by local schoolchildren, demonstrations of traditional Danish arts and crafts, and plenty of *aebleskivers* (Danish fritters) and *medisterpolse* (Danish sausage). Call ☎ 800/GO-SOLVANG for further information.
- **Watts Towers Day of the Drum Festival,** Los Angeles. Celebrating the historic role of drums and drummers, this event features a variety of unique performances, from Afro-Cuban folkloricos to East Indian tabla players. Call ☎ 213/847-4646. Late September.

October

- **Catalina Island Jazz Trax Festival.** Great contemporary jazz artists travel to the island to play in the legendary Avalon Casino Ballroom. The festival is held over two consecutive 3-day weekends. Call ☎ **800/866-TRAX** or 818/347-5299 for more information. Early October.
- **Sonoma County Harvest Fair.** A 3-day celebration of the harvest with exhibitions, art shows, and annual judging of the local wines. At the Sonoma County Fairgrounds. Call ☎ **707/545-4203.** Dates vary.
- **The Half Moon Bay Art & Pumpkin Festival,** Half Moon Bay. The festival features a Great Pumpkin Parade, pie-eating contests, a pumpkin-carving competition, arts and crafts, and all manner of squash cuisine. The highlight of the event is the Giant Pumpkin weigh-in contest, won recently by an 875-pound monster. Colorful to the extreme. For exact date and details, call the **Pumpkin Hotline** at ☎ **650/726-9652.**
- **Western Regional Final Championship Rodeo,** Lakeside. Top cowboys from 11 western states compete in seven rodeo events, including calf roping, barrel racing, bull riding, team roping, and steer wrestling. Held at the Lakeside Rodeo Grounds, Calif. 67 and Mapleview Avenue, Lakeside. Call ☎ **619/561-4331.** Mid-October.
- **Halloween,** San Francisco. The City by the Bay celebrates with a fantastical parade organized at Market and Castro, and a mixed gay-straight crowd revels in costumes of extraordinary imagination. October 31.

November

- **Doo Dah Parade,** Pasadena. An outrageous spoof of the Rose Parade, featuring participants such as the Precision Briefcase Drill Team and a kazoo band. Call ☎ **626/449-3689.** Sunday before Thanksgiving.
- **Hollywood Christmas Parade.** This spectacular star-studded parade marches through the heart of Hollywood. For information call ☎ **323/469-2337.** Sunday after Thanksgiving.

December

- *How the Grinch Stole Christmas,* San Diego. In honor of the late Theodore Geisel ("Dr. Seuss," a former San Diego resident), the lobby of Loews Coronado Bay Resort is transformed into Whoville, where the Cat in the Hat assembles eager young audiences for regular readings of the beloved Christmas story. Punch and cookies are served at this free event, and carolers also perform following each reading. For more information, call ☎ **619/424-4000.** December 1 to 24.
- **Christmas Boat Parade of Lights.** Following longstanding tradition, sailors love to decorate their craft with colorful lights for the holidays. Several Southern California harbors hold nighttime parades to showcase these creations, which range from tiny dinghies draped with a single strand of lights to showy yachts with entire Nativity scenes twinkling on deck. Call the following for schedules and information: **Ventura Harbor** (☎ 805/642-6746), **Marina Del Rey** (Los Angeles; ☎ 310/821-0555), **Long Beach** (☎ 562/435-4093), **Huntington Harbour** (☎ 714/840-7542), **Mission Bay** (San Diego; ☎ 619/ 276-8200).
- ✪ **New Year's Eve Torchlight Parade,** Big Bear Lake. Watch dozens of nighttime skiers follow a serpentine path down Snow Summit's ski slopes bearing glowing torches—it's one of the state's loveliest traditions. Afterward, the party continues indoors with live bands and plenty to eat and drink. For more information on this 21-and-over event, call ☎ **909/866-5766.**

3 Special-Interest Vacations

BICYCLING TOURS   Combine an interest in biking with California's spectacular scenery by signing up for a weeklong or weekend tour with **Backroads,** 801 Cedar St., Berkeley, CA 94710 (☎ **800/GO-ACTIVE** or 510/527-1555; www.backroads.com). Focusing on coastal routes, wine-country rides, and even a microbrew program, the tours vary in difficulty and comfort; some are camping trips, while others accommodate in luxury B&Bs. Professional leaders accompany each group, while a support van trails with gear, baggage, and provisions. Tours include all meals and overnight accommodations, and range in price from $150 to $275 per day (per person).

WHALE WATCHING   Each winter, pods of California gray whales making their annual migration from their Alaskan feeding grounds to breeding lagoons at the southern tip of Baja pass close by California shores; if you've ever been lucky enough to spot one of these graceful behemoths, you'll understand why whale watching is such an eagerly anticipated activity. From December through March, you can view this spectacular parade from land or sea. Recommended spots include **Point Reyes National Seashore** (☎ 415/669-1534), where an historic lighthouse offers whale- and elephant seal–viewing; **Monterey Peninsula**, where January's WhaleFest (☎ 831/644-7588) celebrates these special mammals from the Monterey Aquarium down through Big Sur; **Point Vicente Lighthouse and Interpretive Center** (☎ 562/377-5370), on the windswept Palos Verdes Peninsula south of Los Angeles; and San Diego's **Cabrillo National Monument** (☎ 619/557-5450; www.nps.gov/cabr), which offers a glassed-in observatory and educational whale exhibits.

Boat excursions depart from a number of locations, including **Morro Bay** (Virg's Landing, ☎ 800/762-5263 or 805/772-1222), **Santa Barbara** (The Condor, ☎ 888/77-WHALE or 805/963-3564), **Ventura Harbor** (Island Packers, ☎ 805/642-1393; www.islandpackers.com), and **San Diego** (San Diego Harbor Excursions, ☎ 800/442-7847 or 619/234-4111). Also in San Diego, the **Natural History Museum** (☎ 619/232-3821, ext. 203; www. sdnhm.org) offers fascinating, naturalist-led, half-day whale-watching trips for passengers 12 and older.

YOGA RETREATS   Serenity, flexibility, and overall well-being await you at a specialized yoga retreat. Try **Master Yoga Academy**, 7592 Fay Ave., La Jolla, CA 92037 (☎ **858/454-6978;** www.masteryoga.org), where 3-, 5-, or 7-day yoga vacations include lodgings in a neighborhood hotel, unlimited yoga classes, private yoga therapy, an instructional video to take home, and the myriad activities available within walking distance in this seaside jewel. Fees range from $169 to $259 for 3 days, and from $319 to $699 for 7 days, depending on accommodations. In Northern California, **Mount Madonna Center,** 445 Summit Rd., Watsonville, CA 95076 (☎ **408/847-0406;** www.mountmadonna.org), offers a variety of seminars and overnight programs designed for personal growth. Weekend and weeklong programs are offered throughout the year, including several all-yoga retreats. The center is located in the Santa Cruz Mountains, enjoying solitude and sweeping views of Monterey Bay. Room rates, which include two vegetarian meals daily, are $42 for dormitory accommodations and range from $69 to $87 for a private room with bath; tuition is another $120 per retreat.

4 Tips for Travelers with Special Needs

FOR TRAVELERS WITH DISABILITIES   A disability shouldn't stop anyone from traveling—there are more resources out there than ever before. *A World of Options,* a 658-page book of resources for travelers with disabilities, covers everything from biking trips to scuba outfitters. It costs $45 (less for members) and is available from **Mobility International USA,** P.O. Box 10767, Eugene, OR 97440 (☎ **541/ 343-1284** voice and TDD; www.miusa.org). Annual membership for Mobility International is $35, which includes its quarterly newsletter, *Over the Rainbow.*

You can join the **Society for the Advancement of Travel for the Handicapped** (SATH), 347 Fifth Ave., Suite 610, New York, NY 10016 (☎ **212/447-7284;** fax 212-725-8253; www.sath.org) for $45 annually, $30 for seniors and students, to gain access to its vast network of connections in the travel industry. It provides information sheets on travel destinations as well as referrals to tour operators that specialize in traveling with disabilities. Its quarterly magazine, *Open World for Disability and Mature Travel,* is full of good information and resources. A year's subscription is $13 ($21 outside the U.S.).

Access-Able Travel Source offers a comprehensive online index of accessible hotels, restaurants, attractions, and service providers for those with disabilities throughout California; log on to **www.access-able.com** or call ☎ **303/232-2979.**

FOR GAY & LESBIAN TRAVELERS   The **International Gay & Lesbian Travel Association** (IGLTA) links travelers up with the appropriate gay-friendly service organization or tour specialist. With around 1,200 members, it offers quarterly newsletters, marketing mailings, and a membership directory that's updated quarterly. Membership often includes gay or lesbian businesses but is open to individuals for $150 yearly, plus a $100 administration fee for new members. Members are kept informed of gay and gay-friendly hoteliers, tour operators, and airline and cruise-line representatives. Contact the IGLTA (☎ **800/448-8550** or 954/776-2626; fax 954/ 776-3303; www.iglta.org) for a list of its member agencies, who will be tied into IGLTA's information resources.

There are also two good, biannual English-language gay guidebooks, both focused on gay men but including information for lesbians as well. You can get the *Spartacus International Gay Guide* or *Odysseus* from most gay and lesbian bookstores, or order them online from **Amazon.com**.

Out and About, 8 W. 19th St. #401, New York, NY 10011 (☎ **800/929-2268** or 212/645-6922), offers guidebooks and a monthly newsletter packed with good information on the global gay and lesbian scene. A year's subscription to the newsletter costs $49. *Our World,* 1104 North Nova Rd., Suite 251, Daytona Beach, FL 32117 (☎ **904/441-5367**), is a slicker monthly magazine promoting and highlighting travel bargains and opportunities. Annual subscription rates are $35 in the United States, $45 outside the United States.

FOR SENIORS   Members of the **American Association of Retired Persons** **(AARP),** 601 E St. NW, Washington, DC 20049 (☎ **800/424-3410** or 202/ 434-2277), get discounts not only on hotels but also on airfares and car rentals. AARP offers members a wide range of special benefits, including *Modern Maturity* magazine and a monthly newsletter.

Mature Outlook, P.O. Box 9390, Des Moines, IA 50306 (☎ **800/336-6330**), began as a travel organization for people over 50, though it now caters to people of all ages. Members receive a bimonthly magazine and discounts on hotels. Annual membership is $19.95, which entitles members to discounts and, often, free coupons for discounted merchandise from Sears.

The Mature Traveler, a monthly 12-page newsletter on senior travel, is a valuable resource. It's available by subscription ($30 a year) from GEM Publishing Group, Box 50400, Reno, NV 89513-0400. GEM also publishes *The Book of Deals,* a collection

of more than 1,000 senior discounts on airlines, lodging,
the country; it's available for $9.95 by calling ☎ 800/46

FOR FAMILIES *Family Travel Times* is published si
or Travel with Your Children (☎ 212/477-5524; 888-
weekly call-in service for subscribers. Subscriptions are $4
tions. A free publication list and a sample issue are availab
request to the above address.

Families Welcome!, 92 N. Main, Ashland, OR 97520 (☎ 800/326-0724 or
541/482-6121), is a travel company specializing in worry-free vacations for families.

5 Getting There

BY PLANE

All major U.S. carriers serve the San Francisco, Sacramento, San Jose, Los Angeles, and
San Diego airports. Domestic airlines flying in and out of these cities include **Alaska**
(☎ 800/426-0333; www.alaskaair.com), **American** (☎ 800/433-7300; www.
americanair.com), **America West** (☎ 800/235-9292; www.americawest.com), **Continental** (☎ 800/525-0280; www.continental.com), **Delta** (☎ 800/221-1212; www.
delta-air.com), **Northwest** (☎ 800/225-2525; www.nwa.com), **Southwest** (☎ 800/
435-9792; www.iflyswa.com), **TWA** (☎ 800/221-2000; www.twa.com), **United**
(☎ 800/241-6522; www.ual.com), and **US Airways** (☎ 800/428-4322; www.usair.
com). The lowest round-trip fares to the West Coast from New York fluctuate between
about $350 and $500; from Chicago, they range from $300 to $400. Foreign travelers
should also see "Getting to the U.S.," in chapter 3, for a list of airlines offering overseas flights into California. For details on air travel within California, see "Getting
Around," below.

FINDING THE BEST AIRFARE Passengers who can book their tickets in
advance, stay over Saturday night, or travel at off-peak hours will pay a fraction of the
full fare. Airlines periodically lower prices on their most popular routes. Check your
newspaper for advertised discounts or call the airlines directly and ask if any **promotional rates** or special fares are available. If your schedule is flexible, ask if you can
secure a cheaper fare by staying an extra day or by flying midweek (many airlines won't
volunteer this information).

Formerly known as "bucket shops," **consolidators** (wholesalers who buy tickets in
bulk at a discount) today are very legitimate and offer some of the best deals around.
Their ads usually run in the Sunday travel section, and many have set up online reservations systems. There are lots of fly-by-night consolidators, though, and problems
can range from disputing never-received tickets to finding you have no seat booked
when you get to the airport. Play it safe by going with a reputable business; we suggest **1-800-FLY-CHEAP** (www.1800flycheap.com), **Cheap Seats** (☎ 800/451-7200;
www.cheapseatstravel.com), or our favorite, **Cheap Tickets** (☎ 800/377-1000;
www.cheaptickets.com).

It's possible to get some great deals on airfares, hotels, and car rentals via **Internet
travel agencies.** Two of the better-respected virtual travel agents are **Travelocity**
(www.travelocity.com) and **Microsoft Expedia** (www.expedia.com). Just enter the
dates you want to fly and the cities you want to visit, and the computer roots out the
lowest fares. The **Internet Travel Network** (www.itn.net) provides one-stop shopping
for air, car, and hotel bookings, and also lets you book packages and cruises. ITN is
great for pricing complex itineraries. (See also the Online Directory, at the end of this
book, for more information on resources on the Web.)

Great last-minute deals are also available through a free e-mail service, provided directly by the airlines, called **E-Savers.** Each week, the airline sends you a list of discounted flights, usually leaving the upcoming Friday or Saturday, and returning the following Monday or Tuesday. You can sign up for all the major airlines at once by logging on to **Smarter Living** (www.smarterliving.com), or go to each individual airline's Web site (see Appendix B, "Useful Toll-Free Numbers & Web Sites").

BY CAR

Here are some handy driving times if you're on one of those see-the-USA car trips. From Phoenix, it's about 6 hours to Los Angeles on I-10. Las Vegas is 265 miles northeast of Los Angeles (about a 4-hour drive).

San Francisco is 227 miles southwest of Reno, Nevada, and 577 miles northwest of Las Vegas. It's a long day's drive 640 miles south from Portland, Oregon, on I-5. The drive between San Francisco and L.A. takes about 6 hours on I-5, closer to 8 hours on the more scenic U.S. 101.

BY TRAIN

Amtrak (☎ **800/USA-RAIL;** www.amtrak.com) connects California with about 500 American cities. The *Sunset Limited* is Amtrak's regularly scheduled transcontinental service, originating in Florida and making 52 stops along the way as it passes through Alabama, Mississippi, Louisiana, Texas, New Mexico, and Arizona before arriving in Los Angeles 2 days later. The train, which runs three times weekly, features reclining seats, a sightseeing car with large windows, and a full-service dining car. Round-trip coach fares begin at around $300; several varieties of sleeping compartments are also available for an extra charge.

Amtrak's *Coast Starlight* travels along the Pacific Coast between Seattle and Los Angeles. This stylish train (and wonderfully scenic route) has been steadily growing in popularity; for more information, see "Getting Around," below.

PACKAGE TOURS

Independent fly/drive packages (no escorted tour groups, just a bulk rate on your airfare, hotel, and possibly your rental car) are offered by **American Airlines Fly AAway Vacations** (☎ 800/321-2121), **American Express Vacations** (☎ 800/241-1700; www.americanexpress.com/travel), **Continental Airlines Vacations** (☎ 800/ 634-5555), **Delta Vacations** (☎ 800/872-7786; www.deltavacations.com), **TWA Getaway Vacations** (☎ 800/438-2929), and **United Vacations** (☎ 800/328-6877; www.unitedvacations.com). Availability varies widely based upon season and demand, but it always pays to investigate what these major air carriers are offering to encourage you to fly with them. Packages are best suited to travelers who can be flexible in the following ways:

- Try not to be too picky about your hotel. That's not to say that packages force you to stay in dumps—quite the contrary, they often include some premier hostelries—but your selection will be limited. Pinpoint roughly where you'd like to stay (within a region or city), and ask if there's a participating hotel there. The biggest hotel chains and resorts also offer package deals. If you already know where you want to stay, call the resort itself and ask if it can offer land/air packages.

- If you can schedule your departure and arrival so that you're not flying on the weekend, airfares will usually be at least $25 to $50 lower per person. And it goes without saying that the popular season is the most restrictive season—meaning summer at the beach, winter in the deserts—though package deals can still save you some money.

- Engage the reservationist in conversation, mentioning all the activities you're considering for your visit. All the companies have access to various "goodies" they can hitch to your package for far less than you'd pay separately. Examples include tickets to major attractions; passes for city tours, harbor cruises, and other excursions; tickets for theater events; rental-car upgrades; and other specials.

6 Getting Around

BY CAR

California's freeway signs frequently indicate direction by naming a town rather than a point on the compass. If you've never heard of Canoga Park, you might be in trouble—unless you have a map. The best state road guide is the comprehensive **Thomas Bros.** *California Road Atlas,* a 300-plus-page book of maps with schematics of towns and cities statewide. It costs $20, a good investment if you plan to do a lot of exploring. Smaller, accordion-style maps are handy for the state as a whole or for individual cities and regions; you'll find a very useful one inserted in the back of this book.

If you're heading into the Sierra or Shasta-Cascades for a winter ski trip, top up on antifreeze and carry snow chains for your tires. (Chains are mandatory in certain areas.)

Here are a few sample distances between key California cities:

San Francisco	
87 miles SW of Sacramento	321 miles NW of Santa Barbara
115 miles NW of Monterey	379 miles NW of Los Angeles
278 miles SE of Eureka	548 miles NW of San Diego

Sacramento	
87 miles NE of San Francisco	383 miles N of Los Angeles
185 miles NE of Monterey	391 miles NE of Santa Barbara
304 miles SE of Eureka	484 miles NW of Palm Springs

Los Angeles	
96 miles SE of Santa Barbara	379 miles SE of San Francisco
103 miles W of Palm Springs	383 miles S of Sacramento
120 miles NW of San Diego	659 miles SE of Eureka
332 miles SE of Monterey	

DRIVING RULES   California law requires both drivers and passengers to wear seat belts. Children under 4 years or 40 pounds must be secured in an approved child safety seat. Motorcyclists must wear a helmet. Auto insurance is mandatory; the car's registration and proof of insurance must be carried in the car.

You can turn right at a red light, unless otherwise indicated—but be sure to come to a complete stop first. Pedestrians always have the right-of-way.

Many California freeways have designated carpool lanes, also known as High Occupancy Vehicle (HOV) lanes or "diamond" lanes. Some require two passengers, others three. Most on-ramps are metered during even light congestion to regulate the flow of traffic onto the freeway; cars in HOV lanes can pass the signal without stopping. All other drivers are required to observe the stoplights—fines begin around $271.

CAR-RENTAL AGENCIES   California is one of the cheapest places in the United States to rent a car. The best-known firms, with locations throughout the state and at most major airports, include **Alamo** (☎ 800/327-9633), **Avis** (☎ 800/331-1212), **Budget** (☎ 800/527-0700), **Dollar** (☎ 800/421-6868), **Hertz** (☎ 800/654-3131), **National** (☎ 800/328-4567), and **Thrifty** (☎ 800/367-2277). Additional agencies, along with Web sites, are listed in Appendix B at the end of this book.

Many rental agencies have begun offering a variety of essential or just helpful extras, like cellular phones, child seats, and specially equipped vehicles for travelers with disabilities. Ask about additional fees when you make your reservation.

DEMYSTIFYING RENTER'S INSURANCE   Before you drive off in a rental car, be sure you're insured. Hasty assumptions about your personal auto insurance or a rental agency's additional coverage could end up costing you tens of thousands of dollars—even if you're involved in an accident that was clearly the fault of another driver.

If you already hold a **private auto insurance** policy, you are most likely covered in the United States for loss of or damage to a rental car, and liability in case of injury to any other party involved in an accident. Be sure to find out whether you're covered in the area you're visiting, whether your policy extends to all persons who will be driving the rental car, how much liability is covered in case an outside party is injured in an accident, and whether the type of vehicle you are renting is included under your contract. (Rental trucks, sport-utility vehicles, and luxury vehicles or sports cars may not be covered.)

Most **major credit cards** provide some degree of coverage as well—provided they were used to pay for the rental. Terms vary widely, however, so be sure to call your credit-card company directly before you rent.

If you're **uninsured,** your credit card may provide primary coverage as long as you decline the rental agency's insurance. This means that the credit card may cover damage or theft of a rental car for the full cost of the vehicle. (In a few states, however, theft is not covered; ask specifically about state law where you will be renting and driving.) If you already have insurance, your credit card may provide secondary coverage—which basically covers your deductible.

Credit cards **will not cover liability,** or the cost of injury to an outside party and/or damage to an outside party's vehicle. If you do not hold an insurance policy, you may seriously want to consider purchasing additional liability insurance from your rental company. Be sure to check the terms, however: Some rental agencies only cover liability if the renter is not at fault; even then, the rental company's obligation varies from state to state.

The basic insurance coverage offered by most car-rental companies, known as the **Loss/Damage Waiver (LDW)** or **Collision Damage Waiver (CDW),** can cost as much as $20 per day. It usually covers the full value of the vehicle with no deductible if an outside party causes an accident or other damage to the rental car. Liability

The *Coast Starlight:* All Aboard for Nostalgia

If you're traveling by rail along the California coast, extending as far north as Seattle, treat yourself to a ride aboard Amtrak's luxurious *Coast Starlight.* In an effort to recapture the glory days of 1940s Streamline luxury liners, Amtrak is pulling out all the stops on these double-decker Superliners, complete with gourmet dining car, first-class and coach lounge cars, standard and deluxe sleeping compartments, and enough diversions (including feature-length films, live entertainment, games for kids and adults, and a full bar) to make the overnight, 2-day trip a pleasure. All sleeping-car fares include three meals daily, prepared fresh on board with an emphasis on regional flavor—wines from vintners in Washington, Oregon, and California, as well as seasonal specials from along the *Coast Starlight's* route.

The highlight of the journey is the exceptional scenery you'll enjoy from the upper-level, panoramic windows of the coach and observation cars. Sweeping views of lushly green Washington State, California's rugged coastline, rural farmland, bucolic rolling hills, sparkling beaches, and charming railroad stations all provide a memorable travelogue. For travelers who believe the journey itself is as important as the destination, this excursion fits the bill perfectly.

While coach tickets are comparable to airplane fares, the surcharge for sleeping compartments adds considerably to the cost of the trip. All fares quoted are for one-way adult tickets. Children ages 2 to 15 travel for half price, and seniors 62 and older receive a 15% discount. Coach fare buys assigned seating in surprisingly comfortable upper-level reclining chairs. Blankets and pillows are offered in the evening, and fold-up leg rests help make sleeping more comfortable than you might imagine. Between San Francisco and Los Angeles, one-way adult coach fare ranges from $54 to $77; between Seattle and L.A., it's $102 to $170. Based on travel between Seattle and L.A., a standard sleeping compartment for two adds $255, a deluxe with private bathroom is $525, and a family sleeper for two adults and two kids (no bathroom) is $485.

It's advisable to book several months ahead for peak periods (summer, weekends, and holidays). Since the splendid views depend on daylight, also consider carefully before traveling during the very short days of winter. For information and tickets, call **Amtrak** (☎ **800/USA-RAIL**) or visit its special *Coast Starlight* Web site at **www.coaststarlight.com**.

coverage varies according to the company policy and state law, but the minimum is usually at least $15,000. If you are at fault in an accident, however, you will be covered for the full replacement value of the car but not for liability. Some states allow you to buy additional liability coverage for such cases. Most rental companies will require a police report in order to process any claims you file, but your private insurer will not be notified of the accident.

BY PLANE

In addition to the major carriers listed above in "Getting There," several smaller airlines provide service within the state, including **American Eagle** (☎ 800/433-7300), **Skywest** (☎ 800/453-9417), **Shuttle by United** (☎ 800/241-6522), and **US Airways Express** (☎ 800/428-4322). The round-trip fare between Los Angeles and San Francisco ranges from $79 to $200. See "Orientation" in each city's chapter for further information, and this book's Appendix B for a complete list of airlines serving California.

BY TRAIN

Amtrak (☎ **800/USA-RAIL;** www.amtrak.com) runs trains up and down the California coast, connecting San Diego, Los Angeles, and San Francisco and all points in between. There are multiple trains each day, and rates fluctuate according to season and special promotions. One-way fares for popular segments can range from $18 (Los Angeles–Santa Barbara) to $20 (Los Angeles–San Diego) to $85 (San Francisco–Los Angeles).

Fast Facts: California

Earthquakes   In the rare event of an earthquake, you should know about a few simple precautions that every California schoolchild is taught: If you're in a tall building, don't run outside; instead, move away from windows and toward the building's center. Crouch under a desk or table, or stand against a wall or under a doorway. If you're in bed, get under the bed or stand in a doorway, or crouch under a sturdy piece of furniture. When exiting the building, use stairwells, *not* elevators.

If you're in your car, pull over to the side of the road and stop, but wait until you're away from bridges or overpasses, as well as telephone or power poles and lines. Stay in your car.

If you're out walking, stay outside and away from trees, power lines, and the sides of buildings.

Emergencies   To reach the police, ambulance service, or fire department, dial ☎ **911.** No coins are needed at pay phones for 911 calls.

Liquor Laws   Liquor and grocery stores, as well as some drugstores, can legally sell packaged alcoholic beverages between 6am and 2am. Most restaurants, nightclubs, and bars are licensed to serve alcoholic beverages during the same hours. The legal age for the purchase and consumption of alcoholic beverages is 21; proof of age is strictly enforced.

Taxes   California's state sales tax is 7.25%. Some cities include an additional percentage, so tax varies throughout the state. Hotel taxes are almost always higher than tariffs levied on goods and services.

Time   California and the entire West Coast are in the Pacific time zone, 3 hours earlier than the East Coast.

For Foreign Visitors

3

by Matthew R. Poole

The pervasiveness of American culture around the world may make you feel that you know the United States pretty well, but leaving your own country still requires an additional degree of planning. This chapter will help prepare you for the more common problems that visitors to California may encounter.

1 Preparing for Your Trip

ENTRY REQUIREMENTS

Immigration laws are a hot political issue in the United States these days, and the following requirements may have changed somewhat by the time you plan your trip. Check at any U.S. embassy or consulate for current information and requirements. You can also plug into the **U.S. State Department's** Web site at **www.state.gov**.

VISAS The U.S. State Department has a **Visa Waiver Pilot Program** allowing citizens of certain countries to enter the United States without a visa for stays of up to 90 days. At press time these included Andorra, Argentina, Australia, Austria, Belgium, Brunei, Denmark, Finland, France, Germany, Iceland, Ireland, Italy, Japan, Liechtenstein, Luxembourg, Monaco, the Netherlands, New Zealand, Norway, San Marino, Slovenia, Spain, Sweden, Switzerland, and the United Kingdom. Citizens of these countries need only a valid passport and a round-trip air or cruise ticket in their possession upon arrival. If they first enter the United States, they may also visit Mexico, Canada, Bermuda, and/or the Caribbean islands and return to the United States without a visa. Further information is available from any U.S. embassy or consulate. Canadian citizens may enter the United States without visas; they need only proof of residence.

Citizens of all other countries must have (1) a valid passport that expires at least 6 months later than the scheduled end of their visit to the United States, and (2) a tourist visa, which may be obtained without charge from any U.S. consulate.

To obtain a visa, the traveler must submit a completed application form (either in person or by mail) with a 1½-inch-square photo, and must demonstrate binding ties to a residence abroad. Usually you can get a visa at once or within 24 hours, but it may take longer during the summer rush from June through August. If you cannot go in person, contact the nearest U.S. embassy or consulate for directions on applying by mail. Your travel agent or airline office may also be able to provide you with visa applications and instructions. The U.S. consulate or embassy that issues your visa will determine whether you will be issued a multiple- or single-entry visa and any restrictions regarding the length of your stay.

British subjects can obtain up-to-date passport and visa information by calling the **U.S. Embassy Visa Information Line** (☎ 0891/200-290) or the **London Passport Office** (☎ 0990/210-410 for recorded information).

IMMIGRATION QUESTIONS   Telephone operators will answer your inquiries regarding U.S. immigration policies or laws at the **Immigration and Naturalization Service's Customer Information Center** (☎ 800/375-5283). Representatives are available from 9am to 3pm, Monday through Friday. The INS also runs a 24-hour automated information service, for commonly asked questions, at ☎ **800/755-0777.**

MEDICAL REQUIREMENTS   Unless you're arriving from an area known to be suffering from an epidemic (particularly cholera or yellow fever), inoculations or vaccinations are not required for entry into the United States. If you have a disease that requires treatment with narcotics or syringe-administered medications, carry a valid signed prescription from your physician to allay any suspicions that you may be smuggling narcotics (a serious offense that carries severe penalties in the United States).

For HIV-positive visitors, requirements for entering the United States are somewhat vague and change frequently. According to the latest publication of *HIV and Immigrants: A Manual for AIDS Service Providers,* although INS doesn't require a medical exam for every one trying to come into the United States, INS officials may keep out people who they suspect are HIV positive. INS may stop people because they look sick or because they are carrying AIDS/HIV medicine.

If an HIV-positive noncitizen applying for a non-immigrant visa knows that HIV is a communicable disease of public health significance but checks "No" on the question about communicable diseases, INS may deny the visa because it thinks the applicant committed fraud. If a non-immigrant visa applicant checks "Yes," or if INS suspects the person is HIV positive, it will deny the visa unless the applicant asks for a special waiver for visitors. This waiver is for people visiting the United States for a short time, to attend a conference, for instance, to visit close relatives, or to receive medical treatment. It can be a confusing situation, so for up-to-the-minute information concerning HIV-positive travelers, contact the Center for Disease Control's **National Center for HIV** (☎ 404/332-4559; www.hivatis.org) or the **Gay Men's Health Crisis** (☎ 212/367-1000; www.gmhc.org).

DRIVER'S LICENSES   Foreign driver's licenses are recognized in California, although you may want to get an international driver's license if your home license is not written in English.

PASSPORTS   Safeguard your passport in an inconspicuous, inaccessible place like a money belt. If you lose it, visit the nearest consulate of your native country as soon as possible for a replacement. Passport applications are downloadable from the Internet sites listed below.

For Residents of the United States   If you're applying for a first-time passport, you need to do it in person at one of 13 passport offices throughout the United States; a federal, state, or probate court; or a major post office (though not all post offices accept applications; call the number below to find the ones that do). You'll need to present a certified birth certificate as proof of citizenship, and it's wise to bring along your driver's license, state or military ID, and Social Security card as well. You'll also need two identical passport-sized photos (2 in. by 2 in.), taken at any corner photo shop (not one of the strip photos, however, from a photo-vending machine).

For people over 15, a passport is valid for 10 years and costs $60 ($45 plus a $15 handling fee); for those 15 and under, it's valid for 5 years and costs $40. If you're over 15 and have a valid passport that was issued within the past 12 years, you can renew it by mail and bypass the $15 handling fee. Allow plenty of time before your trip to apply; processing normally takes 3 weeks but can take longer during busy periods (especially spring). For general information, call the **National Passport Agency** (☎ 202/647-0518). To find your regional passport office, call the **National Passport Information Center** (☎ 900/225-5674; http://travel.state.gov).

For Residents of Canada   You can pick up a passport application at one of 28 regional passport offices or most travel agencies. The passport is valid for 5 years and costs $60. Children under 16 may be included on a parent's passport but need their own to travel unaccompanied by the parent. Applications, which must be accompanied by two identical passport-sized photographs and proof of Canadian citizenship, are available at travel agencies throughout Canada or from the central **Passport Office, Department of Foreign Affairs and International Trade,** Ottawa K1A 0G3 (☎ 800/567-6868; www.dfait-maeci.gc.ca/passport). Processing takes 5 to 10 days if you apply in person, or about 3 weeks by mail.

For Residents of the United Kingdom   To pick up an application for a regular 10-year passport (the Visitor's Passport has been abolished), visit your nearest passport office, major post office, or travel agency. You can also contact the **London Passport Office** at ☎ 0171/271-3000 or search its Web site at www.open.gov.uk/ukpass/ukpass.htm. Passports are £21 for adults and £11 for children under 16.

For Residents of Ireland   You can apply for a 10-year passport, costing IR£45, at the Passport Office, Setanta Centre, Molesworth Street, Dublin 2 (☎ 01/671-1633; www.irlgov.ie/iveagh/foreignaffairs/services). Those under age 18 and over 65 must apply for a IR£10 3-year passport. You can also apply at 1A South Mall, Cork (☎ 021/272-525), or over the counter at most main post offices.

For Residents of Australia   Apply at your local post office or passport office or search the government Web site at www.dfat.gov.au/passports. Passports for adults are A$126 and for those under 18 A$63.

For Residents of New Zealand   You can pick up a passport application at any travel agency or Link Centre. For more info, contact the Passport Office, P.O. Box 805, Wellington (☎ 0800/225-050). Passports for adults are NZ$80 and for those under 16, NZ$40.

CUSTOMS

WHAT YOU CAN BRING IN   Every visitor over 21 years of age may bring in, free of duty, the following: (1) 1 liter of wine or hard liquor; (2) 200 cigarettes, 100 cigars (but not from Cuba), or 3 pounds of smoking tobacco; and (3) $100 worth of gifts. These exemptions are offered to travelers who spend at least 72 hours in the United States and who have not claimed them within the preceding 6 months. It is altogether forbidden to bring into the country foodstuffs (particularly fruit, cooked meats, and canned goods) and plants (vegetables, seeds, tropical plants, and the like). Foreign tourists may bring in or take out up to $10,000 in U.S. or foreign currency with no formalities; larger sums must be declared to U.S. Customs on entering or leaving, which includes filing form CM 4790. For more specific information regarding U.S. Customs, call your nearest U.S. embassy or consulate, call **U.S. Customs** (☎ 202/927-1770), or see the Web site at **www.customs.ustreas.gov**.

WHAT YOU CAN BRING HOME   **U.K. citizens** returning from a non-EC country have a customs allowance of 200 cigarettes; 50 cigars; 250g of smoking tobacco; 2 liters of still table wine; 1 liter of spirits or strong liqueurs (over 22% volume); 2 liters of fortified wine, sparkling wine or other liqueurs; 60cc (ml) perfume; 250cc (ml) of toilet water; and £145 worth of all other goods, including gifts and souvenirs. People under 17 cannot have the tobacco or alcohol allowance. For more information, contact HM Customs & Excise, Passenger Enquiry Point, 2nd Floor Wayfarer House, Great South West Road, Feltham, Middlesex, TW14 8NP (☎ **0181/910-3744;** from outside the U.K. 44/181-910-3744), or consult the Web site at **www.open.gov.uk**.

For a clear summary of **Canadian** rules, write for the booklet *I Declare,* issued by **Revenue Canada,** 2265 St. Laurent Blvd., Ottawa K1G 4KE (☎ **613/993-0534**). Canada allows its citizens a $500 exemption, and you're allowed to bring back duty-free 200 cigarettes, 2.2 pounds of tobacco, 40 imperial ounces of liquor, and 50 cigars. In addition, you're allowed to mail gifts to Canada from abroad at the rate of Can$60 a day, provided they're unsolicited and don't contain alcohol or tobacco (write on the package "Unsolicited gift, under $60 value"). All valuables should be declared on the Y-38 form before departure from Canada, including serial numbers of valuables you already own, such as expensive foreign cameras. *Note:* The $500 exemption can only be used once a year and only after an absence of 7 days.

The duty-free allowance in **Australia** is A$400 or, for those under 18, A$200. Personal property mailed home should be marked "Australian goods returned" to avoid payment of duty. Upon returning to Australia, citizens can bring in 250 cigarettes or 250 grams of loose tobacco, and 1,125ml of alcohol. If you're returning with valuable goods you already own, such as foreign-made cameras, you should file form B263. A helpful brochure, available from Australian consulates or Customs offices, is *Know Before You Go.* For more information, contact **Australian Customs Services,** GPO Box 8, Sydney NSW 2001 (☎ **02/9213-2000**).

The duty-free allowance for **New Zealand** is NZ$700. Citizens over 17 can bring in 200 cigarettes, or 50 cigars, or 250 grams of tobacco (or a mixture of all three if their combined weight doesn't exceed 250 grams); plus 4.5 liters of wine and beer, or 1.125 liters of liquor. New Zealand currency does not carry import or export restrictions. Fill out a certificate of export, listing the valuables you are taking out of the country; that way, you can bring them back without paying duty. Most questions are answered in a free pamphlet available at New Zealand consulates and Customs offices: *New Zealand Customs Guide for Travellers, Notice no. 4.* For more information, contact New Zealand Customs, 50 Anzac Ave., P.O. Box 29, Auckland (☎ **09/359-6655**).

INSURANCE

Although it's not required of travelers, health insurance is highly recommended. Unlike many European countries, the United States does not usually offer free or low-cost medical care to its citizens or visitors. Doctors and hospitals are expensive, and in most cases will require advance payment or proof of coverage before they render their services. Policies can cover everything from the loss or theft of your baggage and trip cancellation to the guarantee of bail in case you're arrested. Good policies will also cover the costs of an accident, repatriation, or death. Packages such as **Europ Assistance** in Europe are sold by automobile clubs and travel agencies at attractive rates. **Worldwide Assistance Services, Inc.** (☎ **800/821-2828**) is the agent for Europ Assistance in the United States.

Though lack of health insurance may prevent you from being admitted to a hospital in non-emergencies, don't worry about being left on a street corner to die: The American way is to fix you now and bill the living daylights out of you later.

British travelers will notice that most big travel agents offer their own insurance, which they'll probably try to sell you when you book a holiday. Think before you sign. Britain's Consumers' Association recommends that you insist on seeing the policy and reading the fine print before buying travel insurance. The **Association of British Insurers** (☎ **0171/600-3333**) gives advice by phone and publishes the free *Holiday Insurance,* a guide to policy provisions and prices. You might also shop around for better deals: Try **Columbus Travel Insurance Ltd.** (☎ **0171/375-0011**) or, for students, **Campus Travel** (☎ **0171/730-2101**).

Canadians should check with their provincial health plan offices or call **Health-Canada** (☎ **613/957-2991**) to find out the extent of their coverage and what documentation and receipts they must take home in case they are treated in the United States.

MONEY

CURRENCY   The U.S. monetary system is painfully simple: The most common bills (all ugly, all green) are the $1 (colloquially, a "buck"), $5, $10, and $20 denominations. There are also $2 bills (seldom encountered), $50 bills, and $100 bills (the last two are usually not welcome as payment for small purchases). Note that a newly redesigned $100 and $50 bill were introduced in 1996, and a redesigned $20 bill in 1998. Expect to see redesigned $10 and $5 notes in the year 2000. Despite rumors to the contrary, the old-style bills are still legal tender.

There are six denominations of coins: 1¢ (1 cent, or a penny), 5¢ (5 cents, or a nickel), 10¢ (10 cents, or a dime), 25¢ (25 cents, or a quarter), 50¢ (50 cents, or a half dollar), and, prized by collectors, the rare $1 piece (the older, large silver dollar and the newer, small Susan B. Anthony coin). A new gold $1 piece will be introduced by the year 2000.

Note: The "foreign-exchange bureaus" so common in Europe are rare even at airports in the United States, and nonexistent outside major cities. It's best not to change foreign money (or traveler's checks denominated in a currency other than U.S. dollars) at a small-town bank, or even a branch in a big city; in fact, leave any currency other than U.S. dollars at home—it may prove a greater nuisance to you than it's worth.

TRAVELER'S CHECKS   Though traveler's checks are widely accepted, make sure that they're denominated in U.S. dollars, as foreign-currency checks are often difficult to exchange. The three traveler's checks that are most widely recognized—and least likely to be denied—are **Visa, American Express,** and **Thomas Cook.** Be sure to record the numbers of the checks, and keep that information separately in case they get lost or stolen. Most California businesses are pretty good about taking traveler's checks, but you're better off cashing them in at a bank (in small amounts, of course) and paying in cash. *Remember:* You'll need identification, such as a driver's license or passport, to change a traveler's check.

CREDIT CARDS & ATMs   Credit cards are the most widely used form of payment in the United States: **Visa** (BarclayCard in Britain), **MasterCard** (EuroCard in Europe, Access in Britain, Chargex in Canada), **American Express, Diners Club, Discover,** and **Carte Blanche.** You must have a credit or charge card to rent a car. There are a handful of stores and restaurants in California that do not take credit cards, however, so be sure to ask in advance. Most businesses display a sticker near their entrance to let you know which cards they accept. (*Note:* Often businesses require a minimum purchase price, usually around $10, to use a credit card.)

It is strongly recommended that you bring at least one major credit card. Hotels, car-rental companies, and airlines usually require a credit-card imprint as a deposit against expenses, and in an emergency a credit card can be priceless.

You'll find automated teller machines (ATMs) on just about every block—at least in almost every town—in California and across the country. Some ATMs will allow you to draw U.S. currency against your bank and credit cards. Check with your bank before leaving home, and remember that you will need your personal identification number (PIN) to do so. Most accept Visa, MasterCard, and American Express, as well as ATM cards from other U.S. banks. Expect to be charged up to $3 per transaction, however, if you're not using your own bank's ATM. *Tip:* One way around these fees is to ask for cash back at grocery stores that accept ATM cards and don't charge usage fees. Of course, you'll have to purchase something first.

MONEYGRAMS   If the proverbial poop hits the fan, you can also have someone wire money to you very quickly via Western Union. There are numerous offices throughout California; call ☎ **800/325-6000** for the one nearest you.

SAFETY

GENERAL SAFETY   While tourist areas in California are generally safe, crime is on the increase everywhere, and U.S. urban areas tend to be less safe than those in Europe or Japan. You should always stay alert. This is particularly true of large U.S. cities. It's wise to ask your hotel front desk staff or the city's or area's tourist office if you're in doubt about which neighborhoods are safe.

Avoid deserted areas, especially at night, and don't go into public parks at night unless there's a concert or similar occasion that will attract a crowd.

Avoid carrying valuables with you on the street, and don't display expensive cameras or electronic equipment. If you're using a map, consult it inconspicuously—or better yet, try to study it before you leave your room. Hold on to your pocketbook, and place your billfold in an inside pocket. In theaters, restaurants, and other public places, keep your possessions in sight.

Remember also that hotels are open to the public, and in a large hotel, security may not be able to screen everyone entering. Always lock your room door—don't assume that once inside your hotel you are automatically safe and no longer need to be aware of your surroundings.

DRIVING SAFETY   Driving safety is important, too, especially given the highly publicized carjackings of foreign tourists in Florida. Question your rental agency about personal safety and ask for a traveler-safety brochure when you pick up your car. Obtain written directions—or a map with the route clearly marked—from the agency showing how to get to your destination. (Many agencies now offer the option of renting a cellular phone for the duration of your car rental; check with the rental agent when you pick up the car.) And, if possible, arrive and depart during daylight hours.

Recently, more and more crime has involved cars and drivers. If you drive off a highway into a doubtful neighborhood, leave the area as quickly as possible. If you have an accident, even on the highway, stay in your car with the doors locked until you assess the situation or until the police arrive. If you're bumped from behind on the street or are involved in a minor accident with no injuries and the situation appears to be suspicious, motion to the other driver to follow you. Never get out of your car in such situations. Go directly to the nearest police precinct, well-lit service station, or 24-hour store.

Always try to park in well-lit and well-traveled areas if possible. If you leave your rental car unlocked and empty of your valuables, you're probably safer than locking your car with valuables in plain view. Never leave any packages or valuables in sight. If someone attempts to rob you or steal your car, don't try to resist the thief/carjacker—report the incident to the police department immediately by calling ☎ **911.**

2 Getting to the U.S.

Visitors arriving by air, no matter what the port of entry, should cultivate patience and resignation before setting foot on U.S. soil. Getting through immigration control may take as long as 2 hours on some days, especially on summer weekends, so be sure to have this guidebook or something else to read handy. Add the time it takes to clear Customs, and you'll see that you should make a 2- to 3-hour allowance for delays when you plan your connections between international and domestic flights.

In contrast, for the traveler arriving by car or rail from Canada, the border-crossing formalities have been streamlined to the vanishing point. People traveling by air from Canada, Bermuda, and some places in the Caribbean can sometimes clear Customs and Immigration at the point of departure, which is much quicker.

AIRLINES

See "Getting There," in chapter 2, for tips on finding the best airfare. Overseas visitors can also take advantage of the APEX (Advance Purchase Excursion) reductions offered by all major U.S. and European carriers. Refer also to Appendix B, at the back of this book, for a list of airlines' phone numbers and Web sites.

FROM THE UNITED KINGDOM & IRELAND   Many airlines offer service from the United Kingdom or Ireland to the United States. If possible, try to book a direct flight. Airlines that offer direct flights from London include British Airways, United, and Virgin. Airlines that do not have direct flights from London to Los Angeles or San Francisco can book you straight through on a connecting flight. You can make reservations by calling the following numbers in London: **American Airlines** (☎ 0181/572-5555), **British Airways** (☎ 0345/222-111), **Continental Airlines** (☎ 0293/776-464), **Delta Air Lines** (☎ 0800/414-767), **United Airlines** (☎ 0181/990-9900), and **Virgin Atlantic** (☎ 01293/747-747).

Residents of Ireland can call **Aer Lingus** (☎ 01/844-4747 in Dublin or 061/415-556 in Shannon).

FROM AUSTRALIA & NEW ZEALAND   **Qantas** (☎ 008/177-767 in Australia) has direct flights from Sydney to Los Angeles and San Francisco. You can also take **United** (☎ 02/237-8888 in Sydney, 008/230-322 in the rest of Australia) from Australia to Los Angeles and San Francisco.

Air New Zealand (☎ 0800/737-000 in Auckland or 643/379-5200 in Christchurch) offers service to Los Angeles International Airport.

FROM CANADA   Canadian readers might also consider **Air Canada** (☎ 800/268-7240, or 800/361-8620 in Canada), which offers direct service from Toronto, Montreal, Calgary, and Vancouver to San Francisco, Sacramento, Los Angeles, and San Diego. Many American carriers also offer similar routes.

3 Getting Around the U.S.

BY PLANE   Some large airlines (for example, Northwest and Delta) offer travelers on their transatlantic or transpacific flights special discount tickets under the name **Visit USA,** allowing mostly one-way travel from one U.S. destination to another at very low prices. These discount tickets are not sold in the United States and must be purchased abroad in conjunction with your international ticket. This system is the best, easiest, and fastest way to see the United States at low cost. You should get information well in advance from your travel agent or the office of the airline concerned, since the conditions attached to these discount tickets can be changed without advance notice.

BY TRAIN   International visitors can also buy a **USA Railpass,** good for 15 or 30 days of unlimited travel on Amtrak (☎ 800/USA-RAIL). The pass is available through many foreign travel agents. Prices at press time for a 15-day pass are $285 off-peak, $425 peak; a 30-day pass costs $375 off-peak, $535 peak. (With a foreign pass-port, you can also buy passes at some Amtrak offices in the United States, including locations in San Francisco, Los Angeles, Chicago, New York, Miami, Boston, and Washington, D.C.) Reservations are generally required and should be made for each part of your trip as early as possible.

BY BUS   Although bus travel is often the most economical form of public transit for short hops between U.S. cities, it can also be slow and uncomfortable—certainly not an option for everyone (particularly when Amtrak, which is far more luxurious, offers similar rates). **Greyhound/Trailways** (☎ 800/231-2222), the sole nationwide bus line, offers an **Ameripass** for unlimited travel for 7 days at $199, 15 days at $299, 30 days at $409, and 60 days at $599. Passes must be purchased at a Greyhound terminal. Special rates are available for seniors and students.

BY CAR   The most cost-effective, convenient, and comfortable way to travel around the United States—especially California—is by car. The Interstate highway system con-nects cities and towns all over the country; in addition to these high-speed, limited-access roadways, there's an extensive network of federal, state, and local highways and roads. California has no toll roads, but it does charge a toll fee at many major bridges. Some of the national car-rental companies that have offices in California include **Alamo** (☎ 800/327-9633), **Avis** (☎ 800/331-1212), **Budget** (☎ 800/527-0700), **Dollar** (☎ 800/800-4000), **Hertz** (☎ 800/654-3131), **National** (☎ 800/227-7368), and **Thrifty** (☎ 800/367-2277).

If you plan on renting a car in the United States, you probably won't need the ser-vices of an additional automobile organization. If you're planning to buy or borrow a car, automobile-association membership is recommended. **AAA,** the **American Auto-mobile Association** (☎ 800/222-4357), is the country's largest auto club and sup-plies its members with maps, insurance, and, most important, emergency road service. The cost of joining runs from $63 for singles to $87 for two members, but if you're a member of a foreign auto club with reciprocal arrangements, you can enjoy free AAA service in America. See "Getting There" in chapter 2 for more information.

Fast Facts: For the Foreign Traveler

Automobile Organizations   Auto clubs will supply maps, suggested routes, guidebooks, accident and bail-bond insurance, and emergency road service. The **American Automobile Association (AAA)** is the major auto club in the United States. If you belong to an auto club in your home country, inquire about AAA reciprocity before you leave. You may be able to join AAA even if you're not a member of a reciprocal club; to inquire, call AAA (☎ 800/222-4357). AAA is actually an organization of regional auto clubs, so look under "AAA Automobile Club" in the White Pages of the phone directory. The San Francisco AAA head-quarters is at 150 Van Ness Ave., San Francisco, CA 94102; (☎ 800/922-8228). AAA's nationwide emergency road service telephone number is ☎ 800/ AAA-HELP.

Business Hours   Offices are usually open Monday through Friday from 9am to 5pm. Banks are open Monday through Friday from 9am to 3pm or later and sometimes Saturday mornings. Stores, especially those in shopping complexes, tend to stay open late: until about 9pm on weekdays and 6pm on weekends.

Currency & Currency Exchange   See "Entry Requirements" and "Money" under "Preparing for Your Trip," above.

Drinking Laws   The legal age for purchase and consumption of alcoholic beverages is 21; proof of age is required and often requested at bars, nightclubs, and restaurants, so it's always a good idea to bring ID when you go out. In California, liquor is sold in supermarkets and grocery and liquor stores daily from 6am to 2am. Licensed restaurants are permitted to sell alcohol during the same hours. Note that many eateries are licensed only for beer and wine.

Do not carry open containers of alcohol in your car or any public area that isn't zoned for alcohol consumption (and very few exist in California). The police can, and probably will, fine you on the spot. And nothing will ruin your trip faster than getting a citation for DUI ("driving under the influence"), so don't even think about driving while intoxicated.

Electricity   Like Canada, the United States uses 110 to 120 volts AC (60 cycles), compared to 220 to 240 volts AC (50 cycles) in most of Europe, Australia, and New Zealand. If your small appliances use 220 to 240 volts, you'll need a 110-volt transformer and a plug adapter with two flat parallel pins to operate them here. Downward converters that change 220 to 240 volts to 110 to 120 volts are difficult to find in the United States, so bring one with you.

Embassies & Consulates   All embassies are located in the nation's capital, Washington, D.C. Some consulates are located in major U.S. cities, and most nations have a mission to the United Nations in New York City. If your country isn't listed below, call for directory information in Washington, D.C. (☎ 202/ 555-1212) for the number of your national embassy.

The embassy of **Australia** is at 1601 Massachusetts Ave. NW, Washington, DC 20036 (☎ 202/797-3000; www.austemb.org). There are consulates in New York, Honolulu, Houston, Los Angeles, and San Francisco.

The embassy of **Canada** is at 501 Pennsylvania Ave. NW, Washington, DC 20001 (☎ 202/682-1740; www.cdnemb-washdc.org). Other Canadian consulates are in Buffalo (NY), Detroit, Los Angeles, New York, and Seattle.

The embassy of **Ireland** is at 2234 Massachusetts Ave. NW, Washington, DC 20008 (☎ 202/462-3939). Irish consulates are in Boston, Chicago, New York, and San Francisco.

The embassy of **Japan** is at 2520 Massachusetts Ave. NW, Washington, DC 20008 (☎ 202/238-6700; www.embjapan.org). Japanese consulates are located in Atlanta, Kansas City, San Francisco, and Washington D.C.

The embassy of **New Zealand** is at 37 Observatory Circle NW, Washington, DC 20008 (☎ 202/328-4800; www.emb.com/nzemb). New Zealand consulates are in Los Angeles, Salt Lake City, San Francisco, and Seattle.

The embassy of the **United Kingdom** is at 3100 Massachusetts Ave. NW, Washington, DC 20008 (☎ 202/462-1340). Other British consulates are in Atlanta, Boston, Chicago, Cleveland, Houston, Los Angeles, New York, San Francisco, and Seattle.

Emergencies   Call ☎ 911 to report a fire, call the police, or get an ambulance anywhere in the United States. This is a toll-free call (no coins are required at public telephones).

If you encounter traveler's problems, check the local telephone directory to find an office of the **Traveler's Aid Society,** a nationwide, nonprofit, social-service organization geared to helping travelers in difficult straits. Its services might include reuniting families separated while traveling, providing food and/or shelter to people stranded without cash, or even emotional counseling. If you're in trouble, seek them out.

Gasoline (Petrol)   Petrol is known as gasoline (or simply "gas") in the United States, and petrol stations are known as both gas stations and service stations. Gasoline costs about half as much here as it does in Europe (about $1.55 per gallon in California at press time, though it's supposed come down a bit), and taxes are already included in the printed price. One U.S. gallon equals 3.8 liters or .85 Imperial gallons.

Holidays   Banks, government offices, post offices, and many stores, restaurants, and museums are closed on the following legal national holidays: January 1 (New Year's Day), the third Monday in January (Martin Luther King, Jr. Day), the third Monday in February (Presidents' Day, Washington's Birthday), the last Monday in May (Memorial Day), July 4 (Independence Day), the first Monday in September (Labor Day), the second Monday in October (Columbus Day), November 11 (Veterans' Day/Armistice Day), the fourth Thursday in November (Thanksgiving Day), and December 25 (Christmas). Also, the Tuesday following the first Monday in November is Election Day and is a federal government holiday in presidential-election years (held every 4 years, and next in 2000).

Legal Aid   The foreign tourist will probably never become involved with the American legal system. If you are "pulled over" for a minor infraction (for example, of the highway code, such as speeding), never attempt to pay the fine directly to a police officer; this could be construed as attempted bribery, a much more serious crime. Pay fines by mail, or directly into the hands of the clerk of the court. If accused of a more serious offense, say and do nothing before consulting a lawyer. Here the burden is on the state to prove a person's guilt beyond a reasonable doubt, and everyone has the right to remain silent, whether he or she is suspected of a crime or actually arrested. Once arrested, a person can make one telephone call to a party of his or her choice. Call your embassy or consulate.

Mail   If you aren't sure what your address will be in the United States, mail can be sent to you, in your name, c/o General Delivery at the main post office of the city or region where you expect to be (call ☎ **800/275-8777** for information on the nearest post office). The addressee must pick mail up in person and must produce proof of identity (driver's license, passport, etc.). Most post offices will hold your mail for up to 1 month, and are open Monday through Friday from 8am to 6pm, and Saturday from 9am to 3pm.

Generally found at intersections, mailboxes are blue with a red-and-white stripe and carry the inscription U.S. MAIL. If your mail is addressed to a U.S. destination, don't forget to add the five-digit postal code (or zip code) after the two-letter abbreviation of the state to which the mail is addressed (CA for California).

At press time, domestic postage rates are 20¢ for a postcard and 33¢ for a letter. For international mail, a first-class letter of up to one-half ounce costs 60¢ (46¢ to Canada and 40¢ to Mexico); a first-class postcard costs 50¢ (40¢ to Canada and 35¢ Mexico); and a preprinted postal aerogramme costs 50¢.

Smoking   Heavy smokers are in for a tough time in California. There is no smoking allowed in public buildings, sports arenas, elevators, theaters, banks, lobbies, restaurants, offices, stores, bed-and-breakfasts, most small hotels, and bars. Yes, that's right, you can't even smoke in a bar in California—the only exception being a bar where drinks are served solely by the owner of the establishment.

Taxes   In the United States, there is no value-added tax (VAT) or other indirect tax at the national level. Every state, county, and city has the right to levy its own local tax on all purchases (which can vary from 4% to 10%), including hotel and restaurant checks, airport tax, and so on.

Telephone, Telegraph, Telex & Fax   The telephone system in the United States is run by private corporations, so rates, especially for long-distance service and operator-assisted calls, can vary widely. Generally, hotel surcharges on long-distance and local calls are astronomical, so you're usually better off using a **public pay telephone,** which you'll find clearly marked in most public buildings and private establishments as well as on the street. Convenience grocery stores and gas stations always have them. Many convenience groceries and packaging services sell **prepaid calling cards** in denominations up to $50; these can be the least expensive way to call home. Many public phones at airports now accept American Express, MasterCard, and Visa. **Local calls** made from public pay phones in most locales cost 35¢. Pay phones do not accept pennies, and few will take anything larger than a quarter

Most long-distance and international calls can be dialed directly from any phone. **For calls within the United States and to Canada,** dial 1 followed by the area code and the seven-digit number. **For other international calls,** dial 011 followed by the country code, city code, and the telephone number of the person you are calling.

Calls to area codes **800, 888,** and **877** are toll-free. However, calls to numbers in area codes **700** and **900** (chat lines, bulletin boards, "dating" services, and so on) can be very expensive—usually a charge of 95¢ to $3 or more per minute, and they sometimes have minimum charges that can run as high as $15 or more.

For reversed-charge or collect calls, and for person-to-person calls, dial 0 (zero, not the letter O) followed by the area code and number you want; an operator will then come on the line, and you should specify that you are calling collect, or person-to-person, or both. If your operator-assisted call is international, ask for the overseas operator.

For local directory assistance ("information"), dial ☎ 411; for long-distance information, dial 1, then the appropriate area code and 555-1212.

Telegraph and telex services are provided primarily by Western Union. You can bring your telegram into the nearest Western Union office (there are hundreds across the country) or dictate it over the phone (☎ **800/325-6000**). You can also telegraph money or have it telegraphed to you, very quickly over the Western Union system, but this service can cost as much as 15% to 20% of the amount sent.

Most hotels have **fax machines** available for guest use (be sure to ask about the charge to use it), and many hotel rooms are even wired for guests' fax machines. A less-expensive way to send and receive faxes may be at stores such as Mail Boxes, Etc., a national chain of packing service shops (look in the Yellow Pages directory under "Packing Services").

There are two kinds of telephone directories in the United States. The so-called **White Pages** lists private households and business subscribers in alphabetic order. The inside front cover lists emergency numbers for police, fire, ambulance, the Coast Guard, poison-control center, crime-victims hotline, and so on. The first few pages will tell you how to make long-distance and international calls, complete with country codes and area codes. Government numbers are usually printed on blue paper within the White Pages. Printed on yellow paper, the so-called **Yellow Pages** lists all local services, businesses, industries, and houses of worship according to activity with an index at the front or back. (Drugstores/pharmacies and restaurants are also listed by geographic location.) The Yellow Pages also includes city plans or detailed area maps, postal zip codes, and public transportation routes.

Time　The continental United States is divided into **four time zones:** eastern standard time (EST), central standard time (CST), mountain standard time (MST), and Pacific standard time (PST). Alaska and Hawaii have their own zones. For example, noon in New York City (EST) is 11am in Chicago (CST), 10am in Denver (MST), 9am in Los Angeles (PST), 8am in Anchorage (AST), and 7am in Honolulu (HST). All of California is on Pacific standard time, which is 8 hours behind Greenwich mean time.

Daylight saving time is in effect from 1am on the first Sunday in April through 1am the last Sunday in October, except in Arizona, Hawaii, part of Indiana, and Puerto Rico. Daylight saving time moves the clock 1 hour ahead of standard time.

Tipping　Tipping is so ingrained in the American way of life that the annual income tax of tip-earning service personnel is based on how much they should have received in light of their employers' gross revenues. Accordingly, they may have to pay tax on a tip you didn't actually give them.

Here are some rules of thumb:

In hotels, tip **bellhops** at least $1 per bag ($2 to $3 if you have a lot of luggage) and tip the **chamber staff** $1 to $2 per day (more if you've left a disaster area for him or her to clean up, or if you're traveling with kids and/or pets). Tip the **doorman** or **concierge** only if he or she has provided you with some specific service (for example, calling a cab for you or obtaining difficult-to-get theater tickets). Tip the **valet-parking attendant** $1 every time you get your car.

In restaurants, bars, and nightclubs, tip **service staff** 15% to 20% of the check, tip **bartenders** 10% to 15%, tip **checkroom attendants** $1 per garment, and tip **valet-parking attendants** $1 per vehicle. Tip the **doorman** only if he has provided you with some specific service (such as calling a cab for you). Tipping is not expected in cafeterias and fast-food restaurants.

Tip **cab drivers** 15% of the fare.

As for other service personnel, tip **skycaps** at airports at least $1 per bag ($2 to $3 if you have a lot of luggage) and tip **hairdressers** and **barbers** 15% to 20%.

Tipping ushers at movies and theaters, and gas-station attendants, is not expected.

Toilets　You won't find public toilets or "rest rooms" on the streets in most U.S. cities (though San Francisco is experimenting with French-style public toilets), but they can be found in hotel lobbies, bars, restaurants, museums, department stores, railway and bus stations, and service stations. Note, however, that restaurants and bars in resorts or heavily visited areas may reserve their rest rooms for the use of their patrons. Some establishments display a notice that toilets are for the use of patrons only. You can ignore this sign or, better yet, avoid arguments by paying for a cup of coffee or a soft drink, which will qualify you as a patron. Large hotels and fast-food restaurants are probably the best bet for good, clean facilities. If possible, avoid the toilets at parks and beaches, which tend to be dirty.

San Francisco   4

by Erika Lenkert

Consistently rated one of the top tourist destinations in the world, San Francisco abounds in multiple dimensions. Its famous, thrilling streets go up, and they go down; its multifarious citizens—and their adopted cultures, architectures, and cuisines—hail from San Antonio to Singapore; and its politics range from hyper-liberalism to an ever-encroaching wave of conservatism. Even something as mundane as fog takes on a new dimension as it creeps from the ocean and slowly envelops San Francisco in a resplendent blanket of mist.

In a city so multifaceted, so enamored with itself, it's hard not to find what you're looking for. Feel the cool blast of salt air as you stroll across the Golden Gate. Stuff yourself on dim sum in Chinatown. Browse the Haight for incense and crystals. Walk along the beach, pierce your nose, see a play, rent a Harley—the list is endless. It's all happening in San Francisco, and everyone's invited.

1 Orientation

ARRIVING
BY PLANE
Two major airports serve the Bay Area: San Francisco International and Oakland International. All the major car-rental companies have desks at the airports; see "Getting Around," below, for details on car rentals. For a list of airlines, including toll-free phone numbers and Web sites, see Appendix B at the back of this book.

SAN FRANCISCO INTERNATIONAL AIRPORT San Francisco International Airport, located 14 miles south of downtown directly on U.S. 101, is served by almost four dozen major scheduled carriers. Travel time to downtown during commuter rush hours is about 40 minutes; at other times it's about 20 to 25 minutes.

The airport offers a toll-free hot line available Monday through Friday from 7am to 5pm (PST) for information on ground transportation (☎ 800/736-2008). The line is answered by a real person who will provide you with a rundown of all your options for getting into the city from the airport. Each of the three main terminals also has a desk where you can get the same information.

A cab from the airport to downtown will cost $28 to $32, plus tip. **SFO Airporter** buses (☎415/495-8404) depart from outside the lower-level baggage-claim area to downtown San Francisco every 15 to 30 minutes from 6:15am to midnight. They stop at several Union

San Francisco at a Glance

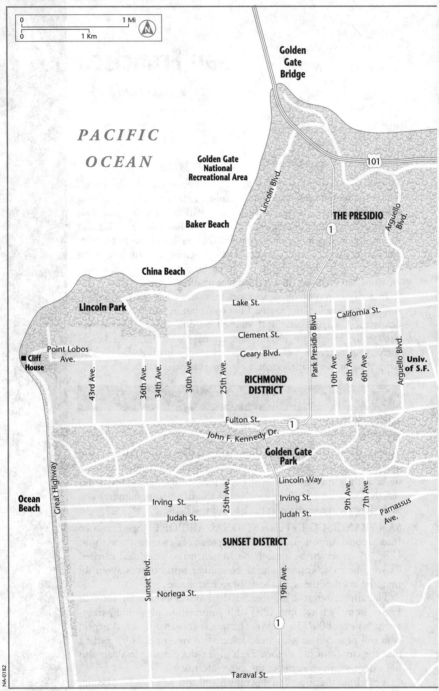

PACIFIC OCEAN

Golden Gate Bridge

101

Golden Gate National Recreational Area

Baker Beach

China Beach

Lincoln Blvd.

THE PRESIDIO

Arguello Blvd.

1

Lincoln Park

Lake St.

California St.

Point Lobos Ave.

Clement St.

Cliff House

Geary Blvd.

43rd Ave.

36th Ave.

34th Ave.

30th Ave.

25th Ave.

RICHMOND DISTRICT

Park Presidio Blvd.

10th Ave.

8th Ave.

6th Ave.

Arguello Blvd.

Univ. of S.F.

Fulton St.

1

John F. Kennedy Dr.

Golden Gate Park

Ocean Beach

Great Highway

Lincoln Way

Irving St.

25th Ave.

Irving St.

9th Ave.

7th Ave.

Parnassus Ave.

Judah St.

Judah St.

SUNSET DISTRICT

Sunset Blvd.

19th Ave.

Noriega St.

1

Taraval St.

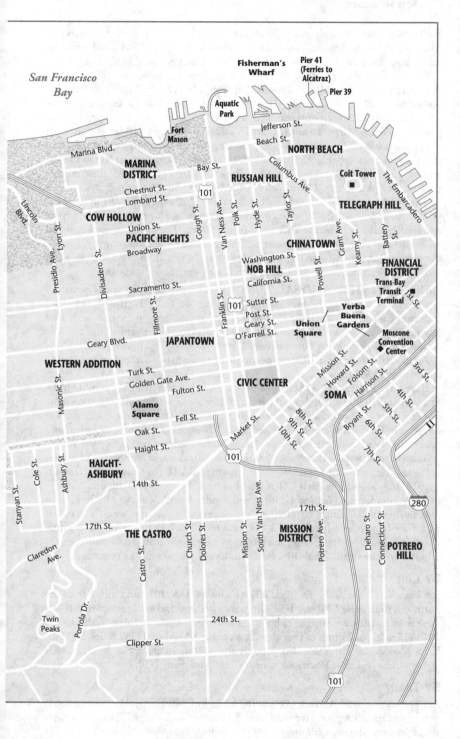

San Francisco Bay

Fisherman's Wharf

Pier 41 (Ferries to Alcatraz)

Pier 39

Aquatic Park

Fort Mason

Jefferson St.

Beach St.

Marina Blvd.

NORTH BEACH

The Embarcadero

MARINA DISTRICT

Bay St.

RUSSIAN HILL

Coit Tower

Chestnut St.

Lombard St.

101

TELEGRAPH HILL

COW HOLLOW

Union St.

PACIFIC HEIGHTS

Broadway

Gough St.

Van Ness Ave.

Polk St.

Hyde St.

Taylor St.

Columbus Ave.

CHINATOWN

Grant Ave.

Kearny St.

Battery St.

FINANCIAL DISTRICT

Lincoln Blvd.

Presidio Ave.

Lyon St.

Divisadero St.

Washington St.

NOB HILL

California St.

Powell St.

Sacramento St.

Fillmore St.

Franklin St.

101

Sutter St.

Post St.

Geary St.

O'Farrell St.

Union Square

Yerba Buena Gardens

Trans-Bay Transit Terminal

St. St.

Moscone Convention Center

Geary Blvd.

JAPANTOWN

WESTERN ADDITION

Masonic St.

Turk St.

Golden Gate Ave.

Fulton St.

Alamo Square

Fell St.

CIVIC CENTER

Mission St.

Howard St.

Folsom St.

Harrison St.

SOMA

3rd St.

4th St.

5th St.

6th St.

Oak St.

Haight St.

Market St.

8th St.

9th St.

10th St.

Bryant St.

7th St.

280

HAIGHT-ASHBURY

Cole St.

Ashbury St.

Stanyan St.

14th St.

17th St.

17th St.

Deharo St.

Connecticut St.

POTRERO HILL

THE CASTRO

Claredon Ave.

Castro St.

Church St.

Dolores St.

Mission St.

South Van Ness Ave.

Potrero Ave.

MISSION DISTRICT

Twin Peaks

Portola Dr.

24th St.

Clipper St.

101

Square–area hotels, including the Grand Hyatt, San Francisco Hilton, San Francisco Marriott, Westin St. Francis, Parc Fifty-Five, Hyatt Regency, and Sheraton Palace. No reservations are needed. The cost is $10 each way; children under 2 ride free.

Other private shuttle companies offer door-to-door airport service, in which you share a van with a few other passengers. **SuperShuttle** (☎ **415/558-8500**) will take you anywhere in the city, charging $10 per person to a hotel; $12 to a residence or business, plus $8 for each additional person; and $40 to charter an entire van for up to seven passengers. **Yellow Airport Shuttle** (☎ **415/282-7433**) charges $10 per person. Each shuttle stops every 20 minutes or so and picks up passengers from the marked areas outside the terminal's upper level. Reservations are required for the return trip to the airport only and should be made 1 day before departure. Keep in mind that these shuttles demand they pick you up 2 hours before your flight, 3 hours during holidays.

The San Mateo County Transit system, **SamTrans** (☎ **800/660-4287** in northern California, or 650/508-6200; www.santrans.com), runs two buses between the airport and the Transbay Terminal at First and Mission streets. The **7B** bus costs $2.20 and makes the trip in about 55 minutes. The **7F** bus costs $3 and takes only 35 minutes, but permits just one carry-on bag. Service begins at 4:45am on the 7B and 5:30am on the 7F. Both run frequently until 8pm, then hourly until about midnight.

OAKLAND INTERNATIONAL AIRPORT   Located about 5 miles south of downtown Oakland, at the Hagenberger Road exit off Calif. 17 (I-880), Oakland International Airport (☎ **510/577-4000**) is used primarily by passengers with East Bay destinations. Some San Franciscans, however, prefer this less-crowded, accessible airport when flying during busy periods.

Again, taxis from the airport to downtown San Francisco are expensive, costing approximately $45, plus tip.

Bayporter Express (☎ **415/467-1800**) is a shuttle service that charges $20 for the first person, $10 for each additional person to downtown San Francisco (it costs more to outer areas of town). Shuttles, usually located to the right of the airport exit, will take you to the city for around $20 per person. These are independently owned and prices vary, so ask and make any negotiations (sometimes possible) before you ride.

The cheapest way to downtown San Francisco (and easiest during traffic snarls) involves taking the shuttle bus from the airport to **BART** (Bay Area Rapid Transit; ☎ **510/464-6000**). The **AirBART** shuttle bus runs about every 15 minutes Monday through Saturday from 6am to 11:30pm and Sunday from 8:30am to 11:30pm, stopping in front of Terminals 1 and 2 near the ground transportation signs. The cost is $2 for the 10-minute ride to BART's Coliseum terminal. BART fares vary, depending on your destination; the trip to downtown San Francisco costs $2.45 and takes 20 minutes once on board. The entire excursion should take around 45 minutes.

BY CAR

San Francisco is accessible via several major highways: **U.S. 101** and **Calif. 1** from the north and south; and **I-80** and **I-580** from the northeast and east, respectively. If you drive from Los Angeles, you can either take the longer coastal route along Calif. 1/U.S. 101 (437 miles, or 11 hr.), or the inland route along I-5 to I-580 (389 miles, or 7 hr.). From Mendocino, it's a little over 3 hours along Calif. 1, and about 3¼ along U.S. 101; and from Sacramento, it's 88 miles, or 1½ hours, along I-80.

BY TRAIN

San Francisco–bound **Amtrak** (☎ **800/872-7245** or 800/USA-RAIL; www.amtrak. com) trains leave from New York and cross the country via Chicago. The journey takes about 3½ days, and seats sell quickly. At this writing, the lowest round-trip fare costs anywhere from $314 to $570 from New York and from $256 to $464 from Chicago. These heavily restricted tickets are good for 45 to 180 days and allow up to three stops along the way, depending on your ticket.

Round-trip tickets from Los Angeles can be purchased for as little as $92 or as much as $140. Trains actually arrive in Emeryville, just north of Oakland, and connect with regularly scheduled buses to San Francisco's Ferry Building and Cal Train station in downtown San Francisco.

Cal Train (☎ **800/660-4287** or 415/546-4461) operates train services between San Francisco and the towns of the peninsula. The city depot is at 700 Fourth St., at Townsend Street.

BY BUS

Greyhound/Trailways (☎ **800/231-2222;** www.greyhound.com) operates to San Francisco from just about anywhere. Round-trip fares vary, depending on your point of origin, but few, if any, ever exceed $300. The main San Francisco bus station is the Transbay Terminal, 425 Mission St., at First Street. For information, call ☎ **800/ 231-2222.**

VISITOR INFORMATION

The **San Francisco Visitor Information Center,** Hallidie Plaza, 900 Market St. (at Powell St.), Lower Level, San Francisco, CA 94102 (☎ **415/391-2000;** www. sfvisitor.org), is the best source for any kind of specialized information about the city. Even if you don't have a specific question, you may want to send them $3 for their 100-page magazine, *The San Francisco Book.* If you just need specific information faxed to you, call ☎ **800/220-5747** and follow the prompts.

CITY LAYOUT

San Francisco occupies the tip of a 32-mile-long peninsula between San Francisco Bay and the Pacific Ocean. Its land area measures about 46 square miles. Twin Peaks, in the geographic center of the city, is more than 900 feet high.

San Francisco may seem confusing at first, but it quickly becomes easy to negotiate. The city's downtown streets are arranged in a simple grid pattern, with the exception of Market Street and Columbus Avenue, which cut across the grid at right angles to each other. Hills appear to distort this pattern, however, and can be disorienting. But as you learn your way around, these same hills will become your landmarks and reference points.

MAIN ARTERIES & STREETS   **Market Street** is San Francisco's main thoroughfare. Most of the city's buses travel this route on their way to the Financial District from the outer neighborhoods to the west and south. The tall office buildings clustered downtown are at the northeast end of Market; 1 block beyond lie the Embarcadero and the Bay.

The **Embarcadero** curves along San Francisco Bay from south of the Bay Bridge to the northeast perimeter of the city and terminates at Fisherman's Wharf, the famous tourist-oriented pier. Aquatic Park, Fort Mason, and the Golden Gate National Recreation Area are located farther on around the bay, occupying the northernmost point of the peninsula.

From the eastern perimeter of Fort Mason, **Van Ness Avenue** runs due south, back to Market Street. The area we have just described forms a rough triangle, with Market Street as its southeastern boundary, the waterfront as its northern boundary, and Van Ness Avenue as its western boundary. Within this triangle lie most of the city's main tourist sights.

Neighborhoods & Districts in Brief

Union Square Union Square is the commercial hub of the city. Most major hotels and department stores are crammed into the area surrounding the actual square (named for a series of violent pro-union mass demonstrations staged here on the eve of the Civil War), with a plethora of upscale boutiques, restaurants, and galleries tucked between the larger buildings.

Nob Hill/Russian Hill Bounded by Bush, Larkin, Pacific, and Stockton streets, Nob Hill is the genteel, well-heeled district of the city, still occupied by the major power brokers and the neighborhood businesses they frequent. Russian Hill extends from Pacific to Bay and from Polk to Mason. It's marked by steep streets, lush gardens, and high-rises occupied by both the moneyed and the more bohemian.

SoMa In recent years, high rents have forced residents and businesses into once desolate South of Market (dubbed "SoMa")—still predominantly warehouses and industrial spaces, but many of them now brimming with life. The area is officially demarcated by the Embarcadero, U.S. 101, and Market Street, with the greatest concentrations of interest around Yerba Buena Center, along Folsom and Harrison streets between Steuart and Sixth, and Brannan and Market. Along the waterfront are an array of restaurants. Farther west, around Folsom between 7th and 11th streets, is where you'll find much of the city's nightclubbing.

Financial District East of Union Square, this area bordered by the Embarcadero, Market, Third, Kearny, and Washington streets is the city's business district and stomping grounds for many major corporations. The pointy TransAmerica Pyramid, at Montgomery and Clay streets, is one of the area's most conspicuous features. To its east stands the sprawling Embarcadero Center, an 8½-acre complex housing offices, shops, and restaurants. Farther east still is the World Trade Center, standing adjacent to the old Ferry Building, the city's pre-bridge transportation hub. Ferries to Sausalito and Larkspur still leave from this point.

Chinatown The official entrance to Chinatown is marked by a large red-and-green gate on Grant Avenue at Bush Street. Beyond lies a 24-block labyrinth, bordered by Broadway, Bush, Kearny, and Stockton streets, filled with restaurants, markets, temples, and shops—and, of course, a substantial percentage of San Francisco's Chinese residents. Chinatown is a great place for urban exploration all along Stockton, Grant, and Portsmouth Square, and the alleys that lead off them like Ross and Waverly. This area is jam-packed, so don't even think about driving around here.

North Beach The Italian quarter, which stretches from Montgomery and Jackson to Bay Street, is one of the best places in the city to grab a coffee, pull up a cafe chair, and do some serious people watching. Nightlife is equally happening: Restaurants, bars, and clubs along Columbus and Grant avenues attract folks from all over the Bay Area to fight for a parking place and romp through the festive neighborhood. Down Columbus toward the Financial District are the remains of the city's Beat generation landmarks, including Ferlinghetti's City Lights Bookstore and Vesuvio's Bar. Broadway—a short strip of sex joints—cuts through the heart of the district. Telegraph Hill looms over the east side of North Beach, topped by Coit Tower, one of San Francisco's best vantage points.

Fisherman's Wharf North Beach runs into Fisherman's Wharf, which was once the busy heart of the city's great harbor and waterfront industries. Today, it is a tacky-but-interesting tourist area with little if any authentic waterfront life, except for recreational boating and some friendly sea lions.

Marina District   Created on landfill for the Pan-Pacific Exposition of 1915, the Marina boasts some of the best views of the Golden Gate, as well as plenty of grassy fields alongside the San Francisco Bay. Streets are lined with elegant Mediterranean-style homes and apartments, which are inhabited by the city's well-to-do singles and wealthy families. Here, too, are the Palace of Fine Arts, the Exploratorium, and Fort Mason Center. The main street is Chestnut between Franklin and Lyon, which is lined with shops, cafes, and boutiques.

Cow Hollow   Located west of Van Ness Avenue, between Russian Hill and the Presidio, this flat, grazable area supported 30 dairy farms in 1861. Today, Cow Hollow is largely residential and occupied by the city's young and yuppie. Its two primary commercial thoroughfares are Lombard Street, known for its many relatively inexpensive motels; and Union Street, a flourishing shopping sector filled with restaurants, pubs, cafes, and shops.

Pacific Heights   The ultra-elite, such as the Gettys and Danielle Steele—and those lucky enough to buy before the real-estate boom—reside in the mansions and homes that make up Pacific Heights. When the rich meander out of their fortresses, they wander down to Union Street, a long stretch of boutiques, restaurants, cafes, and bars.

Japantown   Bounded by Octavia, Fillmore, California, and Geary, Japantown shelters only a small percentage of the city's Japanese population, but it's still a cultural experience to explore these few square blocks and the shops and restaurants within them.

Civic Center   Although millions of dollars have been expended on brick sidewalks, ornate lampposts, and elaborate street plantings, the southwestern section of Market Street remains downright dilapidated. The Civic Center, at the "bottom" of Market Street, is an exception. This large complex of buildings includes the domed City Hall, the Opera House, Davies Symphony Hall, and the city's main library. The landscaped plaza connecting the buildings is the staging area for San Francisco's frequent demonstrations for or against just about everything.

Haight-Ashbury   Part trendy, part nostalgic, part funky, the Haight, as it's most commonly known, was the soul of the psychedelic and free-loving 1960s and the center of the counterculture movement. Today, the neighborhood straddling upper Haight Street on the eastern border of Golden Gate Park is more gentrified, but the commercial area still harbors all walks of life. Leftover aging hippies mingle outside Ben and Jerry's ice-cream shop (where they may still be talking about Jerry Garcia) with grungy, begging street kids, nondescript marijuana dealers, and people with Day-Glo hair. But you don't need to be a freak or wear tie-dye to enjoy the Haight: The food, shops, and bars cover all tastes. From Haight, walk south on Cole Street for a more peaceful and quaint neighborhood experience.

Richmond & Sunset Districts   San Francisco's suburbs of sorts, these are the city's largest and most populous districts, consisting mainly of homes, small shops, and neighborhood restaurants. Though both districts border Golden Gate Park and Ocean Beach, only a small percentage of tourists venture into "The Avenues," as it's referred to by locals.

The Castro   One of the liveliest streets in town, Castro is practically synonymous with San Francisco's gay community, even though technically it is only a street in the Noe Valley District. Located at the very end of Market Street, between 17th and 18th streets, the Castro supports dozens of shops, restaurants, and bars catering to the gay community. Open-minded straight people are welcome, too.

Mission District   The Mexican and Latin American populations, along with their cuisines, traditions, and art, make the Mission District a vibrant area to visit. Because some parts of the neighborhood are poor and sprinkled with the homeless, gangs, and drug addicts, many tourists duck into Mission Dolores, cruise by a few of the 200 amazing murals, and head back downtown. But there's plenty more to the Mission District: a substantial community of lesbians around Valencia Street, several alternative arts organizations, and, most recently, the ultimate in young hipster nightlife. The new bars, clubs, and restaurants that have popped up around Mission between 18th and 24th streets and Valencia at 16th Street have made one magazine dub this area one of the hippest in the United States. Don't be afraid to visit this area, but do use caution at night.

2 Getting Around

BY PUBLIC TRANSPORTATION

The San Francisco Municipal Railway, better known as **Muni** (☎ 415/673-6864), operates the city's cable cars, buses, and Metro streetcars. Together, these three public transportation services crisscross the entire city, making San Francisco fully accessible to everyone. Buses and Metro streetcars cost $1 for adults, 35¢ for ages 5 to 17, and 35¢ for seniors over 65. Cable cars cost $2 ($1 for seniors from 9pm to midnight and from 6 to 7am). Needless to say, they're packed primarily with tourists. Exact change is required on all vehicles except cable cars. Fares quoted here are subject to change.

For detailed route information, phone Muni or consult the bus map at the front of the Yellow Pages. If you plan on making extensive use of public transportation, you may want to invest in a comprehensive route map ($2), sold at the San Francisco Visitor Information Center (see "Visitor Information" in "Orientation," above) and in many downtown retail outlets.

Muni **discount passes,** called "Passports," entitle holders to unlimited rides on buses, Metro streetcars, and cable cars. A Passport costs $6 for 1 day, and $10 or $15 for 3 or 7 consecutive days. As a bonus, your Passport also entitles you to admission discounts at 24 of the city's major attractions, including the M. H. de Young Memorial Museum, the Asian Art Museum, the California Academy of Sciences, and the Japanese Tea Garden (all in Golden Gate Park); the Museum of Modern Art; Coit Tower; the Exploratorium; the zoo; and the National Maritime Museum and Historic Ships. Among the places where you can purchase a Passport are the San Francisco Visitor Information Center, the Holiday Inn Civic Center, and the Tix Bay Area booth at Union Square.

BY CABLE CAR San Francisco's cable cars may not be the most practical means of transport, but these rolling historic landmarks sure are a fun ride. There are only three lines in the city, and they're all concentrated in the downtown area. The most scenic, and exciting, is the **Powell-Hyde line,** which follows a zigzag route from the corner of Powell and Market streets, over both Nob Hill and Russian Hill, to a turntable at gaslit Victorian Square in front of Aquatic Park. The **Powell-Mason line** starts at the same intersection and climbs over Nob Hill before descending to Bay Street, just 3 blocks from Fisherman's Wharf. The least scenic is the **California Street line,** which begins at the foot of Market Street and runs a straight course through Chinatown and over Nob Hill to Van Ness Avenue. All riders must exit at the last stop and wait in line for the return trip. The cable-car system operates from approximately 6:30am to 12:30am.

BY BUS Buses reach almost every corner of San Francisco and travel over the bridges to Marin County and Oakland. All are numbered and display their destinations on the front. Stops are designated by signs, curb markings, and yellow bands on adjacent utility poles, and most bus shelters exhibit Muni's transportation map and schedule. Many buses travel along Market Street or pass near Union Square and run from about 6am to midnight, after which there is infrequent all-night "Owl" service. If you can help it, for safety purposes avoid taking buses late at night.

Popular tourist routes are nos. 5, 7, and 71, all of which run to Golden Gate Park; 41 and 45, which travel along Union Street; and 30, which runs between Union Square and Ghirardelli Square.

BY METRO STREETCAR   Five of Muni's six Metro streetcar lines, designated J, K, L, M, and N, run underground downtown and on the street in the outer neighborhoods. The sleek railcars make the same stops as BART (see below) along Market Street, including Embarcadero Station (in the Financial District), Montgomery and Powell streets (both near Union Square), and the Civic Center (near City Hall). Past the Civic Center, the routes branch off in different directions: The J line will take you to Mission Dolores; the K, L, and M lines to Castro Street; and the N line parallels the north side of Golden Gate Park. Metros run about every 15 minutes—more frequently during rush hours. Service is offered Monday through Friday from 5am to 12:30am, Saturday from 6am to 12:20am, and Sunday from 8am to 12:20am.

The most recent streetcar additions are not newcomers at all, but San Francisco's beloved 1930s streetcars. The beautiful, rejuvenated multicolored cars on the F Market line run from downtown Market Street to the Castro and back. It's a quick and charming way to get up and downtown without any hassle.

BY BART   BART, an acronym for **Bay Area Rapid Transit** (☎ **650/992-2278**), is a futuristic-looking, high-speed rail network that connects San Francisco with the East Bay–Oakland, Richmond, Concord, and Fremont. Four stations are located along Market Street (see "By Metro Streetcar," above). Fares range from $1 to $3.55, depending on how far you go. Tickets are dispensed from machines in the stations and are magnetically encoded with a dollar amount. Computerized exits automatically deduct the correct fare. Children 4 and under ride free. Trains run every 15 to 20 minutes, Monday through Friday from 4am to midnight, Saturday from 6am to midnight, and Sunday from 8am to midnight.

A $2.5-billion, 33-mile BART extension, currently under construction, includes a southern line that is planned to extend all the way to San Francisco International Airport. It will open, presumably, around the year 2000.

BY TAXI

If you're downtown during rush hours or leaving from a major hotel, it won't be hard to hail a cab—just look for the lighted sign on the roof that indicates if one is free. Otherwise, it's a good idea to call one of the following companies to arrange a ride: **Veteran's Cab** (☎ 415/552-1300), **Desoto Cab Co.** (☎ 415/673-1414), **Luxor Cabs** (☎ 415/282-4141), **Yellow Cab** (☎ 415/626-2345), and **Pacific** (☎ 415/986-7220). Rates are approximately $2.50 for the first mile and $1.80 for each mile thereafter.

BY CAR

You don't need a car to explore downtown San Francisco; in fact, in central areas, such as Chinatown, Union Square, and the Financial District, having a car can be your worst nightmare. But if you want to venture outside of the city, driving is the best way to go.

RENTALS   Among the major car-rental companies operating in the city are **Alamo** (☎ 800/327-9633), **Avis** (☎ 800/331-1212), **Budget** (☎ 800/527-0700), **Dollar** (☎ 800/800-4000), **Hertz** (☎ 800/654-3131), **National** (☎ 800/227-7368), and **Thrifty** (☎ 800/367-2277). In addition to the big chains, there are dozens of regional rental places in San Francisco, many of which offer lower rates. These

San Francisco Mass Transit

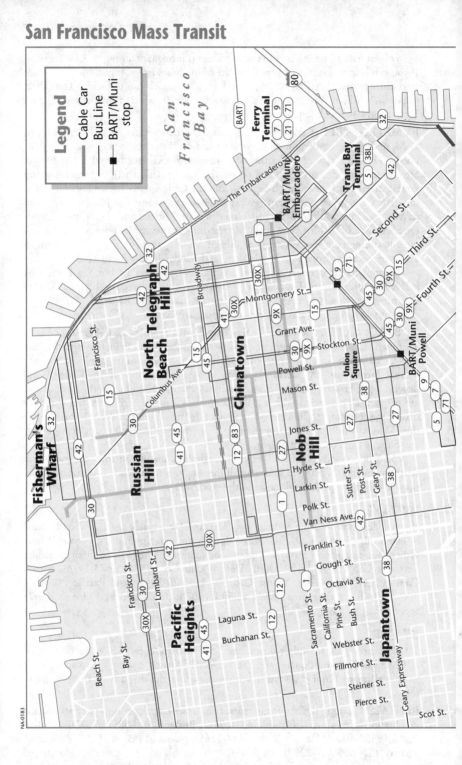

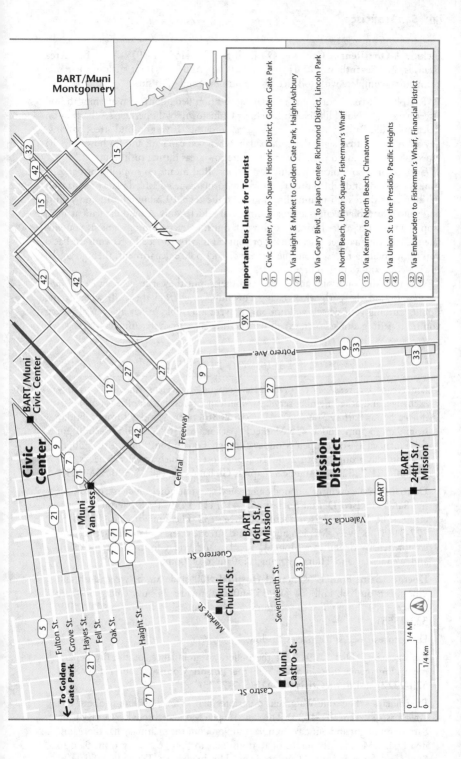

Important Bus Lines for Tourists

5 Civic Center, Alamo Square Historic District, Golden Gate Park
21

7 Via Haight & Market to Golden Gate Park, Haight-Ashbury
71

38 Via Geary Blvd. to Japan Center, Richmond District, Lincoln Park

30 North Beach, Union Square, Fisherman's Wharf

15 Via Kearney to North Beach, Chinatown

41 Via Union St. to the Presidio, Pacific Heights
45

32 Via Embarcadero to Fisherman's Wharf, Financial District
42

BART/Muni
Montgomery

BART/Muni
Civic Center

Civic
Center

Muni
Van Ness

Mission
District

BART
16th St./
Mission

BART
24th St./
Mission

BART

Central   Freeway

Potrero Ave.

Valencia St.

Guerrero St.

Seventeenth St.

Muni
Church St.

Muni
Castro St.

Market St.

Castro St.

Haight St.

Oak St.

Fell St.

Hayes St.

Grove St.

Fulton St.

← To Golden
Gate Park

1/4 Mi

1/4 Km

0

0

include **A-One Rent-A-Car,** 434 O'Farrell St. (☎ 415/771-3977), and **Bay Area Rentals,** 229 Seventh St. (☎ 415/621-8989). See Appendix B for a list of car-rental companies, complete with toll-free phone numbers and Web sites.

PARKING   If you want to have a relaxing vacation here, don't even attempt to find street parking in Nob Hill, North Beach, or Chinatown; by Fisherman's Wharf; or on Telegraph Hill. Park in a garage or take a cab or a bus. If you do find street parking, pay attention to street signs that will explain when you can park and for how long. Be especially careful not to park in zones that are tow areas during rush hours.

Curb colors also indicate parking regulations. **Red** means no stopping or parking; **blue** is reserved for disabled drivers with a California-issued disabled plate or a placard; **white** means there's a 5-minute limit; **green** indicates a 10-minute limit; and **yellow** and **yellow-and-black** curbs are for commercial vehicles only. Also, don't park at a bus stop or in front of a fire hydrant, and watch out for street-cleaning signs. If you violate the law, you may get a hefty ticket or your car may be towed. To get your car back, you must obtain a release from the nearest district police department, then go to the towing company to pick up the vehicle.

When parking on a hill, apply the hand brake, put the car in gear, and *curb your wheels*—toward the curb when facing downhill, away from the curb when facing uphill. Curbing your wheels will not only prevent a possible "runaway," but also keep you from getting a ticket—an expensive fine that is aggressively enforced.

Fast Facts: San Francisco

American Express   For travel arrangements, traveler's checks, currency exchange, and other member services, American Express has an office at 560 California St., at Battery Street (☎ **415/536-2686**), open Monday through Friday from 9am to 5pm, and at 455 Market St., at First Street (☎ **415/536-2600**), in the Financial District, open Monday through Friday from 8:30am to 5:30pm and Saturday from 9am to 2pm. To report lost or stolen traveler's checks, call ☎ **800/221-7282.** For American Express Global Assist, call ☎ **800/554-2639.**

Dentist   In the event of a dental emergency, see your hotel concierge or contact the **San Francisco Dental Society** (☎ **415/421-1435**) for a referral to a specialist. The **San Francisco Dental Office,** 132 The Embarcadero (☎ **415/777-5115**), between Mission and Howard streets, offers emergency service and comprehensive dental care Monday, Tuesday, and Friday from 8am to 4:30pm, and Wednesday and Thursday from 10:30am to 6:30pm.

Doctor   **Saint Francis Memorial Hospital,** 900 Hyde St., between Bush and Pine streets on Nob Hill (☎ **415/353-6000**), provides 24-hour emergency-care service. The hospital also operates a physician-referral service (☎ **800/333-1355**).

Drugstores   See "Pharmacies," below.

Emergencies   Dial ☎ **911** for the police, an ambulance, or the fire department. Emergency hot lines include the **Poison Control Center** (☎ **800/523-2222**) and **Rape Crisis** (☎ **415/647-7273**).

Pharmacies   There are **Walgreens** drugstores all over town, including one at 135 Powell St. (☎ **415/391-4433**). The store is open Monday through Saturday from 8am to midnight and Sunday from 9am to 9pm, but the pharmacy has more limited hours: Monday through Friday from 8am to 9pm, Saturday from 9am to 5pm, and Sunday from 10am to 6pm. The branch on Divisadero Street at

Lombard (☎ **415/931-6415**) has a 24-hour pharmacy. The pharmacy at **Merrill's,** 805 Market St. (☎ **415/431-5466**), is open Monday through Saturday from 8:30am to 6:30pm, while the rest of the drugstore is open Monday through Friday from 7am to 9pm, Saturday from 9am to 7pm, and Sunday from 9:30am to 6pm.

Police For emergencies, dial ☎ **911** from any phone; no coins are needed. For other matters, call ☎ **415/553-0123.**

Post Office There are dozens of post offices located all around the city. The closest office to Union Square is inside Macy's department store, 170 O'Farrell St. (☎ **415/956-3570**).

Safety Few locals would recommend walking alone late at night in certain areas, particularly the Tenderloin, between Union Square and the Civic Center. Compared with similar areas in other cities, however, even this section of San Francisco is relatively tranquil. Other areas where you should be particularly alert are the Mission District, around 16th and Mission streets; the lower Fillmore area, around lower Haight Street; and the SoMa area south of Market Street.

Taxes An 8.5% sales tax is added at t%he register for all goods and services purchased in San Francisco. The city hotel tax is a whopping 14%. There is no airport tax.

Transit Information Call **Muni** at ☎ **415/673-6864** Monday through Friday between 7am and 5pm and Saturday and Sunday between 9am and 5pm. At other times, recorded information is available.

Useful Telephone Numbers **Tourist information** (☎ 415/391-2001); **highway conditions** (☎ 800/427-7623); **KFOG Entertainment Line** (☎ 415/777-1045); **MovieFone** (☎ 415/777-FILM).

Weather Call ☎ **650/364-7974** to find out when the next fog bank is rolling in.

3 Accommodations

San Francisco is an outstanding hotel town, especially considering its relatively small size. We can't cover them all in this guide, so if you'd like a larger selection, check out *Frommer's San Francisco,* which has dozens of other options.

Most of the hotels listed below are within easy walking distance of Union Square, and accessible via cable car. Union Square is near the city's major shops, the Financial District, and all transportation. Prices listed below do not include state and city taxes, which total 14%.

The price categories below reflect the prices of double rooms during the high season, which runs approximately from April through September. (In reality, rates don't vary much because the city is so popular year-round.) But remember: These are rack (or published) rates; you can almost always get a better deal if you inquire about packages, weekend discounts, corporate rates, and family plans.

Bed and Breakfast of California, 12711 McCartysville Pl., Saratoga, CA 95070 (☎ **800/872-4500** or 408/867-9662; fax 408/867-0907; www.bbintl.com; e-mail: info@bbintl.com), offers a selection of accommodations priced from $70 to $300 per night (2-night minimum). Choices range from simple rooms in private homes to luxurious, full-service carriage houses, houseboats, and Victorian homes. **San Francisco Reservations,** 22 Second St., Suite 4, San Francisco, CA 94105 (☎ **800/677-1500** or 415/227-1500; www.hotelres.com), arranges reservations at more than 300 of San Francisco's hotels and often offers discounted rates.

San Francisco Accommodations

Abigail Hotel **18**
Andrews Hotel **22**
Archbishop's Mansion **3**
Bed & Breakfast Inn **9**
Brady Acres **21**
Clarion Bedford Hotel **20**
Commodore International **19**
Edward II Inn & Pub **6**
Fairmont Hotel & Tower **31**
Golden Gate Hotel **33**
Grant Plaza Hotel **40**
Harbor Court **43**
Herb'n Inn **45**
Hotel Bohème **15**
Hotel David Bed & Breakfast **28**
Hotel Diva **29**
Hotel Griffon **43**
Hotel Majestic **5**
Hotel Monaco **24**
Hotel Triton **44**
Huntington Hotel **25**
Inn at the Opera **4**
Inn on Castro **1**
Kensington Park Hotel **34**
King George Hotel **30**
Mandarin Oriental **42**
Marina Inn **10**
Mark Hopkins Intercontinental **32**
Maxwell **36**
Nob Hill Hotel **16**
Nob Hill Lambourne **37**
Parker House **2**
Phoenix Hotel **17**
Prescott Hotel **28**
Queen Anne Hotel **5**
Ritz-Carlton **39**
San Remo Hotel **14**
Savoy Hotel **23**
Sheraton at Fisherman's Wharf **12**
Sheraton Palace Hotel **44**
Sherman House **8**
Tuscan Inn **13**
Union Street Inn **7**
Warwick Regis **27**
Westin St. Francis **35**
Wharf Inn **11**
White Swan Inn **26**

Haight-Ashbury

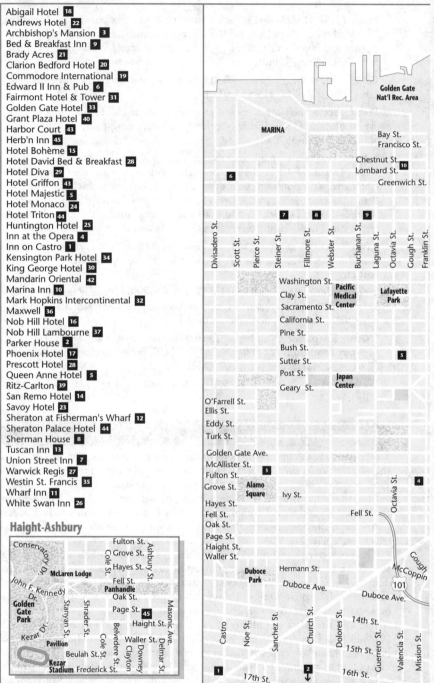

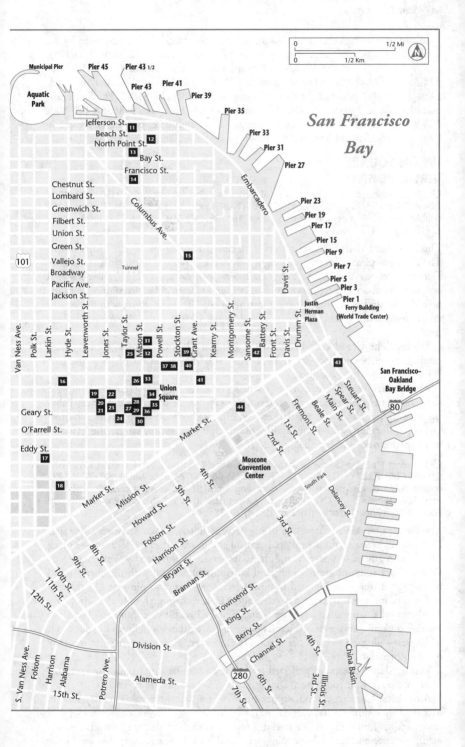

Municipal Pier

Aquatic Park

Pier 45 Pier 43 ½

Pier 43

Pier 41

Pier 39

Pier 35

San Francisco Bay

Pier 33

Pier 31

Pier 27

Jefferson St. **11**

Beach St.

North Point St. **12**

13 Bay St.

Francisco St.

14

Chestnut St.

Lombard St.

Greenwich St.

Filbert St.

Union St.

Green St.

Vallejo St.

Broadway

Pacific Ave.

Jackson St.

Embarcadero

Columbus Ave.

Tunnel

15

Pier 23

Pier 19

Pier 17

Pier 15

Pier 9

Pier 7

Pier 5

Pier 3

Pier 1

Justin Herman Plaza

Ferry Building (World Trade Center)

101

Van Ness Ave.

Polk St.

Larkin St.

Hyde St.

Leavenworth St.

Jones St.

Taylor St.

Mason St.

Powell St.

Stockton St.

Grant Ave.

Kearny St.

Montgomery St.

Sansome St.

Battery St.

Front St.

Davis St.

Drumm St.

Davis St.

31

25 **32**

37 38

39

40

42

43

San Francisco–Oakland Bay Bridge

16

26 **33**

Union Square

19

22

34

20 **28**

23 **27** **29** **35**

21 **24** **30** **36**

41

44

80

Steuart St.

Spear St.

Main St.

Beale St.

Fremont St.

1st St.

2nd St.

Geary St.

O'Farrell St.

Eddy St.

Market St.

17

Moscone Convention Center

South Park

Delancey St.

18

Market St.

Mission St.

Howard St.

Folsom St.

Harrison St.

Bryant St.

Brannan St.

4th St.

5th St.

3rd St.

8th St.

9th St.

10th St.

11th St.

12th St.

Townsend St.

King St.

Berry St.

Channel St.

4th St.

China Basin

S. Van Ness Ave.

Folsom

Harrison

Alabama

Potrero Ave.

15th St.

Division St.

Alameda St.

280

7th St.

6th St.

3rd St.

Illinois St.

0   ½ Mi

0   ½ Km

63

In addition to the hotels listed below, we also recommend those represented by the reasonably priced and fashionable **Joie de Vivre** hotel chain (☎ 800-SF-TRIPS); pricier options from the **Kimpton Group,** such as the **Juliana Hotel** (☎ 800/328-3880) and the new **Hotel Serrano** (☎ 415/885-2500), the latter of which opened in mid–1999; and the stately **Donatello** (☎ 800/227-3184). The **San Francisco Hilton & Towers** (☎ 800/445-8667) and **San Francisco Marriott** (☎ 800/228-9290) both have impersonal convention-hotel ambiance, but are conveniently located downtown and have enough rooms to sleep thousands.

UNION SQUARE
VERY EXPENSIVE

✪ **Hotel Monaco.** 501 Geary Blvd. (at Taylor St.), San Francisco, CA 94102. ☎ **800/214-4220** or 415/292-0100. Fax 415/292-0111. 201 units. A/C MINIBAR TV TEL. From $259 double; from $299 suite. Call for discounted rates. AE, DC, DISC, JCB, MC, V. Valet parking $24. Bus: 2, 3, 4, 27, or 38.

This remodeled 1910 beaux-arts hotel is the new diva of Union Square luxury hotels. The Kimpton Group did this place right—from the cozy main lobby with a two-story French inglenook fireplace to the guest rooms with canopy beds, Chinese-inspired armoires, bamboo writing desks, bold stripes, and vibrant color. Everything is in the best of taste, and as playful as it is comfort-minded. The decor, along with the breathtaking restaurant, makes this a winner—although for the price, the rooms are very small.

Dining: The Grand Cafe is indeed the grandest room downtown, with sky-high ceilings, an elaborate deco-era style, and an amazing collection of local art. (See "Dining," below, for a complete review.)

Amenities: Web TV; concierge; room service; laundry/dry cleaning; overnight shoe-shine; newspaper delivery; in-room massage; twice-daily maid service; babysitting; two-line phones; secretarial services; express checkout; valet parking; courtesy car; complimentary wine-hour nightly; health club with steam, sauna, and massage; meeting, business, and banquet facilities.

✪ **Prescott Hotel.** 545 Post St. (between Mason and Taylor sts.), San Francisco, CA 94102. ☎ **800/283-7322** or 415/563-0303. Fax 415/563-6831. 164 units. MINIBAR TV TEL. $225 double; $275 concierge-level double (including breakfast and evening cocktail reception); from $295 suite. AE, CB, DC, DISC, MC, V. Valet parking $25. Cable car: Powell-Hyde and Powell-Mason lines (1 block east). Bus: 2, 3, 4, 30, 38, or 45.

The Prescott has always been one of our favorite hotels in San Francisco. The staff treats you like royalty, the rooms are beautiful and immaculate, the location—a block from Union Square—is perfect, and the room service is provided by Wolfgang Puck's Postrio. Dark tones of green, plum, and burgundy blend well with the cherry-wood furnishings in the soundproofed rooms; the view, alas, isn't so pleasant. All the tiny bathrooms are supplied with terry robes and hair dryers, though only the suites have whirlpool tubs. Concierge-level guests are pampered with free continental breakfast, evening cocktails, and exercise bicycles or rowing machines brought up to your room on request—all for $30 extra per night. One bummer: The restaurant's not regularly open for breakfast.

Dining: Hotel guests get preferred seating at Postrio; be sure to make reservations when you book your room (see "Dining," below, for a complete review).

Amenities: Concierge; room service from Postrio; same-day valet/laundry service; overnight shoe-shine; newspaper delivery; nightly turndown; twice-daily maid service; valet parking; limousine service weekday mornings to the Financial District; complimentary coffee and tea each morning; wine and hors d'oeuvres every evening in the living room; access to off-premises health club ($10), including pool, free weights, and sauna; conference rooms.

Westin St. Francis. 335 Powell St. (between Geary and Post sts.), San Francisco, CA 94102. ☎ **800/228-3000** or 415/397-7000. Fax 415/503-6865. 1,189 units. A/C MINIBAR TV TEL. Main building: $229–$405 double; from $450 suite. Tower: $360–$405 double; from $525 suite. Extra person $30. Continental breakfast $15–$18 extra. AE, DC, DISC, JCB, MC, V. Valet parking $27. Cable car: Powell-Hyde and Powell-Mason lines (direct stop). Bus: 2, 3, 4, 30, 38, 45, or 76.

Although too massive to offer the personal service you get at the smaller deluxe hotels on Nob Hill, few other hotels in San Francisco can match the majestic aura of the St. Francis. Hordes of VIPs, from Queen Elizabeth II to Mother Teresa, have hung their hats here. The 32-story Tower was added in 1972, doubling the hotel's capacity and adding the requisite banquet and conference centers (as well as a rooftop dance club). The older rooms in the main building vary in size and have more old-world charm than the newer Tower rooms, but the Tower is remarkable for its great views of the city once you rise above the 18th floor. The hotel did a $50-million renovation in 1996 and a $60-million minor overhaul in 1999, so everything looks dapper, from the carpeting, furniture, and bedding in guest rooms to the lobby and Compass Rose tea room.

Dining/Diversions: Even if you stay elsewhere, visit for high tea at the Compass Rose—one of San Francisco's most enduring and enjoyable traditions. It offers one of the city's best tea services and is open daily for lunch and tea (from 3 to 5pm); evenings bring live music, dancing, champagne, cocktails, and caviar tasting. Dewey's, a sports bar, offers a do-it-yourself lunch buffet, with burgers and pizzas at night. There's also a cafe with a basic breakfast menu.

Amenities: Concierge, 24-hour room service, laundry, newspaper delivery, in-room massage, twice-daily maid service, baby-sitting referral, secretarial services, new $2-million fitness center, business center, tour and car-rental desks, American Airlines ticket office, barber/beauty salon, gift shop.

EXPENSIVE

☼ **Hotel Diva.** 440 Geary St. (between Mason and Taylor sts.), San Francisco, CA 94102. ☎ **800/553-1900** or 415/885-0200. Fax 415/346-6613. 111 units. A/C TV TEL. $169 double; $189 junior suite; $400 villa suite. Rates include continental breakfast. AE, DC, DISC, JCB, MC, V. Parking $22. Cable car: Powell-Mason. Bus: 38 or 38L.

Appropriately named, the Diva is the prima donna of San Francisco's modern hotels, and one of our favorites. A showbiz darling when it opened in 1985, the Diva won "Best Hotel Design" by *Interiors* magazine for its sleek, ultra-modern style. A stunning profusion of curvaceous glass, marble, and steel mark the Euro-tech lobby, while the rooms, each spotless and neat, are softened with fashionable Italian Modern furnishings of monochrome color, silver, and wood. Nary a beat is missed with the toys and services either, which range from VCRs (with a discreet video vending machine) and Nintendo to complimentary breakfast delivered to your room. *Insider tip:* Reserve one of the rooms ending in "09," which have extra-large bathrooms with vanity mirrors and makeup tables. The only downside: views that make you want to keep the chic curtains closed.

Amenities: Limited room service, concierge, pay-per-view movies, same-day laundry, on-site 24-hour fitness center, business center.

Hotel Triton. 342 Grant Ave. (at Bush St.), San Francisco, CA 94108. ☎ **800/433-6611** or 415/394-0500. Fax 415/394-0555. 147 units. A/C MINIBAR TV TEL. $169–$260 double; $299–$315 suite. AE, DC, DISC, MC, V. Parking $24. Cable car: Powell-Hyde and Powell-Mason lines (2 blocks west).

Described as chic, retro-futuristic, and even neo-Baroque, the Triton begs attention, from the Dali-esque lobby to the sumptuous designer suites à la Jerry Garcia, Joe Boxer, and Wyland (the ocean artist). Two dozen environmentally sensitive "Eco-Rooms"—with biodegradable soaps, filtered water and air, and all-natural linens—were also installed to please the tree-hugger in all of us. *A mild caveat:* Don't expect perfection; many of the rooms could use a little touching up here and there, and service isn't as snappy as it could be. If you can live with this, and want to inject a little fun and style into your stay, then come join Dorothy and Toto for a trip far from Kansas.

Dining: Café de la Presse, a European-style newsstand and outdoor cafe/restaurant, serves breakfast, lunch, and dinner. In the hotel lobby, complimentary coffee is served each morning and wine each evening.

Amenities: Room service, same-day laundry, business center, exercise room.

Kensington Park Hotel. 450 Post St. (between Powell and Mason sts.), San Francisco, CA 94102. ☎ **800/553-1900** or 415/788-6400. Fax 415/399-9484. 87 units. TV TEL. $175–$205 double; $550 suite. Rates include continental breakfast. Extra person $10. AE, CB, DC, DISC, MC, V. Valet parking $22. Cable car: Powell-Hyde and Powell-Mason lines (½ block east).

The Kensington's age shows, but its cheery, eager-to-please staff, tasteful accommodations, central location, and easy access to downstairs hot-shot restaurant Farallon has made this place so popular that in the past 3 years, the rates have practically doubled. Still, the value is decent. The recently upgraded rooms are indeed handsome with traditional mahogany furniture, enormous armoires, and dark sophisticated colors—far more attractive than most hotel furnishings. Bathrooms may be small, but they're sweetly appointed in brass and marble. For the best view, ask for an upper corner room. One big complaint: Every time we visit, the front desk is understaffed.

The adjoining seafood restaurant, Farallon, is one of the hottest places in town (see "Dining," below, for details). Amenities include room service, concierge, same-day laundry, morning newspaper, and complimentary morning limo to the Financial District; fax and secretarial services are also available.

✪ **White Swan Inn.** 845 Bush St. (between Taylor and Mason sts.), San Francisco, CA 94108. ☎ **800/999-9570** or 415/775-1755. Fax 415/775-5717. 26 units. MINIBAR TV TEL. $165–$185 double; $195 romance suite; $250 2-room suite. Extra person $15. Rates include full breakfast and afternoon wine and hors d'oeuvres. AE, DC, MC, V. Parking $20. Cable car: California St. line (1 block north). Bus: 1, 2, 3, 4, 27, or 45.

From the moment you're buzzed in to this well-secured inn just 2½ blocks from Union Square, you'll know you're not in just any old B&B. Around 50 teddy bears grace the lobby—and if that doesn't cure homesickness, the complimentary homemade cookies, tea, and coffee will. The romantic rooms are warm and cozy; they're also quite big, with rich wood furniture, working fireplaces, and an assortment of books tucked in nooks. The decor is English elegance at its best, if not to excess, with floral prints almost everywhere. The romance suites aren't much better than the regular rooms—just a little bigger, and outfitted with chocolates and champagne. This is a charming choice, with service and style to satisfy the most discriminating traveler. Note that there's no smoking allowed.

Dining: A generous breakfast is served just off a tiny garden. Afternoon tea is also served, with hors d'oeuvres, sherry, wine, and home-baked pastries. Wine and hors d'oeuvres are served every evening.

Amenities: Concierge, laundry, evening turndown, morning newspaper, overnight shoe-shine, access to off-premises health club for $15 per day.

ⓕ Family-Friendly Hotels

Brady Acres *(see p. 69)*   Not only is this one of the city's best budget hotels, but it's also a great place for families; rooms come with microwaves, fridges, and other lifesaving amenities, and weekly rentals are available.

The Wharf Inn *(see p. 75)*   No whining about when you'll get there 'cause you're already there—right smack dab in the middle of the wharf. Plus, parking is free and there's no charge for packing along an extra monster.

MODERATE

Andrews Hotel. 624 Post St. (between Jones and Taylor sts.), San Francisco, CA 94109. ☎ **800/926-3739** or 415/563-6877. Fax 415/928-6919. www.sftrips.com. 48 units. TV TEL. $85–$135 double; $125–$142 petite suite. Rates include continental breakfast and evening wine. AE, DC, JCB, MC, V. Self-parking $15. Cable car: Powell-Hyde and Powell-Mason lines (3 blocks east). Bus: 2, 3, 4, 30, 38, or 45.

As is fitting with Euro-style hotels, the accommodations are small but well maintained and comfortable; lace curtains and fresh flowers in each room add a light touch. Some units have shower only, and bathrooms in general tend to be tiny—but for the location and price, the Andrews is a good, safe bet for an enjoyable stay in the city. An added bonus is the adjoining Fino Bar and Ristorante, which offers complimentary wine to hotel guests in the evening.

Clarion Bedford Hotel. 761 Post St. (between Leavenworth and Jones sts.), San Francisco, CA 94109. ☎ **800/252-7466** or 415/673-6040. Fax 415/563-6739. 144 units. MINIBAR TV TEL. $129–$179 double; from $175 suite. Continental breakfast $8.50 extra. AE, CB, DC, DISC, JCB, MC, V. Parking $20. Cable car: Powell-Hyde and Powell-Mason lines (4 blocks east). Bus: 2, 3, 4, or 27.

For the price and location (3 blocks from Union Square), the 17-story Bedford offers a darn good deal. Your hard-earned dollars will get you a large, spotless, recently renovated room with flowery decor that's not exactly en vogue but definitely in fine taste, as well as service from an enthusiastic, attentive, and professional staff. Each unit is well furnished with a king, a queen, or two double beds; a writing desk; an armchair; in-room coffee; and a well-stocked honor bar with plenty of munchies. Big closets are a trade for the small bathrooms. Most rooms are sunny and bright and have priceless views of the city (the higher the floor, the better the view).

The hotel's bistro, Crushed Tomato's, has a small, beautiful mahogany bar opposite the registration desk. There's also room service (for breakfast only), dry cleaning, laundry, secretarial services, and valet parking.

✪ Commodore International. 825 Sutter St. (at Jones St.), San Francisco, CA 94109. ☎ **800/338-6848** or 415/923-6800. Fax 415/923-6804. 113 units. TV TEL. $99–$139 double or twin. AE, DC, MC, V. Parking $15. Bus: 2, 3, 4, 27, or 76.

If you're looking to pump a little fun and fantasy into your vacation, this is the place. Hot hotelier Chip Conley (who transformed the Phoenix Hotel into a rocker's retreat) let his hip-hop designers do their magic on what was a dilapidated eyesore, and the result is one groovy hotel. Stealing the show is the Red Room, a Big Apple–style bar and lounge that's ruby red through and through (you gotta see this one). The stylish lobby comes in a close second, followed by the Titanic Café, a cute little diner serving buckwheat griddlecakes, Vietnamese tofu sandwiches, and dragon fire salads. Appealing to the masses, Chip left the first four floors as standard no-frills—though quite clean and comfortable—rooms, while decking out the top two floors in neo-deco overtones—well worth the extra $10 a night.

Hotel David Bed & Breakfast. 480 Geary St. (between Taylor and Mason sts.), San Francisco, CA 94102. ☎ **800/524-1888** or 415/771-1600. Fax 415/931-5442. 42 units. TV TEL. $119 double. AE, DISC, MC, V. Rates include full breakfast. Valet parking $20.

No other hotel in the area offers so many amenities for so little money. So what if entering this small, *pensione*-like hotel via the adjoining kosher deli is a little odd. That's the beauty of this place; it's so well hidden that no one knows it's here (not to mention the easy access to a decent matzo-ball soup and hot pastrami on rye). But even beyond that, Hotel David is full of surprises. Whether you come in through the street-side entrance or the restaurant, step off the elevator and you'll find immaculate, smallish rooms with chic-moderne decor, streamlined maple furnishings, and colorful accents. Expect extras like hot towel racks, voice mail, and soundproofed walls. And there's more: free transportation from the San Francisco airport (for guests staying 2 or more nights), valet parking, and a free full and hearty breakfast—served at David's Deli, of course. *Note:* Those whose hotel experience is heightened by entering and lingering in a grand, proper lobby should seek a room elsewhere.

✪ **King George Hotel.** 334 Mason St. (between Geary and O'Farrell sts.), San Francisco, CA 94102. ☎ **800/288-6005** or 415/781-5050. Fax 415/391-6976. 141 units. TV TEL. $160 double; $225 suite. Special-value packages available seasonally. Continental breakfast $5.75 extra. AE, CB, DC, DISC, JCB, MC, V. Self-parking $16.50. Cable car: Powell-Hyde and Powell-Mason lines (1 block west). Bus: 2, 3, 4, 30, 38, or 45.

Built in 1914 for the Panama-Pacific Exhibition when rooms went for $1 per night, this utterly delightful hotel has fared well over the years, continuing to draw a mostly European clientele. The location—surrounded by cable-car lines, the Theater District, Union Square, and dozens of restaurants—is superb, and the rooms are surprisingly quiet for such a busy area. Though rooms can be small, a recent renovation has made the most of the space with new mattresses, desks, data ports, Nintendo, voice mail, and a handsome studylike ambiance. All units are also meticulously neat and clean, and the full private bathrooms have hair dryers and lovely amenities. A big hit since it started a few years back is the hotel's English afternoon tea, served in the Windsor Tea Room from 3 to 6:30pm Wednesday through Sunday. Breakfast, also served in the tea room, runs from $6.50 to $8. (*Note:* Due to elevator renovations, most of the hotel will be closed for a few months in early 2000.)

The Maxwell. 386 Geary St. (at Mason St.), San Francisco, CA 94102. ☎ **888/734-6299** or 415/986-2000. Fax 415/397-2447. 153 units. A/C TV TEL. $155–$215 double; $295–$595 suite. Extra person $15. Corporate discounts available. AE, CB, DC, DISC, MC, V. Parking $18. Cable car: Powell-Hyde and Powell-Mason lines (1 block east). Bus: 2, 3, 4, 30, 38, or 45.

When new management renovated this hotel a few years ago in a style they call "theater-deco-fused-with-Victoriana," the results were a chic-boutique blend of velvets, brocades, and rich color and patterns. Rooms come with upholstered chairs, hand-painted lamps, luxurious pillows, boldly tiled sinks, and respectable prints hanging on the walls. Other pluses are writing desks, hair dryers, and two phones. The adjoining Max's On The Square Restaurant looks great, but its American fare and service are nothing to write home about.

Savoy Hotel. 580 Geary St. (between Taylor and Jones sts.), San Francisco, CA 94102. ☎ **800/227-4223** or 415/441-2700. Fax 415/441-0124. 83 units. MINIBAR TV TEL. $115–$145 double; from $205 suite. Ask about package, government, senior, and corporate rates. AE, CB, DC, DISC, MC, V. Parking $18. Bus: 2, 3, 4, 27, or 38.

When the Savoy opened, *Travel & Leisure* deemed it one of the sweetest affordable options off Union Square. While that's still the case, unfortunately the hotel hasn't kept up with the wear and tear associated with brisk business. However, rooms, which can be small, are still cozy French provincial, with 18th-century period furnishings, featherbeds, and goose-down pillows—plus modern conveniences such as remote-control TVs and hair dryers. Not all rooms are alike, but each has beautiful patterned draperies, triple sheets, turndown service, full-length mirrors, and two-line phones, as well as concierge service and free overnight shoe-shines. Rates include complimentary late-afternoon sherry and tea served in the Brasserie Savoy, an excellent and well-priced downtown restaurant.

Warwick Regis. 490 Geary St. (between Mason and Taylor sts.), San Francisco, CA 94102. ☎ **800/827-3447** or 415/928-7900. Fax 415/441-8788. 80 units. MINIBAR TV TEL. $149–$159 double; $199–$239 suite. Rates include continental breakfast. AE, CB, DC, DISC, MC, V. Parking $23. Cable car: Powell-Hyde and Powell Mason lines. Bus: 2, 3, 4, 27, or 38.

Louis XVI may have been a rotten monarch, but he certainly had taste. Fashioned in the style of pre-Revolutionary France, the Warwick is awash with pristine French and English antiques, Italian marble, chandeliers, four-poster beds, hand-carved head-boards, and the like. The result is an expensive-looking hotel that, for all its pleas-antries and perks, is surprisingly affordable when compared to its Union Square neighbors (singles are as low as $125). All rooms come with VCRs and hair dryers; honeymooners should splurge on a Fireplace room, which has a canopy bed.

Adjoining the lobby is fashionable La Scene Café, the perfect place to start your day with a latte and end it with a nightcap. Amenities include 24-hour room and concierge service, dry cleaning, laundry, twice-daily maid service, complimentary shoe-shine and newspaper, a business center, conference rooms, and access to nearby health club.

INEXPENSIVE

Brady Acres. 649 Jones St. (between Geary and Post sts.), San Francisco, CA 94102. ☎ **800/627-2396** or 415/929-8033. Fax 415/441-8033. www.bradyacres.com. 25 units. TV TEL. $79–$119 double per day May–Sept with special weekly rates. Available only by the week Oct–Apr; special weekly rates. MC, V. Parking garage nearby for $14–$16 per day. Bus: 2, 3, 4, 27, or 38.

Inside this small, four-story brick building is a penny-pincher's dream come true. Enter through a black-and-gold door, and you'll find everything you need to keep costs to a minimum. The small but very clean rooms have microwaves, small fridges, toasters, coffeemakers, hair dryers, alarm clocks, direct-dial phones (with free local calls), answering machines, voice mail, color TVs, and radio/cassette players. Bath-rooms were recently renovated and come stocked with amenities, and a coin-operated washer and dryer are located in the basement, along with free laundry soap and irons. Twice-weekly house cleaning is included. Keep in mind that during the low season, you can only rent by the week. *Note:* New owners intend to make a few changes within the coming year, but promise to continue offering the slew of amenities at affordable rates.

Golden Gate Hotel. 775 Bush St. (between Powell and Mason sts.), San Francisco, CA 94108. ☎ **800/835-1118** or 415/392-3702. Fax 415/392-6202. 23 units, 14 with bath-room. TV. $65–$75 double without bathroom, $99–$115 double with bathroom. Rates include continental breakfast. AE, CB, DC, MC, V. Parking $14. Cable car: Powell-Hyde and Powell-Mason lines (1 block east). Bus: 2, 3, 4, 30, 38, or 45.

Among San Francisco's small hotels occupying historic turn-of-the-century buildings are some real gems, and the Golden Gate Hotel is one of them. It's 2 blocks north of

Union Square and 2 blocks down (literally) from the crest of Nob Hill, with cable-car stops at the corner for easy access to Fisherman's Wharf and Chinatown (the city's theaters and best restaurants are also within walking distance). But the best thing about the Golden Gate Hotel is that it's a family-run establishment: John and Renate Kenaston are hospitable innkeepers who take obvious pleasure in making their guests comfortable. Each individually decorated room has handsome antique furnishings (plenty of wicker) from the early 1900s, quilted bedspreads, and fresh flowers. (Request a room with a clawfoot tub if you enjoy a good, hot soak.) All rooms have phones, and complimentary afternoon tea is served daily from 4 to 7pm.

Grant Plaza Hotel. 465 Grant Ave. (at the corner of Pine St.), San Francisco, CA 94108. ☎ **800/472-6899** or 415/434-3883. Fax 415/434-3886. E-mail: grantplaza@worldnet. att.net. 72 units. TV TEL. $62–$89 double. AE, CB, DC, MC, V. Nearby parking $11.50. Cable car: Powell-Hyde and Powell-Mason lines (2 blocks west).

Grant Plaza offers cheap accommodations and basic—and we mean basic—rooms right in the middle of Union Square/Chinatown action. Many of the small, well-kept units in this six-story building overlook Chinatown's main street, and all of them had new bedspreads, draperies, and hair dryers added in 1997. Corner rooms on higher floors are both larger and brighter. Ask for a room on the top floor—they're the newest and are substantially nicer than the older units. Expect little more than a soap dispenser in the small shower (most bathrooms don't have tubs).

NOB HILL
VERY EXPENSIVE

Fairmont Hotel & Tower. 950 Mason St. (at California St.), San Francisco, CA 94108. ☎ **800/527-4727** or 415/772-5000. Fax 415/772-5013. 600 units. A/C MINIBAR TV TEL. Main building: $229–$279 double; from $530 suite. Tower: $269–$359 double; from $800 suite. Extra person $30. Continental breakfast $14 extra. AE, CB, DC, DISC, MC, V. Parking $29. Cable car: California St. line (direct stop).

The granddaddy of Nob Hill's ritzy hotels, the Fairmont wins top honors for the most awe-inspiring lobby in San Francisco. Even if you're not staying here, it's worth a trip to gape at its massive marble columns, vaulted ceilings, velvet chairs, gilded mirrors, and spectacular wraparound staircase. Unfortunately, such opulence doesn't carry over to the guest rooms, which are surprisingly ordinary (aside from the spectacular views from the top floors). In addition to the expected luxuries, expect such extras as goosedown pillows, electric shoe buffers, large walk-in closets, and multi-line phones with voice mail.

Dining/Diversions: A variety of restaurants ranges from contemporary California cuisine to Chinese and Polynesian specialties to deli favorites. The tropical Hurricane Bar features dancing and a generous happy hour. Afternoon tea is served daily in the lobby.

Amenities: 24-hour room service, 24-hour concierge, twice-daily maid service, evening turndown, laundry/valet, complimentary shoe-shine, complimentary morning limousine to the Financial District, health club, business center, barbershop, beauty salon, pharmacy, shopping arcade.

✪ **Huntington Hotel.** 1075 California St. (between Mason and Taylor sts.), San Francisco, CA 94108. ☎ **800/227-4683**, 800/652-1539 in CA, or 415/474-5400. Fax 415/474-6227. 140 units. A/C MINIBAR TV TEL. $255–$375 double; from $475–$990 suite. Special packages available. Continental breakfast $10.75. AE, CB, DC, DISC, MC, V. Valet parking $19.50. Cable car: California St. line (direct stop). Bus: 1.

The stately Huntington has long been a favorite retreat for Hollywood stars and political VIPs who desire privacy and security. Family owned since 1924—a real rarity among large hotels—this place eschews pomp and circumstance; absolute privacy and unobtrusive service are its mainstay. Though the elaborate 19th-century-style lobby is rather petite, the apartment-like guest rooms are quite large and feature Brunschwig and Fils fabrics, French antiques, and city views. Prices are steep, but special offers like the Romance Package ($240 per couple, including free champagne, sherry, and limousine service) make the Huntington worth considering for a special occasion.

Dining/Diversions: The Big Four restaurant offers expensive seasonal continental cuisine in one of the city's most handsome dining rooms. There's live piano music nightly in the lounge.

Amenities: Concierge, room service, laundry, overnight shoe-shine, evening turndown, complimentary morning newspaper, twice-daily maid service, complimentary limousine to the Financial District and Union Square, complimentary formal tea or sherry upon arrival, access to off-premises health club and spa ($15).

Mark Hopkins Intercontinental. 1 Nob Hill (at California and Mason sts.), San Francisco, CA 94108. ☎ **800/327-0200** or 415/392-3434. Fax 415/421-3302. 390 units. A/C MINIBAR TV TEL. $280–$350 double; from $500 suite. Breakfast buffet $20 extra. AE, CB, DC, DISC, MC, V. Valet parking $25. Cable car: California St. line (direct stop). Bus: 1.

Built in 1926, this 19-story hotel caters mostly to convention-bound executives who can write off the high rates. Each neoclassical room comes with all the fancy amenities you'd expect from a world-class hotel, including custom furniture, plush fabrics, sumptuous bathrooms, and extraordinary views. (*Tip:* The even-numbered rooms on the higher floors overlook the Golden Gate.) A minor caveat is that there are only three guest elevators, making a quick trip up to your room difficult during busy periods.

Dining/Diversions: The plush and decidedly formal Nob Hill Restaurant offers international cuisine with a California flair, plus a continental buffet breakfast; a second restaurant serves lunch, afternoon tea, cocktails, and dinner. The world-renowned Top of the Mark lounge serves cocktails and Sunday brunch, and offers dancing to live music Wednesday through Saturday.

Amenities: Concierge, room service, laundry, overnight shoe-shine, newspaper delivery, evening turndown on request, in-room massage, twice-daily maid service, baby-sitting, valet parking, courtesy limousine weekday mornings, multilingual guest relations, health club, business center, Executive Club floor, car-rental desk.

✪ **Ritz-Carlton.** 600 Stockton St. (between Pine and California sts.), San Francisco, CA 94108. ☎ **800/241-3333** or 415/296-7465. Fax 415/986-1268. 336 units. A/C MINIBAR TV TEL. $365 double; $425 club-level double; from $550 suite. Weekend discounts and packages available. Continental breakfast $15.25 extra; breakfast buffet $14 extra; Sun brunch $42. AE, CB, DC, DISC, MC, V. Parking $29. Cable car: Powell-Hyde and Powell-Mason lines (direct stop).

Ranked among the top hotels in the world (as well as the top hotel in the city) by readers of *Condé Nast Traveler,* the Ritz-Carlton has been the benchmark of San Francisco luxury hotels since it opened in 1991. A Nob Hill landmark, it's outfitted with the finest furnishings, fabrics, and artwork, and the rooms offer every possible amenity and service, from Italian-marble bathrooms with double sinks to plush terry robes. The more expensive rooms offer good views of the city. Club rooms have a dedicated concierge, separate elevator-key access, and complimentary meals throughout the day.

Dining/Diversions: The Ritz-Carlton Dining Room is regarded as one of the city's top restaurants (see "Dining," below, for a complete review). The less formal Terrace Restaurant offers contemporary French cuisine and courtyard dining. The lobby lounge serves afternoon tea and cocktails and sushi, accompanied by low-key live entertainment. Sunday brunch is easily one of the best—and most extensive—in town.

Amenities: Concierge, 24-hour room service, same-day laundry/dry cleaning, valet, shoeshine, complimentary morning newspaper, child care, business center, gift boutique, an outstanding fitness center with pool.

EXPENSIVE

Nob Hill Lambourne. 725 Pine St. (between Powell and Stockton sts.), San Francisco, CA 94108. ☎ **800/274-8466** or 415/433-2287. 20 units. MINIBAR TV TEL. From $200 double; $325 suite. Rates include continental breakfast. AE, CB, DC, DISC, MC, V. Valet parking $24. Cable car: California St. line (1 block north).

One of San Francisco's top "business-boutique" hotels, the Lambourne bills itself as an urban health spa, offering a variety of spa treatments—from massage to yoga lessons—to ease executive-level stress. Even without this hook, the ultra-stylish Lambourne deserves a top-of-the-class rating. Quality, hand-sewn mattresses and goose-down comforters are complemented by such in-room extras as notebook computers with Internet access, fax machines, VCRs, stereos, kitchenettes, and coffeemakers; bathrooms have oversized tubs and hair dryers. Guests are invited to enjoy complimentary wine and hors d'oeuvres at 6pm.

Amenities: Concierge, dry cleaning, laundry, newspaper delivery, in-room massage, twice-daily maid service, evening turndown, business services, spa treatment room.

INEXPENSIVE

Nob Hill Hotel. 835 Hyde St. (between Bush and Sutter sts.), San Francisco, CA 94109. ☎ **415/885-2987.** Fax 415/921-1648. 50 units. TV TEL. Nov–Mar $89 double, $170 suite; Apr–Oct $109 double, $200 suite. Rates include continental breakfast and evening wine reception. AE, DISC, MC, V. Bus: 2, 3, or 4.

Along with long-term apartments, the Nob Hill Hotel also offers 50 hotel rooms geared toward the budget traveler. Most units are small but pleasantly decorated with old-fashioned furnishings such as antique armoires, brass beds, and carved wood nightstands. A recent $1.5-million renovation resulted in new marble bathrooms, textiles, and updated furnishings (though still antique in style). All units offer high-tech amenities such as satellite TV with free HBO; voice mail; and copy, fax, and e-mail services. Complimentary pastries and coffee are served each morning at the adjacent Il Cartoccio Italian restaurant, a good place to refuel before venturing down the street to Union Square, and a wine reception is held each evening.

SOMA
VERY EXPENSIVE

Harbor Court. 165 Steuart St. (between Mission and Howard sts.), San Francisco, CA 94105. ☎ **800/346-0555** in the U.S., or 415/882-1300. Fax 415/882-1313. 131 units. A/C MINIBAR TV TEL. $175–$325 double. Continental breakfast $8 extra. AE, CB, DC, MC, V. Parking $24. Muni Metro: Embarcadero. Bus: 14, 32, or 80x.

When the Embarcadero Freeway was torn down after the Big One in 1989, one of the major benefactors was this hotel, whose backyard view went from a wall of cement to a dazzling view of the Bay Bridge (a bay-view room will cost you $50 extra). Located just off the Embarcadero at the edge of the Financial District, this former YMCA books a lot of corporate travelers, but anyone who prefers stylish, high-quality accommodations—half-canopy beds, large armoires, writing desks, soundproof windows—and a lively scene will be very content here.

Dining: In the evening, the hotel's dark, velvety restaurant, Harry Denton's, transforms into the Financial District's hot spot for festive singles.

Amenities: Concierge, limited room service, dry cleaning, laundry, secretarial services, valet, courtesy car, free refreshments in lobby, free use of the top-quality fitness club with Olympic-size pool.

Hotel Griffon. 155 Steuart St. (between Mission and Howard sts.), San Francisco, CA 94105. ☎ **800/321-2201** or 415/495-2100. Fax 415/495-3522. 62 units. A/C MINIBAR TV TEL. $220–$270 double; $375–$415 suites. Rates include continental breakfast and newspaper. AE, CB, DC, DISC, MC, V. Parking $15. All Market St. buses, BART, and ferries.

After a complete rehab in 1989, the Hotel Griffon emerged as a top contender among San Francisco's small hotels. Ideally situated on the historic waterfront and only steps from the heart of the Financial District, the Griffon is impeccably outfitted with contemporary features such as whitewashed brick walls, lofty ceilings, marble vanities, window seats, cherry-wood furniture, and art deco–style lamps—really, this place is smooth. Be sure to request a bay-view room—the added perks and Bay Bridge view make it well worth the extra $40—and inquire about the excellent weekend packages the hotel occasionally offers.

Dining: As we go to press, restaurant Rôti, which has been a prime lunch spot for the nearby Financial District, is debating a name change. They do, however, claim they'll continue offering California-style food prepared on spit roasts and in wood-burning ovens in a dining room with a view of the Bay Bridge.

Amenities: Limited room service, laundry/valet, concierge, in-room massage, secretarial services, free access to nearby health club, complimentary town car to the Financial District from 7 to 9am.

FINANCIAL DISTRICT
VERY EXPENSIVE

✪ **Mandarin Oriental.** 222 Sansome St. (between Pine and California sts.), San Francisco, CA 94104. ☎ **800/622-0404** or 415/276-9888. Fax 415/433-0289. 158 units. A/C MINIBAR TV TEL. $415–$485 double; from $505–$570 junior suite. Continental breakfast $18 extra. AE, CB, DC, DISC, JCB, MC, V. Valet parking $24. Muni Metro: Montgomery. Bus: All Market St. buses.

The common areas here are a bit cold and impersonal, but the rooms are state-of-the-art and the views divine, making this a top choice for luxury travelers. The large rooms are located between the 38th and 48th floors of a high-rise, which affords them extraordinary views. Not all units have tub-side views (get one that does and you'll never forget it!), but all have well-stocked marble bathrooms that include such luxuries as terry- and cotton-cloth robes, hair dryers, makeup mirrors, and silk slippers. The less opulent rooms are done in a kind of reserved-contemporary decor with Asian accents. Additional amenities include two-line phones with fax hookups and on-command video access to more than 80 movies.

Dining: Silks offers expensive and delicious fine California/Asian dining, though its atmosphere is somber and a little flat.

Amenities: 24-hour room service, complimentary newspaper and shoe-shine, concierge, laundry/valet, business center, fitness center with cardio and Nautilus machines and free weights.

Sheraton Palace Hotel. 2 New Montgomery St. (at Market St.), San Francisco, CA 94105. ☎ **800/325-3535** or 415/512-1111. Fax 415/543-0671. 550 units. A/C MINIBAR TV TEL. $300–$390 double; from $450 suite. Extra person $20. Children under 18 sharing existing bedding stay free in parents' room. Weekend rates and packages available. Continental breakfast $13.50 extra; deluxe continental $15.75 extra. AE, DC, DISC, JCB, MC, V. Parking $22. Muni Metro: Bus: All Market St. trams. All Market St. buses.

Every time you walk through these doors, you'll be reminded how incredibly majestic old luxury really is. The original 1875 Palace was rebuilt after the 1906 quake; the most spectacular attribute is still the old regal lobby and the Garden Court, a San Francisco landmark that has been restored to its original heart-stopping grandeur. Regrettably, the rooms have that standardized, chain-hotel appearance.

Dining/Diversions: On special holidays, the Garden Court serves a $55 brunch worth indulging in, while a scaled-down version takes over on other weekends. The Pied Piper Bar is named for the Maxfield Parrish mural that dominates the room. There's also a traditional San Francisco grill with turn-of-the-century charm, plus an authentic Japanese restaurant.

Amenities: 24-hour room service, concierge, evening turndown, laundry/valet, business center, lobby-level shops, on-site health club with skylight-covered lap pool, whirlpool, sauna, and exercise room.

NORTH BEACH
MODERATE

✪ **Hotel Bohème.** 444 Columbus St. (between Vallejo and Green sts.), San Francisco, CA 94133. ☎ **415/433-9111.** Fax 415/362-6292. 15 units. TV TEL. $139 double. AE, CB, DISC, DC, JCB, MC, V. Parking $23 at nearby public garage. Cable car: Powell-Mason line. Bus: 12, 15, 30, 41, 45, or 83.

North Beach romance awaits you at the Bohème. Although located in the center of North Beach, this recently renovated hotel's style and demeanor are more reminiscent of a prestigious home in upscale Nob Hill. The decor evokes the Beat generation, which flourished here in the 1950s; rooms are small but hopelessly romantic, with gauze-draped canopies and walls artistically accented with lavender, sage green, black, and pumpkin. The staff is ultra-hospitable, and bonuses include hair dryers and free sherry in the lobby each afternoon. Take note: While bathrooms are sweet, they're also absolutely tiny (no tubs). *Tip:* Request a room off the street side; they're quieter.

INEXPENSIVE

San Remo Hotel. 2237 Mason St. (at Chestnut St.) San Francisco, CA 94133. ☎ **800/ 352-REMO** or 415/776-8688. Fax 415/776-2811. www.sanremohotel.com. E-mail: info@ sanremohotel.com. 63 units, 1 with bathroom. $60–$85 double; $125 suite. AE, CB, DC, JCB, MC, V. Parking $10–$12. Cable car: Powell-Mason line. Bus: 15, 22, 30 or 42.

Located in a quiet North Beach neighborhood and within walking distance of Fisherman's Wharf, this small European-style pensione is one of the best budget hotels in San Francisco. The rooms are small and bathrooms shared, but all is forgiven when it comes time to pay the bill. Rooms are decorated in a cozy country style with brass and iron beds, armoires, and wicker furnishings; most have ceiling fans. The shared bathrooms, each immaculately clean, feature clawfoot tubs and brass pull-chain toilets with oak tanks and brass fixtures. If the penthouse is available, book it: You won't find a more romantic place to stay in San Francisco for so little money. (It's got its own bathroom, TV, fridge, and patio.)

FISHERMAN'S WHARF
EXPENSIVE

The Sheraton at Fisherman's Wharf. 2500 Mason St. (between Beach and North Point sts.), San Francisco, CA 94133. ☎ **800/325-3535** or 415/362-5500. Fax 415/956-5275. 525 units. A/C TV TEL. $150–$280 double; from $400 suite. Extra person $20. Continental breakfast $9.50 extra. AE, CB, DC, DISC, MC, V. Self-parking $14. Cable car: Powell-Mason line (1 block east, 2 blocks south). Bus: 15, 32, or 42.

Built in the mid–1970s, this modern, three-story hotel isn't the most visually appealing, but it offers the reliable comforts of a Sheraton in the heart of San Francisco's most popular tourist area. In 1995, the hotel spent $4 million renovating the rooms and adding a Corporate Floor that caters exclusively to business travelers. Additional renovations were made in 1999.

Dining/Diversions: A Victorian-style cafe serves up breakfast, lunch, and dinner, plus live jazz several nights a week along with cocktails and assorted appetizers.

Amenities: Room service, concierge, evening turndown, outdoor heated pool, access to nearby health club, business center, hair salon, car-rental and travel desks.

Tuscan Inn. 425 North Point St. (at Mason St.), San Francisco, CA 94133. ☎ **800/648-4626** or 415/561-1100. Fax 415/561-1199. 221 units. A/C MINIBAR TV TEL. $148–$218 double; $188–$268 suite. Rates include coffee, tea, and evening fireside wine reception. AE, DC, DISC, MC, V. Parking $18. Cable car: Powell-Mason line. Bus: 15, 32, or 42.

The Tuscan is the best hotel at Fisherman's Wharf. Like an island of respectability in a sea of touristy schlock, it offers a level of style and comfort far beyond its neighbors. Splurge on parking—cheaper than the wharf's outrageously priced garages—and then make your way toward the plush lobby warmed by a grand fireplace. Even the rooms, each equipped with writing desks and armchairs, are a cut above competing neighborhood hotels. The only caveat is the lack of views—a small price to pay for a good hotel in a great location.

Dining: Café Pescatore serves standard Italian fare in an airy, partial alfresco setting.

Amenities: Concierge, room service, laundry service, voice mail.

MODERATE

The Wharf Inn. 2601 Mason St. (at Beach St.), San Francisco, CA 94133. ☎ **800/548-9918** or 415/673-7411. Fax 415/776-2181. 51 units. TV TEL. $98–$165 double; penthouse $270–$370. AE, CB, DC, DISC, MC, V. Free parking. Cable car: Powell-Mason. Bus: 15, 32, or 42.

Our top choice for affordable lodging at Fisherman's Wharf, the Wharf Inn offers above-average accommodations amidst one of the most popular tourist attractions in the world. The newly refurbished rooms, done in handsome tones of forest green, burgundy, and pale yellow, come with all the standard amenities, including complimentary coffee and tea. Its main attribute, however, is its location—right smack dab in the middle of the wharf, 2 blocks away from Pier 39 and the cable-car turnaround, and within walking distance of the Embarcadero and North Beach. The inn is ideal for carbound families, as parking is free (there's $25 a day saved) and there's no charge for packing along an extra person.

COW HOLLOW/PACIFIC HEIGHTS
VERY EXPENSIVE

✪ Sherman House. 2160 Green St. (between Webster and Fillmore sts.), San Francisco, CA 94123. ☎ **800/424-5777** or 415/563-3600. Fax 415/563-1882. 14 units. TV TEL. $340–$430 double; $665–$800 suite. Continental breakfast $15 extra. AE, DC, MC, V. Valet parking $16. Cable car: Powell-Hyde line. Bus: 22, 41, or 45.

How expensive is a night at the Sherman House? Put it this way: If you have to ask, you can't afford it. This magnificent 1876 Victorian has been restored to its original splendor, and it now sets the standard in San Francisco for privacy, personal service, and all-around sumptuousness. All rooms are individually decorated with authentic antiques in French Second Empire, Biedermeier, or English Jacobean style; queen-size canopy featherbeds; and ultra-rich tapestry fabrics and down comforters. Extras include VCRs, stereos, and granite bathrooms complete with robes and whirlpools; all rooms except one have fireplaces.

Dining: The dining room has a very fine reputation, but because of a zoning dispute, it has no license to serve food to nonguests and is open only to residents.

Amenities: Room service, butler (who will discreetly unpack luggage), concierge, massage, personalized shopping, chauffeur, dry cleaning/laundry, complimentary newspaper delivery, twice-daily maid service, secretarial services, business center.

EXPENSIVE

Union Street Inn. 2229 Union St. (between Fillmore and Steiner sts.), San Francisco, CA 94123. ☎ **415/346-0424.** Fax 415/922-8046. www.unionstreetinn.com. 5 units, 1 cottage. TV TEL. $135–$245 standard double; $245 cottage. Rates include breakfast, hors d'oeuvres, and evening beverages. AE, MC, V. Parking $15. Bus: 22, 28, 41, 45, or 47.

Who would have guessed that one of the most delightful B&Bs in California would be in San Francisco? This two-story Edwardian may front the perpetually busy (and chichi) Union Street, but it's quiet as a church on the inside. All individually decorated rooms are comfortably furnished, and most come with canopied or brass beds with down comforters, fresh flowers, bay windows (beg for one with a view of the garden), and private bathrooms (a few even have Jacuzzi tubs). An extended continental breakfast is served in the parlor, in your room, or on an outdoor terrace overlooking a lovely English garden. The ultimate honeymoon retreat is the private carriage house behind the inn, but any room at this warm, friendly place is guaranteed to please.

MODERATE

Bed & Breakfast Inn. 4 Charlton Court (off Union St., between Buchanan and Laguna sts.), San Francisco, CA 94123. ☎ **415/921-9784.** Fax 415/921-0544. 13 units, 4 with shared bathroom. $80–$100 double without bathroom; $150 double with bathroom; $250–$300 suite. Rates include continental breakfast. AE, CB, DC, DISC, MC, V. Parking $11 a day at nearby garage. Bus: 41 or 45.

San Francisco's first B&B is composed of a trio of Victorian houses all gussied up in English country style, hidden in a cul-de-sac just off Union Street. While it doesn't have quite the casual ambiance of the neighboring Union Street Inn, it is loaded with charm. Each room is uniquely decorated with family heirlooms, original art, and a profusion of fresh flowers. The Garden Suite—highly recommended for families or groups of four—comes with a fully stocked kitchen, a living room with fireplace, two bedrooms, two bathrooms (one with a Jacuzzi tub), a study, and French doors leading out into the garden. Breakfast—freshly baked croissants, fresh fruit, orange juice, and coffee, tea, or cocoa—is either brought to your room on a tray with flowers and a morning newspaper, or served in a sunny Victorian breakfast room on antique china.

INEXPENSIVE

Edward II Inn & Pub. 3155 Scott St. (at Lombard St.), San Francisco, CA 94123. ☎ **800/473-2846** or 415/922-3000. Fax 415/931-5784. 32 units, 11 with shared bathroom. TV TEL. $75 double with shared bathroom; $99 double with private bathroom; $165–$225 suite/cottage. Rates include continental breakfast and evening sherry. AE, MC, V. Self-parking $10 across the street. Bus: 28, 43, or 76.

This three-story, self-styled "English Country" inn has a room for almost anyone's budget, ranging from pensione rooms with shared bathrooms to luxuriously appointed suites and cottages with living rooms, kitchens, and whirlpool tubs. Originally built to house guests who attended the 1915 Pan-Pacific Exposition, it's now run by innkeepers Denise and Bob Holland, who have done a fantastic job maintaining its worldly charm. Regardless of their rate, all rooms are spotlessly clean and comfortably appointed with cozy antique furnishings and plenty of fresh flowers. The only caveat is that its Lombard Street location is usually congested with traffic, but nearby Chestnut and Union streets offer some of the best shopping and dining in the city. Complimentary breakfast and evening drinks are served in the adjoining pub.

✪ **Marina Inn.** 3110 Octavia St. (at Lombard St.), San Francisco, CA 94123. ☎ **800/274-1420** or 415/928-1000. Fax 415/928-5909. 40 units. TV TEL. Nov 1–Feb 29 $65–$105 double; Mar 1–May 31 $75–$115 double; June 1–Oct 31 $85–$125 double. Rates include continental breakfast, afternoon sherry, and turndown service. AE, MC, V. Bus: 28, 30, 43, or 76.

The Marina Inn is, without question, the best low-priced hotel in San Francisco. How they offer so much for so little is mystifying. Each guest room in this 1924 four-story Victorian looks as though it's been culled from a country-furnishings catalog, complete with rustic pinewood furniture, a four-poster bed with silk-soft comforter, and pretty wallpaper. There are even high-class touches that many expensive hotels don't include: new remote-control TVs discreetly hidden in pine cabinetry, full bathtubs with showers, and nightly turndown service with chocolates on your pillow. Add to that complimentary continental breakfast, afternoon sherry, friendly service, and an armada of nearby shops and restaurants, and there you have it: our number-one choice for Best Overall Value. *Note:* Be sure to request one of the quieter rooms away from busy Lombard Street.

JAPANTOWN & ENVIRONS
EXPENSIVE

The Archbishop's Mansion. 1000 Fulton St. (at Steiner St.), San Francisco, CA 94117. ☎ **800/543-5820** or 415/563-7872. Fax 415/883-3193. 15 units. TEL TV. $139–$385 double. Rates include continental breakfast. AE, CB, DC, MC, V. Limited free parking. Bus: 5 or 22.

One thing is for certain: The Archbishop who built this 1904 belle-epoque beauty was no Puritan. Drippingly romantic, it's one of the most opulent and fabulously adorned B&Bs you could possibly hope to stay in. The Don Giovanni suite—larger than most San Francisco houses—comes with a huge, cherub-encrusted four-poster bed imported from a French castle, a palatial fireplace, elaborately embroidered linens, and a seven-head shower. Slightly closer to earth is the deadly romantic Carmen suite, with a clawfoot tub fronting a toasty, wood-burning fireplace.

Dining: Breakfast is delivered to your room. Complimentary wine is served in the elegant parlor in the evening.

Amenities: Laundry/valet, concierge, limousine service, complimentary morning newspaper, limited room service.

✪ **Hotel Majestic.** 1500 Sutter St. (between Octavia and Gough sts.), San Francisco, CA 94109. ☎ **800/869-8966** or 415/441-1100. Fax 415/673-7331. 60 units. TV TEL. $135–$215 double; from $325 suite. Group, government, corporate, and relocation rates available. Continental breakfast $8.50 extra. AE, CB, DC, DISC, MC, V. Valet parking $18.

The Majestic, built in 1902, meets every professional need while retaining the ambiance of a luxurious old-world hotel. The lobby alone will sweep you into another era with its tapestries, brocades, Corinthian columns, and intricate, lavish detail. Rooms are furnished with French and English antiques, the centerpiece of each being a large four-poster canopy bed; you'll also find mirrored armoires and antique reproductions. All drapes, fabrics, carpet, and bedspreads were replaced in 1997, and half the bathrooms and guest rooms went under a $2-million renovation in 1999, which ensures you'll rest not only in style, but in freshness as well. Extras include a well-lit full-size desk and bathrobes; some rooms also have fireplaces.

Dining/Diversions: Café Majestic and Bar, which serves California/Asian fare in a romantic setting, continues to intrigue a local clientele. Cocktails are offered from the French mahogany marble-topped bar.

Amenities: Room service, laundry/valet, concierge, dry cleaning, laundry service, in-room massage, secretarial service, courtesy car on weekdays, complimentary newspaper, and afternoon sherry and fresh-baked cookies from 6 to 8pm nightly.

MODERATE

Queen Anne Hotel. 1590 Sutter St. (between Gough and Octavia sts.), San Francisco, CA 94109. ☎ **800/227-3970** or 415/441-2828. Fax 415/775-5212. www.queenanne.com.

44 units. TV TEL. $130–$180 double; $185–$295 suite. Extra person $10. Rates include continental breakfast. AE, CB, DC, DISC, MC, V. Parking $12. Bus: 2, 3, or 4.

This majestic 1890 Victorian is a stunning boutique hotel that remains true to its heritage and emulates San Francisco's golden days. The lavish "grand salon" greets you with English oak paneling and antiques; rooms follow suit with antique armoires, marble-top dressers, and other period pieces. Some have corner turret bay windows that look out onto tree-lined streets, plus separate parlor areas and wet bars; others have cozy reading nooks and fireplaces. All rooms have phones in the bathroom, computer hookups, and fridges. You can relax in the parlor, with its impressive floor-to-ceiling fireplace, or in the hotel library. Amenities include room service, concierge, morning newspaper, and complimentary afternoon tea and sherry. There's also access to an off-premises health club with a lap pool. If you're not partial to Union Square, this hotel comes highly recommended.

CIVIC CENTER
EXPENSIVE

The Inn at the Opera. 333 Fulton St. (at Franklin St.), San Francisco, CA 94102. ☎ **800/ 325-2708** or 415/863-8400. Fax 415/861-0821. 48 units. MINIBAR TV TEL. $165–$225 double; from $255 suite. Extra person $15. Rates include European buffet breakfast. AE, DC, MC, V. Parking $22. Bus: 5, 21, 47, or 49.

Judging from its mild-mannered facade and offbeat location, few would ever guess that this is one of San Francisco's—if not California's—finest small hotels. From the minute you walk into a marble- and damask-filled lobby, you know you're about to be spoiled with sumptuousness. But don't take our word for it; Pavarotti, Domingo, Baryshnikov, and dozens of other stars of the stage throw their slumber parties here regularly. Queen beds with huge stuffed pillows are standard in each elegant guest room, along with microwaves, fridges, and bouquets of fresh flowers. The larger rooms and suites are recommended for those who need elbow room; as in most small hotels, the least expensive "standard" rooms are short on space.

Dining/Diversions: Ovation at the Opera, the hotel's fine dining room, provides an intimate setting for dinner, while the adjacent lounge is an excellent place to relax with a cocktail.

Amenities: 24-hour room service, concierge, laundry/valet, evening turndown, complimentary light pressing and overnight shoeshine, complimentary limousine service to the Financial District, morning newspaper, business center.

MODERATE

Phoenix Hotel. 601 Eddy St. (at Larkin St.), San Francisco, CA 94109. ☎ **800/248-9466** or 415/776-1380. Fax 415/885-3109. 44 units. TV TEL. $119–$129 double; $159–$179 suite. Rates include continental breakfast. AE, DC, MC, V. Free parking. Bus: 19, 31, 38, 42, or 47.

Situated on the fringes of the less-than-pleasant Tenderloin District, this retro-1950s-style choice—which has been described by *People* as the hippest hotel in town—is a gathering place for visiting rockers, writers, and filmmakers who crave a dose of Southern California on their trips to San Francisco. The focal point of the pastel-painted Palm Springs–style hotel is a heated, paisley-muraled pool set in a modern-sculpture garden. The rooms, while far from plush, are comfortably outfitted with bamboo furnishings and original local art. In addition to the usual amenities, the inn's own closed-circuit channel shows films exclusively made in or about San Francisco. Services include on-site massage, concierge, laundry/valet, and— whoo hoo!—free parking. Backflip, a superswank cocktail lounge, serves "cocktail cuisine."

INEXPENSIVE

Abigail Hotel. 246 McAllister St. (between Hyde and Larkin sts.), San Francisco, CA 94102. ☎ **800/243-6510** or 415/861-9728. Fax 415/861-5848. 60 units. TV TEL. $79 double standard; $89 deluxe; $149 suite. Extra person $10. Rates include continental breakfast. AE, CB, DC, DISC, MC, V. Valet parking $16. Muni Metro: All Market St. trams. Bus: All Market St. buses.

Although it doesn't get much press, the Abigail is one of the better medium-priced hotels in the city; what it lacks in luxury it more than makes up for in charm. The rooms, while on the small side, are clean, cute, and comfortably furnished with cozy antiques and down comforters. Morning coffee, pastries, and complimentary newspapers greet you in the beautiful faux-marble lobby, while lunch and dinner are served in the hot new organic restaurant, Millennium. Access to a nearby health club, as well as laundry and massage services, are available upon request.

HAIGHT-ASHBURY
INEXPENSIVE

The Herb'n Inn. 525 Ashbury St. (between Page and Haight sts.), San Francisco, CA 94117. ☎ **415/553-8542.** Fax 415/553-8541. 4 units. TV (upon request). $70–$85 double. 2-night minimum. MC, V. Parking with advance notice. Bus: 6, 7, 33, 43, 66, or 71.

For those of you who want to immerse yourself in the sights and sounds of the legendary Haight-Ashbury District without compromising on quality (and cost), there's the Herb'n Inn. Run by sister/brother duo Pam and Bruce Brennan—who know the history and highlights of the Haight better than just about anyone—this modernized Victorian consists of four attractive guest rooms, a huge country-style kitchen, a sunny back garden, and the beginnings of Bruce's Psychedelic History Museum (a.k.a. the dining room). Top choice among the guest rooms is the Cilantro Room, which, besides being the largest, has the only private bathroom and a view of the garden. A hearty full breakfast is included, as well as office services (including forwarded e-mail), personal city tours à la Bruce, and plenty of free advice on how to spend your day in the city. Kids and lesbian and gay couples are welcome.

THE CASTRO
MODERATE

Inn on Castro. 321 Castro St. (at Market St.), San Francisco, CA 94114. ☎ **415/861-0321.** 8 units. TEL. $95–$108 double; from $120–$140 suite. Rates include full breakfast and evening brandy. AE, MC, V. Muni Metro: Castro.

One of the better choices in the Castro, half a block away from all the action, is this Edwardian-style inn decorated with contemporary furnishings, original modern art, and fresh flowers throughout. Almost all rooms have private bathrooms, direct-dial phones, and color TVs. Most rooms share a small back patio, and the suite has its own private outdoor sitting area. There's also a two-bedroom apartment available for $140 to $200.

✪ **The Parker House.** 520 Church St. (between 17th and 18th sts.), San Francisco, CA 94114. ☎ **888/520-PARK** or 415/621-3222. Fax 415/621-4139. members.aol.com/parkerhse/sf.html. E-mail: parkerhse@aol.com. 8 units. $99–$199 double. Rates include breakfast. AE, MC, V. Self-parking $15. Muni Metro: F or J. Bus: 22 or 33.

This is the best B&B option in the Castro. The neighborhood's "newest and grandest guest house" is a 5,000-square-foot, 1909 Edwardian located in a cheery neighborhood a few blocks from the heart of the action and half a block from grassy Dolores Park. Along with a well-decorated common library with fireplace and piano, breakfast room, formal dining room, and garden with patio, there's a lawn, "fern den," fountains, and spa and steam room. Each room features a private bathroom, voice mail, cable TV, and modem hookups.

4 Dining

San Francisco's dining scene is one of the best in the world. Since our space is limited, we had to make tough choices, but the end result is a cross section of San Francisco's best restaurants in every price range. For a greater selection of reviews, see *Frommer's San Francisco*.

Note: If you want a table at a top restaurant, make your reservation weeks in advance.

UNION SQUARE
EXPENSIVE

✪ **Farallon.** 450 Post St. (between Mason and Powell sts.). ☎ **415/956-6969.** Reservations recommended. Main courses $20–$30. AE, DC, DISC, MC, V. Mon–Sat 11:30am–2:30pm (bistro menu); Sun–Thur 5:30–10:30pm, Fri–Sat 5:30–11pm. Valet parking $12. Bus: 2, 3, 4, or 38. COASTAL CUISINE/SEAFOOD.

Here the multimillion-dollar attraction is seafood, from the outrageous decor to the stellar "coastal" cuisine. Handblown jellyfish lamps, kelp-bed-like back-lit columns, glass clam shells, sea-urchin light fixtures, a sea-life mosaic floor, and a tentacle-encircled bar set the scene. Thankfully, during designer Pat Kuleto's impressive renovation of this 1924 building, the original gothic arches were left intact, making the main dining room one of the most impressive in the entire city (although the bright and busy front room and intimate and incognito balcony aren't exactly shabby either). If you think the atmosphere is undeniably appealing and lavish, wait until you try the food. Chef Mark Franz, who opened Stars with Jeremiah Tower, is at the helm of the $5-million kitchen, offering starters ranging from the expected (oysters) to the more ambitious—iced Atlantic and Pacific shellfish indulgence, a cornucopia of oysters, clams, crayfish, prawns, mussels, and scallops with a horseradish mignonette ($16.95 per person), and a grand caviar tasting featuring four varieties with traditional accompaniments. While most main courses, such as the saffron poached sablefish and striped bass "pillows" with prawn mousse, napa cabbage, and foie-gras coulis, stick with the seaside theme, meat and game eaters are also honored with grilled squab breast stuffed with mushrooms and served with braised red chard and grilled veal chop with portobello mushroom galette. Whimsy-meets-sophistication does extend to the food, but the service and wine list (more than 300 by the bottle, 24 by the glass) are serious. This place has been quite the scene since it opened in mid–1997, so reserve well in advance. And if it's available, don't miss the huckleberry bombolini, a refreshingly different dessert.

✪ **Masa's.** In the Hotel Vintage Court, 648 Bush St. (at Stockton St.). ☎ **415/989-7154.** Reservations required and accepted up to 3 weeks in advance. Fixed-price dinner $75–$80. AE, CB, DC, DISC, MC, V. Tues–Sat 6–9:30pm. Closed 1st 2 weeks in Jan and 1st week in July. Cable car: Powell-Mason and Powell-Hyde lines. Bus: 2, 3, 4, 30, or 45. FRENCH.

Despite the departure of chef Julian Serrano, who headed to Vegas's Bellagio in mid–1998, Chad Callahan, who's been in the kitchen for the past 9 years, is matching the culinary magic of his predecessors. Add a flawless wine list and exemplary (even unpretentious) service, and Masa's still ranks as one of the top French outposts in the states. Either fixed-price or à la carte, dinner is a memorable expense-be-damned experience from start to finish. A typical meal might begin with foie gras in a Madeira truffle sauce, or poached lobster with potatoes, fried leek, and a truffle vinaigrette.

Entrees may include medallions of New Zealand fallow deer with zinfandel sauce and caramelized green apples, or Atlantic black bass with a saffron sauce. Desserts, as you might imagine, are heavenly.

✪ **Postrio.** 545 Post St. (between Mason and Taylor sts.). ☎ **415/776-7825.** Reservations recommended. Main courses $6–$15 breakfast, $14–$15 lunch, $19–$30 dinner. AE, CB, DC, DISC, MC, V. Mon–Wed 7–10am, 11:30am–2pm, and 5:30–10pm; Thur–Fri 7–10am, 11:30am–2pm, and 5:30–10:30pm; Sat 11:30am–2pm and 5:30–10:30pm; Sun 9am–2pm and 5:30–10pm; bar daily 11:30am–2am. Cable car: Powell-Mason and Powell-Hyde lines. Bus: 2, 3, 4, or 38. AMERICAN.

They say the higher you climb, the longer it takes to fall, and that's certainly the case with Postrio. All's well in owner Wolfgang Puck's glamourous dining room when brother chefs Mitchell and Steven Rosenthal generally perform to a full house. But eating is only half the reason you come to Postrio. After squeezing through the perpetually swinging bar—which, in its own right, dishes out excellent pizzas from a wood-burning oven—you're forced to make a grand entrance down the antebellum staircase to the cavernous dining room below (it's everyone's 15 seconds of fame, so make sure your fly is zipped). Pure Hollywood, for sure, but fun. The menu combines Italian, Asian, French, and California styles with mixed results. When we last visited, the sautéed salmon, for example, was a bit overcooked, but the accompanying plum glaze, wasabi mashed potatoes, and miso vinaigrette were outstanding. The desserts, each artistically sculpted by pastry chef Susan Brinkley, were the highlight of the evening. Despite the prime-time rush, service was friendly and infallible, as was the presentation.

MODERATE

✪ **Grand Cafe.** 501 Geary St. (at Taylor St., adjacent to the Hotel Monaco). ☎ **415/292-0101.** Reservations recommended. Main courses $15–$27. AE, CB, DC, DISC, MC, V. Mon–Sat 7am–10:30am, 11:30am–2:30pm, and 5:30–11pm; Sun 8–10:30am, 11:30am–2:30pm (brunch), and 5:30–10pm. Valet parking $7 for 3 hr, $3 each additional half hour. Bus: 2, 3, 4, 27, or 38. CALIFORNIA/FRENCH.

Along with Farallon restaurant, the Grand Cafe has one of the grandest dining rooms in San Francisco. The cocktail area alone is impressive, but the pièce de résistance is the enormous turn-of-the-century ballroom, a magnificent combination of old Europe and art nouveau with playful sculptures, original murals, and a cadre of dazzling deco chandeliers. After a shaky start, chef Denis Soriano and his crew are enjoying that most coveted of clientele: the repeat customer. On a recent visit, seated in a plush booth, we feasted on rich and decadent polenta soufflé; tender, pan-seared duck-leg confit with cabbage-walnut dressing; and a delicate baby-spinach salad with sliced pears, feta, walnuts, and fresh raspberry vinaigrette. Recommended entrees are the roasted duck breast with mission figs and huckleberry sauce, and the grilled filet mignon in a mushroom-shallot sauce. Service was both friendly and prompt, making the entire dining experience a pleasure. *Note:* The bar area has its own exhibition kitchen and menu, offering similar dishes for about half the price. The pizzas from the wood-burning oven are excellent, as is the grilled marinated skirt steak with whipped potatoes and red-wine sauce.

Kuleto's. 221 Powell St. (between Geary and O'Farrell sts., in the Villa Florence Hotel). ☎ **415/397-7720.** Reservations recommended. Breakfast $5–$10; main courses $8–$22. AE, CB, DC, DISC, MC, V. Mon–Fri 7–10:30am, Sat–Sun 8–10:30am; daily 11:30am–11pm. Cable car: Powell-Mason and Powell-Hyde lines. Muni Metro: Powell. Bus: 2, 3, 4, or 38. ITALIAN.

Kuleto's is a beautiful place filled with beautiful people who are here to see and be seen (don't come under- or overdressed). The best plan of action is to skip the wait for a table, muscle a seat at the antipasti bar, and fill up on appetizers (which are often better than the entrees). For a main course, try the penne pasta drenched in a tangy lamb-sausage marinara sauce, the clam linguini (generously overloaded with fresh clams), or any of the fresh-fish specials grilled over hardwoods. If you don't arrive by 6pm, expect to wait—this place fills up fast.

Rumpus. 1 Tillman Place (off Grant Ave., between Sutter and Post sts.). ☎ **415/421-2300.** Reservations recommended. Main courses $11.95–$19.95. AE, DC, MC, V. Mon–Sat 11:30am–2:30pm; Sun–Thurs 5:30–10pm; Fri–Sat 5:30–11pm. Bus: 2, 3, 4, 30, 45, or 76. Cable car: Powell-Hyde and Powell-Mason lines. CALIFORNIA.

Tucked into a small cul-de-sac off Grant Avenue, you'll find Rumpus, a fantastic restaurant serving well-prepared California fare at reasonable prices. The perfect place for a business lunch, shopping break, or dinner with friends, Rumpus is architecturally playful, colorful, and buzzing with conversation. The affordable menu offers a wealth of flavorful options, such as pan-roasted chicken, whose crispy and flavorful crust is almost as delightful as the perfectly cooked chicken and mashed potatoes beneath it; and the quality cut of New York steak, which comes with savory mashed potatoes. If nothing else, make sure to stop in here for one of the best desserts we've ever had: the puddinglike chocolate brioche cake.

Scala's Bistro. 432 Powell St. (at Sutter St.). ☎ **415/395-8555.** Reservations recommended. Breakfast $7–$10; lunch and dinner main courses $9–$18. AE, CB, DC, DISC, MC, V. Mon–Fri 7am–midnight; Sat–Sun 8am–midnight. Cable car: Powell-Hyde line. Bus: 2, 3, 4, 30, 45, or 76. FRENCH/ITALIAN.

This latest venture by husband-and-wife team Giovanni (the host) and Donna (the chef) Scala is one of the better restaurants in Union Square. The Parisian-bistro/old-world atmosphere has just the right balance of elegance and informality, which means it's perfectly okay to have some fun here (and apparently most people do). Donna puts together a fantastic array of Italian and French dishes that are priced surprisingly low. We suggest starting with the Earth and Surf calamari appetizer (better than anything we've sampled along the Mediterranean) or grilled portobello mushrooms. Generous portions of the moist, rich duck-leg confit will satisfy hungry appetites, but if you can only order one thing, make it Scala's signature dish: the seared salmon. Resting on a bed of creamy buttermilk mashed potatoes and ensconced with a tomato, chive, and white-wine sauce, it's one of the best salmon dishes we've ever tasted. Finish with the creamy Bostini cream pie, a dreamy combo of vanilla custard and orange chiffon cake with a warm chocolate glaze.

INEXPENSIVE

Tú Lan. 8 Sixth St. (at Market St.). ☎ **415/626-0927.** Main courses $3.50–$7. No credit cards. Mon–Sat 11am–9pm. Bus: 6, 7, 27, 31, 66, or 71. Cable car: Powell-Mason and Powell-Hyde lines. Muni Metro: F, J, K, L, M, N. VIETNAMESE.

You'll have to walk past the winos, weirdos, and street stench to get to this total dive Vietnamese restaurant bordering on Union Square and SoMa, but we do it happily to get our hands on the best imperial rolls on the planet. Even Julia Child (whose face graces the greasy old menus) has been known to pull up a chair at this shack of a restaurant to feast on such goodies as those out-of-this-world imperial rolls on a bed of rice noodles, lettuce, peanuts, and mint (under $5).

NOB HILL
EXPENSIVE

✪ **Charles Nob Hill.** 1250 Jones St. (at Clay St.). ☎ **415/771-5400.** Main courses $25–$35; six-course tasting menu $65. AE, DC, MC, V. Tues–Sun 5:30–10pm. Valet parking $7. Cable car: California St. and Powell-Hyde lines. Bus: 1, 12, 27, or 83. FRENCH.

We never knew beef could actually melt in your mouth until Aqua owner Charles Condy bought historic restaurant "Le Club" and introduced us to Michael Mina's culinary magic. The "classically inspired light French fare" is served in two dining rooms filled with fresh flowers and the loud buzz of an older socialite crowd. For the main course, you might choose lamb with shaved black Périgord truffles, white bean and artichoke ragoût and thyme infused lamb reduction, or an outstanding pan-seared squab breast with wild mushrooms, savoy cabbage, potato gnocchi, and squab-leg confit. Better yet, opt for the $65 six-course tasting menu and let the chef's preference lead you through the meal. Wrap up the evening with the outstanding pear-and-Roquefort tart.

✪ **Ritz-Carlton Dining Room.** 600 Stockton St. (at California St.). ☎ **415/296-7465.** Reservations recommended. Fixed-price menus $61–$87. AE, CB, DC, DISC, MC, V. Mon–Sat 6–9:30pm. Valet parking $11. Cable car: Powell-Hyde and Powell-Mason lines (direct stop). Bus: 1. CALIFORNIA/FRENCH.

Never a hotel to do anything second best, the Ritz-Carlton is renowned for pampering its guests as if they were royalty, and the Dining Room is no exception. The setting, as you would imagine, is quite regal and sumptuous, and the service keenly attentive (no half-empty water glasses in this joint). While the restaurant is less celebrated without renowned chef Gary Danko at the helm, his replacement, chef Sylvain Portay, runs the kitchen with similar aplomb. But the loss is noticeable—dishes such as the roast Maine lobster and striped bass fillet were quite good, but certainly not of the caliber Danko's fans are accustomed to. A few dishes, however, were outstanding, particularly crayfish bisque (one of the best dishes we've ever tasted) and the risotto with butternut squash and roasted squab. Dessert, alas, was also deigned for mere mortals, though the warm port-poached pear in vanilla sauce was superb.

RUSSIAN HILL
INEXPENSIVE

Hard Rock Cafe. 1699 Van Ness Ave. (at Sacramento St.). ☎ **415/885-1699.** Reservations accepted for groups of 15 or more. Main courses $6–$16. AE, DC, DISC, MC, V. Sun–Thurs 11:30am–11pm; Fri–Sat 11:30am–midnight. Valet $4.25 for 2 hr. Cable car: California St. line. Bus: 1. AMERICAN.

We hate to plug chains, and this loud, rock nostalgia–laden place would be no exception if it didn't serve a fine burger and generally decent heaping plates of food at such moderate prices. Music blares to an almost exclusively tourist clientele; for many, the real draw is the merchandise shop, which often has as long a line as the restaurant. Still, there are fine burgers, fajitas, baby-back ribs, grilled fish, chicken, salads, and sandwiches. Although it's nothing unique to San Francisco, the Hard Rock is a fine place to bring the kids and grab a bite.

✪ **Swan Oyster Depot.** 1517 Polk St. (between California and Sacramento sts.). ☎ **415/ 673-1101.** Reservations not accepted. Seafood cocktails $5–$8; clams and oysters on the half shell $6–$7.50 per half dozen. No credit cards. Mon–Sat 8am–5:30pm. Bus: 27. SEAFOOD.

Pushing 90 years of faithful service to Bay Area chowderheads, the Swan Oyster Depot is classic San Francisco, a unique dining experience you shouldn't miss. Opened in 1912, this tiny hole-in-the-wall run by the city's friendliest and most vivacious servers is little more than a narrow fish market that decided to slap down some bar stools. There are only 20 or so seats jammed cheek by jowl along a long marble bar. Most patrons come for a quick cup of chowder or a plate of half-shelled oysters that arrive chilling on crushed ice. The menu is limited to Maine lobster, Boston-style clam chowder, and crab, shrimp, oyster, and clam cocktails, all of which are exceedingly fresh. *Note:* Don't let the lunchtime line dissuade you—it moves fast.

SOMA
EXPENSIVE

✪ **Boulevard.** 1 Mission St. (at Embarcadero and Steuart St.). ☎ **415/543-6084.** Reservations recommended. Main courses $19–$30. AE, CB, DC, DISC, MC, V. Mon–Fri 11:30am–2pm, bistro 2:15–5:15pm; Sun–Wed 5:30–10pm, Thurs–Sat 5:30–10:30pm. Valet parking $8. Bus: 15, 30, 32, 42, or 45. AMERICAN.

Master restaurant designer Pat Kuleto and chef Nancy Oaks teamed up in 1993 to create one of San Francisco's most exciting restaurants, and Boulevard is still one of our—and the city's—all-time favorites. What's the winning combination? The dramatic belle-epoque interior combined with Oaks's well-sculpted, mouth-watering dishes. Starters alone could make a perfect meal, especially if you indulge in the sweetbreads wrapped in prosciutto on watercress and Lola Rose lettuce with garlic croutons and a whole-grain mustard vinaigrette; Sonoma foie gras with Elderberry syrup, toast, and Bosc pear salad; or Maine sea scallops on garlic mashed potato croustade with truffle and portobello mushroom relish. The nine or so main courses are equally creative and might include pan-roasted miso-glazed sea bass with asparagus salad, Japanese rice, and shiitake-mushroom broth, or spit-roasted cider-cured pork loin with sweet potato–swirled mashed potatoes and sautéed baby red chard. Vegetarian items, such as wild-mushroom risotto with fresh chanterelles and Parmesan, are also offered. Three levels of formality—bar, open kitchen, and main dining room—keep things from getting too snobby.

Hawthorne Lane. 22 Hawthorne Lane (at Howard St. between Second and Third sts.). ☎ **415/777-9779.** Reservations recommended. Jacket appropriate but not required. Main courses $10–$14 lunch, $20–$34 dinner. CB, DC, DISC, JCB, MC, V. Mon–Fri 11:30am–2pm; Sun–Thurs 5:30–10pm, Fri–Sat 5:30–10:30pm (bar menu Mon–Fri 2:30–10pm and Sat–Sun from 5:30pm). BART: Montgomery Station. Muni Metro: F, J, K, L, M, or N. Bus: 12, 30, 45, or 76. CALIFORNIA.

Anne and David Gingrass, who launched the famed Postrio, preside over the kitchen at Hawthorne Lane, their haute SoMa restaurant strategically located a block away from the Museum of Modern Art. Menus change with the seasons and reflect the Asian and European influences that made them famous under Wolfgang Puck. The bar area is comfortable and inviting; continue on to the dining room, where earthquake reinforcement beams divide the room in a way that's not only functional but also creates an illusion of intimacy. Dishes are remarkably well balanced; in fact, accompaniments are often more exciting than the main course itself. If it's on the menu, don't pass up the black-cod appetizer served with a miso glaze and spinach rolls. Main courses might include such modern dishes as Miso glazed rack of pork with warm radicchio salad, butternut squash, and fruit mustard sauce. Desserts are as good to look at as they are to eat.

MODERATE

Bizou. 598 Fourth St. (at Brannan St.). ☎ **415/543-2222.** Reservations recommended. Main courses $12.50–$21. AE, MC, V. Mon–Fri 11:30am–2:30pm; Mon–Thurs 5:30–10pm, Fri–Sat 5:30–10:30pm. Bus: 15, 30, 32, 42, or 45. FRENCH/ITALIAN.

Bizou is a quaint neighborhood-style restaurant serving wonderfully flavorful food at very reasonable prices. The restaurant's golden-yellow walls and terra-cotta ceiling are warmly lit by antique light fixtures and art-deco wall sconces, the wait staff is friendly and professional, and all the ingredients are fresh and combined in creative ways. Our only complaint is that literally every dish is so rich and powerfully flavorful (including the salads), it's a bit of a sensory overload. The menu's starters include an Italian flat bread with caramelized onions, fresh herbs, and Parmesan cheese; Sonoma duck-liver terrine; and baked shrimp with white beans, tomato, and feta. Main courses may include a grilled veal chop with broccoli-rabe potato gratin or stuffed chicken with celeriac, apple, and goat cheese. All main-course portions are substantial here, so don't overindulge on appetizers. And save a little room for dessert—the meringue covered in chocolate and topped with coffee ice cream and candied almonds is quite a treat.

☼ **Fringale Restaurant.** 570 Fourth St. (between Brannan and Bryant sts.). ☎ **415/543-0573.** Reservations recommended. Main courses $4–$12 lunch, $11–$19 dinner. AE, MC, V. Mon–Fri 11:30am–3pm; Mon–Sat 5:30–10:30pm. Bus: 30 or 45. FRENCH.

One of San Francisco's best restaurants for the money, Fringale has enjoyed a weeklong waiting list since the day chef/co-owner Gerald Hirigoyen first opened this small SoMa bistro. Sponged eggshell-blue walls and other muted sand and earth tones create a serene dining environment, which is all but shattered when the 18-table room fills with Hirigoyen's fans. For starters, try the steamed mussels with fried-garlic vinaigrette, or the sheep's-milk cheese and prosciutto tureen with figs and greens. Among the dozen or so main courses on the seasonal menu, you might find rack of lamb with potato gratin or pork-tenderloin confit with onion and apple marmalade. Desserts are worth savoring, too, particularly the Basque custard torte (we begged for the recipe) or the signature crème brûlée with vanilla bean. The mostly French waiters provide uncharacteristically charming service, and prices are surprisingly reasonable for such high-quality cuisine.

☼ **Thirsty Bear Brewing Company.** 661 Howard St. (1 block east of the Moscone Center). ☎ **415/974-0905.** Reservations recommended. Main courses $12–$18. AE, DC, MC, V. Mon–Fri 11:30am–11pm, Sat noon–11pm, Sun 4:30–11pm. Bus: 12, 15, 30, 45, or 76. SPANISH.

Despite the dumb name, this brewpub quickly became a favorite of the Financial District/SoMa crowd, who come as much for the excellent house-made brews as they do for the Spanish food. The Paella Valenciana—a sizzling combo of chicken, shrimp, sausage, shellfish, and saffron-laden rice served in a cast-iron skillet—is a hearty favorite. Upscale pub grub includes a variety of hot and cold tapas, a few of our favorites being the Escalivada (roasted vegetables—spicy caramelized onions are wild—served at room temperature) and the Espinacas à la Catalana (spinach sautéed with garlic, pine nuts, and raisins). Almost as impressive is the restaurant's costly conversion, from a high-ceilinged brick warehouse to a two-level, industrial-chic brewpub complete with pool tables, dart boards, and live music that runs the gamut from flamenco to alternative to classical.

INEXPENSIVE

Long Life Noodle Company & Jook Joint. 139 Steuart St. (near Mission St.). ☎ **415/281-3818.** Main courses $5.50–$8.50. MC, V. Mon–Thurs 11:30am–10pm; Fri 11:30am–11pm; Sat 5pm–11am; Sun 5–10pm. Bus: 15, 30, 32, 42, or 45. NOODLES.

Asian noodles are all the rage these days, so it comes as no surprise that big-time restaurateurs such as George Chen (of Betelnut and Shanghai 1930) are willing to invest big bucks into what has traditionally been a small-change business. Long Life serves a wide range of unfamiliar noodle dishes gleaned from China, Korea, Japan, and other Asian lands in a familiar Westernized setting (in this case, a sleek, supermodern interior with lots of neon and Plexiglas). The problem is choosing from the 30 or so noodle dishes, all of which are wildly different. Do you go with the Buddha's Bliss (ramen noodles in miso broth with smoked trout, tofu, and enoki mushrooms) or the Enchanted Heat (a "Chinese hangover cure" comprised of whole-wheat noodles, lily pods, tree ears, and secret healing ginseng herbs)? One thing we *can* recommend is the Ghengis's Buns, crisp sesame biscuits filled with Chinese roast beef, cucumber, cilantro, and hoisin sauce. Wash it all down with either the Cool Cucumber Juice or Ginseng Ginger Ale.

Manora's. 1600 Folsom St. (at 12th St.). ☎ **415/861-6224.** Main courses $5.95–$11.95. MC, V. Mon–Fri 11:30am–2:30pm and 5:30–10:30pm; Sat 5:30–10:30pm; Sun 5:30–10pm. Bus: 9, 12, or 47. THAI.

Manora's cranks out some of the best Thai in town and is well worth a jaunt to its SoMa location. But this is no relaxed dining affair: It's perpetually packed (unless you come early), and you'll be seated sardinelike at one of the cramped but well-appointed tables. Start with a Thai iced tea or coffee and one of the tangy soups or the chicken satay, which comes with a decadent peanut sauce. Follow up with any of the wonderful dinner entrees—which should be shared—and a side of rice. There are endless options, including a vast array of vegetarian plates. Every remarkably flavorful dish arrives seemingly seconds after you order it, which is great if you're hungry, a bummer if you were planning a long, leisurely dinner. Come before 7pm or after 9pm if you don't want a loud, rushed meal.

FINANCIAL DISTRICT
EXPENSIVE

✪ **Aqua.** 252 California St. (between Battery and Front sts.). ☎ **415/956-9662.** Reservations required. Main courses $26–$45; six-course tasting menu $65; vegetarian tasting menu $45. AE, DC, MC, V. Mon–Fri 11:30am–2:15pm; Mon–Sat 5:30–10:30pm. All Market St. buses. SEAFOOD.

Without question, Aqua is San Francisco's finest seafood restaurant. Heralded chef Michael Mina dazzles his customers with a bewildering juxtaposition of earth and sea in his seasonally changing menus. The ahi tartare, for example, is mixed tableside with pears, pine nuts, quail egg, and mint—it's truly divine and one of the best we've ever had. The gulf prawn and lobster dumpling is another work of art, perfectly paired with a heavenly carrot and ginger consommé, while the miso-marinated Chilean sea bass, braised with abalone and served with roasted kabocha squash ravioli and green scallion juice, is another party for the palate. (We weren't big on the crab cakes, though.) Desserts are equally impressive, particularly the Aqua soufflé-of-the-day. Our only complaint: The dining room is rather austere.

MODERATE

✪ **Kokkari.** 200 Jackson St. (at Front St.). ☎ **415/981-0983.** Reservations recommended. Main courses $14.95–$24. AE, DC, MC, V. Mon–Fri 11:30am–2:30pm; Mon–Thurs 5–11pm, Fri–Sat 5pm–midnight. Valet parking $6. Bus: 41, 15, 12, 42, or 83. GREEK.

One of the hottest new restaurants combines the comforts of two rustic-chic dining rooms (one with a huge fireplace), a bar (generally two deep with yuppies), and the stellar Aegean cuisine of executive chef Jean Alberti. A great way to start the meal is with *Pikilia,* a sampling of traditional Greek spreads served with dolmades. There are excellent soups and salads, too, but don't fill up on starters. The moussaka (eggplant, lamb, potato, and bechamel) is to die for and the quail, stuffed with winter greens served on oven-roasted leeks, orzo, and wild-rice pilafi, is phenomenal. In fact, the only complaint we have is the valet-parking situation: The wait at the end of the meal can be tediously long.

Yank Sing. 427 Battery St. (between Clay and Washington sts.). ☎ **415/781-1111.** Dim sum $2.65–$3.40 for three to four pieces. AE, DC, MC, V. Mon–Fri 11am–3pm; Sat–Sun 10am–4pm. Cable car: California St. line. Bus: 1 or 42. CHINESE/DIM SUM.

Loosely translated as "a delight of the heart," Yank Sing does dim sum like few other Chinese restaurant we've visited. Poor quality of ingredients has always been the shortcoming of all but the most expensive Chinese restaurants, but Yank Sing manages to be both affordable and excellent. Confident, experienced servers take the nervousness

Dining with the Sun on Your Face at Belden Place

As cosmopolitan as San Francisco claims to be, it's woefully lacking in alfresco dining options compared to most European cities. One pocket of exceptions, however, is Belden Place, an adorable little brick alley in the heart of the Financial District that is closed to everything but foot traffic. When the weather is agreeable, the restaurants that line the alley break out the big umbrellas, tables, and chairs à la Boulevard Saint-Michel, and voilà—a bit of Paris just off Pine Street.

The four cafes that line Belden Place offer a wide variety of cuisine. From south to north, they are **Cafe Bastille** (22 Belden Place; ☎ 415/986-5673), your classic French bistro serving excellent crepes, mussels, and French onion soup along with live jazz on weekends; **Cafe Tiramisu** (28 Belden Place; ☎ 415/421-7044), a superb—and stylish—Italian hot spot serving addictive risottos and gnocchi; **Plouf** (40 Belden Place; ☎ 415/986-6491), which specializes in big bowls of mussels slathered in a choice of seven sauces as well as fresh seafood; and **Fizz Supper Club** (471 Pine St.; ☎ 415/421-3499), a chic American-Mediterranean bistro serving such entrees as Andouille-stuffed quail with saffron risotto cake and braised rabbit with jalapeño-peach chutney. There's also live jazz nightly at Fizz, but it's those cloudless San Francisco days that draw the city's sun-starved culinary cognoscenti to all four of these wonderful cafes.

out of novices—they're good at guessing your gastric threshold. Most dim sum dishes are dumplings, filled with tasty concoctions of pork, beef, fish, or vegetables. Spareribs, stuffed crab claws, scallion pancakes, pork buns, and other palate-pleasers complete the menu. Like most good dim sum meals, at Yank Sing you get to choose the small dishes from a cart that's continually wheeled around the dining room. *Tip:* Sit by the kitchen and you're guaranteed to get it while it's hot.

CHINATOWN
INEXPENSIVE

Great Eastern. 649 Jackson St. (between Kearny St. and Grant Ave.). ☎ **415/986-2500**. Most main courses $8–$13. AE, MC, V. Daily 11–1am. Bus: 15, 30, 41, or 45. CHINESE.

Great Eastern is famous for its fresh and hard-to-find seafood, pulled straight from the myriad of tanks that line the walls. Rock cod, steelhead, sea chochs, sea bass, shrimp, frogs, softshell turtle, abalone—if it's even remotely aquatic and edible, it's on the menu at this hugely popular Hong Kong–style dinner house. The day's catch, sold by the pound, is listed on a board. Both upper- and lower-level dining rooms are rather stylish, with shiny black and emerald furnishings.

✪ **House of Nanking.** 919 Kearny St. (at Columbus Ave.). ☎ **415/421-1429**. Reservations accepted for 6 or more. Main courses $4.95–$8.95. No credit cards. Mon–Fri 11am–10pm; Sat noon–10pm; Sun 4–10pm. Bus: 9, 12, 15, or 30. CHINESE.

To the unknowing passerby, the House of Nanking has "greasy dive" written all over it. To its legion of fans, however, it's worth the wait—sometimes up to an hour. Located on the edge of Chinatown just off Columbus Avenue, this inconspicuous little diner is one of San Francisco's worst-kept secrets. When the line is reasonable, we drop by for a plate of pot stickers (still the best we've ever tasted) and chef/owner Peter Fang's signature shrimp-and-green-onion pancake served with peanut sauce. Trust the waiter when he recommends a special, or simply point to what looks good on someone else's table. Seating is tight, so prepare to be bumped around a bit, and don't expect good service—it's all part of the Nanking experience.

NORTH BEACH
EXPENSIVE

Moose's. 1652 Stockton St. (between Filbert and Union sts.). ☎ 415/989-7800 or 800/ 28-MOOSE. www.mooses.com. Reservations recommended. Main courses $13–$26. AE, CB, DC, JCB, MC, V. Mon–Wed 5:30–10pm; Thur 11:30am–10pm; Fri 11:30am–11:30pm; Sat 10am–2:30pm and 5:30–11:30pm; Sun 10am–2:30pm and 5–10pm. Valet parking $9 for 3 hr. Bus: 15, 30, 41, or 45. MEDITERRANEAN/CALIFORNIA.

Three years ago Moose's brought on chef Brian Whitmer of Montrio in Carmel, pastry chef Ellen Doren, and sommelier William Sherer—an all-star team that has punched some life back into Moose's menu and already coveted wine list. Aside from such banal things as eating, this is also where Nob Hill socialites and local politicos come to schmooze. Nob Hill's largest dining room is rather sparse and not very intimate, but everything that comes out of the kitchen is way above par. The appetizers are innovative, fresh, and well balanced (try Mediterranean fish soup with rouille and croutons cooked in the wood-fired oven), and the main courses (especially the meats) are perfectly prepared. The menu changes every few months and might include a grilled veal chop with potato galette as well as a variety of pasta, chicken, and fish dishes.

MODERATE

✪ **Black Cat Cafe.** 501 Broadway (at Kearny St.). ☎ 415/981-2233. Reservations highly recommended. Main courses $6–$11 lunch, $8.75–$25 dinner. AE, DC, MC, V. Daily 11:30am–4pm and 5:30pm–2am. Valet parking $6 day, $8 night. Bus: 12, 15, 30, or 83. SAN FRANCISCAN.

With Reed Hearon's latest sexy brasserie, he again proves he knows how to give the people what they want, which in this case is local nostalgia contrived to perfection and celebrated in a combo early-century Parisian brasserie/classic San Francisco restaurant. The dining room is designed for optimum people watching and the menu features cuisines honoring North Beach (Italian), Chinatown, Fisherman's Wharf (seafood), and the Barbary Coast (old-fashioned grill). Executive chef Scott Warner presides over the well-organized, extensive food list, which runs the gamut from fritto misto of artichokes and mushrooms to soups, salads, clay pots, and main courses ranging from a giant T-bone steak for four to grilled sea bass with herb butter and french fries. A seafood section highlights lobster, crab, and shrimp served by the pound and prepared any of five ways. Wash it all down with a wicked Black Cat Martini (with a sake kick) and slink downstairs to the Blue Bar live jazz club, where a limited menu satisfies the lounge lizards, and you'll get why San Franciscans consider this new hot spot—despite its slightly overrated but still tasty cuisine—truly the cat's meow.

Enrico's. 504 Broadway (at Kearny St.). ☎ 415/982-6223. Reservations recommended. Main courses $8–$13 lunch, $13–$19 dinner. AE, DC, DISC, MC, V. Mon–Sun 11:30–11pm; Fri–Sat 11:30–midnight; bar daily noon–2am. Valet parking $5–$10. Bus: 12, 15, 30, or 83. MEDITERRANEAN.

Though North Beach's Broadway has only recently began shirking its bawdy rep, Enrico's has remained the hip glitzy sidewalk restaurant/supper club that was *the* place to hang out before Broadway took its seedy downward spiral. Families may want to skip this one, but anyone with an appreciation for live jazz (offered nightly), late-night noshing, and weirdo watching from the outdoor patio would be quite content spending an alfresco evening under the heat lamps. Chewy brick-oven pizza, a handful of pastas, zesty tapas, and thick steaks are hot items on the monthly changing menu.

The best part? No cover, killer burgers served until midnight on weekends, and valet parking.

❂ **Rose Pistola.** 532 Columbus Ave. (at Union and Green sts.). ☎ **415/399-0499.** Reservations highly recommended. Main courses $6.95–$18.50 lunch; most dishes $9–$24 dinner. AE, DC, MC, V. Sun–Thurs 11:30am–10:30pm (late-night menu until midnight); Fri–Sat 11:30am–11:30pm (late-night menu until 1am). Valet parking $10. Bus: 15, 30, 41, or 45. ITALIAN.

The hottest new restaurant in 1997 is still going strong under the watchful eye of restaurateur extraordinaire Reed Hearon. The smart, bustling-bistro atmosphere features divided dining areas as well as cramped tables next to the bar. Sidewalk seating is favored on sunny afternoons, but inside there's plenty to see as chefs crank out the eclectic food from the open kitchen. The modern Italian fare here is meant to be shared. Aside from sandwiches, everything comes à la carte, including appetizers such as tasty fried chickpeas or savory lemon, prosciutto, sweet pea, and mozzarella risotto fritters, which are wonderful but pricey. Along with meats and foul, the menu features a variety of fish choices such as fabulously flavorful mussels in a rich tomato broth, and most memorably a whole Arctic char, bathed in fennel and tapenade in a big iron skillet with a crispy and perfectly seasoned outside and tender and juicy inside. The "flaming cream" dessert, three fried crème-brûlée–type diamonds that arrived afire with a Bacardi-and-apricot sauce, was creative and very tasty, but not worth the $7.50 asking price.

INEXPENSIVE

L'Osteria del Forno. 519 Columbus Ave. (between Green and Union sts.). ☎ **415/982-1124.** Sandwiches $5.50–$6.50; pizzas $11–$15; main courses $6–$9.75. No credit cards. Mon–Wed 11:30am–10pm; Fri–Sat 11:30am–10:30pm; Sun 1–10pm. Bus: 15 or 41. ITALIAN.

L'Osteria del Forno may be only slightly larger than a walk-in closet, but it's one of the top three Italian restaurants in North Beach. Peer in the window facing Columbus Avenue, and you'll probably see two Italian women with their hair up, sweating from the heat of the brick-lined oven that cranks out the best focaccia (and focaccia sandwiches) in the city. There's no pomp or circumstance involved: Locals come here strictly to eat. The menu features a variety of superb pizzas and fresh pastas, plus a few daily specials (pray for the roast pork braised in milk). Small baskets of warm focaccia bread keep you going 'til the entrees arrive, which should be accompanied by a glass of house red.

Mario's Bohemian Cigar Store. 566 Columbus Ave. ☎ **415/362-0536.** Sandwiches $5–$6.25. No credit cards. Daily 10am–midnight. Closed Dec 24–Jan 1. Bus: 15, 30, 41, or 45. ITALIAN.

Across the street from Washington Square, this is one of North Beach's most popular neighborhood hangouts. The century-old bar—small, well worn, and perpetually busy—is best known for its focaccia sandwiches, including meatball or eggplant. Wash it all down with an excellent cappuccino or a house Campari as you watch the tourists stroll by. And yes, they do sell cigars.

Note: A newer, larger location with live jazz Wednesday and Sunday nights is at 2209 Polk St., between Green and Vallejo streets (☎ 415/776-8226).

FISHERMAN'S WHARF
MODERATE

Cafe Pescatore. 2455 Mason St. (at North Point St.). ☎ **415/561-1111.** Reservations recommended. Main courses $3.95–$8.95 breakfast, $10–$18 lunch and dinner. AE, DC, DISC, MC, V. Sun–Thurs 7am–10pm; Fri–Sat 7am–10:30pm; Sat–Sun 7am–3pm brunch, 3–5pm cafe menu. Cable car: Powell-Mason line. Bus: 42, 15, or 39. ITALIAN.

Though San Francisco locals are a rarity at Cafe Pescatore, most agree that if they had to dine in the Fisherman's Wharf area, this cozy trattoria would be their first choice. Two walls of sliding-glass doors offer almost-alfresco seating when the weather's warm, although heavy traffic can detract from the experience. The general consensus is to order anything that's cooked in the open kitchen's wood-fired oven, such as the pizzas and roasts. A big hit is the *polenta al forno*—oak-roasted cheese polenta with marinara sauce and fresh pesto. Other safe bets are the verde pizza, with pesto-flavored prawns and spinach, and the huge serving of roast chicken.

Crab Cake Lounge at McCormick and Kuleto's. 900 North Point St. (at the corner of Beach and Larkin sts.). ☎ **415/929-1730.** Main courses $8–$12. AE, CB, DC, DISC, MC, V. Mon–Sat 11:30am–11pm; Sun 10:30am–11pm. Cable car: Powell-Hyde line. Bus: 19, 30, or 42. SEAFOOD/ITALIAN.

On the upper level of this glamorous (and expensive) multi-tiered restaurant is a small seafood counter called the Crab Cake Lounge, which offers huge selections of shellfish, sandwiches, and light entrees at very reasonable prices. Case in point: The calzone, made with fresh spinach, mushrooms, tomatoes, and ricotta cheese and baked in the wood-fired brick oven, goes for a mere $7.50. Almost twice the price but worth every penny is the heaping pile of clams, mussels, crayfish, and Dungeness crab in a garlicky broth that's perfect for dipping the crusty French bread in (easily a meal for two). Other menu items range from fresh oysters on the half shell to salmon sandwiches, blackened catfish, and an array of soups and salads. Just about everything served at the lounge is under $10, though you still get a slice of the million-dollar view of the bay.

COW HOLLOW/PACIFIC HEIGHTS/MARINA DISTRICT
EXPENSIVE

✪ **La Folie.** 2316 Polk St. (between Green and Union sts.). ☎ **415/776-5577.** Reservations recommended. Main courses $24–$48; five-course tasting menu $65; vegetarian tasting menu $50. AE, CB, DC, DISC, MC, V. Mon–Sat 5:30–10:30pm. Bus: 19, 41, 45, 47, 49, or 76. FRENCH.

For fantastic French food without attitude, La Folie is the place to feast. The minute you walk through the door, you'll know why this is many locals' favorite restaurant. The country French decor is tasteful but not too serious; the staff is friendly, knowledgeable, and very accommodating; the atmosphere is comfortable and relaxed; and the food is truly outstanding. Unlike many renowned chefs, Roland Passot is in the kitchen nightly—and it shows. Each of his California-influenced French creations is an architectural and culinary masterpiece. We suggest starting with the roast quail and foie gras with salad, wild mushrooms, and roasted garlic—guaranteed to melt in your mouth. Main courses aren't petite as in many French restaurants, and all are accompanied by flavorful and well-balanced sauces. Finish off with any of the delectable desserts.

MODERATE

Betelnut. 2030 Union St. (at Buchanan St.). ☎ **415/929-8855.** Reservations recommended. Main courses $9–$16. CB, DC, DISC, MC, V. Sun–Thurs 11:30am–11pm; Fri–Sat 11:30am–midnight. Bus: 22, 41, or 45. SOUTHEAST ASIAN.

While San Francisco is teeming with Chinese restaurants, few offer the posh environment of this restaurant on upscale Union Street. As the menu explains, the theme is "Pejui Wu," a traditional Asian beer house offering local brews and savory dishes. But with the bamboo paneling, red Formica, and low-hanging lamps, the place feels more like a set out of Madonna's movie *Shanghai Surprise*. Still, the atmosphere is en vogue, with dimly lit booths, ringside seating overlooking the bustling stir-fry chefs, sidewalk tables, and a cramped but festive bar. Starters include sashimi and tasty salt-and-pepper whole gulf prawns; main courses include orange-glazed beef with asparagus and oyster mushrooms and Singapore chili crab. While prices seem reasonable, it's the incidentals such as white rice ($1.50 per person) and tea ($3.50 per pot) that rack up the bill. In our minds, the main reason to choose this restaurant over others is the atmosphere, plus the heavenly signature dessert: mouth-watering tapioca pudding with sweet red azuki beans.

Greens Restaurant. Building A, Fort Mason Center (enter Fort Mason opposite the Safeway at Buchanan and Marina sts.). ☎ **415/771-6222.** Reservations recommended 2 weeks in advance. Main courses $8–$12 lunch, $11–$16 dinner; fixed-priced dinner $40; brunch $8–$11. DISC, MC, V. Mon 5:30–9:30pm; Tues–Fri 11:30am–2pm and 5:30–9:30pm; Sat 11:30am–2:30pm and 5:30–9pm; Sun brunch 10am–2pm. Greens To Go Mon–Fri 8am–9:30pm; Sat 8am–3:30pm; Sun 9am–3:30pm. Bus: 28 or 30. VEGETARIAN.

Knowledgeable locals swear by Greens, where executive chef Annie Somerville (author of *Fields of Greens*) cooks with the seasons, using produce from Green Gulch Farm and other local organic farms. Located in an old warehouse, with enormous windows overlooking the bridge and the bay, the restaurant is both a pioneer and a legend. A weeknight dinner might feature such appetizers as tomato, white-bean, and sorrel soup, or grilled asparagus with lemon, Parmesan cheese, and watercress, followed by spring-vegetable risotto with asparagus, peas, shiitake and crimini mushrooms, and Parmesan cheese, or perhaps Sri Lankan curry made of new potatoes, cauliflower, carrots, peppers, and snap peas stewed with tomatoes, coconut milk, ginger, and Sri Lankan spices. A special four-course dinner is served on Saturday. Adjacent to the restaurant, Greens To Go bakery sells homemade breads, sandwiches, soups, salads, and pastries.

✪ **Pane e Vino.** 3011 Steiner St. (at Union St.). ☎ **415/346-2111.** Reservations recommended. Main courses $8.50–$19.95. AE, MC, V. Mon–Sat 11:30am–10:30pm; Sun 5–10pm. Valet parking Wed–Sat $8. Bus: 41 or 45. ITALIAN.

This is one of the city's top—and most authentic—Italian restaurants, as well as our personal favorite. The food is consistently excellent (try not to fill up on the outstanding breads), the prices reasonable, and the mostly Italian-accented staff always smooth and efficient under pressure. The two small dining rooms—separated by an open kitchen from which heavenly aromas emanate—offer only limited seating, so expect a wait even if you have reservations. The wide selection of appetizers includes a fine carpaccio and the hugely popular chilled artichoke stuffed with bread and tomatoes and served with a vinaigrette. Our favorite, the antipasti of mixed grilled vegetables, always spurs a fork fight. A similarly broad selection of pastas is available, including a flavorful *pennette alla boscaiola* with porcini mushrooms and pancetta in a tomato cream sauce. Other specialties include a chicken breast marinated in lime juice and herbs. Top dessert picks are any of the Italian ice creams, the crème caramel, and the creamy tiramisu.

PlumpJack Café. 3127 Fillmore St. (between Filbert and Greenwich sts.). ☎ **415/563-4755.** Reservations recommended. Main courses $15–$22. AE, DC, DISC, MC, V. Mon–Fri 11:30am–2pm; Mon–Sat 5:30–10:30pm. Bus: 41 or 45. CALIFORNIA/FRENCH/MEDITERRANEAN.

Wildly popular among San Francisco's style-setters, this small Cow Hollow restaurant is one of the neighborhood's "in" places to dine. This is partly due to the fact that it's run by one of the Getty clan (as in offspring of J. Paul), but mostly because chef Maria Helm's food is just plain good, and the whimsical decor is a veritable work of art. Though the menu changes weekly, you might find an appetizer such as grilled day-boat scallops wrapped in pancetta on shaved fennel with citrus vinaigrette and herb-scented Roquefort souffle. Main dishes range from risotto of sweet potato, wild mushrooms, prosciutto, and Grana Parmesan to duck confit and roasted breast with potato rosti, dried sour cherries, and port glaze. Top it off with a bittersweet chocolate soufflé or cinnamon-scented Alsatian apple cake. The extensive California wine list is sold at next-to-retail prices, with many wines available by the glass.

○ **Zinzino.** 2355 Chestnut St. (at Divisadero St.). ☎ **415/346-6623.** Reservations not necessary. Main courses $9.50–$18.50. AE, DC, MC, V. Tues–Thurs 6–10pm; Fri–Sat 5:30–11pm; Sun 5:30–9:30pm. Bus: 22 or 30. ITALIAN.

Owner Ken Zankel and Spago-sired chef Andrea Rappaport combined forces to create one of the city's top Italian restaurants. Italian movie posters, magazines, and furnishings evoke memories of past vacations, but we rarely recall the food in Italy being this good (and certainly not this cheap). Start off with the crispy calamari with a choice of herbed aioli or tomato sauces (second only to Scala's Earth and Surf), the roasted jumbo prawns wrapped in crisp pancetta and bathed in a tangy balsamic reduction sauce, or the peculiar-tasting shaved-fennel-and-mint salad—or try them all. Rappaport is giving Zuni Café a run for its money with her version of roasted half chicken. New to the menu are weekly rotating specials, such as the roasted shellfish platter, oven-roasted half lobster, or baby lamb chops.

INEXPENSIVE

○ **Andalé Taqueria.** 2150 Chestnut St. (between Steiner and Pierce sts.). ☎ **415/ 749-0506.** Most dishes $5.25–$7. No credit cards. Mon–Thurs 11am–10pm; Fri–Sat 11am– 11pm; Sun 11am–9pm. Bus: 22, 28, 30, 30X, 43, 76, or 82X. MEXICAN.

Andalé (Spanish for "hurry up") offers incredible high-end fast food for the health-conscious eater. The freshest of ingredients go into every delicious dish, including a mesquite-roasted chicken with potatoes, salsa, and tortillas ($5.95); giant burritos; and fantastic $2.75 soft tacos. The sophisticated decor, full bar, check-me-out patio seating (complete with corner fireplace), and counter service makes this an all-around budget dream wrapped in an attractive package.

○ **Doidge's.** 2217 Union St. (between Fillmore and Steiner sts.). ☎ **415/921-2149.** Reservations accepted and essential on weekends. Breakfast $4.50–$10; lunch $5.25–$10. MC, V. Mon–Fri 8am–1:45pm; Sat–Sun 8am–2:45pm. Bus: 41 or 45. AMERICAN.

Doidge's is sweet, small, and always packed, serving up one of the better breakfasts in San Francisco since 1971. Its fame is based on its eggs Benedict, while the eggs Florentine, prepared with thinly sliced Motherlode ham, runs a close second. The menu invariably includes a gourmet omelet packed with luscious combinations, and to delight the kid in you, hot chocolate comes in your very own teapot. The six seats at the original mahogany counter are still the most coveted by locals.

Home Plate. 2274 Lombard St. (at Pierce St.). ☎ **415/922-HOME.** Main courses $3.75–$6.50. MC, V. Daily 7am–4pm. Bus: 28, 30, 43, or 76. BREAKFAST.

Dollar for dollar, Home Plate just may be the best breakfast place in San Francisco. Many Marina residents kick off their hectic weekends by carbo-loading at Home Plate on big piles of buttermilk pancakes and waffles smothered with fresh fruit, or hefty omelets stuffed with everything from apple-wood–smoked ham to spinach. Always the first dish to arrive is a coveted plate of freshly baked scones, best eaten with a bit of butter and a dab of jam. Be sure to look over the daily specials scrawled on the little green chalkboard before you order. And as every fan of this tiny cafe knows, it's best to call ahead and ask to have your name put on the waiting list before you slide into Home Plate.

Mel's Diner. 2165 Lombard St. (at Fillmore St.). ☎ **415/921-3039.** Reservations accepted. Main courses $4–$5.50 breakfast, $6–$8 lunch, $8–$12 dinner. No credit cards. Sun–Thurs 6am–3am; Fri–Sat 24 hr. (Lombard location only). Bus: 22, 43, or 30. AMERICAN.

Sure, it's contrived, touristy, and nowhere near healthy, but when you get that urge for a chocolate shake and banana-cream pie at the stroke of midnight, no other place in the city comes through like Mel's Diner. Modeled after a classic 1950s diner right down to the nickel jukebox at each table, Mel's harks back to the halcyon days when cholesterol and fried foods didn't weigh on your guilty conscience with every greasy, wonderful bite.

There's another Mel's at 3355 Geary, at Stanyan Street (☎ **415/387-2244**).

Pluto's. 3258 Scott St. (at Chestnut St.). ☎ **415/7-PLUTOS**. Main courses $3.50–$5.75. MC, V. Mon–Fri 11:30am–10pm; Sat 9:30am–11pm; Sun 9:30am–10pm. Bus: 28, 30, 42, or 76. CALIFORNIA.

Pluto's combines assembly-line efficiency with three-star quality. The result is cheap, fresh, high-quality fare ranging from humongous salads with a dozen choices of toppings to oven-roasted poultry and grilled meats (the flank steak is great), sandwiches, and a wide array of sides like crispy garlic potato rings, seasonal veggies, and barbecued chicken wings. Drinks include cappuccino, tea, sodas, bottled brews, and Napa wines, and desserts are homemade. The ordering system can be bewildering to newcomers: Grab a checklist and hand it to the food servers, who will check off your order and relay it to the cashier. Seating is limited during the rush, but the turnover is fairly fast.

CIVIC CENTER
EXPENSIVE

Jardinière. 300 Grove St. (at Franklin St.). ☎ **415/861-5555.** Reservations recommended. Main courses $19–$29; six-course tasting menu $65. AE, CB, DC, DISC, MC, V. Daily 5:30–10:30pm regular menu; Tues–Sat 10:30pm–midnight late menu. Valet parking $8. Bus: 19 or 21. FRENCH/CALIFORNIA.

Jardinière is one of the favored pre- and post-symphony alternatives to Jeremiah Tower's Stars, but it also happens to be the perfect setting for a cocktail break. The culinary dream team of owner/chef Traci Des Jardins (previously at Rubicon), owner/designer Pat Kuleto (who created the swank champagne-motif-influenced ambiance), and convivial general manager Doug Washington are to thank for the sexy and happening dining room. On most evenings, the two-story brick structure is abuzz with an older crowd who sip cocktails at the centerpiece mahogany bar or watch the scene discreetly from the upstairs circular balcony. But whatever your age, take our word for it: The atmosphere is conducive to throwing back a few in the best of style—especially when there's live jazz. While the daily changing menu is good, many locals argue that it's way pricey, tiny in portion, and not exactly memorable. We're in partial agreement; when we dined here the food was good, but didn't pack the surprise punches necessary to impress us jaded San Francisco diners (although restaurant critic Michael Bauer might disagree). But anyone simply in search of a quality meal will not be disappointed. The sweet onion tart with cured salmon and herb salad was tasty, as was the crisped chicken with chanterelles, ozette potatoes, and apple-wood–smoked bacon. Striped bass with lobster saffron broth, fennel, and potatoes, and fillet of beef with sunchoke gratin, mushrooms, and red-wine sauce are also recommended. Late diners can also come here for a limited menu served Thursday through Sunday from 10:30pm to midnight. Kudos to the great wine selection—many by the glass and more than 300 bottles.

Stars. 555 Golden Gate Avenue (between McAllister and Golden Gate off Van Ness). ☎ **415/861-7827.** Reservations recommended. Main courses $17–$30. AE, MC, V. Daily 5:30–10pm. Bus: 19, 31, or 38. CALIFORNIA.

The large, loud, and vibrant restaurant features the longest bar in the city, which does little to guarantee you'll find a free stool when the place is hopping. Critics complain the quality of the food has slipped (as prices increase), but that hasn't deterred local celebs like Robin Williams and Mayor Willie Brown from making regular appearances. Though the menu changes daily, you might find among the main courses a braised veal ragout with egg noodles, cipollini onions, and wild mushrooms; or sea scallops with braised Belgian endive, lobster cream sauce, and tarragon. *Fair warning:* Prices are high for what little you receive, and the desserts—once considered extraordinary—are not as good as they once were.

MODERATE

Hayes Street Grill. 320 Hayes St. (near Franklin St.). ☎ **415/863-5545.** Reservations recommended. Main courses $9.25–$18.75. AE, DC, DISC, MC, V. Mon–Thurs 11:30am–2pm and 5–9:30pm; Fri 11:30am–2pm and 5–10:30pm; Sat 6–10:30pm; Sun 5–8:30pm. Bus: 19, 31, or 38. SEAFOOD.

This small, no-nonsense seafood restaurant built a solid reputation among San Francisco's picky epicureans for its impeccably fresh fish. Choices ranging from Hawaiian swordfish to Puget Sound salmon—cooked to perfection, naturally—are matched with your sauce of choice (Szechuan peanut, tomatillo salsa, shallot butter) and a side of their signature french fries. Fancier seafood specials are available, too, such as paella with clams, mussels, scallops, calamari, chorizo, and saffron rice, as well as an impressive selection of garden-fresh salads and local grilled meats. Finish with the outstanding crème brûlée.

✪ **Zuni Café.** 1658 Market St. (at Franklin St.). ☎ **415/552-2522.** Reservations recommended. Main courses $15–$22.50. AE, MC, V. Tues–Sat 11:30am–midnight; Sun 11am–11pm. Valet parking $5. Muni Metro: All Market St. trams. Bus: 6, 7, 71, or 75. MEDITERRANEAN.

Even factoring in the sometimes snotty wait staff and absurd prices, Zuni Café is still one of our favorite spots in the city. Its expanse of windows and prime Market Street location guarantee good people watching—a favorite San Francisco pastime—and chef Judy Rodgers's Mediterranean-influenced menu is wonderfully diverse and satisfying. For the full effect, sit at the bustling bar and peruse the foot-long oyster menu (a dozen or so varieties are on hand at all times), or else take a seat in the stylish dining room or on the outdoor patio. Though the changing menu always includes meats and fish, the proven winners are Rodgers's brick-oven-roasted chicken for two with Tuscan-style bread salad, the polenta appetizer with mascarpone, and the hamburger on grilled rosemary focaccia (a strong contender for the city's best burger). Whatever you decide, be sure to order a side of the shoestring potatoes.

HAIGHT-ASHBURY
MODERATE

Eos. 901 Cole (at Carl St.). ☎ **415/566-3063.** Reservations recommended. Main courses $16–$26. AE, MC, V. Mon–Sat 5:30–11pm; Sun 5–11pm. Muni Metro: N. Bus: 6, 33, or 43. EAST-WEST FUSION.

Named after the Greek goddess of dawn, Eos is certainly basking in the spotlight thanks to chef/proprietor Arnold Wong, a master of texture and taste who perfected his craft while working at Masa's and Silks. It's not without a twinge of guilt that one mars the artistic presentation of each dish, such as the tender breast of Peking duck, smoked in ginger-peach tea leaves and served with a plum-kumquat chutney, or the blackened Asian catfish atop a bed of lemongrass risotto. For starters, try the almond-encrusted soft-shell crab dipped in spicy plum ponzu sauce. Unfortunately, the stark, industrial-deco decor does little to dampen the decibels, making a romantic outing nearly impossible unless you're into shouting. There is, however, a quiet, casual wine bar around the corner (same name) which stocks more than 400 vintages from around the globe.

INEXPENSIVE

✪ **Cha Cha Cha.** 1801 Haight St. (at Shrader St.). ☎ **415/386-5758.** Reservations not accepted. Tapas $4.50–$7.75; main courses $9–$13. MC, V. Daily 11:30am–4pm; Sun–Thurs 5–11pm, Fri–Sat 5–11:30pm. Muni Metro: N. Bus: 6, 7, 66, 71, or 73. CARIBBEAN.

This is one of our all-time favorite places to come for a fun night out, but it's not for everybody. Put your name on the mile-long list, crowd into the minuscule bar, and drink sangria while you wait. When you finally get seated (generally at least an hour later), you'll dine in a loud—and we mean *loud*—dining room with Santeria altars, banana trees, and plastic tropical tablecloths. Do as we do and order from the tapas menu, sharing such dishes as one of the city's best fried calamari, fried new potatoes, Cajun shrimp, and mussels in saffron broth, all of which are accompanied by rich, luscious sauces. This is the kind of place where you can take friends in a partying mood, let your hair down, and make an evening of it. If you want all the flavor without the festivities, come during lunch.

A second, larger location is open in the Mission at 2327 Mission St., between 19th and 20th streets (☎ **415/648-0504**).

✪ **Thep. Phanom.** 400 Waller St. (at Fillmore St.). ☎ **415/431-2526.** Reservations recommended. Main courses $6.95–$11.95. AE, CB, DC, DISC, MC, V. Daily 5:30–10:30pm. Bus: 6, 7, 22, 66, or 71. THAI.

By successfully incorporating flavors from India, China, Burma, Malaysia, and more recently the West, Thep Phanom rose the heady ranks to become one of the best Thai restaurants in San Francisco. Case in point: There's almost always a line out the front door. Start with the signature dish, *ped swan*—boneless duck in a light honey sauce served on a bed of spinach. The *larb ped* (minced duck salad), velvety basil-spiked seafood curry served on banana leaves, and spicy *yum plamuk* (calamari salad) are also recommended. The Haight Street location attracts an eclectic crowd and informal atmosphere, though the decor is actually quite tasteful. Reservations are advised, and don't leave anything even remotely valuable in your car.

RICHMOND & SUNSET DISTRICTS
INEXPENSIVE

✪ **Ton Kiang.** 5821 Geary Blvd. (between 22nd and 23rd aves.). ☎ **415/387-8273.** Reservations accepted for parties of eight or more. Dim sum $1.80–$4.50. Daily 10:30am–10pm. AE, MC. V. Bus: 38. DIM SUM.

We still love the Hong Kong Flower Lounge, but Ton Kiang is justifiably the number-one place in the city to do dim sum. Wait in the never-ending line (which is out the door anytime between 11am and 1:30pm on weekends), get a table on either the first or second floor, and get ready to party with your palate. From stuffed crab claws, roast Peking duck, and a gazillion dumpling selections (including scallop and vegetable, shrimp, and beef) to the delicious and hard-to-find *doa miu* (snow pea sprouts, flash sautéed with garlic and peanut oil), shark-fin soup, and a mesmerizing mango pudding, every tray of morsels coming from the kitchen is an absolute delight. This is definitely one of our favorite places to do lunch, and it happens to have an unusually friendly staff.

THE CASTRO
MODERATE

✪ **Mecca.** 2029 Market St. (between Duboce and Church sts.). ☎ **415/621-7000.** www.sfmecca.com. Reservations recommended. Main courses $15–$25. AE, DC, MC, V. Mon–Wed 5pm–midnight; Thurs–Sat 5pm–1:30am; Sun 4–11pm. Valet parking $8. Muni Metro: F, K, L, or M. Bus: 8, 22, 24, or 37. AMERICAN.

In 1996, Mecca entered the scene in a decadent swirl of chocolate-brown velvet, stainless steel, cement, and brown Naugahyde, unveiling the kind of industrial-chic supper club that makes you want to order a martini just so you'll match the ambiance. An eclectic city clientele (with a heavy dash of same-sex couples) mingles at the oval centerpiece bar. A night here promises a live DJ spinning hot grooves and a kitchen turning out fine California meals, served at tables tucked into several dining nooks. Menu options include such classic starters as Osetra caviar, oysters on the half shell, Caesar salad, stir-fried clams with garlic, and minced pork in a black-bean sauce. Main courses include shrimp and lemongrass-crusted Chilean sea bass, rosemary grilled rack of lamb, and soft-shell crabs with white-corn salsa and Creole mustard vinaigrette. The food is good, but it's that only-in-San-Francisco vibe that makes this place the smokin' hot spot to dine in the Castro.

INEXPENSIVE

Firewood Café. 4248 18th St. (at Diamond St.). ☎ **415/252-0999.** Main courses $5.25–$7.95. MC, V. Daily 11am–11pm. Muni Metro: F, K, L, or M line. Bus: 8, 33, 35, or 37. ITALIAN/AMERICAN.

One of the sharpest rooms in the neighborhood, this colorful place put its money in the essentials and eliminated extra overhead. There's no waiter or waitress here—everyone orders at the counter and then relaxes at either the long family-style table or one of the small tables facing the huge, street-side windows. There's no skimping, however, on the cozy-chic atmosphere and inspired-but-limited Mediterranean menu: The fresh salads ($6.25) come with a choice of three "fixin's" ranging from caramelized onions to spiced walnuts. Then there's the pastas—three tortellini selections, such as roasted chicken and mortadella—and gourmet pizzas. Or how about an herb-roasted half or whole chicken ($6.25 or $12.50, respectively) with roasted new potatoes? Wines cost $3.95 to $4.95 by the glass. Draft and bottled beers are also available, and desserts top off at $2.25. (Thank goodness *someone* realized that $7 for an after-dinner treat is bordering on ridiculous.)

MISSION DISTRICT
MODERATE

✪ **Pauline's.** 260 Valencia St. (between 14th St. and Duboce Ave.). ☎ **415/552-2050.** Reservations recommended. Main courses $10.50–$21.50. MC, V. Tues–Sat 5–10pm. Bus: 14, 26, or 49. PIZZA.

The perfect pizza? Quite possibly. At least it's the best we've ever had. Housed in a cheery double-decker yellow building that stands out like a beacon in a somewhat seedy neighborhood, Pauline's only does two things—pizzas and salads—but does them better than any other restaurant in the city. Eclectic toppings range from house-spiced chicken to French goat cheese, roasted eggplant, Danish fontina cheese, and tasso (spiced pork shoulder). Salads are equally amazing: certified organic, hand-picked by California growers, and topped with fresh and dried herbs (including edible flowers) from Pauline's own gardens in Berkeley. The wine list offers a smart selection of low-priced wines, and service is excellent. Yes, prices are a bit steep (small pizzas start at $10.50), but what a paltry price to pay for perfection.

✪ **Universal Café.** 2814 19th St. (at Bryant St.). ☎ **415/821-4608.** Reservations recommended for dinner. Main courses $2–$8 breakfast (full on weekends, continental on weekdays), $5–$12 lunch, $8–$20 dinner. AE, MC, V. Tues–Thur 7:30am–2:30pm and 6–10pm; Fri 9am–11:30pm; Sat 9am–2:30pm and 6–10pm; Sun 9am–2:30pm and 5:30–9:30pm. Bus: 27. AMERICAN/FRENCH.

Not only does this tiny place look good—suave and stylish with floor-to-ceiling windows and a profusion of sculptured metal and marble—but it also attracts a nightly gaggle of locals who come to this drab section of the Mission for the phenomenal focaccia sandwiches (go for the moist and memorable salmon), inventive thin-crust pizzas, and gourmet salads for lunch, and superb dinner dishes such as braised duck leg on a bed of creamy polenta; sea bass served with risotto, spinach, and caramelized onions; and hearty pot roast with lumpy mashed potatoes and fresh veggies. Granted, it's on the way to nowhere, but if you're near the Mission and have a few minutes to spare, it's well worth the detour.

INEXPENSIVE

Taquerias La Cumbre. 515 Valencia St. (between 16th and 17th sts.). ☎ **415/863-8205.** Tacos and burritos $2–$4.25; dinner plates $5–$7. No credit cards. Mon–Sat 11am–10pm; Sun noon–9pm. BART: Mission. Bus: 14, 22, 33, 49, or 53. MEXICAN.

While most restaurants gussy up their gastronomic goods with million-dollar decor and glamorous gimmicks, the fare at this cafeteria-like burrito institution is the main—and only—attraction. The well-crafted burrito needs only fresh pork, steak, chicken, or vegetables, plus cheese, beans, rice, salsa, and maybe a dash of guacamole or sour cream—and practically the whole town will drive to the remotest corners to taste it.

Ti Couz. 3108 16th St. (at Valencia St.). ☎ **415/252-7373.** Crepes $1.95–$8.25. MC, V. Mon–Fri 11am–11pm; Sat 10am–11pm; Sun 10am–10pm. BART: 16th & Mission. Bus: 14, 22, 33, 49, or 53. CREPES.

With fierce culinary competition around every corner, many establishments try to invent new gourmet gimmicks to hook the hungry. Not true for Ti Couz (*tee cooz*), one of the most architecturally stylish and popular restaurants in the Mission. Here the headliner is simple: delicate, paper-thin crepes. And while the fillings are not outrageously original, they are excellently executed and infinite in their combinations. Recommendations are listed, but you can build your own from the 15 main-course selections (such as smoked salmon, mushrooms, sausage, ham, scallops, and onions) and 19 dessert options (such as caramel, fruit, chocolate, and Nutella). Soups and salads solicit the less adventurous palate, but are equally stellar.

5 The Top Attractions

✪ **Alcatraz Island.** Pier 41, near Fisherman's Wharf. ☎ **415/773-1188** (for information only; no ferry reservations accepted at this number). www.nps.gov/alcatraz. Admission (includes ferry trip and audio tour) $11.25 adults, $9.50 seniors 62 and older, $6 children 5–11. Winter daily 9:30am–2:15pm; summer daily 9:15am–4:15pm. Advance purchase advised. Ferries depart every half hour, at 15 and 45 min. after the hour on the weekends, and every 45 min. throughout the week. Arrive at least 20 min. before sailing time.

Visible from Fisherman's Wharf, Alcatraz Island (a.k.a. "The Rock") has seen a checkered history. It was discovered in 1775 by Juan Manuel Ayala, who named it after the many pelicans that nested on the island. From the 1850s to 1933, when the army vacated the island, it served as a military post protecting the bay shoreline. In 1934, the buildings of the military outpost were converted into a maximum-security prison.

Major San Francisco Sights

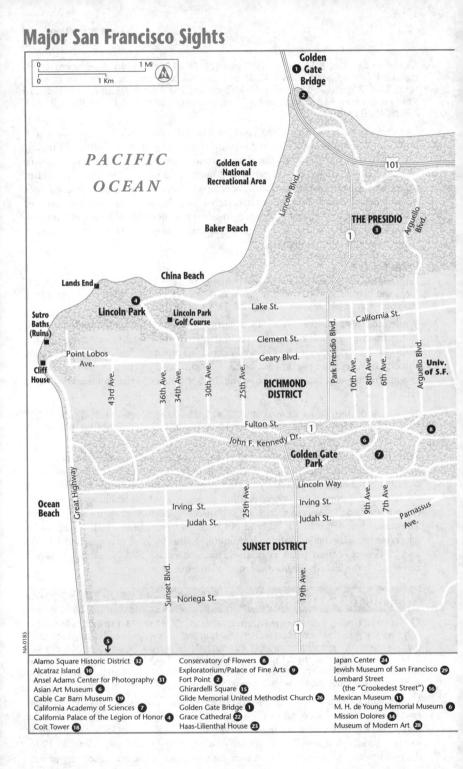

Golden Gate Bridge ❶❷

PACIFIC OCEAN

Golden Gate National Recreational Area

Baker Beach

THE PRESIDIO ❸

Lincoln Blvd.

Arguello Blvd.

101

China Beach

Lands End

Lincoln Park ❹

Lincoln Park Golf Course

Lake St.

California St.

Sutro Baths (Ruins)

Point Lobos Ave.

Clement St.

Geary Blvd.

Park Presidio Blvd.

Arguello Blvd.

Univ. of S.F.

Cliff House

43rd Ave.

36th Ave.

34th Ave.

30th Ave.

25th Ave.

10th Ave.

8th Ave.

6th Ave.

RICHMOND DISTRICT

Fulton St.

John F. Kennedy Dr.

❻ ❽ ❼

Golden Gate Park

Ocean Beach

Great Highway

Lincoln Way

Irving St.

Irving St.

Judah St.

Judah St.

25th Ave.

9th Ave.

7th Ave.

Parnassus Ave.

SUNSET DISTRICT

Sunset Blvd.

19th Ave.

Noriega St.

❺

NA-0185

Alamo Square Historic District ㉜
Alcatraz Island ❿
Ansel Adams Center for Photography ㉛
Asian Art Museum ❻
Cable Car Barn Museum ⑲
California Academy of Sciences ❼
California Palace of the Legion of Honor ❹
Coit Tower ⑱

Conservatory of Flowers ❽
Exploratorium/Palace of Fine Arts ❾
Fort Point ❷
Ghirardelli Square ⑮
Glide Memorial United Methodist Church ㉖
Golden Gate Bridge ❶
Grace Cathedral ㉒
Haas-Lilienthal House ㉓

Japan Center ㉔
Jewish Museum of San Francisco ㉙
Lombard Street (the "Crookedest Street") ⑯
Mexican Museum ⑪
M. H. de Young Memorial Museum ❻
Mission Dolores ㉞
Museum of Modern Art ㉘

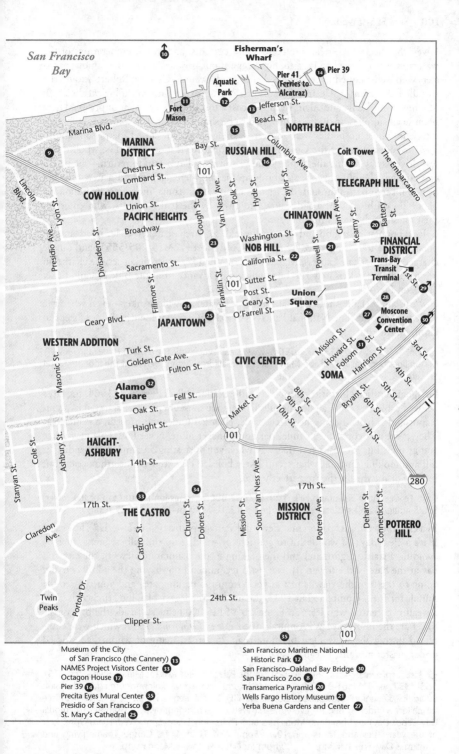

San Francisco Bay

Fisherman's Wharf

↑ 10

Pier 41
(Ferries to
Alcatraz)

14 Pier 39

Aquatic
Park 12

11 Fort
Mason

13 Jefferson St.

Beach St.

NORTH BEACH

Marina Blvd.

15

9

MARINA
DISTRICT

Bay St.

RUSSIAN HILL

16

Coit Tower

18

TELEGRAPH HILL

Chestnut St.

Lombard St.

101

Columbus Ave.

The Embarcadero

COW HOLLOW

Union St.

17

Polk St.

Hyde St.

Taylor St.

Grant Ave.

Kearny St.

Battery St.

PACIFIC HEIGHTS

Broadway

Van Ness Ave.

Gough St.

CHINATOWN

19

20

FINANCIAL
DISTRICT

Lincoln Blvd

Presidio Ave.

Lyon St.

Divisadero St.

23

Washington St.

NOB HILL

22

Powell St.

21

Trans-Bay
Transit
Terminal

1st St.

29

Sacramento St.

Franklin St.

California St.

Fillmore St.

101 Sutter St.

Post St.

Union
Square

28

27

Moscone
Convention
Center

30

Geary Blvd.

24

JAPANTOWN

25

Geary St.

O'Farrell St.

26

Mission St.

Howard St.

31

3rd St.

4th St.

WESTERN ADDITION

Masonic St.

Turk St.

Golden Gate Ave.

Fulton St.

CIVIC CENTER

SOMA

Folsom St.

Harrison St.

Bryant St.

5th St.

6th St.

7th St.

Alamo
Square

32

Fell St.

Oak St.

Haight St.

Market St.

8th St.

9th St.

10th St.

Cole St.

Ashbury St.

Stanyan St.

HAIGHT-
ASHBURY

14th St.

280

33

34

17th St.

South Van Ness Ave.

Mission St.

17th St.

Deharo St.

Connecticut St.

POTRERO
HILL

17th St.

THE CASTRO

Church St.

Dolores St.

Castro St.

MISSION
DISTRICT

Potrero Ave.

Claredon Ave.

Twin
Peaks

Portola Dr.

24th St.

Clipper St.

35

101

Museum of the City
of San Francisco (the Cannery) 13
NAMES Project Visitors Center 33
Octagon House 17
Pier 39 14
Precita Eyes Mural Center 35
Presidio of San Francisco 3
St. Mary's Cathedral 25

San Francisco Maritime National
Historic Park 12
San Francisco–Oakland Bay Bridge 30
San Francisco Zoo 8
Transamerica Pyramid 20
Wells Fargo History Museum 21
Yerba Buena Gardens and Center 27

99

Given the sheer cliffs, treacherous tides and currents, and frigid temperatures of the waters, it was believed to be a totally escape-proof prison. Among the famous gangsters who were penned in cell blocks A through D were Al Capone; Robert Stroud, the so-called Birdman of Alcatraz (because he was an expert in ornithological diseases); Machine Gun Kelly; and Alvin Karpis. It cost a fortune to keep them imprisoned here because all supplies, including water, had to be shipped in. In 1963, after an apparent escape in which no bodies were recovered, the government closed the prison, and in 1972 it became part of the Golden Gate National Recreation Area. The wildlife that was driven away during the military and prison years has begun to return—the black-crested night heron and other seabirds are nesting here again—and a new trail has been built that passes through the island's nature areas. Tours, including an audio tour of the prison block and a slide show, are given by the park's rangers, who entertain their guests with interesting anecdotes.

It's a popular excursion and space is limited, so purchase tickets as far in advance as possible. The tour is operated by **Blue & Gold Fleet** (☎ 415/705-5555) and can be charged to American Express, MasterCard, or Visa ($2.25 per ticket service charge on phone orders). Tickets may also be purchased in advance from the Blue & Gold ticket office on Pier 41.

Wear comfortable shoes and take a heavy sweater or windbreaker—even when the sun's out, it's cold. The National Parks Service also notes that there are a lot of steps to climb on the tour.

✪ **Cable Cars.** ☎ 415/673-6864. www.sfcablecar.com. The Powell-Hyde and Powell-Mason lines begin at Powell and Market sts.; the California St. line begins at the foot of Market St. Fare $3.

Designated official historic landmarks by the National Park Service in 1964, the city's beloved cable cars clank across the hills like mobile museum pieces. Each weighs about 6 tons and is hauled along by a steel cable, enclosed under the street in a center rail. They move at a constant 9½ miles per hour—never more, never less. This may strike you as slow, but it doesn't feel that way when you're cresting an almost perpendicular hill and looking down at what seems like a bobsled dive straight into the ocean. But in spite of the thrills, they're perfectly safe.

Coit Tower. Atop Telegraph Hill. ☎ **415/362-0808.** Admission (to the top of the tower) $3.75 adults, $2.50 seniors, $1.50 children 6–12. Daily 10am–6pm. Bus: 39 (Coit).

In a city known for its panoramic views and vantage points, Coit Tower is "The Peak." If it's a clear day, it's wonderful to get here by walking up the Filbert Steps (thereby avoiding a traffic nightmare) and then taking in the panoramic views of the city and bay at the base of the tower. (In fact, we'd recommend not paying the admission and going to the top; the view is just as good from the parking area and you can see the murals for free.) Completed in 1933, the tower is the legacy of Lillie Hitchcock Coit, a wealthy eccentric who left San Francisco a $125,000 bequest. Inside the base of the tower are the impressive WPA murals titled *Life in California, 1934,* which were completed during the New Deal by more than 25 artists, many of whom had studied under master muralist Diego Rivera.

✪ **The Exploratorium.** 3601 Lyon St., in the Palace of Fine Arts (at Marina Blvd.). ☎ **415/563-7337,** or 415/561-0360 for recorded information. www.exploratorium.edu. Admission $9 adults, $7 seniors and college students with ID, $5 children 6–17, $2.50 children 3–5, free for children under 3; free for everyone 1st Wed of each month. MC, V. Summer (Memorial Day–Labor Day) and holidays, Mon–Tues and Thurs–Sun 10am–6pm, Wed 10am–9pm. Rest of the year, Tues and Thurs–Sun 10am–5pm, Wed 10am–9pm. Closed Thanksgiving and Christmas Day. Free parking. Bus: 30 from Stockton St. to the Marina stop.

This fun, hands-on science fair contains more than 650 permanent exhibits that explore everything from color theory to Einstein's theory of relativity. Optics are demonstrated in booths where you can see a bust of a statue in three dimensions—but when you try to touch it, you discover it isn't there! The same surreal experience occurs with an image of yourself: When you stretch your hand forward, a hand comes out to touch you, and the hands pass in midair. Every exhibit is designed to be used. You can whisper into a concave reflector and have a friend hear you 60 feet away, or you can design your own animated abstract art—using sound.

✪ **Golden Gate Bridge.** ☎ **415/921-5858.** www.goldengate.org. Bridge-bound Golden Gate Transit buses (☎ **415/455-2000**) depart every 30–60 min. during the day for Marin County, starting from the Transbay Terminal at Mission and First sts. and making convenient stops at Market and Seventh sts., at the Civic Center, and along Van Ness Ave. and Lombard St. Consult the route map in the Yellow Pages or phone for schedule information.

With its gracefully swung single span, spidery bracing cables, and sky-high twin towers, the bridge looks more like a work of abstract art than one of the greatest practical engineering feats of the 20th century. Construction began in May 1937 and was completed at the then-colossal cost of $35 million. Contrary to pessimistic predictions, the bridge neither collapsed in a gale or earthquake nor proved to be a white elephant. A symbol of hope when the country was afflicted with widespread unemployment, the Golden Gate single-handedly changed the Bay Area's economic life, encouraging the development of areas north of San Francisco.

The mile-long steel link (longer if you factor in the approach), which reaches a height of 746 feet above the water, is an awesome bridge to cross. You can park in the lot at the foot of the bridge on the city side, then make the crossing by foot. Back in your car, continue to Marin's Vista Point, at the bridge's northern end. Look back and you'll be rewarded with one of the most famous cityscape views in the world. Millions of pedestrians walk across the bridge each year. You can walk out onto the span from either end. Note that it's usually windy and cold, and the bridge vibrates. Still, walking even a short way is one of the best ways to experience the immense scale of the structure.

Museum of Modern Art. 151 Third St. (2 blocks south of Market St., across from Yerba Buena Gardens). ☎ **415/357-4000.** www.sfmoma.org. Admission $8 adults, $5 seniors, $4 for students with ID, free for children 12 and under; half price for everyone Thurs 6–9pm, and free for everyone the first Tues of each month. Labor Day–Memorial Day Thurs 11am–9pm; Fri–Tues 11am–6pm. Memorial Day–Labor Day Thurs 10am–9pm; Fri–Tues 10am–6pm. Closed on major holidays. Muni Metro: J, K, L, or M to Montgomery Station. Bus: 15, 30, or 45.

Swiss architect Mario Botta, in association with Hellmuth, Obata & Kassabaum, designed this $62-million building, which doubled the museum's previous space when it opened in SoMa in 1995. MOMA's collection consists of more than 15,000 works, including close to 5,000 paintings and sculptures by artists such as Henri Matisse, Jackson Pollock, and Willem de Kooning. Other artists represented include Diego Rivera, Georgia O'Keeffe, Paul Klee, the Fauvists, and exceptional holdings of Richard Diebenkorn. MOMA was also one of the first to recognize photography as a major art form; its extensive collection includes more than 9,000 photographs by such notables as Ansel Adams, Alfred Stieglitz, Edward Weston, and Henri Cartier-Bresson. Phone for current details of upcoming special events and whatever you do, check out the fabulous MuseumStore.

✪ **Yerba Buena Gardens and Center.** Between Mission and Howard sts. at Third St., the Yerba Buena Center. ☎ **415/978-2787**. Muni: 30, 45, or 9X. Metro: Powell or Montgomery.

An urban interactive wonderland, Yerba Buena could keep you busy all day with its 5-acre garden and cafes; **Center for the Arts** (www.yerbabuenaarts.org), which presents music, theater, dance, and visual arts; **Galleries and Arts Forum,** which features three galleries and a space designed specially for dance; **Zeum** (☎ 415/777-2800; www.zeum.org), the new children's addition with a cafe, interactive cultural center, ice-skating rink, fabulous 1906 historic carousel, and interactive play and learning garden; Sony's new **Metreon Entertainment Center** (☎ 415/537-3400), a 350,000-square-foot complex housing movie theaters, an **IMAX** theater, small restaurants, interactive attractions (including one that features Maurice Sendak's *Where the Wild Things Are*), and shops; a bowling alley; and a child-care center. For recorded information and tickets, call ☎ 415/978-ARTS.

✪ GOLDEN GATE PARK

Everybody loves Golden Gate Park: people, dogs, birds, frogs, turtles, bison, trees, bushes, and flowers. Literally everything feels unified here in San Francisco's enormous arboreal front yard, conveniently located between Fulton Street and Lincoln Way with the main entrance at Fell and Stanyan streets.

Totaling 1,017 acres, Golden Gate Park is a truly magical place. Spend one sunny day stretched out on the grass along JFK Drive, have a good read in Shakespeare Garden, or stroll around Stow Lake and you, too, will understand the allure. It's an interactive botanical symphony—and everyone is invited to play in the orchestra.

The park is made up of hundreds of gardens and attractions linked by wooded paths and paved roads. While many sites worth seeing are clearly visible, the park has infinite hidden treasures, so make your first stop the **McClaren Lodge and Park Headquarters** (☎ 415/831-2700) if you want detailed information on the park.

Of the dozens of special gardens in the park, most recognized are the Rhododendron Dell, the Rose Garden, the Strybing Arboretum (see below), and, at the western edge of the park, a springtime array of thousands of tulips and daffodils around the Dutch windmill.

In addition to the highlights discussed below, the park contains several recreational facilities: tennis courts; baseball, soccer, and polo fields; a golf course; riding stables; and fly-casting pools.

If you plan to visit all the park's attractions, consider buying the **Culture Pass,** which enables you to visit the park's three museums and the Japanese Tea Garden for $12. Passes are available at each site and at the visitor information center. For further information, call ☎ 415/391-2000. Enter the park at Kezar Drive, an extension of Fell Street. Bus: 16AX, BX, 5, 6, 7, 66, or 71.

MUSEUMS INSIDE THE PARK

Asian Art Museum. In Golden Gate Park, near 10th Ave. and Fulton St. ☎ **415/379-8800;** 415/752-2635 for the hearing impaired. Admission (including the M. H. de Young Memorial Museum and California Palace of the Legion of Honor) $7 adults, $5 seniors 65 and over, $4 youths 12–17, free for children 11 and under (fees may be higher for special exhibitions); free for everyone the 1st Wed of each month. Tues–Sun 9:30am–5pm; 1st Wed each month 10am–8:45pm. Bus: 5, 44, or 71.

This exhibition space, which opened in 1966, can only display about 1,800 of the museum's vast collection of 12,000 pieces. About half the works on exhibit are in the ground-floor Chinese and Korean galleries and include world-class sculptures, paintings, bronzes, ceramics, jades, and decorative objects spanning 6,000 years of history. There's also a wide range of exhibits from more than 40 Asian countries—Pakistan, India, Tibet, Japan, Southeast Asia—including the world's oldest-known "dated" Chinese Buddha. The museum's free daily guided tours are highly informative and sincerely recommended. Call for times.

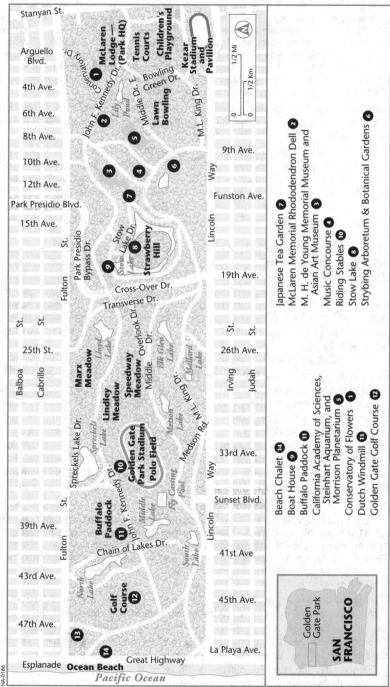

Stanyan St.

Arguello Blvd.

4th Ave.

6th Ave.

8th Ave.

10th Ave.

12th Ave.

Park Presidio Blvd.

15th Ave.

25th St.

Balboa

Cabrillo

33rd Ave.

39th Ave.

43rd Ave.

47th Ave.

Esplanade **Ocean Beach**

Pacific Ocean

9th Ave.

Way

Funston Ave.

Lincoln

19th Ave.

St.

St.

26th Ave.

Irving

Judah

Way

Sunset Blvd.

Lincoln

41st Ave

45th Ave.

La Playa Ave.

Conservatory Dr.

John F. Kennedy Dr.

McLaren Lodge (Park HQ)

Tennis Courts

Children's Playground

Kezar Stadium and Pavilion

Lily Pond

Middle Dr. E.

Bowling Green Dr.

Lawn Bowling

M.L. King Dr.

Park Presidio Bypass Dr.

Stow Lake Dr.

Stow Lake

Strawberry Hill

Cross-Over Dr.

Transverse Dr.

Fulton

St.

St.

Marx Meadow

Lindley Meadow

Speedway Meadow

Overlook Dr.

Middle Dr.

Lloyd Lake

Elk Glen Lake

Mallard Lake

Metson Lake

Medson M.L. King Dr.

Spreckels Lake Dr.

Spreckels Lake

Golden Gate Park Stadium Polo Field

John F. Kennedy Dr.

Fly Casting Pool

Middle Lake

Buffalo Paddock

Fulton

Chain of Lakes Dr.

Golf Course

North Lake

South Lake

Great Highway

SAN FRANCISCO

Golden Gate Park

1/2 Mi

1/2 Km

0

0

Japanese Tea Garden ❼

McLaren Memorial Rhododendron Dell ❷

M. H. de Young Memorial Museum and Asian Art Museum ❸

Music Concourse ❹

Riding Stables ❿

Stow Lake ❽

Strybing Arboretum & Botanical Gardens ❻

Beach Chalet ⓮

Boat House ❾

Buffalo Paddock ⓫

California Academy of Sciences, Steinhart Aquarium, and Morrison Planetarium ❶

Conservatory of Flowers ⓭

Dutch Windmill ⓭

Golden Gate Golf Course ⓬

NA-0186

103

California Academy of Sciences. On the Music Concourse of Golden Gate Park. ☎ **415/ 750-7145** for recorded information. www.calacademy.org. Admission (aquarium and Natural History Museum) $8.50 adults, $5.50 students 12–17 and seniors 65 and over, $2 children 4–11, free for children under 4; free for everyone the 1st Wed of every month. Planetarium shows $2.50 adults, $1.25 children under 18 and seniors 65 and over. Labor Day–Memorial Day daily 10am–5pm; Memorial Day–Labor Day daily 9am–6pm; 1st Wed of every month 10am–9pm. Muni Metro: N to Golden Gate Park. Bus: 5, 71, or 44.

Clustered around the Music Concourse in Golden Gate Park are three outstanding world-class museums and exhibitions that are guaranteed to entertain every member of the family.

The **Steinhart Aquarium** is the most diverse aquarium in the world, housing some 14,000 specimens, including amphibians, reptiles, marine mammals, penguins, and much more. Youngsters will love the California tide pool and a hands-on area where they can touch starfish and sea urchins. The living coral reef is the largest display of its kind in the country. In the Fish Roundabout, visitors are surrounded by fast-swimming schools of fish kept in a 100,000-gallon tank. The penguins are fed at 11:30am and 4pm.

The **Morrison Planetarium** projects sky shows on its 65-foot domed ceiling as well as laser light shows. Approximately four major exhibits, with titles such as *Star Death: The Birth of Black Holes* and *The Universe Unveiled,* are presented each year. Related cosmos exhibits are located in the adjacent Earth and Space Hall. Sky shows are featured at 2pm Monday through Friday and hourly on Saturday, Sunday, and holidays (call ☎ **415/750-7141** for more information). Laserium laser light shows are also presented in the planetarium Thursday through Sunday nights (call ☎ **415/750-7138** for more information).

The **Natural History Museum** includes several halls displaying classic dioramas of fauna in their habitats. The Wattis Hall of Human Cultures traces the evolution of different human cultures and how they adapted to their natural environment; the "Wild California" exhibition in Meyer Hall includes a 14,000-gallon aquarium and seabird rookery, life-size battling elephant seals, and two larger-than-life views of microscopic life forms; in McBean-Peterson Hall, visitors can walk through an exhibit tracing the course of 3½ billion years of evolution, from the earliest life forms to the present day; and in the Hohfeld Earth and Space Hall, visitors can experience a simulation of two of San Francisco's biggest earthquakes, determine what their weight would be on other planets, see a real moon rock, and learn about the rotation of the planet at a replica of Foucault's Pendulum (the original one is in Paris).

M. H. de Young Memorial Museum. In Golden Gate Park (near 10th Ave. and Fulton St.). ☎ **415/750-3600,** or 415/863-3330 for recorded information. Admission (including the Asian Art Museum and California Palace of the Legion of Honor) $7 adults, $5 seniors over 65, $4 youths 12–17, free for children 11 and under (fees may be higher for special exhibitions); free the 1st Wed of each month. Wed–Sun 9:30am–5pm (1st Wed of the month until 8:45pm). Bus: 44.

One of the city's oldest museums, the de Young is best known for its American art dating from colonial times to the 20th century, including paintings, sculptures, furniture, and decorative arts by Paul Revere, Winslow Homer, John Singer Sargent, and Georgia O'Keefe. Special note should be taken of the American landscapes, as well as the fun trompe l'oeil and still-life works from the turn of the century.

Named after the late-19th-century publisher of the *San Francisco Chronicle,* the museum also possesses an important textile collection, with primary emphasis on rugs from central Asia and the Near East. Other collections on view include decorative art from Africa, Oceania, and the Americas. Major traveling exhibitions are equally eclectic, including everything from ancient rugs to great Dutch paintings. Call the museum to find out what's on. Tours are offered daily; call for times.

The museum's **Cafe de Young** serves daily specials that might include Peruvian stew, Chinese chicken salad, and Italian vegetables in tomato-basil sauce. In summer, visitors can dine among bronze statuary in the garden. The cafe is open Wednesday through Sunday from 10am to 4pm.

OTHER PARK HIGHLIGHTS

BEACH CHALET   First listed on the National Register of Historic places in 1981, the Spanish-Colonial Beach Chalet, 1000 Great Hwy., at the west end of Golden Gate Park near Fulton Street (☎ **415/386-8439**), was designed by the architect Willis Polk in 1925. Built with a 200-seat restaurant upstairs and a public lounge and changing rooms on the first floor, it was a popular stopover for generations of beachgoers. In the late 1930s, the federal government's Works Progress Administration (WPA) commissioned Lucien Labaudt (who also painted Coit Tower's frescoes) to create incredible frescoes, mosaics, and wood carvings of San Francisco life. After decades of use, the chalet grew old and worn, forcing its closure in 1981; but in December 1996, the historic Beach Chalet reopened its doors, and through the original mosaics and new literature and displays, it continues to celebrate the city's heritage. The upstairs restaurant is far too modern to wax historical, but it's a great place to stop for a housemade brew and a glimpse of the expansive Pacific.

CONSERVATORY OF FLOWERS (1878)   This striking assemblage of glass and iron, modeled on the famous glass house at Kew Gardens in London, usually exhibits a rotating display of plants and shrubs. Unfortunately, it's closed to visitors until further notice, but the exterior architecture and surrounding gardens alone are worth a look.

JAPANESE TEA GARDEN (1894)   Developed for the 1894 Midwinter Exposition, this garden would be a quiet place with cherry trees, shrubs, and bonsai crisscrossed by winding paths and high-arched bridges crossing over pools of water—were it not for the hordes of tourists and screaming children who can all but destroy any semblance of peace. Come early to enjoy the focal points and places for contemplation, including the massive bronze Buddha that was cast in Japan in 1790 and donated by the Gump family, the Shinto wooden pagoda, and the Wishing Bridge, which reflected in the water looks as though it completes a circle. The garden is open daily, October through February from 8:30am to 6pm (with the teahouse only open until 5:30pm), and March through September from 9am to 6:30pm. For **information** on admissions, call ☎ **415/752-4227.** For the **teahouse,** call ☎ **415/752-1171.**

STRYBING ARBORETUM & BOTANICAL GARDENS   Some 6,000 plant species grow here, among them rare species, very ancient plants in a special "primitive garden," and a grove of California redwoods. Docent tours are given at 1pm daily during operating hours, which are Monday through Friday from 8am to 4:30pm and Saturday and Sunday from 10am to 5pm. For more information, call ☎ **415/753-7089.**

✪ **STOW LAKE/STRAWBERRY HILL**   Rent a paddleboat, rowboat, or motorboat here and cruise around the circular lake as painters create still lifes and joggers pass along the grassy shoreline. Ducks waddle around waiting to be fed and turtles bathe on rocks and logs. Strawberry Hill, the 430-foot-high artificial island that lies at the center of Stow Lake, is a perfect picnic spot and boasts a bird's-eye view of San Francisco and the bay. It also has a waterfall and peace pagoda. To reach the **boathouse,** call ☎ **415/752-0347.** Boat rentals are available daily from 9am to 4pm.

6 Exploring the City

☉ Mission Dolores. 16th St. (at Dolores St.). ☎ **415/621-8203.** Donations appreciated. May–Oct daily 9am–4:30pm; Nov–Apr daily 9am–4pm; Good Friday 10am–noon. Closed Thanksgiving and Christmas Day. BART: Church and 16th sts. Bus: 22.

This is the oldest structure in the city, built on order of Franciscan Father Junípero Serra by Father Francisco Palou. It was constructed of 36,000 sunbaked bricks and dedicated in June 1776 at the northern terminus of El Camino Real, the Spanish road from Mexico to California. It's a moving place to visit, with its cool, serene buildings with thick adobe walls and especially the cemetery/gardens where the early settlers are buried.

The NAMES Project AIDS Memorial Quilt Visitors Center & Panelmaking Workshop. 2362-A Market St. ☎ **415/863-1966.** Mon–Fri noon–7pm; Sun noon–6pm. Muni Metro: J, K, L, or M line to Castro St. Station; F line to Church and Market sts.

The NAMES Project began in 1987 as a memorial to those who have died of AIDS. Sewing machines and fabrics were acquired, and the public was invited to make coffin-sized panels for a giant memorial quilt. More than 40,000 individual panels now commemorate the lives of those who have died. Each has been uniquely designed and sewn by the victims' friends, lovers, and family members.

The quilt, which would cover 24 football fields if laid out end to end, was first displayed on the Capitol Mall in Washington, D.C., during a 1987 national march on Washington for lesbian and gay rights. Although sections of the quilt are often on tour throughout the world, portions of the largest community art project in the world are on display here. A sewing machine and fabrics are also available here, free, for your use.

Lombard Street. Between Hyde and Leavenworth sts.

Known as the "crookedest street in the world," the whimsically winding block of Lombard Street puts smiles on the faces of thousands of visitors each year. The elevation is so steep that the road has to snake back and forth to make a descent possible.

ARCHITECTURAL HIGHLIGHTS

The **Alamo Square Historic District** contains many of the city's 14,000 Victorian ☉ **"Painted Ladies,"** homes that have been restored and ornately painted by residents. The small area—bordered by Divisadero Street on the west, Golden Gate Avenue on the north, Webster Street on the east, and Fell Street on the south, about 10 blocks west of the Civic Center—has one of the city's largest concentrations of these. One of the most famous views of San Francisco, which you'll see on postcards and posters all around the city, depicts sharp-edged Financial District skyscrapers behind a row of Victorians. This view can be seen from Alamo Square at Fulton and Steiner streets.

Built in 1881 to a design by Brown and Bakewell, **City Hall** and the ☉ **Civic Center** are part of a "City Beautiful" complex done in the beaux-arts style. The dome rises to a height of 308 feet on the exterior and is ornamented with occuli and topped by a lantern. The interior rotunda soars 112 feet and is finished in oak, marble, and limestone with a monumental marble staircase leading to the second floor; City Hall is worth seeking as it just underwent a total renovation and retrofitting.

The **Flood Mansion,** 1000 California St., at Mason Street, was built between 1885 and 1886 for James Clair Flood, who, thanks to the Comstock Lode, rose from being a bartender to being one of the city's wealthiest men. The house cost $1.5 million (the fence alone carried a price tag of $30,000!). It was designed by Augustus Laver and modified by Willis Polk after the earthquake to accommodate the Pacific Union Club.

The **Octagon House,** 2645 Gough St., at Union Street (☎ **415/441-7512**), is an eight-sided, cupola-topped house dating from 1861. Its features are extraordinary, especially the circular staircase and ceiling medallion. Inside, you'll find furniture, silverware, and American pewter from the colonial and Federal periods. There are also some historic documents, including signatures of 54 of the 56 signers of the Declaration of Independence. Even if you're not able to visit during open hours, this strange structure is worth a look. It's open on the second Sunday and second and fourth Thursdays of each month (except January) from noon to 3pm; closed January and holidays.

The **Palace of Fine Arts,** on Baker between Jefferson and Bay streets, is the only building to survive from the Pan-Pacific Exhibition of 1915. Constructed by Bernard Maybeck, it was rebuilt in concrete using molds taken from the original in the 1950s. It now houses the Exploratorium (see "The Top Attractions," above).

The **TransAmerica Pyramid,** 600 Montgomery St., between Clay and Washington streets, is the tallest structure in San Francisco's skyline—48 stories tall and capped by a 212-foot spire.

Although the **San Francisco–Oakland Bay Bridge** is visually less appealing than the Golden Gate Bridge (see "The Top Attractions," above), it is in many ways more spectacular. Opened in 1936, before the Golden Gate, it's 8¼ miles long, one of the world's longest steel bridges. It's not a single bridge at all, but actually a dovetailed series of spans joined in midbay—at Yerba Buena Island—by one of the world's largest (in diameter) tunnels. To the west of Yerba Buena, the bridge is really two separate suspension bridges, joined at a central anchorage. East of the island is a 1,400-foot cantilever span, followed by a succession of truss bridges.

CHURCHES

Glide Memorial United Methodist Church. 330 Ellis St. ☎ **415/771-6300.** Services held Sun 9 and 11am. Muni Metro: Powell. Bus: 37.

There would be nothing special about this plain, Tenderloin-area church if it weren't for its exhilarating pastor, Cecil Williams. Williams's enthusiastic and uplifting preaching and singing with the homeless and poor people of the neighborhood crosses all socioeconomic boundaries and has attracted nationwide fame. Go for an uplifting experience.

MUSEUMS

Also see "The Top Attractions," above.

Ansel Adams Center for Photography. 250 Fourth St. ☎ **415/495-7000.** Admission $5 adults, $3 students, $2 seniors and children 13–17, free for children 12 and under. Daily 11am–5pm; until 8pm the 1st Thurs of each month. Muni Metro: Powell St. lines. Bus: 30, 45, or 9X.

This popular SoMa museum features five separate galleries for changing exhibitions of contemporary and historical photography. One area is dedicated to displaying the works and exploring the legacy of Ansel Adams.

Cable Car Barn Museum. Washington and Mason sts. ☎ **415/474-1887.** Free admission. Apr–Oct daily 10am–6pm; Nov–Mar daily 10am–5pm. Cable car: Both Powell St. lines stop by the museum.

If you've ever wondered how cable cars work, this nifty museum will explain (and demonstrate!) it all to you. Yes, this is a museum, but the Cable Car Barn is no stuffed shirt. It's the living powerhouse, repair shop, and storage place of the cable-car system and is in full operation. The exposed machinery, which pulls the cables under San Francisco's streets, looks like a Rube Goldberg invention. Watch the massive groaning and vibrating winches as they thread the cable that hauls the cars through a huge figure eight and back into the system via slack-absorbing tension wheels. In the lower-level viewing room, you can see the cables operating underground. There's also a shop where you can buy a variety of cable-car gifts.

۞ California Palace of the Legion of Honor. In Lincoln Park (at 34th Ave. and Clement St.). ☎ **415/750-3600,** or 415/863-3330 for recorded information. Admission (including the Asian Art Museum and M. H. de Young Memorial Museum) $7 adults, $5 seniors 65 and over, $4 youths 12–17, free for children 11 and under (fees may be higher for special exhibitions); free the 2nd Wed of each month. Tues–Sun 9:30am–5pm; 2nd Wed of each month 9:30am–8:45pm. Bus: 18 or 38.

Designed as a memorial to California's World War I casualties, the neoclassical structure is an exact replica of the Legion of Honor Palace in Paris, right down to the inscription *honneur et patrie* above the portal. Reopened after a 2-year, $29-million renovation and seismic upgrading project that was stalled by the discovery of almost 300 turn-of-the-century coffins, the museum's collection contains paintings, sculpture, and decorative arts from Europe, as well as international tapestries, prints, and drawings. The chronological display of more than 800 years of European art includes a fine collection of Rodin sculpture.

Jewish Museum San Francisco. 121 Steuart St. (between Mission and Howard sts.). ☎ **415/543-8880.** Admission $5 adults, $2.50 students and seniors; free the 1st Mon of each month. Sun–Wed 11am–5pm; Thurs 11am–8pm. Bus: 14, 32.

This museum hosts a variety of shows that concentrate on immigration, assimilation, and identity of the Jewish community in the United States and around the world. They are illustrated by paintings, sculptures, photographs, and installation art.

Mexican Museum. Bldg. D, Fort Mason, Marina Blvd. (at Laguna St.). ☎ **415/202-9700.** Admission $3 adults, $2 children. Free 1st Wed of the month. Wed–Fri noon–5pm; Sat–Sun 11am–5pm. Bus: 76 or 28.

The gallery maintains a collection of art covering pre-Hispanic, colonial, folk, and Mexican fine art, plus Chicano/Mexican-American art. A recent show featured religious works by New Mexican women. *Note:* The museum is scheduled to relocate to the Yerba Buena Center at Third and Mission streets sometime in 2000.

San Francisco Maritime National Historical Park. At the foot of Polk St. (near Fisherman's Wharf). ☎ **415/556-3002.** Museum free; ships $4 adults, $2 children 12–17, free for children 11 and under and seniors over 62. Museum daily 10am–5pm. Ships on Hyde St. Pier daily 9:30am–5pm. Closed Thanksgiving, Christmas Day, and New Year's Day. Cable car: Hyde St. line to the last stop. Bus: 19, 30, 32, 42, or 47.

Shaped like an art-deco ship and located near Fisherman's Wharf, the National Maritime Museum is filled with sailing, whaling, and fishing lore. Exhibits include intricate model craft, scrimshaw, and a collection of shipwreck photographs and historic marine scenes, including an 1851 snapshot of hundreds of abandoned ships, deserted en masse by crews dashing off to participate in the gold rush. The museum's walls are lined with finely carved, painted wooden figureheads from old windjammers.

Two blocks east, at Aquatic Park's Hyde Street Pier, are several historic ships that are open to the public. The *Balclutha,* one of the last surviving square-riggers, was built in Glasgow, Scotland, in 1886 and was used to carry grain from California around Cape Horn at a near-record speed of 300 miles a day; it rounded the treacherous Cape 17 times in its career. Visitors are invited to spin the wheel, squint at the compass, and imagine they're weathering a mighty storm. Kids can climb into the bunking quarters, visit the "slop chest" (galley to you, matey), and read the sea chanties (clean ones only) that decorate the walls.

The 1890 *Eureka* still carries a cargo of nostalgia for San Franciscans. It was the last of 50 paddle-wheeled ferries that regularly plied the bay; it made its final trip in 1957.

Restored to its original splendor, the side-wheeler is loaded with deck cargo, including antique cars and trucks.

At the pier's small-boat shop, visitors can follow the restoration progress of historic boats from the museum's collection. It's behind the maritime bookstore on your right as you approach the ships.

Wells Fargo History Museum. 420 Montgomery St. (at California St.). ☎ **415/ 396-2619.** Free admission. Mon–Fri 9am–5pm. Closed major holidays. Muni Metro: Montgomery St. Bus: any to Market St.

Wells Fargo, one of California's largest banks, was founded on the frontier; this museum displays hundreds of frontier relics. In the center of the main room stands a Concord stagecoach, which opened the West as surely as the Winchester rifle and the iron-horse locomotive. On the mezzanine, you can take an imaginary ride in a replica stagecoach or send a telegraph message in code using a telegraph key and the code books, just the way the Wells Fargo agents did more than a century ago.

NEIGHBORHOODS WORTH SEEKING OUT

THE CASTRO   Castro Street around Market and 18th streets is the center of the city's gay community, which is catered to by the many stores, restaurants, bars, and other institutions here. Among the landmarks are Harvey Milk Plaza, the Quilt Project, and the Castro Theatre, a 1920s movie palace. (See "Organized Tours," below, for details on a walking tour of the area.)

CHINATOWN   California Street to Broadway and Kearny to Stockton Street are the boundaries of today's Chinatown. San Francisco is home to the second-largest community of Chinese in the United States, but the majority of them do not live and work in these 24 blocks, although they do return to shop and dine here on weekends.

The gateway at Grant and Bush marks the entry to Chinatown. Walk up Grant, which has become the tourist face of Chinatown, to California Street and Old St. Mary's.

The **Chinese Historical Society of America,** at 650 Commercial St. (☎ **415/ 391-1188**), has a small but interesting collection relating to the Chinese in San Francisco, which can be viewed for free Tuesday through Friday from 10am to 4pm.

The heart of Chinatown is at **Portsmouth Square,** where you'll find Chinese locals playing board games (often gambling) or just sitting quietly. This square was the center of early San Francisco and the spot where the American flag was first raised on July 9, 1846. From the square, Washington Street leads up to Waverly Place, where you can see three temples.

Explore the area at your leisure, or see "Organized Tours," below, if you'd like to join a walking tour.

FISHERMAN'S WHARF & THE NORTHERN WATERFRONT   Few cities in America are as adept at wholesaling their historical sites as San Francisco, which has converted Fisherman's Wharf into one of the most popular tourist destinations in the world. Unless you come really early in the morning, you won't find any traces of the traditional waterfront life that once existed here; the only serious fishing going on is for tourist dollars. A small fleet of fewer than 30 boats still operates from here, but basically Fisherman's Wharf has been converted into one long shopping mall stretching from Ghirardelli Square at the west end to Pier 39 at the east. Some people love it, others can't get far enough away from it, but most agree that Fisherman's Wharf, for better or for worse, has to be seen at least once in a lifetime.

Ghirardelli Square, at 900 North Point, between Polk and Larkin streets (☎ **415/ 775-5500**), is best known as the former chocolate-and-spice factory of Domingo Ghirardelli. The factory has been converted into a 10-level mall containing more than

50 stores and 11 dining establishments. Scheduled street performers play regularly in the West Plaza. The stores generally stay open until 8 or 9pm in the summer and 6 or 7pm in the winter.

The Cannery, at 2801 Leavenworth St. (☎ **415/771-3112;** www.thecannery. com), was built in 1894 as a fruit-canning plant and converted in the 1960s into a mall containing more than 50 shops and several restaurants and galleries. Vendors' stalls and sidewalk cafes are set up in the courtyard amid a grove of century-old olive trees, and on summer weekends, street performers are out in force entertaining tourists. The **Museum of the City of San Francisco** (☎ **415/928-0289;** www.sfmuseum.org), which traces the city's development with displays and artifacts, is on the third floor. Admission is free; hours are Wednesday through Sunday from 10am to 4pm.

Pier 39, on the waterfront at Embarcadero and Beach Street (☎ **415/981-8030**), is a 4½-acre waterfront complex, a few blocks east of Fisherman's Wharf. Ostensibly a re-creation of a turn-of-the-century street scene, it features walkways of aged and weathered wood salvaged from demolished piers. But don't expect a slice of old-time maritime life. This is the busiest mall of the group, with more than 100 stores. In addition, there are 20 or so restaurants and snack outlets, some with good views of the bay.

In recent years some 600 California **sea lions** have taken up residence on the adjacent floating docks. They sun themselves and honk and bellow playfully. The latest major addition to Fisherman's Wharf is **Underwater World,** a $38-million, 707,000-gallon marine attraction filled with sharks, stingrays, and more, all witnessed via a moving footpath that transports visitors through clear acrylic tunnels.

The shops are open daily from 10:30am to 8:30pm. Cable car: Powell-Mason line to Bay Street.

THE MISSION DISTRICT   Once inhabited almost entirely by Irish immigrants, the Mission is now the center of the city's Latino community, an oblong area stretching roughly from 14th to 30th streets between Potrero Avenue in the east and Dolores on the west. Some of the city's finest Victorians still stand in the outer areas, though many seem strangely out of place in the mostly lower-income neighborhoods. The heart of the community lies along 24th Street between Van Ness and Potrero, where dozens of excellent ethnic restaurants, bakeries, bars, and specialty stores attract a hip crowd from all over the city. Strolling through the Mission District at night isn't a good idea, but it's usually quite safe during the day and highly recommended.

For even better insight into the community, go to the **Precita Eyes Mural Arts Center,** 348 Precita Ave., at Folsom Street (☎ **415/285-2287**), and take one of the hour-long tours conducted on Saturdays, which cost $7 for adults, $4 for seniors, and $1 for children under 18. You'll see 85 murals in an 8-block walk. Tours are also given daily during the annual Mural Awareness Week (usually the second week in May). All tours leave from the center's second and newer location, 2981 24th St., at Harrison Street (☎ **415/285-2287**). Other signs of cultural life include a number of progressive theaters—Eureka, Theater Rhinoceros, and Theater Artaud, to name only a few.

Amazing Graze at the Farmers Market

There's no better way to enjoy a bright San Francisco morning than strolling and snacking through this gourmet street market. Every Saturday from 8:30am to 1:30pm, Northern California fruit, vegetable, bread, and dairy vendors join local restaurateurs in selling fresh, delicious edibles along the Embarcadero at Green Street (about a 15-min. walk from Fisherman's Wharf). You can also pick up locally made vinegars and oils, which make wonderful gifts. Call ☎ **510/528-6987** for more information. Bus: 2, 7, 8, 9, 14, 21, 31, 32, 66, or 71.

At 16th and Dolores is the **Mission San Francisco de Assisi** (better known as **Mission Dolores**), which is the city's oldest surviving building (see the separate listing, above) and the district's namesake.

NOB HILL   When the cable car was invented in 1873, this hill became the most exclusive residential area in the city. The Big Four and the Comstock Bonanza kings built their mansions here, but the structures were all destroyed by the 1906 earthquake and fire. Only the Flood Mansion, which serves today as the Pacific Union Club, and the Fairmont (which was under construction when the earthquake struck) were spared. The area is now home to some of the city's most upscale hotels as well as Grace Cathedral, which stands on the Crocker Mansion site. Stroll around and enjoy the views, and perhaps pay a visit to Huntington Park.

NORTH BEACH   In the late 1800s, an enormous influx of Italian immigrants into North Beach firmly established this aromatic area as San Francisco's "Little Italy." Today, dozens of Italian restaurants and coffeehouses continue to flourish in what is still the center of the city's Italian community. Walk down Columbus Avenue any given morning and you're bound to be bombarded with the wonderful aromas of roasting coffee and savory pasta sauces. Though there are some interesting shops and bookstores in the area, it's the eclectic little cafes, delis, bakeries, and coffee shops that give North Beach its Italian-bohemian character.

For a proper perspective of North Beach, sign up for a guided Javawalk with coffee-nut Elaine Sosa (see "Organized Tours," below).

PARKS, GARDENS & ZOOS

In addition to **Golden Gate Park** (see section 5, above) and **Golden Gate National Recreation Area** and the **Presidio** (see section 8, below), San Francisco boasts more than 2,000 additional acres of parkland, most of which are perfect for picnicking.

Lincoln Park, at Clement Street and 34th Avenue, a personal favorite of ours, occupies 270 acres on the northwestern side of the city and contains the California Palace of the Legion of Honor (see "Museums," above) and a scenic 18-hole municipal golf course. But the most dramatic features of the park are the 200-foot cliffs that overlook the Golden Gate Bridge and San Francisco Bay. Take bus no. 38 from Union Square to 33rd and Geary streets, then transfer to bus no. 18 into the park.

San Francisco Zoo & Children's Zoo. Sloat Blvd. and 45th Ave. ☎ **415/753-7080.** www.sfzoo.org. Main zoo $9 adults, $6.50 seniors and youths 12–17, $3 children 3–11, free for children 2 and under if accompanied by an adult; free for everyone the 1st Wed of each month. Carousel $2. Main zoo daily 10am–5pm. Children's zoo Mon–Fri 11am–4pm; Sat–Sun 10:30am–4:30pm. Muni Metro: L from downtown Market St. to the end of the line.

Located between the Pacific Ocean and Lake Merced, in the southwest corner of the city, the San Francisco Zoo houses more than 1,000 inhabitants, which are contained in landscaped enclosures guarded by concealed moats. The Primate Discovery Center is particularly noteworthy for its many rare and endangered species. Expansive outdoor atriums, sprawling meadows, and a midnight world for exotic nocturnal primates house such species as the ruffed-tailed lemur, black-and-white colobus monkeys, patas monkeys, and emperor tamarins, pint-size primates distinguished by their long, majestic mustaches.

Other highlights include Koala Crossing, housing kangaroos, emus, and walleroos; Gorilla World, one of the world's largest exhibits of these gentle giants; and Penguin Island, home to a large breeding colony of Magellanic penguins. The Feline Conservation Center is a wooded sanctuary and breeding facility for the zoo's endangered snow leopards, Persian leopards, and other jungle cats. And the Lion House is home to rare Sumatran and Siberian tigers, a rare white Bengal tiger, and the African lions (you can watch them being fed at 2pm Tuesday through Sunday).

At the Children's Zoo, adjacent to the main park, the barnyard is alive with strokable domestic animals such as sheep, goats, ponies, and a llama. Also of interest is the Insect Zoo, which showcases a multitude of insect species, including the hissing cockroach and walking sticks.

A free, informal walking tour of the zoo is available on Saturday and Sunday at 11am. The Zebra Zephyr train tour takes visitors on a 30-minute "safari" daily (only on weekends in winter). The tour is $2.50 for adults, $1.50 for seniors and children 15 and under.

7 Organized Tours

ORIENTATION TOURS

Gray Line, Transbay Terminal, First and Mission streets (☎ **800/826-0202** or 415/558-9400), offers several daily itineraries with free transfers from centrally located hotels to departure points. Reservations are required for most tours.

THE 49-MILE SCENIC DRIVE

The self-guided, 49-mile drive is one easy way to orient yourself and to grasp the beauty of San Francisco and its extraordinary location. Beginning in the city, it follows a rough circle around the bay and passes virtually all the best-known sights, from Chinatown and the Golden Gate Bridge to Ocean Beach, Seal Rocks, Golden Gate Park, and Twin Peaks. Originally designed for the benefit of visitors to San Francisco's 1939 and 1940 Golden Gate International Exposition, the route is marked with blue-and-white seagull signs. Although it makes an excellent half-day tour, this mini-excursion can easily take longer if you decide, for example, to stop to walk across the Golden Gate Bridge or to have tea in Golden Gate Park's Japanese Tea Garden.

The San Francisco Visitor Information Center, at Powell and Market streets, distributes free route maps. Since a few of the Scenic Drive marker signs are missing, the map will come in handy. Try to avoid the downtown area during the weekday rush hours from 7 to 9am and 4 to 6pm.

BOAT TOURS

One of the best ways to look at San Francisco is from a boat bobbing on the bay. The **Blue & Gold Fleet** tours the bay year-round in a sleek, 400-passenger sightseeing boat, complete with food and beverage facilities. The fully narrated, 1¼-hour cruise passes beneath the Golden Gate and Bay bridges, and comes within yards of Alcatraz Island. Frequent daily departures from Pier 41 begin at 10am in summer and 11am in winter. Tickets cost $17 for adults, $13 for kids 12 to 18 and seniors over 62, $9 for kids 5 to 11; children under 5 sail free. For recorded information, call ☎ **415/773-1188;** for tickets, which cost an additional $2.25 each when ordered via phone, call ☎ **415/705-5555.**

The **Red & White Fleet** also offers daily bay cruises, which depart from Pier 43½ and travel under the Golden Gate Bridge and past the Marin Headlands, Sausalito, Tiburon, Angel Island, and Alcatraz. Prices are $17 for adults, $13 for seniors, $13 for teens 12 to 18, and $9 for children 6 to 11. Call ☎ **415/447-0597** for information, or check out the Web site at **www.redandwhite.com**.

SPECIAL-INTEREST WALKING TOURS

AN INSIDER'S TOUR OF CHINATOWN   Founded by author, TV personality, cooking instructor, and restaurant critic Shirley Fong-Torres, **Wok Wiz Chinatown**

Walking Tours (☎ **800/281-9255** or 415/981-8989) takes you into nooks and crannies not usually seen by tourists. Each guide is intimately acquainted with all of Chinatown's back ways, alleys, and small businesses as well as the area's history, folklore, culture, and food. Tours are conducted daily from 10am to 1:30pm and include a dim sum lunch. There's also a less expensive tour that does not include lunch. It's an easy walk, fun and fascinating, and you're bound to make new friends. Groups are generally held to a maximum of 12, and reservations are essential. Prices (including lunch) are $37 for adults, $35 for seniors 60 and older, and $30 for children under 12.

Shirley Fong-Torres also operates an **I Can't Believe I Ate My Way Through Chinatown** tour that starts with a Chinese breakfast in a noodle house, moves to a wok shop, and then makes further stops for nibbles at a vegetarian restaurant, rice-noodle factory, and a supermarket before taking a break for a sumptuous luncheon (most Saturdays; $65 per person), as well as a **Walk & Wok** tour that includes shopping for food in Chinatown, then cooking (and eating) it together at Shirley's Cooking Center (most Saturdays; $75 per person).

NORTH BEACH CAFE SOIREE   Self-described "coffeehouse lizard" Elaine Sosa leads **Javawalk,** a 2-hour walking tour. Aside from visiting cafes, Javawalk also serves up a good share of historical and architectural trivia. Sosa keeps the tour interactive and fun, and it's obvious that she knows a wealth of tales and trivia about the history of coffee and its North Beach roots. Tours are given Tuesday through Saturday at 10am. The price is $20 for adults and $10 for kids 12 and under. For information and reservations, call ☎ **415/673-9255.**

THE VICTORIAN LEGACY   Jay Gifford, founder of **Victorian Homes Historical Walking Tour** (☎ **415/252-9485**) and San Francisco resident for two decades, portrays his enthusiasm and love of San Francisco throughout this highly entertaining 2½-hour tour. Set at a very leisurely place, it incorporates a wealth of interesting knowledge about San Francisco's Victorian architecture, as well as the city's storied history—particularly the periods just before and after the great earthquake and fire of 1906. You'll stroll through the neighborhoods of Japantown, the Western Addition (where you can take a break to cruise the trendy shops on Fillmore Street), and onward to Pacific Heights and Cow Hollow. In the process you'll see more than 200 meticulously restored Victorians, including the one where *Mrs. Doubtfire* was filmed. Jay's guests often find they are the only ones on the quiet neighborhood streets, where tour buses are forbidden. The tour ends with a trolley ride back to Union Square, passing though North Beach and Chinatown. Tours, which start at Union Square at 11am, are offered daily year-round and cost $20 per person. Reservations are required. You can preview the tour at **www.victorianwalk.com**.

A TRIP BACK TO THE SUMMER OF LOVE   If you're nostalgic for the 1960s, the **Haight-Ashbury Flower Power Walking Tour** will take you to the city's hippie haunts, including the Grateful Dead's crash pad and Janis Joplin's house. Tours begin at 9:30am Tuesday and Saturday and cost $15 per person. For reservations, call ☎ **415/863-1621.**

A LOOK AT THE CASTRO   For a totally new insight into the gay community's contribution to the political maturity, growth, and beauty of San Francisco, contact **Cruisin' the Castro** (☎ **415/550-8110**). Tours are personally led by Ms. Trevor Hailey, who was involved in the development of the Castro in the 1970s and knew Harvey Milk—the first openly gay politician elected to office in the United States. Call for tour times, but expect to pay $40 for adults, $35 for seniors 62 and older, and a negotiable price for children 16 and under; the price includes lunch at one of the Castro's restaurants.

Golden Gate National Recreation Area & the Presidio

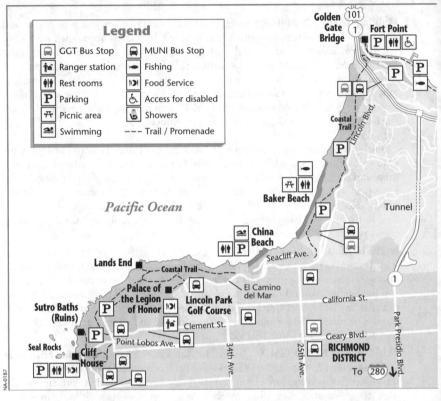

8 Golden Gate National Recreation Area & the Presidio

GOLDEN GATE NATIONAL RECREATION AREA

No urban shoreline is as stunning as San Francisco's. Golden Gate National Recreation Area, which wraps around the northern and western edges of the city and is run by the National Park Service, lets visitors fully enjoy it. Along this shoreline are several landmarks, and from its edge visitors have views of the bay and the ocean. Muni provides transportation to most sites, including Aquatic Park, the Cliff House, and Ocean Beach. For more information, see "Outdoor Pursuits," below, or contact the **National Park Service** (☎ **415/556-0560**).

Here's a brief rundown of the major features of the recreation area, starting at the northern section and moving westward around the coastline:

Aquatic Park, adjacent to the Hyde Street Pier, is a small swimming beach, although it's not that appealing and the water's ridiculously cold.

Fort Mason Center occupies an area from Bay Street to the shoreline and consists of several buildings and piers, which were used during World War II. Today, they're occupied by a variety of museums, theaters, and organizations, as well as by **Greens** vegetarian restaurant (see "Dining," above), which affords views of the Golden Gate Bridge. For information on Fort Mason Center events, call ☎ **415/441-5706.**

Farther west along the bay at the northern end of Fillmore, **Marina Green** is a favorite spot for flying kites or watching the sailboats on the bay. Next stop along the

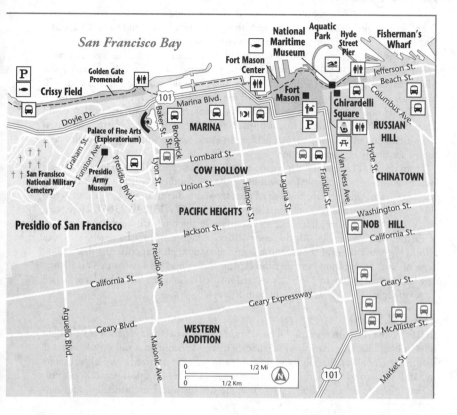

bay is the St. Francis Yacht Club. From here begins the 3½-mile paved **Golden Gate Promenade,** a favorite biking and hiking path, which sweeps along Crissy Field, leading ultimately to Fort Point under the Golden Gate Bridge. This Promenade defines the outer limits of the Presidio (see below).

Fort Point (☎ 415/556-1693), a National Historic Site sitting directly under the Golden Gate Bridge, was built in 1853 to protect the narrow entrance to the harbor. You might recognize it from Alfred Hitchcock's *Vertigo;* the master of suspense filmed some of the most important scenes here. During the Civil War, the brick Fort Point was manned by 140 men and 90 pieces of artillery to prevent a Confederate takeover of California. Rangers in Civil War regalia lead regular tours and sometimes fire the old cannons.

Lincoln Boulevard sweeps around the western edge of the bay to two of the most popular beaches in San Francisco. **Baker Beach,** a small and beautiful strand just outside the Golden Gate where the waves roll ashore, is a fine spot for sunbathing, walking, or fishing—it's packed on sunny days. Because of the cold water and the roaring currents that pour out of the bay twice a day, swimming is not advised here for any but the most confident. (You'll also see some nude sunbathers here.) Here you can pick up the **Coastal Trail,** which leads through the Presidio (see below). A short distance from Baker, **China Beach** is a small cove where swimming is permitted. Changing rooms, showers, a sundeck, and rest rooms are available.

A little farther around the coast appears **Land's End,** looking out to Pyramid Rock. Both a lower and an upper trail provide hiking opportunities amid windswept cypress and pines on the cliffs above the Pacific.

Still farther along the coast lies **Point Lobos,** the **Sutro Baths,** and the **Cliff House.** The latter has been serving refreshments to visitors since 1863. Here you can view the **Seal Rocks,** home to a colony of sea lions and many marine birds. The **visitor center** here (☎ 415/556-8642) is open daily from 10am to 5pm. The kids will enjoy the **Musée Mecanique** (☎ 415/386-1170), an authentic old-fashioned arcade with 150 coin-operated amusements. Only traces of the Sutro Baths remain today northeast of the Cliff House. This swimming facility was a major summer attraction that could accommodate 24,000 people, but it burned down in 1966. A little farther inland at the western end of California Street is **Lincoln Park,** which contains a golf course and the Palace of the Legion of Honor.

From the Cliff House, the Esplanade continues south along the 4-mile-long **Ocean Beach,** which is not suitable for swimming. At the southern end of Ocean Beach is another area of the park around **Fort Funston** where there's an easy loop trail across the cliffs (for information, call the ranger station at ☎ 415/239-2366). Here, too, you can watch the hang gliders taking advantage of the high cliffs and strong winds.

Farther south along I-280, **Sweeney Ridge,** which can only be reached by car, affords sweeping views of the coastline from the many trails that crisscross these 1,000 acres of land. It was from here that the expedition led by Don Gaspar de Portolá first saw San Francisco Bay in 1769. It's located in Pacifica and can be reached via Sneath Lane off Calif. 35 (Skyline Blvd.) in San Bruno.

THE PRESIDIO

In 1989, the Department of Defense announced what many had long thought impossible: The U.S. Army, which had held the Presidio as a military base since before the Civil War, was pulling out and leaving the most prized piece of real estate in San Francisco to the National Park Service as an example of post–Cold War retrofitting. Now an urban national park, it combines historical, architectural, and natural aspects.

The 1,480-acre area incorporates a variety of terrain—coastal scrub, dunes, and prairie grasslands that shelter many rare plants and more than 150 species of birds, some of which nest here. There are also more than 350 historic buildings, a scenic golf course, a national cemetery, and a variety of terrains and natural habitats. The Park Service offers a number of walking and biking tours around the Presidio; reservations are required.

Walkers and joggers will enjoy the forests of the Presidio. It was once a bleak field of wind-blasted rock, sand, and grass, but in a strangely humanitarian gesture, 60,000 trees were planted in the 1880s to make the place more livable for the troops. Today, on the 2-mile **Ecology Loop Trail,** walkers can see more than 30 different species of those trees, including redwood, spruce, cypress, and acacias. Hikers can follow the 2½-mile **Coastal Trail** from Fort Point along this part of the coastline all the way to Land's End. It follows the bluff top from Baker Beach to the southern base of the Golden Gate Bridge.

Crissy Field is a former airfield that in recent years has become known as one of the see-and-be-seen proving grounds of California's windsurfing culture. Between March and October, hundreds come to try their hand. The beach here provides easy water access and plenty of room to rig up, but is not recommended for the inexperienced. This is also a popular place for joggers en route from the Marina District to Fort Point and back. At the west end of Crissy Field is a pier that can be used for fishing and crabbing.

The Presidio is undergoing major changes so that it may pay for its upkeep. At press time, the old military buildings were to be rented to nonprofit organizations. For schedules, maps, and general information about ongoing developments at the Presidio, the best source is the **Golden Gate National Recreation Area Headquarters** at Fort Mason, Building 102, San Francisco, CA 94123 (☎ **415/556-0560**). The **Presidio Visitors Center** (☎ **415/561-4323**) is located on the west side of Montgomery Street, in the Presidio on the main parade ground, and is open daily from 10am to 5pm. Bus: 82X, 28, or 76.

9 Outdoor Pursuits

The prime places to enjoy all kinds of recreational activities in San Francisco have already been described earlier in this chapter. See section 5 for a complete description of Golden Gate Park, and the above section for complete details on Golden Gate National Recreation Area and the Presidio.

BEACHES   There are only two beaches in San Francisco that are safe for swimming: **Aquatic Park,** which is a ridiculously small patch of sand adjacent to the Hyde Park Pier, and **China Beach,** a small cove on the western edge of the South Bay. But dip in at your own risk—there are no lifeguards on duty, and the water is painfully cold.

Baker Beach, a small, beautiful strand just outside the Golden Gate, isn't the best place for swimming due to strong currents, but it's great for sunning, walking, picnicking, or fishing. It's wonderful to sit here on a sunny day and take in the view of the bridge. You'll climb down a very long flight of stairs from the street to reach the beach.

Ocean Beach, at the end of Golden Gate Park, on the westernmost side of the city, is San Francisco's largest beach (4 miles long). Just offshore, at the northern end of the beach in front of the Cliff House, are the jagged Seal Rocks, which are inhabited by various shore birds and a large colony of barking sea lions. Bring binoculars for a close-up view. Ocean Beach is for strolling or sunning, but don't swim here—tides are tricky, and each year bathers and surfers drown in the rough waters.

BICYCLING   Two city-designated bike routes are maintained by the Recreation and Parks Department. One winds for 7½ miles through Golden Gate Park to Lake Merced; the other traverses the city, starting in the south, and follows a route over the Golden Gate Bridge. A bike map is available from the San Francisco Visitor Information Center and from bicycle shops all around town.

A massive new seawall, constructed to buffer Ocean Beach from storm-driven waves, doubles as a public walk and bikeway along 5 waterfront blocks of the Great Highway between Noriega and Santiago streets. It's an easy ride from the Cliff House or Golden Gate Park.

Park Cyclery, 1749 Waller St. (☎ **415/751-7368**), is a shop in the Haight Street area that rent bikes. Located near Golden Gate Park, the cyclery rents mountain bikes exclusively, along with helmets, locks, and accessories. The charge is $5 per hour or $25 per day.

There's also great biking in the Presidio. From here, you can venture across the Golden Gate Bridge and into the Marin hills.

CITY STAIR-CLIMBING   You don't need a Stairmaster in San Francisco. The **Filbert Street Steps,** 377 of them running between Sansome Street and Telegraph Hill, scale the eastern face of Telegraph Hill, from Sansome and Filbert past charming 19th-century cottages and lush gardens. Napier Lane, a narrow wooden plank walkway, leads to Montgomery Street. Turn right and follow the path to the end of the cul-de-sac, where another stairway continues to Telegraph's panoramic summit.

The **Lyon Street Steps,** between Green Street and Broadway, comprise another historic stairway street, containing four steep sets of stairs totaling 288 steps. Begin at Green Street and climb all the way up, past manicured hedges and flower gardens, to an iron gate that opens into the Presidio. A block east, on Baker Street, another set of 369 steps descends to Green Street.

GOLF   Golden Gate Park Course, 47th Avenue and Fulton Street (☎ **415/ 751-8987**), is a nine-hole, par-27 course over 1,357 yards. All holes are par 3, tightly set, and well trapped with small greens. Greens fees are very reasonable: $10 per person Monday through Friday and $13 Saturday and Sunday. The course is open daily from 6am to dusk.

Lincoln Park Golf Course, 34th Avenue and Clement Street (☎ **415/221-9911**), San Francisco's prettiest municipal course, has terrific views and fairways lined with Monterey cypress trees. Its 18 holes encompass 5,081 yards, for a par 68. Greens fees are $23 per person Monday through Friday and $27 Saturday and Sunday. The course is open daily from 6:30am to dusk.

SKATING   Although people skate in Golden Gate Park all week long, Sunday is best, when John F. Kennedy Drive, between Kezar Drive and Transverse Road, is closed to cars. A smooth "skate pad" is located on your right, just past the Conservatory. **Skates on Haight,** 1818 Haight St. (☎ **415/752-8376**), is the best place to rent either in-line or conventional skates and is located only a block from the park. Protective wrist guards and knee pads are included free. The cost is $8 per hour for in-line or "conventionals," $28 for all-day use. A major credit card and ID deposit are required.

10 Shopping

Store hours vary, but are generally Monday through Saturday from 10am to 6pm and Sunday from noon to 5pm. Most department stores stay open later, as do shops around Fisherman's Wharf.

Sales tax in San Francisco is 8½%. If you live out of state and buy an expensive item, consider having the store ship it home for you. You'll have to pay for its transport, but will escape paying the sales tax.

UNION SQUARE & ENVIRONS   San Francisco's most congested and popular shopping mecca is centered around Union Square. Most of the big department stores and many high-end specialty shops are in this area. Be sure to venture to Grant Avenue, Post and Sutter streets, and Maiden Lane.

If you're into art, pick up *The San Francisco Gallery Guide,* a comprehensive, bimonthly publication listing the city's current shows (most of which are downtown). It's available free by mail; send a self-addressed stamped envelope to San Francisco Bay Area Gallery Guide, 1369 Fulton St., San Francisco, CA 94117 (☎ **415/921-1600**). You can also pick one up at the San Francisco Visitor Information Center at 900 Market St. (at Powell Street).

One of our favorite galleries is the ✪ **Catharine Clark Gallery,** on the second floor at 49 Geary St., between Kearny and Grant streets (☎ **415/399-1439**). It exhibits up-and-coming contemporary artists, mainly from California, and nurtures beginning collectors by offering an unusual interest-free purchasing plan.

Of the area's specialty stores, century-old ✪ **Gump's,** 135 Post St., between Kearny Street and Grant Avenue (☎ **415/982-1616**), is a must-visit. A virtual treasure trove of household items and gifts, it offers a collection of Asian antiquities, contemporary art glass, exquisite jade and pearl jewelry, and more.

Music aficionados will choose to get lost in **Virgin Megastore,** Market Street at Stockton (☎ **415/397-4525**), with thousands of CDs (including an impressive collection of imports), videos, laser discs, and a multimedia department. Its literary equivalent is nearby **Borders Books & Music,** 400 Post St., at Powell (☎ **415/ 399-1633**), which has thousands of titles and a cafe.

While the department stores have plenty of clothes, real fashion fiends will want to check out the boutiques. For men, **Cable Car Clothiers,** 246 Sutter St., between Grant Avenue and Kearny Street (☎ **415/397-4740**), is a popular stop for traditional attire, such as three-button suits with natural shoulders, Aquascutum coats, McGeorge sweaters, and Atkinson ties. The more-modern-than-corporate man heads to **MAC,** 5 Claude Lane, off Sutter Street between Grant Avenue and Kearny Street (☎ **415/ 837-0615**), where imported tailored suits come in designs by London's Katharine Hamnett, Belgium's SO, Italy's Alberto Biani, and New York's John Bartlett. (Their women's store is located at 1543 Grant Ave., between Filbert and Union streets; ☎ **415/837-1604.**)

Wilkes Bashford, 375 Sutter St., at Stockton Street (☎ **415/986-4380**), is one of the most expensive and well-known clothing stores in the city offering fashions for both sexes. It stocks only the finest clothes (which can often be seen on Mayor Willie Brown), including men's Kiton and Brioni suits (at $2,500 and up, they're considered some of the most expensive suits in the world).

For what we consider the best in women's fashions, check out **Métier,** 355 Sutter St., between Grant and Stockton streets (☎ **415/989-5395**). Its inventory of European ready-to-wear lines is expensive, but in the best taste; featured designers include Peter Cohen, Georgina Von Etzdorf, and Alberto Biani. There's also a distinguished collection of antique-style, high-end jewelry from L.A.'s Kathie Waterman.

CHINATOWN When you pass under the gate to Chinatown on Grant Avenue, say good-bye to the world of fashion and hello to a swarm of cheap tourist shops selling everything from linen and jade to plastic toys and $2 slippers. The real gems are tucked on side streets or in small, one-person shops selling Chinese herbs, original art, and jewelry. Grant Avenue is the area's main thoroughfare, and side streets between Bush Street and Columbus Avenue are full of restaurants, markets, and eclectic shops. Walking is best, since traffic through this area is slow at best and parking is next to impossible. Most of the stores in Chinatown are open daily from 10am to 10pm. The area is serviced by bus lines 9X, 15, 30, 41, and 45.

Of the endless array of trinket shops scattered through the compact neighborhood, two worth noting are **Eastwind Books & Arts,** 1435 Stockton St., at Columbus Avenue (☎ **415/772-5877** Chinese department, 415/772-5899 English department; e-mail: info@eastwindsf.com), which carries an incredible selection of Chinese books, stationery, and stamps, as well as Asian-American and English books covering everything from health and cooking to martial arts and medicine. At the mystical ✪ **Ten Ren Tea Company,** 949 Grant Ave., between Washington and Jackson streets (☎ **415/362-0656**), you can enjoy a steaming cup of roselle tea, made of black tea and hibiscus, while you browse the selection of almost 50 traditional and herbal teas and related paraphernalia.

SOMA Though this area isn't suitable for strolling, you'll find almost all the discount shopping in warehouse spaces south of Market. You can pick up a discount-shopping guide at most major hotels. Many buses pass through this area, including routes 9, 12, 14, 15, 19, 26, 27, 30, 42, 45, and 76.

One of our favorite gift shops in the city is ✪ **Dandelion,** 55 Potrero Ave., at Alameda Street (☎ **415/436-9500**), which borders on the Mission and offers something for every taste and budget: collectibles, furnishings, and knickknacks including an excellent selection of teapots, decorative dishes, and gourmet foods, as well as books, cards, and picture frames. (Don't miss the Zen-like second floor, with its variety of peaceful furnishings in Indian, Japanese, and Western styles.) Equally cool is ✪ **SFMOMA MuseumStore,** 151 Third St., 2 blocks south of Market Street, across from Yerba Buena Gardens (☎ 415/ 357-4035). Its array of artistic cards, books, jewelry, housewares, knickknacks, and creative tokens of San Francisco makes this one of the locals' favorite shops. It also offers far more tasteful mementos than most Fisherman's Wharf options.

Fashionable bargain hunters head to ✪ **Jeremys,** 2 South Park, at Second Street between Bryant and Brannan streets (☎ **415/882-4929**), where top designer fashions from shoes to suits come at rock-bottom prices. For the more adventurous thrift-shopper, there's the **North Face** discount outlet, 1325 Howard St., between 9th and 10th streets (☎ **415/626-6444**). The sporting, camping, and hiking equipment is still expensive, but the skiwear, boots, sweaters, and goods such as tents, packs, and sleeping bags are far less expensive than if you buy them at a retail shop.

Another worthy stop is the **Wine Club San Francisco,** 953 Harrison St., between Fifth and Sixth streets (☎ **415/512-9086**), which offers bargain prices on more than 1,200 domestic and foreign wines. Bottles cost from $4 to $1,100.

HAYES VALLEY   It may not be the prettiest area in town (with some of the shadier housing projects a few blocks away), but while most neighborhoods cater to more conservative or trendy shoppers, lower Hayes Street, between Octavia and Gough, celebrates anything vintage, artistic, or downright funky. Though still in its developmental stage, it's definitely the most interesting new shopping area in town, with furniture and glass stores, thrift shops, trendy shoe stores, and men's and women's clothiers. There are also lots of great antiques shops south on Octavia and on nearby Market Street. Bus lines include nos. 16AX, 16BX, and 21.

For women's wear, **Bella Donna,** 539 Hayes St., between Laguna and Octavia streets (☎ **415/861-7182**), is our favorite in the area, offering expensive, quality clothes such as hand-knit sweaters, silky slip dresses, and fashionable knit hats. There's also a wonderful (albeit expensive) collection of vases and other household trinkets, a small selection of remainder fabrics, and an excellent wedding and bridal section, which focuses on the vintage look.

If you have a fetish for foot fashions, you must check out **Bulo,** 437A Hayes St., at Gough Street (☎ **415/864-3244**), which carries nothing but imported Italian men's and women's shoes that run the gamut from casual to dressy, reserved to wildly funky. Shop for the sale items unless you're ready to drop around $200 per pair.

THE CASTRO   You could easily spend all day wandering through the home and men's-clothing shops of the Castro. Buses serving this area include nos. 8, 24, 33, 35, and 37.

Citizen Clothing, 536 Castro St., between 18th and 19th streets (☎ **415/ 558-9429**), is a popular shop for stylish casual clothing.

Our favorite chocolate shop, ✪ **Joseph Schmidt Confections,** 3489 16th St., at Sanchez Street (☎ **415/861-8682**), adds a whole new dimension to designer chocolate. Here the sinful sweets take the shape of exquisite sculptural masterpieces that are so beautiful, you'll be hesitant to bite the head off your adorable chocolate panda bear. Prices are also remarkably reasonable.

UNION STREET   Union Street, from Fillmore to Van Ness, caters to the upper-middle-class crowd. It's a great place to stroll; to window-shop the plethora of boutiques, cafes, and restaurants; and to watch the beautiful people parade by. Bus lines include nos. 22, 41, 42, and 45.

In case you want to see the world.

At American Express, we're here to make your journey a smooth one. So we have over 1,700 travel service locations in over 130 countries ready to help. What else would you expect from the world's largest travel agency?

do more **AMERICAN EXPRESS**

Travel

Call 1 800 AXP-3429 or visit
www.americanexpress.com/travel

In case you want to be welcomed there.

We're here to see that you're always welcomed at establishments everywhere. That's why millions of people carry the American Express® Card – for peace of mind, confidence, and security, around the world or just around the corner.

do more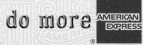

Cards

To apply, call 1 800 THE-CARD
or visit www.americanexpress.com

In case you're running low.

We're here to help with more than 190,000 Express Cash locations around the world. In order to enroll, just call American Express at 1 800 CASH-NOW before you start your vacation.

do more

Express Cash

And in case you'd rather be safe than sorry.

We're here with American Express® Travelers Cheques. They're the safe way to carry money on your vacation, because if they're ever lost or stolen you can get a refund, practically anywhere or anytime. To find the nearest place to buy Travelers Cheques, call 1 800 495-1153. Another way we help you do more.

do more

AMERICAN EXPRESS

Travelers Cheques

Among the dozens of fashion and home boutiques is **Three Bags Full,** 2181 Union St., at Fillmore (☎ **415/567-5753**), where expensive, handmade, and one-of-a-kind knitwear is both playful and extravagant.

CHESTNUT STREET Parallel to and a few blocks north of Union Street, Chestnut is a younger Union Street, with endless shopping and dining choices, and the ever-tanned, superfit population of postgraduate singles who hang around cafes and scope each other out. The area is serviced by bus lines 22, 28, 30, 41, 42, 43, and 76.

FISHERMAN'S WHARF & ENVIRONS The tourist-oriented malls—Ghirardelli Square, Pier 39, the Cannery, and the Anchorage—run along Jefferson Street and include hundreds of shops, restaurants, and attractions.

Locals tend to avoid this part of town, but do venture to **Cost Plus Imports,** 2552 Taylor St., between North Point and Bay streets (☎ **415/928-6200**), a vast warehouse crammed to the rafters with Chinese baskets, Indian camel bells, Malaysian batik scarves, and innumerable other items from Algeria to Zanzibar. There's also a decent wine section. Adjoining is a **Barnes & Noble** "superstore," at 2550 Taylor, between Bay and North Point (☎ **415/292-6762**).

FILLMORE STREET Some of the best shopping in town is packed into 5 blocks of Fillmore Street in Pacific Heights. From Jackson to Sutter streets, Fillmore is the perfect place to grab a bite and peruse the high-priced boutiques, crafts shops, and incredible houseware stores. It's serviced by bus lines 1, 2, 3, 4, 12, 22, and 24.

One of our absolute favorite housewares shops is ✪ **Fillamento,** 2185 Fillmore St., at Sacramento Street (☎ **415/931-2224**), which is always packed with shoppers searching for the most classic, artistic, and refined home items. Whether you're looking to set a good table or revamp your bedroom, you'll find it all here. Head south a few blocks on Fillmore to incredible ✪ **Zinc Details,** 1905 Fillmore St., between Bush and Pine streets (☎ **415/776-2100**), which has an amazing collection of locally handcrafted glass vases, pendant lights, ceramics, and furniture. Each piece is a true work of art created specifically for the store (except vintage items).

HAIGHT STREET Green hair, spiked hair, no hair, or mohair—even the hippies look conservative next to Haight Street's dramatic fashion freaks. The shopping in the 6 blocks of upper Haight Street, between Central Avenue and Stanyan Street, reflects its clientele and offers everything from incense and European and American street styles to furniture and antique clothing. Bus lines 7, 66, 71, and 73 run down Haight Street. The Muni Metro N line stops at Waller Street and at Cole Street.

In the used-clothing-store mecca of the Haight, one of San Francisco's largest secondhand dealers is **Aardvark's,** 1501 Haight St., at Ashbury Street (☎ **415/621-3141**). Shirts, pants, dresses, skirts, and hats from the last 30 years are packed into the ever-busy shop. Another favorite is **Buffalo Exchange,** 1555 Haight St., between Clayton and Ashbury streets (☎ **415/431-7733**), which is crammed with racks of antique and new fashions from the 1960s, 1970s, and 1990s. A second shop is located at 1800 Polk St., at Washington Street (☎ **415/346-5741**).

Of the "vintage" options, **La Rosa,** 1711 Haight St., at Cole Street (☎ **415/668-3744**), is one of the more upscale options, featuring a selection of high-quality, dry-cleaned, secondhand goods. Formal suits and dresses are its specialty, but you'll also find sport coats, slacks, and shoes. For brand-new threads, stop by **Solo Fashion,** 1599 Haight St., at Clayton Street (☎ **415/621-0342**), which has a good selection of upbeat, contemporary, English-style street wear, along with a collection of dresses designed exclusively for this shop.

Also vintage, but less wearable, are the oldies-but-goodies at **Recycled Records,** 1377 Haight St., between Central and Masonic streets (☎ **415/626-4075**). Easily one of the best used-record stores in the city, this loud shop has a good selection of promotional CDs and cases of used classic rock LPs. Sheet music, tour programs, and old *TV Guides* are also sold.

NORTH BEACH Along with a great cup of coffee, Grant and Columbus avenues cater to their hip clientele with a small but worthy selection of boutiques and specialty shops.

You can pick up a great gift for yourself or anyone else at **Biordi Art Imports,** 412 Columbus Ave., at Vallejo Street (☎ 415/392-8096). Its Italian Majolica pottery is both exquisite and unique.

For a dose of local color, join the brooding literary types who browse **City Lights Booksellers & Publishers,** 261 Columbus Ave., at Broadway (☎ 415/362-8193), the famous bookstore owned by renowned Beat-generation poet Lawrence Fer-linghetti. The shelves here are stocked with a comprehensive collection of art, poetry, and political paperbacks, as well as more mainstream books.

Fun mementos are for sale at **Quantity Postcards,** 1441 Grant St., at Green Street (☎ 415/986-8866), where you'll find the perfect postcard for literally everyone you know, as well as some depictions of old San Francisco and movie stars, plus Day-Glo posters featuring concert-poster artist Frank Kozik.

CHINA BASIN The only reason to come to the southeastern tip of the city is to dine at one of the shipyard-front restaurants or to shop at the **Esprit Outlet Store,** 499 Illinois St., at 16th Street (☎ 415/957-2550). Fashionable bargain hunters will revel in the Esprit collections and Susie Tompkins merchandise, which are available here at 30% or more off regular prices. In addition to clothes, there are accessories, shoes, and assorted other items.

11 San Francisco After Dark

For up-to-date nightlife information, turn to the *San Francisco Weekly* and the *San Francisco Bay Guardian,* both of which contain comprehensive current listings. They're available free at bars and restaurants, and from street-corner boxes all around the city. *Where,* a free tourist monthly, also has information on programs and performance times; it's available in most of the city's finer hotels. The Sunday edition of the *San Francisco Examiner and Chronicle* also features a "Datebook" section, printed on pink paper, with information and listings on the week's upcoming events.

GETTING TICKETS Half-price tickets to theater, dance, and music performances are available from **Tix Bay Area** (☎ 415/433-7827) on the day of the show only; tickets for Sunday and Monday events, if available, are sold on Saturday. Tix also sells advance, full-price tickets for most performance halls, sporting events, concerts, and clubs. A service charge, ranging from $1 to $3, is levied on each ticket. Only cash or traveler's checks are accepted for half-price tickets; Visa and MasterCard are accepted for full-price tickets. Tix is located on Stockton Street, between Post and Geary streets on the east side of Union Square (opposite Maiden Lane). It's open Tuesday through Thursday from 11am to 6pm, Friday and Saturday from 11am to 7pm.

Tickets to most theater and dance events can also be obtained through **City Box Office,** 153 Kearny St., Suite 402 (☎ 415/392-4400). American Express, Master-Card, and Visa are accepted.

BASS Ticketmaster (☎ 510/762-2277) sells tickets to concerts, sporting events, plays, and special events. Downtown BASS Ticketmaster outlets can be found at Tix Bay Area (see above) and at **Warehouse** stores throughout the city. The most convenient location is at 30 Powell St.

THE PERFORMING ARTS

✪ **American Conservatory Theatre (A.C.T.).** Performances at the Geary Theater, 415 Geary St. (at Mason St.). ☎ **415/749-2228.** Tickets $14–$55.

American Conservatory Theatre (A.C.T.) made its debut in 1967 and quickly established itself as the city's premier resident theater group. The troupe is so venerated that A.C.T. has been compared to the superb British National Theatre, the Berliner Ensemble, and the Comédie Française. The A.C.T. season runs from September through July and features both classical and experimental works.

The Magic Theatre. Performances at Building D, Fort Mason Center, Marina Blvd. (at Buchanan St.). ☎ **415/441-8822.** Tickets $18–$32. Discounts for students and seniors.

The highly acclaimed Magic Theatre continues to be a major West Coast company dedicated to presenting the works of new playwrights; over the years it has nurtured the talents of such luminaries as Sam Shepard and Jon Robin Baitz. Shepard's Pulitzer Prize–winning play *Buried Child* premiered here. More recent productions have included works by Athol Fugard, Claire Chafee, and Nilo Cruz. The season usually runs from September through July; performances are offered Wednesday through Sunday.

Philharmonia Baroque Orchestra. Performances in the Herbst Theatre, 401 Van Ness Ave. ☎ **415/392-4400** (box office) or 415/495-7445 (offices). www.philparmonia.org. E-mail: info@philharmonia.org. Tickets $30–$42.

Acclaimed by the *New York Times* as "the country's leading early-music orchestra," Philharmonia Baroque performs in San Francisco and all around the Bay Area. The season lasts from September through April.

San Francisco Ballet. Performances at War Memorial Opera House, 301 Van Ness Ave. (at Grove St.). ☎ **415/865-2000.** www.sfballet.org. Tickets $7–$100.

Founded in 1933, the San Francisco Ballet is the oldest professional ballet company in the United States and regarded as one of the country's finest, performing an eclectic repertoire of full-length, neoclassical, and contemporary ballets. Even the *New York Times* proclaimed, "The San Francisco Ballet under Helgi Tomasson's leadership is one of the spectacular success stories of the arts in America." The season runs from February through June. All performances are accompanied by the San Francisco Ballet Orchestra.

✪ **San Francisco Opera.** Performances at the newly refurbished War Memorial Opera House, 301 Van Ness Ave. (at Grove St.). ☎ **415/864-3330** (box office). www.sfopera.org. Tickets $10–$140.

The San Francisco Opera was the first municipal opera in the United States, and is one of the city's cultural icons. All productions have English supertitles. The season starts in September and lasts just 14 weeks. Performances are held most evenings, except Monday, with matinees on Sundays. Tickets go on sale as early as June, and the best seats quickly sell out. Unless Pavarotti or Domingo is in town, some less-coveted seats are usually available until curtain time.

San Francisco Symphony. Performing at Davies Symphony Hall, 201 Van Ness Ave. (at Grove St.). ☎ **415/864-6000** (box office). www.sfsymphony.org. Tickets $12–$73.

Founded in 1911, the internationally respected San Francisco Symphony has long been an important part of this city's cultural life under such legendary conductors as Pierre Monteux and Seiji Ozawa. In 1995, Michael Tilson Thomas took over from Herbert Blomstedt and has already led the orchestra to new heights, crafting an exciting repertoire of classical and modern music. The season runs from September through June.

COMEDY & CABARET

⊙ **Beach Blanket Babylon.** At Club Fugazi, 678 Green St./Beach Blanket Babylon Blvd. (between Powell St. and Columbus Ave.). ☎ **415/421-4222.** Tickets $20–$55.

Now a San Francisco tradition, Beach Blanket Babylon is best known for its outrageous costumes and oversize headdresses. It's been playing almost 22 years now, and still almost every performance sells out. Those under 21 are welcome only at Sunday matinees, when no alcohol is served; photo ID is required for evening performances. It's wise to write for tickets at least 3 weeks in advance, or obtain them through Tix (see above).

Cobb's Comedy Club. 2801 Beach St. (between Leavenworth and Hyde sts.). ☎ **415/ 928-4320.** Cover $5 Mon–Wed, $10–$13 Fri–Sat, $10 Thurs and Sun (plus a two-beverage minimum nightly). Validated parking.

Located in the Cannery at Fisherman's Wharf, Cobb's features such national headliners as George Wallace, Emo Philips, and Jake Johannsen. There's comedy every night, including a 15-comedian All-Pro Monday showcase (a 3-hour marathon). Cobb's is open to those 18 and over, and occasionally to kids ages 16 and 17 if they're accompanied by a parent or legal guardian (call ahead first).

Finocchio's. 506 Broadway (at Kearny St.). ☎ **415/982-9388.** Cover $14.50 (two-drink minimum). Parking available next door at the Flying Dutchman.

For more than 50 years, this family-run cabaret club has showcased the best female impersonators in a funny, kitschy show. Three different revues are presented nightly (usually Thursday through Saturday at 8:30, 10, and 11:30pm), and a single cover is good for the entire evening. Guests must be 21 or older.

THE CLUB & MUSIC SCENE
ROCK & BLUES CLUBS

Biscuits & Blues. 401 Mason St. (at Geary St.). ☎ **415/292-2583.** Cover $5–$25 during performances; no cover during happy hour (Mon–Fri 5–7pm).

With a crisp, blow-your-eardrums-out sound system, a New Orleans–speakeasy (albeit commercial) appeal, and a nightly line-up of live entertainment, there's no better place to muse the blues than at this basement-cum-nightclub.

⊙ **Blue Bar.** 501 Broadway (at Kearny St.), below the Black Cat Cafe. ☎ **415/981-2233.** Cover Wed–Sun $5.

Whether you're passing by North Beach or finishing a night at Reed Hearon's Black Cat Cafe (see "Dining," above, for a review), you should drop into this cozy-chic live jazz/blues venue with cushy couches and laid-back atmosphere. The restaurant's full menu is available here—a plus for late-night eaters and a bummer for those who come exclusively for the music.

The Fillmore. 1805 Geary Blvd. (at Fillmore St.). ☎ **415/346-6000.** www.thefillmore.com. Tickets $9–$25.

Reopened after years of neglect, The Fillmore, made famous by promoter Bill Graham in the 1960s, is once again attracting big names. Check the local listings in magazines, or call the theater for information on upcoming events.

Lou's Pier 47 Club. 300 Jefferson St. (at Jones St). ☎ **415/771-5687.** Cover $5–$10.

There are few locals in the place, but Lou's happens to be a good old-fashioned casual spot where you can let your hair down with Cajun seafood (downstairs), other tourists, and live jazz, blues, rock, and country bands (upstairs). Major happy-hour specials (Monday through Friday from 4 to 7pm) and a vacation attitude make the place one of the more sloppy happy spots near the Wharf. There's no cover for the first band, which plays nightly from 4 to 8pm, but it will cost you for the second, which comes on at 9pm.

Slim's. 333 11th St. (at Folsom St.). ☎ **415/522-0333.** Cover free to $20 (plus a 2-drink minimum when seated at table).

Co-owned by musician Boz Scaggs, who sometimes takes the stage under the name "Presidio Slim," this glitzy restaurant/bar seats 300, serves California cuisine, and specializes in excellent American music—homegrown rock, jazz, blues, and alternative—almost nightly. Menu items range from $3 to $8.50.

Jazz & Latin Clubs

✪ **Cafe du Nord.** 2170 Market St. (at Sanchez St.). ☎ **415/861-5016.** Nominal cover varies.

Although it's been around since 1907, this basement-cum-supper-club has finally been recognized as a respectable jazz venue. With a younger generation now appreciating the music, the place is often packed, from the 40-foot mahogany bar to the back room with a pool table. Du Nord is even putting out its own compilation CDs now, which are definitely worth purchasing.

Jazz at Pearl's. 256 Columbus Ave. (at Broadway). ☎ **415/291-8255.** No cover; 2-drink minimum. Valet parking $3.

This is one of the best venues for jazz in the city. Ribs and chicken are served with the sounds, too, with prices ranging from $4 to $8.95. The live jams last until 2am nightly.

Up & Down Club. 1151 Folsom St. (between Seventh and Eighth sts.). ☎ **415/626-2388.** Cover varies, usually $5–$10.

One of the original homes for SoMa's now-familiar new-jazz scene, the Up & Down supper club attracts a trendy crowd to both its restaurant and dance floor. Dinner is at 8pm (reservations required), the music starts at 9:30pm, and dancing begins at 10pm.aDance Clubs

Dance Clubs

Club Ten 15. 1015 Folsom St. (at Sixth St.). ☎ **415/431-1200.** Cover $5–$15.

Get decked out and plan for a late-nighter if you're headed to this enormous party warehouse. Three levels and dance floors offer a variety of venues, complete with a 20- and 30-something gyrating mass who live for the DJs' pounding house, disco, and acid-jazz music. Each night is a different club that attracts its own crowd, ranging from yuppie to hip-hop.

Nickie's Bar-be-cue. 460 Haight St. (between Fillmore and Webster sts.). ☎ **415/621-6508.** www.nickies.com. Cover $3–$5.

Don't show up here for dinner; the only hot thing you'll find is the small, crowded dance floor. But don't let that stop you from checking it out. Nickie's is a sure thing. Every time we come here, the old-school disco hits are in full force, casually dressed happy dancers lose all inhibitions, and the crowd is mixed with all types of friendly San Franciscans. This place is perpetually hot, so dress accordingly and don't expect a full bar—it's beer and wine only.

Paradise Lounge. 1501 Folsom St. (at 11th St.). ☎ **415/861-6906.** Cover $3–$15.

Labyrinthine Paradise features three dance floors simultaneously vibrating to different beats. Smaller, auxiliary spaces include a pool room with half a dozen tables. Poetry readings are also given.

SUPPER CLUBS

If you can eat dinner, listen to live music, and dance (or at least wiggle in your chair) in the same room, it's a supper club—that's our criteria.

✪ **Harry Denton's Starlight Room.** At the Sir Francis Drake Hotel, 450 Powell St., 21st floor. ☎ **415/395-8595.** Cover $5 Wed–Thurs after 7pm, $10 Fri–Sat after 8pm.

Come dressed to the nines or in casual attire to this old-fashioned cocktail-lounge-turned-nightclub, where tourists and locals sip drinks at sunset and boogie down to live swing and big-band tunes after dark. The room is classic 1930s San Francisco, with red-velvet banquettes, chandeliers, and fabulous views. But what really attracts flocks of all ages is a night of Harry Denton–style fun, which usually includes plenty of drinking and unrestrained dancing.

Julie's Supper Club. 1123 Folsom St. (at Seventh St.). ☎ **415/861-0707.** No cover.

Julie's is a longtime standby for cocktails and late dining. Divided into two rooms, the vibe is very 1950s cartoon, with a space-aged *Jetsons* appeal. Good-looking singles prowl, cocktails in hand, as live music plays by the front door. The food is hit-or-miss, but the atmosphere is definitely a casual and playful winner with a little interesting history—this building is one location where the Symbionese Liberation Army held Patty Hearst hostage back in the 1970s. Menu items range from $7.50 to $16.

✪ **Murcury.** 540 Howard St. (between First and Second sts.). ☎ **415/777-1419.** Cover (without dinner to downstairs club) Wed–Sat $20.

Celebrated nightclub master Dr. Winkie revamped the tired and long-closed multi-level DV8 club space into a sexy visual wonder well worth a jaunt to its discreet SoMa locale. The glittering and glamourous retro-modern interior is one of San Francisco's swankiest (to match the equally image-conscious clientele), with supper-club dining and jazz leading to basement disco dancing. The wildly silver Mirror Bar mimics the bubbly and other libations served there. The Pearl Bar looks like it sounds, and the dining room is an elegant diversion. With jazz and disco and an eclectic clientele, you're sure to find your type of action within the maze of amazing venues at this must-see.

RETRO CLUBS

Bruno's. 2389 Mission St. (at 20th St.). ☎ **415/550-7455.** Cover $3–$7 after 9:30pm.

Before its recognition as a destination restaurant, Mission District hipsters were already keen on this retro hot spot. Live music is played nightly in the back lounge, and the long, 1950s–style full bar is almost always crowded with a mixture of wanna-bes, the cool, and the curious. Appetizers and dessert are served until 1am.

Club Deluxe. 1511 Haight St. (at Ashbury St.). ☎ **415/552-6949.** Cover $2–$10.

Before the recent 1940s trend hit the city, Deluxe and its fedora-wearing clientele had been celebrating the bygone era for years. And fortunately, even with all the retro-hype, the vibe here hasn't changed. Expect an eclectic mix of throw-backs and generic San Franciscans in the intimate, smoky bar and adjoining lounge, and live jazz or blues most nights. Although many regulars dress the part, there's no attitude here—so come as you like.

✪ **HiBall Lounge.** 473 Broadway (between Kearny and Montgomery sts.). ☎ **415/397-9464.** Cover $2–$8.

Retro-jazz is in full swing in the city, and one of the most popular places to hear it—and dance to it—is at this North Beach joint. Harking back to Broadway at its best, the vibe is full-on 1940s and 1950s, from the red banquettes and stage curtains to the small, dark room. Live bands perform nightly to a young, swingin' crowd. There's also a swing-dance class one night a week and an adjoining tropical cocktail lounge.

THE BAR SCENE

Albion. 3139 16th St. (between Valencia and Guerrero sts.). ☎ **415/552-8558.**

This Mission District club is a grit-and-leather in-crowd place packed with artistic types and SoMa hipsters. There's live music—ranging from ragtime and blues to jazz and swing—Sundays between 5 and 8pm.

Backflip. 601 Eddy St. (at Larkin St.). ☎ **415/771-FLIP.**

Adjoining the rock-and-roll Phoenix Hotel, this shimmering aqua-blue cocktail lounge—designed to induce the illusion that you're carousing in the deep end—serves "cocktail fare" to mostly young, fashionable types, so please don't order a Cosmopolitan.

The Bubble Lounge. 714 Montgomery St. (at Columbus Ave.). ☎ **415/434-4204.**

Toasting the town is a nightly event at this relatively new champagne bar. With 300 champagnes (and around 30 by the glass), brick walls, couches, velvet curtains, and a pool table within its two levels, there's plenty of pop in this fizzy lounge.

Persian Aub Zam Zam. 1633 Haight St. (at Clayton St.). ☎ **415/861-2545.**

If you make it through the forbidding metal doors, you'll feel as if you're in *Casablanca,* but the catch is that most people don't even get that far. The owner/bartender Bruno, who has poured here for more than 40 years, opens the place when he wants some company and arbitrarily chooses who's allowed to join him at the bar. If you meet his random requirements, play it safe and order a martini—a drink Bruno likes to serve (we've been 86ed for ordering a Coors Light).

The Red Room. 825 Sutter St. (at Jones St.). ☎ **415/346-7666.**

At one time the hottest cocktail lounge in town (though it's cooled off a bit), this ultra-modern, Big Apple–style bar and lounge reflects no other spectrum but ruby red. Really, you gotta see this one.

Spec's. 12 Saroyan Place (off Columbus Ave.). ☎ **415/421-4112.**

Its incognito locale on Saroyan Place, a tiny alley at 250 Columbus Ave., makes Spec's less of a walk-in bar and more of a lively locals' hangout. Its funky decor—maritime flags that hang from the ceiling, exposed brick walls lined with posters, photos, and various oddities—gives it character that intrigues every visitor. A "museum," displayed under glass, contains memorabilia and items brought back by seamen who drop in between sails, and the clientele is funky enough to keep you preoccupied while you drink a beer.

✪ **Vesuvio.** 255 Columbus Ave. (at Broadway). ☎ **415/362-3370.**

Situated along Jack Kerouac Alley across from the famed City Lights Bookstore, this renowned literary beatnik hangout isn't just riding its historic coattails. Popular with neighborhood writers, artists, songsters, and wanna-bes, Vesuvio is crowded with self-proclaimed philosophers, along with everyone else ranging from longshoremen and cab drivers to businesspeople.

BREWPUBS

Gordon-Biersch Brewery. 2 Harrison St. (on the Embarcadero). ☎ **415/243-8246.**

Popular with the young Republican crowd (loose ties and tight skirts predominate), this modern, two-tiered brewery and restaurant attracts a more upscale clientele than your typical beer garden. The food—beer-braised lamb shank, baby-back ribs, lemon roasted half chicken—is pretty good, but it's the gourmet lagers and ales that account for the line out the door. *One caveat:* When the lower-level bar fills up, you practically have to shout to be heard.

San Francisco Brewing Company. 155 Columbus Ave. (at Pacific St.). ☎ **415/434-3344.** www.sfbrewing.com.

The bar is one of the city's few remaining old saloons, aglow with stained-glass windows, tile floors, skylights, a mahogany bar, and a massive overhead fan running the full length of the bar—a bizarre contraption crafted from brass and palm fronds. Menu items range from $3.25 to $16. The happy-hour special, a dollar per 10-ounce microbrew beer (or $1.75 a pint), runs daily from 4 to 6pm and midnight to 1am.

Thirsty Bear Brewing Company. 661 Howard St. (1 block east of the Moscone Center). ☎ **415/974-0905.**

Seven superb, handcrafted varieties of brew, ranging from a fruit-flavored Strawberry Ale to a steak-in-a-cup stout, are always on tap at this stylish high-ceilinged brick edifice. Excellent Spanish food, too (see "Dining," earlier in this chapter, for a complete review). Pool tables and dart boards are upstairs, and live music (jazz, flamenco, blues, alternative, and classical) can be heard most nights.

20 Tank Brewery. 316 11th St. (at Folsom St.). ☎ **415/255-9455.**

Right in the heart of SoMa's popular strip, this huge, come-as-you-are bar is known for serving good beer at fair prices. Pizzas, sandwiches, chilies, and assorted appetizers are also available. Menu items range from $1.95 to $12.95. Pub games include darts, shuffleboard, and dice.

COCKTAILS WITH A VIEW

The Carnelian Room. 555 California St., in the Bank of America Building (between Kearny and Montgomery sts.). ☎ **415/433-7500.** Jacket and tie required for men.

On the 52nd floor of the Bank of America building, the Carnelian Room offers uninterrupted views of the city. From a window-front table you feel as if you can reach out, pluck up the TransAmerica Pyramid, and stir your martini with it. In addition to cocktails, "Discovery Dinners" are offered for $35 per person. *Note:* The restaurant has the most extensive wine list in the city—1,275 selections to be exact.

Cityscape. Atop Hilton Tower I, 333 O'Farrell St. (at Mason St.), 46th floor. ☎ **415/923-5002.**

When you sit under the glass roof and sip a drink here, it feels as though you're out under the stars and enjoying views of the bay. There's nightly dancing to a DJ's picks from 10pm. The mirrored columns and floor-to-ceiling draperies help create an elegant and romantic ambiance.

Crown Room. In the Fairmont Hotel, 950 Mason St., 24th floor. ☎ **415/772-5131.**

Of all the bars listed here, the Crown Room is definitely the plushest. Reached by an external glass elevator, the panoramic view from the top will encourage you to linger. In addition to drinks (steep at $7 to $9), dinner buffets are served for $34.

Equinox. In the Hyatt Regency Hotel, 5 Embarcadero Center. ☎ **415/788-1234.**

The sales "hook" of the Hyatt's rooftop Equinox is a revolving floor that gives each table a 360° panoramic view of the city every 45 minutes. In addition to cocktails, dinner is served daily.

Harry Denton's Starlight Room. Atop the Sir Francis Drake Hotel, 450 Powell St., 21st floor. ☎ **415/395-8595.**

See "Supper Clubs," above, for a full review.

Top of the Mark. In the Mark Hopkins Intercontinental, 1 Nob Hill (between California and Mason sts.). ☎ **415/616-6916.**

This is one of the most famous cocktail lounges in the world. During World War II, it was considered de rigueur for Pacific-bound servicemen to toast their good-byes to the States here. The spectacular glass-walled room features an unparalleled view. Live entertainment is offered at 8:30pm nightly, when there's a $6 to $10 cover. Drink prices range from $6 to $8.

GAY AND LESBIAN BARS & CLUBS

✪ **The Café.** 2367 Market St. (at Castro St.). ☎ **415/861-3846.**

When this place first got jumping, it was the only predominantly lesbian dance club on Saturday nights in the city. But once the guys found out how much fun the girls were having, they joined the party. Today it's still a very happening mixed gay and lesbian scene with two bars; a steamy, free-spirited dance floor; and a small patio.

The EndUp. 401 Sixth St. (at Harrison St.). ☎ **415/357-0827.** Cover varies.

It's a different nightclub every night of the week, but regardless of who's throwing the party, the place is always jumping with the DJs blasting tunes. There are two pool tables, a flaming fireplace, an outdoor patio, and a mob of gyrating souls on the dance floor. Some nights are straight, so call for gay nights.

The Stud. 399 Ninth St. (at Harrison St.). ☎ **415/863-6623.** Cover $2–$6 Fri–Sat.

The Stud has been around for 30 years, is one of the most successful gay establishments in town, and is mellow enough for straights as well as gays. The interior has an antiques-shop look and a miniature train circling over the bar and dance floor. Music here is a balanced mix of old and new, and nights vary from cabaret and oldies to disco. Call in advance for the evening's venue. Drink prices range from $1.25 to $5.75.

Twin Peaks Tavern. 401 Castro St. (at 17th and Market sts.). ☎ **415/864-9470.** No cover.

Right at the intersection of Castro, 17th, and Market streets is one of the Castro's most famous gay hangouts, which caters to an older crowd and is considered the first gay bar in America. Because of its relatively small size and desirable location, the place becomes fairly crowded and convivial by 8pm, earlier than many neighboring bars.

FILM
REPERTORY CINEMAS

Castro Theatre. 429 Castro St. (near Market St.). ☎ **415/621-6120.**

Built in 1922, the beautiful Castro Theatre is known for its screenings of classic cinema and for its Wurlitzer organ, which is played before each show. There's a different feature here almost nightly, and more often than not it's a double feature. Bargain matinees are usually offered on Wednesdays, Saturdays, Sundays, and holidays. Phone for schedules, prices, and show times.

Red Vic. 1727 Haight St. (between Cole and Shrader sts.). ☎ **415/668-3994.** Tickets $6 adults, $3 seniors 65 and over and children 12 and under.

The worker-owned Red Vic movie collective recently moved from the Victorian building that gave it its name. The theater specializes in independent releases and contemporary cultish hits. Phone for schedules and show times.

Roxie. 3117 16th St. (at Valencia St.). ☎ **415/863-1087.**

The Roxie consistently screens the best new alternative films anywhere. The low-budget contemporary features shown here are largely devoid of Hollywood candy coating; many are West Coast premieres. Films change weekly, sometimes sooner. Phone for schedules, prices, and show times.

The San Francisco Bay Area

by Erika Lenkert & Matthew R. Poole

Without question, the Bay City is captivating. But don't let it ensnare you to the point of ignoring its environs, which contain a multitude of natural spectacles like Mount Tamalpais and Muir Woods; scenic communities like Tiburon, Sausalito, and Half Moon Bay; and cities like gritty Oakland and its youth-oriented next-door neighbor, Berkeley. A little farther north stretch the valleys of Napa and Sonoma, the finest wine region in the nation (see chapter 6). And to the south lies high-tech Silicon Valley and San Jose, Northern California's largest city.

1 Berkeley

10 miles NE of San Francisco

Berkeley would be little more than a quaint, sleepy town east of the big city if it weren't for the University of California at Berkeley, which is world renowned for its first-rate academic standards, 16 Nobel Prize winners, and protests that led to the most well-known student riots in U.S. history. Today, there's still hippie idealism in the air, but the radicals have aged; the 1960s are only present in tie-dye and paraphernalia shops (which are rapidly being taken over by national chains along Telegraph Ave.), and the students suffer from less angst. The most evident change in recent years is due to the young professionals who are moving into the area to avoid San Francisco's absurdly high housing costs. Still, it's an entertaining town with all types of people, a beautiful campus, vast parks, and some incredible restaurants.

ESSENTIALS

GETTING THERE   The Berkeley **BART (Bay Area Rapid Transit)** station is 2 blocks from the university. The fare from San Francisco is less than $3. For information, call BART at ☎ **510/793-2278.**

If you're coming **by car** from San Francisco, take I-80 east to the University Avenue exit. Count on walking some distance, as you won't find a parking spot near the university.

VISITOR INFORMATION   The **Berkeley Convention and Visitors Bureau,** 2015 Center St., Berkeley, CA 94703 (☎ **800/847-4823** or 510/549-7040), can answer your questions and even find accommodations for you. Call the **Visitor Hotline** (☎ **510/549-8710**) for information on events and happenings in Berkeley.

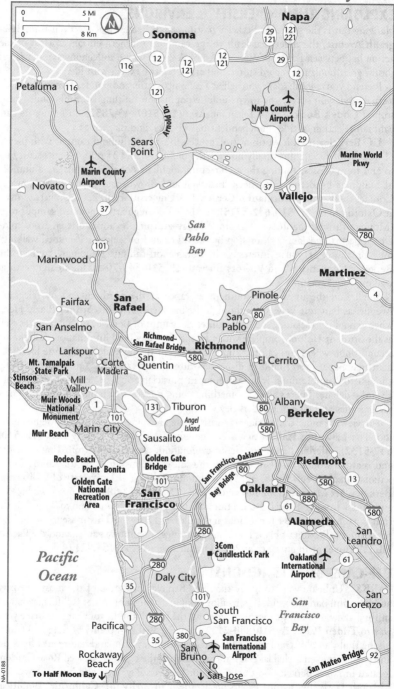

The San Francisco Bay Area

0   5 Mi
0   8 Km

Napa

Sonoma

29
121

121
221

116

12

12
121

12
121

12
121

29

12

121

Petaluma   116

Arnold Dr.

Napa County
Airport

12

Sears
Point

29

Marine World
Pkwy

Marin County
Airport

Novato

37

Vallejo

San
Pablo
Bay

780

101

Marinwood

37

Martinez

Pinole

4

Fairfax

**San
Rafael**

San
Pablo

80

San Anselmo

Richmond–
San Rafael Bridge

Richmond

El Cerrito

Larkspur

580

Mt. Tamalpais
State Park

Corte
Madera

San
Quentin

Stinson
Beach

Mill
Valley

Albany

80

Muir Woods
National
Monument

1

131

Tiburon

Berkeley

101

Angel
Island

580

Muir Beach

Marin City

Sausalito

Rodeo Beach

Golden Gate
Bridge

Piedmont

Point Bonita

San Francisco–Oakland Bay Bridge

80

580

13

Golden Gate
National
Recreation
Area

101

Oakland

880

580

**San
Francisco**

61

1

Alameda

San
Leandro

280

3Com
Candlestick Park

Oakland
International
Airport

61

**Pacific
Ocean**

35

Daly City

San
Lorenzo

1

101

*San
Francisco
Bay*

Pacifica

1

280

35

380

South
San Francisco

Rockaway
Beach

San
Bruno

San Francisco
International
Airport

San Mateo Bridge

92

To Half Moon Bay ↓

To
↓ San Jose

NA-0188

131

EXPLORING THE UNIVERSITY & ENVIRONS

Hanging out is the preferred Berkeley pastime, and the best place to do it is on **Telegraph Avenue,** the street that leads to the campus's southern entrance. Most of the action lies between Bancroft Way and Ashby Avenue, where coffeehouses, restaurants, shops, great book and record stores, and crafts booths swarm with life.

Pretend you're local: Plant yourself at a cafe, sip a latte, and ponder something intellectual while you survey the town's unique population bustling by. Bibliophiles must stop at **Cody's Books,** 2454 Telegraph Ave. (☎ **510/845-7852**), to peruse its gargantuan selection of titles, independent-press books, and magazines.

UC Berkeley itself is worth a stroll as well. It's a beautiful old campus with plenty of woodsy paths, architecturally noteworthy buildings, and 31,000 students scurrying to and from classes. Among the architectural highlights of the campus are a number of buildings by Bernard Maybeck, Bakewell and Brown, and John Galen Howard. Contact the **Visitor Information Center,** 101 University Hall, 2200 University Ave., at Oxford Street (☎ **510/642-5215**), to join a free, regularly scheduled campus tour (Monday through Saturday at 10am, Sunday at 1pm; no tours offered from mid-December to mid-January), or stop by the office and pick up a self-guided walking-tour brochure. If you're interested in notable off-campus buildings, contact the **Berkeley Convention and Visitors Bureau** (☎ **510/549-7040**) for an architectural walking-tour brochure.

You'll find the university's southern entrance at the northern end of Telegraph Avenue, at Bancroft Way. Walk through the main entrance into **Sproul Plaza.** Here, when school is in session, you'll encounter the gamut of Berkeley's inhabitants as well as the **Student Union,** complete with a bookstore, cafes, and information desk on the second floor, where you can pick up a free map of Berkeley along with the local student newspaper (also found in dispensers throughout campus). You might be lucky enough to stumble upon some impromptu musicians or a heated—and sometimes absurd—debate. There's always something going on, so stretch out on the grass for a few minutes and take in the Berkeley vibe.

For viewing more traditional art forms, there are some noteworthy museums here, too. The **Lawrence Hall of Science,** Centennial Drive near Grizzly Peak (☎ **510/642-5132**), offering hands-on science exploration, is open daily from 10am to 5pm and is also a wonderful place to watch the sunset. Admission is $6 for adults, $4 for seniors and children 7 to 18, and $2 for children 3 to 6. The **University of California, Berkeley Art Museum,** 2626 Bancroft Way (☎ **510/642-0808**), is open Wednesday and Friday through Sunday from 11am to 5pm, Thursday from 11am to 9pm. Admission is $6 for adults, $4 for seniors and children 12 to 17. This museum includes a substantial collection of Hans Hofmann paintings, a sculpture garden, and the **Pacific Film Archive,** main entrance at 2625 Durant Ave. (☎ **510/642-1124**).

OFF-CAMPUS ATTRACTIONS

PARKS Unbeknownst to many travelers, Berkeley has some of the most extensive and beautiful parks around. If you enjoy hiking, getting a breath of California air, and sniffing a few roses, or just want to wear out the kids, jump in your car and make your way to **Tilden Park** (☎ **510/843-2137**), where you'll find plenty of flora and fauna, hiking trails, an old steam train and merry-go-round, a farm and nature area for kids, and a chilly tree-encircled lake. On the way, stop at the colorful terraced **Rose Garden,** located in north Berkeley on Euclid Avenue between Bay View and Eunice Street.

Another worthy nature excursion is the **University of California Botanical Garden,** in Strawberry Canyon on Centennial Drive (☎ **510/642-3343**), which features a vast collection of plant life ranging from cacti to redwoods.

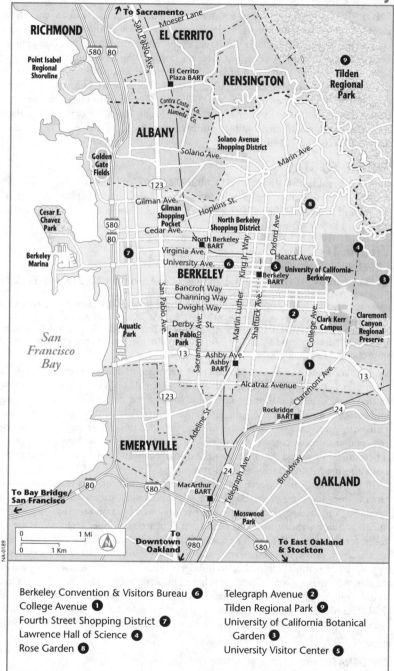

Berkeley

RICHMOND

EL CERRITO

KENSINGTON

580 80

Point Isabel
Regional
Shoreline

To Sacramento

Moeser Lane

San Pablo Ave.

El Cerrito
Plaza BART

Tilden
Regional
Park ➒

Contra Costa Co.
Alameda Co.

ALBANY

Solano Avenue
Shopping District

Golden
Gate
Fields

Solano Ave.

Marin Ave.

Cesar E.
Chavez
Park

123

Gilman Ave.

Hopkins St.

Gilman
Shopping
Pocket

580
80

Cedar Ave.

North Berkeley
Shopping District

➑

Berkeley
Marina

North Berkeley
BART

Oxford Ave.

➐

Virginia Ave.

Hearst Ave.

University Ave.

➏

➎

University of California–
Berkeley

BERKELEY

Berkeley
BART

➍

Bancroft Way

➌

San Pablo Ave.

Channing Way

Dwight Way

King Jr. Way

Martin Luther

Shattuck Ave.

Aquatic
Park

Derby St.

Clark Kerr
Campus

Claremont
Canyon
Regional
Preserve

San
Francisco
Bay

San Pablo
Park

Sacramento Ave.

13

Ashby Ave.

Ashby
BART

➋

College Ave.

➊

123

Alcatraz Avenue

Claremont Ave.

13

Rockridge
BART

24

EMERYVILLE

Adeline St.

MacArthur
BART

24

Telegraph Ave.

Broadway

OAKLAND

80

580

To Bay Bridge/
San Francisco

Mosswood
Park

NA-0189

0   1 Mi
0   1 Km

To
Downtown
Oakland

980

580

To East Oakland
& Stockton

Berkeley Convention & Visitors Bureau ➏

College Avenue ➊

Fourth Street Shopping District ➐

Lawrence Hall of Science ➍

Rose Garden ➑

Telegraph Avenue ➋

Tilden Regional Park ➒

University of California Botanical
Garden ➌

University Visitor Center ➎

SHOPPING If you're itching to exercise your credit cards, head to one of two places. **College Avenue** from Dwight all the way down to the Oakland border is crammed with eclectic boutiques, antiques shops, and restaurants. The other option is **Fourth Street** in west Berkeley, just 2 blocks north of the University Avenue exit off I-80, where you can grab a cup of java, read the paper at a patio table, and then hit the ✪ **Crate & Barrel Outlet,** 1785 Fourth St., between Hearst and Virginia (☎ **510/528-5500**), where prices are 30% to 70% off retail, or any of the small, wonderful stores crammed with imported and locally made housewares. Nearby is **REI,** the Bay Area's favorite outdoor outfitter, at 1338 San Pablo Ave., near Gilman Street (☎ **510/ 527-4140**).

WHERE TO STAY

Bed-and-Breakfast California (☎ **800/872-4500** or 408/867-9662; fax 408/ 867-0907; www.bbintl.com; e-mail: info@bbintl.com), books visitors into private homes and apartments in the Berkeley area. The cost ranges from $65 to $300 per night, and there's a 2-night minimum.

WHERE TO DINE
EXPENSIVE

✪ **Chez Panisse.** 1517 Shattuck Ave. (between Cedar and Vine). ☎ **510/548-5525.** Fax 510/548-0140. Reservations essential for restaurant and accepted a month in advance; for cafe, accepted for lunch (and dinner if available) after 9am on the same day. Main courses $13–$18; fixed-price dinner $38–$68. AE, CB, DC, DISC, MC, V. Restaurant dinner seatings Mon–Sat at 6–6:30pm and 8:30–9:15pm. Cafe Mon–Thurs 11:30am–3pm and 5–10:30pm; Fri–Sat 11:30am–4pm and 5–11:30pm. From I-80 north, take the University exit and turn left onto Shattuck Ave. BART: Berkeley. CALIFORNIA.

California cuisine is so much a product of Waters's genius that all other restaurants following in her wake should be dated "AAW" (After Alice Waters). Read the menus posted outside, and you'll understand why. Most of the produce and meat is organic and comes from local farms, and after all these years, Alice still attends to her restaurant with great integrity and innovation. Her creations are served in a delightful redwood-and-stucco cottage with a brick terrace filled with flowering potted plants. There are two separate dining areas—the upstairs cafe and the downstairs restaurant, both offering Mediterranean-inspired cuisine.

In the upstairs cafe, there are displays of pastries and fruit, and large bouquets of fresh flowers adorning an oak bar. Lunch or dinner might feature a delicately smoked gravlax or a roasted eggplant soup with pesto, followed by lamb ragout garnished with apricots, onions, and spices, and served with couscous. Dinner reservations are not taken for the cafe, so there will be a wait, but it's worth it.

The cozy downstairs restaurant, strewn with blossoming floral bouquets, is an appropriately warm environment to indulge in the fixed-price, four-course gourmet dinner, which is served Tuesday through Thursday. Friday and Saturday, it's four courses plus an aperitif, and Monday is bargain night with a three-course dinner for $39. The menu, which changes daily, is posted outside the restaurant each Saturday for the following week. Meals are complemented by an excellent wine list, with choices ranging anywhere from $20 to $200.

MODERATE

✪ **Cafe Rouge.** 1782 Fourth St. (between Delaware and Hearst). ☎ **510/525-1440.** Reservations recommended. Main courses $9.50–$20. MC, V. Mon 11:30am–3pm; Tues–Sat 11:30am–3pm; interim menu 3–5pm; 5:30–9:30pm; Sun 5–9pm. BISTRO.

After cooking at San Francisco's renowned Zuni Cafe for 10 years, chef/owner Marsha McBride launched her own restaurant, a sort of Zuni East. She brought ex-Zuni staff and some of the restaurant's flavor with her to this sparse, loft-like dining room, which now serves salads, rotisserie chicken with oil and thyme, grilled lamb chops, steaks, and house-made sausages. East Bay carnivores are especially happy with the burger; just like Zuni's, it's top notch.

O Chamé. 1830 Fourth St. (near Hearst). ☎ **510/841-8783.** Reservations recommended Fri–Sat. Main courses $7–$17.50. AE, DC, MC, V. Mon–Sat 11:30am–3pm; Mon–Thurs 5:30–9pm; Fri–Sat 5:30–9:30pm. JAPANESE.

Spare and plain in its decor, with ochre-colored walls marked with etched patterns, this spot has a meditative air to complement the traditional and experimental Japanese-inspired cuisine. The menu, which changes daily, offers meal-in-a-bowl dishes (from $7 to $11) that allow a choice of soba or udon noodles in a clear soup with a variety of toppings—from shrimp and wakame seaweed to beef with burdock root and carrot; appetizers and salads, which include a flavorsome melding of grilled shiitake mushrooms and sweet peppers and portobello mushrooms, watercress, and green-onion pancakes; a sashimi of the day; and specials that range in price from $10 to $17.50 and always include a delicious roasted salmon.

✪ **Rivoli.** 1539 Solano. ☎ **510/526-2542.** Reservations recommended. Main courses $14–$16. AE, DC, MC, V. Mon–Thurs 5:30–9:30pm; Fri 5:30–10pm; Sat 5–10pm; Sun 5–9pm. CALIFORNIA.

One of the favored dinner destinations in the East Bay, Rivoli's winning combination is top-notch food at amazingly reasonable prices. The owners have done the most with an otherwise uninteresting space by creating a warm, intimate dining room that over-looks a sweet little garden with visiting raccoons and possums; a wine bar was recently added near the entrance. Aside from a few house favorites, the menu changes every 3 weeks in order to serve whatever's freshest and in season; the wine list follows suit with around a dozen by-the-glass options hand-picked to match the food. While many love it, we weren't thrilled with the portobello-mushroom fritter, which in our mind was a glorified variation on the fried zucchini stick. However, we did have an absolute A+ dish here (very rare): the hearty oven-braised pork ragout with butternut squash and dandelion greens intermingled with tender and crispy semolina gnocchi. Perfection at this price ($13.50) is enough to put most high-end San Francisco restaurants to shame. Finish the evening with the Meyer lemon cheesecake; it's a decadent sour cream–like affair with a subtle pistachio crust.

INEXPENSIVE

Blue Nile. 2525 Telegraph Ave. ☎ **510/540-6777.** Reservations required Fri–Sat. Main courses $6.50–$8.95. MC, V. Tues–Sat 11:30am–10pm; Sun 5–10pm. ETHIOPIAN.

Step through the beaded curtains into the Blue Nile, and the African paintings and music will summon your appetite to other parts of the world. But the journey doesn't end there—be prepared to savor the flavorful specialties such as *doro wat* (a spiced stew of beef, lamb, or chicken, served with a fluffy crepe injera) or *gomen wat* (mus-tard greens sautéed in cream) with no utensils other than your fingers. Sure, you could convince the wait staff to drum up a fork or two, but don't bother. After all, when in Africa. . . .

Cambodiana's. 2156 University Ave. (between Shattuck and Oxford). ☎ **510/843-4630.** Reservations recommended, especially Fri–Sat. Main courses $7.50–$13; fixed-price dinner $11.25. AE, CB, DC, JCB, MC, V. Mon–Fri 11:30am–3pm; Mon–Thurs and Sun 5–9:30pm; Fri–Sat 5–10:30pm. CAMBODIAN.

For those who relish the spicy cuisine of Cambodia, this is quite a find. The decor is as colorful as the fare—amidst brilliant blue, yellow, and green walls with Breuer-style chairs set at tables, you can feast on a variety of dishes. Especially tasty are the curry or naga dishes—salmon, prawns, chicken, or steak—smothered with a sauce of tamarind, turmeric, lemongrass, shrimp paste, coconut-milk galinga, shallot, lemon leaf, sugar, and green chili. Another tempting dish is the chicken *chaktomuk* prepared with pineapple, red peppers, and zucchini in soy and oyster sauce. There are plenty of vegetarian and low-cal options, and the three-course, fixed-price dinner is an excellent value.

2 Oakland

10 miles E of San Francisco

Although it's less than a dozen miles from San Francisco, the city of Oakland is worlds apart from its sister city across the bay. Originally little more than a cluster of ranches and farms, Oakland's size and stature exploded practically overnight as the last mile of transcontinental railroad track was laid down. Major shipping ports soon followed, and to this day Oakland has retained its hold as one of the busiest industrial ports on the West Coast.

The price for all this economic success, however, is Oakland's lowbrow reputation as a predominantly working-class city, forever in the shadow of San Francisco's chic spotlight. But with all its shortcomings and bad press, Oakland still manages to have a few pleasant surprises up its sleeve for those who venture this way. Rent a sailboat on Lake Merritt, stroll along the waterfront, explore the fantastic Oakland Museum—they're all great reasons to hop the bay and spend a fog-free day exploring one of California's largest and most ethnically diverse cities.

ESSENTIALS

GETTING THERE   Bay Area Rapid Transit (BART) makes the trip from San Francisco to Oakland through one of the longest underwater transit tunnels in the world. Fares range from $1 to $4, depending on your station of origin; children 4 and under ride free. BART trains operate Monday through Friday from 4am to midnight, Saturday from 6am to midnight, and Sunday from 8am to midnight. Exit at the 12th Street station for downtown Oakland.

By car from San Francisco, take I-80 across the San Francisco–Oakland Bay Bridge and follow the signs to downtown Oakland. Exit at Grand Avenue South for the Lake Merritt area.

CITY LAYOUT   Downtown Oakland is bordered by Grand Avenue on the north, I-980 on the west, Inner Harbor on the south, and Lake Merritt on the east. Between these landmarks are three BART stations (12th Street, 19th Street, and Lake Merritt), City Hall, the Oakland Museum, Jack London Square, and several other sights.

WHAT TO SEE & DO

Lake Merritt is Oakland's primary tourist attraction along with Jack London Square (see below). Three and a half miles in circumference, the tidal lagoon was bridged and dammed in the 1860s and is now a wildlife refuge that's home to flocks of migrating ducks, herons, and geese. It's surrounded on three sides by the 122-acre **Lakeside Park,** a popular place to picnic, feed the ducks, and escape the fog. At the **Sailboat House** (☎ 510/444-3807), in Lakeside Park along the north shore, you can rent sailboats, rowboats, pedal boats, and canoes for $6 to $12 per hour.

Another site worth visiting is Oakland's **Paramount Theatre** (☎ 510/893-2300), an outstanding example of art-deco architecture and decor. Built in

1931 and authentically restored in 1973, it now functions as the city's main performing-arts center. Guided tours of the 3,000-seat theater are given the first and third Saturdays of each month, excluding holidays. No reservations are necessary; just show up at 10am at the box-office entrance on 21st Street at Broadway. Cameras are allowed, and admission is $1.

If you take pleasure from strolling sailboat-filled wharves or are a die-hard fan of Jack London, you might actually enjoy a visit to **Jack London Square.** Oakland's only patent tourist area, this low-key version of San Francisco's Fisherman's Wharf shamelessly plays up the fact that Jack London spent most of his youth along this waterfront. The square fronts the harbor, housing a tourist-tacky complex of boutiques and eateries that are about as far away from the "call of the wild" as you can get. Most are open Monday through Saturday from 10am to 7pm (some restaurants stay open later). In the center of the square is a small reconstructed version of the Yukon cabin in which Jack London lived while prospecting in the Klondike during the gold rush of 1897.

In the middle of Jack London Square you'll find a more authentic memorial, **Heinold's First and Last Chance Saloon**—a funky, friendly little bar and historic landmark that's actually worth a visit. This is where London did some of his writing and most of his drinking; the corner table he used has remained exactly as it was nearly a century ago. Also in the square are the mast and nameplate from the **USS** *Oakland,* a ship that saw extensive action in the Pacific during World War II, and a wonderful museum filled with interesting London memorabilia.

The square is located at Broadway and Embarcadero. Take I-880 to Broadway, turn south, and go to the end. Via BART, get off at the 12th Street station, then walk south along Broadway (about half a mile) or take bus no. 51a to the foot of Broadway.

It took the Potomac Association's hundreds of volunteers more than 12 years—at a cost of $5 million—to restore the 165-foot presidential yacht **USS** *Potomac,* Franklin D. Roosevelt's beloved "Floating White House." Now a proud and permanent memorial berthed at the Port of Oakland's FDR Pier at Jack London Square, the revitalized *Potomac* is open to the public for dockside tours, as well as 2-hour public-education cruises along the San Francisco waterfront and around Treasure Island. Prior to departure, a 15-minute video, shown at the nearby Potomac Visitor Center, provides background on FDR's presidency and his legacy concerning the Bay Area.

Dockside tours are available year-round on Wednesday and Friday from 10am to 2pm and Sunday from 11am to 4pm. Admission is $5 for families with children under 18, $3 for adults, $2 for seniors, $1 for children ages 6 to 17, and free for children age 5 and under. Due to popularity of the cruises, advance purchase is strongly recommended. Hours and days are subject to change (especially in bad weather), so be sure to call the 24-hour information line (☎ **510/839-8256**). Tickets can be purchased in advance by calling the **Potomac Association** office (☎ **510/839-7533,** ext. 1). The **Potomac Visitor Center** is at 540 Water St., at the corner of Clay and Water streets adjacent to the FDR pier at the north end of Jack London Square.

✪ **Oakland Museum of California.** 1000 Oak St. ☎ **888/625-6873** or 510/238-2200 for recorded information. Admission $6 adults, $4 students and seniors, free for children 5 and under. Wed–Sat 10am–5pm; Sun noon–5pm. Closed Thanksgiving, Christmas, New Year's Day, and July 4. From I-880 north, take the Oak St. exit; the museum is 5 blocks east at Oak and 10th sts. Alternatively, take I-580 to I-980 and exit at the Jackson St. ramp. BART: Lake Merritt station (1 block south of the museum).

Located 2 blocks south of the lake, this museum includes just about everything you'd want to know about the state and its people, history, culture, geology, art, environment, and ecology. Inside a low-swept, modern building set among sweeping gardens and terraces, it's actually three museums in one: exhibitions of works by California artists from Bierstadt to Diebenkorn; collections of artifacts from California's history, from Pomo Indian basketry to Country Joe McDonald's guitar; and re-creations of California habitats from the coast to the White Mountains. The museum holds major shows of California artists, like the recent exhibit of the work of ceramic sculptor Peter Voulkos, or shows dedicated to major California movements, such as arts and crafts from 1890 to 1930. There are 45-minute guided tours leaving the gallery information desks on request or by appointment. On site are a fine cafe (open Wednesday through Saturday from 10am to 4pm, Sunday from noon to 5pm), a gallery (☎ 510/834-2329) selling works by California artists, and a book and gift shop.

WHERE TO DINE

Bay Wolf. 3853 Piedmont Ave. (off Broadway between 40th St. and MacArthur Blvd.). ☎ 510/655-6004. Reservations recommended. Main courses $15–$18. AE, MC, V. Mon–Fri 11:30am–2pm and 6–9pm; Sat–Sun 5:30–9:30pm. CALIFORNIA.

The life span of most Bay Area restaurants is about a year; Bay Wolf, one of Oakland's most venerable and revered restaurants, has been going strong for nearly 2 decades. This converted brown Victorian is a comfortably familiar sight for most East Bay diners, who have been coming here for years to let chef/owner Michael Wilds do the cooking. Though Wilds has passed his apron on to chef Lauren Lyle, Bay Wolf's reputation for simple yet sagacious preparations using only fresh ingredients remains. Main courses range from a much-revered Liberty Ranch duck with sweet potato flan and chard, flavorful seafood stew seasoned with saffron, and brimful of cracked Dungeness crab, prawns, rockfish, and mussels, to tender braised lamb shanks with white beans, artichokes, and rosemary. Informal service means you can leave the tie at home. Heat lamps on the front deck allow for open-air evening dining—a treat San Franciscans rarely experience.

Citron. 5484 College Ave. (off the northeastern end of Broadway between Taft and Lawton sts.). ☎ 510/653-5484. Reservations recommended. Three-course fixed-price menu Sun–Wed $20. Main courses $15–$21. AE, DC, DISC, MC, V. Mon–Thurs 5:30–9:30pm; Fri 5:30–10pm; Sat 5–10pm; Sun 5–9pm. FRENCH/MEDITERRANEAN.

This petite, adorable French bistro was an instant smash when it first opened in 1992, and it continues to draw raves for its small yet enticingly eclectic menu. Chef Chris Rossi draws the flavors of France, Italy, and Spain together with fresh California produce for Chez Panisse–like results. Though the menu changes every few weeks, dishes range from grilled Colorado lamb sirloin, with wild-mushroom spoon bread and rosemary jus, to osso buco of lamb on a bed of flageolet bean and sun-dried tomato ragout and sprinkled with a pistachio gremolata garnish. The fresh salads and Citron "40-clove" chicken are also superb.

✪ Oliveto Restaurant. Rockridge Market Hall, 5655 College Ave. (off the northeastern end of Broadway at Shafter/Keith St., across from the Rockridge BART station). ☎ 510/547-5356. Reservations recommended for upstairs restaurant. Main courses $16–$22. AE, DC, MC, V. Mon–Fri 11:30am–2pm; Mon–Sat 5:30–10pm, Sun 5–9pm. ITALIAN.

Paul Bertolli, former chef at the world-renowned Chez Panisse restaurant, was recently awarded recognition as one of the top chefs in California by the James Beard Foundation. During the week, his dining room is a madhouse at lunchtime, when BART commuters pile in for the wood-fired pizzas and tapas served at the restaurant's lower-level cafe. The upstairs restaurant—suavely bedecked with neo-Florentine decor and partially open kitchen—is slightly more civil, packed nightly with fans of Bertolli's house-made pastas, sausages, and prosciutto. Noteworthy additions include a wood-burning oven, flame-broiled rotisserie, high-end liquor cabinet (that is, hard alcohol, but no mixed drinks), and an expanded kitchen. An assortment of pricey grills, braises, and roasts anchors the daily changing menu, but it's the reasonably priced pastas, pizzetas, and awesome salads that offer the most bang for your buck. *Tip:* There's free parking in the lot at the rear of the Market Hall building.

3 Sausalito

5 miles N of San Francisco

Just off the northern end of the Golden Gate Bridge is the eclectic little town of Sausalito, a slightly bohemian, nonchalant, and studiedly quaint adjunct to San Francisco. With approximately 7,500 residents, Sausalito feels rather like St. Tropez on the French Riviera—minus the starlets and the social rat race. It has its quota of paper millionaires, but they rub their permanently suntanned shoulders with a good number of hard-up artists, struggling authors, shipyard workers, and fishers. Next to the swank restaurants, plush bars, and antiques shops and galleries, you'll see hamburger joints, beer parlors, and secondhand bookstores.

Above all, Sausalito has scenery and sunshine, for once you cross the Golden Gate Bridge you're out of the San Francisco fog patch and under blue California sky (we hope). Almost all the tourist action, which is basically limited to window-shopping and eating, takes place at sea level on Bridgeway.

ESSENTIALS

The **Golden Gate Ferry Service** fleet, Ferry Building (☎ 415/923-2000), operates between the San Francisco Ferry Building (at the foot of Market Street) and downtown Sausalito. Service is frequent, departing at reasonable intervals every day of the year except New Year's Day, Thanksgiving Day, and Christmas Day. Phone for exact schedule. The ride takes a half hour; one-way fares are $4.75 for adults and $3.55 for kids 6 to 12. Seniors and passengers with disabilities ride for $2.35; children 5 and under ride free. Family rates are also available.

Ferries of the **Blue & Gold Fleet** (☎ 415/773-1188 for recorded info, ☎ 415/705-5555 for tickets) leave from Pier 41 and cost $11 round-trip, half price for kids 5 to 11, free for kids under 5. Boats run on a seasonal schedule; phone for departure information.

By car from San Francisco, take U.S. 101 north, then the first right after the Golden Gate Bridge (Alexander exit). Alexander becomes Bridgeway in Sausalito.

EXPLORING THE TOWN

Sausalito is a mecca for shoppers seeking handmade, original, and offbeat clothes and footwear, as well as arts and crafts. The town's best shops are found in the alleys, malls, and second-floor boutiques reached by steep, narrow staircases on and off **Bridgeway,** Sausalito's main touring strip, which runs along the water. Those in the know make a quick detour to **Caledonia Street,** which runs parallel to and 1 block inland from Bridgeway. Not only is it less congested, but there's also a far better selection of cafes and shops.

Village Fair, at 777 Bridgeway, is Sausalito's closest approximation to a mall. It's a complex of 30 shops, souvenir stores, coffee bars, and gardens. The complex is open daily from 10am to 6pm; restaurants stay open later.

Bay Model Visitors Center. 2100 Bridgeway ☎ 415/332-3871. Free admission. Labor Day–Memorial Day Tues–Sat 9am–4pm; Memorial Day–Labor Day Tues–Fri 9am–4pm, Sat–Sun and holidays 10am–5pm.

The U.S. Army Corps of Engineers uses this high-tech, 1½-acre model of San Francisco's bay and delta to resolve problems and observe what impact any changes in water flow will have. The model indicates trends in sediment movement and reproduces (in scale) the rise and fall of tides, the flows and currents of water, and the mixing of fresh- and salt water. A tour and a 10-minute film explain it all, but the most interesting time to visit is when it's actually being used, so call ahead.

WHERE TO STAY

Casa Madrona. 801 Bridgeway, Sausalito, CA 94965. ☎ **800/567-9524** or 415/332-0502. Fax 415/332-2537. 35 units. MINIBAR TEL. $168–$260 double; $448 Madrona Villa suite. Free breakfast from 7:30–9:30am. 2-night minimum on weekends. AE, MC, V. Parking $7. Ferry: Walk across the street from the landing. From U.S. 101 north, take the first right after the Golden Gate Bridge (Alexander exit); Alexander becomes Bridgeway in Sausalito.

Sooner or later, most visitors to Sausalito look up and wonder at the ornate mansion on the hill. It's part of Casa Madrona, a hideaway by the bay built in 1885 by a wealthy lumber baron. The epitome of luxury in its day, the mansion had slipped into decay when it was saved by Henri Deschamps and converted into a hotel and restaurant. Successive renovations and extensions have added a rambling, New England–style building to the hillside below the main house. Now a certified historic landmark, the hotel offers rooms, suites, and cottages. The 16 newest units are each uniquely deco- rated by different local designers and boast panoramic views of the San Francisco sky- line and bay. The mansion rooms are also appointed in a variety of styles; some have Jacuzzis, while others have fireplaces.

Within the Casa Madrona is **Mikayla Restaurant** (☎ **415/331-5888**), which serves superb American West Coast cuisine—scallopine of leg of lamb with grilled leeks, caramelized scallops with crispy onion rings—in an unbelievably beautiful set- ting overlooking the bay and San Francisco skyline (its decor was orchestrated by renowned local artist/designer Laurel Burch). It's open for dinner nightly from 6 to 10pm and for Sunday brunch from 10am to 2:30pm.

✪ **Inn Above The Tide.** 30 El Portal (next to the Sausalito Ferry Landing), Sausalito, CA 94965. ☎ **800/893-8433** or 415/332-9535. Fax 415/332-6714. 30 units. A/C TV TEL. $195–$485 double. Rates include continental breakfast and evening wine and cheese. 2-night minimum on weekends. AE, DC, MC, V. Valet parking $8.

Perched directly over the bay atop well-grounded pilings, this former luxury apartment complex underwent a $4-million transformation into one of Sausalito's—if not the Bay Area's—finest accommodations. It's the view that clinches it: Every room comes with an unparalleled panorama of the San Francisco Bay, including a postcard-quality vista of the city glimmering in the distance. Should you manage to tear yourself away from your private deck (we were tempted to drag our mattress outside), you'll find that your sumptuously appointed room sports a romantic little fireplace, a vast sunken tub with Jacuzzi jets, remote-control air-conditioning, and wondrously comfortable queen- or king-size beds. Soothing shades of pale green and blue highlight the decor, which blends in well with the bayscape outside. Be sure to request that your breakfast and newspaper be delivered to your deck, then cancel your early appointments: On sunny mornings, nobody checks out early.

WHERE TO DINE

Guernica. 2009 Bridgeway. ☎ **415/332-1512.** Reservations recommended. Main courses $10–$17. AE, MC, V. Daily 5–10pm. From U.S. 101 north, take the first right after the Golden Gate Bridge (Alexander exit); Alexander becomes Bridgeway in Sausalito. FRENCH/BASQUE.

Established in 1976, Guernica is one of those funky old kinds of restaurants that you'd probably pass up for something more chic and modern down the street—if you didn't know better. Be sure to call ahead and order Guernica's legendary Paella Valenciana in advance, then bring a partner, 'cause it's served for two but will feed three. Other main courses range from grilled rabbit with a spicy red diablo sauce to a hearty rack of lamb Guernica and medaillons of pork loin with baked apples and calvados. Rich desserts include such in-season specialties as strawberry tart, peach Melba, and Basque-style rice pudding.

Horizons. 558 Bridgeway. ☎ **415/331-3232.** Reservations accepted weekdays only. Main courses $9–$21; salads and sandwiches $6–$11. AE, MC, V. Mon–Fri 11am–11pm; Sat–Sun 10am–11pm. Valet parking $4. SEAFOOD/AMERICAN.

Eventually, every San Franciscan ends up at Horizons to meet a friend for Sunday Bloody Marys. It's not much to look at from the outside, but it gets better as you head past the funky dark-wood interior toward the waterside terrace. On warm days, it's worth the wait for alfresco seating, if only to watch dreamy sailboats glide past San Francisco's distant skyline. The food here can't touch the view, but it's well portioned and satisfying enough. Seafood dishes are the main items, including steamed clams and mussels, freshly shucked oysters, and a variety of seafood pastas. In fine Marin tradition, Horizons has an "herb tea and espresso" bar.

PICNIC FARE & WHERE TO EAT IT

Even Sausalito's naysayers have to admit that it's hard not to enjoy eating your way down Bridgeway on a warm, sunny day. If the crowds are too much or the prices too steep at the bayside restaurants, grab a bite to go for an impromptu picnic in the park fronting the marina.

Caledonia Kitchen, 400 Caledonia St. (☎ **415/331-0220**), is the sort of place you wish were just around the corner from your house—a beautiful little cafe serving a huge assortment of fresh salads, soups, chili, gourmet sandwiches, and inexpensive entrees like herbed roast chicken or vegetarian lasagna for only $4.95. Continental-style breakfast items and good coffee and espresso drinks are also on the menu.

Like the name says, the specialty at tiny, narrow **Hamburgers,** 737 Bridgeway (☎ **415/332-9471**), is juicy flame-broiled burgers, arguably Marin County's best. Look for the rotating grill in the window off Bridgeway, then stand in line and salivate with the rest. Chicken burgers are a slightly healthier option. Order a side of fries, grab a bunch of napkins, then head over to the park across the street.

4 Angel Island & Tiburon

8 miles N of San Francisco

A federal and state wildlife refuge, **Angel Island** is the largest of the San Francisco Bay's three islets (the others being Alcatraz and Yerba Buena). The island has been, at various times, a prison, a quarantine station for immigrants, a missile base, and even a favorite site for duels. Nowadays, though, most of the people who visit here are content with picnicking on the large green lawn that fronts the docking area; loaded with the appropriate recreational supplies, they claim a barbecue, plop their fannies down on the lush green grass, and while away an afternoon free of phones, televisions, and traffic. Hiking, mountain biking, and guided tram tours are also popular activities.

Tiburon, situated on a peninsula of the same name, looks like a cross between a fishing village and a Hollywood western set—imagine San Francisco reduced to toy dimensions. This seacoast town rambles over a series of green hills and ends up at a spindly, multicolored pier on the waterfront, like a Fisherman's Wharf in miniature. But in reality, it's an extremely plush patch of yacht-club suburbia, as you'll see by both the marine craft and the homes of their owners. **Main Street** is lined with ramshackle, color-splashed old frame houses that shelter chic boutiques, souvenir stores, antiques shops, and art galleries. Other roads are narrow, winding, and hilly, leading up to dramatically situated homes. The view of San Francisco's skyline and the islands in the bay is a good enough reason to pay the precious price to live here.

ESSENTIALS

Ferries of the **Blue & Gold Fleet** (☎ 415/773-1188 for recorded info, ☎ 415/705-5555 for tickets) leave from San Francisco's Pier 41 and travel to both Angel Island and Tiburon. Boats run on a seasonal schedule; call for departure information. The round-trip fare is $10 to Angel Island, $11 to Tiburon; half price for kids 5 to 11, free for kids under 5.

By car from San Francisco, take U.S. 101 to the Tiburon/Calif. 131 exit, then follow Tiburon Boulevard all the way into downtown, a 40-minute drive from San Francisco. Catch **Tiburon–Angel Island Ferry** (☎ 415/435-2131 or 415/388-6770) to Angel Island from the dock located at Tiburon Boulevard and Main Street. The 15-minute round-trip, which only runs on weekends, is $6 for adults, $4 for children 5 to 11, free for kids under 5, and $1 for bikes. One child under 5 rides free per each paying adult.

ANGEL ISLAND

Passengers disembark from the ferry at **Ayala Cove,** a small marina abutting a huge lawn area equipped with tables, benches, barbecue pits, and rest rooms. Also at Ayala Cove are a small store, gift shop, cafe (with surprisingly good grub), and overpriced mountain-bike rental shop (helmets included).

Among the 12 miles of Angel Island's hiking and mountain-bike trails is the **Perimeter Road,** a partly paved path that circles the island and winds its way past disused troop barracks, former gun emplacements, and other military buildings; several turnoffs lead up to the top of Mount Livermore, 776 feet above the bay. Sometimes referred to as the "Ellis Island of the West," from 1910 to 1940 Angel Island was used as a holding area for Chinese immigrants awaiting their citizenship papers. You can still see some faded Chinese characters on the walls of the barracks where the immigrants were held. During the warmer months, you can camp at a limited number of sites; reservations are required and can be obtained by calling ☎ 800/444-7275.

Also offered at Angel Island are guided **sea-kayak tours.** The all-day trips, which include a catered lunch, combine the thrill of paddling stable one-, two-, or three-person kayaks with an informative, naturalist-led tour that encircles the island (conditions permitting). All equipment is provided, kids are welcome, and no experience is necessary. Rates run about $100 per person. For more information, call **Sea Trek** (☎ 415/332-8494).

The most recent tour addition is the 1-hour **Angel Island Tram Tour** (☎ 925/426-3058), which costs $10 for adults, $6 for children 9 to 12, and $9 for seniors; children under 9 ride free.

For recorded information on **Angel Island State Park,** call ☎ 415/435-1915.

TIBURON

The main thing to do in Tiburon is stroll along the waterfront, pop into the stores, and spend an easy $50 on drinks and appetizers before heading back to the city. For a taste of the wine country, stop in at **Windsor Vineyards,** 72 Main St. (☎ 800/214-9463 or 415/435-3113), which has a Victorian tasting room dating back to 1888. Thirty-five choices are available for a free tasting. Wine accessories and gifts— glasses, cork pullers, gourmet sauces, posters, and maps—are also for sale. Carry-packs (which hold six bottles) are available; ask about personalized labels for your own selections. The shop is open Sunday through Thursday from 10am to 6pm, Friday and Saturday until 7pm.

WHERE TO DINE

Guaymas. 5 Main St. ☎ **415/435-6300.** Reservations recommended. Main courses $12–$18. AE, CB, DC, DISC, MC, V. Mon–Thurs 11:30am–10pm; Fri–Sat 11:30am–11pm; Sun 10:30am–10pm. Ferry: Walk about 10 paces from the landing. From U.S. 101, exit at Tiburon/Hwy. 131; follow Tiburon Blvd. 5 miles and turn right onto Main St. The restaurant is situated directly behind the bakery. MEXICAN.

Guaymas offers authentic Mexican regional cuisine and a spectacular panoramic view of San Francisco and the bay. In good weather, the two outdoor patios are almost always packed with diners soaking in the sun and the scene. Inside, a beehive-shaped adobe fireplace warms the dining room, whose walls are hung with colorful Mexican artwork.

Guaymas is named after a fishing village on Mexico's Sea of Cortez, and both the town and the restaurant are famous for their *camarones* (giant shrimp). Other featured dishes are ceviche, handmade tamales, and charcoal-grilled beef, seafood, and fowl. Save room for dessert, especially the outrageously scrumptious fritter with "drunken" bananas and ice cream. In addition to a good selection of California wines, the restaurant offers an exceptional variety of tequilas, Mexican beers, and mineral waters flavored with flowers, grains, and fruits.

Sam's Anchor Café. 27 Main St. ☎ **415/435-4527.** Reservations accepted for dinner nightly and lunch Mon–Fri only. Main courses $8–$16. AE, DC, DISC, MC, V. Mon–Thurs 11am–10pm; Fri 11am–10:30pm; Sat 10am–10:30pm; Sun 9:30am–10pm. Ferry: Walk from the landing. From U.S. 101, exit at Tiburon/Hwy. 131, follow Tiburon Blvd. 4 miles and turn right onto Main St. SEAFOOD.

Summer Sundays are liveliest in Tiburon, when weekend boaters tie up to the docks at waterside restaurants like this one, the kind of place where you and your cronies can take off your shoes and have a fun, relaxed time eating burgers and drinking margaritas outside on the pier. The fare is pretty typical—sandwiches, salads, and seafood such as deep-fried oysters—but the quality and selection of the food is inconsequential: Beers, burgers, and a designated driver are all you really need.

5 Muir Woods & Mount Tamalpais

12 miles N of the Golden Gate Bridge

While the rest of Marin County's redwood forests were being devoured to feed the building spree in San Francisco around the turn of the century, the trees of Muir Woods, in a remote ravine on the flanks of Mount Tamalpais, escaped destruction in favor of easier pickings.

MUIR WOODS

Although the magnificent California redwoods have been successfully transplanted to five continents, their homeland is a 500-mile strip along the mountainous coast of southwestern Oregon and Northern California. The coast redwood, or *Sequoia sempervirens,* is the tallest tree in the immediate region, and the largest-known specimen (located in the Redwood National Forest) towers 367.8 feet. It has an even larger relative, the *Sequoiadendron giganteum* of the California Sierra Nevada, but the coastal variety is stunning enough. Soaring toward the sky like a wooden cathedral, seeing it is an experience you won't soon forget.

Granted, Muir Woods is tiny compared to the Redwood National Forest farther north, but you can still get a pretty good idea of what it must have been like when these redwood giants dominated the entire coastal region. What is truly amazing is that they exist a mere 6 miles (as the crow flies) from San Francisco; close enough, unfortunately, that tour buses arrive in droves on the weekends. You can, however, avoid the masses by hiking up the **Ocean View Trail** and returning via the **Fern Creek Trail**—a moderate hike that shows off the woods' best sides and leaves the lazy-butts behind.

To reach Muir Woods from San Francisco, cross the Golden Gate Bridge heading north on U.S. 101, take the Stinson Beach/Calif. 1 exit heading west, and follow the signs (and the traffic). The park is open daily from 8am to sunset; the entrance fee is $2 per person 17 years or older. There's a small gift shop, educational displays, and docent-led tours that you're welcome to stand in on. For more information, call the **Muir Woods information line** (☎ **415/388-2595**).

If you don't have a car, you can book a bus trip with the **Red & White Fleet** (☎ **800/229-2784** or 415/447-0597), which takes you straight to Muir Woods via the Golden Gate Bridge, and on the way back makes a short stop in Sausalito. The 3½-hour tours run several times daily, and cost $30 for adults, $14 for children. Call for more information and specific departure times.

MOUNT TAMALPAIS

The birthplace of mountain biking, Mount Tam—as the locals call it—is the Bay Area's favorite outdoor playground and the most dominant mountain in the region. Most every local has his or her secret trail and scenic overlook, as well as an opinion on the dilemma between mountain bikers and hikers (a touchy subject around here). The main trails—mostly fire roads—see a lot of foot and bicycle traffic on the weekends, particularly on clear, sunny days when you can see a hundred miles in all directions, from the foothills of the Sierra to the western horizon. It's a great place to escape from the city for a leisurely hike and to soak in the breathtaking views of the bay.

To get to Mount Tamalpais **by car,** cross the Golden Gate Bridge heading north on U.S. 101 and take the Stinson Beach/Calif. 1 exit. Follow the shoreline highway about 2½ miles and turn onto the Panoramic Highway heading west. After about 5½ miles, turn onto Pantoll Road and continue for about a mile to Ridgecrest Boulevard. Ridgecrest winds to a parking lot below East Peak. From here, it's a 15-minute hike up to the top.

6 Half Moon Bay

28 miles SW of San Francisco

A mere 45-minute drive from the teeming streets of San Francisco is a heavenly little seaside hamlet called Half Moon Bay, one of the finest—and friendliest—small towns on the California coast. While other coastal communities like Bolinas take strides to make tourists unwelcome, Half Moon Bay residents are disarmingly amicable, bestowing greeting to anyone and everyone who stops for a visit.

Only in the last decade has Half Moon Bay begun to capitalize on its golden beaches, mild climate, and close proximity to San Francisco, so you won't find the ultra-touristy machinations that result in gaudy theme parks and time-share condos. What you will find, however, is a peaceful, unfettered slice of textbook California: pristine beaches, redwood forests, nature preserves, rustic fishing harbors, horse ranches, organic farms, and a host of superb inns and restaurants—everything you need for the perfect weekend getaway.

ESSENTIALS

There's no public transportation from San Francisco to Half Moon Bay. There are two ways to get here by car: the fast way and the scenic way. To save time, take Calif. 92

west from either I-280 or U.S. 101 out of San Francisco, which will take you over a small mountain range and drop you directly into Half Moon Bay. A better—and far prettier—route is via Calif. 1, which technically starts at the south end of the Golden Gate Bridge and veers southwest to the shoreline a few miles south of Daly City. Both routes to Half Moon Bay are clearly marked with numerous signs, so don't worry about getting lost.

Downtown Half Moon Bay, however, is easy to miss since it's not on Calif. 1, but a few hundred yards inland. Head 2 blocks up Calif. 92 from the Calif. 1 intersection, then turn south at the Shell gas station onto Main Street until you cross a small bridge.

For more information, call the **Half Moon Bay Coastside Chamber of Commerce** (☎ **650/726-8380**).

Note: Temperatures rarely venture into the 70s in Half Moon Bay, so be sure to pack for cool (and often wet) weather.

EXPLORING HALF MOON BAY & ENVIRONS

The best things to do in Half Moon Bay are the same things the locals do. For example, there's a wonderful **paved beach trail** that winds 3 miles from Half Moon Bay to picturesque Pillar Point Harbor, where you can watch the trawlers unload their daily catch. Walking, biking, jogging, and skating are all kosher, and be sure to keep a lookout for dolphins and whales. Bicycles can be rented from the **Bicyclery,** 432 Main St. (☎ **650/726-6000**). Prices range from $8 to $12 an hour to $25 to $30 per day.

Half Moon Bay is also known for its organically grown produce, and the best place to stock up on fruits and vegetables is the **Andreotti Family Farm,** 329 Kelly Ave., off Calif. 1 (☎ **650/726-9461**), a charming old-fashioned outfit that's been in business since 1926. Every Friday, Saturday, and Sunday, a member of the Andreotti family slides open the door to their weathered old barn at 10am sharp to reveal a cornucopia of strawberries, artichokes, cucumbers, and more. Head toward the beach and you'll see the barn on your right-hand side. It's open until 6pm year-round.

BEACHES & PRESERVES   The 4-mile arc of golden-colored sand that rings Half Moon Bay is broken up into three state-run beaches—Dunes, Venice, and Francis—all part of **Half Moon Bay State Beach.** There's a $5-per-vehicle entrance fee for all three beaches. Though surfing is allowed, swimming isn't a good idea unless you happen to be cold-blooded.

A few miles farther north on Calif. 1 is the **Fitzgerald Marine Reserve,** one of the most diverse tidal basins on the West Coast, as well as one of the safest, thanks to a wave-buffering rock terrace 50 yards from the beach. Call ☎ **650/728-3584** before coming to find out when it's low tide (all the sea creatures are hidden at high tide) and to get information on the docent-led tour schedules (usually offered on Saturdays). Rubber-soled shoes are recommended. It's located at the west end of California Avenue off Calif. 1 in Moss Beach.

Sixteen miles south of Half Moon Bay on Calif. 1 (at the turnoff to Pescadero) is the **Pescadero Marsh Natural Preserve,** one of the few remaining natural marshes left on the central California coast. Part of the Pacific flyway, it's a resting stop for nearly 200 bird species, including great blue herons that nest in the northern row of eucalyptus trees. Passing through the marsh is the mile-long **Sequoia Audubon Trail,** accessible from the parking lot at Pescadero State Beach on Calif. 1 (the trail starts below the Pescadero Creek Bridge). Docent-led tours take place every Saturday at 10:30am and every Sunday at 1pm, weather permitting.

Starting in December and continuing through March, the ✪ **Año Nuevo State Reserve** is home to one of California's most amazing animal attractions: the hallowed breeding grounds of the northern elephant seal. Every winter, people reserve tickets months in advance for a chance to witness a fearsome clash between the 2½-ton bulls over mating privileges among the harems of females. Reservations are required for the 2½-hour naturalist-led tours (held rain or shine, December 15 to March 31). For tickets and tour information, call ☎ **800/444-4445.** Even if it's not mating season, you can still see the elephant seals lolling around the shore almost year-round, particularly between April and August when they come ashore to molt.

OUTDOOR PURSUITS   One of the most popular activities in town is horseback riding along the beach. **Sea Horse Ranch** (a.k.a. Friendly Acres Horse Ranch), on Calif. 1 a mile north of Half Moon Bay (☎ **650/726-2362** or 650/726-8550), offers guided and unguided rides along the beach or on well-worn trails for about $35. Hours are daily from 8am to 6pm.

For golfers, there's **Half Moon Bay Golf Links,** 2000 Fairway Dr., at the south end of Half Moon Bay next to the Half Moon Bay Lodge (☎ **650/726-6384**). Designed by Arnold Palmer, the oceanside 18-hole course has been rated among the top 100 courses in the country, as well as the best in the Bay Area. Greens fees range from $95 to $135. Reserve your tee time as far in advance as possible.

SHOPPING   Main Street is a shopper's paradise. Dozens of small stores and boutiques line the quarter-mile strip, selling everything from feed and tack to custom furniture and camping gear. From north to south, must-see stops include the **Buffalo Shirt Company,** 315 Main St. (☎ 650/726-3194), which carries a fine selection of casual wear, Indian rugs, and outdoor gear; **Cartwheels,** 330 Main St. (☎ 650/726-6060), a nifty store specializing in rustic wood furniture, rugs, and toys; and **Half Moon Bay Feed & Fuel,** 331 Main St. (☎ 650/726-4814), a great place to pick up a treat for your pet.

Cunha's Country Store, 448 Main St. (☎ 650/726-4071), the town's beloved grocery and general store, is a mandatory stop for regular visitors from the Bay Area. And, of course, what would Half Moon Bay be without a good bookstore like **Coastside Books,** 432 Main St. (☎ 650/726-5889), which also carries a fair selection of children's books and postcards. End your shopping spree with a stop at **Cottage Industries,** 621 Main St. (☎ 650/712-8078), to marvel at the high-quality handcrafted furniture.

WHERE TO STAY

Beach House Inn. 4100 N. Cabrillo Hwy. (3 miles north of Half Moon Bay on Hwy. 1), Half Moon Bay, CA 94019. ☎ **800/315-9366** or 650/712-0220. Fax 650/712-0693. 54 units. MINIBAR TV TEL. $175–$350 double. Rates include continental breakfast and evening wine tasting on Fri and Sat only. AE, DC, DISC, MC, V.

It was only a matter of time before big-time developers clued in to the potential of Half Moon Bay, so no one was surprised when ground was broken for the three-story Beach House Inn & Conference Center. While the facade has a rather unimaginative Cape Cod look, the rooms are surprisingly well designed and decorated with modern prints, stylish furnishings, soothing yellow tones, and spectacular views of the bay and harbor. Every room comes fully loaded with a wood-burning fireplace, king-size bed and sleeper sofa, large bathroom, stereo with CD player, private patio or deck access, two color TVs and a VCR, *four* telephones with data ports and voice mail, and a kitchenette with microwave and fridge. Facilities include a heated pool, oceanview whirlpool, fitness room, and sauna. *Tip:* Opt for one of the corner rooms, which offer a more expansive view for the same price.

✪ **Cypress Inn on Miramar Beach.** 407 Mirada Rd., Half Moon Bay, CA 94019. ☎ **800/83-BEACH** or 650/726-6002. Fax 650/712-0380. 12 units. TV TEL (in Beach House rooms only). $170–$275 double. Rates include breakfast and afternoon tea, wine, and hors d'oeuvres.

AE, DISC, MC, V. Go 3 miles north of the junction of Calif. 92 and Calif. 1, then turn west on Medio to the end.

Easily our favorite place to stay in Half Moon Bay, the Cypress Inn is blissfully free of Victorian charm (nary a lace curtain in *this* joint). Instead you have a modern, artistically designed and decorated building infused with colorful native folk art and rustic furniture made of pine and heavy wicker. Each room has a billowy feather bed, private balcony, gas fireplace, private bathroom, and an unobstructed ocean view. Adjacent to the inn are four Beach House rooms equipped with built-in stereo systems and hidden TVs, though they lack the Santa-Fe-meets-California effect that we adore in the main house. The ace in the hole is, however, that it's the only B&B perched right on the beach.

✪ **Seal Cove Inn.** 221 Cypress Ave., Half Moon Bay, CA 94038. ☎ **650/728-4114.** Fax 650/728-4116. 10 units. MINIBAR TV TEL. $190–$270 double. Rates include breakfast and complimentary wine/sherry. DISC, MC, V. The inn is 6 miles north of Half Moon Bay off Calif. 1; follow signs to Moss Beach Distillery.

Before Karen Herbert and her husband, Rick, opened this top-notch B&B, she was the writer and publisher of *Karen Brown's Country Inns Series,* so you can bet that she knows what it takes to create and run a superior bed-and-breakfast. The result is a stately, sophisticated inn that harmoniously blends California, New England, and European influences in a spectacular seacoast setting. All rooms have wood-burning fireplaces, country antiques, original watercolors, grandfather clocks, hidden TVs with VCRs, fridges stocked with free beverages, and views overlooking the distant cypress trees and a colorful half-acre wildflower garden dotted with birdhouses. In the morning you'll find coffee and a newspaper outside your door, in the evening there's brandy and sherry by the living-room fireplace, and at night a plate of chocolates sits beside your turned-down bed. The ocean is just a short walk away.

WHERE TO DINE

Pasta Moon. 315 Main St., Half Moon Bay. ☎ **650/726-5125.** Reservations recommended. Main courses $8–$23. AE, DISC, MC, V. Mon–Fri 11:30am–2:30pm; Sat noon–3pm; Sun–Thurs 5:30–9:30pm; Fri–Sat 5:30–10pm; Sun brunch 11am–2:30pm. ITALIAN.

When visitors ask, "Where's the best place to eat around here?" the inevitable answer is Pasta Moon, a handsome nouveau-Italian restaurant in downtown Half Moon Bay that specializes in making everything from scratch and using only the freshest ingredients. Chef Sean Lynd's pasta dishes, always freshly made and perfectly cooked, earn the highest recommendations. We love the house-made black-pepper fettuccine with spicy calabrese sausage and braised winter greens, or the hand-cut pappardelle with sweet fennel sausage, tomatoes, and cream. For dessert, try the wonderful tiramisu.

Sushi Main Street. 696 Mill St., Half Moon Bay. ☎ **650/726-6336.** Main courses $5–$10. MC, V. Mon–Sat 11:30am–2:30pm and 5–9pm; Sun 5–9pm. JAPANESE.

Chef/owner Hirohito Shigeta started out this gem of a Japanese restaurant a decade ago in a tiny space on Main Street and kept the old name when he moved into larger digs down the street. His wife, Karolynne (an interior designer with impeccable taste), in turn decorated the new space with her vast collection of museum-quality Balinese artifacts, and the result is astoundingly beautiful. But even if it looked like the inside of a trailer home, it would still be worth a visit for the exceptional sushi, tempura, and soba, prepared in part by Andrew, one of the few *gai-jin* (white man) sushi chefs on the West Coast. Adventurous sushi warriors will want to try the New Zealand roll (mussels, radish, sprouts, avocado, and teriyaki), the unagi papaya, and the marinated salmon roll with cream cheese and spinach. For a traditional shoeless Japanese meal, request the knee-high table perched in the corner.

7 San Jose

45 miles SE of San Francisco

Some may mourn the San Jose of yesterday, a sleepy small town of orchards, crops, and cattle, but those days are long gone. Founded in 1717 and previously dwelling in the shadows of San Francisco, San Jose is now Northern California's largest city. With surveys that declare it one of the safest and sunniest cities in the country and rank it the fifth most popular place to live in America, San Jose is a force to be reckoned with. Today, the prosperity of Silicon Valley has transformed what was once an agricultural backwater into a thriving city of restaurants, shops, a state-of-the-art light-rail system, a sports arena (go Sharks!), and a reputable art scene.

ESSENTIALS

GETTING THERE   BART (☎ 510/465-2278) travels from San Francisco to Fremont in 1¼ hours; you can take a bus from there. **Cal Train** (☎ 800/660-4287 or 408/271-4980) operates frequently from San Francisco and takes about an hour and 25 minutes.

VISITOR INFORMATION   For information, contact the **San Jose Visitors Information & Business Center,** located in the San Jose McEvery Convention Center, 150 W. San Carlos St., San Jose, CA 95113 (☎ **408/977-0900**).

GETTING AROUND   Light Rail (☎ **408/321-2300**) is your best option for getting around. A ticket is good for 2 hours, and stops include Paramount's Great America, the Convention Center, and downtown museums. Or you can use the historic trolleys, which operate in a loop around downtown (in summer only). Tickets can be purchased at Light Rail stations.

MUSEUMS WORTH SEEKING OUT

Children's Discovery Museum. 180 Woz Way. ☎ **408/298-5437.** Admission $6 adults, $5 seniors, $4 children 2 to 18. Tues–Sat 10am–5pm; Sun noon–5pm (also open Mon 10am–5pm in July and Aug).

Here the kids will find more than 150 interactive exhibits, as well as shows and workshops, which explore science, humanities, arts, and technology. ZoomZone consists of science and art activities designed by kids for kids; Bubbalogna, an exhibit that explores the whimsical and scientifically intriguing world of bubbles, draws rave reviews. Smaller kids enjoy dressing up in costumes and playing on the fire truck.

San Jose Historical Museum. 1650 Senter Rd. ☎ **408/287-2290.** www.sjhistory.org. Admission $6 adults, $5 seniors, $4 children 6 to 17, free for children under 6. Mon–Fri 10am–4:30pm; Sat–Sun noon–4:30pm.

Twenty-six original and replica buildings on 25 acres in Kelley Park have been restored to represent life in 1880s San Jose. The usual cast of characters is here—the doctor, the printer, the postmaster—with an occasional local surprise, such as the 1888 Chinese temple and the original Stevens fruit barn.

San Jose Museum of Art. 110 S. Market St. ☎ **408/294-2787** or 408/271-6840. www.sjmusart.org. Admission $7 adults, $4 children 6 to 17 and seniors, free for children under 6. Tues–Sun 10am–5pm; Thurs 10am–8pm.

This museum is collaborating with New York's Whitney Museum for shows that trace the development of 20th-century American art. In 1999, the final exhibition (running through June 11, 2000), "Surrounding: Responses to the American Landscape," will include works by Georgia O'Keefe, Edward Hopper, and Richard Diebenkorn. Other exhibits include "Bill Owens: The Suburban '70s" (January 23, 2000 to April 2, 2000)

On the Way to San Jose:
A Stop at *The Gates of Hell*

If you're heading down the Peninsula from San Francisco to San Jose or points south, you might want to stop at the new **Iris & B. Gerald Cantor Center for Visual Arts,** on the Stanford University campus at Lomita Drive and Museum Way (☎ **650/723-4177**; www.stanford.edu/dept/ccva). The original Stanford Museum of Art, established in 1894 as the largest privately owned museum in the country, shut its doors after the 1989 Loma Prieta earthquake. It reopened in January 1999 after undergoing a 9-year, $36.8-million facelift, which added a stunning new modern wing to the original 19th-century neoclassical structure.

Highlights include the newly enhanced Rodin Sculpture Garden, with *The Gates of Hell* and 19 other pieces; sculpture by Willem de Kooning; pieces from Asia, Africa, Oceania, and the Americas; and contemporary galleries housing works by Richard Diebenkorn, Robert Rauschenberg, Jasper Johns, and others, some of these on long-term loan. One room of Stanford family memorabilia contains the death mask of Leland Junior, whose death of typhoid fever as a teenager inspired Leland Senior and his wife, Jane, to establish a university in his memory.

Hours are Wednesday through Sunday from 11am to 5pm, Thursday until 8pm. Admission is free; call for information on tours. From San Francisco, take either U.S. 101 or I-280 south (the latter is a far more scenic drive); the exits to Stanford will be clearly marked.

After taking in the exhibits, you can enjoy lunch in the museum cafe—which serves soups, sandwiches, salads, hot entrees, and desserts on a terrace overlooking the sculpture gardens—or settle in at a picnic table in one of the nearby grassy, shaded areas. Stock up on gourmet picnic fare at **Whole Foods Market,** 774 Emerson St., in downtown Palo Alto (☎ **650/326-8676**), or **Draeger's,** 1010 University Dr., Menlo Park (☎ **650/688-0688**).

The surrounding campus is perfect for a leisurely post-lunch stroll—especially in spring, when the California poppies and other wildflowers are in full bloom, carpeting everything from the traffic dividers to the Stanford foothills.

—Leslie Shen

and "Innuendo Non Troppo: The Work of Gregory Barsanian" (April 16, 2000 to June 25, 2000). The renovated Historic Wing now includes a cafe, bookstore, and education center.

Rosicrucian Egyptian Museum & Planetarium. 1342 Naglee Ave. ☎ **408/947-3636.** Museum admission $7 adults, $5 seniors, $3.50 children 7 to 15, free for children under 7. Daily 10am–5pm; closed major holidays. Planetarium admission $4 adults, $3 children; call for show times.

The Rosicrucian is associated with an educational organization that traces its origins back to the ancient Egyptians, who strongly believed in the afterlife and reincarnation. On display are human and animal mummies, funerary boats, and canopic jars, as well as jewelry, pottery, and bronze tools. There's also a replica of a noble Egyptian's tomb. *Note:* At press time, the Planetarium was closed for repairs; call for more information.

✪ **Tech Museum of Innovation.** 201 S. Market St., downtown at the corner of Park and Market sts. ☎ **408/294-TECH.** www.thetech.org. Admission $8 adults, $7 seniors 65 and over, $6 children 3 to 12, free for children under 3; additional fee for IMAX shows. Daily 10am–5pm.

The Winchester Mystery House:
A Monument to One Woman's Paranoia

Begun in 1884, the **Winchester Mystery House,** 525 S. Winchester Blvd., at the intersection of I-280 and I-880, San Jose (☎ **408/247-2101**), is the legacy of Sarah L. Winchester, widow of the son of the famous rifle magnate. After the deaths of her husband and baby daughter, Mrs. Winchester consulted with a seer, who proclaimed that the family had been targeted by the evil spirits of those killed with Winchester repeaters, who would only be appeased by perpetual construction on the Winchester mansion. Convinced that she'd live as long as the building continued, the widow used much of her $20-million inheritance to finance the construction, which went on 24 hours a day, 7 days a week, 365 days a year, for 38 years. (Ricki Lake would love to have her as a guest, we're sure.)

As you can probably guess, this is no ordinary home. With 160 rooms, it sprawls across a half-dozen acres. And it's full of disturbing features: a staircase leading nowhere, a Tiffany window with a spiderweb design, and doors that open onto blank walls. There are 13 bathrooms, 13 windows and doors in the old sewing room, 13 palms lining the main driveway, 13 hooks in the seance room, and chandeliers with 13 lights. Such schemes were designed to confound the spirits that seemed to plague the heiress.

Tours of the house and grounds are $13.95 for adults, $10.95 for seniors 65 and over, $7.95 for children 6 to 12, and free for kids 5 and under; a behind-the-scenes tour is also offered for guests over 12. Tours leave about every 20 to 30 minutes. The house is open daily from 9am to 8pm in the summer (winter hours vary; call ahead).

This museum recently relocated into a 132,000-square-foot facility, which allows visitors to grapple with the latest in modern technology. You can create your own virtual roller-coaster ride, survive an earthquake on a giant shake table, operate an underwater ROV (remotely operated vehicle) à la *Titanic,* and play with tons of other cool high-tech stuff. There's also an IMAX Dome Theater, Jet Pack simulator, and Virtual Bobsled ride, the same used to train Olympic competitors.

THEME PARK THRILLS

✪ **Paramount's Great America,** Great America Parkway (off U.S. 101), Santa Clara (☎ **408/988-1776**), provides 100 acres of family entertainment. A pretty cool place to lose your lunch, the park includes such favorites as the *Top Gun* suspended jet coaster, the *Days of Thunder* auto-racing simulator, a 3-acre Nickelodeon Center for children, "Drop Zone" (the world's tallest free-fall ride), and the new Xtreme Skyflyer, which combines skydiving with hang gliding. Be sure to check for concerts and special events. Admission is $32.99 for adults, $21.99 for seniors 60 and over, and $19.50 for children 3 to 6. Parking is $6 per vehicle. Open Saturday and Sunday from 10am to 9pm from March 15 to May 29; daily from 10am to 9pm from June through August; and Saturday and Sunday from 10am to 9pm from August 30 to October 18. (The park closes earlier than 9pm on weekdays, and the schedule is subject to change due to weather, so be sure to call ahead.) From San Francisco, take U.S. 101 south for about 45 miles to the Great America Parkway exit.

WHERE TO STAY

Fairmont. 170 S. Market St., San Jose, CA 95113. ☎ **800/527-4727** or 408/998-1900. Fax 408/287-1648. 541 units. A/C MINIBAR TV TEL. $169–$229 double; $325–$1,500 suite. AE, DC, DISC, JCB, MC, V.

Ideally situated near the Convention Center and the Center of Performing Arts, this hotel is in a landmark building. A popular spot to have afternoon tea or cocktails, the lobby attracts many who are just passing through. The hotel places an emphasis on comfort: The guest rooms offer many modern features such as fax and high-speed modem lines, while other amenities include 24-hour room service, a concierge, laundry/valet service, and a rooftop pool surrounded by tropical foliage. There are three restaurants: Les Saisons for fine French/continental cuisine, a Chinese restaurant, and a coffee shop that's nicely accented with a massive marble soda fountain.

Hotel De Anza. 233 W. Santa Clara St., San Jose, CA 95113. ☎ **800/843-3700** or 408/286-1000. Fax 408/286-0500. www.hoteldeanza.com. 100 units. A/C MINIBAR TV TEL. $225–$294 double; from $375 suite. Special weekend rates available. AE, DC, DISC, MC, V.

Located downtown in a landmark art-deco building, this hotel is small enough to provide personal service. The room decor may reflect a 1930s style, but the amenities are state-of-the-art. There are three phones in each room, including one with data line and fax port, plus voice-mail service. Computers and fax machines are supplied on request. Additional amenities include VCRs and complimentary video rentals, as well as irons and ironing boards. Bathrobes, a hair dryer, a makeup mirror, a TV, and a phone are also available in each bathroom. There's room service, laundry/valet, complimentary shoe-shine, nightly turndown, and a health club with Nautilus machines. Guests can dine in the club lounge or in La Pastaia restaurant, which serves fine Italian cuisine.

WHERE TO DINE

Emile's. 545 S. Second St. ☎ **408/289-1960.** www.emiles.com. Reservations recommended. Main courses $25–$34. AE, DC, DISC, MC, V. Fri 11:30am–2pm; Tues–Sat 6:30–9:30pm. CONTEMPORARY EUROPEAN.

Chef Michael Schibler uses the Bay Area's bounty of local produce to create exceptional contemporary cuisine at Emile's, a San Jose institution for fine dining for the last 25 years. Mirrors, recessed lighting, and large, bold floral arrangements create an elegant atmosphere. To start, try the seared and peppered Sonoma foie gras with seared apples and arugula salad, or Schibler's interesting variation on French onion soup, made with Parmesan and Gruyère cheese. Follow with a roasted pork tenderloin served with toasted pearl couscous, or perhaps the seared salmon with baby artichokes, trumpet mushrooms, and a veal stock reduction. For dessert, go with the warm chocolate truffle cake with raspberry sorbet.

Paolo's. 333 W. San Carlos St. ☎ **408/294-2558.** Reservations recommended. Main courses $13–$28. AE, CB, DC, DISC, MC, V. Mon–Fri 11am–2:30pm; Mon–Sat 5:30–10pm. REGIONAL/NORTHERN ITALIAN.

Paolo's attracts a business crowd at lunchtime and a rather cultured crowd in the evening. The cuisine is refined northern Italian, with innovative flourishes. Among the appetizers, for instance, the beef carpaccio is served with a piquant vegetable sauce. The main dishes might include sea scallops roasted with whole garlic, cherry tomatoes, and thyme, or a classic roasted quail with white raisins, grappa, and natural juices. Desserts also stretch beyond the typical Italian favorites to include a chocolate torte with orange-caramel sauce, or lemon-curd tart with toasted coconut and pistachio nuts. An extensive wine list features more than 600 selections.

6 The Wine Country

by Erika Lenkert

California's Napa and Sonoma valleys are two of the most famous wine-growing regions in the world, and two of our favorite places to visit in the state. The workaday valleys that are a way of life for thousands of vintners are also the ultimate retreat for wine lovers and romantics. Hundreds of wineries are nestled among the vines, and most are open to visitors. But even if you don't want to wine-taste, the fresh country air, beautiful rolling countryside, and world-class restaurants and spas are reason enough to come. If you can, plan on spending more than a day here; you'll need a couple of days just to get to know one of the valleys. No matter how long you stay, you'll probably never get enough of the Wine Country's romantic, indulgent atmosphere.

While Napa and Sonoma are close to each other (about a half-hour drive apart), each is attraction-packed enough that your best bet is to focus on just one of the valleys, especially if your time is limited. We recommend that you read about each below, then decide which one is right for you—unless, of course, you're lucky enough to have time to explore both.

1 Napa Valley

The most obvious distinction between the two valleys is size—Napa Valley dwarfs Sonoma Valley both in population, number of wineries, and sheer volume of tourism (and in summertime, serious traffic). Napa is definitely the more commercial of the two, with dozens more wineries, spas (at far cheaper rates), and a far superior selection of fine restaurants, hotels, and quintessential Wine Country activities like hot-air ballooning, all of which are set amidst rolling, mustard flower–covered hills and vast stretches of vineyards. And if your goal is to really learn about the wonderful world of wine making, world-class wineries such as Sterling and Robert Mondavi offer the most interesting and edifying wine tours in North America, if not the world. The combined attractions make Napa the place to come for the ultimate Wine Country experience.

Napa Valley is relatively condensed. It's just 25 miles long, which means you can venture from one end to the other in less than a half hour (traffic permitting). Conveniently, most of the large wineries—as well as most of the hotels, shops, and restaurants—are located along a single road, Calif. 29, which starts at the mouth of the Napa River,

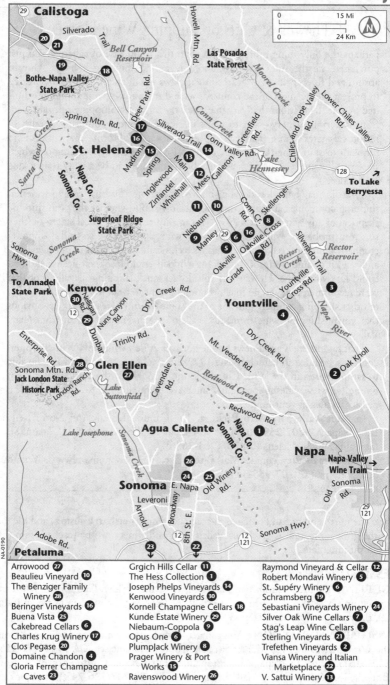

The Wine Country

29 **Calistoga**

Silverado

20
21

19

**Bothe–Napa Valley
State Park**

18

Bell Canyon
Reservoir

Deer Park Rd.

Spring Mtn. Rd.

17

16

St. Helena

15 Madrona

13

12

Spring
Inglewood
Zinfandel
Whitehall

11

**Sugarloaf Ridge
State Park**

10

Niebaum

9
Manley

Howell Mtn. Rd.

**Las Posadas
State Forest**

Conn Creek

Conn Valley Rd.

Greenfield
Rd.

Moorel Creek

Chiles and Pope Valley
Rd.

Lower Chiles Valley
Rd.

Silverado Trail

Conn Valley Rd.

14
Galleron
Mees

Lake
Hennessey

128

**To Lake
Berryessa**

Skellenger

Conn Cr. Rd.

8

16
Oakville Cross

Rd.

7

Rector
Creek

Silverado Trail

Rector
Reservoir

**To Annadel
State Park**

Kenwood

30
29
12

Neligan
Rd.

Nuns Canyon
Rd.

Dunbar

Trinity Rd.

Dry Creek Rd.

Santa Rosa Creek

Napa Co.
Sonoma Co.

Sonoma
Hwy.

Sonoma
Creek

Oakville

5
Oakville
Grade

29

6

Yountville

4

Yountville
Cross Rd.

3

Napa River

2 Oak Knoll

Enterprise Rd.

Sonoma Mtn. Rd.

**Jack London State
Historic Park**

London Ranch
Rd.

28 **Glen Ellen**
27

Lake
Suttonfield

Cavendale
Rd.

Mt. Veeder Rd.

Dry Creek Rd.

Redwood Creek

Redwood Rd.

Lake Josephone

Sonoma Creek

Agua Caliente

Napa Co.
Sonoma Co.

1

Napa

**Napa Valley
Wine Train**

26

24
25

Sonoma
Leveroni

Arnold

Broadway

8th St. E.

E. Napa
Old Winery
Rd.

Sonoma
Old Rd.

29
121

Petaluma

Adobe Rd.

12
8th St. E.

22

12
121

Sonoma Hwy.

NA-0190

Arrowood 27	Grgich Hills Cellar 11	Raymond Vineyard & Cellar 12
Beaulieu Vineyard 10	The Hess Collection 1	Robert Mondavi Winery 5
The Benziger Family Winery 28	Joseph Phelps Vineyards 14	St. Supéry Winery 6
Beringer Vineyards 16	Kenwood Vineyards 30	Schramsberg 19
Buena Vista 25	Kornell Champagne Cellars 18	Sebastiani Vineyards Winery 24
Cakebread Cellars 6	Kunde Estate Winery 29	Silver Oak Wine Cellars 7
Charles Krug Winery 17	Niebaum-Coppola 9	Stag's Leap Wine Cellars 3
Clos Pegase 20	Opus One 6	Sterling Vineyards 21
Domaine Chandon 4	PlumpJack Winery 8	Trefethen Vineyards 2
Gloria Ferrer Champagne Caves 23	Prager Winery & Port Works 22	Viansa Winery and Italian Marketplace 22
	Ravenswood Winery 26	V. Sattui Winery 13

153

The Ins & Outs of Shipping Wine Home

Perhaps the only thing more complex than that $400 case of cabernet you just purchased are the rules and regulations regarding shipping it home. Due to absurd and forever fluctuating "reciprocity laws"—which are supposedly created to protect the business of the country's wine distributors—wine shipping is limited by state regulations that vary in each of the 50 states. Shipping rules also vary from winery to winery—and to make matters even more confusing, the list of reciprocal states (those that have agreements with California that make it no problem to ship wine there) changes almost daily! Hence, depending on which state you live in, sending even a single bottle of wine can be a truly Kafkaesque experience.

To avoid major hassles, do your homework before you buy. Talk to wineries, shipping companies, and the companies below about whether they can ship. Be skeptical of any winery that tells you it can ship to nonreciprocal states—if they run into problems, you'll never get your wine. If you have to find a shipping company yourself, keep in mind that it's technically illegal to box your own wine and send it to a nonreciprocal state; the shippers could lose their license and you could lose your wine. However, if you do get stuck shipping illegally (not that we're recommending you do that), you might want to head to a post office, UPS, or other shipping company outside of the Wine Country area; it's far less obvious that you're shipping wine from, say, Vallejo or San Francisco than from Napa Valley.

That said, there is good news on the horizon. A new company, **WineShopper. com,** is scheduled to launch in late 1999 and if all goes smoothly, you'll be able to sample wines in the Wine Country—and throughout the world, order them online (at www.wineshopper.com), and have them shipped to your home or a nearby retailer in your hometown.

In **Napa Valley,** try **Aero Packing,** 163 Camino Dorado (off North Kelly Rd.), Napa (☎ **707/255-8025**), or **St. Helena Mailing Center,** 1241 Adams St. (at Calif. 29), St. Helena (☎ **707/963-2686**).

In **Sonoma Valley,** contact **Mail Boxes, Etc.,** 19229 Sonoma Hwy. (at Verano St.), Sonoma (☎ **707/935-3438**).

near the north end of San Francisco Bay, and continues north to Calistoga and the top of the growing region. Every Napa Valley town and winery can be reached from this main thoroughfare.

ESSENTIALS

GETTING THERE   From San Francisco, cross the Golden Gate Bridge and continue north on U.S. 101. Turn east on Calif. 37 (toward Vallejo), then north on Calif. 29, the main road through Napa Valley.

VISITOR INFORMATION   You can get Wine Country maps and brochures from the **Wine Institute** at 425 Market St., Suite 1000, San Francisco, CA 94105 (☎ **415/ 512-0151**). Once in Napa Valley, stop first at the **Napa Conference & Visitors Bureau,** 1310 Town Center Mall, Napa, CA 94559 (☎ **707/226-7459**), and pick up the slick *Napa Valley Guide,* or call in advance to order their $10 package, which includes the guide plus a bunch of brochures, a map, a *Four Perfect Days in the Wine Country Itinerary,* and hot-air balloon discount coupons. If you want less to recycle, call **Vintage Publications,** 2929 Conifer Court, Napa, CA 94558 (☎ **800/ 651-8953**), to order just the guide, which costs $6, plus $3 for shipping within the United States. If you don't want to pay the bucks for the official publications, point your browser to **www.napavalley.com/nvcvb.html,** the NVCVB's official site, which has much of the same information for free.

WHEN TO GO   The beauty of the valley is striking any time of the year, but it's most memorable in September and October when the grapes are being pressed and the wineries are in full production. Another great time to come is the spring, when the mustard flowers are in full bloom and the tourist season hasn't yet begun; you'll find less traffic and fewer crowds at the wineries and restaurants, and better deals on hotel rooms. While winter is beautiful and promises the best budget rates, the vines are dormant and rain is likely, so bring appropriate shoes and an umbrella. Summer? Say hello to hot weather and lots of traffic.

TOURING THE VALLEY & WINERIES

The Napa Valley has more than 250 wineries, each offering distinct wines, atmosphere, and experience—so touring the valley takes a little planning. Decide what you're most interested in and chart your path from there. Ask locals which vintners have the type of experience you're looking for. Whatever you do, plan to visit no more than four or five wineries in one day. Above all, take it slowly. The Wine Country should never be rushed; like a great glass of wine, it should be savored.

Most wineries offer tours daily from 10am to 5pm. Tours usually chart the process of wine making from the grafting and harvesting of the vines to the pressing of the grapes and the blending and aging of the wines in oak casks. They vary in length, detail, and formality, depending on the winery. Most tours are free.

The towns and wineries below are organized geographically, from south to north along Calif. 29, from Napa village to Calistoga. We've included a handful of our favorites below; for a complete list of wineries, be sure to pick up one of the free guides to the valley (see "Essentials," above).

THE TOWN OF NAPA

The village of Napa serves as the commercial center of the Wine Country and the gateway to Napa Valley. Most visitors whiz right past it on their way the to the heart of the valley, but if you do veer off the highway, you'll be surprised to discover a small but burgeoning community of 63,000 residents and some of the most affordable accommodations in the area. Unfortunately, any small-town charm Napa may exude is all but squelched by the used-car lots and warehouse superstores surrounding the turn-of-the-century neighborhoods. Just a few minutes north of town, the real Wine Country atmosphere envelops you instantly.

Anyone with an appreciation for art absolutely must visit the ✪ **di Rosa Preserve,** which until recently was closed to the public. Rene and Veronica di Rosa, who have been collecting contemporary American art for more than 40 years, converted 53 acres of prime Wine Country property into a monument to northern California's regional art and nature. Their world-renowned collection features 1,500 works in all media by more than 600 Greater Bay Area artists. Their treasures are displayed practically everywhere, from along the shores of their 30-acre lake to each nook and cranny of their 110-year-old winery-turned-residence, adjoining building, two new galleries, and gardens. With hundreds of surrounding acres of rolling hills protected under the Napa County Land Trust, this place is truly a must-see for both art and nature lovers. It's located at 5200 Sonoma Hwy. (Calif. 121/12)—look for the blue-colored gate. Visits are by appointment only, when a maximum of 25 guests are guided through the

Riding the Napa Valley Wine Train

You don't have to worry about drinking and driving if you tour the Wine Country aboard the **Napa Valley Wine Train,** a rolling restaurant that makes a leisurely 3-hour, 36-mile journey through the vineyards of Napa, Yountville, Oakville, Rutherford, and St. Helena. You'll love riding in the vintage-style cars, each finished with polished mahogany paneling and etched-glass partitions.

During the trip, optional gourmet meals are served complete with all the finery—damask linen, bone china, silver flatware, and etched crystal. The fixed menus consist of three to five courses. In addition to the dining rooms, the train pulls a Wine Tasting Car, a Deli Car, and four 50-passenger lounges. A recent addition to the daytime rides is an optional stop in Yountville and at the Grgich Winery in Rutherford for a tour of the barreling, bottling, and wine-making process, followed by a tasting.

The train departs from the **McKinstry Street Depot,** 1275 McKinstry St. (near First St. and Soscol Ave.), Napa (☎ **800/427-4124** or 707/253-2111; www.winetrain.com). Train fare without meals is $27.50 for daytime rides and evening rides in the Deli Car; fare with meals is $56.50 for brunch, $65 for lunch, and $69.50 for a four-course dinner. A more expensive ride is offered in the 1950s Vista Dome Car, which offers only upstairs seating, has a glass top, and can be ridden only if you opt for the pricier lunch or dinner served within it. Including train fare, dinner is $85 and lunch is $77. Departures are Monday through Friday at 11:30am; Saturday, Sunday, and holidays at 9am and 12:30pm; Wednesday through Friday and Sunday and holidays at 6:30pm; and Saturday and Sunday at 6pm. (The schedule is reduced in January and February.) *Tip:* Sit on the west side for the best views. *Fair warning:* Photos are taken before you board (to be sold to you later); so if you want this moment captured on film, be prepared.

preserve. Each tour lasts 2 to 2½ hours and costs $10 per person. Call ☎ **707/ 226-5991** to make reservations.

SHOPPING   Plan to spend at least an hour if you make a visit to **Red Hen's** co-op collection of antiques. You'll find everything from baseball cards to living-room sets, and prices are remarkably affordable. You can't miss this enormous red barn–style building at 5091 St. Helena Hwy., on Calif. 29 at Oak Knoll Avenue West (☎ **707/ 257-0822**). It's open daily from 10am to 5:30pm.

HITTING THE LINKS   South of downtown Napa, 1.3 miles east of Calif. 29 on Calif. 12, is the **Chardonnay Golf Club** (☎ **707/257-8950**), a challenging 36-hole land-links golf complex with first-class service. There are three nines of similar challenge, all starting at the clubhouse so that you can play the 18 of your choice. You pay just one fee, which makes you a member for the day. Privileges include the use of a golf cart, the practice range (including a bucket of balls), and services usually found only at a private club. Starting times can be reserved up to 2 weeks in advance. Greens fees (including mandatory cart and practice balls) are $60 Monday through Friday, $85 weekends and holidays; at 2pm, fees go down to $45 and $55 respectively, and at 4pm they go to $25.

✪ **The Hess Collection.** 4411 Redwood Rd., Napa. ☎ **707/255-1144.** Daily 10am–4pm. From Calif. 29 north, exit Redwood Rd. west, and follow Redwood Rd. for 6½ miles.

No place in the valley brings together art and wine better than this combination winery/art gallery on the side of Mount Veeder. Swiss art collector Donald Hess acquired the old Christian Brothers Winery in 1978; along with producing wine, he also funded a huge restoration and expansion project to honor wine and the fine arts. The result is a working winery interspersed with gloriously lit rooms that exhibit his truly stunning art collection; the free self-guided tour takes you through these galleries as it introduces you to the wine-making process.

For a $3 fee, you can sample the winery's current cabernet and chardonnay as well as one other featured wine. If you want to take some with you, by-the-bottle prices start at $9.95 for the second-label Hess select brand, while most other selections range from $15 to $35.

Trefethen Vineyards. 1160 Oak Knoll Ave., P.O. Box 2460, Napa, CA 94558. ☎ **707/ 255-7700.** Daily 10am–4:30pm; tours by appointment. From Calif. 29, take Oak Knoll Ave. E.

Listed on the National Register of Historic Places, the vineyard's main building was constructed in 1886 and remains Napa's only wooden, gravity-powered winery. The bucolic brick courtyard is surrounded by oak and cork trees, and free wine samples are distributed in the brick-floored, wood-beamed tasting room. Although Trefethen is one of the valley's oldest wineries, it did not produce its first chardonnay until 1973—but thank goodness it did. Its whites and reds are both award-winners and a pleasure to the palate.

Stag's Leap Wine Cellars. 5766 Silverado Trail, Napa. ☎ **707/944-2020.** Daily 10am–4:30pm. Tours by appointment only. From Calif. 29, go east on Trancas St. or Oak Knoll Ave., then north to the cellars.

Founded in 1972, Stag's Leap shocked the oenological world in 1976 when its 1973 cabernet won first place over French wines in a Parisian blind tasting. For $5 per person, you can be the judge of the winery's current releases, or you can fork over another fiver for one of Stag's Leap's best-known wines, Cabernet Sauvignon Cask 23 (when available). The 1-hour tour runs through everything from the vineyard to production facilities and ends with a tasting; by late 1999, it could also include their new caves, which are currently under construction.

YOUNTVILLE

The town of Yountville, currently with a population of 3,500, was founded by the first white American to settle in the valley, George Calvert Yount. While it lacks the small-town charm of neighboring St. Helena and Calistoga—primarily because it has no rambunctious main street—it does serve as a good base for exploring the valley, and it's home to a handful of excellent wineries, inns, and restaurants, including James Beard's 1997 top dining spot in the nation, the French Laundry.

Domaine Chandon. 1 California Dr. (at Calif. 29), Yountville. ☎ **707/944-2280.** Nov–Dec Wed–Sun 10am–7pm, Mon–Tues 10am–6pm; Jan–Apr 10am–7pm; May–Oct Wed–Sun 10am–8pm. Free tours every hour on the hour 11am–5pm; no reservations necessary.

The valley's most renowned sparkling winery was founded in 1973 by French champagne house Moët et Chandon. The grounds suit Domaine Chandon's reputation perfectly—this is the kind of place where the world's wealthy might stroll the beautifully manicured gardens under the shade of a delicate parasol, stop at the outdoor patio for sips of the famous sparkling wine, then glide into the dining room for a world-class luncheon.

Bubbly is sold by the glass ($8 to $12) and served with complimentary bread and spread. The comprehensive tour of the facilities is worth the time. In addition to a shop, there's a small gallery housing artifacts from Moët et Chandon that depict the history of champagnes.

Hot-Air Ballooning over the Valley

Admit it—floating across lush green pastures in a hot-air balloon is something you've always dreamed of doing. Well, here's your chance, because believe it or not, Napa Valley is the busiest hot-air balloon "flight corridor" in the *world*. Northern California's temperate weather allows for ballooning year-round, and on summer weekends in the valley, it's a rare day when you don't see at least one of the colorful airships floating above the vineyards.

Trips usually depart early in the morning, when the air is cooler and the balloons have better lift. Flight paths vary with the direction and speed of the changing breezes, so "chase" crews on the ground must follow the balloons to their undetermined destinations. Most flights last about an hour and end with a traditional champagne celebration and breakfast. Reservations are required and should be made far in advance. Prices range from $165 to $195 per person for the basic package (which includes shuttle service from your hotel); wedding, wine-tasting, picnic, and lodging packages are also available. For more information or reservations, call Napa's **Bonaventura Balloon Company** (☎ **800/FLY-NAPA**), a highly reputable organization owned and operated by master pilot Joyce Bowen. Another good choice is **Adventures Aloft** (☎ **800/944-4408** or 707/944-4408; www.nvaloft.com), Napa Valley's oldest hot-air-balloon company.

OAKVILLE

Driving farther north on the St. Helena Highway (Calif. 29) brings you to the Oakville Cross Road and the gourmet triangle of the ✪ **Oakville Grocery Café** (see p. 175), **Oakville Grocery Co.** (see p. 176), and **Dean & Deluca** (see p. 176).

Robert Mondavi Winery. 7801 St. Helena Hwy. (Calif. 29), Oakville. ☎ **888/R-MONDAVI** or 707/226-1395. May–Oct daily 9:30am–5:30pm; Nov–Apr daily 9:30am–4:30pm. Reservations recommended for the guided tour (book 1 week in advance, especially for weekend tours).

At Mondavi's magnificent mission-style facility, almost every variable in the winemaking process is controlled by computer (fascinating to watch!). After the tour, you can taste the results in selected current wines, free of charge. You can also taste without taking the tour, but it will cost you: The Rose Garden (an outdoor tasting area open in summer) offers an etched Reidel glass and three wines for $10; tastings in the ToKalon Room go from $3 for a 3-ounce taste to $15 for a rare library wine.

Fridays feature an "Art of Wine and Food" program, which includes a slide presentation on wine history, a tour, and a $65 three-course luncheon with wine pairing; you must reserve in advance. The Vineyard Room usually features an art show; in summer, the winery also hosts some great outdoor jazz concerts. Call to learn about upcoming events. There's no picnicking here.

Opus One. 7900 St. Helena Hwy. (Calif. 29), Oakville. ☎ **707/944-9442.** Daily 10:30am–3:30pm. Tours by appointment only (in high season, book 3 weeks in advance).

A visit to Opus One is a serious and stuffy affair. Robert Mondavi and Baroness Phillipe de Rothschild are to thank for this winery, which caters to one ultra-premium wine offered here for a whopping $25 per 4-ounce taste (and a painful $120 per bottle). Architecture buffs in particular will appreciate the tour, which takes in both the impressive Greco-Roman-meets-20th-century building and the no-holds-barred ultra-high-tech production and aging facilities.

Wine lovers happily fork over the cash for a taste: It's likely to be one of the most memorable reds you'll ever sample. Grab your glass and head to the redwood rooftop deck to enjoy the view.

RUTHERFORD

If you so much as blink after Oakville, you're likely to overlook Rutherford, the next small town that borders on St. Helena. Still, each has its share of spectacular wineries, but you won't see most of them while driving along Calif. 29.

Silver Oak Wine Cellars. 915 Oakville Cross Rd. (at Money Rd.), Oakville. ☎ **800/ 273-8809** or 707/944-8808. Tasting room Mon–Sat 9am–4pm; closed holiday weekends. Tours Mon–Thurs at 1:30pm, by appointment only Mon–Fri at 1:30pm. Tasting fee $5.

Twenty-five years ago, an oil man from Colorado, Ray Duncan, and a former Christian Brothers monk, Justin Meyer, formed a partnership and a mission to create the finest cabernet sauvignon in the world. "We still haven't produced the best bottle of cabernet sauvignon of which Silver Oak is capable," admits Meyer, but this small winery is still the Wine Country's undisputed king of cabernet.

A narrow tree-lined road leads you to the handsome Mediterranean-style winery, where roughly 44,000 cases of 100% varietal cab are produced annually. The elegant tasting room, adorned with redwood panels stripped from old wine tanks and warmed by a wood fire, is quiet and soothing. Tastings and tours are $5, which includes a beautiful German-made burgundy glass. Recently released were a 1994 Alexander Valley and a 1994 Napa Valley. No picnic facilities are available.

۞ PlumpJack Winery. 620 Oakville Cross Rd. (just west of Silverado Trail), Oakville. ☎ **707/945-1220.** Daily 10am–4pm.

If most wineries are like a traditional and refined Brooks Brothers suit, PlumpJack stands out as the Todd Oldham of wine tasting—chic, colorful, a little wild, and popular with a young, hip crowd. This playfully medieval winery is a welcome diversion from the same old, same old. But with Getty bucks behind what was once Villa Mt. Eden Winery, the budget covers far more than just atmosphere: There's some serious wine making going on here, too, and for $5 you can sample the cabernet, chardonnay, and sangiovese—each an impressive product from a winery that's only been open to the public since mid–1997. The few vintages for sale currently range from $15 to $32, and average around $25 per bottle. There are no tours or picnic spots, but this refreshingly stylized and friendly facility will make you want to hang out for awhile nonetheless.

Cakebread Cellars. 8300 St. Helena Hwy. (Calif. 29), Rutherford. ☎ **800/588-0298** or 707/963-5222. Daily 10am–4:30pm. Tasting $5–$10. Tours by appointment only.

This winery's moniker is actually the owners' surname, but it suits the wines produced here, where the focus is on making wine that pairs well with food. They've done such a good job that 70% of their 65,000 annual cases go directly to restaurants, which means only a select few wine drinkers get to take home a bottle. Even if you've found their label in your local wine store, your choice has been limited: Just three varieties are distributed nationally. Here you can sample the sauvignon blanc, chardonnay, cabernet, merlot, zinfandel, pinot noir, the Rubaiyat blend wine, and the dry rose Vin de Porche, which are all made from Napa Valley grapes. Prices range from an affordable $14.25 for a bottle of the 1998 sauvignon blanc to a pricey $53 for the 1996 reserve cab, but the average bottle sells for just a little more than $20. In the tasting room, a large barnlike space, the hospitable hosts pour either a $5 or $10 sampling; both include a keepsake wineglass.

St. Supéry Winery. 8440 St. Helena Hwy. (Calif. 29), Rutherford. ☎ **800/942-0809** or 707/963-4507. Daily 9:30am–4:30pm.

The outside may look like a modern corporate office building, but inside you'll find a functional and welcoming winery that encourages first-time wine tasters to learn more about oenology. On the self-guided tour, you can wander through the demonstration vineyard and learn about growing techniques. Inside, kids gravitate toward "Smella Vision," an interactive display that teaches you how to identify different wine ingredients. Adjoining is the Atkinson House, which chronicles more than 100 years of wine-making history. For $3 you'll get lifetime tasting privileges, and though they probably won't be pouring their ever-popular Moscato dessert wine, the sauvignon blanc and chardonnay flow freely. Even the prices make visitors feel at home: Many bottles go for around $10, although the 1995 Meritage cabernet will set you back $40.

Niebaum-Coppola. 1991 St. Helena Hwy. (Calif. 29), Rutherford. ☎ **707/968-1100.** Daily 10am–5pm. Tours offered daily at 11am and 2pm.

Hollywood meets Napa Valley at Francis Ford Coppola's historic winery (pronounced *nee*-bomb *coh*-pa-la), previously Inglenook Vineyards. Coppola bought and restored the beautiful 1880s ivy-draped stone winery and surrounding property to its historic dimensions, gilding it with the glitz and glamour you'd expect from Tinseltown in the process. On display are Academy Awards and memorabilia from his movies.

In spite of all the Hollywood hullabaloo, wine is not forgotten. Available for tasting are a Rubicon (a blend of estate-grown cabernet, cabernet franc, and merlot, aged for more than 5 years), cabernet franc, merlot, chardonnay, zinfandel, and others, all made from organically grown grapes and ranging from around $12 to more than $80. There's also a wide variety of expensive and affordable gift items. The steep $7.50-per-person tasting fee might make you wonder whether a movie is included in the price—it's not (but you'll at least get to keep the souvenir glass). And at $20 a pop for the château and garden tour (which includes tastings in their private cellars), you've gotta wonder whether you're *funding* his next film. But the grounds are indeed spectacular, and the 1½-hour journey includes private tasting and glass.

Regardless, do visit the grounds—they're absolutely stunning, it costs nothing to stroll, and you're welcome to picnic at any of the designated garden sites.

Beaulieu Vineyard. 1960 S. St. Helena Hwy. (Calif. 29), Rutherford. ☎ **707/963-2411.** Daily 10am–5pm. Tours daily 11am–4pm; in summer, roughly every half hour; call for winter schedule.

Bordeaux native Georges de Latour founded the third-oldest continuously operating winery in Napa Valley in 1900—and, with the help of legendary oenologist André Tchelistcheff, produced world-class, award-winning wines that have been served by every president of the United States since Franklin D. Roosevelt. The brick-and-redwood tasting room isn't much to look at, but with Beaulieu's (pronounced *bowl*-you) stellar reputation, they have no need to impress visually. They do, however, offer a complimentary glass of chardonnay the minute you walk through the door as well as a variety of bottles under $15. The Private Reserve Tasting Room offers a "flight" of reserve wines to taste for $18—but if you want to take a bottle to go, it may cost as much as $50. A free tour explains the wine-making process and the vineyard's history. No reservations are necessary.

Grgich Hills Cellar. 1829 St. Helena Hwy. (Calif. 29, north of Rutherford Cross Rd.), Rutherford. ☎ **707/963-2784.** Daily 9:30am–4:30pm. Free tours by appointment only Mon–Fri 11am and 2pm; Sat–Sun 11am and 1:30pm.

Yugoslavian émigré Miljenko (Mike) Grgich made his presence known to the world when his Château Montelena chardonnay bested the top French white burgundies at the famous 1976 Paris tasting. Since then, this master vintner has teamed up with Austin Hills (of the Hills Brothers coffee fortune) and started this extremely successful and respected winery in Rutherford.

The ivy-covered stucco building isn't much to behold, and the tasting room is even less appealing, but people don't come here for the scenery: As you might expect, Grgich's (pronounced *grr*-gitch) chardonnays are legendary—and priced accordingly. The smart buys, however, are Grgich's outstanding zinfandel and cabernet sauvignon, which are very reasonably priced at around $18 and $25, respectively. The winery also produces a fantastic fumé blanc for as little as $15 a bottle. Before you leave, be sure to poke your head into the barrel-aging room and inhale the divine aroma. Tastings cost $3 on weekends, which includes the glass, and are free on weekdays. No picnic facilities are available.

St. Helena

This quiet, attractive little town, located 17 miles north of Napa on Calif. 29, is home to a slew of beautiful old homes as well as first-rate restaurants and accommodations. The former Seventh Day Adventist village manages to maintain a pseudo–Old West feel while simultaneously catering to upscale shoppers with deep pockets— hence ✪ **Vanderbilt and Company,** 1429 Main St., between Adams and Pine streets (☎ 707/963-1010), purveyor of gorgeous cookware and fine housewares; open daily from 9:30am to 5:30pm.

Shopaholics won't be able to avoid at least one sharp turn off Calif. 29 for a stop at the **St. Helena Premium Outlets,** located 2 miles north of downtown St. Helena (☎ 707/963-7282), whose stores include Donna Karan, Coach, Movado, London Fog, and more; open daily from 10am to 6pm.

One last favorite stop: **Napa Valley Olive Oil Manufacturing Company,** 835 Charter Oak Rd., at the end of the road behind Tra Vigne restaurant (☎ 707/ 963-4173). This tiny market presses and bottles its own oils and sells them at a fraction of the price you'll pay elsewhere. They also have an extensive selection of Italian cooking ingredients, imported snacks, and excellent deals on exotic mushrooms.

If you'd like to go **bicycling,** the quieter northern end of the valley is an ideal place to rent a bike and ride the Silverado Trail. **St. Helena Cyclery,** 1156 Main St. (☎ 707/963-7736), rents bikes for $7 per hour or $25 a day, including rear rack and picnic bag.

Raymond Vineyard & Cellar. 849 Zinfandel Lane (off Calif. 29 or the Silverado Trail), St. Helena. ☎ **800/525-2659** or 707/963-3141. www.raymondwine.com. Daily 10am–4pm. Tours by appointment only.

As fourth-generation vintners from Napa Valley and relations of the Beringers, brothers Walter and Roy Raymond have had plenty of time to develop terrific wines— and an excellent wine-tasting experience. Passing the heavy-hanging grapes on the way to the tasting room makes you feel you're really in the thick of things before you even get in the door. The spacious, warm room, complete with dining table and chairs, is a perfect setting for sampling the four tiers of wines, most of which are free for the tasting and well priced to appeal to all levels of wine drinkers. The Amber Hill label starts at $10 a bottle for the chardonnay and $11 for the cab; the reserves are priced in the mid-teens, while the "Generations" cab costs $50. Private reserve tastings cost $2.50. Sorry, there are no picnic facilities.

✪ **V. Sattui Winery.** 1111 White Lane (at Calif. 29), St. Helena. ☎ **707/963-7774.** www. vsattui.com. Winter daily 9am–5pm; summer daily 9am–6pm.

At this combination winery and enormous gourmet deli (pronounced vee sa-*too*-ee), you can fill up on wine, pâté, and cheese samples without ever reaching for your pocketbook. The gourmet store stocks more than 200 cheeses, sandwich meats, breads, exotic salads, and delicious desserts such as a white-chocolate cheesecake.

Meanwhile, the long wine bar in the back offers everything from chardonnay, sauvignon blanc, Riesling, cabernet, and zinfandel to a tasty Madeira and a muscat dessert wine. Their wines aren't distributed, so if you taste something you simply must have, buy it. (If you buy a case, ask to talk with a manager, who'll give you access to the less crowded, more exclusive private tasting room.) Wine prices start around $9, with many in the $13 range; reserves top out at around $95. V. Sattui's expansive, lively, and grassy picnic facilities make this a favorite for families. *Note:* To use the facilities, food and wine must be purchased here.

✪ **Joseph Phelps Vineyards.** 200 Taplin Rd. (off the Silverado Trail), P.O. Box 1031, St. Helena. ☎ **800/707-5789.** Mon–Sat 10am–5pm; Sun 10am–4pm. Tours and tastings by appointment only.

Joseph Phelps is a favorite stop for serious wine lovers. The winery was founded in 1973 and has since become a major player in both the region and the worldwide wine market. Phelps himself is attributed with a long list of valley firsts, including launching the syrah varietal in the valley and extending the 1970s Berkeley food revolution (led by Alice Waters) up to the Wine Country via his store, the Oakville Grocery (see p. 176). The intimate, comprehensive tour and knockout tasting are only available via reservation, and the location—a quick and unmarked turn off the Silverado Trail in Spring Valley—makes it impossible to find unless you're looking for it.

Those in the know come to this modern, state-of-the-art winery and find an air of seriousness that hangs heavier than harvest grapes. Fortunately, the mood lightens as the well-educated tour guide explains the details of what you're tasting while pouring samples of five to six wines, which may include Riesling, sauvignon blanc, gewürztraminer, syrah, merlot, zin, and cab. (Unfortunately, some wines are so popular that they sell out quickly; come late in the season and you may not be able to taste or buy them.) The three excellently located picnic tables, on the terrace overlooking the valley, are available by reservation.

✪ **Prager Winery & Port Works.** 1281 Lewelling Lane (just west of Calif. 29, behind Sutter Home), St. Helena. ☎ **800/969-PORT** or 707/963-7678. Daily 10:30am– 4:30pm.

If you want a real down-home, off-the-beaten-track experience, Prager's can't be beat. Turn the corner from Sutter Home and roll into the small gravel parking lot. Pull open the creaky old wooden door, pass the oak barrels, and you'll quickly come upon the clapboard tasting room. Most days, your host will be Jim Prager himself, who's a sort of modern-day Santa Claus in both looks and demeanor. But you won't have to sit on his lap for your wish to come true: Just fork over $5 (refundable with purchase) and he'll pour you samples of his delicious $25 Madeline dessert wine, a late-harvest Johannisberg Riesling, the recently released 10-year-old port (which costs close to $50 per bottle), and a few other yummy selections like chardonnay and cab, which retail in the mid-$30s. Also available is Prager Chocolate Drizzle, a chocolate liqueur that tops ice creams and other desserts.

Beringer Vineyards. 2000 Main St. (Calif. 29), St. Helena. ☎ **707/963-7115.** Off-season daily 9:30am–5pm (last tour 4pm); summer 9:30am–6pm (last tour 5pm). Free 45-min. tours offered every hour between 9:30am–4pm; no reservations necessary.

Follow the line of cars just north of St. Helena's business district to Beringer Vineyards, where everyone stops at the remarkable Rhine House to taste wine and view the hand-dug tunnels carved out of the mountainside. Founded in 1876 by brothers Jacob and Frederick, this is the oldest continuously operating winery in the Napa Valley—it was open even during Prohibition, when Beringer kept afloat by making "sacramental" wines. While their white zinfandel is still the winery's most popular nationwide seller, their reserve chardonnay is regularly high-ranked among top California wines. Free tastings of current vintages are conducted in the upstairs gift shop, where there's also a large selection of bottles for less than $20. Reserve wines are available in the Rhine House for a fee of $2 to $6 per taste.

Charles Krug Winery. 2800 St. Helena Hwy. (just north of the tunnel of trees at the northern end of St. Helena), St. Helena. ☎ **707/963-5057.** Daily 10:30am–5:30pm. Tours daily at 11:30am, 1:30, and 3:30pm.

Founded in 1861, Krug was the first winery built in the valley and is today owned by the family of Peter Mondavi (yes, Robert is his brother). It's worth paying your respects here with a $3 tour, which takes just under an hour and encompasses a walk through the historical redwood Italianate wine cellar, built in 1874, as well as the vineyards, where you'll learn more about grapes and varietals. The tour ends with a tasting in the retail center. But you don't have to tour to taste: Just stop by and fork over $3 to sip current releases, $5 to sample reserves; you'll also get a souvenir glass. On the grounds are picnic facilities with umbrella-shaded tables overlooking vineyards or the historic wine cellar.

CALISTOGA

The last tourist town in Napa Valley was named by Sam Brannan, entrepreneur extraordinaire and California's first millionaire. After making a bundle supplying miners during the gold rush, he went on to take advantage of the natural geothermal springs at the north end of the Napa Valley by building a hotel and spa here in 1859. Flubbing up a speech in which he compared this natural California wonder to New York State's Saratoga Springs resort, he serendipitously coined the name "Calistoga," and it stuck. Today, this small, simple resort town with 4,713 residents and an old-time main street (no building along the 6-block stretch is more than two stories high) is popular with city folk who come here to unwind. Calistoga is a great place to relax and indulge in mineral waters, mud baths, Jacuzzis, massages, and, of course, wine. The vibe is more casual—and a little more groovy—than you'll find in neighboring towns to the south.

NATURAL WONDERS   Old Faithful Geyser of California, 1299 Tubbs Lane (☎ 707/942-6463), is one of only three "old faithful" geysers in the world. It's been blowing off steam at regular intervals for as long as anyone can remember. The 350°F water spews out to a height of about 60 feet every 40 minutes, day and night (varying with natural influences such as barometric pressure, the moon, tides, and tectonic stresses). The performance lasts about a minute, and you can watch the show as many times as you wish. Bring along a picnic lunch to munch on between spews. An exhibit hall, gift shop, and snack bar are open every day. Admission is $6 for adults, $5 for seniors, $2 for children 6 to 12, and free for children under 6. Open daily from 9am to 6pm (to 5pm in winter). To get here, follow the signs from downtown Calistoga; it's between Calif. 29 and Calif. 128.

You won't see thousands of trees turned into stone, but you'll still find many interesting petrified specimens at the **Petrified Forest,** 4100 Petrified Forest Rd. (☎ 707/942-6667). Volcanic ash blanketed this area after the eruption of Mount St. Helena 3 million years ago. As a result, you'll find redwoods that have turned to rock through the slow infiltration of silicas and other minerals, as well as petrified seashells, clams, and marine life indicating that water covered this area even before the redwood forest. Admission is $4 for adults, $3 for seniors and children 11 to 17, $1 for children 4 to 11, and free for children under 4. Open daily from 10am to 5:30pm (to 4:30pm in winter). Heading north from Calistoga on Calif. 128, turn left onto Petrified Forest Road, just past Lincoln Street.

BICYCLING Cycling enthusiasts can rent bikes from **Getaway Adventures BHK** (Biking, Hiking, and Kayaking), 1117 Lincoln Ave. (☎ **800/499-BIKE** or 707/ 942-0332; www.getawayadventures.com). Full-day tours cost $89 and include lunch and a visit to four or five wineries; downhill cruises ($49) are available for people who hate to pedal. On weekdays, they'll even deliver bikes to you.

HORSEBACK RIDING If you like horses and venturing through cool, misty forests, then $40 will seem like a bargain for a 1½-hour ride with a friendly tour guide from **Napa Valley Trail Rides** (☎ **707/996-8566;** www.thegridnet/trailrides). After you've been saddled and schooled in the basics of horse handling at the stable, you'll be led on a leisurely stroll (with the occasional trot thrown in for excitement) through beautiful Bothe–Napa Valley State Park, located off Calif. 29 near Calistoga. Also offered are a Western Barbecue Ride, Sunset Ride, Full Moon Ride, and Gourmet Boxed Lunch Ride & Winery Tour. We've taken the trip ourselves and loved every minute of it—sore butts and all.

✪ **Kornell Champagne Cellars.** 1091 Larkmead Lane (just off the Silverado Trail), Calistoga. ☎ **707/942-0859.** Daily 10am–5pm.

Kornell's wine dudes—Dennis, Bob, and Rich—will do practically anything to maintain their self-proclaimed reputation as the "friendliest winery in the valley." They'll serve you all the bubbly you want (four to six varieties: brut, blanc de blanc, blanc de noir, and extra-dry reserve, all ranging from $17 to $23 a bottle). They guarantee that you'll never wait more than 10 minutes to take the 20-minute tour of the oldest champagne cellar in the region, and even offer up a great story about Marie Antoinette's champagne-glass design.

The tasting room is casual-modern, but the stone cellar (listed on the National Register of Historic Places) captures the essence of the Wine Country's history. Meander into the Back Room, where chardonnay, zinfandel, and cabernet are poured. Behind the tasting room is a choice picnic area, situated under the oaks and overlooking the vineyards.

✪ **Schramsberg.** 1400 Schramsberg Rd. (off Calif. 29), Calistoga. ☎ **707/942-4558.** Daily 10am–4pm. Tours and tastings by appointment only.

This 200-acre champagne estate, a landmark once frequented by Robert Louis Stevenson, has a wonderful old-world feel and is one of our all-time favorite places to explore. Schramsberg is the label that presidents serve when toasting dignitaries from around the globe, and there's plenty of historic memorabilia in the front room to prove it. But the real mystique begins when you enter the champagne caves, which wind 2½ miles (the longest in North America, they say) and were partly hand-carved by Chinese laborers in the 1800s. The caves have an authentic Tom Sawyer ambiance, complete with dangling cobwebs and seemingly endless passageways; you can't help but feel you're on an adventure. The comprehensive, unintimidating tour ends in a charming tasting room, where you'll sit around a big table and sample several surprisingly varied selections of bubbly. Tasting prices are a bit dear at $7.50 per person, but it's money well spent. Note, however, that tastings are only offered to those who take the free tour, and you must reserve a spot in advance.

✪ **Clos Pegase.** 1060 Dunaweal Lane (off Calif. 29 or the Silverado Trail), Calistoga. ☎ **707/942-4981.** Daily 10:30am–5pm. Tours daily at 11am and 2pm.

Renowned architect Michael Graves designed this incredible oasis, which integrates art, 20,000 square feet of aging caves, and a luxurious hilltop private home on its 450 acres. Viewing the art here is as much the point as tasting the wines—which, by the way, don't come cheap: Prices range from $18.50 for the 1996 Mitsuko's chardonnay to as much

---

Find the New You—In a Calistoga Mud Bath

The one thing you should do while you're in Calistoga is what people have been doing here for the last 150 years: Take a mud bath. The natural baths are composed of local volcanic ash, imported peat, and naturally boiling mineral hot-springs water, all mulled together to produce a thick mud that simmers at a temperature of about 104°F. Follow your soak in the mud with a warm mineral-water shower, a whirlpool bath, a visit to the steam room, and a relaxing blanket-wrap. The outcome: a rejuvenated, revitalized, squeaky-clean new you.

Indulge yourself at any of these Calistoga spas: **Dr. Wilkinson's Hot Springs,** 1507 Lincoln Ave. (☎ 707/942-4102); **Lincoln Avenue Spa,** 1339 Lincoln Ave. (☎ 707/942-5296); **Golden Haven Hot Springs Spa,** 1713 Lake St. (☎ 707/942-6793); **Calistoga Spa Hot Springs,** 1006 Washington St. (☎ 707/942-6269); **Calistoga Village Inn & Spa,** 1880 Lincoln Ave. (☎ 707/942-0991); **Eurospa & Inn,** 1202 Pine St. (☎ 707/942-6829); **Indian Springs Resort,** 1712 Lincoln Ave. (☎ 707/942-4913); **Lavender Hill Spa,** 1015 Foothill Blvd. (☎ 800/528-4772); **Mount View Spa,** 1457 Lincoln Ave. (☎ 707/942-5789); **Nance's Hot Springs,** 1614 Lincoln Ave. (☎ 707/942-6211); and the **Roman Spa Motel,** 1300 Washington St. (☎ 707/942-4441).

---

as $50 for the 1995 Hommage Artist Series Reserve, an extremely limited blend of the winery's finest lots of cabernet sauvignon and merlot. Tasting all the current releases will cost $2.50, and reserves are $2 each. The grounds at Clos Pegase (pronounced *clo* pay-*goss*) feature an impressive sculpture garden as well as scenic picnic spots.

Sterling Vineyards. 1111 Dunaweal Lane (off Calif. 29, just south of Calistoga), Calistoga. ☎ **800/977-3242** or 707/942-3345. Daily 10:30am–4:30pm.

No, you don't need climbing shoes to reach this dazzling white Mediterranean-style winery, perched 300 feet up on a rocky knoll. Just hand over $6 and you'll arrive via aerial tram, which offers dazzling bucolic views along the way. Once on land, follow the self-guided tour (the most comprehensive in the entire Wine Country) of the wine-making process. Currently owned by the Seagram company, the winery produces more than 200,000 cases per year. Samples at the panoramic tasting room are included in the tram fare. If you can find a bottle of their 1995 Napa Valley chardonnay (currently going for about $14), buy it—it's already garnered a septuplet of awards.

WHERE TO STAY

Accommodations here run the gamut—from motels and B&Bs to world-class luxury retreats—and all are easily accessible from the main highway. While we recommend shacking up in the more romantically pastoral areas such as St. Helena, there's no question you're going to find better deals in the towns of Napa or laid-back Calistoga.

Keep in mind that during the high season—between June and November—most hotels charge peak rates and sell out completely on weekends; many have a 2-night minimum. If you need help organizing your Wine Country vacation, contact one of the following companies: **Accommodation Referral Bed & Breakfast Exchange** (☎ 800/240-8466, 800/499-8466 in Calif., or 707/963-8466), which also represents hotels and inns; **Bed & Breakfast Inns of Napa Valley** (☎ 707/944-4444), an association of 26 Napa Valley B&Bs that provides inn descriptions and makes reservations; or **Napa Valley Reservations Unlimited** (☎ 800/251-NAPA or 707/252-1985), which is also a source for everything from hot-air balloon and glider rides to wine-tasting tours by limousine.

VERY EXPENSIVE

✪ **Auberge du Soleil.** 180 Rutherford Hill Rd., Rutherford, CA 94573. ☎ **707/963-1211.** Fax 707/963-8764. 50 units. A/C MINIBAR TV TEL. $350–$525 double; $750–$1,000 suite; $2,000–$2,500 cottage suite. Rates discounted Dec–Mar. AE, CB, DC, DISC, MC, V. From Rutherford, turn right on Calif. 128 and go 3 miles to the Silverado Trail; turn left and head north about 200 yd. to Rutherford Hill Rd.; turn right.

This spectacular Relais & Châteaux member is quiet, indulgent, and luxuriously romantic. The Mediterranean-style rooms are large enough to get lost in—and you might want to once you discover all the amenities. The bathtub alone—an enormous hot tub with a skylight overhead—will entice you to grab a glass of California red and settle in for a while. The wood-burning fireplace, cushy furniture, stereo with CD player, VCR, fresh flowers, original art, terra-cotta floors, and natural wood and leather furnishings round out the perfect romantic retreat. Each sun-washed private deck has views of the valley that are nothing less than spectacular. All guests have access to a celestial swimming pool and a tiny exercise room, plus an array of spa services. Those with money to burn should opt for the $2,000-per-night cottage suite. This is one of the best places we've ever stayed.

Dining: Another ethereal experience. See "Where to Dine," below.

Amenities: Concierge, newspaper delivery, valet parking, 24-hour room service, twice-daily maid service, laundry/valet, complimentary shoeshine, outdoor pool with sundeck, massage rooms, three tennis courts, exercise room, beauty salon. A nature trail with picnic areas and sculpture crisscrosses the property.

Harvest Inn. 1 Main St., St. Helena, CA 94574. ☎ **800/950-8466** or 707/963-9463. 54 units. A/C TV TEL. Dec–Apr $149–$189 double; $349–$399 suite. May–Nov $249–$289 double; $449–$599 suite. AE, DC, DISC, MC, V.

If you like your accommodations loaded with 20th-century luxuries yet reminiscent of Old England, you'll like the Harvest Inn. Ornate brick walkways lead through beautifully landscaped grounds to this Tudor-style inn. Each of the immaculate rooms—with names like "The Earl of Ecstasy" and "Camelot"—is outfitted in Tudor style with dark oak beds and dressers, black leather chairs, and antique furnishings; most have brick fireplaces, wet bars, and fridges. Facilities include a wine bar, heated pools, and outdoor spas. *A word of caution:* This is a large, big-business hotel, and though it does its best to set a charming stage, you can't help but notice the corporate vibe and accoutrements permeating the place.

The Inn at Southbridge. 1020 Main St., St. Helena, CA 94574. ☎ 800/520-6800 or 707/967-9400. Fax 707/967-9486. MINIBAR TV TEL. Nov–Mar $225–$425 double; Mar to mid-June $245–$475 double; mid-June to Nov $260–$490 double. AE, CB, DC, JCB, MC, V.

Eschewing the lace-and-latticework theme that plagues most Wine Country inns, the Inn at Southbridge takes an unswervingly modern, pragmatic approach to accommodating its guests. Instead of stuffed teddy bears, you'll find terry-cloth robes, fireplaces, bathroom skylights, down comforters, private balconies, and a host of other little luxuries. The decor is upscale Pottery Barn—trendy, and for some a welcome departure from quaintly traditional hotel-style stuff. Functional touches include voice mail and fax modems. One notable bummer—the hotel is located along the highway, so it lacks that reclusive feel many other upscale hotels offer.

Dining: On the premises is Tomatina, owned and run by the owners of Tra Vigne, an Italian restaurant conveniently located next door (see "Where to Dine," below).

Amenities: Concierge, limited room service, dry cleaning, laundry, newspaper delivery, in-room massage, twice-daily maid service, baby-sitting, secretarial services, complimentary refreshments in lobby. The spa offers access to an excellent gym (including classes), steam room, sauna, outdoor heated pool, Jacuzzi, and spa treatments.

✪ **Meadowood Napa Valley.** 900 Meadowood Lane, St. Helena, CA 94574. ☎ **800/ 458-8080** or 707/963-3646. Fax 707/963-3532. 85 units. A/C MINIBAR TV TEL. $395–$670 double; 1-bedroom lodge from $645; 2-bedroom from $1,010; 3-bedroom from $1,410; 4-bedroom from $1,810. Ask about promotional offers and off-season rates. 2-night minimum on weekends. AE, DISC, DC, MC, V.

Less reclusive than Auberge du Soleil, Meadowood is the summer camp for wealthy grown-ups. The resort, tucked away on 250 acres of pristine mountainside amidst a forest of madrone and oak trees, is quiet and exclusive enough to make you forget that busy wineries are just 10 minutes away. Rooms, furnished with American country classics, have beamed ceilings, private patios, stone fireplaces, and wilderness views; many are individual suite-lodges that are so far removed from the common areas that you must drive to get to them (lazier folks can opt for more centrally located accommodations). You can spend your days playing golf, tennis, or croquet; lounging around the pools or spa; or hiking the surrounding areas. Those who actually want to leave the property to do some wine tasting can check in with John Thoreen, the hotel's wine tutor, whose sole purpose is to help guests better understand and enjoy Napa Valley wines.

Amenities: Concierge, room service, dry cleaning and laundry, full-service spa, newspaper delivery, secretarial service, baby-sitting, 9-hole golf course, croquet lawns, two outdoor pools with sundeck, massage rooms, seven tennis courts, exercise room, hiking trails, executive conference center.

MODERATE

✪ **Cedar Gables Inn.** 486 Coombs St., Napa, CA 94559. ☎ **800/309-7969** or 707/ 224-7969. Fax 707/224-4838. www.CedarGablesInn.com. 6 units. $139–$199 double ($10 less in winter). Rates include breakfast. AE, DISC, MC, V. From Calif. 29 north, exit onto First St. and follow signs to downtown; turn right onto Jefferson St.; go 2 blocks and turn left on Oak St.

Innkeepers Margaret and Craig Snasdell have developed quite a following with their cozy, romantic B&B in Old Town Napa. The Victorian was built in 1892, and rooms reflect the era with rich tapestries and stunning gilded antiques. Five rooms have fireplaces; four have whirlpool tubs; and all feature queen-size brass, wooden, or iron beds. Guests meet each evening in front of the roaring fireplace in the family room for complimentary wine and cheese. At other times, it's a perfect place to cuddle up and watch the large-screen TV.

✪ **Cottage Grove Inn.** 1711 Lincoln Ave., Calistoga, CA 94515. ☎ **800/799-2284** or 707/942-8400. Fax 707/942-2653. 16 cottages. A/C TV TEL. $195–$245 double. Rates include continental breakfast and evening wine and cheese. AE, DC, DISC, MC, V.

Standing in two parallel rows at the end of the main strip in Calistoga are the perfect couples' retreats—brand-spanking-new cottages that, although located on a residential street, seem well removed from the action once you've stepped across the threshold. Each compact guest house comes complete with a wood-burning fireplace, homey furnishings (perfect for curling up in front of the fire), cozy quilts, and an enormous bathroom with a skylight and a deep, two-person Jacuzzi tub, plus such niceties as gourmet coffee, stereo with CD player, VCR (a video library is on-site), wet bar, and fridge. Smokers beware—it's not allowed inside, but you can puff all you want on the small front porch. Several major spas are within walking distance. This is our top pick if you want to do the Calistoga spa scene in comfort and style. One cabin is accessible for travelers with disabilities.

✪ **Maison Fleurie.** 6529 Yount St. (between Finnel Rd. and Humboldt St.), Yountville, CA 94599. ☎ **800/788-0369** or 707/944-2056. 13 units. A/C TV TEL. $110–$245 double. Rates include full breakfast and afternoon hors d'oeuvres. AE, DC, MC, V.

Maison Fleurie is one of the prettiest hotels in the Wine Country, a trio of beautiful 1873 brick-and-fieldstone buildings overlaid with ivy. Seven rooms are located in the main house—a charming Provençal replica complete with thick brick walls, terra-cotta tile, and paned windows—while the remaining rooms are split between the old bakery building and the carriage house. All have private bathrooms, and some feature private balconies, patios, sitting areas, Jacuzzis, and fireplaces. Breakfast is served in the quaint little dining room; afterwards, you're welcome to wander the landscaped grounds, use the pool or outdoor spa, or borrow a mountain bike (free of charge) to ride around town, returning in time for afternoon hors d'oeuvres. It's truly impossible not to enjoy your stay at Maison Fleurie.

Napa Valley Lodge. 2230 Madison St., Yountville, CA 94599. ☎ **800/368-2468** or 707/944-2468. Fax 707/944-9362. www.woodsidehotels.com. 55 units. A/C MINIBAR TV TEL. $202–$352 double. Rates include champagne breakfast buffet. AE, CB, DC, DISC, MC, V.

Many frequent visitors compare this contemporary hotel to the town's popular Vintage Inn, noting that it's even more personable and accommodating. The lodge is just off Calif. 29, though they do a good job of disguising it. Facilities include a pool, redwood sauna, and small exercise room; the newly upgraded guest rooms are large, ultra-clean, and better appointed than many in the area. Many have vaulted ceilings and 33 have fireplaces. All come with a king- or queen-size bed, wicker furnishings, coffeemaker, robes, and either a private balcony or a patio. In 1997, all the bathrooms were also upgraded to include a vanity area and nice tile work. The cheapest rooms are at ground level; these are smaller and get less sunlight than those on the second floor. Extras include concierge, on-demand video, afternoon tea and cookies in the lobby, Friday-evening wine tasting in the library, and a full champagne breakfast—with all this, it's no wonder AAA gave the Napa Valley Lodge the four-diamond award for excellence. Ask about winter discounts—they can be as much as 30%.

Rancho Caymus. 1140 Rutherford Rd. (P.O. Box 78), Rutherford, CA 94573. ☎ **800/ 845-1777** or 707/963-1777. Fax 707/963-5387. 26 suites. A/C MINIBAR TV TEL. $175–$205 double; from $265 Master Suite; $355 2-bedroom suite. Rates include continental breakfast. AE, DC, MC, V. From Calif. 29 north, turn right onto Rutherford Rd./Calif. 128 E.; the hotel is ahead on your left.

This Spanish-style hacienda, with two floors opening onto wisteria-covered balconies, was the creation of sculptor Mary Tilden Morton (of Morton Salt). Morton wanted each room in the hacienda to be a work of art, so she hired the most skilled crafts-people of her day. She designed the adobe fireplaces herself, and wandered through Mexico and South America purchasing artifacts for the property.

   Guest rooms are situated around a whimsical garden courtyard with an enormous outdoor fireplace. The mix-and-match interior decor is on the funky side, with overly varnished dark-wood furnishings and braided rugs. The inn is cozy, however, and rooms are decent-size, split-level suites with queen beds. Other amenities include wet bars, sofa beds in the sitting areas, and small private patios. Most of the suites have fireplaces, and five have kitchenettes and whirlpool tubs. Breakfast, which includes fresh fruit, granola, orange juice, and breads, is served in the inn's dining room.

   L.A.'s celebrity chef Ken Frank opened La Toque, a 50-seat in-house restaurant where a five-course fixed-price menu is offered Wednesday through Sunday (with lunch on Sunday as well); it might feature truffled egg "barely scrambled and back in its shell," seared Muscovy foie gras with apples and balsamic vinegar, and roasted monkfish with lentils du puy and Rutherford red wine.

Wine Country Inn. 1152 Lodi Lane, St. Helena, CA 94574. ☎ **707/963-7077.** Fax 707/963-9018. E-mail: romance@winecountryinn.com. 24 units, all with bathroom (12 with shower only). A/C TEL. $148–$275 double. Rates include breakfast. MC, V.

Just off the highway behind Freemark Abbey Vineyard, this attractive wood-and-stone inn, complete with a French-style mansard roof and turret, overlooks a pastoral landscape of Napa Valley vineyards. The individually decorated rooms are outfitted with iron or brass beds, antique furnishings, and handmade quilts; most have fireplaces and private terraces overlooking the valley, while others have private hot tubs. One of the inn's best features, besides the absence of TVs, is the outdoor pool (heated year-round), which is attractively landscaped into the hillside.

Another favorite is the selection of suites, which come with stereos, plenty of space, and lots of privacy. Wine and appetizers are served nightly, along with a big dash of hotel-staff hospitality in the inviting living room. A full buffet breakfast is served there, too. *Note:* Half the bathrooms have showers only.

INEXPENSIVE

Along with the listings below, we also recommend **Napa Valley Railway Inn,** 6503 Washington St., adjacent to the Vintage 1870 shopping complex, Yountville (☎ **707/ 944-2000**), which rents private railway cars converted into adorable hotel rooms; and **Dr. Wilkinson's Hot Springs,** 1507 Lincoln Ave. (☎ **707/942-4102**), which just underwent a soft-goods renovation.

Calistoga Spa Hot Springs. 1006 Washington St. (at Gerrard St.), Calistoga, CA 94515. ☎ **707/942-6269.** 57 units, 1 family unit. A/C TV TEL. Winter $72 double; $97 family unit; $112 suite. Summer $87 double; $112 family unit; $132 suite. MC, V.

Very few hotels in the Wine Country welcome children, which is why we strongly recommend the Calistoga Spa Hot Springs for families. Even if you don't have kids in tow, it's still a great bargain, offering unpretentious yet clean and comfortable rooms with kitchenettes, as well as a plethora of spa facilities ranging from exercise rooms to four naturally heated outdoor mineral pools, aerobic facilities, volcanic-ash mud baths, mineral baths, steam baths, blanket wraps, massage sessions, and more. All of Calistoga's best shops and restaurants are within easy walking distance, and you can even whip up your own grub at the barbecues set up near the large pool and patio area.

Chablis Inn. 3360 Solano Ave., Napa, CA 94558. ☎**800/443-3490** or 707/257-1944. Fax 707/226-6862. www.chablisinn.com. E-mail: chablisinn@aol.com. 34 units. A/C TV TEL. Early Nov to Mar $60–$95 double; Apr to early Nov $80–$130 double. AE, DC, DISC, MC, V.

There's no way around it. If you want to sleep cheaply in a town where the average room goes for upwards of $200 per night in high season, you're going to have to motel it. But look on the bright side: Since your room is likely to be little more than a crashing pad after a day of eating and drinking, a clean bed and a remote control are all you'll really need. But Chablis offers much more than that. Each of the superclean motel-style rooms has a new mattress, fridge, and coffeemaker; some even boast kitchenettes and/or whirlpool tubs. Guests have access to an outdoor heated pool and hot tub, plus a basic continental breakfast. Friendly owner Ken Patel is on hand most of the time and is constantly upgrading his tidy highway-side hostelry.

✪ Deer Run Bed & Breakfast. 3995 Spring Mountain Rd., P.O. Box 311, St. Helena, CA 94574. ☎ **800/843-3408** or 707/963-3794. Fax 707/963-9026. 4 units, all with bathroom (shower only). A/C TV. $140–$195 double. AE, MC, V.

Regardless of your budget, if romantic solitude is a big part of your vacation plan, Deer Run had better be on your itinerary. Situated 4½ miles (10 minutes by car) from downtown St. Helena along a winding mountain road, this four-room B&B is the ultimate heavenly hideaway. Each of the wood-paneled rooms looks onto owners Tom and Carol Wilson's 4 acres of forest, and all feature gorgeous antiques, feather beds, private entrance, deck, decanter of brandy, fridge, coffee and tea, robes, hair dryer, and access to hiking trails. Deer often meander by the Honeymoon Suite (the most secluded), a sweet split-level cottage with a separate bedroom and gas fireplace; its price includes breakfast delivered to your doorstep. The full breakfast served in the main house may include a frittata or apple crepes with chicken-apple sausage. Outside you'll find Cody, the resident chocolate Labrador, hanging out by the very small pool.

✪ **El Bonita Motel.** 195 Main St. (at El Bonita Ave.), St. Helena, CA 94574. ☎ **800/ 541-3284** or 707/963-3216. Fax 707/963-8838. 41 units. A/C MINIBAR TV TEL. Dec–Feb $100–$150 double; Mar–Apr and Nov $120–$220; May–Oct $99–$250 double. AE, CB, DC, DISC, MC, V.

This 1930s art-deco motel was built a bit too close to Calif. 29 for comfort, but the 2½ acres of beautifully landscaped gardens behind the place (away from the road) help even the score. The rooms, while small, are spotlessly clean and decorated with new furnishings; all have microwaves and coffeemakers, and some have kitchens or whirlpool bathtubs. Families, attracted to the larger bungalows with kitchenettes, often regard El Bonita as one of the best values in Napa Valley—especially considering the heated outdoor pool, Jacuzzi, sauna, and massage facility.

✪ **White Sulphur Springs Retreat & Spa.** 3100 White Sulphur Springs Rd., St. Helena, 94574. ☎ **800/593-8873** (in California and Nevada) or 707/963-8588. Fax 707/963-2890. 28 units, 9 cottages. Carriage House (shared bathroom) $95–$125 double; The Inn $115–$145 double; small Creekside Cottages $155–$185; large Creekside Cottages $185–$200. Extra person $15. Discounts available during off-season and midweek. Single-night stays accepted in Carriage House rooms, but cottages require a 2-night minimum weekends from Apr–Oct and all holidays. MC, V.

If your idea of the ultimate vacation is a cozy cabin set among 330 acres of creeks, waterfalls, hot springs, hiking trails, and redwood, madrone, and fir trees, paradise is a short winding drive away from downtown St. Helena. Established in 1852, Sulphur Springs claims to be the oldest resort in California. Guests stay at the inn or in small and large creek-side cabins, which were renovated just last year. Each is decorated with simple but homey furnishings; some have fireplaces or wood-burning stoves, and/or kitchenettes. From here you can venture off on a hike; take a dip in the natural hot sulphur spring; lounge by the pool; sit under a tree and watch for deer, fox, raccoon, spotted owl, or woodpecker; or schedule a day of massage, aromatherapy, and other spa treatments. *Note:* No RVs are allowed without advance notice.

Wine Valley Lodge. 200 S. Coombs St. (between First and Imola sts.), Napa, CA 94559. ☎ **707/224-7911.** Fax 707/224-9152. 53 units. A/C TV TEL. $60–$94 double; $110–$165 suite. AE, CB, DC, DISC, MC, V.

Dollar for dollar, the Wine Valley Lodge offers the most for the least in all of Wine Country. Located at the south end of town in a quiet residential neighborhood, the mission-style motel is extremely well kept and accessible, just a short drive from Calif. 29 and the wineries to the north. Soft pastels dominate the color scheme, featured prominently in the matching quilted bedspreads, furniture, and objets d'art. Its decor is reminiscent of Grandma's house, to be sure, but at these prices, who cares? The clincher on the whole deal is a fetching little oasis in the center courtyard, consisting of a sundeck, barbecue, and pool flanked by a cadre of odd teacup-shaped hedges.

WHERE TO DINE

To best enjoy Napa's restaurant scene, keep one thing in mind: *reserve*—especially for seats in a more renowned room.

The Race for Restaurant Reservations

Over the past few years, the Napa Valley has garnered a widespread reputation for hosting some of the best restaurants in the United States. And with dining considered a major Wine Country attraction in itself, part of your pre-trip planning should include making restaurant reservations—especially if you want to eat at the town's new hot spots. Two years after French Laundry's Thomas Keller was deemed "Chef of the Nation" by the James Beard Foundation, it's still virtually impossible to get beyond the restaurant telephone's busy signal, let alone secure a reservation. But with several new restaurants launched by high-profile chefs in the past year, there's more than one reason to continually hit the redial button with the hopes of booking a table.

Perhaps to appease the crowds who never get a reservation for the French Laundry, Thomas Keller teamed up with his brother Joseph to open a far more casual, but still fabulous, French brasserie called **Bouchon**, 6534 Washington St. (at Humbolt), Yountville (☎ **707/944-8037**). Diners call far in advance for an opportunity to sample the chef's French fare, which is served in a dining room designed by Adam Tihany (who also conceptualized New York's Le Cirque 2000) that has lovely tile floors and mohair banquettes. Along with a raw seafood bar, you can expect superb renditions of steak frites, mussels marinieres, and other heavenly French classics at far more down-to-earth prices. Main courses range from $11.95 to $16.95.

Another rising Yountville star is the restaurant of chef Phillipe Jeanty, who a few years back left his highly reputed 18-year post at Domaine Chandon to open one of the hottest (and most moderately priced) new spots in town. While Jeanty was previously known for formal French cooking and atmosphere, his charming and cheery bistro, simply called **Bistro Jeanty,** 6510 Washington St. (near Mulberry), Yountville (☎ **707/944-0103**), is far more intimate and inviting, with such delicious and classic French bistro fare as foie gras terrine; steak frites; daube de boeuf simmered in red wine and served with mashed potatoes, fresh peas, and baby carrots; and cassoulet with white beans, fennel sausage, pork, and duck leg. But don't let the casual atmosphere fool you—this is world-class cooking and a must-stop on most San Franciscans' itineraries. In other words, start dialing. Main courses range from $10.50 to $16.50.

EXPENSIVE

Auberge du Soleil. 180 Rutherford Hill Rd., Rutherford. ☎ **707/963-1211.** Reservations recommended. Main courses $25–$30. AE, DISC, MC, V. Daily 7–11am, 11:30am–2:30pm, and 6–9:30pm. MEDITERRANEAN/WINE COUNTRY CUISINE.

Alfresco dining is taken to an entirely new level here, particularly on warm summer nights when diners are rewarded with a gorgeous sunset view of the mountains. Inside, a magnificent fireplace, huge wood pillars, and fresh flowers create a warm, rustic ambiance. Chef Andrew Sutton characterizes his cooking as "Wine Country cuisine," a reflection of the region's produce and international influences: Pacific Rim, Southwestern, and Mediterranean styles predominate. Signature dishes include a tasting platter of truffled deviled quail egg, smoked sturgeon, Thai lobster salad, caviar, and more; and a grapevine smoked salmon with walnut-wheat croutons and roasted shallot-caper relish. Regardless of what you order, be sure to arrive before sunset and beg for terrace seating.

Brix. 7377 St. Helena Hwy. (Calif. 29), Yountville. ☎ **707/944-2749.** Reservations recommended. Main courses $17–$24. AE, DC, DISC, MC, V. Sun–Thurs 11:30am–9:30pm; Fri–Sat 11:30am–10pm. ASIAN FUSION.

Executive chef Tod Michael Kawachi does a wonderful job integrating Asian flavors with California cuisine, and the result is a rich culinary adventure. While starters—such as a very tasty grilled portobello-mushroom salad with blue cheese and sherry walnut vinaigrette (ask them not to go too heavy on the dressing!)—are interesting, only the starved should indulge, as portions tend to be large. We tried the Hawaiian ono with a ragout of rock shrimp and shiitake-coconut curry, and a Thai pesto smoked rack of lamb with spicy peanut saté and zinfandel glaze. Both were very good, with knockout sauces, but what really impressed us was the Chinese-style whole crispy fish with cilantro/black-bean sauce—an absolute must-have.

✪ The French Laundry. 6640 Washington St. (at Creek St.), Yountville. ☎ **707/944-2380.** Reservations required. Fixed-price lunch $80; five-course dinner $80; nine-course dinner $95. AE, MC, V. Sat–Sun 11:30am–1pm; Wed–Sun 5:30–9:30pm. CALIFORNIA/FRENCH.

If your restaurant has the chutzpah to post neither a sign nor an address, it had better be good. Fortunately, this Yountville institution *is* that good. Though it's been around since 1978, it wasn't until renowned chef/owner Thomas Keller bought the place a few years back that it caught the attention of epicureans worldwide (including the judges of the James Beard awards, who dubbed him 1997's "Chef of the Nation"). Dinner is an all-night affair; when it's finally over, you'll be ready to sit down and do it all over again—it's truly that wonderful. There's only one catch: You'll either have to reserve a month in advance (no joke—and it's almost impossible to get through to the reservationist since the phone is always busy) or go standby to sample the most coveted cooking in the United States.

   Technically, the prix-fixe menu offers a choice of five or nine courses (including a vegetarian menu), but after a slew of cameo appearances from the kitchen, everyone starts to lose count. Signature dishes include Keller's "tongue in cheek" (a marinated and braised round of sliced lamb tongue and tender beef cheeks) and "macaroni and cheese" (sweet butter-poached Maine lobster with creamy lobster broth and orzo with mascarpone cheese). Portions are small, but only because Keller wants his guests to taste as many different things as possible—nobody leaves hungry. The excellent staff is well acquainted with the wide selection of regional wines; the house charges a $20 corkage fee if you choose to bring your own bottle. On warm summer nights, request a table in the flower-filled garden.

✪ Pinot Blanc. 641 Main St., St. Helena. ☎ **707/963-6191.** Most main courses $9–$20 lunch, $16–$22 dinner. AE, DC, DISC, JCB, MC, V. Tues–Thurs 11:30am–3pm and 5–9pm; Fri–Sun 11:30am–10pm. Extended summer hours. FRENCH BISTRO.

L.A.'s famed Joachim Splichal opened this northern California outpost a few years back and today it remains a beautiful place—recently renovated to depict a more country French atmosphere—to sample the gastronomic glories of executive chef Sean Knight. Lunch offerings might include curry chicken salad with sun-dried Napa grapes and apples. The unique menu features such entrees as coq au vin, cannelloni with roasted vegetables, a pot of mussels with pernod broth and rouille, and planked Atlantic salmon with shallot and apple smoked bacon crust. Attention is paid to every detail at this restaurant, including the wine list, which features over 200 selections. There's patio seating during the summer.

✪ Terra. 1345 Railroad Ave. (between Adams and Hunt sts.), St. Helena. ☎ **707/963-8931.** Reservations recommended. Main courses $15–$26. CB, DC, MC, V. Sun–Mon and Wed–Thurs 6–9pm; Fri–Sat 6–10pm. CONTEMPORARY AMERICAN.

St. Helena's restaurant of choice is the creation of Lissa Doumani and her husband, Hiro Sone, a master chef who hails from Japan and once worked with Wolfgang Puck at L.A.'s original Spago. Sone makes full use of the region's bounty; he seems to know how to coax every nuance of flavor from his fine local ingredients. The simple dining room is a perfect foil for the extraordinary food. Among the appetizers, the terrine of foie gras with apple, walnut, and endive salad and the home-smoked salmon with spring rolls, caviar, and sour cream are the stars of the show. The main dishes successfully fuse different cooking styles: Try the grilled salmon with Thai red-curry sauce or the sake-marinated sea bass with shrimp dumplings in shiso broth. A recommended finale? The chocolate bread pudding with sun-dried sour cherries and crème fraîche.

MODERATE

All Seasons Café. 1400 Lincoln Ave. (at Washington St.), Calistoga. ☎ **707/942-9111.** Reservations recommended on weekends. Main courses $10.25–$20 dinner. MC, V. Thurs–Tues 11am–2:30pm; daily 5:30–10pm. Wine shop daily 11am–10pm. CALIFORNIA.

Wine Country devotees often wend their way to the All Seasons Café in downtown Calistoga because of its extensive wine list and knowledgeable staff. The trick here is to buy a bottle of wine from the cafe's wine shop, then bring it to your table; the cafe adds a corkage fee of $10 instead of tripling the price of the bottle (as they do at most restaurants). The diverse menu ranges from pizzas and pastas to such main courses as braised lamb shank osso bucco in an orange, Madeira, and tomato sauce. Anything with the house-smoked salmon or spiced sausages is also a safe bet. Chef John Coss saves his guests from any major faux pas by matching wines to his dishes on the menu, so you know what's just right for smoked salmon and Crescenza cheese pizza.

Bistro Don Giovanni. 4110 St. Helena Hwy. (on Calif. 29, just north of Salvador Ave.), Napa. ☎ **707/224-3300.** Reservations recommended Fri–Sat. Main courses $11–$17. AE, DC, DISC, MC, V. Sun–Thurs 11:30am–10pm; Fri–Sat 11:30am–11pm. NORTHERN ITALIAN.

Donna and Giovanni Scala—who also run the fantastic Scala's Bistro in San Francisco—serve refined Italian fare prepared with top-quality ingredients and California flair at this large, lively, Mediterranean-style restaurant. The menu features pastas, risottos, pizzas (baked in a wood-burning oven), and a half dozen other main courses, such as braised lamb shank and Niman Schell bistro burgers. Less traditional appetizers include a grilled pear with a frisee-and-arugula salad with bleu cheese, caramelized walnuts, and bacon. Pasta lovers should go for the farfalle with asparagus, porcini, wild mushrooms, pecorino cheese, and truffle oil. Alfresco dining among the vineyards is available—and highly recommended on a warm, sunny day.

✪ **Catahoula.** 1457 Lincoln Ave. (between Washington and Fairway sts.), Calistoga. ☎ **707/942-2275.** Reservations recommended. Main courses $11–$20. DISC, MC, V. Breakfast Sat–Sun 8:30–1:30pm in winter, Fri–Sun 8:30–1:30pm in summer; lunch Mon and Wed–Sun 11:30am–3:30pm; dinner daily 5:30–10:30pm. AMERICAN/SOUTHERN.

The domain of chef Jan Birnbaum, formerly of New York's Quilted Giraffe and San Francisco's Campton Place, this restaurant is the current favorite in town. And for good reason—it's the only place in Napa where you can get a decent rooster gumbo. You'd have to travel all over Louisiana to find another pan-fried jalapeño-pecan catfish like this one. Catahoula is funky and fun, and the food that comes out of the wood-burning oven—like the roast duck with chili-cilantro potatoes or the whole roasted fish with lemon broth, orzo, and escarole—is exciting (and usually spicy). Start with the spicy gumbo ya ya with andouille sausage, and finish with what may be a first for many non-Southerners—buttermilk ice cream.

Mustards Grill. 7399 St. Helena Hwy. (Calif. 29), Yountville. ☎ **707/944-2424.** Reservations recommended. Main courses $11–$17. CB, DC, DISC, MC, V. Sun–Thurs 11:30am–9pm, Fri–Sat 11:30am–10pm. CALIFORNIA.

Mustards is a safe bet for anyone in search of a casual atmosphere and quality food that's not overly adventurous. Housed in a convivial, barn-style space, it offers an 11-page wine list and an ambitious chalkboard list of specials. We started out with a wonderfully light seared ahi tuna that melted in our mouths the way ahi should. Although the hoisin quail with apricot sauce and bok choy and the lamb shank braised in syrah with fennel and onions were tempting, we opted for a moist, perfectly flavored grilled chicken breast with mashed potatoes and fresh herbs. The menu includes something for everyone, from gourmands and vegetarians to good old burger lovers.

✪ **Piatti.** 6480 Washington St. (corner of Oak Circle), Yountville. ☎ **707/944-2070.** Reservations recommended. Main courses $11–$18. AE, DC, MC, V. Mon–Thurs and Sun 11:30am–10pm; Fri–Sat 11:30am–11pm. ITALIAN/CALIFORNIA.

This local favorite—the first (and best) of a swiftly growing northern California chain—is known for serving excellent, reasonably priced food in a rustic Italian-style setting. Chef Peter Hall, a seasoned Napa Valley cook who honed his culinary art at Tra Vigne and Mustards before taking over the helm here, performs to a mostly sold-out crowd nightly. For the perfect meal, start with a salad of morning-cut field greens mixed with white corn and Napa Valley strawberry crostini, accompanied by a bowl of the spaghetti-squash-and-sweet-potato soup. Though Hall offers a wide array of superb pastas and pizzas, it's the wood-oven-roasted duck—basted with a sweet cherry sauce and served over a bed of citrus risotto—that brings back the regulars. There are far fancier and more intimate restaurants in the valley, but we can't think of any that can fill you up on such outstanding fare at these prices. *Note:* Piatti also offers patio dining year-round, weather permitting.

Tra Vigne Restaurant. 1050 Charter Oak Ave., St. Helena. ☎ **707/963-4444.** Reservations recommended. Main courses $12.50–$22; Cantinetta $4–$8. CB, DC, DISC, MC, V. Daily 11:30am–10pm; Cantinetta daily 11:30am–6pm. ITALIAN.

Tra Vigne's combination of good food, high-energy atmosphere, and "reasonable" prices (reasonable being a relative term) makes this restaurant a longstanding favorite among visitors. The enormous dining room packs 'em in every night—and whether seated on the veranda (heated on cold nights) or in the center of the bustling scene, diners are usually thrilled just to have a seat. Even though the wonderful bread served with house-made flavored olive oils is tempting, save room for the robust California dishes, cooked Italian style, that have made this place everyone's favorite. The menu features about five or so pizzas, including a succulent caramelized onion, thyme, and Gorgonzola version. The dishes of the day might include grilled Sonoma rabbit with teleme-layered potatoes, oven-dried tomatoes, and mustard pan sauce, and a dozen or so antipasti. Equally tempting are the pastas—which include ceppo with sausage, spinach, potatoes, sun-dried tomatoes, and Pecorino—and the delicious desserts. When ordering, plan wisely—most dishes are very rich.

The adjoining Cantinetta offers a small selection of sandwiches, pizzas, and lighter meals (see below).

Wappo Bar & Bistro. 1226B Washington St. (off Lincoln Ave.), Calistoga. ☎ **707/942-4712.** Main courses $8.50–$14.50. AE, MC, V. Wed–Mon 11:30am–2:30pm and 6–9:30pm. INTERNATIONAL.

One of the best alfresco dining experiences in the Wine Country is under Wappo's honeysuckle-and-vine-covered arbor, but you'll also be comfortable inside this small bistro at one of the well-spaced, well-polished tables. The menu offers a wide range of choices, from Chilean sea bass with mint chutney to roast rabbit with potato gnocchi. The desserts of choice are the black-bottom coconut-cream pie and the strawberry-rhubarb pie.

Wine Spectator Greystone Restaurant. At the Culinary Institute of America at Greystone, 2555 Main St., St. Helena. ☎ **707/967-1010.** Reservations strongly recommended. Tapas $3–$7; main courses $16–$26 (same prices at both lunch and dinner). AE, CB, DC, DISC, MC, V. Daily 11:30am–3pm; 3:30–5:30pm tapas at the bar; 5:30–10pm. MEDITERRANEAN.

This place offers a visual and culinary feast that's unparalleled in the area, if not the state. The room itself is an enormous stone-walled former winery, but the festive decor and heavenly aromas warm the space up. Cooking islands—complete with scurrying chefs, steaming pots, and rotating chicken—provide edible entertainment. The tapas menu focuses on Mediterranean-inspired dishes, including an excellent pork kebab and stuffed calamari that contradicts the sea dweller's rubbery reputation with every moist and savory bite. Tapas portions are small but affordable; pastas and salads are a bit heftier. Main courses, such as roasted lamb marinated in pomegranate and red wine and served with compote of quince and carmelized onions, are well-portioned and good, but we recommend you opt for a barrage of appetizers for your table to share. You should also order the "Flights of Fancy," where for $14 to $25 you can sample three 3-ounce pours of local wines such as white rhones, pinot, or zinfandel. While the food is serious, the atmosphere is playful—casual enough that you'll feel comfortable in jeans or shorts. If you want to ensure a meal here, reserve far in advance.

INEXPENSIVE

✪ **The Cantinetta.** At Tra Vigne Restaurant, 1050 Charter Oak Ave., St. Helena. ☎ **707/963-8888.** Main courses $4–$8. CB, DC, DISC, MC, V. Daily 11:30am–6pm. ITALIAN.

Regardless of where we dine while in the valley, we always make a point of stopping at The Cantinetta for an espresso and a snack. Part cafe, part shop, it's a casual place with a few tables and a counter. The focaccias (we've never had better in our lives!), pasta salads, and pastries are outstanding, and there's also a selection of cookies and other wonderful treats, flavored oils (free tastings), wines, and an array of gourmet items, many of which were created here. You can also get great picnic grub to go.

✪ **Oakville Grocery Café.** 7848 St. Helena Hwy. (Hwy. 29, at the Oakville Cross Rd.), Oakville. ☎ **707/944-0111.** Reservations available for parties of 8 or more. Breakfast $4–$7.50; lunch main courses $5.50–$9. AE, MC, V. Daily 7:30am–11am and 11am–4pm; hours vary for dinner. CALIFORNIA.

This is one of our favorite places to come for delicious, relatively cheap food. The ovation-worthy lunch menu features a melt-in-your-mouth salmon, watercress, and herb-aioli sandwich ($8); soups, such as a hearty vegetable barley; salads (Niçoise, goat cheese with field greens and peach-chardonnay vinaigrette, and hearts of romaine); pizzas, such as wild mushroom; and lasagna. Breakfast is celebrated with "Small Plates" such as granola ($3.75), toasted breads with house preserves ($2), and a breakfast fruit tart; and "Big Plates" of chicken hash ($7), eggs, omelets, and frittatas. Counter service keeps the prices down, thick windows keep traffic noise out, and an absolutely fab meal and sweet ambiance keep the local constituency coming back for more. As this book goes to press, they're doing a trial run for dinner.

Smokehouse Café. 1458 Lincoln Ave., Calistoga. ☎ **707/942-6060.** Main courses $8–$17. MC, V. Daily 7:30am–10pm (Jan–Feb, closed Tues and only open for lunch on Wed). REGIONAL AMERICAN BBQ.

Who would have guessed that some of the best spareribs and house-smoked meats in northern California would come from this little kitchen in Calistoga? Here's the

Gourmet Picnics, Napa Style

You could easily plan your whole trip around restaurant reservations. But put together one of the world's best gourmet picnics, and the valley's your oyster.

One of the finest gourmet food stores in the Wine Country, if not all of California, is the ✪**Oakville Grocery Co.,** 7856 St. Helena Hwy., at Oakville Cross Road (☎ **707/944-8802**). Here you can put together the provisions for a memorable picnic—or, if you give them at least 24 hours' notice, the staff can prepare a picnic basket for you. The store, with its small-town vibe and claustrophobia-inducing crowds, is crammed with the best breads and the choicest selection of cheeses in the northern Bay Area, as well as pâtés, cold cuts, crackers, top-quality olive oils, fresh foie gras, smoked Norwegian salmon, fresh caviar (Beluga, Sevruga, Osetra), and, of course, an exceptional selection of California wines. The store is open daily from 9am to 6pm; it also has an espresso bar tucked in the corner (open daily from 7am to 3pm), offering breakfast and lunch items, house-baked pastries, and 15 wines available by the glass or for tasting.

Another of our favorite places to fill a picnic basket is New York City's version of a swank European marketplace, ✪ **Dean & Deluca,** 607 South Main St. (Calif. 29), north of Zinfandel Lane and south of Sulphur Springs Road in St. Helena (☎ **707/967-9980**). The ultimate gourmet grocery store is more like a world's fair of foods, where everything is beautifully displayed and often painfully pricey. But even if you choose not to buy, this place is definitely worth a browse. Check out the 200 domestic and imported cheeses; shelves of tapenades, pastas, oils, hand-packed dried herbs and spices, chocolates, sauces, and cookware; an espresso bar; one hell of a bakery section; and more. The wine shop boasts a 1,200-label collection. Hours are Monday through Saturday from 10am to 7pm (the espresso bar opens at 8am), Sunday from 10am to 6pm.

winning game plan: Start with the Sacramento delta crawfish cakes (better than any wimpy crab cakes you'll find in San Francisco) and husk-roasted Cheyenne corn, then move on to the slow pig sandwich, a half slab of ribs, or homemade sausages—all of which take up to a week to prepare (not while you wait, luckily). The clincher, though, is the fluffy all-you-can-eat cornbread dipped in pure cane syrup, which comes with every full-plate dinner. Kids are especially catered to—a rarity in these parts—and patio dining is available during the summer for breakfast, lunch, and dinner.

2 Sonoma Valley

Sonoma is often thought of as the "other" Wine Country, forever in the shadow of Napa Valley. Truth is, even though there are far fewer wineries here (and far fewer tourists), Sonoma's wines have actually won more awards than Napa's. Sonoma County, which stretches west to the coast, still manages to maintain a backcountry ambiance thanks to its much lower density of wineries, restaurants, and hotels; because it's far less traveled than its neighbor to the east, it offers a more genuine "escape from it all" experience. Small, family-owned wineries are its mainstay, just like in the old days of wine making, when everyone started with the intention of going broke and loved every minute of it. Unlike the rigidly structured tours at many of Napa Valley's corporate-owned wineries, tastings and tours on the Sonoma side of the Mayacamas Mountains are usually free and low-key, and come with plenty of friendly banter between the winemakers and their guests.

ESSENTIALS

GETTING THERE   From San Francisco, cross the Golden Gate Bridge and stay on U.S. 101 north. Exit at Calif. 37; after 10 miles, turn north onto Calif. 121. After another 10 miles, turn north onto Calif. 12 (Broadway), which will take you directly into the town of Sonoma.

VISITOR INFORMATION   While you're in Sonoma, stop by the **Sonoma Valley Visitors Bureau,** 453 First St. E. (☎ **707/996-1090;** www.sonomavalley.com). It's open daily from 9am to 7pm in summer and from 9am to 5pm in winter. An additional **Visitors Bureau** is located a few miles south of the square at 25200 Arnold Dr. (Calif. 121), at the entrance to Viansa Winery (☎ **707/996-5793**); it's open daily from 9am to 5pm.

If you prefer some advance information, the free, pocket-size *Sonoma Valley Visitors Guide* covers most every hotel, winery, and restaurant in the valley. Contact the Sonoma Valley Visitors Bureau to order one.

WHEN TO GO   See "When to Go" in the Napa section, above.

TOURING THE VALLEY & WINERIES

Sonoma Valley is currently home to about 35 wineries (including California's first winery, Buena Vista, founded in 1857) and 13,000 acres of vineyards, which produce roughly 25 types of wines totaling more than 5 million cases a year.

The towns and wineries covered below are organized geographically from south to north, starting at the intersection of Calif. 37 and Calif. 121 in the Carneros District and ending in Kenwood. The wineries here tend to be a little more spread out than they are in Napa, but they're easy to find. Still, it's best to decide which wineries you're most interested in and devise a touring strategy before you set out so you don't find yourself doing a lot of backtracking.

We've reviewed our favorite Sonoma Valley wineries here—more than enough to keep you busy tasting wine for a long weekend. For a complete list of local wineries, pick up one of the free guides to the valley available at the Sonoma Valley Visitors Bureau (see "Visitor Information," above).

THE CARNEROS DISTRICT

As you approach the Wine Country from the south, you must first pass through the Carneros District, a cool, windswept region that borders the San Pablo Bay and marks the entrance to both Napa and Sonoma valleys. Until the latter part of the 20th century, this mixture of marsh, sloughs, and rolling hills was mainly used as sheep pasture (*carneros* means sheep in Spanish). After experimental plantings yielded slow-growing yet high-quality grapes—particularly chardonnay and pinot noir—several Napa and Sonoma wineries expanded their plantings here, eventually establishing the Carneros District as an American Viticultural Appellation.

✪ **Viansa Winery and Italian Marketplace.** 25200 Arnold Dr. (Calif. 121), Sonoma. ☎ **800/995-4740** or 707/935-4700. Daily 10am–5pm. Guided tours by appointment only.

The first major winery you'll encounter as you enter Sonoma Valley from the south, this sprawling Tuscany-style villa is perched atop a knoll overlooking the entire lower valley. Viansa is the brainchild of Sam and Vicki Sebastiani, who left the family dynasty to create their own temple to food and wine (Viansa being a contraction of Vicki and Sam). The marketplace is crammed with a cornucopia of high-quality preserves, mustards, olive oils, pastas, salads, breads, desserts, Italian tableware, cookbooks, and other wine-related gifts. The winery, which does an extensive mail-order business through its Tuscany Club (worth joining if you love getting mail and good wine), has quickly established a favorable reputation for its cabernet, sauvignon blanc, and chardonnay, blended from premium Napa and Sonoma grapes. The vineyard is also experimenting with Italian grape varieties such as muscat canelli, sangiovese, and nebbiolo, most of which are sold exclusively at the winery. Free tastings are poured at the east end of the marketplace, and the self-guided tour includes a trip through the underground barrel-aging cellar adorned with colorful hand-painted murals.

Gloria Ferrer Champagne Caves. 23555 Carneros Hwy. (Calif. 121), Sonoma. ☎ **707/ 996-7256.** Daily 10am–5:30pm. Tours daily; call for schedule.

When you've had it up to here with chardonnays and pinots, pay a visit to Gloria Ferrer. (Gloria is the wife of José Ferrer, whose family has been making sparkling wine for the past 5 centuries and whose company, Freixenet, is the largest producer of sparkling wine in the world.) Glimmering like Oz high atop a gently sloping hill, the winery overlooks the verdant Carneros District; on a sunny day, it's impossible not to enjoy a glass of dry Brut while soaking in the magnificent views of the vineyards and valley below.

If you're unfamiliar with the term *méthode champenoise,* be sure to take the free 30-minute tour of the fermenting tanks, bottling line, and caves brimming with racks of yeast-laden bottles. Afterward, retire to the elegant tasting room for a flute of Brut or Cuvée ($3 to $5.50 a glass, $16 and up per bottle). There are picnic tables, but it's usually too windy up here for comfort—plus you have to purchase a bottle of their sparkling wine to reserve a table.

SONOMA

At the northern boundary of the Carneros District along Calif. 12 is the centerpiece of Sonoma Valley, the midsized town of Sonoma, which owes much of its appeal to Mexican general Mariano Guadalupe Vallejo. It was Vallejo who fashioned this pleasant, slow-paced community after a typical Mexican village—right down to its central plaza, Sonoma's geographical and commercial center. The plaza sits at the top of a T formed by Broadway (Calif. 12) and Napa Street. Most of the surrounding streets form a grid pattern around this axis, making Sonoma easy to negotiate. The plaza's Bear Flag Monument marks the spot where the crude Bear Flag was raised in 1846, signaling the end of Mexican rule; the symbol was later adopted by the state of California and placed on its flag. The 8-acre park at the center of the plaza, complete with two ponds populated with ducks and geese, is perfect for an afternoon siesta in the cool shade. Our favorite attraction, however, is the gaggle of brilliantly feathered chickens that roam unfettered through the streets of Sonoma—a sight you'll definitely never see in Napa.

The best way to see the town of Sonoma is to follow the **Sonoma Walking Tour** map, provided by the Sonoma League for Historic Preservation. Tour highlights include General Vallejo's 1852 Victorian-style home; the Sonoma Barracks, erected in 1836 to house Mexican army troops; and the Blue Wing Inn, an 1840 hostelry built to accommodate travelers—including John Fremont, Kit Carson, and Ulysses S. Grant—and new settlers while they erected homes in Sonoma. You can purchase the $2.75 map at the Vasquez House, located at 414 First St. E., between East Napa and East Spain streets (☎ **707/938-0510**), open Wednesday through Sunday from 1:30 to 4:30pm.

The **Mission San Francisco Solano de Sonoma,** on Sonoma Plaza at the corner of First Street East and Spain Street (☎ **707/938-9560**), was founded in 1823. It was the northernmost, and last, mission built in California. It was also the only one established on the northern coast by the Mexican rulers, who wished to protect their territory from expansionist Russian fur traders. It's now part of Sonoma State Historic

Park. Admission is $2 for adults, $1 for children 6 to 12, and free for children under 6. It's open daily from 10am to 5pm except Thanksgiving, Christmas, and New Year's Day.

Sebastiani Vineyards Winery. 389 Fourth St. E., Sonoma. ☎ **800/888-5532** or 707/938-5532. Daily 10am–5pm. Tours offered 10:30am–4pm, every half hour in summer, every 45 min. to an hour in winter; no reservations necessary.

What started in 1904, when Samuele Sebastiani began producing his first wines, has, in three successive generations, now grown into a small empire and Sonoma County's largest winery, producing some 6 *million* cases a year. The 25-minute tour is interesting, informative, and well worth the time. You can see the winery's original turn-of-the-century crusher and press as well as the world's largest collection of oak-barrel carvings, crafted by local artist Earle Brown. If you don't want to take the tour, head straight for the charmingly rustic tasting room, where you can sample an extensive selection of wines sans tasting fee. Bottle prices are very reasonable, ranging from $5 for a 1996 white zin to $15 for a 1994 cabernet sauvignon. A picnic area is adjacent to the cellars, though a far more scenic spot is located across the parking lot in Sebastiani's Cherryblock Vineyards.

Buena Vista. 18000 Old Winery Rd. (off E. Napa St., slightly northeast of downtown), Sonoma. ☎ **800/926-1266** or 707/938-1266. Daily 10:30am–5pm. Self-guided tours only.

The patriarch of California wineries was founded in 1857 by Count Agoston Haraszthy, the Hungarian émigré who is universally regarded as the father of California's wine industry. A close friend of General Vallejo, Haraszthy returned from Europe in 1861 with 100,000 of the finest vine cuttings, which he made available to all winegrowers. Although Buena Vista's wine making now takes place at an ultra-modern facility in the Carneros District, the winery still maintains a complimentary tasting room inside the restored 1862 Press House—a beautiful stone-crafted room brimming with wines, wine-related gifts, and accessories (as well as a small art gallery along the inner balcony).

Tastings are free for most wines, $3 for the really good stuff; bottle prices range from as low as $8.75 for a buttery 1996 sauvignon blanc to $35 for the Carneros Grand Reserve cabernet sauvignon. There's also a self-guided tour that you can follow any time during operating hours; a "Historical Presentation," offered daily at 2pm, details the life and times of the count.

Ravenswood Winery. 18701 Gehricke Rd. (off Lovall Valley Rd.), Sonoma. ☎ **888/669-4679** or 707/938-1960. Daily 10am–4:30pm. Tours by reservation only.

Compared to old heavies like Sebastiani and Buena Vista, Ravenswood is a relative newcomer to the Sonoma wine scene, but it has quickly established itself as the sine qua non of zinfandel. In fact, Ravenswood is the first winery in the United States to focus primarily on zins, which make up about three-quarters of its 150,000-case production; it also produces merlot, cabernet sauvignon, and a small amount of chardonnay.

The winery is smartly designed—recessed into the Sonoma hillside to protect its treasures from the simmering summers. Tours follow the wine-making process from grape to glass, and include a visit into the aromatic oak-barrel-aging rooms. A gourmet "Barbecue Overlooking the Vineyards" is held each weekend (from 11am to 4:40pm, from Memorial Day to the end of September; call for details and reservations), though you're welcome to enjoy your own picnic at any of their tables. Tastings are free and generous, though you may not find some of the pourers to be as witty as they think they are (ours was a jerk, though we've known people who have had great experiences here). Bottle prices range from $8.50 for a light and crisp 1998 French Colombard to

$31.50 for a Pickberry Proprietary Blend, but it's the kick-butt zins—priced well in the low to mid-20s—that you'll want to stock up on.

GLEN ELLEN

About 7 miles north of Sonoma on Calif. 12 is the town of Glen Ellen, which, though just a fraction of the size of Sonoma, is home to several of the valley's finest wineries, restaurants, and inns. Aside from the addition of a few new restaurants, this charming Wine Country town hasn't changed much since the days when Jack London settled on his Beauty Ranch, about a mile west. If you haven't yet decided where you want to set up camp during your visit to the Wine Country, we highly recommend this lovable little town.

Hikers, horseback riders, and picnickers will enjoy **Jack London State Historic Park,** 2400 London Ranch Rd., off Arnold Drive (☎ 707/938-5216). Within its 800 acres, which were once home to the renowned writer, you'll find 9 miles of trails, the remains of London's burned-down dream house, preserved structures, a museum, and plenty of ideal picnic spots. The park is open daily from 9:30am to 7pm in summer, from 9:30am to 5pm in winter; the museum is open from 10am to 5pm. Admission is $6 per car, $5 per car for seniors 62 and over.

Arrowood. 14347 Sonoma Hwy. (Calif. 12), Glen Ellen. ☎ **707/938-5170.** Daily 10am–4:30pm. Tours daily. Tasting $3.

Richard Arrowood had already established a reputation as a master winemaker at Château St. Jean before he and his wife, Alis Demers Arrowood, set out on their own in 1986. Their utterly picturesque winery is perched on a gently rising hillside lined with perfectly manicured vineyards. Tastings take place in the Hospitality House, the newest of Arrowood's two stately gray-and-white buildings that were fashioned after New England farmhouses, complete with wraparound porches. Richard's focus is on making world-class wines with minimal intervention, and his results are impressive: Four out of his five current releases have scored over 90 points. Mind you, such excellence doesn't come cheaply; prices start at $26 for a 1997 chardonnay and quickly climb to the mid- to high $40s. No picnic facilities are available.

✪ **The Benziger Family Winery.** 1883 London Ranch Rd. (off Arnold Dr., on the way to Jack London State Historic Park), Glen Ellen. ☎ **800/989-8890** or 707/935-3000. Tasting room daily 10am–5pm. Tram tours daily (weather permitting) at 11:30am, 12:30pm, 2pm, and 3:30pm.

A visit here confirms that you are indeed visiting a "family" winery; at any given time three generations of Benzigers (pronounced *ben*-zigger) may be running around tending to chores, and you're instantly made to feel as if you're part of the clan. The pastoral, user-friendly property features an exceptional self-guided tour ("The most comprehensive tour in the wine industry," exclaims *Wine Spectator*), gardens, an art gallery, and a spacious tasting room manned by an amiable staff. The free 40-minute tram tour, pulled by a beefy tractor, is both informative and fun as it winds through the estate vineyards before making a champagne-tasting pit stop on a scenic bluff. *Tip:* Tram tickets—a hot item in the summer—are available on a first-come, first-served basis, so either arrive early or stop by in the morning to pick up afternoon tickets.

Tastings of the standard release wines are free, and bottle prices range from $10.99 for a 1997 fumé blanc to $18 for a 1996 pinot noir. You can also purchase a full glass of wine for $4 to $6 and tour the estate in style. The winery offers several scenic picnic spots.

KENWOOD

A few miles north of Glen Ellen along Calif. 12 is the tiny town of Kenwood, the northernmost outpost of the Sonoma Valley. The town itself consists of little more than a few restaurants, wineries, and modest homes recessed into the wooded hillsides.

Kunde Estate Winery. 10155 Sonoma Hwy., Kenwood. ☎ **707/833-5501.** www. kunde.com. Tastings daily 11am–5pm. Cave tours Fri–Sun approximately every half hour from 11am–4pm.

Expect a friendly, unintimidating welcome at this scenic winery, run by four generations of the Kundes since 1904. One of the largest grape suppliers in the area, the Kunde family (pronounced *kun*-dee) converted 800 acres of their 2,000-acre ranch to growing ultra-premium-quality grapes, which they provide to about 30 Sonoma and Napa wineries. Hence, all their wines are "estate" (made from grapes grown on their own property). The tour includes the details and the winery's history. The free new-release tastings are offered in a spiffy new 17,000-square-foot wine-making facility; bottle prices range from $11 to $24. Private tours are available by appointment, but the picnic tables and man-made pond can be spontaneously enjoyed.

Kenwood Vineyards. 9592 Sonoma Hwy. (Calif. 12), Kenwood. ☎ **707/833-5891.** Daily 10am–4:30pm. Tours by appointment only.

Kenwood's history dates back to 1906, when the Pagani brothers made their living selling wine straight from the barrel and into the jug. In 1970, the Lee family bought the place and converted the aging winery into a modern, high-production facility concealed in the original barnlike buildings. Since then, Kenwood's wines have earned a solid reputation for consistent quality with each of their varietals: cabernet sauvignon, chardonnay, zinfandel, pinot noir, merlot, and their most popular wine, sauvignon blanc—a crisp, light wine with hints of melon.

Though the winery looks rather modest in size, its output is staggering: 360,000 cases of ultra-premium wines fermented in 60 steel tanks and 7,000 French and American oak barrels. Popular with wine collectors is winemaker Michael Lee's Artist Series cabernet sauvignon, a limited production from the winery's best vineyards featuring labels with original artwork by renowned artists. The tasting room, housed in one of the old barns, offers free tastings of most varieties, as well as gift items for sale. Wine prices are moderate, ranging from $8 to $25; the Artist Series, on the other hand, runs anywhere from $70 to $250.

WHERE TO STAY

If you're having trouble finding a vacancy, try calling the **Sonoma Valley Visitors Bureau** at ☎ **707/996-1090.** They'll try to refer you to a lodging that has a room to spare, but they won't make reservations for you. Another option is calling the **Bed and Breakfast Association of Sonoma Valley** (☎ **800/969-4667**), which will refer you to a member B&B and make reservations for you as well.

VERY EXPENSIVE

✪ **Kenwood Inn & Spa.** 10400 Sonoma Hwy., Kenwood, CA 95452. ☎ **800/353-6966** or 707/833-1293. Fax 707/833-1247. 12 units. Apr–Oct $255–$395 double (2-night minimum on weekends). Nov–Mar $225–$365. Rates include gourmet breakfast and bottle of wine. AE, MC, V.

Inspired by the villas of Tuscany, the honey-colored Italian-style buildings, flower-filled flagstone courtyard, and pastoral views of vineyard-covered hills are enough to make any northern Italian homesick. Every spacious room here is lavishly and exquisitely decorated with imported tapestries, velvets, and antiques; each has a fireplace, balcony (unless you're on the ground floor), feather bed, CD player, and down comforter—but no phone or TV, so you can relax. A minor caveat is road noise, which you're unlikely to hear from your room, but can be slightly heard over the tranquil pumped-in music around the courtyard and pool.

An impressive two-course gourmet breakfast is served poolside or in the Mediterranean-style dining room; ours consisted of a poached egg accompanied by light, flavorful potatoes, red bell peppers, and other roasted vegetables, all artfully arranged, followed by a delicious homemade scone with fresh berries and a small lemon tart.

Amenities: The inn's own full-service spa offers aromatherapy, massage (one of the best we've had in a long time), and various skin and body treatments such as a Mediterranean salt scrub of lemon rind, rosemary, and salt.

○ **Sonoma Mission Inn & Spa.** 18140 Sonoma Hwy. (Calif. 12), P.O. Box 1447, Sonoma, CA 94546. ☎ **800/862-4945** or 707/938-9000. Fax 707/938-4250. 228 units. A/C MINIBAR TV TEL. Nov–Apr $295 Historic Inn room; $225–$370 Wine Country room; $325 suite. May–Oct $220–$325 Historic Inn room; $285–$385 Wine Country room; $395–$900 suite. AE, CB, DC, MC, V. From central Sonoma, drive 3 miles north on Calif. 12.

The inn consists of a massive three-story replica of a Spanish mission (well, aside from the pink paint job), satellite wings housing 30 superluxury suites, and, most important, the spa facilities. Set on 12 meticulously groomed acres, it's a popular retreat for the wealthy (mostly older folks) and the well-known. The original attraction was the naturally heated artesian mineral water, which is pumped from directly underneath the spa into the temperature-controlled pools and whirlpools. But equally enticing is the slew of luxury-spa amenities: massages, facials, yoga, manicures, tennis courts, hot tub, and two swimming pools.

Accommodations are furnished in modern style with such extras as down comforters, bathroom scales, hair dryers, and oversize bath towels. The Wine Country rooms, in a newer building, feature king-size beds, desks, fridges, and huge limestone-and-marble bathrooms; some offer wood-burning fireplaces, and many have balconies. The older, slightly smaller Historic Inn rooms are sweetly appointed with homey furnishings, and most have queen-size beds; they are, however, overpriced for what you get, and in serious need of renovation. All rooms have video access on command and come with a complimentary bottle of wine.

While the spa is truly fantastic, the rooms were looking a bit tired during our last visit—but thanks to new owners and a $25-million renovation, it's not just the clientele that's being rejuvenated here. The spa itself is undergoing an expansion that will double its size and include a new Roman bath; the property will soon be home to an 18-hole golf course.

Dining: We highly recommend The Grille (see "Where to Dine," below). There's also a casual cafe that serves American cuisine at lunch and is renowned for its bountiful breakfasts.

Amenities: Room service, concierge, laundry, dry cleaning, newspaper delivery, baby-sitting, secretarial services, valet parking, complimentary refreshments, health club, tennis courts. Full spa facilities with a range of treatments and nutritional consultation (individual spa and salon services priced from $35 to $134). The use of the spa's bathhouse (which includes a sauna, steam room, whirlpool, outdoor exercise pool, and gym with weight equipment) costs $10 weekdays, $20 weekends, but is complimentary with any spa service.

MODERATE

Beltane Ranch. 11775 Sonoma Hwy. (Hwy. 12), Glen Ellen, CA 95442. ☎ **707/996-6501.** 6 units. TEL. $130–$170 double; $210 cottage. Rates include full breakfast. No credit cards (though checks are accepted).

The word "Ranch" conjures up an image of a big ol' two-story house in the middle of hundreds of rolling acres, the kind of place where you laze away the day in a hammock watching the grass grow or pitching horseshoes in the garden. Well, friend, you can have all that and more at the Beltane Ranch, a century-old buttercup-yellow manor that's been everything from a bunkhouse to a brothel to a turkey farm. You simply can't help but feel your tensions ease away as you kick your feet up on the shady wrap-around porch overlooking the vineyards, sipping a cool, fruity chardonnay. Each room is uniquely decorated with American and European antiques; all have private bathrooms, sitting areas, and separate entrances. A big country breakfast is served in the garden on the porch overlooking the vineyards. For exercise, you can play tennis on the private court or hike the trails meandering through the 1,600-acre estate. *Tip:* Request one of the upstairs rooms, which have the best views.

El Dorado Hotel. 405 First St. W., Sonoma, CA 95476. ☎ **800/289-3031** or 707/996-3030. Fax 707/996-3148. 26 units. A/C TV TEL. Summer $130–$160 double; winter $100–$130 double. Rates include continental breakfast and a split of wine. AE, MC, V.

This place may look like a 19th-century Wild West relic from the outside, but inside it's all 20th-century deluxe. Each modern guest room—designed by the same folks who put together the ultra-exclusive Auberge du Soleil resort in Rutherford (see "Where to Stay" in Napa Valley section, above)—has French windows and tiny terraces; some offer lovely views of the plaza, while others overlook the hotel's private courtyard and heated lap pool. Each room has a private bathroom with plush towels and hair dryer. Services include a concierge, laundry, in-room massage, bicycle rental, and access to a nearby health club. Breakfast, served either inside or out in the courtyard, includes coffee, fruits, and freshly baked breads and pastries. Within the hotel is Piatti, a popular restaurant serving regional Italian cuisine (see "Where to Dine," below).

✪ Gaige House Inn. 13540 Arnold Dr., Glen Ellen, CA 95442. ☎ **800/935-0237** or 707/935-0237. Fax 707/935-6411. 11 units. A/C TEL. Winter $170–$325 double; summer $195–$355 double. Rates include full breakfast and evening wines. AE, DISC, MC, V.

The Gaige House is the best B&B we've ever stayed in. The inn's owners, Ken Burnet, Jr., and Greg Nemrow, turned what was already a fine bed-and-breakfast into the finest in the Wine Country, and they've done it by offering a level of service, amenities, and decor normally associated with outrageously expensive resorts (and without the snobbery). Breakfast is made with herbs from the inn's garden and prepared by a chef who commutes daily from San Francisco. Firm mattresses are graced with wondrously silk-soft linens and premium down comforters, and even the furniture and artwork are of museum quality. Behind the inn is a 1½-acre oasis with perfectly manicured lawns, a 40-foot-long swimming pool, and a creek-side hammock shaded by a majestic Heritage oak. All 11 rooms, each artistically designed in a plantation theme with Asian and Indonesian influences, have private bathrooms, direct-dial phones, and king- or queen-size beds; two rooms have Jacuzzi tubs, and several have fireplaces. On sunny days, breakfast is served at individual tables on the large terrace. Evenings are best spent in the reading parlor sipping premium wines. In the past year, they've added an outdoor hot tub and two additional suites in the creek-side house.

INEXPENSIVE

✪ Glenelly Inn. 5131 Warm Springs Rd. (off Arnold Dr.), Glen Ellen, CA 95442. ☎ **707/996-6720.** www.glenelly.com. Fax 707/996-5227. 8 units. $115–$150 double. Rates include full breakfast, ever-available cookies, and hot and cold beverages. MC, V.

This former 1916 railroad inn is positively drenched in serenity. Located well off the main highway on an oak-studded hillside, the inn comes with everything you would expect from a country retreat—long verandas with comfy wicker chairs and views of the verdant Sonoma hillsides; a hearty country breakfast served beside a large cobblestone fireplace; and bright, immaculate rooms with private entrances, authentic antiques, old-fashioned clawfoot tubs, Scandinavian down comforters, firm mattresses, and ceiling fans. The simmering hot tub is ensconced within a grapevine- and rose-covered arbor.

Victorian Garden Inn. 316 E. Napa St., Sonoma, CA 95476. ☎ **800/543-5339** or 707/996-5339. Fax 707/996-1689. 4 units. $95–$185 double. Rates include breakfast and afternoon wine and sherry. AE, DC, MC, V.

Proprietor Donna Lewis runs what is easily the cutest B&B in Sonoma Valley. A small picket fence and wall of trees enclose an adorable Victorian garden brimming with bowers of violets, roses, camellias, and peonies, all shaded under flowering fruit trees. Four guest rooms—three in the century-old water tower and one in the main house, an 1870s Greek Revival farmhouse—are in keeping with the Victorian theme: white wicker furniture, floral prints, padded armchairs, and clawfoot tubs. The most popular rooms are in the Top o' the Tower, which has its own entrance and view overlooking the garden, and the Woodcutter's Cottage, which has its own entrance and garden view, plus a sofa and armchairs set in front of the fireplace. A breakfast of croissants, muffins, gourmet coffee, and fruit picked from the garden is served at the dining table, in the garden, or in your room; evening wine and sherry are served in the parlor. Leisure time can be spent in the pool or along the shaded wraparound porch.

Sonoma Hotel. 110 W. Spain St., Sonoma, CA 95476. ☎ **800/468-6016** or 707/996-2996. Fax 707/996-7014. 16 units. $155–$220 double/suite. Rates include afternoon wine tasting. AE, DC, DISC, MC, V.

This cute little historic hotel on Sonoma's tree-lined Town Square underwent a change of ownership and renovation within the past year. Now all of the rooms, which are appointed with purchasable furniture from Harvest Home Stores, are decorated in a style combining French, Mexican, and American antiques and new furnishings. New additions include bathrooms and phones in each room, plus a new California cuisine restaurant, Heirloom's, whose chef, Michael Dotson, hails from San Francisco's PlumpJack.

WHERE TO DINE

Though Sonoma Valley has far fewer visitors than Napa Valley, its restaurants are often equally as crowded, so be sure to make reservations in advance.

EXPENSIVE

Babette's Cafe. 464 First St. E. (at the square), Sonoma. ☎ **707/939-8921.** Reservations recommended for both cafe and dining room. Cafe main courses $12–$19; dining room fixed-price menu $63. MC, V. Cafe daily noon–10pm; dining room Tues–Sat 6–10pm. FRENCH.

Although rave reviews have secured Babette's reputation as one of the hottest places to dine in Sonoma, this quaint little spot across from the plaza has managed to maintain its homey atmosphere. Babette's is both intimate and casual; its front-room cafe feels like a cozy French bistro, while the main dining room is a smaller, more formal space. But its down-home appeal doesn't extend to the food, which continues to garner rave reviews while remaining affordably priced. Along with soups, salads, and sandwiches (all less than $8), main courses include cassoulet baked with duck confit, house-made pork sausage, lamb, and white beans; and Moroccan spiced vegetables on couscous. Chef Daniel Patterson (formerly of Domaine Chandon and Mustards Grill) also offers a fantastic six-course fixed-price dinner (main dining room only). Be sure to start your feast with the fresh goat cheese on toast and end with the warm peach-and-blueberry napoleon. Wines can be paired with each course for an additional $50.

Gourmet Picnics, Sonoma Style

Sure, Sonoma has plenty of restaurants, but when the weather's warm, there's no better way to have lunch in the Wine Country than by toting a picnic basket to your favorite winery and basking under the sweet Sonoma sunshine. Even Sonoma's central plaza, with its many picnic tables, is a good spot to set up a gourmet spread.

But first you need grub, so head to the venerable **Sonoma Cheese Factory,** on the plaza at 2 Spain St. (☎ **707/996-1000**), to stock up for an alfresco fete. The factory offers award-winning house-made cheeses and an extraordinary variety of imported meats and cheeses; a few are set out for tasting every day. Also available are caviar, gourmet salads, pâté, and homemade Sonoma Jack cheese. Pick up some good, inexpensive sandwiches, such as fire-roasted pork loin or New York steak. While you're there, you can watch a narrated slide show about the cheese-making process. The factory is open Monday through Friday from 8:30am to 5:30pm, Saturday and Sunday from 8:30am to 6pm.

✪ **The Girl & the Fig.** 13690 Arnold Dr., Glen Ellen. ☎ **707/938-3634.** www. thegirlandthefig.com. Reservations recommended. Main courses $12–$19. AE, MC, V. Daily 5:30–9pm; Sun brunch 10am–2:30pm. COUNTRY FRENCH.

This modern, attractive cafe with an open kitchen is the creation of Sondra Bernstein (The Girl), who convinced San Francisco chefs/couple Gina Marie Armanini and John Gillis to come work for her. "They make a fantastic team," boasts Bernstein, and if the ever-crowded dining room is any indication, both tourists and locals agree. The cuisine is nouveau-country with French nuances, and yes, figs are sure to be on the menu in one form or another, such as the wonderful winter fig salad made with arugula, pecans, dried figs, Laura Chenel goat cheese, and a fig-and-port vinaigrette. Garden-fresh produce and local meats, poultry, and fish are used whenever possible, in dishes such as roasted root vegetables that accompany the braised lamb shank with polenta and wilted greens or the hearty grilled portobello sandwich with a side salad—a bargain at just $8.95. For dessert, try the warm pear galette topped with gingered crème fraîche, a glass of the Quady Essensia Orange Muscat, and a sliver of raclette from the cheese cart. Sondra knows her wines, and will be happy to choose the best accompaniment to your meal. *Note:* Monday nights in Glen Ellen are a whole lot more fun since Sondra introduced Fondue Night.

Glen Ellen Inn Restaurant. 13670 Arnold Dr., Glen Ellen. ☎ **707/996-6409.** Reservations recommended. Main courses $12–$22. AE, MC, V. Off-season Thurs–Tues 5:30pm–closing (depending on reservations); summer nightly 5:30pm–closing. CALIFORNIA.

Christian and Karen Bertrand run this popular Glen Ellen restaurant. The dining room is so small and cozy that you feel as if you're dining in their home, but that's exactly the place's charm. Garden seating is the favored choice on sunny days, but the covered, heated patio is always welcoming. First courses from Christian's open kitchen might include a wild-mushroom-and-sausage "purse" served in a brandy cream sauce and warm goat-cheese croquettes. Main courses change with the seasons, but might range from linguini with artichoke hearts and feta to a stellar late-harvest ravioli, which is stuffed with pumpkin, walnuts, and sun-dried cranberries and served on a bed of butternut squash. Other favorites include the marinated pork tenderloin on smoked mozzarella polenta, topped with roasted-pepper/onion compote; and, of course, the classic filet mignon accompanied by a full-bodied cabernet sauvignon. On our last visit, the Sonoma Valley mixed green salad, seared ahi tuna, and homemade French vanilla ice cream floating in bittersweet caramel sauce made a perfect meal. The wine list offers numerous Sonoma selections, as well as more than a dozen wines by the glass.

✪ The Grille. At Sonoma Mission Inn, 18140 Sonoma Hwy., Sonoma. ☎ **707/938-9000.** Reservations recommended. Main courses $21–$26. AE, MC, V. Sun brunch 10am–2pm; daily 6pm–9:30pm. CALIFORNIA/SPA.

The Grille, one of the most well-known restaurants in the Wine Country, has long suffered from a solid reputation for serving high-caliber spa cuisine. The problem, of course, is the word "spa," which conjures up visions of boiled vegetables and soybean salads. Fortunately, The Grille has found a solution: Toni Robertson. One bite of the corn risotto flavored with wild mushrooms and molten *reggiano parmigiano* cheese is testament enough. About half of Robertson's menu is spa-conscious, with the calorie and cholesterol percentages listed below selected entrees ranging from roasted medallions of ostrich in apple sauce (11mg cholesterol, 18.1g fat) to oven-roasted breast of Petaluma chicken in a crimini-mushroom cabernet sauce (105mg cholesterol, 4.6g fat). He mercifully spares us the cholesterol and fat gram counts, however, for the dishes we *really* want, such as the seared Sonoma foie gras with caramelized apples, white truffle oil, and a zinfandel reduction sauce (yes, it's as good—and as bad for you—as it sounds), or the rack of herb-marinated lamb, roasted in Levain crumbs and pistachios and served with garlic mashed potatoes. Desserts, such as the tart lemon chiffon topped with a sweet berry purée, are equally as adept at the less-is-more approach. The restaurant's soothing decor features peach-colored walls, bentwood chairs, and just the right amount of elbow room. Service is professional yet friendly. The wine list is extensive and expensive.

Kenwood Restaurant & Bar. 9900 Sonoma Hwy., Kenwood. ☎ **707/833-6326.** Reservations recommended. Main courses $12.50–$26. MC, V. Wed–Sun 11:30am–9pm. CALIFORNIA/CONTINENTAL.

This is what California Wine Country dining should be. From the terrace of the Kenwood Restaurant, diners enjoy a view of the vineyards set against Sugar Loaf Ridge as they imbibe Sonoma's finest at umbrella-covered tables. On nippy days, you can retreat inside to the Sonoma-style roadhouse, with its shiny wood floors, pine ceiling, vibrant artwork, and cushioned rattan chairs set at white-cloth–covered tables. Chef Max Schacher serves first-rate cuisine, perfectly balanced between tradition and innovation, and complemented by a reasonably priced wine list. Great starters are the Dungeness crab cake with herb mayonnaise; superfresh sashimi with ginger, soy, and wasabi; and the wonderful Caesar salad. Main-dish choices might include poached salmon in a creamy caper sauce, prawns with saffron Pernod sauce, or braised Sonoma rabbit with grilled polenta. But the Kenwood doesn't take itself too seriously—sandwiches and burgers are also available.

MODERATE

Della Santina's. 133 E. Napa St. (just east of the square), Sonoma. ☎ **707/935-0576.** Reservations recommended. Main courses $8.95–$14.75. AE, DISC, MC, V. Daily 11:30am–3pm and 5–9:30pm. ITALIAN.

Those of you who just can't take another expensive, chichi California meal should follow the locals to this friendly, traditional Italian restaurant. Every classic Tuscan dish we tried was refreshingly authentic and well flavored—without overbearing sauces or one *hint* of California pretentiousness. Start with traditional antipasti, especially the sliced mozzarella and tomatoes or the delicious white beans. The nine pasta dishes are, again, wonderfully authentic (gnocchi lovers, rejoice!). The spit-roasted meat dishes are a local favorite (though we found them a bit overcooked), and for those who can't choose among chicken, pork, turkey, rabbit, or duck, there's a selection that offers a choice of three. Don't worry about breaking your bank on a bottle of wine, as most of the savory choices here go for under $25.

Piatti. 405 First St. W., Sonoma. ☎ **707/996-2351.** Reservations recommended. Main courses $9.95–$18.95. AE, DC, MC, V. Sun–Thurs 11:30am–10pm; Fri–Sat 11:30am–11pm. ITALIAN.

Part of a Northern California chain that originated in Napa, Piatti has built a steadfast and true clientele by consistently serving large portions of good Italian food at a fair price in a fun and festive setting (got all that?). Good pizzas and braised meats—such as the superb lamb shank flavored with a rich port-wine sauce and fresh mint—emerge from a wood-burning oven. Other recommended dishes include a wonderful roast-vegetable appetizer, the teeming pile of fresh mussels in a tomato-and-herb broth, the rotisserie chicken with garlic mashed potatoes, and the veal scallopine. Also offered is an array of satisfying pastas. Granted, there are fancier and more intimate restaurants in the valley, but none that can fill you up with such good food at these prices. And, if the sun is out, there's no prettier place in Sonoma to dine alfresco than Piatti's courtyard.

INEXPENSIVE

Basque Boulangerie Cafe. 460 First St. E., Sonoma. ☎ **707/935-7687.** Menu items $3–$7. No credit cards. Daily 7am–6pm. BAKERY/DELI.

If you prefer a lighter morning meal and strong coffee, stand in line with the locals at the Basque Boulangerie Cafe, the most popular gathering spot in the Sonoma Valley. Most everything—sourdough Basque breads, pastries, quiche, soups, salads, desserts, sandwiches, cookies—is made in-house, and made well. Daily lunch specials, such as a grilled-veggie sandwich with smoked mozzarella cheese ($4.75), are listed on the chalkboard out front. Seating is scarce, and if you can score a sidewalk table on a sunny day, consider yourself one lucky person. A popular option is ordering to go and eating in the shady plaza across the street. The cafe also sells wine by the glass, as well as a wonderful cinnamon bread by the loaf that's ideal for making French toast.

✪ **Lo Spuntino.** 400 First St. E., Sonoma. ☎ **707/935-5656.** Deli items $5–$9. AE, CB, DISC, MC, V. Sun–Thurs 10am–6pm; Fri–Sat 10am–10pm. ITALIAN DELI.

Lo Spuntino, Italian for "snack" or a tiny taste, is the sexiest thing going in Sonoma, a suave deli and wine bar owned by Sam and Vicki Sebastiani, who also run Viansa Winery. It's a visual masterpiece, with shiny black-and-white-checkered flooring, long counters of Italian marble, track lighting, and a center deli and wine bar where a crew of young men slices meats, pours wines, and scoops gelato. Start by sampling the preserves and jams near the entrance, and then choose among the armada of cured meats, cheeses, fruits, pastas, salads, and breads lining the deli. Popular choices are the hefty sandwiches on herbed focaccia bread or the herb-marinated rotisserie chickens served by the half with your choice of pasta or salad. Roasted turkey, duck, pork, lamb, and rabbit are also available. Opposite the deli is the wine bar, featuring all of Viansa's current releases for both tasting and purchase, as well as a small selection of microbrewed beers on tap. On your way out, stop at the gelateria and treat yourself to some intense Italian ice cream. *Note:* Lo Spuntino also hosts live jazz bands every Friday night from 6 to 9pm.

7

The Northern Coast

by Matthew R. Poole

Heading north from San Francisco, you'll come upon a California that hardly resembles the southern part of the state. It's an entirely different landscape, in climate as well as flora and fauna. You can forget about California's fabled surfing-and-bikini scene this far north; instead, you'll find miles and miles of rugged coastline with broad beaches and tiny bays harboring dramatic rock formations—from chimney stacks to bridges and blowholes—carved by the ocean waves.

The best time to visit is in the spring or fall. In spring, the headlands are carpeted with wildflowers—golden poppy, iris, and sea foam—and in fall, the sun shines clear and bright. Summers are typically cool and windy, with the ubiquitous fog burning off by the afternoon.

You may think you've arrived in Alaska when you hit the beaches of Northern California. Take a dip in the sea and you'll soon agree with the locals: When it comes to swimming, the Arctic waters along the north coast are best left to the sea lions. But that doesn't mean you can't enjoy the beaches, whether by strolling along the water or taking in the panoramic views of towering cliffs and seascapes. And unlike their southern counterparts, the beaches along the north coast are not likely to be crowded, even in summer.

The most scenic way to reach Stinson Beach, Gualala, Mendocino, and points north is to drive along the coast via Calif. 1. The larger freeway, U.S. 101, runs inland through Healdsburg and Cloverdale and is much faster, but doesn't provide the spectacular views of coastal cliffs and windswept beaches you will see on Calif. 1. A good compromise if you're headed to, say, Mendocino, is to take U.S. 101 to Cloverdale, then cut over on Calif. 128 to the coast.

Oh, and one last thing: Dress warmly.

1 Point Reyes National Seashore

35 miles N of San Francisco

The National Seashore system was created to protect rural and undeveloped stretches of the coast from the pressures brought on by soaring real-estate values and increasing population. Nowhere is the success of the system more evident that at Point Reyes. Residents of the surrounding towns—**Inverness, Point Reyes Station,** and **Olema**—have steadfastly resisted runaway development. You won't find any strip malls or fast-food joints here—just a laid-back coastal town with cafes and country inns where gentle living prevails.

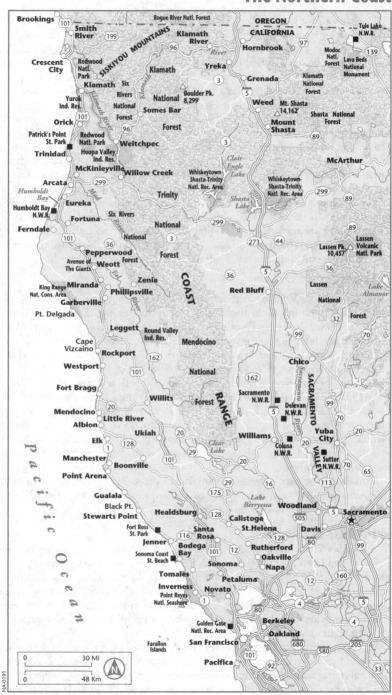

The Northern Coast

The park, a 71,000-acre hammer-shaped peninsula jutting 10 miles into the Pacific and backed by Tomales Bay, is loaded with wildlife, ranging from tule elk, birds, and bobcats to gray whales, sea lions, and great white sharks. Aside from its beautiful scenery, it also boasts historical treasures that offer a window into California's coastal past, including lighthouses, turn-of-the-century dairies and ranches, the site of Sir Francis Drake's 1579 landing, plus a complete replica of a coastal Miwok Indian village.

Though the peninsula's people and wildlife live in harmony above the ground, the situation beneath the soil is much more volatile. The infamous San Andreas Fault separates Point Reyes—the northernmost landmass on the Pacific Plate—from the rest of California, which rests on the North American Plate. Point Reyes is making its way toward Alaska at a rate of about 2 inches per year, but there have been times when it has moved much faster. In 1906, Point Reyes jumped north almost 20 feet in an instant, leveling San Francisco and jolting the rest of the state. The half-mile **Earthquake Trail,** near the Bear Valley Visitor Center, illustrates this geological drama with a loop through an area torn by the slipping fault. Shattered fences, rifts in the ground, and a barn knocked off its foundation by the quake illustrate how alive the earth is here. If that doesn't convince you, a seismograph in the visitor center will.

ESSENTIALS

Point Reyes is only 30 miles northwest of San Francisco, but it takes at least 90 minutes to reach by car (it's all the small towns, not the topography, that slow you down). The easiest route is via Sir Francis Drake Boulevard from U.S. 101 south of San Rafael; it takes its bloody time getting to Point Reyes, but does so without any detours. For a much longer but more scenic route, take the Stinson Beach/Calif. 1 exit off U.S. 101 just south of Sausalito and follow Calif. 1 north.

As soon as you arrive at Point Reyes, stop at the **Bear Valley Visitor Center** (☎ 415/663-1092) on Bear Valley Road (look for the small sign posted just north of Olema on Calif. 1) and pick up a free Point Reyes trail map. The rangers here are extremely friendly and helpful, and can answer any questions you have about the National Seashore. Be sure to check out the great natural-history and cultural displays as well. It's open Monday through Friday from 9am to 5pm, Saturday and Sunday from 8am to 5pm.

Entrance to the park is free. Camping is $10 per site per night, and permits are required; reservations can be made up to 2 months in advance by calling ☎ 415/663-8054, Monday through Friday from 9am to 2pm.

WHAT TO SEE & DO

In November 1995, the Bay Area suffered a great loss when 12,354 acres of Point Reyes burned in an uncontrollable brush fire. However, there's still plenty of pristine property in this 65,000-acre park; even the areas that suffered the worst are quickly replenishing themselves with spectacular blankets of wildflowers. The park encompasses several surf-pounded beaches, bird estuaries, open swaths of land with roaming elk, and the Point Reyes lighthouse—a favorite among visitors who are awestruck by the spectacular views of the coast.

When heading out to any part of the Point Reyes coast, expect to spend the day surrounded by nature at its finest. But bear in mind that as beautiful as the wilderness can be, it's also untamable. Waters in these areas are not only bone chilling and home to a vast array of sea life, including sharks, but are also unpredictable and dangerous. There are no lifeguards on duty and waves and riptides make swimming strongly discouraged. Pets are not permitted on any of the area's trails.

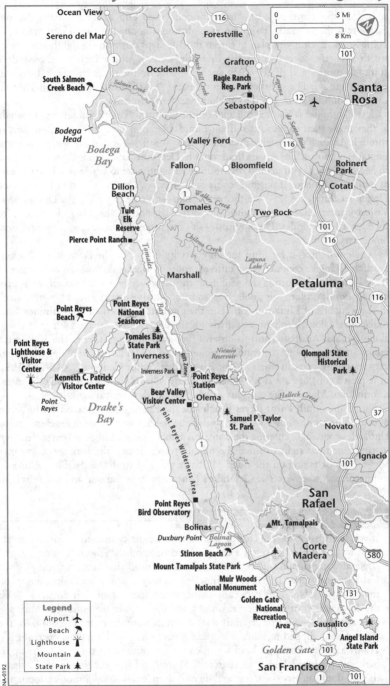

Ocean View

Sereno del Mar

116

Forestville

1

Occidental

Grafton

South Salmon
Creek Beach

Salmon Creek

Ragle Ranch
Reg. Park

Dutch Bill Creek

Laguna de Santa Rosa

101

Santa
Rosa

12

Sebastopol

Bodega
Head

Bodega
Bay

Valley Ford

116

Rohnert
Park

Fallon

Bloomfield

Cotati

Dillon
Beach

1

Walker Creek

Tomales

Two Rock

101

Tule
Elk
Reserve

116

Pierce Point Ranch

Chileno Creek

Laguna
Lake

Marshall

Petaluma

Point Reyes
Beach

Point Reyes
National
Seashore

Tomales Bay
State Park

116

Tomales Bay

1

Rift Zone

Nicasio
Reservoir

101

Olompali State
Historical
Park

Point Reyes
Lighthouse &
Visitor Center

Inverness

Inverness Park

Kenneth C. Patrick
Visitor Center

Point Reyes
Station

Point
Reyes

Bear Valley
Visitor Center

Olema

Halleck Creek

37

Drake's
Bay

Samuel P. Taylor
St. Park

Novato

1

101

Ignacio

Point Reyes Wilderness Area

101

Point Reyes
Bird Observatory

San
Rafael

Bolinas

Mt. Tamalpais

Duxbury Point

Bolinas
Lagoon

Corte
Madera

Stinson Beach

580

Mount Tamalpais State Park

Muir Woods
National Monument

1

131

Golden Gate
National
Recreation
Area

Richardson Bay

Sausalito

1

Angel Island
State Park

Golden Gate

101

San Francisco

1

101

Legend
- ✈ Airport
- 🌴 Beach
- 🗼 Lighthouse
- ▲ Mountain
- 🌲 State Park

NA-0192

By far the most popular—and crowded—attraction at Point Reyes National Seashore is the venerable **Point Reyes Lighthouse,** located at the westernmost tip of Point Reyes. Even if you plan to forego the 308 steps down to the lighthouse, it's still worth the visit to marvel at the dramatic scenery, which includes thousands of common murres and prides of sea lions that bask on the rocks far below (binoculars come in handy). The lighthouse visitor center (☎ **415/669-1534**) is open Thursday through Monday from 10am to 4:30pm, weather permitting.

The lighthouse is also the top spot on the California coast to observe **gray whales** as they make their southward and northward migration along the coast from January through April. The annual round-trip is 10,000 miles—one of the longest mammal migrations known. The whales head south in December and January, and return north in March. *Note:* If you plan to drive out to the lighthouse to whale-watch, arrive early as parking is limited. If possible, come on a weekday. On a weekend or holiday from December through April—weather permitting—it's wise to park at the Drake's Beach Visitor Center and take the shuttle bus to the lighthouse, which is $3 for adults, free for kids 13 and under. Dress warmly—it's often quite cold and windy—and bring binoculars.

Whale watching is far from the only activity offered at the Point Reyes National Seashore. Rangers conduct many different tours on weekends: You can walk along the **Bear Valley Trail,** spotting the wildlife at the ocean's edge; see the waterfowl at **Five-brooks Pond;** explore tide pools; view some of North America's most beautiful ducks in the wetlands of **Limantour;** hike to the promontory overlooking **Chimney Rock** to see the sea lions, elephant seals, harbor seals, and seabirds; or take a self-guided walk along the **San Andreas Fault** to observe the site of the epicenter of the 1906 earth-quake and learn about the regional geology. And this is just a sampling. Since tours vary seasonally, you can either call the **Bear Valley Visitor Center** (☎ **415/663-1092**) or request a copy of *Park Paper,* which includes a schedule of activities and other useful information. Many of the tours are suitable for travelers with disabilities.

North and South **Point Reyes Beach** face the Pacific and withstand the full brunt of ocean tides and winds—so much so that the water is far too rough for even wading. Until a few years ago, entering the water was actually illegal, but persistent surfers went to court for their right to shred the mighty waves. Today, the park service strongly advises against taking on the tides, so play it safe and stroll the coastline. Along the southern coast, the waters of ✪ **Drake's Beach** can be as tranquil and serene as Point

---

Stinky Fun . . . on the Half Shell

If you want to escape the crowds and enjoy some stinky man-made entertainment, head to ✪ **Johnson's Oyster Farm.** Located right on the edge of Drakes Estero (a large saltwater lagoon within the Point Reyes peninsula that produces nearly 20% of California's commercial oyster yield), Johnson's may look and smell like a dump, but those tasty bivalves don't come any fresher or cheaper. Granted, it doesn't look like much—a cluster of trailer homes, shacks, and oyster tanks surrounded by huge piles of oyster shells—but that certainly doesn't detract from the taste of fresh-out-of-the-water oysters dipped in Johnson's special sauce. The popular modus operandi is to 1) buy a couple dozen, 2) head for an empty campsite along the bay, 3) fire up the barbecue pit (don't forget the charcoal), 4) split and 'cue the little guys, 5) slather them in Johnson's special sauce, and then 6) slurp 'em down. Johnson's is located off Sir Francis Drake Boulevard, about 6 miles west(ish) of Inverness; open Tuesday through Sunday from 8am to 4:30pm (☎ **415/669-1149**).

Reyes's are turbulent. Locals come here to sun and picnic; occasionally a hearty soul ventures into the cold waters of Drake's Bay. But keep in mind that storms generally come inland from the south and almost always hit Drake's before moving north or south. A powerful weather front can turn wispy waves into torrential tides.

Some of the park's best—and least crowded—highlights can only be approached on foot, such as **Alamere Falls,** a freshwater stream that cascades down a 40-foot bluff onto Wildcat Beach, or **Tomales Point Trail,** which passes through the Tule Elk Reserve, a protected haven for roaming herds of tule elk that once numbered in the thousands. Hiking most of the trails usually ends up being an all-day outing, however, so it's best to split a 2-day trip within Point Reyes National Seashore into a "by car" day and a "by foot" day.

If you're into bird watching, you definitely want to visit the **Point Reyes Bird Observatory** (☎ **415/868-1221**), one of the few full-time ornithological research stations in the United States, located at the southeast end of the park on Mesa Road. This is where ornithologists keep an eye on more than 400 feathered species. Admission to the visitor center and nature trail is free, and visitors are welcome to observe the tricky process of catching and banding the birds. It's open daily from 15 minutes after sunrise until sunset. Banding hours vary; call ☎ **415/868-0655** for exact times.

One of our favorite things to do in Point Reyes is paddling through placid **Tomales Bay,** a haven for migrating birds and marine mammals. Kayak trips, including sunset outings, full-moon paddles, and day trips, are organized by **Tomales Bay Sea Kayaking** (☎ **415/663-1743;** www.tamalsaka.com). Instruction, clinics, and boat delivery are available, and all ages and levels are welcome. Prices start at $45 for tours. Half-day rentals begin at $25 for one, $35 for two. Don't worry, the kayaks are very stable and there are no waves to contend with. The launching point is located on Calif. 1 at the Marshall Boatworks in Marshall, 8 miles north of Point Reyes Station. Open in the summer, Friday through Sunday from 9am to 6pm and by appointment.

WHERE TO STAY

If you're having trouble finding a vacancy, **Inns of Marin** (☎ **800/887-2880** or 415/663-2000) and **West Marin Network** (☎ **415/663-9543**) are two reputable services that will help you find accommodations, ranging from one-room cottages to inns and complete vacation homes. Keep in mind that many places here have a 2-night minimum, although in slow season they may make an exception. They'll also refer you to restaurants, hiking, and attractions in the area.

EXPENSIVE

Blackthorne Inn. 266 Vallejo Ave. (off Sir Francis Drake Blvd., south of Inverness), Inverness Park, P.O. Box 712, Inverness, CA 94937. ☎ **415/663-8621.** www.blackthorneinn.com. 5 units. $175–$300 double. Rates include buffet breakfast. MC, V.

This elaborate redwood home with its octagonal widow's walk, spiral staircase, turrets, and multiple decks looks more like a superdeluxe tree house than a B&B. Our favorite—and the most expensive—unit is the Eagle's Nest, an octagonal room enclosed by glass and topped with a private sundeck with a catwalk leading to the private outhouse. The largest room is the Forest View Studio, a virtual suite complete with deck, while the smallest room is the Hideaway, which has a private entrance and a sitting area facing the woods; both are furnished with wicker and decorated with floral fabrics and modern lithographs. All have private baths. The main sitting room in the house features a large stone fireplace, skylight, and stained-glass windows and is surrounded by a huge deck. Guests have use of the hot tub on the top deck.

✪ **Manka's Inverness Lodge.** On Argyle St. (off Sir Francis Drake Blvd., 1½ blocks north of downtown Inverness), P.O. Box 1110, Inverness, CA 94937. ☎ **800/58-LODGE** or 415/669-1034. 10 units. $145–$245 double room, $265–$450 cabin. MC, V.

If there were ever a reason to pack your bags and leave San Francisco for a day or two, this is it. A former hunting and fishing lodge, Manka's Inverness Lodge looks like something out of a Hans Christian Andersen fairy tale, right down to the tree-limb bedsteads and cooks roasting venison sausage in front of the hearth. It's all terribly romantic in a Jack London sort of way, and tastefully done as well. The lodge consists of a superb restaurant on the first floor, four rooms upstairs (*Tip:* Room nos. 1 and 2 come with large private decks), four rooms in the Redwood Annex, and two spacious one-bedroom cabins located behind the lodge that come with living rooms and kitchenettes. For the ultimate romantic splurge, inquire about their three secluded guest houses: Grizzly Lodge, Boat House, and Chicken Ranch.

Dining: The lodge's reputation is built on its restaurant, which dominates the bottom floor. The specialty of the house is game and fish, including oysters from Tomales Bay. Prices range from $18 to $28. The limited menu might feature pheasant with a Madeira jus, mashed potatoes, and a wild huckleberry jam; black buck antelope chops with sweet-corn salsa; or everybody's favorite, pan-seared elk tenderloin. It's open for dinner Thursday through Monday; in winter, however, it's open on weekends only.

Moderate

Bear Valley Inn. 88 Bear Valley Rd., Olema, CA 94950. ☎ **415/663-1777.** 3 units, none with private bathroom. $75–$135 double. Rates include breakfast. AE, DISC, MC, V.

Ron and JoAnne Nowell's venerable two-story 1899 Victorian has survived everything from a major earthquake to a recent forest fire, which is lucky for you because you'll be hard-pressed to find a better B&B for the price in Point Reyes. Granted, the Bear Valley Inn isn't perfect—the rooms lack private bathrooms and the main highway is a tad too close—but it's loaded with Victorian charm, right down to the profusion of flowers and vines outside and comfy chairs fronting a toasty-warm woodstove inside. It's in a great location, too, with three good restaurants only a block away and the entire National Seashore at your doorstep. Ron, who also runs a mountain-bike rental shop next door, can set you up wheel-wise for about $25 a day and point you in the right direction.

Point Reyes Country Inn & Stables. 12050 Calif. 1, P.O. Box 501, Point Reyes Station, CA 94956. ☎ **415/663-9696.** www.ptreyescountryinn.com. 7 units. $85–$210 double. Extra human guest $25; $10–$15 per horse. Rates include breakfast. MC, V.

Are you and your horsey dreaming of a country getaway? Then book a room at Point Reyes Country Inn & Stables, a five-bedroom, ranch-style home on 4 acres that offers pastoral accommodations for two- and four-legged guests (horses only), plus access to plenty of hiking and riding trails. Each room has a private bathroom and either a balcony or a garden. The innkeepers have also added two studios (with kitchens) above the stables, and rent out two cottages on Tomales Bay equipped with decks, stocked kitchens, fireplaces, and a shared dock.

Inexpensive

Point Reyes Hostel. Off Limantour Rd., P.O. Box 247, Point Reyes Station, CA 94956. ☎ **415/663-8811.** 44 bunks, 1 private room. $13–$15 per person. 3-night maximum stay. MC, V. Reception hours 7:30–9:30am and 4:30–9:30pm daily.

Located deep within Point Reyes National Seashore, this beautiful old ranch-style complex has 44 dormitory-style accommodations, including one room that's reserved for families (though at least one child must be 5 years old or younger). There are also two common rooms, each warmed by wood-burning stoves on chilly nights, as well as a fully equipped kitchen, barbecue (BYO charcoal), and patio. If you don't mind sharing your sleeping quarters with strangers, this is a deal that can't be beat. Reservations (and earplugs) are strongly recommended.

WHERE TO DINE

In addition to the following choices, see "Where to Stay," above, for a description of ✪ **Manka's Inverness Lodge & Restaurant.**

The Gray Whale. 12781 Sir Francis Drake Blvd., Inverness. ☎ **415/669-1244.** Main courses $5–$10. MC, V. Daily 11am–8pm. ITALIAN.

For more than a decade, the Gray Whale has been a popular pit stop for Bay Areans heading to the lighthouse at Point Reyes. Why so popular? First off, it's cheap: Sandwiches—such as the roasted eggplant with pesto and mozzarella—are under $6, as are most of the salads and pastas. Second, it's pretty good: Personal favorites are the specialty pizzas, such as the Californian (artichoke hearts, fresh basil, and tomatoes) and the Vegetarian (baked eggplant, roasted onions and romas, broccoli, and piles of freshly grated Parmesan cheese). Don't miss the homemade desserts, especially the French apple pie. Veteran hikers and mountain bikers stop by for an espresso booster, sipped on the small patio overlooking the block-long town of Inverness.

Station House Café. Main St., Point Reyes Station. ☎ **415/663-1515.** Reservations recommended. Breakfast $4.45–$7.50; main courses $9–$17.50. DISC, MC, V. Sun–Thurs 8am–9pm; Fri–Sat 8am–10pm. AMERICAN.

This friendly, low-key establishment has been a local favorite for more than 2 decades, thanks to its open kitchen, outdoor garden dining area (key on sunny days), and live music on weekends. Breakfast dishes range from a hangtown fry with local Johnson's oysters and bacon to eggs served with creamed spinach to mashed-potato pancakes. Lunch and dinner specials might include fettuccine with fresh local mussels steamed in a white-wine-and-butter sauce, or two-cheese polenta served with fresh spinach sauté and grilled garlic-buttered tomato—all made from local produce, seafood, and organically raised Niman-Schell Farms beef. Fresh salmon is also always on the menu. The cafe has an extensive list of fine California wines, plus local imported beers.

Taqueria La Quinta. 11285 Calif. 1 (at Third and Main sts.), Point Reyes Station. ☎ **415/663-8868.** Main courses $4–$6. No credit cards. Wed–Mon 11:30am–7:30pm. MEXICAN.

Fresh, fast, good, and cheap: What more could you ask for in a restaurant? Taqueria La Quinta has been one of our favorite lunch stops in downtown Point Reyes for years and years. A huge selection of Mexican-American standards are posted above the counter. Our favorite is chili verde in a spicy tomatillo sauce with a side of handmade corn tortillas. Those in the know inquire about the seafood specials. Since it's all self-serve, you can skip the tip, but watch out for the salsa—that sucker's hot.

2 Along the Sonoma Coast

BODEGA BAY

Beyond the tip of the Point Reyes peninsula, the road curves around toward the coastal village of Bodega Bay, which supports a fishing fleet of around 300 boats. It's a good place to stop for lunch or a stroll around town. Despite the droves of tourists who arrive on summer weekends, Bodega Bay is still a mostly working-class fishing town—the sort of place where most people start their day before dawn mending nets, rigging fishing poles, and talking shop. There are several interesting shops and galleries, though the best show in town—especially for kids—is at **Tides Wharf,** where the fishing boats come in to unload their daily catch, which is promptly gutted and packed in ice.

Bodega Head State Park is a great vantage point for whale watching during the annual migration season from January through April. At **Doran Beach,** there's a large bird sanctuary (willets, curlews, godwits, and more), and the University of California Marine Biology Lab (☎ 707/875-2211) next door conducts guided tours of its lab projects on Friday afternoons between 2 and 4pm (suggested donation is $2).

The **Bodega Harbour Golf Links,** at 21301 Heron Dr. (☎ 707/875-3538), enjoys a panoramic ocean-side setting. It's an 18-hole Scottish-style course designed by Robert Trent Jones, Jr. A new warm-up center and practice facility have been added; it's free of charge to registered golfers. Rates range from $50 with cart on weekdays to $80 with cart on weekends. If golfing isn't your thing, you can go horseback riding through some spectacular coastal scenery by contacting **Chanslor Horse Stables** (☎ 707/875-2721), which also has a petting zoo and pony rides for the kids. Open daily from 8am to 8pm.

One of the bay's major events is the **Fisherman's Festival**, in April. Local fishing boats, decorated with ribbons and banners, sail out for a Blessing of the Fleet, while up to 25,000 landlubbers enjoy music, a lamb-and-oyster barbecue, and an arts-and-crafts fair.

A few miles inland on Calif. 1 (toward Petaluma) is the tiny town of **Bodega** (pop. 100), famous as the setting of Alfred Hitchcock's *The Birds,* which was filmed here in 1961. Fans will want to visit the Potter School House and St. Teresa's Church.

For more information about these festivals and other goings-on in Bodega Bay, call or stop in at the **Bodega Bay Area Visitors Center,** 850 Calif. 1, Bodega Bay, CA 94923 (☎ 707/875-3422). It has lots of brochures about the town and the surrounding area, including maps of the Sonoma Coast State Beaches and the best local fishing spots.

WHERE TO STAY

✪ **Bodega Bay Lodge.** 103 Calif. 1, Bodega Bay, CA 94923. ☎ **800/368-2468** or 707/ 875-3525. 83 units. TV TEL. Mon–Thurs $150–$200 double, $295 suite; Fri–Sun $175–$225 double, $375 suite. 2-night minimum on weekends. AE, CB, DC, DISC, MC, V.

This is easily the best hotel in Bodega Bay. Every room has a private balcony with sweeping views of the bay and bird-filled marshes. As if that weren't enough, they even throw in a fireplace, stocked minibar, and plush furnishings and fabrics. If you can afford the elbow room, opt for one of the luxury suites. As a bonus, guests have complimentary access to a fitness center and sauna, as well as to a beautiful fieldstone spa and heated pool perched above the bay and surrounded by flower gardens.

The lodge's Duck Club Restaurant also enjoys a reputation as Bodega Bay's finest. Large picture windows take advantage of the bay view, a sublimely romantic setting for chef Jeff Reilly's Sonoma County cuisine. Entrees include farm-fresh asparagus strudel, roasted Petaluma duck, and fresh fish caught by the Bodega fleet. Breakfast and dinner are served daily.

Inn at the Tides. 800 Coast Hwy. 1, P.O. Box 640, Bodega Bay, CA 94923. ☎ **800/ 541-7788** or 707/875-2751. Fax 707/875-3023. www.innatthetides.com. 86 units. TV TEL. Summer Sun–Thurs $132–$232; Fri–Sat $154–$259. Winter rates drop about 20%. Rates include continental breakfast. Golf packages available. AE, DISC, MC, V.

The larger (and, in our opinion, less appealing) of Bodega Bay's two upscale lodgings, the other being Bodega Bay Lodge, the Inn at the Tides consists of a cluster of condo-like wood complexes perched on the side of a gently sloping hill. The selling point here is the view; each unit is staggered just enough to guarantee a view of the bay across the highway. The amenities are first-rate, such as the heated indoor/outdoor pool, Jacuzzi, Finnish sauna, and exercise room. While all the rooms are large and comfortably furnished, the decor is rather dated and uninspiring.

The Bay View Restaurant is open Wednesday through Sunday for dinner only. It offers ocean views and has a romantic, somewhat formal ambiance. Dishes range from rack of lamb to smoked chicken risotto, seared scallops, and filet mignon. Though the owners, to their credit, have poured a bundle of money into revitalizing it, it still suffers from a so-so reputation.

WHERE TO DINE

In addition to the following choices, see "Where to Stay," above, for descriptions of the hotel restaurants.

Breakers Cafe. 1400 Calif. 1, Bodega Bay. ☎ **707/875-2513.** Main courses $6–$16. MC, V. Daily 9am–9pm. CALIFORNIA.

If you're a big breakfast eater, the Breakers Cafe is your best bet in Bodega Bay. Omelets, Belgian waffles, baked polenta, house-baked muffins, and even good ol' biscuits and gravy are served in a pleasant greenhouse-style dining room filled with a profusion of healthy plants and diffused sunlight. The cafe also offers a modest lunch-and-dinner menu, ranging from above-average sandwiches and burgers to fresh pastas, locally caught seafood, and a small selection of vegetarian dishes. Prices run a bit steep for the seafood choices, but most items are under $10. If the weather's warm, ask for a table on the patio.

Lucas Wharf Deli. 595 Calif. 1, Bodega Bay. ☎ **707/875-3562.** Deli items $4–$10. DISC, MC, V. Daily 10am–7pm July–Aug; 10am–6pm Sept–June. DELI.

We always stop here whenever we pass through Bodega Bay. Most visitors don't even give it a glance as they head into the adjacent restaurant, but that's because they don't know about the big bowls of fresh, tangy crab cioppino doled out for only $5 a pint—a third of the restaurant price. It's a fabulously messy affair, best devoured at the nearby picnic tables. When crab season is over, the cioppino special is replaced by an equally awesome pile of fresh fish-and-chips (easily big enough for two).

Tides Wharf Restaurant. 835 Calif. 1. ☎ **707/875-3652.** Main courses $12.50–$24.50. AE, DISC, MC, V. Daily 7:30am–10pm. SEAFOOD.

In summer, as many as 1,000 diners a day pass through the Tides Wharf. Back in the early 1960s, it served as one of the settings for Hitchcock's *The Birds,* but don't expect the weather-beaten, board-and-batten luncheonette you saw in the movie—a recent $6-million renovation has gentrified, enlarged, and redecorated the place beyond recognition. The best tables offer views overlooking the ocean, and the bill of fare is what you might expect at a seaside eatery: oysters on the half shell, clam chowder, and all the fish that the owners (who send their own fishing boat out into the Pacific every day) can dredge up from the cold blue waters offshore. Prime rib, pasta, and poultry dishes are available as well. Adjacent to the restaurant are a fish-processing plant, snack bar, and gift shop.

THE SONOMA COAST STATE BEACHES, JENNER & FORT ROSS STATE HISTORIC PARK

Along 13 winding miles of Calif. 1—from Bodega Bay to Goat Rock Beach in Jenner—stretch the Sonoma Coast State Beaches. These beaches are ideal for walking, tide pooling, abalone picking, fishing, and bird watching for such species as great blue heron, cormorant, osprey, and pelican. Each beach is clearly marked from the road, and numerous pullouts are provided for parking. Even if you don't stop at any of the beaches, the drive alone is spectacular.

At **Jenner,** the Russian River empties into the ocean. **Penny Island,** in the river's estuary, is home to otters and many species of birds; a colony of harbor seals lives out on the ocean rocks. **Goat Rock Beach** is a popular breeding ground for the seals; pupping season begins in March and lasts until June.

From Jenner, a 12-mile drive along some very dramatic coastline will bring you to **Fort Ross State Historic Park** (☎ 707/847-3286), a reconstruction of the fort that was established here in 1812 by the Russians as a base for seal and otter hunting (it was abandoned in 1842). At the visitor center, you can view the silver samovars and elaborate table services that the Russians used. The fenced compound contains several buildings, including the first Russian Orthodox church ever built on the North American continent outside Alaska. A short history lesson about the fort is offered at 11:30am, 1:30pm, and 3:30pm in the summer, and noon and 2pm in the winter. The park also offers beach trails and picnic grounds on more than 1,000 acres. Admission is free, but parking is $6.

North from Fort Ross, the road continues to **Salt Point State Park.** This 3,500-acre expanse contains 30 campsites, 14 miles of hiking trails, dozens of tide pools, a pygmy forest, and old Pomo village sites. Your best bet is to pull off the highway any place that catches your eye and start exploring on foot. At the north end of the park, head inland on Kruse Ranch Road to the 317-acre **Kruse Rhododendron Reserve** (☎ 707/847-3221), a forested grove of wild pink and purple flowers where the *Rhododendron californicum* grow up to a height of 18 feet under the redwood-and-fir canopy.

WHERE TO STAY

Jenner Inn & Cottage. 10400 Calif. 1, Jenner, CA 95450. ☎ **800/732-2377** or 707/865-2377. Fax 707/865-0829. www.jennerinn.com. 16 units. $95–$235 double. Rates include extended continental breakfast. AE, MC, V.

The worst-kept secret on the north coast is Jenner Inn, a hodgepodge of individually designed and decorated houses and cottages scattered along the coast and inland along Russian River. Couples from the Bay Area who want to stay along the coast for a night, but dread the long drive to Mendocino, usually wend their way here for an easy weekend getaway. Most of the houses are subdivided into suites, while second honeymooners vie for the ultra private oceanfront cottages. Wicker furniture, wood paneling, and private bathrooms and entrances are standard, though each lodging has its own distinct personality: Some have kitchens, while others have fireplaces, porches, or private decks. Naturally, the private cottages overlooking the Pacific are the priciest, but for about $100 most people are content with one of the small suites. A complimentary continental breakfast is served in the main lodge. In addition to the bed-and-breakfast accommodations, the inn rents out five vacation homes located along the river, within Jenner Canyon, or overlooking the ocean. For a sneak peek at some of the cottages, visit the Web site at **www.jennerinn.com**.

WHERE TO DINE

River's End. Calif. 1, Jenner. ☎ **707/865-2484.** Reservations recommended. Main courses $13–$28. MC, V. Summer daily 11am–9:30pm. Winter (Nov–Apr) Fri–Mon 11am–9:30pm. INTERNATIONAL.

Outwardly unpretentious yet deceptively urbane, this small seaside restaurant offers an artfully rustic setting, with big windows overlooking the coast (seals and sea lions might happen to be cavorting offshore). The menu is wonderfully eclectic, offering everything from Indonesian *bahmi goreng* to a selection of Indian curries, beef saté, beef Wellington, seafood, and steaks. Local Sonoma products—game, lamb, poultry, vegetables—are used whenever possible, including Sonoma microbrews and wines. After dinner, take the remainder of your wine to the outside deck and enjoy the sunset.

Sizzling Tandoor. 9960 Calif. 1, at the south end of the Russian River Bridge, Jenner. ☎ **707/865-0625.** Main courses $8.50–$13.50. AE, DISC, MC, V. Daily 11:30am–3pm; Mon–Thurs 5–9:30pm, Fri–Sun 5–10pm. Closed Tues in winter. INDIAN.

Something of a non sequitur along a rather desolate stretch of Calif. 1 between Bodega Bay and Jenner, the Sizzling Tandoor serves huge, inexpensive plates of classic Indian cuisine. The lonely location, though peculiar, is superb: Perched high atop a windswept hill, the restaurant boasts an exquisite view of the Russian River far below. The large array of curries and kabobs are accompanied by soup, vegetables, pulao rice, and the best nan (Indian bread) we've ever had. Even if you're not hungry, order some nan to go—it makes the perfect road snack.

GUALALA & POINT ARENA

Back on Calif. 1 heading north, you'll pass through Sea Ranch, a series of condominium beach developments, before you reach the small coastal community of Gualala (pronounced wah-*la*-la). Back in the old days, Gualala was an industrious, vivacious logging town. A few real-life suspender-wearing lumberjacks still end their day at the Gualala Hotel's saloon, but for the most part this coastal town's main role is providing gas, groceries, and hardware for area residents. Just outside of town are several excellent parks, hiking trails, and about 10 or so public beaches that are ideal for sunbathing.

The **Gualala River,** adjacent to the town of the same name, is suitable for canoeing, rafting, and kayaking, since all powerboats and jet skis are forbidden. Along its banks you're likely to see osprey, herons, egrets, and ducks; steelhead, salmon, and river otters make their home in the waters. Canoes, kayaks, and bicycles can be rented in Gualala for 2 hours, a half day, or a full day from **Adventure Rents** (☎ **888/881-4386** or 707/884-4386), in downtown Gualala on Calif. 1 north of the Chevron. A bike costs $15 for 2 hours; a double kayak or canoe (which seats two to five persons) costs $40 for 2 hours, $50 for a half day, and $60 for a whole day (single kayaks cost half as much).

Point Arena lies a few miles north of Gualala. Most folks stop here for the view at the **Point Arena Lighthouse** (☎ **707/882-2777**), which was built in 1870 after 10 ships ran aground here on a single night during a storm. A $3-per-person fee ($1 for children under 12) covers parking, entrance to the lighthouse museum, and a surprisingly interesting tour of the six-story, 145-step lighthouse. It's open in summer, Monday through Friday from 11am to 3:30pm and Saturday and Sunday from 10am to 3:30pm; in winter, daily from 11am to 3:30pm (but closed weekdays in December and January).

WHERE TO STAY

✪ **Old Milano Hotel & Restaurant.** 38300 Calif. 1, Gualala, CA 95445. ☎ **707/ 884-3256.** Fax 707/884-4249. 6 units (sharing 2 bathrooms), 1 suite, 6 cottages. $80 double with garden view, $115 double with ocean view; $175 master suite; $135–$210 cottage. Rates include full breakfast. MC, V.

This romantic hotel lies just north of Gualala and has a spellbinding view of Castle Rock from the front porch and sloping lawn. The inn was built in 1905 on 3 acres and is listed on the National Register of Historic Places. It has enchanting flower and herb gardens and a superbly situated hot tub, from which you can look directly out to the ocean. The rooms are each decorated uniquely, often with rare antiques. Upstairs, six rooms share two bathrooms, each with double showers. The most alluring units are the cottages, which have sleeping alcoves, reading lofts, ocean views, and fireplaces or woodstoves; two have Jacuzzis. Our favorite is the honest-to-Betsy train caboose, a romantically private space with woodstove and two upstairs brakeman's seats.

A full breakfast is served either in your room or in the parlor. Chef Brain Knutson offers pricey California cuisine—rack of Sonoma lamb, pan-roasted salmon, breast of Muscovy duck—served nightly in an intimate dining room lit by candlelight and, on cool nights, roaring fires in the stone fireplaces.

✪ **St. Orres.** 36601 Calif. 1, P.O. Box 523, Gualala, CA 95445. ☎ **707/884-3303.** Fax 707/884-1840. 8 units (sharing 3 bathrooms), 12 cottages. $60 double without ocean view, $75 double with ocean view; $85–$225 cottage double. MC, V.

An extraordinary Russian-style building—complete with two onion-domed towers—St. Orres lies 1½ miles north of Gualala. The complex was built in 1972 with century-old timbers salvaged from a nearby mill. It offers secluded cottage-style accommodations on 42 acres, as well as eight rooms in the main building (these rooms are handcrafted and share three bathrooms decorated in brilliant colors). Other units are very private. Some have full bathrooms, wet bars, sitting areas with Franklin stoves, and French doors leading to decks with a distant ocean view. Seven cottages border St. Orres Creek and have exclusive use of a spa facility that includes a hot tub, sauna, and sundeck. The most luxurious is Pine Haven, with two bedrooms, two redwood decks, two bathrooms, a tiled breakfast area, beach-stone fireplace, and wet bar.

The hotel is especially well known for its intimate restaurant (the St. Orres), a 17-seat charmer set below one of the main building's onion domes. Light filters through stained-glass windows onto strands of ivy that cascade down from the upper balcony. The only offering is a $30 three-course fixed-price meal that features game from the surrounding fields and forests. Dishes are inspired by Pacific Northwest cuisine and include wild boar, pheasant, venison, quail, and rack of lamb. Reservations are essential. It's open daily for dinner only; closed Tuesday and Wednesday from January through May. MasterCard and Visa are accepted for hotel guests only; otherwise, no credit cards.

WHERE TO DINE

The Food Company. 38411 Calif. 1 at Robinsons Reef Rd., Gualala. ☎ **707/884-1800.** Deli items $3–$9. MC, V. Daily 8–10:30am; Sun–Thurs 11am–7pm; Fri–Sat 11am–8pm. DELI.

If the St. Orres restaurant (see above) is out of your price range, you'll be happy to know that you can have an equally romantic lunch or dinner just down the road for a fraction of the price. Place your order at the deli counter, grab a bottle of wine from the rack, then head to the adjacent garden and plop your collective fannies at one of the picnic tables. The menu offers a dizzying array of specials from around the globe—corn tamales, Greek moussaka, lamb curry, quiche lorraine, pasta puttanesca—as well as fresh-baked breads, pastries, and sandwiches. Better yet, order it all to go and head for the beach.

✪ **Pangaea.** 250 Main St., Point Arena. ☎ **707/882-3001.** Reservations recommended. Main courses $8–$20. No credit cards. Thur–Sun 5:30–9pm. ECLECTIC.

North-coast locals have been raving about this place since the day it opened. Chef/owner Shannon Hughes, an expatriate of both the St. Orres and Old Milano Hotel restaurants, decided it was time to do her own thing, and boy is she doing it well. Everything that comes out of her kitchen is wondrously fresh, inventive, and organically grown and/or raised. Try the succulent pork confit, served on a potato tart with homemade apricot chutney. And how's this for a $4.50 salad: organic greens in a vinaigrette of toasted shallots, sherry vinegar, and Italian mountain Gorgonzola. Hughes has become famous for her Thai-style crab cakes made with ginger scallions and served with a Thai green-curry coconut sauce. Even her burgers are beyond reproach, made with Niman-Schell beef, organic cheese and greens, caramelized onions and Thai chili sauce, garlic-roasted red potatoes, and homemade ketchup. Desserts—strawberry-rhubarb crisp à la mode, lemon-curd tart with a blood-orange sauce—are equally impressive, as is the hip decor. Highly recommended.

NORTH FROM POINT ARENA

Driving north from Point Arena, you'll pass Elk (a good place to stop for lunch), Manchester, Albion, and Little River on your way to Mendocino.

WHERE TO STAY

Greenwood Pier Inn. 5928 Calif. 1, P.O. Box 336, Elk, CA 95432. ☎ **707/877-9997.** Fax 707/877-3439. 12 units. $120–$235 double. Rates include continental breakfast. AE, MC, V.

The Greenwood Pier Inn, perched on the edge of a dramatic bluff, is an eclectic, New Age kind of place. It's the unique domain of Kendrick Petty, who owns and operates this quartet of cafe, country store, garden shop, and accommodations. Kendrick is an artist and passionate gardener whose collages, tiles, and marble work can be seen in the interiors of several of the buildings in the complex and also outside in the gardens. Of the accommodations, which are in various buildings in addition to the main inn, the Cliffhouse is our top choice: a seaside redwood cabin complete with a fireplace, a large deck, and an upper-level bathtub with ocean views. All the rooms have private decks, fireplaces, or wood burners, and lie within 100 feet of the cliff edge; they have no TVs or phones, but each has access to a hot tub overlooking the ocean. A continental breakfast is delivered to your room; lunch and dinner—roast pork loin, grilled rack of lamb, grilled Chilean sea bass—are served daily in the cafe (weekends only November through May).

✪ **Harbor House.** 5600 S. Calif. 1 (P.O. Box 369), Elk, CA 95432. ☎ **800/720-7474** or 707/877-3203. www.theharborhouseinn.com. 6 units, 4 cottages. $195–$315 double (winter rates are considerably less). Extra person $100. Rates include full breakfast and four-course dinner. No credit cards.

While the Greenwood Pier Inn is New Age, the redwood-sided two-story Harbor House is very, very traditional. It was built in 1916 by the president of the Goodyear Redwood Lumber Co. as a hideaway for corporate executives and their wives. This is not a hotel, but an upscale B&B offering 3 acres of gardens, access to a private beach, and views overlooking the Pacific. None of the units has a TV or phone, and that's how guests here like it. Five of the rooms in the main building have their own fireplaces, many are furnished with antiques originally purchased by the lumber executives, and all have private bathrooms. Cottages tend to be small, but have fireplaces and private decks.

The restaurant here always maintains two of its tables for nonguests, who should make reservations as far in advance as possible. Set dinners, which change nightly, cost $32 and feature both California and Pacific Northwest cuisine, making use of local herbs, freshly baked breads, and vegetables from the inn's own gardens.

✪ **KOA Kamping Kabins.** On Kinney Rd. (off Calif. 1, 5 miles north of Point Arena). ☎ **800/562-4188** or 707/882-2375. 24 cabins, 2 cottages. $41–$49 cabin, $115 cottage (up to four persons). AE, DISC, MC, V.

What? You expect me to stay at a Kampgrounds of America?!? You bet. Once you see these adorable little log cabins, you can't help but admit that, rich or poor, this is one great way to spend a weekend on the coast. The cabins have one or two bedrooms with log-frame double beds or bunk beds for the kids and sleep four to six people respectively. Rustic is the key word here: mattresses, a heater, and a light bulb are your standard amenities. Beyond that, you're on your own, but basically all you need is some bedding or a sleeping bag, cooking and eating utensils, and a bag of charcoal for the barbecue out on the front porch (next to the log porch swing). If this is all a little too spartan for you, opt for one of the cottages, both decked out with private bathrooms, fireplaces, comfy beds and other creature comforts. Hot showers, bathrooms, laundry facilities, a small store, and a swimming pool are a short walk away, as is Manchester Beach.

WHERE TO DINE

Ledford House. 3000 N. Calif. 1, Albion. ☎ **707/937-0282.** www.ledfordhouse.com. Reservations recommended. Main courses $18–$26. AE, DC, MC, V. Wed–Sun 5–9pm. CALIFORNIA/FRENCH.

If James Beard were alive today, he'd feel right at home at this innovative but simply decorated restaurant overlooking the pounding surf of the Pacific from a bluff above. The kitchen offers self-styled "New American cuisine," experimenting with the bounty of the Golden State to fashion rich combinations and harmonious flavors. One part of the menu is reserved primarily for the pastas and hearty stews suitable to this far northern setting, such as Antoine's cassoulet, a jumble of pork, lamb, garlic sausage, and duck confit slowly cooked with white beans. Although the menu changes seasonally, for a taste of California try the salmon primavera with lemon-caper butter, or the crisp-roasted duckling with wild huckleberry sauce. Evenings bring live jazz in the cocktail lounge.

3 Mendocino

166 miles N of San Francisco

Mendocino is, to our minds, *the* premier destination on California's north coast. Despite (or because of) its relative isolation, it emerged as one of Northern California's major centers for the arts in the 1950s. It's easy to see why artists were—and still are—attracted to this idyllic community, a cluster of New England–style sea captain's homes and small stores set on headlands overlooking the ocean.

At the height of the logging boom, Mendocino became an important and active port. Its population was about 3,500, and eight hotels were built, along with 17 saloons and more than a dozen bordellos. Today, it has only about 1,000 residents, most of whom reside on the north end of town. On summer weekends, the population seems more like 10,000, as hordes of tourists drive up from the Bay Area—but despite the crowds, Mendocino still manages to retain its small-town charm.

ESSENTIALS

GETTING THERE The fastest route from San Francisco is via U.S. 101 north to Cloverdale. Then take Calif. 128 west to Calif. 1, then go north along the coast. It's about a 4-hour drive. (You could also take U.S. 101 all the way to Ukiah or Willits, and cut over to the west from there.) The most scenic route from the Bay Area, if you have the time and your stomach doesn't mind the twists and turns, is to take Calif. 1 north along the coast the entire way; it's at least a 5- to 6-hour drive.

VISITOR INFORMATION You can stock up on lots of free brochures and maps at the **Fort Bragg/Mendocino Coast Chamber of Commerce,** 332 N. Main St. (P.O. Box 1141), Fort Bragg, CA 95437 (☎ **800/726-2780** or 707/961-6300; www.mendocinocoast.com). Pick up a copy of the center's monthly magazine, *Arts and Entertainment,* which lists upcoming events throughout Mendocino. It's available at numerous stores and cafes, including the Mendocino Bakery, Gallery Bookshop, and the Mendocino Art Center.

EXPLORING THE TOWN

Stroll through town, enjoy the architecture, and browse through the dozens of galleries and shops. Our favorites include the **Highlight Gallery,** 45052 Main St. (☎ 707/ 937-3132), for its handmade furniture, pottery, and other craft work; and the **Gallery Bookshop & Bookwinkle's Children's Books,** at Main and Kasten streets (☎ 707/ 937-2665), one of the best independent bookstores in northern California, with a wonderful selection of books for children and adults. Another popular stop is **Mendocino Jams & Preserves,** 440 Main St. (☎ 800/708-1196 or 707/937-1037), which offers free tastings of its natural, locally made gourmet wares on little bread chips.

After exploring the town, walk out on the headlands that wrap around the town and constitute ✪ **Mendocino Headlands State Park.** (The visitor center for the park is in Ford House on Main Street.) Three miles of trails wind through the park, giving visitors panoramic views of sea arches and hidden grottoes. If you're here at the right time of year, the area will be blanketed with wildflowers; when we last stopped by, we could pick fresh blackberries beside the trails. The headlands are home to many unique species of birds, including black oystercatchers. Behind the Mendocino Presbyterian Church on Main Street is a trail leading to stairs that take you down to the beach, a small but picturesque stretch of sand where driftwood formations have washed ashore.

On the south side of town, **Big River Beach** is accessible from Calif. 1; it's good for picnicking, walking, and sunbathing.

In town, stop by the **Mendocino Art Center,** 45200 Little Lake Rd. (☎ 707/ 937-5818), the town's unofficial cultural headquarters. It's also known for its gardens, three galleries, and shops that display and sell local fine arts and crafts. Admission is free; open daily from 10am to 5pm.

For a special treat, go to **Sweetwater Spa & Inn,** 955 Ukiah St. (☎ 800/300-4140 or 707/937-4140; www.sweetwaterspa.com), which offers group and private saunas and hot-tub soaks by the hour. Additional services include Swedish or deep-tissue massages. Reservations are recommended. Private tub prices are $9 per person per half hour, $12 per person per hour. Group tub prices are $8 per person with no time limit. Special discounts are available on Wednesdays. Open Monday through Thursday from 2 to 10pm and Friday through Sunday from noon to 11pm.

OUTDOOR PURSUITS

Explore the Big River by renting a canoe, sea cycle, kayak, or outrigger from **Catch a Canoe & Bicycles Too** (☎ 707/937-0273), located on the grounds of the Stanford Inn by the Sea (see "Where to Stay," below). If you're lucky, you'll see some osprey, blue herons, harbor seals, deer, and wood ducks. These same folks will also rent you a mountain bike (of much better quality than your usual bike rental), so you can head up Calif. 1 and explore the nearby state parks on two wheels.

Horseback riding (both English and western) on the beach and into the redwoods is offered by **Ricochet Ridge Ranch,** 24201 N. Calif. 1, Fort Bragg (☎ 888/ 873-5777 or 707/964-PONY; www.horse-vacation.com). Prices range from $35 for a 2-hour beach ride to $195 for an all-day private beach/redwoods trail ride with lunch.

In addition to Mendocino Headlands State Park (see "Exploring the Town," above), there are several other state parks near Mendocino; all are within an easy drive or bike ride and make for a good day's outing. Information on all the parks' features, including maps of each one, is found in a brochure called *Mendocino Coast State Parks,* available from the visitor center in Fort Bragg. These areas include **Manchester State Park,** located where the San Andreas Fault sweeps to the sea; **Jughandle State Reserve;** and **Van Damme State Park,** with a sheltered, easily accessible beach.

Our favorite of these parks, located directly on Calif. 1 just north of Mendocino, is **Russian Gulch State Park** (☎ 707/937-5804). It's one of the region's most spectacular parks, where roaring waves crash against the cliffs that protect the park's California coastal redwoods. The most popular attraction is the **Punch Bowl,** a collapsed sea cave that forms a tunnel through which waves crash, creating throaty echoes. Inland, there's a scenic paved bike path, and visitors can also hike along miles of trails, including a gentle, well-marked 3-mile **Waterfall Loop** that winds past tall redwoods and damp green foliage to a 36-foot-high waterfall. Admission is $5. Thirty camping sites enjoy a beautiful setting and are available from April to mid-October ($14 to $16 per night). Phone ☎ 800/444-7275 for reservations.

Fort Bragg is just a short distance up the coast; deep-sea fishing charters are available from its harbor.

WHERE TO STAY
EXPENSIVE

✪ **Stanford Inn by the Sea.** N. Calif. 1 and Comptche Ukiah Rd. (P.O. Box 487), Mendocino, CA 95460. ☎ **800/331-8884** or 707/937-5615. Fax 707/937-0305. www.stanfordinn. com. 33 units. TV TEL. $215–$275 double; $235–$550 suite. Rates include cooked-to-order breakfast and evening hors d'oeuvres. AE, CB, DC, DISC, MC, V. Pets accepted.

Just south of Mendocino, this rustic but ever-so-sumptuous lodge occupies 11 acres of land abutting the Big River. The grounds are captivating, with tiers of elaborate gardens, a pond for ducks and geese, and fenced pastures containing horses, curious llamas, and old gnarled apple trees. There's a gorgeous solarium-style indoor hot tub and pool surrounded by tropical plants, as well as an exercise room. Mountain bikes and canoes are available on the property from Catch a Canoe & Bicycles Too (see above); bike rentals are complimentary with your stay.

The rooms are luxuriously furnished in forest green and burgundy tones, and offer such special touches as thick terry-cloth robes and heavenly down comforters. They're made even more appealing with fresh flowers and works by local artists. All have fireplaces or stoves, stereos and VCRs (an extensive library of tapes is available from the front desk), and private decks from which you can look out onto the Pacific. Second honeymooners should inquire about the romantic River Cottage; families will want the big ol' renovated barn. Pets are welcome here and receive the royal treatment.

Dining: The inn recently added the only totally vegetarian restaurant on the Mendocino coast, and it's become a big hit with both guests and locals. Entrees—which are quite good—range from a calzone of roasted butternut squash with leeks to eggplant gratin with goat gouda cheese. Vegan dishes are also available. It's open daily for dinner. A breakfast buffet is served every morning in the breakfast room (you can take a tray back to your room), and afternoon wine and hors d'oeuvres are offered as well.

Amenities: Concierge, laundry, newspaper delivery, secretarial services, in-room massage, courtesy car, baby-sitting, complimentary coffee, video rentals, business center.

MODERATE

✪ **Agate Cove Inn.** 11201 N. Lansing St. (P.O. Box 1150), Mendocino, CA 95460; ☎ **800/ 527-3111** or 707/937-0551. www.agatecove.com. 10 units. TV. $109–$250 double. Rates include full breakfast. AE, MC, V.

Good luck trying to find an accommodation with a more beautiful coastal setting than Agate Cove Inn's. Words can barely convey the almost surreal splendor of the view from the inn's front lawn, a sweeping, unfettered vista of the sea and its surging waves crashing onto the dramatic bluffs. Situate yourself on one of the Adirondack chairs with a good book, and you'll never want to leave. The inn consists of a main house trimmed in blue and white, surrounded by a bevy of single and duplex cottages decorated in a "casual country" style with light pine furnishings. All but one of the 10 spacious units have views of the ocean, firm king- or queen-size beds, down comforters, CD players, TVs with VCRs (and a free video and CD library), wood-burning stoves or gas fireplaces, and private decks. In the morning, a fantastic country breakfast is served in the main house's enclosed porch at individual tables (yes, with the same ocean view). Although the guest rooms aren't quite as impressive as those in most other B&Bs in Mendocino, overall the Agate Cove offer seclusion, privacy, and views that the other lodgings in town just can't match.

✪ **Joshua Grindle Inn.** 44800 Little Lake Rd. (P.O. Box 647), Mendocino, CA 95460. ☎ **800/GRINDLE** or 707/937-4143. www.joshgrin.com. 10 units. June–Oct and Fri–Sun year-round $105–$195 double; Nov–May Mon–Thurs $100–$175. Rates include full breakfast. MC, V.

When it was built in 1879, this stately Victorian was one of the most substantial and impressive houses in Mendocino, owned by the town's wealthiest banker. Now the oldest B&B in Mendocino, it features redwood siding, a wraparound porch, and large emerald lawns. From its prettily planted gardens, there's a view across the village to the distant bay. There are five rooms in the main house, two in the cottage, and three in the water tower. All have well-lit, comfortably arranged sitting areas; some offer fireplaces, two have deep-soak tubs, and one has a whirlpool tub. Each is individually decorated: The library, for example, has a New England feel with its four-poster pine bed, floor-to-ceiling bookcase, and 19th-century tiles around the fireplace depicting Aesop's fables. Sherry is served in the parlor in front of the fireplace; breakfast is offered in the dining room.

In addition to the inn, the proprietors also have a beautiful two-bedroom, two-bathroom ocean-view rental home with floor-to-ceiling windows, a large kitchen, and a wood-burning fireplace. It's located a few minutes north of Mendocino, and rates range from $200 to $250 depending on occupancy.

MacCallum House. 45020 Albion St. (P.O. Box 206), Mendocino, CA 95460. ☎ **800/609-0492** or 707/937-0289. Fax 707/964-2243. 19 units. $100–$190 double. Extra person $15. DISC, MC, V. From U.S. 101, turn right onto Albion St. in downtown Mendocino.

An historic 1882 gingerbread Victorian mansion, MacCallum House is one of Mendocino's top accommodations. Originally owned by local matriarch Daisy MacCallum, the house still bears the imprint of this daughter of the town's richest lumber baron. It remained in the family until 1974, when it was turned into a B&B. Now owned by resident proprietors Melanie and Joe Redding, the home has been preserved with all of its original furnishings and contents—right down to Daisy's Christmas cards and books of pressed flowers. Boasting the occasional Tiffany lamp or authentic Persian carpet, each uniquely decorated guest room is exquisitely furnished with many original pieces—a Franklin stove, a handmade quilt, a cushioned rocking chair, or a child's cradle. All have private bathrooms, many equipped with clawfoot or spa tubs for two. The luxurious barn suite, complete with a stone fireplace, can accommodate up to six adults.

The **MacCallum House Restaurant** (☎ 707/937-5763) has a sterling reputation. The menu changes seasonally, but a meal might start with broiled oysters bathed in garlic-basil butter and move on to a local salmon fillet or pan-broiled tenderloin with shiitake mushrooms. It's open daily from 5:30 to 9pm; closed January to mid-February.

Mendocino Hotel & Garden Suites. 45080 Main St., Mendocino, CA 95460. ☎ **800/ 548-0513** or 707/937-0511. Fax 707/937-0513. 51 units, 37 with bathroom. TEL. $85 double without bathroom, $90–$205 double with bathroom; $275 suite. Extra person $20. AE, MC, V.

Right in the heart of town, this 1878 hotel evokes California's gold-rush days. Beveled-glass doors open into a Victorian-style lobby and parlor where you might expect to see Mae West. The hotel's decor combines antiques and reproductions, like the oak reception desk from a demolished Kansas bank. Remington paintings, stained-glass lamps, and Persian carpets contribute to the Wild West aura. Guest rooms feature hand-painted French porcelain sinks with floral designs, quaint wallpaper, old-fashioned beds and armoires, and photographs and memorabilia of historic Mendocino. About half the rooms are located in four handsome small buildings behind the main house. Many of the deluxe rooms have fireplaces or wood-burning stoves, as well as modern bathrooms and good views. Suites have an additional parlor, as well as a fireplace or balcony.

Breakfast and lunch are served daily in the Garden Room, while dinner is offered daily in the Victorian-style dining room. Room service is also available daily from 8am to 9pm.

INEXPENSIVE

✪ **Mendocino Village Inn.** 44860 Main St. (P.O. Box 626), Mendocino, CA 95460. ☎ **800/882-7029** or 707/937-0246. www.mendocinoinn.com. 10 units, 8 with private bathroom. $75 double with shared bathroom; $95–$175 double with private bathroom; $175 suite. Rates include full breakfast and evening refreshments. No credit cards.

Although a street separates the Mendocino Village Inn from the ocean, it's still close to the water. A garden of flowers, plants, and frog ponds fronts the large blue-and-white guest house, which was built in 1882 by a local doctor and later occupied by famed local artist Emmy Lou Packard.

Innkeeper Kathleen Erwin has decorated each room differently. The Queen Anne Room features a four-poster canopy bed and other Victorian furnishings, and the sentimental Maggie's Room is named for a child who etched her name in the window glass almost a century ago (you can still see it). Except for two attic units, all have private bathrooms, and four rooms have private outside entrances. Complimentary beverages are served in the evening.

IN NEARBY ALBION & LITTLE RIVER

✪ **Albion River Inn and Restaurant.** N. Calif. 1 (P.O. Box 100), Albion, CA 95410. ☎ **800/479-7944** or 707/937-1919. www.albionriverinn.com. 20 units. TEL. $170–$200 double; $240–$260 Jacuzzi suite. Rates include full breakfast. AE, DC, DISC, MC, V.

A quarter mile north of Albion, this modern choice overlooks the mouth of the Albion River from a bluff some 90 feet above the Pacific. The rooms are attractively decorated in a contemporary style with comfortable furnishings; all have ocean views and most have decks. You'll find wingbacks placed in front of the fireplaces, down comforters on the king-size beds, well-lit desks, and earthenware lamps beside the beds. Additional amenities include coffeemakers, refrigerators, CD stereos, and bathrobes. *Insider tip:* If you really want to impress your sweetie, reserve one of the rooms with a Jacuzzi tub or oversized tub for two, which have large picture windows that offer dazzling views of the coast.

The cuisine at the inn's restaurant changes daily, but the view from the tables remains the same: stellar. Chef Stephen Smith uses fresh local produce whenever possible with each dish. Entree favorites include grilled Chilean sea bass, ginger-barbecued salmon, and wild mushroom and butternut risotto. The award-winning wine list is also impressive. For dessert, the homemade ice cream is smooth and loaded with flavor. On weekends, soft piano music adds to the romantic atmosphere.

✪ **Glendeven.** 8221 N. Calif. 1, Little River, CA 95456. ☎ **800/822-4536** or 707/937-0083. Fax 707/937-6108. www.glendeven.com. 10 units. Main house Mon–Thurs $98–$220 double; Fri–Sun and Aug $118–$240. Rates include full breakfast. AE, MC, V.

Named one of the 12 best inns in America by *Country Inns* magazine, this 1867 farmhouse has been converted into a place of exceptional styling and comfort. Accommodations are spread across 2½ acres that encompass the main house, the Barn, and an addition known as Stevenscroft. Each room is individually decorated with a well-balanced mixture of antiques and contemporary pieces. We prefer two rooms in the farmhouse (misleadingly called suites, they're really just large rooms). The King's Room suite includes an antique walnut bed, while the Eastlin suite is furnished with a French rosewood bed. Five rooms in the modern annex are large and spacious, but perhaps less charming. Guests are also housed in a fantastic converted Barn House Suite, which can accommodate up to five (perfect for families or groups). Adjacent to the inn are the numerous fern-lined canyon trails of Van Damme State Park.

Heritage House. 5200 N. Calif. 1, Little River, CA 95456. ☎ **800/235-5885** or 707/937-5885. Fax 707/937-0318. 66 units. Summer $125–$350 double; winter $110–$275 double. Extra person $20. MC, V. Closed after Thanksgiving until Christmas, and again from Jan 2 to mid-Feb.

Most of the rooms at this traditional country club–style property have views of the ocean and rugged coastline. Built in 1877 as a farmhouse and surrounded by 37 seafront acres, the main building's most infamous moment came when it served as a hideout for bandit "Baby Face" Nelson. Much of the inn as you see it dates from 1949; it has been renovated several times since. Only three guest rooms are located in the ivy-covered New England–style main building; the rest are in cottages grouped two to four under one common roof. Rooms are individually decorated with original antiques and locally made furnishings, and include such amenities as bathrobes, hair dryers, umbrellas, wine splits, and newspaper delivery (TVs and phones are intentionally missing). Most have wood-burning fireplaces or stoves, private decks, sitting areas, and ocean views, and several suites have wet bars and Jacuzzis. Wooded trails wind along the dramatic coastline, offering spectacular views.

The Heritage House dining room offers cuisine in a magnificent setting overlooking the ocean. The menu changes seasonally, but might include braised lamb shank with white beans and roasted root vegetables, or pan-seared salmon with spinach, crispy potatoes, and wild mushrooms. Prices are surprisingly reasonable, ranging from $15.50 to $17.50. Breakfast and lunch are also served daily.

WHERE TO DINE
EXPENSIVE

✪ **Café Beaujolais.** 961 Ukiah St. ☎ **707/937-5614.** www.cafebeaujolais.com. Reservations recommended. Main courses $16–$25. DISC, MC, V. Daily 5:45–9pm. AMERICAN/FRENCH.

This is one of Mendocino's—if not northern California's—top dining choices, owned and managed since 1977 by chef and entrepreneur Margaret Fox. The venerable French country–style tavern is set in a turn-of-the-century house; rose-colored carnival-glass chandeliers add a burnish to the oak floors and the heavy oak tables adorned with flowers. On warm summer nights, request a table at the enclosed deck overlooking the "designer" gardens.

Though Café Beaujolais started out as a breakfast and lunch place, it's strictly a dinner house now (yes, their famed weekend brunch has been discontinued). The menu changes weekly and usually lists about five main courses, such as wild sturgeon fillet pan-roasted with truffle emulsion sauce, roast free-range duck with wild-huckleberry sauce, or broiled Wildwood Ranch pork loin chop with yam purée. Tuesday through Thursday, the cafe offers a prix-fixe country menu for $25 that's a pretty darn good deal.

The 955 Ukiah Street Restaurant. 955 Ukiah St. ☎ **707/937-1955.** Reservations recommended. Main courses $12–$19. MC, V. Daily Wed–Sun 6–10pm. CALIFORNIA/FRENCH.

Shortly after this building's construction in the 1960s, the region's most famous painter, Emmy Lou Packard, commandeered its premises as an art studio for the creation of a series of giant murals. Today, it's a large but surprisingly cozy restaurant, accented with massive railway ties and vaulted ceilings. The tables on the mezzanine level can get a little cramped; we usually ask for a window table overlooking the gardens. The cuisine is creative and reasonably priced, a worthy alternative to the perpetually booked Café Beaujolais next door. It's hard to recommend a particular main dish, although the phyllo-wrapped red snapper with pesto and lime has a zesty tang, while the crispy duck with ginger, apples, and a calvados sauce would earn enthusiastic friends in Normandy.

MODERATE

Bay View Café. 45040 Main St. ☎ **707/937-4197.** Reservations not accepted. Main courses $6–$15. No credit cards. Summer daily 8am–9pm. Winter daily 8am–3pm; Fri–Sun 8am–9pm. AMERICAN.

This reasonably priced cafe is one of the most popular in town and the only place around besides the Mendocino Hotel that serves breakfast ("And we're way better," says the owner). From the second-floor dining area of the cafe, there's a sweeping view of the Pacific and faraway headlands; to reach it, climb a flight of stairs running up the outside of the town's antique water tower, then detour sideways. Surrounded by dozens of ferns suspended from the ceiling, you'll find a menu with Southwestern selections (the marinated chicken breast is very popular), a good array of sandwiches (our favorite is the hot crabmeat with avocado slices), fish-and-chips, and the fresh catch of the day. Breakfast ranges from the basic bacon 'n' eggs to eggs Florentine and honey-wheat pancakes.

The Moosse Cafe. 390 Kasten St. (at Albion St.). ☎ **707/937-4323.** Reservations recommended for dinner. Main courses $11–$17. MC, V. Mon–Thurs 11:30am–3:30pm and 5:30–9pm; Fri–Sat 11:30am–3:30pm and 5:30–10pm; Sun 11:30am–3:30pm and 5:30–9pm. CONTINENTAL/CALIFORNIA.

This petite cafe set in a New England–style home is one the most popular restaurants in Mendocino. In 1995, the place was gutted and redone, resulting in an attractive, modern interior. The menu boasts many local items such as organic herbs and vegetables, as in the kick-butt Caesar salad. We also enjoyed the roast chicken with garlic mashed potatoes and the swordfish special, which came with a pile of fresh vegetables. Other popular entrees are the mixed seafood cakes served over basmati rice with a roasted red pepper remoulade, and the lavender-smoked double-thick pork chop served with roasted yam and apple puree. The Blackout cake is a chocoholic's fantasy. Service is friendly; our only complaint is that the tables are a bit too close together, especially if it's crowded.

INEXPENSIVE

You'd be surprised what $5 will get you for lunch if you know where to go. **Tote Fete Bakery** (☎ 707/937-3383) has a wonderful little carry-out booth at the corner of Albion and Lansing streets. We like the foil-wrapped barbecue chicken sandwiches, but the pizza, focaccia bread, and twice-baked potatoes are also good choices. Dine at the stand-up counter, or opt for a picnic at the headlands down the street.

Regardless of preference—beef, chicken, turkey, or veggie—burger lovers won't be let down at **Mendo Burgers** (☎ 707/937-1111), arguably the best burger joint on the north coast. A side of thick, fresh-cut fries is mandatory, as is a pile of napkins. Hidden behind the Mendocino Bakery and Café at 10483 Lansing St., it's a little hard to find, but well worth searching out.

In the back of the **Little River Market** (☎ 707/937-5133), located directly across from the Little River Inn on Calif. 1, is a trio of small tables overlooking the beautiful Mendocino coastline. Order a tamale, sandwich, or whatever else is on the menu at the tiny deli inside the market, or buy a loaf of legendary Café Beaujolais bread sold at the front counter and your favorite spread.

IN NEARBY LITTLE RIVER

Little River Restaurant. 7750 N. Calif. 1, Little River. ☎ **707/937-4945.** Reservations required. Main courses $18.50–$27. No credit cards. July 11–Oct 15 Fri–Tues dinner seatings at 6 and 8:30pm; rest of the year Fri–Mon dinner seatings at 6 and 8:30pm. CALIFORNIA/FRENCH.

Charming, small-scale, and personal, this restaurant is part of a complex that contains a general market and the village's only post office. (Don't get it confused with the larger Little River Inn across the road.) The Little River Restaurant is the personal culinary statement of Jeri Barrett (now joined by her son, Troy), who might be the only chef in the neighborhood who routinely quotes Elizabeth Barrett Browning. It enjoys a winning reputation for dishes like tenderloin of pork with a ginger-flavored scallion sauce and red snapper sautéed with lemon-dill butter and shallots. Beer and wine are served, but no hard liquor. Because there are only seven tables, making and keeping your reservations here is extremely important.

4 Fort Bragg

10 miles N of Mendocino, 176 miles N of San Francisco

As Mendocino coast's commercial center—hence the site of most of the area's fast-food restaurants and supermarkets—Fort Bragg is far more down to earth than Mendocino. Inexpensive motels and cheap eats used to be its only attraction, but over the past few years, gentrification has quickly spread throughout the town as the logging and fishing industries have continued to decline. With no room left to open new shops in Mendocino, many gallery, boutique, and restaurant owners have moved up the road. The result is a huge increase in Fort Bragg's tourist trade, particularly during the annual Whale Festival in March and Paul Bunyan Days over Labor Day weekend.

To explore the town properly, make your first stop at the **Fort Bragg/Mendocino Coast Chamber of Commerce,** 332 N. Main St. (P.O. Box 1141), Fort Bragg, CA 95437 (☎ **800/726-2780** or 707/961-6300), and pick up a free walking map. The friendly staff can answer any questions about Mendocino, Fort Bragg, and the surrounding region.

SHOPPING & EXPLORING THE AREA

The town doesn't boast as many well-coiffed stores and galleries as its dainty cousin to the south, but it does have some worthwhile shopping spots. **Antiques shops** line Franklin Street between Laurel and Redwood (a.k.a. "Antiques Row"), while several boutiques are housed within the newly refurbished **Union Lumber Company Store,** an impressive edifice built almost entirely with handcrafted redwoods (on the corner of Main and Redwood sts.).

For the Shell of It, 344 N. Main St. (☎ **707/961-0461**), stocks handmade jewelry, chimes, and collectibles made of shells or designed around a nautical theme, as well as rocks, gems, minerals, and fossils. The **Hot Pepper Jelly Company,** 330 N. Main St. (☎ **707/961-1422**), is famous for its assortment of Mendocino food products— dozens of varieties of pepper jelly, plus local mustards, syrups, and biscotti along with hand-painted porcelain bowls, unusual baskets, and more. The **Mendocino Chocolate Company,** 542 N. Main St. (☎ **707/964-8800**), makes and sells homemade choco- lates and truffles, which it ships all over the world. Painters, jewelers, sculptors, weavers, potters, woodworkers, and other local artists display their works at **Northcoast Artists,** 362 N. Main St. (☎ **707/964-8266**). At **Windsong,** 324 N. Main St. (☎ **707/ 964-2050**), you'll find a clutter of colorful kites, cards, candles, and other gifts.

Fort Bragg is also the home of the **Mendocino Coast Botanical Gardens,** 18220 N. Calif. 1 (☎ **707/964-4352**), about 7 miles north of Mendocino. This cliff-top public garden, set among the pines along the rugged coast, nurtures rhododendrons, fuchsias, azaleas, and a multitude of flowering shrubs. The area contains bridges, streams, canyons, dells, picnic areas, and trails for easy walking. A popular cafe, the Gardens Grill, is also located here (see "Where to Dine," below). Admission is $6 for adults, $5 for seniors 60 and over, $3 for children 13 to 17, $1 for children 6 to 12, and free for children 5 and under. (Children under 18 must be accompanied by an adult.) Open March through October daily from 9am to 5pm, November through February daily from 9am to 4pm.

From Fort Bragg, the **Skunk Train** (☎ **800/77-SKUNK** or 707/964-6371) gives riders a fine tour of the area's redwoods. Locals have always said of the logging trains, "You can smell 'em before you can see 'em," which explains the nickname. The trains, which can be boarded at the Fort Bragg Depot at the foot of Laurel Avenue in Fort Bragg (2 blocks from the Grey Whale Inn), travel 40 miles inland along the Redwood Highway (U.S. 101) to Willits. It's a scenic route through the redwood forest, crossing 31 bridges and trestles and cutting through two deep tunnels. The round-trip takes 6 to 7 hours, allowing plenty of time for lunch in Willits before you return on the after- noon train. The trains run full-day trips daily from Memorial Day weekend through the last weekend in September, but call for exact times, as schedules vary. Half-day trips are offered daily from March 1 through the end of November. During the summer months, it's a good idea to make advance reservations. Tickets cost $35 for a full-day trip, $27 for a half-day trip; children ages 3 to 11 board for $18 full-day, $14 half-day. Serious train buffs can ride in the locomotive cab with the engineer for $100. Family packages are also available.

Also worth checking out is the **North Coast Brewing Company** (☎ **707/ 964-2739**), which offers free tours of the brewery Monday through Friday at 1:30pm. Since the tours are limited to 12 persons, be sure to sign up in advance at the gift store downstairs at 455 N. Main St. Across the street is the Brewing Company's pub, open for lunch and dinner (see "Where to Dine," below).

OUTDOOR PURSUITS

Fort Bragg is the county's sportfishing center. Just south of town, **Noyo Fishing Center,** 32450 N. Harbor, Noyo (☎ **707/964-7609**), is a good place to buy tackle and the best source of information on local fishing boats. Lots of party boats leave from the town's harbor, as do whale-watching tours.

Lost Coast Kayaking, located in Van Damme State Park (☎ **707/937-2434**), offers kayak tours of the coastline's numerous sea caves. All the necessary equipment is provided; all you need to bring is a bathing suit and about $45 for the 2-hour tour (closed during the winter).

Cutting-Edge Theater

Living proof that poor, maligned ol' Fort Bragg is on the road to respect is its much-heralded theatrical company, ✪ **Warehouse Repertory Theatre,** 319A N. Main Street. Determined to make Fort Bragg the Ashland of California, this cadre of highly talented professional actors from around the country has finally answered the age-old Mendocino County question of "So, what is there to do around here at night?" From Shakespeare to Shepard, no play is too shocking or sultry for this gifted gaggle of thespians, who have received heaps of kudos for the fresh, significant interpretations they have brought to the north coast. The Warehouse's season runs from late February through December, Thursday through Saturday (and sometimes Monday) at 8pm, with the occasional Sunday matinee at 2pm. For information about current shows and future plays, or to reserve tickets (which range from $10 to $15), call the box office at ☎ **707/961-2940** or visit their Web site at **www.mcn.org/c/warerep.**

Three miles north of Fort Bragg, off Calif. 1, lies **Mackerricher State Park** (☎ **707/937-5804**), a popular place for biking, hiking, and horseback riding. This enormous 1,700-acre park has 142 campsites and 8 miles of shoreline. For a true biking or hiking venture, travel the 8-mile-long "Haul Road," an old logging road that provides fine ocean vistas all the way to Ten Mile River. Harbor seals make their home at the park's Laguna Point Seal Watching Station, reached via an elevated wooden gangway (truly a pleasant walk).

WHERE TO STAY

Beachcomber Motel. 1111 N. Main St., Fort Bragg, CA 95437. ☎ **800/400-7873** or 707/964-2402. 75 units. TV. $59–$195 double. AE, DIS, MC, V. Pets welcome with $10 fee.

If the room rates in Mendocino have you reconsidering a visit to the coast, the Beachcomber Motel may be just what you're looking for. Granted, the rather plain guest rooms lack the fancy antique and lace accouterments you'll find at most B&Bs in the area, but they are definitely spacious, comfortable, and equipped with the basic necessities such as cable TV and private bathrooms. None of this really matters, though, since you'll be spending most of your time on the huge back deck that overlooks the cool blue Pacific and gorgeous sunsets. Better yet, directly across from the motel is MacKerricher State Park's miles of beaches and dunes. If you really want to save a bundle, get a room with a kitchenette, stock up on groceries, and make use of the large barbecue area. Rates range from $59 for a standard room with no ocean view to $195 for the deluxe suite with king bed, hot tub, fireplace, and ocean view. A huge 45-room expansion opened in May 1999; four of the new units are accessible to the disabled, and there are two suites with hot tub.

Columbi Motel. 647 Oak St., Fort Bragg, CA 95437. ☎ **707/964-5773.** 21 units. A/C TV TEL. $50–$55 double. MC, V.

Considering a room here costs about a quarter of the average room rate in Mendocino, the Columbi Motel is what we travel writers call a real score. For only 50 bones, you get a plethora of lodging perks at this humble little motel just off Fort Bragg's main strip: cable TV, queen-size bed, bathroom, a kitchenette complete with full-size fridge, sink, and stove, and even your own covered carport. Families will want to reserve one of the two-bedroom units that sleep up to six. Across the street is a Laundromat, a small cafe serving good Mexican food, and the Columbi Market, which is where the motel's guest check in.

Grey Whale Inn. 615 N. Main St., Fort Bragg, CA 95437. ☎ **800/382-7244** or 707/
964-0640. Fax 707/964-4408. www.greywhaleinn.com. 14 units. TV TEL. $110–$200 double.
Discounted winter rates available midweek Nov–Mar. Rates include buffet breakfast. AE, DISC,
MC, V.

This cozy B&B, located in downtown Fort Bragg and a short walk from the beach,
was originally built as a hospital in 1915, hence the wide hallways and large guest
rooms. The handsome redwood building is now a well-run, relaxed inn, furnished
with antiques, handmade quilts, and plenty of local art. Each room is unique: Two
have ocean views, three have fireplaces, one has a whirlpool tub, two have private
decks, and one offers a shower with wheelchair access. The buffet breakfast includes a
hot entree, homemade bread or coffee cake, and fresh fruit.

WHERE TO DINE
Gardens Grill. 18220 N. Calif. 1 (1 mile south of Fort Bragg, within the Mendocino Coast
Botanical Gardens). ☎ **707/964-7474**. Main courses $9–$16. MC, V. Mon–Sat
11am–2:30pm, Thurs–Sat 5–9pm, Sun brunch 10am–2:30pm. CALIFORNIA.

Though the locals will tell you that the quality of food at Gardens Grill changes from
week to week, that still doesn't stop carloads of visitors from enjoying a relaxing lunch
or dinner among the multitude of flowers. On sunny days, dining on the elevated deck
overlooking the flower gardens is the main attraction. At lunch, you'll find a wide array
of salads, sandwiches (try the fresh snapper dusted in cornmeal), and entrees such as
fresh grilled salmon served with basmati rice or grilled vegetable lasagna. Dinner
entrees range from fresh local fish, such as blackened local snapper served with kiwi
salsa, to heartier dishes such as wood-grilled New York steak served with roasted garlic
mashed potatoes.

North Coast Brewing Company. 444 N. Main St. ☎ **707/964-3400**. Reservations
accepted for large parties only. Main courses $6–$17. DISC, MC, V. Tues–Sun noon–11pm.
AMERICAN.

This homey brewpub is the most happening place in town, especially during happy
hour, when the bar and dark-wood tables are occupied by boisterous locals. The
building that houses the pub is a dignified, century-old redwood structure, which in
previous lives has functioned as a mortuary, an annex to the local Presbyterian
church, an art studio, and administration offices for the College of the Redwoods.
Beer is brewed on the premises in large copper vats, which are displayed behind plate
glass. A pale ale, a pilsner, a stout, and a fourth seasonal brew are always available.
Standard fare such as burgers and barbecued chicken sandwiches are supplemented
by more substantial dishes, ranging from linguini with smoked mushrooms to a
hefty pile of country-style Carolina barbecued pork. After lunch, browse the retail
shop or take a free tour of the brewery (see "Shopping & Exploring the Area,"
above).

The Restaurant. 418 N. Main St. ☎ **707/964-9800**. Reservations recommended. Lunch
$6.50–$8.50; dinner $12.50–$19.50. MC, V. Thurs–Fri 11:30am–2pm; Sun brunch
10am–1pm; Thurs–Tues 5–9pm. PACIFIC NORTHWEST/CALIFORNIA.

One of the oldest family-run restaurants on the coast, this small, unpretentious Fort
Bragg landmark is known for its good dinners and Sunday brunches. The eclectic
menu offers dishes from just about every corner of the planet: blackened New York
strip steak, sweet-and-sour stir-fry, Livorno-style shellfish stew, and even shrimp rellenos. There are also a few vegetarian specialties, including grilled polenta with melted
mozzarella and sautéed mushrooms, topped with tomato-herb sauce and Parmesan
cheese. The comfortable booth section is the best place to sit if you want to keep an

eye on the entertainment—courtesy of ebullient chef Jim Larsen—in the kitchen. On weekends, additional entertainment comes in the form of live music.

Viraporn's Thai Café. 500 S. Main St. (across from PayLess off Calif. 1). ☎ **707/964-7931.** Main courses $5.50–$7.50. No credit cards. Wed–Mon 11:30am–2:30pm and 5–9pm. THAI.

Born in northern Thailand, Viraporn Lobell attended cooking school and apprenticed in restaurants in her homeland before coming to the United States. After working at Mendocino's premier restaurant, Café Beaujolais, she opened her own restaurant in Fort Bragg in 1991, giving local Thai-food fans good reason to cheer. Viraporn works wonders with Thai mainstays such as pad thai, lemongrass soup, spring rolls, and satays, all of which have a pleasant balance of the five traditional Thai flavors of tart, bitter, hot, sweet, and salty. Viraporn also whips up some wonderful curry dishes, best washed down with a cool, super-sweet Thai iced tea.

5 The Avenue of the Giants & Ferndale

From Fort Bragg, Calif. 1 continues north along the shoreline for about 30 miles before turning inland to Leggett and U.S. 101, a.k.a. the Redwood Highway, which runs north to Garberville. Six miles beyond Garberville, the Avenue of the Giants begins around Phillipsville; it's an alternate route that roughly parallels U.S. 101, and there are about a half dozen interchanges between U.S. 101 and the Avenue of the Giants if you don't want to drive the whole thing. It's one of the most spectacular scenic routes in the West (Calif. 254), cutting along the Eel River through the 51,000-acre Humboldt Redwoods State Park. The Avenue ends just south of Scotia; from here, it's only about 10 miles to the turnoff to Ferndale, about 5 miles west of U.S. 101.

For more information or a detailed map of the area, go to the **Humboldt Redwood State Park Visitor Center,** P.O. Box 276, Weott, CA 95571 (☎ **707/946-2263**), just north of Hidden Springs State Campground, 2 miles south of Weott, in the center of the Avenue of the Giants.

Thirty-three miles long, the Avenue of the Giants was left intact for sightseers when the freeway was built. The giants, of course, are the majestic coast redwoods (*Sequoia sempervirens*); more than 50,000 acres of them make up the most outstanding display in the redwood belt. Their rough-bark columns climb 100 feet or more without a branch and soar to a total height of more than 340 feet. With their immunity to insects and fire-resistant bark, they have survived for thousands of years. The oldest dated coast redwood is more than 2,200 years old.

The state park has three **campgrounds** with 248 campsites: Hidden Springs, half a mile south of Myers Flat; Burlington, 2 miles south of Weott, near park headquarters; and Albee Creek State Campground, 5 miles west of U.S. 101 on the Mattole Road north of Weott. You'll also come across picnic and swimming facilities, motels, resorts, restaurants, and numerous rest and parking areas.

Sadly, the route has several tacky attractions that attempt to turn the trees into some kind of freak show. Our suggestion is to skip these and appreciate the trees by taking advantage of the trails and the campgrounds off the beaten path. As you drive along, you'll see numerous parking areas with short loop trails leading into the forest. From south to north, the first of these "attractions" is the **Chimney Tree,** where J. R. R. Tolkien's Hobbit is rumored to reside. This living, hollow redwood is more than 1,500 years old. Nearby is a gift shop and a burger place. Then there's the **One-Log House,** a small apartment-like house built inside a log. At Myers Flat midway along the Avenue, you can also drive your car through a living redwood at the **Shrine Drive-Thru Tree.**

A few miles north of Weott is **Founders Grove,** named in honor of those who established the Save the Redwoods League in 1918. Farther north, close to the end of the Avenue, stands the 950-year-old **Immortal Tree,** just north of Redcrest. Near Pepperwood at the end of the Avenue, the **Drury Trail** and the **Percy French Trail** are two good short hikes. The park itself is also good for mountain biking. Ask the rangers for details. For more information, contact Humboldt Redwoods State Park, P.O. Box 100, Weott, CA 95571 (☎ **707/946-2409**).

WHERE TO STAY & DINE NEAR THE SOUTHERN ENTRANCE TO THE AVENUE OF THE GIANTS

Benbow Inn. 445 Lake Benbow Dr., Garberville, CA 95542. ☎ **800/355-3301** or 707/923-2124. Fax 707/923-2897. 55 units. A/C TEL. $120–$220 double; $295 cottage. AE, DISC, MC, V.

This elegant National Historic Landmark, overlooking the Eel River and surrounded by marvelous gardens, has housed such notable persons as Eleanor Roosevelt, Herbert Hoover, and Charles Laughton. Constructed in 1926 in a mock Tudor style, it's named after the well-to-do family who built it. Guests enter through a grand hall and into the sumptuous lobby with its huge fireplace surrounded by cushy sofas, grand father clocks, Oriental carpets, and cherry-wood wainscoting. Rooms vary in size and amenities, though all are tastefully decorated with period antiques; the deluxe units have fireplaces, Jacuzzis, private entrances and patios, and VCRs. A comfortable annex with elegant woodwork was added in the 1980s. Bicycles are available, and beautiful Benbow Lake State Park is right out the front door.

Complimentary afternoon tea and scones are served in the lobby at 4pm, hors d'oeuvres in the lounge at 5pm, and port wine at 9pm—all very proper, of course. The dramatic high-ceilinged dining room opens onto a spacious terrace and offers internationally inspired main courses from $12 to $20.

FERNDALE

The village of Ferndale, beyond the Avenue of the Giants and west of U.S. 101, has been declared a historic landmark because of its many Victorian homes and storefronts (which include a smithy and a saddlery). About 5 miles inland from the coast and close to the redwood belt, Ferndale is one of the best-preserved Victorian hamlets in northern California. Despite its unbearably cute shops, it is nonetheless a vital part of the northern coastal tourist circuit. The small town has a number of artists in residence and is also home to one of California's oddest events, the **World Championship Great Arcata to Ferndale Cross-Country Kinetic Sculpture Race,** a bizarre 3-day event held every Memorial Day weekend. The race, which draws more than 10,000 spectators, is run over land and water in whimsically designed human-powered vehicles. Stop in at the museum at 780 Main St. if you want to see some recent race entries.

WHERE TO STAY

✪ **Gingerbread Mansion.** 400 Berding St. (P.O. Box 40), Ferndale, CA 95536. ☎ **800/952-4136** or 707/786-4000. Fax 707/786-4381. www.gingerbread-mansion.com. 11 units. $140–$350 double; $150–$350 suite. Extra person $40. Rates include full breakfast and afternoon tea. AE, MC, V.

This peach-and-yellow structure with stained glass and other fine architectural details is one of Ferndale's most frequently photographed Victorians, built in 1899 as the home of a local doctor and his family. Run by Ken Torbert, it's beautifully furnished with antiques. Some of the large guest rooms have two old-fashioned clawfoot tubs for bubble baths for two, and others offer fireplaces. Our favorite room is the attic-level

Empire Suite, a lavish spare-no-expense blowout with Ionic columns, massage-jet shower, two fireplaces, and a king-size bed draped with Royal Sateen fabric. The new ultra-luxurious Veneto Room is also very impressive. Bathrobes and thick, extra-large towels are provided. Beds are turned down for the night, and you'll find hand-dipped chocolates on the nightstand. When you rise, there's morning coffee or tea outside your door, enough to sustain you until your breakfast of fruit, cheese, muffins, breads, cakes, and a baked egg dish. Afternoon tea with sandwiches, pastries, fresh fruit, and Devonshire cream is also served.

WHERE TO DINE

Curley's Grill. 460 Main St. ☎ **707/786-9696.** Main courses $9–$18. DISC, MC, V. Daily 11:30am–9pm; breakfast Sat–Sun 8–11am. CALIFORNIA GRILL.

Set in what looks like a clapboard-sided Victorian farmhouse, across the street from Ferndale's Repertory Theater, this bright and lively restaurant specializes exclusively in California-inspired grilled foods. Don't think for a moment that the menu is limited to steaks, prime rib, and barbecued baby-back ribs, however. Owner Curley Tait also grills up such items as polenta with a sausage-tomato sauce, a medley of Pacific seafish, crab cakes, and some of the freshest vegetables on the California coast. Curley has added homemade breads and desserts to the menu as well. The interior decor is vaguely art deco and showcases local artists' works, but the best seating is behind the kitchen in the secluded back patio. Curley's also offers a small but interesting selection of California wines.

6 Eureka & Environs

Eureka: 296 miles N of San Francisco

EUREKA

On first glance, Eureka (pop. 27,000) doesn't look very appealing: Fast-food restaurants, cheap motels, and shopping malls predominate on the main thoroughfare. But if you turn west off U.S. 101 anywhere between A and M streets, you'll discover **Old Town Eureka** along the waterfront, which is worth exploring. It has a large number of Victorian buildings, a museum, and some good-quality stores and restaurants.

The **Clarke Memorial Museum,** 240 E St. (☎ 707/443-1947), has a fine collection of Native American baskets and other historic artifacts. The other popular attraction is the extraordinary architectural gem, the ✪ **Carson House,** built from 1884 to 1886 for lumber baron William Carson. A three-story conglomeration of ornamentation, its design is a mélange of styles—Queen Anne, Italianate, Stick, and Eastlake. It took 100 men more than 2 years to build. Today it's a private club, so you can only marvel at the exterior of this 18-room mansion—said to be the most photographed Victorian home in the United States—from the sidewalk. Across the street stands the **"Pink Lady,"** designed for William Carson as a wedding present for his son. Both testify to the wealth that was once made in Eureka's lumber trade. As early as 1856, there were already seven sawmills producing 2 million board feet of lumber every month.

Humboldt Bay, where the town stands, was discovered by whites in 1850. In 1853, Fort Humboldt was established to protect settlers from local Native American tribes. Ulysses S. Grant was stationed here for 5 months until he resigned after serious disputes with his commanding officer about his drinking. The fort was abandoned in 1870. Today, the fort offers a self-guided trail past a series of logging exhibits, plus a reconstructed surgeon's quarters and a restored fort hospital, used today as a museum housing Native American artifacts and military and pioneer paraphernalia. **Fort**

Humboldt State Historic Park is located at 3431 Fort Ave. (☎ 707/445-6567). Admission is free; it's open daily from 9am to 4pm.

Humboldt Bay supplies a large portion of California's fish, and Eureka has a fishing fleet of about 200 boats. To get a better view (and perspective) of the bay and surrounding waters, you can board skipper Leroy Zerlang's *Madaket*—said to be the oldest passenger-carrying vessel in operation in the United States—for a 75-minute **Humboldt Bay Harbor Cruise** (☎ 707/445-1910), departing daily from the foot of C Street in downtown Eureka.

More active water recreation includes fishing for halibut, king salmon, steelhead, and even shark, depending on the season. A license is required and can be secured for one day; for more information, contact the **Eureka Fly Shop,** 505 H St. (☎ 707/444-2000). Kayaks and sailboats can be rented from **Hum Boats,** on F Street (☎ 707/443-5157), which also provides tours and lessons.

Humboldt County is also suitable for biking because it's relatively uncongested. Bikes can be rented from **Pro Sport Center,** 508 Myrtle Ave. (☎ 707/443-6328). Fishing, diving, biking, and hiking information are also available here.

Humboldt Bay is an important stopover point along the Pacific Flyway and is the winter home for thousands of migratory birds. South of town, the **Humboldt Bay National Wildlife Refuge,** 1020 Ranch Rd., Loleta (☎ 707/733-5406), provides an opportunity to see many of the 200 or so species that live in the marshes and willow groves—including Pacific black brant, western sandpiper, northern harrier, great blue heron, and green-winged teal. The egret rookery on the bay, best viewed from Woodley Island Marina across the bay en route to Samoa, is spectacular. Peak viewing for most species of waterbirds and raptors is between September and March. The refuge's entrance is off U.S. 101 north at the Hookton Road exit. Cross the overpass and turn right onto Ranch Road.

For information, contact the **Eureka/Humboldt County Convention and Visitors Bureau,** 1034 Second St., Eureka, CA 95501 (☎ 800/346-3482 or 707/443-5097; fax 707/443-5115; www.redwoodvisitor.org), or the **Eureka Chamber of Commerce,** 2112 Broadway, Eureka, CA 95501 (☎ 800/356-6381 or 707/442-3738).

WHERE TO STAY

✪ **An Elegant Victorian Mansion Bed & Breakfast Experience.** 1406 C St. (at 14th St.), Eureka, CA 95501. ☎ 707/444-3144. Fax 707/442-5594. 5 units. $95–$185 double. Rates include breakfast. MC, V.

For anyone interested in Victorian history and design, this is a special experience; those who just want comfort, service, a true gourmet breakfast, and a lovely garden will also find this lodging ideal. The 1888 house is the labor of love of owners Doug and Lily Vieyra, who have combed the country for the fabrics and designs that now provide the most authentic Victorian atmosphere we have ever encountered in the United States. The wallpapers are extraordinary—brilliant blues, golds, jades, and reds in intricate patterns that feature peacocks and mythological figures. Doug has paid attention to every detail, from the butler who greets you in morning dress to the silent movies and period music on the phonograph. Each unit is individually furnished: The Van Gogh room contains the Belgian bedroom suite of Lily's mother. The Lily Langtry room, named after the actress and king's mistress who stayed here when she performed locally, features a four-poster bed and Langtry memorabilia. There's laundry service, and Swedish massage is offered. Bikes and a sauna are available, and croquet is played on the manicured lawn, where ice-cream sodas and lemonade are served in the afternoon.

✪ **Hotel Carter, Carter House, Carter Cottage, and Bell Cottage.** 301 L St., Eureka, CA 95501. ☎ **800/404-1390** or 707/445-1390. Fax 707/444-8067. 42 units. TV TEL. $154–$187 double; $154–$397 suite. AE, DC, DISC, MC, V. From U.S. 101 north, turn left onto L St. and go to Third.

At the north end of Eureka's Old Town is the original building that launched Carter's renowned hostelry empire: the Carter House. Copied from a famous 1884 San Francisco Victorian, it was constructed by Mark Carter as a family home in 1982. Soon afterwards, Mark and his wife, Christi Carter, began taking guests, and before long they built another 20-room hotel across the street, the Hotel Carter. Later, the pretty Victorian Bell Cottage was acquired, and most recently the ultra-luxurious Carter Cottage.

The 23 rooms in the large, full-service Hotel Carter have modern furnishings and pine four-posters. The suites have such luxury appointments as VCRs, fireplaces, and Jacuzzis; distant views of the waterfront can be seen from the tubs. There are seven rooms in the original Carter House, which is furnished with antiques, Oriental rugs, and modern artwork. The Bell Cottage's rooms are also individually decorated in grand Victorian fashion. If you really want to splurge, however, reserve the Carter Cottage, a small home that's been converted into one of the most luxurious lodgings in northern California, a mini-mansion replete with a chef's kitchen, two fireplaces, a grand bathroom with a whirlpool tub for two, a private deck, and even an honor wine cellar. On the ground level of the Hotel Carter is one of Eureka's finest restaurants, Restaurant 301 (see "Where to Dine," below).

WHERE TO DINE

Ramone's Bakery & Cafe. 209 E St. (in Old Town). ☎ **707/445-2923.** Main courses $4–$6. No credit cards. Cafe Mon–Sat 7am–5:15pm; Sun 8am–4pm. BAKERY.

Ramone's combines a bakery on one side with a small cafe on the other. The baked items are extraordinary—try any one of the croissants, Danish, or muffins, and you won't be disappointed. Alas, the once-popular restaurant has closed down, but you can still find a few lunch specials to choose from among the breads and pastries, such as soups, salads, burgers, and more. At any time of the day, it's a great place to stop in for a light, inexpensive meal and cup of coffee.

There's a second bakery location at 2223 Harrison St., in Eureka, as well as one in Arcata at 747 13th St., at Wildberries Marketplace.

✪ **Restaurant 301.** In the Hotel Carter, 301 L St. ☎ **800/404-1390** or 707/444-8062. Reservations required. Main courses $17–$24. AE, DC, DISC, MC, V. Daily 6–9pm. CALIFORNIA.

The large, light, and airy dining room adjacent to the hotel's lobby has tall windows looking out on the waterfront. It's one of the best restaurants in the area, with most of the herbs and many of the vegetables picked fresh from the hotel's organic gardens across the street. Diners may order either à la carte or off the Discovery Menu, a highly recommended prix-fixe five-course dinner menu that pairs each course with suggested wines by the glass. A typical dinner may begin with an artichoke, green lentil, and fennel salad, followed by a warm chèvre cake appetizer, then on to a roasted chanterelle tian and grilled duck breast served with a seasonal fruit and zinfandel sauce. The cuisine also displays Asian accents, as in the chicken with spicy peanut sauce and the tiger prawns with sesame, ginger, and soy. If you're an oyster lover, start with a few Humboldt Bay oysters roasted with barbecue sauce. There's an excellent and extensive wine list, courtesy of the 301 Wine Shop within the hotel.

Samoa Cookhouse. Cookhouse Rd., Samoa. ☎ **707/442-1659.** Reservations accepted for large groups only. Main courses $6.95–$11.95. AE, DISC, MC, V. Mon–Sat 7am–3:30pm and

5–10pm, Sun 7am–10pm (closes an hour earlier in winter). From U.S. 101, take Samoa Bridge to the end and turn left on Samoa Rd.; then take the 1st left. AMERICAN.

When lumber was king, cookhouses (like this one dating from 1885) were common, serving as community hubs. Here the mill men and longshoremen at the Hammond Lumber Company came to chow down on three hot meals before, during, and after their 12-hour workday. The food is still hearty—though not particularly healthy—and served family style at long tables covered with red-checkered cloths. Nobody leaves hungry. The price includes soup, salad, fresh-baked bread, the main course, and dessert (usually pie). The lunch-and-dinner menu still features a different dish each day—roast beef, fried chicken, or pork chops. Breakfast typically includes eggs, sausages, bacon, pancakes, and all the orange juice and coffee you can drink. Adjacent to the dining room is a small museum featuring memorabilia from the lumbering era.

ARCATA

From Eureka it's only 7 miles to Arcata, one of our favorite towns on the northern coast. Sort of a cross between Mayberry and Berkeley, it has an undeniable small-town flavor—right down to the bucolic town square—yet possesses that intellectual and environmentally conscious esprit de corps so characteristic of university towns (Arcata is the home of Humboldt State University).

There are loads of things to do here. On Wednesday, Friday, and Saturday evenings between June and July, Arcata's semipro baseball team, the **Humboldt Crabs,** partake in America's favorite pastime at Arcata Ballpark, at Ninth and F streets. Also worth a stop: the kid-friendly **Humboldt State University Natural History Museum,** 1315 G St. (☎ 707/826-4479), which is open Tuesday through Saturday from 10am to 4pm; **Tin Can Mailman,** at 10th and H streets (☎ 707/822-1307), a wonderful used-book store with more than 130,000 titles; **Redwood Park** (east end of 11th Street), which has an outstanding playground for kids and miles of forested hiking trails; and the **Humboldt Brewing Company,** 10th and I streets (☎ 707/826-BREW), creators of the heavenly Red Nectar Ale (call for tour information).

The **Arcata Marsh and Wildlife Sanctuary,** at the foot of South I Street (☎ 707/826-2359), is another worthwhile excursion. The 154-acre sanctuary—which doubles as Arcata's integrated wetland wastewater treatment plant—is a popular stopover for marsh wrens, egrets, and other waterfowl, including the rare Arctic loon. Each Saturday at 8:30am (rain or shine), the Audubon Society gives free 1-hour guided tours at the cul-de-sac at the foot of South I Street.

Heading east from Arcata, Calif. 299 leads to the Trinity River in the heart of **Six Rivers National Forest.** Willow Creek and Somes Bar are the prime recreational centers for the area. Here visitors can sign up for canoeing, rafting, and kayaking trips with such outfitters as **Aurora River Adventures,** in Willow Creek (☎ 800/562-8475), which offers some offbeat, educationally oriented excursions that are great for kids, as well as gnarly Class V trips for the more daring.

A few miles north of Willow Creek lies the Hoopa Indian Reservation. In the Hoopa Shopping Center, the **Hoopa Tribal Museum** (☎ 530/625-4110) archives the culture and history of the native people of Northern California—their ceremonial regalia, basketry, canoes, and tools. Hours are Monday through Friday from 8am to noon and 1 to 5pm.

WHERE TO STAY

Hotel Arcata. 708 Ninth St., Arcata, CA 95521. ☎ 800/344-1221 or 707/826-0217. Fax 707/826-1737. 32 units. TV TEL. $66–$110 double. Rates include continental breakfast. AE, CB, DC, DISC, MC, V.

This is the town's most prominent hotel, and many guests are parents visiting their ungrateful offspring at Humboldt State University. Located at the northeast corner of the town plaza, the Hotel Arcata consists of a handsome turn-of-the-century brick facade and an equally charming lobby (the staff is quite friendly as well). The individually decorated rooms range from small singles starting at a modest $66, and twice that amount for a large Executive Suite that overlooks the plaza. The mini-suites are the quietest, and a bargain at $88. On the premises, under different management, is a Japanese restaurant, Tomo. The hotel also offers its guests free passes to the health club and indoor pool just a few blocks down the street. If you can't afford the more sumptuous Lady Anne B&B (see below), this is definitely the next best choice.

✪ **The Lady Anne.** 902 14th St., Arcata, CA 95521. ☎ **707/822-2797.** 5 units. $90–$110 double. Rates include breakfast. MC, V.

Easily Arcata's finest lodging, this Queen Anne–style bed-and-breakfast is kept in top-notch condition by innkeepers Sharon Ferrett and Sam Pennisi, who also served a term as Arcata's mayor. The large, cozy guest rooms are individually decorated with period antiques, lace curtains, Oriental rugs, and English stained glass. For second honeymooners, there's the Lady Sarah Angela Room with its four-poster bed and pleasant bay view. The Cinnamon Bear Room sleeps up to four on its king-size trundle beds, which makes it an obvious choice for parents with kids in tow. Breakfast is served in the grand dining room, warmed on winter mornings by a toasty fire. On summer afternoons, you can lounge on the veranda with a book or play a game of croquet on the front lawn. Several good dining options are only a few blocks away at Arcata Plaza.

WHERE TO DINE

Abruzzi. Jacoby's Storehouse (at the corner of Eighth and H sts.). ☎ 707/826-2345. Reservations recommended. Main courses $9–$22. AE, DISC, MC, V. Sun–Mon 5:30–9pm. ITALIAN.

The best way to review your dining options in Arcata is to stroll downtown to Jacoby's Storehouse, a converted mid-19th-century brick warehouse located at the southwest corner of the town plaza, and ponder the menus posted outside of the Abruzzi and Plaza Grill (see below). Abruzzi is generally acknowledged as the best Italian restaurant in town. Replete with dark woods and dim lighting, it has all the makings for a romantic dinner. Specialties include a roasted lamb loin served with three-cheese polenta and ratatouille, and baked halibut in a white-wine/butter sauce served over fettuccine. Chicken, pastas, veal dishes, and well-seasoned fillet steaks are available as well. The standout dessert is the chocolate paradiso, a dense chocolate cake set in a pool of champagne mousseline. All meals begin with a basket of warm bread sticks, focaccia, and a baguette that you can smell all the way down the street.

✪ **Folie Douce.** 1551 G St (between 15th and 16th sts). ☎ **707/822-1042.** Reservations recommended. Main courses $11–$23. DISC, MC, V. Tues–Thurs 5:30–9pm, Fri–Sat 5:30–10pm. BISTRO.

Humboldt Hip meets Cuisine Chic at Folie Douce, the most energized and inventive restaurant in town. Designer wood-oven-fired pizza is its mainstay, such as the Thai pizza with marinated bits of chicken breast topped with fontina, ginger, and peanut, or the house-smoked salmon pie made with chèvre, Brie, and wild mushrooms. But the appetizers and entrees are equally as intriguing. The highlight of your vacation may well be the artichoke-heart cheesecake appetizer, followed by a plate of macadamia-encrusted scallops served in a light cream. The ultra-moist Monk's Chicken—a full boneless breast sautéed in butter, flambéed in brandy, and simmered in white wine, mustard, and cream—is equally enrapturing. Other heartier menu items range from a fat filet mignon to roast duck. This small, festive off-street eatery is extremely popular, so be sure to make reservations.

Plaza Grill. Jacoby's Storehouse (at the corner of Eighth and H sts.). ☎ **707/826-0860.** Appetizers and main courses $5–$15. AE, DISC, MC, V. Sun–Mon 5–8pm; Tue–Thurs 5–10pm; Fri–Sat 5–11pm. AMERICAN.

If the prices at Abruzzi are a bit more than you care to spend, consider the Plaza Grill, located directly above Abruzzi. Despite efforts to make it more upscale, it can't seem to shake its image as a college-student burger joint. The menu, however, is more substantial than you'd think, with a choice of salads, sandwiches, fish platters, and burgers.

TRINIDAD & PATRICK'S POINT STATE PARK

Back on U.S. 101 north of Arcata, you'll come to **Trinidad,** a tiny coastal fishing village of some 400 people. One of the smallest incorporated cities in California, it occupies a peninsula 25 miles north of Eureka. If you're not into fishing, there's little to do in town except poke around at the handful of shops, walk along the busy pier, and wish you owned a house here.

Five miles north of Trinidad takes you to the 640-acre **Patrick's Point State Park,** 4150 Patrick's Point Dr. (☎ **707/677-3570**), which has one of the finest ocean access points in the north at sandy **Agate Beach.** It's suitable for driftwood picking, rockhounding, and camping on a sheltered bluff. The park contains a re-creation of a Sumeg Village, which is actively used by the Yurok people and neighboring tribes. A self-guided tour takes you to replicas of family homes and sweat houses.

WHERE TO STAY

✪ **The Lost Whale Inn.** 3452 Patrick's Point Dr., Trinidad, CA 95570. ☎ **800/677-7859** or 707/677-3425. Fax 707/677-0284. www.lostwhaleinn.com. 8 units. Summer $140–$170 double; winter $110–$140 double. Rates include country breakfast. AE, DISC, MC, V.

This modern version of a blue-and-gray Cape Cod–style house is set on 4 acres of seafront land studded with firs, alders, spruces, and redwoods. Its owners cater to children (there's a playground on the premises and mini-zoo up the street) and adults (there's also a Jacuzzi with a view of the sea), and claim (arguably) that it's the only hotel in the state of California with its own private beach. Afternoon tea and an artfully prepared and presented breakfast are included in the rates.

The decor is eclectic, with lots of statuary and paintings, plus an outdoor deck facing the surf. Part of the grounds is devoted to a kitchen garden with fresh herbs and vegetables. The comfortable rooms lack phones and TVs, so you can peacefully escape from the rest of the world. Families should inquire about the furnished homes—including a wonderful farmhouse—that the innkeepers also rent out. Recent additions include a rebuilt beach trail with stairs and handrails, as well as a six-person outdoor spa overlooking the ocean. For a better perspective of the inn's ambiance, check out their Web site at **www.lostwhaleinn.com.**

Trinidad Bay Bed & Breakfast. 560 Edwards St. (P.O. Box 849), Trinidad, CA 95570. ☎ **707/677-0840.** 4 units. $125 double; $155 suite. Rates include breakfast. MC, V. Closed Dec–Jan.

Set 175 feet above the ocean, all rooms at this picturesque Cape Cod–style home have sweeping views of Trinidad Bay. On a clear day, you can see up to 65 miles of the rugged coastline. Your hosts are Paul and Carol Kirk, two seasoned innkeepers who have created what many visitors think is the most charming inn around. Rare for an older B&B, both the rooms and suites have private bathrooms. Decor throughout is an eclectic mix of New England–style antiques and more recent reproductions. If it's available, opt for the Mauve Fireplace Suite, with its wraparound window, large woodburning fireplace, king-size bed, and private entrance.

Trinidad Inn. 1170 Patrick's Point Dr., Trinidad, CA 95570. ☎ **707/677-3349**. 10 units. TV. $65–$110 double. Rates include continental breakfast. AE, MC, V. From U.S. 101, take the Trinidad exit and head 2 miles north on Patrick's Point Dr.

There's a bevy of inexpensive motels in these parts, but the Trinidad Inn is the best of the lot. It's located 2 miles north of Trinidad on a serene stretch of road ensconced by a towering cadre of aromatic redwoods. Both the motel's exterior—trimmed in pretty shades of white and blue—and guest rooms are impeccably maintained. Each room is unique: Some are family units that hold up to four persons, while others offer a comfortable queen bed, large TV, and private bath for as little as $65 per night (access to the adjoining kitchen is an extra $10). Our favorite room for couples is no. 10, an adorable little cottage complete with a full kitchen, living room, private bath, bedroom, and small patio. Each morning, Pearl, the manager, serves fresh coffee, tea, and homemade raspberry scones and muffins under the gazebo in the flower-filled garden. Guests are free to use the picnic table and barbecue, or wander through the adjacent forest to the beaches a short stroll away.

WHERE TO DINE

✪ **Larrupin Café.** 1658 Patrick's Point Dr. ☎ **707/677-0230**. Reservations recommended. Main courses $15–$20. No credit cards. Summer Wed–Mon 5–9pm; winter Wed–Sun 5–9pm. AMERICAN.

Located on a quiet country road 2 miles north of Trinidad, this highly popular and wondrously decorated restaurant sports an eclectic blend of Indonesian and African artifacts mingled with colorful urns full of exotic flowers and romantic candlelit tables. Dinner starts with an appetizer board stocked with gravlax, pâté, dark pumpernickel, apple slices, and sauce, followed by a red- and green-leaf salad tossed with a Gorgonzola vinaigrette. Many menu items are barbecued over mesquite fires, such as a hefty cut of halibut that's been basted with lemon butter and served with mustard-flavored dill sauce, and the fantastic pork ribs served with a side of sweet and spicy barbecue sauce. Another recommended dish is the barbecued Cornish game hen served with an orange-and-brandy glaze. For appetizers, the barbecued oysters are divine, especially in winter, when the fireplace casts a welcome warmth. Heaven is a slice of pecan-chocolate pie topped with hot buttered rum sauce, or the sinfully good triple-layer chocolate cake layered with caramel and whipped cream.

The Seascape Restaurant. Beside the Pier at the foot of Bay St. ☎ **707/677-3762**. Reservations accepted. Full dinners $9–$20. MC, V. Daily 7am–8:30pm. CALIFORNIA.

Established in the 1940s, this is an unpretentious cross between a cafe and a diner, with three dining rooms, overworked but cheerful waitresses, and a nostalgic aura. Folks pop in for coffee or snacks from early morning until after sundown, but by far the biggest seller here is the Trinidad Bay Platter ($17.95). Heaped with halibut, scallops, and shrimp, and accompanied by salad and rice pilaf, it's even more popular than the prawn brochette, which draws a close second.

ORICK

From Trinidad, it's about another 15 miles to Orick. You can't miss it: Just look for the dozens of burl stands alongside the road. Carved with chisels and chain saws, these former redwood logs have been transformed into just about every creature you can imagine—perhaps a gift for your mother-in-law?

At the south end of Orick is the town's only saving grace, the sleek **Redwood National Park Information Center** (☎ **707/464-6101,** ext. 5265). If you plan to spend any amount of time exploring the park, stop here first and pick up a free map; the displays of fauna and wildlife aren't too bad, either. It's open daily from 9am to 5pm.

The first of the parks that make up Redwood National Park, Prairie Creek, is 6 miles north of Orick. About 14 miles farther on is the mouth of the **Klamath River,** famous for its salmon, trout, and steelhead. Tours aboard a jet boat take visitors upriver from the estuary to view bear, deer, elk, osprey, hawks, otters, and more along the riverbanks. Rates for the 30-mile scenic trip (offered May 1 to October 30) are $20 for adults, $10 for children 4 to 11, and free for kids under 4. For more information and reservations, contact **Klamath River Jet Boat Tours,** Klamath (☎ 800/ 887-JETS or 707/482-7775).

A more serene alternative to exploring the Klamath is taking a ranger-led **kayak tour.** Offered only during the summer months (and only if they have enough money in their budget), the half-day trip costs only $20 and includes all the requisite kayak gear. For more information, call the Redwood National Park Information Center at the phone number listed above.

From Klamath, it's another 20 miles to Crescent City, gateway to the other parks that make up Redwood National Park.

7　Crescent City, Gateway to Redwood National Park

79 miles N of Eureka, 375 miles N of San Francisco

Crescent City itself has little to offer, but it makes a good base for exploring Redwood National Park and the Smith River, one of the great recreational rivers of the West. The **Battery Point Lighthouse,** at the foot of A Street (☎ 707/464-3089), which is accessible on foot only at low tide, houses a museum with exhibits on the coast's history. Tours of the lighthouse ($2 for adults, 50¢ for children) are offered Wednesday through Sunday from 10am to 4pm, tides and weather permitting (so call ahead in questionable weather), from April through September.

Another draw is the **Smith River National Recreation Area,** east of Jedediah Smith State Park and part of Six Rivers National Forest. The Area Headquarters is at 10600 U.S. 199, Gasquet (☎ 707/457-3131), which is reached via U.S. 199 from Crescent City (19 miles; about a 30-minute drive). Maps of the forest can be obtained here, at the Supervisor's Office in Eureka, or at either of the Redwood National Park centers in Orick and Crescent City.

The 300,000-plus acres of wilderness offer camping at five modest-sized campgrounds (all with fewer than 50 sites) along the Smith River. Sixteen trails attract hikers from across the country. The easiest short trail is the **McClendon Ford,** which is 2 miles long and drops from 1,000 to 800 feet in elevation to the south fork of the river. Other activities include mountain biking, white-water rafting, kayaking, and fishing for salmon and trout.

For information, contact the **Crescent City–Del Norte County Chamber of Commerce,** 1001 Front St., Crescent City, CA 95531 (☎ 800/343-8300 or 707/ 464-3174).

WHERE TO STAY

Crescent Beach Motel. 1455 Redwood Hwy. S. (U.S. 101), Crescent City, CA 95531. ☎ **707/464-5436.** 27 units. TV. Summer $67–$75 double; winter $49–$55 double. AE, DISC, MC, V.

Crescent City has the dubious distinction of being the only city along the coast without a fancy hotel or bed-and-breakfast. There is, however, an armada of cheap motels, the best of which is the Crescent Beach Motel. Near the highway, about 1 mile south of town, this single-story structure is the only local motel set directly on the beach. The freshly remodeled and refurbished rooms are clean and simple. Four of the units face the highway; try to get one of the others, all of which have sliding-glass doors to decks and a small lawn area overlooking the bay. There's no restaurant or bar on the premises, but one of the city's most popular restaurants, the Beachcomber (see "Where to Dine," below), is located next door.

Curly Redwood Lodge. 701 Redwood Hwy. S. (U.S. 101), Crescent City, CA 95531. ☎ **707/464-2137.** www.curlyredwoodlodge.com. 36 units. TV TEL. Summer $60–$65 double; winter $37–$39 double. AE, CB, DC, MC, V.

This is a blast from the past, the kind of place where you might have stayed as a kid during one of those cross-country vacations in the family station wagon. It was built in 1959 on grasslands across from the town's harbor, and completely trimmed with lumber from a single ancient redwood. Although they're not full of the latest high-tech gadgets, the bedrooms are among the largest and best-soundproofed in town, and certainly the most evocative of a bygone, more innocent age. In winter, about a third of the rooms (the ones upstairs) are locked and sealed. Overall, the aura is more akin to Oregon than anything you might imagine in California.

WHERE TO DINE

Beachcomber. 1400 U.S. 101. ☎ **707/464-2205.** Reservations recommended. Main courses $6–$15. MC, V. Thurs–Tues 5–9pm (call ahead during winter months). SEAFOOD.

The decor is as predictably nautical as the name implies: rough-cut planking, a scattering of artfully arranged driftwood, fishnets, and buoys dangling above a dimly lit space. The restaurant lies beside the beach, 2 miles south of Crescent City's center. The cuisine is a joy to fish lovers who prefer not to mask the flavor of their seafood with complicated sauces. Most of the dishes are grilled over madrone-wood barbecue pits, a technique perfected since this place was established in 1975. Pacific salmon, halibut, lingcod, shark, sturgeon, Pacific snapper, oysters, and steamer clams are house specialties that have visitors lining up, especially on Friday and Saturday nights.

Harbor View Grotto Restaurant & Lounge. 150 Starfish Way. ☎ **707/464-3815.** Reservations recommended. Main courses $6–$9 lunch, $4.25–$50 dinner. MC, V. Daily 11:30am–9pm. SEAFOOD/STEAKS.

This is the best-established non-chain restaurant in town, specializing in fresh seafood at market prices since 1961. Completely renovated in December 1995, it has pleasant views of the ocean and harbor from both the dining room and lounge. It's capped with a miniature lighthouse inspired by Crescent City's Battery Point Lighthouse. The "light eaters" menu includes a cup of white chowder (made fresh daily), salad, a main course, and vegetables; heartier appetites can choose from among three different cuts of prime rib. Menu items include fresh, locally caught fish like Pacific snapper and salmon. Crab or shrimp Louis, as well as crabmeat or shrimp sandwiches are popular in season.

8 Redwood National & State Parks

40 miles N of Eureka, 336 miles N of San Francisco

It's impossible to explain the feeling you get in the old-growth forests of Redwood National and State Parks without resorting to Alice-in-Wonderland comparisons. Like a tropical rain forest, the redwood forest is a multistoried affair, the tall trees being only the top layer. Everything seems big, misty, and primeval—flowering bushes cover the ground, 10-foot-tall ferns line the creeks, and the smells are rich and musty. It's so *Jurassic Park* that you can't help but half expect to turn the corner and see a dinosaur.

When Archibald Menzies first noted the botanical existence of the coast redwood in 1794, more than 2 million acres of redwood forest carpeted California and Oregon. By 1965, heavy logging had reduced that to 300,000 acres, and it was obvious something had to be done if any redwoods were to survive. The state created several parks around individual groves in the 1920s, and in 1968, the federal government created Redwood National Park. In May 1994, the National Park Service and the California Department of Parks and Recreation signed an agreement to manage these four redwood parks cooperatively, hence the Redwood National *and* State Parks.

Although logging of old-growth redwoods in the region is still a major bone of contention among the government, private landowners, and environmentalists, it's an auspicious sign that contention even exists, a sign that perhaps we have all learned to see the forest *and* the trees for what they are—the undisputed monarchs of all living things, a thriving link to the age of dinosaurs, and a humble reminder that the age of mankind is but a hiccup in time to the venerable *Sequoia sempervirens.*

JUST THE FACTS

The southern gateway to the Redwood National and State Parks is the town of Orick, which you can identify by the dozens of burl stands alongside the road. Here you'll find the sleek **Redwood Information Center,** P.O. Box 7, Orick, CA 95555 (☎ **707/ 464-6101,** ext. 5265), one of California's rare examples of well-placed tax dollars (though some may dispute this since it's located near a floodplain and within a tsunami zone). Stop here and pick up a free map; it's open daily from 9am to 5pm. If you missed the Orick center, don't worry: About 10 miles farther north on U.S. 101 is the **Prairie Creek Visitor Center** (☎ **707/464-6101,** ext. 5300), which carries all the same maps and information. It's open daily from 9am to 5pm in summer, daily from 10am to 2pm in winter.

The northern gateway to the park is Crescent City, your best bet for a cheap motel, gas, fast food, and outdoor supplies. Before touring the park, pick up a free guide at the **Redwood National and State Parks Headquarters and Information Center,** 1111 Second St. (at K St.), Crescent City, CA 95531 (☎ **707/464-6101,** ext. 5064). It's open daily from 9am to 5pm.

If you happen to be arriving via U.S. 199 from Oregon, the rangers manning the **Hiouchi Information Station** (☎ **707/464-6101,** ext. 5067) and **Jedediah Smith Visitor Center** (☎ **707/464-6101,** ext. 5113) can also supply you with the necessary maps and advice. Both are open daily in summer from 9am to 5pm, and in winter when staffing is available.

Admission to the national park is free, but to enter any of the three state parks (which contain the best redwood groves), you'll have to pay a $6 day-use fee, which is good at all three. Camping fees range from $10 to $14 for drive-in sites, not including the $6.75 reservation fee (highly recommended in summer). Walk-in sites, however, are free, though a permit is required.

For more information about the Redwood National and State Parks, visit their Web site at **www.nps.gov/redw.**

SEEING THE HIGHLIGHTS

If you're approaching the park from the south, be sure to take the detour along U.S. 101 called the **Newton B. Drury Scenic Parkway,** which passes through dazzling groves of redwoods and elk-filled meadows before leading back onto the highway 8 miles later. Another spectacular route is the **Coastal Drive,** which winds through stands of redwoods and offers grand views of the Pacific.

Redwood National & State Parks

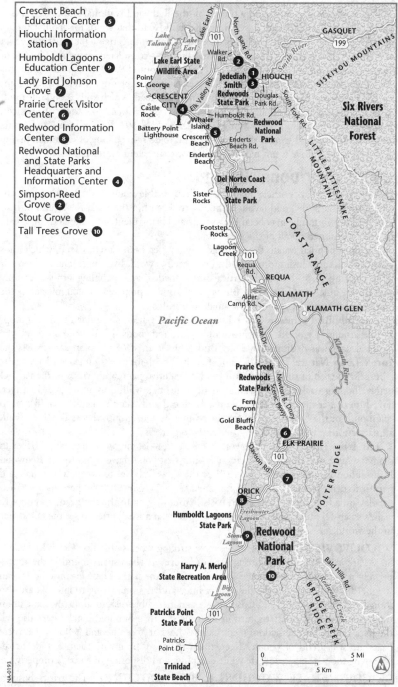

Lake Earl Dr.
Lake Earl
Lake Talawa
North Band Rd.
Smith River
GASQUET
199
SISKIYOU MOUNTAINS
Walker Rd.
101
2
Point St. George
Lake Earl State Wildlife Area
Jedediah Smith Redwoods State Park
1 HIOUCHI
3
Douglas Park Rd.
South Fork Rd.
Six Rivers National Forest
CRESCENT CITY
Castle Rock
Elk Valley Rd.
4
Humboldt Rd.
LITTLE RATTLESNAKE MOUNTAIN
Battery Point Lighthouse
Whaler Island
Crescent Beach
5
Enderts Beach Rd.
Redwood National Park
Enderts Beach
Del Norte Coast Redwoods State Park
Sister Rocks
COAST RANGE
Footstep Rocks
Lagoon Creek
101
Requa Rd.
REQUA
KLAMATH
Alder Camp Rd.
KLAMATH GLEN
Pacific Ocean
Coastal Dr.
Klamath River
Prarie Creek Redwoods State Park
Newton B. Drury Scenic Pkwy.
Fern Canyon
Gold Bluffs Beach
6 ELK PRAIRIE
101
HOLTER RIDGE
Davison Rd.
7
8 ORICK
Freshwater Lagoon
Humboldt Lagoons State Park
Stone Lagoon
9
Redwood National Park
Bald Hills Rd.
Redwood Creek
Harry A. Merlo State Recreation Area
10
Big Lagoon
BRIDGE CREEK RIDGE
Patricks Point State Park
101
Patricks Point Dr.
Trinidad State Beach

0   5 Mi
0   5 Km

NA-0193

225

The most amazing car-friendly trail in all the Redwood National and State Parks is the hidden, well-maintained gravel **Howland Hill Road** that winds for about 12 miles through Jedediah Smith Redwoods State Park. It's an unforgettable journey through an unbelievably spectacular old-growth redwood forest—considered by many to be one of the most beautiful areas in the world. To get here from U.S. 101, keep an eye out for the BP gas station at the south end of Crescent City; just before the station, turn right on Elk Valley Road, and follow it to Howland Hill Road, which will be on your right. After driving through the park, you'll end up at U.S. 199 near the town of Hiouchi, and from here it's a short jaunt west to get back to U.S. 101. Plan at least 2 to 3 hours for the 45-mile round-trip, or all day if you want to do some hiking or mountain biking in the park. This drive is not recommended for trailers and motor homes.

SPORTS & OUTDOOR PURSUITS

HIKING The park's official map and guide, available at any of the information centers, provides a fairly good layout of hiking trails within the park. Regardless of how short or long your hike may be, dress warmly and bring plenty of water and sunscreen. Pets are prohibited on all of the park's trails.

The most popular walk is the short, heavily traveled **Fern Canyon Trail,** which leads to an unbelievably lush grotto of lady, deer, chain, sword, five-finger, and maidenhair ferns clinging to 50-foot-high vertical walls divided by a babbling brook. It's only about a 1½-mile walk from Gold Bluffs Beach, but be prepared to scramble across the creek several times on your way via small footbridges.

The **Lady Bird Johnson Grove Loop** is an easy, 1-hour self-guided tour that loops 1 mile around a glorious lush grove of mature redwoods. It's the site at which the national park was dedicated by Lady Bird Johnson in 1968. Also an easy trek is the **Yurok Loop Nature Trail** at Lagoon Creek. The 1-mile self-guided trail gradually climbs to the top of rugged sea bluff (with wonderful panoramic views of the Pacific) before looping back to the parking lot. If someone's willing to act as shuttle driver, have him or her meet you at the Requa Trailhead and take the 4-mile coastal trail to the mouth of the Klamath. And for the whiner in your group, there's **Big Tree Trail,** a quarter-mile paved trail leading to a really big tree.

Tall Trees Trail leads to the world's tallest tree—some 365½ feet tall, 14 feet in diameter, and more than 600 years old—but first you'll have to go to the Redwood Information Center near Orick (see "Just the Facts," above) to obtain a free map and permit to drive to the trailhead of Tall Trees Grove. (*Note:* Only 50 permits are issued per day on a first-come, first-served basis.) After driving to the trailhead, you have to walk a steep 1⅓ miles down into the grove, but what a small price to see the tallest tree in the world.

WILDLIFE VIEWING One of the most striking aspects of Prairie Creek Redwoods State Park is its 200- to 300-strong herd of **Roosevelt elk,** usually found in the appropriately named Elk Prairie in the southern end of the park. These gigantic beasts can weigh 1,000 pounds, and the bulls carry huge antlers from spring to fall. Elk are also sometimes found at Gold Bluffs Beach—it's an incredible rush to suddenly come upon them out of the fog or after a turn in the trail. Nearly a hundred **black bears** also call the park home, but are seldom seen. Unlike those at Yosemite and Yellowstone, these bears are still afraid of people. Keep them that way by giving them a wide berth, observing food-storage etiquette while camping, and disposing of garbage properly.

BEACHES, WHALE WATCHING & BIRD WATCHING The park's beaches vary from long white-sand strands to cobblestone pocket coves. The water temperature is in the high 40s to low 50s year-round; it's often rough out there, so swimmers and surfers should be prepared for adverse conditions.

Crescent Beach is a long sandy beach just 2 miles south of Crescent City that's popular with beachcombers, surf fishermen, and surfers. Just south of Crescent Beach is **Endert's Beach,** a protected spot with a hike-in campground and tide pools at the southern end of the beach.

High coastal overlooks (like Klamath overlook and Crescent Beach overlook) make great whale-watching outposts during the southern migration in December and January and the return migration in March and April. The northern sea cliffs also provide valuable nesting sites for marine birds like auklets, puffins, murres, and cormorants. Birders will thrill at the park's freshwater lagoons as well. These coastal lagoons are some of the most pristine shorebird and waterfowl habitat left and are chock-full of hundreds of different species.

MOUNTAIN BIKING   Unfortunately, most of the hiking trails throughout the Redwood National and State Parks are off-limits to mountain bikers. However, Prairie Creek Redwoods State Park has a fantastic 19-mile mountain-bike trail through dense forest, elk-filled meadows, and glorious mud holes. Parts of it are a real thigh burner, though, so beginners should sit this one out. Pick up a 25¢ trail map at the Elk Prairie campground ranger station.

There are a few other mountain-bike loops in the 20-mile range, but they are *serious* thigh burners and make the one above look easy. These loops are the Holter Ridge Trail and Little Bald Hills. Mountain biking is also available on Old U.S. 101, now the coastal trail within Del Norte Coast Redwoods State Park.

RANGER PROGRAMS   The park service runs interpretive programs—from trees to tide pools, legends to landforms—at the Hiouchi, Crescent Beach, and Redwood information centers during summer months, as well as year-round at the park headquarters in Crescent City. State rangers lead campfire programs and numerous other activities throughout the year as well. Call the **Parks Information** service for both the national and state parks (☎ **707/464-6101,** ext. 5265) to get current schedules and events.

CAMPING & ACCOMMODATIONS

Five small campgrounds are located in the national park proper. Four of the walk-in (more like backpack-in) camps—Little Bald Hills, Nickel Creek, Flint Ridge, and Butler Creek—are free, and only one (the Redwood Creek Gravel Bar) requires a permit from the visitor center in advance.

Most car campsites are in the **Prairie Creek** and **Jedediah Smith state parks,** which lie entirely inside the national park. Prairie Creek contains two campgrounds, at Elk Prairie and Gold Bluffs Beach. Sites are $14 per night and can be reserved by calling the state's **Park-Net** reservations system (☎ **800/444-7275;** www. park-net.com), which requires an additional $7.50 reservation fee. Be prepared to deal with a truly annoying computer before you call, and know exactly what campground and if possible which site you would like. (The state park service has promised improvements in this system, but we'll see.)

If the camping areas above are all filled, try the **Mill Creek Campground,** in Del Norte Coast Redwoods State Park (part of RNSP), located 7 miles south of Crescent City on U.S. 101, which has 145 tent or RV sites. The walk-in tent sites are actually quite nice, situated amidst the forest. Fees range from $14 to $16 per night. The Park-Net system (see above) handles reservations for this campground as well.

A number of bed-and-breakfasts and funky roadside motels are available in the surrounding communities of Crescent City, Orick, and Klamath. The **Crescent City/Del Norte Chamber of Commerce** (☎ 800/343-8300) can probably steer you toward the proper match.

Redwood AYH Hostel—Demartin House. 14480 U.S. 101 (at U.S. 101 and Wilson Creek Rd., across from False Klamath Cove), Klamath, CA 95548. ☎ **707/482-8265.** 28 bunks, 1 couples room. $13–$15. MC, V.

The only lodging actually within the park, this turn-of-the-century logger's mansion was remodeled in 1987 to accommodate 30 guests dormitory style (that is, bunks and shared bathrooms). What it lacks in creature comforts, it makes up for in location—a mere 100 yards from the beach, and surrounded by hiking trails leading along the Redwood Coast (the staff leads nature walks and is well versed in local history). A couple's room is available with advance notice, and the hostel even takes reservations by credit card (strongly recommended in the summer). The nightly rate includes use of the showers, common room with VCR and videos, redwood deck, self-help common kitchen, laundry room, dining room, woodstove, and bicycle storage.

The Far North: Lake Tahoe, the Shasta Cascades & Lassen Volcanic National Park

by Matthew R. Poole

Dominated by the eternally snowcapped Mt. Shasta—visible for 100 miles around on a clear day—California's upper northern territory is among the least-touristed sections of the state. Often referred to as "the Far North," this vast region stretches from the rice fields north of Sacramento all the way to the Oregon border. In fact, the area is so immense that the state of Ohio would fit comfortably within its borders.

The Far North is a virtual outdoor playground for the adventurous traveler, offering myriad inexpensive recreational activities such as hiking, climbing, skiing, white-water rafting, and mountain biking. Other attractions, both artificial and natural, range from the amazing Shasta Dam to Lava Beds National Monument, which has dozens of caves to explore, and Lassen Volcanic National Park, a towering laboratory of volcanic phenomena.

Directly south of the Cascade Range is one of the most popular recreational regions in the Golden State: Lake Tahoe. Situated at 6,225 feet above sea level in the Sierra Nevada Mountains, it straddles the border between Nevada and California. Although the lake has been marred by overdevelopment—particularly along the casino-riddled southern shore—the western and eastern coastlines still provide quiet havens for hiking and cycling. The surrounding mountains offer some of the best skiing in the United States at more than a dozen resorts.

1 Lava Beds National Monument

324 miles NE of San Francisco, 50 miles NE of Mount Shasta

Lava Beds takes a while to grow on you. It's a seemingly desolate place with high plateaus, cinder cones, and rolling hills covered with lava cinders, sagebrush, and twisted junipers. Miles of land just like it cover most of this corner of California. So why, asks the first-time visitor, is this a national monument? The answer lies underground.

The earth here is like Swiss cheese, so porous in places that it actually makes a hollow sound. When lava pours from a shield volcano, it doesn't cool all at once; the outer edges cool first and the core keeps flowing, forming underground tunnels like a giant pipeline system.

More than 330 lava-tube caves lace the earth at Lava Beds—caves that are open to the public to explore on their own or with park rangers. Whereas most caves lend themselves to a fear of getting lost with their huge chambers, multiple entrances, and bizarre topography, these are simple, relatively easy-to-follow tunnels with little room to go wrong. Once inside, you'll feel that this would be a great place for a game of hide-and-seek.

JUST THE FACTS

Park elevations range from 4,000 to 5,700 feet, and this part of California can get cold any time of year. Summer is the best time to visit, with average temperatures in the 70s; winter temperatures plunge down to about 40°F in the day and as low as 20°F by night. Summer is also the best time to participate in ranger-led hikes, cave trips, and campfire programs. Check at the visitor center for schedules or call the **Lava Beds National Monument** headquarters (☎ 530/667-2282).

SEEING THE HIGHLIGHTS

A hike to **Schonchin Butte** (three-quarters of a mile each way) will give you a good perspective on the wildly stark beauty of the monument and nearby Tule Lake Valley. Wildlife lovers should keep their eyes peeled for terrestrial animals like mule deer, coyote, marmots, and squirrels, while watching overhead for bald eagles, 24 species of hawks, and enormous flocks of ducks and geese headed to the Klamath Basin, one of the largest waterfowl wintering grounds in the Lower 48. Sometimes the sky goes dark with ducks and geese during the peak migrations.

The caves at **Lava Beds** are open to the public with very little restriction or hassle. All you need to see most of them are a good flashlight or headlamp, sturdy walking shoes, and a sense of adventure. Many of the caves are entered by ladders or stairs, others still by holes in the side of a hill. Once inside, walk far enough to round a corner, and then shut off your light—a chilling experience, to say the least.

One-way **Cave Loop Road,** just southwest of the visitor center, is where you'll find many of the best cave hikes. About 15 lava tubes have been marked and made accessible. Two are ice caves, where the air temperature remains below freezing all year and ice crystals form on the walls. If exploring on your own gives you the creeps, check out **Mushpot Cave.** Almost adjacent to the visitor center, this cave has been outfitted with lights and a smooth walkway; you'll have plenty of company.

Hardened spelunkers will find enough remote and relatively unexplored caves in the monument, many requiring specialized climbing gear, to keep themselves busy.

Above ground, several trails crisscross the monument. The longest of these, the 8.2-mile (one-way) **Lyons Trail,** spans the wildest part of the monument, where you are likely to see plenty of animals. The 3.4-mile (one-way) **Whitney Butte Trail** leads from Merill Cave along the shoulder of 5,000-foot Whitney Butte to the edge of the Callahan Lava Flow and monument boundary.

PICNICKING, CAMPING & ACCOMMODATIONS

The 43-unit **Indian Well Campground** near the visitor center has spaces for tents and small RVs year-round, with water available only during the summer. The rest of the year, you'll have to carry water from the nearby visitor center.

Two **picnic grounds,** Fleener Chimneys and Captain Jacks Stronghold, have tables but no water; open fires are prohibited.

There are no hotels or lodges in the monument, but numerous services are available in nearby Tulelake and Klamath Falls. For more information, call or write **Lava Beds National Monument,** P.O. Box 867, Tulelake, CA 96134 (☎ 530/667-2282).

2 Mount Shasta & the Cascades

274 miles N of San Francisco

Chances are, your first glimpse of Mt. Shasta's majestic, snowcapped peak will result in a twang of awe. A dormant volcano with a 17-mile-diameter base, it stands in virtual isolation 14,162 feet above the sea. When John Muir first saw Shasta from 50 miles away in 1874, he wrote: "[I] was alone and weary. Yet my blood turned to wine, and I have not been weary since." He went on to describe it as "the pole star of the landscape," which indeed it is.

Keep in mind, however, that dining and lodging in these parts lean more toward sustenance than indulgence: It's the fresh air, not fresh fish, that lures visitors this far north. You can leave the dinner jacket at home—all that's really required when visiting the Far North are a pair of broken-in hiking boots, binoculars (the bald eagle is a common sight in these parts), some warm clothing, and an adventurous spirit.

ESSENTIALS

GETTING THERE   From San Francisco, take I-80 to I-505 to I-5 to Redding. From the coast, pick up Calif. 299 east a few miles north of Arcata to Redding.

Redding Municipal Airport, 6751 Woodrum Circle (☎ 530/224-4320), is serviced by **United Express** (☎ 800/241-6522) and **Horizon Air** (☎ 800/547-9308). **Amtrak** (☎ 800/USA-RAIL) stops in Dunsmuir and Redding.

VISITOR INFORMATION   Regional information can be obtained from the following organizations: **Shasta Cascade Wonderland Association,** 1699 Calif. 273., Anderson, CA 96007 (☎ 800/474-2782 or 530/365-7500); **Mount Shasta Visitors Bureau,** 300 Pine St., Mount Shasta, CA 96067 (☎ 800/926-4865 or 530/926-4865); **Redding Convention and Visitors Bureau,** 777 Auditorium Dr., Redding, CA 96001 (☎ 800/874-7562 or 530/225-4100); **Trinity County Chamber of Commerce,** 210 N. Main St., P.O. Box 517, Weaverville, CA 96093 (☎ 800/487-4648 or 530/623-6101).

WILLIAM B. IDE ADOBE STATE HISTORIC PARK

En route to Mount Shasta from the south, you may want to stop near Red Bluff at **William B. Ide Adobe State Historic Park,** 21659 Adobe Rd. (☎ **530/529-8599**), for a picnic along the Sacramento River. The 4-acre park commemorates William B. Ide, the Republic of California's first and only president, proclaimed on June 14, 1846, by those who led the Bear Flag Rebellion against the Mexicans who were excluding the Americans from California. The republic lasted only 3 weeks, until the American victory in the Mexican-American War made California a state in the Union. The adobe home dates from 1852. Some historians claim it was not Ide's home, but it does give visitors an idea of frontier life. In summer, the park is open from 8am to sunset, the house from noon to 4pm; call ahead in winter. Parking is $3 per vehicle.

REDDING & SHASTA

The major town and gateway to the region is Redding, the hub of the panoramic Shasta-Cascade region, lying at the top of the Sacramento Valley. From here, you can

Shasta Versus Shasta

Don't confuse the old mining town, Shasta, located a few miles west of Redding, with the much larger community, Mount Shasta, a major tourist destination located on Interstate 5 near the base of Mt. Shasta.

either turn westward into the wilderness forest of Trinity and the Klamath Mountains, or north and east into the Cascades and Shasta Trinity National Forest.

In Redding, with its fast-food joints, gas stations, and cheap motels, summer heat generally hovers around 100°F. A city of some 60,000, Redding is the transportation hub of the upper reaches of northern California. It has little of interest; it's mainly useful as a base for exploring the natural wonders nearby. Information is available from the **Redding Convention and Visitors Bureau,** 777 Auditorium Dr., Redding, CA 96001 (☎ **800/874-7562** or 530/225-4100), west of I-5 on Calif. 299. It's open Monday through Friday from 8am to 5pm, Saturday and Sunday from 9am to 5pm.

Ahead and northeast, Mt. Shasta rises to a height of more than 14,000 feet. From Redding, I-5 cuts north over the Pit River Bridge, crossing Lake Shasta and leading eventually to the mount itself. Before striking north, however, you may want to explore **Lake Shasta** and see **Shasta Dam.** Another option is to take a detour west of Redding to Weaverville, Whiskeytown–Shasta Trinity National Recreation Area, and Trinity Lake (see below).

About 3 miles west, stop at the old mining town of **Shasta,** which has been converted into a state historic park (☎ **530/243-8194**). Shasta was founded on gold and was the "Queen City" of the northern mines in the Klamath Range. Its life was short, and it expired in 1872 when the Central Pacific Railroad bypassed it in favor of Redding. Today, the business district is a ghost town, complete with a restored general store and a Masonic hall. The 1861 courthouse has been converted into a museum where you can view the jail and a gallows out back, as well as a remarkable collection of California art assembled by Mae Helen Bacon Boggs. The collection includes works by Maynard Dixon, Grace Hudson, and many others. It's open Wednesday through Sunday from 10am to 5pm. Admission is $2 for adults, $1 for children 6 to 12, and free for children 5 and under.

Continue along Calif. 299 west to Calif. 3 north, which will take you to Weaverville and then to the west side of the lake and Trinity Center.

WHERE TO STAY

In addition to the choices below, Redding has a **Doubletree Motor Inn** (☎ **800/ 222-8733** or **530/221-8700**) and a **La Quinta Inn** (☎ **800/NU-ROOMS** or 530/ 221-8200). Both are fine choices.

Tiffany House Bed and Breakfast Inn. 1510 Barbara Rd., Redding, CA 96003. ☎ **530/ 244-3225.** 4 units. $85–$105 double; $135 cottage. Rates include breakfast. AE, DISC, MC, V.

Despite the fact that this two-story gray-and-white house wasn't built until 1939, everyone in town refers to it as a Victorian. A sweeping view of the Lassen Mountain Range is visible from every guest room and cottage, as well as from the oversize deck, which seems to float above the garden in back. There's also a Music Room with piano, Victorian Parlor with fireplace, games and puzzles, and even a swimming pool. Each guest room is appointed with a queen-size bed and antique furnishings, and all have private baths and soft robes. Top choice is the secluded Lavinia's Cottage, which has a 7-foot spa tub, sitting area, and magnificent laurel-wreath iron bed.

WHERE TO DINE

Jack's Grill. 1743 California St. ☎ **530/241-9705.** Reservations not accepted. Main courses $8.25–$18.95. AE, DISC, MC, V. Mon–Sat 4–11pm. STEAK HOUSE.

This building was originally constructed in 1835 as a secondhand-clothing store. The second floor served as a whorehouse in the late 1930s, and an entrepreneur named Jack Young set up the main floor as a steak house (his establishment serviced all of a body's needs, you might say). Today, it's a local favorite. Waiting for a table over drinks

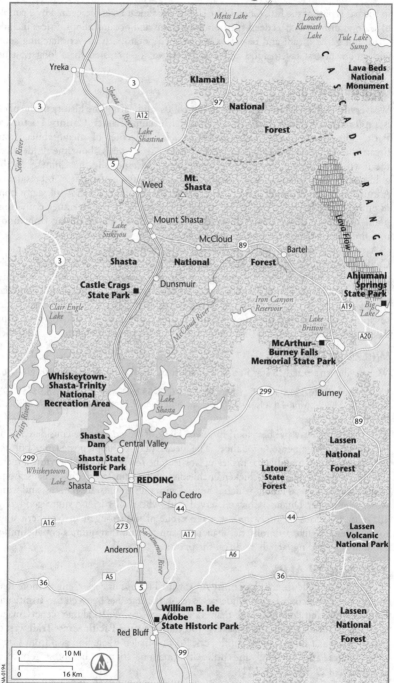

Meiss Lake

Lower Klamath Lake

Tule Lake Sump

CASCADE RANGE

Yreka

Lava Beds National Monument

3

Shasta River

Klamath

97

National

A12

Lake Shastina

Forest

5

Weed

Mt. Shasta

Scott River

Lake Siskiyou

Mount Shasta

McCloud

89

Bartel

Lava Flow

3

Shasta

National

Forest

Ahjumani Springs State Park

Castle Crags State Park

Dunsmuir

A19

Big Lake

Clair Engle Lake

McCloud River

Iron Canyon Reservoir

Lake Britton

A20

McArthur–Burney Falls Memorial State Park

Whiskeytown-Shasta-Trinity National Recreation Area

Trinity River

Lake Shasta

299

Burney

89

Shasta Dam

Central Valley

Lassen

National

Forest

299

Shasta State Historic Park

Whiskeytown Lake

Shasta

REDDING

Palo Cedro

Latour State Forest

44

44

A16

273

A17

Lassen Volcanic National Park

Anderson

Sacramento River

A6

A5

36

36

5

Lassen

William B. Ide Adobe State Historic Park

National

Red Bluff

Forest

99

0   10 Mi
0   16 Km

N

NA-0194

233

in the bar is part of the fun. Good old-fashioned red meat is supplemented by a couple of seafood dishes, such as deep-fried jumbo prawns and ocean scallops. Prices include salad, hot garlic bread, and baked or french-fried potatoes. It's a very fetching spot, with good, honest tavern food and a jovial crowd. Be prepared for a long wait on weekends.

WEAVERVILLE

Weaverville was a gold-mining town in the 1850s, and part of the history of the place is captured at the **Jake Jackson Memorial Museum–Trinity County Historical Park,** 508 Main St. (☎ **530/623-5211**). The collection of memorabilia, from firearms to household items, is interesting for what it reveals about the residents of the town—Native Americans, miners, pioneers, and especially the Chinese. In the gold-rush era, the town was half Chinese, with a Chinatown of about 2,500 residents. Admission is free, although a $1 donation is suggested. It's open in April, daily from noon to 4pm; May 1 to October 31, daily from 10am to 5pm; November, daily from noon to 4pm; and December through March, Tuesday and Saturday from noon to 4pm.

Across the parking lot, you can view the oldest continuously used Taoist temple in California at the **Joss House State Historic Park** (☎ **530/623-5284**). This well-preserved temple was built by immigrant Chinese miners in 1874. It's open June through August, daily from 10am to 5pm; September through November, Wednesday through Sunday from 10am to 5pm; December through March, Saturdays from 10am to 5pm; and April through May, Wednesday through Sunday from 10am to 5pm. Admission is $2 for adults, $1 for children 6 to 12, and free for children 5 and under.

WHERE TO DINE

Weaverville isn't exactly a star in the culinary firmament, but there is one bright spot.

La Grange Café. 315 N. Main St. ☎ **530/623-5325.** Main courses $6.95–$18.95. AE, DISC, MC, V. Mon–Fri 11am–9:30pm; Sat–Sun 7am–9:30pm. CREATIVE TRADITIONAL CUISINE.

This is far and away the best food in town. Heck, it would even be considered good in Redding, Sacramento, or Tahoe. The decor may be unprepossessing, but the friendly small-town ambiance makes up for it. Chef/owner Sharon Heryford's menu includes the local favorite—chicken enchiladas with marinated tri-tip—plus seasonal items such as the local rabbit, which is braised with mushrooms, fresh herbs, and white wine. The tender Duane's Chicken served with wheat pilaf is also quite good. The 135-plus selections on the wine list make it one of the strongest in Northern California. Desserts, like a sinfully rich banana cream pie and that quintessential comfort food, bread pudding, are all made on the premises.

THE TRINITY ALPS

West of Weaverville stretch the Trinity Alps, with Thompson Peak rising to more than 9,000 feet. The second-largest wilderness area in the state lies between the Trinity and Salmon rivers and contains more than 55 lakes and streams. Its alpine scenery makes it popular with hikers and backpackers. You can access the **Pacific Crest Trail** west of Mount Shasta at Parks Creek, South Fork Road, Whalen Road, and also from Castle Crags State Park. For trail and other information, contact the forest service at Weaverville (☎ 530/623-2121).

The Fifth Season, 300 N. Mount Shasta Blvd. (☎ 530/926-3606), offers mountaineering and backpack rentals and will provide trail maps and other information concerning Shasta's outdoor activities.

Living Waters Recreation (☎ 530/926-5446) offers half-day to 2-day rafting trips on the Upper Sacramento, Klamath, Trinity, and Salmon rivers. **Trinity River Rafting Company,** on Calif. 299W in Big Flat (☎ **800/30-RIVER** or 530/623-3033), also operates local white-water trips.

For additional outfitters and information, contact the **Trinity County Chamber of Commerce,** 210 N. Main St., P.O. Box 517, Weaverville, CA 96093 (☎ **800/ 487-4648** or 530/623-6101).

WHISKEYTOWN NATIONAL RECREATION AREA

In adjacent Shasta County, Whiskeytown National Recreation Area is on the eastern shore of Trinity Lake, a quiet and relatively uncrowded lake with 157 miles of shoreline. When this reservoir was created, it was officially named Clair Engle, after the politician who created it. But locals insist on calling it Trinity after the name of the river that used to rush through the region past the towns of Minersville, Stringtown, and an earlier Whiskeytown. All of these were destroyed when the river was dammed. They now lie submerged under the lake's glassy surface.

Both Trinity Lake and the Whiskeytown National Recreation Area are in the Shasta Trinity National Forest, 1.3 million acres of wilderness with 1,269 miles of hiking trails. For information on trails, contact **Shasta Trinity National Forest** (☎ 530/ 246-5222).

LAKE SHASTA

Heading north on I-5 from Redding, travel about 12 miles and take the Shasta Dam Boulevard exit to the ✪ **Shasta Dam and Power Plant** (☎ 530/275-4463), which has an overflow spillway that is three times higher than Niagara Falls. The huge dam— 3,460 feet long, 602 feet high, and 883 feet thick at its base—holds back the waters of the Sacramento, Pit, and McCloud rivers. A dramatic sight indeed, it is a vital component of the Central Valley water project. At the visitor center is a series of photographs and displays covering the dam's construction period. You can either walk or drive over the dam, but far more interesting are the free 1-hour tours given daily from 9am to 5pm on the hour in the summer, and at 10am, noon, and 2pm from Labor Day to Memorial Day. The guided tour takes you deep within the dam's many chilly corridors (not a good place for claustrophobes) and below the spillway. It's an entertaining way to beat the summer heat.

Lake Shasta has 370 miles of shoreline and attracts anglers (bass, trout, and king salmon), water-skiers, and other boating enthusiasts—two million, in fact, in summer. The best way to enjoy the lake is aboard a houseboat; they can be rented from several companies, including **Antlers Resort & Marina,** P.O. Box 140, Antlers Rd., Lakehead, CA 96051 (☎ **800/238-3924**); and **Packers Bay Marina,** 16814 Packers Bay Rd., Lakehead, CA 96051 (☎ **800/331-3137** or 530/275-5570). Prices range from $150 to $300 a day, but if you split it up among five friends, that's only $30 a pop for a full day of fun.

While you're here, you can visit **Lake Shasta Caverns** (☎ 530/238-2341). These caves contain 20-foot-high stalactite and stalagmite formations—60-foot-wide curtains of them in the great Cathedral Room. To see the caves, drive about 15 miles north of Redding on I-5 to the O'Brien/Shasta Caverns exit. A ferry will take you across the lake and a short bus ride will follow to the cave entrance for a 2-hour-long tour. Admission is $14 for adults, $7 for children, and free for kids 3 and under. The caverns are open daily year-round, with tours every half hour from 9am to 4pm Memorial Day to Labor Day; every hour from 9am to 3pm in April, May, and September; and at 10am, noon, and 2pm October through March.

Farther north, off I-5 about 50 miles north of Redding, you'll reach **Castle Crags State Park** (☎ **530/235-2684**), a 4,300-acre park with 64 campsites and 28 miles of hiking trails. Here, granite crags that were formed 225 million years ago tower more than 6,500 feet above the Sacramento River. The park is filled with dogwood, oak, cedar, and pine as well as tiger lilies, azaleas, and orchids in summer. You can walk the 1-mile Indian Creek nature trail or take the easy 1-mile Root Creek Trail. The entrance fee is $5 per vehicle per day.

For information about the Lake Shasta region, contact the **Redding Convention and Visitors Bureau,** 777 Auditorium Dr., Redding, CA 96001 (☎ **800/874-7562** or 530/225-4100), west of 1-5 on Calif. 299. It's open Monday through Friday from 8am to 5pm, Saturday and Sunday from 9am to 5pm.

MOUNT SHASTA

A volcanic mountain with eight glaciers, ✪ **Mt. Shasta** is a towering peak of legend and lore. It stands alone, always snowcapped, unshadowed by other mountains—visible from 125 miles away. Although it's been dormant since 1786, eruptions cannot be ruled out, and indeed, hot sulfur springs bubble at the summit. The springs saved John Muir on his third ascent of the mountain in 1875. Caught in a severe snowstorm, he and his partner took turns submersing themselves in the hot mud to survive.

Many New Agers are convinced that Mt. Shasta is the center of an incredible energy vortex. These devotees flock to the foot of the mountain. In 1987, the foothills were host to the worldwide Harmonic Convergence, calling for a planetary union and a new phase of universal harmony. Yoga, massage, meditation, and metaphysics are all the rage here. These New Agers seem to coexist harmoniously with those whose metaphysical leanings begin and end with Dolly Parton song lyrics.

Those who don't want to climb can drive up to about 7,900 feet. From Mount Shasta City, drive 14 miles up the Everitt Memorial Highway to the end of the road near Panther Meadow. At the **Everitt Vista Turnout,** you'll be able to stop and see the Sacramento River Canyon, the Eddy Mountains to the west, and glimpses of Mount Lassen to the south. You can also take the short hike through the forests to a lava outcrop overlooking the McCloud area.

Continue on to **Bunny Flat,** a major access point for climbing in summer and also for cross-country skiing and sledding in winter. The highway ends at the Old Ski Bowl Vista, providing panoramic views of Mount Lassen, Castle Crags, and the Trinity Mountains.

While in Mount Shasta, visit the **Fish Hatchery** at 3 N. Old State Rd. (☎ **530/ 926-2215**), which was built in 1888. Here you can observe rainbow and brown trout being hatched to stock rivers and streams statewide—millions are born here annually. You can feed them via coin-operated food dispensers, and observe the spawning process on certain Tuesdays during the fall and winter. Admission is free; hours are daily from 8am to sunset. Adjacent to the hatchery is the **Sisson Museum** (☎ **530/ 926-5508**), which displays a smattering of local-history exhibits. It's open daily year-round, from 10am to 4pm in summer, from 1 to 4pm in winter; admission is free.

MOUNTAIN CLIMBING   Mt. Shasta attracts thousands of hikers from around the world each year, from timid first-timers to serious mountaineers who search for the most difficult paths up. The hike isn't technically difficult, but it's a demanding ascent that takes about 8 hours of continuous exertion, particularly when the snow softens up. (*Tip:* Start early, while the snow is still firm.) Before setting out, hikers must secure a permit by signing in at the trailhead or at the **Mount Shasta Ranger District** office, which also gives out plenty of good advice for amateur climbers. The office is at 204 W. Alma St., off North Mount Shasta Boulevard in Mount Shasta (☎ **530/**

926-4511). Be sure to wear good hiking shoes and carry crampons and an ice ax, a first-aid kit, a quart of water per person, and a flashlight in case it takes longer than anticipated. Sunblock is an absolute necessity. All the requisite equipment can be rented at **The Fifth Season,** 300 N. Mount Shasta Blvd. (☎ **530/926-3606**).

Weather can be extremely unpredictable, and every year hikers die on this dormant volcano, usually from making stupid mistakes. For **weather and climbing conditions,** call ☎ **530/926-5555** for recorded information. Traditionally, climbers make the ascent from the Sierra Lodge at Horse Camp, which can be reached from the town of Shasta via Alma Street and the Everitt Memorial Highway or from Bunny Flat.

For more information as well as supervised trips, contact **Shasta Mountain Guides,** 1938 Hill Rd. (☎ **530/926-3117**). This outfitter offers a 2-day climb that follows the traditional John Muir route and costs about $240. It also offers a glacier climb and rock climbing in Castle Crags State Park, plus cross-country and telemark skiing.

SKIING   In winter, visitors can ski at **Mount Shasta Ski Park,** 104 Siskiyou Ave., Mount Shasta (☎ **530/926-8610**), which has 25 runs with 80% snowmaking, three triple-seat chairlifts, and a surface lift. A day-pass costs less than $30. There's also a Nordic ski center with 15½ miles of groomed trails, as well as a Terrain Park that's geared toward snowboarders. In summer, you can ride the chairlifts to scenic views, mountain-bike down the trails (an all-day pass is $10), or practice on the two-story climbing wall. Access to the chairlifts is 10 miles east on Mount Shasta (the town) on its southern slopes via Calif. 89 from McCloud. For information, call ☎ **530/ 926-8600.** The ski lodge's number is ☎ **530/926-8612.**

WATER SPORTS   The source of the headwaters of the Sacramento River accumulates in **Lake Siskiyou,** a popular spot for boating, swimming, and fishing—and a great vantage point for photographs of Mt. Shasta and its reflection. Water-skiing and jet-skiing are not allowed, but windsurfing is, and boat rentals are offered at **Lake Siskiyou Camp Resort,** 4239 W. A. Barr Rd., Mount Shasta (☎ **888/926-2618** or 530/926-2618).

GOLF & TENNIS   Golfers should head for the 27-hole Robert Trent Jones, Jr., golf course at **Lake Shastina Golf Resort,** 5925 Country Club Dr., Weed (☎ **530/ 938-3201**), or the 18-hole course at **Mount Shasta Resort,** 1000 Siskiyou Lake Blvd., Mount Shasta (☎ **530/926-3030**); the resort also has tennis courts.

OTHER WARM-WEATHER ACTIVITIES   Mount Shasta offers some excellent **mountain biking.** In the summer, ride the chairlifts to the top of Mount Shasta Ski Park and bike down the trails. An all-day chairlift pass is only $10 (☎ **530/926-8610**). Another good source for renting mountain bikes and getting trail information is **Shasta Cycling** (☎ **530/938-3002**).

For fishing information or guided trips, call **Jack Trout Flyfishing Guide** (☎ **530/ 926-4540**). Two other recommended sources are **Mount Shasta Fly Fishing** (☎ **530/926-6648**) and **Hart's Guide Service** (☎ **530/926-2431**).

For a really offbeat experience, contact **Rainbow Ridge Ranch** (☎ **530/926-5794**) and join one of their **llama-trekking** trips. Trips last from 3 to 5 days and cost $400 and up.

WHERE TO STAY

Best Western Tree House. 111 Morgan Way (at I-5 and Lake St.), Mount Shasta, CA 96067. ☎ **800/545-7164** or 530/926-3101. Fax 530/926-3542. 98 units. A/C TV TEL. $79–$160 double. AE, CB, DC, MC, V.

Just off the main highway, this motor inn is the best place to stay in the town of Mount Shasta, and it keeps its prices low. New this year is a remodeled lobby, plus new

TVs and furniture in all the rooms. Some units have decks and fridges, making them family favorites. Facilities include a rustic dining room and lounge with a stone fireplace, a new spa, a huge indoor pool that's usually deserted, and an exercise room. Downhill and cross-country ski areas are 10 miles away.

McCloud Guest House. 606 W. Colombero Dr. (P.O. Box 1510), McCloud, CA 96057. ☎ **530/964-3160.** 5 units, 2 with shower only. $80–$95 double. Rates include continental breakfast. MC, V.

Off Calif. 89, west of McCloud, and set among the oak and pine trees of Mt. Shasta's lower slopes, this bungalow-style house has a wraparound veranda and dormer windows. Built in 1907 as a residence for the president of the McCloud River Lumber Company, the house was nicely restored in 1984 by innkeepers Bill and Patti Leigh and Dennis and Pat Abreu. Upstairs, there's a large comfortable parlor with a pool table for guests. Off the parlor are five individually decorated rooms with white iron beds. Three of the rooms have clawfoot tubs; the other two have showers only.

On the ground floor is an atmospheric dining room with leaded- and stained-glass interior decoration. The menu offers a fine selection of Italian chicken, veal, pasta, and seafood dishes several nights a week.

Mt. Shasta Ranch B&B. 1008 W. A. Barr Rd., Mount Shasta, CA 96067. ☎ **530/ 926-3870.** Fax 530/926-6882. 9 units, 4 with private bathroom; 1 cottage. TV. $50–$70 double with shared bathroom; $95 double with bathroom; $95 cottage for 2. Room rates include breakfast. AE, DISC, MC, V. Take Central Mount Shasta exit off I-5 to W. A. Barr Rd.

Mt. Shasta Ranch was conceived and built in 1923 by one of the country's most famous horse trainers and racing tycoons, H. D. ("Curley") Brown, as the centerpiece of a private retreat and thoroughbred-horse ranch. Despite the encroachment of nearby buildings, the main house and its annex are still available as a cozy B&B with touches of nostalgia, the occasional antique, and spectacular views of Mt. Shasta. Four bedrooms (the ones with private bathrooms) lie in the main house; the remaining five share two bathrooms in the carriage house. It's a 3-minute trek to the shores of nearby Lake Siskiyou (15 minutes to the ski slopes), or you could stay here to enjoy the hot tub, Ping-Pong tables, pool table, darts, and horseshoes.

Railroad Park Resort. 100 Railroad Park Rd., Dunsmuir, CA 96025. ☎ **800/974-RAIL** or 530/235-4440. Fax 530/235-4470. www.rrp.com. 23 units, 4 cabins. A/C TV TEL. $60–$85 double. Extra person/pets $8. AE, DISC, MC, V. Take Railroad Park exit off I-5, 1 mile south of Dunsmuir.

Lying a quarter of a mile from the Sacramento River, this is an offbeat place that kids will enjoy. It's located at the foot of Castle Crags and contains several facilities—a restaurant and lounge, campground and RV park, rustic cabins, and the Caboose Motel. The railroad cabooses have been converted into rooms, leaving their pipes, ladders, and lofts in place. Located around the fenced-in kidney-shaped pool and whirlpool, they're furnished with modern brass beds, table and chairs, dressers, and TVs. The restaurant and lounge are also in vintage railroad cars.

Stewart Mineral Springs Resort. 4617 Stewart Springs Rd., Weed, CA 96094. ☎ **530/ 938-2222.** www.starhawk.com. 6 teepees (for up to 4 persons), 4 dorm rooms (for up to 5), 6 motel rooms (for up to 6), 5 cabins with kitchens (for 1 or 2 persons), 1 large A-frame house (suitable for 10 persons). $15 teepee for 1, $5 for each extra person; $30 dorm room for 1, $10 for each extra person; $40 motel room double; $45 cabin double; $300 A-frame house for up to 15. DISC, MC, V. Closed Dec 1–Mar 1 or even later, depending on snow.

Stewart Mineral Springs is one of the most unusual health spas in California, loaded with lore and legends. It lies above cold-water springs that Native Americans valued for their healing powers. Don't expect anything approaching a European spa or big-city luxury here. Everything is deliberately rustic, with as few intrusions from the urban world as possible (no phones or TVs). Designed in a somewhat haphazard compound of about a dozen buildings, 4 miles west of the town of Weed, it occupies a 37-acre site of sloping, forested land accented with ponds, gazebos, and decorative bridges and riddled with hiking and nature trails, freshwater streams, and a swimming hole. There are no restaurants on-site, and the spa facilities are often beside campers and RVs.

Activities revolve around hiking, nature watching, and taking the healing waters of the legendary springs. The bathhouse is the curative headquarters of the resort and contains 13 private rooms where water from the springs is heated and run into tubs for soaking. A staff member will describe the rituals for you: A 20-minute soak is followed by a visit to a nearby sauna and an immersion in the chilly waters of Parks Creek, just outside the bathhouse. Other feel-good options include massages ($30 per half-hour session). On Saturdays, medicine man Walking Eagle guides guests on a spiritual journey within the Native American Purification Sweat Lodge. If you opt for treatment and R&R here, you won't be alone. Despite its rusticity, the place has been discovered by young Hollywood, including many soap actors, San Francisco 49ers football players, and local newscasters.

Wagon Creek Inn. 1239 Woodland Park Dr., Mount Shasta, CA 96067. ☎ **530/926-0838.** 3 units. $75–$85 double with shared bathroom; $90 double with private bathroom. Rates include buffet breakfast. AE, DC, DISC, MC, V. From I-5, take the Central Mount Shasta exit to Old Stage Rd. Go 1½ miles and turn right at Woodland Park Dr. Pets accepted.

Loretta Lynn would feel at home in one of the rustic Southwestern-style rooms within this log-cabin home, located about 2½ miles from Mount Shasta. The King Room has its own bathroom; the other two share. Guests can use the living room with fireplace, TV, and VCR. It's a homey, inexpensive place where pets and kids are welcome.

WHERE TO DINE

The Bagel Cafe and Bakery. 105 E. Alma St., Mount Shasta. ☎ **530/926-1414.** Main courses $4–$6. No credit cards. Mon–Sat 6am–4pm; Sun 7am–2pm. AMERICAN.

This is the hands-down winner for a low-cost meal in Mount Shasta. Packed daily with locals, the lively little cafe serves the best coffee in the region, as well as wonderful vegetarian pizzas, soups, salads, sandwiches, and healthy entrees such as wok-fried veggies with tofu served over brown rice. If you're planning on spending the day out in the great outdoors, stop here first for a large coffee and sandwich to go.

✪ **Café Maddalena.** 5801 Sacramento Ave., Dunsmuir. ☎ **530/235-2725.** Main courses $9–$17. MC, V. Thurs–Sun 5:30–9:30pm. Closed mid-Dec–April. SARDINIAN/MEDITERRANEAN COUNTRY COOKING.

Owner/chef Maddalena Serra, who hails from Sardinia, has created a wonderful restaurant in the refurbished old railroad quarter of Dunsmuir. The smells wafting from this small place will literally draw you in. Maddalena cooks in full sight of the happy, satisfied (and stuffed) customers, preparing dishes like pasta Marco—fresh fettuccine with shrimp, tomatoes, cream, and herbs all wrapped in a flaky dough and baked in a pizza oven. Everything is made fresh daily, including the breads and desserts. Try the deceptively simple yet utterly scrumptious *panna cotta,* a cream flan with lemon, vanilla, and caramelized sugar. A memorable and special place.

Lily's. 1013 S. Mt. Shasta Blvd., Mount Shasta. ☎ **530/926-3372.** Reservations recommended. Main courses $9.95–$18.95. AE, DISC, MC, V. Mon–Fri 7am–9pm; Sat–Sun 7am–9:30pm. AMERICAN.

Set within a white-clapboard, turn-of-the-century house in a residential neighborhood south of the town center, this friendly little restaurant has a front porch, a picket fence, a back garden, and dining in two rooms inside and two patios out. It's popular for breakfast, when chunky breads, omelets, and polenta fritters start the morning off right. Lunch and dinner dishes—spicy Thai noodles, prime rib, scampi al roma, kung-pao shrimp salad—span the globe. Popular dishes are the enchiladas *suizas* stuffed with shrimp, crab, and fresh spinach, and Chicken Rosie, a tender breast of chicken simmered with raspberries, hazelnut liqueur, and cream.

MCARTHUR–BURNEY FALLS MEMORIAL STATE PARK

On its way to Lassen Volcanic National Park (see below) from Mount Shasta, Calif. 89 east loops back south to ✪ **McArthur–Burney Falls Memorial State Park** (☎ **530/335-2777**). One of the most spectacular features of this 910-acre park is **Burney Falls,** an absolutely gorgeous waterfall that cascades over a 129-foot cliff. Theodore Roosevelt once called the falls "the eighth wonder of the world." Giant springs lying a few hundred yards upstream feed the falls and keep them flowing—100 million gallons every day—even during California's legendary dry spells.

The half-mile **Headwater Trail** will take you to a good vantage point above the falls. If you're lucky, you can observe the black swift that nest in the mossy crevices behind the cascade. Other birds to look for include barn and great horned owls, the belted kingfisher, the common flicker, and even the Oregon junco. The year-round park also has 5 miles of nature trails, 128 campsites, picnicking grounds, and good fishing for bass, crappie, brown trout, rainbow trout, and brook trout. For **camping reservations,** call ☎ **800/444-PARK (7275).**

From here, Lassen Volcanic National Park lies about 40 miles south.

3 Lassen Volcanic National Park

45 miles E of Redding, 255 miles NE of San Francisco

Stashed away in the far northeastern corner of California, Lassen Volcanic National Park is a remarkable reminder that North America is still forming, and that the ground below is alive with the forces of creation and, sometimes, destruction. Lassen Peak is the southernmost peak in a chain of volcanoes (including Mt. Saint Helens) that stretches all the way from British Columbia.

Although it's dormant, 10,457-foot **Lassen Peak** is still very much alive. It last awakened in May 1914, beginning a cycle of eruptions that spit lava, steam, and ash until 1921. The eruption climaxed in 1915 when Lassen blew its top, sending a mushroom cloud of ash 7 miles high that was seen from hundreds of miles away. The peak itself has been dormant for nearly three-quarters of a century now, but the area still boils with a ferocious intensity: Hot springs, fumaroles, geysers, and mud pots are all indicators that Lassen hasn't had its last word. Monitoring of geothermal features in the park shows that they are getting hotter, not cooler, and some scientists take this as a sign that the next big eruption in the Cascades is likely to happen here.

Until then, the park gives visitors an interesting chance to watch a landscape recover from the massive destruction brought on by an eruption. To the north of Lassen Peak is the aptly named **Devastated Area,** a huge swath of volcanic destruction steadily repopulating with conifer forests. Forest botanists have revised their earlier theories that forests must be preceded by herbaceous growth after watching the Devastated Area immediately revegetate with a diverse mix of eight different conifer species, four more than were present before the blast.

The 108,000-acre park is a place of great beauty. The flora and fauna here are an interesting mix of species from the Cascade Range, which stretches north from Lassen, and species from the Sierra Nevada Range, which stretches south. The resulting blend

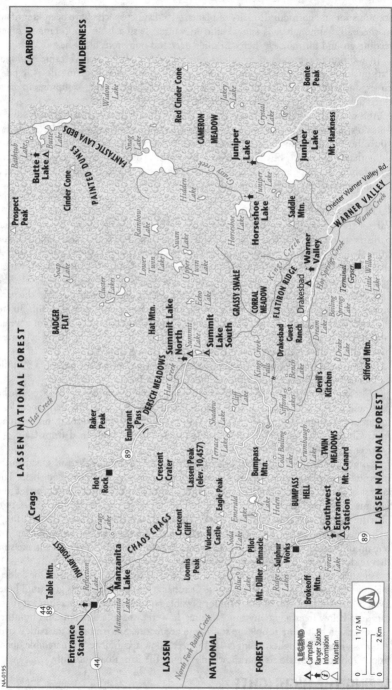

NA-0195

accounts for an enormous diversity of plants: 715 distinct species have been identified in the park. Although it is snowbound in winter, Lassen is an important summer feeding ground for transient herds of mule deer and numerous black bears.

In addition to the volcano and all its geothermal features, Lassen Volcanic National Park includes miles of hiking trails, 50 beautiful alpine lakes, large meadows, cinder cones, lush forests, cross-country skiing, and great backcountry camping. In fact, three-quarters of the park is designated wilderness.

And crowds? Forget it. Lassen is one of the least-visited national parks in the lower 48 states, so crowd control isn't as big a consideration here as in other places. Unless you're here on the Fourth of July or Labor Day weekend, you won't encounter anything that could rightly be called a crowd. Even then, you can escape the hordes simply by skipping the popular sites like Bumpass Hell or the Sulphur Works and heading a few miles down any of the backcountry trails.

JUST THE FACTS

Part of the reason Lassen Volcanic National Park is one of the least visited national parks is its remote location. The most foolproof route here is to take Calif. 44 east from Redding (via I-5), which leads directly to the northern gateway to the park. A shortcut if you're coming from the south along I-5 is Calif. 36 in Red Bluff, which leads to the park's southern gateway. If you're arriving from the east via I-80, take the U.S. 395 turnoff at Reno and head to Susanville. Depending on which end of the park you're shooting for, take either Calif. 44 (to the northwest entrance) or Calif. 36 (to the southwest entrance) from Susanville. The $5-per-car entrance fee, valid for a week, comes with a copy of the *Lassen Park Guide,* a handy little newsletter listing activities, hikes, and points of interest. Camping fees range from $8 to $12.

Only one major road, Calif. 89 (a.k.a. the Park Road), crosses the park in a 39-mile half circle with entrances and visitor centers at either end.

Most visitors enter the park at the southwest entrance station, drive through the park, and leave through the northwest entrance, or vice versa. Two other entrances lead to remote portions of the park. Warner Valley is reached from the south on the road from Chester. The Butte Lake entrance is reached by a cut-off road from Calif. 44 between Calif. 89 and Susanville.

Ranger stations are clustered near each entrance and provide the full spectrum of interpretive displays, ranger-led walks, informational leaflets, and emergency help. The largest **visitor center** is located just inside the northwest entrance station at the Loomis Museum. The park information number for all requests is ☎ **530/595-4444,** or write **Lassen Volcanic National Park,** P.O. Box 100, Mineral, CA 96063-0100.

Because of the dangers posed by the park's thermal features, rangers ask that you remain on trails at all times. Fires are allowed in campgrounds only; please make sure they're dead before leaving them. Mountain bikes are prohibited on all trails.

Another concern is the weather: Lassen Volcanic National Park is in one of the coldest places in California. Winter begins in late October and doesn't release its grip until June. Even in the summer, you should plan for possible rain and snow. Temperatures at night can drop below freezing at any time. Winter, however, shows a different and beautiful side of Lassen that more people are starting to appreciate. Since most of the park is over a mile high and the highest point is 10,457 feet, snow accumulates in incredible quantities. Don't be surprised to find snowbanks lining the Park Road into July.

SEEING THE HIGHLIGHTS

The highlight of Lassen is, of course, the volcano and all of its offshoots: boiling springs, fumaroles, mud pots, and more. You can see many of the most interesting sites in a day, making it possible to visit Lassen as a short detour from I-5 or U.S. 395 on the way to or from Oregon. Available at park visitor centers, the *Road Guide to Lassen Park* is a great traveling companion that will explain a lot of the features you'll see as you traverse the park.

Bumpass Hell, a 1½-mile walk off the Park Road in the southern part of the park, is the largest single geothermal site in the park—16 acres of bubbling mud pots cloaked in a stench of rotten-egg-smelling sulfur. The name comes from an early Lassen traveler, Bumpass, who lost a leg after he took a shortcut through the area while hunting and plunged into a boiling pool. Don't make the same error.

Sulphur Works is another stinky, steamy example of Lassen's residual heat. Two miles from the southwest park exit, the ground roars with seething gases escaping from the ground.

Boiling Springs Lake and **Devil's Kitchen** are two of the more remote geothermal sites; they're located in the Warner Valley section of the park, which can be reached by hiking from the main road or entering the park through Warner Valley Road from the small town of Chester.

OUTDOOR PURSUITS

In addition to the activities below, free naturalist programs are offered daily in the summer, highlighting everything from flora and fauna to geologic history and volcanic processes. For more information, call the **park headquarters** at ☎ **530/595-4444.**

HIKING   Most Lassen visitors drive through in a day or two, see the geothermal hot spots, and move on. That leaves 150 miles of trails and expanses of backcountry to the few who take the time to get off-road. The *Lassen Trails* booklet available at the visitor centers gives good descriptions of some of the most popular hikes and backpacking destinations. Anyone spending the night in the backcountry must have a wilderness permit issued at the ranger stations. And don't forget to bring plenty of water, sunscreen, and warm clothing.

The most popular hike in the park is the **Lassen Peak Trail,** a 2½-mile climb from the Park Road to the top of the peak. The trail may sound short, but it's steep and generally covered with snow until late summer. At an elevation of 10,457 feet, though, you'll get a view of the surrounding wilderness that's worth every step of the way. On clear days, you can see south all the way to Sutter Buttes near Yuba City and north into the Cascades. The round-trip takes about 4 to 5 hours.

Running a close second in popularity is **Bumpass Hell Trail.** This 1½-mile walk off the Park Road in the southern part of the park leads you through a quiet and peaceful meadow of wildflowers and chirping birds before depositing you right in the middle of the largest single geothermal site in the park. The name comes from an early—and unlucky—Lassen traveler, Bumpass (see "Seeing the Highlights," above). Stay on the wooden catwalks that safely guide visitors past the pyrite pools, steam vents, and noisy fumaroles, and you won't suffer Bumpass's fate.

The **Cinder Cone Trail,** located in the northeast corner of the park, is another worthy hike, best reached from Butte Lake Campground at the far northeast corner of the park. If 4 miles seems too short, you can extend the hike (and shorten the drive) by walking in about 8 miles from Summit Lake on the Park Road. Now dormant, Cinder Cone is generally accepted as the source of mysterious flashing lights that were seen by early settlers to the area in the 1850s. Black and charred-looking, Cinder Cone is bare of any sort of life and surrounded by dunes of multihued volcanic ash.

CANOEING & KAYAKING   Paddlers can take canoes, rowboats, and kayaks on any of the park lakes except Reflection, Emerald, Helen, and Boiling Springs. Motors, including electric motors, are strictly prohibited on all park waters. Park lakes are full of trout, and fishing is popular. You must have a current California fishing license.

CROSS-COUNTRY SKIING The park road usually closes due to snow in November, and most years it doesn't open until June, so cross-country skiers have their run of the park. Snowmobiles were once allowed but are now forbidden. Marked trails of all skill levels leave from Manzanita Lake at the north end of the park and Lassen Chalet at the south. Most visitors come to the southwest entrance, where the ski chalet offers lessons, rental gear, and a warm place to stay. Popular trips are the beginners' trails to Lake Helen or Summit Lake. More advanced skiers can make the trek into Bumpass Hell, a steaming valley of sulfuric mud pots and fumaroles.

You can also ski the popular 30-mile course of the Park Road in an overnight trek, but doing this involves a long car shuttle. For safety reasons, the park requires all skiers to register at the ranger stations before heading into the backcountry, whether for an overnight or just the day. For more information or to hire a guide, call **Lassen Ski Touring** (☎ **530/595-3376**).

SNOWSHOEING From January through March, park naturalists give free 2-hour eco-adventure snowshoe hikes across Lassen's snowpacked hills. The tours take place on Saturdays at 1:30pm at the Lassen Chalet, located at the park's southwestern entrance. You must be at least 8 years old, be warmly dressed, and be wearing boots. Snowshoes are provided free of charge on a first-come, first-served basis, although a $1 donation is requested for upkeep. For more details, call park headquarters (☎ **530/595-4444,** ext. 5133).

CAMPING

Car campers have their choice of seven park campgrounds with a total of 375 sites, more than enough to handle the trickle of visitors who come to Lassen every summer. In fact, so few people camp in Lassen that there is no reservations system except for at the **Lost Creek Group Campground,** and stays are granted a generous 14-day limit. Sites do fill up on weekends, so your best bet is to get to the park early on Friday to secure a place to stay. If the park is packed, there are 43 campgrounds in surrounding Lassen National Forest, so you're bound to find a site somewhere.

By far the most "civilized" campground in the park is at **Manzanita Lake,** where you can find hot showers, electrical hookups, flush toilets, and a camper store. When Manzanita fills up, rangers open the **Crags Campground** overflow camp, about 5 miles away and much more basic. Further within the park along Calif. 89 are **Summit Lake Campgrounds,** located on the north and south ends of Summit Lake. It's a pretty spot, often frequented by deer, and is a launching point for some excellent day hikes.

On the southern end of the park you'll find **Southwest Campground,** a walk-in camp directly adjacent to the Lassen Chalet parking lot.

The two remote entrances to Lassen and Warner Valley have their own primitive campgrounds with pit toilets and no water, but the price is right—free.

Backcountry camping is allowed almost everywhere, and traffic is light. Ask about closed areas when you get your wilderness permit, which are issued at the ranger stations and required for anyone spending the night in the backcountry.

ACCOMMODATIONS
INSIDE THE PARK

✪ **Drakesbad Guest Ranch.** ℅ California Guest Services, 2150 N. Main St. #5, Red Bluff, CA 96080. ☎ **530/529-9820.** 19 units. $105–$129 per person, double occupancy. Rates include meals. DISC, MC, V. Open 1st week in June to 2nd weekend in Oct, weather permitting.

The only lodge operating within Lassen Park is Drakesbad Guest Ranch, hidden in a high mountain valley inside the park and surrounded by meadows, lakes, and streams.

It's famous for its rustic cabins, lodge, and steaming thermal swimming pool, fed by a natural hot spring and open 24 hours a day. Drakesbad is deluxe as only a place with some electricity and no phones can be, with handmade quilts on every bed and kerosene lamps to read by. Full meal service is available—and it's very good. Since the lodge is extremely popular and only open from June through mid-October, reservations are booked as far as 2 years in advance (although May or June are good times to call to take advantage of cancellations).

NEAR THE PARK

✪ **The Bidwell House.** 1 Main St., P.O. Box 1790, Chester, CA 96020. ☎ **530/258-3338.** 14 units, 12 with private bathroom; 1 cottage with kitchenette. $82 double without bathroom; $103 double with bathroom; $163 cottage (sleeps up to 6). Rates include full breakfast. MC, V.

In 1901, General John Bidwell, a California senator who made three unsuccessful bids for the U.S. presidency, built a country retreat and summer home for his beloved young wife, Annie. After her death, when Chester had developed into a prosperous logging hamlet, the building, with its farmhouse-style design and spacious veranda, was converted into the headquarters for a local ranch. Today, the house sits at the extreme eastern end of Chester, adjacent to a rolling meadow. The lake is visible across the road, and inside, Ian and Kim James maintain one of the most charming B&Bs in the region. Seven of the rooms have Jacuzzi tubs, and three offer wood-burning stoves. Breakfast is presented with fanfare and incorporates many gourmet touches, including home-baked breads and scrumptious omelets. The Jameses also serve a terrific gourmet dinner Thursday through Saturday.

Lassen Mineral Lodge. On Calif. 36, P.O. Box 160, Mineral, CA 96063. ☎ **530/595-4422.** Fax 530/595-4452. 20 units. $65–$85 double. AE, DISC, MC, V.

A mere 9 miles south of Lassen Volcanic National Park's southern entrance, the Lassen Mineral Lodge offers 20 motel-style accommodations in a forested setting. In summer, the lodge is almost always bustling with guests and customers who venture into the gift shop, ski shop, general store, and full-service restaurant and bar. Also on the grounds are a pool and tennis court that are available during the summer months. For families, this is probably your best lodging option in the Lassen area.

Mill Creek Resort. On Calif. 172 (3 miles south of Calif. 36), Mill Creek, CA 96061. ☎ **530/595-4449.** 9 units. $50–$70 per cabin. No credit cards. Pets accepted.

Set deep within the forest, the Mill Creek Resort is that rustic mountain retreat you've always dreamed of while slaving away in the office. A homey country general store and coffee shop serve as the resort's center, a good place to stock up on food while exploring Lassen Volcanic National Park. Nine housekeeping cabins, available on a daily or weekly basis, are clean, cute, and outfitted with vintage 1930s and 1940s furniture, including kitchens (a good thing, since restaurants are scarce in this region). Pets are welcome, too.

DINING

INSIDE THE PARK

The only restaurant within Lassen Volcanic National Park (besides the Drakesbad Guest Ranch; see above) is the **Summer Chalet Café** (☎ 530/595-3376), which serves inexpensive, basic breakfasts, as well as sandwiches and burgers for lunch. Located at the park's south entrance, it's open daily from 8am to 6pm (grill closed at 4pm, however), May to mid-October, weather permitting.

NEAR THE PARK

When you're this far into the wilderness, the question isn't *which* restaurant to choose, but *if* there even is a restaurant to choose. If bacon and eggs, sandwiches, steaks, chicken, burgers, pizza, and salads aren't part of your diet, you're in big trouble unless you packed your own grub.

Deciding where you're going to eat near Lassen Volcanic National Park depends mostly on which side you're on, north or south. Near the north entrance to the park in the town of Old Station is **Uncle Runt's Place** (☎ 530/335-7177), which serves your standard steaks, chicken, burgers, and sandwiches for lunch and dinner. At the south entrance to the park, the closest restaurant is the **Lassen Mineral Lodge** (see "Accommodations," above) in the town of Mineral, which serves the usual uninspired American fare.

The best approach, however, is to stay at a B&B or lodge that offers meals to its guests—such as the **Bidwell House** or **Drakesbad Guest Ranch**—or at least provides a kitchen to cook your own meals, such as the **Mill Creek Resort** (see above). Food and camping supplies are available at the **Manzanita Lake Camper Store** (☎ 530/335-7557; closed in winter) located at the north entrance to the park, or **Lassen Mineral Lodge,** on Calif. 36 in Mineral, at the southern end of the park (☎ 530/595-4422). They also sell or rent just about every outdoor toy you'd ever want to play with in Lassen Park, including cross-country and alpine ski equipment.

4 Lake Tahoe

107 miles E of Sacramento, 192 miles E of San Francisco

Lake Tahoe has long been California's most popular recreational playground. In summer, you can enjoy boating and water sports, in-line skating, bungee jumping, camping, ballooning, horseback riding, bicycling, parasailing—the list is endless. In winter, Lake Tahoe becomes one of the nation's premier ski destinations with its 15 downhill resorts and 10 cross-country skiing centers. There's also sleigh riding, ice-skating, snowmobiling, and snowshoeing. Year-round activities include tennis, fishing, Vegas-style gambling, and big-name entertainment on the Nevada border.

Then there's the lake. It's disputable whether Lake Tahoe is the most beautiful lake in the world, but it's certainly near the top of the list. It's famous for its 99.997% pure water (a white dinner plate at a depth of 75 feet would be clearly visible from the surface), and its size: The lake is so immense that the water it contains—close to 40 trillion gallons—could cover the entire state of California to a depth of 14½ inches. Its average depth is 989 feet, although it reaches 1,645 feet in places, making it the second-deepest lake in the United States (after Crater Lake, Oregon) and the eighth-deepest in the world.

More important to the visitor, however, is this region's pristine beauty: the play of light during the day, which transforms the color of the lake from a dazzling emerald to blues and rich purples; the snowy mountaintops reflecting off the water; the fresh, crisp air; and the deep green of the trees carpeting the expanse of the valley. It's a sight that no one should miss and that nobody ever forgets.

ESSENTIALS

GETTING THERE　It's a 4-hour drive from San Francisco; take I-80 east to Sacramento, then U.S. 50 to the lake's south shore, or I-80 east to Calif. 89 or 267 south to reach the lake's north shore.

From Los Angeles, it's a grueling 9-hour drive; take I-5 through the Central Valley to I-80 east at Sacramento, then U.S. 50 east. If the weather's good and you can spare

A Tale of Two Shores

You wouldn't think the people and places on one end of Lake Tahoe would be much different from the other, but ask any local: North Shore and South Shore—Tahoe's two main destinations—have about as much in common as snow cones and sandcastles.

Don't let the "City" in North Shore's "Tahoe City" fool you: The entire town can be driven through in about 40 seconds, whereas South Lake Tahoe is brimming with high-rise casinos, condominiums, and mini-malls. Which side you choose to stay on is important, as driving from one end of the lake to the other is a 1- to 2-hour affair on summer weekends and downright treacherous during snowstorms, so don't make the common mistake of thinking you can sleep for cheap on the South Shore and party all day on the North.

So which side is for you? If you're here to gamble, stay south: The selection of casinos is better and the lodging more abundant. If it's the great outdoors you're after, or simply a little R&R in the shade of a Douglas fir, head north. The North Shore offers a far better selection of quality lodgings, restaurants, and scenery, while the South Shore shoots for quantity, offering three times as many lodgings and restaurants at better rates.

a few additional hours, it's really worth avoiding the interstate for the scenic drive on U.S. 395 and U.S. 50, which lie along the corridor between the towering peaks of the eastern Sierra and the Inyo Mountain Range.

Reno/Tahoe International Airport, 40 miles northeast of Lake Tahoe (about a 50-minute drive), offers regularly scheduled service from 12 national airlines, including **American** (☎ 800/433-7300), **Delta** (☎ 800/221-1212), and **United/United Express** (☎ 800/241-6522).

Amtrak (☎ 800/USA-RAIL) services Truckee, 10 miles north of the lake; shuttle service is available to North Lake Tahoe from the station. Trains connect with the rest of the state through Sacramento.

VISITOR INFORMATION   Call the **North Lake Tahoe Resort Association** in Tahoe City (☎ 800/824-6348 or 530/583-3494; www.tahoefun.org), or stop by the Resort Association's **Visitor Service Center** at 245 North Lake Blvd., Tahoe City (☎ 800/824-6348). It's open Monday through Friday from 9am to 5pm, Saturday and Sunday from 9am to 4pm.

In South Lake Tahoe, there's the **Lake Tahoe Visitors Authority,** 1156 Ski Run Blvd. (☎ 800/367-7366 or 530/544-5050), and the **South Lake Tahoe Chamber of Commerce,** 3066 Lake Tahoe Blvd. (☎ 530/541-5255), which is open Monday through Friday from 8:30am to 5pm and Saturday from 9am to 4pm (closed on major holidays).

SKIING

Tahoe offers California's best skiing, with 15 downhill-ski resorts and 10 cross-country centers. The ski season usually lasts from November through May, but frequently extends into the early summer (in 1995, there was skiing until July 4!). Lift tickets usually cost about $45 to $50 per day, $30 to $35 per half day, and $6 to $10 for children under 13. Six of the top areas—Alpine Meadows, Heavenly Resort, Kirkwood, Northstar-at-Tahoe, Sierra-at-Tahoe, and Squaw Valley USA—offer an interchangeable Ski Lake Tahoe lift ticket for about $220 for 5 days.

Lake Tahoe & Environs

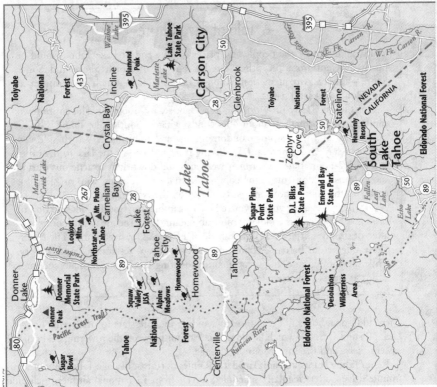

If you've come to ski, contact both visitor offices (see above) for information about the ski packages offered by almost every hotel and resort on the lake—you're likely to save a bundle. The following are some of Tahoe's most popular resorts.

✪ **Alpine Meadows.** P.O. Box 5279, 2600 Alpine Meadows Rd., Tahoe City, CA 96145. ☎ **800/441-4423** or 530/583-4232. www.skialpine.com.

Six miles from Tahoe City, Alpine has a high elevation (8,637 feet) that gives it a long skiing season, often lasting until Memorial Day. The midsize resort—ranked by readers of *Snow Country* magazine as their favorite resort in California—is a great all-around performer, with 40% of the terrain groomed for intermediate skiers, 35% for advanced, and 25% for beginners. Recent additions include a six-passenger high-speed chair, a Family Ski Zone, and a new terrain park and half-pipe for snowboarders.

Diamond Peak. 1210 Ski Way, Incline Village, NV 89451. ☎ **775/832-1177** or 775/831-3249. www.diamondpeak.com.

One of Tahoe's smaller—and less crowded, less expensive—ski resorts, Diamond Peak plugs itself as the "premier family ski resort." It's primarily a mountain for intermediates (49%), with 33% of the mountain groomed for advanced, and 18% for beginners. Kids love the new snowboard park and sledding area. There's also cross-country skiing and snowshoeing, as well as dining and lodging in nearby Incline Village.

Heavenly Resort. P.O. Box 2180, Stateline, NV 89449. ☎ **775/586-7000.** www.skiheavenly.com.

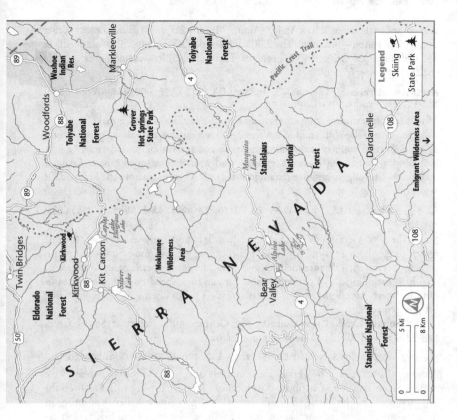

Heavenly is one of the area's largest ski resorts, with 4,800 acres of ski terrain and snowmaking on 66% of the trails. The vertical drop is 3,500 feet, the steepest in the region, with incredible views of the lake basin. The terrain is 45% intermediate, 35% advanced, and 20% beginner. There are 25 lifts, including a 50-passenger aerial tram and three high-speed detachable quads. The resort straddles the state borders; Heavenly West on the California side has easier trails than Heavenly North, which is predominantly intermediate territory. It's less crowded, however, on the Nevada side.

Homewood Mountain Resort. P.O. Box 165, 5145 W. Lake Blvd., Homewood, CA 96141. ☎ **530/525-2992.** www.skihomewood.com.

Homewood is one of our favorite small ski areas, a homey little resort with lean lift lines and gorgeous views of the lake. The ski area covers 1,260 acres and offers 56 trails and 8 lifts. It's a good family resort, with child care for 2- to 6-year-olds and a special Snow Stars program for kids 6 to 12. It's 6 miles south of Tahoe City and 19 miles north of South Lake Tahoe. *Hot Tip:* The best ski deal in Tahoe is the two-for-one special on Wild Wednesdays, which usually starts in January—buy one all-day adult lift ticket and receive one free.

Kirkwood. Off Calif. 88, P.O. Box 1, Kirkwood, CA 95646. ☎ **209/258-6000.** www.skikirkwood.com.

Kirkwood's only drawback is that it's 30 miles (45 minutes) from South Lake Tahoe on Calif. 88; otherwise, this is one of the top ski areas in Tahoe, with one of the highest average snowfalls after Squaw Valley (Alpine Meadows is third) and excellent spring skiing often running into June. The 2,300 acres of skiable terrain is 50% intermediate, 35% advanced/expert, and 15% beginner. There are 12 lifts—including three triple chairs—accessing 65 trails.

Northstar-at-Tahoe. P.O. Box 129, Truckee, CA 96160. ☎ **800/466-6784** or 530/562-1010. www.skinorthstar.com.

More than 50% snowmaking coverage and a full-time kids' program make Northstar a top choice in Tahoe for families. It offers 2,420 acres of downhill skiing with 63 runs, 37 miles of cross-country trails, plus sleigh rides and snowmobiling. There are 12 lifts, including a six-passenger express gondola and four express quad chairs. Facilities include on-site lodging and five restaurants. It's only 45 minutes from the Reno-Tahoe airport.

✪ **Squaw Valley USA.** Squaw Valley, CA 96146. ☎ **800/545-4350** or 530/583-6985. www.squaw.com.

Site of the 1960 Olympic Winter Games, Squaw is almost every serious skier's favorite resort, simply because it offers the most challenging array of runs. Squaw's terrain is 25% for beginners, 45% intermediate, and 30% advanced/expert/insane. There are 30 chairlifts, including a 110-passenger cable car and high-speed Funitel, the first of its kind in North America. Skiing is spread across six peaks offering a whopping 4,000 lift-serviced acres.

The **Squaw Creek Cross-Country Ski Center** at the Resort at Squaw Creek (☎ **530/583-6300**) has 11 miles of groomed trails.

Sugar Bowl. P.O. Box 5, Norden, CA 95724. ☎ **530/426-4000.** www.sugarbowl.com.

Although it was ranked by *Ski* magazine in 1994 as one of the top 30 resorts in the nation, Sugar Bowl's best attribute is its location: If you're driving to Tahoe from the Bay Area via I-80, it's about an hour's drive closer than Squaw Valley. Known for its deep snowpack (does "powder skiing" mean anything to you?), the midsized resort has 80 runs serviced by nine lifts. Whether it's worth the drive from the lake is questionable, but anyone coming up from the valley should seriously consider this one. Should you choose to stay, lodging is available at the base of the resort.

OTHER WINTER FUN

CROSS-COUNTRY SKIING **Lakeview Cross Country** (☎ **530/583-9353**) has 37 miles of groomed trails, a full-service day lodge, and three warming huts. It's only 2 miles from Tahoe City off Calif. 28 at Dollar Point Shell, making it very accessible.

The **Royal Gorge Cross-Country Ski Resort,** Soda Springs (☎ **800/500-3871** or 530/426-3871; www.royalgorge.com), is one of the largest cross-country facilities anywhere, with 88 trails (203 miles), including 28 novice trails and four ski lifts. Facilities include a day lodge, wilderness lodge, ski school, 10 warming huts, and four trailside cafes. It's 1 mile off I-80 at the Soda Springs exit.

Sugar Pine Point State Park (☎ **530/525-7982**) also has cross-country skiing on well-maintained trails. The park is located on the west side of the lake, halfway between North and South Lake Tahoe on Calif. 89. You can't miss it—just look for the big sign on the side of the road.

ICE-SKATING One of the world's most unusual ice rinks is at Squaw Valley's **High Camp** (☎ **530/583-6985**). The ice is accessible only by tram—a scenic ride that's included with admission. Skating costs $19 for adults and $10 for children, including the cable-car ride and skate rentals. After 4pm, the prices drop to $11 for adults and $8 for children. The rink is open year-round, daily from 11am to 9pm. Call first, as the rink closes a few days in the spring and fall for maintenance.

SNOWMOBILING   Snowmobiles are available for rent at several locations in the Lake Tahoe area. The **Zephyr Cove Snowmobile Center** (☎ 775/882-0788) is about 4 miles north of Stateline, Nevada, on the lake's east side. It offers 2-hour guided snowmobile tours from November 26 to April 15 (weather permitting). Tours are scheduled usually thrice daily—at 10am, 12:15pm, and 2:30pm—and cost $74 for a single rider and $99 for two people on one snowmobile (limit 400 pounds). Special moonlight tours are also offered.

   High Sierra Snowmobiling, Calif. 267 and Calif. 28, Kings Beach (☎ 530/546-9909), is open from November 15 to April 1 (again, weather permitting). It offers no trail tours, just a manicured track, for which it charges $30 per half hour. High Sierra is open daily from 9am to 5pm.

SUMMER ACTIVITIES

BALLOONING   View the lake and the Sierra from 10,000 to 12,000 feet above. **Lake Tahoe Balloons,** South Lake Tahoe (☎ 530/544-1221), offers 1- to 1½-hour flights year-round, followed by a champagne brunch at Café Roma at Caesar's.

BICYCLING   There are miles of excellent paved bike paths around the lake. The 3.4-mile **Pope-Baldwin Bike Path** on the south shore runs parallel to Calif. 89 and through Camp Richardson and the Tallac Historic Site. In South Lake Tahoe, another paved path runs from El Dorado Beach along the lake, paralleling U.S. 50. Along the west shore there are 15 miles of paved pathways, extending from Tahoe City in three directions. On the northeast shore, Incline Village has a 2½-mile trail from Gateway Park on Calif. 28.

   You can rent bikes in Tahoe City at **Porter's Ski and Sport,** 501 N. Lake Blvd. (☎ 530/583-2314), and in Incline Village at another Porter's location, 885 Tahoe Blvd. (☎ 775/831-3500). In South Lake Tahoe, go to **Anderson's Bike Rental,** on the lake side of Calif. 89 at 13th Street (☎ 530/541-0500). Bike rentals usually cost $7 per hour, $20 for 4 hours, and $25 per day.

BOAT RENTALS   Several companies rent a variety of boats—canoes, powerboats, and pedalboats. Among them are: **Zephyr Cove Resort Marina** (☎ 775/588-3833), which rents all three; **Paradise Watercraft** at Camp Richardson Resort (☎ 530/541-1801); **Tahoe Keys Boat Rentals** at Tahoe Keys Marina (☎ 530/544-8888 or 530/541-8405), which only rents powerboats; and **North Tahoe Marina,** Calif. 28, 1 mile west of Calif. 267, Tahoe Vista (☎ 530/546-8248), which rents skis and tow lines along with 18- to 21-foot motorboats. Canoes and kayaks can be rented from **Tahoe Paddle & Oar** in Tahoe City (☎ 530/581-3029).

FISHING   Fishing in the crystal-clear waters of the lake presents a special challenge to anglers. Deep-water fishing for mackinaw trout is good year-round. Surface fishing for kokanee salmon is best in May and June, whereas fishing for rainbow trout is ideal in the fall and winter months.

   There are dozens of charter companies offering daily excursions on Lake Tahoe year-round. **Mickey's Big Mack Charters,** Tahoe City (☎ 800/877-1462 after 6pm, or 530/546-4444), is a well-respected outfit, led by experienced guide Mickey Daniels. All the fishing gear is provided, but you'll need a license, which can be purchased on the boat. Call for requirements and reservations. Mickey's boats depart from Sierra Boat Company, in Carnelian Bay, about 5 miles north of Tahoe City. Five-hour trips cost $65 per person (or 3 hours for $45) and depart daily year-round, in the early morning and late afternoon; exact times vary according to season. Other fishing specialists include **Blue Ribbon Fishing Charters,** South Lake Tahoe (☎ 530/541-8801), and **Tahoe Sportfishing,** Ski Run Marina, 900 Ski Run Blvd., South Lake Tahoe (☎ 530/541-5448).

FITNESS CENTERS & SPAS   At the end of the day, soak your sore bones at the **North Tahoe Beach Center,** 7860 North Lake Blvd., at Kings Beach (☎ 530/546-2566). Besides offering a full line of exercise equipment, the center also boasts the largest spa on the lake, some 26 feet in diameter. It's all yours for $7 for adults and $3 for kids under 12; kids under 4 are free. It's open daily from 10am to 10pm (on Mondays, Wednesdays, and Fridays it opens at 7am). Another spa that's popular with the locals is **Walley's Hot Springs Resort** (☎ 775/782-8155), located 2 miles north of the east end of Kingsbury Grade at 2001 Foothill Rd. in Nevada. It's worth the drive to indulge in their six open-air pools (each a bit warmer than the next) and massage center. Admission is $12.

GOLF   There are two Robert Trent Jones, Jr., championship courses in the area: **Incline Village Championship Course,** 955 Fairway Blvd. (☎ 775/832-1144), and **Squaw Creek Golf Course,** at the Resort at Squaw Creek (☎ 530/583-6300), which is the most expensive course at Tahoe ($110 on weekends, $85 in the off-season). Other challenging courses include the **Northstar Golf Course,** Basque Drive (☎ 530/562-2490), which has water hazards on 14 holes and was designed by Robert Muir Graves, and South Lake's **Edgewood Tahoe,** site of the Isuzu Celebrity Gold Championship, with 18 holes and a driving range (☎ 775/588-3566).

HIKING   The mountains surrounding Lake Tahoe are crisscrossed with hiking trails graded for all levels of experience. Before setting out, you may wish to contact the local visitors bureau for a map and more in-depth information on particular trails, or hire a guide. From $25 to $60 per person—depending on the hike, group size, and transportation—an experienced mountaineer from **Tahoe Trips & Trails** (☎ 800/581-HIKE or 530/583-4506) will take anyone, from Grandpa to Rambo, on a guided hike specifically suited to each person's ability, ranging from super-easy to hard-core hoofin' it. Everything is provided, including a gourmet vegetarian-friendly lunch, drinks, transportation, and answers to any questions you have about the history and geology of Lake Tahoe. It's truly a great outfit that guarantees a good time at a fair price.

Some of the most popular trails in the area are:

Eagle Falls/Eagle Lake: One of the best trails for novice hikers, the Eagle Falls walk offers a cascading reward. The trail begins at Eagle Picnic Area, directly on Calif. 89 across from Emerald Bay.

Emerald Bay/Vikingsholm: From the parking area, 1½ miles above Tahoe's prettiest inlet, you can hike down to Vikingsholm, a 38-room replica of a medieval Scandinavian castle. The trail begins at the parking area on the north side of Emerald Bay, on Calif. 89.

Loch Levon Lakes: An easy but beautiful walk to three lakes, the Loch Levon trail is perfect for hikers who wish to stay on the beaten path. To reach the trailhead, take I-80 to the Big Bend exit and look for the sign PRIVATE ROAD PUBLIC TRAIL across from the Big Bend Ranger Station.

Shirley Lake: In Squaw Valley, near the tram line, this excellent hike has the advantage of a one-way adventure: You can take the tram up and hike down, or vice versa. The trail begins at the end of Squaw Peak Road, next to the cable-car building.

HORSEBACK RIDING   **Camp Richardson Corral,** South Lake Tahoe (☎ 530/541-3113), offers a variety of trail rides and pack trips. A 2-hour trail ride is $35, whereas pack trips cost $150 per day, including packer, livestock, food, boat, and tackle. Sleigh rides are offered from December through March.

Northstar Stables, 2499 Northstar Dr. and Calif. 267 (☎ 530/562-2267), at the resort of the same name, offers a variety of trail rides, lessons, and pack trips. Special breakfast and dinner rides are also available. Children under the age of 7 are not allowed on trail rides. Northstar is on the north side of Lake Tahoe, between Kings Beach and Truckee. Prices range from $5 for pony rides to $28 for 1½ hours, $50 for half-day rides, and $100 for a full day. Call for pack-trip information. Open year-round daily from 9am to 5pm; when winter prohibits trail rides, sleigh rides are available.

Squaw Valley Stables, 1525 Squaw Valley Rd. (☎ **530/583-7433**), offers trail rides and lessons for all ages and riding levels. Squaw Valley is about 5 miles north of Tahoe City. Prices range from $19 for a 1-hour guided ride to $55 for a half-day ride. Pony rides are $6 per half hour. Open mid-May to early September, daily from 8:30am to 4:30pm.

Sunset Ranch, U.S. 50, South Lake Tahoe (☎ **530/541-9001**), is the only stable to allow unescorted riding. A quarter of a mile west of the Lake Tahoe Airport, Sunset Ranch offers rides to both children and adults along the open meadows that abut the Truckee River. Prices are $21 per hour, or $31 per hour for two people on a single horse; children 12 and under are $16. Open year-round daily from 9am to 6pm.

IN-LINE SKATING   Although there are trails all around Lake Tahoe, the best ones for blading are the well-paved bicycle-and-pedestrian-only paths that hug the Truckee River and Calif. 89, between Tahoe City and Squaw Valley. Rollerblades and other in-line skates can be rented from the nearby **Squaw Valley Sport Shop,** Tahoe City (☎ **530/583-6278**). The shop charges $12 for a half day, $18 full day (including wrist guards and other protective gear). The shop is open Sunday through Thursday from 9am to 6pm, Friday and Saturday from 9am to 7pm.

JET-SKIING   The **Lighthouse Watersports Center,** 950 N. Lake Blvd., Tahoe City (☎ **530/583-7245**), rents jet skis, paddleboats, and canoes in summer only. Reservations are recommended for jet-ski rentals. Jet skis cost $35 per half hour and $60 per hour; paddleboats and canoes go for $15 per half hour and $20 for 2 hours. The water-sports center is open June through September, daily from 9am to 6pm.

In South Lake Tahoe, the place to rent is **Lakeview Sports,** 3131 U.S. 50, across from the El Dorado Campground (☎ **530/544-0183** or 530/541-8405). It also rents mountain bikes, in-line skates, and boats.

MOUNTAIN BIKING   At both **Northstar** (☎ **530/562-1010**) and **Squaw Valley** (☎ **530/583-6985**), you can take the cable car (Squaw) or chairlift (Northstar) up with your bike and ride the trails all the way down (call for complete information). However, for a far more rewarding experience, set up a guided off-road tour with **Cyclepaths Mountain Bike Adventures,** 1785 West Lake Blvd. in Tahoe Park, a few miles south of Tahoe City (☎ **800/780-BIKE** or 530/581-1171; www.tahoecountry. com/cyclepaths). Whether you're into hardcore downhill singletrack or easy-going scenic outings, the expert guides will provide you with all the necessary equipment, food, and transportation.

If you would rather go it on your own, the numerous sports stores in Tahoe City and South Lake Tahoe all carry books and maps to the mountain-biking trails around the lake. Be sure to carry plenty of water and wear strong sunscreen.

PARASAILING   **Lake Tahoe Parasailing,** Tahoe City (☎ **530/583-7245**), charges $40 to $50 (depending on your time aloft), and $70 for tandem flights. Rides are offered from Memorial Day to September 20, daily from 8am to 3pm. Boats operate from Tahoe City Marina. Boat and WaveRunner rentals are also available, as are water-skiing and sailboat charters.

RIVER RAFTING   The Truckee River—Lake Tahoe's only outlet—dumps plenty of water for a swift but gentle ride. Rafts seat anywhere between 2 to 14 people and cost about $25 for adults and $20 for kids (no kids under 5); the season runs from Memorial Day weekend to Labor Day. Rafting outfits include **Truckee River Raft Rental** (☎ 530/583-0123), **Fanny Bridge Rafts** (☎ 530/581-0123), and **Truckee River Rafting/Mountain Air Sports** (☎ 530/583-7238).

TENNIS All the major resorts have tennis courts open to the public on a fee basis. Call the **Resort at Squaw Creek** (☎ 530/583-6300) or **Northstar** (☎ 530/562-0321) for information and reservations.

Budget-minded players looking for good local courts should visit Tahoe Lake School, Grove Street, Tahoe City, where two lighted courts are available free on a first-come, first-served basis. South Tahoe Intermediate School, Lyons Avenue, off U.S. 50, has eight lighted courts. It charges a manageable $3 per hour.

WATER-SKIING **North Tahoe Marina,** Calif. 28, 1 mile west of Calif. 267, Tahoe Vista (☎ 530/546-8248), rents skis and tow lines along with 18- to 24-foot motorboats. Other powerboat toys, including tubes, knee boards, and wet suits, are also available. Rates are $65 to $110 per hour. Open May 1 to October 1, daily from 8am to 6pm.

WINDSURFING Easy winds and relatively calm conditions make Lake Tahoe an ideal place to learn. **Lakeside Chalets,** 5240 N. Lake Blvd., Carnelian Bay (☎ 530/546-5857), rents boards and offers lessons by appointment from June through September. Windsurfers cost $20 per initial hour and $10 per hour thereafter ($50 to $60 a day).

LAKE CRUISES

The best way to experience the lake is to get out on it. *M.S. Dixie II,* Zephyr Cove Marina, Nevada (☎ 775/588-3508), a 570-passenger vessel with bars, a dance floor, and a full dining room, offers daily cruises year-round, which may include breakfast, champagne brunch, or dinner. Zephyr Cove Marina is on U.S. 50, 4 miles north of Stateline in South Lake Tahoe. Bay cruises cost $16 for adults and $5 for children 11 and under; breakfast and brunch cruises, $18 for adults and $9 for children; dinner cruises, $28 to $38 for adults and $12 for children. Call for schedules.

The *Tahoe Queen* (☎ 800/238-2463 or 530/541-3364), a 500-passenger stern-wheeler, operates year-round, offering daily Emerald Bay cruises, sunset dinner-dance cruises, and shuttle service between the lake's north and south shores during the ski season. There are large outdoor and indoor viewing decks and a glass bottom for peering deep into the lake. The Emerald Bay Cruise costs $14 for adults and $5 for children 11 and under; dinner cruise, $18 for adults and $9.50 for children (dinner optional, menu selections from $15); round-trip North/South Shore Ski Shuttle, $18 for adults and $9 for children. The *Tahoe Queen* departs from Ski Run Marina, just west of Stateline. Call to confirm rates and schedules.

The North Shore version of the Tahoe Queen is the *Tahoe Gal* (☎ 800/218-2464 or 530/583-0141), a Mississippi River paddle wheeler that departs from the Lighthouse Marina in Tahoe City (behind Safeway). Cruises include Emerald Bay ($20 for adults and $8 for children) and Scenic Shoreline ($15 for adults and $5 for children). Dinner is available for an additional $15 for adults and $5 for children.

Woodwind **Sailing Cruises**, in the Zephyr Cove Resort, on U.S. 50, Zephyr Cove, Nevada (☎ 775/588-3000), offers daily sailing trips aboard a 41-foot tri-hull craft that takes up to 30 passengers, as well as a new 55-foot catamaran. Both boats have glass bottoms that allow good underwater viewing. Reservations are recommended. Trips are $18 for adults, $9 for children under 12, and free for children under 2. Trips start daily at 11:30am, 1pm, 2:30pm, and 4pm from April through October. There's also a sunset champagne cruise for $26 (adults only).

Travel Tip

If your car sports a tape deck, consider buying *Drive Around the Lake,* a drive-along audio cassette that contains facts, tales and legends, places of interest, and just about everything else you could possibly want to know about the lake. It's available at numerous gift shops or at the **South Lake Tahoe Chamber of Commerce,** 3066 Lake Tahoe Blvd. (☎ **530/541-5255**), which is open Monday through Friday from 8:30am to 5pm and Saturday from 9am to 4pm (closed on major holidays).

A DRIVE AROUND THE LAKE

Other than cruising over it, the next best way to contemplate the lake is to drive the 72 miles around it, although at times the route can be completely clogged with traffic. And while the lake has never frozen over, the roads that surround it do; many are closed in winter, making this trip possible during summer only.

We'll start at the California/Nevada border in South Lake Tahoe and loop around the western shore on Calif. 89 to Tahoe City and beyond. U.S. 50, which runs along the south shore, is an ugly, overdeveloped strip that obliterates any view of the lake unless you're staying at one of these motels. Keep heading west and you'll soon be free of this ugly zone.

First stop is the **Tallac Historic Site,** a cluster of rustic mansions that were built 100 years ago and are currently being restored by the forest service. A little farther on you'll find the forest services' **Lake Tahoe Visitors Center,** located along Taylor Creek, which offers nature trails as well as an opportunity to view kokanee salmon making their way upstream to spawn.

From here, Calif. 89 climbs northward. Soon you'll be peering down into beautiful **Emerald Bay,** a 3-mile-long inlet containing tiny Fanette Island, which has an old stone teahouse clearly situated at its peak. It was built by Lora Knight, who also built Vikingsholm (see below).

Across Calif. 89 from Emerald Bay, there's another parking area. From here, it's a short, steep, quarter-mile hike to a footbridge above Eagle Falls. Then it's about 1 mile to Eagle Lake. Register at the trailhead. **Emerald Bay State Park** (☎ **530/988-0205**) offers 100 camping sites on the south side of the bay.

It's not surprising that someone chose to build a mansion right here overlooking the bay—**Vikingsholm,** Emerald Bay, Calif. 89 (☎ **530/525-7277** or 530/525-7232). Constructed in 1929, this 38-room mansion is a replica of a medieval Viking castle. It is so striking that a paved parking area on the highway had to be built for all the gawkers. Tree branches shaped like spears jut out from the gutters to ward off evil spirits. Inside, carved dragon heads decorate the ceiling beams. A layer of sod blankets the roof, which sprouts wildflowers in the spring. You can visit Vikingsholm by hiking down a steep 1-mile trail (but remember, you have to come back up, too). The mansion is open for tours, every half hour on the hour and half hour. Admission is $3 for adults, $2 for children 6 to 12, and free for kids under 6. It's open June 3 to Labor Day, daily from 10am to 4pm.

From here, it's only about 2 miles to **D. L. Bliss State Park** (☎ **530/525-7277**), where you'll find one of the lake's best beaches. It gets very crowded in summer, so arrive early before all the parking places are occupied. The park also contains 168 campsites and several trails, including one along the shoreline.

About 7 miles farther on, **Sugar Pine Point State Park** (☎ **530/525-7982**) is the largest (2,000 acres) of the lake's parks and also the only one that has year-round camping. In summer, you can visit one of several beaches in the park plus a nature trail; in winter, there's cross-country skiing on well-maintained trails.

It's a clear drive through the small town of Homewood (site of the ski resort of the same name) to **Tahoe City,** which is smaller and much more appealing than South Lake Tahoe, although it, too, has its share of strip development.

At Tahoe City, Calif. 89 turns off to **Truckee** and to Alpine Meadows and Squaw Valley ski resorts. Squaw Valley is only 5 miles out, and a ride on the **Squaw Valley cable car** (☎ **530/583-6985**) rewards visitors with incredible vistas from 2,000 feet above the valley floor. The cable car operates year-round, daily from 8am to 4pm. A ticket is $12 for adults, $9 for seniors 65 and over, $5 for children 4 to 12, and free for children under 3. From Squaw Valley, it's another 5 or so miles to the railroad town of Truckee and **Donner State Park,** with its museum and monument to the Donner Party Expedition of 1846.

If you continue around the lake on Calif. 28, you'll reach Carnelian Bay, Tahoe Vista, and Kings Beach before crossing the state line into Nevada to Crystal Bay, Incline Village, the Ponderosa Ranch, and Sand Harbor Beach. **Kings Beach State Recreation Area** (☎ **530/546-7248**), 12 miles east of Tahoe City, is jammed in summer with sunbathers and swimmers. From Incline Village, a 4-mile side trip up the Mount Rose Highway leads to an overlook of the entire Tahoe Basin.

Remember Hoss and Little Joe Cartwright? The **Ponderosa Ranch,** Calif. 28, Incline Village (☎ **775/831-0691**), is a theme park inspired by the popular 1960s television show *Bonanza.* You can visit the original 1959 Cartwright Ranch House along with a western township complete with blacksmith's shop and staged gun battles. There are also such activities as pony rides and a petting farm. The barbecue grill is almost always fired up, and breakfast hayrides on tractor-pulled wagons are offered for an extra $2. Admission is $9.50 for adults, $5.50 for children 5 to 11, and free for children under 5. It's open mid-April to October only, daily from 9:30am to 5pm.

Also at Incline Village is **Sand Harbor,** one of the best beaches on the lake (though it can get incredibly crowded in summer).

South of Sand Harbor, if you wish, you can turn inland to Spooner Lake and Carson City, the capital of Nevada, or continue south along Calif. 28 to an outcropping called **Cave Rock,** where the highway passes through 25 yards of solid stone. Farther along is **Zephyr Cove,** from which the tour boats depart. You'll then return to Stateline and South Lake Tahoe, your original starting point.

WHERE TO STAY
SOUTH SHORE/SOUTH LAKE TAHOE
Expensive

Caesar's Tahoe. 55 U.S. 50, P.O. Box 5800, Lake Tahoe, NV 89449. ☎ **800/648-3353** or 775/588-3515. 440 units. A/C TV TEL. $110–$195 double; $375 minisuite; $650 theme suite. Extra person $10. AE, DC, MC, V.

This 16-story hotel, built in the early 1980s, has the glitter, the glitz, and the campy references to Roman mythology that Caesar's Palace in Las Vegas has perfected for decades. It's a more intimate version of its Las Vegas counterpart, spruced up with a mere $16-million renovation. The guest rooms, many of which offer beautiful views of the lake, are furnished with contemporary hardwood pieces and fully equipped with extra-large tubs (Roman-style, of course) and two phones. Firm king- or queen-size beds await you, often with padded scalloped headboards à la Mae West. Suites have unique themes, such as the Hollywood Suite, which comes complete with faux palm trees. Suites can only be guaranteed at check-in, presumably because high rollers are difficult to evict on schedule.

Dining/Diversions: There are six in-house restaurants, one of the most popular being the Broiler Room. It's all here: grill, yogurt shop, buffets, an Asian dining room, and even an Italian restaurant. But Planet Hollywood is the venue that packs them in—everyone from tourists to the occasional visiting pop star. The 24-hour casino and showrooms provide major entertainment.

Amenities: 24-hour room service, concierge, laundry/valet, baby-sitting, indoor lagoon-style swimming pool, tennis courts, fitness room with Universal machines plus massage therapists.

✪ **Embassy Suites Resort Lake Tahoe.** 4130 Lake Tahoe Blvd., South Lake Tahoe, CA 96150. ☎ **800/988-9820** or 530/544-5400. Fax 530/544-4900. 400 suites. A/C MINIBAR TV TEL. $150–$300 double. Extra person $30. Rates include cooked-to-order breakfast and evening cocktail reception. Packages available. AE, CB, DC, DISC, MC, V.

Standing near the state line, this is the only major hotel on California's south shore, and it's in a class by itself, competing for the upscale gambling crowd and the convention business with Nevada's glittering casino hotels across the way. Family skiers fill up the place in winter. A Bavarian-style hotel of character, it rises nine floors, the roofline pierced with a double layer of dormers. Accommodations are nothing unusual for those who've stayed at Embassy Suites before: dark hardwood furniture, tasteful fabrics, well-chosen carpets, microwaves, VCRs, and Nintendo.

Dining/Diversions: Zackary's restaurant serves American and international dishes around the clock. Turtles sport bar opens onto an outdoor deck; it keeps its wood-fired pizza oven busy at night and turns into a disco later in the evening.

Amenities: Concierge, room service, laundry service, newspaper delivery, in-room massage, maid service, baby-sitting, valet parking, whirlpool, indoor pool, basic gym.

✪ **Fantasy Inn.** 3696 Lake Tahoe Blvd., South Lake Tahoe, CA 96150. ☎ **800/367-7736** or 530/541-4200. Fax 530/541-6798. www.fantasy-inn.com. 53 units. A/C TV TEL. Sun–Thurs $159–$259 double; Fri–Sat $219–$319 double. All rooms $30 less Sept 8–June 17. Packages available. AE, CB, DC, DISC, MC, V.

Even the "fantasy" industry is downsizing: At one time, there were five Fantasy Inns around Lake Tahoe and Reno, but, alas, now there is only one hotel left in Tahoe that caters exclusively to the adults-only, all-romance market. Despite a theme that in less-skilled hands would be tacky and leering, this place is actually outfitted in relatively good taste with goodly amounts of fun. Its erotic undercurrent isn't particularly discreet, thanks to sexually provocative art and a choice of porno flicks coming over the VCR. Nonetheless, the place has provided love nests for hundreds of couples (of all persuasions). Set on the California side, about 1½ miles from the state line, it offers little in the way of outside diversions (presumably, you'll bring your own). There's no restaurant, no breakfast served, and no casino on-site.

The decor mingles camp with a sense of fun and (usually) taste. All units have one king-size or round bed, lots of mirrors (on both walls and ceilings), surround-sound stereo systems, cable TV with in-house adult-movie rentals, twin showerheads, whirlpool spa, provocative art, and accoutrements designed for two. Theme suites (Antony and Cleopatra, Romeo and Juliet, Caesar's Indulgence, and the Sultan's Tent, for example) might have round beds or "waveless waterbeds." Our favorite of all, Graceland, has a bed shaped like a heart and enough Elvis memorabilia to give you something to talk about after your passions have been satiated.

Harrah's Casino Hotel. U.S. 50 at Stateline Ave. (P.O. Box 8), Lake Tahoe, NV 89449. ☎ **800/427-7247** or 775/588-6611. Fax 775/586-6607. 532 units. A/C TV TEL. $119–$180 double; $179–$280 junior suite; $486–$918 suite. AE, CB, DC, DISC, MC, V.

In hot competition with Caesar's, this modern Vegas-style palace in an 18-story concrete-and-glass tower is deliberately glitzy and flashy. It stands astride the California–Nevada state line, and for legal reasons, all the gambling facilities are on the

Nevada side. Connected to Harvey's Casino Resort (see below) by tunnel, it's a consistently high-rated hotel, an impressive achievement for such a sprawling complex.

Rooms are among the largest in Tahoe—each with two bathrooms and those thick, fluffy, white towels Sinatra was always demanding. Most have bay windows overlooking the lake or the Sierra Mountain Range, and all have soundproofing and walk-in closets. The casino has full no-smoking floors (this is California, after all), as well as an enormous Family Fun Center designed to keep the kids busy while Mom and Dad work the one-armed bandits.

Dining/Diversions: There are seven restaurants, the most glamorous of which are on the upper floors. Big names in showbiz headline at the casino's South Shore Room. The dinner-only Summit Restaurant on the 16th floor offers panoramic views of the lake and mountains, which are often better than the food. Other choices include a 24-hour coffee shop, an Italian cafe, and a split-level rooftop steak house. Buffets are also served on the rooftop. A sports bar is just one of many drinking meccas.

Amenities: 24-hour room service, concierge, valet, overnight laundry, shoe-shine, ski shuttle, baby-sitting, car-rental desk, casino, glass-enclosed swimming pool, health club, arcade.

Harvey's Casino Resort, Lake Tahoe. U.S. 50 at Stateline Ave., Stateline, NV 89449. ☎ **800/HARVEYS** or 775/588-2411. www.harveystahoe.com. Fax 775/588-6643. 740 units. TV TEL. Sun–Thurs $119–$209 double; Fri–Sat $149–$259 double. Year-round $299–$659 suite. Rates include continental breakfast. AE, CB, DC, DISC, MC, V.

Harvey's was built in Lake Tahoe in the 1940s, during the great expansion of Las Vegas, and its design reflects a Vegas sensibility (though with far better surroundings). Originally, the resort contained only a 12-story tower, referred to today as the Mountain Tower, but in 1986, the hotel's size more than doubled with the addition of a 19-story Lake Tower. Today, it's the largest hotel in Tahoe, boasting an 88,000-square-foot casino (Tahoe's largest), eight restaurants, and a cabaret with some of the most glittering, bespangled entertainment in town. More than a hotel, Harvey's is like a city unto itself, with a connecting tunnel to the neighboring Harrah's. Try to get a room between the 15th and 19th floors in the newer tower, where every unit has a view of both Lake Tahoe and the surrounding Sierra.

Dining/Diversions: There are eight restaurants, often filled with convention revelers. Llewellyn's, on the 19th floor with panoramic views of the lake, is the premier restaurant and serves contemporary cuisine. There's also the Sage Room, a traditional western steak house (rib eye to venison), a Hard Rock Café, a coffee shop, a buffet restaurant, a seafood grotto, a fast-food stop, and the very popular Mexican venue, El Vaquero. The Emerald Theater showroom features live revues.

Amenities: 24-hour room service, concierge, laundry/valet, shoe-shine, ski shuttle, shopping shuttle, car-rental desk, casino, pool, arcade, health club and spa, children's day camp, family fun center. The hotel also has its own wedding chapel, whose view of the lake has been the backdrop for thousands of marriages.

Tahoe Seasons Resort. 3901 Saddle Rd., off Ski Run Blvd. (P.O. Box 5656), South Lake Tahoe, CA 96157. ☎ **800/540-4874** or 530/541-6700. Fax 530/541-0653. 183 suites. A/C TV TEL. Summer $160–$225 double; winter $170–$240 double; spring and fall $115–$190 double. Seasonal "Romance" packages available. AE, DC, MC, V.

Big, modern, and loaded with luxuries, the Tahoe Seasons lies in a relatively uncongested residential neighborhood at the base of the Heavenly Valley Ski Resort, 2 miles from Tahoe's casinos. Every unit here is a suite; all but 10 have gas fireplaces, and all have huge whirlpool spas, VCRs, fridges, microwaves, and coffeemakers. Skiing isn't the only activity around here: Play a round of tennis on the roof, swim in the heated outdoor pool, or hop aboard the free casino shuttles. The ambiance is rustic Californian, a style appreciated by the droves of second honeymooners who come here to lose their shirts, in more ways than one. An on-site restaurant and cocktail lounge provides, among other things, room service.

Moderate

Best Western Station House Inn. 901 Park Ave., South Lake Tahoe, CA 96150. ☎ **800/822-5953** or 530/542-1101. Fax 530/542-1714. 100 units. A/C TV TEL. $98–$118 double; $125–$150 suite; $175–$200 chalet. Rates include full breakfast. AE, DC, DISC, MC, V.

Trimmed with redwood, the Best Western Station House Inn was built in the late 1970s, nestled amid pines 2 blocks off U.S. 50. It's one of the few hotels in town that has its own private "gated" beach on the lake. It's not a particularly exciting hotel, but it's clean and very acceptable. Guest rooms are done in a modern style with oak furnishings. The staff is friendly and competent, the hotel offers free shuttle service to the casinos and most ski resorts, and there's an in-house restaurant called Lew Mar-Nell's.

Horizon Casino Resort. U.S. 50 (P.O. Box C), Lake Tahoe, NV 89449. ☎ **800/648-3322** or 775/588-6211. Fax 775/588-0349. 539 units. A/C TV TEL. Summer $99–$149 double; winter $69–$119 double; year-round from $325 suite. Children under 12 stay free in parents' room. Extra person $10. AE, DISC, DC, MC, V.

This massive hotel stands next to the even larger and better-known Harvey's; it's definitely a runner-up in the hotel sweepstakes, but it charges a lot less for basically the same facilities. Rising in a pair of towers (with 8 and 15 floors, respectively), the Horizon was radically renovated in 1994. Its original core, built in the 1960s, was the High Sierra Hotel, whose trademark Old West trappings were ripped out in favor of a glitzy yet bland modern decor. The lobby is now a sea of white marble and mirrors. The rooms are smoother and more tasteful (and for lovers of kitsch, less amusing). The upper floors, naturally, open onto the best views of mountains and lake. The place is so big that if you've had too much to drink, you may never find your way to the room with your number on it.

The 24-hour coffee shop often attracts hard-core gamblers in the wee hours. There's also a buffet room and a run-of-the-mill steak house (many guests head over to the Planet Hollywood across the way at Caesar's). Second-string performers, often from Los Angeles, perform in the cabaret room, which charges a one-drink minimum. Amenities include valet parking, 24-hour room service, a fitness center, an outdoor pool and hot tubs, a ski-rental shop, an arcade, and a wedding chapel.

Lakeland Village Beach & Ski Resort. 3535 Lake Tahoe Blvd., South Lake Tahoe, CA 96150. ☎ **800/822-5969** or 530/544-1685. www.lakeland-village.com. Fax 530/541-6278. 210 condo units. A/C (except in town house). TV TEL. $90–$175 double. AE, MC, V.

Clustered on 19 lightly forested acres of prime shoreline property is this half–residential apartment/half–holiday resort complex, built in the 1970s as one of South Lake Tahoe's most ambitious developments. The layout is a complicated labyrinth of buildings whose wood sides blend into the surrounding landscape. The only drawback is the proximity to traffic headed into Lake Tahoe, although some units, placed out among the grounds, are quieter than those in the main lodge, which lies adjacent to the road. When you check in, be prepared for a baffling choice of layouts; the staff will present an array of floor plans. The units, ranging from studios to four-bedroom lakeside apartments, are streamlined California architecture, and many have upstairs sleeping lofts.

There are no restaurants on the premises, though all rooms come with fully equipped kitchens, as well as fireplaces, cable TV with HBO, hair dryers, and daily maid service. Complimentary shuttle buses carry gamblers to the nearby casinos/ski resorts; a grocery store is within walking distance. Perks include two outdoor pools, three saunas, tennis and volleyball courts, a large private beach opening directly onto the lake, and access to a boat dock. It's a good choice for families.

NORTH SHORE/TAHOE CITY
Expensive

Chinquapin Resort. 3600 N. Lake Blvd., P.O. Box 1923, Tahoe City, CA 96145. ☎ **800/ 732-6721** or 530/583-6991. Fax 530/583-0937. 172 town houses/condos. TV TEL. $150– $270 1-bedroom unit; $135–$275 2-bedroom; $180–$460 3-bedroom; $165–$600 four-bed-room. DISC, MC, V.

Built in the 1970s on 95 acres of land on the north shore of Lake Tahoe, this complex lies 3 miles east of Tahoe City and offers easy access to the area's ski resorts, golf courses, restaurants, and shopping. It consists of a series of town houses and condos on forested lakefront land, including 1 mile of shoreline with two sandy beaches. One-to four-bedroom units range in size from 950 to 2,800 square feet. The development offers some 20 different floor plans, and redwood trim and fireplaces are featured in every accommodation, some of which have their own saunas. All are fully furnished, containing an equipped kitchen, fireplace, washer/dryer, and attractive decor. Some one-bedroom units are more expensive than the two-bedroom units because of their lakefront location. At all times, about a third of the units are available to rent; the rest are in use by their owners.

Amenities: Seven tennis courts, newly remodeled pool area, pier, saunas, sand vol-leyball court, and numerous jogging, walking, and hiking trails.

Hyatt Regency Lake Tahoe. Country Club at Lakeshore (P.O. Box 3239), Incline Village, NV 89450. ☎ **800/233-1234** or 775/832-1234. Fax 775/831-7508. 458 units, 24 cottages. A/C TV TEL. $145–$280 double; $395–$850 cottages. AE, DC, DISC, MC, V.

If you like to gamble but hate those gauche, racy casinos that line the California–Nevada border, you might want to consider this Hyatt in Incline Village. Far, far classier and quieter than the casino/hotels you'll find along Stateline, the Hyatt is a resort hotel first and casino second. Infinitely more inviting than the baccarat tables (okay, so we're not big gamblers) is the resort's exquisite private beach, loaded with water toys—catamaran cruises, jet skis, parasailing—available to guests.

While the hotel itself isn't exactly an architectural masterpiece inside or out, the adjoining Lakeside Cottages are a wee bit o' heaven for families—or honeymooners—who want beachfront access and large, comfortable rooms with unobstructed panoramas of the lake. A bonus for families is the popular Camp Hyatt, which lets kids ages 3 to 12 get a break from their parents for the day.

Dining/Diversions: The Hyatt's Lone Eagle Grill offers fine American cuisine and lakefront dining in a rustic "lodge" atmosphere with large wooden beams and an enor-mous 20-foot fireplace. There's also the intimate Ciao Mein Trattoria, which mixes Pacific Rim and Italian styles, and Sierra Café, which serves inexpensive burgers, soups, fajitas, buffets, and breakfasts. The small casino runs 24 hours a day and includes an arcade and cabaret entertainment.

Amenities: 24-hour room service, Camp Hyatt for kids, business services, valet, outdoor heated pool and spa, health club, tennis courts, 55-foot catamaran, ski-rental shop.

✪ **PlumpJack Squaw Valley Inn.** 1920 Squaw Valley Rd., off Calif. 89 (P.O. Box 2407), Squaw Valley, CA 96146. ☎ **800/323-7666** or 530/583-1576. 61 units. A/C TV TEL. Summer $130–$510; winter $180–$995. Rates include continental breakfast. AE, DC, DISC, MC, V. Free parking.

Part ski chalet, part boutique hotel, PlumpJack Squaw Valley Inn is easily Tahoe's most stylish and sophisticated hotel and restaurant. Granted, it lacks the fancy toys offered by its competitor across the valley, the Resort at Squaw Creek (see below), but the PlumpJack is unquestionably more suave, a tribute to the melding of artistry and hostelry. The entire hotel is draped in muted, earthy tones; swirling sconces and sculpted metal accents are brain-candy for the eyes, while the rest of our body parts are soothingly enveloped in thick hooded robes, terry-cloth slippers, and down comforters atop expensive mattresses. Each room has mountain views.

Dining: See "Where to Dine," below, for a complete review of the hotel's highly regarded restaurant.

Amenities: Room service via the restaurant from 7am to 10pm, ski rentals and storage, pool, two spas, in-room massage, concierge, retail sports shop.

✪ **The Resort at Squaw Creek.** 400 Squaw Creek Rd. (P.O. Box 3333), Olympic Valley, CA 96146. ☎ **800/327-3353** or 530/583-6300. Fax 530/581-6632. 405 units. A/C MINIBAR TV TEL. $250–$375 double; $375–$1,900 suite. AE, DC, DISC, MC, V. Valet parking $15; free self-parking.

The only deluxe resort on the California side of the lake, the $130-million Resort at Squaw Creek opened in 1990 amidst controversy about its impact on the environment. It's located in an inconspicuous corner of the valley at the base of Snow King Mountain, and you can't beat the resort's ski-in/ski-out access to Squaw Valley skiing. In fact, a chairlift lands just outside the door. Don't ski? Don't worry. There are lots of other sports facilities to keep active travelers happy.

The resort, 6 miles northwest of Tahoe City, encompasses two buildings connected by a shopping promenade, evocative of a luxurious Sierra lodge. One, featuring a harmonious design inspired by Frank Lloyd Wright, houses public areas, restaurants, and meeting areas. In jarring contrast, the other multistory building is made of black glass and steel; it contains the guest rooms, often filled with well-heeled skiers or business types on expense accounts. A waterfall cascades from the lobby to the pool area.

The accommodations are not particularly spacious, but they're well equipped with ample closets, good lighting, ironing boards, hair dryers, and speakerphones. (If only they had desks.) Suites, with spacious entertaining areas and additional TVs and phones, come in a baffling array of sizes, each with a name the staff expects everyone to understand instantly (executive suites, panorama suites, vista suites, junior suites).

Dining/Diversions: Glissandi, the resort's top restaurant, serves California-French cuisine in a window-wrapped dining room. Cascades is open for all-day, buffet-style casual dining. Ristorante Montagna, which serves California-Italian cuisine, has tables both indoors and out. Sweet Potatoes Deli is open early for coffee, light bites, and picnic-style lunches. Bullwhackers Pub is a combination steak house and sports bar with pool table, regular live entertainment, and happy-hour specials.

Amenities: Room service, concierge, overnight laundry, supervised children's activities, 18-hole golf course, three heated pools, three outdoor whirlpools, eight tennis courts, fitness center, shopping arcade, 18½ miles of groomed cross-country skiing trails (marked for hiking and biking in the summer), ice-skating rink (in winter only), equestrian center with riding stables.

✪ **The Shore House.** 7170 N. Lake Blvd., Tahoe Vista, CA 96148. ☎ **800/207-5160** or 530/546-7270. Fax 530/546-7130. 9 units. $150–$225 double. Rates include breakfast. DISC, MC, V.

If you're looking for a cozy, romantic bed-and-breakfast right on Lake Tahoe's shoreline, you'll be hard-pressed to find a better one than the Shore House. Hosts Marty and Barb are an immediately likable pair who have made pampering an art form, whether they're personally cooking your breakfast—Marty's a former chef—or planning a foolproof itinerary for your day.

Each individually decorated room has its own entrance, fabulous rough-hewn log furniture (handmade in Idaho), a minifridge, a gas-log fireplace, and a blissfully comfortable feather bed. All guests have access to a private and pristine patch of lakeside beach and landscaped lawn that overlook the entire lake, as well as a common hot tub. Boat owners can even make use of their six buoys and private dock. Planning on tying the knot? No problem: Marty's a minister of the Universal Life Church; Barb can provide the marriage license; they have a pretty area for small, romantic weddings, and even a Honeymoon cottage with a two-person spa tub (talk about a full-service B&B). If you're looking for a romantic weekend you won't soon forget, this place is worth every penny.

Moderate

Meeks Bay Resort. P.O. Box 787, Tahoma, CA 96142. ☎ 877/326-3357 or **530/525-6946.** Fax 530/525-4028. 21 units. $75–$215 double per night; $650–$3,300 per week. AE, MC, V. Closed early Oct through end of May.

Lying 10 miles south of Tahoe City on Calif. 89, Meeks Bay Resort is one of the oldest hostelries on the lake and something of a historical landmark. This wide, sweeping lakefront boasts the best fine-sand beach in Tahoe. Known centuries ago to the Washoe Indians, Meeks Bay was opened as a public campground in 1920. During the next 50 years, the resort grew to include cabins and other improvements, and attracted many celebrities from southern California. Acquired by the U.S. Forest Service in 1974 under a special-use year-round permit, the property is open during summer only. Most rentals are on a weekly basis and consist of cabins perched near the lake. Units vary in size, sleeping from 2 to 12, and are modest without being austere. Each has a full kitchen, and some have fireplaces. Facilities include a full marina with boat slips, campground with RV access, beachfront snack bar, and visitor center with a cultural display, coffee bar, and retail store.

On the grounds, the Kehlet House is the resort's first-rate accommodation. Owned at one time by William Hewlett, co-founder of the Hewlett-Packard Corporation, and later the summer residence of billionaire Gordon Getty, this pretty little house, on a rock that juts out into the lake, is one of the best places to stay in all of Tahoe. The House has seven bedrooms, three bathrooms, a large kitchen, living room, and water on three sides. The entire house is rented by the week, sleeps a dozen, and costs $3,300 for Wednesday-to-Wednesday bookings.

✪ **River Ranch Lodge & Restaurant.** On Calif. 89, at Alpine Meadows Rd. (P.O. Box 197), Tahoe City, CA 96145, Alpine Meadows. ☎ **800/535-9900** or 530/583-4264. www.riverranchlodge.com. 19 units. TV TEL. Winter $60–$140 double; spring and fall $50–$95 double; summer $60–$125 double. Rates include continental breakfast. AE, MC, V.

The River Ranch Lodge has long been one of our favorite places to stay in Lake Tahoe. Situated alongside the Truckee River, the lodge is mere minutes away from Alpine Meadows and Squaw Valley ski resorts, and a short drive (or ride along the bike path) into Tahoe City. The best rooms in this rustic lodge feature private balconies that overlook the river. All have a handsome mountain home decor. Room nos. 9 and 10, the farthest from the road, are our top choices.

In summer, guests relax under umbrellas on the huge patio overlooking the river, working down burgers and beer while watching the rafters float by. During the ski season, the River Ranch's spectacular circular cocktail lounge and dining area, which cantilevers over the river, is an immensely popular après-ski hangout. Also a big hit is the handsome River Ranch Lodge Restaurant, which serves fresh seafood, steaks, rack of lamb, and more exotic meats such as wood-oven-roasted Montana elk loin with a dried-cherry/port sauce.

Sunnyside Lodge. 1850 W. Lake Blvd., off Calif. 89 (P.O. Box 5969), Tahoe City, CA 96145. ☎ **800/822-2754** or 530/583-7200. 23 units. Apr 4–May 20 $100–$165 double; May 21–Oct 9 $170–$210 double; Dec 11–Apr 3 $120–$175 double. Rates include continental breakfast. AE, MC, V.

Built as a private home in 1908, this hotel and restaurant, one of the grand old lodges still left on the lake, stands 2 miles south of Tahoe City. With its typical northern California architecture, it looks very much like a giant wooden cabin, complete with dormers, steep pitched roofs, and natural-wood siding. Stretching across the building, a large deck fronts a tiny marina. The place is rustic but fairly sophisticated, with about two dozen individually decorated bedrooms with homey bark-covered timber tables and chairs as well as both contemporary and antique-style prints. The newly remodeled Lakefront rooms, the most desirable, go for about $15 more than the others, and are well worth the added expense. Only four have no views at all (unless you find parked cars attractive). Five units have rock fireplaces, while three have wet bars; 20 are no-smoking rooms. Most of the lodge's ground floor is dominated by the popular Sunnyside Restaurant (see "Where to Dine," below).

✪ Tahoma Meadows Bed & Breakfast. 6821 W. Lake Blvd., on Calif. 89, 8½ miles from Tahoe City (P.O. Box 810), Homewood, CA 96141. ☎ **800/355-1596** or 530/525-1553. 13 units. TV. $85–$145 double. Rates include breakfast. AE, DISC, MC, V.

Owners/innkeepers Bill and Missy Sanderman—two of the friendliest folks you'll ever meet—offer one of Tahoe's best B&B bargains: accommodations in cabins, most of which are private, perched on a gentle forest slope amongst a cadre of sugar pines and flowers. Missy, a talented watercolorist, has individually decorated each cabin in a decidedly warm and cozy style that is enhanced by her framed paintings of bucolic settings (many are bought by guests). All rooms have comfy king-, queen-, or twin-size beds; most have gas fireplaces. Favorites are the cheery Sunflower and Fox Glove cabins, both equipped with clawfoot tubs. The largest cabin, Columbine, sleeps six and is ideal for families.

A full breakfast is served at the main lodge upstairs, by the independently owned (and highly recommended) Stoneyridge Cafe. Nearby activities include skiing at Ski Homewood (including shuttle service), fly-fishing at the Sandermans' friend's private trout-stocked lake, and sunbathing at the lakeshore just across the street.

Inexpensive

Lake of the Sky Motor Inn. 955 N. Lake Blvd. (P.O. Box 227), Tahoe City, CA 96145. ☎ **530/583-3305.** 23 units. Apr 30–June 13 $50–$65 double; June 14–Sept 21 $75–$90 double; winter $50–$90 double; holidays $100–$105 double. AE, DC, DISC, MC, V.

Not much more than a 1960s-style A-frame motel in the heart of Tahoe City, the Lake of the Sky Motor Inn offers decent accommodations in a central location, only steps away from shops and restaurants. The place is popular with budget travelers and skiers, some of whom can be seen grabbing a very early morning cup of coffee and obviously itching to get out and tackle the wilderness. Rooms throughout have almost no style, but the housekeeping is good and the comfort level in tiptop motor-inn tradition. There's a heated pool as well as a barbecue area.

WHERE TO DINE
SOUTH SHORE/SOUTH LAKE TAHOE
Expensive

Fresh Ketch. 2433 Venice Dr. ☎ **530/541-5683.** Main courses $16–$22. AE, CB, DC, DISC, MC, V. Daily 11:30am–10pm (bar open until midnight). SEAFOOD.

Ensconced in a small marina at the foot of Tahoe Keys Boulevard, Fresh Ketch has long been regarded as South Lake's premier seafood restaurant. The most coveted tables at this attractive, modern spot are situated alongside a row of large windows overlooking an armada of expensive watercraft. For starters, we always order half a dozen oysters and the seared ahi tuna with ponzu and wasabi dipping sauces. Then it's on to the sautéed sea bass encrusted with pistachio, herbs, and garlic, or the big ol' Alaskan King Crab, steamed in the shell and served with the requisite drawn butter. There's also a modest selection of meat and poultry dishes, including a great surf-and-turf of petite mignon and lobster. For dessert, the calorie fest continues with a big slice of Kimo's Hula Pie. Prices are a bit steep due to the expense of getting fresh seafood this far up, but you can always join the locals at the bar and order off the extensive bar menu, which offers everything from blackened mahimahi to fresh-fish tacos and fish-and-chips, all for under $10. There's also live music Friday and Saturday evenings.

Moderate

Cantina Bar & Grill. 765 Emerald Bay Rd. ☎ **530/544-1233.** Main courses $7–$13. MC, V. Daily 11:30am–10:30pm (bar open until midnight). MEXICAN.

Sporting a new Southwestern look, the Cantina Bar & Grill (formerly Cantina Los Tres Hombres) serves the best Mexican food in South Lake. The bar and adjacent dining area are two of the busiest rooms in South Lake Tahoe. The menu is well priced and extensive, offering tried-and-true Cal-Mex specialties such as tacos, burritos, and enchiladas along with a half-dozen Southwestern dishes such as Texas crab cakes, smoked chicken polenta, and grilled pork chops with jalapeño mashed potatoes. The steak fajitas (with shrimp, sweet peppers, and onions) get a thumbs-up, as does the half chicken smothered in rich mole sauce, served with rice, black beans, and tortillas. A few vegetarian selections are offered as well. Service is brisk but not unfriendly, and some patrons may have had more than their share of tequila.

Scusa! 1142 Ski Run Blvd. ☎ **530/542-0100.** Main courses $9–$18. AE, DISC, MC, V. Daily 5–10pm. ITALIAN.

Located on the trail to the Heavenly Ski Resort, this cozy Italian spot may have a decor that errs a little garishly on the neon side, but the food more than compensates. Dishes are interspersed with enough surprises to keep the locals happy. The place is civilized, basic but clean, and the staff is usually cheerful and knowledgeable. Among the specialties are a savory baked penne with smoked mozzarella, prosciutto, roasted garlic, and focaccia crust.

The Swiss House. 787 Emerald Bay Rd. ☎ **530/542-1717.** Main courses $10–$17. AE, MC, V. Daily 11:30am–2pm and 5–9pm. SWISS/CONTINENTAL.

The ambiance of this South Lake Tahoe spot is genuine enough and warmly appreciated by diners, especially those arriving from the ski slopes in winter to find a fire blazing away. Despite its name, the place is not exactly into yodeling and cowbells, but the dishes are often alpine. The operation seems to run like Swiss clockwork, and, although we've had better Wiener schnitzel, the one served here is perfectly adequate. There's also cheese fondue and raclette to take you back to the old country; it's warmly flavored but so filling you might not be able to finish.

Inexpensive

✪ **Sprouts Natural Foods Cafe.** 3123 Harrison Ave. (at U.S. 50 and Alameda St., next to Lakeview Sports). ☎ **530/541-6969.** Meals $3.75–$6.50. No credit cards. Daily 8am–10pm. HEALTH FOOD/JUICES.

Sprouts owner Tyler Cannon has filled a much-needed niche in South Lake, serving wholesome food that looks good, tastes good, and *is* good. Most everything is made in-house, including the soups, smoothies, and fresh-squeezed juices. Menu items range from rice bowls to sandwiches (try the Real Tahoe Turkey), huge burritos, coffee drinks, muffins, fresh-fruit smoothies, and a marvelous mayo-free tuna sandwich made with yogurt and packed with fresh veggies. Order from the counter, then scramble for a vacant seat (outdoor tables are coveted), and listen for your name as Tyler's buff and beautiful servers bring out your tray of earthy delights. This is also an excellent place to pack a picnic lunch, whether skiing, hiking, or mountain biking.

Yellow Sub. 983 Tallac Ave. (at U.S. 50). ☎ **530/541-8808.** Sandwiches $3–$7. No credit cards. Daily 10:30am–10pm. SANDWICHES.

When it comes to picnic supplies, there's stiff competition in South Lake Tahoe: three sandwich shops on this single block alone. Still, our favorite is Yellow Sub, voted Best Deli Sandwich Shop by readers of the *Tahoe Daily Tribune.* It offers a whopping 21 versions of overstuffed subs—made in 6-inch and 12-inch varieties—as well as several kinds of wraps. The shop is hidden in a small shopping center across from the El Dorado Campground.

NORTH SHORE/TAHOE CITY
Expensive
✪ **PlumpJack Cafe.** In the PlumpJack Squaw Valley Inn, 1920 Squaw Valley Rd., Squaw Valley. ☎ **530/583-1576.** Reservations recommended. Main courses $17–$20. AE, MC, V. Daily 7–11am, 11:30am–2:30pm, and 5:30–10pm. COUNTRY MEDITERRANEAN.

Squaw Valley's investors have spent oodles of money trying to turn the ski resort into a world-class destination, and one major step in the right direction is the sleek and sexy PlumpJack Cafe. Although dinner prices have dropped slightly (guests balked at the original outrageous rates), none of PlumpJack's high standards have diminished. Expect impeccable service regardless of your attire (this is, after all, a ski resort), and heady menu choices ranging from risotto with shiitake mushrooms and fava beans to roasted rabbit atop a golden potato purée, plus a fabulous dish of braised oxtail paired with horseradish mashed potatoes and carrots. Those already familiar with PlumpJack in San Francisco know that the reasonably priced wine list is among the nation's best.

✪ **Sunsets on the Lake.** 7320 N. Lake Blvd. (on Calif. 28 at the west end of Tahoe Vista), Tahoe Vista. ☎ **530/546-3640.** Reservations recommended. Main courses $15–$23. AE, CB, DC, DISC, MC, V. Winter daily 5–10pm; June 25–Sept 7 daily 11:30am–midnight. NORTHERN ITALIAN/CALIFORNIA.

Here's something new: a lakeside restaurant in Tahoe where the food is as spectacular as the view. Chef Lew Orlady works wonders in the kitchen of this hugely popular restaurant built of gleaming pine. The rustic, romantic ambiance is helped along by a large fireplace, white-clothed tables, and—of course—a panoramic lake view. Recommended dishes include Orlady's fantastic braised lamb shank, a hefty hunk of tender lamb perfectly complemented by shiitake mushrooms, caramelized vegetables, and garlic mashed potatoes. If the duck is among the daily specials, order it: Each tender slice explodes with flavor. So does the portobello-mushroom entree, an enormous serving of house-baked focaccia stuffed with succulent wood-fried mushrooms, roasted chilies, goat cheese, glazed red onions, and sun-dried-tomato aioli. Pretty much everything on the large menu is a winner, which explains the large crowds that arrive via car or boat. When the snow melts, the heated outdoor deck and "Island Bar" are open for dining and drinks. Heck, they even provide blankets for an especially cozy sunset cocktail hour.

Wolfdale's. 640 N. Lake Blvd., Tahoe City. ☎ **530/583-5700.** Reservations recommended. Main courses $16–$21. MC, V. Wed–Mon 5:30–10pm (open daily July–Aug). CALIFORNIA/ JAPANESE.

Although it's long been one of Tahoe's top restaurants, situated in an idyllic lakeside setting, Wolfdale's is visually low-key. Behind a rather unassuming wood-shingle exterior is a simple, clean interior that combines country-style American furnishings with Japanese-style blond woods and screens. The innovative chefs know how to put a personal spin on regional ingredients, fusing flavors and textures of the East and the West. Although the menu changes frequently, a "cuisine unique" experience—as they're fond of calling it— might begin with tea-smoked duck with peanut noodles and mango chutney or sashimi with ginger and wasabi. The spinach salad tossed with smoked local trout, olives, and grated eggs is particularly memorable. Main courses are equally inventive, such as grilled game hen with Thai dipping sauce, or Alaskan halibut and sea scallops wrapped in Swiss chard with leek sauce.

Moderate

Sunnyside Restaurant. At the Sunnyside Lodge, 1850 W. Lake Blvd., Tahoe City. ☎ **530/ 583-7200.** Main courses $13–$19. AE, MC, V. Oct–June Sun–Thurs 4–9:30pm; Fri–Sat 4–10pm. July–Sept daily 11am–10:30pm; Sun brunch 9am–2pm. SEAFOOD/AMERICAN.

Located about 2 miles south of Tahoe City on Calif. 89, the Sunnyside Restaurant is worth a detour. In summer, when the sun is shining, there's no more highly coveted table in Tahoe than one on Sunnyside's lakeside veranda. Guests can also dine in the lodge's more traditional dining room with its 1930s aura.

Nothing out of the ordinary here: The lunch menu has fresh pastas, burgers, chicken, and fish sandwiches, together with a variety of soups and salads. Dinners are fancier, with such main courses as Australian lobster tail, lamb chops with roasted-garlic chutney butter, and fresh salmon oven-baked on a cedar plank. All dinners come with San Francisco–style sourdough bread, the chef's starch of the day, and a Caesar/Napa Valley salad or cup of creamy chowder.

Tahoe House Restaurant and Bäckerei. 625 W. Lake Blvd., Tahoe City. ☎ **530/583-1377.** Main courses $9–$19.50. AE, DISC, MC, V. Bakery daily 6am–10pm; deli 11am–4pm and 5–10pm. SWISS/CALIFORNIA.

Serving Tahoe's skiers, boaters, and sunbathers for nearly 2 decades, Tahoe House is one of the oldest Swiss restaurants on the lake, located at the Y in Tahoe City. Although not a trendsetter, it is known locally as a reliable venue for good food at reasonable prices. Chef/owner Barbara Vogt's menu features some Swiss-German dishes such as Wiener schnitzel, *Rahmschnitzel* (veal with creamy mushroom sauce), grilled bratwurst, and pork cordon bleu. Steaks and fresh seafood also satisfy, as do several house-made pastas and vegetarian choices. The full-service European-style bakery items and desserts are wonderful, as exemplified by home-baked tortes, truffles, and chocolates. Dishes are based on the seasonal availability of ingredients, and usually only the freshest and best are used. Vogt has added a selection of lighter choices, including vegetarian dishes straight from the family farm.

Inexpensive

Bridgetender Tavern and Grill. 30 W. Lake Blvd. (at Fanny Bridge), Tahoe City. ☎ **530/ 583-3342.** Burgers, salads, and ribs $5–$7. MC, V. Daily 11am–2am. PUB FARE.

Although it's located in one of the most popular tourist areas in North Lake, the Bridgetender is a locals' hangout through and through. Still, they're surprisingly tolerant of out-of-towners, who come for the cheap grub and huge selection of draft beers. The tavern is built around a trio of Ponderosa pines that meld in with the decor so well you hardly notice them. Big burly burgers, salads, pork ribs, and such round out the menu, and the daily beer specials—posted on the wall in Day-Glo colors—are definitely worth going over. In summer, dine outside among the pines.

✪ **Fire Sign Café.** 1785 W. Lake Blvd., Tahoe City. ☎ **530/583-0871.** Breakfast and lunch $4–$9. MC, V. Daily 7am–3pm. AMERICAN.

Choosing a place to have breakfast in North Tahoe is a no-brainer. Since the late 1970s, the Fire Sign Café has been the locals' choice—which explains the lines out the door on weekends. Just about everything is made from scratch, such as the delicious coffee cake that accompanies the big ol' plates of bacon and eggs or blackberry-buckwheat pancakes. Even the salmon for chef/owner Bob Young's legendary salmon omelet is smoked in-house. Lunch—burgers, salads, sandwiches, burritos, and more—is also quite popular, particularly when the outdoor patio is open.

Izzy's Burger Spa. 100 W. Lake Blvd. (at Fanny Bridge), Tahoe City. ☎ **530/583-4111.** Burgers $3.50–$6. No credit cards. Daily 11am–7pm. BURGERS.

It's just a simple, wooden A-frame building containing a small short-order grill, but Izzy's Burger Spa flips an unusually hefty and tasty burger and an equally enticing grilled chicken-breast sandwich. On a sunny day, the best seats are at the picnic tables set out front. The restaurant is directly across from the Tahoe Yogurt Factory.

Tahoe Yogurt Factory. 125 W. Lake Blvd., Tahoe City. ☎ **530/581-5253.** Coffee/espresso $1–$2.60; yogurt $1.50–$3.25; sandwiches $2–$4. No credit cards. Daily 6am–6pm (summer daily until 8pm). YOGURT/SANDWICHES.

This small coffee shack, located near Fanny Bridge in Tahoe City, is frequently written up as "the best little cafe in Tahoe"—perhaps an overstatement, but it *does* have its fans, who line up out the door for a quick caffeine fix before going off to work or ski. There's not much more to it than basic croissants, bagels, muffins, sandwiches, smoothies, and excellent java. A few small tables are available inside and outdoors in summer.

✪ **Za's.** 395 N. Lake Blvd. (across from the fire station), Tahoe City. ☎ **530/583-1812.** Main courses $6–$10. MC, V. Daily 4:30–9:30pm. ITALIAN.

The sign used to say PIZZA'S until half of it fell off, which is just as well because there's a whole lot more to Za's than just pizza. One of the most popular restaurants in North Tahoe, this little gem serves great Italian food at bargain prices. Example: A hefty plate of smoked chicken fettuccine in a garlic-cream sauce with roasted bell peppers, fresh artichoke hearts, and mushrooms is under $10. Start with Pudge's Plate—a pleasing platter of fresh-roasted veggies doused in a balsamic vinaigrette—and a bottle or two of Chianti, then pick from the wide range of superb pasta, calzones (the sausage calzone is particularly good), and pizza. Za's is a bit hard to find (look behind Pete-n-Peter's Saloon), but *mama mia,* is it worth the search.

TAHOE AFTER DARK

Tahoe is not particularly known for its nightlife, although there's always something going on in the showrooms of the major casino hotels located in Stateline, just east of South Lake Tahoe. Call **Harrah's** (☎ **775/588-6611**), **Harvey's** (☎ **775/588-2411**), **Caesar's** (☎ **775/588-3515**), and the Lake Tahoe **Horizon** (☎ **775/588-6211**) for current show schedules and prices. Most cocktail shows cost $12 to $40, and headliners are likely to include the likes of Jay Leno or Johnny Mathis.

There's usually live music nightly in **Bullwhackers Pub,** at the Resort at Squaw Creek (☎ **530/583-6300**), 5 miles west of Tahoe City. The **Pierce Street Annex,** 850 North Lake Blvd. (☎ **530/583-5800**), behind the Safeway in Tahoe City, has pool tables, shuffleboard, and DJ dancing every night. It's one of the livelier places around.

The college crowd will feel at home at **Elevation,** 877 North Lake Blvd., across from Safeway (☎ **530/583-4867**), which has the cheapest drinks in town and live rock music most nights. If it's just a casual cocktail you're after, our favorite spot is the handsome fireside lounge at **River Ranch Lodge,** which cantilevers over a turbulent stretch of the Truckee River, on Calif. 89 at the entrance to Alpine Meadows, about 10 miles northwest of Tahoe City (☎ **530/583-4264**).

9

The High Sierra: Yosemite, Mammoth Lakes & Sequoia/Kings Canyon

by Erika Lenkert

The national parks of California's Sierra are a mecca for travelers from around the globe. The big attraction is Yosemite, of course, but the entire region is packed with natural wonders and adventures.

It was in Yosemite that naturalist John Muir found "the most songful streams in the world . . . the noblest forests, the loftiest granite domes, the deepest ice sculptured canyons." Even today, few visitors would disagree with Muir's early impressions as they explore this land of towering cliffs, snowfields, alpine lakes, and river beaches. Yosemite Valley is riddled with dramatic waterfalls, sheer walls, and domes and peaks reaching toward the sky. The valley is the most central and accessible part of the park, stretching for some 7 miles from Wawona Tunnel in the west to Curry Village in the east. If you visit during spring or early fall, you'll encounter fewer problems with crowds.

Across the heart of the Sierra Nevada, in east-central California, sprawl Sequoia and Kings Canyon national parks, which are administered as one entity. Their peaks stretch across some 1,300 square miles, taking in the giant sequoias for which they're fabled. This is a land of alpine lakes, granite peaks, and deep canyons. At 14,495 feet, Mount Whitney is the highest point in the Lower 48.

Another big attraction in the area is Mammoth Lakes, one of the major playgrounds of California, where you can enjoy dozens of recreational activities in a setting of lakes, streams, waterfalls, and rugged meadows that bring the Austrian countryside to mind.

1 Yosemite's Gateways

Yosemite could not accommodate its 4.1 million annual guests even before a severe storm and flood struck Yosemite Valley in January 1997, eliminating 400 campsites and at least 250 guest rooms. (Reservations are usually booked up to a year in advance.) The good news: Towns on each gateway's periphery are virtually built around the tourism industry. They offer plenty of places to stay and eat (though the food up here is hardly a gourmet experience) and have natural wonders of their own. The bad news: If you stay here, reaching any point within the park requires at least a half-hour drive (usually closer to an hour), which is especially frustrating during high season, when motor homes and overall congestion cause traffic to move at a snail's pace.

The Flood of 1997

A severe storm in January 1997 flooded Yosemite Valley, stranding visitors and wreaking havoc on campsites, cabins, and trails. The raging Merced River eroded 1½ miles of riverbank, washed over 550 acres of meadow, moved building-size boulders, and chewed up huge portions of highway.

The storm ruined hundreds of campsites, flooded more than 350 motel and lodge units, and left 440 employees homeless. Throughout the park, the storm damaged 800 miles of trails, destroyed nine road bridges, and washed out 33 trail bridges. When the water receded, much of the valley floor was buried beneath a fine layer of silt more than a foot deep. Picnic tables, bear-proof storage boxes, garbage cans, and fire grates were found miles downstream.

Two years later, the trails and bridges have long been repaired and the valley shows few signs of nature's wrath. However, restoration of the park's lost amenities is far from complete. Construction began in 1998 and is scheduled to continue through 2001. Accommodations and campgrounds are still severely limited.

Should you need to reserve outside the park, choose based on which gate offers you easiest access. Our selections below are grouped by the three most popular entrances: The west entrances are Big Oak Flat (via Calif. 120), which is 88 miles east of Manteca and accommodates traffic from San Francisco, and Arch Rock (via Calif. 140), which is 75 miles northeast of Merced and is the easiest route from central California. The South Entrance is Wawona (via Calif. 41), which is 64 miles north of Fresno and the passage leading from southern California.

BIG OAK FLAT ENTRANCE

This is our favorite entrance to the park. It's 150 miles east of San Francisco and 130 miles southeast of Sacramento. Among the string of small communities along the way is charming **Groveland** (23 miles from the park's entrance), a throwback to gold-mining days, complete with rednecks, the oldest saloon in the state, and at least some semblance of a real town. It'll take around an hour to reach the park entrance from Groveland, but at least there's some extracurricular activity should you choose to hang around. Big Oak Flat has a few hotels as well, but no town. Call the visitor information number below for details.

GETTING THERE   If you're driving from San Francisco, take I-580 (which turns into I-205) to Manteca, then Calif. 120 east.

VISITOR INFORMATION   Contact the Hwy. 120 Chamber of Commerce (☎ 800/ 449-9120) for information on lodging.

WHERE TO STAY & DINE

Besides the places mentioned below, there are only a few other dining options—none of which are worth writing home about. Ask anyone in town, and they'll point you to the following offerings.

✪ **Evergreen Lodge.** 33160 Evergreen Rd. (at Calif. 120), Groveland, CA 95321. ☎ **800/ 935-6343** or 209/379-2606. Fax 209/379-2607. www.evergreenlodge.com. 22 units. TV. Apr–Oct $69 double; $79–$85 cabin (with one queen and two single beds); $89–$95 2 -bedroom cottage. DISC, MC, V. Closed in winter. From San Francisco, take I-580 E. (which turns into I-205) to Manteca; take Calif. 120 E. through Groveland; turn left at Hetch Hetchy/Evergreen Rd.

This has been a favorite rustic retreat for everyone from families to bikers for over 75 years. The 22 cabins, which look very cheap and motel-like from the inside, offer the basic necessities and are well dispersed along a wooded grove. But what's great about this place is its surroundings: It's only 8 miles from Yosemite's entrance and has a fun log-cabin lodge/bar where dinner is served and where dudes in 10-gallon hats shoot pool. (On warm nights, it's best to enjoy a pitcher of beer and some barbecue on the outdoor patio.) There are endless hiking trails and, in summer, access to Camp Mather's tennis courts, pool (major family action), and horseback riding. Though officially in Groveland, the lodge is 40 minutes east of downtown.

The Groveland Hotel. 18767 Main St., Groveland, CA 95321. ☎ **800/273-3314** or 209/962-4000. Fax 209/962-6674. 18 units, 4 with shower only. A/C TEL. $115–$135 double; $195 suite. Rates include extended continental breakfast. AE, DC, DISC, MC, V.

Constructed around 1850, this adorable historic hotel complements the surroundings of the Wild West–like town. Rooms are sweetly appointed with antiques as well as modern amenities like hair dryers and coffeemakers; the suite has a spa tub and fireplace. The staff is both friendly and accommodating. The most expensive and fanciest (a far cry from big-city fancy, mind you) restaurant in town is on the premises, and the supercool Iron Door Saloon (the other place to eat well) is across the street. Smoking is not permitted in this hotel.

ARCH ROCK ENTRANCE
GETTING THERE   Arch Rock is 75 miles northeast of Merced. If you're driving from central California, take I-5 to Calif. 99 to Merced, then Calif. 140 east.

WHERE TO STAY
Yosemite View Lodge. 11136 Calif. 140, P.O. Box D, El Portal, CA 95318. ☎ **800/ 321-5261** or 209/379-2681. Fax 209/379-2704. www.yosemite-motels.com. 308 units. TV TEL. Apr–Oct $99–$139 double; Nov–Mar $82–$104 double. 2-night minimum during holidays. MC, V.

Once you've come this far, you're practically at the gate, so it's literally shocking to drive onto this gargantuan pink compound amidst the otherwise awesome natural surroundings. But the crowds need to stay somewhere, and with the ongoing construction, this mega-motel is scheduled to offer around 500 rooms within the coming year. The attractively decorated units include fridges, microwaves, and HBO; some offer river views, balconies, and fireplaces. There's also a general store, two well-priced restaurants, two pools, three hot tubs, laundry facilities, and more public areas in the works. If this place is booked, they also represent three other properties in the vicinity, although they're not nearly as close to the entrance. Call the number above for information.

SOUTH ENTRANCE
The South Entrance is 332 miles north of Los Angeles, 190 miles east of San Francisco, 59 miles north of Fresno, and 33 miles south of Yosemite Valley. Fish Camp and Oakhurst are the closest towns to the South Entrance at Wawona.

Warning

If you plan on entering or exiting the park via Calif. 140 (the Merced route), be forewarned that due to damage from the 1997 storms, repairs began on that road in October 1998 and may continue until late 2000. Driving will be restricted to certain times of day, and you should expect delays. For complete details, listen to the National Park Service Road & Weather Recording at ☎ **209/372-0200.**

White-Water Rafting on the Tuolumne

One of the most depressing facts about Yosemite tourism is that few folks do more than get out of their car, take a brief walk around the valley floor, "ooh" and "ah," snap some photos, and go back to their hotel. But if you really want to experience the wonders of the outdoors, contact **Ahwahnee Whitewater,** P.O. Box 1161, Columbia, CA 95310 (☎ **800/359-9790** or 209/533-1401). Its rafting trips offer one of the best ways to truly interact with nature—especially if you're not the type to throw on a backpack and hoof it. The 1- to 3-day trips are ideal for white-water rebels in the spring (when the melting snow makes the ride most exciting) and for families later in the season. Although the trip doesn't go through the park, it's still an all-wilderness adventure—except they make the arrangements, provide and cook the food (gourmet by camping standards), steer the rafts, and practically hand you an experience you'll never forget. All you need to do is reserve well in advance, and if you're going on an overnight trip (highly recommended!), bring a tent, sleeping bag, and a few other camping accoutrements—and get ready for the time of your life.

GETTING THERE   If you're driving from Los Angeles, take I-5 to Calif. 99 north, then Calif. 41 north.

WHERE TO STAY & DINE

For more options, contact the **Yosemite Sierra Visitors Center,** 41729 Calif. 41, Oakhurst, CA 93644 (☎ **209/683-4636;** www.yosemite-sierra.org). Ask for the helpful brochure on the area, and be sure to check out its excellent online guide.

○ The Estate by the Elderberries. 48688 Victoria Lane (P.O. Box 577), Oakhurst, CA 93644. ☎ **559/683-6860** (Château du Sureau), or 559/683-6800 (Erna's Elderberry House restaurant). Fax 559/683-0800. 10 units. A/C TEL. $315–$515 double. Rates include full breakfast. Extra person $75. AE, MC, V.

Its kudos say it all: five diamonds, five stars, and hailed by *Zagat* as one of the top three small hotels in the United States. This is the ultimate in luxurious lodging, decadent dining, and exclusivity, and it's only a 20-minute drive from the South Entrance to Yosemite along Calif. 41. The château—"built to look old"—dates only from 1991 and is set back off the road on the crest of a hill. From the renowned restaurant, a pathway leads through fragrant gardens to the house, which resembles a French château, complete with turret and terra-cotta tile roof.

The interior is exquisitely furnished with fine antiques, rugs, and fabrics. Each individually decorated room has a wood-burning fireplace, wrought-iron balcony, and CD player with a selection of CDs; TVs are available on request. Beds are covered in the finest Italian linens and down comforters; some rooms have whirlpool tubs. This is where Hollywood's elite often head for their escapes. Celebrities escaping Los Angeles will be especially fond of the new $2,500-per-night Villa Sureau, a two-bedroom, two-bathroom luxury villa with a library, full kitchen, and 24-hour butler service.

The restaurant offers impeccable food, ambiance, and service. The six-course prix-fixe menu (from $64 to $68) changes daily. A smaller three-course menu is available for $45. Amenities include twice-daily maid service, 24-hour room service, coffee and refreshments in the lobby, an outdoor pool, and a sundeck.

The Narrow Gauge Inn. 48571 Calif. 41, Fish Camp, CA 93623. ☎ **559/683-7720.** Fax 559/683-2139. www.narrowgaugeinn.com. 25 units, all but 1 with shower only. TV TEL. Memorial Day–Labor Day: Nelder Ridge rooms $85–$95 double; Courtyard rooms $95 double; Creekside rooms $120; Clover Hill rooms $120–$130. Labor Day–Memorial Day:

Nelder Ridge $70–$80; Courtyard $85; Creekside $100; Clover Hill $80–$130. Extra person $10. Children under 6 stay free in parents' room. AE, DISC, MC, V.

If you want to stay in a place that celebrates the mountain atmosphere, book a room at this very friendly inn, just 4 miles south of the park entrance. All of the superclean motel-style units have a rustic cabin feel, complete with A-frame ceilings, little balconies or decks, antiques, quilts, lace curtains, and coffeemakers; some have wood-paneled walls. The higher the price of the room, the cuter it gets (rooms nos. 16 through 26 are the best and most secluded; they look directly into forest). On the property are a pool, hot tub, and hiking trails, as well as a wonderfully old-fashioned, lodge-style restaurant/buffalo bar serving "Old California Rancho Cuisine." One downside: Some of the mattresses are soft. *Note:* The inn closes in winter; the restaurant is closed on Tuesday and Wednesday, even during high-season.

Tenaya Lodge. 1122 Calif. 41, Fish Camp, CA 93623. ☎ **800/635-5807** or 559/683-6555. Fax 559/683-8684. 244 units. A/C MINIBAR TV TEL. Winter from $109 double Sun–Thurs; from $149 double Fri–Sat. Summer from $229 double. Add $20–$80 for suite. Buffet breakfast $13.50 per person. Children 17 and under stay free in parents' room. AE, DC, DISC, MC, V.

Tenaya Lodge is the best resort outside the southern entrance to Yosemite; it's particularly idyllic for families. The three- and four-story complex, which is run by the Marriott chain, is set on a 35-acre tract of forested land a few miles outside the national park. Inside, the decor is a cross between an Adirondack hunting lodge and a Southwestern pueblo, with a lobby dominated by a massive river-rock fireplace rising three stories. There's an indoor pool and three restaurants (which leave much to be desired). The ultra-modern rooms, however, definitely do the trick, with three phones; roomy, well-appointed bathrooms; and other amenities like in-room safes. Other extras include room service, a health club, on-site massage, a games room, and sleigh and hay rides (depending on the season). At press time, the property was undergoing a $4.2-million renovation, which can only improve the already fine digs.

2 Yosemite National Park

Yosemite is a place of record-setting statistics: the highest waterfall in North America and three of the world's 10 tallest (Upper Yosemite Fall, Ribbon Fall, and Sentinel Falls); the tallest and largest single granite monolith in the world (El Capitan); the most recognizable mountain (Half Dome); one of the world's largest trees (the Grizzly Giant in the Mariposa Grove); and literally thousands of rare plant and animal species. But trying to explain its majesty is impossible: This is a place you simply must experience firsthand. Even after extensive world travel, it's still one of the most awe-inspiring places we've ever been—every single time we visit.

What sets the valley apart is its incredible geology. The Sierra Nevada was formed between 10 and 80 million years ago, when a tremendous geological uplift pushed layers of granite lying under the ocean up into an impressive mountain range. Cracks and rifts in the rock gave erosion a start at carving canyons and valleys. Then, during the last ice age, at least three glaciers flowed through the valley, shearing vertical faces of stone and hauling away the rubble. The last glacier retreated 10,000 to 15,000 years ago, but left its legacy in the incredible number and size of the waterfalls pouring into the valley from hanging side canyons. From the 4,000-foot-high valley floor, the 8,000-foot tops of El Capitan, Half Dome, and Glacier Point look like the top of the world, but they're small in comparison to the highest mountains in the park, some of which reach over 13,000 feet. The 7-square-mile valley is really a huge bathtub drain for the combined runoff of hundreds of square miles of snow-covered peaks (which explains why the valley flooded during the great storm of 1997).

High-country creeks flush with snowmelt catapult over the abyss left by the glaciers and form an outrageous variety of falls, from tiny ribbons that never reach the ground to the torrents of Nevada and Vernal falls. Combined with the shadows and lighting of the deep valley, the effect of all this falling water is mesmerizing. All that vertical stone gets put to use by hundreds who flock to the park for some of the finest climbing anywhere.

The valley is also home to beautiful meadows and the Merced River. When the last glacier retreated, its debris dammed the Merced and formed a lake. Eventually, sediment from the river filled the lake and created the rich and level valley floor we see today. Tiny Mirror Lake was created later by rockfall that dammed up Tenaya Creek; the addition of a man-made dam in 1890 made it more of a lake than a pond. Rafters and inner-tubers enjoy the slow-moving Merced during the heat of summer.

Deer and coyote frequent the valley, often causing vehicular mayhem as one heavy-footed tourist slams on brakes to whip out the Handi-cam while another rubber-necker, also mesmerized, drives right into him. Metal crunches, tempers flare, and the deer daintily hops away.

Bears, too, are at home in the valley. Grizzlies are gone from the park now, but black bears are plentiful—and hungry for your "pic-a-nic" baskets. They don't actually come begging by daylight, but they make their presence known through late-night ransacking of ice chests, and have even been known to rip into cars that have even the smallest treats inside.

Right in the middle of the valley's thickest urban cluster is the **Valley Visitor Center** (☎ **209/372-0200**), with exhibits that will teach you about glacial geology, history, and the park's flora and fauna. Check out the **Indian Cultural Museum** next door for insight into what life in the park was once like. Excellent exhibits highlight the Miwok and Paiute cultures that thrived here. The Ansel Adams Gallery displays the famous photographer's prints as well as other artists' works. You'll also find much history and memorabilia from the career of nature writer John Muir, one of the founders of the conservation movement.

While it's easy to let the tremendous beauty of the valley monopolize your attention, remember that 95% of Yosemite is wilderness. Of the 4 million visitors who come to the park each year, very few ever venture more than a mile from their cars. That leaves most of Yosemite's 750,000 acres open for anyone adventurous enough to hike a few miles. Even though the valley is a hands-down winner for dramatic freak-of-nature displays, the high country offers a more subtle kind of beauty: glacial lakes, roaring rivers, and miles of granite spires and domes. In the park's southwest corner, the Mariposa Grove is a striking forest of rare sequoias, the world's largest trees, as well as several meadows and the rushing south fork of the Merced River.

Tenaya Lake and Tuolumne Meadows are two of the most popular high-country destinations, as well as starting points for many great trails to the backcountry. Since this area of the park is under snow from November through June, summer is really more like spring. From snowmelt to the first snowfall, the high country explodes with wildflowers and long-dormant wildlife trying to make the most of the short season.

JUST THE FACTS

ENTRY POINTS There are four main entrances to the park. Most valley visitors enter through the **Arch Rock Entrance** on Calif. 140. The best entrance for Wawona is the **South Entrance** on Calif. 41 from Oakhurst. If you're going to the high country, you'll save a lot of time by coming in through the **Big Oak Flat Entrance,** which puts you straight onto Tioga Road without forcing you to deal with the congested valley. The **Tioga Pass Entrance** is open only in summer and is only really relevant if you're

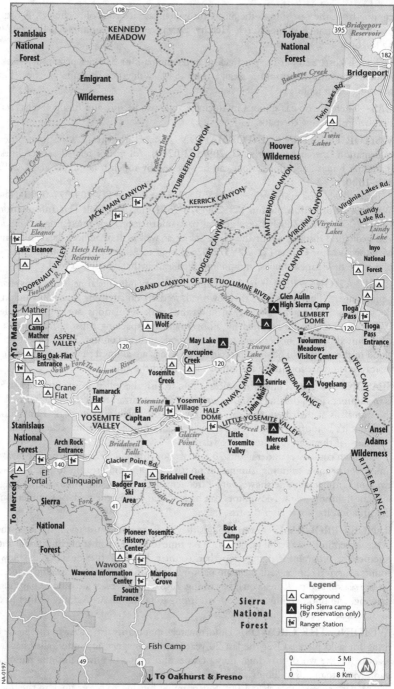

Yosemite National Park

Stanislaus National Forest

Toiyabe National Forest

Bridgeport Reservoir

KENNEDY MEADOW

Emigrant Wilderness

Buckeye Creek

Bridgeport

Cherry Creek

Twin Lakes Rd.

Twin Lakes

Hoover Wilderness

STUBBLEFIELD CANYON

Pacific Crest Trail

JACK MAIN CANYON

KERRICK CANYON

MATTERHORN CANYON

VIRGINIA CANYON

Virginia Lakes Rd.

Virginia Lakes

Lundy Lake Rd.

Lundy Lake

Lake Eleanor

RODGERS CANYON

COLD CANYON

Inyo National Forest

POOPENAUT VALLEY

Hetch Hetchy Reservoir

Tuolumne R.

GRAND CANYON OF THE TUOLUMNE RIVER

Tuolumne River

Glen Aulin High Sierra Camp

LEMBERT DOME

Tioga Pass

Tioga Pass Entrance

To Manteca

Mather

Camp Mather

ASPEN VALLEY

Big Oak-Flat Entrance

White Wolf

May Lake

Porcupine Creek

Tuolumne Meadows Visitor Center

LYELL CANYON

South Fork Tuolumne River

Crane Flat

Tamarack Flat

Yosemite Creek

Tenaya Lake

Sunrise

Vogelsang

CATHEDRAL RANGE

John Muir Trail

YOSEMITE VALLEY

Yosemite Falls

El Capitan

Yosemite Village

HALF DOME

TENAYA CANYON

LITTLE YOSEMITE VALLEY

Merced R.

Ansel Adams Wilderness

Stanislaus National Forest

Arch Rock Entrance

El Portal

Chinquapin

Bridalveil Falls

Glacier Point

Glacier Point Rd.

Bridalveil Creek

Little Yosemite Valley

Merced Lake

RITTER RANGE

To Merced

Sierra National Forest

Badger Pass Ski Area

S. Fork Merced R.

Bridalveil Creek

Buck Camp

Pioneer Yosemite History Center

Wawona

Wawona Information Center

Mariposa Grove

South Entrance

Sierra National Forest

Fish Camp

To Oakhurst & Fresno

Legend

⛺	Campground
▲	High Sierra camp (By reservation only)
🏠	Ranger Station

0   5 Mi
0   8 Km

NA-0197

275

coming from the east side of the Sierra (in which case it's your only choice). A fifth, little-used entrance is the **Hetch Hetchy Entrance** in the euphonious Poopenaut Valley, on a dead-end road.

FEES It costs $20 per car per week to enter the park or $10 per person per week. Annual Yosemite Passes are a steal at only $40. Wilderness permits are free, but reserving them requires a $3 fee per person.

GAS There are no gas stations in Yosemite Valley, so be sure and fill up at a gas station before entering the park.

VISITOR CENTERS & INFORMATION There's a central, 24-hour recorded information line for the park (☎ 209/372-0200). All visitor-related service lines, including hotels and information, can be accessed by touch-tone phone at ☎ 209/372-1000.

By far, the biggest visitor center is the **Valley Visitor Center** (☎ 209/372-0200). The **Wawona Information Station** (☎ 209/375-9501) and **Big Oak Flat Information Center** (☎ 209/372-0615) give general park information. For interesting biological and geological displays about the High Sierra, as well as trail advice, the **Tuolumne Meadows Visitor Center** (☎ 209/372-0263) is great. All can provide you with maps, plus more newspapers, books, and photocopied leaflets than you'll ever read.

REGULATIONS Rangers in the Yosemite Valley spend more time being cops than being rangers. They even have their own jail, so don't do anything here you wouldn't do in your hometown. Despite the pressure, park regulations are pretty simple. Wilderness permits are required for all overnight backpacking trips. Fishing licenses are required. Utilize proper food-storage methods in bear country. Don't collect firewood in the valley. No off-road bicycle riding. Dogs are allowed in the park but must be leashed and are forbidden from trails. Don't feed the animals.

SEASONS Winter is one of the nicest times to visit the valley. It isn't crowded, as it is in summer, and a dusting of snow provides a stark contrast to all that granite. To see the waterfalls at their best, come in spring when snowmelt is at its peak. Fall can be cool, but it's beautiful and much less crowded than summer. Sunshine seekers will love summer—if they can tolerate the crowds.

The high country is under about 20 feet of snow from November through May, so unless you're snow camping, summer is pretty much the only season to pitch a tent. Even in summer, thundershowers are a frequent occurrence, sometimes with a magnificent lightning show. Mosquitoes can be a plague during the peak of summer, but the situation improves after the first freeze.

RANGER PROGRAMS Even though they're overworked just trying to keep the peace, Yosemite's wonderful rangers also take time to lead a number of educational and interpretive programs ranging from backcountry hikes to fireside talks to snow-country survival clinics. Call the main park-information number with specific requests for the season and park area you'll be visiting. Also a great service are the free painting, drawing, and photography classes offered spring to fall at the Art Activity Center next to the Museum Gallery in the valley.

AVOIDING THE CROWDS Unfortunately, popularity isn't always the greatest thing for wild places. Over the last 20 years, tourist-magnet Yosemite Valley has set records for the worst crowding, noise, crime, and traffic in any California national park. More than 3.8 million visitors came in 1998.

The park covers more than 1,000 square miles, but most visitors flock to the floor of Yosemite Valley, a 1-mile-wide, 7-mile-long freak of glacial scouring that tore a deep and steep valley from the solid granite of the Sierra Nevada. It's still one of the most beautiful places on earth, but the Yosemite Valley becomes a total zoo between Memorial Day and Labor Day.

Cars line up bumper to bumper on almost any busy weekend. Until now, federal authorities did not show enough courage to implement one of several plans that would reduce traffic. But in 1995, Yosemite's new superintendent closed the entrances to the park 11 times between Memorial Day and mid-August when the number of visitors reached the park's quota; she turned away 10,000 vehicles.

In the meantime, our best advice is to try to come before Memorial Day or after Labor Day. If you must go in summer, try to do your part to help out. It's not so much the numbers of people that are ruining the valley, but their insistence on driving from attraction to attraction within the valley. Once you're here, park your car, then bike, hike, or ride the shuttle buses. Curry Village and Yosemite Lodge both offer **bicycle rentals** in summer (☎ **209/372-1240**). It may take longer to get from point A to point B, but you're in one of the most gorgeous places on earth—so why hurry?

SEEING THE HIGHLIGHTS
THE VALLEY

First-time visitors are often completely dumbstruck as they enter the valley from the west. The first two things you'll see are the delicate and beautiful **Bridalveil Fall** and the immense face of **El Capitan,** a stunning and anything-but-delicate 3,593-foot-tall solid-granite rock. A short trail leads to the base of Bridalveil, which at 620 feet tall is only a medium-size fall by park standards, but one of the prettiest.

This is a perfect chance to get those knee-jerk tourist impulses under control early: Resist the temptation to rush around bagging sights like they're feathers for your cap. Instead, take your time and look around. One of the best things about the valley is that many of its most famous features are visible from all over. Instead of rushing to the base of every waterfall or famous rock face and getting a crick in your neck from staring straight up, go to the visitor center and spend a half hour learning something about the features of the valley. Buy the excellent *Map and Guide to Yosemite Valley* for $2.50; it describes many hikes and short nature walks. Then go take a look. Walking and biking are the best ways to get around. To cover longer distances, the park shuttles run frequently around the east end of the valley.

If you absolutely must see it all and want to have someone tell you what you're seeing, the **Valley Floor Tour** is a 2-hour narrated bus or open-air tram tour (depending on the season) that provides an introduction to the valley's natural history, geology, and human culture for $17.50. Purchase tickets at valley hotels or call ☎ **209/372-1240** for advance reservations.

Three-quarters of a mile from the visitor center is the **Ahwahnee.** Unlike the rest of the hotel accommodations in the park (see "Accommodations in the Park," below), the Ahwahnee actually lives up to its surroundings. The native granite-and-timber lodge was built in 1927 and reflects an era when grand hotels were, well, grand. Fireplaces bigger than most Manhattan studio apartments warm the immense common rooms. Parlors and halls are filled with antique Native American rugs. Don't worry about what you're wearing unless you're going to dinner—this is Yosemite, after all.

The best single view in the valley is from **Sentinel Bridge** over the Merced River. At sunset, Half Dome's face functions as a projection screen for all the sinking sun's hues from yellow to pink to dark purple, and the river reflects it all. Ansel Adams took one of his most famous photographs from this very spot.

VALLEY WALKS & HIKES Yosemite Falls is within a short stroll of the visitor center. You can actually see it better elsewhere in the valley, but it's really impressive to stand at the base of all that falling water. The wind, noise, and blowing spray generated when millions of gallons catapult 2,425 feet through space onto the rocks below are sometimes so overwhelming you can barely stand on the bridge.

If you want more, the **Upper Yosemite Fall Trail** zigzags 3½ miles from Sunnyside Campground to the top of Upper Yosemite Fall. This trail gives you an inkling of the weird, vertically oriented world climbers enter when they head up Yosemite's sheer walls. As you climb this narrow switchback trail, the valley floor drops away until people below look like ants, but the top doesn't appear any closer. It's a little unnerving at first, but braving it promises indescribable rewards. Plan on spending all day on this 7-mile round-trip because of the incredibly steep climb.

A mile-long trail leads from the Valley Stables (shuttle-bus stop 17; no car parking) to **Mirror Lake.** The already tiny lake is gradually becoming a meadow as it fills with silt, but the reflections of the valley walls and sky on its surface remain one of the park's most introspective sights.

Also accessible from the Valley Stables or nearby Happy Isles is the best valley hike of all—the **John Muir Trail** to Vernal and Nevada falls. It follows the Sierra crest 200 miles south to Mount Whitney, but you only need go 1½ miles round-trip to get a great view of 317-foot Vernal Fall. Add another 1½ miles and 1,000 vertical feet for the climb to the top of Vernal Fall on the **Mist Trail,** where you'll get wet as you climb directly alongside the falls. On top of Vernal and before the base of Nevada Fall is a beautiful little valley and deep pool. For a truly outrageous view of the valley and one heck of a workout, continue on up the Mist Trail to the top of Nevada Fall. From 2,000 feet above Happy Isles where you began, it's a dizzying view straight down the face of the fall. To the east is an interesting profile perspective of Half Dome. Return either by the Mist Trail or the slightly easier John Muir Trail for a 7-mile round-trip hike.

Half Dome may look insurmountable to anyone but an expert rock climber, but thousands every year take the popular cable route up the backside. It's almost 17 miles round-trip and a 4,900-foot elevation gain from Happy Isle on the John Muir Trail. Many do it in a day, starting at first light and rushing home to beat nightfall. A more relaxed strategy is to camp in the backpacking campground in Little Yosemite Valley just past Nevada Fall. From here, the summit is within easy striking distance of the base of Half Dome. If you plan to spend the night, you need a Wilderness Pass (see "Camping," below). You must climb up a very steep granite face using steel cables installed by the park service. In summer, boards are installed as crossbeams, but they're still far apart. Wear shoes with lots of traction and bring your own leather gloves for the cables (your hands will thank you). The view from the top is an unbeatable vista of the high country, Tenaya Canyon, Glacier Point, and the awe-inspiring abyss of the valley below. When you shuffle up to the overhanging lip for a look down the face, be extremely careful not to kick rocks or anything else onto the climbers below, who are earning this view the hard way.

THE SOUTHWEST CORNER

This corner of the park is densely forested and gently sculpted in comparison to the stark granite that makes up so much of Yosemite. Coming from the valley, Calif. 41 passes through a long tunnel. Just prior to the entrance is **Tunnel View,** site of another famous Ansel Adams photograph, and the best scenic outlook of the valley accessible by car. Virtually the whole valley is laid out below: Half Dome and Yosemite Falls straight ahead in the distance, Bridalveil to the right, and El Capitan to the left.

A few miles past the tunnel, Glacier Point Road turns off to the east. Closed in winter, this winding road leads to a picnic area at **Glacier Point,** site of another fabulous view of the valley, this time 3,000 feet below. Schedule at least an hour to drive here from the valley and an hour or two to absorb the view. This is a good place to study the glacial scouring of the valley below; the Glacier Point perspective makes it easy to picture the valley filled with sheets of ice.

Some 30 miles south of the valley on Calif. 41 is the **Wawona Hotel** and the **Pioneer Yosemite History Center.** The Wawona was built in 1879 and is the oldest hotel in the park. Its Victorian architecture evokes a time when travelers spent several days in horse-drawn wagons to get here. The Pioneer Center is a collection of early homesteading log buildings across the river from the Wawona.

One of the primary reasons Yosemite was first set aside as a park was the **Mariposa Grove** of giant sequoias. (Many good trails lead through the grove.) These huge trees have personalities that match their gargantuan size. Single limbs on the biggest tree in the grove, the Grizzly Giant, are 10 feet thick. The tree itself is 209 feet tall, 32 feet in diameter, and more than 2,700 years old. Totally out of proportion with the size of the trees are the tiny cones of the sequoia. Smaller than a baseball and tightly closed, the cones won't release their cargo of seeds until opened by fire.

THE HIGH COUNTRY

The high country of Yosemite has the most grandiose landscape in the entire Sierra Nevada. Dome after dome of beautifully crystalline granite reflects the sunlight above deep-green meadows and icy-cold rivers.

Tioga Pass is the gateway to the high country. At times, it clings to the side of steep rock faces; in other places, it weaves through canyon bottoms. Several good campgrounds make it a pleasing overnight alternative to fighting summertime crowds in the valley, although use is increasing here, too. Unlike the valley, a car is vital to getting around here, as the only public transportation is the once-a-day Tuolumne Shuttle. This bus travels to and from Tenaya Lake and Tioga Pass, leaving the valley at 8am and letting you off anywhere along the way. The driver waits 2 hours at Tuolumne Meadows, which isn't much time to see anything, then heads back down to the valley, returning around 4pm. The one-way fare is $13, slightly less to intermediate destinations.

Tenaya Lake is a popular windsurfing, fishing, canoeing, sailing, and swimming spot. The water is very chilly. Many good hikes lead into the high country from here, and the granite domes surrounding the lake are popular with climbers. Fishing here varies greatly from year to year.

Near the top of Tioga Pass is stunning **Tuolumne Meadows.** This enormous meadow covering several square miles is bordered by the Tuolumne River on one side and spectacular granite peaks on the other. The meadow is cut by many stream channels full of trout, and herds of mule deer are almost always present. The **Tuolumne Meadows Lodge** and store are a welcome counterpoint to the overdeveloped valley. In winter, the canvas roofs are removed and the buildings fill with snow. You can buy last-minute backpacking supplies here, and there's a basic burgers-and-fries cafe.

TUOLUMNE MEADOWS HIKES & WALKS   So many hikes lead from here into the backcountry that it's impossible to do them justice. A good trail passes an icy-cold spring and traverses several meadows.

On the far bank of the Tuolumne from the meadow, a trail leads downriver, eventually passing through the grand canyon of the Tuolumne and exiting at Hetch Hetchy. Shorter hikes will take you downriver past rapids and cascades.

An interesting geological quirk is the **Soda Spring** on the far side of Tuolumne Meadow from the road. This bubbling spring gushes carbonated water from a hole in the ground; a small log cabin marks its site.

For a great selection of Yosemite high-country hikes and backpacking trips, consult some of the specialized guidebooks to the area. Two of the best are published by Wilderness Press: *Tuolumne Meadows,* a hiking guide by Jeffrey B. Shaffer and Thomas Winnett; and *Yosemite National Park,* by Thomas Winnett and Jason Winnett.

SPORTS & OUTDOOR PURSUITS

BICYCLING   With 10 miles of bike paths in addition to the valley roads, biking is the perfect way to go. You can rent one-speeds at the **Yosemite Lodge or Curry Village** (☎ **209/372-1240**) for $5.25 per hour or $20 per day. Six-speed bikes with trailers for kids are also available. If you want a fancier bike, you'll have to bring it from home. All trails in the park are closed to mountain bikes.

FISHING   The Merced River in the valley is catch-and-release only, and barbless hooks are required. High-country lakes and streams are literally leaping with trout. A California license is required and available in the park at the Yosemite Village Sport Shop.

HORSEBACK RIDING   Three stables offer scenic day rides and multi-day pack excursions in the park. **Yosemite Valley Stables** (☎ **209/372-8348**) is open spring through fall. The other two—**Wawona** (☎ **209/375-6502**) and **Tuolumne Stables** (☎ **209/372-8427**)—operate only in summer. Day rides run from $35 to $70, depending on length. Multi-day backcountry trips cost roughly $100 per day and must be booked almost a year in advance. The park wranglers can also be hired to make resupply drops at any of the backcountry High Sierra Camps if you want to arrange for a food drop while on an extended trip.

ICE-SKATING   In winter, the **Curry Village Ice Rink** (☎ **209/372-8341**) is a lot of fun. It's outdoors and melts quickly when the weather warms up. Rates are $5 for adults and $4.50 for children. Skate rentals are available for $2.

ROCK CLIMBING   Much of the most important technical advancement in rock climbing came out of the highly competitive Yosemite Valley climbing scene of the 1970s and 1980s. Though other places have taken some of the limelight, Yosemite is still one of the most desirable climbing destinations in the world.

The **Yosemite Mountaineering School** (☎ **209/372-8444** in the valley, or 209/372-8435 at Tuolumne Meadows) runs classes for beginners through advanced climbers. Considered one of the best climbing schools in the world, it offers a basic lesson for $100 per person per day that will teach you basic body moves and rappelling, and will take you on a single-pitch climb. Classes run from early spring to early October in the valley; during summer in Tuolumne Meadows.

SKIING & SNOWSHOEING   Yes, there is an alpine ski area in Yosemite, but it isn't much of one. Opened in 1935, **Badger Pass** (☎ **209/372-8430**) is the oldest operating ski area in California. Four chairs and one rope tow cover a compact mountain of beginner and intermediate runs. At $28 per weekend day for adults and $13 for children (about 20% cheaper midweek), it's a great place to learn how to ski or snowboard. If you're a good skier or boarder already, don't bother.

Yosemite is a better destination for cross-country skiers and snowshoers. Both the Badger Pass ski school and the mountaineering school run trips and lessons for all abilities, ranging from basic technique to trans-Sierra crossings. If you're on your own, Crane Flat is a good place to go, as is the groomed track up to Glacier Point, a 20-mile round-trip.

CAMPING

Campgrounds in Yosemite can be reserved up to 3 months in advance through the **National Park Reservation Service** (☎ **800/436-7275;** www.reservations.nps.gov). During the busy season, all valley campsites sell out within hours of becoming available on the service.

Backpacking into the wilderness and camping is always the least crowded option and takes less planning than reserving a campground. If you plan to backpack and camp in the wilderness, you must get a free **Wilderness Pass** (and still pay the park entrance fee). Half are allocated up to 24 hours in advance; the other half are available through mail. Write to the Wilderness Center, P.O. Box 545, Yosemite, CA 95389, and specify the dates and trailheads of entry and exit, principal destination, number of people, and any accompanying animals; include a $3 advance-registration fee. You may also secure a pass by calling ☎ 209/372-0740.

VALLEY CAMPGROUNDS

Until January 1997, the park had five car campgrounds that were always full except in the dead of winter. Now the park has half the number of campsites available, and getting a reservation on short notice takes a minor miracle. (Yosemite Valley lost almost half of its 900 camping spaces in a freak winter storm that washed several campsites downstream and buried hundreds more beneath a foot of silt.)

The 2½ campgrounds that remain—**North Pines, Upper Pines,** and half of **Lower Pines**—charge $15 per night. All have drinking water, flush toilets, pay phones, fire pits, and a heavy ranger presence. Showers are available for a small fee at Curry Village. Upper Pines, North Pines, and Lower Pines allow small RVs (less than 40 feet long). If you're expecting a real nature experience, skip camping in the valley unless you like doing so with 4,000 strangers.

Sunnyside Campground is the only walk-in campground in the valley and fills up with climbers since it's only $3 per night. Hard-core climbers used to live here for months at a time, but the park service has cracked down on that. It still has a much more bohemian atmosphere than any of the other campgrounds.

CAMPGROUNDS ELSEWHERE IN THE PARK

Outside the valley, things start looking up for campers. Two campgrounds near the south entrance of the park, **Wawona** and **Bridalveil Creek,** offer a total of 210 sites with all the amenities. Wawona is open year-round, and reservations are required May through October; otherwise, it's first-come, first-served (call the National Park Reservation Service at ☎ 800/436-7275). Because it sits well above snow line at more than 7,000 feet, Bridalveil is open in summer only. Both cost $10 per night.

Crane Flat, Hodgdon Meadow, and Tamarack Flat are all in the western corner of the park near the Big Oak Flat Entrance.

Crane Flat is the nearest to the valley, about a half-hour drive, with 166 sites, water, flush toilets, and fire pits. Its rates are $15 per night, and it's open from June through October. **Hodgdon Meadow** is directly adjacent to the Big Oak Flat Entrance at 4,800 feet elevation. It's open year-round, charges $15 per night, and requires reservations May through October through NPRS (☎ 800/436-7275). Facilities include flush toilets, running water, a ranger station, and pay phones. It's one of the least crowded low-elevation car campgrounds, but there's not a lot to do here. **Tamarack Flat** is a waterless, 52-site campground with pit toilets; open June through October. It's a bargain at $6 per night.

Tuolumne Meadows, White Wolf, Yosemite Creek, and Porcupine Flat are all above 8,000 feet and open in summer only. ✪**Tuolumne Meadows** is the largest campground in the park, with more than 300 spaces, but it absorbs the crowd well and has all the amenities, including campfire programs and slide shows in the outdoor amphitheater. You will, however, feel sardine-packed between hundreds of other visitors. Half of the sites are reserved in advance; the rest are set aside on a first-come, first-served basis. Rates are $15 per night.

White Wolf, west of Tuolumne Meadows, is the other full-service campground in the high country, with 87 sites available for $10 per night. It offers a drier climate than the meadow and doesn't fill up as quickly.

Tips for Securing Accommodations

All hotel reservations can be made exactly 366 days in advance. Call ☎ **209/ 252-4848** in the morning 366 days before your intended arrival for the best chance of securing your reservation. If you don't plan far in advance, it's good to call anyway—cancellations may leave new openings. Winter reservations may also be booked through the Yosemite Concession Services at **www.yosemitepark.com**. Keep in mind that reservations held without deposit must be confirmed on the scheduled day of arrival by 4pm. Otherwise, you'll lose your reservation.

Two primitive camps, **Porcupine Flat** and **Yosemite Creek,** are the last to fill up in the park. Both have pit toilets but no running water, and charge $6 per night.

ACCOMMODATIONS IN THE PARK

Yosemite Concessions Services, 5410 E. Home Ave., Fresno, CA 93727 (☎ **559/ 252-4848**), operates all accommodations within the park and accepts all major credit cards. The reservations office is open Monday through Friday from 8am to 5pm. For more lodging options and information or to make an online reservation request, visit their Web page at **www.yosemiteparks.com**.

An intriguing option bridging the gap between backpacking and staying in a hotel is Yosemite's five backcountry **High Sierra Camps** (☎ **559/253-5674**). The five camps—Glen Aulin, May Lake, Sunrise, Merced Lake, and Vogelsang—make for good individual destinations. Or you can link several together, since they're arranged in a loose loop about a 10-mile hike from one another. Guests bunk dormitory style in canvas tents; each camp has bathrooms and showers. Unguided stays cost $94 per night, per person; guided trips start at $375 for 4 nights. Rates include breakfast and dinner. Due to the enormous popularity of these camps, reservations are booked by lottery. Applications are accepted from October 15 to November 30. The lottery is then held in December and the winning applicants are notified by the end of March. For more information, call the above number or write Yosemite Concession Services (see above for address).

✪ The Ahwahnee Hotel. ☎ **559/252-4848.** 123 units. A/C TV TEL. $226–$287 double, from $345 suite.

A National Historic Landmark noted for its striking architecture, the grand Ahwahnee is one of the most romantic and beautiful hotels in California. With its great lounge, grand gourmet dining room, outstanding views, and high-digit prices, it's a special-occasion sort of affair. Try to reserve one of the more spacious cottages, which cost the same as rooms in the main hotel. Tennis courts, a pool, and a full-time concierge add to the experience.

Curry Village. ☎ **559/252-4848.** 668 units. $46–$101 double.

Accommodations at Curry Village, which celebrated its 100th birthday in 1999, range from a few motel-type rooms or heated wood cabins with private bathrooms to canvas tent cabins with central baths. Ironically, the older wood cabins are the nicest. The tent cabins have wood floors and canvas walls; without a real wall to stop noise, they lack any sort of privacy, but they're fun in that summer-camp sort of way. You'll have to sustain yourself with fast food from the village concessions, as no cooking is allowed in the rooms.

Wawona Hotel. ☎ **559/252-4848.** 104 units. $84–$94 double without bathroom, $115–$120 double with bathroom.

If the Ahwahnee doesn't fit your plans or your pocketbook, the Wawona is the next best thing. Also a National Historic Landmark, the Wawona is a romantic throwback to another century. However, old-world charm has its ups and downs. Private bathrooms were not a big hit in the 19th century, rooms were small to hold in heat, there were no TVs or telephones, and walls were thin—and all of the above still applies today. Still, the Wawona is charming and less commercial than other accommodations on the valley floor. On-site amenities include a restaurant, lounge, pool, stables, and golf course.

Yosemite Lodge. ☎ **559/252-4848.** 250 units. TEL. $82–$115 double.

The next step down in valley accommodations, Yosemite Lodge is not actually a lodge but a large, more modern complex with two types of accommodations. The larger "Lodge" rooms with outdoor balconies have striking views of Yosemite falls. Indeed the largest bonus—and curse—is that every room's front yard is the valley floor, which means you're near glorious larger-than-life natural attractions and equally gargantuan crowds. Unfortunately, the lodge has had only 250 of its 495 rooms in use since the 1997 flood; they have no plans to replace the rooms, but say there are potential plans to add new hotel rooms within a few years. In addition to a pool and bar, the lodge has two restaurants and a cafeteria that serve mediocre meals.

3 Mammoth Lakes

40 miles E of Yosemite, 319 miles E of San Francisco, 325 miles NE of Los Angeles

High in the Sierra, just southeast of Yosemite, Mammoth Lakes is surrounded by glacier-carved, pine-covered peaks that soar up from flower-filled meadows. It's an alpine region of sweeping beauty and one of California's favorite playgrounds for hiking, biking, horseback riding, skiing, and more. It's also home to one of the top-rated ski resorts in the world, which makes it a great place to frolic any time of year.

ESSENTIALS

GETTING THERE   It's a 6-hour drive from San Francisco via Calif. 120 over the Tioga Pass in Yosemite (closed in winter); 5 hours north of Los Angeles via Calif. 14 and U.S. 395; and 3 hours south of Reno, Nevada, via U.S. 395. In winter, Mammoth is accessible via U.S. 395 from the north or the south.

Mammoth Air Charter (☎ **760/934-4279**) and **Ralston Aviation** (☎ **760/934-1633**) offer charter flights to the area. Both service Mammoth Lakes Airport on U.S. 395. The closest international airport is Reno-Tahoe Airport (☎ **775/328-6870**).

VISITOR INFORMATION   Contact the **Mammoth Lakes Visitors Bureau,** Calif. 203 (P.O. Box 48), Mammoth Lakes, CA 93546 (☎ **800/367-6572** or 760/ 934-2712; www.visitmammoth.com).

ENJOYING THE OUTDOORS

Mammoth Lakes is at the heart of several wilderness areas and is cut through by the San Joaquin and Owens rivers. Mammoth Mountain overlooks the Ansel Adams Wilderness Area to the west and the John Muir Wilderness Area to the southeast, and beyond to the Inyo National Forest and the Sierra National Forest.

The **Mammoth Mountain Ski Area** (☎ **888/462-6668** or 760/934-2571) is the central focus for both summer and winter activities. Visitors can ride the lifts to see panoramic vistas; those who want an active adventure have a world of options.

DOWNHILL SKIING, CROSS-COUNTRY SKIING & SNOWBOARDING In winter, Mammoth Mountain has more than 3,500 skiable acres, a 3,100-foot vertical drop, 150 trails (32 with snowmaking), and 30 lifts, including seven high-speed

Get on Board

If you're like me, when you first saw those junior skate-rats dressed in baggy garb barreling down the slopes on snowboards, you stuck your nose up in disdain and murmured "punks." And if you, like me, in all fairness attempted the sport, only to find yourself lying in a pile of your own limbs while some young brat yelled from the chairlift, "Give it up, Grandma; you could *walk* down the hill faster!" you probably loved your skis all the more. But that was then. Today, snowboarding has become such the rage that it's not just those pesky renegades who are into it. In fact, there are plenty of polite, mature boarders who swear by the sport, as well as the many beginners on the mountain who offer moral support as you flounder your way toward boarding bliss.

After my first (treacherous) boarding encounter, it took a while to get the nerve up to try it again. But my second time out, I didn't just charge the mountain with my boarder friends, praying that determination and masochism would pay off. No, this time I swallowed my pride—and signed up for Mammoth's group lesson.

Packed in padding (including the ultimate fashion embarrassment, the fanny-protecting "duck butt"), I met my group at the wimpiest bunny slope, which was so flat, a rope pull wasn't even necessary. Our instructor, cool-guy Rich, was wonderfully encouraging as we hobbled up the joke of a hill (with our boards strapped tightly to one foot) and then attempted to imitate his elementary moves during our descent. This went on all morning—dragging ourselves up the hill and intentionally falling back down. Though progression was slow, it was worlds better than my prior experience, when I never traveled more than 2 feet without eating it.

After lunch break (and a few loosen-me-up beers), we headed to the "Sesame Street" chairlift for our first true bunny-slope bonanza. I was ready and determined: I fantasized of getting a shredding from a group of chairlift hecklers and laughing with 30-something delight. And believe it or not, I not only made it off the chairlift, but also found myself zigzagging down the run, euphoric and triumphant. By the time I reached the bottom, I already knew that I'd abandoned my skis forever.

Take it from an avid skier: Snowboarding is less clumsy, easy to learn, and an absolute must-try. But if you want to do it relatively painlessly, keep in mind the following: Take a lesson, don't start out on an ice-packed day (your butt will thank you), and leave your fear behind. Soon enough, you, too, will be shredding past the crowds yelling, "Look out kiddies, here comes Grandma!" (Grandpas are equally encouraged.)

quads. The terrain is 30% beginner, 40% intermediate, and 30% advanced. It's known for power sun, ideal spring skiing conditions, and anywhere from 8 to 12 feet of snow.

Cross-country ski centers are at **Tamarack Lodge** (☎ 760/934-2442) and **Sierra Meadows Ski Touring Center** (☎ 760/934-6161). There's also snowmobiling, dog sledding, snowshoeing, and sleigh rides.

If you're renting equipment, you'll save money if you do it in town instead of at the resort. Try **Sandy's Ski & Sports** (☎ 760/934-7518), on Calif. 203 next to Schat's Bakery, for all types of winter equipment, and **Wave Rave Snowboard Shop,** on Main Street (Calif. 203; ☎ 760/934-2471), for snowboards and accessories.

Mammoth Lakes Region

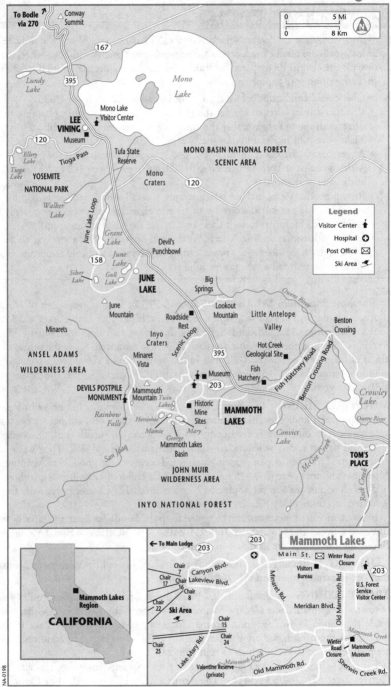

To Bodie via 270
Conway Summit

167

Mono Lake

Lundy Lake

395

Mono Lake Visitor Center

LEE VINING
Museum

120

Ellery Lake

Tioga Pass

Tioga Lake

Tufa State Reserve

MONO BASIN NATIONAL FOREST SCENIC AREA

Mono Craters

120

YOSEMITE NATIONAL PARK

Walker Lake

June Lake Loop

Grant Lake

Devil's Punchbowl

158

June Lake

Silver Lake

Gull Lake

JUNE LAKE

Big Springs

Legend

Visitor Center	
Hospital	
Post Office	
Ski Area	

June Mountain

Minarets

Roadside Rest

Lookout Mountain

Little Antelope Valley

Owen River

Benton Crossing

Inyo Craters

Scenic Loop

395

Hot Creek Geological Site

Fish Hatchery Road

Benton Crossing Road

ANSEL ADAMS WILDERNESS AREA

Minaret Vista

Museum

203

Fish Hatchery

Crowley Lake

DEVILS POSTPILE MONUMENT

Mammoth Mountain

Twin Lakes

Historic Mine Sites

MAMMOTH LAKES

Owen River

Rainbow Falls

Horseshoe

Mamie

Mary

George

Mammoth Lakes Basin

Convict Lake

McGee Creek

TOM'S PLACE

San Joaq

JOHN MUIR WILDERNESS AREA

Rock Creek

INYO NATIONAL FOREST

CALIFORNIA

Mammoth Lakes Region

Mammoth Lakes

← To Main Lodge

203

203

Main St.   Winter Road Closure

Chair 7

Canyon Blvd.

Chair 17

Chair 16

Lakeview Blvd.

Chair 8

Chair 22

Ski Area

Chair 15

Chair 24

Chair 25

Lake Mary Rd.

Valentine Reserve (private)

Minaret Rd.

Visitors Bureau

203

U.S. Forest Service Visitor Center

Meridian Blvd.

Old Mammoth Rd.

Mammoth Creek

Winter Road Closure

Mammoth Museum

Old Mammoth Rd.

Sherwin Creek Rd.

Winter Driving in the Sierra

Winter driving in the Sierra Nevada Range can be dangerous. While the most hazardous roads are often closed, others are negotiable by vehicles with four-wheel drive or with tire chains. Be prepared for sudden blizzards, and protect yourself by taking these important pre-trip precautions:

- Check road conditions before setting out by calling ☎ **800/427-7623.**
- If you're driving a rental car, let the rental company know you're planning to drive in snow, and ask whether the antifreeze is prepared for cold climates.
- Make sure your heater and defroster work.
- Always carry chains. If there's a blizzard, the police will not allow vehicles without chains on certain highways. You'll have to pay about $40 to "chain up" at the side of the road.
- Recommended items include an ice scraper, a small shovel, sand or burlap for traction if you get stuck, warm blankets, and an extra car key (it's surprisingly common for motorists to lock their keys in the car while chaining up).
- Don't think winter ends in March. At the end of April 1998, snow was up to 7 feet high on the sides of the roads leading to the valley, and cold temperatures made more snowfall a very real possibility.

The **June Mountain Ski Area** (☎ 760/648-7733), 20 minutes north of Mammoth, is smaller and offers many summer activities. It has 500 skiable acres, a 2,590-foot vertical drop, 35 trails, and eight lifts, including two high-speed quads. The terrain is 35% beginner, 45% intermediate, and 20% advanced. It's at the center of a chain of lakes—Grant, Silver, Gull, and June—which can be viewed on a scenic driving loop around Calif. 158. It's especially beautiful in the fall when the aspens are ablaze with gold.

MOUNTAIN BIKING   In summer, the mountain becomes one huge bike park and climbing playground. The **Bike Center** at the base of the mountain has rentals and accessories. The bike park is famous for its **Kamikaze Downhill Trail,** an obstacle arena and slalom course where riders can test their balance and skill. There's also an area designed for kids. A pass granting unlimited access to the gondola at Mammoth Mountain and trail systems is $25 for adults, $13 for children 12 and under; with limited uphill access, it's $20 for adults, $12 for children. The park operates daily from 9am to 6pm, from about June 26 to September 26.

In town, mountain bikes can also be rented from the **Footloose Sports Center,** at the corner of Canyon and Minaret (☎ 760/934-2400). The **NORBA National Mountain Bike Championships** are held here in summer.

CLIMBING   Climbing and orienteering courses are offered by **Mammoth Mountain Adventure Connection** (☎ 760/934-0606).

TROUT FISHING   Mammoth Lakes Basin sits in a canyon a couple of miles west of town. Here are the lakes—Mary, Mamie, Horseshoe, George, and Twin—that have made the region known for trout fishing. Southeast of town, Crowley Lake is also famous for trout fishing, as are the San Joaquin and Owens rivers. In addition, there are plenty of other lakes in which to spin your reel.

For fishing information and guides, contact **Rick's Sport Center,** at Calif. 203 and Center Street (☎ 760/934-3416); **The Trout Fitter,** in the Shell Mart Center at Main Street and Old Mammoth Road (☎ 760/924-3676); or **Kittredge Sports,** Main Street and Forest Trail (☎ 760/934-7566), which rents equipment, supplies guides, teaches fly-fishing, and offers backcountry trips and packages.

KAYAKING Kayaks are available at Crowley Lake from **Caldera Kayaks** (☎ 760/935-4942) starting at $30 a day. This outfitter also offers tours on Crowley and Mono lakes and provides instruction as well.

PACK TRIPS The region is also an equestrian's paradise, and numerous outfitters offer pack trips. Among them are **Red's Meadows Pack Station,** Red's Meadows, past Minaret Vista (☎ 800/292-7758 or 760/934-2345); **Mammoth Lakes Pack Outfit,** Lake Mary Road, past Twin Lakes (☎ 760/934-2434), which offers 1- to 6-day riding trips and semiannual horse drives, plus other wilderness workshops; and **McGee Creek Pack Station,** McGee Creek Road, Crowley Lake (☎ 760/935-4324).

HIKING Trails abound in the Mammoth Lakes Basin area. They include the half-mile-long **Panorama Dome Trail,** which is just past the turnoff to Twin Lakes on Lake Mary Road, leading to the top of a plateau that provides a view of the Owens Valley and Lakes Basin. Another trail of interest is the 5-mile-long **Duck Lake Trail,** starting at the end of the Coldwater Creek parking lot with switchbacks across Duck Pass past several lakes to Duck Lake. The head of the **Inyo Craters Trail** is reached via gravel road, off the Mammoth Scenic Loop Road. This trail takes you to the edge of these craters and a sign that explains how they were created.

For additional trail information and maps, contact the **Mammoth Ranger Station** (☎ 760/924-5500). For equipment and maps, go to **Footloose Sports Center,** at the corner of Canyon and Minaret (☎ 760/934-2400), which also rents in-line skates and mountain bikes.

OTHER SUMMERTIME FUN Golf can be enjoyed at **Snowcreek Golf Course,** Old Mammoth Road (☎ 760/934-6633). Adventurers can also go hot-air ballooning with the **Mammoth Ballooning Co.** (☎ 760/934-7188).

EXPLORING THE SURROUNDING AREA

Bodie, one of the most authentic ghost towns in the West, lies about an hour's drive north of Mammoth, past the Tioga Pass entrance to Yosemite. In 1870, more than 10,000 people lived in Bodie; today, it's an eerie shell. En route to Bodie, you'll pass **Mono Lake,** near Lee Vining, which has startling tufa towers arising from its surface—limestone deposits formed by underground springs. It's a major bird-watching area—about 300 species nest or stop here during their migrations.

WHERE TO STAY

If you stay at the resort, you'll be steps from the lifts each morning. If you opt for the town, you're closer to the restaurants and nightlife. Regardless, they're within a 5-minute drive from each other, so whatever you choose, you're never too far from the action.

There are more than 700 **campsites** available in the area. These sites open on varying dates in June, depending on the weather. The largest campgrounds are at Convict Lake, Twin Lakes and Cold Water (both in the Mammoth Lakes Basin), and Red's Meadow. For additional information, call the **Mammoth Ranger Station** (☎ 760/924-5500).

Holiday Inn. 3236 Main St. (behind the Chevron station), Mammoth Lakes, CA 93546. ☎ **800/HOLIDAY** or 760/924-1234. Fax 760/934-3626. 72 units. TV TEL. Double from $129 year-round. Honeymoon suite from $299 winter, from $149 summer. AE, DC, DISC, MC, V.

Opened in the summer of 1999, this faux alpine lodge is Mammoth's newest hotel and only 4-star property. A woodsy exterior with a river-rock base gives the three-story hotel a rustic appeal, while the interior boasts a more contemporary atmosphere. Refrigerators, microwaves, coffeemakers and irons/ironing boards are provided in the generically decorated guest rooms. Suites offer a little extra room, kitchenettes, and Jacuzzi tubs. A spacious honeymoon suite caters to those who want a little romance in the great outdoors. There's no restaurant, but a food court with Pizza Hut and Mrs. Field's Cookies is situated just off the lobby. An indoor pool and spa and a small fitness center with a treadmill and weights are available.

Mammoth Mountain Inn. Minaret Rd. (P.O. Box 353), Mammoth Lakes, CA 93546. ☎ **800/228-4947** or 760/934-2581. Fax 760/934-0701. 173 units, 40 condos (some suitable for up to 13 people). TV TEL. Winter $115–$235 double; from $260–$485 condo. Summer $99–$130 double; from $145 condo. Special ski and mountain-biking packages available. AE, MC, V.

Located opposite the ski lodge at the base of the ski resort, the inn started out in 1954 as only one building, but was expanded a decade later into a larger, glossier complex. Though it was remodeled in the early 1990s, it still retains the rustic charm you'd expect from a mountain resort. Rooms, which were recently upgraded with new carpets and furnishings, are well equipped and pleasantly furnished, but not exactly inspired. Families love this place for its day-care activities, cribs ($10 one-time charge), playground, box lunches for picnics, games room, and even picnic tables. There's also an array of sports facilities, including bicycles, fishing or hiking guides, downhill or cross-country skiing, sleighing, horseback riding, and hay-wagon rides. The hotel has a general store/coffee bar and offers barbecues and room service. The rather standard restaurant serves breakfast, lunch, and dinner. Extras include free airport transportation and occasional entertainment. A whirlpool spa is also on the property.

Motel 6. 3372 Main St. (P.O. Box 1260), Mammoth Lakes, CA 93546. ☎ **800/4-MOTEL-6** or 760/934-6660. Fax 760/934-6989. 151 units. A/C TV TEL. Winter $50–$60 double; summer from $55 double. Extra person $6. AARP discounts. AE, DC, DISC, MC, V.

The rooms may be small, but after a $1.5-million renovation in 1997, accommodations here are the nicest around in this price range. Although quarters are a bit more cramped than some other options, factor in the heated pool (summer only), vending machines, and free coffee in the lobby, and you've got all you really need to set up camp.

Sherwin Villas. P.O. Box 2249, Mammoth Lakes, CA 93546. ☎ **800/228-5291** or 760/934-4773. 70 condos. TV. 1-bedroom unit for up to 4 people $95–$110 winter; $70 summer. 2-bedroom loft for up to 6 people $130–$180 winter; $85 summer. Extra person $10. MC, V.

Just outside the center of town on Old Mammoth Road is this cluster of woodsy condos, perfect for larger families or groups of friends traveling together. Here you'll find one-, two-, three-, and four-bedroom units, each with a fully stocked kitchen, fireplace, linens, and access to the sauna, Jacuzzi, pool, tennis courts, and free ski shuttle that will take you to the slopes (a 5-minute drive away). Considering how many people you can pack into these apartments—and that if you stay 4 weekday nights, the fifth night is free—it's a good deal. When making reservations, make sure you specify exactly what you're looking for; each condo is independently owned and varies dramatically in both decor and quality. You can also request a phone.

Sierra Lodge. 3540 Main St. (Calif. 203), Mammoth Lakes, CA 93546. ☎ **800/356-5711** or 760/934-8881. Fax 760/934-7231. 36 units. TV TEL. Winter $85–$95 double; holidays $110–$130 double. Summer $75–$89 double; holidays $89 double. MC, V.

In the heart of the resort town near the ski shuttle, this two-story inn offers clean, modern surroundings; rock-built fireplaces in the public areas; and a sincere effort to please its guests. Rooms are large and equipped with a kitchenette and utensils, but are unfortunately decorated in upscale-motel style. Still, everything is spotless, rooms have small patios or balconies, and although there's no proper closet, there is a nook to hang your things as well as a few drawers. Facilities include an outdoor Jacuzzi and a fireside room for relaxing. Continental breakfast is the only meal served, but many restaurants are nearby. Smoking is not permitted.

Snow Goose Inn. 57 Forest Trail (P.O. Box 387), Mammoth Lakes, CA 93546. ☎ **800/874-7368** or 760/934-2660. Fax 760/934-5655. 19 units. TV TEL. Winter Sun–Thurs $78 double, $148 suite; Fri–Sat $98 double, $168 suite. Summer $68 double; $98 suite. Rates include breakfast, evening wine, and appetizers. Doubles with kitchens $10 extra. Special packages available. AE, DISC, MC, V.

Scott and Denise Robertson run this place as if it were a B&B rather than a traditional hotel. Set half a block off the main street near a number of restaurants, the Snow Goose consists of two separate two-story buildings. Rooms are comfortably and attractively furnished, and two come with kitchens. The two-bedroom suites can accommodate up to seven in a two-story space with dinette, kitchen, and living room complete with fireplace; some have Jacuzzi tubs. Antiques add a graceful note to some of the public rooms, and the helpful staff can direct you to cross-country and downhill skiing possibilities 3 miles away or, better yet, the property's hot tub just outside.

Tamarack Lodge. Twin Lakes Rd., off Lake Mary Rd. (P.O. Box 69), Mammoth Lakes, CA 93546. ☎ **800/237-6879** or 760/934-2442. Fax 760/934-2281. 11 units, 6 with bathroom; 25 cabins. TEL. Winter $80 double without bathroom, $95–$140 double with bathroom; $110–$300 cabin. Summer $70 double without bathroom, $85–$105 double with bathroom; $85–$260 cabin. Special packages available. AE, MC, V.

The lodge and cabin accommodations at this rustic lakeside retreat are nothing fancy, but that's exactly what's kept guests coming here since the 1920s. Folks relax in front of the fire in the sitting room or hang out in their rooms, which are intentionally rustic with knotty-pine walls and modern furnishings. The cabins, which can accommodate two to nine people, are dotted around the property and offer a variety of configurations, from studios with wood-burning stove and shower to two-bedroom/two-bathroom accommodations with fireplace. Each cabin has a fully equipped kitchen, but there's no daily maid service (fresh towels are provided at the front desk). In the main lodge, there are rooms both with private bathrooms and with shared bathrooms.

The lodge has a very popular cross-country ski center with more than 25 miles of trails and skating lanes, ski rentals, and a ski school. Boat and canoe rentals are also available. The dining room, overlooking Twin Lakes, offers California and continental fare. *Note:* Mammoth Mountain purchased the lodge in 1998 and has plans to expand and renovate in coming years.

WHERE TO DINE

✪ **Nevados.** Main St. (at Minaret Rd.). ☎ **760/934-4466.** Reservations recommended. Main courses $14–$23; fixed-price meal $27. AE, CB, DC, DISC, MC, V. Daily 5:30–9:30pm. EUROPEAN/CALIFORNIA.

What makes this restaurant a favorite with the locals? Well, owner/host Tim Dawson is on hand nightly to ensure that their every need is met; the innovative cuisine is fresh and homemade; and the tasty bread is house-baked. The clincher, though, is the fixed-price meal, which consists of a first course such as potato-crusted crab cake, salad of duck confit and baby lettuces, or seared tuna sashimi; a main course featuring the likes of rosemary rack of lamb or grilled New York steak; and dessert (love that warm-pear-and-almond tart). Throw in the casual-but-sweet ambiance (white tablecloths, candles, and French country murals) and the extensive selection of wines, single-malt scotches, and single-batch bourbons, and it's no wonder this is the hangout for ski instructors and race coaches.

⚫ **The Restaurant at Convict Lake.** Convict Lake Rd. ☎ **760/934-3803.** Reservations recommended. Main courses $14–$28. AE, MC, V. Summer daily 11am–2pm; year-round daily 5:30–9:30pm. CONTINENTAL/FRENCH.

After years of remaining a local secret, this place was awarded 4-star status by AAA. With only 20 others in the state enjoying similar recognition, you can bet you'd better make reservations. The rustic-but-elegant dining room's ambiance—surrounded by mountains amidst tiny wood cabins and a lake—makes for one heck of a special backdrop for this romantic dining diversion 5 miles south of the town of Mammoth Lakes. Within the woodsy, plank-sided cabin with a copper-hooded, freestanding fireplace and windows overlooking a forest of aspen, you can try such classic dishes as duck breast with Grand Marnier and sun-dried-cherry sauce, garnished with candied-orange zest. In season, the venison, pan-seared with kalamata olives, toasted cumin, and oven-dried tomatoes and served with a fine herb glaze, is worth the trip here.

Shogun. Old Mammoth Rd. (in the Sierra Center Mall) ☎ **760/934-3970.** Reservations recommended. Main courses $8.95–$17.50. AE, CB, DC, DISC, MC, V. Mon–Sun 5:30–9:30pm. JAPANESE.

Sushi and tempura in an alpine setting may seem out of context, but this authentic Japanese restaurant, located on the second floor of a strip mall, consistently packs in both tourists and locals. Diners at the eight-seat sushi bar sup on sashimi, handrolls, and a variety of sushi creations. Delicate tempura, sweet and tangy teriyaki dishes, and grilled yakitori skewers are offered individually or as combination dinners. Those with a hearty appetite can order the Boat Dinner, which includes beef and chicken teriyaki, tempura, tonkatsu, sashimi or salmon, and dessert for $17.50 per person (minimum two people). Sake, beer, and cocktails are also available.

Skadi. 587 Old Mammoth Rd. (in the Sherwin Plaza III shopping mall). ☎ **760/934-3902.** Reservations recommended. Main courses $14–$22. AE, MC, V. Wed–Mon 5:30–10pm. ECLECTIC.

The mini-mall where this restaurant is located (half a mile south of Mammoth Lake's center) may not be the home of the Viking goddess of skiing and hunting whose name this restaurant bears, but she wouldn't have cared once she saw the view—it encompasses most of the mountains for miles around. This universal favorite is perfect for an après-ski cocktail at the 14-seat bar, a snack from the substantial selection of appetizers and desserts, or a full-blown dinner on the town.

The decor has a big-city postmodern aura that's a welcome change after all that local alpine rusticity. Main courses are self-proclaimed "Alpine cuisine" and include such dishes as smoked trout napoleon or grilled venison with lingonberries and a game sauce. Finish the evening with crème brûlée or the frozen macadamia-nut parfait.

Whiskey Creek. 24 Lake Mary Rd. (at Minaret Rd.). ☎ **760/934-2555.** Reservations recommended. Main courses $12–$18. AE, DC, DISC, MC, V. Daily 5–10pm; bar stays open until 2am. AMERICAN.

If you favor surf-and-turf fare combined with alpine atmosphere, you've found your dining spot. The building's wraparound windows encompass a view of the snow-clad mountains, and the menu is known for its beef, baby-back ribs, tequila shrimp, and lemon-garlic chicken. While this is better than many options in town, it's our least favorite of those listed.

Although the dining room may offer a peaceful experience, the upstairs brewpub is a whole different world. The upstairs Mammoth Brewing Company and its live music (every night from 9pm until at least 1am) make this place the number one spot to mingle, slam suds, and get happy. (Think very crowded, post-collegiate frat party.) The cover ranges from free to $5.

4 Devils Postpile National Monument

10 miles W of Mammoth, 50 miles E of Yosemite's eastern boundary

Just a few miles outside the town of Mammoth Lakes, Devils Postpile National Monument is home to one of nature's most curious geological spectacles. Formed when molten lava cracked as it cooled, the 60-foot-high, blue-gray basalt columns that form the postpile look more like some sort of enormous eerie pipe organ or a jumble of giant pencil leads than anything you'd expect to see made from stone. The mostly six-sided columns formed underground and were exposed when glaciers scoured this valley in the last ice age, some 10,000 years ago. Similar examples of columnar basalt are found in Ireland and Scotland.

Because of its high elevation (7,900 feet) and heavy snowfall, the monument is open only from summer until early fall. The weather in summer is usually clear and warm, but afternoon thundershowers can soak the unprepared. Nights are still cold, so bring good tents and sleeping bags if you'll be camping. The Mammoth Lakes region is famous for its beautiful lakes—but unfortunately all that water also means lots of mosquitoes. Plan for them.

From late June to early September, cars are prohibited in the monument between 7:30am and 5:30pm because of the small roads' inability to handle the traffic. Visitors must take a shuttle bus from the Mammoth Mountain Inn to and from locations in the monument. While it takes some planning, the resulting peace and quiet are well worth the trouble and make you wonder why the park service hasn't implemented similar programs at Yosemite Valley and other traffic hot spots.

HIKING   There's more to Devils Postpile than a bunch of rocks, no matter how impressive they might be. Located on the banks of the San Joaquin River in the heart of a landscape of granite peaks and crystalline mountain lakes, the 800-acre park is a gateway to a hiker's paradise. Short paths lead from here to the top of the postpile and to **Soda Springs,** a spring of cold carbonated water.

A longer hike (about 1¼ miles) from the separate Rainbow Falls Trailhead will take you to spectacular **Rainbow Falls,** where the entire middle fork of the San Joaquin plunges 101 feet from a lava cliff. From the trail, a stairway and short trail lead to the base of the falls and swimming holes below.

The **John Muir Trail,** which connects Yosemite National Park with Kings Canyon and Sequoia national parks, and the **Pacific Crest Trail** both run through here. Named after the famous conservationist and author who is largely credited with saving Yosemite and popularizing the Sierra Nevada as a place worth preserving, the 211-mile John Muir Trail traverses some of the most rugged and remote parts of the Sierra. There are two accesses to it in Devils Postpile, one via the ranger station, the other from the Rainbow Falls Trailhead. From here, you can hike as far as your feet will take you north or south. *Note:* Mountain bikes are not permitted on trails.

CAMPING   While most visitors stay in or around Mammoth Lakes, the monument does maintain a 21-site campground with piped water, flush toilets, fire pits, and picnic tables on a first-come, first-served basis. Rates are $8 per night. Bears are common in the park, so take proper food-storage measures. Leashed pets are permitted on trails and in camp. Call the **National Park Service** (☎ **760/934-2289**) for details, but don't expect an answer during winter—the park is closed. There are several other U.S. Forest Service campgrounds nearby, including **Red's Meadow** and **Upper Soda Springs.**

5 En Route to Sequoia & Kings Canyon

Though Visalia is the official "gateway" and the city closest to Sequoia and Kings Canyon national parks, it's still 40 minutes to the park entrance. Much closer to the entrance is the small town of **Three Rivers,** which has little more than a restaurant, coffee shops, and motels. However, we've included information on both areas, should you decide to make Visalia your home base.

ESSENTIALS

GETTING THERE   If you're driving from San Francisco, take I-580 east to I-5 south to Calif. 198 east.

The **Visalia Municipal Airport,** 9500 Airport Dr. No. 1 (☎ 209/651-1131), is served by **Shuttle by United** (☎ 800/241-6522).

Amtrak (☎ 800/USA-RAIL) stops at nearby Hanford, and there's a shuttle from there to Visalia.

VISITOR INFORMATION   Contact the **Visalia Convention and Visitors Bureau,** 301 E. Acequia St., Visalia, CA 93291 (☎ 800/524-0303 or 559/738-3435; www.cvbvasilia.com). Since Three Rivers has no tourist office, you should call here for information on the town.

VISALIA
WHERE TO STAY

Ben Maddox House. 601 N. Encina St., Visalia, CA 93291. ☎ 800/401-9800 or 559/739-0721. Fax 559/625-0420. www.bizweb.lightspeed.net/benmaddox. 4 units. A/C TV TEL. $75–$95 double. Rates include breakfast. AE, DISC, MC, V.

Set on a residential street of Victorian homes, 4 blocks from the town's main street, the Ben Maddox House is an impressive sight. Its triangular gable is punctuated with a round window and two extremely tall palm trees looming over the front yard. The house, built in 1876, is constructed of redwood, and its rooms retain their original dark-oak trim and white-oak floors. The guest rooms contain fridges and 18th- and 19th-century furnishings, and the two front rooms have French doors leading to two small porch sitting areas. A pool and hot tub in the back are open to guests, and a full made-to-order breakfast is served.

Radisson Hotel. 300 S. Court St., Visalia, CA 93291. ☎ 800/333-3333 or 559/636-1111. Fax 559/636-8224. 208 units. A/C MINIBAR TV TEL. $119–$144 double; $229–$329 suite. Extra person $15. Cribs provided free. AE, CB, DC, MC, V.

Seven blocks from the town center, the eight-story Radisson is the finest hotel in Visalia and a family favorite for those en route to Sequoia and Kings Canyon national parks. Some of the attractively furnished rooms open onto balconies. This is certainly not the most glamorous Radisson in California, but it's serviceable in every way, offering a whirlpool, exercise equipment, a pool with poolside service, a fleet of bikes, room service until 2am, and free airport transfers. The restaurant serves breakfast, lunch, and dinner, with last seating at 10pm. The local bar provides entertainment on Friday and Saturday nights.

WHERE TO DINE

✪ **The Vintage Press.** 216 N. Willis St. ☎ 559/733-3033. Reservations recommended. Main courses $13–$30. AE, CB, DC, MC, V. Mon–Thurs 11:30am–2pm and 6–10:30pm; Fri–Sat 11:30am–2pm and 6–11pm; Sun 10am–2pm and 5–9pm. AMERICAN/CONTINENTAL.

This is the best restaurant within a surrounding 100-mile radius, a culinary stopover of widely acknowledged merit in the gastronomic wasteland between Los Angeles and San Francisco. The design is reminiscent of a fin de siècle gin mill in gold-rush San Francisco, with a bar imported from that city manufactured by the Brunswick Company (of bowling-alley fame), lots of antiques bought at local auctions, and glittering panels of leaded glass and mirrors. The place is big enough (250 seats) to feed a boat-load of gold-rush hopefuls and has a bustling bar/lounge where a pianist presents live music Thursday through Saturday from 5:30 to 9pm.

The menu is supplemented by daily specials—a zesty rack of lamb roasted in a cabernet sauce with rosemary and pistachios, for example. The regular menu offers about a dozen meat and fish dishes, with steaks as well as such choices as red snapper with lemon, almonds, and capers, or pork tenderloin with Dijon mustard, red chili, and honey. To start, we recommend farm-raised fresh oysters on the half shell or the wild mushrooms with cognac in puff pastry.

THREE RIVERS
WHERE TO STAY

The **Holiday Inn Express,** 40820 Sierra Dr. (Calif. 198), Three Rivers, CA 93271 (☎ **800/HOLIDAY** or 559/561-9000), has an outpost here. For other options, contact **The Reservation Centre** (☎ **559/561-0410;** www.sequoiapark.com).

6 Sequoia & Kings Canyon National Parks

30 miles E of Visalia

Only 200 road miles separate Yosemite from Sequoia and Kings Canyon national parks, but they're worlds apart. While the National Park Service has taken every opportunity to modernize, accessorize, and urbanize Yosemite, resulting in a frenetic tourist scene much like the cities so many of us strive to escape, at Sequoia and Kings Canyon, they've treated the wilderness beauty of the parks with respect and care. Only one road, the Generals Highway, loops through the area, and no road traverses the Sierra here. The park service recommends that vehicles over 22 feet long avoid the steep and windy stretch between Potwisha Campground and the Giant Forest in Sequoia National Park. Generally speaking, the park is much less accessible by car than most, but spectacular for those willing to head out on foot.

The Sierra Nevada tilts upward as it runs south. **Mount Whitney,** at 14,494 feet the highest point in the lower 48 states, is just one of many high peaks in Sequoia and Kings Canyon. The **Pacific Crest Trail** also reaches its highest point here, crossing north to south through both parks. In addition to rocky, snow-covered peaks, Sequoia and Kings Canyon are home to the largest groves of giant sequoias in the Sierra Nevada, as well as the headwaters of the Kern, Kaweah, and Kings rivers. A few small, high-country lakes are home to some of the only remaining pure-strain golden trout. Bears, deer, and numerous smaller animals and birds depend on the parks' miles of wild habitat for year-round breeding and feeding grounds.

Technically two separate parks, Sequoia and Kings Canyon are contiguous and managed jointly from the park headquarters at Ash Mountain, just past the entrance on Calif. 198 east of Visalia.

JUST THE FACTS

Most visitors make a loop through the parks by entering at Grant Grove and leaving through Ash Mountain, or vice versa.

Note that there are no gas stations in the parks, so be sure to fill up your gas tank before you enter.

ENTRANCE FEES   A $10-per-car fee is good for 7 days' entry at any park entrance. An annual pass costs $20; the Golden Age pass offers lifetime access for seniors 62 and over for $10; and blind or permanently disabled visitors get free entry with the Golden Access pass.

VISITOR CENTERS & INFORMATION   The **Lodgepole** and **Grant Grove** visitor centers are the largest, with a full selection of park information and displays about the history, biology, and geology of this incredible place. Some time spent here will pay off by letting you decide which parts of the parks you most want to concentrate on. For visitor information before you go, call ☎ **559/565-3341.**

AVOIDING THE CROWDS   To escape the crowds and see less-used areas of the parks, enter on one of the dead-end roads to Mineral King or Cedar Grove (open only in summer), or South Fork. The lack of through traffic makes these parts of the parks incredibly peaceful even at full capacity, and they're gateways to some of the best hiking.

RANGER PROGRAMS   Park rangers offer hikes, campfire talks, and slide shows at several campgrounds and visitor centers during the summer.

REGULATIONS   Mountain bikes and dogs are forbidden on all park trails (dogs are only permitted in developed areas, but must be leashed). The park service allows firewood gathering at campgrounds, although supplies can be scarce. Removing wood from living or standing trees is forbidden.

RESERVATIONS FOR CAMPING   Wilderness permits are required for all overnight trips in the parks. You can reserve the $10 permits in advance by writing the Wilderness Office, Superintendent, Sequoia and Kings Canyon National Parks, HCR 89 Box 60, Three Rivers, CA 93271. You must reserve backpacking permits for climbing Mount Whitney via the Inyo National Forest. Reservations can be made by phone, fax, or mail through **Wilderness Reservations,** P.O. Box 430, Big Pine, CA 93513 (☎ **888/374-3773** or 760/938-1136; fax 760/938-1137).

THE SEASONS   In the high altitudes, where most Sequoia and Kings Canyon visitors are headed, the summers are short and the winters cold. Snow in July and August, although rare, is not unheard of. At mid-elevations, where the sequoias grow, spring can come as early as April and as late as June. Afternoon showers are occasional. In winter, only the main roads into the parks are usually open; the climate can range from bitter cold to pleasant and can change minute by minute. The Generals Highway between Sequoia and Kings Canyon closes for plowing during and after snowstorms. Be ready for anything if you head into the backcountry on skis. In summer, poison oak and rattlesnakes are common in lower elevations, and mosquitoes are plentiful in all wet areas.

SEEING THE HIGHLIGHTS

There are some 75 groves of giant sequoias in the parks, but the easiest places to see the trees are **Grant Grove,** in Kings Canyon near the park entrance on Calif. 180 from Fresno, or **Giant Forest,** a huge grove of trees containing 40 miles of footpaths, located 16 miles from the entrance to Sequoia National Park on Calif. 198. Saving the sequoias was one of the reasons Sequoia National Park was created in 1890 at the request of San Joaquin Valley residents, making it the second-oldest national park in the United States.

Sequoia & Kings Canyon National Parks

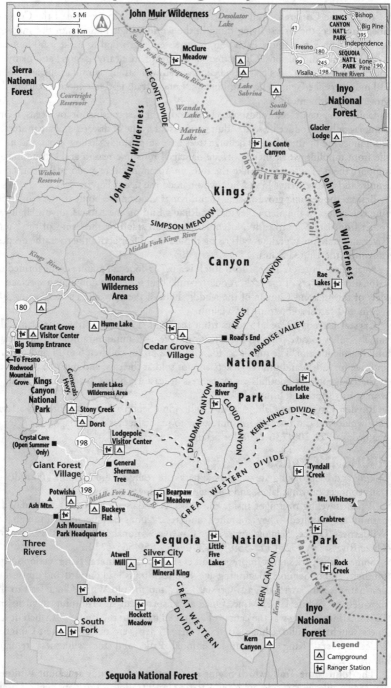

The 2-mile **Congress Trail** loop in Giant Forest starts at the base of the **General Sherman Tree,** the largest living thing in the world. Single branches of this monster are more than 7 feet thick. Each year, it grows enough wood to make a 60-foot-tall tree of normal dimensions. Other trees in the grove are nearly as large, and many of the peaceful-looking trees have also been saddled with strangely militaristic and political monikers like General Lee and Lincoln. Longer trails lead to remote reaches of the grove and nearby meadows.

Unlike the coast redwoods, which reproduce by sprouting or by seeds, giant sequoias only reproduce by seed. Adult sequoias rarely die of diseases and are protected from most fire by thick bark. The huge trees have surprisingly shallow roots, and most die from toppling when their roots are damaged for some reason and can no longer support them. These groves, like the ones in Yosemite, were explored by conservationist and nature writer John Muir, who named the Giant Forest.

Besides the sequoia groves, Sequoia and Kings Canyon are home to the most pristine wilderness in the Sierra Nevada. At **Road's End** on the Kings Canyon Highway (open from late May to early November), you can stand by the banks of the Kings River and stare up at granite walls rising thousands of feet above the river, the deepest canyon in the United States.

Near Giant Forest Village, **Moro Rock** is a 6,725-foot-tall granite dome formed by exfoliation of layers of the rock. A quarter-mile trail scales the dome for a spectacular view of the adjacent Canyon of the Middle Fork of the Kaweah. The trail gains 300 feet in 400 yards, so be ready for a climb.

Crystal Cave is located 15 miles from the Calif. 198 park entrance and an additional 7 miles to cave parking. Here you can take a 50-minute tour of Crystal's beautiful marble interior. The tour is $5 for adults, $2.50 for children 6 to 11 and seniors, and free for kids 5 and under. Tickets are not sold at the cave and must be purchased at the Lodgepole or Foothills visitor centers at least 1½ hours in advance. Be sure to wear sturdy shoes and bring a jacket.

Boyden Cavern, on Calif. 180 in neighboring Sequoia National Forest, is a large cave where you can take a 45-minute tour to see stalactites and stalagmites. A fee is charged; call ☎ **209/736-2708** for details.

HIKING THE PARKS

Hiking and backpacking are what these parks are really all about. Some 700 miles of trails connect canyons, lakes, and high alpine meadows and snowfields.

When traveling overnight inside the parks' boundaries, overnight and/or day-use permits are required. They're limited and reservations can be made through the **Wilderness Office,** Sequoia and Kings Canyon National Parks, HCR 89 Box 60, Three Rivers, CA 93271 (☎ **559/565-3708;** fax 559/565-4239).

Some of the park's most impressive hikes start in the **Mineral King** section in the southern end of Sequoia. Beginning at 7,800 feet, trails lead onward and upward to destinations like Sawtooth Pass, Crystal Lake, and the old White Chief Trail to the now-defunct White Chief Mine. Once an unsuccessful silver-mining town in the 1870s, Mineral King was the center of a pitched battle in the late 1970s when developers sought to build a huge ski resort here. They were defeated when Congress added Mineral King to Sequoia National Park, and the wilderness remains unspoiled.

The **John Muir Trail,** which begins in Yosemite Valley, ends at Mount Whitney. For many miles it coincides with the **Pacific Crest Trail** as it skirts the highest peaks in the park. This is the most difficult part of the Pacific Crest, remaining above 10,000 feet most of the time and crossing 12,000-foot-tall passes.

Other hikers like to explore the northern part of Kings Canyon from **Cedar Grove** and **Road's End.** The **Paradise Valley Trail,** leading to beautiful Mist Falls, is a fairly easy day trip by park standards. The **Copper Creek Trail** immediately rises into the high wilderness around Granite Pass at 10,673 feet, one of the most strenuous day hikes in the parks.

If the altitude and steepness are too much for you at these trailheads, try some of the longer hikes in **Giant Forest** or **Grant Grove.** These forests are woven with inter-locking loops that allow you to take as short or as long a hike as you want. The 6-mile **Trail of the Sequoias** in Giant Forest will take you to the grove's far-eastern end, where you'll find some of the finest trees. In Grant Grove, a 100-foot walk through the hollow trunk of the **Fallen Monarch** makes a fascinating side trip. The tree has been used for shelter for more than 100 years and is tall enough inside that you can walk through without bending over.

Perhaps the most traversed trail to the park is the **Whitney Portal Trail.** It runs from east of Sequoia near Lone Pine, through Inyo National Forest, to Sequoia's boundary, the summit of Mount Whitney. Though it's a straightforward walk to the summit and it's possible to bag it in a very long day hike, you'd better be in really good shape before attempting it. Almost half the people who attempt Whitney, including those who camp partway up, don't reach the summit. Weather, altitude, and fatigue can conspire to stop even the most prepared party. If you're interested in an overnight trip into the backcountry, contact **Whitney Portal reservations** (☎ 888/374-3730) 6 months in advance.

The official park map and guide has good road maps for the parks, but for serious hiking you'll want to check out *Sierra South: 100 Back-Country Trips,* by Thomas Win-nett and Jason Winnett (Wilderness Press). Another good guide is *Kings Canyon Country,* a hiking handbook by Ginny and Lew Clark. The Grant Grove, Lodgepole, Cedar Grove, Foothills, and Mineral King visitor centers all sell a complete selection of maps and guidebooks to the parks. Books and maps are also available by mail through the **Sequoia Natural History Association** (☎ 559/565-3768).

OTHER OUTDOOR PURSUITS

FISHING   Trout fishing in the lower altitudes is fairly limited; most fishing takes place along the banks of the Kings and Kaweah rivers. A few high-country lakes are refuges for trout and are not stocked with hatchery fish. Before venturing into the high country, inquire at a ranger station about the area you'll be visiting to find out about closures or specific regulations. A California fishing license is required for everyone over 16 years old. Tackle and licenses are available at several park stores.

RAFTING & KAYAKING   Only recently have professional outfitters begun taking experienced rafters and kayakers down the Class IV and V Kaweah and Upper Kings rivers outside the parks. Contact **Sequoia National Forest** (☎ 559/784-1500) for a current listing of companies running trips. This is only for the very adventurous.

SKIING & SNOWSHOEING   In Kings Canyon, **Sequoia Ski Touring,** in Grant Grove (☎ 559/335-2314), offers complete rentals and trail maps for 35 miles of Sequoia backcountry trails. People with their own equipment are welcome on all trails in the parks at no cost. Trail maps are available at the visitor centers. On winter week-ends, park rangers lead introductory snowshoe hikes at Giant Forest and Grant Grove. The roads to Cedar Grove and Mineral King are closed in winter.

CAMPING & ACCOMMODATIONS

There are 13 campgrounds in the parks, offering the most convenient and economical accommodations here, although none have hookups. Only two accept reservations: **Lodgepole Campground** and **Dorst Campground** in Sequoia (☎ 800/365-2267). Others are first-come, first-served, and often fill up on weekends. Three campgrounds—Azalea, Lodgepole, and Potwisha—are open year-round. The rest are open from snowmelt through September. Call ☎ 559/565-3341 for camping information. Even in summer, campers should prepare for rain and cold temperatures. Bring a good tent and warm sleeping bags. Also note that due to bears, proper food storage is required.

Two large campgrounds in Sequoia are **Dorst** and **Lodgepole.** Both are close to Giant Forest. Lodgepole is within a short stroll of a restaurant, market, showers, laundry, and visitor center. With more than 200 sites each, they tend to be the noisiest campgrounds in Sequoia. Lodgepole and Dorst charge $16 per night.

Smaller and more peaceful are **South Fork, Potwisha, Buckeye Flat, Atwell Mill,** and **Cold Springs.** South Fork, Atwell Mill, and Cold Springs have pit toilets and cost $6 per night. The others, with flush toilets and sinks, charge from $8 to $16.

Campers in the remote Cedar Grove area of Kings Canyon National Park in the Kings River gorge can choose from **Moraine, Sentinel, Sheep Creek,** and **Canyon View,** which also has a group camp. All four have flush toilets and are convenient to some of the parks' best hiking. The small **Cedar Grove Village** offers a restaurant, motel, showers, and store. Sites are $14.

Three campgrounds in the Grant Grove area will put you near the sequoias without the noise and crowds of Giant Forest Village. All three—**Sunset, Azalea,** and **Crystal Springs**—have flush toilets and phones. The area has an RV disposal site, a visitor center, and showers nearby. The charge is $12 per site.

Lodging in the parks ranges from rustic cabins (with no bathrooms or heat) to brand-new rooms. Lodging in Kings Canyon is operated by the park concessionaire, Kings Canyon Park Services Co., P.O. Box 909, **Kings Canyon National Park,** CA 93633 (☎ 559/335-5500 for information and reservations).

Cedar Grove is the site of an 18-room motel. Each room has its own bathroom and two queen-size beds. Grant Grove offers a variety of cabins with private or shared bathrooms. **Grant Grove Village,** on Calif. 180 (☎ 559/335-5500), brings brandspankingnew overnight digs to Kings Canyon. Opening at press time, it plans to offer 30 rooms and six suites in a two-story building in the forest.

Sequoia National Park is in the process of eliminating the old lodgings at Giant Forest and replacing them with a new development. **Wuksachi Village & Lodge,** 64740 Wuksachi Way in Lodgepole, Sequoia National Park (☎ 888/252-5757 or 559/565-0340), is Sequoia's newest addition, opening as this book goes to press and offering 102 rooms within the park.

Sacramento, the Gold Country & the Central Valley

by Matthew R. Poole

On the morning of January 24, 1848, a carpenter named James Marshall was working on John Sutter's mill in Coloma when he made an exciting discovery: He stumbled upon a gold nugget on the south fork of the American River. Despite Sutter's wishes to keep the find a secret, word leaked out—a word that would change the fate of California almost overnight: *Gold!*

The news spread like wildfire, and a frenzy seized the nation: The gold rush was on. Within 3 years, the population of the state grew from a meager 15,000 to more than 265,000. Most of these newcomers were single men under the age of 40, and not far behind were the thousands of merchants, bankers, and women who made their fortunes catering to the miners, most of whom went bust in their search for instant wealth.

Sacramento grew quickly as a supply town at the base of the surrounding goldfields. The Gold Country boom lasted less than a decade; the gold supply was quickly exhausted and many towns shrank or disappeared. Sacramento, however, continued to grow as the fertile Central Valley south of it exploited another source of wealth, becoming the vegetable and fruit garden of the nation.

A trip along Calif. 49 from the northern mines to the southern mines will give visitors a sense of what life might have been like on the rough mining frontier. The towns along this route seem frozen in time, with the main streets boasting raised wooden sidewalks, double-porched buildings, ornate saloons, and Victorian storefronts. Each town tells a similar story of sudden wealth and explosive growth, yet each has also left behind its own unique imprint. Any fan of movie westerns will recognize the setting—hundreds, perhaps even thousands, of films have been shot in these parts.

At the base of the Gold Country's rolling hills is the sprawling and decidedly flat Central Valley. Some 240 miles long and 50 miles wide, it's California's agricultural bread basket, the source of much of the bounty that is shipped across the nation and overseas. Much of the history of California has revolved around the struggle for control of the water used to irrigate the valley (it receives less than 10 inches of rainfall per year) and make this inland desert bloom. Despite the scarcity of water, a breathtaking panorama of orange and pistachio groves, grape vines, and strawberry fields stretches uninterrupted for miles.

1 Sacramento

90 miles E of San Francisco

Sacramento, with a metropolitan population of 1,782,000, is one of the state's fastest growing areas. In addition to being the state capital, it is a thriving shipping and processing center for the fruit, vegetables, rice, wheat, and dairy goods that are produced in the fertile Central Valley. In the past decade, it's also become an area of high-tech spillover from Silicon Valley. This prosperous and politically charged city has broad, tree-shaded streets lined with some impressive Victorians and well-crafted bungalows. At its heart sits the capitol building—Sacramento's main attraction—in a well-maintained park replete with flower gardens and curious squirrels. It's far from a tourist town, but it does have its share of touristy activities. Visitors and locals alike enjoy spending the day walking through Old Sacramento or floating down the American River.

ESSENTIALS

GETTING THERE If you're driving from San Francisco, Sacramento is located about 90 miles east on I-80. From Los Angeles, take I-5 through the Central Valley directly into Sacramento. From North Lake Tahoe, get on I-80 west, and from South Lake Tahoe take U.S. 50.

Sacramento Metropolitan Airport (☎ 916/929-5411), 12 miles northwest of downtown Sacramento, is served by about a dozen airlines, including **American** (☎ 800/433-7300), **Delta** (☎ 800/221-1212), **Northwest** (☎ 800/225-2525), **Southwest** (☎ 800/435-9792), and **United** (☎ 800/241-6522).

AAA Taxi and Shuttle Service (☎ **916/362-5525**) will get you from the airport to downtown; it charges a flat rate of $15 to the capital, a bargain compared to the $30 a conventional taxi would cost.

Amtrak (☎ **800/USA-RAIL**) trains serve Sacramento daily.

VISITOR INFORMATION The **Sacramento Convention and Visitors Bureau,** 1303 J St., Sacramento, CA 95814 (☎ **916/264-7777;** fax 916/264-7788), provides plenty of helpful information for tourists. Once in the city, visitors can also stop by the **Sacramento Visitor Center,** 1101 Second St. (☎ **916/442-7644**), in Old Sacramento; it's usually open daily from 9am to 5pm.

ORIENTATION Suburbia sprawls around Sacramento, but its downtown area is relatively compact. Getting around the city is made easy by a gridlike pattern of streets that are designated by numbers or letters. The capitol building, on 10th Street between N and L streets, is the key landmark. From the front of the capitol, M Street—which is at this point called Capitol Mall—runs 10 straight blocks to Old Sacramento, the oldest section of the city.

EXPLORING THE CAPITAL & ENVIRONS

In town, you'll want to stroll around **Old Sacramento,** 4 square blocks at the foot of the downtown area that have become a major attraction. These blocks contain more than 100 restored buildings (California's largest restoration project), including restaurants and shops. Although the area has cobblestone streets, wooden sidewalks, and gold rush–era architecture, the high concentration of T-shirt shops and other gimmicky stores has turned it into a sort of historical Disneyland. Nonetheless, there's a lot to see here, such as where the Pony Express ended and the transcontinental railroad—and the Republican Party—began. While you're at it, be sure to stop at the **Discovery Museum** at 101 I St. (☎ 916/264-7057; www.thediscovery.org), which houses hands-on exhibits of California's history, highlighting the valley's agricultural gold rush as well as the real one in 1849. It's open Tuesday through Sunday from 10am to 5pm. Admission is $4 for adults, $2 for kids 6 to 12, and free for kids 5 and under.

Downtown Sacramento

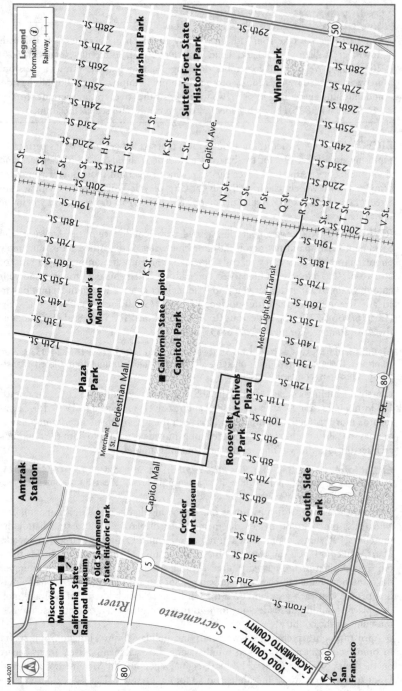

Legend
- Information ⓘ
- Railway ┼┼┼

Marshall Park

Sutter's Fort State Historic Park

Winn Park

28th St.
27th St.
26th St.
25th St.
24th St.
23rd St.
22nd St.
21st St.
20th St.
19th St.
18th St.
17th St.
16th St.
15th St.
14th St.
13th St.
12th St.

D St.
E St.
F St.
G St.
H St.
I St.
J St.
K St.
L St.

I St.
J St.
K St.
L St.
Capitol Ave.

N St.
O St.
P St.
Q St.
R St.
S St.
T St.
U St.
V St.

29th St.
28th St.
27th St.
26th St.
25th St.
24th St.
23rd St.
22nd St.
21st St.
20th St.
19th St.
18th St.
17th St.
16th St.
15th St.
14th St.
13th St.
12th St.
11th St.
10th St.
9th St.
8th St.
7th St.
6th St.
5th St.
4th St.
3rd St.
2nd St.
Front St.

Governor's Mansion ■

ⓘ

K St.

■ California State Capitol
Capitol Park

Plaza Park

Pedestrian Mall

Merchant St.

Capitol Mall

Amtrak Station

Discovery Museum ■
California State Railroad Museum ■

Old Sacramento State Historic Park

Crocker Art Museum ■

Roosevelt Park

Archives Plaza

Metro Light Rail Transit

South Side Park

Sacramento River

YOLO COUNTY
SACRAMENTO COUNTY

To San Francisco

50

5

80

80

W St.

NA-0201

301

For Kids: Where the Wild Things Are

The best place to take your kids on a sunny afternoon in Sacramento is **Fairytale Town,** at William Land Park, Land Park Drive and Sutterville Road (☎ 916/264-5233). We can still remember dragging our poor parents through the stone archway, guarded by a perilously perched Humpty Dumpty. After riding all the rides and climbing everything in sight, we would cross the street to the **Sacramento Zoo** (☎ 916/264-5885), buy a big spool of cotton candy, and see *all* the animals.

BICYCLING   One good thing about a town that's as flat as a tortilla: It's perfect for exploring on a bike. One of the best places to ride is through Old Sacramento and along the 22-mile American River Parkway, which runs right though it. If you didn't bring your own wheels, the friendly guys at **City Bicycle Works,** 2419 K St., at 24th Street (☎ 916/447-2453), will rent you one for about $15 a day and point you in the right direction.

RIVER RAFTING   Sacramento lies nestled at the confluence of the American and Sacramento rivers, and rafting on the clear blue water of the American is immensely popular, especially on warm weekends. Several Sacramento-area outfitters rent rafts for 4 to 15 persons, along with life jackets and paddles. Their shuttles drop you and your entourage upstream and meet you 3 to 4 hours later at a predetermined point downstream. Recommended outfitters include **River Rat,** 9840 Fair Oaks Blvd., Fair Oaks (☎ 916/966-6777), and **American River Raft Rentals,** 11257 S. Bridge St. (at Sunrise Ave), Rancho Cordova (☎ 916/635-6400).

✪ **California State Capitol.** 10th St. (between N and L sts.). ☎ 916/324-0333. Free admission. Daily 9am–5pm. Tours offered every hour on the hour until 4pm. Closed Thanksgiving, Christmas, and New Year's Day.

Closely resembling a scale model of the U.S. Capitol in Washington, D.C., the domed California state capitol was built in 1869 and massively renovated in 1976. It is Sacramento's most distinctive landmark and has been the stage of many important political dramas in California history. The guided tours provide insight into both the building's architecture and the workings of the government it houses.

✪ **California State Railroad Museum.** 125 I St. (at Second St.). ☎ 916/445-6645. www.csrmf.org. Admission $6 adults, $3 children 6–12. Daily 10am–5pm. Closed Thanksgiving, Christmas, and New Year's Day.

Well worth visiting, this museum is one of the highlights of Old Sacramento. You won't miss much if you bypass the memorabilia displays and head straight for the museum's 105 shiny locomotives and rail cars, beautiful antiques that are true works of art. Afterward, you can watch a film on the history of the western railroads that's quite good, then peruse related exhibits that tell the amazing story of the building of the transcontinental railroad. This museum is not just for train buffs: Over half a million people visit each year, and even the hordes of schoolchildren that typically mob this place shouldn't dissuade you from visiting one of the largest and best railroad museums in the country.

April through September, on weekends and holidays from 11am to 5pm, **steam locomotive rides** carry passengers 6 miles along the Sacramento River. Trains depart on the hour from the Central Pacific Freight Depot in Old Sacramento, at K and Front streets. Fares are $6 for adults and $3 for children 6 to 12.

✪ **Crocker Art Museum.** 216 O St. (at Third St.). ☎ 916/264-5423. Admission $4.50 adults, $2 children 7–17, free for children 6 and under. Tues–Wed and Fri–Sun 10am–5pm; Thurs 10am–9pm. Closed major holidays.

This museum houses a truly outstanding collection of California art, as well as tempo- rary exhibits from around the world. The museum itself is an imposing century-old Ital- ianate building, with an ornate interior of carved and inlaid woods. The Crocker Mansion Wing, the museum's most recent addition, is modeled after the Crocker family home and contains works by Northern California artists from 1945 to the present.

Sutter's Fort State Historic Park. 2701 L St. ☎ **916/445-4422.** Admission $3 adults, $1.50 children 6–12, free for children 5 and under. Daily 10am–5pm.

John Sutter established this outpost in 1839, and the park, restored to its 1846 appear- ance, aims to recapture the pioneering spirit of 19th-century California. The usual exhibits are on hand—a blacksmith's forge, cooperage, bakery, and jail—and a self- guided audio tour is available. Historic demonstrations and live reenactments in cos- tume are staged daily from Memorial Day to Labor Day, when admissions are bumped to $6 for adults and $3 for children.

WHERE TO STAY
EXPENSIVE

✪ **Hyatt Regency Sacramento.** 1209 L St., Sacramento, CA 95814. ☎ **800/233-1234** or 916/443-1234. Fax 916/321-6699. 500 units. A/C MINIBAR TV TEL. $220–$260 double; from $375 suite. AE, CB, DC, DISC, MC, V. Self-parking $7; valet parking $12.

Sacramento's top hotel stands right in the heart of downtown, directly across from the California state capitol and adjacent to the convention center. It's the high-status address for visiting politicos and is popular with conventioneers as well, as its facilities and services are unmatched in the city. While the rooms themselves are not terribly distinctive, they conform to a very high standard and come with all the amenities you expect from Hyatt. The best are the corner units with views facing the state capitol.

Dining: Dawson's, the hotel's top restaurant, is an inviting grill decorated with luminous paintings of the city. For lunch or dinner, it's worth a visit even if you're not staying at the Hyatt. Ciao Yama is a very successful hybrid that serves Italian/Japanese cuisine, and is much better than it sounds.

Amenities: Room service, concierge, evening turndown, car-rental desk, overnight laundry, lobby shoe-shines, pool, Jacuzzi, exercise room, gift shop.

MODERATE

✪ **Amber House Bed-and-Breakfast.** 1315 22nd St., Sacramento, CA 95816. ☎ **800/ 755-6526** or 916/444-8085. Fax 916/552-6529. 14 units. A/C TV TEL. $139–$289 double. Rates include breakfast. AE, CB, DC, DISC, MC, V.

Just 8 blocks from the capitol, Amber House, a bucolic old home built in 1905, offers individually decorated rooms named for famous artists, musicians, and writers. Accom- modations are located in two adjacent historic houses: the Poet's Refuge, a well-crafted 1905 home with five rooms, and the Artist's Retreat, a Mediterranean-style house built in 1913. A third addition—an old colonial-revival home called the Musician's Manor— is across the street, and its Mozart Room is the B&B's best, containing a four-poster queen bed, a heart-shaped Jacuzzi, a private patio, and three bay windows overlooking the quiet tree-shaded street. All rooms have hair dryers, VCRs, phones with computer jacks and voice mail, and marble bathrooms—11 with Jacuzzi bathtubs for two.

Amber House effectively combines elegant surroundings with impeccable service. A beautiful living room and intimate library are available for guests' use. A full breakfast is served at the time and location you request—either in your room, in the large dining room, or outside on the veranda. Coffee and a newspaper are brought to your door early every morning, as are freshly baked cookies and wine or champagne every evening. Additional perks include concierge and room and laundry service, as well as free use of bicycles kept on the premises.

Best Western Sutter House. 1100 H St., Sacramento, CA 95814. ☎ **800/830-1314** or 916/441-1314. Fax 916/441-5961. 98 units. A/C TV TEL. $85–$160 double. Rates include continental breakfast. AE, CB, DC, DISC, MC, V.

You would never know from the plain, motel-like exterior that this is one of the best values in Sacramento. Rooms here are as up-to-date as any offered by upscale hotels such as the Hilton or the Sheraton; they include well-coordinated furnishings, cable TV, phone with voice mail, and valet and laundry service. There's also a pool in the courtyard, and complimentary coffee and pastries are served each morning in the lobby.

✪ *Delta King* **Riverboat.** 1000 Front St., Old Sacramento, CA 95814. ☎ **800/825-5464** or 916/444-5464. 44 units. A/C TV TEL. Sun–Thurs $109–$129 double; $400 captain's quarters. Fri–Sat $149 double; $400 captain's quarters. Rates include continental breakfast. AE, DC, DISC, MC, V.

The *Delta King* carried passengers between San Francisco and Sacramento in the 1930s. Permanently moored in Sacramento since 1984, the riverboat is now a gimmicky but nonetheless charming hotel. Staying here can be quite a novelty, but the boat's cramped quarters may wear thin, especially if you're planning to spend a lot of time in your room. All units are nearly identical and have private bathrooms and low ceilings. The captain's quarters, a particularly pricey suite, is a unique, mahogany-paneled stateroom, complete with an observation platform and private deck.

The Pilothouse Restaurant is popular for local office parties. When the weather is nice, there's dining on outside decks with views of Old Sacramento. The Delta Lounge features regular live entertainment. On Friday and Saturday nights, the *Delta King* hosts "Suspect's Murder Mystery," an interactive whodunit that challenges the audience to reveal the true murderer, played by period actors. It's $35 per person to attend, but that includes dinner, tax, and gratuity. Drinks, of course, are extra.

✪ **Sterling Hotel.** 1300 H St., Sacramento, CA 95814. ☎ **800/365-7660** or 916/448-1300. Fax 916/448-8066. 16 units. A/C TV TEL. Sun–Thurs $149–$179 double; $325 suite. Fri–Sat $179–$229 double; $325 suite. Rates include continental breakfast. AE, DC, MC, V.

Set in the heart of Sacramento, 3 blocks from the capitol, this inn occupies a white-fronted Victorian mansion originally built in the 1890s and heavily renovated in 1995. The Sterling has all the charm of a small, well-managed, sophisticated inn, with a carefully tended flowering yard, tasteful decor, designer furnishings, Italian marble, and a Jacuzzi in every room.

The Chanterelle, which serves well-prepared California regional cuisine in a dignified setting, is known as one of Sacramento's better restaurants. Main courses range from $13 to $19, and reservations are recommended.

INEXPENSIVE

The Sacramento Vagabond Inn. 909 Third St., Sacramento, CA 95814. ☎ **800/522-1555** or 916/446-1481. Fax 916/448-0364. 108 units. A/C TV TEL. $83 double. Extra person $7. Children under 19 stay free in parents' room. Rates include continental breakfast. AE, DC, DISC, MC, V.

A reliable choice within walking distance of the state capitol, the Vagabond Inn has a heated pool and a host of free features, including local phone calls, weekday newspapers, and continental breakfast. Bedrooms are clean and comfortable, but not exceptional—it's the economical rates and the convenient location that make it worth your while. There's an adjoining 24-hour Denny's coffee shop as well.

WHERE TO DINE
EXPENSIVE

✪ **Biba.** 2801 Capitol Ave. ☎ **916/455-2422.** Main courses $16–$20. AE, MC, V. Mon–Fri 11:30am–2:30pm; Mon–Thurs 5:30–9:30pm; Fri–Sat 5:30–10:30pm. ITALIAN.

Locals flock to this sleek neo-art-deco restaurant to sample the classical Italian cuisine of Bologna-born owner Biba Caggiano, who has published her sixth cookbook. Although the menu changes seasonally, you can expect to find about 10 pastas and an equal number of main courses. There might be a delicate pappardelle with a fresh-seafood sauce, or a more pungent spaghetti alla Siciliana, which combines eggplant, tomatoes, capers, garlic, and anchovies. For a main course, the osso bucco with Madeira wine is excellent, but save room for the double-chocolate trifle made with dark and white chocolate, Grand Marnier–soaked pound cake, and raspberry purée.

Twenty Eight. 2730 N St. ☎ **916/456-2800.** Reservations recommended. Main courses $15–$24. AE, DISC, MC, V. Mon–Fri 11:30am–10pm; Sat 5–10pm. CALIFORNIA.

Named after the restaurant's cross street, Twenty Eight has quickly become a contender for the city's best restaurant. This place is serious about food, going so far as to bake their own bread and grow many of the veggies served. The menu, which changes seasonally, serves such tempting fare as pork loin carefully grilled to that magic spot between rare and overdone, served on a bed of polenta with sage and blue cheese. Other notable entrees include sweet-pea ravioli with hedgehog mushrooms; pan-seared fresh daily scallops with mashed potatoes, caramelized shallots, and vanilla oil; and grilled quail with an artichoke and a salad of mustard greens and blood oranges. It's a popular hangout for lobbyists and legislators, and because it only seats 55, reservations are a must.

MODERATE

✪ **Harlow's.** 2708 J St. ☎ **916/441-4693.** Main courses $12–$24. AE, MC, V. Tues–Fri 11:30am–2pm; Tues–Sat 6–9pm. ITALIAN/CALIFORNIA.

This comfortable, casual, and very popular supper club has a 1930s air that might have pleased Jean Harlow herself. If you've got a hot date for the night, suggest meeting at the bar: It's one of Sacramento's most fashionable places to see and be seen. The Italian dishes are superb here—ranging from the simple house-made smoked-chicken ravioli to the elaborate veal Portofino stuffed with chicken, hot salami, and Parmesan and baked in a sherry-mushroom-cream sauce. Top it all off with the chocolate pâté, and lean back and enjoy the live music (swing, salsa, reggae, and R&B) that starts nightly at 10pm. After dinner, join the party upstairs at the MoMo Lounge, where you can often find some of Sacramento's best jazz groups.

Jammin' Salmon. 1801 Garden Hwy. (north of downtown on the Sacramento River). ☎ **916/929-6232.** Reservations recommended. Main courses $9–18. AE, DC, DISC, MC, V. Mon–Thurs 11:30am–9pm; Fri–Sat 10am–10pm; Sun 9am–9pm (closed from 2 to 5pm in winter). CALIFORNIA.

The Jammin' Salmon, a small restaurant built on a barge right on the Sacramento River, offers some of the best food—and riverside views—in River City (as the locals call Sacramento). Part of the experience is rocking gently while dining on locally grown produce, fresh fish, and imaginatively prepared entrees. Try the grilled salmon fillet with a red curry sauce or the macadamia-crusted chicken breast topped with a fresh strawberry balsamic vinaigrette. Desserts include a seasonal fresh-fruit crisp with house-made vanilla ice cream or a silky chocolate crème brûlée.

Paragary's Bar and Oven. 1401 28th St. ☎ **916/452-3335.** Main courses $10–$17. AE, DC, DISC, MC, V. Mon–Thurs 11:30am–11pm; Fri 11:30am–midnight; Sat 4:30pm–midnight; Sun 4:30–10pm. ITALIAN/CALIFORNIA.

Occupying two distinct dining rooms just across the street from Twenty Eight, Paragary's is widely considered the best moderately priced restaurant in Sacramento's downtown area. During good weather, the best seats are outside amid the gorgeous fountains and plantings of the courtyard; other seating options include the formal fireplace room and the brightly lit cafe. The same menu is served no matter where you sit, with some of the best dishes coming from the kitchen's wood-burning pizza oven. But this is more than a gourmet pizza parlor, as evidenced by the grilled rib-eye steak with mashed potatoes, portobello mushrooms, and grilled leeks, or the hand-cut rosemary noodles with seared chicken, pancetta, artichokes, leeks, and garlic.

33rd Street Bistro. 3301 Folsom Blvd. (at 33rd St.). ☎ **916/455-2282.** Main courses $8–$15. AE, MC, V. Mon–Wed 7am–10pm; Thurs–Fri 7am–midnight; Sat 8am–midnight; Sun 8am–9pm. BISTRO.

Seattle transplants Fred Haynes (chef) and his brother Matt (manager) have taken an old brick building and transformed it into a bistro that's been a raging success from the day it opened. And it's popular for all the right reasons—the food is wonderful (and priced right), the staff is friendly and helpful, and the ambiance is warm and cheerful. Selections include a variety of Italian grilled sandwiches and house favorites such as wood-roasted vegetables with sun-dried tomatoes and goat-cheese crostini; Uncle Bum's jerk ribs with Jamaican barbecue sauce and key-lime crème fraîche; and wood-roasted pork loin with ancho-chili butter and linguisa risotto.

INEXPENSIVE

Fox & Goose Public House. 1001 R St. (at 10th St.). ☎ **916/443-8825.** Main courses $4–$7. AE, MC, V. Mon–Fri 7am–2pm; Sat–Sun 8am–1pm. Bar stays open until midnight Mon–Thurs, until 2am Fri–Sat. ENGLISH PUB.

The Fox is your classic British pub, right down to the dartboard, giant picture of the queen, and numerous varieties of beers from across the pond. The soups at lunch are excellent, and the specials often include bangers and mash, Welsh rarebit, and Cornish pasties. The burnt cream dessert is famous. Either arrive early for lunch or be prepared for a wait, as locals love this place. Equally popular breakfasts include kippers, grilled tomatoes, and crumpets, as well as the ubiquitous waffles, omelets, and French toast. There's live entertainment by local bands 6 nights a week, as well as serve-yourself pub grub Monday through Friday from 5:30 to 9:30pm.

Tower Café. 1518 Broadway. ☎ **916/441-0222.** Main courses $7–$12. AE, MC, V. Mon–Fri 7–11am and 11:30am–4pm; Sun–Thurs 4:30–10pm; Fri–Sat 4:30–11pm; Sat 8am–4pm; Sun 8am–2pm. Open later for dessert and drinks only. INTERNATIONAL.

The Tower Café gets its name from the building in which it's located: a grand old 1939 movie house with a tall art-deco spire. The restaurant occupies the same space in which a small mom-and-pop music store once stood. This former resident, Tower Records, has since grown into America's second-largest record retailer. While it's unlikely that Tower Café will share the phenomenal success of its predecessor, it's not for the lack of effort. Both the food and the ambiance are pleasant, and even with its perpetually sluggish service, this restaurant remains our favorite Sacramento lunch spot. On warm days, it seems as if everyone in the city is lunching here (in fact, recent patrons included the president and his staff), and people watching can be a real treat. Dishes reflect a variety of international flavors, from the Jamaican jerk chicken to Brazilian chicken salad.

2 The Gold Country

Cutting a serpentine swath for nearly 350 miles along aptly numbered Calif. 49, the Gold Country stretches from Sierra City to the foothills of Yosemite. Much of this rugged region still retains its '49er ambiance: Mining sites, horse ranches, and Wild West saloons are common sights in these parts. Along with its numerous ghost towns and gold rush–era architecture, it's enough to make Gene Autry or Roy Rogers feel right at home.

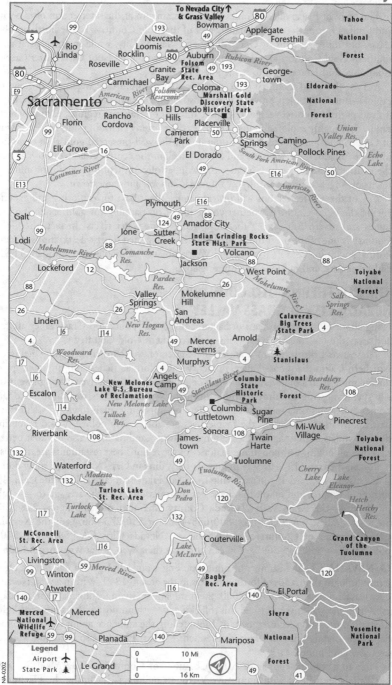

The Gold Country

To Nevada City ↑
& Grass Valley
Tahoe
National
Forest

Bowman
Applegate
Foresthill
80

Newcastle
Loomis
Rocklin
Auburn
Folsom
State
Rec. Area
Georgetown
Eldorado
National
Forest

Rio
Linda
Roseville
Granite
Bay
193

Carmichael
Folsom
Reservoir
Coloma
Marshall Gold
Discovery State
Historic Park

Sacramento
American River
Rancho
Cordova
Folsom
Hills
El Dorado
Hills
Placerville
Diamond
Springs
Camino
Union
Valley Res.
Echo
Lake

Florin
Cameron
Park
50
Pollock Pines
50

Elk Grove
16
El Dorado
South Fork American River
American River

Cosumnes River
49

Galt
Plymouth
E16

Lodi
Ione
Sutter
Creek
124
Amador City
88

Mokelumne River
Comanche
Res.
Indian Grinding Rocks
State Hist. Park
Volcano
Tolyabe
National
Forest

Lockeford
12
Jackson
88
West Point
88

Pardee
Res.
26
Mokelumne River
Salt
Springs
Res.

Valley
Springs
Mokelumne
Hill
San
Andreas
Calaveras
Big Trees
State Park
4

Linden
26
New Hogan
Res.
Mercer
Caverns
Arnold

J6
J14
Murphys
Stanislaus

Woodward
Res.
Angels
Camp
Columbia
State
Historic
Park
National
Beardsleys
Res.
108

Escalon
New Melones
Lake U.S. Bureau
of Reclamation
New Melones Lake
Stanislaus River
Forest

Oakdale
Tullock
Res.
Columbia
Tuttletown
Sugar
Pine
Pinecrest

Riverbank
108
James-
town
Sonora
108
Twain
Harte
Mi-Wuk
Village
Tolyabe
National
Forest

Waterford
132
Modesto
Lake
49
Tuolumne River
Tuolumne
Cherry
Lake
Lake
Eleanor
Hetch
Hetchy
Res.

Turlock Lake
St. Rec. Area
Turlock
Lake
Lake
Don
Pedro
120

McConnell
St. Rec. Area
J16
Couterville
Grand Canyon
of the
Tuolumne

Livingston
59
Merced River
Lake
McLure
120

Winton
Bagby
Rec. Area

Atwater
140
J16
El Portal

Merced
National
WHdlife
Refuge
Merced
140
Sierra
Yosemite
National
Park

Planada
140
Mariposa
National

Legend
Airport ✈
State Park 🌲

0 ——— 10 Mi
0 ——— 16 Km

Le Grand
Forest
49
41

NA-0202

The town of Placerville, 44 miles east of Sacramento at the intersection of U.S. 50 and Calif. 49, is in the approximate center of the Gold Country. To the north are the classic old mining towns of Grass Valley and Nevada City, while in the central and southern Gold Country are such well-preserved towns as Amador City, Sutter Creek, Columbia, and Jamestown, to name just a few.

In fact, the Gold Country is so immense that it would take weeks to thoroughly explore. But rather than provide an exhaustive list of each and every town, we have instead narrowed our coverage to include three of our favorite regions, each of which can be thoroughly explored in just 2 or 3 days: the utterly charming side-by-side towns of Grass Valley and Nevada City to the north; the well-preserved gold-rush communities of Amador City, Jackson, and Sutter Creek in the central Gold Country; and at the southern end of Gold Country, the wonderfully authentic neighboring mining towns of Angels Camp, Murphys, Columbia, Sonora, and Jamestown.

Any of these three regions will provide an excellent base for exploring and experiencing the Gold Country, whether you're intent on panning for gold, exploring old mines and caverns, or rafting the area's many white-water rivers. In fact, the Gold Country is one of the most underrated and least congested tourist destinations in California, a winning combination of Old West ambiance, adorable (and affordable) bed-and-breakfasts, and outdoor adventures galore.

THE NORTHERN GOLD COUNTRY: NEVADA CITY & GRASS VALLEY

Lying about 60 miles northeast of Sacramento, Nevada City and Grass Valley are far and away the top tourist destinations of the northern Gold Country.

These two historic towns were at the center of the hard-rock mining fields of Northern California. Grass Valley, in fact, was California's richest mining town, producing more than a billion dollars worth of gold. Both are attractive, although we usually spend most of our time traipsing through Nevada City. Its wealth of Victorian homes and storefronts makes it one of the most appealing small towns in California, particularly in the fall when the maple trees are ablaze with color (in fact, its entire downtown has been designated a National Historic Landmark). It also has a far better selection of lodgings, although the majority of the region's best restaurants are in Grass Valley. So there you have it: Stay in Nevada City, dine in Grass Valley, and enjoy both.

It's easy to get here. If you're driving from San Francisco, take I-80 to the Calif. 49 turnoff in Auburn and follow the signs. For information about the area, go to—or call in advance—the **Grass Valley/Nevada County Chamber of Commerce,** 248 Mill St., Grass Valley, CA 95945 (☎ **800/655-4667** or 530/273-4667), or the **Nevada City Chamber of Commerce,** 132 Main St., Nevada City, CA 95959 (☎ **800/ 655-NJOY** or 530/265-2692). You can also visit their Web site at **www.ncgold.com.**

✪ **NEVADA CITY** Rumors of miners pulling a pound of gold a day out of Deer Creek brought thousands of fortune seekers to the area in 1849. Within a year, Nevada City was a boisterous town of 10,000, the third largest city in California. In its heyday, everyone who was anyone visited this rollicking western outpost with its busy red-light district. Mark Twain lectured here in 1866, telling the audience about his trips to the Sandwich Islands (Hawaii). Former President Herbert Hoover also lived and worked here as a gold miner.

Pick up a walking-tour map at the **Chamber of Commerce,** 132 Main St., and stroll the streets lined with impressive Victorian buildings, including the **Firehouse Number 1 Museum,** 214 Main St. (☎ **530/265-5468**), complete with bell tower, gingerbread decoration, a small museum that displays mementos from the Donner Party, a Maidu Indian basket collection, and an altar from a temple originally located in the Chinese section of Grass Valley. Admission is free. It's open in summer daily from 11am to 4pm; winter hours (from November 1 to April 1) are Thursday through Sunday from 11am to 4pm. The **National Hotel** (built between 1854 and 1856) is here (we always stop in at the handsome gold rush–era bar for a refresher), as is the **Nevada Theatre** (1865), one of the oldest theaters in the nation and still operating as such, today home to the Foothill Theatre Company.

If you want to see the source of much of the city's wealth, visit **Malakoff Diggins State Historic Park,** 23579 N. Bloomfield Rd. (☎ **530/265-2740**), 28 miles northeast of Nevada City. Once the world's largest hydraulic gold mine, it's an awesome (some might say disturbing) spectacle of hydraulic mining—nearly half a mountain has been washed away by powerful jets of water, leaving behind a 600-foot-deep canyon of exposed rock. In the 1870s, North Bloomfield, then located in the middle of this park, had a population of 1,500. Some of the buildings have been reconstructed and refurnished to show what life was like then. The 3,000-acre park also offers several hiking trails, swimming at Blair Lake, and 30 campsites that can be reserved through **Park-Net** (☎ **800/444-7275**; www.park-net.com). The museum is open daily in summer from 10am to 5pm, in winter on weekends only from 10am to 4pm. To reach the park, take Calif. 49 toward Downieville for 11 miles. Turn right onto Tyler-Foote Crossing Road for 17 miles. The name will change to Curzon Grade and then to Backbone. Turn right onto Derbec Road and into the park. The fee is $5 per car.

Another 6 miles up Calif. 49 from the Malakoff Diggins turnoff will bring you to Pleasant Valley Road, the exit that will take you (in about 7 miles) to one of the most impressive **covered bridges** in the country. Built in 1862, it's 225 feet long and was crossed by many a stagecoach (in autumn, it makes for a spectacular photo opportunity).

GRASS VALLEY In contrast to Nevada City's "tourist town" image, Grass Valley is the commercial/retail center of the region. The **Empire Mine State Historic Park,** 10791 E. Empire St., Grass Valley (☎ **530/273-8522**), the largest and richest gold mine in California, is just outside of town. This mine, which once had 367 miles of underground shafts, produced an estimated 5.8 million ounces of gold between 1850 and 1956, when it closed. Here you can look down the shaft of the mine, walk around the mine yard, and stroll through the gardens of the mine owner. March through November, tours are given daily and a mining movie is shown. You can also enjoy picnicking, cycling, mountain biking, or hiking in the 784-acre park. It's open year-round except for Thanksgiving, Christmas, and New Year's Day. Admission to the park, tour, and museum is $3 for adults and $1 for children and dogs.

In town, visitors can pick up a walking-tour map at the **Chamber of Commerce,** 248 Mill St., and explore the historic downtown area along Mill and Main streets. There are also a few museums that California-history and gold-mining buffs will want to visit: the **Grass Valley Museum,** 410 S. Church St., adjacent to St. Joseph's Cultural Center (☎ **530/273-5509**); the **North Star Mining Museum,** at the south end of Mill Street at McCourtney Road (☎ **530/273-4255**); and the **Video History Museum,** in the center of Memorial Park off Calif. 174 (☎ **530/274-1126**), which houses a collection of old films of the region from the 1920s.

Grass Valley was, for a time, the home of **Lola Montez,** singer, dancer, and paramour of the rich and famous. A fully restored home that she bought and occupied in 1853 can be viewed at 248 Mill St., now the site of Grass Valley's Chamber of Commerce. **Lotta Crabtree,** Montez's famous protégé, lived down the street at 238 Mill St., now an apartment house. Also pop into the **Holbrooke Hotel,** 212 Main St., to see the signature of Mark Twain, who stayed here, as did five U.S. presidents. The saloon has been in continuous use since 1852, and it's the place to meet the locals and have a tall cold one.

The surrounding region offers many recreational opportunities on its rivers and lakes and in the Tahoe National Forest. You can enjoy fishing, swimming, and boating at **Scotts Flat Lake** near Nevada City (east on Calif. 20) and at **Rollins Lake** on Calif. 174, between Grass Valley and Colfax. White-water rafting is available on several rivers. **Tributary Whitewater Tours,** 20480 Woodbury Dr., Grass Valley, CA 95949 (☎ **800/672-3846** or 530/346-6812; www.whitewatertours.com), offers half- to 3-day trips from March through October. The region is also ideal for **mountain biking.** The chambers of commerce publish a trail guide, but there's nowhere to rent a bike in either Nevada City or Grass Valley, so bring your own wheels. For regional **hiking** information, contact **Tahoe National Forest Headquarters**, at Coyote Street and Calif. 49 in Nevada City (☎ **530/265-4531**).

WHERE TO STAY
Nevada City
Deer Creek Inn Bed & Breakfast. 116 Nevada St., Nevada City, CA 95959. ☎ **800/655-0363** or 530/265-0363. Fax 530/265-0980. 5 units. A/C. $95–$145 double. Rates include breakfast. AE, MC, V.

An 1860 three-floor Victorian overlooking Deer Creek and within walking distance of downtown Nevada City, this inn feels like a warm home-away-from-home. The individually decorated rooms, most with private verandas facing the creek or town, are furnished with assorted antiques and four-poster or canopy beds with down comforters. The ceiling fans provide adequate cooling in summer; most bathrooms have clawfoot tubs. A full breakfast is served either out on the deck or in the formal dining room. Guests are invited to try a little panning of their own, fish, play croquet, or simply relax and enjoy the lawn and landscaped rose gardens along the creek.

✪ **Emma Nevada House.** 528 E. Broad St., Nevada City, CA 95959. ☎ **800/916-EMMA** or 530/265-4415. www.nevadacityinns.com. 6 units. $100–$150 double. Rates include breakfast. AE, DC, MC, V.

Innkeeper Ruth Ann Riese runs one of the finest—and prettiest—B&Bs in the Gold Country, a picture-perfect Victorian that was once the childhood home of 19th-century opera star Emma Nevada. You'll like everything about this place: the quiet location, sun-drenched decks, wraparound porch, understated decor, and particularly breakfast, which is served in the beautiful hexagonal Sun Room. The guest rooms range from small and intimate to large and luxurious; all have private bathrooms and queen-size beds, and most are available with phone and TV upon request. Top choice for honeymooners is the Empress's Chamber, with its large wall of windows, soothing ivory and burgundy tones, and—of course—the Jacuzzi tub for two. You'll also like the fact that the shops and restaurants of Nevada City's Historic District are only a short walk away.

National Hotel. 211 Broad St., Nevada City, CA 95959. ☎ **530/265-4551.** 42 units, 30 with private bathroom. A/C TV TEL. $68 double with bathroom; from $113 suite with bathroom. AE, MC, V.

You can't miss this classic three-story Victorian, the oldest hotel in continuous operation west of the Rocky Mountains. It's located near what was once the center of the town's red-light district. The lobby is full of mementos from that era, hence the grandfather clock and early square piano. The suites are replete with gold rush–era antiques and large, cozy beds. Most rooms have private bathrooms, and some come with canopy beds and romantic love seats. A definite bonus during typically sweltering summers is the secluded swimming pool filled with cool mountain water.

The hotel's Victorian dining room, which serves traditional items such as prime rib, steaks, lobster tail, and homemade desserts, also has a gold-rush atmosphere; tables, for example, are lit with coal oil lamps. The hotel provides live entertainment on

Friday and Saturday nights. There's also a popular Sunday brunch, one of the best in the county.

Red Castle Historic Lodgings. 109 Prospect St., Nevada City, CA 95959. ☎ **800/ 761-4766** or 530/265-5135. 7 units. $75–$150 double. Rates include breakfast. MC, V.

This elegant, comfortable hillside inn occupies a four-story Gothic Revival brick house built in 1860; it's situated in a secluded spot with a panoramic view of the town. The highlight of the week is the Sunday-afternoon "Conversations with Mark Twain," in which guests can engage the great author (or at least a reasonable facsimile) in conversation while enjoying such specialties as lemon tarts and a choice cup of tea. The house has retained its original woodwork, plaster moldings, ceiling medallions, and much of the handmade glass; it lacks any modern intrusions, such as TVs and phones. Guests enjoy bountiful five-course buffet breakfasts and relax on the verandas that encircle the first two floors of the house and overlook the rose gardens. Our favorite rooms are the Garden Room, with a canopy bed and French doors leading into the gardens, and the air-conditioned three-room garret suite tucked under the eaves, furnished with sleigh beds and featuring Gothic arched windows.

Grass Valley

Holbrooke Hotel. 212 W. Main St., Grass Valley, CA 95945. ☎ **800/933-7077** or 530/ 273-1353. Fax 530/273-0434. 28 units. A/C TV TEL. $75–$115 double; $130–$155 suite. AE, DC, DISC, MC, V.

This Victorian-era white-clapboard building was a rollicking saloon during the gold-rush days, and then evolved into a place for exhausted miners to "rack out." The oldest and most historic hotel in town, it has hosted a number of legendary figures since opening its doors: Ulysses Grant, Mark Twain, Benjamin Harrison, and Grover Cleveland, among others. Seventeen of the rooms lie within the main building. The remainder are in an adjacent annex, a house occupied long ago by the hotel's owner. Each guest room is decorated with an eclectic collection of gold rush–era furniture and antiques. All have cable TVs tucked away in armoires, and most bathrooms have claw-foot tubs. If you can, reserve one of the larger Veranda rooms, which face Main Street and have access to the balconies; it's well worth the few extra dollars.

Murphy's Inn. 318 Neal St., Grass Valley, CA 95945. ☎ **800/895-2488** or 530/273-6873. www.murphysinn.com. 8 units. A/C TV. $100–$155 double. Rates include breakfast. AE, MC, V.

This 1866 colonial-revival house that was built for Edward Coleman, owner of the North Star mine, has been turned into a crackerjack B&B. Today, it stands at the center of well-tended gardens complete with fountains, a large deck, and a tall sequoia. Guests can relax in the gardens, on the porch, or in two very well-furnished and comfortable living rooms with fireplaces. The rooms are equally alluring, all decorated in a chintzy Victorian style, but each with its own unique charm. Some have fireplaces, all have VCRs, and others, such as the Sequoia Room and Karena's Room, have skylights. Two of the most spacious units, both with fireplaces and one with a full kitchen, are in the Donation Day House.

WHERE TO DINE

Nevada City

✪ **Country Rose Cafe.** 300 Commercial St. ☎ **530/265-6252.** Reservations recommended. Main courses $14–$22. Daily 11am–2:30pm; Mon–Thurs 5–9pm; Fri–Sun 5– 9:30pm; Sun brunch 11am–2:30pm. AE, MC, V. COUNTRY FRENCH.

The flowery country-French atmosphere of this popular Nevada City restaurant belies a serious (and seriously priced) menu put together by owner/chef Michael Johns. Dinner selections, written on a huge board that's lugged over to your table soon after you've been seated, are mostly French with a dash of Italian, Mexican, and American dishes. Skip the lifeless pastas and head straight for John's specialty—fresh fish prepared in a myriad of classic styles such as fillet of sole dore, swordfish oskar, and sea bass with garlic-basil sauce. Other regular menu items include filet mignon, lobster, rack of lamb, and roast game hen, all served with soup and salad. Both lunch (handled by Michael's son Dave) and dinner are served on the pretty walled-in patio in the summer, so be sure to request alfresco seating when making a reservation.

Friar Tucks. 111 N. Pine St. ☎ **530/265-9093.** Main courses $14–$20. AE, MC, V. Sun–Thurs 5–9:30pm; Fri–Sat 5–10pm. INTERNATIONAL.

A local favorite for nearly a quarter of a century, this restaurant consists of a series of rustic, dimly lit rooms furnished with high-backed oak booths. The eclectic menu changes weekly, offering everything from French fondues and Swiss meatballs to teriyaki steak, Tuck's bouillabaisse, fresh seafood, filet mignon, and roast duck. Request a table in the dining room that overlooks Nevada City's Historic District. The accompanying wine list is surprisingly impressive. With the flavor and ambiance of a British pub, the bar is a popular local hangout; a guitar player entertains nightly from 7pm.

Kirby's Creekside Restaurant & Bar. 101 Broad St. ☎ **530/265-3445.** Main courses $14–$20. AE, MC, V. Reservations suggested. Mon–Thurs 11:30am–2:30pm and 5–9:30pm; Fri–Sat 11:30am–2:30pm and 5–10pm; Sun 10am–2:30pm and 5–8:30pm. INTERNATIONAL.

After being royally thumped by the floods of 1997, Kirby's Creekside is back in business serving a wide variety of steak, seafood, pasta, and chicken to the sights and sounds of Deer Creek, which literally flows underneath the restaurant's large wood deck. If possible, forego the low-ceilinged, low-budget dining room for a far more romantic table outdoors. For starters, try the fresh-pumpkin ravioli in sage cream sauce or steamed mussels with chive sauce and sherry aioli. Recommended dinner choices include the oven-roasted leg of lamb with honey-thyme sauce, the stuffed pork chop with orange port sauce, or take a chance with the "Chef's Grand Creation: unique and exotic creations supremely chosen by the chef." Lunch is more modest—sandwiches, burgers, salads, and half a dozen hot entrees, all surprisingly inexpensive.

Grass Valley

Arletta's at the Holbrooke. 212 W. Main St. ☎ **530/273-1353.** Reservations recommended Fri–Sat nights. Main courses $12.50–$18.50. AE, DC, DISC, MC, V. Daily 11:30am–2pm and 5–8:30pm; Sun brunch 10am–2pm. AMERICAN.

This elegant hotel dining room is the most formal place in town—an ironic twist, given its past life as a gold-rush saloon and a flophouse for drunken miners. In its way, it's the most authentic and nostalgic restaurant in a town filled with worthy hard-working competitors. Items on chef Peter Jackson's ever-changing menu range from smoked duck breast with a dried-blueberry bourbon sauce to free-range roast pork loin served with wild rice and pecan fritters. Lunch prices are significantly lower, ranging from $5.75 for a portobello-mushroom-and-tomato sandwich to $6.50 for a tasty chicken-breast sandwich with apple-wood-smoked bacon, herbed mayonnaise, and Monterey Jack on focaccia bread.

Tofanelli's. 302 W. Main St. ☎ **530/272-1468.** Main courses $7–$12. AE, MC, V. Mon–Fri 7am–8:30pm; Sat–Sat brunch 8:30am–3pm, dinner 5–9pm. INTERNATIONAL.

If a diet of meat and potatoes isn't your cup of tea, head to Tofanelli's, which specializes in good—and good for you—entrees for brunch, lunch, and dinner. You'll like the setting, a bright, cheery trio of dining areas (outdoor patio, atrium room, and dining room) separated by exposed brick walls and decorated with beautiful prints and paintings. Specials on the menu, such as Gorgonzola ravioli topped with garlic cream sauce or mu-shu vegetables with baked tofu, change weekly, but you can always rely on Tofanelli classics like Linda's famous vegetarian lasagna and the popular veggie burger.

And yes, they serve good ol' New York steak, too. Don't you dare depart without a slice of Katherine's chocolate cake.

THE CENTRAL GOLD COUNTRY: AMADOR CITY, SUTTER CREEK & JACKSON

Though Placerville is technically the center of the Gold Country, it's the small trio of towns a few miles to the south—Amador City, Sutter Creek, and Jackson—that are far and away the most appealing destination in this beautiful region of rolling hills, dotted with solitary oaks and granite outcroppings. When the mining boom went bust, most of the towns were abandoned; nowadays, most of these restored gold-rush towns rely solely on tourism (hence the rapid conversion of many Victorian homes into B&Bs), though a few mines have reopened recently and are reportedly making a profit.

One of the advantages of staying in this area, 55 miles southeast of Sacramento, is that both the northern and southern regions of the Gold Country are only a few hours' drive away (via very winding roads, however). If you're intent on seeing as much of the Gold Country as possible in a few days' time, any one of these three towns will suffice as a good home base.

To reach Amador City, Sutter Creek, or Jackson from Placerville, head south along Calif. 49 past Plymouth and Drytown. If you're coming straight here from Sacramento, take U.S. 50 to Placerville and head south on Calif. 49; Calif. 16 from Sacramento is another option, but only slightly faster. For more information about any of these towns, contact the **Amador County Chamber of Commerce,** 125 Peek St., Jackson (☎ **209/223-0350**).

AMADOR CITY   Once a bustling mining town, Amador City is now devoted mostly to dredging up tourist dollars. Although Amador City sounds large and impressive, it is in fact so tiny that it holds the title as the smallest incorporated city in California. Local merchants have made the most of a refurbished block-long boardwalk, converting the historic false-fronted buildings into a gallery of sorts; the stores sell everything from turn-of-the-century antiques and folk art to handcrafted furniture, gold-rush memorabilia, rare books, and Native American crafts. Parking can be difficult, however, especially in summer.

SUTTER CREEK   The self-proclaimed "nicest little town in the Mother Lode," Sutter Creek was named after sawmill owner John Sutter, employer of James Marshall (the first white man to discover gold in California). Railroad baron Leland Stanford made his fortune at Sutter Creek's Lincoln Mine, then invested his millions to both build the transcontinental railroad and fund his successful campaign to become governor of California.

The town is a real charmer, lined with beautiful 19th-century buildings in pristine condition, including **Downs Mansion,** the former home of the foreman at Stanford's mine (now a private residence on Spanish St., across from the Immaculate Conception Church), and the landmark **Knight's Foundry,** 81 Eureka St., off Main Street (no phone), the last water-powered foundry and machine shop in the nation. There are also numerous shops and galleries along Main Street, though finding a free parking space can be a real challenge on summer weekends.

JACKSON   Jackson, the county seat of Amador County, is far livelier than its neighboring towns to the north (it was the last place in California to outlaw prostitution). Be sure to take time to stroll through the center of town, browsing in the stores and admiring the Victorian architecture. Although the Kennedy and Argonaut mines ultimately produced more than $140 million in gold, Jackson initially earned its place in the gold rush as a supply center. That history is apparent in the town's wide Main Street, lined by tall buildings adorned with intricate iron railings.

Coloma: Where the Gold Rush Began

Located on Calif. 49 between Auburn and Placerville, the town of Coloma is so small, placid, and unpretentious that it's hard to imagine the significant role it played in the rapid development of California and the West. For it was here that James Marshall, working on John Sutter's mill, first discovered that there was gold aplenty in the foothills of California. Over the next 50 years, 125 *million* ounces of gold were taken from the Sierra foothills, an amount worth a staggering $50 billion today.

Although Marshall and Sutter tried to keep the discovery secret, word soon leaked out. Sam Brannan, who ran a general store at Fort Sutter, secured some gold samples himself—as well as significant amounts of choice Coloma real estate—and then headed for San Francisco, where he ran through the streets shouting, "Gold! Gold! Gold! From the American River!" San Francisco rapidly emptied as men rushed off to seek their fortunes at the mines (and make Sam Brannan's as well).

Coloma was quickly mined out, but its boom brought 10,000 people to the settlement and lasted long enough for residents to build a schoolhouse, a gunsmith, a general store, and a tiny, tin-roofed post office. The miners also planted oak and mimosa trees that shade the street during hot summers. About 70% of this quiet, pretty town lies in the **Marshall Gold Discovery State Historic Park** (☎ **530/622-3470**), which preserves the spot where James Wilson Marshall discovered gold along the banks of the south fork of the American River.

Farther up Main Street is a huge replica of the mill Marshall was building when he made his discovery. The largest building in town, the mill is powered by electricity during the summer. Other attractions in the park include the **Gold Discovery Museum,** which relates the story of the gold rush, and a number of Chinese stores, all that remain of the once sizable local Chinese community. The park also has three picnic areas, four trails, recreational gold panning, and a number of buildings and exhibits relating the way of life that prevailed here in the 19th century. Admission is $5 per vehicle; hours are daily from 10am to 5pm, except on major holidays.

Folks also come here for white-water thrills on the American River (Coloma is a popular launching point). **White Water Connection,** in Coloma (☎ **530/622-6446**), offers half- to 2-day trips down the frothy forks of the American River. It's great fun and one of the Gold Country's best outdoor attractions.

Make no mistake: This is not a ghost town, but rather a modern minicity that has worked to preserve its pre-Victorian influence. At the southern end of the street is the famous **National Hotel,** 2 Water St., at Main Street (☎ **209/223-0500**), rumored to be California's oldest continuously operating hotel since it opened its doors in 1862. Will Rogers, John Wayne, Leland Stanford, and many other celebrities and big-time politicos of the previous century stayed here. Today, the hotel's **Louisiana House Bar**—a cool, dark establishment where weary travelers can rest while a honky-tonk pianist beats out ragtime tunes and classic oldies—does a brisk business (alas, the guest rooms aren't nearly as enjoyable).

Also worth a look is the **Wells Fargo Club and Charcoal Broiler,** located diagonally across the street from the hotel. This two-story brick structure with its wooden balcony and awning is an original 1851 Wells Fargo building. The **Amador County Museum,** a huge brick building at 225 Church St. (☎ **209/223-6386**), is where Will Rogers filmed *Boys Will Be Boys* in 1920. Today, the former home of Armistead Calvin Brown and his

11 children is filled with mining memorabilia and information on two local mines, the Kennedy and the Argonaut, that were among the deepest and richest in the nation. Within the museum is a working large-scale model of the Kennedy. The museum is open Wednesday through Sunday from 10am to 4pm; requested donation is $2. Tours of the museum cost $1 and are offered Saturday and Sunday on the hour from 11am to 3pm.

If you would rather see the real thing, head to the **Kennedy Tailing Wheels Park,** site of the famous Kennedy and Argonaut mines, the deepest in the Mother Lode. The mines have been closed for decades, but the huge tailing wheels and head frames, used to convey mine debris over the hills to a settling pond, remain. To reach the park, take Main Street to Jackson Gate Road, just north of Jackson (no phone).

A few miles south of Jackson on Calif. 49 is one of the most evocative mining towns of the region: **Mokelumne Hill.** The town basically consists of one street overlooking a valley with a few old buildings, and somehow its sad, abandoned air has the mark of authenticity. At one time, the hill was dotted with tents and wood-and-tar-paper shacks, and the town boasted a population of 15,000, including an old French quarter and a Chinatown. But now many of its former residents are merely memorialized in the town's Protestant, Jewish, and Catholic cemeteries.

WHERE TO STAY
Amador City
Imperial Hotel. Main St. (Calif. 49), P.O. Box 195, Amador City, CA 95601. ☎ **800/ 242-5594** or 209/267-9172. 6 units. A/C. $75–$105 double. AE, DISC, MC, V. Located right on Calif. 49, in an 1879 brick Victorian building.

Proprietors Bruce Sherrill and Dale Martin did a brilliant job restoring this stately century-old brick hotel and restaurant, located at the foot of Main Street overlooking Amador City. The individually decorated rooms—all with private bathrooms—are furnished with brass, iron, or pine beds and numerous antiques; two come with private balconies. Our favorite room features hand-painted furnishings by local artist John Johannsen. Amenities include hair dryers and heated towel bars, as well as newspaper delivery and in-room massage upon request. The restaurant, serving Mediterranean/ California cuisine, has a sterling reputation, and hotel guests can take advantage of room service when it's open (see restaurant hours below).

Sutter Creek
✪ **The Foxes.** 77 Main St. (P.O. Box 159), Sutter Creek, CA 95685. ☎ **800/987-3344** or 209/267-5882. www.foxesinn.com. Fax 209/267-0712. 7 units. A/C. $125–$185 double. Rates include breakfast. DISC, MC, V.

This clapboard house, built in 1857, is Sutter Creek's most elegant hostelry. The seven rooms are all uniquely decorated, each with a queen-size bed and down comforters. Four rooms, including the Garden Room and the Fox Den, have wood-burning fireplaces. The Fox Den also has a little library of its own, while the Victorian suite features a 9-foot-tall Renaissance Revival bed and a separate sitting room. Three of the rooms have TVs tucked in armoires, and all have private bathrooms. Breakfast, cooked to order and delivered on silver service along with the morning paper, can be served in your room or in the gazebo in the garden.

✪ **Grey Gables Inn.** 161 Hanford St., Sutter Creek, CA 95685. ☎ **800/473-9422** or 209/ 267-1039. www.greygables.com. 8 units. A/C. $100–$150 double. AE, DC, DISC, MC, V.

A newcomer to Sutter Creek is the Grey Gables Inn, a postcard-perfect replica of a Victorian manor made all the more English by Roger and Sue Garlick, two amicable British expatriates who relish being innkeepers. The two-story B&B is surrounded by terraces of colorful gardens embellished with fountains and vine-covered arbors ("A touch of the English countryside," says Sue). Each of the plushly carpeted guest rooms is named after

A Visit to Volcano

About a dozen miles east of Jackson on Calif. 88 is the enchantingly decrepit town of Volcano—one of the most authentic ghost towns in the central Sierra. The town got its name in 1848, after miners mistook the origins of the enormous craggy boulders that lie in the center of town. The dark rock and blind window frames of a few backless, ivy-covered buildings give the town's main thoroughfare a haunted look. Sprinkled between boarded-up buildings, about a hundred residents do business in the same sagging storefronts that a population of 8,000 frequented nearly 150 years ago.

One thing you'll notice about Volcano is the overwhelming silence of its streets. But the tiny, now-quiet burg has a rich history: Not only was this boomtown once home to 17 hotels, courts of quick justice, and the state's first lending library and astronomical observatory, but Volcano gold also supported the Union during the Civil War. Residents even smuggled a huge cannon to the front line in a hearse (it was never used). The story goes that had the enthusiastic blues fired it, it was so overcharged that "Old Abe" would have exploded. The cannon sits in the town center today, under a rusting weather vane.

Looming over the small buildings is the stately **St. George Hotel** (☎ **209/296-4458**), a three-story, balconied building that testifies to the $90 million in gold mined in and around the town. Its ivy-covered brick and shuttered windows will remind you of colonial New England. The 20-room hotel is still in operation (though not particularly recommended), as is the restaurant, which serves brunch on Sunday, lunch on Saturday, and dinner Tuesday through Sunday. Even if you're not hungry, stop in for a libation at the classic old bar.

In summer, the **Volcano Theatre Company** performs at the town's outdoor amphitheater, hidden behind stone facades on Main Street, a block north of the St. George Hotel. It's a wonderful Gold Country experience. For information on upcoming performances, call ☎ **209/296-2525.** And in early spring, hundreds of people come from all around to picnic amid the nearly half million daffodils in bloom on **Daffodil Hill,** a 4-acre ranch 3 miles north of Volcano (follow the sign on Ram's Horn Grade; no phone).

a British poet; the Byron Room, for example, features hues of deep green and burgundy, dark-wood furnishings, and a Renaissance Revival bed. Aside from the king-size bed in the Brontë Room and Victorian Suite, all rooms have queen beds, gas-log fireplaces, large armoires, and private bathrooms (a few with clawfoot tubs). Breakfast, delivered on fine English bone china, is served either in the formal dining room adjacent to the Victorian parlor or in your room. The only flaw in an otherwise perfect B&B is the bit-too-close proximity to heavily traveled Calif. 49, but once inside you'll hardly notice. *Note:* The shops and restaurants of Sutter Creek are within walking distance.

Jackson

Court Street Inn. 215 Court St., Jackson, CA 95642. ☎ **800/200-0416** or 209/223-0416. www.courtstreetinn.com. 7 units. A/C. $95–$190 double. Rates include breakfast. AE, DISC, MC, V.

Two blocks from Main Street, this Victorian beauty—listed on the National Register of Historic Places—was built in 1870 and is brimming with elegant details such as eyelash shutters, embossed ceilings, and a Carrara-marble fireplace. Our favorite room is Angel Court, with its oak-mantled fireplace and handsome four-poster king-size bed. Romantics will like the Rose Court's private sitting room and four-poster wicker bed, or the separate and secluded Garden Court with its own private terrace, skylight, and corner fireplace. The guest rooms are very nicely decorated; all have down bedding, and some have fireplaces and whirlpool or clawfoot tubs. The separate two-story/two-bedroom Indian House cottage can accommodate up to four guests. There's a porch where guests can relax on the swing, and an outdoor hot tub that's ideal for stargazing. A full home-made breakfast (served outside on the terrace on sunny days) and complimentary evening refreshments are included in the room rate. TVs are available on request.

WHERE TO DINE
Amador City
✪ **Imperial Hotel.** Main St. (Calif. 49). ☎ **209/267-9172.** Reservations recommended. Main courses $14–$24. AE, MC, V. Daily 5–9pm. MEDITERRANEAN/CALIFORNIA.

This restored 1879 hotel has been recommended already, but even if you aren't staying here, its restaurant is worth a detour. There are only about seven main dishes offered on executive chef Rhonda Uhlmann's seasonally changing menu, but whatever you choose will undoubtedly be good. You might try the sea bass with honey soy glaze and ginger butter sauce, or a pan-roasted rib-eye steak topped with gorgonzola Maui onion sauce. People with smaller appetites can order a lighter version of each entree, all of which come with soup or tossed green salad and fresh seasonal vegetables. The desserts are equally impressive. And if you put your name on the waiting list for their New Year's celebration, you might get a seat by the year 2004—it's that popular.

Sutter Creek
✪ **Zinfandels.** 51 Hanford St. ☎ **209/267-5008.** Reservations recommended. Main courses $12.95–$19.95. AE, DC, DISC, MC, V. Thurs–Sun 5:30–9:30pm. CALIFORNIA.

Greg and Kelley West's Zinfandels has received nothing but kudos since it first opened in July 1996. Greg, a 6-year veteran of Greens (a highly respected vegetarian restaurant in San Francisco; see chapter 4), is responsible for the entrees, while his wife, Kelley, bakes the breads and pastries. Though the emphasis is on low-fat vegetarian fare such as butternut-squash risotto with pancetta, leeks, crimini mushrooms, and spinach, West also offers a trio of fresh fish, chicken, and beef dishes ranging from cannelloni filled with lamb sausage, chard, and smoked mozzarella to Patrale sole with a citrus-ginger beurre blanc. The menu changes weekly to take advantage of seasonal produce from local farms, and even the wines—paired with each dish—are provided by local wineries such as Stevenot and Ironstone. An appealing alternative to a full sit-down dinner is the wine tasting/appetizer/dessert/espresso room downstairs.

Jackson
Mel and Faye's Diner. 205 Calif. 49 (at Main St.). ☎ **209/223-0853.** Menu items $3–$6. No credit cards. Daily 4:45am–10pm. AMERICAN.

How can anybody not love a classic old diner? In business since 1956, Mel and Faye have been cranking out the best diner food in the Gold Country for so long that it's okay to not feel guilty for salivating over the thought of a sloppy double cheeseburger smothered with onions and special sauce and washed down with a large chocolate shake, and could you please add a large side of fries with that and how much is a slice of pie? It's a time-honored Jackson tradition.

Upstairs Restaurant & Streetside Bistro. 164 Main St. ☎ **209/223-3342.** Reservations recommended. Main courses $15–$27. AE, DISC, MC, V. Tues–Fri 11:30am–2:30pm; Sat–Sun 11:30am–3:30pm; daily 5:30–9pm. INTERNATIONAL.

This adorable little restaurant offers a limited menu that changes weekly, but you might stumble on some true culinary gems, such as pasta puttanesca with tomato-basil fettuccine and fresh Roma tomatoes, or duck julienned and served with a blackberry-ginger port sauce. Layne McCollum, a graduate of California's Culinary Academy, is known as the town's finest and most sophisticated chef, with a reputation for imaginative and innovative cuisine. Crisp white linens, bowls of fresh flowers, and background music provide a romantic backdrop to the restaurant's 12 candlelit tables. Lunch—quiche, soups, salads, and gourmet sandwiches such as smoked pork loin with red chili pesto on chipotle—is served until about 3pm in the bright, cheery Streetside Bistro, which is tastefully outfitted with wrought-iron furniture, tile flooring, and colorful oil paintings.

THE SOUTHERN GOLD COUNTRY: ANGELS CAMP, MURPHYS, COLUMBIA, SONORA & JAMESTOWN

No other region in the Gold Country offers more to see and do than these towns in the south, 86 miles southeast of Sacramento. From exploring enormous caverns to riding in the stagecoach and panning for real gold, the neighboring towns of Angels Camp, Murphys, Columbia, Sonora, and Jamestown offer a cornucopia of gold rush–related sites, museums, and activities. It's a great place to bring the family (kids love roaming around the dusty car-free streets of Columbia), and the region offers some of the best lodgings and restaurants in the Gold Country. In short, if you're the Type-A sort who needs to stay active, the southern Gold Country is for you.

To reach any of these towns from Sacramento, head south on Calif. 99 to Stockton, then take Calif. 4 east directly into Angels Camp (from here, it's a short, scenic drive to all the other towns). For a much longer but more scenic route, take U.S. 50 east to Placerville and head south on Calif. 49, which also takes you directly to Angels Camp.

ANGELS CAMP You've probably heard of Angels Camp, the town that inspired Mark Twain to pen "The Celebrated Jumping Frog of Calaveras County."

This pretty, peaceful Gold Country community is built on hills that are honeycombed with mine tunnels. In the 1880s and 1890s, five mines were located along Main Street—Sultana, Angel's, Lightner, Utica, and Stickle—and the town echoed with noise as more than 200 stamps crushed the ore. Between 1886 and 1910, the five mines generated close to $20 million.

But a far-more lasting legacy than the town's gold production is the **Jumping Frog Jubilee,** started in 1928 to mark the paving of the town's streets. To this day, the ribbiting competition takes place every third weekend in May. The record, 21 feet, 5¾ inches, was jumped in 1986 by "Rosie the Ribiter," beating the old world record by 4½ inches. Livestock exhibitions, pageants, cook-offs, arm-wrestling tournaments, live music, carnival rides, a rodeo, and plenty of beer and wine keep the thousands of spectators entertained between jump-offs (heck, you can even rent a frog if you forget to pack one). For more information and entry forms ($5 per frog), call the Jumping Frog Jubilee headquarters at ☎ **209/736-2561.**

MURPHYS From Angels Camp, a 20-minute drive east along Calif. 4 takes you to Murphys, one of our favorite Gold Country towns. Legend has it Murphys started as a former trading post set up by brothers Dan and John Murphy in cooperation with local Indians (John married the chief's daughter). These days, its peaceful community is made up of gingerbread Victorians shaded by tall locust trees bordering narrow streets. Be sure to take a stroll down Main Street, stopping in **Grounds** for a bite to eat (see "Where to Dine," below) and perhaps a cool draft of Murphys Red—direct from **Murphys Brewing Company**—at the rustic saloon within Murphys Historic Hotel and Lodge.

While you're here, you might also want to check out **Ironstone Vineyards,** 1894 Six Mile Rd., 1 mile south of downtown Murphys (☎ **209/728-1251**), a veritable wine theme park built by the Kautz family. It boasts an enormous tasting room, jewelry shop, museum housing the largest crystalline gold piece in existence, gallery, amphitheater, music room, caverns, park and gardens, and even a culinary center. It's open daily from 10am to 5pm.

How to Pan for Gold

Find a gold pan, ideally a 12- to 15-inch steel pan. Place the pan over an oven burner, or better yet, in a campfire. This will darken the pan, making it easier to see any flakes of placer gold (many gold pans come already blackened). Find some gravel, sand, or dirt in a stream that looks promising or feels lucky. Scoop dirt into the pan until it's nearly full, then place it under water and keep it there while you break up the clumps of mud and clay and toss out any stones. Then grasp the pan with both hands. Holding it level, rotate it in swirling motions. This will cause the heavier gold to loosen and settle to the bottom of the pan. Drain off the dirty water and loose stuff. Keep doing this until gold and heavier minerals called "black sand" are left in the pan. Carefully inspect the black sand for nuggets or speck traces of gold. Who knows? You just might get lucky.

If this all seems too much to try on your own, you can sign up for a gold-panning lesson with Jamestown's ✪**Gold Prospecting Expeditions** (☎ **800/596-0009** or 209/984-4653). The hour-long instruction costs about $15, and yes, you get to keep any gold you might find.

Also in the vicinity—just off Calif. 4, 1 mile north of Murphys off Sheep Ranch Road—are the **Mercer Caverns** (☎ **209/728-2101**). These caverns, discovered in 1885 by Walter Mercer, contain a variety of geological formations—crystalline stalactites and stalagmites—in a series of descending chambers. Tours of the well-lit caverns take about 55 minutes. From Memorial Day through September, hours are Sunday through Thursday from 9am to 6pm, Friday and Saturday from 9am to 8pm; October through May, Sunday through Thursday from 10am to 4:30pm, Friday and Saturday from 10am to 6pm. Admission is $7 for adults, $3.50 for children 5 to 11, and free for children 4 and under.

Fifteen miles east of Murphys up Calif. 4 is **Calaveras Big Trees State Park** (☎ 209/795-2334), where you can witness giant sequoias that are among the biggest and oldest living things on earth. It's a popular summer retreat that offers camping, swimming, hiking, and fishing along the Stanislaus River. It's open daily; admission is $5 per car for day use.

COLUMBIA   Though somewhat hokey and contrived, **Columbia State Historic Park** (☎ 209/532-4301 for the museum) is the best maintained gold-rush town in the Mother Lode (as well as one of the most popular, so expect crowds in the summer). At one point, this boisterous mining town was the state's second largest city (and only two votes shy of becoming the state capital over Sacramento). When gold mining no longer panned out in the late 1850s, most of the town's 15,000 residents departed, leaving much of the mining equipment and buildings in place. In 1945, the entire town was turned into a Historic Park.

As a result, Columbia has been preserved and functions much as it did in the 1850s, with stagecoach rides, western-style Victorian hotels and saloons, a newspaper office, a working blacksmith's forge, a Wells Fargo express office, and numerous other relics of California's early mining days. Cars are banned from its dusty streets, giving the shady town an authentic and uncommercial feel. Merchants still do business behind some storefronts, as horse, stagecoach, and pedestrian traffic wanders by.

If Columbia's heat and dust get to you, pull up a stool at the **Jack Douglass Saloon** (☎ 209/533-2355) on Main Street, open daily from 10am to 5pm. Inside the swinging doors of the classic western bar, you can sample homemade sarsaparilla and wild cherry, drinks the saloon has been serving since 1857. The storefront's large shuttered windows open onto a dusty main street, so put up your boots, relax awhile, and watch the stagecoach go by.

SONORA   Located a few miles south of Columbia, Sonora is the largest town in southern Gold Country (you'll know you've arrived when traffic starts to crawl). Back in the gold-rush days, Sonora and Columbia were the two richest towns in the Mother Lode. Dozens of stores and small cafes line the main thoroughfare. If you can find a parking space, it's worth your while to spend an hour or two checking out the sites, including the 19th-century **St. James Episcopal Church,** at the top of Washington Street, and the **Tuolumne County Museum and History Center,** 158 W. Bradford Ave. (☎ 209/532-1317), located in the 1857 County Jail. Admission is free, and it's open daily year-round: Sunday, Monday, and Wednesday from 9am to 4pm; Tuesday and Thursday from 10am to 4pm; and Saturday from 10am to 3:30pm.

JAMESTOWN   About 4 miles southwest of Sonora on Calif. 49 is Jamestown, a 4-block-long town of old-fashioned storefronts and two charming turn-of-the-century hotels. Yes, there's gold in these parts, too, as the marker commemorating the discovery of a 75-pound nugget will attest (panning nearby Woods Creek is a popular pastime among both locals and tourists). If Jamestown looks eerily familiar to you, that's probably because you've seen it in the movies or on television. It's one of Hollywood's favorite western movie sets; scenes from such films as *Butch Cassidy and the Sundance Kid* were shot here.

Jamestown's most popular attraction is the **Railtown 1897 State Historic Park,** a train buff's paradise featuring three original Sierra steam locomotives. These great machines were used in many a movie and television show, including *High Noon, Little House on the Prairie, Bonanza,* and *My Little Chickadee.* The trains at the roundhouse are on display daily year-round. Call for information on weekend rides and guided tours. The Depot Store and Museum are open daily from 9:30am to 4:30pm. The park is located near the center of town, on Fifth Avenue at Reservoir Road (☎ 209/ 984-3953).

WHERE TO STAY
Angels Camp
Cooper House Bed & Breakfast Inn. 1184 Church St. (P.O. Box 1388), Angels Camp, CA 95222. ☎ **800/225-3764,** ext. 326, or 209/736-2145. 3 units. A/C. $105 double. Rates include breakfast. DISC, MC, V.

Once the home and office of a prominent community physician, Dr. George P. Cooper, the Cooper House is now Angels Camp's only B&B. This small Arts and Crafts home is mercifully positioned well away from the hustle and bustle of the town's Main Street. Owner/innkeeper Kathy Reese maintains three units, all with private bathrooms. The Zinfandel Suite has its own private entrance and deck, and the Chardonnay Suite has a king-size bed, antique clawfoot bathtub, and a private deck. The third bedroom, the Cabernet Suite, is midsized, with a queen bed, adjoining sunroom, and splendid garden view.

Murphys
✪ **Dunbar House, 1880.** 271 Jones St., Murphys, CA 95247. ☎ **800/692-6006** or 209/ 728-2897. www.dunbarhouse.com. 4 units. A/C TV TEL. $135 double; $195 suite. Rates include breakfast. AE, MC, V.

This pretty Italianate home, built in 1880 for the bride of a local businessman, is one of the finest B&Bs in the Gold Country. The inviting front porch, which overlooks the exquisite gardens, is decorated with wicker furniture and hanging baskets of ivy. Inside, the emphasis is on comfort and elegance. The rooms are furnished with quality antiques and equipped with every possible amenity. Beds have lace-trimmed linens and down comforters, and each room has a wood-burning stove and personal fridge stocked with mineral water and a complimentary bottle of wine. Other extras include a TV/VCR, makeup mirror, and hair dryer, plus his-and-her reading lamps. Our favorite room, the

Cedar, is a fabulous two-room suite with a private sunporch, whirlpool tub, and complimentary champagne. We also like the Sugar Pine suite, with its private balcony in the trees. Lemonade and cookies are offered in the afternoon, appetizers and wine in the early evening. Breakfast is served in your room, the dining room, or the garden.

Columbia
City Hotel. Main St. (P.O. Box 1870), Columbia State Park, CA 95310. ☎ **800/532-1479** or 209/532-1479. Fax 209/532-7027. 10 units, all with shared bathroom. A/C. $85–$105 double. Rates include breakfast. AE, DISC, MC, V.

Established in 1856, the historic City Hotel was fully restored in 1975 by the State of California, the nonprofit City Hotel Corporation, and Columbia College, and is now run as a sort of on-the-job training center for hospitality-management students (hence the eager-to-please staff). It's a big, beautiful building, complete with a stately parlor furnished with Victorian sofas, antiques, and Oriental rugs. The largest guest rooms have two balconies overlooking Main Street; the units off the parlor are also spacious. The hallway rooms are smaller, but still nicely furnished with Renaissance Revival beds and antiques. Each room has a sink and toilet. A large buffet breakfast is served in the dining room. The hotel also runs a fine-dining restaurant serving classic continental cuisine (roast rack of lamb, grilled salmon, smoked duck breast) Tuesday through Sunday, as well as the What Cheer saloon.

Fallon Hotel. Washington St. (P.O. Box 1870), Columbia State Park, CA 95310. ☎ **800/532-1479** or 209/532-1470. www.cityhotel.com. 14 units, 13 with shared bathroom. A/C. $50–$115 double. Rates include breakfast. AE, DISC, MC, V.

This hotel, which opened in 1857, has been restored and decorated to evoke the 1890s. The classic two-story building has retained many of its original antiques and furniture. The largest rooms are those along the front upper balcony. Only one unit has a full bathroom; the rest have a private sink and toilet, and showers are down the hall. The rooms are furnished with high-backed Victorian beds, marble-topped dressers, rockers, and similar oak pieces. A full breakfast is served in the downstairs parlor.

Sonora
✪ Serenity. 15305 Bear Cub Dr., Sonora, CA 95370. ☎ **800/426-1441** or 209/533-1441. 4 units. A/C. $100–$135 double. Rates include breakfast. AE, DISC, MC, V. From Sonora, take Business 108 east to Calif. 108 to Phoenix Lake Rd. Turn left and proceed for 3 miles to Bear Cub Dr.; turn right.

This B&B, set on 6 acres outside of town, affords an opportunity to enjoy the beauty, peace, and quiet of the area's deer-filled oak and pine forest. A traditional wood house with a wraparound porch, it has all the comforts of home—and then some. Beds are made with lace-trimmed linens, and each room has a sitting area and private bathroom; two have remote-control gas-log fireplaces. One unit has a four-poster, another a white-iron bed. Breakfast, served in the formal dining room, is a veritable feast. If it's a soothing, serene respite that you desire, this is the place.

Jamestown
Jamestown Hotel. Main St. (P.O. Box 539), Jamestown, CA 95327. ☎ **800/205-4901** or 209/984-3902. Fax 209/984-4149. 10 units. A/C. $70–$135 double; $125 suite. Rates include continental breakfast. AE, DISC, MC, V.

The most worked-over building in town, the Jamestown was originally built in 1858; it burned down and was rebuilt twice before 1915. To achieve the old-fashioned, brick-fronted Victorian look it sports today, its current owners ripped out a lot of stucco and Spanish-revival paraphernalia. Much of the lower floor is devoted to the front office, bar, and restaurant (see "Where to Dine," below). The second floor contains a cadre of cozy bedrooms outfitted with antiques acquired along both coasts of North America. All of the spacious rooms are loaded with nostalgic charm; a few have sitting rooms, and all have a private bathroom (some with clawfoot tubs). The street-level rooms are the most luxurious, outfitted with whirlpool tubs, TV/VCRs, private patios, and individual heat/AC controls.

National Hotel. 77 Main St. (P.O. Box 502), Jamestown, CA 95327. ☎ **800/894-3446** or 209/984-3446. Fax 209/984-5620. 11 units. A/C. $80–$120 double. Rates include continental breakfast. AE, CB, DC, DISC, MC, V.

Located in the center of town, this two-story classic western hotel has been operating since 1859, making it one of the ten oldest continuously operating hotels in the state. The saloon has its original 19th-century redwood bar, and you can imagine what it must have been like when miners traded gold dust for drinks. The rooms above are outfitted with numerous period antiques, as well as oak furnishings and brass beds made up with quilts. A recent addition is an authentic "Soaking Room," a private room equipped with a sort of 1800s clawfoot Jacuzzi for two (when cowboys longed for a good, hot soak). All units have private bathrooms. The restaurant on the main floor serves continental cuisine with a California influence, such as brandy-apple pork, ruby trout amandine, and blackened prime rib with sautéed prawns.

WHERE TO DINE
Angels Camp

B of A Cafe. 1262 S. Main St. ☎ **209/736-0765.** Main courses $9–$15. MC, V. Daily 11am– 3pm; Thurs and Sun 5:30–8pm; Fri–Sat 5:30–9pm. Cafe opens daily at 8am. AMERICAN.

Katherine Reese, who also runs the Cooper House Bed & Breakfast Inn, has done a marvelous job restoring and converting this 1936 Bank of America building into a bright, cheerful cafe. Using leftover banking curios, she decorated the walls with polished teller windows and converted the vault into a wine-tasting room. Lunch items range from country-style quiche du jour and gourmet baby-green salad to roasted eggplant sandwiches on multigrain bread. Dinners include sliced pork loin marinated with Australian maple wood, lemon rosemary chicken, prime rib, and mesquite-marinated baby-back ribs. Daily specials include fresh fish, pasta, and vegetables, and all entrees come with fresh bread, soup or salad, and Kathy's Famous Herbed Roasted Red Potatoes. Basque-style dinners (steak, chicken, or lamb with tureens of soup, salad, and pasta for $15 per person) are served Sunday between 5 and 8pm, but be sure to make a reservation—tables fill up fast.

✪ Camps. 676 McCauley Ranch Rd. (a half mile west of Calif. 4/Calif. 49 junction off Angel Oaks Dr.). ☎ **209/736-8181.** Reservations recommended. Main courses $12.50–$22.50. AE, MC, V. Tues–Sat 11:30am–3pm; Wed–Sun 5:30–9pm; Sun brunch 11am–3pm. FUSION.

Located on the edge of a sprawling golf resort on the western fringes of Angels Camp is Camps, the culinary feather in the cap of Greenhorn Creek, one of northern California's newest destination retreats. The restaurant's architects have successfully integrated the building into its natural surroundings by constructing the outer walls with locally mined ryolite and painting it in natural earth tones. The interior is furnished with leather armchairs, wicker, and antique woods. The best seats in the house are on the spacious veranda overlooking the golf course, the perfect setting for executive chef Renee Gianettoni's fusion cuisine, a culinary composition that pairs local produce with European, Asian, and Caribbean influences. Though the menu changes seasonally, a typical dish may be a roti of duck with kumquat and sun-dried cherries, cooked crisp and basted with rosemary jus. The wildflower salad with American field greens, toasted pine nuts, and a raspberry hazelnut vinaigrette is marvelous, as is the marinated demi-rack of lamb, grilled with an essence of sweet bay and fresh thyme and served with a vegetable couscous.

Murphys

✪ **Grounds.** 402 Main St. ☎ **209/728-8663.** Reservations recommended. Main courses $7.50–$15.50. DISC, MC, V. Tue 7am–4pm; Wed–Mon 7am–9pm. ECLECTIC.

When River Klass moved here from the East Coast to open his own place, Murphys' restaurant-challenged residents heaved a collective sigh of relief. Its nickname is the "Rude Boy Cafe," but you'll find only happy smiles and friendly service from the energetic staff. The majority of Klass's business is with the locals, who have become addicted to the potato pancakes that come with every made-to-order omelet. For lunch, try the sausage sandwich on house-baked bread or the grilled eggplant sandwich stuffed with smoked mozzarella and fresh basil. Although the menus change twice a week, typical dinner choices include fettuccine topped with sautéed shrimp, halibut, and mussels in a garlic cream sauce; grilled halibut served with rock shrimp and spinach dumplings; and a big, fat Angus rib eye served with fresh grilled vegetables and garlic mashed potatoes. The wine list is equally impressive (and reasonably priced). The long, narrow dining rooms are bright and airy with pinewood furnishings, wood floors, and an open kitchen. On sunny days, request a table on the back patio.

Sonora

Good Heavens. 49 N. Washington St. ☎ **209/532-3663.** Main courses $5–$10 lunch, $10–$15 dinner. DISC, MC, V. Wed–Mon 11am–3pm; summer Thurs–Sun 5–9pm; winter Fri–Sat 5–9pm. AMERICAN.

This small, homey cafe is one of our favorite places to eat in the Gold Country. The lunch menu features a variety of unusual yet wonderful sandwiches—cucumber and pesto cream, turkey and cranberry orange—plus an array of delicious soups, salads, and desserts. There are several daily lunch specials as well, ranging from chiles rellenos to crepes and pastas. They've just recently added a dinner menu, featuring such dishes as a hearty beef loin pot roast with potatoes, carrots, and gravy; Cornish game hen with fresh cornbread and vegetables; and a wonderful honey-fried chicken with a crispy buttermilk crust. Each meal starts with fresh herb-and-cheese biscuits and a choice of freshly made jams, such as the decadent raspberry chocolate or the tart orange marmalade. Don't leave without purchasing a jar or two; they're sold at the counter.

North Beach Cafe. 14317 Mono Way/Calif. 108 (from central Sonora, go 3 miles east on Calif. 108 to John's Sierra Market, turn right into parking lot). ☎ **209/536-1852.** Main courses $7.50–$12.50. Daily 11am–9pm. AE, MC V. ITALIAN.

Chef/owner Terry La Torre has turned this former auto-parts store into one of the most popular restaurants in Sonora. A longtime local and progeny of San Francisco restaurateurs, the well-rounded, mustachioed La Torre can usually be found draped in chef's whites, barking orders to his amiable staff. The place is almost always abuzz with customers who come to eat La Torre's cooking and to bask in his infectious pomposity. The menu is predominantly Italian, including a dozen or so pastas, fresh fish, veal, chicken, and steaks. The lunch menu is less complex, ranging from chicken or steak sandwiches to burgers, soups, and salads. La Torre tends to be a bit heavy-handed with the sauces; we usually request that he halves the regular amount. Otherwise, the combination of fair prices, good food, and classic La Torre histrionics makes North Beach Cafe worth searching out.

3 The Central Valley & Sierra National Forest

The Central Valley (also known as the San Joaquin Valley) is about as far as you can get from California's glamorous movie-stars-in-stretch-limos image. This hot, flat strip of farms, dairies, fast-food joints, cheap motels, and truck stops stretches for some 225 miles from Bakersfield to Redding. The 18,000-square-mile valley is central to the economy of the Golden State, in part because of its cultivated and irrigated fields, orchards, pastures, and vineyards.

The major traffic arteries through the valley are Calif. 99 and I-5. Calif. 99 links the agricultural communities, while I-5 provides access routes to the roadside attractions in the valley. Rivers cutting through the valley offer fishing, boating, houseboating on the delta, and white-water rafting on the rapids. And the valley's spectacular landscapes provide unrivaled natural beauty; many visitors drive through in spring just to view the orchards in bloom.

The Central Valley also stands on the doorstep of some of America's greatest attractions, the most well known being Yosemite National Park. See chapter 9 for coverage of two Central Valley towns, Merced and Visalia, which are good gateways to Yosemite, Sequoia, and Kings Canyon, respectively.

Fresno, although not much in itself, is on the doorstep of the Sierra National Forest and nearby natural attractions like the Millerton Lake State Recreation Area.

FRESNO

The running joke in California is that Fresno is the "gateway to Bakersfield." For most visitors, Fresno, located 185 miles southeast of San Francisco, is just a place to pass through en route to the state parks; it can, however, be a good place to stop for food and lodging, and it makes a good base for exploring the Sierra National Forest (see below). But be careful if you're looking for a bargain at one of the cheap motels along the highway—security may be questionable.

Founded in 1874 in the geographic center of the state, Fresno lies in the heart of the Central Valley and has experienced incredible growth in recent years. Like most growing cities, it has been plagued by an increase in crime, drugs, and urban sprawl.

As the seat of Fresno County, the city handles more than $3 billion annually in agricultural production. It also contains Sun Maid, the world's largest dried-fruit packing plant, and Guild, one of the country's largest wineries.

If you have any reason at all to be in Fresno, try to visit between late February and late March so you can drive the **Fresno County Blossom Trail**. This 62-mile, self-guided tour takes in the beauty of California's agrarian bounty at its peak. The trail courses through fruit orchards in full bloom and citrus groves with lovely orange blossoms and a heady natural perfume. The **Fresno Convention and Visitors Bureau,** 808 M St. in Fresno (☎ **800/788-0836** or 559/233-0836), supplies full details, including a map.

WHERE TO STAY

San Joaquin. 1309 W. Shaw Ave., Fresno, CA 93711. ☎ **800/775-1309** or 559/225-1309. Fax 559/225-6021. 68 suites. A/C TV TEL. $82–$89 junior suite; $125 1-bedroom suite with kitchen; $165 2-bedroom suite with kitchen; $185 3-bedroom suite with kitchen. Rates include breakfast. AE, DC, DISC, MC, V.

Set on the northern edge of Fresno, this full-service hotel was conceived as an apartment complex in the 1970s. Around 1985, a lobby was added, the floor plans were adjusted, and the place was reconfigured as an all-suite hotel. Each suite is outfitted in a slightly different style, with light, contemporary colors and furniture. Room service is available from an independently managed restaurant down the street.

WHERE TO DINE

✪ **Veni, Vidi, Vici.** 1116 N. Fulton. ☎ **559/266-5510.** Reservations recommended. Main courses $16–$23. AE, CB, MC, V. Tue–Sun 5:30–10pm (late-night menu Fri–Sat 10pm–midnight). NORTHERN CALIFORNIA.

The most innovative and creative restaurant in Fresno occupies a prominent position about 6 miles south of the commercial center, in a funky neighborhood known as the

Tower District. The place's rustic exterior strikes an interesting contrast to the polished and artful interior on the other side of the 15-foot doors, where the decor is accented with exposed brick walls, hanging mirrors, and chandeliers fashioned from twisted wire and metal leaves.

The menu changes often, but might include roasted loin of pork with Chinese black beans and citrus-flavored glaze, served with grilled portobello mushrooms, sun-dried tomatoes, risotto, and red-pepper coulis; or a wild-mushroom lasagna with preserved tomato sauce. There are also fresh-fish specials nightly. This is the only restaurant in Fresno that makes its own ice cream (the flavor of the day when we arrived was Technicolor lime sorbet). Have a scoop or two with the restaurant's perennial dessert favorite: bittersweet chocolate cake.

SIERRA NATIONAL FOREST

Leaving Fresno's taco joints, used-car lots, and tract houses behind, an hour's drive and 45 miles northeast gets you to the Sierra National Forest, a land of lakes and coniferous forests lying between Yosemite, Sequoia, and Kings Canyon national parks. The entire eastern portion of the park is still unspoiled wilderness protected by the government. Development—some of it, unfortunately, beside the bigger lakes and reservoirs—is confined to the western side.

The 1.3-million-acre forest contains 528,000 acres of wilderness. The Sierra's five wilderness areas include Ansel Adams, Dinkey Lakes, John Muir, Kaiser, and Monarch (see below). The forest offers plenty of opportunities for fishing, swimming, sailing, boating, camping, water-skiing, white-water rafting, kayaking, and horseback riding, all regulated by certain guidelines. Downhill and cross-country skiing, as well as hunting, are also available, depending on the season. Backpackers looking to retreat to the wilderness will find solace here, as the park is traversed by some 1,100 miles of forest hiking trails.

In the lower elevations, summer temperatures can frequently reach 100°F, but in the higher elevations, more comfortable temperatures in the 70s and 80s are the norm.

After visiting the ranger station at Oakhurst, take Calif. 41 to Calif. 49, the major road into the northern part of the national forest. This is more convenient for visitors approaching the park from northern California. Calif. 168 via Clovis is the primary route from Fresno if you're headed for Shaver Lake. There is no approach road from the eastern Sierra, only from the west.

To learn about hiking, camping, or other activities, or to obtain the fire and wilderness permits needed for backcountry jaunts, visit one of the ranger stations in the park's western section. These include **Minarets Ranger Station,** 57003 North Fork (☎ **559/877-2218**); **Kings River Ranger District,** 34849 Maxon Rd., Sanger, near the Pine Flat Reservoir (☎ **559/855-8321**); and the **Pineridge Ranger Station,** 29688 Auberry Rd., Prather (☎ **559/855-5360**).

Shaver Lake is one place where you can stock up on goods and supplies if you're going into the wilderness, but stores in Fresno carry much of the same stuff at lower prices. Cheaper supplies are also available in the town of Clovis outside Fresno (which you must pass through en route to the forest), especially at the **Peacock Market,** at Tollhouse Road (Third St.) and Sunnyside Avenue (☎ **559/299-6627**).

THE MAJOR WILDERNESS & RECREATION AREAS

ANSEL ADAMS WILDERNESS   Divided between the Sierra and Inyo national forests, this wilderness area covers 228,500 acres. Elevations range from 3,500 to 13,157 feet. The frost-free period extends from mid-July through August, the best time for a visit to the park's upper altitudes.

Ansel Adams is dotted with scenic alpine vistas, including steep-walled gorges and barren granite peaks. There are several small glaciers in the north and some fairly large lakes on the eastern slope of the precipitous Ritter Range. This vast wilderness has excellent stream and lake fishing, especially for rainbow, golden, and brook trout, and offers challenging mountain climbing on the Minarets Range. The wilderness is accessed by the Tioga Pass Road in the north, U.S. 395 and Reds Meadow Road in the east, the Minarets Highway in the west, and Calif. 168 to High Sierra in the south.

DINKEY LAKES WILDERNESS   The 30,000-acre Dinkey Lakes area was created in 1984 and occupies the western slope of the Sierra Nevada, southeast of Huntington Lake and just northwest of Courtright Reservoir. Most of the timbered, rolling terrain here is 8,000 feet above sea level, reaching its highest point (10,619 feet) at Three Sisters Peak. Sixteen lakes are clustered in the west-central region. You can reach the area on Kaiser Pass Road (north), Red/Coyote Jeep Road (west), Rock Creek Road (southwest), or Courtright Reservoir (southeast), generally from mid-June to late October.

JOHN MUIR WILDERNESS   Occupying 584,000 acres in the Sierra and Inyo national forests, John Muir Wilderness—named after the turn-of-the-century naturalist—extends southeast from Mammoth Lakes along the crest of the Sierra Nevada for 30 miles before forking around the boundary of Kings Canyon National Park to Crown Valley and Mount Whitney. Elevations range from 4,000 to 14,496 feet at Mount Whitney, with many of the area's peaks surpassing 12,000 feet.

Split by deep canyons, the wilderness is also a land of meadows (especially beautiful when wildflowers bloom), lakes, and streams. The south and middle forks of the San Joaquin River, the north fork of Kings River, and many creeks draining into Owens Valley originate in the John Muir Wilderness. Mountain hemlock, red and white fir, and whitebark and western pine dot the park's landscape. Temperatures vary wildly throughout any 24-hour period: Summer temperatures range from 25°F to 85°F, and the only really frost-free period is between mid-July and August. The higher elevations are marked by barren expanses of granite splashed with many glacially carved lakes.

KAISER WILDERNESS   Immediately north of Huntington Lake and some 70 miles northeast of Fresno, Kaiser is a 22,700-acre forest tract commanding a view of the central Sierra Nevada. It was named after Kaiser Ridge, which divides the area into two different regions. Four trailheads provide easy access to the wilderness, but the northern half is much more open than the forested southern half; the primary point of entry is the Sample Meadow Campground. All other lakes are approached cross-country. Winter storms begin to blow in late October, and the grounds are generally snow-covered until early June.

MONARCH WILDERNESS   This area extends across 45,000 acres in the Sierra and Sequoia national forests. The Sierra National Forest portion of the region—about 21,000 acres—is very rugged and hard to traverse. Steep slopes climb from the middle and main forks of Kings River, with elevations increasing from 2,400 to more than 10,000 feet. Rock outcroppings are found throughout Monarch, and most of the lower elevations are mainly chaparral covered with pine stands near the tops of the higher peaks.

HUNTINGTON LAKE RECREATION AREA   At 7,000 feet, this area is a 2-hour drive east of Fresno via Calif. 168. The lake is one of the reservoirs in the Big Creek Hydroelectric System and has 14 miles of shoreline. It's a popular recreational area, offering camping, hiking, picnicking, sailing, swimming, windsurfing, fishing, and horseback riding—or you can just appreciate the beauty. The main summer season stretches from Memorial Day to Labor Day. There are seven campgrounds and four picnic areas in the Huntington Lake Basin, plus numerous hiking and riding trails.

○ NEIDER GROVE OF GIANT SEQUOIAS This 1,540-acre tract in the Sierra National Forest contains 101 mature giant sequoias in the center of the Sequoia Range, south of Yosemite National Park. A visitor center stands near the Neider Grove Campground, with historical relics and displays, including two restored log cabins. The Bull Buck Tree—at one time thought to be the largest in the world—is 246 feet high and has a circumference at ground level of 99 feet. There's a mile-long, self-guided walk along the "Shadow of the Giants" National Recreational Trail in the southwest corner of the grove.

OUTDOOR PURSUITS

CAMPING The Sierra National Forest seems like one vast campsite. Options range from unembellished, primitive wilderness camps to developed and often crowded campgrounds with snack bars, flush toilets, bathhouses, and hookups for RVs. For information and reservations, call the **National Recreation Reservation Service** toll-free at ☎ 877/444-6777, or visit their Web site at **www.reserveusa.com**.

The major campgrounds are the Shaver Lake area; the Huntington Lake area (which has seven family campgrounds open from the end of June to Labor Day that must be reserved in advance); the Florence and Edison Lake area (first-come, first-served); the Dinkey Creek area (family and group camping); the Wishon and Courtright area (four campgrounds; first-come, first-served); the Pine Flat Reservoir (in the Sierra foothills, with two first-come, first-served campgrounds); and Upper Kings River, east of Pine Flat Reservoir (family campgrounds; first-come, first-served).

FISHING The many streams of the Sierra are home to rainbow, golden, brown, and brook trout. The best freshwater angling is in the Pineridge and Kings River Rangers District. At the lower elevations, Shaver Lake, Bass Lake, and Pine Flat Reservoirs are known for their black-bass fishing. Questions about fishing in the national forest can be directed to the **California Department of Fish and Game,** 1234 E. Shaw Ave., Fresno, CA 93710 (☎ 559/243-4005).

SKIING Lying 65 miles northeast of Fresno on Calif. 168 in the Sierra National Forest, the **Sierra Summit Ski Area** offers mildly challenging alpine skiing, as well as marked trails for cross-country skiing and snowmobiling. The resort area has two triple and three double chairlifts, plus four surface lifts and 30 runs, the longest of which extends for 2¼ miles. There's a vertical drop-off at 1,600 feet. Other facilities include a lodge, snack bar, cafeteria, restaurant, and bar, all open daily from mid-November until mid-April. For resort information or a ski report, call ☎ 559/893-3311.

The **Pineridge Ranger Station** (☎ 559/855-5360) also maintains several marked cross-country trails along Calif. 168, ranging from a 1-mile tour for beginners to a 6-mile trail for more advanced skiers.

WHITE-WATER RAFTING The Upper Kings River, east of Pine Flat Reservoir, offers a 10-mile rafting run through Garnet Dike to Kirch Flat Campground. Rafting season is from late April to mid-July, with the highest waters in late May and early June. To get there, take Belmont Avenue in Fresno east (toward Pine Flat Reservoir) for about 63 miles. For more information about guided rafting trips on the Kings River, call **Kings River Expeditions** (☎ 559/233-4881).

11 The Monterey Peninsula & the Big Sur Coast

by Matthew R. Poole

The Monterey Peninsula and the Big Sur coast comprise one of the world's most spectacular shorelines, skirted with cypress trees, rugged shores, and crescent-shaped bays. Monterey reels in visitors with its world-class aquarium and array of outdoor activities. Pacific Grove is so peaceful and quaint that the butterflies choose it as their yearly mating ground. Pebble Beach attracts the world's golfing elite, and although packed with tourists who come for the beaches, shops, and restaurants, tiny Carmel-by-the-Sea somehow remains romantic and sweet. Big Sur's dramatic and majestic coast, backed by pristine redwood forests and rolling hills, is one of the most breathtaking and tranquil environments on earth. And if you're traveling on Calif. 1 (which you should be), the magnificent coastline will guide you all the way through the region.

This chapter begins with Santa Cruz, located at the northwestern end of Monterey Bay. It's one of our favorite coastal destinations and home of the famous Santa Cruz Beach Boardwalk. Across Monterey Bay at the northern tip of the Monterey Peninsula are the seaside communities of Monterey and Pacific Grove, while Pebble Beach and Carmel-by-the-Sea hug the peninsula's south coast along Carmel Bay. Between the north and south coasts, which are only about 5 miles apart, are numerous golf courses, some of the state's most stunning homes and hotels, and 17-Mile Drive, one of the most scenic coastal roads in the world.

Inland lies Carmel Valley, with its elegant inns and resorts, golf courses, and guaranteed sunshine, even when the coast is socked in with fog. Farther down the coast along Calif. 1 is Big Sur, a stunning 90-mile stretch of coast south of the Monterey Peninsula and west of the Santa Lucia Mountains.

1 Santa Cruz

77 miles SE of San Francisco

For a small bayside city, Santa Cruz has a lot to offer. The main show, of course, is the Beach Boardwalk, the West Coast's only seaside amusement park, which attracts millions of visitors each year. But past the arcades and cotton candy is a surprisingly diverse and energetic city that has a little something for everyone. Shopping, hiking, mountain biking, sailing, fishing, kayaking, surfing, wine tasting, golfing, whale watching—the list of things to do here is almost endless, making Santa Cruz one of the premier family destinations on the California coast.

ESSENTIALS

GETTING THERE   Santa Cruz is 77 miles southeast of San Francisco. The most scenic route to Santa Cruz is along Calif. 1 from San Francisco, which, aside from the "you fall, you die" stretch called Devil's Slide, allows you to cruise at a steady 50 m.p.h. along the coast. Faster but far less romantic is Calif. 17, which is accessed near San Jose from I-280, I-880, or U.S. 101, and literally ends at the foot of the boardwalk. The exception to this rule is on weekend mornings, when Calif. 17 tends to logjam with Bay Area beachgoers while Calif. 1 remains relatively uncrowded.

VISITOR INFORMATION   For information, contact the **Santa Cruz County Conference and Visitors Council,** 701 Front St., Santa Cruz, CA 95060 (☎ **800/ 833-3494** or 831/425-1234; www.scccvc.org), open Monday through Saturday from 9am to 5pm, Sunday from 10am to 4pm.

SPECIAL EVENTS   Special events include the Santa Cruz Hot and Cool Jazz Festival in July (☎ 831/662-1912), Shakespeare Santa Cruz in July and August (☎ 831/ 459-2121), and the Cabrillo Music Festival in August (☎ 831/426-6966).

WHAT TO SEE & DO: BEACHES, HIKING, FISHING & MORE

One of the top amusement parks in the nation, the privately owned **Santa Cruz Beach Boardwalk** (☎ **831/426-7433**) draws more than 3 million visitors a year to its 28 rides and multitudes of arcades, shops, and restaurants. The park has two national landmarks—a 1924 wooden Giant Dipper roller coaster and a 1911 carousel complete with hand-carved wooden horses and a 342-pipe organ band. It's open daily in the summer (from Memorial Day weekend through Labor Day) and on weekends and holidays throughout the spring and fall, from 11am (noon sometimes in winter). Admission to the boardwalk is free, but an all-day "unlimited rides" pass will set you back about $19.

Here, too, is **Neptune's Kingdom**, 400 Beach St. (☎ **831/426-7433**), an enormous indoor family recreation center whose main feature is a two-story miniature golf course. Also on Beach Street is the **Municipal Wharf** (☎ **831/429-3628**), lined with shops and restaurants—a beachfront strip that is serenaded by the sea lions below. You can also crab and fish from here. Most shops are open daily from 7am to 9pm, the wharf daily from 5am to 2am. **Stagnaro's** (☎ **831/427-2334**) operates fishing and whale-watching trips from the wharf year-round, as well as hour-long narrated bay cruises for a mere $6.

Farther down on West Cliff Drive, you'll come to a favorite surfing spot, **Steamer Lane,** where you can watch pro surfers shredding the waves. If you want to find out more about this local sport that's been practiced here for 100 years, go to the **Santa Cruz Surfing Museum,** at the memorial lighthouse (☎ **831/429-3429**), open Thursday through Tuesday from noon to 5pm. Antique surfboards, videos, photographs, and other memorabilia depict the history and evolution of surfing around the world.

Continue along West Cliff and you'll eventually reach **Natural Bridges State Beach,** 2531 W. Cliff Dr. (☎ **831/423-4609**), a large sandy beach with nearby tide pools and hiking trails. It's also home to a large colony of monarch butterflies that cluster and mate in the nearby eucalyptus grove.

Other Santa Cruz beaches worth noting are **Bonny Doon,** at Bonny Doon Road and Calif. 1, an uncrowded sandy beach and a major surfing spot accessible by a steep walkway; **Pleasure Point Beach,** East Cliff Drive at Pleasure Point Drive; and **Twin Lakes State Beach,** which is ideal for sunning and also provides access to Schwann Lagoon, a bird sanctuary.

In addition to hosting many cultural and sporting events, the University of California at Santa Cruz also features the **Long Marine Laboratory and Aquarium,**

The Monterey Peninsula

 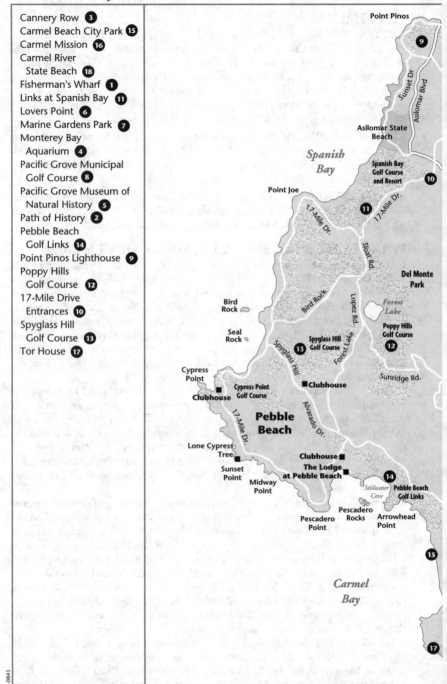
330

1-0843

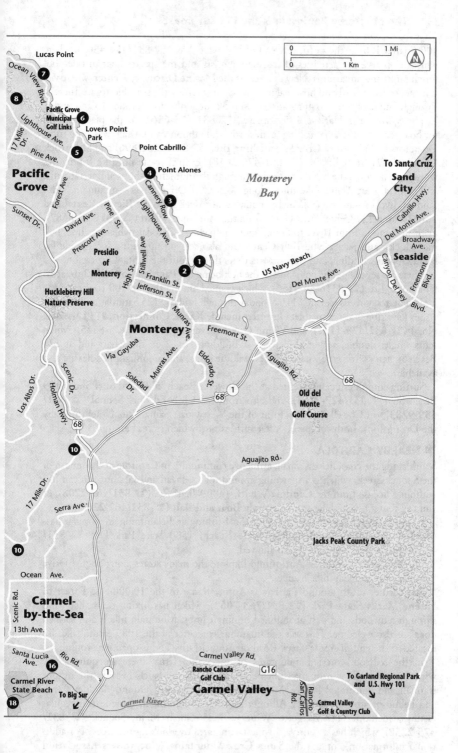

Lucas Point

Ocean View Blvd.

7

8

Pacific Grove
Municipal
Golf Links **6**

Lovers Point
Park

Lighthouse Ave.

5

17 Mile Dr.

Pine Ave.

**Pacific
Grove**

Point Cabrillo

4 Point Alones

Cannery Row

3

Lighthouse Ave.

*Monterey
Bay*

To Santa Cruz

**Sand
City**

Cabrillo Hwy.

Del Monte Ave.

Broadway
Ave.

Seaside

Sunset Dr.

Forest Ave.

David Ave.

Prescott Ave.

Pine St.

**Presidio
of
Monterey**

Stillwell Ave.

High St.

Franklin St.

2 **1**

Jefferson St.

US Navy Beach

Del Monte Ave.

1

Canyon Del Rey

Freemont Blvd.

**Huckleberry Hill
Nature Preserve**

Monterey

Via Gayuba

Munras Ave.

Munras Ave.

Freemont St.

Eldorado St.

Aguajito Rd.

**Old del
Monte
Golf Course**

68

Los Altos Dr.

Scenic Dr.

Holman Hwy.

Soledad Dr.

68

68 **1**

10

Aguajito Rd.

Jacks Peak County Park

17 Mile Dr.

1

Serra Ave.

10

Ocean Ave.

**Carmel-
by-the-Sea**

Scenic Rd.

13th Ave.

Santa Lucia
Ave.

16

Rio Rd.

1

Carmel Valley Rd.

Rancho Cañada
Golf Club

G16

Carmel Valley

To Garland Regional Park
and U.S. Hwy 101

**Carmel River
State Beach**

18

To Big Sur

Carmel River

Rancho San Carlos Rd.

Carmel Valley
Golf & Country Club

0   1 Mi
0   1 Km

331

100 Shaffer Rd., at the northwest end of Delaware Ave. (☎ 831/459-4308), where you can observe the activities of marine scientists and the species kept in tide-pool touch tanks and aquariums. New this year is the **Marine Discovery Center,** where visitors get to learn firsthand how real marine scientists study the seas. Hours are Tuesday through Sunday from 1 to 4pm; admission is $2 for adults, free for kids 16 and under.

The **Santa Cruz Harbor,** 135 5th Ave. (☎ 831/475-6161), is the place to head for boat rentals, open boat fishing (cod, shark, and salmon), and whale-watching trips. Operators include **Santa Cruz Sportfishing Inc.** (☎ 831/426-4690) and **Shamrock Charters,** 2210 E. Cliff Dr. (☎ 831/476-2648). Even if you're not into fishing, it's worth a walk down the harbor to browse through the numerous shops and restaurants.

There's a great 2-mile bike route along West Cliff Drive. Bikes—mountain, kids', tandem, hybrid—are available by the hour, day, or week from the **Bicycle Rental and Tour Center,** 131 Center St., 2 blocks from the Municipal Wharf (☎ 831/426-8687), open in summer from 10am to 6pm. Figure on paying $25 a day, which includes helmets, locks, and packs. The Tour Center can also set you up with a local guide for hiking, biking, birding, and water-sports tours throughout the Santa Cruz region.

There are several public golf courses, the best being the **Pasatiempo Golf Club,** at 18 Clubhouse Rd. (☎ 831/459-9155), which is rated among the top 100 courses in the United States. Greens fees are $115 Monday through Friday, $125 Saturday and Sunday.

Sea kayaking is also available. Outfitters include **Kayak Connection,** 413 Lake Ave. No. 4 (☎ 831/479-1121), and **Vision Quest Kayaking** (☎ 831/425-8445), which rents single, double, and triple kayaks at Building No. 2 on the wharf and at 125 Beach St. across from the wharf. Classes, wildlife tours, and moonlight paddles are also available.

Surfing equipment can be rented at the **Cowell's Beach 'n' Bikini Surf Shop,** 109 Beach St. (☎ 831/427-2355), and also from the **Club Ed Surf School** (☎ 831/459-9283), on Cowell Beach in front of the West Coast Santa Cruz Hotel (formally the Dream Inn). Both companies offer surf lessons, which start at around $50.

IN NEARBY CAPITOLA

South along the coast lies the small, attractive community of **Capitola** at the mouth of the Soquel Creek, which is a spawning ground for steelhead and salmon. You can fish without a license from the **Capitola Wharf,** 1400 Wharf Rd. (☎ 831/462-2208), or you can rent a fishing boat from **Capitola Boat and Bait** (☎ 831/462-2208).

Capitola Beach fronts the Esplanade. Surf-fishing and clamming are popular pastimes at Capitola's **New Brighton State Beach,** 1500 State Park Dr. (☎ 831/475-4850), where camping is also allowed.

Other Capitola pastimes? **Antiquing!** Explore the many stores along Soquel Drive between 41st and Capitola avenues.

Still farther south around the bay is **Aptos,** home to the 10,000-acre **Forest of Nisene Marks State Park** (☎ 831/763-7062), which has hiking trails that wind through redwoods and past abandoned mining camps. Mountain bikers and leashed dogs are also welcome. This was the infamous epicenter of the 1989 earthquake. It's located at the end of Aptos Creek Road off Soquel Drive and is open year-round.

In the redwood-forested mountains behind Santa Cruz, there are quite a few wineries, although visitors may not be familiar with the labels because the output is small and consumed locally. Most wineries are clustered around Boulder Creek and Felton or around Capitola. All offer tours by appointment; some feature regular tastings, including the **Bargetto Winery,** 3535 North Main, Soquel (☎ 831/475-2258), which has a courtyard wine-tasting area overlooking the creek. For additional information, contact the **Santa Cruz Mountains Winegrowers Association** (☎ 831/479-WINE).

WHERE TO STAY

Two **Travelodges** (☎ 800/578-7878), two **Best Westerns** (☎ 800/528-1234), two **Super 8s** (☎ 800/800-8000), and an **Econolodge** (☎ 800/553-2666) provide moderate- and budget-priced accommodations in addition to the more inspiring choices below.

Casa Blanca Inn. 101 Main St. (at the corner of Beach), Santa Cruz, CA 95060. ☎ **800/644-1570** or 831/423-1570. Fax 831/423-0235. 34 units. TV TEL. High-season (summer) $105–$300 double; low-season $68–$295 double. AE, CB, DC, DISC, MC, V.

Across from the wharf in a heavily trafficked area, this motel along the waterfront was once the Mediterranean-style Cerf Mansion, dating from 1918. Other motel-style accommodations have grown up around the main building. Originally the home of a federal judge, it offers individually decorated bedrooms, some with brass beds and velvet draperies. Some units contain fireplaces and terraces, and all are equipped with microwaves and coffeemakers. Most of the rooms have views of the water. A restaurant on the premises (see "Where to Dine," below) serves California-continental cuisine in a romantic ocean-view setting.

✪ Darling House. 314 W. Cliff Dr., Santa Cruz, CA 95060. ☎ **831/458-1958.** 8 units (2 with private bathroom). $95 double without bathroom; $260 double with bathroom. AE, DISC, MC, V.

This lovely Spanish-style house, designed in 1910 by William Weeks (architect of Santa Cruz's Coconut Grove), has a panoramic view of the Pacific Ocean and is situated in a quiet residential area within walking distance of the Boardwalk and lighthouse. The gardens are fragrant with citrus and orchids, and contain some stately palms as well. From the tiled front veranda, guests enter an elegant interior, the focal point of which is the dining room hand-crafted from tiger oak. The house boasts fine architectural features throughout, such as beveled glass, antiques, and handsome fireplaces. Each of the eight rooms is individually decorated; although all have sinks, only two come with private bathrooms. The Pacific Ocean room, decorated like a sea captain's quarters, features a fireplace, telescope, and one of the finest ocean views in Santa Cruz. A backyard hot tub is available for guests. Breakfast includes oven-fresh breads and pastries, fruit, and homemade granola made with walnuts from the Darling's own farm.

Edgewater Beach Motel. 525 Second St., Santa Cruz, CA 95060. ☎ **831/423-0440.** 17 units. TV TEL. $105–$185 double. AE, DC, DISC, MC, V.

If the other two inns listed here are booked, consider the Edgewater Beach Motel. It looks like a time capsule from the 1960s, which, oddly enough, makes it all the more appealing (how they kept the furnishings in such prime condition is a mystery). The motel offers a range of accommodations, from family suites with kitchens to rooms with fireplaces; most have microwaves and all have fridges. The Edgewater also sports a heated pool, sundeck, and barbecue area, but the real bonus is the location—the Santa Cruz Beach Boardwalk is only a block away. *Tip:* Inquire about the Edgewater's off-season mini-vacation packages, which can save you a bundle on room rates. Smoking is not permitted in any of the rooms.

IN NEARBY CAPITOLA

✪ The Inn at Depot Hill. 250 Monterey Ave. (near Park Ave.), Capitola, CA 95010. ☎ **800/57-B-AND-B** or 831/462-3376. Fax 831/462-3697. www.innatdepothill.com. 12 units. A/C TV TEL. $190–$275 double. Rates include breakfast, afternoon tea or wine, hors d'oeuvres, and after-dinner dessert. AE, DC, DISC, MC, V.

Located a few blocks from the bay front, this converted railroad station has been beautifully designed and decorated with great attention to detail, thanks to innkeeper-extraordinaire Suzanne Lankes. Sporting fine fabrics and linens, all rooms and suites have wood-burning fireplaces, VCRs and stereos, phones with fax/modem capability, bathrobes, hair dryers, two-person showers, and full bathrooms. Most have private patios with private hot tubs (guests in the other rooms share a common hot tub, and sign up for times). Perhaps you'll check into the Portofino Room, patterned after an Italian villa right down to the frescoes and stone cherub, or the Stratford-on-Avon, a replica of an English cottage.

The evening wine and hors d'oeuvres and the breakfast are of similar prime quality, and can be enjoyed either in your room or out back in the garden courtyard on wrought-iron tables shaded by market umbrellas.

WHERE TO DINE

✪ **Bittersweet Bistro.** 787 Rio Del Mar Blvd. (about 10 miles SE of Santa Cruz on Calif. 1), Rio Del Mar. ☎ **831/662-9799.** www.bittersweetbistro.com. Reservations recommended. Main courses $15–$18. AE, MC, V. Wed–Fri 11:30am–3pm, Tues–Sun 5:30–10pm, Sun brunch 10am–2pm. CALIFORNIA.

What started out as a tiny operation within a small strip development has grown into one of the most popular restaurants in the Santa Cruz region. The relocation to bigger digs in Rio Del Mar hasn't tarnished chef/owner Thomas Vinolus's reputation for serving exceptional cuisine. The menu offers a wide array of carefully crafted dishes, ranging from pizzas from the wood-fired oven to grilled lamb porterhouse in a sun-dried cranberry demi glace. Fresh fish is Vinolus's forte, however, such as the Monterey Bay halibut, baked in parchment over fresh vegetables, or the roasted Chelis River wild sturgeon finished with an exotic mushroom sauce. Co-proprietor and wine director Elizabeth Vinolus has put together an exceptional wine list and often hosts winemaker dinners. The bistro's lunch and Sunday brunch are also exceptional.

Café El Palomar. 2222 E. Cliff Dr. (at the Santa Cruz Harbor). ☎ **831/462-4248**. Main courses $4–$6. MC, V. Fri–Wed 7am–7pm, Thurs 7am–8:30pm (closes earlier in winter). MEXICAN.

If both O'Mei and Café Bittersweet are out of your price range, then head to the Santa Cruz Harbor and seat yourself at one of the seven tables at Café El Palomar. An off-shoot of the far fancier El Palomar restaurant in the Pacific Garden Mall, the Café serves the standard Mexican fare—chimichangas, burritos, tacos, chorizo, and more—for breakfast, lunch, and dinner. For the money, it's mucho bueno grub.

Casablanca Restaurant. 101 Main St. (at Beach). ☎ **831/426-9063.** Reservations recommended. Main courses $14–$23. AE, DC, DIS, MC, V. Sun–Thurs 5–9pm, Fri–Sat 5–10pm. CALIFORNIA/CONTINENTAL.

The candlelit dining room at the Casa Blanca Inn was obviously built for romance, right down to the stellar views of the shimmering bay. The menu offers your classic fancy fare such as rack of lamb, grilled salmon, and sautéed chicken breast, but most folks here primarily for the ambiance. For a fiery start, try the fire-roasted Anaheim chili stuffed with herbed chèvre and served with tomatillo salsa. Among the 10 or so main courses, we'd recommend any of the fresh seafood dishes, perhaps the red snapper sautéed with capers, scallions, and lime sauce. The award-winning book-length wine list is excellent.

✪ **O'Mei.** 2316 Mission St. (where Calif. 1 turns into Mission St.). ☎ **831/425-8458.** Reservations recommended. Main courses $8–$14. AE, MC, V. Mon–Fri 11:30am–2pm; Sun–Thurs 5–9pm, Fri–Sat 5–10pm. PROVINCIAL SICHUAN.

O'Mei's (pronounced *oh-may*) minimall location may not be very inviting, but the fantastic food served here more than makes up for it. The menu features some unusual specialties such as Chengdu-bean-curd sea bass in a spicy *dou-ban* sauce (a rich, velvety wine-chili sauce), apricot-almond chicken, and lichee pi-pa bean-curd balls, along with more familiar dishes like chicken with cashews or beef with asparagus. Dinner starts with a dim sum–style tray of exotic vegetarian offerings such as sesame-cilantro-eggplant salad or pan-roasted peppers with feta cheese. A recommended dish is the sliced rock cod in black-bean/sweet-pepper sauce, followed by a scoop of black-sesame ice cream.

IN NEARBY CAPITOLA

Shadowbrook. 1750 Wharf Rd., Capitola. ☎ **831/475-1511.** Reservations recommended. Main courses $12–$22. AE, CB, DC, DISC, MC, V. Mon–Fri 11:30am–9:30pm, Sat 4:30–10:30pm, Sun 10am–2:30pm and 4:30–9pm. AMERICAN/CONTINENTAL.

Shadowbrook, one of Capitola's most venerable and romantic restaurants, occupies a serene setting above Soquel Creek. To reach the restaurant, diners either have to take the cable-driven "hillavator" down or walk the long, steep bank of steps beside a running waterfall. At the bottom is a log cabin built in the 1920s, which has been enlarged and now contains a series of dining rooms on different levels: the wood-paneled Wine Cellar, the airy Garden Room, the Fireplace Room, and the creek-side Greenhouse.

The menu doesn't hold many surprises, featuring thick-cut prime rib and steaks along with seafood such as scampi and grilled trout, plus pasta dishes including shellfish linguine and porcini ravioli. Prawn cocktail, deep-fried artichoke hearts, and baked brie are among the appetizers. Standout desserts are the mud pie and chocolate torte with raspberry sauce. If you don't have the time, appetite, or budget for a big sit-down dinner, grab a seat in the lounge and nosh on appetizers and light entrees prepared in the restaurant's wood-fired oven.

A SIDE TRIP TO MISSION SAN JUAN BAUTISTA

On U.S. 101, **San Juan Bautista** is a charming mission town that works hard to honor its pioneer heritage by retaining the flavor of a 19th-century village. The mission complex is perched in a picturesque farming valley, surrounded by the restored buildings of the original city plaza.

From U.S. 101, take Calif. 156 east (south) to the center of town to the mission itself, which was founded in 1797. Here you'll see the largest church in the mission chain and the only one in continuous service since its founding. The padres here inspired many Native Americans to convert, creating one of the largest congregations in all of California. The small museum contains many musical instruments and transcriptions, evidence of the mission's musical focus—it once boasted a formidable Native American boys' choir. Mission San Juan Bautista is open daily year-round from 9:30am to 4:45pm. Suggested donation is $2 per person, $1 per child. For further information, call ☎ **831/623-4528.**

East of the church, perched at the edge of an abrupt drop created by the movement of the San Andreas Fault, is a marker pointing out the path of the old **El Camino Real.** Accompanying the marker are seismographic measuring equipment and an earthquake science exhibit.

In addition to the mission, there's much to see on the restored city plaza. Be sure to visit the **San Juan Bautista State Historic Park.** The park is comprised of not only the old Plaza Hotel with its classic frontier barroom and furnished rooms, but also the Plaza Hall, its adjoining stables and blacksmith shop, and the Castro House, where the Breen family lived after traveling here with the ill-fated Donner Party in 1846. Allow 1½ to 2 hours to see the entire plaza. Admission to the park buildings is $2 per person,

$1 for kids ages 6 to 12 (separate from your charge to the mission). For further information (including events schedules), call ☎ **831/623-4881.**

2 Monterey

45 miles S of Santa Cruz, 116 miles S of San Francisco, 335 miles N of Los Angeles

Originally settled in 1770, Monterey was one of the West Coast's first European settlements, and the capital of California under the Spanish, Mexican, and American flags. California's state constitution was drafted here in 1849, paving the way for admission to the Union a year later. In fact, many buildings from the early colonial era still stand. A major whaling center in the 1800s, Monterey eventually became the sardine capital of the Western Hemisphere when the first packing plant was built in 1900. By 1913, the boats were bringing in 25 tons of sardines a night to the 18 canneries. The gritty lives of the mostly working-class residents were forever captured by local hero John Steinbeck in his 1945 novel *Cannery Row.*

After the sardines disappeared, Monterey was forced to fish for tourist dollars instead; hence, the numerous array of boutiques, knickknack stores, and theme restaurants that now reside in converted sardine factories along the bay. Granted, plenty of history and heritage remains along Cannery Row, but you'll have to weed though the tourist schlock to find them. Its saving grace is the world-class aquarium and beautiful Monterey Bay, where sea lions and otters still frolic in abundance.

As you distance yourself from the Row, however, you'll soon discover that Monterey is a pleasant seaside community, replete with magnificent vistas, historic architecture, stately Victorians, and a number of quality lodgings and restaurants. More important, Monterey is only a short drive from Pacific Grove, Carmel, Pebble Beach, and Big Sur, and the lodgings here are far less expensive, which makes it a great place to set up base while exploring the Monterey coast.

ESSENTIALS

GETTING THERE   The region's most convenient runway, at the **Monterey Peninsula Airport** (☎ 831/373-1704), is 3 miles east of Monterey on Calif. 68. **American Eagle** (☎ 800/433-7300), **Northwest** (☎ 800/225-2525), **United** (☎ 800/241-6522), and **US Air** (☎ 800/428-4322) have daily flights in and out of Monterey.

Many area hotels offer free airport shuttle service. If you take a taxi, it will cost about $10 to $15 to get to a peninsula hotel. Several national car-rental companies have airport locations, including **Dollar** (☎ 800/800-4000) and **Hertz** (☎ 800/654-3131).

VISITOR INFORMATION   The **Monterey Peninsula Visitors and Convention Bureau** (☎ **831/649-1770;** www.monterey.com) has two visitor centers: one located in the lobby of the Maritime Museum at Custom House Plaza near Fisherman's Wharf, and the other at Lake El Estero on Camino El Estero. Both locations, open daily, offer an array of good maps, as well as free pamphlets and publications, including an excellent visitors' guide and the magazine *Coast Weekly.*

GETTING AROUND   The **Waterfront Area Visitor Express (WAVE)** operates each year from Memorial Day weekend through Labor Day and takes passengers to and from the aquarium and other waterfront attractions. Stops are located at many hotels and motels in Monterey and Pacific Grove. The cost of $1.50 for adults and 75¢ for kids and seniors gets you unlimited rides all day between 9am and 6pm and eliminates the stress of parking in crowded downtown. For further information, call **Monterey Salinas Transit** (☎ 831/899-2555).

SEEING THE SIGHTS

The **National Steinbeck Center** is not in town, but if you're a fan, you'll want to make the 20-mile drive northeast from Monterey on Calif. 68 to One Main St. in Salinas (☎ **831/775-4720;** www.steinbeck.org). A new $11-million, 37,000-square-foot museum opened in mid-1998, offering walk-through interactive exhibits, a changing exhibition gallery, an orientation theater presenting a 10-minute video on Steinbeck's life, educational programs, a gift shop, and cafe. Admission is $7 for adults, $6 for seniors over 62, $4 for ages 11 to 17, and free for kids 10 and under. Hours are daily from 10am to 5pm.

If you're traipsing through Monterey on a Tuesday afternoon, be sure to check out the **Old Monterey Marketplace** on Alvarado Street, from Pearl to Del Monte streets, open from 4 to 8pm (until 7pm in winter). More than 100 vendors participate in this farmers' market, bringing food, music, crafts, and entertainment together for an afternoon of flavorful festivities.

✪ **Monterey Bay Aquarium.** 886 Cannery Row. ☎ **800/756-3737** or 831/648-4888. www.mbayaq.org. Admission $15.95 adults, $12.95 students and seniors 65 and over, $7.95 visitors with disabilities and children 3–12, free for children 2 and under. AE, MC, V. Daily 10am–6pm (opens at 9:30am summer and holidays).

The site of one of the world's most spectacular aquariums was not chosen at random. It sits on the border of one of the largest underwater canyons on earth (wider and deeper than even the Grand Canyon) and is surrounded by incredibly diverse local marine life. The Monterey Bay Aquarium is one of the best exhibit aquariums in the world, and one of the largest, too—home to more than 350,000 marine animals and plants. One of the living museum's main exhibits is a three-story, 335,000-gallon tank, with clear acrylic walls that give visitors an unmatched look at local sea life. A towering kelp forest, which rises from the floor of this oceanic zoo, gently waves with the water as hundreds of leopard sharks, sardines, anchovies, and other fish swim back and forth in an endless game of hide-and-seek.

In 1996, the outstanding Outer Bay exhibit opened, which features creatures that inhabit the open ocean. This tank—holding a million gallons of water—houses yellow-fin tuna, large green sea turtles, barracuda, sharks, the very cool giant ocean sunfish, and schools of bonito. The Outer Bay's jellyfish exhibit is guaranteed to amaze, and kids will love Flippers, Flukes, and Fun, a learning area for families.

New this year is the Mysteries of the Deep exhibit, the largest collection of live deep-sea species in the world—many of which have never been on display anywhere. The 7,000-square-foot exhibit highlights the underwater life collected from waters as deep as 3,300 feet, including such creatures as spider crabs, ratfish, filetail catsharks, predatory tunicates, mushroom corals, and California king crabs.

Additional exhibits re-create other undersea habitats found in Monterey Bay. Everyone falls in love with the sea otters playing in their two-story exhibit. There are also coastal streams, tidal pools, a sand beach, and a petting pool, where you can touch living bat rays and handle sea stars. Visitors can also watch a live video link that regularly transmits from a deep-sea research submarine maneuvering thousands of feet below the surface of Monterey Bay.

Avoid lines at the gate by calling the above numbers and ordering tickets in advance.

Fisherman's Wharf. 99 Pacific St.

Just like San Francisco's Fisherman's Wharf, this wooden pier is jam-packed with craft and gift shops, boating and fishing operations, fish markets, and seafood restaurants—all trawling for tourist dollars. But Monterey's wharf does have redeeming qualities: The natural surroundings are so beautiful that if you cast your view toward the bobbing boats and surfacing sea lions, you might not even notice the hordes of tourists around you. Grab some clam chowder in a sourdough bread bowl and find a seaside perch along the pier. Or, when the wind picks up, find a bayfront seat at one of the seafood restaurants (see "Where to Dine," below).

If the seaside sights have got you itching to set sail, boats depart regularly from Fisherman's Wharf and will lead you on a number of ocean adventures. See "Outdoor Pursuits," below, for details on some of the offerings.

Cannery Row. Between David and Drake aves. ☎ **831/649-6690.**

Once the center for an industrial sardine-packing operation immortalized by John Steinbeck as "a poem, a stink, a grating noise, a quality of light, a tone, a habit, a nostalgia, a dream," this area today is better described as a strip congested with wandering tourists, tacky gift shops, overpriced seafood restaurants, and an overall parking nightmare. What changed it so dramatically? The silver sardines suddenly disappeared from Monterey's waters in 1948 as a result of overfishing, changing currents, and pollution. Fishermen left, canneries closed, and the Row fell into disrepair. But curious tourists continued to visit Steinbeck's fabled area, and where there are tourists, there are capitalists.

After visiting Cannery Row in the 1960s, Steinbeck wrote, "The beaches are clean where they once festered with fish guts and flies. The canneries that once put up a sickening stench are gone, their places filled with restaurants, antique shops, and the like. They fish for tourists now, not pilchards, and that species they are not likely to wipe out." And we couldn't put it any better.

FOLLOWING THE PATH OF HISTORY

The dozen or so historic buildings clustered around Fisherman's Wharf and the adjacent town collectively comprise the "Path of History," a tour that examines 1800s architecture and lifestyle. Many of the buildings are a part of the **Monterey State Historic Park,** 20 Custom House Plaza (☎ **831/649-7118**). Highlights include the **Custom House,** which was constructed around 1827 and is the oldest government building in California, and the **Maritime Museum of Monterey,** 5 Custom House Plaza (☎ **831/ 372-2608**), which showcases ship models and other collections that relate the area's seafaring history, including a two-story-high, 10,000-pound Fresnel lens, used for nearly 80 years at the Point Sur lighthouse. Admission is $3 for adults, $2 for seniors and youths 13 to 18, children free 12 and under; open daily from 10am to 5pm.

You can go the self-guided route by picking up a free tour booklet at the Monterey Peninsula Visitors and Convention Bureau (see above), the Cooper-Molera Adobe (at the corner of Polk and Munras sts.), and various other locations. You may also opt to take the guided tour, which departs several times daily. The price is $5 for adults, $3

Monterey Wine Country

The congestion and price of Napa and Sonoma vineyards and the increasingly lucrative and romantic occupation of wine making have forced industry newcomers to plant their grapes elsewhere. Fortunately, much of the California coast offers perfect growing conditions. Nowadays, if you visit any area between Monterey and Santa Barbara, there's easy access to new appellations and a variety of boutique vintners making respectable wines. Stop by **A Taste of Monterey,** 700 Cannery Row (☎ **831/646-5446**), between 11am and 6pm to learn about and taste locally produced wines in front of huge bayfront windows. This is also the place to get a map and winery touring information.

for youths 13 to 18, $2 for children 6 to 12, 5 and under free. Call ☎ 831/649-7118 for exact schedule information, or visit the **State Park Visitor Center** at Stanton Center, 5 Custom House Plaza. A free film on the history of Monterey is shown here every 20 minutes.

OUTDOOR PURSUITS

Cast your hook on a deep-sea–fishing expedition. Among the operators are **Chris' Fishing Trips,** 48 Fisherman's Wharf (☎ 831/375-5951), which offers large party boats. Cod and salmon are the main catches, with separate boats leaving daily. Full-day excursions cost $32 to $40 per person. Call for a complete price list and departure schedule.

Sam's Fishing Fleet, 84 Fisherman's Wharf (☎ 831/372-0577), offers fishing excursions for cod, salmon, and whatever else is running, as well as whale-watching tours. Make reservations and bring a lunch. Departures are Monday through Friday at 7:30am (salmon-fishing boats leave earlier), Saturday and Sunday at 7am. Check-in is 45 minutes prior to departure. Weekday prices are $30 for adults, $17 for children 11 and under; weekend and holiday rates are $34 for adults, $20 for children. Equipment rental costs a bit extra.

Kayaks can be rented from several outfitters for a spin around the bay. Contact **Monterey Bay Kayaks,** 693 Del Monte Ave. (☎ 800/649-5357 or 831/373-5357; www.montereykayaks.com), on Del Monte Beach north of Fisherman's Wharf, which offers instruction as well as natural-history tours that introduce visitors to the Monterey Bay National Marine Sanctuary. Prices start at $45 for the tours, $25 for rentals. A second store is at nearby Moss Landing, offering guided tours of Elkhorn Slough, one of the last remaining estuaries in California. Call ☎ 800/655-6367 for more information.

For bikes and in-line skates as well as kayak tours and rentals, contact **Adventures by the Sea,** 299 Cannery Row (☎ 831/372-1807). Bikes cost $6 per hour or $24 per day; kayaks are $25 per person, or $45 for a 2½-hour tour; and skates are $12 for 2 hours, $24 for a day. Adventures also has other locations at 201 Alvarado Mall (☎ 831/648-7235) at the Doubletree Hotel, and on the beach at Lovers Point in Pacific Grove.

Experienced scuba divers wishing to go out on an excursion can contact **Monterey Bay Dive Center,** 225 Cannery Row (☎ 831/656-0454), which arranges personal dives with a divemaster and has scheduled weekend dives. **Aquarius Dive Shop,** 2040 Del Monte Ave. (☎ 831/375-1933), also has regularly scheduled trips and divemasters. Certification cards are essential.

A popular—and exhilarating—way to view Monterey Bay's spectacular scenery is via hot-air balloon. **Balloons-by-the-Sea** (☎ 831/384-3483) offers sunrise flights daily by appointment, and sunset flights in fall and winter only. Call for additional information.

North of Monterey at Marina State Beach, you can learn to hang glide during a 3-hour course that includes a minimum of five flights with **Western Hang Gliders,** Calif. 1 at Reservation Road, Marina (☎ 831/384-2622). The cost is $98. Tandem flights, paragliding, and ultralights are available, too.

Need to keep the kids busy, or feeling playful yourself? The **Dennis the Menace Playground** at Camino El Estero and Del Monte Avenue, near Lake Estero, is an old-fashioned playground created by Pacific Grove resident and famous cartoonist Hank Ketcham. It has bridges to cross, tunnels to climb through, and an authentic Southern Pacific Railroad engine teeming with wanna-be conductors. There's also a hot dog and burger stand, and a big lake where you can rent paddleboats or feed the ducks. The park is open daily from 10am to sunset.

Sensational Safari Stopover: The Otters, Seals & Birds of the Elkhorn Slough

One of our favorite stops along the coast is Moss Landing, which is 25 minutes north of Monterey on Calif. 1. Along the virtually one-street town are a few adorable down-home restaurants and antiques shops. But what really attracts us is Captain Yohn Gideon's ✪ **Elkhorn Slough Safari.** For $24 for adults or $18 for children under 15, friendly Cap'n Gideon loads guests onto a 27-foot pontoon boat (safe for old and young) and embarks on a 2-hour tour of the wondrous Elkhorn Slough Wildlife Reserve, which, by the way, is like jumping into a *National Geographic* special. It's not uncommon to see a "raft" of up to 50 otters feet-up and sunning themselves, an abundance of lounging harbor seals, and hundreds of species of waterfowl and migratory shorebirds. An onboard naturalist answers questions, Cap'n educates on the surroundings, and binoculars are available. For reservations, schedules, and information, call ☎ **831/633-5555** or check out **www.elkhornslough.com**.

WHERE TO STAY

It seems there are only three types of choices for accommodations in Monterey: lace-and-flowers B&Bs, large corporate hotels with only a slight beachy feel (if even that), or run-of-the-mill motel digs. Consider which area you'd like to be in—beach, Cannery Row, wharf, secluded, central, and so forth—as well as how much you want to spend; then check out the options below or contact the reservations service **Time to Coast** (☎ **800/555-WAVE**; www.timetocoast.com), which represents about 30 lodging facilities in Monterey.

EXPENSIVE

In addition to the choices below, there are two chain hotels conveniently located near Fisherman's Wharf: The **Monterey Marriott,** 350 Calle Principal, at Del Monte Blvd. (☎ **800/228-9290** or 831/649-4234), offers some rooms with bay views, an outdoor pool, health club, whirlpool, and saunas. There's also the **Doubletree Hotel at Fisherman's Wharf,** 2 Portola Plaza (☎ **800/222-8733** or 831/649-4511). Less centrally located, but great for families and golfers, is the enormous **Hyatt Regency Monterey** resort, 1 Old Golf Course Rd. (☎ **800/233-1234** or 831/372-1234). It adjoins the Del Monte Golf Course and has three pools, two whirlpools, a gym, tennis courts, and two restaurants. All three hotels are popular with business travelers and conventioneers.

✪ **Hotel Pacific.** 300 Pacific St., Monterey, CA 93940. ☎ **800/554-5542** or 831/373-5700. Fax 831/373-6921. 105 suites. TV TEL. $199–$349 suite for two. Rates include continental breakfast and afternoon tea. AE, CB, DC, DISC, MC, V. Free parking.

Although it's not even remotely waterfront (it's close to the wharf and across the street from the Monterey Conference Center), this is our favorite upscale choice in Monterey. Beyond the elegant Spanish/Mediterranean architecture of the common areas, each unit is situated in one of 16 buildings clustered around courtyards and compact gardens complete with spas and fountains. The cozy Southwestern-style junior suites have overly fluffy down comforters atop four-poster feather beds (for the full effect, request a canopied bed), rustically stylish decor, terra-cotta–tiled floors, and a fireplace surrounded by a cushy couch and seats. Add to that two TVs, three phones, and gourmet coffee and tea—all make this a place where you'll want to hibernate awhile. Tiny closets are one of the few downsides.

Amenities: Room service (evenings only), video rentals, laundry/valet, two Jacuzzis.

Monterey Bay Inn. 242 Cannery Row, Monterey, CA 93940. ☎ **800/424-6242** or 831/373-6242. Fax 831/373-7603. 47 units. MINIBAR TV TEL. $199–$399 double. Rates include continental breakfast delivered to your room. AE, CB, DC, DISC, MC, V. Free parking. From Calif. 1, take the Pacific Grove/Del Monte Ave. exit and follow the signs to Cannery Row; the hotel is near the aquarium.

The private patios overlooking Monterey Bay—complete with otters splashing around below—are almost enough to make you forget you're in the middle of touristy Cannery Row. But if you don't fork over the big bucks for the Monterey Bay Inn's oceanfront accommodations, you may wonder why you're handing over a chunk of the kids' college fund for a good night's sleep. If, however, you simply must be in the thick of things, you've got your choice between this and the Spindrift (see below), and you'll be pleased to discover that the spacious rooms here aren't corporate-chain-hotel-like, but rather light and beachy with old Monterey photos on the walls. Most have king-size beds and convertible sofas, as well as dressing areas and combination tub/shower bathrooms stocked with terry robes. Extras include fridges, VCRs, and binoculars. Parents with small children should take precautions with the sliding-glass doors, which open to minimal balustrades.

Amenities: Room service (from 5 to 10pm), dry cleaning, laundry, sauna, fitness room, scuba facilities, beach and dive access, two hot tubs (one is open 24 hours; the other boasts romantic bay views), conference rooms.

Monterey Plaza Hotel and Spa. 400 Cannery Row, Monterey, CA 93940. ☎ **800/334-3999** in California, 800/631-1339 outside of California, or 831/646-1700. Fax 831/646-5937. 289 units. MINIBAR TV TEL. $170–$360 double; $425–$2400 suite. Children 17 and under stay free in parents' room. Packages available. AE, CB, DC, DISC, MC, V. Parking $13. From Calif. 1, take the Soledad Dr. exit and follow the signs to Cannery Row.

One of the most formal hotels in town, the Monterey Plaza is comprised of three buildings—two on the water and one across the street—that are connected by a second-story enclosed "skywalk." The public areas are elegantly decorated with imported marble, Brazilian teak, and attractive artwork. The stately bedrooms are more upscale-corporate than most around town and have double or king beds, decor reminiscent of 19th-century Biedermeier, and Italian marble bathrooms. Many units have balconies overlooking the water (sea otters included in the view). The least desirable rooms are across the street from the ocean. Extras include terry robes and an attentive and professional staff.

Dining: The Duck Club, the hotel's flagship dining room, has splendid views of the bay and serves an à la carte, primarily Italian menu prepared in an open Genovese exhibition kitchen. Schooners Bistro on the Bay, with an outdoor terrace, is a yacht-themed lounge/restaurant.

Amenities: Concierge, dry cleaning, room service, newspaper delivery, twice-daily maid service, conference rooms. New this year is a full service European-style spa, featuring a sundeck, whirlpool spas, top-of-the-line fitness room, and a full range of spa treatments.

○ **Old Monterey Inn.** 500 Martin St. (off Pacific Ave.), Monterey, CA 93940. ☎ **800/350-2344** or 831/375-8284. Fax 831/375-6730. 9 units, 1 cottage. $250–$350 double; from $350 cottage. Rates include full breakfast. MC, V. Free parking. From Calif. 1, take the Soledad Dr. exit and turn right onto Pacific Ave., then left onto Martin St.

Proprietors Ann and Gene Swett did a masterful job of converting their comfortable three-story family home into a vine-covered Tudor-style country inn. Although it's away from the surf, it's a perfect choice for romantics, with rose gardens, a bubbling brook, and brick-and-flagstone walkways shaded by a panoply of oaks. All but one guest room enjoy peaceful garden views and cozy beds with goose-down comforters and pillows. Most units also have feather beds and wood-burning fireplaces, and two open onto private patios. The guest rooms are all charmingly furnished and unique in character; two of our favorites are the Library and the Serengeti Room. Special touches are evident throughout, including fresh fruit, flowers, and candies; sachets by the pillow; and books and magazines. The bathrooms come with hair dryers and complete toiletries. The private cottage out back has an English country look and comes with a double Jacuzzi, linen-and-lace-draped king-size bed, wood-burning fireplace, sitting area, and private patio.

Breakfast, prepared by Gene, is also stellar, consisting of perhaps orange French toast, soufflé, or Belgian waffles. It's served in your room, the dining room, or the rose garden. The Swetts will also provide picnic blanket and towels for the beach, as well as passes to a nearby health club. At 5pm, guests retire to the living room for wine and hors d'oeuvres in front of a blazing fire.

Spindrift Inn. 652 Cannery Row, Monterey, CA 93940. ☎ **800/841-1879** or 831/ 646-8900. Fax 831/646-5342. 42 units. MINIBAR TV TEL. $199–$299 double with Cannery Row view; $329–$429 double with ocean view. Rates include continental breakfast delivered to your room and afternoon tea. Parking $6. AE, CB, DISC, DISC, MC, V.

Down in the middle of honky-tonk Cannery Row, but right along a narrow stretch of beach, this four-story hotel is an island of continental style in a sea of commercialism. It's elegant and well maintained, and the rooms are sweetly decorated with feather beds (a few with canopies), hardwood floors, wood-burning fireplaces, and either cushioned window seats or private balconies. The luxurious bathrooms are adorned with marble and brass fixtures. Extras include terry robes and two phones. The ocean views are definitely worth the additional cost, although the place is still painfully expensive for what it offers—unless, of course, you get a deal (same goes for the Monterey Bay Inn).

Amenities: Nightly turndown, daily newspaper, video rentals, laundry service, room service from an Italian restaurant next door.

MODERATE

Munras Avenue and northern Fremont Avenue are lined with moderate and inexpensive family-style motels, some independently owned and some chains. They're not as central as the downtown options, and atmosphere is seriously lacking on Fremont Avenue, but if transportation's not an issue, you can save a bundle by staying in one of these areas. If the selections below are full, try calling **Best Western** (☎ **800/ 528-1234**) for several other options. There's also the **Cypress Gardens Inn,** 1150 Munras Ave. (☎ **831/373-2761**), with a pool, hot tub, free movie channel, and continental breakfast; dogs are welcome.

Fireside Lodge. 1131 10th St., Monterey, CA 93940. ☎ **831/373-4172.** Fax 831/ 655-5640. 24 units. TV TEL. $69–$225 double. Rates include continental breakfast. AE, CB, DC, DISC, MC, V.

Location is the primary advantage of this hotel near Fisherman's Wharf and downtown. The room furnishings are relatively standard, but make an attempt at coziness with wicker chairs set around the gas-heated brick fireplace; six have kitchenettes, which go for an extra $10 per night. Amenities include an in-room tea/coffeemaker, a hot tub on the premises, and continental breakfast served daily in the hotel's lobby.

✪ **The Jabberwock Bed & Breakfast.** 598 Laine St., Monterey, CA 93940. ☎ **888/ 428-7253** or 831/372-4777. Fax 831/655-2946. 7 units (5 with bathroom). $110 double without bathroom, $210 double with bathroom. Rates include full breakfast, afternoon aperitifs, and bedtime cookies. MC, V.

One of the better B&Bs in the area, the Jabberwock (named after an episode in Lewis Carroll's *Through the Looking Glass*) is 4 short blocks from Cannery Row. Although centrally located, the property is tranquil, and its half-acre garden with waterfalls offers a welcome respite from the downtown crowds. The seven rooms are individually furnished, some more elegantly than others, but all with goose-down comforters and pillows. The Toves Room has a huge walnut Victorian bed; the Borogrove has a fireplace and a view of Monterey Bay; the Mimsey has a fine ocean view from its window seat; and the Wabe has an Austrian carved bed. A full breakfast is served in the dining room or in your own room. Evening hors d'oeuvres are offered on the veranda, and a Vorpal rabbit tucks each guest in with cookies and milk.

INEXPENSIVE

Opt for a motel to get the best rates in this town. Some reliable options are **Motel 6** (☎ **800/4-MOTEL6**), **Super 8** (☎ **800/800-8000**), or **Best Western** (☎ **800/ 528-1234**).

Cypress Tree Inn. 2227 N. Fremont St., Monterey, CA 93940. ☎ **831/372-7586.** Fax 831/372-2940. 55 units. TV TEL. $62–$102 double. AE, DC, DSIC, MC, V.

Although it's not centrally located (2 miles from downtown), if you're on a budget and have transportation, you won't be sorry if you stay here. The large rooms are spotless, and all but one has a combination tub/shower. Nine also have hot tubs. There's no shampoo, hair dryer, or in-room treats other than the taffy left by the maid, but the hostelry does have a hot tub, sauna, and coin-op laundry. RV spaces are also available.

WHERE TO DINE

Bubba Gump Shrimp Co. Restaurant & Market. 720 Cannery Row (at Prescott). ☎ **831/373-1884.** Main courses $8.95–$18.95. AE, DC, DISC, MC, V. Sun–Thurs 11am– 10pm, Fri–Sat 11am–11pm. AMERICAN.

Culinary cognoscenti will flee in disgust at the sight of this tourist haven, but the fact is, lots of folks love this place. It could be the location—near the aquarium and offering a million-dollar unobstructed bayfront view—or the old boatyard decor that attracts visitors in droves. But it's more likely the entertainment value: Gump's (as in Forrest Gump) is packed with movie gimmicks and memorabilia.

The food, unfortunately, is far less exciting. As the roll of paper towels at each table suggests, you're guaranteed a go with grease, which is likely to arrive in the form of fried and buttered-up seafood. The "Bucket of Boat Trash," for example, is shrimp and lobster tails cooked and served in a bucket with a side of fries and coleslaw. There are also pork chops, a veggie dish, salads, and burgers. The "market" referred to in the moniker is a gift shop packed with T-shirts, caps, and, of course, boxes of chocolate.

Cafe Fina. 47 Fisherman's Wharf. ☎ **831/372-5200.** Reservations recommended. Main courses $13–$17. AE, CB, DC, DISC, MC, V. Mon–Fri 11:30am–2:30pm, Sat–Sun 11:30am–3pm; daily 5pm–closing. ITALIAN/SEAFOOD.

While other pier-side restaurants lure tourists with little more than an outstanding view, Cafe Fina's mesquite-grilled meats, well-prepared fresh fish, brick-oven pizzas, and an array of delicious salads and pastas give even locals a reason to head to the wharf. Combine the food with a million-dollar vista and a casual atmosphere, and Cafe Fina ranks hands down as the best choice on the pier.

John Pisto's Whaling Station Prime Steaks & Seafood. 763 Wave St. (between Prescott and Irving aves.). ☎ **831/373-3778.** Reservations recommended on weekends. Main courses $15–$30. AE, CB, DC, DISC, MC, V. Daily 5–10pm. From Calif. 1, take the Soledad Dr. exit and follow the signs toward Cannery Row; turn left on Wave St. 1 block before Cannery Row. Free valet parking on weekends. AMERICAN/STEAK HOUSE.

If you insist on eating on Cannery Row, come to this touristy restaurant known for its New York, porterhouse, and other steaks grilled over oak and mesquite. A 28-year tradition guarantees you an artichoke vinaigrette appetizer before your main course, which ranges from pasta and chicken to jumbo live Maine lobsters and live local abalone.

✪ **Montrio**. 414 Calle Principal (at Franklin). ☎ **831/648-8880**. Reservations recommended. Main courses $14–$19. AE, DISC, MC, V. Sun–Thurs 11:30am–10pm, Fri–Sat 11:30am–11pm. AMERICAN BISTRO.

Big-city sophistication met old Monterey when Montrio hit the ground running here in March 1995. The enormous dining room is definitely the sharpest in town, mixing chic style with a playful canopied vineyard of modern light fixtures, clouds hanging from the ceiling, and the buzz of well-dressed diners. You can watch chefs scurry around in the open kitchen, but you're more likely to keep your eyes on the tasty dishes, such as the crispy Dungeness crab cakes with spicy rémoulade; succulent grilled pork chops with apple, pear, and currant compôte; or an oven-roasted portobello mushroom with polenta and ragoût of vegetables. Finish the evening with passion-fruit gratin with wild-berry coulis.

✪ **Stokes Adobe**. 500 Hartnell St. (at Madison St). ☎ **831/373-1110**. Reservations recommended. Main courses $12–$19. AE, DC, MC, V. Mon–Sat 11:30am–10pm, Sun 4–10pm. CALIFORNIA/MEDITERRANEAN.

This historic adobe and board-and-batten house, built in 1833 for the town doctor, has been converted into one of Monterey's finest restaurants. It's quite the handsome establishment, consisting of a bar and several large dining rooms, all outfitted with terra-cotta floors, bleached-wood plank ceilings, and Southwestern-style wood chairs and tables. It's the perfect rustic-yet-contemporary showcase for chef Brandon Miller's carefully crafted California-Mediterranean fare—butternut-squash soup with apple cider and maple crème fraîche, cassoulet of duck confit and homemade currant sausage with chestnut beans, grilled lavender-infused pork chops with savory bread pudding and pear chutney. Desserts are equally dreamy, such as the warm apricot clafouti and the warm banana-rum bread pudding with vanilla crème Anglaise. Highly recommended is the prix-fixe dinner, offered nightly for around $35. The wine list is excellent as well.

✪ **Tarpy's Roadhouse**. 2999 Monterey-Salinas Hwy. (at Calif. 68 and Canyon del Rey near the Monterey Airport). ☎ **831/647-1444**. Reservations recommended for dinner. Most main courses $12–$20. AE, DISC, MC, V. Daily 11:30am–10pm. CALIFORNIA/AMERICAN.

Always a mandatory stop when we're passing through Monterey is this lively Southwestern-style restaurant located a few miles east of downtown (and definitely worth the detour). The very handsome dining room has stylish yet soothingly rustic decor. On sunny afternoons, patrons relax under market umbrellas on the huge outdoor patio, sipping margaritas and munching on Tarpy's legendary Caesar salad. Come nightfall, the place fills quickly with tourists and locals who pile in for the hefty plate of bourbon-molasses pork chops or Dijon-crusted lamb loin. There's also a modest selection of fresh fish, shellfish, and vegetable dishes, but it's the good ol' meat 'n' potato mainstays that sell the best. (The thick, juicy meatloaf with garlic mashers and fresh veggies is a bargain at $12.)

Wharfside Restaurant & Lounge. 60 Fisherman's Wharf. ☎ **831/375-3956**. Reservations recommended. Main courses $11–$20. AE, DC, DISC, MC, V. Daily 11am–9:30pm. Closed the first 2 weeks of Dec. SEAFOOD.

While the fresh seafood is okay, the real attraction is the Wharfside's casual upstairs dining room, which offers a nautical decor and a great view from the end of Fisherman's Wharf (there's also downstairs and upper-deck outdoor seating). Choose from six different varieties of ravioli (made on the premises), such specialties as a combination bouillabaisse, and any of the house-made desserts. Daily specials usually include fresh seasonal fish, beef, and pasta. Clam chowder, sandwiches (including hot crab), and pizzas are on the regular menu.

3 Pacific Grove

42 miles S of Santa Cruz, 113 miles S of San Francisco, 338 miles N of Los Angeles

Some compare 2.6-square-mile Pacific Grove—the locals call it "P.G."—to Carmel as it was 20 years ago. Although tourists wind their way through here on oceanfront trails and dining excursions, the town remains quaint and peaceful—amazing considering that Monterey is a stone's throw away (a quarter of the Monterey Bay Aquarium is actually in Pacific Grove). While neighboring Monterey is comparatively congested and cosmopolitan, Pacific Grove is a community sprinkled with historic homes, blooming flowers, and the kind of tranquillity that inspires butterflies to flutter about and deer to meander fearlessly across the road in search of another garden to graze.

ESSENTIALS

VISITOR INFORMATION   Although the town is small, there is the **Pacific Grove Chamber of Commerce,** at the corner of Forest and Central avenues (☎ **831/ 373-3304**).

ORIENTATION   Lighthouse Avenue is the Grove's principal thoroughfare, running from Monterey to the lighthouse at the very point of the peninsula. Lighthouse Avenue is bisected by Forest Avenue, which runs from Calif. 1 (where it's called Holman Highway, or Calif. 68) to Lover's Point, an extension of land that sticks out into the bay in the middle of Pacific Grove.

EXPLORING THE TOWN

Pacific Grove is a town to be strolled, so park the car, put on your walking shoes, and make an afternoon of it. Meander around George Washington Park and along the waterfront around the point.

The **Point Pinos Lighthouse,** at the tip of the peninsula on Ocean View Boulevard (☎ **831/648-3116**), is the oldest working lighthouse on the West Coast. Its 50,000-candlepower beacon has illuminated the rocky shores since February 1, 1855, when Pacific Grove was little more than a pine forest. The museum and grounds are open, free to visitors, Thursday through Sunday from 1 to 4pm.

Marine Gardens Park, a stretch of shoreline along Ocean View Boulevard on Monterey Bay and the Pacific, is renowned not only for its ocean views and colorful flowers, but also for its fascinating tide-pool seaweed beds. Walk out to **Lover's Point** (named after Lovers of Jesus, not groping teenagers) and watch the sea otters playing in the kelp beds and cracking open an occasional abalone for lunch.

An excellent shorter alternative, or complement, to the 17-Mile Drive (see section 4 on Pebble Beach, later in this chapter) is the scenic drive or bike ride along Pacific Grove's **Ocean View Boulevard.** This coastal stretch starts near Monterey's Cannery Row and follows the Pacific around to the lighthouse point. Here it turns into Sunset Drive, which runs along secluded **Asilomar State Beach.** Park on Sunset and explore the trails, dunes, and tide pools of this sandy stretch of shore. You might find purple shore crabs, green anemone, sea bats, starfish, and limpets, as well as all kinds of kelp and algae. The 11 buildings of the conference center established here by the YWCA in 1913 are historic landmarks that were designed by noted architect Julia Morgan. If you follow this route during winter, a furious sea rages and crashes against the rocks.

To learn more about the marine and other natural life of the region, stop in at the **Pacific Grove Museum of Natural History,** 165 Forest Ave. (☎ **831/648-3116**). It has displays on the monarch butterflies and their migration, stuffed examples of the local birds and mammals, and temporary exhibits and special events. Admission is free; hours are Tuesday through Sunday from 10am to 4:30pm.

Pacific Grove is widely known as "Butterfly Town, USA.," a reference to the thousands of **monarch butterflies** that migrate here from November to February, traveling from as far away as Alaska. Many settle in the Monarch Grove sanctuary, a eucalyptus stand on Grove Acre Avenue off Lighthouse Avenue. George Washington Park, at Pine Avenue and Alder Street, is also famous for its "butterfly trees." To reach these sites, the butterflies may travel as far as 2,000 miles, covering 100 miles a day at an altitude of 10,000 feet. Collectors beware: The town imposes strict fines for molesting butterflies.

Just as Ocean View Boulevard serves as an alternative to the 17-Mile Drive, the **Pacific Grove Municipal Golf Course,** 77 Asilomar Ave. (☎ **831/648-3177**), serves as a reasonably priced alternative to the high-priced courses at Pebble Beach. The back nine holes of this 5,500-yard, par-70 course overlook the sea and offer the added challenge of coping with the winds. Views are panoramic, and the fairways and greens are better maintained than most semiprivate courses. There's a restaurant, pro shop, and driving range. Greens fees are $30 Monday through Thursday and $35 Friday through Sunday and holidays; twilight rates are available. Optional carts cost $25.

The **American Tin Cannery Factory Premium Outlets,** 125 Ocean View Blvd., around the corner from the Monterey Bay Aquarium (☎ **831/372-1442**), is a huge converted warehouse housing 40 factory-outlet shops. Labels represented here include Anne Klein, Joan & David, Bass Shoes, Reebok, Carter's Childrenswear, Royal Doulton, Jones New York, Maidenform, London Fog, Woolrich, and Carole Little. It's open Sunday through Thursday from 10am to 6pm, Friday and Saturday from 10am to 8pm.

WHERE TO STAY

If you're having trouble finding a vacancy, try calling **Resort II Me** (☎ **800/757-5646**), a local reservations service that offers free recommendations of Monterey Bay—area hotels in all price ranges.

EXPENSIVE & MODERATE

Centrella Inn. 612 Central Ave., Pacific Grove, CA 93950. ☎ **800/233-3372** or 831/372-3372. Fax 831/372-2036. 26 units. $109–$229 double; from $189 cottage and suite. Rates include buffet breakfast and evening hors d'oeuvres. AE, DISC, MC, V.

A couple of blocks from the waterfront and from Lover's Point Beach, the two-story Centrella is an old turreted Victorian that was built as a boardinghouse in 1889. Today, the rooms are decorated in Victorian style, but they're somewhat plain—iron beds, side table, floor lamp, and armoire—although the bathrooms do have clawfoot tubs. In the back, connected to the house by brick walkways, are several private cottages and suites with fireplaces, wet bars, TVs, and separate bedrooms and bathrooms. Two have private decks; the others offer decks facing the rose garden and patio, which is set with umbrella tables and chairs.

Gosby House. 643 Lighthouse Ave., Pacific Grove, CA 93950. ☎ **800/527-8828** or 831/375-1287. Fax 831/655-9621. 22 units (20 with bathroom). $105 double without bathroom, $90–$160 double with bathroom. Rates include full breakfast. AE, DC, MC, V. From Calif. 1, take Calif. 68 to Pacific Grove, where it turns into Forest Ave., continue on Forest to Lighthouse Ave., turn left, and go 3 blocks.

Originally a boardinghouse for Methodist ministers, this Victorian was built in 1887, 3 blocks from the bay. It's still one of the most charming Victorians in town, with individually decorated rooms, floral-print wallpapers, lacy pillows, and antique furnishings. Twelve guest rooms have fireplaces, and all come with the inn's trademark teddy bears. Especially noteworthy are the two Carriage House rooms, which come with fireplace, deck, and extra-large bathroom with spa tub. The house has a separate dining room and parlor, where guests gather for breakfast and complimentary wine and snacks in the afternoon. Other amenities include complimentary newspaper, twice-daily maid service, and bicycles.

Green Gables Inn. 104 5th St., Pacific Grove, CA 93950. ☎ **800/722-1774** or 831/ 375-2095. Fax 831/375-5437. 11 units (7 with bathroom). $110–$135 double without bathroom, $145–$180 double with bathroom; $180–$225 suite. Rates include buffet breakfast. AE, MC, V. From Calif. 1, take the Pacific Grove exit (Calif. 68) and continue to the Pacific Ocean; turn right on Ocean View Blvd. and drive half a mile to 5th St.

This 1888 Queen Anne–style mansion, which is decorated like an English country inn, forgoes opulence (and in some cases private bathrooms) to allow for reasonable rates and more homey accommodations. The rooms are divided between the main building and the carriage houses behind it; teddy bears populate every nook and cranny. The Carriage House rooms, which are better for families, have large private bathrooms with Jacuzzi tubs. All accommodations are individually decorated with dainty furnishings, including some antiques and an occasional poster bed. Most rooms in the original home have ocean views and share two immaculate bathrooms. There's an antique carousel horse in the comfortable parlor, where complimentary wine, tea, and hors d'oeuvres are served each afternoon.

۞ Martine Inn. 255 Ocean View Blvd., Pacific Grove, CA 93950. ☎ **800/852-5588** or 831/373-3388. Fax 831/373-3896. 23 units. $150–$260 double; $300 suite. Rates include full breakfast and evening hors d'oeuvres. AE, DISC, MC, V.

One glance at the lavish Victorian interior and the incredible bay views and you'll know why this Mediterranean-style inn is one of the best B&Bs in the area. Enjoy the vista via binoculars that the management leaves out for guests, or stroll the bayfront promenade. You'll have to pay more if you want a fireplace and ocean view, though every room is a winner. Request a room with a bathtub if it matters to you; some have only a shower. The inn also maintains an adjacent Victorian cottage, which has been converted into a luxury suite. A full breakfast is served at lace-covered tables in the large front room; hors d'oeuvres are served in the evening. Guests also have access to two additional sitting quarters: a small room downstairs overlooking the ocean and a larger room with shelves of books. Amenities include newspaper delivery, free coffee and refreshments, a Jacuzzi, and a billiards table.

Pacific Grove Inn. 581 Pine Ave., Pacific Grove, CA 93950, ☎ **800/732-2825** or 831/ 375-2825. 16 units. TV TEL. $98–$138 double; $135–$200 suite. Rates include buffet breakfast. AE, DC, DISC, MC, V. From Calif. 1, take the Pacific Grove exit (Calif. 68) to the corner of Pine and Forest aves.

Five blocks from the beach, this stately, renovated 1904 Queen Anne–style mansion is one of the town's architectural gems. Despite heavy Victorian embellishments, the elegant accommodations feel light, airy, and spacious. Rooms come with queen- or king-size beds, fridges, safes, and fireplaces. Afternoon tea is served in the parlor.

✪ **Seven Gables Inn.** 555 Ocean View Blvd., Pacific Grove, CA 93950. ☎ **831/372-4341.** 14 units. $155–$350 double. Rates include breakfast and afternoon tea. 2-night minimum on weekends. MC, V.

This is one of the most opulent B&Bs we've ever seen. Named after the seven gables that cap the hotel, the compound of Victorian buildings was constructed in 1886 by the Chase family (as in Chase Manhattan Bank). Outside is the coast road overlooking the sea; inside is a valuable collection of mostly European antiques. Everything here is luxurious and gilded, including the ocean-view rooms, which are scattered among the main house, cottages (including a two-bedroom option), and the guest house. The accommodations are linked by verdant gardens filled with roses and marble sculpture. Afternoon tea is accompanied by an array of pastries and homemade chocolates. If the hotel's booked, ask about the Grand View Inn, a newer, comparable B&B next door that's run by the same owners.

INEXPENSIVE

✪ **The Wilkies Inn.** 1038 Lighthouse Ave., Pacific Grove, CA 93950. ☎ **800/253-5707** or 831/372-5960. Fax 831/655-1681. 24 units. $55–$105 double. Extra person $8. 2-night minimum on weekends. AE, CB, DC, DISC, MC, V.

This motel is a great value: It consistently charges less than the other hotels in town, gets an A+ for service, and is located on a quiet tree-lined street with a resident deer who often drops by for breakfast. The motel boasts well-kept furnishings and carpets, stylish bedspreads, and special amenities for divers. All the squeaky-clean rooms come with coffeemakers and free movies and local calls. Some have VCRs (free movies!), microwaves, and partial ocean views; two have full kitchens; and you can have a fridge for a few extra dollars.

WHERE TO DINE
EXPENSIVE

✪ **Cypress Grove.** 663 Lighthouse Ave. (at 19th St.). ☎ **831/375-1743.** Reservations recommended. Main courses $15–$29. AE, MC, V. Tues–Fri 11:30am–2:30pm and 5–9:30pm, Sat–Sun 11am–2:30pm and 5:30–9:30pm. CALIFORNIA/FRENCH.

This area has few seriously gourmet restaurants, so when chef/proprietor Kurt Steeber opened Cypress Grove (in Melac's old spot) in early 1998, gourmands breathed a collective sigh of relief. Steeber, who hails from San Francisco's Campton Place and Zuni and New York's Tapastry, is a creative chef who knows how to make a dish work. The sophisticated menu, which is California-farm-fresh French, offers sautéed foie gras with port poached pear and Maytag blue cheese; onion and fennel tart; roasted quail with morels, mango, and leeks; and oxtail ragout with orzo. With a romantic dining room and an enthusiastic start, we're guessing Cypress Grove will continue to be worth a visit.

✪ **Fandango.** 223 17th St. ☎ **831/372-3456.** Reservations recommended. Main courses $11–$24. AE, CB, DC, DISC, MC, V. Mon–Sat 11am–3pm, Sun 10am–2:30pm; daily 5–9:30pm. From Calif. 1, take the Pacific Grove exit (Calif. 68), turn left on Lighthouse Ave., and continue a block to 17th St. MEDITERRANEAN.

Provincial Mediterranean specialties from Spain to Greece to North Africa spice up the menu with such offerings as seafood paella with North African couscous (the recipe has been in the owner's family for almost 200 years), cassoulet maison, cannelloni niçoise, and a Greek-style lamb shank. You'll feel transported straight to Europe in one of the five upstairs and downstairs dining rooms, cozied by roaring fires, wood tables, and antiqued walls. There's an award-winning international wine list with 450 options and a dessert menu that includes a Grand Marnier soufflé with fresh raspberry purée

---

Readers Recommend

Red House Café, *662 Lighthouse Ave. (at 19th), Pacific Grove.* ☎ **831/643-1060.**
*"This restaurant is a rustic turn-of-the-century cottage painted a delightful shade of red.
In the backyard is Mrs. Trawick's Garden Shop, a wonderful collection of garden orna-
ments, tools, and whimsies. The neighborhood birds seem very pleased to stay and add a
bit of local color. Inside the restaurant, an eclectic mix of clients is served a wonderful
changing menu for breakfast, lunch, or pastries. We sampled a pork loin sandwich on
focaccia bread, café au lait served in its traditional bowl, and an exquisite pear tart. The
young couple, Laura and Chris, opened this jewel in 1996, but you can tell from the
crowd that they have won over the hearts and tummies of the town."*

—Karla Baer Cohen and Jim Cohen, Huntington Beach, CA

Authors' Note: Main courses are $5.95 to $8.95; hours are Tuesday through Sunday
from 8am to 3pm.

---

sauce and profiteroles. In winter, ask to be seated in the fireplace dining room, and in
summer, request the terrace room—but whenever you come, expect everything here
to be lively and colorful, from the regional decor to the owner himself.

Joe Rombi's. 208 17th St. (at Lighthouse Ave.). ☎ **831/373-2416.** Reservations recommended. Main courses $12–$19. AE, MC, V. Wed–Sun 5–10pm. ITALIAN.

In an area where most restaurants pack 'em in, Joe Rombi's offers a refreshingly intimate dining room with dimmed lights and enormous French antique posters. The
food here is very fresh (lasagnas and pastas are made that day). Once seated at one of
the 11 tables, you'll immediately be served a basket of fresh house-made focaccia to
munch while you peruse the limited menu of appetizers, soups, salads, pizzas, pastas,
and four main courses (some of which come with soup and salad). Go with the fish of
the day—we had a halibut dish that any upscale San Francisco restaurant would be
proud to serve.

The Old Bath House. 620 Ocean View Blvd. ☎ **831/375-5195.** Reservations required.
Main courses $17.50–$29.50. AE, CB, DC, DISC, MC, V. Mon–Fri 5–10:30pm, Sat 4–11pm,
Sun 4–10:30pm. CONTINENTAL.

Romance is in the air at this restored Victorian restaurant, perched on the edge of the
earth overlooking Lover's Point. It may be pricey and frequented by tourists, but
dinner here is a stately affair with knockout bay views, superb service, and compe-
tently prepared cuisine. Popular starters are the grilled prawns and wild-boar sausage.
Main courses range from soy-ginger-glazed filet mignon to braised petrale sole and
veal medallions crusted with pistachios. The signature dish is the duck merlot, served
with apples and a raspberry-merlot sauce. End your decadent dinner with a plate of
hot pecan ice-cream fritters.

MODERATE & INEXPENSIVE

First Awakenings. In the American Tin Cannery, 125 Ocean View Blvd. ☎ **831/372-1125.**
Reservations not accepted. Breakfast $4–$7; lunch $5–$7. AE, CB, DISC, MC, V. Daily
7am–2:30pm. From Calif. 1, take the Pacific Grove exit (Calif. 68) and turn right onto Lighthouse Ave.; after a mile turn left onto Eardley Ave., and take it to the corner of Ocean View.
AMERICAN.

What was once a dank canning factory is now a bright, huge, open restaurant offering
one of the cheapest and healthiest breakfasts in the area. Eye-openers include eight
varieties of omelets; granola with nuts, fruit, and yogurt; walnut and wheat pancakes;

"gourmet" pancakes; and raisin French toast. At lunch, there's a fine choice of salads and a slew of sandwiches ranging from albacore to zucchini. On sunny days, take advantage of the outdoor patio tables.

The Fishwife at Asilomar Beach. 1996½ Sunset Dr. (at Asilomar Beach). ☎ **831/ 375-7107.** Main courses $8.75–$13.25. AE, DC, DISC, MC, V. Mon–Sat 11am–10pm, Sun 10am–10pm. From Calif. 1, take the Pacific Grove exit (Calif. 68) and stay left until it becomes Sunset Dr.; the restaurant will be on your left about 1 mile ahead, as you approach Asilomar Beach. SEAFOOD.

The Fishwife is the ideal dining spot for anyone looking for a casual, affordable, and quality meal. The restaurant dates from the 1830s, when a sailor's wife started a small food market that became famous for its Boston clam chowder. Today, locals still return for the savory soup as well as some of the finest seafood in Pacific Grove. Two bestsellers at dinner are calamari steak sautéed with shallots, garlic, tomatoes, and white wine; and prawns Belize, served sizzling with red onions, tomatoes, fresh serrano chiles, jicama, lime juice, and cashews. Steak and pasta dishes are also available, and all main courses come with vegetables, bread, black beans, and rice or potatoes. Kids get their own color-in menu, which has smaller portions for less than $6.

Peppers Mexicali Cafe. 170 Forest Ave. ☎ **831/373-6892.** Reservations recommended. Main courses $6–$13. AE, CB, DC, DISC, MC, V. Mon and Wed–Thurs 11:30am–10pm, Fri–Sat 11:30am–10:30pm, Sun 4–10pm. MEXICAN/LATIN AMERICAN.

Peppers is a casual, festive place serving good food at reasonable prices. The inviting dining room has wooden floors and tables, pepper art visible from every vantage point, and a perpetual crowd of diners who come to suck up beers and savor spicy specialties such as well-balanced seafood tacos and fajitas or house-made tamales and chile rellenos. Other fire-starters include the snapper Yucatán, which is cooked with chiles, citrus cilantro, and tomatoes; and grilled prawns with lime-cilantro dressing. More than a dozen daily specials are offered as well, such as Mexican seafood paella and grilled mahimahi tacos. Add a substantial selection of cervezas, an addicting compilation of chips and salsa, and a friendly staff, and your taste buds are bound to bellow "Ole!"

4 Pebble Beach & the 17-Mile Drive

Pebble Beach is a world unto itself. Polo shirts, golf shoes, and big bankrolls are standard here, and if you have to ask how much accommodations and greens fees are, you definitely can't afford them. In this elite golfers' paradise, endless grassy fairways are interrupted only by a few luxury resorts and cliffs where the ocean meets the land. In winter, it's also the site of the AT&T Pebble Beach National Pro-Am, a celebrity tournament originally launched in 1937 by crooner Bing Crosby.

THE 17-MILE DRIVE

The beautiful 17-Mile Drive demands a leisurely afternoon. Pack a picnic or make lunch reservations at pricey Roy's in the Inn at Spanish Bay (see "Where to Stay & Dine," below), fork over $7.50 to enter the drive, and prepare to see some of the most exclusive coastal real estate in California.

The drive can be entered from any of five gates: two from Pacific Grove to the north, one from Carmel to the south, or two from Monterey to the east. The most convenient entrance from Calif. 1 is just off the main road at the Holman Highway exit. You may beat traffic by entering at the Carmel Gate and doing the tour backward.

Admission to the drive includes an informative map that lists 26 points of interest along the way. Aside from homes of the ultra-rich, highlights include **Seal and Bird**

Rocks, where you can see countless gulls, cormorants, and other offshore birds as well as seals and sea lions; and **Cypress Point Lookout,** which affords a 20-mile view all the way to the Big Sur Lighthouse on a clear day. Also visible is the famous **Lone Cypress** tree, inspiration to so many artists and photographers, which you can admire from afar but to which you can no longer walk. The drive also traverses the **Del Monte Forest,** thick with tame blacktail deer and often described as some "billionaire's private game preserve."

One of the best ways to see 17-Mile Drive is by bike, but the ride toward Carmel is all downhill, so unless you're in great shape, arrange for a ride back.

GREAT GOLF COURSES

Locals tell us it's almost impossible to get a tee time unless you're staying at the golf resort. If you're one of the lucky few, you can choose from several famous courses along the 17-Mile Drive.

✪ **PEBBLE BEACH GOLF LINKS**   The most famous course is Pebble Beach Golf Links (☎ **800/654-9300**), at the Lodge at Pebble Beach (see "Where to Stay & Dine," below). It's home in winter to the AT&T Pebble Beach National Pro-Am, a celebrity-laden tournament televised around the world. Jack Nicklaus has claimed, "If I could play only one course for the rest of my life, this would be it." He should know; he won both the 1961 U.S. Amateur and the 1972 U.S. Open here. Indeed, 10 national championships have been decided here. Herbert Warren Wind, dean of this century's golf writers, said, "There is no finer seaside golf course in creation"—and that includes the legendary Old Course at St. Andrews in Scotland. Built in 1919, this 18-hole course is 6,799 yards and par 72. It's precariously perched over a rugged ocean. Greens fees are a staggering $255 for resort guests, $295 for nonguests—if they can get a slot (it's almost impossible for anyone else to play here).

✪ **SPYGLASS HILL GOLF COURSE**   Also frequented by celebrities is this course at Stevenson Drive and Spyglass Hill Road (☎ **800/654-9300**). Its slope rating of 143 means that it's one of the toughest courses in California. It's a justifiably famous links: 6,859 yards and par 72 with five oceanfront holes. The rest reach deep into the Del Monte Forest. Greens fees are $225, $195 for guests of the Lodge or the Inn (see "Where to Stay & Dine," below). Reservations for nonguests should be made a month in advance. There's an excellent Grill Room on the grounds.

✪ **POPPY HILLS**   This 18-hole, 6,219-yard course, on 17-Mile Drive (☎ **831/625-1513**), was named one of the world's top 20 by *Golf Digest.* It was designed by Robert Trent Jones, Jr., in 1986. Greens fees are $115 Monday through Friday, $130 Saturday and Sunday, plus $30 for the cart rental. You can make reservations 30 days in advance.

✪ **THE LINKS AT SPANISH BAY**   Lying on the north end of 17-Mile Drive at the Pebble Beach Resort/Inn at Spanish Bay (☎ **800/654-9300**), this is the most easily booked course. Serious golfers say it's the most challenging of the Pebble Beach links. Robert Trent Jones, Jr., Tom Watson, and Frank Tatum (former USGA president) designed it to duplicate a Scottish links course. Greens fees are $165 (including cart) for resort guests, $185 for nonguests. Cart rental is an additional $25. Reservations can be made 60 days in advance.

DEL MONTE GOLF COURSE   At 1300 Sylvan Rd. (☎ **831/373-2700**) lies the oldest course west of the Mississippi, charging some of the most "reasonable" greens fees: $80 per player ($70 for resort guests), plus a cart rental of $18. The course, often cited in magazines for its "grace and charm," is relatively short— only 6,339 yards.

This seldom-advertised course, which is located at the Hyatt east of Monterey, is part of the Pebble Beach complex, but is not along 17-Mile Drive.

WHERE TO STAY & DINE

✪ **The Inn at Spanish Bay.** 2700 17-Mile Dr., Pebble Beach, CA 93953. ☎ **800/654-9300** or 831/647-7500. Fax 831/644-7960. 276 units. MINIBAR TV TEL. $330–$500 double; from $650 suite. $17 gratuity added. AE, CB, DC, JCB, MC, V. From Calif. 1 south, turn west onto Calif. 68 and south onto 17-Mile Dr.; the hotel is on your right, just past the toll plaza.

Surrounded by the renowned Links at Spanish Bay golf course, the Inn at Spanish Bay is a plush three- and four-story low-rise, set on 236 manicured acres 10 miles north of the Lodge at Pebble Beach. Approximately half the rooms face the ocean and are more expensive than their counterparts, which overlook the forest. Each unit contains about 600 square feet of floor space and has a private fireplace and either an outdoor deck or a patio. The bathrooms are finished in Italian marble; the custom-made furnishings include four-poster beds with down comforters.

Dining/Diversions: Roy Yamaguchi, Hawaii's celebrity chef, opened Roy's, his first mainland outpost, in April 1995. The Euro-Asian menu offers many of his signature dishes, plus some new ones inspired by California's regional ingredients. Roy has a way with sauces, and although he's probably not in the kitchen, his protégés whip up some of the best food in Pebble Beach. The adjacent Lobby Lounge serves light meals; the Bay Club serves gourmet Mediterranean fare. You can also have breakfast or lunch at the nearby Clubhouse Bar and Grill, overlooking the first fairway. A jazz band performs in the Lobby Lounge Thursday through Sunday, but our favorite time is at dusk, when a bagpiper strolls the terrace with a skirling tribute to Scotland.

Amenities: Concierge, 24-hour room service, massage, evening turndown, overnight shoe shine, laundry/valet. World-class golf course, eight tennis courts (two lighted), a first-rate Ansel Adams gallery, pro shops, award-winning fitness center, equestrian center, bicycles, heated pool.

The Lodge at Pebble Beach. 17-Mile Dr., Pebble Beach, CA 93953. ☎ **800/654-9300** or 831/624-3811. Fax 831/644-7960. 173 units. MINIBAR TV TEL. $370–$500 double; from $950 suite. $15 gratuity added. AE, CB, DC, DISC, MC, V. From Calif. 1 south, turn west on Calif. 68, turn south onto 17-Mile Dr., and follow the coastal road to the hotel.

For the combined cost of greens fees and a room here, you could easily create a professional putting green in your own backyard—and still have some money left over. But if you're a dedicated hacker, you've got to play here at least once. Look on the bright side—at least you can expect ultra-plush, recently revamped rooms, which are equipped with every conceivable amenity, including fridges and wood-burning fireplaces. Most are in two-story cottage clusters, with anywhere from eight to a dozen units in each. Those opening onto the ocean carry the highest price tags.

Dining: The Stillwater Bar & Grill, which overlooks the 18th green and the bay, serves seafood. The Tap Room, patterned after an English pub and decorated with golfing memorabilia, offers everything from prime rib to thick-crust pizza. The Gallery, overlooking the first tee, is open only for breakfast and lunch. Club XIX, which overlooks the 18th green at Carmel Bay, serves light California-French cuisine for lunch and dinner.

Amenities: Concierge, 24-hour room service, supervised children's facilities, barber, evening turndown, complimentary airport transportation, massage, laundry/valet. Outstanding golf course and priority tee times, 12 tennis courts, fitness room, horseback riding, bicycles for rent, heated pool, sauna, hiking trails, shopping arcade.

5 Carmel-by-the-Sea

5 miles S of Monterey, 121 miles S of San Francisco, 33 miles N of Big Sur

If you visited the town officially known as Carmel-by-the-Sea dozens of years ago, you're likely to be of the school that criticizes its present-day overcommercialization. Carmel began as an artists' colony that attracted such luminaries as Robinson Jeffers, Sinclair Lewis, Robert Louis Stevenson, Ansel Adams, William Rose Benet, and Mary Austin. It was a nonconformist enclave where residents resisted assigned street numbers and lighting (they carried lanterns, which they considered more romantic).

Today, Carmel may not be the bohemian artists' village of seasoned travelers' memories, but it's still an adorable (albeit touristy) town that knows how to celebrate its surroundings. Vibrant wildflower gardens flourish along each residential street, gnarled cypress trees reach up from white sandy beaches, and at the end of each day tourists magically disappear and the town—for a split second—feels undiscovered.

It's still intimate enough that there's no need for street numbers. Carmel's inns, restaurants, boutiques, and art galleries all identify their locations only by cross streets. A few hints such as Saks Fifth Avenue, convertible roadsters cruising through town, intolerable traffic, and lofty B&B rates indicate we're not in Kansas anymore, but rather a well-preserved upscale tourist haven.

If you're interested in saving a few dollars, we recommend staying in quaint Pacific Grove. It's only a few miles away, has better rates, and you can easily day-trip into crowded Carmel.

ESSENTIALS

The **Carmel Business Association,** P.O. Box 4444, Carmel, CA 93921 (☎ 831/624-2522), is located on San Carlos between 5th and 6th streets. It distributes local maps, brochures, and publications. Pick up a copy of the *Guide to Carmel* and a schedule of local events. Hours are Monday through Friday from 9am to 5pm. On weekends, an information booth is set up from 11am to 3pm at Carmel Plaza, on Ocean Avenue between Junipero and San Carlos streets.

EXPLORING THE TOWN

A wonderful stretch of white sand backed by cypress trees, **Carmel Beach City Park** is a wee bit o' heaven on earth (though the jammed parking lot can feel more like a visit to a car rally). There's plenty of room for families, surfers, and dogs with their owners (yes, pooches are allowed to run off-leash here). If the parking lot is full, there are some spaces on Ocean Avenue, but take heed: They're generally good for 90-minute parking only, and you will get a ticket if you park for the day.

Farther south around the promontory, **Carmel River State Beach** is a less crowded option, with white sand and dunes, plus a bird sanctuary where brown pelicans, black oystercatchers, cormorants, gulls, curlews, godwits, and sanderlings make their home.

The ✪ **Mission San Carlos Borromeo del Rio Carmelo,** on Basilica Rio Road at Lasuen Drive, off Calif. 1 (☎ 831/624-3600), is the burial ground of Father Junípero Serra and the second-oldest of the 21 Spanish missions he established. Founded in 1771 on a scenic site overlooking the Carmel River, it remains one of the largest and most interesting of California's missions. The stone church, with its gracefully curving walls and Moorish bell tower, was begun in 1793. Its walls are covered with a lime plaster made of burnt seashells. The old mission kitchen, the first library in California, the high altar, and the flower gardens are all worth visiting. More than 3,000 Native Americans are buried in the adjacent cemetery; their graves are decorated with seashells. The mission is open June through August, Monday through Saturday from

9:30am to 7:30pm, Sunday from 10:30am to 7:30pm; in other months, Monday through Saturday from 9:30am to 4:30pm, Sunday from 10:30am to 4:30pm. A $2 donation is requested.

One of Carmel's prettiest homes and gardens is **Tor House,** 26304 Ocean View Ave. (☎ **831/624-1813;** www.torhouse.org), built by California poet Robinson Jeffers. Situated on Carmel Point, the house dates from 1918 and includes a 40-foot tower containing stones from around the world, which are embedded in the walls (there's even one from the Great Wall of China). Inside, an old porthole is reputed to have come from the ship on which Napoleon escaped from Elba in 1815. No photography is allowed. Admission is by guided tour only, and reservations are requested. It's $7 for adults, $4 for college students, and $2 for high-school students (no children under 12). Open on Friday and Saturday from 10am to 3pm.

If the tourists aren't lying on the beach in Carmel, then they're probably **shopping**—the sine qua non of Carmel activities. You'll be surprised at the number of shops packed into this small town—more than 500 boutiques offering unique fashions, baskets, housewares, imported goods, and a veritable cornucopia of art galleries. Most of the commercial action is packed along the small stretch of Ocean Avenue between Junipero and San Antonio avenues.

If you want to tour the galleries, pick up a copy of the *Carmel Gallery Guide* from the Carmel Business Association (see "Essentials," above).

Serious shoppers should also head south a few miles to the **Crossroads Shopping Center** (from Calif. 1 south, take the Rio Rd. exit west for 1 block and turn right onto Crossroads Blvd.). As far as malls go, this is a great one, with oodles of shopping and a few good restaurants.

WHERE TO STAY

If you're traveling with pets, your best bet is **The Cypress Inn,** Lincoln and 7th (P.O. Box Y), Carmel-by-the-Sea, CA 93921 (☎ **800/443-7443** or 831/624-3871; www.cypress-inn.com), which is a moderately priced option run by owner/actress Doris Day.

EXPENSIVE

✪ **Carriage House Inn.** Junipero St., between 7th and 8th aves. (P.O. Box 1900), Carmel, CA 93921. ☎ **800/433-4732** or 831/625-2585. Fax 831/624-0974. 13 units. MINIBAR TV TEL. $189–$315 double; $315 suite. Rates include continental breakfast. Extra person $15. AE, DISC, MC, V. From Calif. 1, exit onto Ocean Ave. and turn left onto Junipero St.

The luxurious atmosphere and superfluous pampering make this one of our top picks in the "downtown" area. Each room comes with a VCR (and free movies from the video library), wood-burning fireplace, small fridge, and king-size bed with down comforter. Most of the second-floor rooms have sunken tubs and vaulted beam ceilings; first-floor rooms have single whirlpool tubs. Not only is breakfast delivered to guest rooms, but there's also wine and hors d'oeuvres served in the afternoon and cappuccino in the evening. Plus, while almost all choices in the area are frill-and-lace, the Carriage House is a more mature, formal, yet cozy environment.

Highlands Inn. Calif. 1 (P.O. Box 1700), Carmel, CA 93921. ☎ **800/682-4811** or 831/624-3801. Fax 831/626-1574. 42 units, 100 spa suites. TV TEL. $295 double; $375–$450 spa suite; $900 2-bedroom, full ocean-view spa suite. AE, CB, DC, DISC, MC, V.

Four miles south of Carmel on a 12-acre cliff overlooking Point Lobos, this one- and two-story inn attracts everyone from celebrities—Madonna, Sammy Hagar, Walt Disney, Marlon Brando—to honeymooners and business executives. It's rustic yet luxurious, with wildflowers gracing its pathways, plenty of character, and a charming, exclusive atmosphere. The old-style main lounge dates from 1916 and has panoramic coastal vistas. The guest rooms are distributed throughout a cluster of buildings terraced into the hillside. Since they were renovated in 1996, expect modern decor with natural-wood furnishings, VCRs, coffeemakers, and hair dryers. Most units have decks or balconies and wood-burning fireplaces. The suites come with Jacuzzi tubs and fully equipped kitchens; four rooms have showers only.

Dining: The two restaurants are well known for their fine cuisine. The Pacific's Edge Restaurant, which hosts an annual Masters of Food and Wine event, offers dramatic views and memorable cuisine. The California Market is more casual, and you can dine inside by the potbelly stove or outdoors on the redwood deck.

Amenities: Concierge, room service, dry cleaning/laundry, valet, newspaper delivery, in-room massage, twice-daily maid service, baby-sitting, secretarial services, free shuttle. Three outdoor spas, free bicycle use, small gym, and sundeck. The well-landscaped, kidney-shaped pool is fringed by pine and cypress and reached via stairways cut into the hillside.

La Playa. Camino Real and 8th Ave. (P.O. Box 900), Carmel, CA 93921. ☎ **800/582-8900** or 831/624-6476. Fax 831/624-7966. 80 units. MINIBAR TV TEL. $135–$235 double; $235–$525 suite or cottage. Complimentary valet parking. AE, DC, MC, V.

Only 2 blocks from the beach and yet within walking distance of town, the four-story La Playa is a romantic Mediterranean-style villa built in 1904. Norwegian artist Christopher Jorgensen ordered its construction for his bride, an heiress of the Ghirardelli chocolate dynasty. The stylish lobby sets the elegant tone with its terra-cotta floors, Oriental rugs, and white marble fireplace. In the courtyard, walkways lead through beautifully landscaped grounds that surround a heated pool. Unfortunately, this is where the compliments end: Compared to the splendor of the lobby and grounds, the standard guest rooms are a real disappointment. The walls are thin, the furnishings are unappealing, the amenities scarce, and the profusion of terra-cotta pink is a visual eyesore (a green plant or two wouldn't hurt). The luxury cottages are an improvement—all have kitchens, wet bars, and garden patios, and most have wood-burning fireplaces—but yes, they're expensive.

Dining: The moderately priced Terrace Grill serves California cuisine; for a very relaxing summertime meal, dine out on the alfresco terrace overlooking the gardens.

Amenities: Room service (limited to breakfast and lunch in cottages), dry cleaning, newspaper delivery, twice-daily maid service, and nightly turndown (excluding cottages).

✪ **Mission Ranch.** 26270 Dolores St., Carmel, CA 93923. ☎ **800/538-8221** or 831/ 624-6436. Fax 831/626-4163. 31 units. TV TEL. $85–$225 double. Rates include continental breakfast. AE, MC, V.

If you want to stay a bit off the beaten track, consider this converted 1850s dairy farm, which was purchased and restored by Clint Eastwood to preserve the vista of the nearby wetlands stretching out to the bay. The ranch's accommodations are spaciously scattered amid different structures, both old and new, and surrounded by wetlands and grazing sheep. Guest rooms range from "regulars" in the main barn (which are less desirable) to meadow-view units, each with a vista across the fields to the bay. As befits a ranch, rooms are decorated in a provincial style, with carved wooden beds bedecked with handmade quilts. Most are equipped with whirlpool baths, fireplaces, and decks or patios. The Martin Family farmhouse contains six units, all arranged around a central parlor, while the Bunkhouse (the oldest structure on the property) contains separate living and dining areas, bedrooms, and a fridge.

Dining: Even if you're not staying here, call for a table at the Restaurant at Mission Ranch; see "Where to Dine," below.

Amenities: Tennis courts, exercise room, putting green, pro shop.

MODERATE

Carmel Sands Lodge. San Carlos and 5th (P.O. Box 951), Carmel, CA 93921. ☎ **800/ 252-1255** or 831/624-1255. Fax 831/624-2576. 38 units. TV TEL. Apr–Sept $125–$145 double; Oct–Mar $69–$98 double. AE, DC, DISC, MC, V. From Ocean Ave., take a right onto San Carlos and go 2 blocks.

The Sands is a motor lodge, but it's decorated better than most and is located on a quiet street in Carmel. The modern rooms have pretty bedspreads and updated furnishings; some have fireplaces, fridges, and wet bars. There's a small pool here, but it's practically in the center courtyard parking lot. Adjoining the property is Simpson's restaurant, and several more restaurants are within walking distance. We like the quaint location here better than that of the comparable Carmel Village Inn.

Carmel Village Inn. Ocean Ave. and Junipero St. (P.O. Box 5275), Carmel, CA 93921. ☎ **800/346-3864** or 831/624-3864. Fax 831/626-6763. 58 units. TV TEL. $69–$165 double; $89–$300 triple or quad; from $89 suite. Rates include continental breakfast. AE, MC, V. From Calif. 1, exit onto Ocean Ave. and continue straight to Junipero St.

Well run and centrally located, the Village Inn is nothing more than a motor lodge. The rooms, arranged around a courtyard/parking lot lined with potted geraniums, are outfitted with bland but functional decor. The guest rooms come equipped with fridges. Breakfast, accompanied by the morning newspaper, is served in the downstairs lounge.

Cobblestone Inn. Junipero St., between 7th and 8th aves., 1½ blocks from Ocean Ave. (P.O. Box 3185), Carmel, CA 93921. ☎ **800/833-8836** or 831/625-5222. Fax 831/625-0478. 24 units. TV TEL. $125–$165 double; from $200 suite. Rates include full breakfast and afternoon hors d'oeuvres. AE, DC, MC, V.

The Cobblestone may not be Victorian like other properties owned by the Four Sisters Inns, but it's just as flowery, well kept, and cute, with hand-stenciled wall decorations, fireplaces, and a trademark abundance of teddy bears. The first floor is completely constructed of stones taken from the Carmel River (hence the inn's name), and the rooms encircle a slate courtyard; some look out onto the brick patio where breakfast is occasionally served. The guest rooms vary in size; some can be small and none come with bathtubs, but the largest units include a wet bar, sofa, and separate bedroom. Guests have the use of a comfortable living room with large stone fireplace and enjoy complimentary wine, hors d'oeuvres, coffee, and cookies. Extras include twice-daily maid service, morning newspaper, free videos, and bicycle rentals.

Normandy Inn. Ocean Ave., between Monte Verde and Casanova sts. (P.O. Box 1706), Carmel, CA 93921. ☎ **800/343-3825** or 831/624-3825. Fax 831/624-4614. 48 units. TV TEL. $98–$200 double; $165–$500 suites and cottages. Rates include continental breakfast. Extra person $10. AE, MC, V. From Calif. 1, exit onto Ocean Ave. and continue straight for 5 blocks past Junipero St.

Three blocks from the beach, this Tudor-style hotel is like something out of a storybook, especially with the array of colorful flowers that brighten up the property. The guest rooms show their age a little, but are well appointed with French country decor, down comforters, and coffeemakers; some also have fireplaces and/or kitchenettes. The tiny heated pool is banked by a sweet flower garden. Other perks include a self-service laundry and newspapers delivered to your room daily.

The three large family-style units are an especially good deal and accommodate up to eight; each one has three bedrooms, two bathrooms, a fully equipped kitchen, a dining room, a living room with a fireplace, and a back porch. Be sure to reserve far in advance, especially in summer.

Sandpiper Inn by the Sea. 2408 Bay View Ave., Carmel, CA 93923. ☎ **800/633-6433** or 831/624-6433. Fax 831/624-5964. www.sandpiper-inn.com. 16 units. $140–$235 double.

Value-season rates are available in off-season. Rates include extended continental breakfast and afternoon sherry/tea. AE, DISC, MC, V.

A garden of flowers welcomes visitors to this quiet, midscale Carmel standby that's been in business for more than 60 years. The inn's rooms, from which you can hear the surf, offer a range of well-kept accommodations. The highest priced are corner rooms with four-poster beds and plenty of windows framing the ocean view. All are decorated with handsome country antiques and fresh flowers that are changed daily; three have fireplaces. Carmel's fabled white-sand beaches are a mere 100 yards away.

WHERE TO DINE
EXPENSIVE

Anton & Michel. At Court of the Fountain, Mission St. (between Ocean and 7th aves.). ☎ **831/624-2406.** Reservations recommended. Main courses $17.75–$27.50. AE, DC, DISC, MC, V. Daily 11:30am–3pm and 5:30–9:30pm. EUROPEAN/CONTINENTAL.

This elegant restaurant, just across from Carmel Plaza, serves traditional French cuisine in one of the most formal rooms in town. During the day, it's best to dine fountain-side on the patio or encased in the glass-wrapped terrace. The view is equally charming in the evening, when the courtyard is lit and the fountain's water sparkles with reflections. Decorated with French chandelier lamps and original oil paintings, the main dining room is a formal affair—but, as in most restaurants in town, patrons' attire need not match it. Appetizers include crab cakes with cilantro-pesto aioli or delicate ravioli filled with ricotta cheese and spinach. Specialties include rack of lamb with an herb-Dijon mustard au jus, medallions of ahi tuna with a black-pepper-and-sesame-seed crust, and more eclectic items such as a flavorful chicken breast Jerusalem, sautéed with olive oil, white wine, cream, mushrooms, and artichoke hearts. The award-winning wine list is also impressive.

Casanova. 5th Ave. (between San Carlos and Mission sts.). ☎ **831/625-0501.** Reservations recommended. Three-course dinner $21.75–$35.75. MC, V. Mon–Sat 11:30am–3pm, Sun 9am–3pm; Sun–Thurs 5–10pm, Fri–Sat 5–10:30pm. From Calif. 1, take the Ocean Ave. exit and turn right on Mission, then left onto 5th Ave. NORTHERN ITALIAN/SOUTHERN FRENCH.

It's the European ambiance that makes this place special. The building, which once belonged to Charlie Chaplin's cook, is divided into three Belgian chalet–style dining rooms that serve as the perfect setting for leaning over a bottle of red wine and creating vacation memories. More festive folk step back to the Old World–style covered patio where it's bustling and crowded. Since all dinner entrees include antipasto and a choice of appetizers (such as baked stuffed eggplant with rice, herbs, cheese, and tomatoes), $30 is not such a bad deal (at least in overpriced Carmel). The menu features typical Mediterranean cuisine: paella, homemade pastas, meats, and fish. Casanova also boasts an award-winning wine cellar featuring more than 1,600 French, California, German, and Italian wines.

✪ **The Restaurant at Mission Ranch.** At Mission Ranch, 26270 Dolores St. ☎ **831/625-9040.** Reservations recommended. Most main courses $15–$29. MC, V. Mon–Fri 4:30–9:45pm; Sat 11am–2:30pm and 4:30–9:45pm; Sun 9:30am–1:30pm and 4:30–9:45pm; bar stays open until midnight. AMERICAN.

Clint Eastwood bought this rustic out-of-the-way property in 1986 and restored the ranch-style building to its original integrity, and although the chance of seeing him brings in some folks, it's the views, quality food, and merry atmosphere that really make the place special. The wooden building is encased with large windows that accentuate the wonderful view of the marshlands, grazing sheep, and bay beyond. Warm days make patio dining the prime choice, but the key time to come is at sunset, when the sky is transforming and happy hour is in full swing (you'll find some of the cheapest drinks around, and Clint often stops by when he's in town). As you'd expect from the ranch motif, meat is king here: Burgers are freshly ground on-site, and prime rib with twice-baked potato and vegetables is the favored dish. There are, of course, wonderful seafood, chicken, and vegetarian options as well; and all dinners include soup or salad. Entertainment is provided at the piano bar, where locals and tourists have been known to croon their favorites. The Sunday buffet brunch with live jazz piano is also hugely popular; be sure to reserve.

Robert Kincaid's Bistro on the Boulevard. Crossroads Shopping Center, 217 Crossroads Blvd. ☎ **831/624-9626.** Reservations recommended for dinner. Fixed-price lunch $16; dinner main courses $19–$28. AE, CB, DC, DISC, MC, V. Mon–Fri 11:30am–2pm and 5:30–10pm, Sat–Sun 5:30–10pm. From Calif. 1, turn east on Rio Rd.; go 1 block and turn right into Crossroads Center, then left on Crossroads Blvd. FRENCH.

Chef/owner Robert Kincaid was at renowned Fresh Cream before he went solo and wowed locals with hard-to-beat ambiance and quality food. The decor—sophisticated country French with antiqued walls, dried flowers, and divided dining rooms—is cozy and romantic (especially if you grab a booth), and the three-course lunch deal has got to be one of the best in town ($16 gets you a starter such as country sausage in a puff pastry, one of five main courses such as spicy blackened swordfish, and a dessert). There are no deals at dinner, just delightful offerings such as crab dumplings, award-winning crisp roast duck, roast rack of lamb with a mustard crust, and serious desserts that may almost be worth the $7 price tag.

✪ Zig Zag. Mission Street, between 5th and 6th aves. ☎ **831/622-9949.** Reservations recommended. Main courses $17.50–$21.50. AE, MC, V. Daily 5–10pm (closed Mon–Tues Nov–March). ECLECTIC AMERICAN.

With its highly fashionable dining room and a cuisine that launches trends rather than sticks with the classics, Zig Zag is a welcome departure from traditional Carmel dining—a successful amalgamation of a friendly village dining room and an adventurous big-city restaurant. The 12-table dining room, like the fare, eschews Carmel's generic cute cottage antics. Here modern design, streamlined furnishings, and strategic track lighting set the stage for executive chef Wendy Little's bold take on California comfort food, which celebrates Central California's bounty of fresh ingredients. Little's seasonal American menu is a robust culinary adventure. Always outstanding is the daily risotto special, such as the seared quail risotto made with sun-dried cherries, snap peas, artichokes, and port sauce. The Asian Duck Bowl, a colorful combination of grilled ginger-soy duck breast, udon noodles, shiitake mushrooms, snow peas, and vegetable strips in a smoky sherry duck broth reduction, is an exercise in decadence and delicacy. If you're still not convinced, stop by during the weekday happy hour for free tastes of Little's handiwork, such as her seared rare albacore tuna with roasted garlic, hummus, and cured olives.

MODERATE

Flying Fish Grill. In Carmel Plaza, Mission St. (between Ocean and 7th aves.). ☎ **831/ 625-1962.** Reservations recommended. Main courses $13.75–$19.75. AE, DISC, MC, V. Daily 5–10pm. Closed Tues in winter. PACIFIC RIM/SEAFOOD.

We always feel more confident when a restaurant's kitchen is actually run by its owner—and a dinner experience here will confirm that chef/proprietor Kenny Fukumoto is in the house. Dark, romantic, and Asian-influenced, the dining room has an intimate atmosphere with redwood booths (built by Kenny) and fish hanging (flying?) from the ceiling. The cuisine features fresh seafood with exquisite Japanese accents. Start with sushi, tempura, or any of the other exotic and tantalizing taste teasers. Then prepare your tongue for seriously sensational main courses. House favorites include a savory rare peppered ahi, blackened and served with mustard/sesame-soy vinaigrette and angel-hair pasta, and a pan-fried almond sea bass with whipped potatoes, Chinese cabbage, and rock shrimp stir-fry.

Grasing's Coastal Cuisine. Sixth St. (at Mission St.). ☎ **831/624-6562.** Reservations recommended. Main courses $12.50–$21.50. AE, MC, V. Daily 11am–4pm, 5–10pm. CALIFORNIA.

When chef Kurt Grasing and renowned Bay Area restaurateur Narsai David teamed together to open Grasing's Coastal Cuisine, the result was one of Carmel's best new restaurants. The bright, split-room dining area is simple yet stylish, with buttercup yellow walls, beaded lamps, and colorful artwork. Grasing's menu also reflects a stylish simplicity; ultra-fresh ingredients gleaned from California's coast and central valley regions are displayed in a modest fashion that belie an intense combination of textures and flavors. The warm Napa Salad, for example, appears ordinary enough, but "when I took it off the menu," says Grasing, "I still made 30 a night." Two other dishes that have generated such interest are the lobster risotto made with pearl pasta (rather than aborio rice, for a smoother texture) and the Bronzed Salmon served in a garlic cream sauce. Even the bread, which comes fresh from Gail's Bakery in Aptos, is fantastic. When the sun's out, request a table at the dog-friendly patio, and be sure to inquire about the very reasonable $25 prix-fixe meal.

Il Fornaio. Ocean Ave. (at Monte Verde). ☎ **831/622-5100,** or 831/622-5115 for the bakery. Main courses $8.50–$21.50. AE, DC, MC, V. Mon–Thurs 7am–10pm, Fri 7am–11pm, Sat 8am–11pm, Sun 8am–10pm. ITALIAN.

We don't care if it is a chain—Il Fornaio is still one of our favorite restaurants because we know we're guaranteed a well-prepared mocha and thick chocolate-dipped biscotti at every outpost. There's also a great selection of salads (go with the simple house salad with shaved Parmesan, croutons, and a tangy light dressing), pastas, pizzas, and rotisserie chicken, duck, and rabbit fresh from the brick oven. The house-made breads and seeded breadsticks alone are reason enough to come. We must admit that we were disappointed with the tasty-but-measly $11 lasagna, so skip it and start with the seared swordfish antipasto with roast pepper and Dijon mustard, or decadent grilled polenta with sautéed wild mushrooms, provolone, and Italian truffle oil. Move on to a gourmet pizza or pasta. The large airy dining room and sunny terrace offer charming and diverse atmosphere. The Panetteria, a retail bakery, is the perfect place to pick up a gourmet picnic or have a breakfast snack.

La Bohème. Dolores St. and 7th Ave. ☎ **831/624-7500.** www.laboheme.com. Reservations not accepted. Fixed-price, three-course dinner $23.75. MC, V. Daily 5:30–10pm. Closed 2 weeks before Christmas. From Calif. 1, exit onto Ocean Ave. and turn left onto Dolores St. FRENCH COUNTRY.

Like a set from Disney's "It's a Small World," La Bohème mimics a French street with cartoony asymmetrical shingled house facades and a painted blue sky overhead. Thankfully, the similarity stops with the decor, and there are no dolls singing anywhere—in French or English. Dinner here is utterly romantic French, served at cramped tables set with floral-print cloths in bright colors, hand-painted dinnerware, and vibrant bouquets. Dinner is a three-course, fixed-price feast consisting of a large salad, a tureen of soup, and a main dish (perhaps roast breast of duckling with green peppercorn sauce or filet mignon with cognac-cream sauce). Vegetarian specials are also available nightly. Homemade desserts and fresh coffee are sold separately, and are usually worth the extra expense. Dress is casual.

✪ **Rio Grill.** Crossroads Shopping Center, 101 Crossroads Blvd. ☎ **831/625-5436.** Reservations recommended. Main courses $10–$25. AE, DISC, MC, V. Sun–Thurs 11:30am–10pm,

Fri–Sat 11:30am–11pm. From Calif. 1, take the Rio Rd. exit west for 1 block and turn right onto Crossroads Blvd. AMERICAN.

The food or the festive atmosphere (a cartoon mural of famous locals such as Clint Eastwood and the late Bing Crosby, plus playful sculpture, cactus, and other vibrant art) have kept this place popular with even the locals for the past several years. The whimsical nature of the modern Santa Fe–style dining room belies the kitchen's serious preparations, which include homemade soups; a rich quesadilla with almonds, cheeses, and smoked-tomato salsa; barbecued baby-back ribs from a wood-burning oven; and fresh fish from an open oak grill. The restaurant's good selection of wines includes some rare California vintages and covers a broad price range. As usual in this town, dress is casual.

INEXPENSIVE

Caffè Napoli. Ocean Ave. (between Dolores and Lincoln). ☎ **831/625-4033.** Reservations recommended. Main courses $8–$15. MC, V. Daily 11:30am–4pm and 5–9:30pm. ITALIAN.

The decor here is so quintessentially Italiana, with flags, gingham tablecloths, garlic, and baskets overhead, that we expected a flour-coated pot-bellied Padrino Napoli to emerge from the kitchen, embrace us wholeheartedly, and exclaim "Mangia! Mangia!" as he slapped down a bowl overflowing with sauce-drenched pasta. Of course there is no Padrino here, and we received no welcoming hug, but we did indulge in the fine Italian fare that keeps locals coming back for more.

6 Carmel Valley

3 miles SE of Carmel-by-the-Sea

Inland from Carmel stretches Carmel Valley, where wealthy folks retreat beyond the reach of the coastal fog and mist. It's a scenic and perpetually sunny valley of rolling hills dotted with manicured golf courses and many a horse ranch.

Hike the trails in **Garland Regional Park,** 8 miles east of Carmel on Carmel Valley Road (dogs are welcome off-leash). The sun really bakes you out here, so bring lots of water. You could also sign up for a trail ride or riding lesson at the **Holman Ranch,** 60 Holman Rd. (☎ **831/659-2640**), 12 miles east of Calif. 1.

Golf is offered at several resorts and courses in the valley, notably at **Quail Lodge,** 8000 Valley Green Dr. (☎ **831/624-2770**), and **Rancho Cañada Golf Club,** Carmel Valley Rd. (☎ **831/624-0111**).

While you're in the valley, taste the wines at the **Château Julien Winery,** 8940 Carmel Valley Rd. (☎ **831/624-2600**), which is open daily.

WHERE TO STAY

✪ **Quail Lodge Resort and Golf Club.** 8205 Valley Greens Dr., Carmel, CA 93923. ☎ **888/828-8787** or 831/624-2888. Fax 831/624-3726. 100 units. MINIBAR TV TEL. Apr–Nov $245–$345 double; $395–$800 deluxe room/suite. Dec–Mar $188–$225 double; $255–$800 suite. Extra person $25. AE, MC, V. From Calif. 1 north, past the Carmel exits (after which the highway narrows to 2 lanes), turn left on Carmel Valley Rd. and continue 3 miles to Valley Greens Dr.

The ultra-elite Peninsula Hotel Group, which acquired the Quail Lodge in 1997, is currently executing a 5-year, $43-million renovation plan. However, considering this resort's reputation as an executive golf haven—and one of the most highly regarded resort hotels in the country—the upgrades can only mean one thing: superfluous luxury. Lying in the foothills of the Santa Lucia Range, Quail Lodge has already received five-star ratings for 20 years running. Its pastoral setting encompasses more than 850 acres of sparkling lakes, secluded woodlands, and rolling meadows. The guest rooms are in two-story balconied wings, with terraces overlooking the pool or one of the 10 man-made lakes, or in cottages holding five units each. Executive villas are the most expensive and luxurious accommodations.

Remodeled in 1996, the guest rooms are decorated in warm earth tones jazzed up with floral and striped patterns. Higher-priced accommodations, on the upper floors, have cathedral ceilings. Every room has a separate dressing area and an ample balcony; some have fireplaces and wet bars. All units have coffeemakers, supplied with freshly ground beans; a fresh-fruit plate is delivered to each room per day as well. Afternoon tea is served in the lobby from 3 to 5pm.

Dining: The renowned Covey Restaurant serves European fare in warmly elegant surroundings; renovation plans include alfresco lakeside dining. Jackets are requested for men, and reservations are essential.

Amenities: Concierge, room service, evening turndown, complimentary morning newspaper, 18-hole golf course designed by Robert Muir Graves, pro shop, four tennis courts, two pools, sauna, hot tub, hiking and jogging trails, gift shops.

7 The Big Sur Coast

3 miles S of Carmel-by-the-Sea, 123 miles S of San Francisco, 87 miles N of Hearst Castle

Big Sur is more than a drive along one of the most dramatic coastlines on earth or a peaceful repose amid a forest of towering California redwoods. It's a stretch of vast wilderness so overwhelmingly beautiful—especially when the fog glows in the moonlight—that it enchants all who walk its majestic paths. It's also home to a particular breed of nature lover who prefers a rustic lifestyle over the rest of California's offerings. When the 1997 and 1998 El Niño storms caused landslides and major road damage, cutting the area off from civilization for months, reports from Big Sur were unusual: Some residents fled, vowing never to return; others loved it even though their incomes were temporarily all but eliminated. The remaining residents rejoiced in the temporary solitude; while Post Ranch, the area's ultimate luxury resort, shared the impromptu intimacy with deep-pocketed guests by flying them in via helicopter (for an extra fee, of course). Such is the price paid for living among the untamable California wilderness. Since the roads reopened, they're packed again, and driving through the region is painfully slow; rubber-neckers admiring the view and nervous Nellys fearing the cliffs can't help but drive with their foot on the brakes.

Although there is an actual Big Sur Village approximately 25 miles south of Carmel, "Big Sur" refers to the entire 90-mile stretch of coastline between Carmel and San Simeon, blessed on one side by the majestic Santa Lucia Range and on the other by the rocky Pacific coastline. It's one of the most romantic and relaxing places on earth, and if you need respite from the rat race, we can recommend no better place to find it (although Yosemite, if you hike past the crowds, is equally rejuvenating). There's little more to do than explore the mountains and beaches, or just perch yourself atop the cliffs and take in the California sea air—but spend a few days here and you'll find that you need nothing else.

ESSENTIALS

VISITOR INFORMATION   Contact the **Monterey Peninsula Visitors and Convention Bureau** (☎ 831/649-1770; www.monterey.com) for specialized information on places and events in Big Sur.

ORIENTATION   Most of this stretch is state park, and Calif. 1 runs its entire length, hugging the ocean the whole way. Restaurants, hotels, and sights are easy to spot—most are situated directly on the highway—but without major towns as reference points, their addresses can be obscure. For the purposes of orientation, we'll use the River Inn as our mileage guide. Located 29 miles south of Monterey on Calif. 1, the inn is generally considered to mark the northern end of Big Sur.

EXPLORING THE BIG SUR COAST

Big Sur offers visitors a profusion of tranquillity and natural beauty—ideal for hiking, picnicking, camping, fishing, and beachcombing.

The first settlers arrived here only a century ago, and the present highway was built in 1937, making the area accessible by car. (Electricity arrived only in the 1950s, and it's still not available in the remote inland mountains.) Big Sur's mysterious, misty beauty has inspired several modern spiritual movements (the Esalen Institute was the birthplace of the human potential movement). Even the tourist bureau bills the area as a place in which "to slow down . . . to meditate . . . to catch up with your soul." Take the board's advice and take your time—nothing better lies ahead.

The region affords a bounty of wilderness adventure opportunities. The inland **Ventana Wilderness,** which is maintained by the U.S. Forest Service, contains 167,323 acres straddling the Santa Lucia Mountains and is characterized by steep-sided ridges separated by V-shaped valleys. The streams that cascade through the area are marked by waterfalls, deep pools, and thermal springs. The wilderness offers 237 miles of hiking trails that lead to 55 designated trail camps—a backpacker's paradise. One of the easiest trails to access is the **Pine Ridge Trail** at Big Sur station (☎ 831/ 667-2315).

From Carmel, the first stop along Calif. 1 is ✪ **Point Lobos State Reserve** (☎ 831/ 624-4909), 3 miles south of Carmel. Sea lions, harbor seals, sea otters, and thousands of seabirds reside in this 1,276-acre reserve. Between December and May, you can also spot migrating California gray whales just offshore. Trails follow the shoreline and lead to hidden coves. Note that parking is limited; on weekends especially, you need to arrive early to secure a place.

From here, cross the Soberanes Creek, passing **Garrapata State Park,** a 2,879-acre preserve with 4 miles of coastline. It's unmarked and undeveloped, though the trails are maintained. To explore them, you'll need to park at one of the turnouts on Calif. 1 near Soberanes Point and hike in.

Ten miles south of Carmel, you'll arrive at North Abalone Cove. From here, Palo Colorado Road leads back into the wilderness to the first of the Forest Service camping areas at **Bottchers Gap** ($10 to camp, $5 to park overnight).

Continuing south, about 13 miles from of Carmel, you'll cross the **Bixby Bridge** and see the **Point Sur Lighthouse** off in the distance. The Bixby Bridge, one of the world's highest single-span concrete bridges, towers nearly 270 feet above Bixby Creek Canyon, and offers gorgeous canyon and ocean views from several observation alcoves at regular intervals along the bridge. The lighthouse, which sits 361 feet above the surf on a volcanic rock promontory, was built in 1889, when only a horse trail provided access to this part of the world. Tours, which take 2 to 3 hours and involve a steep half-mile hike each way, are scheduled on most weekends. For information, call ☎ 831/ 625-4419. Admission is $5 for adults, $3 for youths 13 to 17, $2 for children 5 to 12, and free for kids 4 and under.

About 3 miles south of the lighthouse is **Andrew Molera State Park** (☎ 831/ 667-2315), the largest state park on the Big Sur Coast at 4,800 acres. It's much less crowded than Pfeiffer–Big Sur (see below). Miles of trails meander through meadows and along beaches and bluffs. Hikers and cyclists use the primitive trail camp about a third of a mile from the parking area. **Molera Big Sur Trail Rides** (☎ 800/942-5486 or 831/625-5486) offers coastal trail rides through the park for horseback riders of all

Map: The Big Sur Coast

- To Monterey
- Point Sur Lighthouse
- Point Sur State Historic Park
- Point Sur
- False Sur
- California Sea Otter Game Refuge
- South Fork Santa Lucia Range
- Little Sur River
- Ventana Wilderness
- Gate
- Andrew Molera State Park
- Adams Hill
- Los Padres
- Gate
- Gate
- Camp Parking
- Gate
- Molera Point
- Gate
- Big Sur
- National Forest
- Big Sur River
- Gate
- Gate
- Pfeiffer Falls
- Pfeiffer Big Sur State Park
- Cooper Point
- Park Headquarters
- Pfeiffer Beach
- Big Sur Lodge
- Sawmill Flat
- Weyland
- South Park Entrance
- Pfeiffer Point
- Wreck Beach
- To San Luis Obispo
- California Sea Otter Game Refuge
- Pacific Ocean
- 0   1 Mi
- 0   1 Km
- N
- NA-0204

levels of experience. The 2½-mile-long beach, which is sheltered from the wind by a bluff, is accessible via a mile-long path flanked in spring by wildflowers and offers excellent tide pooling. You can walk the entire length of the beach at low tide; otherwise take the bluff trail above the beach. The park also has campgrounds.

Back on Calif. 1, you'll soon reach the village of Big Sur, where commercial services are available.

About 26 miles south of Carmel you'll come to **Big Sur Station** (☎ **831/667-2315**), where you can pick up maps and other information about the region. It's located a quarter mile past the entrance to **Pfeiffer–Big Sur State Park** (☎ **800/444-7275** or 831/667-2315), an 810-acre park that offers 218 camping sites along the Big Sur River, picnicking, fishing, and hiking. It's a scenic park of redwoods, conifers, oaks, and open meadows. For this reason, it gets very crowded. The Lodge in the park has cabins with fireplaces and other facilities (see "Where to Stay" and the "Camping in Big Sur," box below). Admission to the park is $5, and it's open daily from dawn to dusk.

Exactly 1⅒-mile south of the entrance to Pfeiffer–Big Sur State Park is the turnoff to Sycamore Canyon Road (unmarked), which will take you two winding miles down to beautiful **Pfeiffer Beach,** a great place to soak in the sun on the wide expanse of golden sand. It's open for day-use only, there's no fee, and it's the only beach accessible by car (but not motorhomes).

Back on Calif. 1, the road travels 11 miles past Sea Lion Cove to Julia Pfeiffer Burns State Park. High above the ocean is the famous **Nepenthe** restaurant (see "Where to Dine" below), the retreat bought by Orson Welles for Rita Hayworth in 1944. A few miles farther south is the **Coast Gallery** (☎ 831/667-2301), the premier local art gallery, which shows lithographs of works by Henry Miller. The gallery's casual Coast Cafe offers simple serve-yourself lunches of soup, sandwiches, baked goods, and coffee drinks. Miller fans will also want to stop at the **Henry Miller Memorial Library** (☎ 831/667-2574) on Calif. 1, 30 miles south of Carmel and a quarter mile south of Nepenthe restaurant. The library displays and sells books and artwork by Miller and houses a permanent collection of first editions. It also serves as a community art center, hosting concerts, poetry readings, and art exhibitions (check their upcoming events at **www.henrymiller.org**). The rear gallery room is a video-viewing space where films about Henry Miller can be seen. There's a sculpture garden, plus tables on the adjacent lawn where visitors can rest and enjoy the surroundings. Admission is free; hours are Tuesday through Sunday from 11am to 5pm.

   Julia Pfeiffer Burns State Park (☎ 831/667-2315) encompasses some of Big Sur's most spectacular coastline. To get a closer look, take the trail from the parking area at McWay Canyon, which leads under the highway to a bluff overlooking an 80-foot-high McWay Waterfall dropping directly into the ocean. It's less crowded here than at Pfeiffer–Big Sur, and there are miles of trails to explore in the 3,580-acre park. Scuba divers can apply for permits to explore the 1,680-acre underwater reserve.

   From here, the road skirts the Ventana Wilderness, passing Anderson and Marble Peaks and the Esalen Institute, before crossing the Big Creek Bridge to Lucia and several campgrounds farther south. **Kirk Creek Campground,** about 3 miles north of Pacific Valley, offers camping with ocean views and beach access. Beyond Pacific Valley, the ✪ **Sand Dollar Beach** picnic area is a good place to stop and enjoy the coastal view and take a stroll. A half-mile trail leads down to the sheltered beach, from which there's a fine view of Cone Peak, one of the coast's highest mountains. Two miles south of Sand Dollar is **Jade Cove,** a popular spot for rock hounds. From here, it's about another 27 miles past the Piedras Blancas Light Station to San Simeon.

WHERE TO STAY

Only a handful of Big Sur's accommodations offer the kind of pampering and luxury you'd expect in a fine urban hotel; even direct-dial phones and TVs (often considered gauche in these parts) are rare. Big Sur hotels are especially busy in summer, when advance reservations are required. There are more accommodations than those listed here; so if you're having trouble securing a room or a site, contact the Visitors Bureau for other options.

Big Sur Lodge. In Pfeiffer–Big Sur State Park, Calif. 1 (P.O. Box 190), Big Sur, CA 93920. ☎ **800/424-4787** or 831/667-3100. Fax 831/667-3110. www.bigsurlodge.com. 61 cottages. $79–$139 cottage for two; $99–$169 cottage with kitchen or fireplace; $119–$189 cabin with kitchen and fireplace. Rates include park entrance fees. AE, MC, V. From Carmel, take Calif. 1 south 26 miles.

A family-friendly place, the Big Sur Lodge—sheltered by towering redwoods, sycamores, and broad-leafed maples—is situated in the enormous state park. The rustic motel-style cabins are huge, with high peaked cedar- and redwood-beamed ceilings. They're clean and heated, and have private bathrooms and reserved parking spaces. Some have fireplaces and/or kitchenettes (bring your own cooking utensils, though). All offer porches or decks with views of the redwoods or the Santa Lucia Range. Cabin nos. 34 to 50 will put you in Siberia.

   An advantage to staying here is that you're entitled to free use of all the facilities of the park, including hiking, barbecue pits, and picnic areas. In addition, the lodge has its own outdoor heated pool, gift shop, grocery stores, and laundry facilities.

The lodge dining room is open for breakfast, lunch, and dinner, but it doesn't have the ambiance of other nearby options. Evening menus feature fresh seafood, steaks, and pasta dishes.

Deetjen's Big Sur Inn. Calif. 1, Big Sur, CA 93920. ☎ **831/667-2377.** 20 units (15 with bathroom). Sun–Thurs from $75 double without bathroom, from $100 double with bathroom; Fri–Sat from $85 double without bathroom, from $180 double with bathroom. MC, V.

Man, is this place cute. In the 1930s, before Calif. 1 was built, this homestead was an overnight stopping place on the coastal wagon road. It was begun by Norwegian homesteader Helmuth Deetjen, who over the years built several units constructed from hand-hewn logs and lumber. Folks either love or hate the accommodations, which are set in a redwood canyon. They're rustic, cozy, and adorable with their old-fashioned furnishings and down-home feel. But those who want extensive creature comforts should go elsewhere. Single-wall construction means that the rooms are far from soundproof, so children under 12 are allowed only if families reserve both rooms of a two-room building. There's no insulation, so prepare to crank up the fire or wood-burning stove. *Tip:* The cabins near the river offer the most privacy.

The restaurant is a local favorite and consists of four intimate, English country inn–style rooms lit by candlelight (See "Where to Dine," below).

✪ **Post Ranch Inn.** Calif. 1 (P.O. Box 219), Big Sur, CA 93920. ☎ **800/527-2200** or 831/667-2200. Fax 831/667-2824. 31 units, 1 suite. TEL. $365–$645 double. Rates include breakfast. AE, MC, V.

This is one of our very favorite places to stay on the planet. Perched on 98 acres of pristine seaside ridges 1,200 feet above the Pacific, this romantic resort opened in 1992 and was instantly declared one of the world's finest retreats. What's the big deal? The Post Ranch doesn't attempt to beat its stunning natural surroundings, but rather to join them. The wood-and-glass guest cottages are built around existing trees—some are elevated on stilts to avoid damaging native redwood root structures—and the ultra-private Ocean and Coast cottages are so close to the edge of the earth, you get the impression that you've joined the clouds (imagine that from your private spa tub). Other cottages face the woodlands and are equally impressive in design. Each room contains a fireplace, terrace, massage table, cassette and CD player, and wet bar filled with complimentary goodies. The bathrooms, fashioned out of slate and granite, feature spa tubs. There's also a small workout room, the best "hot tub" we've ever encountered (it's on a cliff and seems to join the sky), a mediocre pool, and sundecks on the premises. The only drawback is that the vibe can be stuffy, which is due more to the clientele than the staff.

Dining: The Sierra Mar restaurant is open only to guests for continental breakfasts, and to the public nightly for dinner (when there's a four-course, fixed-price meal for $58). It, too, has floor-to-ceiling views of the ocean and is one of the best (and most expensive) dining choices in the area.

Amenities: Room service, twice-daily maid service, complimentary newspaper, concierge, complimentary valet, massage, yoga, spa services, guided hikes, tarot reading, aromatherapy, and facials. Library, fitness room, pool, Jacuzzi, nature trails.

✪ **Ventana Big Sur Resort.** Calif. 1, Big Sur, CA 93920. ☎ **800/628-6500** or 831/ 667-2331. Fax 831/667-2419. 59 units. A/C MINIBAR TV TEL. $340–$725 double; from $485 suite. Rates include continental breakfast and afternoon wine and cheese. AE, CB, DC, DISC, MC, V.

Luxuriously rustic and utterly romantic, Ventana has been a wildly popular wilderness outpost for more than 20 years, and with good reason. Located on 243 mountainous

Camping in Big Sur

Big Sur is one of the most spectacular places in the state for camping. One of the most glorious settings can be found at **Pfeiffer–Big Sur State Park,** on Calif. 1, 26 miles south of Carmel (☎ **800/444-7275** or 831/667-2315; fax 831/ 667-2886). The 810-acre state park offers hundreds of secluded, woodsy sites, each tucked into the property's hundreds of acres of redwood forest. Hiking trails, streams, and the river are steps away from your sleeping bag, and the most modern amenities are the 25¢ showers (for 3 minutes). Water faucets are located between sites, and each spot has its own picnic table and fire pit. There are, however, no RV hookups or electricity. Riverfront sites are most coveted, but others promise more seclusion among the shaded hillsides of the park. Campfire programs and nature walks are also offered. At the entrance are a store, gift shop, restaurant, and cafe. There's a total of 218 sites (fees are $20 for regular sites, $23 for riverside sites). Rates include park entrance fees. Senior discounts are available, and dogs are permitted ($1 per night extra).

The entrance to the **Ventana Campground,** on Calif. 1, 28 miles south of Carmel and 4¼ miles south of the River Inn (☎ **831/667-2688**), is adjacent to the entrance to the resort of the same name, but the comparison stops there. This is pure rusticity. The 75 campsites, on 40 acres of a redwood canyon, are set along a hillside and spaced well apart for privacy. Each is shaded by towering trees and has a picnic table and fire ring, but offers no electricity, RV hookups, or river access. There are, however, three bathhouses with hot showers (25¢ fee), which are conveniently located. To reserve a space, call and charge on a credit card (MasterCard or Visa) one night's deposit. Or you can mail a check for the deposit along with the dates you'd like to stay and a stamped, self-addressed envelope at least 2 weeks in advance (earlier during peak months). Rates are $25 for a site for two with one vehicle; $30 per night with a 3-night minimum during holiday weekends. An additional person is $5 extra, and it'll cost you $5 to bring Fido. Rates include entrance fee for your car. Open year-round.

Big Sur Campground and Cabins is on Calif. 1, 26 miles south of Carmel (a half mile south of the River Inn; ☎ **831/667-2322**). The sites are cramped, so the feel is more like a camping village than an intimate retreat. However, it's very well maintained and perfect for families, who love the playground, river swimming, and inner-tube rentals. Each campsite has its own wood-burning fire pit, picnic table, and freshwater faucet within 25 feet of the pitching area. There are also RV water and electric hookups available. Facilities include bathhouses with hot showers, laundry facilities, an aged volleyball/basketball court, and a grocery store. There are 81 tent sites (30 RV-ready with electricity and water hookup), plus 13 cabins (all with shower). The all-wood cabins are absolutely adorable, with stylish country furnishings, wood-burning ovens, patios, and full kitchens. Rates are $26 for a tent site for two, $26 for an RV hookup (plus $3 extra for electricity and water), $45 for a tent cabin (bed, but no heat or plumbing), or $82 to $165 for a cabin for two. Rates include entrance for your car. MasterCard and Visa are accepted. Pets cost $3 for campsites and $12 for tent-cabins; pets are not allowed in the other cabins. Open year-round.

oceanfront acres, Ventana has an elegance that's atypical of the region, and has continually attracted famous guests such as Barbra Streisand, Goldie Hawn, and Francis Ford Coppola since its opening in 1975.

The accommodations, in one- and two-story, natural-wood buildings along winding, wildflower-flanked paths, blend in with the magical Big Sur countryside. The extensive grounds are dotted with hammocks and hand-carved benches, which are strategically located under shady trees and at vista points. The guest rooms are divinely decorated in warm, cozy luxury, with such amenities as a VCR, refrigerator, and private terrace or balcony overlooking the ocean or forest. Most rooms offer wood-burning fireplaces, and some have hot tubs and high cathedral ceilings. A small fitness center offers the basics—but you'll be more inspired to hike the grounds, where you'll not only find plenty of pastoral respite, but also a pool, a rustic library, and clothing-optional tanning decks and spa tubs. This, along with Post Ranch, is one of the best retreats in the region, if not the state. But we can't say which is better. We prefer the rooms at Post Ranch, but the laid-back energy and the extensive grounds at Ventana. Families take heed: Children are permitted, but not exactly embraced.

Dining: Ventana's restaurant, Cielo, is an incredibly romantic and first-rate dining experience (see "Where to Dine," below, for complete details).

Amenities: Concierge, massage, newspaper delivery, twice-daily maid service, free coffee. Two 90-foot heated outdoor pools, bathhouse, Japanese hot bath, sauna, fitness room, gift store, art gallery.

WHERE TO DINE

In addition to the following choices, you might want to stop by **Big Sur Cafe,** on Calif. 1, just past the post office and a mile south of Pfeiffer–Big Sur State Park (☎ **831/667-2450**; e-mail: BigSurCafe@aol.com). It offers friendly service and healthy fare, ranging from omelets and breakfast burritos to lunchtime soups, salads, and sandwiches (with tofu options for vegetarians). Dinner brings entrees such as grilled salmon with baby greens or grilled vegetable lasagna, plus daily specials.

Big Sur River Inn. On Calif. 1, 2 miles north of Pfeiffer–Big Sur State Park. ☎ **831/667-2700.** Main courses $7.95–$12.25 lunch, $8.25–$20 dinner. AE, DC, DISC, MC, V. Daily 8am–9pm. CALIFORNIA/AMERICAN.

Popular with everyone from families to bikers, the River Inn is an unpretentious, rustic, down-home restaurant that's got something for all tastes. Trying to seat a small army? No problem. Want to watch sports on TV at a local bar? Pull up a stool. Looking to snag a few rays from a deck right beside the Big Sur River? Break out the suntan lotion. In winter, the wooden dining room is the prime spot; on summer days, some folks grab their patio chair and a cocktail and hang out literally midstream. Along with the local color, attractions include a full bar and good ol' American breakfasts (steak and eggs, omelets, pancakes, etc., plus espresso with most dishes for around $6), lunches (an array of salads, sandwiches, and baby-back ribs, or fish-and-chips), and dinners (fresh catch, pastas, burgers, or ribs).

Café Kevah. Calif. 1, 28 miles south of Carmel (5 miles south of the River Inn). ☎ **831/667-2344.** Main courses $5.75–$10.75. Daily 9am–3pm. AE, MC, V. SOUTHWEST/CALIFORNIA.

Located one level below Nepenthe, Café Kevah offers the same celestial view (at a fraction of the price), a more casual environment, and—depending on your taste—better food. Seating is entirely outdoors—a downside when the biting fog rolls in, but perfect on a clear day. You can order breakfast or lunch from the small shack of a kitchen, then grab an umbrella-shaded table, and enjoy the feast for your eyes and taste buds. Fare here is more eclectic than Nepenthe's, with such choices as homemade granola, pastries, baby greens with broiled salmon and papaya, chicken brochettes, omelets, and new potato hash. It ain't cheap, but innovative cuisine, the view, and a surprisingly decent mocha make it a worthwhile stopover. Don't forget to bring a coat.

✪ **Cielo Restaurant.** At Ventana Big Sur Resort, Calif. 1, Big Sur. ☎ **831/667-4242.** Reservations recommended for dinner. Main courses $9.50–$15 lunch, $20–$25 dinner. AE, CB, DC, DISC, MC, V. Mon–Fri 11am–3pm, Sat–Sun noon–3pm; daily 6–10pm. CALIFORNIA.

Like the resort, Ventana's restaurant is woodsy but extravagant, and is an excellent place to dine alfresco at lunch or à la romance at dinner. The airy cedar interior is divided into two spaces: the lounge, where a wooden bar and cocktail tables look onto a roaring fire and through picturesque windows; and the dining room, which overlooks the mountains and/or the ocean. But in summer it's the outdoor patio, with its views of the ocean expanse and 50 miles of Big Sur coast, that's the coveted lunch spot. Unlike some costly restaurants in the area, a meal here is as gratifying as the surroundings. Lunch offers sandwiches, burgers, and an array of gourmet salads, as well as main courses such as grilled Atlantic salmon; dinner includes stellar starters like a perfectly dressed Caesar salad and a well-balanced chanterelle mushroom risotto, and main courses such as seared ahi tuna or roasted duck breast with hazelnut risotto and sun-dried cherry sauce.

Deetjen's Big Sur Inn Restaurant. On Calif. 1. ☎ **831/667-2377.** Reservations recommended. Main courses $7–$9.50 breakfast, $14.50–$24 dinner. MC, V. Daily 8am–noon and 6–9pm. AMERICAN.

With the feel of an English farmhouse, this cozy, country setting is the perfect venue for the delicious comfort food and friendly service that you'll find here. Mornings start off with a jump after a cup of the delicious and strong coffee, and breakfast offers all the basics: omelets, eggs Benedict, pancakes, and granola, most of which come piled high with breakfast potatoes. Dinner is highly regarded by locals, and might include lamb au jus and twice-baked potato; grilled chicken with mushrooms and a garlic marsala sauce; and roast duckling with brandy, peppercorn, and molasses sauce.

Nepenthe. Calif. 1, 28 miles south of Carmel (5 miles south of the River Inn). ☎ **831/667-2345.** Reservations accepted only for parties of five or more. Main courses $9–$25. AE, MC, V. Daily 11:30am–10pm. AMERICAN.

Stop by Nepenthe for two reasons: The views are outrageous and the atmosphere rocks. Sitting 808 feet above sea level along the cliffs overlooking the ocean, Nepenthe is naturally celestial—especially when fog lingers above the water below. On a warm day, join the crowds on the terrace. On colder days, go the indoor route—the redwood-and-adobe structure offers a warmer and equally magical view, and with its big wood-burning fireplace, redwood ceilings, and large bayfront windows, the atmosphere is something you can't find anywhere else.

Unfortunately, that's not been our experience with the fare. We would scoff at a $11 burger (without fries!), $16 swordfish sandwich, and a $4 draft Budweiser anywhere else—but we'd cough up the cash all over again for an afternoon here. (Think of it as nominal admission to dine at heights only angels usually enjoy.) Lunch is adequate and basic: burgers, sandwiches, and salads. Dinner main courses include steak, broiled chicken, and fresh fish prepared any number of ways, though we suggest you come only for lunch and spend big dinner bucks elsewhere.

8 Pinnacles National Monument

58 miles SE of Monterey

Once a little-known outpost of the national park system, Pinnacles National Monument has become one of the most popular weekend climbing destinations in central California over the past decade. The mild winter climate and plentiful routes make this a perfect off-season training ground for climbers (with the except of 1997–1998's

El Niño winter, which hit the area hard). It's also a popular haven for campers, hikers, and nature lovers. One of the unique chaparral ecosystems in the world supports a large community of plant and animal life here, including one of California's largest breeding populations of raptors.

The Pinnacles themselves—hundreds of towering crags, spires, and hoodoos—are seemingly out of place in the voluptuously rolling hills of the coast range. And they are, in fact, out of place, part of the eroded remains of a volcano formed 23 million years ago 195 miles south in the middle of the Mojave Desert. It was carried here by the movement of the San Andreas Fault, which runs just east of the park. (The other half of the volcano remains in the Mojave.)

You could spend days here without getting bored, but it's possible to cover the most interesting features in a weekend. With a single hike, you can go from the lush oak woodland around the Bear Gulch Visitor Center to the dry and desolate crags of the high peaks, then back down through a half-mile-long cave complete with underground waterfalls.

JUST THE FACTS

ACCESS POINTS Two entrances lead to the park. The **West Entrance** from Soledad and U.S. 101 is a dry, dusty, winding single-lane road (not suitable for trailers) with the best drive-up view of the park. It doesn't connect with the east side.

The alternative route is via the **East Entrance.** Unless you're coming from nearby, take the longer drive on Calif. 25 to enter through the east. Because most of the peaks of the Pinnacles face east and the watershed drains east, most of the interesting hikes and geologic features are on this side. No road crosses the park.

FEES Park entrance fees, which are good for 7 days, are $2 per person or $5 per car.

VISITOR CENTER The first place you should go upon entering the park from the east is the **Bear Gulch Visitor Center** (☎ 831/389-4485). This small center is rich with exhibits about the park's history, wildlife, and geology, and also has a great selection of nature handbooks and climbing guides for the Pinnacles. Climbers should check with rangers about closures and other information before heading out: Many routes are closed during hawk- and falcon-nesting season, and rangers like to know how many climbers are in the park.

Adjacent to the visitor center, the Bear Gulch picnic ground is a great place to fuel up before setting out on a hike or, if you're not planning to leave your car, one of the best places to gaze up at dramatic spires of the high peaks (the ultimate spot is from the west side).

REGULATIONS & WARNINGS Beware of poison oak, particularly in Bear Gulch. Rattlesnakes are common throughout the park but rarely seen. Bikes and dogs are prohibited on all trails, and no backcountry camping is allowed anywhere in the park.

Hiking through this variety of landscapes demands versatility. Come prepared with a good pair of hiking shoes, snacks, lots of water, and a flashlight.

Daytime temperatures often exceed 100°F in summer, so the best time of year to visit is spring, when the wildflowers are blooming, followed by fall. Crowds are common during spring weekends.

HIKING/SEEING THE HIGHLIGHTS

To see most of the park in a single, moderately strenuous morning, take the **Condor Gulch Trail** from the visitor center. As you climb quickly out of the parking area, the Pinnacles' wind-sculpted spires seem to grow taller. In less than 2 miles, you're among them, and Condor Gulch intersects with the **High Peaks Trail.** The view from the top spans miles: the Salinas Valley to your west, the Pinnacles below, and miles of coast to the east. After traversing the high peaks (including stretches of footholds carved in steep rock faces) for about a mile, the trail drops back toward the visitor center via a valley filled with eerie-looking hoodoos.

In another 1½ miles, you'll reach the reservoir marking the top of **Bear Gulch Cave** (which closes occasionally: in 1998, it closed due both to storm damage and to accommodate migrating Townsend bats, who in the past 2 years have come here to have their babies). It's usually open, but if you want to explore, you'll need your flashlight and you might get wet; still, this .6-mile-long talus cave is a thrill. From the end of the cave you're just a short walk (through the most popular climbing area of the park) away from the visitor center. It's also possible to hike just Bear Gulch and the cave, then return via the **Moses Spring Trail**. It's about 2 miles round-trip, but you'll miss the view from the top.

If you're coming from the West Entrance, the **Juniper Canyon Trail** is a short (1.2 miles), but very steep, blast to the top of the high peaks. You'll definitely earn the view. Otherwise, try the short **Balconies Trail** to the monument's other talus cave, **Balconies Cave.** Flashlights are required here, too.

CAMPING

The park's campground on the west side was demolished by El Niño storms in 1997 and 1998 and is not scheduled for repair. Now the only campground is the privately run **Pinnacles Campground, Inc.,** on the east side (☎ **831/389-4462;** www. pinncamp.com), which charges $7 per person, $14 minimum on Friday and Saturday nights. It's just outside the park (off Calif. 25, 32 miles south of Hollister), with lots of privacy and space between sites, plus showers, a store, and a pool. It's close enough so you can hike into the park from the campground, though it will add a few miles to your outing. Though private campgrounds are often overdeveloped, the management here saw the benefits of leaving the surroundings natural. Dogs are not recommended, but you can bring them if you're willing to pay a $10 leash deposit. *Note:* No animals are allowed at Pinnacles.

The Central Coast   **12**

by Erika Lenkert & Stephanie Avnet Yates

California's Central Coast—a spectacular amalgam of beaches, lakes, and mountains—is the state's most diverse region. The narrow strip of coast that runs for more than 100 miles from San Simeon to Ventura spans several climate zones and is home to an eclectic mix of students, middle-class workers, retirees, farmers, computer techies, and fishermen. The ride along Calif. 1, which follows the ocean cliffs, is almost always packed with rental cars, RVs, and bicycles. Traffic may give your brakes a workout, but it also allows you to take longer looks at one of the most spectacular vistas in the world.

Whether you're driving up from Los Angeles or down from San Francisco, Calif. 1 is the most scenic and leisurely route. (U.S. 101 gets you there faster, but is less picturesque.) Most bicyclists pedal from north to south, the direction of the prevailing winds. Those in cars may prefer to drive south to north, so they can get a better look at the coastline as it unfolds toward the west. No matter which direction you drive, break out the camera—you're about to experience unparalleled beauty, California style.

1 San Simeon: Hearst Castle

205 miles S of San Francisco (via Calif. 1), 254 miles NW of Los Angeles

Few places on earth compare to Hearst Castle. The 165-room estate of publishing magnate William Randolph Hearst, situated high above the coastal village of San Simeon atop a hill he called La Cuesta Encantada ("the Enchanted Hill"), is an ego trip par excellence. One of the last great estates of America's Gilded Age, it's an astounding, completely over-the-top monument to wealth—and to the power that money brings.

Hearst Castle is a sprawling compound of structures, constructed over 28 years in a Mediterranean Revival architectural style, set in undeniably magical surroundings. The focal point of the estate is the you-have-to-see-it-to-believe-it **Casa Grande,** a 100-plus-room mansion brimming with priceless art and antiques. Hearst acquired most of his vast European collection via New York auction houses, where he bought entire rooms (including walls, ceilings, and floors) and shipped them here. The result is an old-world castle done in a priceless mix-and-match style. You'll see fantastic 400-year-old Spanish and Italian ceilings, enormous 500-year-old fireplace mantels, 16th-century Florentine bedsteads, Renaissance paintings, Flemish tapestries, and innumerable other treasures.

Three opulent "guest houses" also contain magnificent works of art. A lavish private movie theater was used to screen first-run films twice nightly—once for employees, and again for the guests and host.

And then there are the swimming pools. The Roman-inspired indoor pool has intricate mosaic work, Carrara-marble replicas of Greek gods and goddesses, and alabaster globe lamps that create the illusion of moonlight. The breathtaking outdoor Greco-Roman Neptune pool, flanked by marble colonnades that frame the distant sea, is one of the mansion's most memorable features.

In 1957, in exchange for a massive tax write-off, the Hearst Corporation donated the estate to the state of California (while retaining ownership of approximately 80,000 acres); the California Department of Parks and Recreation now administers it as a State Historic Monument.

TOURING THE ESTATE

✪ **Hearst Castle** can be visited only by guided tour. Four distinct daytime tours are offered on a daily basis, each lasting almost 2 hours. **Tour 1** is usually recommended for first-time visitors and is the first to get booked up. In addition to the swimming pools, this tour visits several rooms on the ground floor of the main house (known as Casa Grande), including Hearst's private theater, where you'll see some home movies taken during the castle's heyday. You'll get to see the sculptures and flowers in the gardens and the formal esplanade, as well as the largest guest house, Casa del Sol.

Tour 2 focuses on Casa Grande's upper floors, including Hearst's opulent library, private suite of rooms, and lots of fabulous bathrooms. Ongoing efforts are made to lend a lived-in look to the house; examples are the lifelike food displayed in the kitchen and pantry, and vintage sewing equipment in Marion Davies's suite. Although Tour 1 is commonly recommended for first-timers, Tour 2 is a perfectly fine choice if you're only planning to take one tour, particularly if your interest lies more in the home's private areas.

Tour 3 delves into the complex construction and subsequent alterations of Hearst Castle. You'll visit Casa del Monte, a guest house unaltered from its original design, then head to the North Wing of Casa Grande, the last portion of the property to be completed, to see the contrast in styles. A video called *The Building of a Dream,* which uses film and photographs from the 1920s and 1930s to go behind the scenes of the construction process, is shown. Tour 3 is especially fascinating for architecture buffs and detail hounds, but shouldn't be the first and only tour you take if you've never visited the castle before.

Tour 4 is dedicated to the estate's gardens, terraces, and walkways, and is only offered from April through October. You'll also tour the Casa del Mar guest house, the wine cellar of Casa Grande, and the colorful dressing rooms at the Neptune Pool. Like Tour 3, this one is best taken after you've seen some of the more essential areas of the estate.

Evening tours are held most Friday and Saturday nights during spring and fall. These last about 30 minutes longer than the daytime tours, and visit highlights of the main house, the largest and most elaborate guest house, and the estate's pools and gardens, which are illuminated by hundreds of restored light fixtures. The pools in particular are most breathtaking when seen this way. The entire living-history experience is enhanced by docents dressed in period costume assuming a variety of roles.

Tip: Because these are walking tours, be sure to wear comfortable shoes—you'll be walking about a half mile per tour, which includes between 150 and 400 steps to climb or descend. (Wheelchair tours are available by calling ☎ **805/927-2020** at least 10 days in advance.)

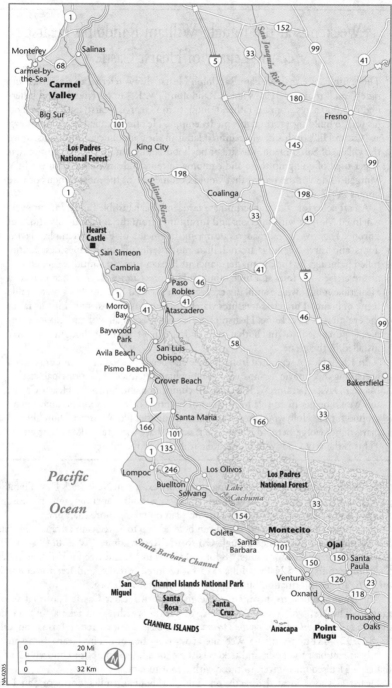

Pacific

Ocean

Weekends at the Ranch: William Randolph Hearst & the Legacy of Hearst Castle

The lavish palace that William Randolph Hearst always referred to simply as "the ranch" took root in 1919. William Randolph ("W. R." to his friends) had inherited 275,000 acres from his father, mining baron George Hearst, and was well on his way to building a formidable media empire. He often escaped to a spot known as "Camp Hill" on his newly acquired lands in the Santa Lucia Mountains above the village of San Simeon, the site of boyhood family outings. Complaining that "I get tired of going up there and camping in tents," Hearst hired architect Julia Morgan to design the retreat that would become one of the most famous private homes in the world.

An art collector with indiscriminate taste and inexhaustible funds, Hearst overwhelmed Morgan with interiors and furnishings from the ancestral collections of Europe. Each week, railroad cars carrying fragments of Roman temples, lavish doors and carved ceilings from Italian monasteries, Flemish tapestries, hastily rolled paintings by the old masters, ancient Persian rugs, and antique French furniture arrived—5 tons at a time—in San Simeon. *Citizen Kane,* which depicts a Hearstlike mogul with a similarly excessive estate called Xanadu, has a memorable scene of hoarded priceless treasures warehoused in dusty piles, stretching as far as the eye can see. Like Kane, Hearst, once described as a man with an "edifice complex," purchased so much that only a fraction of what he bought was ever installed in the estate.

In 1925, Hearst separated from his wife and began to spend time in Los Angeles overseeing his movie company, Cosmopolitan Pictures. His principal starlet, Marion Davies, became W. R.'s constant companion and hostess at Hearst Castle; this would be her main role for the rest of his life. The ranch soon became a playground for the Hollywood crowd as well as dignitaries like Winston Churchill and playwright George Bernard Shaw, who is said to have wryly remarked of the estate, "This is the way God would have done it if He had the money."

Tours are conducted daily beginning at 8:20am, except on New Year's Day, Thanksgiving, and Christmas. Two to six tours leave every hour, depending on the season. Allow 2 hours between starting times if you plan on taking more than one tour.

Reservations are recommended and can be made up to 8 weeks in advance. Tickets can be purchased by phone through **California Reservations** (☎ **800/444-4445**). Daytime tours are $14 for adults, $8 for children 6 to 12, and free for children under 6. Evening tours are $25 for adults, $13 for children 6 to 12, and free for children under 6. To get information online, go to **www.hearstcastle.org**.

The latest addition to the estate is the giant-screen **Hearst Castle National Geographic Theatre,** which you can visit regardless of whether you take a tour. Films include *Hearst Castle: Building the Dream,* among others. For current information, call ☎ **805/927-6811** or visit the Web site at **www.ngthc.com**. The Hearst film shows hourly at half past the hour, and tickets cost $7 for adults and $5 for children 12 and under; a $1 discount is given to those with a tour receipt.

Hearst Castle is located directly on Calif. 1, about 42 miles north of San Luis Obispo and 94 miles south of Monterey. From San Francisco or Monterey, take U.S. 101 south to Paso Robles, then Calif. 46 west to Calif. 1, and Calif. 1 north to the castle. From Los Angeles, take U.S. 101 north to San Luis Obispo, then Calif. 1 north

Despite its opulence, Hearst promoted "the ranch" as a casual weekend home. He regularly laid the massive refectory table in the dining room with paper napkins and bottled ketchup and pickles to evoke a rustic camplike atmosphere. In Hearst's beautiful library, his priceless collection of ancient Greek pottery—one of the greatest collections of its kind in the world—is arranged casually among the rare volumes, like knickknacks.

The Hollywood crowd would take Hearst's private railway car from Los Angeles to San Luis Obispo, where a fleet of limousines waited to transport them to San Simeon. Those who didn't come by train were treated to a flight on Hearst's private plane from the Burbank airport (MGM head Irving Thalberg and his wife, Norma Shearer, preferred this mode of transportation). Hearst, an avid aviator, had a sizable landing strip built; Charles Lindbergh used it when he flew up for a visit in the summer of 1928.

Oh, if the walls could talk. Atop one of the castle's looming towers are the hexagonal Celestial Suites. One was a favorite of Clark Gable and Carole Lombard, who would be startled out of their romantic slumber by the clamor of 18 carillon bells directly overhead. David Niven, a frequent guest, was one of the unknown number who defied teetotaler Hearst's edict against liquor in private rooms; Niven was called upon more than once to explain the several "empties" under the bed (which Cardinal Richelieu once owned and slept in) in his customary suite.

W. R. Hearst and Marion Davies hosted frequent costume parties at the ranch, which were as intricately planned as a movie production. The most legendary, the Circus Party, was held to celebrate W. R.'s 75th birthday on April 29, 1938. Much of Hollywood attended to honor the tycoon, including grande dame Bette Davis—dressed as a bearded lady.

to the castle. Park in the visitor-center parking lot; a bus will take you the 5 miles up the hill to the estate. The movie theater and visitor center adjoin the parking lot and are easily accessible without heading up to the actual estate.

WHAT TO SEE & DO IN NEARBY CAMBRIA

After driving for close to an hour without passing anything but lush green hills and nature at its most glorious (especially from Calif. 46 off U.S. 101), it's a remarkably quaint surprise to roll into the adorable coastal minitown of Cambria, just south of San Simeon. Cambria, known as an artists' colony, is so charming that the town itself is reason enough to make the drive. With little more than 3 blocks worth of charming shops, restaurants, and a handful of B&Bs, Cambria is the perfect place to escape the everyday, enjoy the endless expanses of pristine coastal terrain, and meander through little shops selling local artwork and antiques.

Gray whales pass through the area from late December to early February, and for the past few years hundreds of elephant seals have made the shore just north of the Hearst Castle entrance their year-round playground—much to the delight of locals and nature enthusiasts. Keep your distance from these mammoth mammals: They're a protected species and can be dangerous if molested. There is a parking lot and docents are usually on hand to answer questions. The beaches and coves are also wonderful places for humans to frolic as well. For more information on Cambria, check out **www.cambria-online.com**.

SHOPPING

Cambria has some great boutique shopping. In the West Village is **Maison de Marie,** 768 Main St. (☎ **805/927-7234**), which offers one-stop shopping for French imports ranging from Provincial fabric to herbs d' Provence. Another good stop is **Home Arts,** 707 Main St. (☎ **805/927-2781**), which has an eclectic mix of furnishings and gifts. After blocks of antiques shops and country collectibles, this place renews your faith that someone hip might actually live in Cambria. In the East Village is **Seekers Collection and Gallery,** 4090 Burton Dr. (☎ **800/841-5250** or 805/927-4352), which has one of the finest collections of museum-quality art glass to be found anywhere. Seekers represents more than 200 leading artists from the American art-glass movement. You can also visit its virtual gallery online at www.seekersglass.com. ✪ **Heart's Ease,** 4101 Burton Dr. (☎ **800/266-4372** or 805/927-5224), is located inside a quaint historic cottage and is packed with an abundance of garden delights, apothecary herbs, and custom-blended potpourris.

WHERE TO STAY

Best Western Cavalier Oceanfront Resort. 9415 Hearst Dr. (Calif. 1), San Simeon, CA 93452. ☎ **800/826-8168** or 805/927-4688. Fax 805/927-4688. 90 units. TV TEL. $89–$185 double. AE, CB, DC, DISC, MC, V.

"Oceanfront" and "budget" are generally a contradiction, but this family-friendly hotel offers the best of both. Aside from the basics, the rooms are all outfitted with VCRs (video rentals are available next door), fridges, computer jacks, and hair dryers; some even have fireplaces. Other bonuses include two outdoor heated pools, an exercise room, two restaurants, a laundry, a shopping center, a video arcade, and three oceanfront fire pits lit daily by the resort. This also happens to be the only true oceanfront resort in the area.

Blue Dolphin Inn. 6470 Moonstone Beach Dr., Cambria, CA 93428. ☎ **805/927-3300.** Fax 805/927-7311. 18 units. TV. $75–$210 double. Rates include continental breakfast. AE, DC, DISC, MC, V.

Voted one of the best moderately priced California accommodations by *Los Angeles Times* readers in 1996, the Blue Dolphin offers high-quality rooms along the Cambria coastline. Designed in English country style, the guest rooms brim with frilly opulence and include gas fireplaces, fridges, hair dryers, and VCRs. Room nos. 111, 112, and 114 have good ocean views from their private patios.

✪ **Olallieberry Inn.** 2476 Main St., Cambria, CA 93428. ☎ **888/927-3222** or 805/ 927-3222. Fax 805/927-0202. www.olallieberry.com. 9 units. $90–$160 double; $175–$185 cottage suite. Rates include full breakfast and evening wine and hors d'oeuvres. AE, MC, V.

This 1873 Greek Revival house is our favorite B&B in the area. The grounds are perfectly manicured but bloom whimsically, in the afternoon the aromas of baked brie and homemade bread (served during the wine hour) waft through the main house, and the staff does everything imaginable to make your stay special. They also have a passion for cooking and gardening, but the decor doesn't fall by the wayside: Victorian floral-and-lace reigns, and the guest rooms are lovingly and individually appointed. Each has its own private bathroom, although some are across or down the hall. Rooms in a newer adjoining building overlook a creek; they're remarkably charming and have a fireplace and private deck. The delicious full breakfast—accompanied by Olallieberry jam, of course—is gourmet all the way.

Ragged Point Inn. P.O. Box 110 (15 miles north of Hearst Castle), San Simeon, CA 93452. ☎ **805/927-4502.** Fax 805/927-8862. 20 units. TV. $89–$150 double. Extra person $10. AE, DISC, MC, V.

There would be little reason to stay here if it weren't for the surroundings: grassy, oceanfront grounds on a cliff at the base of Big Sur country. Rooms, although newish, are just a step above motel style. But if you get one with a view that looks directly onto the ocean, you probably won't care. A visit here promises more seclusion than staying in Cambria or San Simeon. The only establishments in the area are a restaurant, snack bar, gift ship, minimart, and gas station that belong to the hotel.

The Squibb House Bed & Breakfast. 4063 Burton Dr., Cambria, CA 93428. ☎ **805/927-9600.** Fax 805/927-9606. 5 units. $95–$140 double. Rates include continental breakfast. AE, MC, V.

If you don't mind small rooms without TV or telephone, the Squibb House is second only to the Olallieberry. Each room in this compact and lovingly restored 1877 Victorian reflects its history, with beautiful wooden reproductions, wood-burning stoves, and attention to detail. Even the garden is worthy of perusal. Owner/renovator Bruce Black makes sure everything is in the finest of taste and that a night here is a romantic step back in time.

WHERE TO DINE

Bistro Sole. 1980 Main St., Cambria. ☎ **805/927-0887.** Reservations recommended. Main courses $7–$10 lunch, $8–$18 dinner. MC, V. Daily 11am–3pm and 5pm–9 or 10pm. ECLECTIC.

"Quaint" is the best word to describe Cambria, and the same goes for this restaurant located in an old house in the town's East Village. The cozy California bungalow and tree-filled back garden are the ideal settings for to-die-for oysters Rockefeller, tasty wontons with baked yam and goat cheese, lobster bisque, one of five lovely salads, and a selection of contemporary California cuisine dinner main courses. When we dined here, the calamari picatta was superb and the filet mignon was on the money. Among the 20 or so main courses are a handful of pastas (chicken artichoke linguini and cannelloni, for example) balanced with a selection of chicken and seafood dishes. Lunch heads south of the border with enchiladas, fish tacos, chicken mole, and a selection of gourmet sandwiches. This is one of the most contemporary places to eat in town—in both decor and cuisine.

Moonstone Beach Bar & Grill. 6550 Moonstone Beach Dr, Cambria. ☎ **805/927-3859.** Reservations recommended in summer. Entrees $8–$13 lunch and brunch, $14–$30 dinner. Daily 8am–9pm. MC, V. AMERICAN.

On a warm, sunny day, nothing beats this place for lunch, brunch, or a late afternoon snack, enjoyed out on the large heated patio that overlooks beautiful Moonstone Beach. Lunch offers some respectable sandwiches and tasty salads as well as one of the best clam chowders we've had. Our favorite was the truly authentic fish tacos. Dine here for brunch and you can indulge in the Grand Marnier–laced Pacific Coast french toast topped with Chantilly cream. Dinner entrees range from lobster to steak to pasta and include four fresh fish choices; the salmon with pesto cream was delicious. It's on the expensive side for such a casual place, but the view is priceless.

Robin's. 4095 Burton Dr., Cambria. ☎ **805/927-5007.** www.robinsrestaurant.com. Reservations recommended. Main courses $9–$18. MC, V. Daily 11am–9pm. ECLECTIC.

Robin's is a restaurant with something for everyone, from exotic dishes from Mexico, Thailand, India, and beyond to more straightforward preparations like a tasty salad or juicy steak and an array of vegetarian dishes. Offerings include a salmon-bisque appetizer; porcini ravioli with roasted-pepper/cream sauce, fresh spinach, basil, and Parmesan; and other flavorful combinations such as Tandoori prawns with basmati brown rice, fruit chutney, and chapati. Don't miss dessert—try the espresso-soaked cake with mascarpone mousse and shaved chocolate or vanilla-custard bread pudding.

2 Morro Bay

124 miles S of Monterey, 235 miles S of San Francisco (via Calif. 1), 220 miles N of Los Angeles

Morro Bay is separated from the ocean by a long peninsula of towering sand dunes. It's best known for dramatic **Morro Rock,** an enormous egg-shaped monolith that juts out of the water just offshore. Part of a chain of long-extinct volcanoes, the huge domed rock is a winter and fall sanctuary for thousands of migrating birds, including cormorants, pelicans, sandpipers, and two rare peregrine falcons.

But other than gawking at the amazing "Gibraltar of the Pacific," there's not all that much to see in the town itself. The motel strip and the gigantic, absurdly placed ocean-front electrical plant (directly blocking the view of the rock) put a damper on the sleepy town's appeal, although fortunately the new electric company that bought the plant has plans to remove the old obtrusive stacks and replace them with shorter ones.

If you do stay for more than a quick stop to snap a few photos, you'll find a touristy bayfront strip of stores and a makeshift aquarium, which displays a few fish, but more interestingly hosts rescued seals that beg for fish. The town's best feature is its natural surroundings; the beaches and wildlife sanctuaries can be quite peaceful and wondrous.

ESSENTIALS

The **Morro Bay Chamber of Commerce,** 880 Main St., Morro Bay, CA 93442 (☎ **800/231-0592** or 805/772-4467), offers armfuls of area information. It's open Monday through Friday from 8:30am to 5pm and Saturday from 10am to 3pm.

EXPLORING THE AREA

Most visitors come to Morro Bay to ogle **Morro Rock,** the much-photographed Central Coast icon. It's definitely worth a gander (you couldn't miss it even if you wanted to).

BEACHES   Popular **Atascadero State Beach,** just north of Morro Rock, has gentle waves and lovely views. Rest rooms, showers, and dressing rooms are available. Just north of Atascadero is **Morro Strand State Beach,** a long, sandy stretch with normally gentle surf. Rest rooms and picnic tables are available here. Morro Strand has its own campgrounds; for information, call ☎ **805/772-2560,** or reserve a spot through Park-Net (☎ **800/444-7275;** www.park-net.com).

STATE PARKS   Cabrillo Peak, located in the lovely **Morro Bay State Park** (☎ **805/772-7434**), makes for a terrific day hike and offers fantastic 360° views from its summit. There's a faint zigzagging trail, but the best way to reach the top is by bush-whacking straight up the gentle slope—a hike that takes about 2 hours round-trip. To reach the trailhead, take Calif. 1 south and turn left at the Morro Bay State Park/Montana de Oro State Park exit. Follow South Bay Boulevard for three-quarters of a mile, then take the left fork another half a mile to the Cabrillo Peak dirt parking lot, located on your left. The park also offers camping and a decent public **golf** course called Morro Bay, which charges $28 to $35 for greens fees (☎ **805/782-8060**).

South of Morro Bay in Los Osos is **Montana de Oro State Park** ("Mountain of Gold"), fondly known as "petite Big Sur" because of its stony cliffs and rugged terrain. There's great swimming at Spooner's Cove and lots of easy hiking trails here, including a number that lead to spectacular coastal vistas or hidden forest streams. The Hazard Reef Trail will take you up on the Morro Bay Sandspit dunes. The park's campground is in the trees, across from the beach. For information, call the park rangers (☎ 805/528-0513 or 805/772-7434), or reserve a spot through Park-Net (☎ 800/444-7275; www.park-net.com).

IN TOWN   You can escape being landlocked by renting a kayak through **Kayak Horizons** (☎ 805/772-6444), which is located at 551 Embarcadero at the end of Marina Street. Rentals range from $8 to $14 per hour or from $35 for a half-day, depending on the kind of boat you want and the length of time you use it.

WHERE TO STAY

Baywood Bed & Breakfast Inn. 1370 Second St., Baywood Park, CA 93042. ☎ 805/528-8888. Fax 805/528-8887. www.baywoodinn.com. 15 units. TV TEL. $80–$110 double; $110–$160 suite. Rates include breakfast. Extra person $15. MC, V.

Rarely will you find such affordable accommodations with so many extras. Each room at the two-story bayfront inn, located in Baywood Park just south of Morro Bay, is decorated with a distinct (over-the-top) theme and Grandma-style flair. Guests can cuddle in a floral and light-wood country cottage, stretch out in a 19th-century English affair, or saddle down in a Southwestern suite. Every room has a private entrance, gas fireplace, microwave, coffeemaker, and a fridge stocked with complimentary sodas and snacks; all but a few have ocean views. Breakfast is brought to your room, wine and cheese are served each evening, and turndown service includes cookies.

The Inn at Morro Bay. 60 State Park Rd., Morro Bay, CA 93442. ☎ 800/321-9566 or 805/772-5651. Fax 805/772-4779. 98 units. TV TEL. $98–$265 double (highest rates on weekends). AE, MC, V.

One of the most upscale hotels on the San Luis coast is strategically sandwiched along the shoreline between monumental Morro Bay and Morro Bay's 18-hole golf course (see above, under "State Parks"). Two-story Cape Cod–style buildings house guests and have contemporary interiors tempered by blond-wood cabinetry, polished-brass fittings and beds, and reproduction 19th-century European furnishings. The best rooms enjoy unobstructed views of Morro Rock; those in back face the swimming pool and gardens.

WHERE TO DINE

Hofbrau. 571 Embarcadero, Morro Bay. ☎ 805/772-2411. Reservations not accepted. Most items $4.25–$8.75. Sun–Thurs 11am–8:30pm; Fri–Sat 11am–9pm. AE, DISC, MC, V. GERMAN/AMERICAN.

If you're hungry in Morro Bay and want something other than fish-and-chips, Hofbrau is the place. Although they do serve the standard wharfside fare, the star here is the roast beef French Dip (their strategically placed carving station ensures its popularity). Those in the know order the mini sandwich, which is a dollar less and just an inch shorter. As the name would suggest, they have a nice selection of beers as well as a kids' menu with six choices at $3.49, making this a great value for families.

Hoppe's at Marina Square. 699 Embarcadero (at Pacific). ☎ 805/772-9012. Reservations recommended. Main courses $13–$25. AE, DC, DISC, MC, V. Sun–Thurs 5–9pm; Fri–Sat 5–10pm; Sun 11am–2pm. CALIFORNIA.

Ask locals where to go for the best meal in Morro Bay and they're likely to send you to Hoppe's. Here you get a stellar view of Morro Rock, as well as such dishes as potato-crusted free-range chicken with mushroom sauce, rack of lamb with white beans and homemade curry sausage, and a variety of fresh seafood. The service can be slow, but the atmosphere is surprisingly upscale, and the food respectable. Considering the neighboring options, Hoppe's is as good as it gets.

3 San Luis Obispo

38 miles S of Cambria, 226 miles S of San Francisco, 198 miles N of Los Angeles

Because the actual town of San Luis Obispo is not visible from U.S. 101, even many Californians don't know that it's more than a McDonald's-and-gasoline stopover on the way to Southern California. But its secret location is exactly what keeps it a quaint little Central Coast jewel.

San Luis Obispo is neatly tucked into the mountains about halfway between San Francisco and Los Angeles. It's surrounded by green, pristine mountain ranges and filled with college kids and friendly locals; the atmosphere is small-town casual.

The town grew up around an 18th-century mission, and its dozens of historic landmarks, Victorian homes, shops, and restaurants are its primary attractions. Today, it's still quaint, almost undiscovered, and best ventured on foot. It also makes a good base for an extensive exploration of the region as a whole. To the west of town, a short drive away, are some of the state's prettiest swimming beaches; turning northeast, you enter the Central Coast's wine country, home to dozens of respectable wineries.

ESSENTIALS

GETTING THERE   U.S. 101, one of the state's primary north-south roadways, runs right through San Luis Obispo; it's the fastest land route here from anywhere. If you're driving down along the coast, Calif. 1 is the way to go for its natural beauty and oceanfront cliffs. If you're entering the city from the east, take Calif. 46 or 41 to U.S. 101, then go south.

VISITOR INFORMATION   The **San Luis Obispo Visitors Center,** 1039 Chorro St., Suite E, San Luis Obispo, CA 93401 (☎ **805/781-2777;** fax 805/543-1255), is located downtown, between Monterey and Higuera streets. This helpful office is one of the best-run visitors bureaus we've ever come across. Drop in to ask questions and to pick up maps, a calendar of events, or specialized information on local sights. Ask for a "Path of History" map, which details many of the sights listed below. The center is open Sunday and Monday from 10am to 5pm, Tuesday and Wednesday from 8am to 5pm, Thursday and Friday from 8am to 8pm, and Saturday from 10am to 8pm.

ORIENTATION   San Luis Obispo is about 10 miles inland, at the junction of Calif. 1 and U.S. 101. The downtown is laid out in a grid, roughly centered around the historic mission and its Mission Plaza (see below). Most of the main tourist sights are around the mission, within the small triangle created by U.S. 101 and Santa Rosa and Marsh streets.

EXPLORING THE TOWN

Before heading downtown, definitely make a pit stop at the perpetually pink **Madonna Inn,** 100 Madonna Rd., off U.S. 101 (☎ **805/543-3000**), if for no other reason than to use its unique public rest rooms (the men's has a waterfall urinal; the women's is a barrage of crimson and pink). Every over-the-top inch of this place is an exercise in excess, from the dining room, complete with pink leather booths, pink table linens, and colored sugar that's—you guessed it—piquantly pink, to the rock-walled, cavelike guest rooms (see "Where to Stay," below, for a complete review).

Once downtown, you can check out the minitown via the free trolley that does a repeat loop through the downtown area daily from noon to 5pm. (Stops are well marked.)

Ah Louis Store. 800 Palm St. (at Chorro St.). ☎ **805/543-4332.** Whenever the owner feels like opening (rarely).

Mr. Ah Louis was a Cantonese immigrant who was lured to California by gold fever in 1856. Emerging from the mines empty handed, he soon began a lucrative career as a labor contractor, hiring and organizing Chinese crews that built the railroad. In 1874, he opened this store. Today, the store is rarely open, but if it is you can chat with Ah Louis's only living heir, 91-year-old Howard, while you browse the clutter of Asian merchandise.

✪ **Farmers Market.** Higuera St. (between Osos and Nipomo sts.). Thurs 6:30–9pm.

If you're lucky enough to be in town on a Thursday, take an evening stroll down Higuera Street, when the county's largest weekly street fair fills four downtown city blocks. You'll find much more here than fresh-picked produce—there's an ever-changing array of street entertainment, open-pit barbecues, food stands, and market stalls selling fresh flowers, cider, and other seasonal goodies. Surrounding stores stay open until 9pm.

Mission San Luis Obispo de Tolosa. 751 Palm St. ☎ **805/543-6850.** www.thegrid.net/slomission. Free admission ($2 donation requested). Summer daily 9am–5pm (sometimes later); winter daily 9am–4pm.

Founded by Father Junípero Serra in 1772, California's fifth mission was built with adobe bricks by Native American Chumash people. It remains one of the prettiest and most interesting structures in the Franciscan chain. Serra chose this valley for the site of his fifth mission based on tales told to him of friendly natives and bountiful food (including grizzly bears). Here the traditional red-tile roof was first used atop a California mission, after the original thatched tule roofs repeatedly fell to hostile Native Americans' burning arrows. The former padres' quarters are now an excellent museum chronicling both Native American and missionary life through all eras of the mission's use. Allow about 30 to 45 minutes to tour the mission and its grounds.

Mission Plaza, a pretty garden with brick paths and park benches fronting a meandering creek in which children love to wade, still functions as San Luis Obispo's town square. It's the focal point for local festivities and activities, from live concerts to poetry readings and dance and theater productions. Check at the visitor center (see "Essentials," above) to find out what's on when you're in town.

At the south end of Mission Plaza you'll find the **San Luis Obispo Art Center** (☎ 805/543-8562), whose three galleries display and sell an array of California-made art. Admission is free; hours are Tuesday through Sunday from 11am to 5pm.

San Luis Obispo Children's Museum. 1010 Nipomo St. (at Monterey St.). ☎ **805/544-KIDS.** Admission $4 adults and children 2 and older, free for children under 2. Daily 11am–5pm.

This terrific children's museum features a playhouse of interesting manipulatives for toddlers, an authentic reproduction of a Native American Chumash cave dwelling, a music room, a computer corner, a pint-sized bank and post office, and over 20 interactive exhibits rotated on a regular basis. Special events like mask making, sing-alongs, and stage-makeup classes are scheduled regularly; call for a list of events.

San Luis Obispo County Historical Museum. Mission Plaza, 696 Monterey St. ☎ **805/543-0638.** Free admission. Wed–Sun 10am–4pm.

This little museum, run by the San Luis Obispo County Historical Society in a Carnegie library, houses an extensive research library and historical photograph collection. The permanent exhibit includes artifacts from Native American Chumash and early European settlers. Unfortunately, the building will be undergoing major retrofitting in late

1999 and will be closed indefinitely. They will, however, offer a historical walking tour for large groups. Call the above number for information.

SHOPPING

Don't expect Rodeo Drive here, but rather a few charming boutiques (among many uninteresting ones) scattered throughout town. The best place to exercise your credit cards is on the downtown streets surrounding the mission, specifically the 5 blocks of **Higuera Street** from Nipomo to Osos streets, as well as a short stretch of **Monterey Street** between Chorro and Osos streets.

On Higuera Street, check out **Hands Gallery,** 777 Higuera St. (☎ 805/ 543-1921), which has a playful, bright collection of local and international art. Trinkets range from glass candies to vases, jewelry, and ceramics and can be viewed or purchased Monday through Wednesday from 10am to 6pm, Thursday through Saturday from 10am to 9pm, and Sunday from 11am to 5pm.

The **Downtown Centre,** between Higuera, Marsh, Broad, and Chorro streets, is the hot spot for locals and anyone else who wants even the most remote cosmopolitan (a.k.a. chain store) feeling. This place is considered the town square because families, pets, teens, and everyone else come here for one reason or another. The outdoor mall has a movie theater, the Gap, a few restaurants, shops, and a bookstore. Cartoons and trailers are projected outside the theater, so if you need a break, grab a latte and watch free flicks.

ATTRACTIONS OUTSIDE OF TOWN

There are dozens of **wineries** in the area that offer tastings and tours daily and make for a fun country diversion. See "The Central Coast Wine Country: Paso Robles & the Santa Ynez Valley," later in this chapter, for further details. If you don't have time to tour the wineries or would like more information before heading out to taste, you can visit the **Central Coast Wine Room,** 10 Old Creamery Rd., Harmony, around 8 miles south of Cambria (☎ 805/927-7337), which offers excellent selections from Paso Robles and the Edna Valley. The tasting room is open daily from 10am to 5pm (closed Tuesday in winter); tastings are $2.

If you're into history and architecture, another worthy side trip is the **Mission San Miguel Arcangel,** 775 Mission St., in San Miguel (7 miles north of Paso Robles on U.S. 101). Founded in 1824, this mission is less spoiled by restoration than many others in the state and is still run by the Franciscan order and inhabited by brown-robed friars. The modest exterior belies one of the most elaborate and best-preserved interiors of the entire central California chain. Painted and decorated by area Native Americans under the supervision of Spanish designer Estevan Munras, the walls and woodwork glow with luminous colors untouched since their original application. Behind the altar and its statue of San Miguel (St. Michael) is splendid tile work featuring a radiant Eye of God.

Mission San Miguel is open to the public daily from 9:30am to 4:30pm; the church remains open until 5pm. The requested donation is $1 per family, 50¢ per person; allow 30 minutes to see the sights. For further information, call ☎ 805/467-3256.

WHERE TO STAY

In addition to what's listed below, there's a pristine branch of **Holiday Inn Express** (☎ 800/465-4329 or 805/544-8600), a reliable **Motel 6** (☎ 800/4-MOTEL-6 or 805/541-6992), and 34 sweet motel-style units at the **Apple Farm Trellis Court** (☎ 800/255-2040 or 805/544-2040).

If you'd like free help making reservations in the area, contact the **Accommodations Reservation Service** (☎ 800/292-2222).

✪ **Adobe Inn.** 1473 Monterey St., San Luis Obispo, CA 93401. ☎ **800/676-1588** or 805/549-0321. Fax 805/549-0383. www.adobeinns.com. 15 units (8 with kitchenette, but no stove). TV TEL. $55–$105 double. Rates include breakfast. Extra person $6 in winter, $10 in summer. Seasonal discounts available. AE, DISC, MC, V.

Okay, it's not *actually* adobe—or even remotely close for that matter—but Michael and Ann Dinshaw have taken this old motor inn and given it a creatively homey atmosphere at unbeatable prices. Each spotless room is individually decorated in Southwestern style with quirky additions such as playfully painted cupboards or a window-side reading nook. Breakfast is served in a clean dining area that unfortunately faces the street, but coffee snobs will delight in the strong, locally roasted blend. Plants adorn the inn's exterior. The owners go out of their way to make guests happy and offer a slew of packages that explore the surrounding areas and attractions.

✪ **Apple Farm Inn.** 2015 Monterey St., San Luis Obispo, CA 93401. ☎ **800/255-2040** or 805/544-2040. Fax 805/546-9495. 69 units. A/C TV TEL. $139–$269 double. AE, DISC, MC, V.

Ultra-popular, the Apple Farm Inn is a peaceful getaway in a Disney-plantation kind of way. Every square inch of the immaculate Victorian-style farmhouse is cheek-pinchingly cute with floral wallpaper, fresh flowers, and sugar-sweet colorful touches. No two rooms are alike, although each has a gas fireplace, large well-equipped bathroom, pine antiques, lavish country decor, and either a canopy four-poster or brass bed. Some bedrooms open onto cozy turreted sitting areas with romantic window seats; others have bay windows and a view of San Luis Creek, where a working mill spins its huge wheel to power an apple press. The outstanding service here includes nightly turndown and a morning wake-up knock, delivered with complimentary coffee or tea and a newspaper. Other features include complimentary cribs and train and airport shuttle service. Cider is always on hand in the lobby. An outdoor heated pool and Jacuzzi are open year-round. There's an on-site restaurant as well.

Those who want the bang without the requisite bucks can opt for the adjoining motel-style Apple Farm Trellis Court, which shares the inn's wonderful grounds. Rooms are smaller, but are well decorated and have gas fireplaces; rates include a continental breakfast and are just half as much as the inn.

Lamp Lighter Inn. 1604 Monterey St. (at Grove St.), San Luis Obispo, CA 93401. ☎ **805/547-7777.** Fax 805/547-7787. 40 units. A/C TV TEL. $49–$80 double; from $109 suite. Rates include continental breakfast. AE, DISC, MC, V.

Even if you're not looking for a bargain, you'll be pleasantly surprised with the value you get at this motel. The rooms boast traditional motel style and colors, but look brand-new, are squeaky clean, and have firm mattresses. Other bonuses are coffeemakers, fridges (except in three rooms), and a heated pool and whirlpool. Breakfast is served in the lobby by an amazingly enthusiastic staff.

Madonna Inn. 100 Madonna Rd. (off U.S. 101), San Luis Obispo, CA 93405. ☎ **800/543-9666** or 805/543-3000. www.madonnainn.com. Fax 805/543-1800. 134 units. TV TEL. $117–$218 double; from $188 suite. AE, MC, V.

This one you've got to see for yourself. The creative imaginations of owners Alex and Phyllis Madonna gave birth to the wildest—and most superfluously garish—fantasy world this side of Graceland. The only decor consistency throughout the hotel is its color scheme, which is perpetual pink. Beyond that, it's a free-for-all. Although tongue-in-cheek, this place can seem tired and tacky and some of the rooms could use updating. However, the lobby men's room with its rock-waterfall urinal and clam-shell sinks is a must-see. Each unit offers a different thematic fantasy far beyond a creative paint job. One room features a trapezoidal bed—it's 5 feet long on one side and 6 feet long on the other. "Rock" rooms with zebra- or tiger-patterned bedspreads and stone-like showers and fireplaces conjure up thoughts of a Flintstones' Playboy palace. There are also blue rooms, red rooms, and over-the-top Spanish, Italian, Irish, Alps, Currier and Ives, Native American, Swiss, and hunting rooms. The coffee shop, dining room, and two cocktail lounges are also outlandishly ornate. Even if you don't stay here, stop by and check it out. One major bummer: There's no pool here, and there definitely should be one.

WHERE TO DINE

Big Sky Cafe. 1121 Broad St. ☎ **805/545-5401.** Reservations not necessary. Main courses $7–$12; salads and sandwiches $5–$8; breakfast $4–$8. AE, MC, V. Mon–Sat 7am–10pm; Sun 8am–9pm. AMERICAN.

The folk-artsy fervor of San Luis really shines at this Southwestern mirage, where local art and a blue, star-studded ceiling surround diners who come for fresh, healthy food. Most everything on the menu, like shrimp tacos and herb-infused roasted chicken, is created with local ingredients. Lighter meals, such as black-bean vegetarian chili, charcoal-broiled eggplant sandwich, and the chilled sesame-ginger noodles with shrimp, chicken, or veggies, are local favorites. Breakfasts include buttermilk pancakes, a jambalaya omelet, turkey hash, and black-bean huevos rancheros.

✪ **Buona Tavola.** 1037 Monterey St. ☎ **805/545-8000.** Reservations recommended. Main courses $8.25–$17. AE, DISC, MC, V. Mon–Fri 11:30am–2:30pm; Sun–Thurs 5:30–9:30pm; Fri–Sat 5:30–10pm. NORTHERN ITALIAN.

While most choices in town are burger-and-sandwich casual, Buona Tavola offers well-prepared Italian food in a more upscale setting. You can stroll in wearing jeans, but the dining room, with checkerboard floors and original artwork, is warmer and more intimate than other spots in town. There's also backyard-terrace seating where you can enjoy your meal surrounded by magnolias, ficus, and grapevines. The menu boasts a number of salads on the antipasti list. Favorite pastas include *agnolotti de scampi allo zafferand,* which is homemade, filled with scampi, and served in a cream-saffron sauce. The *spaghettini scoglio d'oro* comes with lobster, sea scallops, clams, mussels, shrimp, and diced tomatoes in a saffron sauce. Don't worry—once you've gotten past trying to pronounce your desired dish, the rest of the evening should be both relaxing and satisfying.

Mondéo Pronto. 893 Hugeura St., #D4. ☎ **805/544-2956.** Reservations not necessary. Wraps and "fusion bowls" $5.25–$6.25. MC, V. Sun–Wed 11am–9pm; Thurs–Sat 11am–10pm. INTERNATIONAL.

Mondéo Pronto provides patrons an affordable bite of international fillings in a burrito-type wrap. But unlike most "wrap" restaurants in California, this place goes a step beyond by paying attention to detail with presentation and freshness. Choices range from Americana versions like the Mardi Gras, a tomato tortilla packed with Cajun sausage, rock shrimp, Creole veggies, and jambalaya sauce, to Mediterranean selections like the Sicilian, with grilled portobello mushrooms, herb polenta, veggies, goat cheese, olives, capers, and sun-dried tomato pesto. "Fusion bowls" satisfy non-wrappers with such combinations as basil scampi, a lovely shrimp dish over bow-tie pasta with pesto, marinara, pine nuts, and herbs. Big bonuses: Everything on the kids' menu is under $3, and as the menu states, "Substitutions and sides are no problem."

Mo's Smokehouse BBQ. 970 Higuera St. (at Osos St.). ☎ **805/544-6193.** Reservations not necessary. Most items $4.95–$13. AE, MC, V. Sun–Wed 11am–9pm; Thurs–Sat 11am–10pm. BARBECUE.

Friends of ours who moved from San Francisco to San Luis Obispo insisted we dine at Mo's, the town's top choice for great barbecue. It's not fancy, but you name it, it's here—pork or baby-back ribs, BBQ beef, and chicken in either a mild or hot sauce, all accompanied by baked beans, bread, potato salad, or coleslaw. To top off this delectable deal, practically everything on the menu is under $10.

Thai-rrific. 206 Higuera St. ☎ **805/541-THAI**. Reservations not necessary. Most dishes $7–$13. MC, V. Mon–Fri 11am–2pm; Mon–Sat 5–9pm. THAI.

Although on Higuera Street, Thai-rrific is a bit removed from the downtown action—but once you step inside this cute, ivy-covered building, the aroma will convince you you've made a worthy diversion. Fine examples of authentic Bangkok-style cuisine are the ginger beef, garlic noodles, and our favorite, lemongrass chicken (grilled chicken breasts topped with lemongrass cream sauce, roasted chilies, and peanuts). Don't overlook the great array of tasty appetizers and salads, including the grilled shrimp or beef with cucumber, lime, and chili. An impressive wine list rounds out the offerings. Prices here are a little higher than at most Thai restaurants, but well worth it.

4 Pismo Beach

13 miles S of San Luis Obispo

Just outside San Luis Obispo, on Pismo's 23-mile stretch of prime beachfront, flip-flops are the shoes of choice and surf wear is the dominant fashion. It's all about beach life here, so bring your bathing suit, your board, and a good book.

If building sandcastles or tanning aren't your idea of a tantalizing time, you can explore isolated dunes, cliff-sheltered tide pools, and old pirate coves. Bring your dog (Fido's welcome here) and play an endless game of fetch, or go fishing—it's permitted from Pismo Beach Pier, which also offers arcade entertainment, bowling, and billiards. Pismo is also the only beach in the area that allows all-terrain vehicles on the dunes.

Since the town itself consists of little more than tourist shops and surf-and-turf restaurants, nearby San Luis Obispo is a far more charming place to stay. But if all you want are a few lazy days on a beautiful beach at half the price of an oceanfront room in Santa Barbara, Pismo is the perfect choice.

ESSENTIALS

The **Pismo Beach Chamber of Commerce and Visitors Bureau,** 581 Dolliver St., Pismo Beach, CA 93449 (☎ **800/443-7778** in California, or 805/773-4382), offers free brochures and information on local attractions, lodging, and dining. The office is open Monday through Saturday from 9am to 5pm and Sunday from 10am to 4pm. You can peruse their information on the Web at **www.pismobeach.com**.

WHAT TO SEE & DO

Beaches in Pismo are exceptionally wide, making them some of the best in the state for sunning and playing. The beach north of Grand Avenue is popular with families and joggers. North of Wadsworth Street, the coast becomes dramatically rugged as it rambles northward to Shell Beach and Pirates Cove.

Pismo Beach was once one of the most famous places in America for **clamming,** but the clam population was depleted almost to extinction. Government intervention has saved the "Pismo clam," and if you have a fishing license, you're now permitted to pick them in limited numbers directly from the sand. If you're into it, clam forks can be rented from a number of locations around the pier.

If **fishing** is more your style, you'll be pleased to know that no license is required to fish from Pismo Beach Pier. Catches here are largely bottom fish like red snapper and lingcod. There's a bait-and-tackle shop on the pier.

Livery Stables, 1207 Silver Spur Place (☎ **805/489-8100**), in Oceano (about 5 minutes south of Pismo Beach), is one of the very few places in the state that rents horses for riding on the beach. Horses go for $15 per hour and can be ridden at your own pace, or you can opt for a guided ride.

You can hike along the **Guadalupe-Nipomo Dunes** year-round. This 18-mile strip of coastline 20 minutes south of Pismo has the highest beach dunes in the West. It's a great place for observing native plants and birds, including the California brown pelican, one of 200 species that migrate here each year.

From late November to February, tens of thousands of migrating **monarch butterflies** take up residence in the area's eucalyptus and Monterey pine-tree groves. The colorful butterflies form dense clusters on the trees, each hanging with its wings over the one below it, providing warmth and shelter for the entire group. During the monarchs' stay, naturalists at Pismo State Beach conduct 45-minute narrative walks every Saturday and Sunday at 11am and 2pm (call ☎ 805/772-2694 for tour information). Most of the "butterfly trees" are located on Calif. 1, between Pismo Beach and Grover Beach, to the south.

WHERE TO STAY

Cottage Inn by the Sea. 2351 Price St., Pismo Beach, CA 93449. ☎ **888/440-8400** or 805/7734617. Fax 805/773-8336. 80 units. TV TEL. $79–$199 double. Rates include deluxe continental breakfast. Extra person $10. AE, DC, DISC, MC, V.

One of Pismo Beach's newest cliffside lodgings, the Cottage Inn is a good, moderately priced choice for couples and families alike. With its rounded thatched roofs and Laura Ashley–style decor, the country charm is evident both inside and out. Rooms, which are refreshingly clean and spacious, range both in price and style from traditional to ocean view. All come with the amenities of a romantic inn (fireplace, bathrobes, deluxe continental breakfast), yet have the modern conveniences as well (coffeemaker, fridge, microwave, hair dryer, movies, and Nintendo). An oceanfront pool and spa round out this seaside retreat.

SeaVenture Resort. 100 Ocean View Ave., Pismo Beach, CA 93449. ☎ **800/662-5545** or 805/773-4994. Fax 805/773-0924. www.seaventure.com. 50 units. MINIBAR TV TEL. $119–$349 double. Rates include continental breakfast. AE, DC, DISC, MC, V. Take U.S. 101 to the Price St. exit and turn west onto Ocean View (at the beach).

If luxury accommodations overlooking the beach and an outdoor spa on your private deck sound like heaven to you, head for SeaVenture, a 4-year-old resort providing the most luxurious accommodations in Pismo. Once in your room, you need only drag your tired traveling feet through the thick forest-green carpeting and past the white country furnishings and feather bed, and turn on your gas fireplace to begin what promises to be a relaxing stay. Then rent a movie from the video library, schedule a massage, or simply bathe your weary bones in your own outdoor hydrotherapy spa tub. With the beach right outside your door, there's not much more you could ask for—although there is, in fact, more provided: plush robes, a wet bar, a fridge, a coffeemaker, continental breakfast delivered to your room, and a restaurant on the premises with a lovely brunch. Most rooms have ocean views and many have a private balcony overlooking the beach. Extras include room service from 4 to 9pm, laundry, massage, and a pool.

Surf Motel. 250 Main St., Pismo Beach, CA 93449. ☎ **800/472-7873** or 805/773-2070. 33 units. TV TEL. $65–$85 double (lower on off-season weekends). Rates include continental breakfast. AE, MC, V.

Strategically located just half a block from the beach, the Surf Motel is a good bet if you want basic, clean accommodations. All rooms have refrigerators; some have fully stocked kitchenettes. The indoor pool is open year-round.

WHERE TO DINE

Giuseppe's. 891 Price St. ☎ **805/773-2870.** Reservations not accepted. Main courses $6–$10 lunch, $9–$22 dinner. AE, DISC, MC, V. Daily 11:30am–3pm; Sun–Thurs 4:30–10pm; Fri–Sat 4:30–11pm. ITALIAN.

This is the region's best southern Italian restaurant. Along with the fresh homemade bread baked in their wood-burning oven imported from Italy, the classic fare comes with a clutter of Italian culinary accoutrements and an atmosphere reminiscent of a busy Columbus Avenue restaurant in San Francisco's North Beach. The extensive menu of antipasti, salads, pizzas, pastas, fish, and steak makes it virtually impossible to not find something you like. Highlights of our meal included linguini with shrimp, scallops, pancetta, and garlic in a vodka cream sauce and seared ahi with a peppercorn crust and garlic-caper aioli.

Splash Cafe. 197 Pomeroy St. (near Pismo Beach Pier). ☎ **805/773-4653.** Most items $2.50–$5.75. No credit cards. Daily 10am–8pm. AMERICAN.

This beachy burger stand, with a short menu and just a few tables, gets high marks for its award-winning clam chowder, served in a sourdough bread bowl. Fish-and-chips, burgers, hot dogs, and grilled-ahi sandwiches are also available.

5 The Central Coast Wine Country: Paso Robles & the Santa Ynez Valley

Paso Robles: 29 miles N of San Luis Obispo; Solvang: 60 miles S of San Luis Obispo

When people talk about California wines, you can normally assume they mean those from the Napa and Sonoma regions north of San Francisco. But here in California, and increasingly across the country, wine lovers are becoming more aware of vintages coming from California's Central Coast wineries, located in the dewy green hills and sun-kissed valleys of San Luis Obispo and Santa Barbara counties. Closer and more convenient than the Napa Valley, the Central Coast is coming into its own as a respected wine region, and offers another excuse to visit some of the state's most beautifully scenic countryside. Wine snobs might tell you that Central Coast wines cannot compare to those from the northern appellations, where precious vintages can age to sublime flavor and astronomical price, but if you're in the market for bottles in the $12-to-$25 range that are ready to drink within 5 years, then trust us—you'll love what this up-and-comer has to offer.

PASO ROBLES

Welcome to Paso Robles—"pass through the oaks"—so named for the clusters of oak trees liberally scattered throughout the rolling hills of this inland region. The town has a faintly checkered past: It was established in 1870 by Drury James, uncle of outlaw Jesse James (who reportedly hid out in tunnels under the original Paso Robles Inn). In 1913, pianist Ignace Paderewski came to live in Paso Robles, where he brought zinfandel vines for his ranch (zinfandel is now the most successful varietal among area wineries) and played often in the Paso Robles Inn, which today maintains a small exhibit in his honor in the lobby. Paderewski really wasn't here for long, returning to Poland after World War I, but the town today treats him like a native son, and fans gather each year at the Paderewski Festival in March.

ESSENTIALS

GETTING THERE/ORIENTATION   Paso Robles lies along U.S. 101; there's an exit for the town's main business thoroughfare, Spring Street. Calif. 46 intersects, and briefly joins, U.S. 101. Many wineries are located on the winding roads off Calif. 46 on either side—try to cluster your visit according to this destination, visiting one side and then the other. You'll be able to feel how the weather on the western side, which is cooler due to higher elevations and frequent coastal fog, differs from the hotter east side, on a flat plain leading inland; winemakers bicker constantly over which conditions are "better" for wine grapes.

VISITOR INFORMATION   For a complete list of area wineries, tasting rooms, and seasonal events, contact the **Paso Robles Vintners and Growers Association,** 1940 Spring St. (P.O. Box 324), Paso Robles, CA 93447 (☎ **800/549-WINE** or 805/ 239-8463; fax 805/237-6439; www.pasowine.com). Additional information on the area is offered by the **Paso Robles Chamber of Commerce,** 1225 Park St., Paso Robles, CA 93446 (☎ **800/406-4040** or 805/238-0506; fax 805/238-0527; www.pasorobleschamber.com).

TOURING THE LOCAL WINERIES

They've been tending vines in Paso Robles's fertile foothills since the turn of the century—the 19th century, that is. For decades, the area was overlooked by wine aficionados, even though in 1983 it was granted its own "Paso Robles" appellation (the official government designation of a recognized wine-producing region; "Napa Valley" and "Sonoma County" are probably more familiar appellations). But somewhere around 1992, wine grapes surpassed lettuce as San Luis Obispo County's primary cash crop, and there are now almost 40 wineries and more than 100 vineyards (which grow grapes but do not produce their own wine from them).

Wine touring in Paso Robles is reminiscent of another, unhurried time. Since not all wine enthusiasts are wine experts, an advantage of the area is its friendly attitude and small crowds, which make it easy to learn more about the wine-making process as you go along. Enjoy the relaxed rural atmosphere along two-lane country roads, driving leisurely from winery to winery and, more often than not, chatting with the winemaker while tasting their product.

Eberle Winery. Calif. 46 E. (3½ miles east of U.S. 101). ☎ **805/238-9607.** Complimentary tastings daily 10am–5pm (until 6pm in summer).

Owner Gary Eberle, who's been making Paso Robles wine since 1973, is sometimes called the "grandfather of Paso Robles's wine country" because many of the recent new vintners in the area honed their craft working under his tutelage. A visit to Eberle Winery includes a tour through its underground caves, where hundreds of aging barrels share space with the Wild Boar Room, site of Eberle's monthly winemaker dinners featuring guest chefs from around the country (always held on Saturday nights; the prix-fixe meal is around $80, including wine). Call for a current-events schedule.

EOS Estate Winery at Arciero Vineyards. Calif. 46 E. (6 miles east of U.S. 101). ☎ **805/ 239-2562**. www.eosvintage.com. Complimentary tastings daily 10am–5pm (until 6pm summer weekends).

Follow the checkered flag to the 800 acres of wine grapes owned by former race-car driver Frank Arciero, Sr. Arciero was drawn to the area by its resemblance to his native Italy; he passed through on his way to Laguna Seca, a racetrack near Salinas (trivia buffs will know it as James Dean's intended destination in 1955, when he was killed in nearby Cholame driving his silver Porsche). The label specializes in Italian varietals

The Paso Robles Wine Country

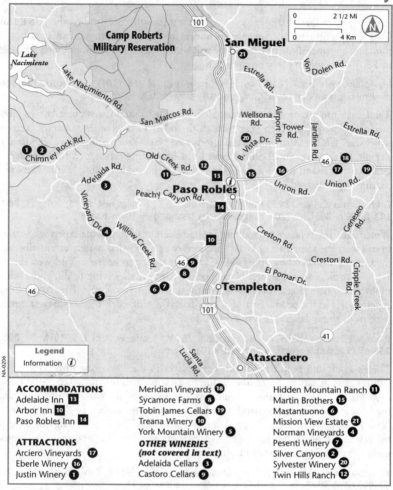

ACCOMMODATIONS
Adelaide Inn **13**
Arbor Inn **10**
Paso Robles Inn **14**

ATTRACTIONS
Arciero Vineyards **17**
Eberle Winery **16**
Justin Winery **1**

Meridian Vineyards **18**
Sycamore Farms **8**
Tobin James Cellars **19**
Treana Winery **10**
York Mountain Winery **5**

OTHER WINERIES
(not covered in text)
Adelaida Cellars **3**
Castoro Cellars **9**

Hidden Mountain Ranch **11**
Martin Brothers **15**
Mastantuono **6**
Mission View Estate **21**
Norman Vineyards **4**
Pesenti Winery **7**
Silver Canyon **2**
Sylvester Winery **20**
Twin Hills Ranch **12**

(nebbiolo, sangiovese) and blends; the facility includes a self-guided tour, race-car exhibit, spectacular rose gardens, and a picnic area.

Justin Vineyards & Winery. 11680 Chimney Rock Rd. (15 miles west of U.S. 101). ☎ **805/ 237-4150**; www.justinwine.com. Tastings Mon–Fri 11am–4pm; Sat–Sun 10am–5pm. Tasting fee $3, includes souvenir glass.

At the end of a scenic country road lies Justin and Deborah Baldwin's boutique winery, and even a casual glance shows how much love and dedication the ex–Los Angelenos have put into their operation. The tasting room, dining room, offices, and even wine-making barns have a stylish Tuscan flair. Justin's flagship wine is Isosceles, a Bordeaux-style blend that's pricier than most area wines but exudes both sophistication and superior aging potential. Also worth a try is their port-style dessert wine, called Obtuse. Since 1987, the Baldwins have commissioned a different artist each year to interpret their property for the label; you can see the framed results throughout the complex.

For an extra-special treat, the winery has a three-suite B&B called the **JUST Inn.** Impeccably outfitted, the inn has an undeniable serenity, and you can even have a romantic gourmet dinner prepared for you with advance notice. Room rates are $225 to $275—and worth every precious penny.

Meridian Vineyards. Calif. 46 E. (7 miles east of U.S. 101). ☎ **805/237-6000;** www.meridianvineyards.com. Complimentary tastings daily 10am–5pm.

The local vintner with the largest profile is also the Central Coast's best-known label, producing more cases each year than all the other Paso wineries *combined.* Veteran winemaker Chuck Ortman brought a respected Napa Valley pedigree to Meridian; as a result, here's where you'll get the most Napa-like tasting experience. In addition to a grand tasting room, there's a man-made lake surrounded by rolling lawns, where picnicking is encouraged.

Tobin James Cellars. 8950 Union Rd. (at Calif. 46 E., 8 miles east of U.S. 101). ☎ **800/543-0256** or 805/239-2204. Complimentary tastings daily 10am–6pm.

Winemaker Tobin James is a walking contradiction. A lifelong wine expert who claims to still wear the same pair of khaki shorts every day, Toby has patterned his winery in the spirit of local bad boys, the James Gang. The tasting room has a Wild West theme, a 100-year-old saloon bar, and blaring country music, all serving to dispel the wine-snob atmosphere that prevails at so many other wineries. Tobin James's particular expertise lies in the production of a "user-friendly" zinfandel; the late-harvest dessert wine from zinfandel grapes is smooth and spicy.

Treana Winery. 2175 Arbor Rd. (at Calif. 46 W., 1 mile west of U.S. 101). ☎ **805/238-6979.** Complimentary tastings daily 10am–5pm.

There's a spit and polish about this sleek player in the Paso wine game. The Hope family's elegant tasting room now features a gourmet deli for picnickers, an adjacent cigar gazebo (a relaxed room of tropical palms and wicker invoking 1950s Cuba), and the luxurious Arbor Inn bed-and-breakfast set among the vines (see "Where to Stay," below). With the help of a Napa-alumnus winemaker, Treana is turning out some of the best reds around, including cabernets rich in character, plus a portlike late-harvest merlot that's sweet, smooth, and complex.

York Mountain Winery. 7505 York Mountain Rd. (off Calif. 46 W., 7 miles west of U.S. 101). ☎ **805/238-3925.** Tastings daily 10am–5pm. Tasting fee $1.

If you're impressed by "firsts" and "onlys," don't miss York Mountain. It was the first winery established in the area (in 1882 by Andrew York, on land originally deeded by President Ulysses S. Grant) and is the oldest continuously operating vintner, as well as the only producer in the "York Mountain" viticulture appellation. In the 100-year-old stone tasting room, look for a dry chardonnay with a complex, spicy aroma, and award-winning cabernet sauvignons, the best of which are the Reserve bottlings from hand-chosen grapes.

OTHER DIVERSIONS IN THE PASO ROBLES AREA

The fragrance emanating from **Sycamore Farms,** Calif. 46 West, 3 miles west of U.S. 101 (☎ **800/576-5288** or 805/238-5288), is that of hundreds of herbs, grown for culinary, medicinal, and decorative purposes. Learn about them at the farm's walk-through garden; it also sells fresh-cut and dried herbs, nursery seedlings to transplant at home, and a bevy of herbal vinegars, olive oils, mustards, herbal soaps, and potpourri. Hours are daily from 10:30am to 5:30pm, except Christmas Day and from January 4 to 14.

It requires some advance planning, but nothing beats the exhilaration of seeing the wine country at sunrise from the serenity of a hot-air balloon. **Seventh Heaven Balloons** (☎ 805/687-8459) operates on select weekends throughout the year, offering two flights daily followed by champagne brunch. The package price is $139 per person; reservations are suggested at least 4 weeks in advance.

WHERE TO STAY

Adelaide Inn. 1215 Ysabel Ave., Paso Robles, CA 93446. ☎ **800/549-PASO** or 805/238-2770. Fax 805/238-3497. www.adelaideinn.com. 67 units. A/C TV TEL. $45–$65 double. Extra person $5. AE, CB, DC, DISC, JCB, MC, V. From U.S. 101, exit Calif. 46 E. Turn west at 24th St.; the hotel is just west of the freeway.

Tended with a loving care that's rare among lower-priced accommodations, the Adelaide Inn stands out from other motels. Although it's situated adjacent to freeway-close gas stations and coffee shops, special attention has been given to isolate this quiet, lushly landscaped property from its bustling surroundings. The rooms are clean and comfortable with extra warmth, and the motel has a safe, welcoming ambiance. Unexpected comforts include fridges, coffeemakers, hair dryers, complimentary newspaper, fruit and muffins, and in-room amenities for the business traveler. Facilities include a heated outdoor pool, a spa, a sauna, and even a putting green.

The Arbor Inn. 2130 Arbor Rd. (P.O. Box 3260), Paso Robles, CA 93447. ☎ **805/227-4673.** 9 units. A/C TV TEL. $140–$205 double; $245 suite. Extra person $65. Rates include full breakfast, afternoon wine and hors d'oeuvres, and evening cookies. MC, V. From U.S. 101, exit Calif. 46 W. 1 mile to Arbor Rd.

The guest book at this elegant B&B sports more than its share of honeymooners drawn by the splendid setting and luxurious treatment. Located at Treana Winery (see "Touring the Local Wineries," above), this three-story clapboard house looks like a cross between Queen Anne and Southern-plantation styles, but is furnished in formal English country. It's a brand-new building (the inn opened in 1995), so rooms are spacious and bathrooms ultra-modern; the main floor (including two guest rooms) is fully wheelchair accessible. Every room has a private balcony overlooking Treana's vineyards, plus a gas fireplace, fresh flowers, and terry robes; morning coffee is left discreetly outside your door in insulated carafes.

Paso Robles Inn. 1103 Spring St., Paso Robles, CA 93446. ☎ **805/238-2660.** 68 units. A/C TV TEL. $70–$75 double. Extra person $5. AE, CB, DC, DISC, JCB, MC, V.

This Mission Revival–style inn was built to replace the 1891 Stanford White masterpiece, El Paso De Robles Hotel, that burned to the ground in 1940. Photos of the grand landmark in its heyday line the Spanish-tiled lobby and adjacent dining room and cocktail lounge. A creek meanders through the oak-shaded property, and bungalow-style motel units are scattered across the tranquil and lovely grounds. Well shielded from street noise, these rooms are simple and plain; many guests will find them charming and nostalgic, but if you demand modern amenities and appointments, you'll be disappointed. There's a large heated pool near the creek, and convenient carports located behind each building. *Insider tip:* Avoid room numbers beginning with 1 or 2—they're too near the street.

WHERE TO DINE

Bistro Laurent. 1202 Pine St., Paso Robles. ☎ **805/226-8191.** Reservations recommended. Main courses $14–$19. MC, V. Mon–Sat 4:30–10pm. FRENCH/CALIFORNIA.

Executive chef Laurent Grangien's sophisticated bistro initially caused quite a stir in this town unaccustomed to such innovations as a chef's tasting menu. But once the

Gourmet Picnics, Paso Robles Style

You'll find everything you need for a casual snack or sophisticated picnic at Paso Robles's new **Odyssey Culinary Provisions,** 1214 Pine St. (☎ **805/237-7516**). A sandwich board features gourmet deli selections on focaccia and other fresh-baked breads, and refrigerated cases yield up inventive salads, cheeses, salami, olives, and other delicacies. Mustards, crackers, chocolates, and pastries line the shelves, along with baskets and knapsacks to hold your feast. Odyssey is also the place to come for fresh-brewed coffee and espresso drinks. It's open Sunday through Thursday from 7am to 7pm, Friday and Saturday from 7am to 11pm.

dust settled, everyone kept returning for the unpretentious neighborhood atmosphere, delicious recipes, and reasonable (by L.A. or San Francisco standards) prices. Whet your appetite with a complimentary teaser hors d'oeuvre (goat-cheese toasts, for example) before plunging into dishes like rosemary-garlic chicken, pork loin bathed in peppercorn sauce, or ahi tuna in red-wine reduction. "Twilight dinners" are served nightly until 6:30pm.

Busi's on the Park. 1122 Pine St., Paso Robles. ☎ **805/238-1390.** Reservations recommended on weekends. Main courses $10–$25. AE, MC, V. Tues–Fri 5–9pm; Sat–Sun 10am–2pm and 5–9pm. CALIFORNIA ECLECTIC.

The name may sound snooty and scenic, but Busi's is neither. It's just a comfortable, tavernlike joint across the street from downtown's City Park, but the capable kitchen draws a big local crowd. A short seasonal menu highlights fresh local ingredients; eclectic offerings include Southwestern chicken salad with refreshing cilantro-lime crema; Chinese stir-fried beef tinged with orange and sesame; pan-roasted salmon with oriental salsa; and a superior cannelloni that utilizes freshly made basil-egg pasta, roasted tomato sauce, and sautéed spinach. Weekend brunch runs the gamut from french toast or Spanish frittata to Thai noodle salad or saffron mussels.

✪ **McPhee's Grill.** 416 Main St., Templeton. ☎ **805/434-3204.** Reservations recommended. Main courses $6–$12 lunch, $12–$24 dinner; brunch $12.95 adults, $6.95 for kids under 10. MC, V. Daily 11:30–2pm and 5–9pm. CALIFORNIA GRILL.

When Ian McPhee left Ian's restaurant in Cambria and launched this one, it didn't take long for word to get out: McPhee's is worth the short drive to the historic town of Templeton. The converted old saloon features contemporary country decor, an open kitchen, and indoor and outdoor dining. The menu offers a half-dozen appetizers such as a duck quesadilla, artichoke fritters, and a zingy greens-and-grapefruit salad with Maytag bleu cheese and spiced nuts. Gourmet pizza, pasta, an amazing macadamia-crusted salmon, and four varieties of tender, juicy steaks cooked to perfection round out the Americana-with-a-twist style menu. Especially impressive are the prices; it's rare that a restaurant "dedicated to great food and great service" offers the majority of their dishes for under $16; it's the steaks and rack of lamb that hover closer to $20. The menu is accompanied by a fine selection of local wines. A champagne buffet brunch is offered on Sundays. This is definitely one of the very best restaurants in the region. Families should head here for the kids' menu, which includes five entree options and finishes with an ice-cream sundae with homemade chocolate sauce for $2.95.

THE SANTA YNEZ VALLEY

Welcome to the Santa Ynez Valley, an idyllic domain of oak-covered hills and uncrowded roads set against a mountain backdrop. This is beautiful country, where the clear blue sky achieves a brilliance unheard of in California's smog-clogged cities.

In the Santa Ynez Valley, the pace is a little slower, the locals a little friendlier. Don't expect to find yokels gnawing on hay, though—this is gentleman-farmer country, where some of the nicest ranches are gated and have video surveillance, and even Disney's Davy Crockett is a respected winemaker. This balance of old-fashioned living and modern sophistication is what makes the area enjoyable; you can wallow in simple pleasures one day and go wine tasting the next.

Los Olivos is a good ol'-fashioned country town right in the middle of wine country. There's a big flagpole in the center of the town's intersection, and stretches of boardwalk stand in for sidewalk here and there, giving the town a Wild West air. If you saw TV's *Return to Mayberry,* that was Los Olivos standing in for Andy Griffith's sentimental Southern hamlet. But these days, the town's storefronts feature art galleries, stylish cafes, and wine-tasting rooms; you'll see more Land Rovers than John Deeres in this upscale retreat.

Just minutes away from one another, Los Olivos, Santa Ynez, Ballard, Solvang, and Buellton each make an excellent base for touring the wineries of this fertile area.

ESSENTIALS

GETTING THERE   From U.S. 101, take Calif. 246 east 4 miles to reach Solvang, Santa Ynez, and Ballard. Los Olivos is located on Calif. 154 about 2 miles from U.S. 101. Lake Cachuma is also on Calif. 154, traveling southeast toward Santa Barbara.

VISITOR INFORMATION   Contact the **Santa Barbara County Vintners Association,** 3669 Sagunto St., Unit 101 (P.O. Box 1558), Santa Ynez, CA 93460 (☎ **800/218-0881** or 805/688-0881; www.sbcountywines.com), for its *Winery Touring Map.* Hours are Monday through Friday from 9am to 5pm. The **Solvang Visitor Bureau,** 1511 Mission Dr., at Fifth Street (P.O. Box 70), Solvang, CA 93464 (☎ **800/GO-SOLVANG** or 805/688-6144; www.solvangca.com), has additional information on the Santa Ynez Valley. It's open daily from 10am to 4pm.

ORIENTATION   U.S. 101, Calif. 246, and Calif. 154 form a triangle enclosing the towns of the Santa Ynez Valley. Calif. 246 becomes Mission Drive within Solvang city limits, then continues east past the mission toward Santa Ynez. Alamo Pintado Road connects Solvang with Los Olivos, whose commercial stretch is located along 3 blocks of Grand Avenue. Foxen Canyon Road continues north from downtown Los Olivos.

TOURING THE LOCAL WINERIES

Santa Barbara County has a 200-year tradition of growing grapes and making wine—an art originally practiced by Franciscan friars at the area's missions—but only in the past 20 to 30 years have wine-grape fields begun to approach the size of other crops that do so well in these fertile inland valleys.

Geography makes the area well suited for successful vineyards: The Santa Ynez and San Rafael mountain ranges are transverse (east-west) ranges, which allows ocean breezes to flow through, keeping the climate temperate. Variations in temperature and humidity within the valley create many microclimates, and vintners have learned how to cultivate nearly all the classic grape varietals. Today, you'll find about 25 vintners in the Santa Ynez Valley area, most of which have tasting rooms—a few offer tours of their operations as well. If you'd like to start with a winery tour to acquaint yourself with viticulture, Gainey Vineyard or Firestone Vineyard are good bets (see below). And if you'd like to sample wines without driving around, head to **Los Olivos Tasting Room & Wine Shop,** 2905 Grand Ave. (☎ **805/688-7406**), located in the heart of town, or **Los Olivos Wine & Spirits Emporium,** 2531 Grand Ave. (☎ **805/688-4409;** www. sbwines.com), a friendly barn in a field half a mile away. Both offer a wide selection of vintners, including those—like Au Bon Climat and Qupé—who don't have their own tasting rooms.

The Brander Vineyard. 2401 Refugio Rd., Los Olivos. ☎ **805/688-2455.** Tastings daily 10am–5pm. Tasting fee of $2.50 includes souvenir glass and is applied toward any purchase.

Winemaker Fred Brander has been making a name for himself since 1976; although the winery's production is small, his is a name you'll see frequently on local wine lists. Brander is among the valley's most pleasant wineries, with a friendly family of staff. The best bets are Cuvee Nicolas, which is a 100% sauvignon blanc from low-yielding vines; or choose a high-density cabernet from the cellar for full-bodied perfection.

Fess Parker Winery & Vineyard. 6200 Foxen Canyon Rd., Los Olivos. ☎ **800/841-1104** or 805/688-1545. Tastings daily 10am–5pm; tours daily at 11am, 1, and 3pm. Tasting fee $3.

You loved him as a child, now see what Hollywood's Davy Crockett/Daniel Boone is up to. Fess Parker has made a big name for himself in Santa Barbara County, with resort hotels, cattle ranches, and now an eponymous winery that's turning out some critically acclaimed syrahs, among other varietals. Look for the syrah and chardonnay American Tradition Reserve vintages in the tasting room. Parker's grandiose complex, shaded by the largest oak tree we've ever seen, also features picnic tables on a breezy terrace and an extensive gift shop where you can even buy—you guessed it—'coon-skin caps!

Firestone Vineyard. 5017 Zaca Station Rd., Los Olivos. ☎ **805/688-3940.** Tastings daily 10am–5pm; tours hourly Sat–Sun.

Probably the largest producers in Santa Barbara County, this operation started by Brooks Firestone (of tire-manufacturing fame) now includes two "second" labels. Their wines are affordable and reasonably good, and they've started experimenting with Chilean-grown grapes, some of which can be excellent. Firestone's tasting room and gift shop are a three-ring circus of merchandise, but they offer a quick, worthwhile tour and free tastings.

The Gainey Vineyard. 3950 E. Calif. 246, Santa Ynez. ☎ **805/688-0558.** Tastings daily 10am–5pm; tours daily 11am, 1, 2, and 3pm. No reservations required. Tasting fee $3, includes souvenir glass.

This slick operation is one of the most-visited wineries in the valley, thanks to its prime location on Calif. 246 and its in-depth tours, offered daily. They've got every hallmark of a visitor-oriented winery: a terra-cotta–tiled tasting room, plenty of logo merchandise, and a deli case for impromptu lunches at the picnic tables in a secluded vineyard garden. They bottle the most popular varietals—chardonnay, cabernet sauvignon, pinot noir, sauvignon blanc—and offer them at moderate prices.

Sunstone Vineyards and Winery. 125 Refugio Rd., Santa Ynez. ☎ **800/313-WINE** or 805/688-WINE. Tastings daily 10am–4pm. Tasting fee $3–$5, includes souvenir glass.

Take a rambling drive down to this locally well-known winery, whose gracious wisteria-wrapped stone tasting room belies the dirt road you take to reach it. Sunstone is nestled in an oak grove overlooking the river, boasting a splendid view from the lavender-fringed picnic courtyard. Inside, try their flagship merlot or treasured reserve vintages; there's also a fine selection of gourmet foods, logo ware, and cigars.

Zaca Mesa Winery. 6905 Foxen Canyon Rd., Los Olivos. ☎ **800/350-7972** or 805/688-9339. Complimentary tastings daily 10am–4pm; call for tour schedule.

One of the region's old-timers, Zaca Mesa has been in business since 1972, so we can forgive them the hippie/New Age mumbo-jumbo pleasantly interwoven with the well-honed vintages. Situated on a unique plateau that the Spanish named *la zaca mesa* (the restful place), this winery's 750 acres are uniquely beautiful—a fact they celebrate with two easy nature trails for visitors. You'll also find picnic tables and a giant lawn chessboard. Inside, look for the usual syrah and chardonnay offerings jazzed up with experimental Rhône varietals like grenache, roussanne, and voignier.

A TASTE OF DENMARK: SOLVANG

The valley's largest town is also one of the state's most popular tourist stops, and Solvang takes a lot of flack for being a Disney-fied version of its founders' vision. Everything here that *can* be Danish *is* Danish: You've never seen so many windmills, cobblestone streets, wooden shoes, and so much gingerbread trim—even the sidewalk trash cans look like little Danish farmhouses with pitched-roof lids.

To reach Solvang from U.S. 101 south, turn east (left) onto Calif. 246 at Buellton; it's a well-marked 20-minute drive along an extremely scenic two-lane road. From Santa Barbara, take U.S. 101 north to Calif. 154, a truly breathtaking 45-minute drive over San Marcos Pass. For a destination guide or hotel information, contact the **Solvang Conference and Visitors Bureau,** 1511 Mission Dr. (Calif. 246), Solvang (☎ 805/688-6144).

One way to weed through the unabashed tourism here for a little authentic history is to visit the **Elverhøj Museum,** 1624 Elverhoy Way (☎ 805/686-1211), a warm and welcoming place devoted to Danish culture and Solvang history. Set in a traditional handcrafted Scandinavian-style home, and featuring many original old-world furnishings, this little museum can be fully appreciated in 30 minutes or less. Hours are Wednesday through Sunday from 1 to 4pm; a $2 donation is suggested.

Solvang has always been renowned for its traditional and delectable pastries, and the best bakery in town is **Birkholm's Bakery,** 1555 Mission Dr. (☎ 805/688-3872). It's the oldest, opened in 1951 and still family-run. In addition to sticky pastries, sweet rolls, fresh bread, and fresh-brewed coffee, Birkholm's sells its trademark blue-and-white waxed tub of Danish butter cookies ($7.95 each). Hours are daily from 8am to 5:30pm.

Old Mission Santa Ines. 1760 Mission Dr., Solvang. ☎ 805/688-4815. $3 donation requested, free for children under 16. Summer Mon–Fri 9am–7pm; Sat 9am–4pm; Sun 1:30–5:30pm. Winter Sun–Fri 9am–5:30pm; Sat 9am–4pm. From downtown Solvang, take Calif. 246 1 mile east to Mission Dr.

Just on the edge of town, and one of the few buildings without a windmill or other Scandinavian fanfare, this Spanish mission was founded by Franciscan friars in 1804 and is still in use for daily services. Most of the original structure, painstakingly constructed of adobe by Native Americans, has been destroyed; the reconstruction features the ornately tiled and painted chapel typical of the Spanish missions and an extensive museum display of mission artifacts and Franciscan vestment robes.

✪ CACHUMA LAKE: A BALD-EAGLE HABITAT

Created in 1953 by damming the Santa Ynez River, this picturesque reservoir running along Calif. 154 is the primary water source for Santa Barbara County. It's also the centerpiece of a 6,600-acre county park with a flourishing wildlife population and well-developed recreational facilities. Cachuma has, through both agreeable climate and diligent ranger efforts, become a notable habitat for resident and migratory birds, including rarely sighted bald eagles, which migrate south from as far as Alaska in search of food.

One of the best ways to appreciate this fine-feathered bounty is to take one of the naturalist-led **Eagle Cruises** of the lake, offered between November and February. The 48-foot *Osprey* was specially designed for wildlife observation, with unobstructed views from nearly every seat. During the rest of the year, rangers lead **Wildlife Cruises** around the lake, helping you spot resident waterfowl, grazing deer, and the elusive bobcats and mountain lions that live here. Eagle Cruises depart Wednesday through Sunday at 10am, with additional cruises Friday and Saturday at 2pm. Wildlife Cruises run Friday and Saturday at 3pm, and Saturday and Sunday at 10am. All cruises are 2 hours long. In addition to the park day-use fee of $5 per car, the fare is $10 for adults and $5 for children 12 and under. Reservations are recommended for all cruises; call the **Santa Barbara County Parks Department** (☎ **805/686-5050**).

The recreational opportunities at Cachuma don't stop there; campers, boaters, and fishermen will find abundant facilities. Contact the **Lake Cachuma Recreation Area** (☎ **805/686-5054**) for more information.

WHERE TO STAY

Ballard Inn. 2436 Baseline Ave., Ballard, CA 93463. ☎ **800/638-2466** or 805/688-7770. Fax 805/688-9560. www.ballardinn.com. 15 units. A/C. $170–$250 double. Rates include full breakfast, afternoon wine and hors d'oeuvres, and evening coffee and tea. AE, MC, V. Take Alamo Pintado Rd. to Baseline; the inn is half a block east of the intersection.

This two-story inn may look 100 years old, but it's actually of modern construction, offering both contemporary comforts and charming country details like wicker rockers on a wraparound porch. The entry and parlors are tastefully furnished with a comfortable mix of antiques and reproductions; sumptuous wallpaper and fabrics lend a cozy touch, and hand-hooked rugs, bent-twig furniture, and vintage accessories lend character to the house. The guest rooms upstairs are similarly unique—some have fireplaces and/or private balconies, and all have well-stocked bathrooms, many featuring a separate antique washbasin in the bedroom. The best (and most expensive) unit is the Mountain Room, a minisuite decorated in rich forest green and outfitted with a fireplace and private balcony. In addition to cooked-to-order breakfast and a wine-and-hors d'oeuvres reception, you'll be treated to evening coffee and tea, plus addictive chocolate cookies on your nightstand at bedtime.

The inn's restaurant, Cafe Chardonnay, is tucked into a cozy room downstairs by a crackling fire; the California-style seasonal menu can include grilled meats, seafood pastas, and catch-of-the-day specials. *Note:* The Inn staff doesn't accept gratuities; instead, a 10% service charge is added at checkout.

Inn at Petersen Village. 1576 Mission Dr., Solvang, CA 93463. ☎ **800/321-8985** or 805/688-3121. Fax 805/688-5732. 42 units. A/C TV TEL. $125–$195 double. Extra person $15. Rates include generous breakfast buffet, evening wine and hors d'oeuvres, and dessert buffet. Midweek and auto-club discounts available. AE, MC, V.

If you think every hotel in Solvang has a kitschy, Danish theme, then step off the street right into this quiet, tasteful, and affordable hotel. Rooms are decorated in a European country motif, with print wallpaper, canopy beds, and mahogany-hued furniture. But it's the little touches that impress the most, like lighted magnifying mirrors, bathroom lights controlled by dimmers, free coffee and tea service to your room, and the complimentary food that's nearly always laid out in the hotel's friendly piano lounge. Some rooms overlook a bustling courtyard of shops, while others face Solvang's scenic hills. All are designed so everyone's happy: Smaller units have private balconies, those with noisier views are more spacious, and so on.

Royal Scandinavian Inn. 400 Alisal Rd. (P.O. Box 30), Solvang, CA 93464. ☎ **800/624-5572** or 805/688-8000. Fax 805/688-0761. www.solvangrsi.com. 133 units. A/C TV TEL. Mar–Nov $91–$141 double; from $136 suite. Dec–Feb $81–$121 double; from $126 suite. Extra person $10. AE, DC, DISC, MC, V.

If you're looking for a traditional, full-service hotel, this attractive and comfortable mainstay in Solvang is nicely located away from the congested main drag. Popular with business conventions and leisure groups, the Royal Scandinavian Inn has an all-day restaurant and cocktail lounge and is within walking distance of downtown Solvang; the championship Alisal River Golf Course is next door. Rooms are furnished in a vaguely Danish country decor, but are otherwise unremarkable; bathrooms are up-to-date. Ask for a room overlooking the courtyard, with its heated pool and spa; the view extends to the foothills beyond.

WHERE TO DINE

If you're looking for traditional Danish fare in Solvang, head for **Bit o' Denmark,** 473 Alisal Rd. (☎ **805/688-5426**). Its smorgasbord may not be the largest in town, but it's the freshest and highest quality; you can also order from the regular menu. It's open daily from 9am to 9pm; the smorgasbord costs $8.95 at lunch, $12.95 at dinner.

✪ **Brothers Restaurant.** 409 First St. (in the Storybook Inn), Solvang. ☎ **805/688-9934.** Reservations recommended. Main courses $15–$23. Wed–Sun 5–9pm. CALIFORNIA.

Jeff and Matt Nichols are the brothers; although young, the two chefs nevertheless bring more than 30 combined years of culinary experience to this intimate parlor of only nine tables. Since opening in 1996, Brothers has quickly won the hearts of smorgasbord-weary Solvangites with a California/international menu that changes seasonally according to the chefs' whims. You can always count on selections from the grill, such as swordfish resting on vegetable rice, splashed with Thai curry sauce, and accented with mango salsa. A tender rack of lamb is fanned over mashed potatoes studded with tangy black olives on a rich rosemary sauce. And we always like a restaurant with as many dessert offerings as entrees; two to try are the fudge brownie with homemade roasted-banana ice cream and the passion-fruit cheesecake. A carefully chosen, moderately priced list of Central Coast wines complements the menu.

Mattei's Tavern. Calif. 154, Los Olivos. ☎ **805/688-4820.** Reservations suggested on week-ends. Dinner $15–$35. Daily 5:30–9pm; Sat–Sun noon–2:30pm. AE, DISC, MC, V. AMERICAN/ CONTINENTAL.

Mattei's is proud of its stagecoach past, and this rambling white Victorian submerged in climbing wisteria has successfully retained its historic charm. It's well known throughout the county for fun and good food; rumors abound of high-stakes poker games in Mattei's back room, where many an early rancher literally "lost the farm."

Picnicking in the Santa Ynez Valley

You can assemble a picnic lunch at the **Santa Ynez Valley Market,** on Calif. 154 about a mile east of Los Olivos (☎ **805/688-5115**), where a fresh deli counter prepares simple sandwiches and side salads, plus buckets of fried chicken. With a little advance notice, they'll prepare box lunches that include a sandwich, chips, a piece of fruit, and a cookie, for $7.50 each. The market is open daily from 7am to 8pm.

Los Olivos offers easy-to-carry, eat-at-room-temperature goodies packed up with all the necessary utensils. At **Panino,** 2900 Grand Ave. (☎ **805/688-9304**), choose from 31 gourmet sandwiches priced from $5 to $7, all served on Panino's fresh-baked, Italian-style bread; varieties include grilled chicken with sun-dried tomatoes, fresh basil, and provolone, or English Stilton with Asian pear on fresh walnut bread. Open Monday through Friday from 10am to 4pm, Saturday and Sunday from 9am to 5pm.

You'll find fine steaks on the menu, along with Australian lobster tail, rainbow trout, burgers, prime-rib chili, a dill-tinged tomato bisque, and chicken picatta, marsala, or teriyaki.

Paula's Pancake House. 1531 Mission Dr., Solvang. ☎ **805/688-2867.** Most menu items under $7. Daily 6am–3pm. AE, DISC, MC, V. AMERICAN/DANISH.

Morning means one thing in Solvang, and that's Paula's three-page menu of *just break-fast!* There are wafer-thin Danish pancakes, served plain and simple, sweet and fruity, or with sausage and eggs; plus buttermilk pancakes, whole-wheat/honey pancakes, fresh-baked waffles, sourdough French toast, and every omelet and egg dish imaginable, including some south-of-the-border salsa-fied specials. Paula's is friendly and casual, plunked in the heart of town so that patio diners can watch the whole wacky world go by.

6 Santa Barbara

45 miles S of Solvang, 105 miles S of San Luis Obispo, 92 miles NW of Los Angeles

Between the Santa Ynez Mountains and the Pacific, charming, spoiled Santa Barbara is coddled by wooded mountains, caressed by baby breakers, and sheltered from tempestuous seas by rocky offshore islands. And it's just far enough from Los Angeles to make the big city seem at once remote and accessible. There are few employment opportunities and real estate is expensive here, so demographics favor college students and rich retirees (referred to by the locals as the "almost wed and almost dead"), and most recently, Hollywood heavyweights.

Downtown Santa Barbara is distinctive for its Spanish-Mediterranean architecture; all the structures sport matching red-tile roofs. But it wasn't always this way. Santa Barbara had a thriving Native American Chumash population for hundreds, if not thousands, of years. The European era began in the late 18th century, around a presidio (fort) that's been reconstructed in its original spot. The earliest architectural hodgepodge was destroyed in 1925 by a powerful earthquake that leveled the business district. Out of the rubble rose the Spanish-Mediterranean town of today, a stylish planned community that continues to rigidly enforce its strict building codes.

ESSENTIALS

GETTING THERE   U.S. 101 runs right through Santa Barbara; it's the fastest and most direct route from north or south (2 hours from Los Angeles, 6 hours from San Francisco).

The **Santa Barbara Municipal Airport** (☎ 805/967-7111) is located in Goleta, about 10 minutes north of downtown Santa Barbara. Airlines serving Santa Barbara include **American Eagle** (☎ 800/433-7300), **AmericaWest Airlines** (☎ 800/235-9292), **United** (☎ 800/241-6522), and **US Airways Express** (☎ 800/428-4322). **Yellow Cab** (☎ 805/965-5111) and other metered taxis line up outside the terminal; the fare is about $22 (without tip) to downtown.

Amtrak (☎ 800/USA-RAIL) offers daily service to Santa Barbara. Trains arrive at and depart from the **Santa Barbara Rail Station,** 209 State St. (☎ 805/963-1015). Fares can be as low as $16 from Los Angeles.

VISITOR INFORMATION   The **Santa Barbara Visitor Information Center,** 1 Santa Barbara St., Santa Barbara, CA 93101 (☎ **800/927-4688,** or 805/965-3021 to order a free destination guide), is on the ocean, on Cabrillo Street. The center offers maps with points of interest and a scenic drive, literature, an events calendar, and excellent advice. Hours are Monday through Saturday from 9am to 5pm and Sunday

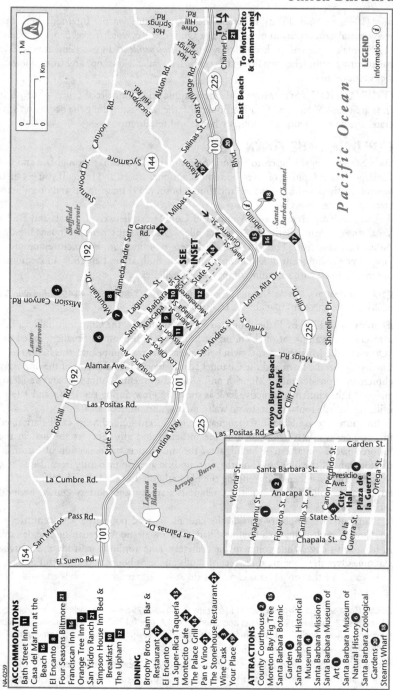

Santa Barbara

Pacific Ocean

East Beach

To Montecito & Summerland

To LA

Santa Barbara Channel

LEGEND ⓘ
Information ⓘ

Pacific Ocean

SEE INSET

INSET
Garden St.
Victoria St.
Santa Barbara St.
Anapausa St.
Anacapa St.
Figueroa St.
Carrillo St.
State St.
Chapala St.
De la Guerra St.
Canon Perdido St.
Presidio Ave.
Ortega St.
City Hall
Plaza de la Guerra

NA-0259

399

from 10am to 5pm. Plenty of details are also available via the Internet; check out **www.santabarbaraca.com** or on America Online at Keyword: Travel Santa Barbara.

Also make sure you pick up a copy of the *Independent,* an excellent, free weekly paper with a comprehensive listing of events. It's available in shops and from sidewalk racks around town.

ORIENTATION   State Street is the geographic and commercial center of town. It ends at Stearns Wharf and Cabrillo Boulevard; the latter runs along the ocean and separates the city's beaches from touristy hotels and restaurants.

EXPLORING THE TOWN

State Street from the beach to Victoria Street is the city's main thoroughfare and has the largest concentration of cafes, boutiques, antiques stores, and more. If you get tired of strolling, hop on one of the electric shuttle buses (25¢) that run up and down State Street at regular intervals.

Also check out **Brinkerhoff Avenue** (off Cota Street, between Chapala and De La Vina streets), Santa Barbara's "antiques alley." Most shops here are open Tuesday through Sunday from 11am to 5pm. **El Paseo,** 814 State St., is a picturesque shopping arcade reminiscent of an old Spanish street. Built around an 1827 adobe home, the mall is lined with charming shops and art galleries.

✪ **Santa Barbara Mission.** Laguna and Los Olivos sts. ☎ **805/682-4149.** Admission $3 adults, free for children 11 and under. Daily 9am–5pm.

Established in 1786 by Father Junípero Serra and built by the Chumash Indians, this is a very rare example of the blending of Indian and Hispanic spirituality. Called the "Queen of the Missions" for its twin bell towers and graceful beauty, this hilltop mission overlooks the town and the Channel Islands beyond. The design of the imposing church incorporates many Moorish and classical elements. Santa Barbara's residents embraced the church's distinctive look as the town grew during the 1920s and 1930s, utilizing red-tile roofs, thick stucco walls, arches, and outdoor arcades.

Brochures are available in six languages, and docent-guided tours can be arranged in advance. It's worthwhile to tour the museum and gift shop, established in the restored padres' quarters. A highlight of the museum is the collection of historical photographs of the buildings and the surrounding area, some dating from the 1850s, featuring brown-robed friars tending the old orchards and gardens. The gift shop has an extensive collection of crucifixes, religious statuary, and pottery crafted by local artisans.

Don't miss the cemetery outside the church, its yard populated with centuries of headstones, vaults, and mausoleums. Shaded by a majestic Australian fig tree, it's still in use to this day. While you're in the cemetery, take a minute to study the church's exterior. Over the door are three sets of skulls and crossbones. Upon careful observation, you'll see that only one is carved in stone—two sets are real bones embedded in the plaster.

Santa Barbara Museum of Art. 1130 State St. ☎ **805/963-4364.** Admission $5 adults, $3 seniors 62 and over, $2 students and children 6–17, free for children 5 and under; free for everyone Thurs and the first Sun of each month. Tues–Thurs and Sat 11am–5pm; Fri 11am–8pm; Sun noon–5pm.

A trip here feels like a visit to the private galleries of a wealthy art collector. Works by Monet and other mid-quality oils by Dalí, Picasso, Matisse, Chagall, and Rousseau are displayed on a rotating basis in rooms that, for the most part, are ample, airy, and well lit. Quantitatively, the museum's strengths lie in early-20th-century western American paintings and 19th- and 20th-century Asian art. Qualitatively, the best are the antiquities and Chinese ceramics collections. Many pieces are often on loan to other museums, but good temporary exhibits show a high degree of reciprocity. Some awkward arrangements don't always make sense, and lighting could be improved on the placards. For the most part, though, this is a jewel of a museum. Free docent-led tours are given Tuesday through Sunday at 1pm. Focus tours are held on Wednesday and Saturday at noon. The new Peck Wing, completed in 1998, includes more galleries, a larger gift shop, and a cafe, which is operated by the Wine Cask folks.

County Courthouse. 1100 Anacapa St. ☎ **805/962-6464.** Free admission. Mon–Fri 8am–5pm; Sat–Sun and holidays 10am–4:45pm. Free guided tours Mon–Sat at 2pm and Fri at 10:30am. Closed Christmas.

Even the accused are afforded exquisite surroundings in stunning Santa Barbara—the courthouse is the most flamboyant example of Spanish-Mediterranean architecture in the entire city. Built in 1929 to mimic a much older style, the ornate building is Santa Barbara's literal and figurative centerpiece. The observation deck atop the clock tower affords great views of the ocean, the mountains, and the city's terra-cotta tile roofs. There's also an outstanding collection of palms, specimen trees, and exotic plantings from around the world.

Moreton Bay Fig Tree. Chapala and Montecito sts.

Santa Barbara's best-known tree has a branch spread that would cover half a football field, and its roots run under more than an acre of ground. It is, hands down, the largest of its kind in the world. It's so broad, in fact, that an estimated 10,000 people could stand in its shade. Planted in 1877, it's a native of Moreton Bay in eastern Australia. The tree is related to both the fig and the rubber trees, but produces neither. Don't be surprised if you see some of Santa Barbara's homeless here; it's been a long-time hangout, although in recent years they've begun frequenting the pier area, where there are better panhandling opportunities.

Santa Barbara Botanic Garden. 1212 Mission Canyon Rd. ☎ **805/682-4726.** Admission $5 adults, $3 seniors 60 and over and children 13–19, $1 children 5–12, free for children 4 and under. Mon–Fri 9am–5pm; Sat–Sun 9am–6pm.

The gardens, about 1½ miles north of the mission, encompass 65 acres of native trees, shrubs, cacti, and wildflowers, and more than 5 miles of trails. They're at their aromatic peak just after spring showers. Docent tours are offered daily at 2pm, with additional tours on the weekends at 10:30am.

Santa Barbara Historical Museum. 136 E. De La Guerra St. ☎ **805/966-1601.** Free admission; donations requested. Tues–Sat 10am–5pm; Sun noon–5pm.

Local-lore exhibits include late-19th-century paintings of the California missions by Edwin Deakin; a 16th-century carved Spanish coffer from Majorca, home of Junípero Serra; and objects from the Chinese community that once flourished here, including a magnificent carved shrine from the turn of the century. A knowledgeable docent leads an interesting free tour every Wednesday, Saturday, and Sunday at 1:30pm.

Santa Barbara Museum of Natural History. 2559 Puesta del Sol Rd. (2 blocks uphill from the mission). ☎ **805/682-4711.** Admission $5 adults, $4 seniors and teens, $3 children; free last Sun of each month. Mon–Sat 9am–5pm; Sun and holidays 10am–5pm.

This museum focuses on the study and interpretation of Pacific Coast natural history, which includes mammals, birds, marine life, plants, and insects; displays range from fossil ferns to the complete skeleton of a blue whale. Native American history is emphasized in exhibits including basketry, textiles, and a full-size replica of a Chumash canoe. Recent additions include a replica of a pygmy mammoth skeleton and the

"Lizard Lounge," featuring live reptiles and amphibians. An adjacent planetarium projects sky shows every Saturday and Sunday.

Santa Barbara Zoological Gardens. 500 Niños Dr. ☎ **805/962-5339,** or 805/962-6310 for a recording. Admission $7 adults, $5 seniors and children 2–12, free for children under 2. Daily 10am–5pm (last admission is 1 hr. before closing). Closed Thanksgiving and Christmas.

This is a thoroughly charming, pint-sized place, where all 600 animals can be seen in about 30 minutes. Most of the animals live in natural, open settings. The zoo has a children's Discovery Area, a miniature train ride, a small carousel, and recent additions including a new lion habitat and aquarium grotto. The picnic areas (complete with barbecue pits) are underutilized and especially recommended.

Stearns Wharf. At the end of State St.

In addition to a small collection of second-rate shops, attractions, and restaurants, the city's 1872-vintage pier offers terrific inland views and good drop-line fishing. The Dolphin Fountain at the foot of the wharf was created by local artist Bud Bottoms for the city's 1982 bicentennial.

BEACHES & OUTDOOR PURSUITS

BEACHES   Santa Barbara has an array of beaches perfect for stretching out on a towel, playing volleyball, or frolicking seaside. Arroyo Burro, a.k.a. **Hendry's Beach,** at the end of Cliff Drive, is popular with families, boogie boarders who come to ride the excellent beach breaks, and sunset strollers. ✪ **East Beach** is a wide swath of clean white sand that hosts beach umbrellas, sandcastle builders, and spirited volleyball games. A grassy, parklike median keeps the noise of busy Cabrillo Boulevard away. On Sundays, local artists set up shop beneath the palms.

Note: A tragic oil spill off the coast of Santa Barbara in 1969 left surfers and sea critters dodging gobs of floating tar for the next 20 years. Although the area has finally cleared up, the staining brown substance still finds its way onto clothes and skin from time to time, even if you don't go in the water (that's why the Four Seasons Biltmore hotel includes "Tar Off" in its baskets of toiletry goodies).

BICYCLING   A relatively flat, palm-lined, 2-mile coastal pathway runs along the beach and is perfect for biking. More adventurous riders can pedal through town, up to the mission, or to Montecito, the next town over. The best mountain-bike trail begins at the end of Tunnel Road and climbs up along a paved fire road before turning into a dirt trail to the mountaintop.

Beach Rentals, 22 State St. (☎ **805/966-6733**), rents well-maintained one-speeds. It also has tandem bikes and surrey cycles that can hold as many as four adults and two children. Rates vary depending on equipment. Bring your driver's license or passport to expedite your rental. It's open daily from 8am to dusk.

GOLF   At the **Santa Barbara Golf Club,** 3500 McCaw Ave., at Las Positas Road Exit from U.S. 101 (☎ **805/687-7087**), there's a great 18-hole, 6,009-yard course and driving range. Unlike many municipal courses, the Santa Barbara Golf Course is well maintained and was designed to present a moderate challenge for the average golfer. Greens fees are $25 Monday through Friday, $35 Saturday and Sunday (discounts for residents and seniors); twilight discounts are offered after 2pm. Optional carts are $22 for 18 holes, $12 for 9 holes.

The 18-hole, 7,068-yard **Sandpiper,** 7925 Hollister Ave. (☎ **805/968-1541**), is a scenic oceanside course with a pro shop and driving range, plus an enormous new clubhouse. Greens fees are $68 Monday through Thursday, $108 Friday through Sunday and holidays; twilight discounts are available. Carts are $12 per person.

HIKING   The hills and mountains surrounding Santa Barbara have excellent hiking trails. One of our favorites begins at the end of Tunnel Road. Take Mission Canyon Road past the mission, turn right onto Foothill Road, and take the first left onto Mission Canyon Drive. Bear left onto Tunnel Road and park at the end (where all the other cars are). You can buy a trail map at the Santa Barbara Visitor Information Center (see "Essentials," above).

HORSEBACK RIDING   Several area stables rent horses, including the **Circle Bar B Ranch,** 1800 Refugio Rd. (☎ 805/968-3901). A 1-hour trail ride is offered for $22 at **Rancho Oso,** Paradise Road, off Calif. 154 (☎ **805/964-8985**).

POWERBOATING & SAILING   The **Sailing Center of Santa Barbara,** at the Santa Barbara Breakwater (☎ **800/350-9090** or 805/962-2826; www.sbsailctr.com), rents sailboats from 13 to 50 feet, as well as powerboats, kayaks, and jet skis. Both crewed and bare-boat charters are available by the day or hour. Sailing instruction for all levels of experience is also offered. Coastal, island, whale watching, and dinner tours are available on the 50-foot sailing catamaran *Double Dolphin.*

SKATING   The paved beach path that runs along Santa Barbara's waterfront is perfect for skating. **Beach Rentals,** 22 State St. (☎ 805/966-6733), located nearby, rents in-line skates. The $6-per-hour fee includes wrist and knee pads.

SPORTFISHING, DIVE CRUISES & WHALE WATCHING   **Sea Landing,** at the foot of Bath Street and Cabrillo Boulevard (☎ 805/963-3564), makes regular sportfishing runs from specialized boats. It also offers a wide variety of other fishing and diving cruises and camping trips to the Channel Islands. Food and drinks are served on board, and rental rods and tackle are available. Rates vary according to excursion; call for reservations.

Whale-watching cruises are offered from February to April, when California gray whales make their migratory journey from Baja California, Mexico, to Alaska. Tours are $24 for adults and $14 for children; sightings of large marine mammals are guaranteed.

WHERE TO STAY

Before you even begin calling around for reservations, keep in mind that Santa Barbara's accommodations are expensive—especially in summer. Then decide whether you'd like to stay beachside (even more expensive) or downtown. The town is small, but not small enough to happily stroll between the two areas.

Hot Spots Accommodations, 36 State St., Santa Barbara, CA 93101 (☎ **800/ 793-7666** or 805/564-1637), a one-stop shop for hotel, motel, and B&B rooms, keeps an updated list of what's available in all price categories. There's no charge for their services. Significantly discounted rates are often available at the last minute, when hotels need to fill their rooms.

Another option is **Coastal Escapes Accommodations** (☎ 800/292-2222; www.coastalescapes@linkline.com), a company that books rooms in all price ranges along California's coast, from Ventura to Monterey. The service is free.

VERY EXPENSIVE

✪ **Four Seasons Biltmore.** 1260 Channel Dr. (at the end of Olive Mill Rd.), Santa Barbara, CA 93108. ☎ **800/332-3442** or 805/969-2261. Fax 805/565-8326. 234 units. MINIBAR TV TEL. $405–$575 double; from $795 suite. Extra person $30. Special midweek and package rates available. AE, DC, MC, V.

This is the largest of what we consider the top three places to stay in the area (the other two are San Ysidro Ranch and the Simpson House). The now-divorced king and queen of tattoo and lace, Tommy Lee (Mötley Crüe) and Heather Locklear (*Melrose Place*), tied the knot with class at the beach club next door and later indulged in the hotel's infamously decadent Sunday brunch. They weren't the first to celebrate here—other Hollywood highbrows such as Greta Garbo, Errol Flynn, and Bing Crosby also knew that the Biltmore is one of the most beautiful hotels in the country. Although the hotel debuted in 1927, Four Seasons acquired the property in 1987 and brought its beauty to its full potential with a $20-million renovation.

Today, the hotel still captivates guests with its Spanish revival architecture, hand-painted Mexican tiles, and 19 acres of incredibly landscaped oceanfront gardens. It has a light, warm aura, with flora and fauna almost everywhere you look. The guest rooms are less elaborate but are newly renovated, and come complete with comfortable beds, fluffy towels and robes, and bath soaps you can't help but stow away in your luggage when you depart. They also boast striking views of the mountains or the ocean, and some have Spanish balconies, fireplaces, or private patios; all come with VCRs.

Dining/Diversions: This is resort dining at its finest. The elegant La Marina offers surprisingly innovative specialties. The Patio is more casual, serving three meals daily and Santa Barbara's best Sunday brunch; it's a beautiful setting, with an oceanfront view, indoor and outdoor seating, and a retractable atrium roof. La Sala is a comfortable lounge serving afternoon tea and evening cocktails; there's live jazz on Wednesday and Friday nights.

Amenities: Concierge, 24-hour room service, laundry service, nightly turndown, twice-daily maid service, overnight shoe shine, two outdoor heated pools, two health clubs, sundeck, three lighted tennis courts, shuffleboard and croquet courts, complimentary bicycle use, putting green, beachfront cabanas, special children's programs, beauty salon, gift shop.

✪ **San Ysidro Ranch.** 900 San Ysidro Lane (off U.S. 101), Montecito, CA 93108. ☎ **800/ 368-6788** or 805/969-5046. Fax 805/565-1995. 38 units. MINIBAR TV TEL. $399–$575 cottage for two; from $950 suite. AE, DC, MC, V.

For 100 years, this has been the ultimate retreat for the rich (Vivien Leigh and Laurence Olivier) and the royal (JFK and Jackie hung out here, too). It's one of our favorite places in the state, winning us over every time with its quaint winding trails overgrown with wildflowers and trees, peaceful rolling hills beyond, 540 acres of lush countryside all around, and rustically luxurious accommodations. This is the kind of place where the noisiest time of day is when the sun comes up and birds begin to celebrate their surroundings; a strenuous afternoon consists of leaning up from a poolside lounge chair to accept a bowl of complimentary berries from an accommodating pool hand.

Upon arrival, guests are escorted to their freestanding "cottages" (with their last name posted in rustic block letters next to the door), which are impeccably outfitted in country luxury, with a wood-burning stove or fireplace, outdoor terrace, goose-down comforter and Frette linens, VCR, and dozens of other amenities that'll pamper every aspect of your being. Each individually decorated accommodation feels more like a rich uncle's country home than a resort and boasts such personal touches as books and magazines, fresh flowers, and a stereo with CDs. The brand-new 2,200-square-foot Eucalyptus Cottage is a private luxury home complete with two bedrooms, kitchen, pool, hot tub, and total privacy.

Dining: The Stonehouse, the renowned restaurant on the property, is our top dining choice (see "Where to Dine," below, for complete details).

Amenities: Tennis courts, a fitness center and exercise course, spa treatments.

EXPENSIVE

El Encanto. 1900 Lasuen Rd., Santa Barbara, CA 93103. ☎ **800/346-7039** or 805/687-5000. Fax 805/687-3903. 84 units. MINIBAR TV TEL. $190–$269 double; $229–$1,000 suite. AE, DC, MC, V.

On 10 acres of hillside overlooking Santa Barbara, El Encanto is a romantic retreat perched high enough above the city to afford incredible Pacific Ocean and town views, but low enough that it's still a short drive to all the action. This vintage getaway was built in 1915 in a combination of Craftsman cottage and Spanish colonial revival styles. Enchanting gardens with sitting nooks and lush landscaping surround the bungalow and cottage-style accommodations, which are tastefully decorated with wood furnishings, Oriental carpets, and English-country prints. Many rooms have fireplaces, hardwood floors, and patios or balconies. With renovations wrapping up in late 1999, including the addition of in-room fax machines, coffeemakers, and air-conditioning, the property can only improve.

The romantic restaurant is highly regarded for both its view and its fare (see "Where to Dine," below, for details). Facilities include a pool, tennis court, and library.

✪ Simpson House Inn Bed & Breakfast. 121 E. Arrellaga St. (between Santa Barbara and Anacapa sts.), Santa Barbara, CA 93101. ☎ **800/676-1280** or 805/963-7067. Fax 805/564-4811. www.simpsonhouseinn.com. 14 units. TV TEL. $175–$275 double; $325–$395 suite and cottage. 2-night minimum on weekends. Rates include full gourmet breakfast, evening hors d'oeuvres, and wine. AE, DISC, MC, V.

Simpson House is North America's first and only AAA 5-diamond B&B, so you can bet this place is something special. Rooms within the 1874 Historic Landmark main house are decorated to Victorian perfection, with extras ranging from a clawfoot tub and antique brass shower to skylight and French doors opening to the masterfully manicured gardens. During our visit, we stayed in a two-level cottage nestled in the acre of English gardens; it was decorated in country-luxury style with a fireplace, spa tub, wet bar, and private fountain courtyard. The rooms have everything you could possibly need (even makeup remover!), but most impressive are the extras: the extensive selection of gourmet Mediterranean hors d'oeuvres and Santa Barbara wines served in the luxurious main house's living room; the enormous video library; in-room massage; and the absolutely heavenly full gourmet breakfast delivered to your room each morning on delicate china. (Breakfast delivery is only available for some rooms.) Fact is, the Simpson House goes the distance—and then some—to create the perfect stay. Although this property is packed into a relatively small space, it still manages an ambiance of country elegance and exclusivity—especially if you book one of the cottages. *Note:* Some rooms don't come with a TV/VCR, but you can have one by request.

The Upham. 1404 De La Vina St. (at Sola St.), Santa Barbara, CA 93101. ☎ **800/727-0876** or 805/962-0058. Fax 805/963-2825. 54 units. TV TEL. $140–$215 double; from $260 suite. Rates include continental breakfast. AE, CB, DC, DISC, MC, V.

This upscale B&B right in the heart of town celebrated its 125th anniversary in 1996. Its longtime popularity is due to great service, which keeps businesspeople happy; European atmosphere, which makes foreigners feel comfortable; and the accommodations themselves. The rooms have private entrances and are distinctively outfitted with some impressive antiques and brass or four-poster beds; many even have private porches and fireplaces. (We do wish they'd add to the decor, though; it can be a bit sparse.) Combined with the complimentary continental breakfast and evening wine and cheese served in the lobby and garden, the Upham is a charming alternative to other downtown hotels (although if you want the real royal treatment you should head to the Simpson House). Louie's at the Upham, a cozy restaurant, is open for lunch and dinner.

MODERATE

In addition to the listing below, there are moderately priced rooms at the **Best Western Encina Lodge and Suites** (☎ **800/526-2282** or 805/682-7277) and **Tropicana Inn and Suites** (☎ **800/468-1988** or 805/966-2219).

◐ Bath Street Inn. 1720 Bath St. (north of Valerio St.), Santa Barbara, CA 93101. ☎ **800/341-BATH**, 800/549-BATH in Calif., or 805/682-9680. Fax 805/569-1281. 12 units. TV TEL. $110–$210 double. Rates include breakfast. Midweek rates up to 20% off. AE, MC, V.

This is one of the cutest, most meticulously cared for B&Bs we've ever seen. The minute we walked in, a gracious innkeeper guided us to the redwood patio to see an amazing wisteria canopy in bloom (lucky guests can have breakfast beneath it). We were then treated to fresh-baked cookies, which are served with tea and wine each afternoon. After our snack, we wandered from room to room, astonished by the exquisite details of each nook and cranny throughout the three-story Victorian (two unique features include a semicircular "eyelid" balcony and a hipped roof). Each adorable (and immaculate) unit is intimately and individually decorated with antiques, colorful wallpaper, and fresh flowers. Some come with a Jacuzzi and/or VCR. The equally attractive common areas include a third-floor reading nook with VCR (there's a video library downstairs). No smoking is permitted.

INEXPENSIVE

All the best buys fill up fast in summer, so be sure to reserve your room well in advance—even if you're just planning to stay at the nice, reliable **Motel 6** (☎ **800/4-MOTEL6** or 805/564-1392) near the beach, or the good-value **Sandpiper Lodge** (☎ **805/687-5326**) just a little farther away.

✪ Casa del Mar Inn at the Beach. 18 Bath St., Santa Barbara, CA 93101. ☎ **800/433-3097** or 805/963-4418. Fax 805/966-4240. www.casadelmar.com. 21 units. TV TEL. $69–$179 double; from $114 suite. Rates include continental breakfast and wine-and-cheese social. Extra person $10. Midweek discounts available. AE, DC, DISC, MC, V. From northbound U.S. 101, exit at Cabrillo, turn left onto Cabrillo, and head toward the beach; Bath is the second street on the right after the wharf. From southbound U.S. 101, take the Castillo exit and turn right on Castillo, left on Cabrillo, and left on Bath. Pets $10.

A half block from the beach (sorry, no views), Casa del Mar is an excellent-value motel with one- and two-room suites. The largish rooms have brand-new furnishings, with plenty of pastels. The flower-sprinkled grounds are well maintained, and the staff is eager to please. Many rooms have kitchenettes, fridges, and stoves. The Jacuzzi here stays open half an hour later than the neighboring Franciscan's. Considering the prices of hotels in this town, Casa del Mar is a great bargain.

✪ Franciscan Inn. 109 Bath St. (at Mason St.), Santa Barbara, CA 93101. ☎ **805/963-8845.** Fax 805/564-3295. 53 units. TV TEL. $65–$99 double; from $85 suite. Rates include continental breakfast and afternoon cookies and drinks. Extra person $8. AE, CB, DC, MC, V.

One of the best bargains beachside can be found a block from the shore at the Franciscan Inn. The exterior is motel-like. Inside, the rooms are looking dapper, especially since the motel poured $400,000 into redecorating in 1997. Several units have fully equipped kitchenettes and/or balconies, and most bathrooms come with a tub. All rooms have coffeemakers, computer jacks, and VCRs; hair dryers are available upon request. Each suite comes complete with a living room, a separate kitchen, and sleeping quarters for up to four adults; one has a fireplace. Breakfast, afternoon appetizers, and a complimentary newspaper are included in the price, as is the use of the heated outdoor pool, Jacuzzi, video library, and coin-operated laundry. Reserve well in advance, especially for May through September.

Orange Tree Inn. 1920 State St. (at Alamar St.), Santa Barbara, CA 93101. ☎ **805/ 569-1521.** 46 units. A/C TV TEL. $75–$150 double; from $150 suite. AE, CB, DC, DISC, MC, V.

We'd personally prefer to stay by the beach, but if you want cheap downtown accommodations, you're safe with the Orange Tree. Don't get too excited, though—it's a motel. Still, the rooms were recently renovated and have nice carpets and bedspreads. Most have a balcony or patio, and some have bathtubs. Guests also get free local calls and use of the pool.

WHERE TO DINE
EXPENSIVE

El Encanto. 1900 Lasuen Rd. ☎ **805/687-5000.** Main courses $14–$35. AE, CB, DC, MC, V. Daily 7–11am, 11:45am–2:30pm, and 6–10pm. CALIFORNIA/MEDITERRANEAN.

Clinging to the hillside above Santa Barbara is El Encanto, a hotel and restaurant known for its romantic ambiance and breathtaking ocean views. But the fare doesn't take a back seat: Chef Vincent Vanhecke, who flies his salmon in from Scotland and the wood from the south of England, obviously takes his food seriously, as does S.B. resident Julia Child, who dines here frequently. Starters might include a superb lobster bisque and an incredible mussels à la mariniere (white wine, onions, and parsley sauce). Main courses include a perfectly cooked, roasted breast of free-range pheasant with pinot-noir sauce, or a tender sautéed sea bass with tarragon crust and garlic mashed potatoes with tomato and basil coulis. Don't miss the fantastic napoleon of chocolate—a perfect, sinful treat. The restaurant also has an excellent wine selection.

✪ **The Palace Grill.** 8 E. Cota St. (at State St.). ☎ **805/963-5000.** www.palacegrill.com. Reservations accepted for lunch daily and dinner Sun–Thurs and Fri–Sat for 5:30 seating only. Main courses $9–$25. AE, MC, V. Sun–Thurs 11am–3pm and 5:30–10pm; Fri–Sat 11am–3pm and 5:30–11pm. CAJUN/CREOLE/ITALIAN.

If you're looking for a festive scene, great food, and an all-around fun evening, this is the place to find it. Even when there's a line out the door (always the case on weekends), the Palace makes the wait enjoyable with free appetizers and live entertainment (weekends only) by a local saxophonist. Inside the divided dining room, amidst the jazz memorabilia and lively music, the staff pampers you silly as they provide you with an overflow of Cajun, Creole, and the recent addition of Italian favorites (that is, pasta dishes). We tried a knockout rum punch, splendid oysters Rockefeller, an outstanding blackened filet mignon, an absolutely divine blackened salmon, and tasty crispy Louisiana soft-shell crabs. Portions are large, but we did manage to squeeze in a few bites of the key lime pie and bread pudding soufflé—both very tasty.

Pan e Vino. 1482 E. Valley Rd., Montecito. ☎ **805/969-9274.** Reservations required. Pastas $8–$10; meat and fish dishes $11–$18. AE, MC, V. Mon–Sat 11:30am–10pm; Sun 5:30–9pm. ITALIAN.

The perfect Italian trattoria, Pan e Vino offers food as authentic as you'd find in Rome. The simplest dish, spaghetti topped with basil-tomato sauce, is so delicious it's hard to understand why diners would want to occupy their taste buds with more complicated concoctions. But this kitchen is capable of almost anything. Pasta puttanesca, with tomatoes, anchovies, black olives, and capers, is always tops. Pan e Vino also gets high marks for its reasonable prices, attentive service, and casual atmosphere. Although many diners prefer to eat outside on the intimate patio, some of the best tables are in the charming, cluttered dining room.

✪ **The Stonehouse Restaurant.** At San Ysidro Ranch, 900 San Ysidro Lane (off U.S. 101), Montecito. ☎ **805/969-5046.** Reservations recommended. Most main courses $22–$39.50. AE, DC, DISC, MC, V. Daily 8am–2:30pm and 6–10pm. REGIONAL AMERICAN.

If you fork over the big bucks in one restaurant while in Santa Barbara, make it the Stonehouse. Executive chef David Adjey, who arrived here from Toronto in early 1998, is in our opinion the best new chef in California. At first glance, we worried the globally influenced menu was too ambitious. We were dead wrong. Everything that came out of the kitchen was sheer genius—in both flavor and intricate presentation. The chicken Havana with arching banana strips: a knockout; lobster skewer with sugarcane "spike" and pad Thai: to die for; the rack of lamb with red-wine-cherry demi glace served atop a vegetable-filled, "zebra-striped" acorn squash: an absolute work of art. Adjey manages to be respectful of the cuisines' cultural origins, while putting his own magical touch to every delicious dish. The decor, though mildly formal and comfortable, is far less impressive than the food. But no matter; this is still our number-one choice in the area. By the way, desserts rock, too.

☺ Wine Cask. 813 Anacapa St. (in El Paseo Center). ☎ **805/966-9463.** Reservations recommended. Main courses $8–$12 lunch, $17–$26 dinner. AE, DC, MC, V. Mon–Fri 11:30am–3pm; Sat–Sun 10am–3pm; Sun–Thurs 5:30–9pm; Fri–Sat 5:30–10pm. Valet parking $4. ITALIAN.

This is one of Santa Barbara's most popular upscale restaurants, which evolved out of the adjoining 17-year-old wine shop. The large dining room with a hand-stenciled, gold-leaf, 1920s historic-landmark ceiling is the backdrop for fine Italian fare and bustling atmosphere. Whether you go for the dining room (request fireside for romance) or the patio (yes, there are heat lamps), you'll be treated to such creations as lamb sirloin with red-wine and wild-mushroom risotto or porcini-crusted salmon with toasted pearl couscous. The wine list reads like a novel, with more than 1,000 wines (ranging from $14 to $1,400); it has deservedly received the *Wine Spectator* award for excellence. There's also a happy hour at the adjoining Intermezzo from 4 to 6pm daily. If choosing between here and Stonehouse, consider the following: Stonehouse's atmosphere is more reserved and quiet, and the menu, far more expensive.

MODERATE

Brophy Bros. Clam Bar & Restaurant. Yacht Basin and Marina (at Harbor Way). ☎ **805/966-4418.** Reservations not accepted. Main courses $9–$16. AE, MC, V. Sun–Thurs 11am–10pm; Fri–Sat 11am–11pm. SEAFOOD.

This place is most known for its unbeatable view of the marina, but the dependable fresh seafood keeps tourists and locals coming back. Dress is casual, portions are huge, and favorites include New England clam chowder, cioppino, and any one of an assortment of seafood salads. The scampi is consistently good, as is all the fresh fish, which comes with soup or salad, coleslaw, and pilaf or French fries. A nice assortment of beers and wines is available. *Be forewarned:* The wait at this small place can be up to 2 hours on a weekend night.

Montecito Cafe. 1295 Coast Village Rd. (off Olive Mill Rd.). ☎ **805/969-3392.** Reservations recommended for dinner. Main courses $7–$13. AE, MC, V. Daily 11:30am–2:30pm and 5:30–10pm. CALIFORNIA NOUVEAU.

Overlooking Montecito's shopping street, the light and airy Montecito Cafe offers diners a high-quality culinary experience at an affordable price (some say it's the best value in the area). Menu items include a watercress salad with sesame vinaigrette and broiled oysters; an Emmentaler-cheese-filled pork chop with lemon-wine-herb sauce; and capellini with mushrooms, tomato, basil, olive oil, and wine. The petite dining room itself is pleasantly simple, with well-set tables, a wall of windows, plants, a small fountain, and original art—it's the perfect place to impress a date.

Your Place. 22-A N. Milpas St. (at Mason St.). ☎ **805/966-5151.** Reservations recommended. Main courses $7–$13. AE, MC, V. Tues–Thurs and Sun 11am–10pm, Fri–Sat 11am–11pm. THAI.

There are lots of Thai restaurants in Santa Barbara, but when locals argue about which one is best, Your Place invariably ranks high on the list. Traditional dishes are prepared with the freshest ingredients and represent a wide cross-section of Thai cuisine. It's best to begin with *tom kah kai,* a hot-and-sour chicken soup with coconut milk and mushrooms, ladled out of a hot pot table-side—enough for two or more. Siamese duckling, a top main dish, is prepared with sautéed vegetables, mushrooms, and ginger sauce. Like other dishes, it can be made mild, medium, hot, or very hot.

INEXPENSIVE

✪ **La Super-Rica Taquería.** 622 N. Milpas St. (between Cota and Ortega sts.). ☎ **805/ 963-4940.** Reservations not accepted. Main courses $3–$6. No credit cards. Daily 11am–9:30pm. MEXICAN.

Following celebrity chef Julia Child's lead, aficionados have deemed this place the state's best Mexican restaurant, or to be more specific, taco stand. Excellent soft tacos are the shack's real forte. Unfortunately, portions are quite small—you must order two or three items in order to satisfy an average hunger, which can easily turn a meal for two into a $20 excursion. Still, there's no denying this place is *muy fantastico!*

SANTA BARBARA AFTER DARK

To find out what's going on while you're in town, check the free weekly the *Independent,* or call the following venues: the **Center Stage Theater,** upstairs at the Paseo Nuevo Shopping Center, Chapala and De La Guerra streets (☎ 805/963-0408); the **Lobero Theater,** 33 E. Canon Perdido St. (☎ 805/963-0761); the **Arlington Theater,** 1317 State St. (☎ 805/963-4408); and the **Earl Warren Showgrounds,** at Las Positas Road and U.S. 101 (☎ 805/687-0766).

At night, a young crowd spills out of the bars on lower State Street. Unless you're aching to relive your college days, it isn't likely to be your bag.

7 The Ojai Valley

35 miles E of Santa Barbara, 88 miles NW of Los Angeles

In a crescent-shaped valley between Santa Barbara and Ventura, surrounded by mountain peaks, lies Ojai (pronounced *o*-hi). It's a magical place, selected by Frank Capra as Shangri-La, the legendary utopia of his 1936 classic *Lost Horizon.* The spectacularly tranquil setting has made Ojai a mecca for artists and a particularly large population of New Age spiritualists, both drawn by the area's mystical beauty.

Life is low-key in the peaceful Ojai Valley. Perhaps the most excitement generated all year happens during the first week of June, when the **Ojai Music Festival** draws world-renowned contemporary jazz artists to perform in the Libbey Bowl amphitheater.

While in Ojai, you're bound to hear folks wax poetic about something called the "pink moment." It's a phenomenon first noticed by the earliest Native American valley dwellers, when the brilliant sunset over the nearby Pacific is reflected onto the mountainside, creating an eerie and beautiful pink glow.

ESSENTIALS

GETTING THERE   The 45-minute drive south from Santa Barbara to Ojai is along two-lane Calif. 150, a beautiful road that's as curvaceous as it is stunning. From Los Angeles, take U.S. 101 north to Calif. 33, which winds through eucalyptus groves to meet Calif. 150—the trip takes about 90 minutes. Calif. 150 is called Ojai Avenue in the town center and is the village's primary thoroughfare.

VISITOR INFORMATION   The **Ojai Valley Chamber of Commerce,** 150 W. Ojai Ave., Ojai, CA 93023 (☎ **805/646-8126;** www.the-ojai.org), distributes free area maps, brochures, and a *Visitor's Guide to the Ojai Valley,* which lists galleries and current events. It's open Monday through Friday from 9:30am to 4:30pm, Saturday and Sunday from 10am to 4pm. For information on the **Ojai Music Festival,** call ☎ **805/646-2094.**

EXPLORING THE TOWN & VALLEY

Small Ojai is home to more than 35 artists working in a variety of media; most have home studios and are represented in one of several galleries in town. The best for jewelry and smaller pieces is **HumanArts,** 310 E. Ojai Ave. (☎ **805/646-1525**). It also has a home-accessories annex, **HumanArts Home,** 246 E. Ojai Ave. (☎ **805/ 646-8245**). Artisans band together each October for an organized **Artists' Studio Tour** (☎ **805/646-8126** for information). It's fun to drive from studio to studio at your own pace, meeting various artists and perhaps purchasing some of their work. Ojai's most famous resident is world-renowned **Beatrice Wood,** who worked up until her death in 1998 at 104 years of age. Her whimsical sculpture and luminous pottery are internationally acclaimed, and her spirit is still a driving force in Ojai.

Strolling the Spanish arcade shops downtown and the surrounding area will yield a treasure trove, including open-air **Bart's Books,** Matilija Street at Canada Street (☎ **805/646-3755**), an Ojai fixture for many years. Antiques hounds head for **The Antique Collection,** 236 W. Ojai Ave. (☎ **805/646-6688**), an indoor antiques mall packed to the rafters with treasures, trash, and everything in between.

Residents of the Ojai Valley *love* their equine companions—miles of bridle paths are painstakingly maintained, and horse-crossing signs are everywhere. If you'd like to explore the equestrian way, call the **Ojai Valley Inn's Ranch & Stables** (☎ **805/ 646-5511,** ext. 456).

Ojai has long been a haven for several esoteric sects of metaphysical and philosophical beliefs. The **Krotona Institute and School of Theosophy,** Calif. 33 and Calif. 150 at Hermosa Road (☎ **805/646-2653**), has been in the valley since moving from Hollywood in 1926, and visitors are welcome at their library and bookstore.

In the **Lake Casitas Recreation Area** (☎ **805/649-2233** for visitor information), the incredibly beautiful Lake Casitas boasts nearly 32 miles of shoreline and was the site of the 1984 Olympic canoeing and rowing events. You can rent rowboats and small powerboats year-round from the **boathouse** (☎ **805/649-2043**) or enjoy picnicking and camping by the lakeside. Because the lake serves as a domestic water supply, swimming is not allowed. From Calif. 150, turn left onto Santa Ana Road, then follow the signs to the recreation area.

When Ronald Coleman saw Shangri-La in *Lost Horizon,* he was really admiring the Ojai Valley. To visit the breathtakingly beautiful spot where Coleman stood for his view of **Shangri-La,** drive east on Ojai Avenue, up the hill, and stop at the stone bench near the top; the view is spectacular.

WHERE TO STAY

The Moon's Nest Inn. 210 E. Matilija, Ojai, CA 93023. ☎ **805/646-6635.** Fax 805/ 646-5665. www.moonsnestinn.com. 7 units, 5 with bathroom. A/C. $95–$135 double. Rates include breakfast and evening wine and spirits. Midweek discounts available. AE, MC, V.

Conveniently located a block off Ojai Avenue, this comfortable clapboard B&B was built as a schoolhouse in 1874 and is Ojai's oldest building, newly reborn as a charming bed-and-breakfast. Renovated in 1998 by innkeepers Rich and Joan Assenberg, who carefully preserved, replaced, or complemented the inn's historic details, the building now boasts every modern comfort, including four private balconies. Throughout the house, from a cozy fireplace parlor to the sunny breakfast room, architectural features like crown moulding are highlighted by dramatically painted walls, and the entire Inn is furnished with a mix of carefully chosen antiques and high-quality contemporary pieces. A once-neglected side lawn has been transformed into a restful, tree-shaded garden retreat, complete with rock-lined pond and large trellised veranda (where breakfast is served on pleasant days). A cottage on the grounds houses a friendly beauty-and-massage salon (in-room massage is available), and guests enjoy full privileges at the Ojai Valley Athletic Club for a nominal day-use fee.

Ojai Rancho Motel. 615 W. Ojai Ave. (at Country Club Dr.), Ojai, CA 93023. ☎ **805/ 646-1434**. 18 units. A/C TV TEL. $95–$155 double. AE, DISC, MC, V.

This classic ranch-style motel has been well maintained and presents an attractively rustic alternative to the pricey country club around the corner (but don't expect the same gracious service from their cranky front office). The rooms all come with microwave, refrigerator, and coffeemaker, and there's a heated outdoor pool, sauna, and Jacuzzi; two units have fireplaces. The rooms in back look out on ranch land and tend to be quieter than the front rooms near the street.

✪ **Ojai Valley Inn and Spa.** Country Club Dr. (off Calif. 33), Ojai, CA 93023. ☎ **800/ 422-OJAI** or 805/646-5511. Fax 805/646-7969. www.ojairesort.com. 222 units. A/C MINIBAR TV TEL. $195–$260 double; from $345 suite. Packages available. AE, DC, DISC, MC, V. Pets permitted for $25 per night, with advance notice.

In 1923, famous Hollywood architect Wallace Neff designed the clubhouse that's now the focal point of this quintessentially Californian, colonial Spanish–style resort. The inn has carefully kept a sprawling ranch ambiance while providing gracious, elegant service and amenities, along with a beautifully oak-studded Senior PGA Tour golf course. Next to the golf course, the jewel of the resort is pampering **Spa Ojai,** where stylish spa treatments—many modeled after Native American traditions—are administered inside a beautifully designed and exquisitely tiled Spanish-Moorish complex. Mind/body fitness classes, art classes, nifty workout machines, and a sparkling outdoor pool complete the relaxation choices. Many guest rooms have fireplaces; most have sofas, writing desks, and secluded terraces or balconies that open onto expansive views of the valley and the magnificent Sierra Madre. Added comforts include coffeemakers, plush terry robes, and hair dryers. The Inn is worth the trip. (At press time, it was even offering a midweek, AAA-member rate of $109.)

Dining/Diversions: The formal Maravilla has an excellent and intriguing Mediterranean/California menu if you're looking for a supremely gourmet splurge. There's also a terrace grill overlooking the golf course and two lounges.

Amenities: Concierge; 24-hour room service; two outdoor heated pools (including a 60-foot lap pool); state-of-the-art fitness center with exercise room, Jacuzzi, sauna, steam room; jogging trails; complimentary bicycles; horseback riding. Eight hard-surface tennis courts (four lit for night play), available for $12 per hour. Golf on the championship 18-hole, 6,258-yard course costs $95 for guests; greens fees include the use of a cart. "Camp Ojai" offers special children's programs including a supervised play area and activities during peak holiday periods.

WHERE TO DINE
EXPENSIVE

L'Auberge. 314 El Paseo (at Rincon St.). ☎ **805/646-2288.** Reservations recommended. Main courses $15–$20. AE, MC, V. Sat–Sun 11am–2:30pm; daily 5:30–9pm. FRENCH/ BELGIAN.

Possibly the most romantic restaurant in the Ojai Valley, L'Auberge is located in a 1910 mansion with a fireplace, chandeliers, and a charming terrace with an excellent view of Ojai's famous sunset "pink moment." The dinner menu is traditional, featuring scampi, frog legs, poached sole, tournedos of beef, sweetbreads, and duckling à l'orange. The weekend brunch menu offers a selection of crepes. Service is expert and friendly, and this elegant house is an easy walk from downtown.

✪ **The Ranch House.** S. Lomita Ave. ☎ **805/646-2360.** www.TheRanchHouse.com. Reservations recommended. Main courses $19–$26. AE, CB, DC, DISC, MC, V. Wed–Sat 6–8:30pm; Sun 11am–7:30pm. CALIFORNIA.

This restaurant has been placing an emphasis on the freshest vegetables, fruits, and herbs in its cuisine since opening its doors in 1965, long before this practice became a national craze. Freshly snipped sprigs from the restaurant's lush herb garden will aromatically transform your simple meat, fish, or game dish into a work of art. From an appetizer of cognac-laced liver pâté served with their own chewy rye bread to leave-room-for desserts like fresh raspberries with sweet Chambord cream, the ingredients always shine through. And you'll dine in a magical setting, for the Ranch House offers alfresco dining year-round on the wooden porch facing the scenic valley, as well as in the romantic garden amid twinkling lights and stone fountains.

MODERATE

Blue Moon Cafe. 401 E. Ojai Ave. ☎ **805/646-1766.** Reservations recommended for dinner. Main courses $4–$9 breakfast and lunch, $9–$15 dinner. AE, DISC, MC, V. Wed–Mon 7am–9pm. AMERICAN.

This casual cafe is perfectly situated at the heart of Ojai, within walking distance of the Arcade and all downtown. Recently opened in an awkward little building with more tables on the patio than indoors, it's not much to look at. But their convenient hours—from early breakfast through late dinner—and tasty, affordable menu make the Blue Moon one to watch. They serve a typical American breakfast of pancakes, omelets, roast beef hash, and more; lunch features some burgers, sandwiches, and lunchroom-style salads; at dinnertime, they fire up the grill for steaks and chops plus a home-style meatloaf and cheese-fondue appetizer. Call it coffee-shop fare raised to Ojai's rigorous culinary standards.

Suzanne's Cuisine. 502 W. Ojai Ave. ☎ **805/640-1961.** Reservations recommended for dinner. Main courses $7–$13 lunch, $11–$22 dinner. MC, V. Wed–Mon 11:30am–3pm and 5:30–8:30pm. CONTEMPORARY EUROPEAN.

Enjoy a great meal in a comfortably sophisticated setting at this local fave, where every little touch bespeaks a preoccupation with quality details. Ask for a table on the covered outdoor patio, where lush greenery frames a casual setting warmed by a fireplace; when it rains, a plastic curtain descends to keep water out without losing that airy garden feel. Favorites from a seasonally changing menu include the lunch-only Southwest salad (wild, brown, and jasmine rices tossed with smoked turkey, feta cheese, veggies, and green chilies) and pepper-and-sesame-crusted ahi, served at dinner either sautéed or seared (your choice). From seafood specialties to Italian recipes from chef/owner Suzanne Roll's family, everything is fresh and natural; veggies are crisply al dente, and even the occasional cream sauce tastes light and healthy. Don't skip dessert.

INEXPENSIVE

Boccali's. 3277 Ojai–Santa Paula Rd. ☎ **805/646-6116.** Reservations recommended for dinner. Pizza $9–$19; pasta $6–$12. No credit cards. Mon–Tues 4–9pm; Wed–Sun noon–9pm. ITALIAN.

This small, wood-frame restaurant, set among citrus groves, is a pastoral pleasure spot where patrons eat outside at picnic tables under umbrellas and twisted oak trees, or inside at tables covered with red-and-white–checked oilcloths. Pizza is the main dish served here, topped California-style with the likes of crab, garlic, shrimp, and chicken. We think Boccali's lasagna (served piping hot *en casserole*) would win a statewide contest hands down. Fresh lemonade, squeezed from fruit plucked from local trees, is the usual drink of choice. Come hungry, and plan on sharing.

Oak Pit BBQ. 820 N. Ventura Ave. (Calif. 33), Oak View. ☎ **805/649-9903.** Reservations not accepted. Sandwiches $4; main courses $8–$12. Tues–Thurs and Sun 11:30am–8:30pm; Fri–Sat 11am–9pm. BARBECUE.

This stick-to-your-ribs joint on the road between Ojai and Ventura is worth building up an appetite for. The rust-colored shack doesn't have much going for it—just some gingham curtains, a few tables indoors and out, and stacks of wood for firing up the BBQ—but generous portions of slowly oak-smoked meats will have dedicated carnivores coming back for more. BBQ tri-tip brisket, ham, pork, Cajun sausage, chicken—they're all served up in sandwiches or full dinners, with available sides of coleslaw, potato salad, french fries, baked beans, and corn-on-the-cob.

8 En Route to Los Angeles: Ventura

15 miles SW of Ojai, 74 miles NW of Los Angeles

Nestled between gently rolling foothills and the sparkling blue Pacific Ocean, Ventura may not have the cultural and gastronomic appeal of Los Angeles or even nearby Santa Barbara, but it does boast the picturesque setting and clean sea breezes typical of California coastal towns. Southland antiques hounds know about Ventura's quirky collectible shops, and time-pressed vacationers zip up to charming bed-and-breakfasts just an hour from Los Angeles. Ventura is also the headquarters and main point of embarkation for Channel Islands National Park (see the following section).

Most travelers don't bother exiting U.S. 101 for a closer look. But think about stopping to while away a couple of hours around lunchtime; sleepy Ventura's charm might even convince you to spend a night.

ESSENTIALS

GETTING THERE If you're traveling northbound on U.S. 101, exit at California Street; southbound, take the Main Street exit. If you're coming west on Calif. 33 from Ojai, there's also a convenient Main Street exit. By the way, don't let the directions throw you off; because of the curve of the coastline, the ocean is not always to the west, but often southward.

VISITOR INFORMATION For a visitor's guide and genial answers to any questions you might have, stop in at the **Ventura Visitors & Convention Bureau,** 89-C S. California St., Ventura, CA 93001 (☎ **800/333-2989** or 805/648-2075; www. ventura-usa.com).

EXPLORING THE TOWN

Much of Ventura's recent development has taken place inland and to the south, so many folks overlook the charming seaside **Main Street,** the town's historic center, which grew outward from the Spanish mission of San Buenaventura (see below). The best section for strolling is between the mission (to the north) and Fir Street (to the south). Both sides of the street are lined almost entirely with antiques stores, used-book stores, and charity thrift stores, making it perfect for browsing.

Although Ventura stretches south to one of California's most picturesque little harbors (the jumping-off point for the Channel Islands; see the following section), the town has its own simple **pier** at the end of California Street. Exceptionally well maintained and favored by area fishers, the charming wooden pier is the longest of its kind in California.

Mission San Buenaventura. 225 E. Main St. ☎ **805/643-4318.** Free admission; donations appreciated. Mon–Sat 10am–5pm; Sun 10am–4pm.

Founded in 1782 (current buildings date from 1815) and still in use for daily services, this whitewashed and red-tile church lent its style to the contemporary civic buildings across the street. Step back in time by touring the mission's inside garden, where you can examine the antique water pump and olive press once essential to daily life here. Good for a quick history fix, the mission is small and near the rest of Ventura's action. Pick up a self-guided tour brochure in the adjacent gift shop for the modest donation of $1 per adult, 50¢ per child.

San Buenaventura City Hall. 501 Poli St. ☎ **805/658-4726.** Guided tours $4 adults, $3 seniors, free for children 6 and under. 1-hr. tours given May–Sept Sat 11am–1pm.

This majestic neoclassical building was constructed in 1912 to serve as the Ventura County Courthouse. It sits on the hillside, regally overlooking old downtown and the ocean. To either side on Poli Street are some of Ventura's best-preserved and most ornate late-19th- and early-20th-century houses. Full of architectural detail (like the carved heads of Franciscan friars adorning the facade) inside and out, City Hall can be fully explored by escorted tour.

Ventura County Museum of History & Art. 100 E. Main St. ☎ **805/653-0323.** Admission $3 adults, free for children 16 and under. Tues–Sun 10am–5pm.

This museum is worth visiting for its rich Native American Room, filled with Chumash treasures, and its Pioneer Room, which contains a collection of artifacts from the Mexican-American War (1846 to 1848). The art gallery features revolving exhibits of local painters and photographers, and the museum has an enormous archive (20,000 and counting) of photos depicting Ventura County from its origins to the present. There is also a small archaeological museum across Main Street from the main building.

WHERE TO STAY

Bella Maggiore Inn. 67 S. California St. (half a block south of Main St.), Ventura, CA 93001. ☎ **800/523-8479** or 805/652-0277. 24 units. TV TEL. $75–$150 double; $100–$130 suite. Extra adult $10; extra child (under 12) $5. Rates include full breakfast and afternoon refreshments and appetizers. Ask about midweek specials. AE, DISC, MC, V.

The Bella Maggiore is an intimate Italian-style small hotel whose simply furnished rooms (some with fireplaces, balconies, or bay window seats) overlook a romantic courtyard or roof garden. The style is Mediterranean casual, with shuttered windows, ceiling fans, and fresh flowers in every room. An open-air center courtyard is the inn's focal point, with stone fountains and flowering trees. Complimentary breakfast is served downstairs at Nona's Courtyard Cafe, which also offers dinner and weekday lunches. A kind of European elegance pervades all but the reasonable rates here.

Holiday Inn Beach Resort. 450 E. Harbor Blvd. (at California St.), Ventura, CA 93001. ☎ **800-HOLIDAY** or 805/648-7731. Fax 805/653-6202. 260 units. $100–$110 double. Midweek and off-season rates available. AE, CB, DC, DISC, JCB, MC, V.

One of the nicer Holiday Inns we've seen, this waterfront high-rise enjoys some spectacular views courtesy of its 12 stories. Because there's little else around as tall, nearly every room has a panoramic view of the sea or Ventura's pretty foothills—or both! Situated on the boardwalk that runs between the pier and the fairgrounds, the hotel is also within easy walking distance of historic downtown Ventura. There's excellent beach access, a heated outdoor pool facing the ocean, a couple of nearby restaurants in addition to the hotel's coffee shop, plus bike and surrey rentals right outside the front door. Ride up to the top floor and check out the hotel's circular ballroom; its adjacent cocktail lounge is oh-so-perfect for sunset gazing. Guest rooms are decent, thoroughly renovated, but otherwise unremarkable.

La Mer European Bed & Breakfast. 411 Poli St. (west of City Hall), Ventura, CA 93001. ☎ **805/643-3600.** Fax 805/653-7329. www.vcol.net/LaMer. 5 units (4 with private entrance). $105–$185 double. Rates include full breakfast and complimentary wine in room. Packages available. AE, MC, V. No children accepted.

Perfect for a romantic getaway, La Mer is an 1890 Cape Cod–style home with a spectacular view of the ocean from the parlor and two of the five guest rooms, each of which is furnished in a different international style. Whether you choose the "Madame Pompadour" French chamber with wood-burning stove, the "Vienna Woods" Austrian hideaway with sunken bathtub, or one of three other rooms, you'll love this cozy little cottage. It offers generous midweek packages for couples, which can include gourmet candlelit dinners, cruises to Anacapa Island, country carriage rides, therapeutic massages . . . or all of the above.

WHERE TO DINE

Eric Ericsson's. 668 Harbor Blvd. (on the Ventura Pier). ☎ **805/643-4783.** Reservations suggested on weekends. Main courses $7–$15 lunch; most full dinners $12–$28. AE, MC, V. Sun–Thurs 11am–10pm; Fri–Sat 11am–11pm. SEAFOOD/AMERICAN.

Having already established a reputation in Ventura for crowd-pleasing seafood, Ericsson's moved to the pier-top spot in 1997. Here scruffy beachgoers mingle with suited business folk at lunch, sports fans and 20-somethings scarf down appetizers at cocktail hour, families come early for generous dinners, and couples on dates linger at window tables until closing. The staggering array of seafood includes clams, oysters, mussels, shrimp, scallops, cod, halibut, lobster, and calamari. Add specialties like Mexican cioppino or traditional clambake, plus plenty of nonfish and vegetarian dishes, and it's impossible to imagine anyone being stumped by this menu.

Rosarito Beach Cafe. 692 E. Main St. (at Fir St.). ☎ **805/653-7343.** Main courses $10–$19. AE, DISC, MC, V. Tues–Sat 11:30am–2pm; Tues–Thurs and Sun 5:30–9pm; Fri–Sat 5–10pm. MEXICAN.

The Rosarito Beach Cafe really packs them into this 1938 Aztec Revival Moderne building and its welcoming outdoor patio. In-the-know diners bring their palates for superb Baja-style cuisine (whose tangy elements are borrowed from the Caribbean), delicious handmade tortillas, and a culinary sophistication rare in modest Ventura.

71 Palm Restaurant. 71 N. Palm St. (between Main and Poli sts.). ☎ **805/653-7222.** Reservations recommended. Main courses $11–$19. AE, DC, DISC, MC, V. Mon–Fri 11:30am–2:30pm and 5–9:30pm, Sat 5–9:30pm. COUNTRY FRENCH.

Situated in a charmingly restored 1905 Craftsman, this ambitious new restaurant is still working out some of the details, but their country French menu is a pleasant change of pace in town. Upstairs tables have an ocean view, while downstairs diners are warmed by a crackling fire. Stick with bistro basics like steak au poivre with crispy pommes frites, Provençal lamb stew, or country pâté served with crusty bread and tangy cornichons, and don't miss the antique-filled original rest rooms.

9 Channel Islands National Park

Approximately 40 miles W (offshore) of Ventura

There's nothing like a visit to the Channel Islands for discovering the sense of awe explorers must have felt more than 400 years ago. It's miraculous what 25 miles of ocean can do; for compared to the mainland, this is wild and empty land. Whether you approach the islands by sea or air, you'll be bowled over by how untrammeled they remain despite neighboring southern California's teeming masses.

Channel Islands National Park encompasses the five northernmost islands of the eight-island chain: Santa Barbara, Anacapa, Santa Cruz, Santa Rosa, and San Miguel. The park also protects the ocean 1 nautical mile offshore from each island, thereby prohibiting oil drilling, shipping, and other industrial uses.

The islands are the meeting point of two distinct marine ecosystems: The cold waters of northern California and the warmer currents of southern California swirl together here, creating an awesome array of marine life. On land, the relative isolation from mainland influences has allowed distinct species, like the island fox and the night lizard, to develop and survive here. The islands are also the most important seabird nesting area in California and home to the biggest seal and sea lion breeding colony in the United States.

JUST THE FACTS

GETTING THERE   Each of the five islands is relatively distinct and difficult to reach. Odds are, you're only going to visit one island on a given trip, so it's a good idea to study your options before going.

Visit the **Channel Islands National Park Headquarters and Visitor Center,** 1901 Spinnaker Dr., Ventura, CA 93001 (☎ **805/658-5700;** www.nps.gov/chis), to get acquainted with the various programs and individual personalities of the islands through maps and displays. Rangers run interpretive programs both on the islands and at the center year-round.

Island Packers, next door to the visitor center at 1867 Spinnaker Dr. (☎ **805/ 642-7688** for recorded information, 805/642-1393 for reservations; www.islandpackers. com), is the park's concessionaire for boat transportation to and from the islands. It's another great source of information.

There are no park fees, but getting to the islands is expensive—anywhere from $32 to $120 per person—since you must go by boat or plane. Island Packers will take you on a range of regularly scheduled boat excursions, from 3½-hour nonlanding tours of the islands ($21 per person) or full-day tours of individual islands led by naturalists ($49 per person) to 2-day excursions to two islands ($245). Private yachts and commercial dive and tour boats from all over Southern California also visit the park on a regular basis.

If you want to get to Santa Rosa in a hurry, **Channel Islands Aviation,** 305 Durley Ave., Camarillo (☎ **805/987-1678**), will fly you there in one of its small, fixed-wing aircraft. If you just want a quick overflight and maybe a picnic stop with a short hike, **Heli-Tours, Inc.,** at the Santa Barbara Airport (☎ **805/964-0684**), offers 3- to 4-hour flights to Santa Cruz Island.

THE WEATHER   While the climate is mild, with little variation in temperature year-round, the weather in the islands is always unpredictable. Thirty-mile-per-hour winds can blow for days, or sometimes a fog bank will settle in and smother the islands for weeks at a time. Winter rains can turn island trails into mud baths. In general, plan on wind, lots of sun (bring sunscreen), cool nights, and the possibility of hot days. Water temperatures are in the 50s and 60s year-round. If you're camping, bring a good tent—if you don't know the difference between a good and a bad tent, the island wind will gladly demonstrate it for you.

CAMPING   Camping is permitted on all the park-owned islands, but is limited to a certain number of campers per night, depending on the island. Fires and pets are prohibited on all the islands. You must bring everything you'll need; there are no supplies on any of the islands. To reserve free camping permits for any of the islands, call ☎ **800/365-CAMP.**

EXPLORING THE ISLANDS

SANTA BARBARA   As you come upon Santa Barbara Island after a typical 3-hour crossing, you'll think that someone took a single, medium-sized, grassy hill, ringed it with cliffs, and plunked it down in the middle of the ocean. When you drop anchor, you'll realize that your initial perception is basically on target. Landwise, there's just not a lot here. But the upside is that, of all the islands, Santa Barbara gives you the best sense of what it's like to be stranded on a desert isle. Being on Santa Barbara, far enough out to sea that the mainland is almost invisible, gives you an idea of just how immense the Pacific really is.

Other than the landing cove, there's no access to the water's edge. The snorkeling in the chilly cove is great. You can hike the entire 640-acre island in a few hours; then it's time to stare out to sea. You won't be let down. The cliffs and rocks are home to elephant seals, sea lions, and swarms of seabirds such as you'll never see on the mainland. There's also a small campground, pit toilets, and a tiny museum chronicling island history. Camping is available year-round, but Island Packers only schedules boats to Santa Barbara in summer and fall (see "Getting There," above).

ANACAPA   Most people who visit the park come to Anacapa. It's only 14½ nautical miles from Ventura, an easy half-day trip. At only 1.1 square miles, Anacapa—actually three small islets divided by narrow stretches of ocean—is only marginally larger than Santa Barbara and, consequently, not a place for those who need a lot of space to roam around. Only East Anacapa is open to visitors, as the other two islets are important brown-pelican breeding areas. Several trails on the island will take you to beautiful overlooks of clear-watered coves and wild ocean. **Arch Rock,** a natural land bridge, is visible from the landing cove, where you'll clamber up 154 stairs to the island's flat top.

Camping is allowed on East Anacapa year-round, but don't bring more than you can carry the half mile from the landing cove. Bring earplugs and steer clear of the foghorn, which can leave permanent hearing damage. Most of the waters around the island, including the landing cove, are protected as a National Marine Preserve, where divers can look but not take anything. Pack a good wet suit, mask, fins, and snorkel; you can dive right off the landing cove dock.

SANTA CRUZ   By far the biggest of the islands—nearly 100 square miles—Santa Cruz is also the most diverse. It has huge canyons, year-round streams, beaches, cliffs, the highest mountain in the Channel Islands (2,400 feet), now-defunct early cattle and sheep ranches, and Native American Chumash village sites—2,000 Chumash were probably living on the island when Cabrillo first visited in 1542. The island also hosts seemingly endless displays of flora and fauna, including 650 species of plants, nine of which are endemic; 140 land-bird species; and a small group of other land animals, including the island fox.

Most of the island is still privately owned: The Nature Conservancy holds the western nine-tenths. On February 10, 1997, the park service took over the eastern end from the Gherini family, who had owned a sheep ranch here. While this eliminated the island's formerly exorbitant landing and camping fees, it also eliminated the Channel Islands' only noncamping overnight options—lodges that are being converted into interpretive centers.

Valdez Cave (also known as Painted Cave for its colorful rock types, lichens, and algae) is the largest and deepest known sea cave in the world. The huge cave stretches nearly a quarter of a mile into the island and is nearly 100 feet wide. The entrance ceiling rises 160 feet, and in the spring, a waterfall tumbles over the opening. Located on the northwest end of the island, the cave can only be entered via dinghy or kayak.

SANTA ROSA Windy Santa Rosa also has a strong ranching past—one that ended in 1998 in a storm of controversy that pitted the National Park Service against both environmental groups and the 97-year-old Vail & Vickers cattle ranch. The cows are all gone now, taking with them a slice of history and leaving uncertainty that nature's balance can ever be restored on Santa Rosa. Santa Rosa is home to a large concentration of endangered plant species, 34 of which occur only on the islands. And like Santa Cruz, Santa Rosa is home to the diminutive island fox, a tiny cousin of the gray fox that has become nearly fearless as it has evolved in the predator-free island environment. They'll walk right through your camp if you let them. Santa Rosa also has great beaches, a benefit somewhat outweighed by the nearly constant winds.

SAN MIGUEL People often argue about what's the wildest place left in the lower 48 states. They bat around names like Montana, Colorado, and Idaho. Curiously, no one ever thinks to consider San Miguel. They should, for this 9,500-acre island is a wild, wild place. The wind blows constantly, and the island can be shrouded in fog for days at a time. Human presence is definitely not the status quo here.

Visitors land at Cuyler Harbor, a half-moon-shaped cove on the island's east end. Arriving here is like arriving on earth the day it was made: perfect water, perfect sand, outrageously blue water. Seals bask on the offshore rocks. The island's two most interesting features are the **Caliche Forest,** a sort of petrified forest left when the wind exposed sandstone casts of a forest that once stood on the island, and **Point Bennett,** the outrageous-sounding (and smelling) breeding ground of six separate species of seals and sea lions. In winter, thousands carpet the beach; their barking is deafening.

The waters around San Miguel are the richest and most dangerous of all the islands. The island is exposed to wave action from all sides. Many ships have sunk here. A 3-foot-tall stone cross stands in memory of Juan Rodríguez Cabrillo, the Spanish explorer credited with discovering the Channel Islands in 1542. Although his grave has never been found, Cabrillo is believed to be buried on the island.

Island Packers' schedule to San Miguel is sporadic in summer and almost nonexistent in winter, so call ahead. Primitive camping is allowed near the ranger's residence, but no potable water is available, and fires are prohibited.

THE EXTRA MILE: EXPLORING THE COASTLINE & WATERS OFF THE CHANNEL ISLANDS

DIVING A good portion of Channel Islands National Park is underwater. In fact, twice as many visitors come annually to dive the waters than ever set foot on the islands. Scuba divers come here from all over the globe for the chance to explore stunning kelp forests, shipwrecks, and underwater caves, all with the best visibility in California. Everything from sea snails and urchins to orcas and great white sharks call these waters home.

Truth Aquatics, in Santa Barbara (☎ 805/962-1127), is the best provider of single- and multi-day dive trips to all the islands. **Ventura Dive & Sport** (☎ 805/650-6500) also leads trips, including a "Discover Program" that allows novice and uncertified divers to explore the waters accompanied by an instructor. **Channel Islands Scuba** (☎ 805/644-3483) and **Pacific Scuba** (☎ 805/984-2566) also lead regular trips, as do boats from San Pedro and other southern California ports.

SEA KAYAKING One of the best ways to explore the fascinating coastline of the islands is by kayak. Warren Glaser of **OAARS** (Outdoor and Aquatic Recreation Specialist), based in Ventura (☎ 805/642-2912), leads small-group tours by sea kayak to all five Channel Islands. The trips allow you to explore sea caves and rock gardens. Channel crossing by charter boat, brief lessons, and lunch are included. Fares generally run $125 per person. Three-day adventures to Santa Rosa, with meals, campsite, and guide included are offered for $295. **Aqua Sports** (☎ **805/968-7231**) and **Paddle Sports** (☎ **805/899-4925**) also lead similar excursions, or trips can be arranged through **Island Packers** (☎ **805/642-7688** for recorded information, 805/642-1393 for reservations).

13 Los Angeles

by Stephanie Avnet Yates

The entire world knows what Los Angeles looks like. It's a real-life version of one of those souvenir postcard folders, which spills out images accordion style: tall palm trees sweeping an azure sky, the gleaming white HOLLYWOOD sign, freeways flowing like concrete rivers, a lone surfer riding the day's last wave silhouetted against the sunset's glow. These seductive images are just a few of many that bring to mind the city that everyone loves to hate—and to experience, at least once in a lifetime.

Los Angelenos know their city will never have the sophisticated style of Paris or the historical riches of London—but we cheerfully lay claim to being the most fun city in the United States, maybe even the world. Home to the planet's first amusement park, L.A. kind of feels like one, as the line between fantasy and reality is so often obscured. The colors of the city seem just a little bit brighter—and more surreal—than in other cities, the angles just a little sharper. Everything seems larger than life. Drive down Sunset Boulevard, and you'll see what we mean: The billboards are just a little bit taller, the wacky folks just a touch wackier.

Part of the spontaneity and excitement of L.A. comes from the fact that the city is constantly redefining itself. Just like the movies and TV shows that come to life here, the physical landscape, social doctrines, and popular pastimes of the city itself are fluid and unreliable. L.A. gleefully embraces individuality, weirdness, and change. Collectively, the city is like a theatrical actor projecting to the very back row: We want everyone else to sit up and take notice—and we're constantly reinventing ourselves so they will. We'd never want our city to be Paris or London for all the *Mona Lisa*s in the world.

1 Orientation

ARRIVING
BY PLANE
For a list of airlines, including toll-free phone numbers and Web sites, see appendix B at the back of this book.

LOS ANGELES INTERNATIONAL AIRPORT (LAX)   Most visitors to the area fly into Los Angeles International Airport, better known as LAX (☎ **310/646-5252**). Situated ocean-side just off I-405, between Santa Monica and Manhattan Beach, LAX is a convenient place to land; it's minutes away from all the city's beach communities, and about a half-hour drive from the Westside, Hollywood, or downtown. The airport's Web site (**www.lawa.org**) offers a bounty of information, including transportation contacts, nearby lodging, a map of the airport and surrounding streets, and links to related sites (like U.S. Customs, L.A. weather forecasts, and upcoming Southland activities).

You'll probably be renting a **car** from LAX; you'll need one (see "Getting Around," below). All the major car-rental firms provide shuttles from the terminals to their off-site branches. To reach Santa Monica and other northern beach communities, exit the airport, take Sepulveda Boulevard north, then follow the signs to Calif. 1 (Pacific Coast Highway, or PCH) north. To reach the southern beach communities, take Sepulveda Boulevard south, then follow the signs to Calif. 1 (PCH) south. To reach Beverly Hills or Hollywood, exit the airport via Century Boulevard, then take I-405 north to Santa Monica Boulevard east. To reach downtown, exit the airport, turn right onto Sepulveda Boulevard south, then take I-105 east to I-110 north. To reach Pasadena, drive through downtown (following the directions above), and continue north on Calif. 110 (the Pasadena Freeway).

Many city hotels provide free **shuttles** for their guests; ask about transportation when you make reservations. You can also catch a taxi from your terminal. **Taxis** line up outside each terminal, and rides are metered. Expect to pay about $30 to Hollywood and downtown, $25 to Beverly Hills, $20 to Santa Monica, and $45 to Pasadena, including a $2.50 service charge for rides originating at LAX.

SuperShuttle (☎ **800/554-3146** from LAX, or 310/782-6600) offers regularly scheduled minivans from LAX to any location in the city. The set fare can range from about $10 to $50 per person, depending on your destination (you're unlikely to pay more than $35, which will get you as far as Burbank or Universal City). It's cheaper to cab it to most destinations if you're a group of three or more, but the vans are infinitely more comfortable; however, you might have to stop at other passengers' destinations before you reach your own. When you arrive at LAX, you can call SuperShuttle from a pay phone in baggage claim at the toll-free number above or at the courtesy phones at the services information board. If you call during a very busy time, however, expect a wait. Reservations are strongly advised, even if you just make them the day before you arrive; call the 310 number above to book. When traveling to the airport for your trip home, reserve your shuttle at least a day in advance.

City **buses** also go between LAX and many parts of the city; phone **MTA Airport Information** (☎ **800/252-7433** or 213/626-4455) for schedules and fares.

OTHER AREA AIRPORTS   One of the area's smaller airports might be more convenient for you, landing you closer to your destination and allowing you to avoid the traffic and bustle of LAX. **Burbank–Glendale–Pasadena Airport** (☎ **818/840-8840**) is the best place to land if you're going to Hollywood or the Valleys. This small airport has especially good links to Las Vegas and other Southwestern cities. **Long Beach Municipal Airport** (☎ 562/421-8293), south of LAX, is the best place to land if you're visiting Long Beach or northern Orange County, and want to avoid L.A. entirely. The **Orange County/John Wayne International Airport,** in Anaheim (☎ **714/ 252-5200**), is closest to Disneyland, Knott's Berry Farm, and other Anaheim-area attractions (see chapter 14 for details).

BY CAR

If you're driving in **from the north,** you have two choices: the quick route, along I-5 through the middle of the state, or the scenic route along the coast.

Heading south along I-5, you'll pass a small town called Grapevine. This marks the start of a mountain pass known as the Grapevine. Once you've reached the southern

Southern California at a Glance

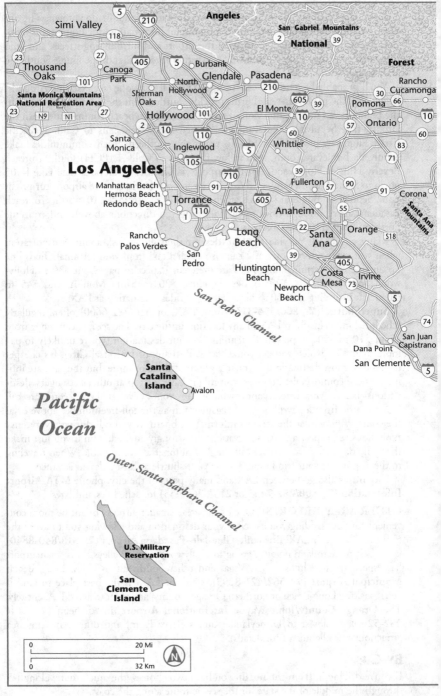

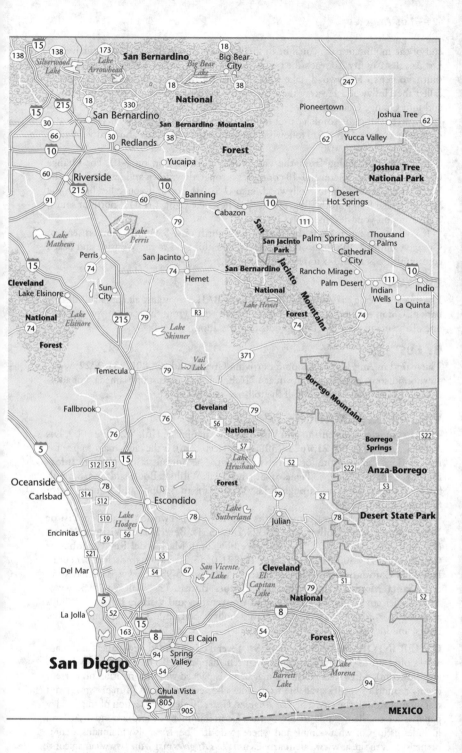

end of the mountain pass, you'll be in the San Fernando Valley, and you've arrived in Los Angeles County. To reach the beach communities and L.A.'s Westside, take I-405 south; to get to Hollywood, take Calif. 170 south to U.S. 101 south (this route is called the Hollywood Freeway the entire way); I-5 will take you through downtown and into Orange County.

If you're taking the scenic coastal route in from the north, take U.S. 101 to I-405 or I-5, or stay on U.S. 101, following the instructions as listed above to your final destination.

If you're approaching **from the east,** you'll be driving in on I-10. For Orange County, take Calif. 57 south. I-10 continues through downtown and terminates at the beach. If you're heading to Hollywood, take U.S. 101 north; if you're heading to the Westside, take I-405 north. To get to the beaches, take Calif. 1 (PCH) north or south, depending on your destination.

If you're coming in **from the south,** head north on I-5. At the southern end of Orange County, I-405 splits off to the west; take this road to the Westside and beach communities. Stay on I-5 to reach downtown.

BY TRAIN

Passengers arriving via **Amtrak** (☎ **800/USA-RAIL**; www.amtrak.com) will disembark at Union Station, on downtown's northern edge. From the station, you can take one of the many taxis that line up outside the station.

BY BUS

The main Los Angeles bus station for arriving **Greyhound** (☎ **800/231-2222**; www.greyhound.com) buses is downtown at 1716 E. Seventh St., east of Alameda. For additional area terminal locations, call the toll-free number above.

VISITOR INFORMATION

The **Los Angeles Convention and Visitors Bureau,** 633 W. Fifth St., Suite 6000, Los Angeles, CA 90071 (☎ **213/624-7300;** www.lacvb.com), is the city's main source for information. Call or write for a free visitor's kit. The bureau staffs a **Visitors Information Center** at 685 S. Figueroa St., between Wilshire Boulevard and Seventh Street; it's open Monday through Friday from 8am to 5:30pm and Saturday from 8:30am to 5pm.

Many Los Angeles–area communities also have their own tourist offices: **Visitor Information Center Hollywood** (☎ 323/236-2331), **Beverly Hills Visitors Bureau** (☎ 800/345-2210 or 310/271-8174; www.bhvb.org), **Marina del Rey Chamber of Commerce** (☎ 800/910-0555 or 310/821-0555; www.wlaxmdrchamber.com), **Pasadena Convention and Visitors Bureau** (☎ 626/795-9311; www.pasadenavisitor.org), **Santa Monica Convention and Visitors Bureau** (☎ 310/393-7593; www.santamonica.com), and **West Hollywood Convention and Visitors Bureau** (☎ 800/368-6020 or 310/289-2525; www.ci.west-hollywood.ca.us). Call for information, hours, and locations.

OTHER INFORMATION SOURCES   Several city-oriented newspapers and magazines offer up-to-date information on current happenings. The *L.A. Weekly* (www.laweekly.com), a free weekly listings magazine, is packed with information on current events around town. It's available from sidewalk news racks and in many stores and restaurants around the city. The *Los Angeles Times* "Calendar" section of the Sunday paper is an excellent guide to the world of entertainment in and around L.A., and includes listings of what's doing and where to do it. The *Times* also maintains a comprehensive Web site at **www.calendarlive.com.** *Los Angeles* magazine (www.lamag.com)

A Note on Area Codes

In 1999, the phone company introduced an "overlay" area code (424) to the part of Los Angeles already served by area code 310. This means *all* calls to *either* code, even if made within the same code, must be dialed using 1 plus the area code and seven-digit number.

is a city-based monthly full of news, information, and previews of L.A.'s art, music, and food scenes. It's available at newsstands around town. Serious cyber-surfers should visit **At L.A.'s** Web site (**www.at-la.com**); one of our favorite tools, its exceptional search engine provides links to over 31,000 sites in thousands of categories relating to all of Southern California.

CITY LAYOUT

Los Angeles is not a single compact city, but a sprawling suburbia comprising dozens of disparate communities. Most of the city's communities are located between mountains and ocean, on the flatlands of a huge basin. Even if you've never visited L.A. before, you'll recognize the names of many of these areas: Hollywood, Beverly Hills, Santa Monica, Malibu. Ocean breezes push the city's infamous smog inland, toward dozens of less well-known residential communities, and through mountain passes into the suburban sprawl of the San Fernando and San Gabriel valleys.

Downtown Los Angeles—which isn't where most tourists will stay—is in the center of the basin, about 12 miles east of the Pacific Ocean. Most visitors will spend the bulk of their time either on the coast or on the city's Westside. (See "Neighborhoods in Brief," below, for details on all the city's sectors, as well as the map on pp. 422 for an overview of the Los Angeles area's neighborhoods and freeway system.)

MAIN ARTERIES & STREETS   L.A.'s extensive freeway system connects the city's patchwork of communities; they work well together to get you where you need to be, although rush-hour traffic can sometimes be bumper to bumper. You might only drive on a couple of L.A.'s freeways, but here's an overview of the entire system:

U.S. 101, called the "Ventura Freeway" in the San Fernando Valley and the "Hollywood Freeway" in the city, runs across L.A. in a roughly northwest-southeast direction, from the San Fernando Valley to the center of downtown.

Calif. 134 continues as the Ventura Freeway after U.S. 101 turns into the city and becomes the Hollywood Freeway. The Calif. 134 branch of the Ventura Freeway continues directly east, through the valley towns of Burbank and Glendale, to I-210 (the "Foothill Freeway"), which will take you through Pasadena and out toward the eastern edge of Los Angeles County.

I-5, otherwise known as the "Golden State Freeway" north of I-10 and the "Santa Ana Freeway" south of I-10, bisects downtown on its way from San Francisco to San Diego.

I-10, labeled the "Santa Monica Freeway" west of I-5 and the "San Bernardino Freeway" east of I-5, is the city's major east-west freeway, connecting the San Gabriel Valley to downtown and Santa Monica.

I-405, also known as the "San Diego Freeway," runs north-south through L.A.'s Westside, connecting the San Fernando Valley with LAX and the southern beach areas.

I-105, Los Angeles's newest freeway—called the "Century Freeway"—extends from LAX east to I-605.

I-110, commonly known as the "Harbor Freeway," starts in Pasadena as **Calif. 110** (the "Pasadena Freeway"); it turns into the Interstate in downtown Los Angeles and runs directly south, where it dead-ends in San Pedro. The section that's now the Pasadena Freeway is Los Angeles's historic first freeway, known as the Arroyo Seco when it opened in 1940.

I-710, also called the "Long Beach Freeway," runs in a north-south direction through East Los Angeles and dead-ends at Long Beach.

I-605, the "San Gabriel River Freeway," runs roughly parallel to I-710 farther east, through the cities of Hawthorne and Lynwood and into the San Gabriel Valley.

Calif. 1—called "Highway 1," the "Pacific Coast Highway," or simply "PCH"—is really a highway (more like a surface thruway) rather than a freeway. It skirts the ocean, linking all of L.A.'s beach communities, from Malibu to the Orange Coast.

The freeways are complemented by a complex web of surface streets. The major east-west thoroughfares connecting downtown to the beaches (listed from north to south) are Sunset Boulevard, Santa Monica Boulevard, Wilshire Boulevard, and Olympic, Pico, and Venice boulevards. The section of Sunset Boulevard that runs between Crescent Heights Boulevard and Doheny Drive is the famed Sunset Strip.

STREET MAPS   Because Los Angeles is so spread out, a good map of the area is essential. Foldout maps are available at gas stations, hotels, bookstores, and tourist-oriented shops around the city. Members of **AAA** should stock up on L.A. maps before they arrive; they're free to members and are the most precise and helpful area maps we've seen. For locations, call ☎ **800/922-8228** or visit online at www.aaa-calif.com; the Hollywood/Wilshire branch is at 5550 Wilshire Blvd., Suite 101 (☎ **323/ 525-0018**). There's also an overview of the L.A. area included on the four-color sheet map in the back of this book.

Neighborhoods in Brief

Los Angeles is a very confusing city, with fluid neighborhood lines and equally elastic labels. We've found that the best way to grasp the city is to break it into six regions—Santa Monica and the Beaches, Westside L.A. and Beverly Hills, Hollywood, Downtown, the San Fernando Valley, and Pasadena and Environs—each of which encompasses a more-or-less distinctive patchwork of city neighborhoods and independently incorporated communities.

SANTA MONICA & THE BEACHES
These are our favorite L.A. communities. The 60-mile beachfront stretching southward from Malibu to the Palos Verdes Peninsula has milder weather and less smog than the inland communities, and traffic is nominally lighter—except on summer weekends, of course. The towns along the coast each have their own mood and charm. We've listed them below from north to south:

Malibu, at the northern border of Los Angeles County, is 25 miles from downtown. Its particularly wide beaches, sparsely populated hills, and relative remoteness from the inner city make it extremely popular with rich recluses. With plenty of green space and dramatic rocky outcroppings, Malibu's rural beauty is unsurpassed in L.A.

Pretty **Santa Monica,** Los Angeles's premier beach community, is known for its long ocean pier, artsy atmosphere, and somewhat wacky residents. The Third Street Promenade, a pedestrians-only thoroughfare lined with great shops and restaurants, is one of the country's most successful revitalization projects.

Venice, a planned community in the spirit of its Italian forebear, was constructed with a series of narrow canals connected by quaint one-lane bridges. The area has been infested with grime and crime, but gentrification is in full swing. Some of L.A.'s most innovative and interesting architecture lines funky Main Street. Without question,

Venice is best known for its Ocean Front Walk, a nonstop circus of skaters, sellers, and poseurs of all ages, colors, and sizes.

Marina del Rey, just south of Venice, is a somewhat quieter, more upscale community best known for its small-craft harbor, one of the largest of its kind in the world.

Manhattan, Hermosa, and **Redondo beaches** are relatively sleepy residential neighborhoods with modest homes, mild weather, and easy parking. These communities have excellent beaches for volleyballers, surfers, and sun worshippers, but there's not much else about these South Bay suburbs for visitors to get very excited about—when it comes to good restaurants or cultural activities, pickings are slim.

L.A.'s Westside & Beverly Hills

The Westside, an imprecise, misshapen L sandwiched between Hollywood and the city's coastal communities, includes some of Los Angeles's most prestigious neighborhoods, all with names you're sure to recognize:

Beverly Hills is roughly bounded by Olympic Boulevard on the south, Robertson Boulevard on the east, and Westwood and Century City on the west; it extends into the hills to the north. Politically distinct from the rest of Los Angeles, this famous enclave is best known for its palm tree–lined streets of palatial homes and high-priced shops (does Rodeo Drive ring a bell?), but it's the healthy mix of the filthy rich, tourists, and wanna-bes that creates a unique—and sometimes bizarre—atmosphere.

West Hollywood is a key-shaped community (go ahead, look at your map) whose epicenter is the intersection of Santa Monica and La Cienega boulevards. It's bounded on the west by Doheny Drive and on the south roughly by Melrose Avenue; the tip of the key extends east for several blocks north and south of Santa Monica Boulevard as far as La Brea Avenue, but it's primarily located to the west of Fairfax Avenue. Nestled between Beverly Hills and Hollywood, this politically independent town can feel either tony or tawdry, depending on which end of it you're in. In addition to being home to the city's best restaurants, shops, and art galleries, West Hollywood is the center of L.A.'s gay community.

Bel Air and **Holmby Hills,** located in the hills north of Westwood and west of the Beverly Hills city limits, comprise a wealthy residential area and feature prominently on most maps to the stars' homes.

Brentwood, the world-famous backdrop for the O. J. Simpson melodrama, is really just a tiny, quiet, relatively upscale neighborhood with the typical L.A. mixture of homes, restaurants, and strip malls. It lies west of I-405 and north of Santa Monica and West Los Angeles.

Westwood, an urban village that the University of California, Los Angeles (UCLA), calls home, is bounded by I-405, Santa Monica Boulevard, Sunset Boulevard, and Beverly Hills. The village, which used to be a hot destination for a night on the town, has lost much of its appeal because of overcrowding, rudeness, and even street violence. There's still a high concentration of movie theaters, but we're all waiting for Westwood to regain the charm it once had.

Century City is a compact, busy, rather bland high-rise area sandwiched between West Los Angeles and Beverly Hills. Once the back lot of 20th Century Fox studios, Century City is home to the Shubert Theater and the outdoor Century City Marketplace. Its three main thoroughfares are Century Park East, Avenue of the Stars, and Century Park West; it's bounded on the north by Santa Monica Boulevard and on the south by Pico Boulevard.

West Los Angeles is a label that basically applies to everything that isn't one of the other Westside neighborhoods. It's generally the area south of Santa Monica Boulevard, north of Venice Boulevard, east of the communities of Santa Monica and Venice, and west and south of Century City.

HOLLYWOOD

Yes, they still come. Young aspirants are attracted to this town like moths fluttering in the glare of neon lights. But Hollywood is now much more a state of mind than a glamour center. Many of the neighborhood's former movie studios have moved to less-expensive, more spacious venues. Hollywood Boulevard has become one of the city's seediest strips. The area is now just a less-than-admirable part of the whole of Los Angeles, but the legend of the neighborhood as the movie capital of the world endures, and it's still home to several important attractions, such as the Walk of Fame and Mann's Chinese Theatre.

For our purposes, the label "Hollywood" extends beyond seedy Hollywood itself—centered around Hollywood and Sunset boulevards—to surrounding neighborhoods. It generally encompasses everything between Western Avenue to the east and Fairfax Avenue to the west and from the Hollywood Hills (with its dazzling homes and million-dollar views) south.

Melrose Avenue, a scruffy but fun neighborhood, is the city's funkiest shopping district.

The stretch of Wilshire Boulevard that runs through the southern part of Holly-wood is known as the **Mid-Wilshire District,** or Miracle Mile. It's lined with con-temporary apartment houses and office buildings; the stretch just east of Fairfax Avenue, now known as **Museum Row,** is home to almost a dozen museums, including the Los Angeles County Museum of Art, the La Brea Tar Pits, and that shrine to L.A. car culture, the Petersen Automotive Museum.

Griffith Park, up Western Avenue in the northernmost reaches of Hollywood, is one of the country's largest urban parks and home to the Los Angeles Zoo and the famous Griffith Observatory.

DOWNTOWN

Roughly bounded by U.S. 101, I-110, I-10, and I-5 freeways, L.A.'s downtown is home to a tight cluster of high-rise offices, the El Pueblo de Los Angeles Historic Dis-trict, and the neighborhoods of **Koreatown, Chinatown,** and **Little Tokyo.** For our purposes, the residential neighborhoods of **Los Feliz** and **Silver Lake** (a grungy bur-geoning artistic community that has been called the "West Coast SoHo"), **Exposition Park** (home to Los Angeles Memorial Coliseum, the L.A. Sports Arena, and several downtown museums), and **East and South-Central L.A.,** the city's famous barrios, all fall under the downtown umbrella.

The construction of skyscrapers—facilitated by earthquake-proof technology—transformed downtown Los Angeles into the business center of the city. Despite the relatively recent construction of numerous cultural centers—including the Music Center and the Museum of Contemporary Art—and a few smart restaurants, down-town is not the hub it would be in most cities; the Westside, Hollywood, and the beach communities are all more popular.

THE SAN FERNANDO VALLEY

The San Fernando Valley, known locally as "the Valley," was nationally popularized in the 1980s by the notorious, mall-loving "Valley Girl" stereotype. Snuggled between the Santa Monica and the San Gabriel mountain ranges, most of the Valley is residential and commercial, and off the beaten tourist track. But there are some attractions bound to draw you over the hill: **Universal City,** located west of Griffith Park between U.S. 101 and Calif. 134, is home to Universal Studios Hollywood and CityWalk, a vast shopping and entertainment complex. And you may want to make a trip to **Burbank,** just north of Universal City, to see one of your favorite TV shows being filmed at the NBC or Warner Bros. studios. There are also many good restaurants and shops along Ventura Boulevard in and around **Studio City.**

PASADENA & ENVIRONS

Best known to the world as the site of the Tournament of Roses Parade each New Year's Day, **Pasadena** was mercifully spared from the tear-down epidemic that swept L.A., so it has a refreshing old-time feel. Once upon a time, Pasadena was every Angeleno's best-kept secret—a quiet community whose slow and careful regentrification meant excellent, unique restaurants and boutique shopping without the crowds, in a revitalized downtown respectful of its old brick and stone commercial buildings. Although the area's natural and architectural beauty still shines through—so much so that Pasadena remains Hollywood's favorite backyard location for countless movies and TV shows—Old Town has become a pedestrian mall similar to Santa Monica's Third Street Promenade, complete with huge crowds, predictable mid-range chain eateries, and standard mall-issue stores. It still gets our vote as a scenic alternative to the congestion of central L.A., but it has lost much of its small-town charm.

The residential neighborhoods in Pasadena and its adjacent communities—Arcadia, La Cañada, San Marino, and South Pasadena—are renowned for well-preserved historic homes, ranging from humble bungalows to lavish mansions. Some present-day uses include public gardens, designated historic neighborhoods, house museums, and bed-and-breakfasts.

2 Getting Around

BY CAR

Despite its hassles, driving is the way to get around L.A. The golden rule is this: Always allow more time to get to your destination than you reasonably think it will take, especially during morning and evening rush hours.

RENTALS   Los Angeles is one of the cheapest places in the United States to rent a car. Among the national firms operating in L.A. are **Alamo** (☎ 800/327-9633), **Avis** (☎ 800/331-1212), **Budget** (☎ 800/527-0700), **Dollar** (☎ 800/800-4000), **Hertz** (☎ 800/654-3131), **National** (☎ 800/328-4567), and **Thrifty** (☎ 800/367-2277). A complete list of rental-car agencies, including toll-free phone numbers and Web sites, can be found in appendix B, at the back of this book.

PARKING   Parking in L.A. is usually ample, but in some sections—most notably downtown and in Santa Monica, West Hollywood, and Hollywood—finding a space can be fraught with frustration. In most places, though, you'll be able to find metered street parking—be sure to carry plenty of quarters. When you can't, expect to valet or garage your car for somewhere between $4 and $10. Many restaurants and nightclubs, and even some shopping centers, offer valet parking; they usually charge about $3 to $5. Most of the hotels listed in this book offer off-street parking; it's often complimentary, but can cost as much as $20 per day in high-density areas.

DRIVING TIPS   Many Southern California freeways have designated carpool lanes, also known as High Occupancy Vehicle (HOV) lanes. Some require two passengers, others three. The minimum fine for an HOV violation is $271. Most on-ramps are metered to control the traffic flow; carpools are exempt and pass in their own lane.

When it comes to radio traffic-reporter jargon, the names of L.A.'s freeways (as opposed to their numbers) are usually used. A "SigAlert" is the term used for an unplanned freeway crisis (a serious accident) that will affect the movement of traffic for 30 minutes or more. When you hear "a big rig is blocking the number-one lane," you can determine the lane by counting out from the center divider.

BY PUBLIC TRANSPORTATION

We've heard rumors about visitors to Los Angeles who have toured the city entirely by public transportation, but they can't be more than just that—rumors. It's hard to believe that visitors can comprehensively tour this Auto Land without a car of their own. Still, if you're in the city for only a short time, are on a very tight budget, or don't expect to be moving around a lot, public transport might be for you. The city's trains and buses are operated by the **Los Angeles County Metropolitan Transit Authority (MTA),** 425 S. Main St., Los Angeles, CA 90013 (☎ **800/COMMUTE** or 213/ 626-4455; www.mta.net).

LOCAL SHUTTLES   Some of L.A.'s more popular (read: more congested) neighborhoods offer the opportunity to park once and take advantage of shuttle service. These include **downtown,** where Downtown Area Short Hop **(DASH)** buses run every 5 to 15 minutes and cost only 25¢. DASH also runs shuttles in **Hollywood** (along Sunset and Hollywood boulevards), and between **Fairfax Avenue** and the **Beverly Center** (via Melrose Ave. and Third St.). Call the MTA for schedules and route information.

In **Pasadena,** free **Arts Buses** run between Old Town and the Lake Avenue shopping district. Shuttles come every 20 minutes (12 minutes during lunchtime) between 11am and 8pm Monday through Saturday; stops are marked with ARTS BUS signs. The Visitor Center can provide additional information, including route maps.

Fast Facts: Los Angeles

American Express   In addition to those at 327 N. Beverly Dr., Beverly Hills (☎ 310/274-8277), and at 8493 W. 3rd St., Los Angeles (☎310/659-1682), offices are located throughout the city. To locate one nearest you, call ☎ **800/ 221-7282.**

Area Codes   Within the past 20 years, L.A. has gone from having a single (213) area code to, by the end of 1999, a whopping seven. Even residents can't keep up with the changes. As of press time, here's the basic layout: Those areas west of La Cienega Boulevard, including Beverly Hills and the city's beach communities, use the **310** and **424** area codes, which coexist in what the phone company calls an "overlay." *Calls to either code, even if made within the same code, must always be dialed using 1 plus the area code and seven-digit number.* Portions of Los Angeles county east and south of the city, including Long Beach, are in the **562** area. The San Fernando Valley has the **818** area code, while points east—including parts of Burbank, Glendale, and Pasadena—use the newly created **626** code. What happened to 213, you ask? Only the downtown business area still uses **213.** All other numbers, including Griffith Park, Hollywood, and parts of West Hollywood (east of La Cienega Blvd.) now use the new area code **323.** If it's all too much to remember, just call directory assistance at ☎ 411.

Baby-Sitters   If you're staying at one of the larger hotels, the concierge can usually recommend a reliable baby-sitter. If not, contact the **Baby-Sitters Guild** in Glendale (☎ 818/552-2229) or **Sitters Unlimited** (☎ 800/328-1191).

Dentist   For a recommendation in the area, call the **Dental Referral Service** (☎ 800/422-8338).

Doctor   Contact the **Uni-Health Information and Referral Hotline** (☎ 800/922-0000) for a free, confidential physician referral.

Emergencies   For police, fire, or highway patrol, or in case of life-threatening medical emergencies, dial ☎ **911.**

Police   For nonemergency police matters, phone ☎ **213/485-2121,** or 310/550-4951 in Beverly Hills.

Post Office   Call ☎ **800/ASK-USPS** to find the one closest to you.

Taxes   The combined Los Angeles County and California state sales taxes amount to 8.25%; hotel taxes range from 12% to 17%, depending on the municipality you're in.

Taxis   You can call a taxi in advance from **Checker Cab** (☎ 213/221-2355), **L.A. Taxi** (☎ 213/627-7000), or **United Independent Taxi** (☎ 213/483-7604).

Useful Telephone Numbers   For the correct **time,** call ☎ 853-1212 (good for all local area codes). Call **Los Angeles Weather Information** (☎ 213/554-1212) for the daily forecast. For beach conditions, call the **Zuma Beach Lifeguard** recorded information (☎ 310/457-9701).

3 Accommodations

Due to space considerations, we've had to limit the number of hotels included here. If you'd like a larger selection, check out *Frommer's Los Angeles,* which has dozens of other options.

CHOOSING A LOCATION   In sprawling Los Angeles, location is everything. Choosing the right neighborhood as a base can make or break your vacation; if you plan to while away a few days at the beach but base yourself downtown, for example, you're going to lose a lot of valuable relaxation time on the freeway. Take into consideration where you'll be wanting to spend your time before you commit yourself to a base. But wherever you stay, count on doing a good deal of driving—no hotel in Los Angeles is convenient to everything.

In general, **downtown** hotels are business oriented; they're sometimes popular with groups, but are largely ignored by independent tourists. The top hotels here are very good, but cheaper ones can be downright nasty. If you're on a budget, locate elsewhere.

Hollywood, which is centrally located between downtown and Beverly Hills and within easy reach of Santa Monica, makes a great base if you're planning to do a lot of touring—but there are fewer hotels here than you'd expect. The accommodations in Hollywood are usually moderately priced and generally well maintained, but otherwise unspectacular.

Most visitors stay on the city's **Westside,** a short drive from the beach and close to many of L.A.'s most colorful sights. The city's most elegant—and expensive—accommodations are in Beverly Hills and Bel Air. You'll find the city's best hotel values in West Hollywood, an exciting and convenient place to settle in.

Trendy, relatively smogless **Santa Monica** and its coastal neighbors are home to lots of hotels; book ahead because they fill up quickly in the summer, when everyone wants to be by the water. Santa Monica also enjoys convenient freeway access to the popular tourist sights inland. Malibu and the South Bay communities (Manhattan, Hermosa, and Redondo beaches) are more out of the way, and hence quieter.

Families might want to head to the **San Fernando Valley** to be near Universal Studios, or straight to Anaheim or Buena Park for easy access to Disneyland and Knott's

Los Angeles Area Accommodations

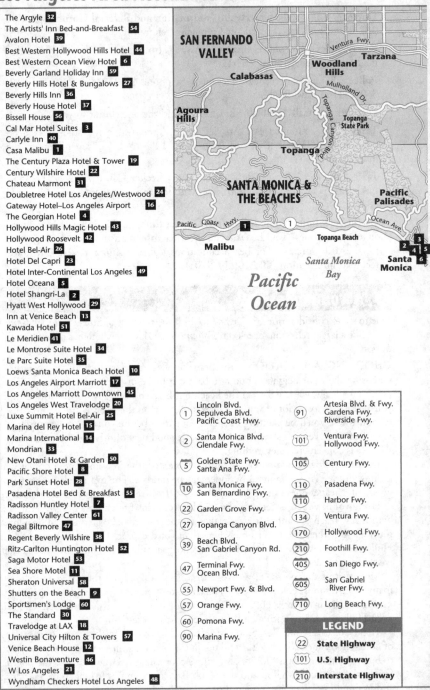

The Argyle 32
The Artists' Inn Bed-and-Breakfast 54
Avalon Hotel 39
Best Western Hollywood Hills Hotel 44
Best Western Ocean View Hotel 6
Beverly Garland Holiday Inn 59
Beverly Hills Hotel & Bungalows 27
Beverly Hills Inn 36
Beverly House Hotel 37
Bissell House 56
Cal Mar Hotel Suites 3
Carlyle Inn 40
Casa Malibu 1
The Century Plaza Hotel & Tower 19
Century Wilshire Hotel 22
Chateau Marmont 31
Doubletree Hotel Los Angeles/Westwood 24
Gateway Hotel–Los Angeles Airport 16
The Georgian Hotel 4
Hollywood Hills Magic Hotel 43
Hollywood Roosevelt 42
Hotel Bel-Air 26
Hotel Del Capri 23
Hotel Inter-Continental Los Angeles 49
Hotel Oceana 5
Hotel Shangri-La 2
Hyatt West Hollywood 29
Inn at Venice Beach 13
Kawada Hotel 51
Le Meridien 41
Le Montrose Suite Hotel 34
Le Parc Suite Hotel 35
Loews Santa Monica Beach Hotel 10
Los Angeles Airport Marriott 17
Los Angeles Marriott Downtown 45
Los Angeles West Travelodge 20
Luxe Summit Hotel Bel-Air 25
Marina del Rey Hotel 15
Marina International 14
Mondrian 33
New Otani Hotel & Garden 50
Pacific Shore Hotel 8
Park Sunset Hotel 28
Pasadena Hotel Bed & Breakfast 55
Radisson Huntley Hotel 7
Radisson Valley Center 61
Regal Biltmore 47
Regent Beverly Wilshire 38
Ritz-Carlton Huntington Hotel 52
Saga Motor Hotel 53
Sea Shore Motel 11
Sheraton Universal 58
Shutters on the Beach 9
Sportsmen's Lodge 60
The Standard 30
Travelodge at LAX 18
Universal City Hilton & Towers 57
Venice Beach House 12
Westin Bonaventure 46
W Los Angeles 21
Wyndham Checkers Hotel Los Angeles 48

1 Lincoln Blvd.
   Sepulveda Blvd.
   Pacific Coast Hwy.

2 Santa Monica Blvd.
   Glendale Fwy.

5 Golden State Fwy.
   Santa Ana Fwy.

10 Santa Monica Fwy.
   San Bernardino Fwy.

22 Garden Grove Fwy.

27 Topanga Canyon Blvd.

39 Beach Blvd.
   San Gabriel Canyon Rd.

47 Terminal Fwy.
   Ocean Blvd.

55 Newport Fwy. & Blvd.

57 Orange Fwy.

60 Pomona Fwy.

90 Marina Fwy.

91 Artesia Blvd. & Fwy.
    Gardena Fwy.
    Riverside Fwy.

101 Ventura Fwy.
    Hollywood Fwy.

105 Century Fwy.

110 Pasadena Fwy.

110 Harbor Fwy.

134 Ventura Fwy.

170 Hollywood Fwy.

210 Foothill Fwy.

405 San Diego Fwy.

605 San Gabriel
    River Fwy.

710 Long Beach Fwy.

LEGEND

22 **State Highway**

101 **U.S. Highway**

210 **Interstate Highway**

NA-0209

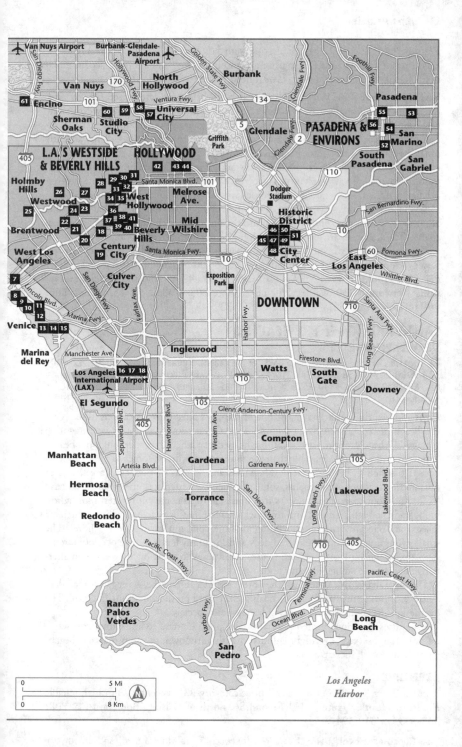

Berry Farm. (See chapter 14, "Side Trips from Los Angeles," for places to stay in the Anaheim area.) **Pasadena** is a charming community with some unique accommodations, but it's not a good choice if you'll need to get back and forth across town.

RATES & RESERVATIONS   The hotels listed below are categorized first by area, then by price. Rates given are the rack rates for a standard room for two with private bathroom (unless otherwise noted); you can often do better. Ask about weekend packages and discounts, AAA or AARP discounts, corporate rates, family plans, and any other special rates that might be available. The prices given do not include state and city hotel taxes, which run from 12% to a whopping 17%, depending on which community you're in. Be aware that many hotels charge extra for parking (with in-and-out privileges, except where noted), and some levy heavy surcharges for telephone use.

Several reservations services offer one-stop shopping; they'll tell you what's available at many of L.A.'s hotels and book you into the one of your choice, all at no additional charge. These services are particularly helpful for last-minute reservations, when rooms are often scarce—or discounted. Two companies that serve the L.A. area are **Central Reservation Service,** 505 Maitland Ave., Suite 100, Altamonte Springs, FL 32701 (☎ **800/548-3311** or 417/339-4116; fax 407/339-4736), and the **Hotel Reservations Network,** 8140 Walnut Hill Lane, Suite 203, Dallas, TX 75231 (☎ **800/ 96-HOTEL** or 214/361-7311; fax 214/361-7299).

SANTA MONICA & THE BEACHES
VERY EXPENSIVE

✪ **Shutters on the Beach.** 1 Pico Blvd. (at the beach), Santa Monica, CA 90405. ☎ **800/ 334-9000** or 310/458-0030. Fax 310/458-4589. www.shuttersonthebeach.com. 198 units. A/C MINIBAR TV TEL. $330–$525 double; from $750 suite. AE, DC, DISC, EURO, MC, V. Parking $16.

Light and luxurious Shutters enjoys one of the city's most prized locations: directly on the beach, a block from Santa Monica Pier. Guest rooms fall into two categories: cottage-like beachfront rooms, and those housed in a taller tower. Although the beach-cottage rooms are more desirable than the tower units, when it comes to rates the hotel doesn't distinguish between them. The views and sounds of the ocean are the most outstanding features of the rooms, some of which have fireplaces and Jacuzzis; all have VCRs and floor-to-ceiling windows that open. Showers come with waterproof radios, biodegradable bath supplies, and toy duckies. Despite this welcome whimsy, there's a relaxed and elegant atmosphere throughout the contemporary art–filled hotel. The small swimming pool on an elevated deck and the sunny lobby lounge overlooking the sand are two great places for spotting the celebrities who swear by Shutters as an alternative hangout to smoggy Hollywood.

Dining/Diversions: One Pico, the hotel's premier restaurant, is very well-regarded. The best meals at the more casual Pedals are prepared on the wood-burning grill. The overdesigned Handle Bar offers good happy-hour specials.

Amenities: Outdoor heated pool and whirlpool, exercise room, sauna, concierge, 24-hour room service, overnight laundry, nightly turndown, in-room massage, beach-equipment rental, bicycle rental.

EXPENSIVE

Another Santa Monica option in this price category is the recently renovated, reliable **Radisson Huntley Hotel,** 1111 Second St., north of Wilshire Boulevard (☎ **800/ 333-3333** or 310/394-5454).

The Georgian Hotel. 1415 Ocean Ave. (between Santa Monica Blvd. and Broadway), Santa Monica, CA 90401. ☎ **800/538-8147** or 310/395-9945. Fax 310/451-3374.

www.georgianhotel.com. 84 units. MINIBAR TV TEL. Summer $195–$235 double; from $295 suite. Off-season $175–$210 double. Rates include continental breakfast. Packages available. AE, CB, DC, MC, V. Parking $12. Small pets accepted with $250 refundable deposit and $150 fee.

This gracious eight-story art-deco grande dame was established in 1933 as the Lady Windermere, frequented by the Hollywood elite who often patronized the infamous nightclubs lining PCH below. In fact, the "Lady" had its own speakeasy, rumored to have been established by mobster Bugsy Siegel; today, guests enjoy breakfast in that historic room. The Georgian was used as a retirement home until 1994, when a tasteful and historically sensitive renovation uncovered the hotel you see today. The juxtaposition of Classical Revival architecture with bold pastels (à la Miami Beach's hotels of the same era) works splendidly, and every comfort is considered, from in-room robes and Starbucks coffee to comfy wicker chaises on the front veranda. Most rooms have a partial or full ocean view; the hotel is perched with an unobstructed coastal vista. Always inquire about available packages; at press time, the combo of oceanfront room and convertible rental car (with parking!) was only $224 per night in high season.

   Amenities: Concierge, room service, complimentary shoe shine and daily newspaper, laundry/dry-cleaning, twice-daily maid service, valet parking.

Hotel Oceana. 849 Ocean Ave., Santa Monica, CA 90403. ☎ **800/777-0758** or 310/393-0486. Fax 310/458-1182. www.smweb.com/oceana. 63 units. TV TEL. $200–$365 suite. Rates include continental breakfast. AE, CB, DC, DISC, MC, V. Parking $17.50.

If you've stayed in the former Oceana Suites Hotel, you won't even recognize the renovated and renamed Hotel Oceana. Excellently located in a residential neighborhood right on Ocean Avenue, this all-suite hotel is great for families. You'll immediately know you've arrived at the beach; light and airy and capped by an enormous skylight, the newly built lobby is completely covered with Jean Cocteau–inspired floor-to-ceiling murals. With the bright Matisse-inspired colors and cushy IKEA-ish furniture, the renovated suites appear to have been decorated by the set designer from *Friends*. Some suites have ocean views; VIP suites feature air-conditioning and two-person Jacuzzi tubs. In-room lunch and dinner service is provided by Wolfgang Puck Cafe, but since all suites come with fully equipped kitchens, cooking for yourself is another option.

   Amenities: Outdoor heated pool, health club, concierge, room service (from 11am to 10pm), continental breakfast in-suite, dry-cleaning/laundry service, self-service Laundromat, LodgeNet movie channels, newspaper delivery, massage, baby-sitting, valet parking.

Loews Santa Monica Beach Hotel. 1700 Ocean Ave. (south of Colorado Blvd.), Santa Monica, CA 90401. ☎ **800/223-0888** or 310/458-6700. Fax 310/458-6761. 341 units. A/C TV TEL. $225–$440 double; from $575 suite. AE, CB, DC, EURO, MC, V. Valet parking $18; self-parking $15. Pets accepted with $200 refundable deposit.

If it weren't for Shutters, this would be the finest hotel in Santa Monica. Loews isn't exactly beachfront; it's on a hill less than a block away, but the unobstructed ocean views are fabulous. While the standard rooms seem a bit, well, standard, for Loews's luxury rates, in return you get great location and the outstanding service of a very friendly staff. A dramatic, multi-story glass-and-steel atrium lobby gives way to amply sized rooms outfitted with the latest luxury amenities. This popular hotel doesn't need our recommendation to stir up business; it's become something of a darling for industry functions, and is booked to capacity in the summer months.

   Dining: There's fine dining in the Provençal-flavored restaurant Lavande; there's also a more casual restaurant and poolside snack service.

Amenities: Outdoor heated pool and whirlpool, fitness center, concierge, 24-hour room service, nightly turndown, bicycle and skate rental, summer kids program, baby-sitting, business center, VCRs on request.

MODERATE

In addition to the hotels recommended below, you may want to consider the **Cal Mar Hotel Suites,** 220 California Ave., Santa Monica (☎ **800/776-6007** or 310/395-5555), whose garden apartments are lovingly cared for and deliver a lot of bang for your vacation buck.

Best Western Ocean View Hotel. 1447 Ocean Ave., Santa Monica, CA 90401. ☎ **800/452-4888** or 310/458-4888. Fax 310/458-0848. 65 units. A/C TV TEL. Summer $159–$219 double. Off-season and midweek discounts available. AE, CB, DC, DISC, JCB, MC, V. Parking $7.

Yes, there are oceanfront bargains to be found, even in high-rent Santa Monica—and this gem is one of them. Clean and modern, the Ocean View boasts the detail-minded touch of Best Western, and offers terrific bargains to those willing to forego an ocean view from their room. Even the view rooms, which all have private balconies looking out across noisy Ocean Avenue, are a steal for this area. Use the rack rates only as a guideline; rooms here can go as low as $89 off-season and $99 in summer. All rooms feature fridges, coffeemakers, and hair dryers; microwaves are available upon request. Within walking distance of many fine restaurants, the hotel offers room service from the Italian cafe La Luna Mare around the corner.

✪ **Casa Malibu.** 22752 Pacific Coast Hwy. (about a quarter-mile south of Malibu Pier), Malibu, CA 90265. ☎ **800/831-0858** or 310/456-2219. Fax 310/456-5418. E-mail: casamalibu@earthlink.net. 21 units. TV TEL. $99–$139 double with garden view; $159 double with ocean view; $189–$199 beachfront double; from $199 suite. Rates include continental breakfast. Room with kitchen $10 extra. AE, EURO, MC, V. Free parking.

Left over from the heyday of Malibu's Golden Age as playground of suntanned surfers and celebs unafraid to get some sand between their toes, this modest two-story motel on the beach isn't rushing to play the sleek resort game—and we're delighted! Wrapped around a palm-studded inner courtyard with well-tended flower beds and cuppa d'oro vines climbing the walls, these 21 rooms are comfortable, charming, and thoughtfully outfitted. As we go to press, Casa Malibu is emerging from a loving renovation and sporting a traditional "California beach cottage" look that's cozy and timeless. Each unit features top-quality bedding, terry bathrobes, coffeemakers, and fridges; some have fire-places, kitchenettes, and/or private balconies. The upstairs Catalina Suite (Lana Turner's old hideout) has the best view while the Malibu Suite offers state-of-the-art pampering. Past the garden is a handsome brick sundeck directly over the sand and shielded from the wind; wooden stairs lead to the hotel's private beach (raked smooth each morning). The blue Pacific provides a mesmerizing backdrop here, from breakfast—fresh coffee and pastries from Wolfgang Puck's nearby Granita restaurant—to the waves that lull you to sleep each night. Book well ahead in summer—this one's a favorite of locals and tourists alike.

Hotel Shangri-La. 1301 Ocean Ave., Santa Monica, CA 90401. ☎ **800/345-STAY** or 310/394-2791. Fax 310/451-3351. www.shangrila-hotel.com. 55 units. A/C TV TEL. $130 studio; from $170 suite. Rates include continental breakfast. AE, CB, DC, DISC, MC, V. Free parking.

Perched right on Ocean Avenue overlooking the Pacific and just 2 blocks from the Third Street Promenade, the Shangri-La has a great location. The small lobby opens to a large plant-filled courtyard (surprisingly lacking a pool), bordered on two sides by the hotel. The rooms—which are accessed motel-style, from outside balconies over-looking the courtyard—are spacious, and almost all offer ocean views. The overall art-deco feel of the hotel carries through into the bedrooms—the lamps and mirrors, even the faucets and doorknobs, evoke the early part of the century. The large Formica-covered furniture, however, evokes the Starship *Enterprise* more than the golden age of Hollywood. There's a small ocean-view exercise room.

Marina del Rey Hotel. 13534 Bali Way (west of Lincoln Blvd.), Marina del Rey, CA 90292. ☎ **800/882-4000** or 310/301-1000. Fax 310/301-8167. www.marinadelreyhotel.com. 160 units. A/C TV TEL. $160–$220 double; from $300 suite. Packages available. AE, CB, DC, EURO, MC, V. Free parking.

This hotel, on a pier jutting into the harbor, is bounded on three sides by the world's largest man-made marina. The guest rooms are surprisingly well decorated, with fine contemporary furnishings and a few nautical nods. Most units have balconies or patios as well as harbor views; ask for one overlooking the main channel for the best daylong parade of boats. The hotel is peaceful and quiet—the only noise you'll hear is the soothing metallic clang of sailboat rigging. The on-site bar and grill overlooks the marina and serves California-style cuisine all day. Services and facilities include a concierge, room service, complimentary airport limousine, an outdoor heated water-side pool, a sundeck, nearby tennis and golf, a putting green, and car-rental service.

Marina International. 4200 Admiralty Way (west of Lincoln Blvd.), Marina del Rey, CA 90292. ☎ **800/529-2525** or 310/301-2000. Fax 310/301-6687. 135 units. A/C TV TEL. $125–$300 double; from $150 bungalow. AE, CB, DC, EURO, MC, V. Free parking.

This hotel's lovely rooms are bright, contemporary, and very, very private. Most units are decorated in a casual California style; all have balconies or patios. The bungalows are plush and absolutely huge—some are even split-level duplexes—with sitting areas and sofa beds. The Crystal Fountain serves continental fare indoors or out, and the hotel offers concierge, room service, and complimentary airport shuttle. Facilities include an outdoor heated pool, whirlpool, sundeck, nearby golf and tennis, a busi-ness center, and a tour desk.

Pacific Shore Hotel. 1819 Ocean Ave. (at Pico Blvd.), Santa Monica, CA 90401. ☎ **800/622-8711** or 310/451-8711. Fax 310/394-6657. 168 units. A/C TV TEL. Summer $145–$200 double. Off-season and mid-week discounts available. AE, CB, DC, DISC, EURO, JCB, MC, V. Parking $5.

This rectangular, eight-story glass-and-concrete monolith, located about a block from the beach, is a good choice for those who want to be in the heart of Santa Monica. The rooms are decent and well priced, and the hotel provides extras like a mini-gym and free area shuttle service. Great sunsets can be seen from the ocean-facing rooms on the high floors, but you'll have to look over busy Ocean Avenue and the roofs of Shutters on the Beach. Consider the discount city-view rooms, which gaze out over the hotel's charming garden, complete with heated pool. A bar and full-service restau-rant are located off the lobby.

INEXPENSIVE

Sea Shore Motel. 2637 Main St. (south Of Ocean Park Blvd.), Santa Monica, CA 90405. ☎ **310/392-2787.** Fax 310/392-5167. www.seashoremotel.com. 20 units. TV TEL. $80–$95 double; $100 suite. Extra person $5. Midweek discounts available. Children under 12 stay free in parents' room. AE, CB, DC, DISC, MC, V. Free parking. Pets accepted for $10 fee per night.

Most denizens of Santa Monica's trendy Main Street area don't even know about this small, family-run motel in the heart of the dining and shopping action. A recent total upgrade of the property (furnishings, fixtures, exterior) has brought it up to standard; rooms are unremarkable, arranged around a parking courtyard, but the management is caring and conscientious, installing extras such as fridges, voice mail, and attractive terra-cotta floor tiles. A stylish little deli sells morning muffins and sandwiches and homemade soup at lunchtime. The beach is a short walk away, and the businesses on Main Street are among the city's chicest; the Sea Shore makes a terrific bargain base for exploring this part of town.

Inn at Venice Beach. 327 Washington Blvd., Marina del Rey, CA 90291. ☎ **800/828-0688** or 310/821-2557. Fax 310/827-0289. www.innatvenicebeach.com. 43 units. A/C TV. $95–$105 double; $135 suite. Extra person $10. Rates include continental breakfast. Children under 12 stay free in parents' room. AE, CB, DC, DISC, EURO, JCB, MC, V. No cash or checks accepted. Free parking.

A charming, friendly, well-located inn with affordable rates that even include breakfast—it sounds too good to be true, but the Inn at Venice Beach is all that and more. Each room has a small balcony and a fridge, along with such thoughtful touches as a hair dryer, complimentary weekday newspapers, free movies, and a separate vanity area. Since the hotel is just 3 blocks from the ocean on the border between Venice and Marina del Rey, there's an endless parade of people out front exploring the marina, the beach, or the nearby canals on foot, bike, or in-line skates (rentals are 2 blocks away; inquire at the front desk). Breakfast is served in a cobblestone outdoor courtyard shielded from the noisy boulevard. About the only thing missing is a pool, but the staff will cheerfully lend you beach towels for an ocean dip. Suites, which have high-ceilinged living rooms and spacious sleeping lofts with queen-size beds, are the best deal here.

✪ **Venice Beach House.** 15 30th Ave. (off Pacific Ave.), Venice, CA 90291. ☎ **310/ 823-1966.** Fax 310/823-1842. 9 units, 5 with bathroom. TV TEL. $95–$165 double. Extra person $20. Rates include continental breakfast. AE, EURO, MC, V. Free parking.

This 1911 Victorian house is now a homey bed-and-breakfast on one of funky Venice's unique sidewalk streets, just a block from the beach. The interiors bear witness to years of family life: well-worn hardwood floors, faded Oriental rugs, and shelves of vintage hardbound books. Ask innkeeper Elaine Alexander to recount the home's colorful history, including its many notable guests. Our favorite room is the upstairs Pier Suite— light and airy, with a fireplace and sunny sitting room, this is as romantic as it gets. An expanded continental breakfast is served in the sunroom overlooking a splendid garden; afternoon tea or cool lemonade is served with fresh-baked cookies every day. The inn lends bicycles and can prepare picnic baskets for day excursions. *Beware:* The inn hums noisily with activity when there's a full house; seekers of absolute quiet and pristine appointments will not be comfortable here. Smoking is not permitted.

NEAR LAX

If you have an early-morning flight and you need an airport hotel, two good, moderately priced choices are **Gateway Hotel–Los Angeles Airport,** 6101 W. Century Blvd., near Sepulveda Boulevard (☎ **800/325-3535** or 310/642-1111), a comfortable, California-style hotel that literally overlooks the runway; and the **Los Angeles Airport Marriott,** Century Boulevard at Airport Boulevard (☎ **800/228-9290** or 310/641-5700), a reliable choice for travelers on-the-fly.

If you're looking for an inexpensive option, try the **Travelodge at LAX,** 5547 W. Century Blvd. (☎ **800/421-3939** or 310/649-4000), an otherwise standard member of the reliable chain with a surprisingly beautiful tropical garden surrounding the pool area.

L.A.'S WESTSIDE & BEVERLY HILLS
VERY EXPENSIVE

✪ **Beverly Hills Hotel & Bungalows.** 9641 Sunset Blvd. (at Rodeo Dr.), Beverly Hills, CA 90210. ☎ **800/283-8885** or 310/276-2251. Fax 310/281-2905. www.thebeverly hillshotel.com. 234 units. A/C TV TEL. $335–$390 double; from $545 bungalow; from $685 suite. AE, DC, JCB, MC, V. Parking $18. Pets under 30 lb. accepted in bungalows only.

Behind the famous facade of the "Pink Palace" (pictured on the Eagles's *Hotel California*) lies the kind of hotel where legends are made, and many were: This was center stage for both deal- and star-making in Hollywood's golden days. Today, plenty of current stars and industry hotshots can be found lazing around the pool, which Katharine Hepburn once dove into fully clothed.

Following a 4½-year, $100-million restoration, the hotel's grand lobby and impeccably landscaped grounds retain their over-the-top glory, while guest rooms now boast every state-of-the-art luxury the first-class traveler demands. Bathrooms are outfitted with double Grecian marble sinks, TVs, and telephones for sink-side deal making; bed linens are of the highest quality. The best original touches have been retained as well, such as a butler at your service with the touch of a button. The bungalows are more luxurious than ever—and who knows whom you'll have as a neighbor?

Dining: The iconic Polo Lounge is back, with the original atmosphere and traditional comfort fare, like Dutch apple pancakes or the signature guacamole. The adjacent Polo Grill takes up the nouvelle torch, specializing in California cuisine. The famous Fountain Coffee Shop has also returned, while the Tea Lounge is a new addition.

Amenities: Large outdoor heated pool and whirlpool, fitness room, VCRs with video delivery, concierge, 24-hour room service, dry-cleaning/laundry service, nightly turndown, massage, valet parking, airport limo service, car-rental desk, beauty salon.

The Century Plaza Hotel & Tower. 2025 Avenue of the Stars (south of Santa Monica Blvd.), Century City, CA 90067. ☎ **800/WESTIN-1** or 310/277-2000. Fax 310/551-3355. www.centuryplazala.com. 1,046 units. A/C TV TEL. $270–$395 double; from $500 suite. Weekend, off-season, and other discounts available. AE, CB, DC, DISC, EURO, MC, V. Valet parking $23; self-parking $12. Pets accepted with $50 deposit.

Located on a former 20th Century Fox back lot, this Westin-managed property sits on 10 of L.A.'s most centrally located acres. It's so close to film and TV's Century City nerve center that it has become the de facto home-away-from-home for countless rank-and-file industry execs and creative types. Because it's so huge (the main building has 19 floors; the tower has 30), the hotel is also a natural for conventions and meetings; there's always something going on here. All this makes it the antithesis of warm and cozy, but the rooms are large, the freeways are nearby, and your anonymity is assured. Recent renovations vastly improved room facilities—and vastly increased rates. Each unit now contains an extra-large, double-sink bathroom and brand-new elegant furnishings. Rooms and suites in the tower are nicer than those in the hotel, and enjoy additional services (daily newspaper, VCRs and video rental, and courtesy shuttles around town).

Dining/Diversions: The hotel has two restaurants and two lounges, but dine in only if you have to.

Amenities: Two large outdoor heated pools, two exercise rooms, Jacuzzi, concierge, 24-hour room service, same-day laundry service, nightly turndown, business center, car-rental desk, airline desk, ticket agency, tour desk.

✪ **Hotel Bel-Air.** 701 Stone Canyon Rd. (north of Sunset Blvd.), Bel Air, CA 90077. ☎ **800/648-4097** or 310/472-1211. Fax 310/476-5890. 92 units. $380–$500 double; from $625 suite. AE, DC, DISC, JCB, MC, V. Parking $13.50.

The Hotel Bel-Air is your address if you want to impress. This mission-style hotel is truly one of the finest—and most beautiful—hotels in Southern California. It regularly wins praise for its attentive service and luxurious rooms. The parklike grounds—lush with ancient trees, fragrant flowers, and a swan-dotted pond—are magical, and the welcoming, richly traditional public rooms are filled with fine antiques. The guest villas, decorated in Mediterranean style with compulsive attention to detail, dot the property. The rooms and garden suites are equally stunning; each has two phones, a VCR, and a CD player. Some units have wood-burning fireplaces. The hotel is a natural for honeymooners and other celebrants, but families might be put off by the Bel-Air's relative formality, which is geared more to the jet set and business professionals.

Dining: It's worth having dinner at the restaurant. Even if you don't stay here, you might consider brunch or lunch on the hotel's outdoor woodsy terrace, or drinks at the cozy bar.

Amenities: Outdoor heated pool, health club, sundeck, nature trails, concierge, 24-hour room service, nightly turndown, valet parking, welcome tea upon arrival.

Le Meridien. 465 S. La Cienega Blvd., Los Angeles, CA 90048. ☎ **800/645-5687** or 310/247-0400. Fax 310/247-0315. 300 units. A/C TV TEL. $315–$440 double; from $600 suite. AE, CB, DC, DISC, JCB, MC, V. Valet parking $18. Pets accepted with $25 fee per stay.

Finally—a hotel designed for business travelers where the primary goal isn't mimicking every other business hotel. The former Hotel Nikko refers to its interior decor as Pacific Rim (Organic Pacific Rim for the suites, which use all-organic textiles), but well-thought-out seems just as appropriate. Thanks to amenities such as in-room fax machines, three two-line phones, and large counter/desk space, the rooms function equally well as sleeping quarters and workspaces. And after a long day at work, the huge Japanese soaking tubs are perfect for unwinding. Shoji screens replace curtains, allowing light to filter through or blocking it out entirely.

Dining/Diversions: Pangaea restaurant blends French and American dishes with Asian influences; it also offers a 14-piece, big-band brunch. A cocktail lounge offers nightly entertainment.

Amenities: Heated pool, exercise room, massage, sauna, concierge, 24-hour room service, same-day dry cleaning and laundry, nightly turndown, business center.

Le Parc Suite Hotel. 733 N. West Knoll Dr., West Hollywood, CA 90069. ☎ **800/5-SUITES** or 310/855-8888. Fax 310/659-7812. www.leparcsuites.com. 154 units. A/C MINIBAR TV TEL. $260–$400 suite. AE, CB, DC, JCB, MC, V. Parking $16. Pets accepted with $75 cleaning fee.

Situated on a quiet residential street, Le Parc is a high-quality, all-suite hotel with a pleasantly mixed clientele. Designers stay here because it's a few minutes' walk to the Pacific Design Center, patients and medical consultants check in because it's close to Cedars-Sinai, and tourists enjoy being near the Farmers Market and Museum Row. The nicely furnished, apartment-like units each have a kitchenette, dining area, living room with fireplace, and balcony. What this hotel lacks in cachet, it more than makes up for in value. Although your L.A. friends may not have heard of this place, thanks to an overall renovation in 1996 they'll be impressed when you invite them up for drinks.

Dining/Diversions: Cafe Le Parc is open from 6:30am to 11pm and features a fully licensed bar.

Amenities: Outdoor heated pool, rooftop night-lit tennis court, basketball hoop, health club with sauna and whirlpool, concierge, room service (from 6:30am to 11pm), dry-cleaning/laundry service, VCRs and video rentals, newspaper delivery, in-room massage, twice-daily maid service, baby-sitting, valet parking, courtesy car, bathrobes, in-room ironing board and iron, self-service laundry, business center, car-rental desk.

Mondrian. 8440 Sunset Blvd., West Hollywood, CA 90069. ☎ **800/525-8029** or 323/650-8999. Fax 323/650-5215. www.mondrianhotel.com. 235 units. A/C TV TEL. $260–$375 double; $325–$545 suite. Weekend rates available. AE, CB, DC, EURO, MC, V. Parking $18.

Theatrical, enchanted, sophisticated—this is the kind of place boutique hotelier Ian Schrager has created from a once-drab apartment building that he transformed in late

1996. Working with French designer Philippe Starck (as he successfully did at Manhattan's Royalton and Miami's Delano), Schrager used the Mondrian's already breathtaking views (from every room) as the starting point for his vision of a "hotel in the clouds."

Because it's a seductive lure for the local scene, the Mondrian's public areas can be off-putting to outsiders, but guest quarters are sophisticated and welcoming. Purposely underlit hallways lead to bright, clean rooms done in shades of white, beige, and pale gray and outfitted with casually slip-covered furniture. Double rooms have minibars, while suites, which comprise the majority of the hotel, have fully outfitted kitchenettes. No luxury is spared; amenities include down comforters and pillows, in-room entertainment centers (including CDs), and tons of the grooviest giveaway hotel notepads and pencils we've ever seen.

Dining/Diversions: In addition to its pricey, ultra-hip restaurant Asia de Cuba, the Mondrian serves light meals off the lobby at a quirky communal table. There's also Skybar, overlooking the pool and cityscape and usually filled with L.A.'s starlets du jour.

Amenities: 24-hour concierge, 24-hour room service, outdoor heated pool, exercise room with sauna and whirlpool, supervised children's play area, dry-cleaning/laundry service, video library, newspaper delivery, valet parking, twice-daily maid service, fresh flowers in room, business center, billiards area, gift shop.

Regent Beverly Wilshire. 9500 Wilshire Blvd. (east of Santa Monica Blvd.), Beverly Hills, CA 90210. ☎ **800/421-4354** or 310/275-5200. Fax 310/274-2851. 396 units. A/C TV TEL. $365–$540 double; from $520 suite. AE, CB, DC, DISC, MC, V. Parking $21. Pets accepted at no extra fee; owner required to sign responsibility agreement.

If the Beverly Hills Hotel is where new money exhibits itself, then this is the place for seasoned sophisticates. But that doesn't mean that it hasn't seen its share of color: Actor Warren Beatty earned his playboy reputation while living here, and parts of *Pretty Woman* were filmed in one of the palatial suites. You just can't beat the location, close to Rodeo Drive shops and an easy cruise down Wilshire to just about anywhere else. The rooms are refined, with a mix of period furniture, three phones, three TVs, and special double-glazed windows that ensure absolute quiet. Wilshire Wing rooms are unusually huge, but those on the Beverly side are prettier and include balconies overlooking the pool. The bathrooms have extra-deep soaking tubs and glass-enclosed showers large enough for two. There's steward service on every floor, and butlers can be called from a bedside bell.

Dining/Diversions: The elegant dining room offers fine dining and live dance music. The Lounge, a European-style salon, serves a terrific tea from 3 to 5pm, light menus, and cocktails; at night, it's packed with media moguls and beautiful hangers-on.

Amenities: Outdoor heated pool and whirlpool, large health club/spa/salon, concierge, 24-hour room service, nightly turndown, express checkout, valet parking, overnight shoe-shine, business center, shops.

EXPENSIVE

The Argyle. 8358 Sunset Blvd., West Hollywood, CA 90069. ☎ **800/225-2637** or 323/654-7100. Fax 323/654-9287. www.argylehotel.com. 64 units. A/C MINIBAR TV TEL. $220 double; from $260 suite. AE, DC, DISC, EURO, MC, V. Valet parking $18.

Completed in 1929, this landmark 15-story, Streamline Moderne–style hotel is one of the most pristine art-deco buildings in the city. It's also terrifically located, at the base of the Hollywood Hills between Beverly Hills and Hollywood. The rooms are on the small side, but they're lovely, with art-deco reproductions and specially commissioned, handcrafted Italian furnishings, such as unique gondola-like beds. Corner rooms have marvelous rounded windows and spectacular city views. Although the hotel appears to be straight out of the 1920s, modern conveniences haven't been overlooked—all rooms come equipped with VCRs, CD players, hair dryers, fax machines, and space-age phones with display screens that do everything from tell the temperature to control the lighting.

Dining: Fenix is the hotel's elegant dining room, serving New American/California cuisine.

Amenities: Heated outdoor pool, exercise room, sundeck, concierge, 24-hour room service, laundry service, secretarial services, car-rental desk.

✪ **Carlyle Inn.** 1119 S. Robertson Blvd. (south of Olympic Blvd.), Los Angeles, CA 90035. ☎ **800/322-7595** or 310/275-4445. Fax 310/859-0496. 40 units. A/C TV TEL. $168–$198 double; $218 suite. Rates include full breakfast and weekday hors d'oeuvres. AE, DC, DISC, JCB, MC, V. Parking $8.

Hidden on an uneventful stretch of Robertson Boulevard just south of Beverly Hills, this four-story inn is one of the best-priced finds in L.A. An exceedingly clever design has transformed an ordinary square lot in a high-density district into a delightfully airy hotel. Despite its small size and unlikely location, architects have managed to create a multi-story interior courtyard, which almost every room faces. Well-planned, contemporary interiors are fitted with recessed lighting, deco wall lamps, pine furnishings, and well-framed, classical architectural monoprints. Extras include coffeemakers and VCRs. The hotel's primary drawback is that it lacks views; curtains must remain drawn at all times to maintain any sense of privacy. The suites are only slightly larger than standard rooms.

✪ **Chateau Marmont.** 8221 Sunset Blvd. (between La Cienega and Crescent Heights blvds.), West Hollywood, CA 90046. ☎ **800/CHATEAU** or 323/656-1010. Fax 323/655-5311. 63 units. A/C MINIBAR TV TEL. $220–$280 double; from $335 suite; from $650 bungalow. AE, CB, DC, EURO, MC, V. Valet parking $19. Pets accepted with $100 fee.

The Norman-style Chateau Marmont, perched in a curve of the Sunset Strip, is a landmark from 1920s–era Hollywood; step inside and you expect to find John Barrymore or Errol Flynn holding inebriated court in the baronial living room. Greta Garbo regularly checked in as "Harriet Brown"; Jim Morrison was one of many to call this home in later years. This historical monument built its reputation on exclusivity and privacy, a posture that was shattered when John Belushi overdosed in Bungalow no. 2. Chateau Marmont is popular because it's close to the Hollywood action and a luxurious world away at the same time. The standard rooms have views of the city and the Hollywood Hills; some have kitchenettes. The suites are large, and most come with cloth-canopied balconies. The poolside Cape Cod–style bungalows—large, secluded, and cozy, with full kitchens—are some of the most coveted in town. Accustomed to the demands of showbiz big shots, the hotel provides a wide array of amenities, including 24-hour room service, same-day laundry and dry-cleaning service, in-room CD players, free use of a cell phone, and a fitness room.

Hyatt West Hollywood. 8401 Sunset Blvd. (2 blocks east of La Cienega Blvd.), West Hollywood, CA 90069. ☎ **800/233-1234** or 323/656-1234. Fax 323/650-7024. 262 units. A/C TV TEL. $185–$220 double; $235–$400 suite. Special weekend and AAA rates available. AE, CB, DC, DISC, EURO, MC, V. Parking $10.

In 1997, this 13-story Sunset Strip hotel completed extensive renovations that erased any last remnants of its former debauched life as the rock-and-roll "Riot Hyatt." It doesn't even look like other Hyatts, since the management eschewed the standard corporate decor and contracted locally; the end result is a stylish cross between the clean black-and-white geometrics of a 1930s movie set and a Scandinavian birch-and-ebony aesthetic. While not as haute couture as the Mondrian across the street, neither is it as haute attitude. Rooms all have beautiful city or hillside views (about half have balconies), but stay away from front-facing rooms on the lower floors—too close to noisy Sunset. The Hyatt woos both business and leisure travelers, providing secure access to guest floors and ergonomic desk chairs in each room; in-room minifridges are an extra $5 a day. *Auto-club members take note:* Special AAA rates are as low as $139.

Dining/Diversions: The casual Silver Screen Bistro is a notch above any good diner. There's also a sports bar and lobby coffee/pastry cart.

Amenities: Rooftop heated pool, concierge, room service (from 6am to midnight), same-day laundry service, business center, tour desk, valet parking.

✪ **Le Montrose Suite Hotel.** 900 Hammond St., West Hollywood, CA 90069. ☎ **800/ 776-0666** or 310/855-1115. Fax 310/657-9192. www.lemontrose.com. 132 units. $240–$270 queen suite, $280–$440 king suite with kitchen. AE, CB, DC, EURO, MC, V. Parking $16. Pets allowed with $250 refundable deposit.

Nestled on a quiet residential street just 2 blocks from the bustling Strip, this all-suite hotel features large one-bedroom apartments that feel more like upscale condos than standard hotel rooms. Each has a large bedroom, kitchenette or kitchen, and bathroom, as well as a sizable sunken living room complete with gas fireplace, fax machine, and Nintendo games. You have to go up to the roof for anything resembling a view, but once you're up there, you can swim in the pool or play on the lighted tennis court. For location, quality, and price, this is one of L.A.'s best values, and it is already popular among music-industry clientele; let's hope that when the place catches on, prices will stay reasonable and reservations won't be hard to come by.

Dining: The Library Restaurant serves continental meals all day. Light bites are served poolside.

Amenities: Outdoor heated pool, whirlpool, sundeck, lighted tennis court, exercise room with sauna, laundry room, concierge, 24-hour room service, nightly turndown, complimentary bicycles, voice mail, currency exchange.

W Los Angeles. 930 Hilgard Ave., Los Angeles, CA 90024-3033. ☎ **800/421-2317** or 310/208-8765. Fax 310/824-0355. 257 units. A/C MINIBAR TV TEL. From $239 suite; from $325 penthouse suite. AE, DC, DISC, JCB, MC, V. Valet parking $18. Pets accepted with $100 fee.

This terrific 15-story all-suite hotel near UCLA was, at press time, undergoing a massive renovation by new owners W Hotels, whose other properties have been described as "Pottery Barns you can sleep in." Hidden behind a severe concrete exterior, this hotel has always attracted behind-the-scenes industry types drawn by the ample amenities; each suite now boasts multi-line cordless phones, stereo, VCR, iron and board, bathrobes, hair dryer, and coffeemaker. South-facing suites have the best city and ocean views. *Beware:* The hotel can be noisy during graduation and other large school events.

Dining/Diversions: The Garden Terrace is open for breakfast, lunch, and Sunday champagne brunch; dinner is served in the Dynasty Room. You can enjoy cocktails or afternoon tea in the lounge, and cocktails and casual fare at the outdoor cafe.

Amenities: Two outdoor heated pools in a quiet garden setting, whirlpool, fitness center, concierge, 24-hour room service, dry-cleaning/laundry service, nightly turndown, gift shop, flower shop.

MODERATE

Two good, moderately priced options near UCLA are the comfortable **Doubletree Hotel Los Angeles/Westwood,** 10740 Wilshire Blvd., at Selby Avenue (☎ **800/ 472-8556** or 310/475-8711), and the **Century Wilshire Hotel,** 10776 Wilshire

Blvd., between Malcolm and Selby avenues (☎ **800/421-7223** outside Calif., or 310/474-4506), with large, somewhat worn units that nevertheless offer great value in an expensive neighborhood.

If you're traveling with a group or as a family, be sure to consider the suite hotels listed in the "Expensive" category, above; since suites can accommodate four (or more), they can become quite a deal.

Avalon Hotel. 9400 W. Olympic Blvd. (at Beverly Dr.), Beverly Hills, CA 90212. ☎ **800/ 535-4715** or 310/277-5221. Fax 310/277-4928. 88 units. A/C MINIBAR TV TEL. $150–$200 double; $275–$325 suite. AE, DC, MC, V. Free valet parking.

A new trend in L.A. accommodations is retro-stylish boutique hotels that sport luxury amenities but appeal to a savvy, financially challenged traveler—and this mid-century modern classic in the heart of Beverly Hills leads the pack. With furnishings that make every unit look like a *Metropolitan Home* photo spread, in-room amenities you can *really* use, and nearly unheard-of low rates, the Avalon has attracted a very chic, low-key clientele since it opened in 1999. It took enormous creativity to transform the former Beverly-Carlton (seen on *I Love Lucy* and once home to Marilyn Monroe and Mae West) into this showplace; since the simple 1950s lines of the structure were enhanced but not changed, it's the high-style period furniture—Eames cabinets, Haywood-Wakefield chairs, Noguchi lamps—that kicks the fashion quotient up several notches. Fax machines, CD players, PC hookups, terry bathrobes, stocked fridges, and top-of-the-line bedding are standard in every room; some also have private balconies or kitchenettes. The hotel's kidney-shaped pool is modernized with simple, Zen-style plantings and edgy (but plush) chaises. There's a friendly poolside cafe off the lobby, and a staff ready to see to your needs, including free shuttle service to Beverly Hills shopping and dining.

Beverly Hills Inn. 125 S. Spalding Dr., Beverly Hills, CA 90212. ☎ **800/463-4466** or 310/278-0303. Fax 310/278-1728. 46 units. A/C TV TEL. $145–$160 double; from $195 suite. Rates include full breakfast, plus afternoon fruit and cheese. AE, DC, EURO, MC, V. Free parking.

The secret to a Beverly Hills lifestyle is knowing how to put on a good appearance—any face-lifted, tummy-tucked socialite will tell you that. So go ahead and brag about your Beverly Hills address to your friends—they'll never know about the bargain you're really enjoying. You can honestly say you've got a quiet, newly decorated room outfitted with cable TV, fridge, hair dryer, and other thoughtful touches—like a bathrobe for strolling down to the small but lushly landscaped garden pool. Popular with Asian business travelers, the hotel is impeccably furnished in a bland but vaguely tropical motif. Most rooms have views of either the pool or quiet, tree-lined street out front. When you're ready to face the world, you'll find yourself ideally located just a block from Rodeo Drive shopping and dining, or an easy walk from Century City. Breakfast is served in the aptly named Garden Hideaway Room (which also serves afternoon snacks and has a full bar). All in all, one of the best deals going in a high-rent neighborhood.

Luxe Summit Hotel Bel-Air. 11461 Sunset Blvd., Los Angeles, CA 90049. ☎ **800/ HOTEL-411** or 310/476-6571. Fax 310/471-6310. www.luxehotels.com. 161 units. A/C TV TEL. $159–$209 double; $189–$259 suite. AE, CB, DC, DISC, EURO, JCB, MC, V. Parking $10.

This two-story hotel on 8 garden acres has one thing going for it: location, location, location. It's just minutes away from Beverly Hills, Brentwood, Westwood Village, and Century City. The conservatively styled rooms and suites are spacious, airy, and comfortably fitted with furniture that was obviously purchased in bulk; each has a large balcony. Since breaking with the Radisson chain in 1996, the hotel has undergone an overall renovation. Facilities include a heated pool, a single unlit tennis court, a recently renovated lobby restaurant and bar, and an advanced facial salon, Summit Aromatasée Retreat.

INEXPENSIVE

In addition to the hotels listed below, the **Los Angeles West Travelodge,** 10740 Santa Monica Blvd., at Overland Avenue (☎ **310/474-4576**), is a terrific option, offering pleasant, modern, recently renovated rooms and friendly service.

Beverly House Hotel. 140 S. Lasky Dr., Beverly Hills, CA 90212. ☎ **800/432-5444** or 310/271-2145. Fax 310/276-8431. www.beverlyhouse.com. 45 units. A/C TV TEL. $109 double; $149–$189 suite. Rates include continental breakfast. AE, CB, DC, JCB, MC, V. Free parking.

Tucked discreetly away on a quiet, tree-shaded residential street, this small European-style hotel is just a half block from the well-heeled streets of Beverly Hills's "Golden Triangle" shopping district. Location and value are the hotel's main draws, but the smallish rooms are nicer than you'd expect: sparsely but comfortably furnished, with brand-new carpeting, upholstery, and wallpaper. Although there's no view to speak of, plenty of sunlight streams in. More than half of the little bathrooms have only a stall shower; if you prefer a combination tub/shower, specify when you reserve your room. The plush, spacious lobby is furnished with antiques plus a checkers and backgammon table; it's a nice place to enjoy your morning coffee. The hotel also provides complimentary morning newspapers, in-room minifridges, and free parking (an amenity virtually unheard of in these parts). *Tip:* Ask for one of the four front rooms—they're larger and have a lovely street view.

✪ **Hotel Del Capri.** 10587 Wilshire Blvd. (at Westholme Ave.), Los Angeles, CA 90024. ☎ **800/444-6835** or 310/474-3511. Fax 310/470-9999. 79 units. A/C TV TEL. $95–$115 double; from $115 suite. Extra person $10. Rates include continental breakfast. AE, CB, DC, EURO, MC, V. Free parking. Pets accepted for additional fee equal to 1 night's stay.

The Del Capri is one of the best values in trendy Westwood. This well-located and fairly priced hotel is popular with tourists, business travelers, and parents visiting their UCLA offspring. There are two parts to the property: a four-story building on the boulevard and a quieter two-story motel that surrounds a kidney-shaped swimming pool. Though the rooms are beginning to show wear and tear, all are of good quality and have electrically adjustable beds—a decidedly novel touch. The more expensive rooms are slightly larger and have whirlpool baths and an extra phone in the bathroom. Most of the suites have kitchenettes. The hotel provides free shuttle service to nearby shopping and attractions in Westwood, Beverly Hills, and Century City.

Park Sunset Hotel. 8462 Sunset Blvd., West Hollywood, CA 90069. ☎ **800/821-3660** or 323/654-6470. Fax 323/654-5918. 82 units. A/C TV TEL. $79–$89 double; $159 suite. AE, CB, DC, DISC, EURO, MC, V. Parking $5.

You'd think that the Park Sunset's location—right on the Strip—would make this one of the noisiest places to sleep in L.A. But all the guest rooms are in the back of the modest three-story hotel, away from the cars and cacophony. The rooms are well kept and surprisingly well decorated, though the carpets are a bit worn and the bathroom color schemes a tad dated. Some rooms have balconies and/or kitchens, and corner rooms have panoramic city views. There's a small heated pool in a lush courtyard and a continental restaurant on the lobby level that also provides room service. Tours can be arranged at the front desk, and many of the Strip's hot spots are within easy walking distance. At press time, the hotel had just been purchased by the owners of chic Le Montrose nearby—and things can only look up (we hope the prices won't, though).

ⓘ Family-Friendly Hotels

The highest concentration of family-friendly accommodations—those that make families with kids their primary concern—are found close to Disneyland (see chapter 14). That doesn't mean that families aren't welcome in L.A. hotels; in fact, a few welcome kids with open arms.

The Century Plaza Hotel & Tower *(see p. 439)*   The Century Plaza offers spacious, family-size rooms and lots of facilities. Because it's a veritable city unto itself, older kids love to explore this labyrinthine hotel.

Hotel Oceana *(see p. 435)*   This spacious all-suite hotel overlooks the beach at Santa Monica. Kids will love the brightly colored walls and cushy furniture, and all suites come with Nintendo video games.

Inn at Venice Beach *(see p. 438)*   Location and value make this a great choice for ocean-loving families. The 3-block walk to the beach is lined with snack bars, surf shops, and bike and skate rentals; the resident ducks of the Venice canals are equally close, as are the attractions of Marina del Rey. The under-12 set is welcomed free of charge, and everyone starts the day with complimentary breakfast.

Le Montrose Suite Hotel *(see p. 443)* and **Le Parc Suite Hotel** *(see p. 440)* These fairly comparable all-suite hotels are centrally located in West Hollywood. Multiple rooms mean privacy for parents, and kitchenettes can cut down on restaurant and room-service bills.

Loews Santa Monica Beach Hotel *(see p. 435)*   Offering comprehensive children's programs throughout the summer, and more like a resort than any other L.A. hotel, Loews boasts an unbeatable location—right by the beach and the boardwalk. What more could make the kids happy? It also offers baby-sitting services, so you can enjoy a kid-free evening on the town.

Sheraton Universal *(see p. 449)*   This Sheraton enjoys a terrifically kid-friendly location, adjacent to Universal Studios and the enormously fun CityWalk mall. Baby-sitting services are available to give Mom and Dad a break, and there's a large games room on the premises.

✪ The Standard. 8300 Sunset Blvd. (at Sweetzer), West Hollywood, CA 90069. ☎ **323/ 650-9090.** Fax 323/650-2820. 140 units. $95–$200 double; from $400 suite. AE, CB, DC, MC, V. Valet parking $15.

There's something different about the Standard, you'll notice right away. Shag carpeting on the lobby *ceiling,* blue Astroturf surrounding the swimming pool, scantily clad performance artists and DJs entertaining alongside the check-in desk . . . this place is definitely left of center. Designed by hotelier André Balazs (also of New York's Mercer Hotel) to appeal to the "shag-a-delic" under-35 crowd, the Standard is sometimes silly, sometimes brilliant, but always provocative (and always crowded!). Carved from the fine bones of a vintage 1962 Sunset Strip hotel, this newcomer boasts comfortably sized guest rooms outfitted with silver beanbag chairs, Andy Warhol curtains, private balconies, cordless phones, CD players, T1 data lines, and minibars that hold everything from sake to condoms to animal crackers. A 24-hour restaurant downstairs features a menu designed by Jean-Georges Vongerichten (of New York's Jean Georges, Vong, and the Mercer Kitchen in the Mercer Hotel); next to it sits a branch of Seattle-based Rudy's barbershop (with resident tattoo artist). Look past the retro clutter and often raucous party scene, though, and you'll find a level of service more often associated with hotels costing twice—or three times—as much.

HOLLYWOOD
MODERATE

✪ **Hollywood Roosevelt.** 7000 Hollywood Blvd., Hollywood, CA 90028. ☎ **800/ 950-7667** or 323/466-7000. Fax 323/469-7006. www.hollywoodroosevelt.com. 330 units. $139–$189 double; from $299 suite. AE, CB, DC, DISC, EURO, MC, V. Valet parking $10.

This 12-story movie-city landmark is located on a slightly seedy, very touristy part of Hollywood Boulevard, across from Mann's Chinese Theatre and just down the street from the Walk of Fame. The Roosevelt was one of the city's grandest hotels when it opened its doors in 1927, and was home to the first Academy Awards ceremony. The exquisitely restored two-story lobby features a Hollywood mini-museum. The rooms, however, are typical of chain hotels, far less appealing—in both size and decor—than the public areas. A few, however, are charmed with their original 1920s-style bathrooms. The suites are named after stars who stayed in them during the glory days; some have grand verandas, while others are rumored to be haunted by the ghosts of Marilyn Monroe and Montgomery Clift. High floors have unbeatable skyline views. David Hockney decorated the famous Olympic-size pool. The Cinegrill supper club draws locals with a zany cabaret show and guest chanteuses from Eartha Kitt to Cybill Shepherd.

INEXPENSIVE

Best Western Hollywood Hills Hotel. 6141 Franklin Ave. (between Vine and Gower sts.), Hollywood, CA 90028. ☎ **800/287-1700** in Calif. only, or 323/464-5181. Fax 323/ 962-0536. 82 units. $79–$89 double. Senior and auto-club discounts available. DC, DISC, MC, V. Free parking. Pets accepted with $20 fee per stay.

Location is a big selling point for this chain representative, just off U.S. 101 (the Hollywood Freeway) and within walking distance of the famed Hollywood and Vine intersection. They know it, too: The walls showcase images from the golden age of movies, and the front desk offers an endless variety of arranged tours, ranging from the Hollywood Walk of Fame to Six Flags Magic Mountain. Ask about package deals for extra value. Rooms are plain and clean, but lack much warmth—outer walls are painted cinder block, and closets are hidden behind institutional metal accordion doors. On the plus side, however, all come with a fridge and free movies. The rooms in back have an attractive view of the neighboring hillside. Facilities include a gleaming blue-tiled, heated outdoor pool, plus one of the city's most trendy retro-eateries, the Hollywood Hills Coffee Shop (see "Dining," below) off the lobby.

Hollywood Hills Magic Hotel. 7025 Franklin Ave. (between La Brea and Highland), Hollywood, CA 90028. ☎ **800/741-4915** or 323/851-0800. Fax 323/874-5246. www. magichotel.com. 49 units. A/C TV TEL. $75 double; $99–$149 suite. Extra person $5. Off-season and other discounts available. AE, DC, DISC, JCB, MC, V. Free secured underground parking.

You'll love being centrally located to all of Hollywood Boulevard's tourist attractions, and we think you'll be surprised by the spacious comfort afforded by this bargain nestled up against the Hollywood Hills. Named for the Magic Castle, the landmark illusionist club just uphill, the hotel was once an apartment building, and hasn't lost that private feeling of being insulated from the street's frenzy. Situated around a courtyard with a pool, most of the rooms are apartment-style suites, but all are roomy and boast kitchens with microwaves and coffeemakers; several units have balconies overlooking the large heated pool. It's ideal for families or long-term stays; it offers self-service laundry, and extras like hair dryers and irons and ironing boards are free for the asking.

DOWNTOWN
EXPENSIVE

In addition to the hotels listed below, downtown is home to the ultra-contemporary **Hotel Inter-Continental Los Angeles,** 251 S. Olive St. (☎ **213/617-3300**), the best-managed property in the neighborhood; the Japanese-style **New Otani Hotel & Garden,** 120 S. Los Angeles St., at First Street (☎ **800/421-8795** or 213/629-1200); and the spacious, warm **Los Angeles Marriott Downtown,** 333 S. Figueroa St., between Third and Fourth streets (☎ **800/228-9290** or 213/617-1133), attractively decorated and located right in the heart of the downtown hustle.

Regal Biltmore. 506 S. Grand Ave. (between Fifth and Sixth sts.), Los Angeles, CA 90071. ☎ **800/245-8673** or 213/624-1011. Fax 213/612-1545. www.thebiltmore.com. 683 units. A/C TV TEL. $225–$245 double; from $370 suite. Super breakfast and weekend discount packages available. AE, CB, DC, DISC, EURO, MC, V. Parking $18.

Built in 1923, the historic and opulent Biltmore is considered the grande dame of L.A. hotels. During the 1930s and 1940s, the Academy Awards were held in the spectacular Crystal Ballroom—the first sketch of the Oscar statuette was scrawled on a linen napkin here—and the hotel was the top choice for presidents and the elite. You've seen the Biltmore in many movies, including *The Fabulous Baker Boys, Beverly Hills Cop,* and Barbra Streisand's *A Star Is Born;* the Crystal Ballroom appeared upside-down in *The Poseidon Adventure.* The 11-story hotel sparkles with Italian marble and traditional French-reproduction furnishings, but the overall elegance has been compromised by an ugly office tower that was added in the mid–1980s. Still, the sense of refinement and graciousness endures, with a vaulted, hand-painted lobby ceiling, and attentively decorated—though small—rooms with marble baths.

Dining/Diversions: Bernard's features high-quality continental cuisine. Smeraldi's serves homemade pastas and lighter California fare. The lunch-only Sai Sai serves sushi, tempura, and traditional Japanese kaiseki. Afternoon tea and evening cocktails are served in the lobby's stately Rendezvous Court; a full bar is also available in the Grand Avenue Sports Bar.

Amenities: Health club with original 1923 inlaid pool (extra charge), concierge, 24-hour room service, dry cleaning, laundry service, newspaper delivery, nightly turndown, business center.

Westin Bonaventure. 404 S. Figueroa St. (between Fourth and Fifth sts.), Los Angeles, CA 90071. ☎ **800/228-3000** or 213/624-1000. Fax 213/612-4800. 1,523 units. A/C TV TEL. $175–$215 double; from $190 suite. AE, CB, DC, EURO, MC, V. Parking $18.50.

The 35-story Bonaventure is the hotel that locals most love to hate. It's certainly architecturally unique: The hotel's five gleaming glass silos–like giant mirrored rolls of paper towels—constitute one of downtown's most distinctive landmarks. This is an enormous convention hotel, designed on the scale of a mini-city. The six-story skylit lobby houses splashing fountains, gardens, trees, and even a large lake. There's a tangle of concrete ramps and 12 glass-enclosed, high-speed elevators that appear to rise from the reflecting pools. The guest rooms begin on the 10th floor; each has a wall of windows offering good views, but they're smaller than similarly priced rooms in the neighborhood. One of the towers is a completely remodeled all-suite facility whose rooms come with an additional parlor room and half bathroom.

Dining/Diversions: The rooftop Top of Five features panoramic views along with adequate, but not distinctive, continental cuisine. Ask for an exterior table—they're the only ones with the view. The views from the Bona Vista cocktail lounge are worth the price of a drink. There's nightly entertainment—jazz combos, cocktail-hour dancing—at the Sidewalk Cafe, a California bistro, and the adjacent Lobby Court.

Amenities: Outdoor pool and sundeck, concierge, 24-hour room service, nightly turndown, express checkout, business center, car-rental desk, valet parking, Executive Club level with upgraded facilities and services, five levels of shops and boutiques.

Wyndham Checkers Hotel Los Angeles. 535 S. Grand Ave., Los Angeles, CA 90071. ☎ **800/996-3426** or 213/624-0000. Fax 213/626-9906. www.wyndham.com. 188 units. A/C TV TEL. $179–$300 double; from $400 suite. AE, DC, DISC, EURO, MC, V. Valet parking $21. Pets accepted with $20 cleaning fee.

The atmosphere at the Wyndham Checkers, a boutique version of the Biltmore across the street, is as removed from "Hollywood" as a top L.A. hotel can get. Built in 1927, the hotel is protected by the City Cultural Heritage Commission as a Historic Cultural Monument. It has the feel of a grand old home, with cozy (and freshly upgraded) public areas such as a wood-paneled library. The top-of-the-line guest rooms are outfitted with oversize beds and coffeemakers.

Dining: Checkers Restaurant is one of downtown's finest dining rooms.

Amenities: Rooftop spa, heated lap pool, whirlpool, sundeck, concierge, 24-hour room service, dry cleaning, laundry service, nightly turndown, express checkout.

INEXPENSIVE

Kawada Hotel. 200 S. Hill St. (at Second St.), Los Angeles, CA 90012. ☎ **800/752-9232** or 213/621-4455. Fax 213/687-4455. www.kawadahotel.com. 116 units. A/C TV TEL. $95–$129 double. Weekend discounts available. AE, DC, DISC, EURO, MC, V. Parking $6.60.

This pretty, well-kept, and efficiently managed hotel is a pleasant oasis in the otherwise gritty heart of downtown, conveniently located near the Civic Center, the Museum of Contemporary Art, and Union Station. Behind the clean three-story, red-brick exterior are more than 100 pristine rooms, all with handy kitchenettes and simple furnishings. The rooms aren't large, but they're extremely functional, each outfitted with a VCR (movies available free of charge) and two phones. No-smoking rooms are available. The hotel's lobby-level restaurant Epicentre features an eclectic international menu all day.

THE SAN FERNANDO VALLEY
EXPENSIVE

Sheraton Universal. 333 Universal Terrace Pkwy., Universal City, CA 91608. ☎ **800/ 325-3535** or 818/980-1212. Fax 818/985-4980. 442 units. A/C TV TEL. $250 double; from $325 suite. AE, CB, DC, DISC, EURO, JCB, MC, V. Valet parking $14; self-parking $10.

This 21-story concrete rectangle, situated on the grounds of Universal Studios, is a good-quality, mixed-use hotel catering to tourists, businesspeople, and industry folks visiting the studios' production offices. A major 1994 renovation updated every room with contemporary fabrics and floor-to-ceiling windows that actually open; each is equipped with Nintendo games. The hotel is very close to the Hollywood Bowl, and you can practically roll out of bed and into the theme park.

Dining/Diversions: The hotel's restaurant serves California cuisine, but the many restaurants and nightspots of Universal City and CityWalk are a quick tram ride away.

Amenities: Outdoor pool and whirlpool, health club, games rooms, concierge, room service (from 6am to 10:30pm), dry-cleaning/laundry service, LodgeNet movie channels, twice-daily maid service, express checkout, valet parking, gift shop.

Universal City Hilton & Towers. 555 Universal Terrace Pkwy., Universal City, CA 91608. ☎ **800/HILTONS** or 818/506-2500. Fax 818/509-2031. 478 units. A/C TV TEL. $175–$225 double; from $250 suite. Weekend discounts available. AE, CB, DC, DISC, MC, V. Valet parking $14; self-parking $10.

Although this 24-story hotel sits right outside the Universal Studios theme park, there's more of a conservative-business-traveler feel here than the raucous family-with-young-children vibe you might expect. The large lobby is built almost entirely of glass, giving it an openness that doesn't seem hollow or empty. The rooms are tastefully decorated in light earth tones with English-style furniture.

Cafe Sierra serves California cuisine all day, as well as Sunday brunch. Amenities include heated pool and whirlpool, free access to health club, concierge, 24-hour room service, dry cleaning, laundry service, and express checkout.

MODERATE

In addition to the choices listed below, another comfortable option close to Universal Studios is the **Radisson Valley Center,** 15433 Ventura Blvd. (at the junction of I-405 and U.S. 101), Sherman Oaks (☎ **818/981-5400**).

Beverly Garland Holiday Inn. 4222 Vineland Ave., North Hollywood, CA 91602. ☎ **800/ BEVERLY** or 818/980-8000. Fax 818/766-5230. www.beverlygarland.com. 255 units. A/C TV TEL. $169 double; from $199 suite. AE, JCB, MC, V. Free parking.

Don't get confused by the name—this hotel is named for its owner, the actress Beverly Garland (of *My Three Sons* fame), not Beverly Hills. Grassy areas and greenery abound at this North Hollywood Holiday Inn, a virtual oasis in the concrete jungle that is most of L.A. The Southern California mission-influenced buildings that make up the hotel are a bit dated, but if you grew up with *Brady Bunch* reruns, this only adds to the charm—it looks like something Mike Brady would have designed. Southwestern-themed fabrics complement the natural-pine furnishings in the recently renovated guest rooms; unfortunately, the painted cinder-block walls give off something of a college-dorm feel. All rooms feature balconies, and facilities include a pool, sauna, and two tennis courts. The Paradise Restaurant serves Polynesian-influenced cuisine throughout the day. A complimentary shuttle to Universal is available.

Sportsmen's Lodge. 12825 Ventura Blvd. (east of Coldwater Canyon), Studio City, CA 91604. ☎ **800/821-8511** or 818/769-4700. Fax 213/877-3898. www.slhotel.com. 191 units. A/C TV TEL. $117–$156 double; from $180 suite. AE, DC, DISC, EURO, MC, V. Free parking.

It's been a long time since this part of Studio City was wilderness enough to justify the lodge's name. This sprawling motel has been enlarged and upgraded since those days, the most recent improvements—sprucing up the worn room furnishings—made within the last 3 years. Relaxing around the heated, Olympic-size pool surrounded by a fleet of chaise longues, you might take advantage of the new pool cabana bar and forget all about busy Ventura Boulevard beyond this garden setting. The guest rooms are large and comfortable, but not luxurious; all have balconies or patios, and fridges are available. There's a well-equipped exercise room and a variety of shops and service desks, and both golf and bowling are nearby. A hunting-lodge motif bar and grill is on the property, adjoining a fine-dining room that serves only weekend dinner and brunch in stunning glass-enclosed surroundings. Don't miss the beautiful black and white swans frolicking out back in the koi-filled ponds.

PASADENA & ENVIRONS
EXPENSIVE

✪ **Ritz-Carlton Huntington Hotel.** 1401 S. Oak Knoll Ave. (west of Elliott), Pasadena, CA 91109. ☎ **800/241-3333** or 626/568-3900. Fax 626/568-3700. 383 units. A/C MINIBAR TV TEL. $145–$240 double; from $350 suite or cottage. AE, DC, MC, V. Parking $12.

Built in 1906 and still one of America's grandest hotels, the Spanish-Mediterranean Huntington gained popularity early on among celebrated writers, entertainers, political and business leaders, even royalty. Set on 23 meticulously landscaped acres, it seems a world apart from downtown Los Angeles, though it's only about 20 minutes away. Closed for 6 years after a particularly destructive earthquake, the hotel reopened in 1991 as a full replica of itself under the Ritz-Carlton banner. Each oversize guest room is dressed in conservatively elegant Ritz-Carlton style, with marble baths, thick carpets, terry robes, and the like. Behind the hotel is a bucolic Japanese garden that's great for strolling.

Dining/Diversions: Local seniors love to celebrate in the Georgian Room, where continental meals are prepared by a classically trained French chef. The less formal Grill serves traditional fare in a comfortable clublike setting. The Cafe serves all day, either indoors or out; it's best on Sunday for champagne brunch. High tea is served daily in the Lobby Lounge.

Amenities: Olympic-size heated outdoor pool, whirlpool, sundeck, three lighted tennis courts, concierge, 24-hour room service, nightly turndown, bicycle rental, pro shop, full-service spa/salon, exercise room, car-rental desk, shopping promenade, baby-sitting.

MODERATE

The Artists' Inn Bed-and-Breakfast. 1038 Magnolia St., South Pasadena, CA 91030. ☎ **888/799-5668** or 626/799-5668. Fax 626/799-3678. www.artistsinns.com. 9 units. A/C. $110–$205 double. Rates include full breakfast and afternoon tea. Extra person $20. AE, MC, V.

This Victorian-style inn, an unpretentious yellow-shingled home pleasantly furnished with wicker throughout, was built in 1895 as a farmhouse, and recently expanded to include a neighboring 1909 home. Each unit is decorated to reflect the style of a particular artist or period, including impressionist, Fauve, and van Gogh. While the three annex suites have deluxe amenities—whirlpool tubs, minibars, coffeemakers, phones, and TVs—every room is thoughtfully arranged with fresh roses (from the front garden), a hair dryer, port wine, and chocolates. The inn is on a quiet residential street 5 minutes from the heart of downtown.

Bissell House. 201 Orange Grove Ave. (at Columbia St.), South Pasadena, CA 91030. ☎ **800/441-3530** or 626/441-3535. Fax 626/441-3671. www.virtualcities.com. 5 units. A/C. $115–$160 double. Rates include full breakfast on weekends, expanded continental breakfast on weekdays, plus afternoon snacks and all-day beverages. AE, MC, V.

Hidden behind tall hedges that carefully isolate it from busy Orange Grove Avenue, this 1887 gingerbread Victorian is furnished with antiques and offers a delightful taste of life on what was once Pasadena's "Millionaire's Row." All rooms have private bathrooms with both shower and tub (one an antique clawfoot, one a private whirlpool). There's a pool and Jacuzzi on the beautifully landscaped grounds, and a downstairs library offers a telephone and fax machine for guests' use.

INEXPENSIVE

Pasadena Hotel Bed & Breakfast. 76 N. Fair Oaks Ave. (between Union and Holly sts.), Pasadena, CA 91103. ☎ **800/653-8886** or 626/568-8172. Fax 626/793-6409. 12 units, 1 with half bathroom. A/C TV TEL. $80–$165 double. Rates include continental breakfast. AE, MC, V. Parking $5.

This old-style hostelry is definitely not for everyone. In true turn-of-the-century rooming-house style, the small but comfortable guest rooms have washbasins, but all but one must share hallway bathrooms (three full, two half). Part of the attraction here is the well-restored National Historic Register building, and part is the hotel's flawless location: It's the only accommodation literally in the heart of lively—and noisy—Old Pasadena. The central sitting room/lounge is elegant and welcoming, and there's a spirited coffeehouse in the courtyard behind the hotel where you can enjoy your breakfast and complimentary afternoon teas. Shuttle buses to the Rose Bowl depart 1 block away during major events.

Saga Motor Hotel. 1633 E. Colorado Blvd. (between Allen and Sierra Bonita aves.), Pasadena, CA 91106. ☎ **800/793-7242** or 626/795-0431. Fax 626/792-0559. 70 units. A/C TV TEL. $62–$69 double; $75 suite. Rates include continental breakfast. AE, CB, DC, MC, V. Free parking.

This 1950s relic of old Route 66 is a little bland by modern standards, but has far more character than most others in its price range. The rooms are small, clean, and simply furnished with just the basics. The best units are in the front building surrounding the gated swimming pool, which is shielded from the street and inviting in warm weather. The grounds are attractive and surprisingly well kept, if you don't count the Astroturf "lawn" around the pool. The motel is about a mile from the Huntington Library and within 10 minutes of both the Rose Bowl and Old Pasadena.

4 Dining

Since the advent of California cuisine, now a staple across the country, trend-watchers have looked to L.A. restaurants for culinary fashion tips. These days, instead of the trattoria of the week, you'll find a wave of pan-Asian eateries fusing Thai, Vietnamese, Szechwan, and Indian elements with often-inspired results. Also look for the return of French cuisine—but in the form of friendly country bistros rather than stuffy formal dining rooms.

The restaurants below are categorized first by geographic area, then by price. Keep in mind that many of the restaurants listed as "Expensive" are moderately priced at lunch. Reservations are recommended almost everywhere, particularly on weekends and during peak lunch (noon to 1:30pm) and dinner (7 to 8:30pm) hours.

If you're looking for L.A.'s theme restaurants, you'll find the **Hard Rock Cafe** at two locations: at the Beverly Center, 8600 Beverly Blvd. (at San Vicente Blvd.), Los Angeles (☎ **310/276-7605**), and at Universal CityWalk, Universal Center Drive exit off U.S. 101 (☎ **818/622-7625**). **Planet Hollywood** is at 9560 Wilshire Blvd. (west of Rodeo Dr.), Beverly Hills (☎ **310/275-7828**).

Our limited space forced us to make tough choices; for a greater selection of reviews, see *Frommer's Los Angeles.* For additional late-night dining options, see "Late-Night Bites" under "Los Angeles After Dark," later in this chapter.

SANTA MONICA & THE BEACHES
EXPENSIVE

Encounter at LAX. 209 World Way (Theme Building, Los Angeles International Airport). ☎ **310/215-5151.** Reservations recommended for dinner. Main courses $7–$14 lunch, $15–$29 dinner. AE, CB, DC, DISC, MC, V. Daily 10:30am–10pm. CALIFORNIA.

There's always been a restaurant in the spacey, circa-1961 Theme Building perched in LAX's midst, but these days it draws as many Angelenos as fly-by travelers (including John Travolta, who had his star-studded birthday party here). The reason? A recent makeover transforming the staid continental dining room (whose best feature was a panoramic view over the runways) into a 1960s *Star Trek* set gone Technicolor. Outer-space lounge music dominates the entire place, and waitresses endure silver satin minidress costumes complete with go-go boots. The menu features art-food, that L.A. specialty that combines too many ingredients and focuses more on creating sculptural arrangements on the plate than culinary delights for the taste buds; that said, the food is entertaining and adequately tasty. We suggest at least coming up and having a blue cocktail at the lava lamp–festooned bar, because quirky Encounter is worth an encounter.

JiRaffe. 502 Santa Monica Blvd. (at Fifth St.), Santa Monica. ☎ **310/917-6671.** Reservations recommended. Main courses $19–$26. AE, DC, MC, V. Tues–Fri noon–2pm and 6–11pm; Sat 5:30–11pm; Sun 5:30–9pm. AMERICAN/FRENCH.

"JiRaffe"—it isn't a long-necked zoo creature, but a blending of names from the two chefs responsible for this overnight sensation. Josiah Citrin has since left former partner Raphael Lunetta to carry on alone at this crowded, upscale bistro in restaurant-hungry Santa Monica. The deafening din of conversation here is usually praise for JiRaffe's artistic treatment of whitefish (spiced and served with sugar snap peas, glazed carrots, and ginger-carrot sauce), roasted rabbit, crispy salmon, or pork chop (grilled with wild rice, smoked bacon, apple chutney, and cider sauce). JiRaffe also wins culinary points for highlighting oft-ignored vegetables like salsify, Swiss chard, and fennel, as well as complex appetizers that are more like miniature main dishes.

Michael's. 1147 Third St. (north of Wilshire Blvd.), Santa Monica. ☎ **310/451-0843.** Reservations recommended. Main courses $16–$22 lunch, $24–$31 dinner. AE, DISC, MC, V. Tues–Fri 11:30am–2:30pm and 6–10:30pm; Sat 6–10:30pm. CALIFORNIA.

Owner Michael McCarty, L.A.'s answer to Alice Waters, is considered by many to be the father of California cuisine. Since the opening of Michael's in 1979 (when McCarty was only 25), several top L.A. restaurants have caught up to it—and Michael handed executive chef responsibilities to Sam Yoon, whose impressive pedigree includes stints at L.A. and San Francisco's most renowned restaurants—but this fetching Santa Monica restaurant remains one of the city's best. The dining room is filled with contemporary art by wife Kim McCarty, and the restaurant's beloved garden is a relaxed setting for always-inventive menu choices like Baqueta sea bass with a chanterelle-mushroom ragout and fresh Provençal herbs, seared Hawaiian ahi accented with braised enoki mushrooms and earthy-tangy sesame wasabi ponzu sauce, or grilled pork chop sweetened with sweet-potato puree and anise-pinot noir sauce. Don't miss Michael's famous warm mushroom salad, tossed with crumbled goat cheese, watercress, caramelized onion, and mustard-sage vinaigrette. *Note:* Michael's automatically adds a 15% service charge to the check.

✪ **Röckenwagner.** 2435 Main St. (north of Ocean Park Blvd.), Santa Monica. ☎ **310/399-6504.** Reservations recommended. Main courses $10–$18 lunch and brunch, $18–$26 dinner. AE, CB, DC, MC, V. Mon–Wed and Fri 6–10pm; Thurs 11:30am–2:30pm and 6–10pm; Sat 10am–3pm and 5:30–11pm; Sun 10am–3pm and 5:30–10pm. CALIFORNIA.

Set in Frank Gehry's starkly modern Edgemar complex (itself a work of art), chef Hans Röckenwagner's eponymous restaurant continues the motif by presenting edible sculpture amid gallerylike decor. Although set in the midst of a popular shopping area, the space manages to be refreshingly quiet. Röckenwagner takes his art—and his food—very seriously, once orchestrating an entire menu around German white asparagus at the height of its short season. The delightfully unpretentious staff carries out deliciously pretentious dishes fusing Pacific Rim ingredients with traditional European preparations; a good example is the langoustine ravioli with mangoes in port-wine reduction and curry oil. The menu tastes as good as it reads, and desserts are to die for. Don't overlook the lunch bargains here, nor the unique European-style breakfast of bread and cheese.

The Wolfgang Puck Experience

For perhaps the quintessential L.A. dining experience, be sure to try at least one of Wolfgang Puck's L.A. restaurants. Of course, there's **Spago Hollywood** (see p. 459). In 1997, Puck opened a second **Spago** in the heart of Beverly Hills, 176 N. Canon Dr., at Wilshire Boulevard (☎ **310/385-0880**). This one is more spacious and formal, but disciple Lee Hefter was brought back from Granita to ensure that the kitchen mimics the original. Puck also has two terrific restaurants near the beach. **Chinois on Main,** 2709 Main St., Santa Monica (☎ **310/392-9025**), serves terrifically quirky East-meets-West Franco-Chinese cuisine. At **Granita,** 23725 W. Malibu Rd. (in the Malibu Colony Mall), Malibu (☎ **310/456-0488**), Puck applies his signature California style to seafood—very successfully, of course. His latest venture is **ObaChine,** 242 N. Beverly Dr. in Beverly Hills (☎ **310/274-4440**), a Pan-Asian bistro and satay bar interpreting exotic Asian for mainstream tastes. If you're dining on a budget, try one of the several **Wolfgang Puck Cafe** branches around town, where Puck's cuisine is interpreted in an affordable style and served up in colorful surroundings. There's one in West Hollywood, at 8000 Sunset Blvd. (☎ **323/ 650-7300**); one in Santa Monica, at 1323 Montana Ave. (☎ **310/393-0290**); and one at Universal CityWalk (☎ **818/985-9653**).

✪ **Valentino.** 3115 Pico Blvd. (west of Bundy Dr.), Santa Monica. ☎ **310/829-4313.** Reservations required. Pasta $14–$18; meat and fish dishes $22–$28. AE, CB, DC, DISC, MC, V. Mon–Thurs 5:30–10:30pm; Fri 11:30am–2:30pm and 5:30–11pm; Sat 5:30–11pm. ITALIAN.

Charming owner Piero Selvaggio oversees two other restaurants, but his distinctive touch still pervades this 25-year-old flagship. Elegant Valentino continues to maintain its position as *Wine Spectator* magazine's top wine cellar, and *New York Times* food critic Ruth Reichl calls this the best Italian restaurant in the United States. The creations of Selvaggio and his brilliant young chef, Angelo Auriana, make dinners here lengthy multicourse affairs (often involving several bottles of wine). You might begin with a crisp pinot grigio paired with caviar-filled cannoli, or crespelle, thin little pancakes with fresh porcini mushrooms and a rich melt of fontina cheese. A rich barolo is the perfect accompaniment to rosemary-infused roasted rabbit; the fantastically fragrant risotto with white truffles is one of the most magnificent dishes we've ever had. Jackets are all but required in the elegant dining room. Valentino is a good choice if you're splurging on just one special dinner.

Vincenti Ristorante. 11930 San Vicente Blvd. (west of Montana Ave.), Brentwood. ☎ **310/207-0127.** Reservations recommended. Main courses $18–$32. AE, MC, V. Tues–Thurs 6–10:30pm; Fri noon–2pm and 5:30–10:30pm; Sat–Sun 5:30–10:30pm. ITALIAN.

Despite newer trends sweeping L.A., the finely executed northern Italian is still going strong, as evidenced by this spot of the moment. Opened by Maureen Vincenti, widow of Mauro (whose downtown Rex ruled the scene for years), with former Rex chef Gino Angelini supervising the kitchen, Vincenti lives up to its promising pedigree. Praised as "authentically Italian," the menu offers such unusual fare as homemade pasta with lobster and a touch of red pepper, pumpkin-squash ravioli sauced with asparagus and sage, plus rotisserie-cooked whole fish, game birds, and meat. Economy-minded diners with upwardly mobile palates can easily stick with hearty appetizers and pastas ($9 to $18) and still have some left for one of Vincenti's tempting *dolci* (sweets).

MODERATE

Aunt Kizzy's Back Porch. 4325 Glencove Ave. (in the Villa Marina shopping center), Marina del Rey. ☎ **310/578-1005.** Reservations not accepted. Main courses $8–$13. AE. Mon–Thurs 11am–11pm; Fri–Sat 11am–midnight; Sun 11am–3pm and 4–11pm. SOUTHERN.

This is a real Southern restaurant, owned by genuine Southerners from Texas and Oklahoma. Kizzy's chicken Creole, jambalaya, and smothered pork chops are just about as good as it gets in this city. Almost everything comes with vegetables, red beans and rice, and corn muffins. Fresh-squeezed lemonade is served by the mason jar. These are huge meals that, as corny as it sounds, are as delicious as they are filling. Sunday brunches are all-you-can-eat affairs, served buffet-style. The biggest problem with Aunt Kizzy's is its location, hidden in a shopping center that has too few parking spaces to accommodate its customers. Look for the restaurant to the right of Vons supermarket.

Border Grill. 1445 Fourth St. (between Broadway and Santa Monica Blvd.), Santa Monica. ☎ **310/451-1655.** www.bordergrill.com. Reservations recommended. Main courses $10–$21. AE, DC, DISC, MC, V. Mon–Thurs 5–10pm; Fri–Sat 11:30am–11pm; Sun 11:30am–10pm. MEXICAN.

Before Mary Sue Milliken and Susan Feniger spiced up cable TV as "Too Hot Tamales," they started this restaurant over in West Hollywood. Now Border Grill has moved to a boldly painted, cavernous (read: loud) space in Santa Monica, and the gals aren't in the kitchen here very much at all (though cookbooks and paraphernalia from their Food Network show are prominently displayed for sale). But their influence on the inspired menu is enough to maintain the cantina's enormous popularity with folks who swear by the authentic flavor of Yucatan fish tacos, rock shrimp with ancho chilies, and meaty *ropa vieja,* the traditional Latin stew. The best meatless dish is *mulitas de hongos,* a layering of portobello mushrooms, poblano chilies, black beans, cheese, and guacamole, spiced up with roasted garlic and seared red chard. Distracting desserts are displayed near the entrance, so you may spend the meal fantasizing about the yummy coconut flan or key lime pie.

Joe's. 1023 Abbot Kinney Blvd., Venice. ☎ **310/399-5811.** Reservations recommended. Main courses $8–$10 lunch, $15–$18 dinner. AE, MC, V. Tues–Fri 11:30am–2:30pm and 6–11pm; Sat–Sun 11am–3pm and 6–11pm. AMERICAN ECLECTIC.

This is one of West L.A.'s best dining bargains. Chef/owner Joe Miller excels in simple New American cuisine, particularly grilled fish and roasted meats accented with piquant herbs. Set in a tiny, quirky storefront, the humble room is a blank palette that belies Joe's popularity; the best tables are tucked away on the enclosed back patio. Lunch is a hidden treasure for those with a champagne palate but seltzer pocketbook: Topping out at $10, all include salad, one of Miller's exquisite soups, and prompt service. Beer and wine are served, except during weekday lunchtime (regulation, due to the elementary school across the street).

INEXPENSIVE

Benny's Bar-B-Q. 4077 Lincoln Blvd. (south of Washington Blvd.), Marina del Rey. ☎ **310/821-6939.** Sandwiches $4–$6; dinner specials $7–$10. AE, MC, V. Mon–Fri 11am–10pm; Sat noon–10pm; Sun 4–10pm. BARBECUE.

It's mostly takeout at this cook-shack dive, but there are a few tables, where the city's luckiest diners gorge themselves on Los Angeles's best barbecued pork and beef ribs and hot-link sausages. Like almost everything on the menu, the barbecued chicken is bathed in a tangy hot sauce and served with baked beans and a choice of coleslaw, potato salad, fries, or corn on the cob. Beef, ham, and pork sandwiches are also available. To reach Benny's, find Lincoln Boulevard, then follow the heavy aroma.

Sea Breezes & Sunsets: Ocean-View Dining in Malibu

Despite fires, mudslides, and high rents, Malibu residents remain enamoured of their precious parcel of beachfront paradise. There really is a beautifully calm, on-vacation vibe to this upscale stretch of coast. One of the best ways to sample a slice of this happiness pie is to (literally) turn your back on the frenzy of L.A. and gaze upon the sparkling Pacific—at least for the duration of a meal.

From south to north, numerous restaurants dot the coastline, all exploiting as much ocean view as their property line allows. Here are some of our favorites:

Gladstone's 4 Fish, 17300 Pacific Coast Hwy., at Sunset Boulevard (☎ **310/454-3474**), a local tradition, is perfectly immersed in the Malibu scene. It shares a parking lot with a public beach, so its wood deck has a constant view of surfers, bikini-clad sunbathers, and other frolicking beachgoers. At busy times, Gladstone's even sets up picnic-style tables right out on the sand. Prices are moderate, and the atmosphere casual. The menu boasts several pages of fresh fish and seafood, augmented by a few salads and other meals for landlubbers. Gladstone's is popular for afternoon and evening drinks, its nearly 20 seafood appetizer platters, and its decadent chocolate-y desserts. Open Monday through Thursday from 11am to 11pm, Friday from 11am to midnight, Saturday from 7am to midnight, and Sunday from 7am to 11pm. Parking $3.50.

The Malibu branch of the surf-and-turf **Chart House** chain, at 18412 Pacific Coast Hwy., south of Topanga Canyon (☎ **310/454-9321**), lets its dramatic location steal the show. Built on a rocky point, suspended over the sand, and often perilously close to the breaking surf, the Chart House's dark, woody dining room is terraced, affording every table a great view. The menu, though predictable (prime rib, steaks, lobster, seafood), is first class. Prices are moderate to expensive. Open Monday and Tuesday from 5 to 9:30pm, Wednesday and Thursday from 11:30am to 9:30pm, Friday and Saturday from 11:30am to 10:30pm, and Sunday from 11am to 9:30pm. Free valet parking.

Duke's Malibu, 21150 Pacific Coast Hwy., at Las Flores Canyon (☎ **310/317-0777**), will appeal to lovers of all things Polynesian. This Hawaiian chain is like a South Pacific TGI Friday's where the food is secondary to the decor; this branch's rocky perch atop breaking waves makes it a surfing-themed crowd-pleaser. Named for Hawaiian surf legend "Duke" Kahanamoku, this place is

---

Bread & Porridge. 2315 Wilshire Blvd. (3 blocks west of 26th St.), Santa Monica. ☎ **310/453-4941.** Main courses $4.50–$9. No credit cards. Daily 7am–2pm. INTERNATIONAL.

A dozen tables are all that comprise this neighborhood cafe, but a steady stream of locals mills outside, reading their newspapers and waiting for a vacant seat. Once inside, surrounded by the vintage fruit-crate labels adorning the walls and tabletops, you can sample the delicious breakfasts, fresh salads and sandwiches, and super-affordable entrees. There's a vaguely international twist to the menu, which leaps from breakfast quesadillas and omelets—all served with black beans and salsa—to the Southern comfort of Cajun crab cakes and coleslaw to typical Italian pastas adorned with roma tomatoes and plenty of garlic. All menu items are cheap—truck-stop cheap—but with an inventive elegance that truly makes this a best-kept secret. Get a short stack of one of five varieties of pancakes with any meal; they thoughtfully serve breakfast all day.

worth a visit for the impressive memorabilia alone. Duke's offers up decent food at inflated, but not outrageous, prices. You'll find good-quality fresh fish prepared in the Hawaiian regional style, hearty surf-and-turf, a smattering of chicken and pasta dishes, and plenty of finger-lickin' appetizers to accompany the Day-Glo tropical cocktails. Open Monday through Thursday from 11:30am to 10pm, Friday and Saturday from 11:30am to 10:30pm, Sunday from 10am to 10pm. Valet parking $2 (dinner and weekends only, otherwise free self-parking).

The appropriately named **Pier View Cafe & Cantina,** 22718 Pacific Coast Hwy. (☎ 310/456-6962), sits on the beach about a half mile south of the pier, and offers huge portions of inexpensive food in an ultra-casual setting. Inside, there's sawdust on the floor and surfboards in the rafters; out on the clunky wooden deck, sun-lovers get to feel the wind in their hair. The comprehensive menu has something for everyone, including giant farm-style breakfasts, burgers served with curly fries, a terrifically meaty chili, and fresh seafood and enormous main-course salads. For the lingering cocktail crowd, there's a long list of appetizer platters. An added bonus is patrons-only direct beach access from the deck. Open Sunday through Thursday from 7am to midnight, Friday and Saturday from 7am to 1am. Valet parking $3 (Friday through Sunday only, otherwise free self-parking).

Although **Beau Rivage,** 26025 Pacific Coast Hwy., at Corral Canyon (☎ 310/456-5733), is our only pick located on the *other* side of PCH from the beach, this romantic Mediterranean restaurant nevertheless has nearly unobstructed ocean views. The baby-pink villa and its flagstone dining patio are overgrown with flowering vines. The place is loveliest at sunset; romantic lighting takes over after dark. The country French and Italian cuisine features plenty of moderately priced pastas, many with seafood. Other main courses are in the expensive range; they include chicken, duck, rabbit, and lamb, all traditionally prepared. You'll dine with an older, nicely dressed crowd at this special-occasion place. Open Monday through Saturday from 5 to 11pm, Sunday from 11am to 11pm. Valet parking $4 (Friday and Saturday only, otherwise free self-parking). *Tip:* Sunday's brunch menu, which isn't limited to breakfast-y dishes, offers a more economic alternative to dinner.

Jody Maroni's Sausage Kingdom. 2011 Ocean Front Walk (north of Venice Blvd.), Venice. ☎ **310/306-1998.** www.maroni.com. Sandwiches $4–$6. No credit cards. Daily 10am–sunset. SANDWICHES/SAUSAGES.

Your cardiologist might not approve, but Jody Maroni's all-natural, preservative-free "haut dogs" are some of the best wieners served anywhere. The grungy walk-up (or inline skate-up) counter looks fairly foreboding—you wouldn't know there was gourmet fare behind that aging hot-dog stand facade, from which at least 14 different grilled-sausage sandwiches are served up. Bypass the traditional hot Italian and try the Toulouse garlic, Bombay curried lamb, all-chicken apple, or orange-garlic-cumin. Each is served on a freshly baked onion roll and smothered with onions and peppers. Burgers, BLTs, and rotisserie chicken are also offered, but why bother?

Other locations include the Valley's **Universal CityWalk** (☎ 818/622-JODY), and inside **LAX Terminals 3, 4,** and **6,** where you can pick up some last-minute vacuum-packed sausages to take home. Having elevated sausage-worship to an art form, Jody's now boasts a helpful and humorous cookbook, plus its own Web site (www.maroni.com).

⊗ **Kay 'n Dave's Cantina.** 262 26th St. (south of San Vicente Blvd.), Santa Monica. ☎ **310/260-1355.** Reservations accepted for parties of 8 or more only. Main courses $5–$10. MC, V. Mon–Thurs 11am–9:30pm; Fri 11am–10pm; Sat 8:30am–10pm; Sun 8:30am–9:30pm. HEALTHY MEXICAN.

A beach community favorite for "really big portions of really good food at really low prices," Kay 'n Dave's cooks with no lard and has a vegetarian-friendly menu with plenty of meat items, too. Come early (and be prepared to wait) for breakfast, as local devotees line up for five kinds of fluffy pancakes, zesty omelets, or one of the best breakfast burritos in town. Grilled tuna Veracruz, spinach and chicken enchiladas in tomatillo salsa, seafood fajitas tostada, vegetable-filled corn tamales, and other Mexican specialties really are served in huge portions, making this mostly-locals minichain a great choice to energize for (or re-energize after) an action-packed day of beach sightseeing. Bring the family—there's a kids' menu and crayons on every table.

L.A.'S WESTSIDE & BEVERLY HILLS
EXPENSIVE

⊗ **Four Oaks.** 2181 N. Beverly Glen Blvd., Los Angeles. ☎ **310/470-2265.** Reservations required. Main courses $22–$29. AE, DISC, MC, V. Mon 6–10pm; Tues–Sat 11:30am–2pm and 6–10pm; Sun 10:30am–2pm and 6–10pm. CALIFORNIA.

Just looking at the menu here makes us swoon. The country-cottage ambiance and chef Peter Roelant's superlative blend of fresh ingredients with luxurious continental flourishes make a meal at the Four Oaks one of our favorite luxuries. Dinner is served beneath trees festooned with twinkling lights. Appetizers such as lavender-smoked salmon with crisp potatoes and horseradish crème fraîche complement mouthwatering dishes like roasted chicken with sage, Oregon forest mushrooms, artichoke hearts, and port-balsamic sauce. If you're looking for someplace special, head to this canyon hideaway—you won't be disappointed.

Jozu. 8360 Melrose Ave. (at Kings Rd.), West Hollywood. ☎ **323/655-5600.** www.jozu.com. Reservations recommended. Main courses $16–$27. AE, MC, V. Thurs–Fri noon–2pm and 5:30–10:30pm; Sat–Wed 5:30–10:30pm. ASIAN/CALIFORNIA.

Jozu means "excellent" in Japanese, and it perfectly describes everything about this tranquil restaurant where everyone's meal begins with a complimentary sake from Jozu's premium sake list. Chef Suzanne Tracht honed her art at Campanile, and the menu presents Asian flavors interpreted with an international inventiveness. Outstanding dishes include pork *charsui*-style, caramelized with tart kumquat sauce and laid on a bed of celery-root purée; delicately roasted sea bass on a bed of crunchy cabbage; and scallops grilled with lemongrass and other Thai flavorings. There's a heavenly tofu-and-daikon salad appetizer lightly dressed with mustard, soy, and scallion oil; the dessert of choice is banana tart, lightly caramelized fruit laid in a buttery crust. The interior is warmly comfortable and subtly lit; plenty of beautiful Hollywood types dine here, but it's quiet enough for real dinner conversation.

Lawry's The Prime Rib. 100 N. La Cienega Blvd. (north of Wilshire Blvd.), Beverly Hills. ☎ **310/652-2827.** Reservations recommended. Main courses $20–$30. AE, CB, DC, DISC, JCB, MC, V. Mon–Thurs 5–10pm; Fri 5–11pm; Sat 4:30–11pm; Sun 4–10pm. PRIME RIB/SEAFOOD.

Most Americans know Lawry's only as a brand of seasoned salt (it was invented at this family-run institution that dates back to 1938). Going to Lawry's is an old-world event; the main menu offerings are four cuts of prime rib that vary in thickness from two fingers to an entire hand. Every standing rib roast is dry-aged for 2 to 3 weeks, sprinkled with Lawry's famous seasoning, then roasted on a bed of rock salt. A carver wheels the cooked beef table-side, then slices it properly, rare to well done. All dinners come with creamy whipped horseradish, Yorkshire pudding, and the Original Spinning Bowl Salad (drenched in Lawry's signature Sherry French dressing). Lawry's moved across the street from its original location a few years ago, but retained its throwback-to-the-1930s clubroom atmosphere, complete with Persian-carpeted oak floors, high-backed chairs, and European oils.

✪ **Matsuhisa.** 129 N. La Cienega Blvd. (north of Wilshire Blvd.), Beverly Hills. ☎ **310/659-9639.** Reservations recommended. Main courses $14–$26; sushi $4–$13 per order; full *omakase* dinner from $65. AE, DC, MC, V. Mon–Fri 11:45am–2:15pm; daily 5:45–10:15pm. JAPANESE/PERUVIAN.

Japanese chef/owner Nobuyuki Matsuhisa arrived in Los Angeles via Peru and opened what may be the most creative restaurant in the entire city. A true master of fish cookery, Matsuhisa creates fantastic, unusual dishes by combining Japanese flavors with South American spices and salsas. Broiled sea bass with black truffles, sautéed squid with garlic and soy, and Dungeness crab tossed with chilies and cream are good examples of the masterfully prepared delicacies that are available, in addition to thickly sliced nigiri and creative sushi rolls. Matsuhisa is perennially popular with celebrities and hard-core foodies, so reserve early for those hard-to-get tables. The small, crowded main dining room suffers from bad lighting and precious lack of privacy; many big names are ushered through to private dining rooms. If you dare, ask for *omakase*, and the chef will personally compose a selection of eccentric dishes.

Mimosa. 8009 Beverly Blvd. (west of Fairfax), Los Angeles. ☎ **323/655-8895.** Reservations recommended. Main courses $13–$24. AE, MC, V. Mon–Fri 11:30am–3pm; daily 5pm–midnight. FRENCH PROVENÇAL.

It takes seasoned maitre d' Silvio de Mori to fend off the throngs clamoring to get into chef Jean-Pierre Bosc's country French bistro—it seems "Provençal" is the magic culinary buzzword these days, and this stylish spot leads the pack. Decked out in traditional bistro garb (butter-yellow walls, artsy photos, French posters), Mimosa also attracts plenty of French expats and Euro-style denizens with a truly authentic menu. Not the classic French of caviar and truffles, but regional peasant specialties like rich veal *daube*, tripe sausage (*andouillette*), perfect steak frites, and a slow-cooked pork roast with horseradish lentils. The appetizer list usually includes a splendid terrine, and bowls of house-cured *cornichons* and spicy Dijon mustard accompany bread to every table. Despite the occasional tinge of trendy attitude, Mimosa should be appreciated for its casual, comforting bistro fare.

Spago Hollywood. 1114 Horn Ave. (at Sunset Blvd.), West Hollywood. ☎ **310/652-4025.** Reservations recommended. Main courses $18–$34. AE, CB, DC, DISC, JCB, MC, V. Sun and Tues–Thurs 6–10pm; Fri–Sat 5:30–11pm. CALIFORNIA.

Wolfgang Puck is more than a great chef: He's also a masterful businessman and publicist who has made Spago one of the best-known restaurants in the United States. Despite all the hoopla—and more than 18 years of service—Spago remains one of L.A.'s top-rated restaurants. German-born Puck originally won fame serving imaginative "gourmet" pizzas. These individually sized thin-crust pies are baked in a wood-burning oven and topped with goodies like duck sausage, shiitake mushrooms, leeks, and artichokes, and other combinations once considered to be on the culinary edge. Of meat dishes, roast Sonoma lamb with braised shallots and grilled chicken with garlic and parsley are two perennial favorites. The celebrated (and far from secret) off-menu meal is Jewish pizza, a crispy pie topped with smoked salmon, crème fraîche, dill, red onion, and dollops of caviar.

MODERATE

✪ **Bombay Cafe.** 12021 W. Pico Blvd. (at Bundy). ☎ **310/820-2070.** Reservations recommended on weekends. Main courses $9–$15. MC, V. Tues–Thurs 11:30am–10pm; Fri–Sat 11:30am–11pm; Sun 11:30am–4pm. INDIAN.

This friendly sleeper may well be L.A.'s best Indian, serving excellent curries and kurmas typical of South Indian street food. Once seated, immediately order *sev puri* for the table; these crispy little chips topped with chopped potatoes, onions, cilantro, and chutneys are the perfect accompaniment to what's sure to be an extended menu-reading session. Also recommended are the burrito-like "frankies," juicy little bread rolls stuffed with lamb, chicken, or cauliflower. The best dishes come from the tandoor, and include spicy yogurt-marinated swordfish, lamb, and chicken. While some dishes are authentically spicy, plenty of others have a mellow flavor for less incendiary palates. The restaurant is phenomenally popular and gets its share of celebrities: Meg Ryan and Dennis Quaid hired the Bombay Cafe to cater an affair at their Montana ranch.

Cava. 8384 W. Third St. (at Orlando Ave., in the Beverly Plaza Hotel). ☎ **323/658-8898.** Reservations recommended on weekends. Main courses $8–$17 dinner, $3–$9 breakfast, $4–$14 lunch. AE, CB, DC, DISC, MC, V. Daily 6:30am–midnight. SPANISH.

Trendy types in the mood for some fun are attracted to Cava's great mambo atmosphere; the tapas bar is made festive with flamboyant colors, and the loud, lively flamenco really is live on weekends. The dining room is less raucous, with velvet drapes and tassels adorning the walls and comfortable booths. The cuisine is Spanish livened up with Caribbean touches, an influence reflected in dishes like black-bean tamales with tomatillo salsa and golden caviar; thick, dark tortilla soup; jerk chicken with sweet yams; and pan-seared shrimp in spicy peppercorn sauce. Spanish paella is stewed up three ways—with seafood, chicken and sausage, or all-vegetable—and is featured in Monday's all-you-can-eat "Paella Festival." If you have room for dessert, try the ruby-colored pears poached in port, the rice pudding, or the flan.

Kate Mantilini. 9101 Wilshire Blvd. (at Doheny Dr.), Beverly Hills. ☎ **310/278-3699.** Reservations accepted only for parties of 6 or more. Main courses $7–$16. AE, MC, V. Mon–Thurs 7:30am–1am; Fri 7:30am–2am; Sat 11am–2am; Sun 10am–midnight. AMERICAN.

It's rare to find a restaurant that feels comfortably familiar yet cutting-edge trendy at the same time—and also happens to be one of L.A.'s few late-night eateries. Kate Mantilini fits the bill perfectly. One of the first to bring meat loaf back into fashion, Kate's offers a huge menu of upscale truck-stop favorites like "white" chili (made with chicken, white beans, and Jack cheese), grilled steaks and fish, a few token pastas, and just about anything you might crave. At 2am, nothing quite beats a steaming bowl of lentil-vegetable soup and some garlic-cheese toast, unless your taste runs to fresh oysters and a dry martini—Kate has it all. The huge mural of the Hagler-Hearns boxing match that dominates the stark, open interior provides the only clue to the namesake's identity: Mantilini was an early female boxing promoter, around 1947.

La Serenata Gourmet. 10924 W. Pico Blvd., West Los Angeles. ☎ **310/441-9667.** Reservations not accepted. Main courses $8–$13. AE, MC, V. Daily 11am–3:30pm; Sun–Thurs 5–10pm; Fri–Sat 5–10:30pm. MEXICAN.

Westsiders rejoiced when this branch of Boyle Heights's award-winning La Serenata de Girabaldi began serving its authentic but innovative Mexican cuisine just a block away from the Westside Pavilion shopping center. It's casual, fun, and intensely delicious; specialties like shrimp enchiladas, fish tacos, and pork *gorditas* are all accented with flavorful salsas and plenty of authentic regional Mexican touches. Always packed to capacity, the restaurant finally expanded in 1998, but try to avoid the prime lunch and dinner hours nonetheless.

There's also a brand-new **La Serenata** in Santa Monica, at 1416 Fourth St. (☎ **310/656-7017**), that boasts a more upscale atmosphere.

✪ **Locanda Veneta.** 8638 W. Third St. (between San Vicente and Robertson blvds.). ☎ **310/274-1893.** Reservations required. Main courses $10–$22. AE, MC, V. Mon–Fri 11:30am–2:30pm; Mon–Sat 5:30–11pm. VENETIAN.

Locanda Veneta's citywide renown belies its tiny size and unpretentious setting. Its location, across from the unsightly monolith that is Cedars-Sinai Hospital, is a far cry from Venice's Grand Canal, and the single loud, tightly packed dining room can sometimes feel like Piazza San Marco at the height of tourist season. But the sensible prices reflect the restaurant's efficient decor. While the dining room is decidedly unfancy, the kitchen is dead serious, making this restaurant a kind of temple for knowledgeable foodies, who flock here to sample the latest creations of chef Massimo Ormani, a gifted artist and culinary technician who's building a national reputation. The soups are excellent, seafood dishes extraordinary, and pastas as good as they can get. Signature dishes include pasta-and-bean soup, veal chops, lobster ravioli, shrimp risotto, and perfectly grilled vegetables. Although the dessert menu is long and tempting, we always order the *crema de vaniglia,* a dense, silky custard topped with caramel and chocolate sauces.

Lucques. 8474 Melrose Ave. (east of La Cienega), West Hollywood ☎ **323/655-6277.** Reservations recommended. Main courses $16–$25. Tues–Sat 6pm–1:30am; Sun 6pm–midnight. FRENCH/MEDITERRANEAN.

Once Los Angeles became accustomed to this restaurant's unusual name—a variety of French olive, pronounced "Luke"—local foodies fell hard for the quietly and comfortably sophisticated new home of former Campanile chef Suzanne Goin. This old brick building, once silent star Harold Lloyd's carriage house, is decorated in a mute, clubby style with subdued lighting that extends to the handsome enclosed patio behind. Goin cooks with bold flavors, fresh-from-the-farm produce, and an instinctive feel for the food of the Mediterranean; the short and oft-changed menu makes the most of unusual ingredients like salt cod and oxtail. Standout dishes include Tuscan bean soup with tangy greens and pistou, grilled chicken served alongside spinach sauteed with pancetta and shallots, rustic mascarpone polenta topped with wildmushroom ragout and wilted greens, and perfect vanilla *pôt de crème* for dessert. Lucques's bar menu, featuring steak frites bearnaise, omelets, and tantalizing hors d'oeuvres (olives, warm almonds, sea salt, chewy bread), is a godsend for late-night diners.

Pastis. 8114 Beverly Blvd. (west of Crescent Heights), Los Angeles. ☎ **323/655-8822.** Reservations recommended. Main courses $15–$20. AE, MC, V. Daily 5:30–10pm. FRENCH PROVENÇAL.

Of the new wave of country French bistros in town, Pastis usually takes a back seat to the ultra-hip, celebrity-frequented Mimosa, which happens to be just a block away. But locals and regulars often prefer this rustic yet civilized spot, named for the licoriceflavored liqueur imbibed throughout the south of France. Intimate and friendly, with sidewalk tables and a warmly ochre-toned dining room, Pastis manages to be elegant yet also the kind of place where you can scrape your chair, raise your voice, or drink a little too much wine. Distinctive menu selections include curly endive salad with bacon and poached-egg garnish, wine-braised rabbit, and Marseilles-style seafood bouillabaisse. For chocolate lovers only: Dessert is chocolat pot au crème, a beautiful thick custard served in rustic glazed pots.

INEXPENSIVE

The Apple Pan. 10801 Pico Blvd. (east of Westwood Blvd.). ☎ **310/475-3585.** Most items under $5. No credit cards. Tues–Thurs and Sun 11am–midnight; Fri–Sat 11am–1am. SANDWICHES/AMERICAN.

There are no tables, just a U-shaped counter, at this classic American burger shack and L.A. landmark. Open since 1947, The Apple Pan is a diner that looks—and acts—the part. It's famous for juicy burgers, bullet-speed service, and its authentic frills-free atmosphere. The hickory burger is best, though the tuna sandwich also has its huge share of fans. Ham, egg-salad, and Swiss-cheese sandwiches round out the menu. Definitely order fries and, if you're in the mood, the home-baked apple pie, too.

✪ Skewers'. 8939 Santa Monica Blvd. (between Robertson and San Vicente blvds.), West Hollywood. ☎ **310/271-0555.** Main courses $7–$9; salads and pitas $4–$7. AE, MC, V. Daily 11am–midnight. MIDDLE EASTERN.

Santa Monica Boulevard is the heart of West Hollywood's commercial strip, and Skewers's sidewalk tables are a great place to see all kinds of neighborhood activity (and audacity). Inside is a New York–like narrow space with changing artwork adorning bare brick walls. From the zesty marinated carrot sticks you get the moment you're seated to the sweet, sticky squares of baklava for dessert, this Mediterranean grill is sure to please. The cuisine features baskets of warm pita bread for scooping up traditional salads like babaghanoush (grilled eggplant with tahini and lemon) and tabbouleh (cracked wheat, parsley, and tomatoes). Try marinated chicken and lamb off the grill, or dolmades (rice- and meat-stuffed grape leaves) seared with a tangy tomato glaze.

Versailles. 1415 S. La Cienega Blvd. (south of Pico Blvd.). ☎ **310/289-0392.** Main courses $5–$11. AE, MC, V. Daily 11am–10pm. CUBAN.

Outfitted with Formica tabletops and looking something like an ethnic IHOP, Versailles feels very much like any number of Miami restaurants that cater to the exiled Cuban community. The menu reads like a veritable survey of Havana-style cookery and includes specialties like "Moors and Christians" (flavorful black beans with white rice), *ropa vieja* (a stringy beef stew), *eastin lechón* (suckling pig with sliced onions), and fried whole fish (usually sea bass). Shredded roast pork is particularly recommendable, especially when tossed with the restaurant's trademark garlic-citrus sauce. But what everyone comes for is the chicken—succulent, slow roasted, smothered in onions and either the garlic-citrus sauce or barbecue sauce. Most everything is served with black beans and rice; wine and beer are available. Because meals are good, bountiful, and cheap, there's often a wait.

Another **Versailles** restaurant is located in Culver City, at 10319 Venice Blvd. (☎ **310/558-3168**).

HOLLYWOOD
EXPENSIVE

Campanile. 624 S. La Brea Ave. (north of Wilshire Blvd.). ☎ **323/938-1447.** Reservations required. Main courses $18–$32. AE, MC, V. Mon–Fri 11:30am–2:30pm; Sat–Sun 9:30am–1:30pm; Mon–Thurs 6–10pm; Fri–Sat 5:30–11pm. Valet parking $3.50. CALIFORNIA/MEDITERRANEAN.

Built as Charlie Chaplin's private offices in 1928, this lovely building has a multilevel layout with flower-bedecked interior balconies, a bubbling fountain, and a skylight through which diners can see the *campanile* (bell tower). The kitchen, headed by Spago alumnus chef/owner Mark Peel, gets a giant leg up from baker (and wife) Nancy Silverton, who runs the now-legendary La Brea Bakery next door. Meals here might begin with fried zucchini flowers drizzled with melted mozzarella or lamb carpaccio surrounded by artichoke leaves—a dish that arrives looking like one of van Gogh's sunflowers. Chef Peel is particularly known for his grills and roasts; try the grilled prime rib smeared with black-olive tapenade or papardelle with braised rabbit, roasted tomato, and collard greens. And don't skip dessert—the restaurant's many enthusiastic sweets fans have turned Nancy's dessert book into a best-seller. Breakfast is a surprising crowd-pleaser, and a terrific way to appreciate this beautiful space on a budget.

✪ **Patina.** 5955 Melrose Ave. (west of Cahuenga Blvd.). ☎ **323/467-1108.** www.patina-pinot.com. Reservations required. Main courses $18–$30. AE, DC, DISC, JCB, MC, V. Tues noon–2pm; Sun–Thurs 6–9:30pm; Fri 6–10:30pm; Sat 5:30–10:30pm. CALIFORNIA/FRENCH.

Joachim Splichal, arguably L.A.'s very best chef, is also a genius at choosing and training top chefs to cook in his kitchens while he jets around the world. Patina routinely wins the highest praise from demanding gourmands, who are happy to empty their bank accounts for unbeatable meals that almost never miss their intended mark. The dining room is straightforwardly attractive, low key, well lit, and professional, without the slightest hint of stuffiness. The menu is equally disarming: "Mallard Duck with Portobello Mushrooms" gives little hint of the brilliant colors and flavors that appear on the plate. The seasonal menu features partridge, pheasant, venison, and other game in winter and spotlights exotic local vegetables in warmer months. Seafood is always available; if Maine lobster cannelloni or asparagus-wrapped John Dory is on the menu, order it. Patina is justifiably famous for its mashed potatoes and potato-truffle chips; be sure to include one (or both) with your meal.

MODERATE

Boxer. 7615 Beverly Blvd. (east of Fairfax), Los Angeles. ☎ **323/932-6178.** Reservations suggested. Main courses $11–$20. AE, MC, V. Tues–Fri 11:30am–2:30pm; Sat–Sun 10:30am–2:30pm; Tues–Sun 6–11pm. CALIFORNIA.

This minimally furnished space on ever-developing Beverly Boulevard has been a favorite of L.A. foodies since opening in 1996. Chef Michael Plapp recently assumed the toque; his style is similar to former star chef Neal Fraser, whose career was launched by the success of Boxer. That style weaves elements of Italian, Moroccan, Mexican, and French cuisine into an eclectic "New American" mélange, producing selections like rack of lamb glazed with pomegranate and paired with couscous and roasted eggplant. The crowd here ranges from suited yuppies to Chanel-garbed socialites to chunky-shoed 20-somethings—all of whom blend inside as well as the menu's varied ingredients. Every plate is artistically arranged, including the splendid desserts. Eschew the valet for always-plentiful street parking, and bring your own wine: Boxer sells no liquor and charges no corkage fee on wines purchased at the shop next door.

Dar Maghreb. 7651 Sunset Blvd. (between Fairfax and La Brea aves.). ☎ **323/876-7651.** Reservations recommended. Fixed-price dinner $34. CB, DC, MC, V. Mon–Fri 6–11pm; Sat 6:30–11pm; Sun 5:30–10:30pm. Valet parking $3.50. MOROCCAN.

If you're a lone diner in search of a quick bite, this isn't the place for you. Dinner at Dar Maghreb is an entertaining dining experience that increases exponentially the larger your party and the longer you linger. Enter an exotic Arab world of genie waitresses who wash your hands with lemon water and belly dancers who shimmy around an exquisite fountain in the center of a Koranic patio. You'll feel like a guest in an ornately tiled palace as you dine at traditional tables on either low sofas or goatskin cushions.

Nothing is available à la carte here. The fixed-price meal is a multicourse feast, starting with bread and traditional Moroccan salads, followed by b'stilla, an appetizer of shredded chicken, eggs, almonds, and spices wrapped in a flaky pastry shell and topped with powdered sugar and cinnamon. The main courses, your choice of lamb, quail, chicken, and more, are each sublimely seasoned and delectable. Perhaps it's the exotic atmosphere that makes everyone eat more than they expected, but you'll be thankful that dessert is a simple fruit-and-nut basket, accompanied by warm spice tea poured dramatically into traditional glasses. All is eaten with your hands—a slithery sensual experience that grows on you as the night progresses.

Georgia. 7250 Melrose Ave. (at Alta Vista Ave.). ☎ **323/933-8420.** Reservations recommended. Main courses $15–$22. AE, MC, V. Mon–Sat 6:30–11pm; Sun 5:30–10pm. SOUTHERN.

Soul food and power ties come together at this calorie-unconscious ode to Southern cooking in the heart of Melrose's funky shopping district. Owned by a group of investors that include Denzel Washington and Eddie Murphy, the restaurant is popular with Hollywood's African-American crowd and others who can afford L.A.'s highest-priced pork chops, fried chicken, and grits. It's great for people watching. The antebellum-style dining room is built to resemble a fine Southern house, complete with mahogany floors, Spanish moss, and wrought-iron gates; a bourbon bar continues the theme. The smoked baby-back ribs are particularly good and, like many other dishes, are smothered in onion gravy or rémoulade, and sided with corn pudding, grits, string beans, or an excellent creamy garlic coleslaw. Other recommendations include turtle soup, grilled gulf shrimp, and a Creole-style catfish that's delicately fried.

Lola's. 945 N. Fairfax Ave. (south of Santa Monica Blvd.), Los Angeles. ☎ **323/736-5652.** Reservations recommended. Main courses $10–$18. AE, MC, V. Daily 5:30pm–2am. Valet parking $3.50. AMERICAN.

As the song goes, "Whatever Lola wants, Lola gets . . ."—and Lola must have wanted to open a stylish restaurant and martini bar that would instantly become the in crowd's darling. This centrally located place has a lot going for it: Not only is the circa-1935 Hollywood building a perfect foil for Lola's semi-Gothic decor, but the menu is reasonably priced (and better than it reads)—and then there's the famed martini bar. All of the several-dozen colorful concoctions are available table-side, served up in individual stainless-steel cocktail shakers with chilled conical glasses. Menu selections are unfussy and flavorful, featuring mesquite-grilled meats, simple pasta dishes, and internationally flavored appetizers. Be sure to try "Domenicks Mashed Potatoes," a creamy dollop of mash atop a nest of crispy shoestring potatoes. The star dessert is Lola's "Chocolate Kiss Cake," a dense and rich treat.

Musso & Frank Grill. 6667 Hollywood Blvd. (at Cahuenga Blvd.). ☎ **323/467-7788.** Reservations recommended. Main courses $13–$28. AE, CB, DC, MC, V. Tues–Sat 11am–11pm. AMERICAN/CONTINENTAL.

A survey of Hollywood restaurants that leaves out Musso & Frank is like a study of Las Vegas showrooms that fails to mention Wayne Newton. As L.A.'s oldest eatery (since 1919), Musso & Frank is the paragon of Old Hollywood grill rooms, an almost kitschy glimpse into a meat-and-potatoes world that has remained the same for generations. This is where Faulkner and Hemingway drank during their screenwriting days, and where Orson Welles used to hold court. The restaurant is still known for its bone-dry martinis and perfectly seasoned Bloody Marys. The setting is what you'd expect: oak-beamed ceilings, red-leather booths and banquettes, mahogany room dividers, chandeliers with tiny shades. The extensive menu is a veritable survey of American/continental cookery. Hearty dinners include veal scallopine marsala, roast spring lamb with mint jelly, and broiled lobster. Grilled meats are the restaurant's specialties, as is the Thursday-only chicken pot pie. Regulars also flock here for Musso's trademark "flannel cakes," crepe-thin pancakes flipped to order.

✪ Tahiti. 7910 W. Third St. (at Fairfax), Los Angeles. ☎ **323/651-1213.** Reservations recommended. Main courses $11–$17. AE, MC, V. Mon–Fri 11:30am–2:30pm; Mon–Thurs 6–10pm; Fri–Sat 6–11pm; Sun 5–9pm. Valet parking $3.75. WORLD CUISINE.

With a rapidly growing fan base of showbiz types and artists who inhabit the eclectic surrounding neighborhood, Tahiti may have only recently joined the L.A. dining scene—but will be instantly familiar to scores who frequented chef/owner Tony DiLembo's late, great Indigo restaurant nearby. DiLembo has imported his distinctive "world cuisine," a provocative mix of zesty influences that create diverse specialties like rare ahi tuna drizzled with lime-ginger butter, sprinkled with toasted sesame seeds, and served with wasabi horseradish and papaya garnish; Argentinean-style T-bone with chimichurri dipping sauce; sherry-sautéed chicken and spinach potstickers accented with mint; and perennial standout rosemary chicken strips with fettuccine in sun-dried tomato/cream sauce. The relaxing decor is sophisticated South Seas with a modern twist, incorporating thatch, batik, rattan, and palm fronds. If the weather is nice, try to sit on the patio. And don't forget to save room for Tahiti's tropical-tinged desserts.

INEXPENSIVE

Authentic Cafe. 7605 Beverly Blvd. (at Curson Ave.). ☎ **323/939-4626.** Main courses $8–$13. AE, MC, V. Mon–Thurs 11am–11pm; Fri–Sat 11am–midnight; Sun 9:30am–11pm. SOUTHWESTERN.

True to its name, this restaurant serves authentic Southwestern food in a casual atmosphere. It's a winning combination that quickly made this place an L.A. favorite, although popularity has dropped off recently due to the decline in Southwestern cuisine and the rush for the next big thing. But Authentic Cafe still has a loyal following of locals who appreciate generous portions and lively flavor combinations. You'll sometimes find an Asian flair to chef Roger Hayot's dishes. Look for Brie, papaya, and chili quesadillas; other worthwhile dishes are the chicken casserole with a corn-bread crust, fresh corn and red peppers in chili-cream sauce, and meat loaf with caramelized onions.

✪ **El Cholo.** 1121 S. Western Ave. (south of Olympic Blvd.). ☎ **213/734-2773.** Reservations recommended. Main courses $8–$14. AE, DC, MC, V. Mon–Thurs 11am–10pm; Fri–Sat 11am–11pm; Sun 11am–9pm. MEXICAN.

There's authentic Mexican and then there's traditional Mexican—El Cholo is comfort food of the latter variety, south-of-the-border cuisine regularly craved by Angelenos. They've been serving it up in this pink adobe hacienda since 1927, even though the once-outlying mid-Wilshire neighborhood around them has turned into Koreatown. El Cholo's expertly blended margaritas, invitingly messy nachos, and classic combination dinners don't break new culinary ground, but the kitchen has perfected these standards over 70 years. We wish they'd bottle their rich enchilada sauce! Other specialties include seasonally available green-corn tamales and creative sizzling vegetarian fajitas that go way beyond just eliminating the meat. The atmosphere is festive, as people from all parts of town dine happily in the many rambling rooms that comprise the restaurant. There's valet parking as well as a free self-park lot directly across the street.

Westsiders head to the new Santa Monica branch of **El Cholo,** at 1025 Wilshire Blvd. (☎ **310/899-1106**).

Hollywood Hills Coffee Shop. 6145 Franklin Ave. (between Gower and Vine sts.). ☎ **323/467-7678.** Most items less than $10. AE, DISC, MC, V. Daily 7am–10pm. DINER. Free parking.

Having for years served as the run-of-the-mill coffee shop for the attached freeway-side Best Western, this place took on a life of its own when chef Susan Fine commandeered the kitchen and spiked the menu with quirky Mexican and Asian touches. Hotel guests spill in from the lobby to rub noses with the actors, screenwriters, and other artistic types who converge from nearby canyons while awaiting that sitcom casting call or feature-film deal—a community immortalized in the 1996 film *Swingers,* which was filmed in the restaurant. Prices have gone up (to pay for the industrial-strength cappuccino maker visible behind the counter?) and the dinner menu features surprisingly sophisticated entrees. But breakfast and lunch are still bargains, and the comfy Americana atmosphere is a nice break from the bright lights of nearby Hollywood Boulevard.

Pink's Hot Dogs. 709 N. La Brea Ave. (at Melrose Ave.). ☎ **323/931-4223.** Hot dogs $2.10. Sun–Thurs 9:30am–2am; Fri–Sat 9:30am–3am. HOT DOGS.

Pink's isn't your usual guidebook recommendation, but then again, this crusty corner stand isn't your usual doggery. The heartburn-inducing chili dogs are so decadent that otherwise-upstanding, health-conscious Angelenos crave them. Bruce Willis reportedly proposed to Demi Moore at the 59-year-old shack that grew around the late Paul Pink's 10¢ wiener cart. Pray the bulldozers stay away from this little nugget of a place.

Roscoe's House of Chicken 'n' Waffles. 1514 N. Gower St. (at Sunset Blvd.). ☎ **323/466-7453.** Main courses $4–$11. No credit cards. Sun–Thurs 9am–midnight; Fri–Sat 9am–4am. AMERICAN.

It sounds like a bad joke: Only chicken and waffle dishes are served here, a rubric that also encompasses eggs and chicken livers. Its close proximity to CBS Television City has turned this simple restaurant into a kind of de facto commissary for the network. A chicken-and-cheese omelet isn't everyone's ideal way to begin the day, but it's de rigueur at Roscoe's. At lunch, few calorie-unconscious diners can resist the chicken smothered in gravy and onions—a house specialty that's served with waffles or grits and biscuits. Large chicken-salad bowls and chicken sandwiches also provide plenty of cluck for the buck. Homemade corn bread, sweet-potato pie, homemade potato salad, and corn on the cob are available as side orders, and wine and beer are sold.

   Roscoe's can also be found at 4907 W. Washington Blvd., at La Brea Avenue (☎ **323/936-3730**), and 5006 W. Pico Blvd. (☎ **323/934-4405**).

Sofi. 8030¾ W. Third St. (between Fairfax Ave. and Crescent Heights Blvd.). ☎ **323/651-0346.** Reservations recommended. Main courses $7–$14. AE, DC, MC, V. Mon–Sat noon– 3pm; daily 5:30–11pm. GREEK.

Look for the simple black awning over the narrow passageway leading from the street to this hidden Aegean treasure. Be sure to ask for a table on the romantic patio amid twinkling lights, and immediately order a plate of the thick, satisfying *tzatziki* (yogurt-cucumber-garlic spread) accompanied by a basket of warm pitas for dipping. Other specialties (recipes courtesy of Sofi's old-world grandmother) include herbed rack of lamb with rice, fried calamari salad, *saganaki* (kasseri cheese flamed with ouzo), and other hearty taverna favorites. Located near the Farmers Market in a popular part of town, Sofi's odd, off-street setting has made it an insiders' secret.

Swingers. 8020 Beverly Blvd. (west of Fairfax Ave.). ☎ **323/653-5858.** Most items less than $8. AE, DISC, MC, V. Sun–Thurs 6am–2am; Fri–Sat 9am–4am. DINER/AMERICAN.

Resurrected from a motel coffee shop so dismal we can't even remember it, Swingers was transformed by a couple of L.A. hipster nightclub owners into a 1990s version of comfy Americana. The interior seems like a slice of the 1950s until you notice the plaid upholstery and Warholesque graphics, which contrast nicely with the retro red-white-and-blue "Swingers" logo adorning *everything*. Guests at the attached Beverly Laurel Motor Hotel chow down alongside body-pierced industry hounds from nearby record companies, while a soundtrack that runs the gamut from punk rock to *Schoolhouse Rock* plays in the background. It's not all attitude here, though—you'll enjoy a menu of high-quality diner favorites spiked with trendy crowd-pleasers: Steel-cut Irish oatmeal, challah French toast, grilled Jamaican jerk chicken, and a nice selection of tofu-enhanced vegetarian dishes are just a few of the eclectic offerings. Sometimes we just "swing" by (ha ha) for a malt or milk shake to go—theirs are among the best in town.

Toi on Sunset. 7505½ Sunset Blvd. (at Gardner). ☎ **323/874-8062.** Reservations accepted for parties of 6 or more. Main courses $6–$11. AE, DISC, MC, V. Daily 11am–4am. THAI.

Because it's open *really* late, Toi has become an instant fave of Hollywood hipsters like Sean Penn and Woody Harrelson, who make post-clubbing excursions to this rock-and-roll eatery a few blocks from the Sunset Strip. After all the hype, we were surprised to find possibly L.A.'s best bargain Thai food, authentically prepared and served in portions so generous the word "enormous" seems inadequate. Menu highlights include hot-and-sour chicken and coconut soup and the house specialty—chicken curry somen, a spicy dish with green curry and mint sauce spooned over thin Japanese rice noodles. Vegetarians will be pleased with the vast selection of meat-free items like *pad kee mao,* rice noodles served spicy with tofu, mint, onions, peppers, and chili. The interior is a noisy amalgam of cultish movie posters, rock memorabilia, and haphazardly placed industrial-issue dinette sets; the plates, flatware, and drinking glasses are cheap coffee-shop issue. In other words, it's all about the food and the scene—neither will disappoint.

Westsiders can opt for **Toi on Wilshire,** 1120 Wilshire Blvd., Santa Monica (☎ 310/394-7804), open daily from 11am to 3am.

DOWNTOWN
EXPENSIVE
Pacific Dining Car. 1310 W. Sixth St. (at Witmer St.). ☎ **213/483-6000.** Reservations recommended. Main courses $20–$42 dinner, $14–$29 lunch, $11–$20 breakfast. AE, CB, DC, MC, V. Daily 24 hours (breakfast 11pm–11am). STEAKS.

It's 4am and you're in the mood for a well-marbled, patiently aged New York steak. Well, even in these health-conscious times, there are still enough nocturnal carnivores in Los Angeles to justify not one, but two all-night Pacific Dining Car steak houses. The flagship location, just a few short blocks from the epicenter of downtown, is dark and clubby, a vestige of an age when diners guiltlessly indulged in fist-sized medaillons of beef. The mesquite-charred steaks are terrific indeed, a cut above the restaurant's other hearty offerings, like lamb and chicken. There's a good wine selection. A separate breakfast menu features egg dishes, salads, and ministeaks.

A second **Pacific Dining Car** is in Santa Monica, at 2700 Wilshire Blvd., a block east of 26th Street (☎ 310/453-4000), but it's only (!) open from 6am to 2am daily.

MODERATE
Cafe Pinot. In the L.A. Public Library, 700 W. Fifth St. (between Grand and Flower sts.). ☎ 213/239-6500. www.patina-pinot.com. Reservations recommended. Main courses $13–$22. AE, DC, DISC, JCB, MC, V. Mon–Fri 11:30am–2:30pm and 5–9pm; Sat–Sun 5–9pm. CALIFORNIA/FRENCH.

A member of superstar-chef Joachim Splichal's L.A. restaurant empire, Cafe Pinot is modeled after the top-ranked Patina, but designed to be less formal and lighter on the palate—and the pocketbook. Situated in the front garden of the L.A. Public Library, Cafe Pinot's tables are mostly on the patio, shaded by umbrellas and the well-landscaped library courtyard. The restaurant's location makes it a natural for downtown business folk; at night, there's a free shuttle to the Music Center.

The best meals come from the giant rotisserie in the kitchen. The tender, mustard-crusted roast chicken is your best bet—unless it's Friday night, when you can order the roast suckling pig with its crackling skin. Other recommended dishes include duck-leg confit, grilled calf's liver, and seared peppered tuna.

Cha Cha Cha. 656 N. Virgil Ave. (at Melrose Ave.), Silver Lake. ☎ **323/664-7723.** Reservations recommended. Main courses $8–$15. AE, DC, DISC, MC, V. Sun–Thurs 8am–10:30pm; Fri–Sat 8am–11:30pm. CARIBBEAN.

Cha Cha Cha serves the West Coast's best Caribbean food in a fun and funky space on the seedy fringe of downtown. The restaurant is a festival of flavors and colors that are both upbeat and offbeat. It's impossible to feel down when you're part of this eclectic hodgepodge of pulsating Caribbean music, wild decor, and kaleidoscopic clutter; still, the intimate dining rooms cater to lively romantics, not obnoxious frat boys. Claustrophobes should choose seats in the airy covered courtyard. The very spicy black-pepper jumbo shrimp gets top marks, as does the paella, a generous mixture of chicken, sausage, and seafood blended with saffron rice. Other Jamaican-, Haitian-, Cuban-, and Puerto Rican–inspired recommendations include jerk pork and mambo gumbo, a zesty soup of okra, shredded chicken, and spices. Hard-core Caribbeanites might visit for breakfast, when the fare ranges from plantain, yucca, onion, and herb omelets to scrambled eggs with fresh tomatillos served on hot-grilled tortillas.

Yang Chow Restaurant. 819 N. Broadway (at Alpine St.), Chinatown. ☎ **213/625-0811.** Reservations recommended on weekends. Main courses $8–$12. AE, MC, V. Daily 11:30am–2:30pm; Sun–Thurs 5–9:30pm, Fri–Sat 5–10:30pm. MANDARIN/SZECHUAN.

Open for more then 30 years, family-operated Yang Chow is one of downtown's more popular Chinese restaurants. It's not the dining room's bland and functional decor that accrues accolades, however; what makes Yang Chow so popular is an interesting menu of seafood specialties complementing well-done Chinese standards. After covering the Mandarin and Szechuan basics—sweet-and-sour pork, shrimp with broccoli, moo shu chicken—the kitchen leaps into high gear, concocting dishes like spicy Dungeness crab; a tangy and hot sautéed squid; and sautéed shellfish with a pungent hoisin-based dipping sauce. The key to having a terrific meal is to first order the house specialty—plump steamed pork dumplings presented on a bed of fresh spinach—and then respectfully ask for recommendations from your server.

INEXPENSIVE

The Original Pantry Cafe. 877 S. Figueroa St. (at Ninth St.). ☎ **213/972-9279.** Main courses $6–$11. No credit cards. Daily 24 hours. AMERICAN.

An L.A. institution if there ever was one, this place has been serving huge portions of comfort food around the clock for more than 60 years. In fact, they don't even have a key to the front door. Owned by L.A. mayor Richard Riordan, the Pantry is especially popular with politicos, who come here for weekday lunches, and conference-goers en route to the nearby L.A. Convention Center. The well-worn restaurant is also a welcoming beacon to clubbers after hours, when downtown becomes a virtual ghost town. A bowl of celery stalks, carrot sticks, and whole radishes greets you at your Formica table, and creamy coleslaw and sourdough bread come free with every meal. Famous for quantity rather than quality, the Pantry serves huge T-bone steaks, densely packed meat loaf, macaroni and cheese, and other American favorites. A typical breakfast (served all day) might consist of a huge stack of hotcakes, a big slab of sweet cured ham, home fries, and coffee.

✪ **Philippe the Original.** 1001 N. Alameda St. (at Ord St.). ☎ **213/628-3781.** Reservations not accepted. Most items under $7. No credit cards. Daily 6am–10pm. SANDWICHES/AMERICAN.

Good old-fashioned value is what this legendary landmark cafeteria is all about. Popular with both South-Central project dwellers and Beverly Hills elite, Philippe's decidedly unspectacular dining room is one of the few places in L.A. where everyone can get along. Philippe claims to have invented the French Dip sandwich at this location in 1908; this remains the most popular menu item. Patrons push trays along the counter and watch while their choice of beef, pork, ham, turkey, or lamb is sliced and layered onto crusty French bread that's been dipped in meat juices. Other menu items include homemade beef stew, chili, and pickled pigs' feet. A hearty breakfast, served daily until 10:30am, is worth attending if only for Philippe's uncommonly good cinnamon-dipped French toast. Beer and wine are available.

THE SAN FERNANDO VALLEY
EXPENSIVE

Pinot Bistro. 12969 Ventura Ave. (west of Coldwater Canyon Ave.), Studio City. ☎ **818/ 990-0500.** www.patina-pinot.com. Reservations required. Main courses $7–$13 lunch, $16–$22 dinner. AE, DC, DISC, MC, V. Mon–Fri 11:30am–2:30pm; Mon–Thurs 6–10pm; Fri 6–10:30pm; Sat 5:30–10:30pm; Sun 5:30–9:30pm. CALIFORNIA/FRENCH.

When the Valley crowd doesn't want to make the drive to Patina, they pack into Pinot Bistro, one of Joachim Splichal's other hugely successful restaurants. The Valley's only great bistro is designed with dark woods, etched glass, and cream-colored walls that scream "trendy French" almost as loudly as the rich, straightforward cooking. The menu, a symphony of California and continental elements, includes a beautiful warm potato tart with smoked whitefish, and baby lobster tails with creamy polenta—both studies in culinary perfection. The most popular dish is chef Octavio Becerra's Frenchified Tuscan bean soup, infused with oven-dried tomatoes and roasted garlic and served over crusty ciabatta bread. The generously portioned main dishes continue the gourmet theme: baby-lobster risotto, braised oxtail with parsley gnocchi, and puff pastry stuffed with bay scallops, Manila clams, and roast duck. The service is good, attentive, and unobtrusive. Many regulars prefer Pinot Bistro at lunch, when a less-expensive menu is served to a more easygoing crowd.

MODERATE

Casa Vega. 13371 Ventura Blvd. (at Fulton Ave.), Sherman Oaks. ☎ **818/788-4868.** Reservations recommended. Main courses $5–$11. AE, CB, DC, MC, V. Mon–Fri 11am–2am; Sat–Sun 4pm–2am. MEXICAN.

We believe that everyone loves a friendly dive, and Casa Vega is one of our local favorites. A faux-weathered adobe exterior conceals red Naugahyde booths lurking amidst fake potted plants and 1960s amateur oil paintings of dark-eyed Mexican children and red cape–waving bullfighters. (The decor achieves critical mass at Christmas, when everything drips with tinsel.) Locals love it for its good, cheap margaritas (order on the rocks), bottomless baskets of hot and salty chips, and traditional combination dinners, which all come with Casa Vega's patented tostada-style dinner salad. Street parking is plentiful, so use the valet only as a last resort.

Miceli's. 3655 Cahuenga Blvd. (east of Lankershim), Los Angeles. ☎ **818/508-1221.** Main courses $7–$12; pizza $9–$15. AE, DC, MC, V. Mon–Thurs 5pm–midnight; Fri 5pm–1am; Sat 4pm–1am; Sun 4–11pm. ITALIAN.

Mostaccioli marinara, lasagna, thin-crust pizza, and eggplant parmigiana are indicative of the Sicilian-style fare at this cavernous, stained glass–windowed Italian restaurant adjacent to Universal City. The wait staff sings show tunes or opera favorites in between serving dinner (and sometimes instead of); make sure you have enough Chianti to get into the spirit of it all. This is a great place for kids, but way too rollicking for romance.

INEXPENSIVE

Du-par's Restaurant & Bakery. 12036 Ventura Blvd. (1 block east of Laurel Canyon Blvd.), Studio City. ☎ **818/766-4437.** www.dupars.com. All items under $10. AE, DC, DISC, MC, V. Sun–Thurs 6am–1am; Fri–Sat 6am–4am. AMERICAN/DINER.

It's been called a "culinary wax museum," the last of a dying breed, the kind of coffee shop Donna Reed took the family to for blue-plate specials. This isn't a trendy new theme place, but the real deal—and that motherly waitress who calls everyone under 60 "hon" has probably been slinging hash here for 20 or 30 years. It's popular among old-timers who made it part of their daily routine decades ago, show-business denizens who eschew the industry watering holes, a new generation that appreciates a tasty, cheap meal . . . well, everyone, really. It's common knowledge that Du-par's makes the best buttermilk pancakes in town, though some prefer the eggy, perfect French toast (extra-crispy around the edges, please). Mouth-watering pies (blueberry cream cheese, coconut cream, and more) line the front display case and can be had for a song.

There's another **Du-par's** in Los Angeles at the Farmers Market, 6333 W. Third St. (☎ **323/933-8446**), but it doesn't stay open as late.

Jerry's Famous Deli. 12655 Ventura Ave. (just east of Coldwater Canyon Ave.), Studio City. ☎ **818/980-4245.** Dinner main courses $9–$14; breakfast $2–$11; sandwiches and salads $4–$12. AE, MC, V. Daily 24 hours. DELI.

Here's a simple yet sizable deli where all the Valley's hipsters go to relieve their late-night munchies. This place probably has one of the largest menus in America—a tome that spans cultures and continents, from Central America to China to New York. From salads to sandwiches to steak-and-seafood platters, everything—including breakfast—is served all day. Jerry's is consistently good at lox and eggs, pastrami sandwiches, potato pancakes, and all the deli staples. It's also an integral part of L.A.'s cultural landscape and a favorite of the show-business types who populate the adjacent foothill neighborhoods. It also has a full bar.

PASADENA & ENVIRONS

During the past decade or so, Pasadena has grown into one of the premier dining destinations for Angelenos in the know. It's now packed with restaurants ranging from elegant art-food dining to casual sidewalk cafes, and Pasadena is no longer anybody's secret.

EXPENSIVE

Parkway Grill. 510 S. Arroyo Pkwy. (at California Blvd.), Pasadena. ☎ **626/795-1001.** Reservations recommended. Main courses $8–$23. AE, CB, DC, MC, V. Mon–Thurs 11:30am–2:30pm and 5:30–11pm, Fri 11:30am–2:30pm and 5pm–midnight, Sat 5pm–midnight, Sun 10am–2pm and 5–11pm. CALIFORNIA ECLECTIC.

This vibrant, quintessentially Southern California restaurant has been one of the L.A. area's top-rated spots since it opened in 1985, quickly gaining a reputation for avant-garde flavor combinations and gourmet pizzas to rival Spago's. Although some critics find many dishes too fussy, others thrill to appetizer innovations like lobster-stuffed cocoa crepes or Dungeness crab cakes with ginger cream and two salsas. The stars of the menu are meat and game from the iron mesquite grill, followed by richly sweet (and substantial) desserts. Located where the old Arroyo Seco Parkway glides into an ordinary city street, the Parkway Grill is within a couple of minutes' drive from Old Pasadena and thoughtfully offers free valet parking.

Pinot Restaurant & Martini Bar. 897 Granite Dr. (behind Lake Ave.), Pasadena. ☎ **626/792-1179.** Reservations recommended. Main courses $14–$20. AE, CB, DC, DISC, MC, V. Mon–Fri 11:30am–2:30pm and 6–10pm; Sat 5:30–10:30pm. CALIFORNIA/FRENCH.

Superstar chef Joachim Splichal is everywhere, opening cousins to his acclaimed Patina in fanciful locations throughout the city. His latest replaces a venerable Pasadena grande dame that for decades was synonymous with dining elegance. The decor is clubby and the crowd tends to be the traditional, jacket-and-tie socialite set that's so common in conservative Pasadena, but the menu is the standard Splichal hybrid of California ingredients and French preparations. With the exception of the spa menu, dishes are rich and saucy, like chicken atop a parsnip-potato pancake with mushroom reduction sauce, or crispy whitefish on cod/garlic-mashed potatoes with buttery cream sauce. Pinot aficionados eagerly end their meal with the profiteroles: three perfect cream puffs drenched in chocolate sauce.

Shiro. 1505 Mission St. (at Fair Oaks Ave.), Pasadena. ☎ **626/799-4774.** Reservations required. Main courses $15–$20. AE, MC, V. Tues–Sun 6pm–closing (usually 9:30–10:30pm). FRANCO-JAPANESE.

Ever since chef/owner Shiro defected from the late, great Cafe Jacoulet, his eponymous restaurant has been consistently ranked at the top of Zagat's lists. Although the menu changes nightly at this minimalist bento box, certain favorites are always among the half-dozen selections. Look first for the whole sizzling catfish in cilantro-tangy ponzu sauce; many devotees insist you should stop reading right there, but there's also Canadian scallops in saffron sauce, and often chicken or lamb charbroiled with inventive herb sauces. Shiro's careful attention to detail extends to desserts like fruit-filled won tons with ginger custard—the perfect sweet follow-up to the savory catfish.

MODERATE

Yujean Kang's Gourmet Chinese Cuisine. 67 N. Raymond Ave. (between Walnut St. and Colorado Blvd.), Pasadena. ☎ **626/585-0855.** Reservations recommended. Main courses $8–$19. AE, MC, V. Daily 11:30am–2:30pm and 5–10pm. CONTEMPORARY CHINESE.

Many Chinese restaurants put the word "gourmet" in their name, but few really mean—or deserve—it. Not so at Yujean Kang's, where Chinese cuisine is taken to an entirely new level. A master of "fusion" cuisine, the eponymous chef/owner snatches bits of techniques and flavors from both China and the West, commingling them in an entirely fresh way. Can you resist such provocative dishes as "Ants on Tree" (beef sautéed with glass noodles in chili and black sesame seeds), or lobster with caviar and fava beans, or Chilean sea bass in passion-fruit sauce? Kang is a wine aficionado and has assembled a magnificent cellar of California, French, and particularly German wines. Try pairing a German Spätlese with tea-smoked duck salad. The red-wrapped dining room is less subtle than the food, but just as elegant.

There's a second **Yujean Kang's** in West Hollywood, at 8826 Melrose Ave. (☎ **310/288-0806**). Even though Kang consulted with a feng shui master on the location and layout of the new space, some Angelenos grumble about the less adventurous menu and higher prices. Others are merely grateful they don't have to trek to Pasadena anymore.

INEXPENSIVE

Goldstein's Bagel Bakery. 86 W. Colorado Blvd. (at Delacey Ave.), Old Pasadena. ☎ **626/79-BAGEL.** Most items under $3. AE, MC, V. Sun–Thurs 5:30am–8:30pm; Fri–Sat 5:30am–10pm. BAKERY/DELI.

Join the locals who storm Goldstein's each morning for freshly baked (in the authentic New York style, they'll assure you) bagels—the reliable plain and onion are as good as exotic honey-oat-raisin or banana-nut. In addition to six flavored cream cheeses, you can choose a bagel sandwich prepared with your choice of every deli ingredient under the sun. Centrally located in the heart of Old Pasadena, this is a good choice for snacks and light meals without interrupting the rhythm of your day.

Old Town Bakery & Restaurant. 166 W. Colorado Blvd. (at Pasadena Ave.), Pasadena. ☎ **626/792-7943.** Main courses $5–$11. DISC, MC, V. Sun–Thurs 7:30am–10pm; Fri–Sat 7:30am–midnight. CONTINENTAL.

Set back from the street in a quaint fountain courtyard, this cheery bakery is an especially popular place to read the morning paper over one of their tasty breakfasts like pumpkin pancakes or zesty omelets. The display counters are packed with cakes, muffins, scones, and other confections, all baked expressly for this shop. The rest of the menu is a mishmash of pastas, salads, and the like, borrowing heavily from Latin and Mediterranean cuisines. A great place to spy on local Pasadenans in their natural habitat.

Pasadena Baking Company/Mi Piace. 25–29 E. Colorado Blvd. (east of Fair Oaks Ave.), Old Pasadena. ☎ **626/796-9966** or 626/795-3131. Main courses $6–$15; bakery items under $3. AE, MC, V. Mon–Thurs 7am–11pm; Fri 7am–midnight; Sat 8am–midnight; Sun 8am–11pm. BAKERY/ITALIAN CAFE.

This little cafe holds just a handful of small tables, which spill out onto the sidewalk during nice weather (which is to say 90% of the time). The large and sweet-smelling selection of fresh pastries, tarts, truffles, cakes, and candies is all proudly displayed. There's also an assortment of fresh breads and a fresh-fruit stand to accompany the breakfast and lunch menu.

Mi Piace is the adjoining casual trattoria, offering the usual pastas and northern Italian dishes done unusually well. The Baking Company commandeers the sidewalk tables at breakfast, but starting around 11:30am, it's not unusual to see Pasadena locals enjoying an espresso with their dogs tethered to a table leg.

5 The Top Attractions

SANTA MONICA & THE BEACHES
✪ **Venice Ocean Front Walk.** On the beach, between Venice Blvd. and Rose Ave.

Venice is one of the world's most engaging bohemias. It's not an exaggeration to say that no visit to L.A. would be complete without a stroll along the famous beach path, an almost surreal assemblage of every L.A. stereotype—and then some. Among stalls and stands selling cheap sunglasses, Mexican blankets, and "herbal ecstasy" pills swirls a carnival of humanity that includes bikini-clad roller skaters, tattooed bikers, muscle-bound pretty boys, panhandling vets, beautiful wanna-bes, and plenty of tourists and gawkers. On any given day, you're bound to come across all kinds of performers: white-faced mimes, breakdancers, buskers, chain-saw jugglers, talking parrots, and an occasional apocalyptic evangelist. Last time we were here, a man stood behind a table and railed against the evils of circumcision: "It's too late for us, guys, but we can save the next generation." But a chubby guy singing "Kokomo"—out of tune but with all his heart—cheered us up.

L.A.'S WESTSIDE & BEVERLY HILLS
J. Paul Getty Museum at the Getty Center. 1200 Getty Center Dr., Los Angeles. ☎ **310/440-7300.** www.getty.edu. Free admission. Tues–Wed 11am–7pm; Thurs–Fri 11am–9pm; Sat–Sun 10am–6pm. Closed major holidays. Advance reservations required. Parking $5.

After 14 years of planning, construction, and endless delays, the über-wealthy Getty Trust finally opened its dramatic, Richard Meier–designed Center overlooking Brentwood. In the months after its front-page-news opening in December 1997, the Getty Center quickly began assuming its place in the L.A. landscape (literally and figuratively) as a cultural cornerstone and international mecca. Headquarters for the Getty Trust's research, education, and conservation concerns, the complex is most frequently visited for the museum galleries displaying collector J. Paul Getty's enormous collection of important art. Always known for antiquities, expanded galleries now allow the display of impressionist paintings, French decorative arts, fine illuminated manuscripts, and contemporary photography and graphic arts that were previously overlooked. A sophisticated system of programmable window louvers allows many outstanding works to be displayed in natural light for the first time in the modern era. One of these is van Gogh's *Irises,* one of the museum's finest holdings. Trivia buffs will enjoy knowing the museum spent $53.9 million to acquire the painting; it's displayed in a complex that cost roughly $1 billion to construct.

Visitors to the center park at the base of the hill and ascend via a cable-driven electric tram. On clear days, the sensation is of being in the clouds, gazing across Los Angeles and the Pacific Ocean (and into a few chic Brentwood backyards). In addition to a casual cafe and several espresso/snack carts, the complex even has a bona fide restaurant on-site, complete with a panoramic view.

At press time, parking reservations were in high demand, particularly on weekends. If you're planning a trip to Los Angeles, make your Getty Center reservations as early as possible. Even visitors without cars—those who arrive by taxi, tour bus, or bicycle—aren't guaranteed admittance during high-volume periods. *Insider tip:* Avoid the crowds by visiting in the late afternoon or evening; the center is open until 9pm Thursdays and Fridays, the nighttime view is breathtaking, and you can finish with a late dinner on the Westside.

Rancho La Brea Tar Pits/George C. Page Museum. 5801 Wilshire Blvd. (east of Fairfax Ave.), Los Angeles. ☎ **323/934-PAGE.** www.tarpits.org. Admission $6 adults, $3.50 seniors 62 and over and students with ID, $2 children 5–12, free for kids 4 and under; free for everyone the first Tues of each month. Museum, Tues–Sun 10am–5pm.

An odorous, murky swamp of congealed oil continuously oozes to the earth's surface in the middle of Los Angeles. No, it's not a low-budget horror-movie set: It's the La Brea Tar Pits, an awesome, primal pool right on Museum Row, where hot tar has been bubbling from the earth for more than 40,000 years. The glistening pools, which look like murky water, have enticed thirsty animals throughout history. Thousands of mammals, birds, amphibians, and insects—many of which are now extinct—mistakenly crawled into the sticky sludge and stayed forever. In 1906, scientists began a systematic removal and classification of entombed specimens, including ground sloths, giant vultures, mastodons, camels, bears, lizards, even prehistoric relatives of today's beloved super-rats. The best finds are on display in the adjacent George C. Page Museum of La Brea Discoveries, where an excellent 15-minute film documenting the recoveries is also shown. Archaeological work is ongoing; you can watch as scientists clean, identify, and catalog new finds in the Paleontology Laboratory.

HOLLYWOOD

Hollywood Sign. At the top of Beachwood Dr., Hollywood.

These 50-foot-high, white sheet-metal letters have come to symbolize both the movie industry and the city itself. Erected in 1923 as an advertisement for a fledgling real-estate development, the full text originally read HOLLYWOODLAND. The recent installation of motion detectors around the sign just made this graffiti tagger's coup a target even more worth boasting about. A thorny hiking trail leads to it from Durand Drive near Beachwood Drive, but the best view is from down below, at the corner of Sunset Boulevard and Bronson Avenue.

Hollywood Walk of Fame. Hollywood Blvd., between Gower St. and La Brea Ave.; and Vine St., between Yucca St. and Sunset Blvd. ☎ **323/469-8311.**

Hollywood Area

NA-0210

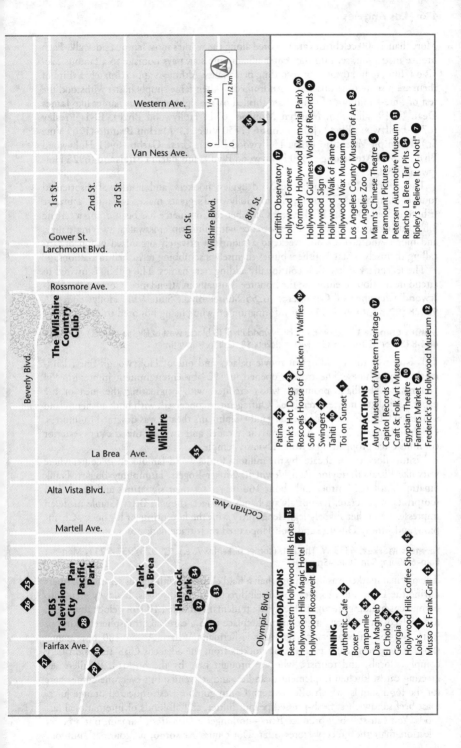

ACCOMMODATIONS
Best Western Hollywood Hills Hotel 15
Hollywood Hills Magic Hotel 6
Hollywood Roosevelt 4

DINING
Authentic Cafe 25
Boxer 26
Campanile 45
Dar Maghreb 2
El Cholo 46
Georgia 24
Hollywood Hills Coffee Shop 45
Lola's 1
Musso & Frank Grill 13
Patina 22
Pink's Hot Dogs 23
Roscoe's House of Chicken 'n' Waffles 19
Sofi 29
Swingers 27
Tahiti 30
Toi on Sunset 3

ATTRACTIONS
Autry Museum of Western Heritage 17
Capitol Records 14
Craft & Folk Art Museum 33
Egyptian Theatre 10
Farmers Market 28
Frederick's of Hollywood Museum 12
Griffith Observatory 17
Hollywood Forever
(formerly Hollywood Memorial Park) 20
Hollywood Guinness World of Records 9
Hollywood Sign 16
Hollywood Walk of Fame 11
Hollywood Wax Museum 8
Los Angeles County Museum of Art 32
Los Angeles Zoo 17
Mann's Chinese Theatre 5
Paramount Pictures 21
Petersen Automotive Museum 31
Rancho La Brea Tar Pits 34
Ripley's "Believe It Or Not!" 7

475

More than 2,500 celebrities are honored along the world's most famous sidewalk. Each bronze medallion, set into the center of a granite star, pays homage to a famous television, film, radio, theater, or recording personality. Although approximately a third of them are just about as obscure as Andromeda—their fame simply hasn't withstood the test of time—millions of visitors are thrilled by the sight of famous names like **James Dean** (1719 Vine St.), **Marilyn Monroe** (6744 Hollywood Blvd.), **Elvis Presley** (6777 Hollywood Blvd.), **John Lennon** (1750 Vine St.), **Marlon Brando** (1765 Vine St.), **Rudolph Valentino** (6164 Hollywood Blvd.), **Greta Garbo** (6901 Hollywood Blvd.), **Louis Armstrong** (7000 Hollywood Blvd.), and **Barbra Streisand** (6925 Hollywood Blvd.).

The sight of bikers, metal heads, druggies, hookers, and hordes of disoriented tourists all treading on memorials to Hollywood's greats makes for quite a bizarre tribute indeed. But the Hollywood Chamber of Commerce has been doing a terrific job sprucing up the pedestrian experience with filmstrip crosswalks, swaying palms, and more. And at least one weekend a month, a privately organized group of fans calling themselves Star Polishers busies themselves scrubbing tarnished medallions.

The legendary sidewalk is continually adding new names. The public is invited to attend dedication ceremonies; the honoree is usually in attendance. Contact the **Hollywood Chamber of Commerce,** 6255 Sunset Blvd., Suite 911, Hollywood, CA 90028 (☎ **323/469-8311**), for information on who's being honored this week.

Mann's Chinese Theatre. 6925 Hollywood Blvd. (3 blocks west of Highland Ave.). ☎ **323/ 464-8111** or 323/461-3331. Movie tickets $8. Call for show times.

This is one of the world's great movie palaces and one of Hollywood's finest landmarks. The Chinese Theatre was opened in 1927 by entertainment impresario Sid Grauman, a brilliant promoter who's credited with originating the idea of the paparazzi-packed movie "premiere." Outrageously conceived, with both authentic and simulated Chinese embellishments, gaudy Grauman's theater was designed to impress. Original Chinese heaven doves top the facade, and two of the theater's exterior columns once propped up a Ming Dynasty temple.

Visitors flock to the theater by the millions for its world-famous entry court, where stars like Elizabeth Taylor, Paul Newman, Ginger Rogers, Humphrey Bogart, Frank Sinatra, Marilyn Monroe, and about 160 others set their signatures and hand- and footprints in concrete. It's not always hands and feet, though: Betty Grable made an impression with her shapely leg, Gene Autry with the hoofprints of his horse, Champion, and Jimmy Durante and Bob Hope used their trademark noses.

Farmers Market. 6333 W. Third St. (corner of Fairfax Ave.). ☎ **323/933-9211.** Mon–Sat 9am–6:30pm; Sun 10am–5pm.

The original market was little more than a field clustered with stands set up by farmers during the Depression so they could sell directly to city dwellers. It slowly grew into permanent buildings recognizable by the trademark shingled 10-story clock tower and has evolved into a sprawling food marketplace with a carnival atmosphere, a kind of "turf" version of San Francisco's surfy Fisherman's Wharf. About 100 restaurants, shops, and grocers cater to a mix of workers from the adjacent CBS Television City complex, locals, and tourists, who are brought here by the busload. Retailers sell greeting cards, kitchen implements, candles, and souvenirs; but everyone comes here for the food stands, which offer oysters, Cajun gumbo, fresh-squeezed orange juice, roast beef sandwiches, fresh-pressed peanut butter, and all kinds of international fast foods. You can still buy produce here—no longer a farm-fresh bargain, but a better selection than the grocery stores offer. Don't miss **Kokomo,** a "gourmet" outdoor coffee shop that has become a power breakfast spot for showbiz types. Red turkey hash and sweet-potato fries are the dishes that keep them coming back.

✪ **Griffith Observatory.** 2800 E. Observatory Rd. (in Griffith Park, at the end of Vermont Ave.). ☎ **323/664-1191,** or 323/663-8171 for the Sky Report, a recorded message on current planet positions and celestial events. www.griffithobservatory.org. Free admission; planetarium show tickets $4 adults, $3 seniors, $2 children. June–Aug daily 12:30–10pm. Sept–May Tues–Fri 2–10pm; Sat–Sun 12:30–10pm.

Made world-famous in the film *Rebel Without a Cause,* Griffith Observatory's bronze domes have been Hollywood Hills landmarks since 1935. Most visitors never actually go inside; they come to this spot on the south slope of Mount Hollywood for unparalleled city views. On warm nights, with the lights twinkling below, this is one of the most romantic places in L.A.

The main dome houses a **planetarium,** where narrated projection shows reveal the stars and planets that are hidden from the naked eye by the city's lights and smog. Mock excursions into space search for extraterrestrial life or examine the causes of earthquakes, moonquakes, and starquakes. Presentations last about an hour. Show times vary, so call for information.

The adjacent **Hall of Science** holds exhibits on galaxies, meteorites, and other cosmic objects, including a telescope trained on the sun, a Foucault pendulum, and earth and moon globes 6 feet in diameter. On clear nights, you can gaze at the heavens through the powerful 12-inch telescope.

DOWNTOWN

El Pueblo de Los Angeles Historic District. Enter on Alameda St. across from Union Station. ☎ **213/628-1274.**

This historic district was built in the 1930s, on the site where the city was founded, as an alternative to the wholesale razing of a particularly unsightly slum. The result is a contrived nostalgic fantasy of the city's beginnings, a kitschy theme park portraying Latino culture in a Disney-esque fashion. Nevertheless, El Pueblo has proven wildly successful, as L.A.'s Latinos have adopted it as an important cultural monument.

El Pueblo is not entirely without authenticity. Some of L.A.'s oldest extant buildings are located here, and the area really does exude the ambiance of Old Mexico. At its core is a Mexican-style marketplace on old Olvera Street. The carnival of sights and sounds is heightened by mariachis, colorful piñatas, and more than occasional folkloric dancing. **Olvera Street,** the district's primary pedestrian thoroughfare, and adjacent Main Street are home to about two-dozen 19th-century buildings; one houses an authentic Mexican restaurant, **La Golondrina.** Stop in at the **Visitor Center,** 622 N. Main St. (☎ 213/628-1274), open Monday through Saturday from 10am to 3pm. Don't miss the **Avila Adobe,** at E-10 Olvera St. (open Monday through Saturday from 10am to 5pm); built in 1818, it's the oldest building in the city.

THE SAN FERNANDO VALLEY

Universal Studios Hollywood. Hollywood Fwy. (Universal Center Dr. or Lankershim Blvd. exits), Universal City. ☎ **818/662-3801.** www.universalstudios.com. Admission $39 adults, $33 seniors 60 and over, $29 children 3–11, free for kids under 3. Parking $7. Summer daily 7am–11pm; rest of the year, daily 9am–7pm.

Believing that filmmaking itself was a bona fide attraction, Universal Studios began offering tours to the public in 1964. The concept worked. Today, Universal is more than just one of the largest movie studios in the world—it's one of the biggest amusement parks.

The main attraction continues to be the **Studio Tour,** a 1-hour guided tram ride around the company's 420 acres. En route, you pass stars' dressing rooms and production offices before visiting famous back-lot sets that include an eerily familiar Old West town, a clean New York City street, and the famous town square from the *Back to the Future* films. Along the way, the tram encounters several staged "disasters," which we won't divulge here lest we ruin the surprise.

Other attractions are more typical of high-tech theme-park fare, but all have a film-oriented slant. On **Back to the Future—The Ride,** you're seated in a mock time-traveling DeLorean and thrust into a fantastic multimedia roller-coasting extravaganza—it's far and away Universal's best ride. The **Waterworld** live-action stunt show is thrilling to watch (and probably more successful than the film that inspired it), while the special-effects showcase, **Jurassic Park—The Ride,** is short in duration but long on dinosaur illusions and computer magic lifted from the Universal blockbuster. The latest thrill is **Terminator 2 3-D,** a virtual adventure utilizing triple-screen technology to impact all the senses. **Totally Nickelodeon** is an interactive live show from the kids' TV network, providing adventure and gallons of green slime.

Universal Studios is a really fun place. But just as in any theme park, lines can be long; the wait for a 5-minute ride can sometimes last more than an hour. In summer, the stifling Valley heat can dog you all day. To avoid the crowds, skip weekends, school vacations, and Japanese holidays.

PASADENA & ENVIRONS

✪ **Huntington Library, Art Collections, and Botanical Gardens.** 1151 Oxford Rd., San Marino. ☎ **626/405-2141.** www.huntington.org. Admission $8.50 adults, $7 seniors 65 and over, $5 students and children 12 and over, free to children under 12; free to all the first Thurs of each month. Tues–Fri noon–4:30pm; Sat–Sun 10:30am–4:30pm. Summer (June–Aug) Tues–Sun 10:30am–4:30pm. Closed major holidays.

The Huntington Library is the jewel in Pasadena's crown. The 207-acre hilltop estate was once home to industrialist and railroad magnate Henry E. Huntington (1850–1927), who bought books on the same massive scale that he acquired businesses. The continually expanding collection includes dozens of Shakespeare's original works, Benjamin Franklin's handwritten autobiography, a Gutenberg Bible from the 1450s, and the earliest known manuscript of Chaucer's *Canterbury Tales.* Although some rarer works are only available to visiting scholars, the library has a regularly changing (and always excellent) exhibit showcasing different items in the collection.

If you prefer canvas to parchment, Huntington also put together a terrific 18th-century British and French art collection. His most celebrated paintings are Gainsborough's *The Blue Boy* and *Pinkie,* a companion piece by Sir Thomas Lawrence depicting the youthful aunt of Elizabeth Barrett Browning. These and other works are displayed in the stately Italianate mansion on the crest of this hillside estate, so you can also get a glimpse of its splendid furnishings.

But it's the botanical gardens that draw most locals to the Huntington. The Japanese Garden is complete with a traditional open-air Japanese house, koi-filled stream, and serene Zen garden; the cactus garden is exotic, the jungle garden intriguing, the lily ponds soothing—and there are plenty of benches scattered about encouraging you to sit and enjoy.

Because the Huntington surprises many with its size and the wealth of activities to choose from, first-timers might want to start by attending one of the regularly scheduled 12-minute introductory slide shows, or taking the more in-depth 1-hour garden tour, given each day at 1pm.

We also recommend that you tailor your visit to include the popular English high tea served Tuesday through Sunday from 1:30 to 3:30pm. The charming tearoom overlooks the Rose Garden (home to 1,000 varieties displayed in chronological order of their breeding), and since the finger sandwiches and desserts are served buffet style, it's a genteel bargain (even for hearty appetites) at $11 per person. Phone ☎ 626/683-8131 for reservations.

6 TV Tapings

Being part of the audience for the taping of a television show might be the quintessential L.A. experience. This is a great way to see Hollywood at work, to find out how your favorite sitcom or talk show is made, and to catch a glimpse of your favorite TV personalities. Timing is important here—remember that most series productions go on hiatus between March and July. And tickets to the top shows, like *Friends* and *Everybody Loves Raymond,* are in greater demand than others, and getting your hands on them usually takes advance planning—and possibly some time waiting in line.

Request tickets as far in advance as possible. Several episodes may be shot on a single day, so you may be required to remain in the theater for up to 4 hours (in addition to the recommended 1-hour early check-in). If you phone at the last moment, you may luck into tickets for your top choice. More likely, however, you'll be given a list of shows that are currently filming, and you won't recognize many of the titles; studios are always taping pilots, few of which end up on the air. But you never know who may be starring in them—look at all the famous faces that have launched new sitcoms in the past couple of years. Tickets are always free, usually limited to two per person, and are distributed on a first-come, first-served basis. Many shows don't admit children under the age of 10; in some cases, no one under the age of 18 is admitted.

In addition to the suppliers listed below, tickets are sometimes given away to the public outside popular tourist sites like Mann's Chinese Theatre in Hollywood and Universal Studios in the Valley; L.A.'s visitor information centers in downtown and Hollywood often have tickets as well (see "Orientation," above). But if you're determined to see a particular show, contact the following sources.

Audiences Unlimited (☎ 818/506-0043 or 818/506-0067) is a good place to start. It distributes tickets for most of the top sitcoms, including *Friends, Saved by the Bell, Caroline in the City, Suddenly Susan, 3rd Rock From The Sun, Everybody Loves Raymond,* and many more. Its service is organized and informative, and fully sanctioned by production companies and networks. ABC, for example, no longer handles ticket distribution directly, but refers all inquiries to Audiences Unlimited. **Television Tickets** (☎ 323/467-4697) distributes tickets for talk and game shows, including the popular *Jeopardy!* You may want to contact the networks directly for information on a specific show, including some whose tickets are not available at the above agencies.

At **ABC,** all ticket inquiries are referred to Audiences Unlimited (see above), but you may want to check out the Web site at **www.abc.com** for a colorful look at the lineup and links to specific shows' sites. For tickets to *Politically Incorrect with Bill Maher,* call the show's ticket line at ☎ 323/852-2655 to make a reservation (taken on a first-come, first-served basis), or order them online at **www.abc.com/pi.**

For **CBS,** 7800 Beverly Blvd., Los Angeles, CA 90036 (☎ 323/852-2458), call to see what's being filmed while you're in town. Tickets for tapings are distributed on a first-come, first-served basis; you can write in advance to reserve them or pick them up directly at the studio up to an hour before taping. Tickets for many CBS sitcoms, including *Everybody Loves Raymond,* are also available from Audiences Unlimited (see

Stargazing in L.A.: Top Spots About Town for Sighting Celebrities

Celebrities pop up everywhere in L.A. If you spend enough time here, you'll surely bump into a few of them. If you're only in the city for a short time, how-ever, it's best to go on the offensive.

Restaurants are your surest bet. Dining out is such popular recreation among Hollywood's elite—along with taking convenient lunch and dinner meetings with agents and lawyers—that you've got to wonder whether frequently sighted folks like Johnny Depp, Nicole Kidman, Bridget Fonda, Nicolas Cage, Brad Pitt, or Cindy Crawford ever actually eat at home. **Matsuhisa, Locanda Veneta, Mimosa, Jozu, Hollywood Hills Cafe, Maple Drive,** and **Lola's** can almost guarantee sightings any night of the week.

The city's stylish hotels can also be good bets—the **Mondrian** draws stars galore to its dining room, Asia de Cuba, as well as the elite Sky Bar; and **Shut-ters's** lobby lounge is rendezvous of choice for famous faces heading to dinner at the hotel's One Pico restaurant. The trendiest clubs and bars—**House of Blues, Viper Room, Sky Bar,** and **The Gate**—are second-best for star sighting, but cover charges can be astronomical and the velvet ropes oppressive. And it's not always Mick and Quentin and Madonna; a recent night on the town only turned up Yanni, Ralph Macchio, and Dr. Ruth.

Often, the best places to see members of the A-list aren't as obvious as a back-alley stage door or the front room of Spago. Shops along Sunset Boulevard, like **Tower Records** and the **Virgin Megastore,** are often star-heavy. **Book Soup,** that browser's paradise across the street from Tower, is usually good for a star or two. A midafternoon stroll along **Melrose Avenue** might also produce a familiar face; likewise the chic European-style shops of **Sunset Plaza.**

Keep your eyes peeled for celebrities—everyone does in L.A.—and you'll more than likely be rewarded. And don't forget to peer through the windows of any Land Rover or Mercedes driving by; even movie stars have errands to run!

above). Tickets for *The Price Is Right* must be requested by mail; allow 4 to 6 weeks. For a virtual visit to CBS's shows, log onto **www.cbs.com**.

For **NBC,** 3000 W. Alameda Ave., Burbank, CA 91523 (☎ **818/840-4444** or 818/840-3537), call to see what's on while you're in L.A. Tickets for NBC tapings, including *The Tonight Show with Jay Leno,* can be obtained in two ways: Pick them up at the NBC ticket counter on the day of the show you want to see (they're distributed on a first-come, first-served basis at the ticket counter off California Ave.); or at least 3 weeks before your visit, send a self-addressed, stamped envelope with your ticket request to the address above. All the NBC shows are represented online at **www.nbc.com**.

7 Exploring the City

ARCHITECTURAL HIGHLIGHTS

Los Angeles is a veritable Disneyland of architecture. The city is home to an amalgam of distinctive styles, from art deco to Spanish revival to coffee-shop kitsch to suburban ranch to postmodern—and much more. Cutting-edge, over-the-top styles that would be out of place in other cities, from the oversize hot dog that is Tail o' the Pup to the mansions lining the streets of Beverly Hills, are perfectly at home in movie city.

SANTA MONICA & THE BEACHES

When you're strolling the historic canals and streets of Venice, be sure to check out **Chiat/Day** offices at 340 Main St. What would otherwise be an unspectacular contemporary office building is made fantastic by a three-story pair of binoculars that frames the entrance to this advertising agency. The sculpture is modeled after a design created by Claes Oldenburg and Coosje van Bruggen.

When you're flying in or out of LAX, be sure to stop for a moment to admire the ✪ **Control Tower and Theme Building.** The spacey *Jetsons*-style "Theme Building," which has always loomed over LAX, has been joined by a brand-new silhouette. The main control tower, designed by local architect Kate Diamond to evoke a stylized palm tree, is tailored to present Southern California in its best light. You can go inside to enjoy the view from the Theme Building's observation deck, or have a space-age cocktail at the Technicolor bachelor pad that is Encounter restaurant (see "Dining," above).

L.A.'S WESTSIDE & BEVERLY HILLS

In addition to **The Argyle** and the **Beverly Hills Hotel** (see "Accommodations," earlier in this chapter), be sure to wind your way through the streets of Beverly Hills off Sunset Boulevard, where you'll see everything the overactive, deep-pocketed imagination can conjure up, from faux Merry-Olde-England hunting lodges to turreted Sleeping Beauty castles.

The **Rudolph M. Schindler House,** 835 N. Kings Rd. (☎ **310/651-1510**), is distinguished by the intermingling of indoors and out, daring modern (1921–22) design, and technological innovations. A protégé of Frank Lloyd Wright and contemporary of Richard Neutra, the Austrian architect was very active in Los Angeles; little survives of his work, and his own home barely escaped the wrecking ball. But Austria's Museum of Applied Arts (MAK) now maintains the restored house as a mini-MAK, and also offers guided tours on weekends.

Postmodern-architecture lovers should check out the **Pacific Design Center** at 8687 Melrose Ave. Designed by Argentinean Cesar Pelli, the bold architecture and overwhelming scale of the center aroused plenty of controversy when it was erected in 1975. Sheathed in gently curving cobalt-blue glass, the seven-story building, housing over 750,000 square feet of wholesale interior-design showrooms, is known to locals as "the blue whale." Nearby on San Vicente Boulevard—on a totally different scale—is the iconic ✪ **Tail o' the Pup.** This is roadside art—and the wiener at its best.

HOLLYWOOD

In addition to the **Griffith Observatory** and **Mann's Chinese Theatre** (see "The Top Attractions," above) and the **Hollywood Roosevelt Hotel** (see "Accommodations," above), check out the old **Egyptian Theatre,** 6712 Hollywood Blvd. Conceived by grandiose Sid Grauman, it's just down the street from Grauman's better-known Chinese Theatre, but remains less altered from its 1922 design based on the then-headline news discovery of hidden treasures in Pharaohs' tombs. It has just undergone a sensitive restoration by American Cinematheque, which now screens rare, classic, and independent films (see "Los Angeles After Dark," later in this chapter, for details).

Farther east is the **Capitol Records Building.** This 12-story tower just north of the legendary intersection of Hollywood and Vine is one of the city's most recognizable buildings. Often, but incorrectly, rumored to have been made to resemble a stack of 45s on a turntable (it kinda does, really), this circular tower is nevertheless unmistakable. Nat "King" Cole, songwriter Johnny Mercer, and other 1950s Capitol artists populate a giant exterior mural.

Stargazing, Part II: The Less-Than-Lively Set

Almost everybody who visits L.A. hopes to see a celebrity—they are, after all, our most common export item. But celebrities usually don't cooperate, failing to gather in readily viewable herds. There's a much, much better alternative, an absolutely guaranteed method of being within 6 feet of your favorite star—cemeteries. Cemeteries are *the* place for star (or at least headstone) gazing: The star is always available, and you're going to get a lot more up close and personal than you probably would to anyone who's actually alive. What follows is a guide to the most fruitful cemeteries, listed in order (more or less) of their friendliness to stargazers.

Weathered Victorian and deco memorials add to the decaying charm of **Hollywood Forever** (formerly Hollywood Memorial Park), 6000 Santa Monica Blvd., Hollywood (☎ **323/469-1181**). Fittingly, there's a terrific view of the Hollywood sign over the graves, as many of the founders of the community rest here. The most notable tenant is Rudolph Valentino, who rests in an interior crypt. Outside are Tyrone Power, Jr.; Douglas Fairbanks, Sr.; Cecil B. DeMille (facing Paramount, his old studio); Alfalfa from *The Little Rascals* (contrary to what you might think, the dog on his grave is not Petey); Hearst mistress Marion Davies; John Huston; and a headstone for Jayne Mansfield (she's really buried in Pennsylvania with her family).

Catholic **Holy Cross Cemetery,** 5835 W. Slauson Ave., Culver City (☎ **310/670-7697**), hands out maps to the stars' graves. In one area, within mere feet of each other, lie Bing Crosby, Bela Lugosi (buried in his Dracula cape), and Sharon Tate; not far away are Rita Hayworth and Jimmy Durante. Also here are "Tin Man" Jack Haley and "Scarecrow" Ray Bolger, Mary Astor, John Ford, and Gloria Morgan Vanderbilt.

The front office at **Hillside Memorial Park,** 6001 Centinela Ave., Baldwin Hills (☎ **310/641-0707**), can provide a guide to this Jewish cemetery, which has an L.A. landmark: the behemoth tomb of Al Jolson, another humble star. His rotunda, complete with a bronze reproduction of Jolson and cascading fountain, is visible from I-405. Also on hand are Jack Benny, Eddie Cantor, and Vic Morrow.

You just know developers get stomach aches looking at **Westwood Memorial Park,** 1218 Glendon Ave., Westwood (☎ **310/474-1579;** the staff can direct

DOWNTOWN

Built in 1928, the 27-story **City Hall,** at 200 N. Spring St., remained the tallest building in the city for more than 30 years. The structure's distinctive ziggurat roof was featured in the film *War of the Worlds,* but is probably best known as the headquarters of the *Daily Planet* in the *Superman* TV series. On a clear day, the top-floor observation deck (open Monday through Friday from 10am to 4pm) offers views of Mount Wilson, 15 miles away.

On West Fifth Street, between Flower Street and Grand Avenue, is one of L.A.'s early architectural achievements, the carefully restored ✪ **Central Library** (the majestic main entrance is actually on Flower St.). Working in the 1920s, architect Bertram G. Goodhue played on the Egyptian motifs and materials popularized by the discovery of King Tut's tomb, combining them with modern concrete block to great effect.

you around), smack-dab in the middle of some of L.A.'s priciest real estate. But it's not going anywhere. Especially when you consider its most famous resident: Marilyn Monroe. It's also got Truman Capote, John Cassavetes, Armand Hammer, Donna Reed, and Natalie Wood.

Forest Lawn Glendale, 1712 S. Glendale Ave. (☎ **323/254-3131**), likes to pretend it has no celebrities. The most prominent of L.A. cemeteries, it's also the most humorless. The place is full of bad art, all part of the continuing vision of founder Hubert Eaton, who thought cemeteries should be happy places. So he banished all those gloomy upright tombstones and monuments in favor of flat, pleasant, character-free, flush-to-the-ground slabs.

Contrary to what you've heard, Walt Disney was *not* frozen and placed under Cinderella's castle at Disneyland. His cremated remains are in a little garden to the left of the Freedom Mausoleum. Turn around, and just behind you are Errol Flynn and Spencer Tracy. In the Freedom Mausoleum are Nat "King" Cole, Chico Marx, Gummo Marx, and Gracie Allen—finally joined by George Burns. In a columbarium near the Mystery of Life is Humphrey Bogart. Unfortunately, some of the best celebs—such as Clark Gable, Carole Lombard, and Jean Harlow—are in the Great Mausoleum, which you often can't get into unless you're visiting a relative.

You'd think a place that encourages people just to visit for fun would understand what the real attraction is. But no—Forest Lawn Glendale won't tell you where any of their illustrious guests are, so don't even bother asking. And this place is immense—and, frankly, dull in comparison to the previous cemeteries, unless you appreciate the kitsch value of the Forest Lawn approach to art.

Forest Lawn Hollywood Hills, 6300 Forest Lawn Dr. (☎ **800/204-3131**), is slightly less anal than the Glendale branch, but the same basic attitude prevails. On the right lawn, beside the wall near the statue of George Washington, is Buster Keaton. In the Courts of Remembrance are Lucille Ball, Charles Laughton, and the not-quite-gaudy-enough tomb of Liberace. Outside, in a vault on the Ascension Road side, is Andy Gibb. Bette Davis's sarcophagus is in front of the wall, to the left of the entrance to the Courts.

—*Mary Susan Herczog*

The 1893 **Bradbury Building,** at South Broadway and Third Street, is Los Angeles's oldest commercial building, and one of the city's most revered architectural landmarks. You've got to go inside to appreciate it. The glass-topped atrium is often used as a movie and TV set; you've seen it in *Chinatown* and *Blade Runner.*

Union Station, at Macy and Alameda streets, is one of the finest examples of California mission–style architecture, built with the opulence and attention to detail that characterize 1930s WPA projects. The cathedral-size, richly paneled ticket lobby and waiting area of this fantastic cream-colored structure stand sadly empty most of the time, but the MTA does use Union Station for Blue Line commuter trains.

For a taste of what downtown's Bunker Hill was like before the bulldozers tore through, visit the residential neighborhood of **Angelino Heights,** near Echo Park. Entire streets are still filled with stately gingerbread Victorian homes; most still enjoy the splendid views which led early L.A.'s elite to build here. The 1300 block of

Downtown Area

ACCOMMODATIONS

Hotel Inter-Continental Los Angeles **16**
Kawada Hotel **20**
Los Angeles Marriott Downtown **12**
New Otani Hotel & Garden **21**
Regal Biltmore **8**
Westin Bonaventure **11**
Wyndham Checkers Hotel
    Los Angeles **7**

DINING

Cafe Pinot **10**
Cha Cha Cha **1**
The Original Pantry Cafe **6**
Pacific Dining Car **3**
Philippe the Original **27**
Yang Chow Restaurant **28**

ATTRACTIONS

Angelino Heights **2**
Angel's Flight **17**
Bradbury Building **19**
California ScienCenter **32**
Central Library **9**
Chinatown **29**
City Hall **14**
El Pueblo de Los Angeles
    Historic District (Olvera Street) **26**
Grand Central Market **18**
Japanese American National Museum **22**
Los Angeles Children's Museum **24**
Museum of Contemporary Art
    Geffen Contemporary at MOCA **23**
    Main Building **15**
Music Center **13**
Natural History Museum of
    Los Angeles County **31**
Staples Center **5**
Union Station **25**
University of Southern
    California (USC) **30**
Watts Towers **4**

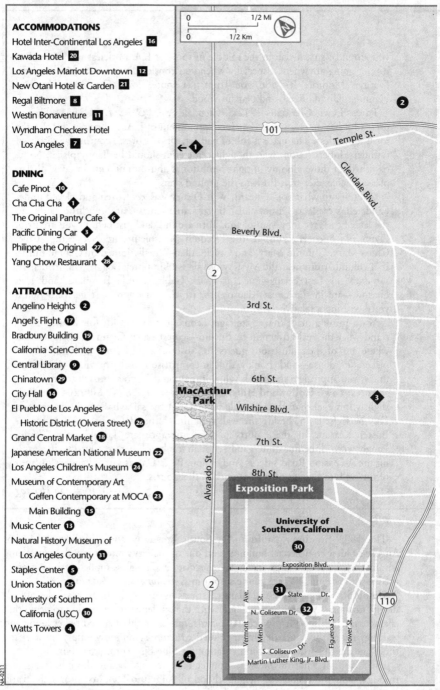

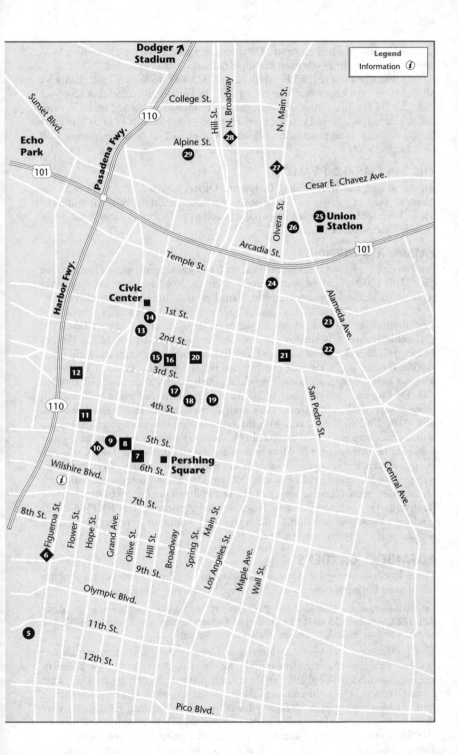

Carroll Avenue is the best preserved. Don't be surprised if a film crew is scouting locations while you're there—these blocks appear often on the silver screen.

The **Watts Towers,** at 1765 E. 107th St. (☎ **323/847-4646**), are more than a bit off the beaten track, but they warrant a visit. The fantastically colorful, 99-foot-tall concrete-and-steel sculptures are ornamented with mosaics of bottles, seashells, cups, plates, generic pottery, and ceramic tiles. They were completed in 1954 by folk artist Simon Rodia, an immigrant Italian tile setter who worked on them for 33 years. Call for a tour schedule.

THE SAN FERNANDO VALLEY

At first glance, the **Walt Disney Corporate Office,** at 500 S. Buena Vista St. (at Alameda Ave.) in Burbank, is just another neoclassical building. But wait a minute: Those aren't Ionic columns holding up the building's pediment . . . they're the Seven Dwarfs—giant-size, of course.

PASADENA & ENVIRONS

For a quick but profound architectural fix, stroll past Pasadena's grandiose and baroque **City Hall,** 100 N. Garfield Ave., 2 blocks north of Colorado; closer inspection will reveal its classical colonnaded courtyard, formal gardens, and spectacular tiled dome.

Architects Charles and Henry Greene built prolifically in Pasadena's Arroyo Seco area (overlooking the Rose Bowl) in the early 1900s, their masterpiece being the ✪**Gamble House,** 4 Westmoreland Place (off Orange Grove, north of the Ventura Freeway). Intricately crafted teakwood interiors, custom furnishings, and California-specific features like a sleeping porch make this a one-stop primer in Craftsman design. One-hour tours are given Thursday through Sunday afternoons; call ☎ **626/793-3334** for more information. Additional elegant Greene & Greene creations (still privately owned) abound 2 blocks away along **Arroyo Terrace,** including address nos. **368, 370, 400, 408, 424,** and **440;** the Gamble House bookshop can give you a walking-tour map and conducts guided neighborhood tours by appointment.

While the Greenes were building retreats for the wealthy, scaled-down Craftsman bungalows were becoming the standard in affordable housing nearby. An exceptionally well-preserved neighborhood of around 900 pre-Depression homes is the Landmark District **Bungalow Heaven,** between Lake and Hill avenues north of Orange Grove Boulevard. The Bungalow Heaven Neighborhood Association (☎ 626/585-2172) conducts a house tour each April, and can give you information on taking a self-guided walking tour of this charming enclave.

BOTANICAL GARDENS

These Pasadena-area gardens are in addition to Pasadena's splendid Huntington Library and Botanical Gardens (see "The Top Attractions," above).

The Arboretum of Los Angeles County. 301 N. Baldwin Ave., Arcadia. ☎ **626/821-3222.** Admission $5 adults, $3 students and seniors 62 and over, $1 children 5–12, free for kids 4 and under. Daily 9am–5pm. Closed Christmas Day.

This horticultural and botanical center was formerly the estate of silver magnate "Lucky" Baldwin—the man responsible for bringing horse racing to Southern California—who lived until 1909 on these lushly planted 127 acres overlooking Santa Anita racetrack. You might recognize Baldwin's red-and-white Queen Anne cottage from the opening sequence of *Fantasy Island* ("de plane, de plane"); the gardens are also a favorite location for movie filming and local weddings. In addition to spectacular flora, the Arboretum boasts a bevy of resident peafowl that seem unafraid of humans—one of the best treats here is being up close when the peacocks, attempting to impress passing hens, unfold their brilliant rainbow plumage. Avid gardeners will want to visit the nurserylike gift shop on the way out.

Descanso Gardens. 1418 Descanso Dr., La Cañada. ☎ **818/952-4400** or 818/952-4401. Admission $5 adults, $3 students and seniors 62 and over, $1 children 5–12, free for kids 4 and under. Daily 9am–4:30pm.

Camellias—evergreen flowering shrubs from China and Japan—were the passion of amateur gardener E. Manchester Boddy, who began planting them here in 1941. Today his Descanso Gardens contain more than 100,000 camellias in over 600 varieties, blooming under a 30-acre canopy of California oak trees. The shrubs now share the limelight with a 5-acre Rose Garden, home to hundreds of varieties. This is really a magical place, with paths and streams that wind through the towering forest, bordering a lake and a bird sanctuary. Each season features different plants: daffodils, azaleas, tulips, and lilacs in the spring; chrysanthemums in the fall; and so on. Monthly art exhibits are held in the garden's hospitality house.

There's also a beautifully landscaped Japanese-style teahouse that serves tea and cookies on Saturdays and Sundays from 11am to 4pm. Free docent-guided walking tours are offered every Sunday at 1pm; guided tram tours, which cost $1.50, run Tuesday through Friday at 1, 2, and 3pm, and on Saturday and Sunday at 11am and 1, 2, and 3pm. Picnicking is allowed in specified areas.

MISSIONS

Two of the 21 missions built by Franciscan missionaries in the late 18th century along the California coast from San Diego to Sonoma are in the Los Angeles area. The valleys in which they're nestled eventually took their names.

Mission San Fernando. 15151 San Fernando Mission Blvd., Mission Hills. ☎ **818/361-0186.** Admission $4 adults, $3 seniors and children 12 and under. Daily 9am–5pm. From I-5, exit at San Fernando Mission Blvd. west and drive 5 blocks to the mission.

Established in 1797, Mission San Fernando in the San Fernando Valley once controlled more than 1½ million acres, employed 1,500 Native Americans, and boasted over 22,000 head of cattle and extensive orchards. The mission complex was destroyed several times, but was always faithfully rebuilt with low buildings surrounding grassy courtyards. The aging church was replaced in the 1940s, and again in the 1970s after a particularly destructive earthquake. The Convento, a 250-foot-long colonnaded structure dating from 1810, is the compound's oldest remaining part. Some of the mission's rooms, including the old library and the private salon of the first bishop of California, have been restored to their late-18th-century appearance. A half-dozen padres and hundreds of Shoshone Indians are buried in the adjacent cemetery.

Mission San Gabriel Arcangel. 537 W. Mission Dr., San Gabriel. ☎ **626/457-3048.** Admission $4 adults, $1 children 6–12 years, free for kids 5 and under. Daily 9am–5pm. Closed Good Friday, Easter, Thanksgiving Day, and Christmas Day.

Founded in 1771, Mission San Gabriel Arcangel still retains its original facade, notable for its high oblong windows and large capped buttresses that are said to have been influenced by the cathedral in Cordova, Spain. The mission's self-contained compound encompasses an aqueduct, a cemetery, a tannery, and a working winery. In the church stands a copper font with the dubious distinction of being the first one used to baptize a native Californian. The most notable contents of the mission's museum are Native American paintings depicting the Stations of the Cross, painted on sailcloth, with colors made from crushed desert-flower petals. The mission is about 15 minutes south of Pasadena.

MUSEUMS & GALLERIES
SANTA MONICA & THE BEACHES
Museum of Flying. Santa Monica Airport, 2772 McDonnell Douglas Loop N., Santa Monica. ☎ **310/392-8822.** www.mof.org/mof. Admission $7 adults, $5 seniors, $3 children under 16. Wed–Sun 10am–5pm.

Once headquarters of the McDonnell Douglas corporation, the Santa Monica Airport is the birthplace of the DC-3 and other pioneers of commercial aviation. The museum celebrates this bit of local history with 24 authentic aircraft displays and some interactive exhibits. In addition to antique Spitfires and Sopwith Camels, there's a new kid-oriented learning area, where hands-on exhibits detail airplane parts, pilot procedures, and the properties of air and aircraft design. The shop is full of scale models of World War II birds; the coffee-table book *The Best of the Past* beautifully illustrates 50 years of aviation history.

L.A.'s WESTSIDE & BEVERLY HILLS
Museum of Tolerance. 9786 W. Pico Blvd. (at Roxbury Dr.). ☎ **310/553-8403.** www.wiesenthal.com. Admission $8.50 adults, $6.50 seniors, $5.50 students, $3.50 children 3–12, free for children 2 and under. Advance purchase recommended. Mon–Thurs 10am–4pm; Fri 10am–3pm (to 1pm Nov–Mar); Sun 11am–5pm (closing hours represent last entry time). Closed many Jewish and secular holidays; call for schedule.

The Museum of Tolerance is designed to expose prejudices and to teach racial and cultural tolerance. It's located in the Simon Wiesenthal Center, an institute founded by the legendary Nazi-hunter. While the Holocaust figures prominently here, this is not just a Jewish museum—it's an academy that broadly campaigns for a live-and-let-live world. Tolerance is an abstract idea that's hard to display, so most of this $50-million museum's exhibits are high tech and conceptual in nature. Fast-paced interactive displays are designed to touch the heart as well as the mind, and engage both serious investigators and the MTV crowd. One of two major museums in America that deal with the Holocaust, the Museum of Tolerance is considered by some to be inferior to its Washington, D.C., counterpart, and visitors can be frustrated by the museum's policy of insisting that you follow a prescribed 2½-hour route through the exhibits.

Museum of Television and Radio. 465 N. Beverly Dr. (at Santa Monica Blvd.), Beverly Hills. ☎ **310/786-1000.** www.mtr.org/camsm. Suggested contribution $6 adults, $4 students and seniors, $3 kids 12 and under. Wed and Fri–Sun noon–5pm; Thurs noon–9pm. Closed New Year's Day, July 4, Thanksgiving Day, and Christmas Day. Valet parking free for 2 hours with validation.

Want to see the Beatles on *The Ed Sullivan Show* (1964) or Edward R. Murrow's examination of Joseph McCarthy (1954), watch Arnold Palmer win the 1958 Masters Tournament, or listen to radio excerpts like FDR's first "Fireside Chat" (1933) and Orson Welles's famous *War of the Worlds* UFO hoax (1938)? All these, plus a gazillion episodes of *The Twilight Zone, I Love Lucy,* and other beloved series, can be viewed within the starkly white walls of architect Richard Meier's neutral, contemporary museum building. Like the ritzy Beverly Hills shopping district that surrounds it, the museum is more flash than substance. Once you gawk at the celebrity and industry-honcho names adorning every hall, room, and miscellaneous area, it becomes quickly apparent that "library" would be a more fitting name for this collection, since the main attractions are requested via sophisticated computer catalogs and viewed in private consoles. Although no one sets out to spend a vacation watching TV, it can be tempting once you start browsing the archives. The West Coast branch of the 20-year-old New York facility succeeds in treating our favorite pastime as a legitimate art form, with the respect history will prove it deserves.

HOLLYWOOD

○ **Autry Museum of Western Heritage.** 4700 Western Heritage Way (in Griffith Park). ☎ **323/667-2000.** www.autry-museum.org. Admission $7.50 adults, $5 seniors 60 and over and students 13–18, $3 children 2–12, free for kids under 2. Tues–Sun 10am–5pm.

If you're under the age of 45, you might not be familiar with Gene Autry, a Texas-born actor who starred in 82 westerns and became known as the "Singing Cowboy." Located north of downtown in Griffith Park, his eponymous museum is one of California's best, a collection of art and artifacts of the European conquest of the West remarkably comprehensive and intelligently displayed. Evocative exhibits illustrate the everyday lives of early pioneers, not only with antique firearms, tools, saddles, and the like, but also with many hands-on exhibits that successfully stir the imagination and the heart. There's footage from Buffalo Bill's Wild West Show, movie clips from the silent days, contemporary films, the works of Wild West artists, and plenty of memorabilia from Autry's own film and TV projects. The "Hall of Merchandising" displays Roy Rogers bedspreads, Hopalong Cassidy radios, and other items from the collective consciousness—and material collections—of baby boomers. Specially curated exhibitions planned for 2000 include the relationship between Chinese immigrants and California's gold rush, plus California's vital citrus agriculture, past and present.

Craft & Folk Art Museum. 5814 Wilshire Blvd. (at Curson Ave.). ☎ **323/937-4230.** Admission $3.50 adults, $2.50 seniors and students, free for children under 12; free to everyone Thurs 5–9pm. Tues, Wed, and Fri noon–5pm; Thurs noon–9pm; Sat 10am–4pm.

This gallery has grown into one of the city's largest, opening in a prominent Museum Row building in 1995. "Craft and folk art" is quite a large rubric that encompasses everything from clothing, tools, religious artifacts, and other everyday objects to wood carvings, papier-mâché, weaving, and metalwork. The museum displays folk objects from around the world, but its strongest collection is masks from India, America, Mexico, Japan, and China. Special exhibitions in 1997 included a retrospective of California woodworker Sam Maloof (whose custom-made chairs grace many a celebrity home) and a collection examining parallels between Italy's rich textile heritage and traditional bread shapes and textures. The museum is well known for its annual International Festival of Masks, a colorful and ethnic celebration held each October in Hancock Park, across the street.

Frederick's of Hollywood Museum. 6608 Hollywood Blvd. ☎ **323/466-8506.** Free admission. Mon–Sat 10am–6pm; Sun noon–5pm.

God bless Frederick Mellinger, inventor of the push-up bra (originally known as the "Rising Star"). Frederick's of Hollywood opened this world-famous purple-and-pink art-deco panty shop in 1947, and dutifully installed a small exhibition saluting all the stars of stage, screen, and television who glamorized lingerie. The collection now includes Madonna's pointy-breasted corset, a pair of Tony Curtis's skivvies, and a Cher-autographed underwire bra (size 32B). Some exhibits were lost during the 1992 L.A. riots, when looters ransacked the exhibit. Mercifully, the bra worn by Milton Berle on his 1950s TV show was saved.

○ **Los Angeles County Museum of Art.** 5905 Wilshire Blvd. ☎ **323/857-6000.** www.lacma.org. Admission $6 adults, $4 students and seniors 62 and over, $1 children 6–17, free for kids 5 and under; regular exhibitions free for everyone the second Tues of each month. Mon–Tues and Thurs noon–8pm; Fri noon–9pm; Sat–Sun 11am–8pm.

This is one of the finest art museums in the United States. The huge complex was designed by three very different architects over a span of 30 years. The architectural fusion can be migraine inducing, but this city landmark is well worth delving into.

The newest wing is the **Japanese Pavilion,** which has exterior walls made of Kalwall, a translucent material that, like shoji screens, permits the entry of soft natural light. Inside is a collection of Japanese Edo paintings that's rivaled only by the holdings of the emperor of Japan.

The **Anderson Building,** the museum's contemporary wing, is home to 20th-century painting and sculpture. Here you'll find works by Matisse, Magritte, and a good number of Dada artists.

The **Ahmanson Building** houses the rest of the museum's permanent collections. Here you'll find everything from 2,000-year-old pre-Columbian Mexican ceramics to 19th-century portraiture to a unique glass collection spanning the centuries. There's also one of the nation's largest holdings of costumes and textiles, and an important Indian and Southeast Asian art collection.

The **Hammer Building** is primarily used for major special-loan exhibitions. Free guided tours covering the museum's highlights depart on a regular basis from here.

The museum recently took over the former May Company department store one block away, converting the historic art-deco building into gallery space that, in 1999, housed the spectacular *Van Gogh's Van Goghs* exhibit.

✪ **Petersen Automotive Museum.** 6060 Wilshire Blvd. (at Fairfax Ave.). ☎ **323/ 930-CARS.** www.petersen.org. Admission $7 adults, $5 seniors and students, $3 children 5–12, free for kids 4 and under. Tues–Sun 10am–6pm. Parking $4.

When the Petersen opened in 1994, many locals were surprised that it had taken this long for the City of Freeways to salute its most important shaper. Indeed, this museum says more about the city than probably any other in L.A. Named for Robert Petersen, the publisher responsible for *Hot Rod* and *Motor Trend* magazines, the four-story museum displays more than 200 cars and motorcycles, from the historic to the futuristic. Cars on the first floor are depicted chronologically, in period settings. Other floors are devoted to frequently changing shows of race cars, early motorcycles, and famous movie vehicles. Past exhibits have included the Flintstones' fiberglass-and-cotton movie car; "woodies" and surf culture; and a three-wheeled scooter that folds into a Samsonite briefcase, created in competition by a Mazda engineer.

DOWNTOWN

California ScienCenter. 700 State Dr., Exposition Park. ☎ **213/SCIENCE,** or 213/ 744-7400; IMAX theater ☎ 213/744-2014. www.casciencectr.org. Free admission to the museum; IMAX theater, $7 adults, $4.75 ages 18–21, $4 seniors and children. Multi-show discounts available. Parking $5. Daily 10am–5pm. Closed Thanksgiving, Christmas, and New Year's Day.

A $130-million reinvention has turned the former Museum of Science and Industry into Exposition Park's newest attraction. Using high-tech sleight-of-hand, the Center stimulates kids of all ages with questions, answers, and lessons about the world. One of the museum's educational highlights is Tess, a 50-foot animatronic woman whose muscles, bones, organs, and blood vessels are revealed, demonstrating how the body reacts to a variety of external conditions and activities. There are nominal fees to enjoy the science center's more thrilling attractions: a 43-foot high-wire bicycle ride, or the zero-gravity Space Docking Simulator. The newly expanded IMAX theater screens breathtaking surround-sound movies in 2D and 3D thoughout the day until 9pm.

Japanese American National Museum. 369 E. First St. (at Central Ave.). ☎ **213/ 625-0414.** Admission $4 adults, $3 seniors and children 6–17, $2 students; free to all the third Thurs of each month. Tues–Wed and Fri–Sun 10am–5pm; Thurs 10am–8pm.

Located in an architecturally acclaimed modern building in Little Tokyo, this museum is a private nonprofit institute created to document and celebrate the history of the

Japanese in America. Its fantastic permanent exhibition chronicles Japanese life in the U.S., while temporary exhibits highlight distinctive aspects of Japanese-American culture, from the internment camp experience to the lives of Japanese Americans in Hawaii. Don't miss the museum store, which carries everything from hand-fired sake sets to mini Zen gardening kits.

Los Angeles Children's Museum. 310 N. Main St. (at Los Angeles St.). ☎ **213/687-8800.** Admission $5 adults, free for kids under 2. Summer (late June to early Sept) Mon–Fri 11:30am–5pm; Sat–Sun 10am–5pm. Rest of the year, Sat–Sun 10am–5pm.

This thoroughly enchanting museum is a place where children learn by doing. Everyday experiences are demystified by interesting interactive exhibits displayed in a playlike atmosphere. In the Art Studio, kids are encouraged to make finger puppets from a variety of media and shiny rockets out of Mylar. Turn the corner and you're in the unrealistically clean and safe City Street, where kids can sit on a police officer's motorcycle or pretend to drive a bus or a fire truck. Kids (and adults) can see their shadows freeze in the Shadow Box and play with giant foam-filled, Velcro-edged building blocks in Sticky City. Because this is Hollywood, the museum wouldn't be complete without its own recording and TV studios, where kids can become "stars."

Museum of Contemporary Art/Geffen Contemporary at MOCA. 250 S. Grand Ave. and 152 N. Central Ave. ☎ **213/626-6222** or 213/621-2766. Admission $6 adults, $4 seniors and students, free for children 11 and under. Tues–Wed and Fri–Sun 11am–5pm; Thurs 11am–8pm.

MOCA is Los Angeles's only institution exclusively devoted to art from 1940 to the present. Displaying works in a variety of media, it's particularly strong in works by Cy Twombly, Jasper Johns, and Mark Rothko, and shows are often superb. For many experts, MOCA's collections are too spotty to be considered world-class, and the conservative museum board blushes when offered controversial shows (it passed on a Whitney exhibit that included photographs by Robert Mapplethorpe). Nevertheless, we've seen some excellent exhibitions here.

MOCA is one museum housed in two buildings that are close to one another but not within walking distance. The Grand Avenue main building is a contemporary red sandstone structure designed by renowned Japanese architect Arata Isozaki. The museum restaurant, **Patinette** (☎ 213/626-1178), located here, is the casual-dining creation of celebrity chef Joachim Splichal (see Patina in "Dining," above).

The museum's second space, on Central Avenue in Little Tokyo, was the "temporary" Contemporary while the Grand structure was being built, and now houses a superior permanent collection in a fittingly neutral warehouse-type space recently renamed for entertainment mogul and passionate art collector David Geffen. An added feature here is a detailed timeline corresponding to the progression of works. Unless there's a visiting exhibit of great interest at the main museum, we recommend that you start at the Geffen building—where it's also easier to park.

Natural History Museum of Los Angeles County. 900 Exposition Blvd., Exposition Park. ☎ 213/763-3466. www.nhm.org. Admission $8 adults; $5.50 children 13–17, seniors, and students with ID; $2 children 5–12; free for kids 4 and under; free for everyone the first Tues of each month. Mon–Fri 9:30am–5pm; Sat–Sun 10am–5pm. Free docent-led tours offered daily at 1pm.

The "Fighting Dinosaurs"—they're not a high-school football team, but rather the trademark symbol of this massive museum, *Tyrannosaurus rex* and triceratops skeletons poised in a stance so realistic that every kid feels inspired to imitate their *Jurassic Park* bellows. Opened in 1913 in a beautiful columned and domed Spanish Renaissance building, the museum is a 35-hall warehouse of the earth's history, chronicling the planet and its inhabitants from 600 million years ago to the present day. There's a mind-numbing number of exhibits of prehistoric fossils, bird and marine life, rocks and minerals, and North American mammals. The best permanent displays include the world's rarest shark, a walk-through vault of priceless gems, and an insect zoo. Between January and April 2000, kids can learn about robotic engineering from an exhibit of larger-than-life animal robots and hands-on displays.

PASADENA & ENVIRONS

✪ **Norton Simon Museum of Art.** 411 W. Colorado Blvd., Pasadena. ☎ **626/449-6840.** www.nortonsimon.org. Admission $4 adults, $2 students and seniors, free for children 12 and under. Museum, Thurs–Sun noon–6pm; bookshop, Thurs–Sun noon–5:45pm.

Named for a food-packing king and financier who reorganized the failing Pasadena Museum of Modern Art, this has become one of California's most important museums. Comprehensive collections of masterpieces by Degas, Picasso, Rembrandt, and Goya are augmented by sculptures by Henry Moore and Auguste Rodin, including *The Burghers of Calais,* which greets you at the gates. The "Blue Four" collection of works by Kandinsky, Jawlensky, Klee, and Feininger is particularly impressive, as is a superb collection of Southeast Asian sculpture. *Still Life with Lemons, Oranges, and a Rose* (1633), an oil by Francisco de Zurbarán, is one of the museum's most important holdings. One of the most popular pieces is Diego Rivera's *The Flower Vendor/Girl with Lilies.* Architect Frank Gehry recently helped remodel the galleries, just in time for 1999's splendid exhibit of works from artist June Wayne's noted Tamarind Lithography Workshop of the 1960s.

Pacific Asia Museum. 46 N. Los Robles Ave., Pasadena. ☎ **626/449-2742.** www. westmuse.org/pacasiamuseum. Admission $5 adults, $3 students and seniors, free for children under 12; free for everyone on the third Sat of each month. Wed–Sun 10am–5pm.

The most striking aspect of this museum is the building itself. Designed in the 1920s in Chinese Imperial Palace style, it's rivaled in flamboyance only by Mann's Chinese Theatre in Hollywood (see "The Top Attractions," above). Rotating exhibits of Asian art span the centuries, from 100 B.C. to the current day. This manageably sized museum is usually worth a peek, particularly for 2000's showcase exhibit of miniature Chinese ceramics from the collection of the former U.S. Ambassador. Other planned highlights include a showing of Chinese carpets and a sampling of contemporary Asian-American artists throughout California.

PARKS

✪ **Griffith Park.** Entrances along Los Feliz Blvd. at Riverside Dr., Vermont Ave., and Western Ave. ☎ **323/665-5188.** Park and museum, free; zoo, $8.25 adults, $5.25 seniors, $3.25 children 2–12, free for kids under 2. Park, daily 24 hours. Zoo, daily 10am–5pm. Museum, Mon–Fri 10am–4pm; Sat–Sun 10am–5pm.

Mining tycoon Griffith J. Griffith donated these 4,000 acres of Hollywood parkland to the city in 1896. Today, Griffith Park is one of the largest city parks in the U.S. There's a lot to do here, including hiking, horseback riding, golfing, swimming, biking, and picnicking (see "Outdoor Pursuits," below). For a general overview, drive the mountainous loop road that winds from the top of Western Avenue, past Griffith Observatory, and down to Vermont Avenue. For a more extensive foray, turn north at the loop road's midsection, onto Mt. Hollywood Drive. To reach the golf courses or Los Angeles Zoo, take Los Feliz Boulevard to Riverside Drive, which runs along the park's western edge.

L.A.'s medium-sized **Los Angeles Zoo** (see below) is an easy place to tote the kids around. Animal habitats are divided by continent. The best features are the new

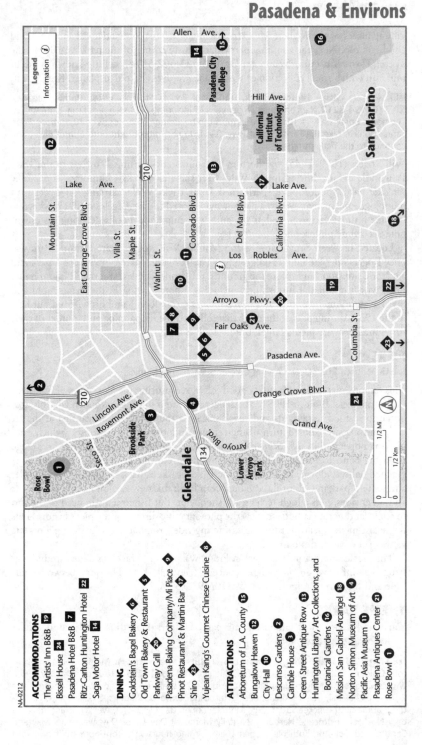

Pasadena & Environs

NA-0212

Legend
Information ⓘ

Allen Ave.

Pasadena City College ⑮ ⑭

⑯

Hill Ave.

California Institute of Technology ⑰

San Marino

⑫

⑬

Lake Ave.

Mountain St.

Lake Ave.

East Orange Grove Blvd.

Villa St.

Maple St.

Walnut St.

Colorado Blvd.

Del Mar Blvd.

California Blvd.

⑱

⑪

Los Robles Ave.

ⓘ

⑩

Arroyo Pkwy.

⑳

⑲

㉒

⑧

⑨

Fair Oaks Ave.

㉑

Columbia St.

⑦

⑤ ⑥

Pasadena Ave.

㉓

②

210

Lincoln Ave.

Rosemont Ave.

④

Orange Grove Blvd.

㉔

Seco St.

Brookside Park

③

Grand Ave.

Glendale

134

Arroyo Blvd.

Lower Arroyo Park

Rose Bowl ①

1/2 Mi

1/2 Km

ACCOMMODATIONS
The Artists' Inn B&B ⑲
Bissell House ㉔
Pasadena Hotel B&B ⑦
Ritz-Carlton Huntington Hotel ㉒
Saga Motor Hotel ⑭

DINING
Goldstein's Bagel Bakery ⑥
Old Town Bakery & Restaurant ⑤
Parkway Grill ⑳
Pasadena Baking Company/Mi Piace ⑨
Pinot Restaurant & Martini Bar ⑰
Shiro ㉓
Yujean Kang's Gourmet Chinese Cuisine ⑧

ATTRACTIONS
Arboretum of L.A. County ⑮
Bungalow Heaven ⑫
City Hall ⑩
Descanso Gardens ②
Gamble House ③
Green Street Antique Row ⑬
Huntington Library, Art Collections, and Botanical Gardens ⑯
Mission San Gabriel Arcangel ⑱
Norton Simon Museum of Art ④
Pacific Asia Museum ⑪
Pasadena Antiques Center ㉑
Rose Bowl ①

Chimpanzees of the Mahale Mountains habitat and the interactive Adventure Island children's zoo. Near the zoo, in a particularly dusty corner of the park, you'll find the **Travel Town Museum,** 5200 Zoo Dr. (☎ **323/662-5874**), a little-known outdoor museum with a small collection of vintage locomotives and old airplanes. Kids love it.

Will Rogers State Historic Park. 1501 Will Rogers State Park Rd., Pacific Palisades. ☎ **310/454-8212.** Park entrance $6 per vehicle, including all passengers. Daily 8am–sunset. The house opens daily at 10am; guided tours can be arranged for groups of 10 or more. From Santa Monica, take the Pacific Coast Hwy. (Calif. 1) north, turn right onto Sunset Blvd., and continue to the park entrance.

Will Rogers (1879–1935) was born in Oklahoma and became a cowboy in the Texas Panhandle before drifting into a Wild West show as a folksy, humorous roper. The "cracker-barrel philosopher" performed lariat tricks while carrying on a deadpan monologue on current events. The showman moved to Los Angeles in 1919, where he become a movie actor as well as the author of numerous books detailing his down-home "cowboy philosophy."

Located between Santa Monica and Malibu, Will Rogers State Historic Park was once Rogers's private ranch and grounds. The 168-acre estate is now both a park and a historic site. You can explore the grounds, the former stables, and the 31-room house filled with the original furnishings, including a porch swing in the living room and many Native American rugs and baskets. Charles Lindbergh and his wife hid out here in the 1930s during part of the craze that followed the kidnapping and murder of their first son. There are picnic tables, but no food is sold.

PIERS

Santa Monica Pier. Ocean Ave. at Colorado Ave., Santa Monica.

This famous pier is doing a pretty good job of recapturing the glory days of Southern California piers. Built in 1909 for passenger and cargo ships, the wooden wharf is now home to seafood restaurants and snack shacks, a touristy Mexican cantina at the far end, and a gaily colored turn-of-the-century indoor wooden carousel (which Paul Newman operated in *The Sting*). Summer evening concerts, which are free and range from big band to Miami-style Latin, draw huge crowds, as does the new fun-zone perched halfway down. Its name, Pacific Park, hearkens back to the granddaddy pier amusement park in California, Pacific Ocean Park; this new version has a roller coaster and other rides, plus a high-tech arcade shoot-out. But fishermen still head to the end to angle, and nostalgia buffs to view the photographic display of the pier's history. This is the last of the great pleasure piers, offering rides, romance, and perfect panoramic views of the bay and mountains.

The pier is about a mile up Ocean Front Walk from Venice; it's a great round-trip stroll. For information on twilight concerts (generally held Thursday between mid-June and the end of August), call ☎ **310/393-7593.**

THEME PARKS

You'll find L.A.'s most famous theme park, **Universal Studios Hollywood,** under "The Top Attractions," above.

Six Flags California (Magic Mountain & Hurricane Harbor). Magic Mountain Pkwy. (off Golden State Fwy. [I-5] north), Valencia. ☎ **661/255-4100** or 818/367-5965. www.sixflags.com. Magic Mountain $36 adults, $20 seniors 55 and over, $18 children age 2 to 48 inches tall, free for kids under 2; Hurricane Harbor $19 adults, $12 seniors, $12 children; adult combo ticket $50. Magic Mountain open daily Mar–Oct, weekends and holidays only Nov–Feb. Hurricane Harbor open daily Memorial Day–Labor Day, weekends May and Sept; closed Oct–Apr. Both parks open 10am, closing hours vary from 6pm–midnight. Take the San Diego Fwy. (I-405) or the Hollywood Fwy. (U.S. 101/170) north; both will eventually merge with I-5; from I-5, take the Magic Mountain Pkwy. exit.

What started as a countrified little amusement park with a couple of relatively tame roller coasters in 1971 has since been transformed by Six Flags into a thrill-a-minute daredevil's paradise. Located about 20 to 30 minutes north of Universal Studios, Magic Mountain is the lesser known of the two attractions, but enormously popular with teenagers and young adults—height-based ride restrictions make the place a big bore for little kids who haven't yet sprouted over 48 inches tall. Likewise those without an iron constitution; rides with names like Ninja, Viper, Colossus, and Psyclone will have your cheeks flapping with the G-force, and queasy expressions are common at the exit. But where else can you experience zero-gravity weightlessness, careen down vertical tracks into relentless hairpin turns, or "race" another train on a side-by-side wooden roller coaster? Some rides are themed to action-film characters (like Superman—The Escape and Batman—The Ride); others are loosely tied to their themed surroundings, like a Far East pagoda or gold-rush mining town. Arcade games and summer-only entertainment (stunt shows, zany carnivals, and parades) round out the park's attractions.

Hurricane Harbor is Six Flags's over-the-top water park. While advertised as a companion to Magic Mountain, you really can't see both in one day—combo tickets allow you to return within a year's time. Bring your own swimsuit; the park has changing rooms with showers and lockers. Like Magic Mountain, areas have themes like a tropical lagoon or African river (complete with ancient temple ruins). The primary activities are swimming, water slides, rafting, volleyball, and lounging; many areas are designed especially for the "little buccaneer."

TOURIST TRAPS

You've heard of all of the following attractions, of course, but you should know exactly what you're in for before you part with your dollars.

Hollywood Guinness World of Records. 6746 Hollywood Blvd., Hollywood. ☎ 323/463-6433. Admission $8.95 adults, $7.50 seniors, $6.95 children 6–11. Sun–Thurs 10am–midnight; Fri–Sat 10am–2am.

Scale models, photographs, and push-button displays of the world's fattest man, biggest plant, smallest woman, fastest animal, and other superlatives don't make for a superlative experience.

The Hollywood Wax Museum. 6767 Hollywood Blvd., Hollywood. ☎ 323/462-8860. Admission $8.95 adults, $7.50 seniors, $6.95 children 6–12, free for kids 5 and under. Sun–Thurs 10am–midnight; Fri–Sat 10am–2am.

Cast in the Madame Tussaud mold, the Hollywood Wax Museum features dozens of lifelike figures of famous movie stars and events. The "museum" is not great, but it can be good for a cheeky laugh or two. A Chamber of Horrors exhibit includes the coffin used in *The Raven*, as well as a diorama from the Vincent Price classic *The House of Wax*. The Movie Awards Theatre exhibit is a short film highlighting Academy Award presentations from the last 4 decades.

Ripley's "Believe It Or Not!" 6780 Hollywood Blvd, Hollywood. ☎ 323/466-6335. Admission $9.95 adults, $8.95 students and seniors, $6.95 children 5–12.

Believe it or not, this amazing and silly "museum" is still open. A bizarre collection of wax figures, photos, and models depicts unnatural oddities from Robert Leroy Ripley's infamous arsenal. Our favorites include the skeleton of a two-headed baby, a statue of Marilyn Monroe sculpted with shredded money, and a portrait of John Wayne made from laundry lint.

THE ZOO

Los Angeles Zoo. Zoo Drive, Griffith Park. ☎ **323/664-6400.** www.lazoo.org. Admission $8.25 adults, $5.25 seniors 65 and over, $3.25 kids 2-12, free to children under 2. Discount for AAA members. Daily 10am–5pm. Closed Christmas Day. Free parking.

Nestled in the foothills of Griffith Park and sharing a parking lot with the Autry Museum (see above), the L.A. Zoo has been welcoming visitors and busloads of school kids since 1966. In 1982, the zoo welcomed a display of cuddly koalas, still one of the biggest attractions, and Chinese pandas, which stayed for only three months during the 1984 Olympics. While mature shade trees now help cool the once-barren grounds, and new habitats are light-years ahead of the cruel concrete roundhouses originally used to exhibit animals, there are still some depressing remnants of the humble old zoo—like a polar bear whose enclosure looks as much like the Arctic as the average suburban swimming pool. Stick with the newer, more humane and authentic exhibits, like the interactive and educational Adventure Island (promoted as the Children's Zoo, it's actually just as cool for grown-ups) and the new Chimpanzees of the Mahale Mountains habitat. Renowned in zoo circles for the successful breeding and releasing of California condors, the zoo occasionally has some of the majestic and endangered birds of prey on exhibit.

8 Organized Tours

STUDIO TOURS

NBC Studios. 3000 W. Alameda Ave., Burbank. ☎ **818/840-3537.** Tours $6 adults, $5.50 seniors, $3.75 children 6–12. Mon–Fri 9am–3pm.

According to a security guard, John Wayne and Redd Foxx once got into a fight here after Wayne refused to ride in the same limousine as Foxx, who called the movie star a "redneck." Well, your NBC experience will probably be a bit more docile than that. The guided 1-hour tour includes a behind-the-scenes look at *The Tonight Show with Jay Leno* set, wardrobe, makeup, and set-building departments, and several sound studios. The tour includes some cool video demonstrations of high-tech special effects.

Paramount Pictures. 5555 Melrose Ave., Hollywood. ☎ **323/956-1777.** Tours $15 per person. Mon–Fri 9am–2pm.

Paramount's 2-hour walking tour around its Hollywood headquarters is both a historical ode to filmmaking and a real-life look at a working studio. Tours depart hourly; the itinerary varies, depending on what productions are in progress. Visits might include a walk through the soundstages of TV shows or feature films, though you can't enter while taping is taking place. Cameras, recording equipment, and children under 10 are not allowed.

✪ **Warner Brothers Studios.** Olive Ave. (at Hollywood Way), Burbank. ☎ **818/972-TOUR.** Reservations required 2-4 weeks in advance. Tours $30 per person. Mon–Fri 9am–4pm.

This is the most comprehensive—and the least theme park–like—of the studio tours. The tour takes visitors on a 2-hour informational drive-and-walk jaunt around the studio's faux streets. After a brief introductory film, you'll pile into glorified golf carts and cruise past parking spaces marked CLINT EASTWOOD, MICHAEL DOUGLAS, and SHARON STONE, then walk through active film and television sets. Whether it's an orchestra scoring a film or a TV show being taped or edited, you'll get a glimpse of how it's all done. Stops may include the wardrobe department or the mills where sets are made. Whenever possible, guests visit working sets to watch actors filming actual productions. Children under 8 are not admitted.

SIGHTSEEING TOURS

Oskar J's Tours (☎ 818/501-2217) operates regularly scheduled, panoramic motor-coach tours of the city. Buses (or plush minivans) pick up passengers from major hotels for morning or afternoon tours of Sunset Strip, the movie studios, Farmers Market, Hollywood, homes of the stars, and other attractions. Tours vary in length from 2 to 5 hours and cost $25 to $50. Call for details and to make reservations.

Next Stage Tour Company (☎ 213/939-2688) offers a unique Insomniacs' Tour of L.A., a 3am tour of the predawn city that usually includes trips to the *Los Angeles Times;* the flower, produce, and fish markets; and the top of a skyscraper to watch the sun rise over the city. The fact-filled tour lasts about 6½ hours and includes breakfast. Tours depart twice monthly and cost $47 per person. Phone for information and reservations.

Grave Line Tours (☎ 323/469-4149) is a terrific journey through Hollywood's darker side. You're picked up in a renovated hearse and taken to the murder sites and final residences of the stars. You'll see the Hollywood Boulevard hotel where female impersonator/actor Divine died, the liquor store where John Belushi threw a temper tantrum shortly before his overdose, and more. Tours are $44 per person and last about 2½ hours. They depart at 9:30am daily from the corner of Orchid Street and Hollywood Boulevard, by Mann's Chinese Theatre. Reservations are required.

The ✪ **L.A. Conservancy** (☎ 213/623-2489) conducts a dozen fascinating, information-packed walking tours of historic downtown L.A., seed of today's sprawling metropolis. The most popular is Broadway Theaters, a loving look at movie palaces. Other intriguing ones include Marble Masterpieces, Art Deco, Mecca for Merchants, Terra-Cotta, and tours of the landmark Biltmore Hotel and City Hall. They're usually held on Saturday mornings and cost $5. Call Monday through Friday between 9am and 5pm for exact schedule and information.

In Pasadena, various tours spotlighting architecture or neighborhoods are lots of fun, given this area's history of wealthy estates and ardent preservation. Call **Pasadena Heritage** (☎ 626/793-0617) for a schedule of guided tours, or pick up "Ten Tours of Pasadena," self-guided walking or driving maps available at the **Pasadena Convention and Visitors Bureau,** 171 S. Los Robles Ave. (☎ 626/795-9311).

9 Beaches

Los Angeles County's 72-mile coastline sports over 30 miles of beaches, most of which are operated by the **Department of Beaches & Harbors,** 13837 Fiji Way, Marina del Rey (☎ 310/305-9503). County-run beaches usually charge for parking ($4 to $8). Alcohol, bonfires, and pets are prohibited, so you'll have to leave Fido at home. For recorded surf conditions (and coastal weather forecast), call ☎ 310/457-9701. The following are the county's best beaches, listed from north to south.

EL PESCADOR, LA PIEDRA & EL MATADOR BEACHES   These relatively rugged and isolated beaches front a 2-mile stretch of the Pacific Coast Highway (Calif. 1) between Broad Beach and Decker Canyon roads, about a 10-minute drive from the Malibu Pier. Picturesque coves with unusual rock formations are perfect for sunbathing and picnicking, but swim with caution as there are no lifeguards or other facilities. These beaches can be difficult to find, marked only by small signs on the highway. Visitors are limited by the small number of parking spots atop the bluffs. Descend to the beach via stairs that cling to the cliffs.

✪ **ZUMA BEACH COUNTY PARK**   Jam-packed on warm weekends, L.A. County's largest beach park is located off the Pacific Coast Highway (Calif. 1), a mile

Los Angeles Beaches & Coastal Attractions

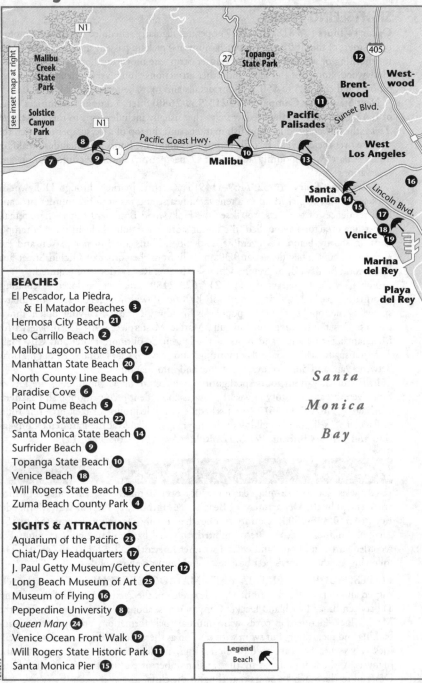

BEACHES

El Pescador, La Piedra,
& El Matador Beaches **3**
Hermosa City Beach **21**
Leo Carrillo Beach **2**
Malibu Lagoon State Beach **7**
Manhattan State Beach **20**
North County Line Beach **1**
Paradise Cove **6**
Point Dume Beach **5**
Redondo State Beach **22**
Santa Monica State Beach **14**
Surfrider Beach **9**
Topanga State Beach **10**
Venice Beach **18**
Will Rogers State Beach **13**
Zuma Beach County Park **4**

SIGHTS & ATTRACTIONS

Aquarium of the Pacific **23**
Chiat/Day Headquarters **17**
J. Paul Getty Museum/Getty Center **12**
Long Beach Museum of Art **25**
Museum of Flying **16**
Pepperdine University **8**
Queen Mary **24**
Venice Ocean Front Walk **19**
Will Rogers State Historic Park **11**
Santa Monica Pier **15**

Legend
Beach

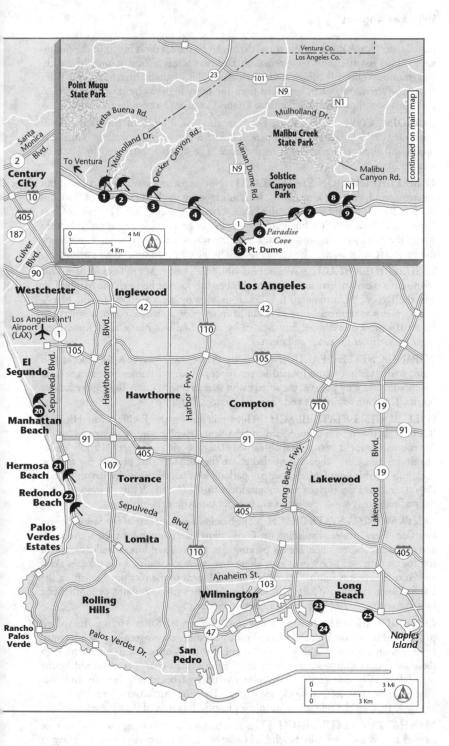

continued on main map

Ventura Co.
Los Angeles Co.

Point Mugu
State Park

Yerba Buena Rd.

Mulholland Dr.

To Ventura

Century
City

Santa
Monica
Blvd.

Culver
Blvd.

Decker Canyon Rd.

Kanan Dume Rd.

Mulholland Dr.

Malibu Creek
State Park

Malibu
Canyon Rd.

Solstice
Canyon
Park

Paradise
Cove

Pt. Dume

0   4 Mi
0   4 Km

Westchester

Inglewood

Los Angeles

Los Angeles Int'l
Airport
(LAX)

El
Segundo

Manhattan
Beach

Hermosa
Beach

Redondo
Beach

Palos
Verdes
Estates

Rancho
Palos
Verde

Sepulveda Blvd.

Hawthorne Blvd.

Hawthorne

Harbor Fwy.

Compton

Long Beach Fwy.

Lakewood

Lakewood Blvd.

Torrance

Sepulveda

Blvd.

Lomita

Rolling
Hills

Palos Verdes Dr.

San
Pedro

Anaheim St.

Wilmington

Long
Beach

Naples
Island

0   3 Mi
0   3 Km

499

past Kanan Dume Road. While it can't claim to be the loveliest beach in the Southland, Zuma has the most comprehensive facilities: plenty of rest rooms, lifeguards, playgrounds, volleyball courts, and snack bars. The southern stretch, toward Point Dume, is Westward Beach, separated from the noisy highway by sandstone cliffs. A trail leads over the point's headlands to Pirate's Cove, once a popular nude beach.

PARADISE COVE This private beach in the 28000 block of the Pacific Coast Highway (Calif. 1) charges $15 to park and $5 per person if you walk in. Changing rooms and showers are included in the price. The beach is often full by noon on weekends.

✪ **MALIBU LAGOON STATE BEACH** Not just a pretty white-sand beach but an estuary and wetlands area as well, Malibu Lagoon is the historic home of the Chumash Indians. The entrance is on the Pacific Coast Highway (Calif. 1) south of Cross Creek Road, and there's a small admission charge. Marine life and shorebirds teem where the creek empties into the sea, and the waves are always mild. The historic Adamson House is here, a showplace of Malibu tile now operating as a museum.

✪ **SURFRIDER BEACH** Without a doubt, L.A.'s best waves roll ashore here. One of the city's most popular surfing spots, this beach is located between the Malibu Pier and the lagoon. In surf lingo, few "locals-only" wave wars are ever fought here—surfing is not as territorial here as it can be in other areas, where out-of-towners can be made to feel unwelcome. Surrounded by all of Malibu's hustle and bustle, don't come to Surfrider for peace and quiet.

TOPANGA STATE BEACH Noise from the highway prevents solitude at this short, narrow strip of sand located where Topanga Canyon Boulevard emerges from the mountains. Why go? Ask the surfers who wait in line to catch Topanga's excellent breaks. There are rest rooms and lifeguard services, but little else.

WILL ROGERS STATE BEACH Three miles along the Pacific Coast Highway (Calif. 1), between Sunset Boulevard and the Santa Monica border, are named for the American humorist whose ranch-turned-state-historic-park (see "Parks" under "Exploring the City," above) is nestled above the palisades that provide the striking backdrop for this popular beach. A pay parking lot extends the entire length of Will Rogers, and facilities include rest rooms, lifeguards, and a snack hut in season. While the surfing is only so-so, the waves are friendly for swimmers of all ages.

SANTA MONICA STATE BEACH The beaches on either side of the Santa Monica Pier (see "Piers" under "Exploring the City," above) are popular for their white sands and easy accessibility. There are big parking lots, eateries, and lots of well-maintained rest rooms. A paved beach path runs along here, allowing you to walk, bike, or skate to Venice and points south. Colorado Boulevard leads to the pier; turn north on the Pacific Coast Highway (Calif. 1) below the coastline's striking bluffs, or south along Ocean Avenue; you'll find parking in both directions.

✪ **VENICE BEACH** Moving south from the city of Santa Monica, the paved pedestrian Promenade becomes Ocean Front Walk and gets progressively weirder until it reaches an apex at Washington Boulevard and the Venice fishing pier. Although there are people who swim and sunbathe, Venice Beach's character is defined by the sea of humanity that gathers here, plus the bevy of boardwalk vendors and old-fashioned "walk-streets" a block away (see "The Top Attractions," earlier in this chapter). Park on the side streets or in the plentiful lots west of Pacific Avenue.

MANHATTAN STATE BEACH The Beach Boys used to hang out (and surf, of course) at this wide, friendly beach backed by beautiful ocean-view homes. Plenty of parking on 36 blocks of side streets (between Rosecrans Avenue and the Hermosa

Beach border) draws weekend crowds from the L.A. area. Manhattan has some of the best surfing around, along with rest rooms, lifeguards, and volleyball courts. Manhattan Beach Boulevard leads west to the fishing pier and adjacent seafood restaurants.

✪ **HERMOSA CITY BEACH**   A very, very wide white-sand beach with tons to recommend it, Hermosa extends to either side of the pier and includes "The Strand," a pedestrian lane that runs its entire length. Main access is at the foot of Pier Avenue, which itself is lined with interesting shops. There's plenty of street parking, rest rooms, lifeguards, volleyball courts, a fishing pier, playgrounds, and good surfing.

REDONDO STATE BEACH   Popular with surfers, bicyclists, and joggers, Redondo's white sand and ice-plant–carpeted dunes are just south of tiny King Harbor, along "The Esplanade" (South Esplanade Dr.). Get here via the Pacific Coast Highway (Calif. 1) or Torrance Boulevard. Facilities include rest rooms, lifeguards, and volleyball courts.

10 Outdoor Pursuits

BICYCLING   L.A. is great for biking. If you're into distance pedaling, you can do no better than the flat, 22-mile paved **Ocean Front Walk** that runs along the sand from Pacific Palisades in the north to Torrance in the south. The path attracts all levels of riders, so it gets pretty busy on weekends. For information on this and other city bike routes, phone the **Metropolitan Transportation Authority** (☎ 213/244-6539).

The best place to mountain-bike is along the trails of **Malibu Creek State Park** (☎ 800/533-7275 or 818/880-0350), in the Santa Monica Mountains between Malibu and the San Fernando Valley. Fifteen miles of trails rise to a maximum of 3,000 feet and are appropriate for intermediate to advanced bikers. Pick up a trail map at the park entrance, 4 miles south of U.S. 101 off Las Virgenes Road, just north of Mulholland Highway. Park admission is $5 per car.

Sea Mist Rental, 1619 Ocean Front Walk, Santa Monica (☎ 310/395-7076), rents 10-speed cruisers for $5 per hour and $14 a day; 15-speed mountain bikes rent for $6 per hour and $20 a day.

FISHING   **Marina del Rey Sports Fishing,** 13759 Fiji Way (☎ 310/822-3625), known locally as "Captain Frenchy's," has four deep-sea boats departing daily on half- and full-day ocean fishing trips. Of course, it depends on what's running when you're out, but bass, barracuda, halibut, and yellowtail tuna are the most-common catches on these party boats. Excursions cost $20 to $25, including bait and tackle. Phone for reservations. No permit is required to cast from shore or to drop a line from a pier.

GOLF   Most of the city's public courses are administered by the Department of Recreation and Parks, which follows a complicated registration/reservation system for tee times. While visitors cannot reserve start times in advance, you're welcome to play any of the courses by showing up and getting on the call sheet. Expect to wait for the most popular tee times, but try to use your flexible vacationer status to your advantage by avoiding the early-morning rush.

Of the city's seven 18-hole and three 9-hole courses, you can't get more central than the **Rancho Park Golf Course,** 10460 W. Pico Blvd. (☎ 310/838-7373), located smack-dab in the middle of L.A.'s Westside. The par-71 course has lots of tall trees, but not enough to blot out the towering Century City buildings next door. Rancho also has a 9-hole, par-3 course.

For a genuinely woodsy experience, try one of the three courses inside Griffith Park, northeast of Hollywood (see "Parks," above; ☎ 323/664-1191). All named for presidents, the courses are extremely well maintained, challenging without being frustrating,

Spectator Sports

The **Los Angeles Dodgers** (☎ **213/224-1500**) play at Dodger Stadium, 1000 Elysian Park, near Sunset Boulevard. L.A.'s baseball fans have put up with a lot lately; not since migrating from their former Brooklyn home have the Dodgers been the center of so much controversy. We hope that, by the time you read this, L.A.'s beloved boys of summer will be back on track—check the *L.A. Times* "Sports" section for the latest. The team's slick, interactive Web site (**www.dodgers.com**) offers everything from game schedules to souvenir merchandise online.

Los Angeles has two NBA franchises, the **L.A. Lakers** (☎310/419-3100; www. nba.com/lakers) and the **L.A. Clippers** (☎ 213/745-0400; www.nba.com/ clippers). Beginning in 1999, both teams moved to their new home in downtown L.A., the $300-million **Staples Center,** 1111 S. Figueroa St. (☎ **877/673-6799;** www.staplescenterla.com). Celebrity fans like Jack Nicholson and Dyan Cannon have the best tickets, but this 20,000-seater should have room for you, too.

and (despite some holes alongside I-5) a great way to leave the city behind. Bucolic pleasures abound, particularly on 9-hole **Roosevelt,** on Vermont Avenue across from the Greek Theatre; early-morning wildlife often includes deer, rabbits, skunks, and raccoons (fore!). **Wilson** and **Harding** are each 18 holes and start from the main clubhouse off Riverside Drive, the park's main entrance.

Greens fees on all city courses are $17 Monday through Friday, $22 Saturday, Sunday, and holidays; 9-hole courses charge $8.50 weekdays, $11.50 on weekends and holidays. For details on other city courses, or to contact the starter directly by phone, call the **Department of Recreation and Parks** (☎ 213/485-5566).

The ✪ **Industry Hills Golf Club,** 1 Industry Hills Pkwy., City of Industry (☎ 818/810-4455), has two 18-hole courses designed by William Bell. Together, they encompass eight lakes, 160 bunkers, and long fairways. The **Eisenhower Course,** which consistently ranks among *Golf Digest's* top-25 public courses, has extra-large, undulating greens and the challenge of thick Kikuyu rough. An adjacent driving range is lit for night use. Greens fees (including cart) are $45 Monday through Friday, $60 Saturday and Sunday.

HIKING   The Santa Monica Mountains, a small range that runs only 50 miles from Griffith Park to Point Mugu, on the coast north of Malibu, makes Los Angeles a great place for day hikes. The mountains peak at 3,111 feet and are part of the **Santa Monica Mountains National Recreation Area,** a contiguous conglomeration of 350 public parks and 65,000 acres. Many animals make their homes in this area, including deer, coyote, rabbit, skunk, rattlesnake, fox, hawk, and quail. The hills are also home to almost 1,000 drought-resistant plant species, including live oak and coastal sage.

Santa Ynez Canyon, in Pacific Palisades, is a long and difficult climb that rises steadily for about 3 miles. At the top, hikers are rewarded with fantastic views over the Pacific. Also at the top is Trippet Ranch, a public facility providing water, rest rooms, and picnic tables. From Santa Monica, take the Pacific Coast Highway (Calif. 1) north. Turn right onto Sunset Boulevard, then left onto Palisades Drive. Continue for 2½ miles, turn left onto Verenda de la Montura, and park at the cul-de-sac at the end of the street, where you'll find the trailhead.

Temescal Canyon, in Pacific Palisades, is far easier than the Santa Ynez Trail and, predictably, far more popular with locals. It's one of the quickest routes into the wilderness. Hikes here are anywhere from 1 to 5 miles. From Santa Monica, take the

Pacific Coast Highway (Calif. 1) north; turn right onto Temescal Canyon Road and follow it to the end. Sign in with the gatekeeper, who can also answer your questions.

Will Rogers State Historic Park, Pacific Palisades, is a terrific place for hiking. An intermediate-level hike from the park's entrance ends at Inspiration Point, a plateau from which you can see a good portion of L.A.'s Westside. See "Parks" under "Exploring the City," above, for complete information.

۞Griffith Park (also discussed in "Parks," above) is an urban hiker's paradise. This 100-year-old park used to have dozens of paved roads popular for weekend motorists, but cuts in funding over the years have forced the park to stop maintenance and close them to car traffic. The good news is that they make great hiking routes—safe, easy to follow, and leading to some of the most spectacular city vistas in L.A. The park also has dozens of dirt trails at every endurance level; you can get a map of both paved roads and hiking trails at the ranger center 1 mile inside the Riverside Drive main entrance.

HORSEBACK RIDING The **Los Angeles Equestrian Center,** 480 Riverside Dr., Burbank (☎ **818/840-9066**), rents horses by the hour for western or English riding through Griffith Park's hills. There's a 200-pound weight limit, and children under 12 are not permitted to ride. Horse rentals cost $13 per hour; there's a 2-hour rental maximum. The stables are open Monday through Friday from 8am to 7pm and on Saturday and Sunday from 8am to 4pm.

SKATING The 22-mile-long **Ocean Front Walk** that runs from Pacific Palisades to Torrance is one of the premier skating spots in the country. In-line skating is especially popular, but conventionals are often seen here, too. Roller-skating is allowed just about everywhere bicycling is, but be aware that cyclists have the right-of-way. **Spokes 'n Stuff,** 4175 Admiralty Way, Marina del Rey (☎ **310/306-3332**), is just one of many places to rent wheels near the Venice portion of Ocean Front Walk. Skates cost $5 per hour; kneepads and wrist guards come with every rental.

SURFING Shops near all top surfing beaches in the L.A. area rent boards, including **Zuma Jay Surfboards,** 22775 Pacific Coast Hwy., Malibu (☎ **310/456-8044**). You'll find the shop about a quarter-mile south of the Malibu Pier. Rentals are $20 per day, plus $8 to $10 for wet suits in winter.

TENNIS You'll find mostly hard-surface courts in California. If your hotel doesn't have a court, try the well-maintained, well-lit **Griffith Park Tennis Courts,** on Commonwealth Road just east of Vermont Avenue. Or call the **City of Los Angeles Department of Recreation and Parks** (☎ **213/485-5555**) to make a reservation at a municipal court near you.

11 Shopping

Here's a rundown of the primary shopping areas, along with descriptions of a few of their best stores. For a more complete guide to shopping in Los Angeles, see *Frommer's Los Angeles.*

The sales tax in Los Angeles is 8¼%, but savvy out-of-state shoppers know how to have more expensive items shipped directly home, thereby avoiding the tax.

SANTA MONICA & THE BEACHES

Third Street Promenade. Third St., from Broadway to Wilshire Blvd., Santa Monica.

Packed with chain stores and boutiques as well as dozens of restaurants and a large movie theater, Santa Monica's pedestrians-only section of Third Street is one of the most popular shopping areas in the city. The Promenade bustles on into the evening with a seemingly endless assortment of street performers and shoppers. Stores stay open late (often until 1 or 2am on the weekends) for the movie-going crowds. There's plenty of metered parking in structures on the adjacent streets, so bring lots of quarters!

Highlights include **Hennessey & Ingalls,** 1254 Third Street Promenade (☎ **310/ 458-9074**), a bookstore devoted to art and architecture, from magnificent coffee-table photography books to graphic-arts titles and obscure biographies of artists and art movements; **Midnight Special Bookstore,** 1318 Third Street Promenade (☎ **310/ 393-2923**), a medium-size general bookshop known for its good small-press selection and regular poetry readings; and **Na Na,** 1245 Third Street Promenade (☎ **310/ 394-9690**), a punk-clothing store featuring clunky shoes, knit hats, narrow-striped shirts, and baggy street wear. At **Puzzle Zoo,** 1413 Third Street Promenade (☎ **310/ 393-9201**), voted "Best in L.A." by *Los Angeles* magazine, you'll find the double-sided World's Most Difficult Puzzle, the Puzzle in a Bottle, and collector's serial-numbered Ravensburger series, among others. Booklovers may also want to stop by the local **Barnes & Noble,** 1201 Third Street Promenade (☎ **310/260-9110**), which carries thousands of titles; or **Borders Books & Music,** which has a branch at 330 S. La Cienega Blvd., at Third Street (☎ **310/659-4045**).

Main Street. Between Pico Blvd. and Rose Ave., in Santa Monica & Venice.

Another good strip for strolling, Main Street boasts a healthy combination of mall standards as well as upscale, left-of-center individual boutiques. You'll also find plenty of casually hip cafes and restaurants. The primary strip connecting Santa Monica and Venice, Main Street has a relaxed, beach-community vibe that sets it apart from similar strips. The stores here straddle the fashion fence between upscale trendy and beach-bum edgy.

Highlights include **C. P. Shades,** 2925 Main St. (☎ **310/392-0949**), a San Francisco women's clothier whose loose and comfy cotton and linen line is carried by many department stores and boutiques. **Horizons West,** 2011 Main St., south of Pico Blvd. (☎ **310/392-1122**), sells brand-name surfboards, wet suits, leashes, magazines, waxes, lotions, and everything else you need to catch the perfect wave. Stop in and say hi to Randy, and pick up a free tide table. If you're looking for some truly sophisticated, finely crafted eyewear, friendly **Pepper's Eyeware,** 2904 Main St., between Ashland and Pier streets (☎ **310/392-0633**), is for you. Ask for frames by cutting-edge L.A. designers Bada and Koh Sakai. If you're lucky enough to have perfect vision, consider some stylish shades. Outdoors types will get lost in 5,600-square-foot **Patagonia,** 2936 Main St. (☎ **310/314-1776**), where climbers, surfers, skiers, and hikers can gear up in the functional, colorful duds that put this environmentally friendly firm on the map.

Montana Avenue. Between Seventh and 17th sts., in Santa Monica.

This breezy stretch of slow-traffic Montana is one of our favorite regentrified parts of the city. Okay, so it's gotten a lot more pricey than in the late 1970s, when tailors and Laundromats ruled the roost, but we're just happy the specialty shops still outnumber the chains. Look around and you'll see upscale Moms with strollers and cell phones shopping for designer fashions, country-home decor, and gourmet takeout.

Montana's biggest selling point is that it's still original enough for residents from across town to make a special trip to shop here, seeking out distinctive shops like **Shabby Chic,** 1013 Montana Ave. (☎ **310/394-1975**), a much-copied purveyor of slipcovered sofas and flea-market furnishings. Vintage jewelry buffs keep coming back to **Brenda Cain,** 1211 Montana Ave. (☎ **310/395-1559**), for platinum rings, bracelets, earrings, and brooches from the 1920s, while clotheshorses shop for designer wear at minimalist **Savannah,** 706 Montana Ave. (☎ **310/458-2095**);

ultra-hip **Jill Roberts,** 920 Montana Ave. (☎ **310/260-1966**); and sleekly professional **Weathervane,** 1209 Montana Ave. (☎ **310/393-5344**). Upscale Moms can find tiny fashions at **Real Threads,** 1527 Montana Ave. (☎ **310/393-3175**), and kid-sized bedroom furnishings at **Little Folk Art,** 1120 Montana Ave. (☎ **310/ 576-0909**). For more grown-up style, head to **Ponte Vecchio,** 702 Montana Ave. (☎ **310/394-0989**), for Italian hand-painted dishes and urns, or to **Cinzia,** 1129 Montana Ave. (☎ **310/393-7751**), which features a smattering of both Tuscan and English home accessories. The stylish choice for lunch is **Wolfgang Puck Cafe,** 1323 Montana Ave. (☎ **310/ 393-0290**).

Bergamot Station. 2525 Michigan Ave., Santa Monica. ☎ **310/829-5854.**

Once a station for the Red Car trolley line, the industrial space of Bergamot Station is now home to the **Santa Monica Museum of Art** plus two dozen art galleries, a cafe, a bookstore, and offices. Most of the galleries are closed Monday; the train yard is located at the terminus of Michigan Avenue west of Cloverfield Boulevard.

Exhibits change often and vary widely, ranging from a Julius Shulman black-and-white photo retrospective of L.A.'s Case Study Houses, to a provocative exhibit of Vietnam War propaganda posters from the United States and Vietnam, to whimsical furniture constructed entirely of corrugated cardboard.

A sampling of offerings includes the **Gallery of Functional Art** (☎ 310/ 829-6990), featuring one-of-a-kind and limited-edition furniture, lighting, bathroom fixtures, and other functional art pieces, as well as smaller items like jewelry, flatware, ceramics, and glass. The **Rosamund Felson Gallery** (☎ 310/828-8488) is well known for showcasing L.A.–based contemporary artists; this is a good place to get a taste of current trends. **Track 16 Gallery** (☎ 310/264-4678) has exhibitions that range from pop art to avant-garde inventiveness—make an effort to see what's going on here.

L.A.'S WESTSIDE & BEVERLY HILLS

◐ West Third Street. Between Fairfax Ave. and Robertson Blvd.

You can shop till you drop on this trendy strip, anchored on the east end by the Farmers Market (see "The Top Attractions," above). Many of Melrose Avenue's shops have relocated here, alongside some terrific up-and-comers, several cafes, and the much-lauded restaurant Locanda Veneta (see "Dining," above). "Fun" is more the catchword here than "funky," and the shops (including the vintage-clothing stores) tend a bit more to the refined than do those along Melrose.

The **Cook's Library,** 8373 W. Third St. (☎ 323/655-3141), is where the city's top chefs find both classic and deliciously offbeat cookbooks and other food-oriented tomes. Browsing is welcomed, even encouraged, with tea, tasty treats, and rocking chairs. **Traveler's Bookcase,** 8375 W. Third St. (☎ 323/655-0575), is truly one of the best travel-book shops in the West, stocking a huge selection of guidebooks and travel literature, as well as maps and travel accessories. A quarterly newsletter chronicles the travel adventures of the genial owners, who know firsthand the most helpful items to carry.

There's a lot more to see along this always-growing street, enough to take up several hours. Refuel at **◐Chado Tea Room,** 8422 W. Third St. (☎ 323/655-2056), a temple for tea lovers. Chado is designed with a nod to Paris's renowned Mariage Frères tea purveyor; one wall is lined with nooks whose recognizable brown tins are filled with over 250 different varieties of tea from around the world. Among the choices are 15 kinds of Darjeeling, Indian teas blended with rose petals, and ceremonial Chinese and Japanese blends. You can also get tea meals here, featuring delightful sandwiches and individual pots of any loose tea in the store.

Sunset Strip. Between La Cienega Blvd. and Doheny Dr., West Hollywood.

The monster-size billboards advertising the latest rock god make it clear that this is rock-and-roll territory. So it makes sense that you'll find legendary **Tower Records,** 8801 W. Sunset Blvd. (☎ **310/657-7300**), in the heart of the action. Tower insists that it has L.A.'s largest selection of CDs—over 125,000 titles—despite the Virgin Megastore's contrary claim. Even if Virgin has more, Tower's collection tends to be more interesting and browser friendly. And the shop's enormous blues, jazz, and classical selections are definitely better than the competition's. It's open 365 days a year. At the east end of the strip sits the gigantic **Virgin Megastore,** 8000 Sunset Blvd., at Crescent Heights (☎ **323/650-8666**). Some 100 CD listening posts and an in-store radio station make this megastore a music lover's paradise. Virgin claims to stock 150,000 titles, including an extensive collection of hard-to-find artists.

The "Strip" is lined with trendy restaurants, industry-oriented hotels, and dozens of shops offering outrageous fashions and chunky stage accessories. One anomaly is **Sunset Plaza,** an upscale cluster of Georgian-style shops resembling Beverly Hills at its snootiest. Here's where you'll find **Billy Martin's,** 8605 Sunset Blvd. (☎ **310/ 289-5000**), which was founded by the legendary Yankee manager in 1978. This chic men's western shop—complete with fireplace and leather sofa—stocks hand-forged silver and gold belt buckles, Lucchese and Liberty boots, and stable staples like flannel shirts. **Book Soup,** 8818 Sunset Blvd. (☎ **310/659-3110**), has long been one of L.A.'s most celebrated bookshops, selling both mainstream and small-press books and hosting regular book signings and author nights. A great browsing shop, it has a large selection of show-biz books and an extensive outdoor news- and magazine stand on one side. The **Book Soup Bistro** has an appealing bar, a charming outdoor patio, and an extensive traditional bistro menu catering to hungry intellectuals.

La Brea Avenue. North of Wilshire Blvd.

This is L.A.'s artsiest shopping strip. Anchored by the giant **American Rag, Cie.** alterna-complex, 150 S. La Brea Ave. (☎ **323/935-3157**), La Brea is home to lots of great urban antiques stores dealing in deco, Arts and Crafts, 1950s modern, and the like. You'll also find vintage clothiers, furniture galleries, and other warehouse-size stores, as well as some of the city's hippest restaurants, such as Campanile.

Bargain hunters find flea-market furnishings at **Nick Metropolis,** 100 S. La Brea Ave. (☎ **323/934-3700**), while more upscale seekers of home decor head to **Mortise & Tenon,** 446 S. La Brea Ave. (☎ **323/937-7654**), where handcrafted heavy wood pieces sit next to overstuffed velvet-upholstered sofas and even vintage steel desks. Stuffed to the rafters with hardware and fixtures of the last 100 years, **Liz's Antique Hardware,** 453 S. La Brea Ave. (☎ **323/939-4403**), thoughtfully keeps a canister of wet-wipes at the register—believe us, you'll need one after sifting through bags and crates of doorknobs, latches, finials, and any other home hardware you can imagine needing. Perfect sets of Bakelite drawer pulls and antique ceramic bathroom fixtures are some of the more intriguing items. Be prepared to browse for hours, whether you're redecorating or not!

Although the art of millinery often seems to have gone the way of white afternoon gloves for ladies, inventive ✪**Drea Kadilak,** 463 S. La Brea Ave., at Sixth Street (☎ **323/931-2051**), charms us with her tiny hat shop. Designing in straw, cotton duck, wool felt, and a number of more unusual fabrics, she does her own blocking, will cheerfully take measurements for custom ladies' headwear, is reasonably priced, and gives away signature hatboxes with your purchase.

The **Swell Store,** 126 N. La Brea Ave. (☎ **323/937-2096**), might be single-handedly responsible for bringing back Hush Puppies; it stocks every configuration and shade of these newly hip-again suede retro loafers. There's also a respectable collection of coordinatingly trendy clothing for men and women.

The best place for a snack is Nancy Silverton's **La Brea Bakery,** 624 S. La Brea Ave. (☎ 323/939-6813), which foodies know from gourmet markets and the attached Campanile restaurant (see "Dining," earlier in this chapter).

○ Rodeo Drive and Beverly Hills' Golden Triangle. Between Santa Monica Blvd., Wilshire Blvd., and Crescent Dr.

Everyone knows about Rodeo Drive, the city's most famous shopping street. Couture shops from high fashion's Old Guard are located along these three hallowed blocks, along with plenty of newer high-end labels. And there are two examples of the Beverly Hills version of minimalls, albeit more insular and attractive—the **Rodeo Collection,** 421 N. Rodeo Dr., and **Two Rodeo,** at Wilshire Boulevard. The 16-square-block area surrounding Rodeo Drive is known as the "Golden Triangle." Shops off Rodeo are generally not as name-conscious as those on the strip (you might actually be able to buy something!), but they're nevertheless plenty upscale. Little Santa Monica Boulevard has a particularly colorful line of specialty stores, and Brighton Way is as young and hip as relatively staid Beverly Hills gets.

The big names to look for here are **Giorgio Beverly Hills,** 327 N. Rodeo Dr. (☎ 800/GIORGIO or 310/274-0200); **Gucci,** 347 N. Rodeo Dr. (☎ 310/278-3451); **Hermès,** 343 N. Rodeo Dr. (☎ 310/278-6440); **Louis Vuitton,** 307 N. Rodeo Dr. (☎ 310/859-0457); **Polo/Ralph Lauren,** 444 N. Rodeo Dr. (☎ 310/281-7200); and **Tiffany & Co.,** 210 N. Rodeo Dr. (☎ 310/273-8880). The newest arrival is **Tommy Hilfiger,** 468 N. Rodeo Dr. (☎ 310/888-0132). **Niketown,** at the corner of Wilshire Boulevard and Rodeo Drive (☎ 310/275-9998), is a behemoth shrine to the reigning athletic-gear king.

Beverly Boulevard. From Robertson Blvd. to La Brea Ave.

Although these businesses are too far apart to be considered adjacent, they are representative of the variety you'll find along this stylish street.

Every Picture Tells a Story, 7525 Beverly Blvd., between Fairfax and La Brea avenues (☎ 323/932-6070), a gallery devoted to the art of children's literature, displays antique children's books as well as the works of more than 100 illustrators, including lithos of *Curious George, Eloise,* and *Charlotte's Web.* Whether you're indulging your inner child or introducing your kids to their first "art gallery," you'll also enjoy the story readings and interactive workshops.

Across the street from Cedars-Sinai Medical Center, the **Mysterious Bookshop,** 8763 Beverly Blvd. (☎ 310/659-2959), carries more than 20,000 used, rare, and out-of-print titles in the field of mystery, espionage, detective stories, and thrillers. Author appearances and other special events are regularly hosted.

If you can name more than three tenors, then pleasantly cluttered **Opera Shop of Los Angeles,** 8384 Beverly Blvd., 3 blocks east of La Cienega Boulevard (☎ 323/658-5811), is for you. Everything imaginable with an opera theme is available: musical motif jewelry, stationery, T-shirts, opera glasses (of course!), and tapes, videos, and CDs of your favorite productions.

If you complain that they just don't make 'em like they used to . . . well, they do at **Re-Mix,** 7605½ Beverly Blvd., between Fairfax and La Brea avenues (☎ 323/936-6210). Selling only vintage (1940s to 1970s) but brand-new (as in unworn) shoes for men and women, it's more like a shoe-store museum featuring wing tips, Hush Puppies, Joan Crawford pumps, and 1970s platforms. A rack of unworn vintage socks all display their original tags and stickers, and the prices are downright reasonable. Celebrity hipsters and hep cats from Madonna to Roseanne are often spotted here.

Other vintage wares are found at **Second Time Around Watch Co.,** 8840 Beverly Blvd., west of Robertson Boulevard (☎ **310/271-6615**). The city's best selection of collectible timepieces includes dozens of classic Tiffanys, Cartiers, Piagets, and Rolexes, plus rare pocket watches. Priced for collectors, but a fascinating browse for the Swatch crowd, too.

HOLLYWOOD

Melrose Avenue. Between Fairfax and La Brea aves.

Melrose is showing some wear—some stretches have become downright ugly—but this is still one of the most exciting shopping streets in the country for cutting-edge fashions—and some eye-popping people watching to boot. There are scores of shops selling the latest in clothes, gifts, jewelry, and accessories. Melrose is a playful stroll, dotted with plenty of hip restaurants and funky shops that are sure to shock. Where else could you find green patent-leather cowboy boots, a working 19th-century pocket watch, an inflatable girlfriend, and glow-in-the-dark condoms in the same shopping spree? From east to west, here are some highlights.

Condomania, 7306 Melrose Ave. (☎ **323/933-7865**), is quintessentially 1990s: A vast selection of condoms, lubricants, and kits creatively encourage safe sex. Curious? Check out the Web site at www.condomania.com. **Retail Slut,** 7308 Melrose Ave. (☎ **323/934-1339**), is a famous rock-and-roll shop carrying new clothing and accessories for men and women. The unique designs are for a select crowd (the name says it all), so don't expect to find anything for your next PTA meeting here. **Betsey Johnson Boutique,** 7311 Melrose Ave. (☎ **323/931-4490**), is a favorite among the young and pencil-thin; the New York–based designer has brought her brand of fashion—trendy, cutesy, body-conscious women's wear in colorful prints and faddish fabrics—to L.A. It's also in Santa Monica at 2929 Main St. (☎ **310/452-7911**).

Across the street, **Off the Wall,** 7325 Melrose Ave. (☎ **323/930-1185**), is filled with neon-flashing, bells-and-whistles kitsch collectibles, from vintage Wurlitzer jukeboxes to life-size fiberglass cows. The L.A. branch of a Bay Area hipster hangout, **Wasteland,** 7428 Melrose Ave. (☎ **323/653-3028**), has an enormous steel-sculpted facade. There's a lot of leather, denim, and some classic vintage—but mostly funky 1970s garb, both vintage and contemporary. This ultra-trendy store is packed with the flamboyantly colorful polyester halters and bell-bottoms from the decade some of us would rather forget. More racks of vintage treasures (and trash) are found at **Aardvark's Odd Ark,** 7579 Melrose Ave. (☎ **323/655-6769**), which stocks everything from suits and dresses to neckties, hats, handbags, and jewelry. This place also manages to anticipate some of the hottest new street fashions. There's another Aardvark's at 85 Market St., Venice (☎ **310/392-2996**).

Hollywood Boulevard. Between Gower St. and La Brea Ave.

One of Los Angeles's most famous streets is, for the most part, a sleazy strip. But along the Walk of Fame, between the T-shirt shops and greasy pizza parlors, you'll find some excellent poster shops, souvenir stores, and Hollywood-memorabilia dealers that are worth getting out of your car for—especially if there's a chance of getting your hands on that long-sought-after Ethel Merman autograph or 200 Motels poster.

Some longstanding purveyors of memorabilia include **Book City Collectibles,** 6631 Hollywood Blvd. (☎ **323/466-0120**), which has more than 70,000 color prints of past and present stars available, along with a good selection of autographs from the likes of Lucille Ball ($175), Anthony Hopkins ($35), and Grace Kelly ($750). **Hollywood Book and Poster Company,** 6349 Hollywood Blvd. (☎ **323/465-8764**), has an excellent collection of movie posters (from about $15 each), particularly strong in

Dressing the Part: Where to Find Hollywood's Hand-Me-Downs

Admit it: You've dreamed of being a glamorous movie or TV star—everyone has. Well, you shouldn't expect to be "discovered" during your L.A. vacation, but you *can* live out your fantasy by dressing the part. Costumes from famous movies, TV-show wardrobes, castoffs from celebrity closets—they're easier to find (and more affordable to own) than you might think.

A good place to start is **Star Wares,** 2817 Main St., Santa Monica (☎ **310/ 399-0224**). This deceptively small shop regularly has leftovers from Cher's closet, as well as celebrity-worn apparel from the likes of Winona Ryder, Tom Cruise, and Sarah Jessica Parker. It also stocks movie-production wardrobes and genuine collectors' items. If the $5,000 *Star Trek* uniform or *Independence Day* flight suit you covet is out of your price range, don't worry: You can still pick up some threads from *Pulp Fiction* or *Jurassic Park,* dresses from the closets of Lucille Ball and Greer Garson, or E.T.'s bathrobe, all of which are surprisingly affordable. Many pieces have accompanying photos or movie stills, so you'll know exactly who wore them before you.

That isn't the case, however, at **The Place & Co.,** 8820 S. Sepulveda Blvd., Westchester (☎ **310/645-1539**), where the anonymity of their well-heeled clientele (sellers and buyers) is strictly honored. Here you'll find men's and women's haute couture—always the latest fashions, gently worn—at a fraction of the Rodeo Drive prices. All the designers are here: Bill Blass, Krizia, Donna Karan, Hugo Boss. You may even have seen that Armani suit or Sonia Rykiel gown on an Academy Awards attendee last year!

For sheer volume, you can't beat **It's a Wrap,** 3315 W. Magnolia Blvd., Burbank (☎ **818/567-7366**). Every item here is marked with its place of origin, and the list is staggering: *Melrose Place, Seinfeld, Baywatch, All My Children, Forrest Gump, The Brady Bunch Movie,* and so on. Many of these wardrobes (which include shoes and accessories) aren't outstanding but for their Hollywood origins: Jerry Seinfeld's trademark polo shirts, for instance, are standard mall-issue. Some collectible pieces, like Sylvester Stallone's *Rocky* stars-and-stripes boxers, are framed and on display.

When you're done at It's A Wrap, stop in across the street at **Junk for Joy,** 3314 W. Magnolia Blvd., Burbank (☎ **818/569-4903**). A Hollywood wardrobe coordinator or two will probably be hunting through this wacky little store right beside you. The emphasis here is on funky items more suitable as costumes than everyday wear (the store is mobbed each year around Halloween). Always strong in 1970s polyester shirts and tacky slacks, it's not surprising that costumers from the *Brady Bunch* movies and *The People vs. Larry Flynt* came here first.

The grande dame of all wardrobe and costume outlets is **Western Costume,** 11041 Vanowen St., North Hollywood (☎ **818/760-0900**). In business since 1912, it still designs and executes entire wardrobes for major motion pictures; when filming is finished, the garments are added to its staggering rental inventory. This place is perhaps best known for outfitting Vivien Leigh in *Gone with the Wind;* several of Scarlett O'Hara's memorable gowns were even available for rent until they were auctioned off at a charity event. Western maintains an outlet store on the premises, where damaged garments are sold at rock-bottom (nothing over $15) prices. If you're willing to do some rescue work, there are definitely some hidden treasures here.

horror and exploitation flicks. Photocopies of about 5,000 movie and television scripts are also sold for $10 to $15 each, and the store carries music posters and photos, too. **The Last Moving Picture Company,** 6307 Hollywood Blvd., near Vine Street (☎ 323/467-0838), sells movie-related merchandise of all kinds, including stills from 1950s movies and authentic production notes from a variety of films.

SILVER LAKE & LOS FELIZ

Located at the eastern end of Hollywood, and technically part of just plain Los Angeles, these two communities have been steadily rising on the hipness meter. Silver Lake, named for the man-made Silver Lake reservoir at its center, is a bohemian community of artists and ethnic families that's popular for nightclubbing and bar-hopping. Los Feliz is northwest of Silver Lake, centered on Vermont and Hillhurst avenues between Sunset Boulevard and Los Feliz Boulevard; it's slightly tamer, and filled with 1920s and 1930s buildings. You'll find tons of unique businesses of all sorts, including artsy boutiques, music stores, and furniture dealers that have inspired some to compare the area to New York's SoHo.

Because so many alternative bands call Silver Lake home, it's not surprising to find cutting-edge music stores around every corner. A neighborhood mainstay is **Rockaway Records,** 2395 Glendale Blvd., south of Silver Lake Boulevard (☎ 323/664-3232), with tons of used CDs, collectible discs, and new releases. **Destroy All Music,** 3818 Sunset Blvd., south of Santa Monica Boulevard (☎ 323/663-9300), covers all bases, from hard-core to ska, indie to lo-fi.

Vintage clothing is another big draw in these parts: The most reliable yet eclectic selections to browse through are at **Ozzie Dots,** 4637 Hollywood Blvd., west of Hillhurst (☎ 323/663-2867); **Pull My Daisy,** 3908 Sunset Blvd., at Griffith Park Boulevard (☎ 323/663-0608); and **Squaresville,** 1800 N. Vermont Ave., south of Franklin (☎ 323/669-8464).

Hollywood set designers know to prowl the vintage furniture stores of Silver Lake. The best for mid-century modern gems are **Edna Hart,** 2945 Rowena Ave., south of Hyperion (☎ 323/661-4070); and **Rubbish,** 1630 Silver Lake Blvd., north of Sunset (☎ 323/661-5575). Plastic decorative items, from the 1950s on, reign at the aptly named **Plastica,** 4685 Hollywood Blvd., east of Hillhurst (☎ 323/644-1212), while ethnic and international furniture, gifts, and clothing blend in the browsers' paradise of **Sol e Luna,** 2910 Rowena Ave., south of Hyperion (☎ 323/664-7254). One not-to-be-missed neighborhood highlight is the wacky and eclectic **Soap Plant/Wacko/ La Luz de Jesus Art Gallery,** 4633 Hollywood Blvd., west of Hillhurst (☎ 323/663-0122), a three-in-one business with candles, art books, erotic toys, soap and bath items, and a large selection of lava lamps.

DOWNTOWN

Since the late, lamented grande dame department store Bullock's closed in 1993 (its deco masterpiece salons were rescued to house the Southwestern Law School's library), downtown has become even less of a shopping destination than ever. But although many of the once-splendid streets are lined with cut-rate luggage and cheap electronics storefronts, shopping downtown can be a rewarding if gritty experience for the adventuresome.

Savvy Angelenos still go for bargains in the garment and fabric districts, florists and bargain hunters arrive at the vast Flower Mart before dawn for the city's best selection of fresh blooms, and families of all ethnicities stroll the ✪**Grand Central Market,** 317 S. Broadway, between Third and Fourth streets (☎ 213/624-2378). Opened in 1917, this bustling market has watched the face of downtown L.A. change while changing little itself. Today, it serves Latino families, enterprising restaurateurs, and home cooks in search of unusual ingredients and bargain-priced fruits and vegetables. On week-ends, you'll be greeted by a lively mariachi band at the Hill Street entrance, near our favorite market feature—the fruit-juice counter, which dispenses 20 fresh varieties from wall spigots and blends up the tastiest, healthiest "shakes" in town. Farther into the market, you'll find produce sellers and prepared-food counters, plus spice vendors who seem straight out of a Turkish alley, and a grain-and-bean seller who will scoop out dozens of exotic rices and dried legumes.

THE SAN FERNANDO VALLEY

Technically an outdoor mall rather than a shopping area, **Universal CityWalk** (☎ 818/622-4455) gets mention here because it's so utterly unique. A pedestrian promenade next door to Universal Studios, CityWalk is dominated by brightly col-ored, outrageously surreal, oversize storefronts. The heavily touristed faux street is home to an inordinate number of restaurants, including B. B. King's Blues Club, the newest Hard Rock Cafe, and a branch of the Hollywood Athletic Club featuring a restaurant and pool hall. This is consumer culture gone haywire, an egotistical eyesore not worth a special visit, unless you have the kids in tow—they'll love it.

PASADENA & ENVIRONS

Compared to L.A.'s behemoth shopping malls, the streets of pretty, compact Pasadena are a true pleasure to stroll. As a general rule, stores are open daily from about 10am, and while some close at the standard 5 or 6pm, many stay open until 8 or 9pm to accommodate the before- and after-dinner/movie crowd.

Old Pasadena. Centered around the intersection of Colorado Blvd. and Fair Oaks Ave.

In our opinion, Old Pasadena has some of the best shopping in L.A., but we hope they retain more of the mom-and-pop businesses currently being pushed out by the likes of Banana Republic and Crate & Barrel. As you move eastward, the mix begins to include more eclectic shops and galleries commingling with dusty, pre-yuppie relics.

At the contemporary crafts gallery **Del Mano,** 33 E. Colorado Blvd. (☎ 626/793-6648), it's a whole lot of fun to see the creations—some whimsical, some exquisite—of American artists working with glass, wood, ceramics, or jewelry. Across the street, **Penny Lane,** 12 W. Colorado Blvd. (☎ 626/564-0161), carries new and used CDs, plus a great selection of music magazines and kitschy postcards. The stock is less picked-over here than at many record stores in Hollywood. Travelers always seem to find something they need at **Distant Lands Bookstore and Outfitters,** 54 and 62 S. Raymond Ave. (☎ 626/449-3220), a duo of related stores. The bookstore has a terrific selection of maps, guides, and travel-related literature, while the recently opened outfitters two doors away offers everything from luggage and pith helmets to space-saving and convenient travel accessories. An Old Town mainstay is **Rebecca's Dream,** 16 S. Fair Oaks Ave. (☎ 626/796-1200), where men and women can find vintage-clothing treasures. The store is small and meticulously organized (by color scheme); be sure to look up at the vintage hats adorning the walls.

OTHER PASADENA SHOPPING

In addition to Old Town Pasadena, there are numerous good hunting grounds in the surrounding area. Antiques hounds might want to head to the **Green Street Antique Row,** 985–1005 E. Green St., east of Lake Avenue; or the **Pasadena Antiques Center,** on South Fair Oaks Boulevard south of Del Mar. Each has a rich concentration of col-lectibles that can captivate for hours.

You never know what you'll find at the **Rose Bowl Flea Market,** at the Rose Bowl, 991 Rosemont Ave., Pasadena (☎ 626/577-3100). Built in 1922, the horseshoe-shaped

Rose Bowl is one of the world's most famous stadiums, home to UCLA's Bruins, the annual Rose Bowl Game, and an occasional Super Bowl. California's largest monthly swap meet, on the second Sunday of every month from 9am to 3pm, is a favorite of Los Angeles antiques hounds (who know to arrive as early as 6am for the best finds). Antique furnishings, clothing, jewelry, and other collectibles are assembled in the parking area to the left of the entrance, while the rest of the flea market surrounds the exterior of the Bowl. Expect everything from used surfboards and car stereos to one-of-a-kind lawn statuary and bargain athletic shoes. Admission is $5 after 9am (early-bird admission is $10 to $15).

STORES WORTH SEEKING OUT ELSEWHERE IN THE CITY

♺**Rhino Records,** 1720 Westwood Blvd., Westwood (☎ 310/474-8685), is L.A.'s premier alternative shop, specializing in new artists and independent-label releases. In addition to new releases, there's a terrific used selection; this is where record-industry types come to trade in the music they don't want for the music they do, so you'll find never-played promotional copies of brand-new releases at half the retail price. You'll also find the definitive collection of records on the Rhino label here.

If you're feeling wanderlust—or just plain lost—check out **California Map and Travel Center,** 3312 Pico Blvd., Santa Monica (☎ 310/396-6277). As the name implies, this store carries a good selection of domestic and international maps and travel accessories, including guides for hiking, biking, and touring. Globes and atlases are also sold. Visit them online at www.mapper.com.

And it just wouldn't be L.A. without **Trashy Lingerie,** 402 N. La Cienega Blvd., Hollywood (☎ 310/652-4543; www.trashy.com). This shop will tailor-fit its house-designed clothes—everything from patent-leather bondage wear to elegant bridal underthings—for you. There's a $2 "membership" fee to enter the store, but, even for browsers, it's worth it.

12 Los Angeles After Dark

by Bryan Yates

The *L.A. Weekly* (www.laweekly.com), a free weekly paper available at sidewalk stands, shops, and restaurants, is the best place to find up-to-date news on what's happening in Los Angeles's playhouses, cinemas, museums, and live-music venues. The "Calendar" section of the *Los Angeles Times* (www.calendarlive.com) is also a good place to see what's going on after dark.

Ticketmaster (☎ 213/480-3232; www.ticketmaster.com) and **Telecharge** (☎ 800/447-7400) are the major charge-by-phone ticket agencies in the city, selling tickets to concerts, sporting events, plays, and special events.

THEATER

Tickets for most plays usually cost $10 to $35, though performances of big-name shows at the major theaters can fetch up to $75 for the best seats. **Theatre LA** (www.theatrela.org), an association of live theaters and producers in Los Angeles (and the organization that puts on the yearly Ovation Awards, L.A.'s answer to Broadway's Tonys), operates a half-price ticket booth modeled after New York's successful TKTS. **Times Tix,** 8701 Beverly Blvd., West Hollywood (☎ 310/659-3678), is a block west of the Beverly Center, attached to Jerry's Famous Deli. It's open Thursday through Sunday from noon to 6pm; tickets are sold on a walk-up, cash-only basis.

MAJOR THEATERS & COMPANIES

The Ahmanson Theater and Mark Taper Forum, the city's top two playhouses and home to the Center Theater Group (www.taperahmanson.com), are located in the all-purpose **Music Center,** 135 N. Grand Ave., downtown. The **Ahmanson Theater** (☎ 213/972-7401) is active year-round, either with shows produced in-house or with traveling Broadway productions. The 1998–99 season opened with the only American run of the Royal National Theatre's standout production of Ibsen's *Enemy of the People,* which starred Sir Ian McKellan. Ahmanson audiences also delighted to *Cinderella* by ballet impresario Matthew Bourne. Choreographed to Prokofiev's 1945 score, Bourne innovatively set the classic fairytale in bomb-besieged, wartime London. The Ahmanson is so huge that you'll want seats in the front third or half of the theater.

The **Mark Taper Forum** (☎ 213/972-0700) is a more intimate, circular theater staging contemporary works by international and local playwrights and often starring big-name actors. Highlights from the 1999 season included Paula Vogel's Pulitzer Prize–winner *How I Learned to Drive* with former brat-packer Molly Ringwald, and Al Pacino making his West Coast–theatrical debut, as director and cast member, in one of Eugene O'Neill's last plays, *Hughie. Insider tip:* Two hours prior to curtain time, the Mark Taper Forum offers specially priced $12 tickets, which must be purchased in person with cash.

Big-time traveling troupes and Broadway-bred musicals that don't go to the Ahmanson head instead for the **Shubert Theater,** in the ABC Entertainment Center, 2020 Avenue of the Stars, Century City (☎ 800/233-3123). This plush playhouse presents major musicals on the scale of *Sunset Boulevard* and *Les Misérables;* the smash hit musical *Rent* reprised in Los Angeles at the Shubert in 1999.

Across town, the moderately sized **Geffen Playhouse,** 10886 Le Conte Ave., Westwood (☎ 310/208-5454; www.geffen.ucla.edu), presents dramatic and comedic productions by prominent and always cutting-edge writers. UCLA purchased the theater—which was originally built as a Masonic temple in 1929, and later served as the Westwood Playhouse—back in '95 with a little help from L.A.'s philanthropic entertainment mogul David Geffen. This charming playhouse is often the West Coast choice of many acclaimed off-Broadway shows, and also attracts locally based TV and movie actors eager for the immediacy of stage work. One recent highlight was Annette Bening in Ibsen's *Hedda Gabler.* Always audience-friendly, the Playhouse prices tickets in the $25-to-$38 range.

SMALLER PLAYHOUSES & COMPANIES

It's a little-known fact that on any given night, there's more live theater to choose from in Los Angeles than in New York, due, in part, to the surfeit of ready actors and writers just chomping at the bit to make it in Tinseltown. The city is home to nearly 200 small- and medium-sized theaters and theater companies. With so many options, navigating the scene can be a monumental undertaking. Your safest bet is to choose one of the following theaters and companies, which have all established excellent reputations for their productions. As always, consult the *L.A. Weekly* for up-to-date performance listings.

The **Colony Studio Theatre,** 1944 Riverside Dr., Silver Lake (☎ 323/665-3011; www.colonytheatre.org), has an excellent resident company that has played in this air-conditioned, 99-seat, converted silent-movie house for more than 20 years. **Actors Circle Theater,** 7313 Santa Monica Blvd., West Hollywood (☎ 323/882-8043), is a 47-seater that's as acclaimed as it is tiny.

Founded in 1965, **East-West Players,** 120 N. Judge John Aiso St., Los Angeles (☎ 323/625-7000; www.eastwestplayers.com), is now the oldest Asian-American theater company in the United States. It's been so successful that the company moved from a 99-seat venue to a 200-seat downtown L.A. theater in March 1998. Since then, East-West Players has performed several musicals, including Sondheim's *Pacific Overtures,* and undertaken a decidedly Asian theme in *Big Hunk of Burnin' Love,* a comedy about a Thai boy whose parents insist he must marry before the age of 30, lest he fall victim to the family curse of spontaneous combustion.

One of the most highly acclaimed professional theaters in L.A., the **Pasadena Playhouse,** 35 S. El Molino Ave., near Colorado Boulevard, Pasadena (☎ 626/356-7529), is a registered historic landmark that has served as the training ground for many theatrical, film, and TV stars, including William Holden and Gene Hackman. Productions are staged on the main theater's elaborate Spanish Colonial revival stage.

CLASSICAL MUSIC & OPERA

Beyond the pop realms, music in Los Angeles generally falls short of that found in other cities. For the most part, Angelenos rely on visiting orchestras and companies to fulfill their classical-music appetites; scan the papers to find out who's performing while you're in the city.

The **Los Angeles Philharmonic** (☎ 323/850-2000; www.laphil.org) isn't just the city's top symphony; it's the only major classical-music company in Los Angeles. Finnish-born music director Esa-Pekka Salonen concentrates on contemporary compositions; despite complaints from traditionalists, he does an excellent job attracting younger audiences. Tickets can be hard to come by when celebrity musicians like Itzhak Perlman, Isaac Stern, Emanuel Ax, and Yo-Yo Ma are in town. In addition to regular performances at the Music Center's **Dorothy Chandler Pavilion,** 135 N. Grand Ave., downtown, the Philharmonic also plays a popular summer season at the **Hollywood Bowl** (see "Concerts Under the Stars," below).

Slowly but surely, the **L.A. Opera** (☎ 213/972-8001; www.laopera.org) is gaining both respect and popularity with inventive stagings of classic operas, usually with guest divas. Highlights from the 1999 season included *Falstaff* and *Don Giovanni.* The Opera also calls the Music Center home.

CONCERTS UNDER THE STARS

✪ **Hollywood Bowl.** 2301 N. Highland Ave. (at Odin St.), Hollywood. ☎ **323/850-2000.** www.hollywoodbowl.org.

Built in the early 1920s, the Hollywood Bowl is an elegant Greek-style natural outdoor amphitheater cradled in a small mountain canyon. This is the summer home of the Los Angeles Philharmonic Orchestra; internationally known conductors and soloists often sit in on Tuesday and Thursday nights. Friday and Saturday concerts often feature orchestral swing or pops concerts. The summer season also includes a jazz series; past performers have included Natalie Cole, Mel Torme, Dionne Warwick, and Chick Corea. Other events, from Tom Petty concerts to an annual Mariachi Festival, frequently appear on the season's schedule.

For many concertgoers, a visit to the Bowl is an excuse for an accompanying picnic dinner, complete with a bottle of wine or two, under the stars—it's one of L.A.'s grandest traditions. You can prepare your own, or order a picnic basket with a choice of hot and cold dishes and a selection of wines and desserts from the theater's catering department. À la carte baskets run from $17 to $26 per person; appetizers and drinks are extra. Call ☎ 323/851-3588 the day before you go.

THE CLUB & MUSIC SCENE

Let's face it: Los Angeles is more or less the center of the entertainment industry. So, on any given night, finding something to satisfy any musical fancy can be a snap. From acoustic rock to jazz fusion, from Judas Priest cover bands to Latin funk, from the up-and-coming to the already gone, L.A.'s got something for everyone. Check out *L.A. Weekly* or the "Calendar" in Sunday's *Los Angeles Times* to see what's up with the music scene.

In addition to the venues listed below, which are popular as attractions in their own right, there are several distinctly L.A. concert venues worth visiting if someone on the bill appeals to you: The alfresco **John Anson Ford Theatre,** 2580 Cahuenga Blvd. East, Hollywood (☎ 323/461-3673), is across the Cahuenga pass from the more highbrow Hollywood Bowl, but features an eclectic mix of jazz, folk, and international music plus dance and family events.

Numerous significant alternative-rock shows—including key appearances by Smashing Pumpkins and Garbage—take place at the vaudeville-era **Palace,** 1735 N. Vine St., Hollywood (☎ 323/467-4571), which doubles as a late-night dance club. The carefully restored **Wiltern Theatre,** 3790 Wilshire Blvd., Los Angeles (☎ 213/380-5005), is a WPA-era art-deco showplace that's hosted countless national and international acts, from Penn and Teller to Radiohead.

B. B. King's Blues Club. CityWalk, Universal City. ☎ **818/622-5464.**

This three-level club/restaurant, where the ribs alone are reputedly worth the trip, hosts plenty of great local and touring national blues acts and is a testament to the establishment's venerable namesake. There's no shortage of good seating, but if you find yourself on one of the top two levels, grab a table along the railing for an ideal view of the stage.

Doug Weston's Troubadour. 9081 Santa Monica Blvd., West Hollywood. ☎ **310/276-6168.** All ages; cover varies.

This infamous West Hollywood mainstay radiates rock history—from the 1960s to the 1990s, the Troub really has seen 'em all. Audiences are consistently treated to memorable shows from the already established or young-and-promising acts that take the stage. But bring your earplugs: This beer- and sweat-soaked club likes it loud.

Dragonfly. 6510 Santa Monica Blvd., Hollywood. ☎ **323/466-6111.** www.dragonfly.com. Cover varies.

Not one to miss a trend, Dragonfly went from being a dance club that offered live music to becoming a live stage that offers dancing. This hip venue in the heart of Hollywood offers "surprise" shows ranging from Rage Against the Machine and Porno for Pyros to surprising national acts—Run-D.M.C. at an alternative music club! These days, Dragonfly is soaring. Overheated guests and smokers enjoy the cool outdoor patio.

House of Blues. 8430 Sunset Blvd., West Hollywood. ☎ **323/848-5100;** www.hob.com.

In spite of its frequently ridiculed, cartoonish "Country Bear Jamboree" facade, there are plenty of reasons the music fans and industry types keep coming back to House of Blues. Night after night, audiences are dazzled by hot acts of national and international acclaim, ranging from Soul Coughing to Paul Westerberg to Randy Newman.

Jack's Sugar Shack. 1707 Vine St., Hollywood. ☎ **323/466-7005.** www.jackssugarshack. com. Cover usually $5.

With its thatched-roof bar and collection of *Gilligan's Island* murals, Jack's has elevated tiki chic to an artform. But it's the great roots rock, alternative, rockabilly, and alt-country from local and national acts, like Russel Scott and the Red Hots or Big Sandy and His Fly-Rite Boys, that keep the fans coming back. Ronnie Mack's Barndance is a free Tuesday-night affair of alternative country music.

Jazz Bakery. 3233 Helms Ave, Culver City. ☎ **310/271-9039.** www.jazznet.com/jazzbakery.

Located in the restored Helms Bakery factory, Ruth Price's nonprofit venue is renowned for attracting some of the most important names in jazz. Hers is a no-frills, all-about-the-music affair, and the place is pretty much BYO in the drinks department. Drummer Jimmy Cobb, the last remaining member of Miles Davis's *Kind of Blue* band, and his band had a four-night stint at JB last year.

LunaPark. 665 N. Robertson Blvd., West Hollywood. ☎ **310/652-0611.** Cover varies, usually around $10.

This bi-level restaurant/performance space is one of the most unpredictable but reliable venues in town. The food here is better than it has to be and the performances from Ani DiFranco to international DJs, plus comedy and cabaret shows are always diverse.

McCabe's. 3101 Pico Blvd., Santa Monica. ☎ **310/828-4403.** www.mccabesguitar.com. Cover varies.

For some 20-plus years, this 40-some-year-old guitar store has opened its backroom for some pretty memorable acoustic sets by the likes of Doc and Merle Watson, Wendy and Lisa, and Peter Case. McCabe's is intimate in the extreme; you'd have to have the gig in your living room to get any cozier. A guitar shop first and music venue second, McCabe's doesn't have a bar.

Roxy. 9009 Sunset Blvd., West Hollywood ☎ **323/276-2222.** Cover varies.

Veteran record producer/executive Lou Adler opened this Sunset Strip club in the mid–1970s with concerts by Neil Young and a lengthy run of the pre-movie *Rocky Horror Show.* Since then, the Roxy has remained among the top showcase venues in Hollywood—though it has lost its unchallenged preeminence among cozy clubs to increased competition from the revitalized Troubadour and such new entries as the House of Blues.

Spaceland at Dreams. 1717 Silver Lake Blvd., Silver Lake. ☎ **323/413-4442.** Cover varies.

Though the wall-to-wall mirrors and shiny brass posts suggest that Spaceland must have been a seedy 1980s strip joint in a past life, the club's current personality offers something entirely different. Host to countless performances by alternative artists, such as Pavement, Mary Lou Lord, Grant Lee Buffalo, Elliott Smith, and the Eels, this hot spot on the fringe of east Hollywood has become one of the most important clubs on the L.A. circuit.

✪ Viper Room. 8852 Sunset Blvd., West Hollywood. ☎ **310/358-1880.** Ages 21 and over; cover varies.

Yes, Johnny Depp owns it (with partner Sal Jenco), and yes, River Phoenix overdosed here—a combo that continues to repulse or attract clubgoers. The advertised lineup ranges from smokin' to snorin', but it's still a great place for celebrity spotting; huge stars like Johnny Cash, Iggy Pop, and David Bowie often perform unannounced, late-night sets when they're in town playing the 6,000-seaters.

DANCE CLUBS

The city's dance scene is burgeoning. The momentous popularity of Latin dance and swing has resulted in the opening of new clubs dedicated to both, taking some of the pressure off the old standbys. DJ club culture is also on the rise locally; such dance clubs, however, can come and go as quickly as you can say "jungle/hip-hop/drum-and-bass/rave." Mere whispers of a happening thing can practically relegate a club to yesterday's news. Check the *L.A. Weekly* for listings on specific club information.

The Conga Room. 5364 Wilshire Blvd., Los Angeles. ☎ **323/938-1696;** www.congaroom.com. Cover varies.

Attracting such Latin-music luminaries as Tito Puente and Pucho & The Latin Soul Brothers, this one-time Jack LaLanne health club on the Miracle Mile is fast becoming *the* nightspot for live salsa and merengue. Break up the evening of heart-melting, sexy Latin dancing with a trip to the dining room, where the chef serves up savory Cuban fare in a setting that conjures up romantic images of pre-Castro Cuba.

The Derby. 4500 Los Feliz Blvd., Los Feliz. ☎ **323/663-8979.** Ages 21 and over; cover $5–$7.

Located at a former Brown Derby restaurant site, this class-A swing club was restored to its original luster and detailed with a heavy 1940s edge. This would explain the inordinate number of guests who come decked out in garb from that era to swing the night away to such musical acts as Big Bad Voodoo Daddy and the Royal Crown Revue (whose popularity soared after weekly bookings at the club). Dance lessons are offered, but it can be impossibly crowded on weekends.

El Floridita. 1253 N. Vine St., Hollywood. ☎ **323/871-8612.** Ages 21 and over; cover varies.

This Cuban restaurant-and-salsa-joint is hot, hot, hot. Despite its modest strip-lot locale, the tiny club attracts the likes of Jennifer Lopez, Sandra Bullock, Jimmy Smits, and Jack Nicholson. The hippest nights continue to be Monday and Thursday, when Johnny Polanco and his swinging New York–flavored salsa band get the dance floor jumping.

Hollywood Athletic Club. 6525 Sunset Blvd., Hollywood. ☎ **323/962-6600.** Ages 21 and over; cover $10–$20.

Built in 1924, this art-deco venue is a cavern of rooms dedicated to drinking, billiards, dining, and dancing. Taking the main room the third Monday of the month, Groove City dazzles tireless clubbers with hip-hop and old school. Friday has DJs spinning in both the main room and the lounge.

The Love Lounge. 657 N. Robertson Blvd., West Hollywood. ☎ **310/659-0472** or 213/896-9099. Ages 21 and over; cover $10.

DJ Mike Messex's Friday-night gig, Cherry, finds him digging deep into the 1980s for loads of glam rock, new wave, and disco. He keeps the dance floor packed all evening. Promoter Bryan Rabin knows how to keep the energy level high, with selective live performances—often with a homoerotic edge—as well as theme nights.

The Pink. 2810 Main St., Santa Monica. ☎ **310/392-1077.** Ages 21 and over; cover $10.

Thursday is the most popular night here, when DJs and label execs Jason Bentley and Bruno Guez spin an eclectic collection, and noteworthy guest DJs round out the mood—which includes electronic, acid jazz, and more. During the rest of the week, musical fare ranges from drum-and-bass to progressive house.

Sugar. 814 Broadway, Santa Monica. ☎ 310/899-1989. Ages 21 and over; cover $10.

Wednesday through Saturday, clubgoers pack this popular Santa Monica spot for its great dance music. If you're into funky house or soul lounge, try Lollipop or Chocolate on Wednesday and Thursday, respectively; hip-hop and funk are Friday's musical fare at In the Raw; or escape to the world of progressive house, trance, and Euro electronica at Pure on Saturdays.

BARS & COCKTAIL LOUNGES

El Carmen. 8138 W. Third St., Los Angeles. ☎ **323/852-1552.** No cover.

Opened by L.A. restaurant and bar impresario Sean Macpherson, the man with the mescal touch, El Carmen conjures the feel of a back-alley Mexican cantina of a bygone era. Vintage Mexican movie posters, vibrant Latin American colors, and oil paintings of masked Mexican wrestlers decorate the Quonset-hut interior, while an eclectic jukebox offers an array of tunes from Desi Arnaz to Tool. The busy bar boasts a gargantuan list of more than 100 tequilas and a small menu of tacos and light fare.

Four Seasons Hotel Los Angeles. 300 S. Doheny Dr. (at Burton Way), Los Angeles. ☎ **310/273-2222.** No cover.

The sprawling lobby bar of this slightly pretentious but always eventful hotel serves as both celebrity magnet and unofficial parlor for moneyed regulars who virtually live in the high-rise. A house pianist plays quietly in the background. The bartenders here have seen it all—no request is too outrageous, from a platter of oysters courtesy of the hotel's restaurant to a bowl of water for a canine companion (dogs are served only on the patio).

Good Luck Bar. 1514 Hillhurst Ave. (between Hollywood and Sunset blvds.), Los Angeles. ☎ **323/666-3524.** No cover.

Until it installed a flashing neon sign outside, only locals and hipsters knew about this kung-fu–themed room in the Los Feliz/Silver Lake area. The dark-red window-less interior boasts Oriental ceiling tiles, fringed Chinese paper lanterns, sweet-but-deadly drinks like the "Yee Mee Loo" (translated as "blue drink"), and a jukebox with selections from Thelonius Monk to Cher's "Half Breed." The spacious sitting room, furnished with mismatched sofas, armchairs, and banquettes, provides a great atmosphere for conversation or romance. Arrive early to avoid the throngs of L.A. scenesters.

Kane. 5574 Melrose Ave., Hollywood. ☎ **323/466-6263.** No cover.

The classic spirit of American lounge is the mainstay at Kane, where sounds from recent decades—ranging from Bobby Darin to the Jackson 5—are spun by a DJ flanked by a duo of go-go dancers in hot pants. Kitsch notwithstanding, owner Ivan Kane has created an atmosphere reminiscent of 1960s Vegas and 1970s funk that is warm, friendly, and inviting to its youthful 20-something crowd.

Lola's. 945 N. Fairfax Ave. (south of Santa Monica Blvd.), Los Angeles. ☎ **213/736-5652.** No cover.

The swimming pool–sized martinis ought to be reason enough to trek over to Lola's. From the classic gin or vodka martini for the purist to the chocolate- or apple-flavored concoctions for the adventurous, this place has a little something for everyone. Two bars, billiards, and plush couches hidden in dark, romantic corners make for an enjoy-able setting, with plenty of celeb spotting. For a full listing, see "Dining," earlier in this chapter.

360. 6290 Sunset Blvd., Hollywood. ☎ **323/871-2995.** No cover.

This 19th-story, penthouse-perched restaurant and lounge is a perfect place to romance that special someone. It's all about the view here—all 360 degrees of it. The understated and softly lit interior emphasizes the scene *outside* the plentiful windows, including a spectacular vista of the famed HOLLYWOOD sign.

GAY AND LESBIAN BARS & CLUBS

Although West Hollywood, often affectionately referred to as "Boys Town," has the densest gay population in Los Angeles, there are several other noteworthy enclaves. Silver Lake, in particular, has a longstanding gay community; Santa Monica and Venice also have a strong gay and lesbian presence.

If you're looking for more specific info on gay culture in L.A., beyond what we've included below, check out one of these resources: *4-Front Magazine* (☎ **323/650-7772**), *Edge Magazine* (☎ **323/962-6994**), or *Frontiers* (☎ **323/848-2222**). Women might want to pick up a copy of *Female FYI* (☎ **323/938-5969**), *LA Girl Guide* (☎ **310/391-8877**), or *Lesbian News* (☎ **310/392-8224**). Edge and Frontiers are the most prominently featured free biweekly gay mags and are readily available in coffeehouses and newsstands citywide. If you're having a difficult time locating any of these magazines, give the good people at **A Different Light Bookstore**, 8853 Santa Monica, West Hollywood (☎ **310/854-6601**), a call, or visit for in-person assistance. The *L.A. Weekly* and *New Times Los Angeles* also contain lesbian and gay articles and listings.

The Abbey. 692 N. Robertson Blvd., West Hollywood. ☎ **310/289-8410.** No cover.

By all accounts, this is *the* gay coffee bar. Whether you sit inside or out, this is the place to enjoy a latte while you watch the passing parade of WeHo boys in muscle shirts. Most of West Hollywood seems to end up here on Saturday nights—even k.d. lang occasionally makes an appearance.

Club 7969. 7969 Santa Monica Blvd., West Hollywood. ☎ **323/654-0280.** Cover varies.

Fashionable of late, Club 7679 is the kind of place where male and female strippers bare it all while mingling with the gay, lesbian, and straight crowd. Each night features a different theme, ranging from drag burlesques to techno parties. On Tuesdays, Michelle's CC revue—with its legion of topless female dancers—attracts a largely lesbian crowd.

Cobalt Cantina. 4326 Sunset Blvd., Silver Lake. ☎ **323/953-9991.** Also at 616 N. Robertson Blvd., West Hollywood. ☎ **310/659-8961.** No cover.

For years, the "Martini Lounge," located in the Silver Lake restaurant, has been one of the hottest gay cocktail bars in town. Around the long bar and zinc-colored cocktail tables, gargantuan margaritas and strong martinis are sipped by the ethnically mixed crowd of buffed-out locals. Cobalt is largely gay but definitely straight-friendly. The WeHo location's "Bluebar" is a quiet alternative to the nearby wild, party-oriented clubs.

Dragstrip 66. The second Saturday of each month at Rudolpho's, 2500 Riverside Dr., Silver Lake. ☎ **323/969-2596.** Ages 21 and over; cover $10–$20.

Note the cover disparity: If you ain't in drag, prepare to pay for it (and wait in line a wee bit longer). This all-time-great drag club, located in a Mexican restaurant, switches themes each month ("Chicks with Dicks" was a standout), and offers up every type of music—except disco and Liza. That's entertainment.

Micky's. 8857 Santa Monica Blvd., West Hollywood. ☎ **310/657-1176.** Cover varies.

A diverse, outgoing, and mostly older crowd cruises back and forth between the front-room bar and the dance floor in back. More women—probably looking to party with the friendly crowd and enjoy the great drink specials—are drawn to Micky's than to some of the neighboring bars.

Rage. 8911 Santa Monica Blvd., West Hollywood. ☎ **310/652-7055.** Cover varies.

For 15 years, this high-energy, high-attitude disco has been the preferred mainstay on WeHo's gay dance-club circuit. Between turns around the dance floor, shirtless muscle boys self-consciously strut about—like peacocks flashing their plumes—looking to exchange vital statistics.

COMEDY & CABARET

Except for the Cinegrill, which is in its own league, each of the following venues claims—and justly so—to have launched the careers of now-famous comics. The funniest up-and-comers play all the clubs (except for the Groundlings, which features improvisation), so you're best off choosing a club for its location.

The Cinegrill. 7000 Hollywood Blvd., in the Hollywood Roosevelt Hotel, Hollywood. ☎ **323/466-7000.** Tickets $10–$25.

The Cinegrill, at one of L.A.'s most historic hotels, draws locals with a zany cabaret show and guest chanteuses from Eartha Kitt to Cybill Shepherd. Some of the country's best cabaret singers pop up here regularly.

Comedy Store. 8433 Sunset Blvd., West Hollywood. ☎ **323/656-6225.** Tickets $8–$15.

You can't go wrong here: New comics develop their material, and established ones work out the kinks, at this landmark venue owned by Mitzi Shore (Pauly's mom). The talent here is always first-rate, and includes comics who regularly appear on *The Tonight Show* and other high-profile TV programs.

✪ **Groundling Theater.** 7307 Melrose Ave., Los Angeles. ☎ **323/934-9700.** Tickets $10–$18.

L.A.'s answer to Chicago's Second City has been around for more than 20 years, yet remains the funniest and most innovative group in town. Their collection of skits changes every year or so, but they take new improvisational twists every night, and the satire is often savage. The Groundlings were the springboard to fame for Pee-Wee Herman, Lisa Kudrow of *Friends,* and former *Saturday Night Live* stars Jon Lovitz, Phil Hartman, and Julia Sweeney. Trust us—you haven't laughed this hard in ages.

The Improvisation. 8162 Melrose Ave., West Hollywood. ☎ **323/651-2583.** Tickets $5–$10.

A showcase for top stand-ups since 1975, the Improv offers something different each night. Owner Budd Freedman's buddies—like Jay Leno, Billy Crystal, and Robin Williams—hone their skills here more often than you would expect. But even if the comedians on the bill are all unknowns, they won't be for long.

COFFEEHOUSES

Anastasia's Asylum. 1028 Wilshire Blvd., Santa Monica. ☎ **310/394-7113.**

Stop by for a cup of joe to go or stick around and while away the hours at this top-notch coffeehouse. Anastasia's boasts an eclectic clientele, diverse live music (from jazz and folk to acoustic and plugged-in rock), vintage furniture in a classy decor, constantly changing art exhibits, and a great menu, making it a favorite draw for folks from around the city.

Bourgeois Pig. 5931 Franklin Ave., Hollywood. ☎ **323/962-6366.**

With a nearly Gothic aversion to natural lighting, this dark cavern has more of a bar atmosphere than the usual coffeehouse: The Bourgeois Pig is to Starbucks what Marilyn Manson is to Celine Dion. This veteran, on a hot business strip at the Hollywood/Los Feliz border, is a favorite among youths and show-biz drones, who enjoy losing themselves on couches tucked into shadowed corners, shooting a game of pool, or perusing the terrific newsstand next door.

Equator. 22 Mills Place, Pasadena. ☎ **626/564-8656.**

Airy and comfy, this brick room, on a busy alleyway in the heart of resurgent Old Town Pasadena, has withstood the challenge of a Starbucks that moved in a block away. The menu—with smoothies, soups, and desserts in addition to a wide variety of coffee drinks—and the friendly service keep people coming back. The post-Haring art on the walls contributes to the distinctive character of the place, which has been used for scenes in such films and TV shows as *A Very Brady Sequel* and *Beverly Hills, 90210.*

Highland Grounds. 742 N. Highland Ave., Hollywood. ☎ **323/466-1507.**

Predating the coffeehouse explosion, this comfortable, relatively unpretentious place set the L.A. standard with a vast assortment of food and drink—not just coffee—and often first-rate live music, ranging from nationally known locals, such as Victoria Williams, to open-mike Wednesdays. The ample patio is often used for readings and record-release parties.

LATE-NIGHT BITES
After-hours snacking is getting easier in L.A., as each year sees more late-night and 24-hour eateries join the culinary landscape.

The Apple Pan. 10801 W. Pico Blvd., West Los Angeles. ☎ **310/475-3585.** Tues–Thurs and Sun 11am–midnight; Fri–Sat 11am–1am.

This classic American burger shack, an L.A. landmark, hasn't changed much since opening in 1947—and its burgers and pies still hit the spot. See "Dining," earlier in this chapter, for a complete review.

Canter's Restaurant & Bakery. 419 N. Fairfax Ave., Los Angeles. ☎ **323/651-2030.** Daily 24 hours.

This Jewish deli has been a hit with late-nighters for more than 65 years. If you show up after the clubs close, you're sure to spot a bleary-eyed celebrity or two alongside the rest of the after-hours crowd, chowing down on a giant pastrami sandwich, matzo-ball soup, potato pancakes, or another deli favorite. Try a potato knish with a side of brown gravy—trust us, you'll love it.

Du-par's Restaurant & Bakery. 12036 Ventura Blvd. (1 block east of Laurel Canyon), Studio City. ☎ **818/766-4437.** Sun–Thurs 6am–1am; Fri–Sat 6am–4am.

During the week, Du-par's serves up blue-plate specials 'til 1am. Come the weekend, they're slinging hash until 4am. See "Dining," earlier in this chapter, for a complete review.

Jerry's Famous Deli. 12655 Ventura Blvd. (at Coldwater Canyon Blvd.), Studio City. ☎ **818/980-4245.** Daily 24 hours.

This is where Valley hipsters go to relieve their late-night munchies. See "Dining," earlier in this chapter, for a complete review.

Kate Mantilini. 9101 Wilshire Blvd. (at Doheny Dr.), Beverly Hills. ☎ **310/278-3699.** Mon–Thurs 7:30am–1am; Fri 7:30am–2am; Sat 11am–2am; Sun 10am–midnight.

Kate's serves stylish nouveau comfort food in a striking setting. See "Dining," earlier in this chapter, for a complete review.

Mel's Drive-In. 8585 Sunset Blvd. (west of La Cienega), West Hollywood. ☎ **310/854-7200.** Daily 24 hours.

Straight out of *Happy Days*, this 1950s diner on the Sunset Strip attracts customers ranging from chic shoppers during the day to rock-and-rollers at night; the fries and shakes here are among the best in town.

✪ Operetta. 8223 W. Third St. (near Harper St.), Los Angeles. ☎ **323/852-7000.** Daily 24 hours.

This French bakery and cafe is a welcome sight to L.A. night owls; even though the kitchen stops serving sandwiches and other light fare at midnight, Operetta's mouthwatering pastries and breads are available around the clock.

The Original Pantry Cafe. 877 S. Figueroa St. (at Ninth St.), downtown. ☎ **213/972-9279.** Daily 24 hours.

Owned by Los Angeles mayor Richard Riordan, this place has been serving huge portions of comfort food around the clock for more than 60 years; in fact, they don't even have a key to the front door. See "Dining," earlier in this chapter, for a complete review.

Pacific Dining Car. 1310 W. Sixth St. (at Witmer St.), downtown. ☎ **213/483-6000.** Daily 24 hours.

This is the place for a well-marbled, patiently aged New York steak any time of the day or night. See "Dining," earlier in this chapter, for a complete review.

Swingers. 8020 Beverly Blvd. (at the Beverly Laurel Motor Hotel), west of Fairfax Ave. ☎ **323/653-5858.** Sun–Thurs 6am–2am; Fri–Sat 9am–4am.

This hip coffee shop keeps L.A. scenesters happy with its retro comfort food. See "Dining," earlier in this chapter, for a complete review.

✪ Toi On Sunset. 7505 Sunset Blvd. (at Gardner), Hollywood. ☎ **323/874-8062.** Daily 11am–4am.

This colorful and *loud* hangout is for those requiring a little more *oomph* from their late-night snack. Garbled pop-culture metaphors mingle with the tastes and aromas of "rockin' Thai" cuisine in delicious ways. Portions are generous, and Toi's menu features plenty of vegetarian treats.

MOVIES

The **American Cinematheque** (☎ **323/466-3456,** www.americancinamatheque. com) presents not-readily-seen videos and films, ranging from the wildly arty to the old classics. It recently moved into its new Hollywood home, the historic and beautifully refurbished 1923 **Egyptian Theater,** 6712 Hollywood Blvd.

The **Bing Theater,** at the **L.A. County Museum of Art**, 5905 Wilshire Blvd., Los Angeles (☎ **323/857-6010**), presents a specially themed film series each month. Past subjects have ranged from 1930s blonde-bombshell films to thinly veiled Cold War–propaganda flicks to a 3-day Monty Python's Flying Circus marathon.

Laemmle's Sunset 5, 8000 Sunset Blvd., West Hollywood (☎ **323/848-3500**), despite being a contemporary multiplex located in a bright outdoor mall, features the films that most theaters of its ilk won't even touch. This is the place to see interesting independent art films that have something to say, as well as a selection of gay-themed movies.

The **Nuart Theater**, 11272 Santa Monica Blvd., Los Angeles (☎ **310/478-6379**), digs deep into the archives for some real classics, from campy to cool. One recent Nuart highlight was "Francois Truffault: A Celebration," in which new 35mm prints of the French director's works were shown during a 2-week retrospective.

Side Trips from Los Angeles

14

by Stephanie Avnet Yates

The area within a 100-mile radius of Los Angeles is one of the most diverse regions in the world: There are arid deserts, rugged mountains, industrial cities, historic towns, alpine lakes, rolling hillsides, and sophisticated seaside resorts. You'll also find an offshore island that's been transformed into the ultimate city-dweller's hideaway, not to mention the Happiest Place on Earth.

1 Long Beach & the *Queen Mary*

21 miles S of downtown Los Angeles

The fifth-largest incorporated city in California, Long Beach is best known as the permanent home of the former cruise liner *Queen Mary*, and in mid-April for the annual Long Beach Grand Prix, whose star-studded warm-up race sends the likes of young hipster Jason Priestly (*Beverly Hills, 90210*) and perennial racer Paul Newman burning rubber through the streets of the city. In 1998, a sleek new aquarium joined the waterfront attractions.

ESSENTIALS

GETTING THERE   From Los Angeles, take either I-5 or I-405 to I-710 south; it follows the Los Angeles River on its path to the ocean and leads directly to both downtown Long Beach and the *Queen Mary* Seaport.

VISITOR INFORMATION   Contact the **Long Beach Area Convention & Visitors Bureau,** One World Trade Center, Suite 300 (☎ **800/4LB-STAY** or 562/436-3645; www.golongbeach.org). For further information on the **Long Beach Grand Prix,** call ☎ **562/981-2600** or check out www.longbeachgp.com.

ORIENTATION   Downtown Long Beach is at the eastern end of the vast Port of Los Angeles; Pine Avenue is the central restaurant and shopping street, which extends south to Shoreline Park and the Aquarium. The *Queen Mary* is docked just across the waterway, gazing south toward tiny Long Beach marina and Naples Island.

THE *QUEEN MARY* & OTHER PORT ATTRACTIONS

✪ *Queen Mary.* Pier J (at the end of I-710), Long Beach. ☎ **562/435-3511.** www.queenmary.com. Admission $15 adults, $13 seniors 55 and over and military, $9 children 4–11, free for kids 3 and under. Daily 10am–6pm (last entry at 5:30pm), with extended summer hours. Parking $6.

It's easy to dismiss the *Queen Mary* as a barnacle-laden tourist trap, but it is the only surviving example of this particular kind of 20th-century elegance and excess. From the staterooms paneled lavishly in now-extinct tropical hardwoods to the perfectly preserved crew quarters and the miles of hallway handrails made of once-pedestrian Bakelite, wonders never cease aboard this deco luxury liner. Stroll the teakwood decks with just a bit of imagination and you're back in 1936 on the maiden voyage from Southampton, England. Don't miss the Streamline Moderne observation lounge, featured often in period motion pictures. Kiosk displays of photographs and memorabilia are everywhere—following the success of *Titanic*, the *Queen Mary* even hosted an exhibit of artifacts from its less fortunate cousin. In 1998, the Cold War–era Soviet submarine *Scorpion* sidled alongside; separate admission is required to tour the sub. Buy both tickets and you'll also get a behind-the-scenes guided tour, peppered with worthwhile anecdotes and details.

Aquarium of the Pacific. 100 Aquarium Way, off Shoreline Dr., Long Beach. ☎ **562/ 590-3100.** www.aquariumofpacific.org. Admission $14.95 adults, $11.95 seniors 60 and over, $7.95 ages 3–11, free to kids under 3. Daily 9:30am–6pm. Closed Christmas. Parking $6 max.

Opened in summer 1998 to much local scrutiny, this enormous facility is the cornerstone of Long Beach's new waterfront destination, designed to stimulate the city's flagging economy. Figuring that what worked in Monterey and Baltimore would work in Long Beach, planners gave their all to this project, creating a crowd-pleasing attraction just across the harbor from Long Beach's other mainstay, the *Queen Mary*. With enough exhibit space to fill three football fields, the aquarium re-creates three areas of the Pacific—the warm Baja and Southern California regions, the Bering Sea and chilly northern Pacific, and faraway tropical climes, including stunning re-creations of a lagoon and barrier reef. There are over 12,000 animals in all, from sharks and sea lions to delicate sea horses and moon jellies. Learn little-known aquatic facts at the many educational exhibits, or thrill to come nose-to-nose with sea lions, eels, sharks, and other inhabitants of giant, three-story-high tanks.

OTHER WATERFRONT DIVERSIONS

A different kind of nautical excursion awaits at the **Tall Ship *Californian***, the flagship of the Nautical Heritage Society. At 145 feet long, this two-masted wooden cutter-class vessel offers barefooters the opportunity to help raise and lower eight sails, steer by compass, and generally experience the "romance of the high seas." Landlubbers will want to choose the 4-hour day sail for $75 ($113 for two), including lunch, while old salts can take 2-, 3-, or 4-day cruises out to Catalina or the Channel Islands at $140 per person per day. The *Californian* sails from Long Beach between late August and mid-April (it's based in northern California in summer). Call ☎ **800/ 432-2201** for schedule and advance reservations.

Situated on a prime waterfront knoll, the **Long Beach Museum of Art**, 2300 East Ocean Ave. (☎ **562/439-2119**; www.lbma.org), was built in 1912 as the summer home of New York philanthropist Elizabeth Milbank Anderson. The grand mansion was designed by the firm who built Los Angeles's landmark Chinese and Egyptian theaters, and functioned as a private social club and WWII officers' club before becoming the museum's home in 1957. In 1999, a yearlong expansion project began to restore the home to its original state and build a complementary gallery annex on the property. In addition to its interest as an historic site, the museum is notable for its collection of 20th-century European Modernists, post-war art from California, and the largest video art archive in the nation. The museum is open Wednesday through Sunday from 10am to 5pm; admission is free until the expansion project is complete in mid-2000.

Take to the waterways Italian style at nearby Naples Island with **Gondola Getaway**, 5437 Ocean Blvd. (☎ **562/433-9595;** http://clever.net/gondolas). Since 1982, these authentic Venetian gondolas have been snaking around the man-made canals of Naples Island, under gracefully arched bridges and past the gardens of resort cottages. Feel free to bring your beverage of choice, as they'll send you out with a nice basket of bread, cheese, and salami, plus wineglasses and a full ice bucket. Perhaps your traditionally clad oarsman will sing an Italian aria or relate the many tales of marriage proposals (some not so successful!) made by romance-minded passengers. Gondola Getaway operates daily between 11am and 11pm; a 1-hour cruise for two is $55.

WHERE TO STAY

✪ **Hotel Queen Mary.** 1126 Queen's Hwy. (end of I-710), Long Beach, CA 90802-6390. ☎ **800/437-2934,** 562/435-3511, or 562/432-6964. Fax 562/437-4531. www.queenmary. com. 365 units. A/C TV TEL. $95–$225 double; from $400 suite. AE, DC, MC, V. Rates include self-parking; valet parking $5.

Although the *Queen Mary* is considered the most luxurious ocean liner ever to sail the Atlantic, with the largest rooms ever built aboard a ship, the quarters aren't exceptional when compared to those on terra firma today, nor are the amenities. The idea is to enjoy the novelty and charm of features like the original bathtub watercocks ("cold salt," "cold fresh," "hot salt," "hot fresh"). The beautifully carved interior is a feast for the eye and fun to explore, and the weekday rates are hard to beat. Three on-board restaurants are overpriced but convenient, and the shopping arcade has a decidedly British feel (one shop sells great *Queen Mary* souvenirs). An elegant Sunday champagne brunch—complete with ice sculpture and harpist—is served in the ship's Grand Salon, and it's always worth having a cocktail in the art-deco Observation Bar. If you're too young or too poor to have traveled on the old luxury liners, this is the perfect opportunity to experience the romance of an Atlantic crossing—and with no seasickness, cabin fever, or week of formal dinners.

Lord Mayor's Inn. 435 Cedar Ave., Long Beach, CA 90802. ☎ **562/436-0324.** www. lordmayors.com. 12 units. $80–$125 double. Rates include full breakfast. AE, DISC, MC, V.

Situated in a formerly elite residential neighborhood downtown, this elegant and impeccably restored Edwardian home was built in 1904 and belonged to Long Beach's first mayor, Charles H. Windham. The main house offers five charming guest rooms, each furnished with impeccably chosen antiques, luxurious high-quality linens, and heirloom bedspreads and accessories. All boast private baths cleverly recreated with vintage fixtures and painstakingly matched materials (the original home had only one bathroom). Seven more rooms—four with private bath—are available in two less-formal adjacent cottages, also dating from the early 20th century; they offer a private option for families or those seeking seclusion and independence. All guests gather at their leisure in the main house's dining room for innkeeper Laura Brasser's lavish breakfasts, which include specialties like old-world pancakes with fried apples, delicate asparagus eggs, and hearty stuffed French toast.

WHERE TO DINE

The Madison Restaurant & Bar. 102 Pine Ave., Long Beach. ☎ **562/628-8866.** www.madisonsteakhouse.com. Reservations recommended. Main courses $10–$22 lunch, $18–$29 dinner. AE, MC, V. Mon–Thurs 11am–11pm, Fri 11am–midnight, Sat 5pm–midnight, Sun 5–11pm. Valet parking $3. STEAKS/SEAFOOD.

This elegant 1920s-style supper club offers fine dining reminiscent of majestic ocean-liner dining salons. A beautifully restored historic bank building (and dinner music from the 1940s) provides the grand backdrop for service that's deferential without being stuffy. The Madison serves exceptional dry aged beef broiled and accompanied by à la carte sides like buttery garlic potatoes or perfectly seasoned creamed spinach. The menu includes seafood dishes like grilled salmon atop mussels and clams with a creamy ginger-citrus sauce, or oyster-stuffed sole breaded and drizzled with buerre blanc and fragrant fresh dill. Desserts are artistic renditions of reliable favorites—a s'mores sundae, or sugary apple crumble.

Papadakis Taverna. 301 W. Sixth St. (at Centre St.), San Pedro. ☎ **310/548-1186.** Reservations recommended. Main courses $12–$35. CB, DC, MC, V. Daily 5–10pm. GREEK.

The food here rates higher than the ambiance—even genial host John Papadakis's hand-kissing greeting doesn't soften the blunt lines and bright lights of this banquet-room–like space decorated with equal parts Aegean murals and football art (in deference to Papadakis's glory days as a University of Southern California football legend). The waiters dance and sing loudly when they're not bringing plates of spanakopita (spinach-filled phyllo pastries) or thick, satisfying tsatziki (garlic-laced cucumber-and-yogurt spread) to your table. Servings are very generous, and the wine list has something for everyone.

Shenandoah Cafe. 4722 E. Second St. (at Park Ave.), Long Beach (Belmont Shore). ☎ **562/ 434-3469.** Reservations recommended. Main courses $13–$25. AE, DISC, MC, V. Mon–Thurs 5–10pm, Fri 5–11pm, Sat 4:30–11pm, Sun 10am–2pm and 4:40–10pm. AMERICAN/ SOUTHERN.

Here's a place where "American" food means regional homestyle cuisines served in a high-ceilinged parlor that's equal parts New Orleans mansion and Grandma's house. Definitely not for vegetarians or light eaters; even fresh fish specialties are given rich and heavy Southern treatments, and meats take up most of the menu. Start by nibbling on irresistible, fresh-from-the-oven apple fritters, and prepare for an enormous meal that also includes soup or salad and sides. Recommended specialties include Texas-sized chicken-fried steak with country gravy, Santa Fe–style baby-back ribs glazed with smoky chipotle, Cajun blackened fresh catch-of-the-day, and Granny's deep-fried chicken.

2 Santa Catalina Island

22 miles W of mainland Los Angeles

Santa Catalina—which everyone calls simply Catalina—is a small, cove-fringed island famous for its laid-back inns, largely unspoiled landscape, and crystal-clear waters. Many devotees consider it southern California's alternative to Capri or Malta. Because of its relative isolation, out-of-state tourists tend to ignore it, but those who do show up have plenty of elbowroom to boat, fish, swim, scuba, and snorkel. There are miles of hiking and biking trails, plus golf, tennis, and horseback riding.

Catalina is so different from the mainland that it almost seems like a different country, remote and unspoiled. In 1915, the island was purchased by William Wrigley, Jr., the chewing-gum manufacturer, who had plans to develop it into a fashionable pleasure resort. To publicize the new vacation land, Wrigley brought big-name bands to the Avalon Ballroom and moved the Chicago Cubs, which he owned, to the island for spring training. His marketing efforts succeeded, and this charming and tranquil retreat became what it still is: a favorite vacation resort for mainlanders.

Today, about 86% of the island remains undeveloped, owned and preserved by the Santa Catalina Island Conservancy. Some of the spectacular outlying areas can only be reached by arranged tour (see "Exploring the Island," below).

ESSENTIALS

GETTING THERE   The most common way to get to and from the island is via the **Catalina Express** (☎ 800/464-4228 or 562/519-1212), which operates up to 22 daily departures year-round from San Pedro and Long Beach. The trip takes about an hour. Round-trip fares are $36 for adults, $32.50 for seniors 55 and over, $27 for children 2 to 11, and $2 for infants. In San Pedro, the Catalina Express departs from the **Sea/Air Terminal,** Berth 95; take the Harbor Freeway (I-110) south to the Harbor Boulevard exit, then follow signs to the terminal. In Long Beach, boats leave from the **Queen Mary Landing;** take the Long Beach Freeway (I-710) south, following the QUEEN MARY signs to the Catalina Express port. Call ahead for reservations. *Note:* Luggage is limited to 50 pounds per person; reservations are necessary for bicycles, surfboards, and dive tanks; and there are restrictions on transporting pets. You can leave your car at designated lots at each departure terminal; the parking fee is around $7 per 24-hour period.

Catalina Cruises (☎ 800/CATALINA) also ferries passengers from Long Beach to Avalon Harbor. It has the best rates going (about $10 cheaper than above) because it runs monstrous 700-passenger boats, which take longer to make the crossing (about 1 hour and 50 minutes). If you want to save money, particularly if you're staying overnight and don't have to maximize your island time, Catalina Cruises is a good choice.

Island Express Helicopter Service, 900 Queens Way Dr., Long Beach (☎ 310/510-2525), flies from Long Beach or San Pedro to Avalon in about 15 minutes. It flies on demand between 8am and sunset year-round, charging $66 each way. It also offers brief air tours over the island; prices vary. Island Express shares terminals with Catalina Express.

VISITOR INFORMATION   The **Catalina Island Chamber of Commerce and Visitors Bureau,** P.O. Box 217, Avalon, CA 90704 (☎ 310/510-1520; fax 310/510-7606), located on the Green Pleasure Pier, distributes brochures and information on island activities, hotels, and transportation. Call for a free 100-page visitors' guide. Its colorful Web site, **www.catalina.com,** offers current news from the *Catalina Islander* newspaper in addition to updated activities, events, and general information.

ORIENTATION   The picturesque town of **Avalon** is both the port of entry for the island and the island's only city. From the ferry dock, you can wander along Crescent Avenue, the main road along the beachfront, and easily explore adjacent side streets.

Northwest of Avalon is the village of **Two Harbors,** accessible by boat or shuttle bus. Its twin bays are favored by pleasure yachts from L.A.'s various marinas, so there's more camaraderie and a less touristy ambiance overall.

GETTING AROUND   There are only a limited number of cars permitted on the island; visitors are not allowed to drive cars on the island, and most residents, in fact, motor around in golf carts (many of the homes only have golf-cart–size driveways). Don't worry, though—you'll be able to get everywhere you want to go by renting a cart yourself or just hoofing it, which is what most visitors do.

If you want to explore the area around Avalon beyond where your feet can comfortably carry you, try renting a mountain bike or tandem from **Brown's Bikes,** 107 Pebbly Beach Rd. (☎ 310/510-0986), or even a gas-powered golf cart from **Cartopia,** on Crescent Avenue at Pebbly Beach Road (☎ 310/510-2493), where rates are about $30 per hour.

EXPLORING THE ISLAND

ORGANIZED TOURS   The Santa Catalina Island Company's **Discovery Tours** (☎ 800/626-7489 or 310/510-TOUR) has a ticket and information office on

Crescent Avenue across from the pier. It offers the greatest variety of excursions from Avalon; many last just a couple of hours, so you don't have to tie up your whole day. In addition to day and night scenic tram tours of Avalon, glass-bottomed boat cruises, and bus trips along Skyline Drive to the Airport in the Sky, Discover conducts some very worthwhile outings none of the other operators offer. Tours are available in money-saving combo packs; inquire when you call.

Noteworthy excursions include the **Undersea Tour,** a slow 1-hour cruise of Lover's Cove Marine Preserve in a semi-submerged boat ($21 for adults and $13 for kids); the ✪ **Casino Tour,** a fascinating 1-hour look at the style and inventive engineering of this elegant ballroom ($8.50 adults, $4.25 kids); nighttime **Flying Fish Boat Trips,** a 70-minute Catalina tradition in searchlight-equipped open boats ($8.50 adults, $4.25 kids); and the ✪ **Inland Motor Tour,** a half-day (4-hour) jaunt through the island's rugged interior, including an Arabian-horse show and refreshments at Wrigley's Rancho Escondido ($30 adults, $15 kids).

VISITING TWO HARBORS If you want to get a better look at the rugged natural beauty of Catalina and escape the throngs of beachgoers, head over to Two Harbors, the quarter-mile "neck" at the island's northwest end that gets its name from the "twin harbors" on each side, known as the Isthmus and Cat Harbor. An excellent starting point for campers and hikers, Two Harbors also offers just enough civilization for the less-intrepid traveler.

The **Banning House Lodge** (☎ 310/510-2800) is an 11-room bed-and-breakfast overlooking the Isthmus. The clapboard house was built in 1910 for Catalina's pre-Wrigley owners and has seen duty as on-location lodging for movie stars like Errol Flynn and Dorothy Lamour. Peaceful and isolated, the simply furnished but comfortable lodge has spectacular views of both Isthmus harbors. Rates range from $77 to $201 (April through October), and they'll even give you a lift from the pier.

Everyone eats at **Doug's Harbor Reef** (☎ 310/510-7265), down on the beach. This nautical/tropical-themed saloon/restaurant serves breakfast, lunch, and dinner, the latter consisting of hearty steaks, ribs, swordfish, chicken teriyaki, and buffalo burgers in summer. The house drink is sweet "buffalo milk," a potent concoction of vodka, crème de cacao, banana liqueur, milk, and whipped cream.

WHAT TO SEE & DO IN AVALON Walk along horseshoe-shaped Crescent Avenue, past **private yachting and fishing clubs,** toward the landmark **Casino** building. You can see the art-deco **theater** for the price of a movie ticket any night; also on the ground floor is the **Catalina Island Museum** (☎ 310/510-2414), which features exhibits on island history, archaeology, and natural history. The museum has a contour relief map of the island that's helpful to hikers. Admission is $1.50 for adults, 50¢ for kids; it's included in the price of Discovery's Casino Tour (see above).

Around the point from the Casino lies **Descanso Beach Club** (☎ 310/510-7410), a mini–Club Med in a private cove. While you can get on the beach year-round, the club's facilities (including showers, restaurant/bar, volleyball lawns, and thatched beach umbrellas) are only open from Easter to September 30. Admission is $1.50.

About 1½ miles from downtown Avalon is the **Wrigley Memorial and Botanical Garden** (☎ 310/510-2288), an invigorating walk or short taxi ride. The specialized gardens, a project of Ada Wrigley, showcase plants endemic to California's coastal islands. Open daily from 8am to 5pm; admission is $1.

SNORKELING, DIVING & KAYAKING

Snorkeling, scuba diving, and sea kayaking are among the main reasons mainlanders head to Catalina. Purists will prefer the less-spoiled waters of Two Harbors, but Avalon's many coves have plenty to offer as well, especially the protected marine life in

Casino Point Underwater Park. **Banana Boat Riders,** 107 Pebbly Beach Rd., Avalon (☎ **800/708-2262** or 310/510-1774), offers snorkel gear and sea-kayak rentals, as well as half- and full-day excursions to Two Harbors and other island coves. **Scuba Luv** (☎ **800/262-DIVE** or 310/510-2350) offers guided half-day to 2-day snorkel and scuba tours with certified instructors. **Descanso Beach Ocean Sports** (☎ **310/ 510-1226**) offers sea kayak and snorkel rentals with instruction, plus specialty expeditions and kids' programs.

At Two Harbors, stop by **West End Dive Center** (☎ **310/510-2800**). Excursions range from half-day introductory dives to complete certification courses to multi-day dive packages. It also rents snorkel gear and offers kayak rental, instruction, and excursions.

WHERE TO STAY

If you plan to stay overnight, be sure to reserve a room in advance, since most places fill up pretty quickly during the summer and holiday seasons. **Catalina Island Accommodations** (☎ **310/510-3000**) might be able to help you out in a pinch; it's a reservations service with updated information on the whole island.

In addition to the choices below, we recommend the **Catalina Island Inn**, 125 Metropole Ave. (☎ **800/246-8134** or 310/510-1623), one of Avalon's historic boardinghouse-style hotels. Rates are inexpensive to moderate and include continental breakfast. Or, for a European ambiance, try the waterfront **Vista del Mar,** 417 Crescent Ave. (☎ **310/510-1452**), situated above the boardwalk and featuring plenty of lounge chairs and thoughtful amenities. Rates are moderate and include breakfast plus afternoon cookies and milk. If you'd like to stay on the less-visited side of the island, see "Visiting Two Harbors" under "Exploring the Island," above.

Hotel Metropole. 205 Crescent Ave. (PO Box 1900), Avalon, CA 90704. ☎ **800/300-8528** or 310/510-1884. Fax 310/510-2534. www.catalina.com/metropole. 48 units. A/C MINIBAR TEL TV. Summer (May–Oct) $129–$209 double; from $249 suite; winter $99–$179 double, from $199 suite. Rates include continental breakfast. AE, MC, V.

Named for Avalon's historic grande dame hotel, today's Metropole is the cornerstone of a shopping plaza that looks like Disneyland's New Orleans Square. Built in the early 1990s, this sleek and well-appointed replacement has the ambiance of a boutique inn, affording nice views from almost every room on its three floors. There's a windshielded rooftop deck and whirlpool overlooking the harbor, and some rooms have luxurious touches like fireplaces, whirlpool tubs, and balconies. Furnishings throughout public areas and guest rooms alike are contemporary with a tropical air, reminiscent of a Florida plantation. Just outside the front door is all of Avalon Bay's activity, starting with the theme-y Metropole Market Place in the ground-floor courtyard. It may look touristy from the outside, but the Metropole shapes up as a classy, comfortable retreat that's equally suitable for romantic interludes or family getaways.

✪ **The Inn on Mt. Ada.** 398 Wrigley Rd. (P.O. Box 2560), Avalon, CA 90704. ☎ **800/ 608-7669** or 310/510-2030. Fax 310/510-2237. www.catalina.com/mtada. 6 units. Nov–May Mon–Thurs $205–$350 double; $350–$455 suite. June–Oct and Fri–Sun year-round $300–$475 double; $475–$580 suite. Rates include three meals daily. MC, V.

When William Wrigley, Jr., purchased Catalina Island in 1921, he built this ornate hilltop Georgian colonial mansion as his summer vacation home; it's now one of the finest small hotels in California. The opulent inn has several ground-floor salons, a club room with fireplace, a deep-seated formal library, and a wickered sunroom where tea, cookies, and fruit are always available. The best guest room is the Grand Suite, fitted with a fireplace and a large private patio. Amenities include bathrobes and the use of a golf cart during your stay. TVs are available on request, but there are no phones in the rooms. A hearty full breakfast, a light deli-style lunch, and a beautiful multicourse dinner complemented by a limited wine selection are included in the tariff.

Zane Grey Pueblo Hotel. Off Chimes Tower Rd., north of Hill St. (P.O. Box 216), Avalon, CA 90704. ☎ **800/3-PUEBLO** or 310/510-0966. www.virtualcities.com. 17 units. June–Sept $90–$175 double; Oct–May $59–$90 double. Rates include continental breakfast. AE, MC, V.

Author and avid fisherman Zane Grey spent his later years in Avalon and wrote many books here, including *Tales of Swordfish and Tuna*, which tells of his local fishing adventures. Perched atop a steep road overlooking the bay, this unfancy house still sports many of the ethnic touches (Tahitian teak, Hopi elements) Grey enjoyed. The simply furnished guest rooms have private bathrooms and ceiling fans; a comfortable living room features a fireplace, grand piano, and TV. The house is one of only two Avalon hotels with its own pool; shuttle service is offered to and from town.

WHERE TO DINE

Other than the choices below, recommended Avalon options include **The Channel House,** 205 Crescent Ave. (☎ **310/510-1617**), where continental fare is served with elegance but without pretension on a romantic outdoor patio or in a quiet dining room. For a special treat, head to the recently reopened **Clubhouse Bar & Grille,** at the historic Catalina Island Country Club (☎ **310/510-7404**). The California/Pacific Rim menu is peppered with abundant anecdotes from the club's star-studded history, and the restaurant is open throughout the day (from 11am to 9pm). On the Two Harbors side of the island, **Doug's Harbor Reef** is the place to eat; see "Exploring the Island," above.

The Busy Bee. 306 Crescent Ave. (north of the Pleasure Pier). ☎ **310/510-1983.** Reservations not accepted. Main courses $7–$15. AE, CB, DC, DISC, MC, V. Summer daily 8am–10pm; winter daily 10am–8pm. AMERICAN.

An Avalon institution, occupying this prime waterfront spot since 1923, this casual deli/diner serves throughout the day; it has a heated and wind-protected patio as well as full bar service. While the food is unremarkable, it's good, reliable, homestyle stuff; the place is always crowded in season because it's right in the middle of the action.

El Galleon. 411 Crescent Ave. ☎ **310/510-1188.** Reservations recommended on weekends. Main courses $6–$12 lunch, $11–$25 dinner. AE, MC, V. Daily 11am–10pm. Bar daily 11am–2am. AMERICAN.

It's Catalina's answer to Disney's *Pirates of the Caribbean.* Red-leather booths, brass portholes, ship's rigging, and wrought-iron conquistador decor are the perfect setting for a hearty menu of steaks and seafood. You can also make a respectable repast from the many appetizer selections, each of which is like a meal. Our favorites are zesty BBQ pork ribs, Cajun crab cakes with Creole sauce, and warm spinach-artichoke dip with chewy sourdough bread.

3 Big Bear Lake & Lake Arrowhead

100 miles NE of Los Angeles

These two deep-blue lakes lie close to each other in the San Bernardino Mountains, and have long been a favorite year-round alpine playground for city-weary Angelenos.

Big Bear Lake has always been popular with skiers as well as avid boaters (it's much larger than Arrowhead, and equipment rentals abound), and in the past decade the area has been given a much-needed face-lift. Big Bear Boulevard was substantially widened to handle high-season traffic, and downtown Big Bear Lake (the "Village")

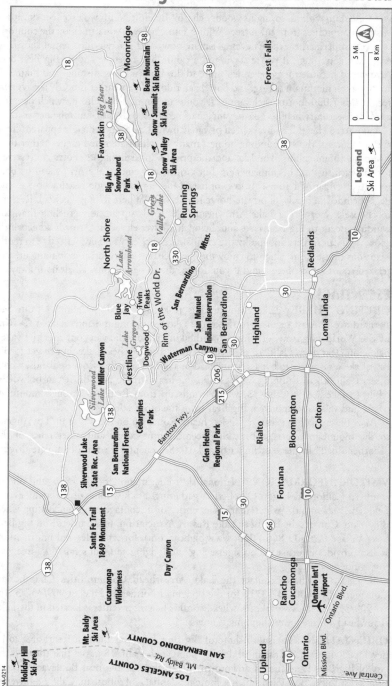

Legend
Ski Area

was spiffed up without losing its woodsy charm. In addition to two excellent ski slopes less than 5 minutes from town (see "Winter Fun," below), you can enjoy the comforts of a real supermarket (there's even a Kmart now) and several video-rental shops, all especially convenient if you're staying in a cabin. Most people choose Big Bear over Arrowhead because there's so much more to do, from boating, fishing, and hiking to snow sports, mountain biking, and horseback riding. The weather is nearly always perfect at this 7,000-foot-plus elevation: If you want proof, ask Caltech, which operates a solar observatory here to take advantage of nearly 300 days of sunshine per year.

Lake Arrowhead has always been privately owned, as is immediately apparent from the affluence of the surrounding homes, many of which are gated estates rather than rustic mountain cabins. The lake and the private docks lining its shores are reserved for the exclusive use of homeowners, but visitors can enjoy Lake Arrowhead by boat tour (see "Organized Tours," below) or use of the summer-season beach clubs, a privilege included in nearly all private-home rentals (see "Where to Stay," below). Reasons to choose a vacation at Lake Arrowhead? The roads up are less grueling than the winding ascent to Big Bear Lake and, being at a lower elevation, Arrowhead gets little snow (you can forget those pesky tire chains). It's very easy and cost effective to rent a luxurious house from which to enjoy the spectacular scenery, crisp mountain air, and relaxed resort atmosphere—and if you do ski, the slopes are only a half hour away.

ESSENTIALS

GETTING THERE Lake Arrowhead is reached by taking Calif. 18 from San Bernardino. The last segment of this route takes you along the aptly named ✪ **Rim of the World Highway,** offering a breathtaking panoramic view out over the valley below on clear days. Calif. 18 then continues east to Big Bear Lake, but to get to Big Bear Lake it's quicker to bypass Arrowhead by taking Calif. 330 from Redlands, which meets Calif. 18 in Running Springs. During heavy-traffic periods, it can be worthwhile to take scenic Calif. 38, which winds up from Redlands through mountain passes and valleys to approach Big Bear from the other side.

Note: Nostalgia lovers can revisit legendary **Route 66** on the way from Los Angeles to the mountain resorts, substituting scenic motor courts and other relics of the "Mother Road" in place of impersonal I-10. See chapter 15 for a complete driving tour.

VISITOR INFORMATION National ski tours, mountain-bike races, and one of southern California's largest Oktoberfest gatherings are just some of the many events held here year-round—which may either entice or discourage you from visiting when they're on. Contact the **Big Bear Lake Resort Association,** 630 Bartlett Rd., Big Bear Lake Village (☎ 909/866-7000; www.bigbear.com), for schedules and information. It also provides information on sightseeing and lodging and will send you a free visitors' guide.

In Lake Arrowhead, contact the **Lake Arrowhead Communities Chamber of Commerce** (☎ 800/337-3716 for the Lodging Information Line, or 909/337-3715; fax 909/336-1548; www.lakearrowhead.com). The visitor center is located in the Lake Arrowhead Village lower shopping center.

ORIENTATION The south shore of Big Bear Lake was the first resort area to be developed and remains the most densely populated. Calif. 18 passes first through the city of Big Bear Lake and its downtown village; then, as Big Bear Boulevard, it continues east to Big Bear City, which is more residential and suburban. Calif. 38 traverses the north shore, home to pristine national forest and great hiking trails, as well as a couple of small marinas (see "Water Sports," below) and a lakefront bed-and-breakfast inn (see "Where to Stay," below).

Arrowhead's main town is Lake Arrowhead Village, located on the south shore at the end of Calif. 173. The village's commercial center is home to factory-outlet stores, about 40 chain and specialty shops, and the Lake Arrowhead Resort Hotel. Minutes away is the town of Blue Jay (along Calif. 189), where the Ice Castle Skating Rink is located (see "Winter Fun," below).

ENJOYING THE OUTDOORS

In addition to the activities below, there's a great recreation spot for families near the heart of Big Bear Lake: **Magic Mountain,** on Calif. 18/Big Bear Boulevard (☎ 909/ 866-4626), has a year-round bobsled-style Alpine Slide, a splashy double water slide open from mid-June to mid-September, and bunny slopes for snow tubing from November to Easter. The dry Alpine Slide is $3 a ride, the water slide is $1 (or $10 for a day-pass), and snow play costs $10 per day including tube and rope tow.

The **Moonridge Animal Park** (☎ 909/866-0183), located at the base of the Bear Mountain Ski Resort, offers an opportunity to roam around and get an up-close look at mountain lions, raccoons, hawks, timber wolves, grazing deer, owls, bobcats, and more. The zoo is a sanctuary for orphaned and injured animals unable to be released into the wild, including grizzly bears. It's open May through October, daily from 10am to 5pm; November through April, weekends and holidays only (weather permitting) from 10am to 4pm. Admission is $2 for adults, $1 for kids 3 to 11, and free for kids under 3.

WATER SPORTS

BOATING   You can rent all kinds of boats—including speedboats, rowboats, paddleboats, pontoons, sailboats, and canoes—at a number of Big Bear Lake marinas. Rates vary only slightly from place to place: A 14-foot dinghy with an outboard runs around $10 per hour or $30 for a half day; pontoon (patio) boats that can hold large groups range in size and price from $25 to $45 per hour or $80 to $150 for a half-day. **Pine Knot Landing** (☎ 909/866-BOAT) is the most centrally located marina, behind the post office at the foot of Pine Knot Boulevard in Big Bear Lake. **Gray's Landing** (☎ 909/866-2443) is just across the dam on the north shore and offers the best prices and the least attitude. **Big Bear Marina,** Paine Road at Lakeview (☎ 909/ 866-3218), is also close to Big Bear Lake Village and provides take-along chicken dinners when you rent a pontoon boat for a sunset cruise ($75 for 3 hours).

FISHING   Big Bear Lake brims with rainbow trout, bass, and catfish in spring and summer, the best fishing seasons. Phone ☎ 310/590-5020 for recorded stocking information. A fishing license is required and costs $8.95 per day, $24.95 per year. Pine Knot Landing, Gray's Landing, and Big Bear Marina (see "Boating," above) all rent fishing boats and have bait and tackle shops that sell licenses.

JET-SKIING   Personal Water Craft (PWCs) are available for rent at **Big Bear Marina** (see "Boating," above) and **Pleasure Point Landing,** 603 Landlock Landing Rd. (☎ 909/866-2455), where you can rent a single-rider SeaDoo for $35 an hour, or opt for a two-seat Waverunner at $55 per hour. **North Shore Landing,** on Calif. 38, 2 miles west of Fawnskin (☎ 909/868-4386), rents jet skis and two- and three-person Waverunners at rates ranging from $55 to $65 per hour. Call ahead to reserve your craft and check age and deposit requirements.

WATER-SKIING   Big Bear Lake, Pine Knot Landing, North Shore Landing, and Big Bear Marina (see "Boating," above) all offer water-ski lessons and speedboat rentals. Lake Arrowhead is home to the **McKenzie Water Ski School,** dockside in Lake Arrowhead Village (☎ 909/337-3814), famous for teaching Kirk Douglas, George Hamilton, and other Hollywood stars to ski. It's open from Memorial Day to the end of September and offers group lessons for $115 per hour, short refresher lessons for $35, and boat charters (including driver) for $95 an hour.

OTHER WARM-WEATHER ACTIVITIES

GOLF The **Bear Mountain Golf Course,** Goldmine Drive, Big Bear Lake (☎ 909/585-8002), is a 9-hole, par-35, links-style course that winds through a gently sloping meadow at the base of the Bear Mountain Ski Resort. The course is open daily from April through November. Greens fees are $17 and $23 for 9 and 18 holes, respectively. Both riding carts and pull carts are available. Phone for tee times.

HIKING Hikers will love the San Bernardino National Forest. The gray squirrel is a popular native; you may see them scurrying around gathering acorns or material for their nest. You can sometimes spot deer, coyotes, and American bald eagles, which come here with their young in winter. The black-crowned stellar jay and the talkative red, white, and black acorn woodpecker are the most common of the great variety of birds in this pine forest.

Stop in at the brand-new **Forest Information Center** on Calif. 38, 3 miles east of Fawnskin on Big Bear Lake's north shore (☎ 909/866-3437). Here you can pick up free trail maps, as well as other information on the area's plants, animals, and geology. The best choice for a short mountain hike is the **Woodland Trail,** which begins near the ranger station. The best long hike is the **Pacific Crest Trail,** which travels 39 miles through the mountains above Big Bear and Arrowhead lakes. The most convenient trailhead is located at Cougar Crest, half a mile west of the Big Bear Ranger Station.

The best place to begin a hike in Lake Arrowhead is at the **Arrowhead Ranger Station,** located in the town of Skyforest on Calif. 18 (☎ 909/337-2444), a quarter mile east of the Lake Arrowhead turnoff (Calif. 173). The staff will provide you with maps and information on the best area trails, which range from easy to difficult. The **Enchanted Loop Trail,** near the town of Blue Jay, is an easy half-hour hike. The **Heaps Peak Arboretum Trail** winds through a grove of redwoods; the trailhead is on the north side of Calif. 18, at an auxiliary ranger kiosk west of Running Springs.

The area is home to a **National Children's Forest,** a 20-acre area developed so that children, the wheelchair-bound, and the visually impaired could enjoy nature. To get to the Children's Forest from Lake Arrowhead, take Calif. 330 to Calif. 18 east, past Deer Lick Station; when you reach a road marked IN96 (open only in summer), turn right and go 3 miles.

HORSEBACK RIDING Horses are permitted on all the mountain trails through the national forest. **Bear Mountain Stables,** at Bear Mountain Ski Resort, City of Big Bear Lake (☎ 909/878-HORSE), offers 1- and 2-hour guided rides for $20 per hour, and sunset hay rides for $45. The stables are open daily from May through December; phone for reservations. **Baldwin Lake Stables,** southeast of Big Bear City (☎ 909/585-6482), conducts hourly, lunch, and sunset rides in addition to offering lessons.

MOUNTAIN BIKING Big Bear Lake has become a mountain-biking center, with most of the action around the **Snow Summit Ski Area** (see "Winter Fun," below), where a $7 lift ticket will take you and your bike to a scenic web of trails, fire roads, and meadows at about 8,000 feet. Call its **Summer Activities Hotline** (☎ 909/866-4621). The lake's north shore is also a popular biking destination; the forest service ranger stations (see "Hiking," above) have maps to the historic gold rush–era Holcomb Valley and the 2-mile Alpine Pedal Path (an easy lakeside ride).

Big Bear Bikes, 41810 Big Bear Blvd. (☎ 909/866-4565), rents mountain bikes for $6 an hour or $21 for 4 hours. **Bear Valley Bikes,** 40298 Big Bear Blvd. (☎ 909/866-8000), rents bikes and offers free lessons on Sundays. **Team Big Bear** is located at the base of Snow Summit (☎ **909/866-4565**); it rents bicycles and provides detailed maps and guides for all Big Bear–area trails.

At Lake Arrowhead, bikes are permitted on all hiking trails and back roads except the Pacific Crest Trail. See the local ranger station for an area map. Gear can be rented from the **Lake Arrowhead Resort** (☎ **909/336-1511**) or **Above & Beyond Sports,** 32877 Calif. 18, Running Springs (☎ **909/867-5517**).

WINTER FUN

SKIING & SNOWBOARDING   When the L.A. basin gets wintertime rain, skiers everywhere rejoice, for they know snow is falling up in the mountains. The last few seasons have seen abundant natural snowfall at Big Bear, augmented by sophisticated snowmaking equipment, which also compensates during drier years. While the slopes can't compare with those in Utah or Colorado, they do offer diversity, difficulty, and convenience.

Snow Summit at Big Bear Lake (☎ **909/866-5766;** www.bigbear.com/summit) is the skier's choice, especially since it installed its second high-speed quad express from the 7,000-foot base to the 8,200-foot summit. Another nice feature is green (easy) runs even from the summit, so beginners can also enjoy the Summit Haus lodge and breathtaking lake views from the top. Advanced risk-takers will appreciate three double-black-diamond runs. Lift tickets range from $30 to $42. The resort offers mid-week, beginner, half-day, night, and family specials, as well as ski and snowboard instruction. Hey, you can even ski free on your birthday here! Other helpful Snow Summit phone numbers include advance lift-ticket sales (☎ **909/866-5841**), the ski school (☎ **909/866-4546**), and a snow report (☎ **310/390-1498** in L.A. County).

The **Bear Mountain Ski Resort** at Big Bear Lake (☎ **909/585-2519,** or 213/683-8100 for a snow report; www.bearmtn.com) is the smallest of the area's three major resorts, but experts flock to the double-black-diamond "Geronimo" run from the 8,805-foot Bear Peak. Natural-terrain skiers and snowboarders will enjoy legal access to off-trail canyons, but the limited beginner slopes and kids' areas get pretty crowded in season. One high-speed quad express rises from the 7,140-foot base to 8,440-foot Goldmine Mountain; most runs from here are intermediate. Bear Mountain has a ski school, abundant dining facilities, and a well-stocked ski shop.

The **Snow Valley Ski Resort** in Arrowbear, midway between Arrowhead and Big Bear (☎ **800/680-SNOW** or 909/867-2751; www.aminews.com/snowvalley), has improved its snowmaking and facilities to be competitive with the other two major ski areas, and is the primary choice of skiers staying at Arrowhead. From a base elevation of 6,800 feet, Snow Valley's 13 chairlifts (including five triples) can take you from the beginner runs all the way up to black-diamond challenges at the 7,898-foot peak. Lift tickets cost $35 to $40 for adults; children's programs, night skiing, and lesson packages are available.

The **Big Air Snowboard Park** in Green Valley (☎ **909/867-2338**)—take Green Valley Lake Road from Arrowbear—is the answer to a snowboarder's dream. No skiers are allowed on Big Air's 50 rideable acres full of hits, bonks, spines, and more. Use the rope tow or take the high-speed chair to untouched forest full of natural hits. It offers equipment rentals, lessons, and package deals. All-day passes are $24 for adults, $18 for kids 12 and under; half-day passes are $20 and $14, respectively.

ICE-SKATING   The **Blue Jay Ice Castle,** at North Bay Road and Calif. 189 (☎ **909/33-SKATE;** www.ice-castle.com), near Lake Arrowhead Village, is a training site for world champion Michelle Kwan and boasts Olympic gold medalist Robin Cousins on its staff. Several public sessions each day—as well as hockey, broomball, group lessons, and book-in-advance private parties—give nonpros a chance to enjoy this impeccably groomed "outdoor" rink (it's open on three sides to the scenery and fresh air).

ORGANIZED TOURS

LAKE TOURS The *Big Bear Queen* (☎ 909/866-3218), a midget Mississippi-style paddle wheeler, cruises Big Bear Lake on 90-minute tours daily from late April through November. The boat departs from Big Bear Marina (at the end of Paine Avenue). Tours are $9.50 for adults, $8 for seniors 65 and older, $5 for children 3 to 12, and free for kids under 3. Call for reservations and information on the special Sunday brunch, champagne sunset, and dinner cruises.

Fifty-minute tours of Lake Arrowhead are offered year-round on the *Arrowhead Queen* (☎ 909/336-6992), a sister ship that departs hourly each day between 10am and 6pm from Lake Arrowhead Village. Tours are $9.50 for adults, $8.50 for seniors, $6.50 for children 2 to 12, and free for kids under 2. It's about the only way to really see this alpine jewel, unless you know a resident with a boat.

FOREST TOURS **Big Bear Jeep Tours** (☎ 909/878-JEEP) journeys into Big Bear Lake's backcountry, including historic Holcomb Valley, relic of the gold rush, plus the panoramic viewpoint Butler Peak. These off-road adventures range in length from 2 to 4½ hours, and cost from $38 to $80 per person. Bring your own snack, though, because although the guide carries ample water, the longer excursions include short but appetite-building hikes. Phone for reservations, particularly on weekends and holidays.

WHERE TO STAY
BIG BEAR LAKE

Vacation rentals are plentiful in the area, from cabins to condos to private homes. Some can accommodate up to 20 people and can be rented on a weekly or monthly basis. The oldest realtor, with seven area offices and a wide range of rental properties, is **Spencer Real Estate** (☎ 800/237-3725 or 909/866-7591). The **Village Reservation Service** (☎ 909/866-8583 or 909/585-5850) can arrange for everything from Jacuzzi condos to lakefront homes, or call the **Big Bear Lake Resort Association** (☎ 909/866-7000) for information and referrals on all types of lodgings.

Besides the places below, other choices we recommend are **Apples Bed & Breakfast Inn,** 42430 Moonridge Rd. (☎ 909/866-0903), a crabapple-red New England–style clapboard that blends hotel-like professionalism with B&B amenities (and lots of cute, frilly touches); and **Gold Mountain Manor,** 1117 Anita Ave. (☎ 909/585-6997), a woodsy 1920s lodge that's now an ultra-cozy (and affordable) B&B.

Grey Squirrel Resort. 39372 Big Bear Blvd., Big Bear Lake, CA 92315. ☎ 800/381-5569 or 909/866-4335. Fax 909/866-6271. www.greysquirrel.com. 18 cabins. TV TEL. $75–$95 1-bedroom cabin; $99–$125 2-bedroom cabin; $125–$275 3-bedroom cabin. Value rates available. Higher rates on holidays. AE, DISC, MC, V. Pets welcome for extra $10 fee per day.

This is the most attractive of the many cabin-cluster-type motels near the city of Big Bear Lake, offering a wide range of rustic cabins, most with fireplace and kitchen. They're adequately, if not attractively, furnished—the appeal here is the flexibility and privacy afforded large or long-term parties. Facilities include a heated pool that's enclosed in winter, an indoor spa, a fire pit and barbecues, volleyball and basketball courts, laundry facilities, and completely equipped kitchens.

Holiday Inn Big Bear Chateau. 42200 Moonridge Rd. (P.O. Box 1814), Big Bear Lake, CA 92315. ☎ 800/BEAR-INN or 909/866-6666. Fax 909/866-8988. 76 units. A/C TV TEL. $120–$180 double; $180–$250 suite. Winter ski and summer-fun packages available. AE, DISC, MC, V.

One of only two traditional full-service hotels in Big Bear, this European-flavored property underwent a complete renovation in 1997. Its highly visible location—just off Big Bear Boulevard, at the base of the road to Bear Mountain—makes the Chateau a popular choice for skiers and families. The rooms are modern but more charming than your average Holiday Inn, with tapestries, brass beds, antique furniture, gas fireplaces, and lavish marble bathrooms, many with whirlpool tubs. There's a heated outdoor pool and spa, and the entire compound is surrounded by tall forest. The restaurant (which also provides room service) is advertised as "casually elegant," which means you can enjoy upscale continental/American cuisine even in après-ski duds.

✪ **Windy Point Inn.** 39015 North Shore Dr., Fawnskin, CA 92333. ☎ **909/866-2746.** Fax 909/866-1593. 5 units. $135–$245 double. Rates include welcome cookies, lavish full breakfast, and afternoon hors d'oeuvres. Midweek discounts available. AE, DISC, MC, V.

A contemporary architectural showpiece on the scenic north shore, the Windy Point is the only shorefront B&B in Big Bear, and all rooms but one have spectacular sunrise/sunset views over the lake. Hosts Val and Kent Kessler's attention to detail is impeccable—if you're tired of knotty pine and Victorian frills, here's a grown-up place for you, with plenty of romance and all the pampering you can stand. Every unit has a wood-burning fireplace, feather bed, private deck, VCR (you can borrow tapes from the Inn's plentiful video library), coffeemaker, and fridge; some also feature whirlpool tubs, CD players, and luxurious state-of-the-art bathrooms. The welcoming Great Room features a casual sunken fireplace nook with floor-to-ceiling windows overlooking the lake, a telescope for stargazing, a baby grand, and up-to-date menus for every local eatery. Many guests never leave the cocoon of their room after Kent's custom gourmet breakfast each day, but if they do, they find a wintertime bald-eagle habitat is just up the road, and the city of Big Bear Lake is only a 10-minute drive around the lake.

LAKE ARROWHEAD

There are far more private homes than tourist accommodations in Arrowhead, but rental properties abound, from cozy cottages to palatial mansions; many can be surprisingly economical for families or other groups. Two of the largest agencies are **Arrowhead Cabin Rentals** (☎ **800/244-5138** or 909/337-2403) and **Arrowhead Mountain Resorts Rentals** (☎ **800/743-0865** or 909/337-4413). Overnight guests in rental properties enjoy some resident lake privileges—be sure to ask when you reserve.

Two other options are **Chateau du Lac,** 911 Hospital Rd. (☎ **909/337-6488**), an elegant and contemporary five-room B&B with stunning views of the lake; and the **Saddleback Inn,** 300 S. Calif. 173 (☎ **800/858-3334** or 909/336-3571), an inn and restaurant that still boasts historic charm while offering up-to-date in-room amenities, all at a prime location in the center of the village.

Bracken Fern Manor. 815 Arrowhead Villas Rd. (P.O. Box 1006), Lake Arrowhead, CA 92352. ☎ **909/337-8557.** Fax 909/337-3323. 10 units. $80–$185 double. Rates include full breakfast. MC, V. Located half a mile north of Calif. 18.

Billing itself as a "House of Now Fine Repute," this off-the-beaten-path inn boasts a registered historical marker as well as a checkered past. The present owners work hard at evoking its 1930s heyday: They've preserved the downstairs public rooms, along with many well-maintained antiques, and named each guest room for one of the "girls." There are many quiet corners for relaxing, including a games room, hidden library, whirlpool gazebo, and wood-lined sauna. Rooms are decorated in a fresh country style and have private bathrooms, a feature not originally included in the house.

Lake Arrowhead Resort. 27984 Calif. 189, Lake Arrowhead, CA 92352. ☎ **800/ 800-6792** or 909/336-1511. Fax 909/336-1378. www.lakearrowheadresort.com. 177 units. A/C MINIBAR TV TEL. $119–$229 double; $299–$399 suite. Inquire about auto-club discounts. AE, CB, DC, DISC, MC, V.

This sprawling resort has been upgraded somewhat since it was part of the Hilton chain, but location is still its most outstanding feature, coupled with unparalleled service and facilities. Situated on the lakeshore adjacent to Lake Arrowhead Village, the hotel has its own beach, plus docks that are ideal for fishing. The rooms are fitted with good-quality, bulk-purchased contemporary furnishings, and most have balconies, king-size beds, and fireplaces. The suites, some in private cottages, are equipped with full kitchens and whirlpool tubs.

The hotel offers a casual restaurant serving all meals (and room service), plus the elegant Seasons, which serves dinner but has only limited hours off-season. Facilities include a fully equipped health club, a heated outdoor pool and whirlpool, racquetball courts, massage, and a video arcade. A full program of supervised children's activities, ranging from nature hikes to T-shirt painting, is offered on weekends year-round.

Pine Rose Cabins. 25994 Calif. 189 (P.O. Box 31), Twin Peaks, CA 92391. ☎ **800/ 429-PINE** or 909/337-2341. Fax 909/337-0258. www.lakearrowheadcabins.com. 17 units. $69–$179 cabin for up to 4 people; $350 5-bedroom lodge. Ski packages offered in season. AE, DISC, MC, V. Pets accepted with $5 fee per night and $100 refundable deposit.

The only place of its kind in Lake Arrowhead, Pine Rose Cabins is a good choice for families. Situated on 5 forested acres about 3 miles from the lake, the wonderful freestanding cabins offer lots of privacy. Innkeepers Tricia and David Dufour have 15 cabins, ranging in size from romantic studios to a large five-bedroom lodge, each decorated in a different theme: The Indian cabin has a tepeelike bed; the bed in Wild Bill's cabin is covered like a wagon. One- and two-bedroom units have fully stocked kitchens and separate living areas. There's a large heated pool on the premises, plus swing sets, croquet, tetherball, and Ping-Pong.

WHERE TO DINE
BIG BEAR LAKE

The Captain's Anchorage. Moonridge Way at Big Bear Blvd., Big Bear Lake. ☎ **909/ 866-3997.** Reservations recommended. Full dinners $10–$25. AE, MC, V. Sun–Thurs 4:30–9pm; Fri–Sat 4:30–10pm. STEAK/SEAFOOD.

Historic and rustic, this knotty-pine restaurant has been serving fine steaks, prime rib, seafood, and lobster since 1947. Inside, the dark, nautical decor and fire-warmed bar are just right on blustery winter nights. It's got one of those mile-long soup-and-salad bars, plus some great early-bird and weeknight specials.

Madlon's. 829 W. Big Bear Blvd., Big Bear City. ☎ **909/585-3762.** Reservations recommended. Main courses $12–$25. DC, DISC, MC, V. Sat–Sun 8am–2pm; Tues–Fri 11am–2pm; Tues–Sun 5–9pm. AMERICAN/CONTINENTAL.

One of the few non-retro-fare dining rooms at the mountain resorts, Madlon's brings a bit of European flair to this fairy-tale cottage. A variety of creative croissant sandwiches at lunch are complemented by dinner selections like black-pepper filet mignon with mushroom-and-brandy sauce, and lemon-pepper-marinated chicken breast over pasta, all of which are prepared with a sophisticated touch.

Mozart's Bistro. 40701 Big Bear Blvd., Big Bear Lake. ☎ **909/866-9497.** Main courses $7–$10 lunch, $14–$25 dinner. AE, DISC, MC, V. Tues–Sun 11:30am–3pm; Tues–Thurs and Sun 5:30–9pm; Fri–Sat 5:30–10pm. CALIFORNIA.

At last, a trendy Big Bear restaurant (the regular weekenders from L.A. must have been complaining). Mozart's, which opened in 1998, isn't perfect—at these prices, the service could be more polished and the bar better stocked—but its immediate surge in popularity shows how starved the community was for a sophisticated menu incorporating American-based fusion and Pacific Rim cuisine. The house specialty is rack of pork glazed with hard-cider molasses sauce and served with chayote squash and garlic mashed potatoes; other seasonal choices include mahimahi in a macadamia-coconut crust on a pool of honey-lime beurre blanc, and breaded veal schnitzel with lingonberry port-wine sauce—a nod to the Bavarian flavor of the building (which was formerly Hansel's Cottage).

Old Country Inn. 41126 Big Bear Blvd., Big Bear Lake. ☎ **909/866-5600.** Main courses $5–$20. AE, CB, DC, DISC, MC, V. Sun–Thurs 8am–9pm; Fri–Sat 8am–10pm. DINER/ GERMAN.

The Old Country Inn has long been a favorite for hearty pre-ski breakfasts and stick-to-your-ribs old-world dinners. The restaurant is casual and welcoming, and the adjacent cocktail lounge is raucous on weekends. At breakfast, enjoy German apple pancakes or colossal omelets, while lunch choices include salads, sandwiches, and burgers. At lunch or dinner, feast on Wiener schnitzel, sauerbraten, and other gravy-topped German standards, along with grilled steaks and chicken.

LAKE ARROWHEAD

For an affluent residential community, there are surprisingly few dining options around Lake Arrowhead. But not surprisingly, what there is tends to run toward pricey elegance—elegant for a rustic mountain resort, that is. Although there is both a California/continental restaurant and a casual family eatery in the Lake Arrowhead Resort (see "Where to Stay," above), you might want to venture out to some of the locals' choices. These include the **Chef's Inn & Tavern,** 29020 Oak Terrace, Cedar Glen (☎ **909/336-4488**), a moderate to expensive continental restaurant in a turn-of-the-century former bordello; the **Antler's Inn,** 26125 Calif. 189, Twin Peaks (☎ **909/337-4020**), serving prime rib, seafood, and buffalo in a historic log lodge; the **Royal Oak,** 27187 Calif. 189, Blue Jay Village (☎ **909/337-6018**), an expensive American/continental steak house with a pub; and **Belgian Waffle Works,** dockside at Lake Arrowhead Village (☎ **909/337-5222**), an inexpensive coffee shop with Victorian decor, known for its generous, crispy waffles with tasty toppings.

4 Disneyland & Other Anaheim-Area Attractions

27 miles SE of downtown Los Angeles

The sleepy Orange County town of Anaheim grew up around Disneyland, the West's most famous theme park. Now, even beyond this Happiest Place on Earth, the city and its neighboring communities are kid-central: Otherwise unspectacular, sprawling suburbs have become a playground of family-oriented hotels, restaurants, and unabashedly tourist-oriented attractions. Among the nearby draws are Knott's Berry Farm, another family-oriented theme park, in nearby Buena Park. At the other end of the scale is the Richard Nixon Library and Birthplace, a surprisingly compelling presidential library and museum, just 7 miles northeast of Disneyland in Yorba Linda.

ESSENTIALS

GETTING THERE   Los Angeles International Airport (LAX) is located about 30 minutes from Anaheim via I-5 south (see "Orientation," in chapter 13). If you're heading directly to Anaheim and want to avoid L.A. altogether, try to land at the

John Wayne International Airport in Irvine (☎ **714/252-5200**), Orange County's largest airport. It's about 15 miles from Disneyland. Check to see if your hotel has a free shuttle to and from either airport, or call one of the following commercial shuttle services (fares are generally $10 one-way from John Wayne): **L.A. Xpress** (☎ 800/I-ARRIVE), **Prime Time** (☎ 800/262-7433), or **SuperShuttle** (☎ 714/517-6600). Car-rental agencies located at the John Wayne Airport include **Budget** (☎ 800/221-1203) and **Hertz** (☎ 800/654-3131).

VISITOR INFORMATION   The **Anaheim/Orange County Visitor and Convention Bureau,** 800 W. Katella Ave. (P.O. Box 4270), Anaheim, CA 92803 (☎ **714/999-8999**), can fill you in on area activities and shopping shuttles. It's located just inside the convention center (across the street from Disneyland), next to the dramatic cantilevered arena, and welcomes visitors Monday through Friday from 8am to 5pm.

The **Buena Park Convention and Visitors Office,** 6280 Manchester Blvd., Suite 103, Buena Park, CA 90621 (☎ **800/541-3953** or 714/562-3560), will provide specialized information on its area, including Knott's Berry Farm.

DISNEYLAND

Opened in 1955, Disneyland—along with its sibling, Florida's Walt Disney World—is the original mega–theme park, and remains unsurpassed despite constant threats from pretenders to the crown. At no other park is fantasy elevated to an art form. Nowhere else is as fresh and fantastic every time you walk through the gates, whether you're 6 or 60—and no matter how many times you've done it before. There's nothing like Disney Magic.

ESSENTIALS

GETTING THERE   Disneyland is located at 1313 Harbor Blvd. in Anaheim. It's about an hour's drive from downtown Los Angeles. Take I-5 south; while construction is being completed on the new Disneyland exit, orange signs will direct visitors off the freeway at either Harbor or Katella boulevards.

ADMISSION, HOURS & INFORMATION   Admission to the park, including unlimited rides and all festivities and entertainment, is $39 for adults and children 12 and over, $37 for seniors 60 and over, and $29 for children 3 to 11; children under 3 enter free. Parking is $6. Also, 2- and 3-day passes are available, and some area accommodations offer lodging packages that include one or more days' park admission.

Disneyland is open every day of the year, but operating hours vary, so we recommend that you call for information that applies to the specific day(s) of your visit (☎ **714/781-4565** or 213/626-8605, ext. 4565). Generally speaking, the park is open from 9 or 10am to 6 or 7pm on weekdays, fall to spring; and from 8 or 9am to midnight or 1am on weekends, holidays, and during winter, spring, or summer vacation periods.

If you've never been to Disneyland before and would like to get a copy of its *Vacation Planner* brochure to orient yourself to the park before you go, call its automated request line at ☎ **800/225-2057.** You can also browse the official park Web site (**www.disneyland.com**) or pick up a copy of *The Unofficial Guide to Disneyland* (Macmillan Travel) at your local bookstore.

DISNEY TIPS   Disneyland is busiest from mid-June to mid-September, and on weekends and school holidays year-round. Peak hours are from noon to 5pm; visit the most popular rides before and after these hours, and you'll cut your waiting times substantially. If you plan on arriving during a busy time, purchase your tickets in advance and get a jump on the crowds at the ticket counters.

New & Noteworthy

Disneyland stays on the cutting edge by continually updating and expanding, while still maintaining the hallmarks that make it the world's top amusement park (a term coined by Walt himself). Look for the most recent additions—1995's **Indiana Jones Adventure** is a high-tech thrill that's not to be missed, no matter how long the wait. It was lights out in 1996 for the beloved Main Street Electrical Parade; today, a changing series of nighttime parades feature larger-than-life fiber-optic and video light displays. At press time, the parade showcased characters and themes from Disney's animated feature *Mulan.* In 1998, **Tomorrowland** blasted off with a bunch of new attractions; the best ride is the high-speed outer-space **Rocket Rods.** And keep your eyes open as Disney prepares to round the century mark: Work has already begun on **California Adventure,** a new, separate sister park and great big hotel/resort that will debut in 2001. Until then, related construction obstructions are likely to add time and frustration to your park experience, so be prepared.

Many visitors tackle Disneyland systematically, beginning at the entrance and working their way clockwise around the park. But a better **plan of attack** is to arrive early and run to the most popular rides first—Rocket Rods, the Indiana Jones Adventure, Star Tours, Space Mountain, Big Thunder Mountain Railroad, Splash Mountain, the Haunted Mansion, and Pirates of the Caribbean. Lines for these rides can last an hour or more in the middle of the day.

If you're going to stay in Anaheim, you might want to consider booking at the ✪ **Disneyland Hotel** (see "Where to Stay," below). Hotel guests get to enter the park early almost every day and enjoy the major rides before the lines form. The amount of time varies from day to day, but usually you can enter 1½ hours early. Call ahead to check the schedule for your specific day.

Disneyland's attendance falls dramatically during the off-season (late fall to early spring), so the park offers **discounted admission** (about 25% off) to southern California residents, who may purchase up to six of these discount tickets by showing proof of their zip code. If you'll be visiting the park with someone who lives here, be sure to take advantage of this money-saving opportunity.

TOURING THE PARK

The Disneyland complex is divided into several themed "lands," each of which has a number of rides and attractions that are, more or less, related to that land's theme.

Main Street, U.S.A., at the park's entrance, is a cinematic version of turn-of-the-century small-town America. This whitewashed Norman Rockwell fantasy is lined with gift shops, candy stores, a soda fountain, and a silent theater that continuously runs early Mickey Mouse films. You'll find the practical things you might need here, too, such as stroller rentals and storage lockers. Because there are no rides here, it's best to tour Main Street during the middle of the afternoon, when lines for rides are longest, and in the evening, when you can rest your feet in the theater that features *Great Moments with Mr. Lincoln,* a patriotic (and Audio-Animatronic) look at America's 16th president. There's always something happening on Main Street; stop in at the information booth to the left of the main entrance for a schedule of the day's events.

You might start your day by circumnavigating the park by train. An authentic 19th-century steam engine pulls open-air cars around the park's perimeter. Board at the Main Street Depot and take a complete turn around the park, or disembark at any one of the lands.

Adventureland is inspired by the most exotic regions of Asia, Africa, India, and the South Pacific. Here's where you can cavort inside Tarzan's Treehouse, a climb-around attraction featuring Disney's latest animated success. Frequent visitors might recognize the former Swiss Family Treehouse, remodeled with jungle vines and moss. Its African-themed neighbor is the Jungle Cruise, passengers board a large authentic-looking Mississippi River paddleboat and float along an Amazon-like river. En route, the boat is threatened by Audio-Animatronic wild animals and hostile natives, while a tour guide entertains with a running patter. A spear's-throw away is the Enchanted Tiki Room, one of the most sedate attractions in Adventureland. Inside, you can sit down and watch a 20-minute musical comedy featuring electronically animated tropical birds, flowers, and "tiki gods."

The Indiana Jones Adventure ride is based on the Steven Spielberg series of films, taking adventurers into the Temple of the Forbidden Eye in joltingly realistic all-terrain vehicles. Riders follow Indy and experience the perils of bubbling lava pits, whizzing arrows, fire-breathing serpents, collapsing bridges, and the familiar cine-matic tumbling boulder (this effect is very realistic in the front seats!). Disney "Imag-ineers" reached new heights with the design of this ride's line, which—take my word for it—has so much detail throughout its twisting path that a half hour or more simply flies by.

New Orleans Square, a large, grassy, gas-lamp–dotted green, is home to the Haunted Mansion, the most high-tech ghost house we've ever seen. The spookiness has been toned down so kids won't get nightmares anymore, and the events inside are as funny as they are scary. Even more fanciful is Pirates of the Caribbean, one of Dis-neyland's most popular rides. Here, visitors float on boats through mock underground caves, entering an enchanting world of swashbuckling, rum-running, and buried trea-sure. Even in the middle of the afternoon, you can dine by the cool moonlight and to the sound of crickets in the Blue Bayou Restaurant, the best eatery in the land.

Critter Country is supposed to be an ode to the backwoods—a sort of Frontierland without those pesky settlers. Little kids like to sing along with the Audio-Animatronic critters in the musical Country Bear Jamboree show. Older kids and grown-ups head straight for Splash Mountain, one of the largest water-flume rides in the world. Loosely based on the Disney movie *Song of the South,* the ride is lined with about 100 characters that won't stop singing "Zip-A-Dee-Doo-Dah." Be prepared to get wet, especially if someone sizable is in the front seat of your log-shaped boat.

Frontierland gets its inspiration from 19th-century America. It's full of dense "forests" and broad "rivers" inhabited by hearty-looking "pioneers." You can take a raft to Tom Sawyer's Island, a do-it-yourself play island with balancing rocks, caves, and a rope bridge, and board the Big Thunder Mountain Railroad, a runaway roller coaster that races through a deserted 1870s gold mine. You'll also find a petting zoo and an Abe Lincoln–style log cabin here; both are great for exploring with the little ones.

On Saturdays, Sundays, holidays, and vacation periods, head to Frontierland's Rivers of America after dark to see the FANTASMIC! show—a mix of magic, music, live performers, and sensational special effects. Just as he did in *The Sorcerer's Appren-tice,* Mickey Mouse appears and uses his magical powers to create giant water foun-tains, enormous flowers, and fantasy creatures. There's plenty of pyrotechnics, lasers, and fog, as well as a 45-foot-tall dragon that breathes fire and sets the water of the Rivers of America aflame. Cool!

Mickey's Toontown is a colorful, wacky, whimsical world inspired by the *Roger Rabbit* films. This is a gag-filled land populated by toons. There are several rides here, including Roger Rabbit's CarToonSpin, but these take a back seat to Toontown itself—a trippy, smile-inducing world without a straight line or right angle in sight.

Disney Dossier

Believe it or not, the Happiest Place on Earth keeps more than a few skeletons—as well as some just plain interesting facts—in its closet. For instance, did you know that:

- Disneyland was carved out of **orange groves,** and the original plans called for carefully chosen individual trees to be left standing and included in the park's landscaping. On groundbreaking day, July 21, 1954, each tree in the orchard was marked with a ribbon—red to be cut and green to be spared. But the bulldozer operator went through and mowed down every tree indiscriminately . . . no one had realized that he was color-blind.

- Disneyland designers utilized forced perspective in the construction of many of the park's structures to give the illusion of height and dramatic proportions while keeping the park a manageable size. The buildings on **Main Street U.S.A.,** for example, are actually 90% scale on the first floor, 80% on the second, and so forth. The stones on Sleeping Beauty Castle are carved in diminishing scale from the bottom to the top, giving it the illusion of towering height.

- The faces of the **Pirates of the Caribbean** were modeled after some of the early staff of Walt Disney Imagineering, who also lent their names to the second-floor "businesses" along Main Street U.S.A.

- Walt Disney maintained two apartments inside Disneyland. His private apartment above the **Town Square Fire Station** has been kept just as it was when he lived there.

- The elaborately carved horses on Fantasyland's **King Arthur Carousel** are between 100 and 120 years old; Walt Disney found them lying neglected in storage at Coney Island in New York and brought them home to be carefully cleaned and restored.

- **It's a Small World** was touted at its opening as "mingling the waters of the oceans and seas around the world with Small World's Seven Seaways." This was more than a publicity hoax—records from that time show such charges as $21.86 for a shipment of seawater from the Caribbean.

- The peaceful demeanor of Disneyland was broken during the summer of 1970 by a group of radical Vietnam War protesters who invaded the park. They seized **Tom Sawyer Island** and raised the Viet Cong flag over the fort before being expelled by riot specialists.

- **Indiana Jones: Temple of the Forbidden Eye,** Disneyland's subterranean thrill ride, won't be experienced the same way by any two groups of riders. Like a sophisticated computer game, the course is programmed with so many variables in the action that there are 160,000 possible combinations of events.

- After the 24-year run of the enormously popular **Main Street Electrical Parade** ended in 1996, 700,000 of the floats' light bulbs were sold, at $10 a piece, with the benefits going to several local charities.

This is a great place to talk with Mickey, Minnie, Goofy, Roger Rabbit, and the rest of your favorite toons. You can even visit their "houses" here. Mickey's red-shingled house and movie barn is filled with props from some of his greatest cartoons.

Fantasyland has a storybook theme and is the catchall "land" for all the stuff that doesn't quite seem to fit anywhere else. Most of the rides here are geared to the under-6 set, including the King Arthur Carousel, Dumbo the Flying Elephant ride, and the Casey Jr. Circus Train, but some, like Mr. Toad's Wild Ride and Peter Pan's Flight, elicit an irrational attachment from grown-ups as well. You'll also find Alice in Wonderland, Snow White's Scary Adventures, Pinocchio's Daring Journey, and more. The most lauded attraction is It's a Small World, a slow-moving indoor river ride through a saccharine nightmare of all the world's children singing the song everybody loves to hate. For a different kind of thrill, try the Matterhorn Bobsleds, a zippy roller coaster through chilled caverns and drifting fog banks. It's one of the park's most popular rides. An indoor live-action theater features a musical extravaganza called "Classic Disney Characters."

Tomorrowland, conceived as an optimistic look at the future, has always had a hard time keeping a jump on real advances. The "Rocket to the Moon" of 1955 became "Mission to Mars" in 1975, only to be a dated laughingstock by the early 1980s. In 1998, Disney architects unveiled a redesigned Tomorrowland that employs an angular, metallic look popularized by futurists like Jules Verne. The high-speed Rocket Rods ride joined Tomorrowland favorites Space Mountain (a pitch-black indoor roller coaster that assaults your equilibrium and ears) and Star Tours (the original Disney/George Lucas joint venture; it's a 40-passenger StarSpeeder that encounters a spaceload of misadventures on the way to the Moon of Endor, achieved with wired seats and video effects—not for the queasy). Other new attractions include a 3-D adventure called "Honey, I Shrunk the Audience," which uses a variety of theatrical effects to impart the sensation that you've shrunk to thumbnail size; and an interactive pavilion of near-future technology called "Innoventions"—a feature close to what old Walt originally envisioned for Tomorrowland, when he created exhibits like the "House of the Future" and "Bathroom of Tomorrow" that showcased imaginative technology of the day.

The "lands" themselves are only half the adventure. Other joys include roaming Disney characters, penny arcades, restaurants and snack bars galore, summer fireworks, mariachi and ragtime bands, parades, shops, marching bands, and much more. Oh, yeah—there's also the storybook Sleeping Beauty Castle. Can you spot the evil witch peering from one of the top windows?

KNOTT'S BERRY FARM

Cynics say that Knott's Berry Farm is for people who aren't smart enough to find Disneyland. Well, there's no doubt that visitors should tour Disney first, but it's worth staying in a hotel nearby so you can play at Knott's during your stay.

Like Disneyland, Knott's Berry Farm is not without its historical merit. Rudolph Boysen crossed a loganberry with a raspberry, calling the resulting hybrid the "boysenberry." In 1933, Buena Park farmer Walter Knott planted the boysenberry, thus launching Knott's berry farm on 10 acres of leased land. When things got tough during the Great Depression, Mrs. Knott set up a roadside stand, selling pies, preserves, and home-cooked chicken dinners. Within a year, she was selling 90 meals a day. Lines became so long that Walter decided to create an Old West Ghost Town as a diversion for waiting customers.

The Knott family now owns the farm that surrounds the world-famous Chicken Dinner Restaurant, an eatery serving more than a million fried meals a year. And Knott's Berry Farm is the nation's third-most-attended family entertainment complex (after the two Disney parks, of course).

During the last half of October, locals flock to Knott's Berry Farm. Why? Because the entire park is revamped as "Knott's *Scary* Farm"—the ordinary attractions are made spooky and haunted, every grassy area is transformed into a graveyard or gallows, and even the already-scary rides get special surprise extras, like costumed ghouls who grab your arm in the middle of a roller-coaster ride!

ESSENTIALS

GETTING THERE   Knott's Berry Farm is located at 8039 Beach Blvd. in Buena Park. It's about a 5-minute drive north on I-5 from Disneyland. From I-5 or Calif. 91, exit south onto Beach Boulevard. The park is located about half a mile south of Calif. 91.

ADMISSION, HOURS & INFORMATION   Admission to the park, including unlimited access to all rides, shows, and attractions, is $35 for adults and children 12 and over, $25 for seniors 60 and over and children 3 to 11, and free for children under 3. Admission is $15 for everyone after 4pm. Parking is $6. Like Disneyland, Knott's offers discounted admission during off-season for southern California residents, so if you're bringing local friends or family members along, be sure to take advantage of the bargain. Also like Disneyland, Knott's Berry Farm's hours vary from week to week, so you should call about the day you plan to visit. Generally speaking, the park is open in summer daily from 9am to midnight. The rest of the year, it opens at 10am and closes at 6 or 8pm, except Friday and Saturday when it stays open until 10pm or midnight. Knott's is closed Christmas Day. Special hours and prices are in effect during Knott's Scary Farm in late October. For recorded information, call ☎ **714/220-5200.** On the Web, go to **www.knotts.com**.

TOURING THE PARK

Knott's Berry Farm still maintains its original Old West motif. It's divided into seven "Old Time Adventures" areas:

Old West Ghost Town, the original attraction, is a collection of refurbished 19th-century buildings that have been relocated from actual deserted Old West towns. You can pan for gold, ride aboard an authentic stagecoach, ride rickety train cars through the Calico Mine, get held up aboard the Denver and Rio Grande Calico Railroad, and hiss at the villain during a melodrama in the Birdcage Theater.

Fiesta Village has a south-of-the-border theme that means festive markets, strolling mariachis, and wild rides like Montezooma's Revenge and Jaguar!, a roller coaster that includes two heart-in-the-mouth drops and a loop that turns you upside down.

The Roaring '20s Amusement Area contains Sky Tower, a parachute jump/drop with a 20-story free fall. Other white-knuckle rides include XK-1, an excellent flight simulator "piloted" by the riders; and Boomerang, a state-of-the-art roller coaster that turns riders upside down six times in less than a minute. Kingdom of the Dinosaurs features extremely realistic *Jurassic Park*–like creatures. It's quite a thrill, but it may scare the little kids.

Wild Water Wilderness is a $10-million, 3½-acre attraction styled like a turn-of-the-century California wilderness park. The top ride here is a white-water adventure called Bigfoot Rapids, featuring a long stretch of artificial rapids; it's the longest ride of its kind in the world.

Camp Snoopy will probably be the youngsters' favorite area. It's meant to re-create a wilderness camp in the picturesque High Sierra. Its 6 rustic acres are the playgrounds of Charles Schulz's beloved beagle and his pals, Charlie Brown and Lucy, who greet guests and pose for pictures. The rides here, including Beary Tales Playhouse, are tailor-made for the 6-and-under set.

Thunder Falls contains Mystery Lodge, a truly amazing high-tech, trick-of-the-eye attraction based on the legends of local Native Americans. Don't miss this wonderful theater piece.

The Boardwalk is Knott's newest themed area, presented as a salute to Southern California's beach culture—its main attraction is Windjammer, a wind-whipping dual roller coaster originally intended to evoke the flips and glides of windsurfing, but often advertised as a twister tornado.

Stage shows and special activities are scheduled throughout the day. Pick up a schedule at the ticket booth.

ATTRACTIONS BEYOND THE THEME PARKS

To locate these attractions, see the map on p. 553.

Crystal Cathedral. 12141 Lewis St., Garden Grove. ☎ **714/971-4000.**

This angular, mirror-sheathed church (think of the Fortress of Solitude in the movie *Superman*), otherwise known as the Garden Grove Community Church, is a shocking architectural oddity, with nine-story-high doors and a vast, open interior that's shaped like a four-pointed star. Opened in 1980, it's the pulpit for televangelist Robert Schuller, who broadcasts sermons and hymns of praise on radio and TV to an international audience of millions. Each Sunday, an overflow crowd listens to the service blaring from loudspeakers into the parking lot. Annual Christmas and Easter pageants feature live animals, floating "angels," and other theatrics. A $5-million stainless-steel carillon, which began ringing in 1991, has prompted some of the cathedral's neighbors to complain that they want less joyful noise and more peace on earth.

Richard Nixon Library and Birthplace. 18001 Yorba Linda Blvd., Yorba Linda. ☎ **714/993-5075.** Fax 714/528-0544. www.nixonfoundation.org. Admission $5.95 adults, $3.95 seniors, $2 children 8–11, free for children 7 and under. Mon–Sat 10am–5pm; Sun 11am–5pm. Closed Thanksgiving and Christmas.

Although he was the most vilified U.S. president in modern history, there has always been a warm place in the hearts of Orange County locals for Richard Nixon. This presidential library, located in Nixon's boyhood town, celebrates the roots, life, and legacy of America's 37th president. The 9-acre site contains the modest farmhouse where Nixon was born, manicured flower gardens, a modern museum housing presidential archives, and the final resting place of Mr. Nixon and his wife, Pat.

Displays include videos of the famous Nixon–Kennedy TV debates, an impressive life-size statuary summit of world leaders, gifts of state (including a gun from Elvis), and exhibits on China and Russia. There's also a display of Pat Nixon's sparkling First Lady gowns and a 12-foot-high graffiti-covered chunk of the Berlin Wall, symbolizing the defeat of Communism, but hardly a mention is made of Nixon's leading role in the anti-Communist witch hunts of the 1950s. Similarly, there are exhibits on Vietnam, yet no mention of Nixon's illegal expansion of that war into neighboring Cambodia. Only the Watergate Gallery is relatively forthright, allowing visitors to listen to actual White House tapes and view a montage of the president's last day in the White House.

WHERE TO STAY
EXPENSIVE

✪ **Disneyland Hotel.** 1150 W. Cerritos Ave. (west of the Disneyland parking lot), Anaheim, CA 92802. ☎ **714/778-6600.** Fax 714/965-6597. 1,198 units. A/C MINIBAR TV TEL. $175–$270 double; from $425 suite. Inquire about multi-day packages that allow you to take on the park at your own pace and usually include free parking for the duration of your stay. AE, MC, V. Parking $10.

The "Official Hotel of the Magic Kingdom," attached to Disneyland via a monorail system that runs right to the hotel, is the perfect place to stay if you're doing the park. You'll be able to return to your room anytime you need to during the day, whether it's to take a much-needed nap or to change your soaked shorts after your Splash Mountain Adventure. Best of all, hotel guests get to enter the park early almost every day and enjoy the major rides before the lines form. The amount of time varies from day to day, but usually you can enter 1½ hours early. Call ahead to check the schedule for your specific day.

The theme hotel is a wild attraction unto itself. The rooms aren't fancy, but they're comfortably and attractively furnished like a good-quality business hotel; in-room amenities include hair dryers, irons and boards, movie channels, and balconies. Many rooms feature framed reproductions of rare Disney conceptual art, and the Disney Channel is free on TV, naturally. The beautifully landscaped hotel is an all-inclusive resort, offering six restaurants, five cocktail lounges, every kind of service desk imaginable, a "wharf-side" bazaar, a walk-under waterfall, and even an artificial white-sand beach. The complex also includes the adjoining Pacific Hotel, which offers a Disney version of Asian tranquillity (including a fine and pricey Japanese restaurant).

Dining: The best restaurant is Stromboli's, an Italian/American eatery that serves all the pasta staples. Kids love Goofy's Kitchen, where the family can enjoy breakfast and dinner with Disney characters.

Amenities: Three large heated outdoor pools, complete health club, putting green, shuffleboard and croquet courts, concierge, room service, laundry, shoe-shine, nightly turndown, baby-sitting, special children's programs, beauty salon, 20 shops and boutiques.

Sheraton Anaheim Hotel. 1015 W. Ball Rd. (at I-5), Anaheim, CA 92802. ☎ **800/ 325-3535** or 714/778-1700. Fax 714/535-3889. 526 units. A/C MINIBAR TV TEL. $170–$190 double; $290–$360 suite. AE, CB, DC, MC, V. Free parking; shuttle to Disneyland.

This hotel rises to the festive theme-park occasion with its fanciful English Tudor architecture; it's a castle that lures business conventions, Disney-bound families, and area high-school proms equally successfully. The public areas are quiet and elegant—intimate gardens with fountains and koi ponds, plush lobby and lounges—which can be a pleasing touch after a frantic day at the amusement park. The rooms are modern and unusually spacious, but otherwise not distinctive; a large swimming pool is located in the center of the complex, surrounded by attractive landscaping. Don't be put off by the high rack rates listed; rooms more commonly go for $100 to $130, even on busy summer weekends.

Dining: The Garden Court Bistro offers indoor and outdoor ambiance, while the California Deli is open from 6am to midnight and serves standard delicatessen fare. There's also a wood-and-tapestry cocktail lounge.

Amenities: Heated outdoor pool, sundeck, room service, laundry services, concierge, overnight shoe-shine, nightly turndown, gift shop.

WestCoast Anaheim Hotel. 1855 S. Harbor Blvd. (south of Katella Ave.), Anaheim, CA 92802. ☎ **800/426-0670** or 714/750-1811. Fax 714/971-2485. 500 units. A/C TV TEL. $160 double. AE, CB, DC, DISC, JCB, MC, V. Parking $8; free shuttle to Disneyland.

Although the hotel is in the Anaheim Convention Center Complex (across the street from Disneyland) and draws primarily a business crowd, there's much to appeal to the leisure traveler. The contemporary and comfortable rooms in the 12-story tower all have balconies overlooking either Disneyland or the hotel's luxurious pool area, which includes a large heated pool, deluxe spa, attractive sundeck, and snack/cocktail bar gazebo. The front desk can provide guests with many in-room amenities upon request (including, free of charge, hair dryers, irons and boards, fax machines, and fridges). The hotel offers guest laundry and valet, an activities desk, room service, and a gift shop, plus an Old West frontier-themed restaurant serving up steak and seafood along with a few colorful game selections.

MODERATE

Anaheim Plaza Hotel. 1700 S. Harbor Blvd., Anaheim, CA 92802. ☎ **800/228-1357** or 714/772-5900. Fax 714/772-8386. 300 units. A/C TV TEL. $79–$119 double; from $175 suite. AE, DC, DISC, MC, V. Free parking; shuttle to Disneyland.

You can easily cross the street to Disneyland's main gate, or you can take advantage of the Anaheim Plaza's free shuttle to the park. Once you return, you'll appreciate the way this 32-year-old hotel's clever design shuts out the noisy world. In fact, the seven two-story garden buildings remind us of 1960s Waikiki more than busy Anaheim. The Olympic-size heated outdoor pool and whirlpool are unfortunately surrounded by Astroturf, but the new management recently completed a total room renovation, so there's always hope. They didn't change a thing about the light-filled modern lobby, nor the friendly rates, which can often drop as low as $49. There's room service from the casual cafe in the lobby, plus valet service and a coin-op laundry.

Best Western Anaheim Stardust. 1057 W. Ball Rd., Anaheim, CA 92802. ☎ **800/ 222-3639** or 714/774-7600. Fax 714/535-6953. 121 units. A/C TV TEL. $70–$85 double; $105 family room. Rates include full breakfast. AE, DC, DISC, MC, V. Free parking.

Located on the back side of Disneyland, this modest hotel will appeal to the budget-conscious traveler who isn't willing to sacrifice everything. All rooms have a fridge and microwave, breakfast is served in a refurbished train dining car, and you can relax by the large outdoor heated pool and spa while doing wash in the laundry room. The extra-large family rooms will accommodate virtually any brood, and shuttles run regularly to the park.

Buena Park Hotel. 7675 Crescent Ave. (at Grand), Buena Park, CA 90620. ☎ **800/ 422-4444** or 714/995-1111. Fax 714/828-8590. www.buenaparkhotel.com. 320 units. A/C TV TEL. $129–$139 double; $199–$279 suite. AE, CB, DC, DISC, MC, V. Free parking; shuttle to Disneyland.

Within easy walking distance of Knott's Berry Farm, the Buena Park Hotel also offers a free shuttle to Disneyland just 7 miles away. The pristine lobby has the look of a business-oriented hotel, and that it is. But vacationers can also benefit from the elevated level of service designed for the business traveler. Be sure to inquire about Executive Club rates as well as Knott's or Disneyland package deals. The rooms in the nine-story tower were tastefully redecorated in 1999; amenities include room service, a charming heated outdoor pool and spa, two restaurants and a 1950s/60s dance club, and a rental-car desk.

Candy Cane Inn. 1747 S. Harbor Blvd., Anaheim, CA 92802. ☎ **800/345-7057** or 714/774-5284. Fax 714/772-5462. 173 units. A/C TV TEL. $74–$129 double. Rates include expanded continental breakfast. AE, DC, DISC, MC, V. Free parking; shuttle to Disneyland.

Take your standard U-shaped motel court with outdoor corridors, spruce it up with cobblestone drive- and walkways, old-time street lamps, and flowering vines engulfing the balconies of attractively painted rooms, and you have the Candy Cane. The face-lift worked, making this motel near Disneyland's main gate a real treat for the stylish bargain hunter. The guest rooms are decorated in bright floral motifs with comfortable furnishings, including queen beds and a separate dressing and vanity area. Complimentary breakfast is served in the courtyard, where you can also splash around in a heated pool, spa, or kids' wading pool.

Howard Johnson Hotel. 1380 S. Harbor Blvd., Anaheim, CA 92802. ☎ **800/422-4228** or 714/776-6120. Fax 714/533-3578. www.hojoanaheim.com. 320 units. A/C TV TEL. $79–$104 double. AE, CB, DC, DISC, JCB, MC, V. Free parking.

This hotel occupies an enviable location, directly opposite Disneyland, and a cute San Francisco trolley car runs to and from the park every 30 minutes. Guest rooms—renovated in 1999—are divided among several low-profile buildings, all with balconies opening onto a central garden with two heated pools for adults and one for children. Garden paths lead under eucalyptus and olive trees to a splashing circular fountain. In summer, you can see the nightly fireworks display at Disneyland from the upper balconies of the park-side rooms. Try to avoid the units in the back buildings, as they get some freeway noise. Amenities include in-room movies, coffeemakers, room service from the attached Coco's Restaurant, gift shop, games room, laundry service plus coin-op laundry, airport shuttle, and family lodging/Disney admission packages. We think it's pretty classy for a HoJo's.

Jolly Roger Inn & Suites. 640 W. Katella Ave. (west of Harbor Blvd.), Anaheim, CA 92802. ☎ **800/446-1555** or 714/772-7621. Fax 714/772-2308. 240 units. A/C TV TEL. $119–$149 double; $259–$289 suite. Ask about midweek, seasonal, and other discounts. AE, DC, DISC, MC, V. Free parking; shuttle to Disneyland.

The only thing still sporting a buccaneer theme here is the adjoining Jolly Roger Restaurant, and even that may fall by the wayside during the Jolly Roger's massive renovation. In early 2000, Jolly Roger expects to unveil its all-suite towers, two five-story annexes to the original two-story L-shaped motel. The comfortable but blandly furnished older rooms have always been our favorites for their quiet and also for the palm-shaded heated pool in their center courtyard, but we hear they'll be converted into suites in the fall of 2000. Get a deal on the older rooms while you can, or check out the brand-new suites (but be sure to get a discounted or package rate). Across the driveway is the swashbuckling restaurant, where dinner will set you back more than a few doubloons. The all-day coffee shop is more reasonable, and there's nightly entertainment and dancing in the lounge. Conveniently located across the street from Disneyland, the Jolly Roger also has meeting and banquet rooms, plus a second pool and a spa, a beauty salon, and a gift shop.

INEXPENSIVE

Colony Inn. 7800 Crescent Ave. (west of Beach Blvd.), Buena Park, CA 90620. ☎ **800/98-COLONY** or 714/527-2201. Fax 714/826-3826. 130 units. A/C TV TEL. $49–$98 double or suite. AE, MC, V. Free parking.

Although it's composed of two modest U-shaped motels, the recently refurbished Colony Inn has a lot to offer. It's the closest lodging to Knott's Berry Farm's south entrance and is just 10 minutes away from Disneyland. It cheerfully offers discount coupons for Knott's and other nearby attractions, as well as complimentary coffee and doughnuts to jump-start your morning. The rooms are spacious (doubles sleep up to four people, and suites sleep up to eight) and comfortably outfitted with conservatively styled furnishings. There are two pools, two wading pools for kids, two saunas, and a coin-operated laundry on the premises.

WHERE TO DINE

If you're visiting just for the day, you'll probably eat at the theme parks, where there are plenty of restaurants to choose from. At Disneyland, in the Creole-themed **Blue Bayou,** you can sit under the stars inside the Pirates of the Caribbean ride—no matter what time of day it is. At Knott's, try the fried-chicken dinners and boysenberry pies at Mrs. Knott's historic **Chicken Dinner Restaurant.** Nearby **Orange** has a charming historic downtown that's home to several of the region's best dining options, listed below.

EXPENSIVE

Chanteclair. 18912 MacArthur Blvd. (opposite John Wayne Airport), Irvine. ☎ **949/752-8001.** Reservations recommended. Main courses $9–$16 lunch, $22–$30 dinner. AE, CB, DC, DISC, JCB, MC, V. Mon–Fri 11:30am–2:30pm and 6–10pm, Sat 5:30–10pm. Valet parking $2. COUNTRY FRENCH.

Chanteclair is expensive and a little difficult to reach, but it's worth seeking out. Designed in the style of a provincial French inn, the rambling stucco structure is built around a central garden court and houses several dining and drinking areas, each with its own unique ambiance. The antique-furnished restaurant has five fireplaces. At lunch, you can try reasonably priced dishes that'd be dinner anywhere else: grilled scallops and prawns on tomato risotto, lamb loin in port-ginger reduction, or pan-seared calf liver. Dinner is a worthwhile splurge that might begin with a lobster bisque with cognac, Beluga caviar, or sautéed foie gras. Main dishes include an elegant mixed grill of filet mignon, lamb, and quail, tournedo of ahi tuna and foie gras with shiitake-merlot sauces, and showy Long Island duckling flamed table-side with Grand Marnier. Many folks dress up for dinner here.

Mr. Stox. 1105 E. Katella Ave. (east of Harbor Blvd.), Anaheim. ☎ **714/634-2994.** www.MrStox.com. Reservations recommended. Main courses $14–$28. AE, CB, DC, DISC, MC, V. Mon–Fri 11:30am–2:30pm and 5:30–10pm, Sat–Sun 5:30–10pm. AMERICAN.

Hearty steaks and fresh seafood are served in an early California manor-house setting here. Specialties include roast prime rib and mesquite-broiled fish, veal, and lamb. Chef Scott Raczek particularly excels at reduction sauces and innovative herbal preparations. Sandwiches and salads are also available. The homemade breads and desserts, such as chocolate-mousse cake, are unexpectedly good. Mr. Stox has an enormous and renowned wine cellar, and there's live entertainment nightly.

MODERATE

Citrus City Grille. 122 No. Glassell St. (1/2 block north of Chapman), Orange. ☎ **714/639-9600.** Reservations recommended. Main courses $8–$13 lunch, $12–$24 dinner. AE, DC, MC, V. Tues–Sat 11:30am–3pm and 5–10pm. CALIFORNIA.

Though housed in Orange's second-oldest brick building, this sophisticated crowd-pleaser is furnished without an antique in sight, paying homage to the town's agricultural (citrus) legacy with a bold industrial chic. World-inspired appetizers range from Hawaiian-style ahi poke to Southeast Asian coconut shrimp tempura accented with spiced apricots. Main courses come from the Mediterranean (pasta and risotto), Mexico (carne asada with avocado-corn relish), the American south (authentic Louisiana gumbo), and Mom's kitchen (meatloaf smothered in gravy and fried onions). Gleaming bar shelves house myriad bottles for the extensive martini menu, while outdoor foyer tables are nicely protected from the street.

Felix Continental Cafe. 36 Plaza Sq. (at the corner of Chapman and Glassell), Orange. ☎ **714/633-5842.** Reservations recommended for dinner. Main courses $6–$14. AE, DC, MC, V. Mon–Thurs 7am–9pm, Fri 7am–10pm, Sat 8am–10pm, Sun 8am–9pm. CUBAN/ SPANISH.

If you like the re-created Main Street in the Magic Kingdom, then you'll love the historic 1886 town square in the city of Orange, on view from the cozy sidewalk tables outside the Felix Continental Cafe. Dining on traditional Cuban specialties and watching traffic spin around the magnificent fountain and rosebushes of the plaza evoke old Havana or Madrid rather than the cookie-cutter Orange County communities just blocks away. The food receives glowing praise from restaurant reviewers and loyal locals alike.

INEXPENSIVE

Watson Drugs & Soda Fountain. 116 E. Chapman Ave. (half a block east of Glassell), Orange. ☎ **714/633-1050.** Reservations not accepted. Most menu items under $7. AE, MC, V. Mon–Sat 6:30am–9pm, Sun 8am–6pm. DINER.

The past lives on at this drugstore established by K. E. Watson in 1899, and still beloved by the nostalgia-mad town of Orange. Remember the diner in Tom Hanks's *That Thing You Do?* It was filmed here . . . in fact, Hollywood comes knocking quite often, and any employee will proudly recite Watson's screen credits. Fully half the historic store is taken up with dinette tables, and the shelf behind the lunch counter gleams with industrial milkshake mixers. You've seen this menu a thousand times—sandwiches, burgers, salads, "blue-plate" dinner specials, and breakfast (served all day)—and it's as comforting as ever.

5 The Orange Coast

Seal Beach is 36 miles S of Los Angeles; Newport Beach, 49 miles; Dana Point, 65 miles

Whatever you do, don't say "Orange County" here. The mere name evokes images of smoggy industrial parks, cookie-cutter housing developments, and the staunch Republicanism that prevails behind the so-called "orange curtain." We're talking instead about the Orange Coast, one of southern California's best-kept secrets, a string of seaside jewels that have been compared with the French Riviera or the Costa del Sol. Here, 42 miles of beaches offer pristine stretches of sand, tide pools teeming with marine life, ecological preserves, charming secluded coves, quaint pleasure-boat harbors, and legendary surfers atop breaking waves. Whether your bare feet want to stroll a funky wooden boardwalk or your gold card gravitates toward a yacht club, you've come to the right place.

ESSENTIALS

GETTING THERE   See "Orientation," in chapter 13 for airport and airline information. By car from Los Angeles, take I-5 or I-405 south. The scenic, shore-hugging Pacific Coast Highway (Calif. 1, or just PCH to the locals) links the Orange Coast communities from Seal Beach in the north to Capistrano Beach just south of Dana Point, where it merges with I-5. To reach the beach communities directly, take the following freeway exits: **Seal Beach,** Seal Beach Boulevard from I-405; **Huntington Beach,** Beach Boulevard/Calif. 39 from either I-405 or I-5; **Newport Beach,** Calif. 55 from either I-405 or I-5; **Laguna Beach,** Calif. 133 from I-5; **San Juan Capistrano,** Ortega Highway/Calif. 74 from I-5; and **Dana Point,** Pacific Coast Highway/Calif. 1 from I-5.

A Special Arts Festival

A tradition for 60-plus years in arts-friendly Laguna, the ✪ **Festival of Arts and Pageant of the Masters** is held each summer throughout July and August. Festivities include a fantastic performance-art production in which live actors re-create famous Old Masters paintings, live music, crafts sales, art demonstrations and workshops, and the grass-roots Sawdust Festival across the street. Grounds admission is $3; pageant tickets range from $15 to $40. Call ☎ **800/487-FEST** or 949/494-1145, or check out **www.foapom.com.**

VISITOR INFORMATION   The **Seal Beach Chamber of Commerce,** 311 Main St. #14A, at Electric (☎ **562/799-0179**; www.seal-beach.com), is open Monday through Friday from 10am to 4pm.

The **Huntington Beach Conference & Visitors Bureau,** 417 Main St., Suite A-2 (☎ **800/SAY-OCEAN** or 714/969-3492; fax 714/969-5592; www.hbvisit.com), genially offers tons of information, enthusiasm, and personal anecdotes. Open Monday through Friday from 9am to 5pm.

The **Newport Beach Conference & Visitors Bureau,** 3300 W. Coast Hwy. (☎ **800/94-COAST** or 949/722-1611; fax 949/722-1612; www.newportbeach-cvb.com), distributes brochures, sample menus, a calendar of events, and its free and helpful *Visitor's Guide.* Call or stop in Monday through Friday from 8am to 5pm (plus weekends in summer).

The **Laguna Beach Visitors Bureau,** 252 Broadway (☎ **800/877-1115** or 949/497-9229; www.lagunabeachinfo.org), is in the heart of town and distributes lodging, dining, and art-gallery guides. It's open Monday through Friday from 9am to 5pm and on Saturday from 10am to 4pm (plus Sundays in summer).

The **San Juan Capistrano Chamber of Commerce,** Franciscan Plaza, 31781 Camino Capistrano, Suite 306 (☎ **949/493-4700;** www.sanjuancapistrano.com), is within walking distance of the mission and offers a walking-tour guide to historic sites. Open Monday through Friday from 8:30am to 4pm.

The **Dana Point Chamber of Commerce,** 24681 La Plaza, Suite 120 (☎ **800/ 290-DANA** or 949/496-1555; www.danapoint-chamber.com), is open Monday through Friday from 9am to 4:30pm and carries some restaurant and lodging information as well as a comprehensive recreation brochure.

DRIVING THE ORANGE COAST

You'll most likely be exploring the coast by car, so we cover the beach communities in order, from north to south. Keep in mind, however, that if you're traveling between Los Angeles and San Diego, the Pacific Coast Highway (Calif. 1) is a splendidly scenic detour that adds less than an hour to the commute—so pick out a couple of destinations and go for it.

Seal Beach, on the border between Los Angeles and Orange counties and neighbor to Long Beach's Naples Harbor, is geographically isolated both by the adjacent U.S. Naval Weapons Station and the self-contained Leisure World retirement community. As a result, the charming beach town appears untouched by modern development—it's Orange County's answer to small-town America. Take a stroll down Main Street for a walk back in time, culminating in the Seal Beach Pier. Although the clusters of sunbathing, squawking seals that gave the town its name aren't around any more, old-timers still fish hopefully, lovers still stroll swooningly, and families still cavort by the seaside, perhaps capping off the afternoon with an old-fashioned double dip from **Main Street Ice Cream & Yogurt** (☎ **562/431-3394**), at the corner of Main Street and Ocean Avenue, where the walls are decorated with sepia-toned photographs of Seal Beach's yesteryear.

Huntington Beach is probably the largest Orange Coast city; it stretches quite a ways inland and has seen the most urbanization. To some extent, this has changed the old boardwalk and pier into a modern outdoor mall where cliques of gang kids coexist with families and the surfers who continue to flock here, drawn by Huntington's legendary place in surf lore. Hawaiian surfer Duke Kahanamoku brought the sport here in the 1920s, and some say the breaks around the pier and Bolsa Chica are the best in California. The world's top wave-riders flock to Huntington each August for the rowdy but professional **U.S. Open of Surfing** (☎ **310/286-3700** for information).

Anaheim Area & Orange Coast Attractions

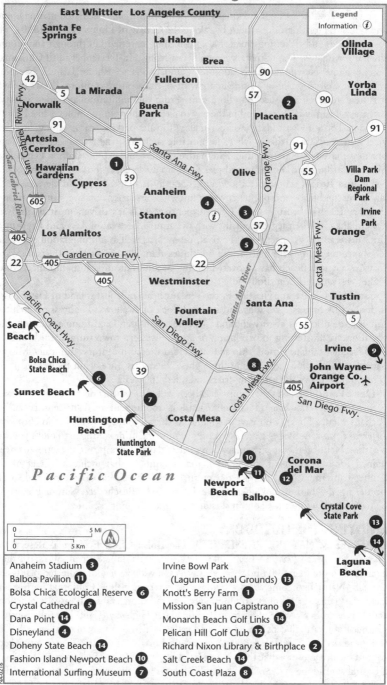

Legend
Information (i)

East Whittier Los Angeles County
Santa Fe Springs
La Habra
Olinda Village
Brea
42
5 La Mirada
Norwalk
Fullerton
90
57
Placentia
2
Yorba Linda
90
91
Artesia Cerritos
Buena Park
5 Santa Ana Fwy.
91
Hawaiian Gardens
Cypress
39
Anaheim
Olive
55
Villa Park Dam Regional Park
605
Stanton
4
(i)
3
57
Irvine Park
Orange
405
Los Alamitos
5
Garden Grove Fwy.
22
Costa Mesa Fwy.
22
405
22
Westminster
405
Fountain Valley
Santa Ana
Tustin
5
Seal Beach
Pacific Coast Hwy.
San Diego Fwy.
55
Irvine
9
Bolsa Chica State Beach
6
39
San Santa Ana River
8
John Wayne–Orange Co. Airport
Sunset Beach
1
7
405
San Diego Fwy.
Huntington Beach
Costa Mesa
Huntington State Park
10
Corona del Mar
11
12

Pacific Ocean

Newport Beach
Balboa
Crystal Cove State Park
13
14
Laguna Beach

0   5 Mi
0   5 Km

Anaheim Stadium 3	Irvine Bowl Park
Balboa Pavilion 11	(Laguna Festival Grounds) 13
Bolsa Chica Ecological Reserve 6	Knott's Berry Farm 1
Crystal Cathedral 5	Mission San Juan Capistrano 9
Dana Point 14	Monarch Beach Golf Links 14
Disneyland 4	Pelican Hill Golf Club 12
Doheny State Beach 14	Richard Nixon Library & Birthplace 2
Fashion Island Newport Beach 10	Salt Creek Beach 14
International Surfing Museum 7	South Coast Plaza 8

NA-0216

If you'll be around during Christmastime, try to see the gaily decorated marina homes and boats in Huntington Harbour by taking the **Cruise of Lights** (☎ 714/840-7542 for schedules and ticket information), a 45-minute narrated sail through and around the harbor islands. The festivities generally last from mid-December until Christmas.

The name **Newport Beach** conjures comparisons to Rhode Island's Newport, where the well-to-do enjoy seaside living with all the creature comforts. That's the way it is here, too, but on a less grandiose scale. From the million-dollar Cape Cod–style cottages on sunny Balboa Island in the bay to elegant shopping complexes like Fashion Island and South Coast Plaza (an über-mall with valet parking, car detailing, limo service, and concierge), this is where fashionable socialites, right-wing celebrities, and business mavens can all be found. Alternatively, you could explore **Balboa Peninsula's** historic Pavilion and old-fashioned pier or board a passenger ferry to Catalina Island.

Laguna Beach, whose breathtaking geography is marked by bold elevated headlands, coastal bluffs, and pocket coves, is known as an artists' enclave, but the truth is that Laguna has became so *in* (read: expensive) that it's driven most of the true bohemians *out.* Their legacy remains with the annual **Festival of Arts and Pageant of the Masters** (see "A Special Arts Festival," above), as well as a proliferation of art galleries intermingling with high-priced boutiques along the town's cozy streets. In warm weather, Laguna Beach has an overwhelming Mediterranean-island ambiance, which makes *everyone* feel beautifully, idly rich.

San Juan Capistrano, nestled in the verdant headlands just inland of Dana Point, is defined by Spanish missions and its loyal flock of swallows. The mission architecture is authentic, and history abounds. Consider San Juan Capistrano a compact, life-size diorama illustrating the evolution of a small western town from Spanish-mission era to secular rancho period, into statehood and the 20th century. Ironically, Mission San Juan Capistrano (see "Seeing the Sights," below) is once again the center of the community, just as the founding friars intended 200 years ago.

Dana Point, the last town south, has been called a "marina development in search of a soul." Overlooking the harbor stands a monument to 19th-century author Richard Henry Dana, who gave his name to the area and described it in *Two Years Before the Mast.* Activities generally center around yachting and Dana Point's jewel of a harbor. Nautical themes are everywhere; particularly charming are the series of streets named for old-fashioned shipboard lights, a rainbow that includes "Street of the Amber Lantern," " . . . the Violet Lantern," " . . . the Golden Lantern," and so on. Bordering the harbor is Doheny State Beach (see "Beaches & Nature Preserves," below), which wrote the book on seaside park and camping facilities.

ENJOYING THE OUTDOORS

BEACHES & NATURE PRESERVES The **Bolsa Chica Ecological Reserve,** in Huntington Beach (☎ 714/897-7003), is a 300-acre restored urban salt marsh that's a haven to more than 200 bird species, as well as a wide variety of protected plants and animals. Naturalists come to spot herons and egrets as well as California horn snails, jackknife clams, sea sponges, common jellyfish, and shore crabs. An easy 1½-mile loop trail begins from a parking lot on the Pacific Coast Highway (Calif. 1) a mile south of Warner Boulevard; docents lead a narrated walk the first Saturday of every month. The trail heads inland, over Inner Bolsa Bay and up Bolsa Chica bluffs. It then loops back toward the ocean over a dike that separates the Inner and Outer Bolsa bays and traverses a coastal sand-dune system. This beautiful hike is a terrific afternoon adventure. The Bolsa Chica Conservancy has been working since 1978 on reclaiming the wetlands from oil companies that began drilling here 70 years ago. It's an ongoing process, and you can still see those "seesaw" drills dotting the outer areas of the reserve. Although

Bolsa Chica State Beach across the road has superb facilities, fantastic surfing, and well-equipped campsites, you might find that the hulking offshore oil rigs spoil the view.

Huntington City Beach, adjacent to Huntington Pier, is a haven for volleyball players and surfers; dense crowds abound, but at least so do amenities like outdoor showers, beach rentals, and rest rooms. Just south of the city beach is 3-mile-long **Huntington State Beach.** Both popular beaches have lifeguards and concession stands seasonally. The state beach also has rest rooms, showers, barbecue pits, and a waterfront bike path. The main entrance is on Beach Boulevard, and there are access points all along the Pacific Coast Highway (Calif. 1).

Newport Beach runs for about 5 miles and includes both Newport and Balboa piers. There are outdoor showers, rest rooms, volleyball nets, and a vintage boardwalk that just may make you feel as though you've stepped 50 years back in time. **Balboa Bike and Beach Stuff** (☎ **949/723-1516**), at the corner of Balboa and Palm near the pier, rents a variety of items, from pier fishing poles to bikes, beach umbrellas, and body boards. The **Southwind Kayak Center,** 2801 W. Pacific Coast Hwy. (☎ **800/768-8494** or 949/261-0200; www.southwindkayaks.com), rents sea kayaks for use in the bay or open ocean at rates of $10 to $14 per hour; instructional classes are available on weekends, with some midweek classes in summer. It also conducts bird-watching kayak expeditions into the Upper Newport Bay Ecological Reserve at rates of $40 to $65.

Crystal Cove State Park, which covers 3 miles of coastline between Corona del Mar and Laguna Beach and then extends up into the hills around El Moro Canyon, is a good alternative to the more popular beaches for you seekers of solitude. (There are, however, lifeguards and rest rooms.) The beach is a winding, sandy strip, backed with grassy terraces; high tide sometimes sections it into coves. The entire area offshore is an underwater nature preserve. There are four entrances, including Pelican Point and El Moro Canyon. For more information, call ☎ **949/494-3539** or 949/ 848-1566.

Salt Creek Beach Park lies below the palatial Ritz-Carlton Laguna Niguel; guests who tire of the pristine swimming pool venture down the staircase on Ritz-Carlton Drive to wiggle their toes in the sand. The setting is marvelous, with wide white-sand beaches looking out toward Catalina Island (why do you think the Ritz-Carlton built here?). There are lifeguards, rest rooms, a snack bar, and convenient parking near the hotel.

Doheny State Beach in Dana Point has long been known as a premier surfing spot and camping site. Just south of lovely Dana Point Marina (enter off Del Abispo St.), Doheny has the friendly vibe of beach parties in days gone by: Tree-shaded lawns give way to wide beaches, and picnicking and beach camping are encouraged. There are 121 sites for both tents and RVs, plus a state-run visitor center featuring several small aquariums of sea and tide-pool life. For more information and camping availability, call ☎ **949/492-0802.**

BICYCLING   Biking is the most popular beach activity up and down the coast. A slower-paced alternative to driving, it allows you to enjoy the clean, fresh air and notice smaller details of these laid-back beach towns and harbors. The Newport Beach Visitor Center (see "Visitor Information," above) offers a free *Bike Ways* map of trails throughout the city and harbor. Bikes and equipment can be rented at **Balboa Bike & Beach Stuff,** 601 Balboa Blvd., Newport Beach (☎ **949/723-1516**); **Laguna Beach Cyclery,** 240 Thalia St. (☎ **949/494-1522**); and **Dana Point Bicycle,** 34155 Pacific Coast Hwy. (☎ **949/661-8356**).

GOLF   Many golf-course architects have used the geography of the Orange Coast to its full advantage, molding challenging and scenic courses from the rolling bluffs. Most courses are private, but two outstanding ones are open to the public. **Monarch**

Beach Golf Links, 33033 Niguel Rd., Dana Point (☎ 949/240-8247), is particularly impressive, a hilly and challenging course designed by Robert Trent Jones, Jr. Most holes offer great ocean views, but afternoon winds can sneak up, so accuracy is essential. Weekend greens fees are $145.

Another challenge is the **Pelican Hill Golf Club,** 22651 Pelican Hill Rd. S., Newport Beach (☎ 949/760-0707 starter; 949/640-0238 pro shop; www.pelicanhill. com), with two Tom Fazio–designed courses. The Ocean North course is heavily bunkered, while the Ocean South course features canyons and rocky ravines; both have difficult, large, multi-tier greens. Weekend greens fees are $210. And remember, when putting near the ocean, the break is always toward the water!

SEEING THE SIGHTS

The charm of the pretty little neighborhood of **Balboa Island** isn't diminished by knowing that the island was man-made—and it certainly hasn't affected the price of real estate. Tiny clapboard cottages in the island's center and modern houses with two-story windows and private docks along the perimeter make a colorful and romantic picture. You can drive onto the island on Jamboree Road to the north or take the three-car ferry from Balboa Peninsula (about $1.50 per vehicle). It's generally more fun to park and take the ferry as a pedestrian, since the tiny alleys they call streets are more suitable for strolling, there are usually crowds, and parking spaces are scarce. **Marine Avenue,** the main commercial street, is lined with small shops and cafes that evoke a New England fishing village. Refreshing shaved ices sold by sidewalk vendors will relieve the heat of summer.

International Surfing Museum. 411 Olive Ave., Huntington Beach. ☎ **714/960-3483.** www.surfingmuseum.org. Admission $2 adults, $1 students, free for kids 6 and under. Mid-June to late Sept daily noon–5pm; rest of the year Wed–Sun noon–5pm.

Nostalgic Gidgets and Moondoggies shouldn't miss this monument to the laid-back sport that has become synonymous with California beaches. There are gargantuan long boards from the sport's early days, memorabilia of Duke Kahanamoku and the other surfing greats represented on the "Walk of Fame" near Huntington Pier, and a gift shop where a copy of the "*Surfin'ary*" can help you bone up on your surfer slang even if you can't hang ten.

Balboa Pavilion. 400 Main St., Balboa, Newport Beach. ☎ **949/673-5245.** From Calif. 1, turn south onto Newport Blvd. (which becomes Balboa Blvd. on the peninsula); turn left at Main St.

This historic cupola-topped structure, a California Historical Landmark, was built in 1905 as a bathhouse for swimmers in their ankle-length bathing costumes. Later, during the Big Band era, dancers rocked the Pavilion doing the "Balboa Hop." Now it serves as the terminal for Catalina Island passenger service, harbor and whale-watching cruises, and fishing charters. The surrounding boardwalk is the Balboa Fun Zone, a collection of carnival rides, game arcades, and vendors of hot dogs and cotton candy. For Newport Harbor or Catalina cruise information, call ☎ **949/673-5245;** for sportfishing and whale watching, call ☎ **949/673-1434.**

Laguna Art Museum. 307 Cliff Dr., Laguna Beach. ☎ **949/494-6531.** www.lagunaart-museum.org. Admission $5 adults, $4 students and seniors, free for kids under 12. Tues–Sun 11am–5pm.

Reopened in 1997, this beloved local institution is working hard to position itself as the artistic cornerstone of the community. In addition to a small but interesting permanent collection, the museum presents installations of regional works definitely worth a detour. Past examples include a display of surf photography from the coast's

1930s and 1940s golden era, and dozens of plein-air impressionist paintings (ca. 1900 to 1930) by the founding artists of the original colony.

Mission San Juan Capistrano. Ortega Hwy. (Calif. 74), San Juan Capistrano. ☎ **949/ 248-2048.** www.missionsjc.com. Admission $5 adults, $4 children and seniors. Daily 8:30am–5pm.

The seventh of the 21 California coastal missions, Mission San Juan Capistrano is continually being restored. The mix of old ruins and working buildings is home to small museum collections and various adobe rooms that are as quaint as they are interesting. The intimate mission chapel with its ornate baroque altar is still regularly used for religious services, and the mission complex is the center of the community, hosting performing arts, children's programs, and other cultural events year-round.

This mission is best known for its swallows, which are said to return to nest each year at their favorite sanctuary. According to legend, the birds wing their way back to the mission annually on March 19, St. Joseph's Day, arriving here at dawn; they are said to take flight again on October 23, after bidding the mission farewell. In reality, however, you can probably see the well-fed birds here any day of the week, winter or summer.

SHOPPING

Just as the communities along the coast range from casually barefoot summer playgrounds to meticulously groomed yacht-clubby enclaves, so does the shopping scene stretch to both ends of the spectrum. **Seal Beach,** indifferent to tourists, has charming low-tech shops designed to service the year-round residents, while **Huntington Beach** offers a plethora of surf and water-sports shops, reflecting its sporty nature. Both Huntington and Balboa have more than their share of T-shirt and souvenir stands, while tony **Newport Beach** has been called "Beverly Hills South" because of its many European designer boutiques and high-priced shops. ✪ **Laguna Beach** is art-gallery intensive; with over 100 at last count, you'll do well to pick up an expanded gallery guide at the Laguna Beach Visitors Bureau (see "Visitor Information," above). Most galleries are clustered along Pacific Coast Highway, particularly at the northern end of town—a stretch that's historically been known as **Gallery Row.** There's little shopping in **Dana Point** and mostly mission-themed souvenirs in **San Juan Capistrano.**

Shoppers from all over the Southland flock to the two excellent malls listed below. If that isn't to your taste, a drive along the Pacific Coast Highway will yield many other opportunities for browsing and souvenir purchases.

Fashion Island Newport Beach. 401 Newport Center Dr., Newport Beach. ☎ **949/ 721-2000;** www.fashionisland-nb.com.

It's actually *not* an island, unless you count the nearly impenetrable sea of skyscrapers that border this posh mall, which is designed to resemble an open-air Mediterranean village. Anchored by Neiman-Marcus, Bloomingdale's, and Macy's, the mall is lined with outdoor artwork, upscale shops, and specialty boutiques including Allen Allen women's casual wear and trendy Optical Shop of Aspen; 12 different restaurants offer something for everyone.

✪ **South Coast Plaza.** 3333 Bristol St. (at I-405), Costa Mesa. ☎ **800/782-8888** or 714/435-2000.

South Coast Plaza is one of the most upscale shopping complexes in the world, and is so big that it's a day's adventure unto itself. This beautifully designed center is home to some of fashion's most prominent boutiques, including Emporio Armani, Chanel, Alfred Dunhill, and Coach; beautiful branches of the nation's top department stores such as Saks Fifth Avenue and Nordstrom; and outposts of the best high-end specialty shops like Williams-Sonoma, L.A. Eyeworks, and Rizzoli Booksellers.

The multidimensional mall is home to many impressive works of modern art, and snacking and dining options are also a cut above. You won't find Hot-Dog-on-a-Stick among the 40 or so restaurants scattered throughout. Wolfgang Puck Cafe, Morton's of Chicago, Ghirardelli Soda Fountain, Planet Hollywood, and Scott's Seafood Grill lure the hungry away from Del Taco and McDonald's.

WHERE TO STAY

Also consider the **Seal Beach Inn** (☎ **800/HIDEAWAY** or 562/493-2416; fax 562/799-0483), a romantic 23-room bed-and-breakfast inn a block from the beach in a charming residential neighborhood.

EXPENSIVE

Portofino Beach Hotel. 2306 W. Ocean Front, Newport Beach, CA 92663. ☎ **949/673-7030.** Fax 949/723-4370. 20 units. TV TEL. Summer $175–$250 double; winter $150–$210 double. AE, CB, DC, DISC, MC, V.

Just steps away from the Newport Pier, this oceanfront inn maintains a calm, European air even in the face of the midsummer beach frenzy. Built in a former seaside rail station, the hotel is located along a stretch of beachy bars and equipment-rental shacks; the beach is across the parking lot. Although it can get noisy in summer, there are advantages to being at the center of the action. The hotel has its own enclosed parking, and sunsets are spectacular when viewed from a plush armchair in the upstairs parlor. Guest rooms, furnished with old-world antique reproductions, are on the second floor—the first is occupied by a guests-only bar and several cozy sitting rooms—and most have luxurious skylit bathrooms.

✪ **Ritz-Carlton Laguna Niguel.** 1 Ritz-Carlton Dr., Dana Point, CA 92629. ☎ **800/241-3333** or 949/240-2000. Fax 949/240-0829. 393 units. A/C MINIBAR TV TEL. $260–$495 double; from $600 suite. Children 17 and under stay free in parents' room. Midweek and special packages available. AE, CB, DC, DISC, MC, V. Parking $20.

The Old World meets the Pacific Rim at this glorious hotel, majestically set among terraces and fountained gardens on a 150-foot-high bluff above a 2-mile-long beach. There's a beautiful limestone fireplace in the elegant, silk-lined lobby, and lush foliage abounds throughout the interior. A ravishingly arched lounge is perfect for watching the sun set over the Pacific. The service, in Ritz-Carlton style, is unassuming and impeccable. Some guests, however, might find the hotel's palatial airs out of keeping with the beachy location.

The spacious guest rooms are outfitted with sumptuous furnishings and fabrics; despite their generous size, some are overfurnished to the point of being cramped. All come with a terrace; an Italian marble bathroom equipped with double vanity, hair dryer, and robes; three phones (with voice mail); and a fridge, shoe polisher, and safe. Some rooms even have fireplaces.

Dining/Diversions: The hotel has four restaurants, each more elegant than the last, and a clubby lounge for nightcaps (in addition to five separate bar areas).

Amenities: Room service (on Rosenthal china, no less), twice-daily maid service (they'll even stick a bookmark in the appropriate page of your *TV Guide*), masseur, baby-sitting, children's programs, regular shuttle to/from the beach and the golf course, games room, lawn games, sauna, steam room, whirlpool, beauty salon, day-care center.

Surf and Sand Hotel. 1555 S. Coast Hwy. (south of Laguna Canyon Rd.), Laguna Beach, CA 92651. ☎ **800/524-8621** or 949/497-4477. Fax 949/494-2897. 164 units. MINIBAR TV TEL. Apr–Oct $260–$400 double; from $475 suite. Nov–Mar $255–$305 double. AE, CB, DC, DISC, MC, V.

The fanciest hotel in Laguna Beach has come a long way since it started life in 1937 as a modest little place with just 13 units. Still occupying the same fantastic ocean-side location, it now features dozens of top-of-the-line luxurious rooms that, despite their standard size, feel enormously decadent. Done entirely in white, they're very bright and beachy, and every one has a private balcony with an ocean view, a marble bathroom, and plush robes; some have whirlpool tubs. Try to get a deluxe corner room.

Dining: Splashes Restaurant (see "Where to Dine," below) serves three meals daily in a beautiful oceanfront setting. Towers offers contemporary northern Italian cuisine for dinner. Because the windows don't open, a sound system was installed to pipe in the sounds of the surf below.

Amenities: Heated outdoor pool and whirlpool, concierge, room service, dry cleaning, overnight laundry, complimentary morning newspaper, nightly turndown.

MODERATE

Blue Lantern Inn. 34343 St. of the Blue Lantern, Dana Point, CA 92629. ☎ 800/950-1236 or 949/661-1304. Fax 949/496-1483. www.foursisters.com. 29 units. A/C TV TEL. $150–$400 double. Rates include full breakfast and afternoon wine and hors d'oeuvres. AE, DC, MC, V.

A newly constructed three-story New England–style gray clapboard inn, the Blue Lantern is a pleasant cross between romantic B&B and sophisticated small hotel. Almost all the rooms, which are decorated with reproduction traditional furniture and plush bedding, have a balcony or deck overlooking the harbor. All have a fireplace and Jacuzzi tub. Have your breakfast here in private (clad perhaps in the fluffy robe provided), or choose to go downstairs to the sunny dining room that also serves complimentary afternoon tea. There's an exercise room and a cozy lounge with menus for many area restaurants. The friendly staff welcomes you with home-baked cookies at the front desk.

Casa Laguna. 2510 S. Coast Hwy, Laguna beach, CA 92651. ☎ 800/233-0449 or 949/494-2996. Fax 949/494-5009. 20 units. TV TEL. $115–$250 double. Rates include breakfast, afternoon wine, and hors d'oeuvres. Off-season and midweek discounts available. AE, DISC, MC, V.

Once you see this romantic terraced complex of Spanish-style cottages amid impossibly lush gardens and secluded patios, which offers all the amenities of a B&B *and* affordable prices, you might wonder: What's the catch? Well, the noise of busy PCH wafts easily into Casa Laguna, a background hum that might prove disturbing to sensitive ears and light sleepers. Still, the Casa has been a favorite hideaway since Laguna's early days. Catalina tile adorns fountains, while bougainvillea spills into paths; there's a shaded pool with ocean views, and each room has an individual charm. Request a room in the rear—not only will the noise be less noticeable, but you'll also enjoy a better view.

Doryman's Inn Bed & Breakfast. 2102 W. Ocean Front, Newport Beach, CA 92663. ☎ 949/675-7300. 10 units. A/C TV TEL. $150–$230 double; from $185 suite. Rates include breakfast. AE, MC, V.

The Doryman's rooms are both luxurious and romantic, making this one of the nicest B&Bs anywhere. The rooms are outfitted with French and American antiques, floral textiles, beveled mirrors, and cozy furnishings. Every unit has a fireplace and a sunken marble tub (some with Jacuzzi jets). King or queen beds, lots of plants, and good ocean views round out the decor. The location, directly on the Newport Beach Pier Promenade, is also enviable, though some may find it a bit too close to the action. Breakfast includes fresh pastries and fruit, brown eggs, yogurt, cheeses, and international coffees and teas.

WHERE TO DINE

Options in Seal Beach are limited, but a good choice for seafood is **Walt's Wharf,** 201 Main St. (☎ **562/598-4433**), a bustling, polished restaurant featuring market-fresh selections either plain or with Pacific Rim accents.

EXPENSIVE

5'0" (Five Feet). 328 Glenneyre, Laguna Beach. ☎ **949/497-4955.** Reservations recommended. Main courses $18–$30. AE, DC, DISC, MC, V. Sun–Thurs 5–10pm; Fri–Sat 5–11pm. CALIFORNIA/ASIAN.

While 5'0" may no longer break culinary ground, chef/proprietor Michael Kang still combines the best in California cuisine with Asian technique and ingredients. The restaurant has a minimalist, almost industrial decor that's brightened by a friendly staff and splendid cuisine. Menu selections run the gamut from tea-smoked filet mignon topped with Roquefort cheese and candied walnuts to a hot Thai-style mixed grill of veal, beef, lamb, and chicken stir-fried with sweet peppers, onions, and mushrooms in curry-mint sauce. While the menu changes daily, you can always find the house specialty, whole braised catfish.

Splashes Restaurant and Bar. In the Surf and Sand Hotel, 1555 S. Coast Hwy., Laguna Beach. ☎ **949/497-4477.** Reservations recommended. Main courses $16–$30. AE, CB, DC, DISC, MC, V. Sun–Thurs 7am–10pm; Fri–Sat 7am–11pm. MEDITERRANEAN.

Splashes is truly stunning. Almost directly on the surf, this light and bright restaurant basks in sunlight and the calming crash of the waves. At dinner, a basket of fresh-baked crusty bread prefaces a long list of appetizers that might include wild-mushroom ravioli with lobster sauce or sautéed Louisiana shrimp with red chilies and lemon. Gourmet pizzas also make great starters; they come topped with interesting combinations like grilled lamb, roasted fennel, artichokes, mushrooms, and feta. Main courses change daily and might offer baked striped bass or braised duck with cabernet.

MODERATE

Crab Cooker. 2200 Newport Blvd., Newport Beach. ☎ **949/673-0100.** Reservations not accepted. Main courses $8–$19 lunch, $10–$25 dinner. AE, MC, V. Sun–Thurs 11am–9pm; Fri–Sat 11am–10pm. SEAFOOD.

Since 1951, folks in search of fresh, well-prepared seafood have headed to this bright-red former bank building. Also a fish market, the Crab Cooker has a casual atmosphere of humble wooden tables, uncomplicated smoked and grilled preparations, and meticulously selected fresh fare. They're especially proud of their Maryland crab cakes, and recently added clams and oysters to the repertoire.

Harbor Grill. 34499 St. of the Golden Lantern, Dana Point. ☎ **949/240-1416.** www. harborgrill.com. Reservations recommended. Main courses $10–$20. AE, CB, DC, DISC, MC, V. Mon–Sat 11:30am–10pm; Sun 9am–10pm. SEAFOOD/STEAK.

In a business/commercial mall right in the center of the pretty Dana Point Marina, the Harbor Grill is enthusiastically recommended by locals for mesquite-broiled, ocean-fresh seafood. Hawaiian mahimahi with a mango-chutney baste is on the menu, along with Pacific swordfish, crab cakes, and beef steaks.

Las Brisas. 361 Cliff Dr. (off the PCH north of Laguna Canyon), Laguna Beach. ☎ **949/497-5434.** Reservations recommended. Main courses $10–$24. AE, CB, DC, DIS, MC, V. Mon–Sat 8am–10:30pm; Sun 9am–10:30pm. MEXICAN/SEAFOOD.

Boasting a breathtaking view of the Pacific, Las Brisas is popular for sunset drinks and alfresco appetizers—so much so that it can get pretty crowded in summer. Affordable during lunch but pricey at dinner, the menu consists mostly of seafood recipes from the Mexican Riviera. Even the standard enchiladas and tacos get a zesty update with crab or lobster meat and fresh herbs. Calamari steak is sautéed with bell peppers, capers, and herbs in a garlic-butter sauce, and king salmon is mesquite broiled and served with a creamy lime sauce. Although a bit on the touristy side, Las Brisas can be a fun part of the Laguna Beach experience.

INEXPENSIVE

El Adobe de Capistrano. 31891 Camino Capistrano (near the mission), San Juan Capistrano. ☎ **949/493-1163** or 949/830-8620. Main courses $5–$10 lunch, $8–$15 dinner. AE, DISC, MC, V. Mon–Thurs 11:30am–10pm; Fri–Sat 11:30am–11pm; Sun 10:30am–2:30pm and 4–10pm. CLASSIC MEXICAN.

This restaurant is housed in a historic landmark 1778 Spanish adobe near San Juan Capistrano's main attraction, the mission. It's understandably touristy, but there's some interesting history inside, like the enclosed lobby that was originally a dirt pathway between two buildings. A former dungeon jail cell makes a fine wine cellar, and El Adobe proudly offers a menu combination named "the President's Choice" after Richard Nixon, who visited often from his Summer White House at the shore nearby. Hot plates overflow with cheesy combinations featuring chiles rellenos, tamales, and enchiladas topped with rich red sauce. Dinner selections also include steak and seafood.

15 The Southern California Desert

by Stephanie Avnet Yates

To the casual observer, Southern California's desert seems desolate—nothing but vast landscapes baking under a relentless sun. Its splendor is subtle, though; you have to discover its beauty in your own time. For some travelers it will be the surprising lushness of trees, flowering cacti, fragrant shrubs, and other plants—many of them unique to the region—that have adapted ingeniously to the harsh climate. The unique Joshua tree, which some deem majestic and others call ugly, thrives in the upper Mojave Desert. Each spring, the ground throughout the Lancaster area is carpeted with brilliant golds and oranges of the poppy, California's state flower. Like the autumn leaves in New England, the poppies draw seasonal tourists in droves.

If it looks as though nothing except insects could survive here, look again: You're bound to see a speedy roadrunner or a tiny gecko dart across your path. Close your eyes and listen for the cry of a hawk or an owl. Check the ground for coyote or bobcat tracks. Notice the sparkle of fish in the streams running through flourishing palm oases. Check the road signs, which warn of desert tortoise crossings. The tortoise is just one of the many endangered species found only here; fortunately, most of the Southern California desert's flora and fauna is protected by the federal government in a wildlife sanctuary.

Perhaps the beauty you seek is that of personal renewal in the spectacular desert landscape. Whether it's in the shadow of purple-tinged mountains, amid otherworldly rock formations, or beside a sparkling swimming pool, you'll find as much or as little to occupy your time as you desire. Destinations range from gloriously untouched national parks to ultra-luxurious resorts—and it's a rare day when the sun doesn't shine out here.

1 En Route to the Palm Springs Resorts

If you're making the drive from Los Angeles via I-10, your first hour or so will be spent just, well, getting out of the L.A. metropolitan sprawl. Soon you'll leave the Inland Empire auto plazas behind, sail past the last of the bedroom-community shopping malls, and edge ever closer to the snow-capped (if you're lucky) San Bernardino and San Jacinto mountain ranges. (Coming from San Diego via I-15, the area discussed below is east of the junction with I-10.)

For frequent travelers on this stretch of highway, there are certain unmistakable signposts. Roadside attractions are part of what makes every moment of the vacation enjoyable. Below are three of our favorites.

Jurassic Park in the Desert

As the cities give way to pale, dry desert, keep your eyes peeled for the dinosaurs that stand guard over the **Wheel Inn Restaurant** (☎ **760/849-7012**), in Cabazon. That's right, a four-story-tall brontosaurus and his Tyrannosaurus rex pal. You can even climb into the belly of the larger one, where you'll find a remarkably spacious gift shop.

Desert Hills Premium Outlets. 48400 Seminole Dr. (off I-10), Cabazon. ☎ **909/849-6641.** Sun–Thurs 10am–8pm, Fri 10am–9pm, Sat 9am–9pm.

Factory-outlet malls are all the rage among bargain-hunters, and this one is truly a cut above the rest—or maybe it's just so massive, the shlock gets lost in the shuffle. Pick up a map to help navigate this two-part behemoth, or you may find yourself browsing Timberland when you'd rather be shopping the Gap. Some of our faves: Kenneth Cole, J. Crew, Eddie Bauer, Coach, Barney's New York, A/X Armani Exchange, Villeroy & Boch, Donna Karan DKNY, Max Studio, Nike, and Quiksilver. The list goes on; there are 15 shoe stores alone here.

Hadley's Fruit Orchards. 48190 Seminole Dr. (off I-10), Cabazon. ☎ **800/854-5655** or 909/849-5255. www.hadleys.com. Mon–Thurs 8am–8pm, Fri–Sun 8am–9pm.

This friendly emporium has been a fixture here since 1931, long before the outlet mall went up down the road. It's always packed with folks shopping for dates, dried fruits, nuts, honey, preserves, and other regional products. A snack bar serves the beloved date shake; there are also plenty of gift-packed treats to carry (or ship) home. (For more about the date mystique, see "Sweet Treat of the Desert: The Coachella Valley Date Gardens," later in this chapter).

Wind Farm Tours. Interstate 10, Indian Ave. exit, Palm Springs. ☎ **760/251-1997.** Admission $23 adults, $20 seniors and students, $10 kids under 10. Tours daily at 9am, 11am, 1pm, and 3pm (can vary seasonally).

Travelers through the San Gorgonio Pass have, for years, been struck by an awesome and otherworldly sight: never-ending windmill fields that harness the powerful force of the wind gusting through this passage and convert it to electricity to power air-conditioners throughout the Coachella Valley. If you really get a charge (!) from them, consider a unique guided tour offering a look into this alternative energy source. Learn how designers have improved the efficiency of wind turbines (technically they're not windmills, which are used in the production of grain) over the years, and measure those long rotors against the average human height (about 10 people could lie along one span).

2 Get Your Kicks—On Historic Route 66

There's a way for nostalgia buffs to take a detour down memory lane on their way to desert destinations: Just eschew the fast-paced, faceless I-10 for a very special interstate highway: Route 66.

It's been immortalized in film, song, literature, memory, and in the popular imagination. But is anything really left of this great snaking highway, this dependable, comforting spirit John Steinbeck called "the Mother Road?" What of the path to adventure traveled by Tod and Buz in their trademark red Corvette on the namesake 1960s TV series?

The answer is, yes, it's still there: You just have to be willing to look for it.

Historic Route 66

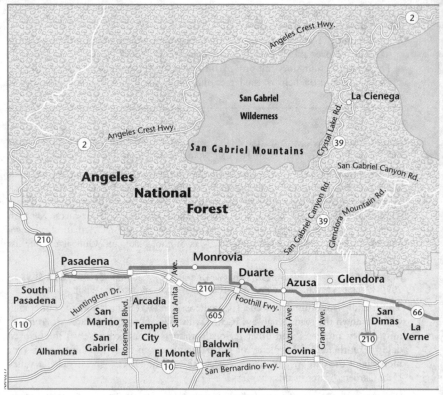

Until the final triumph of the multi-lane superslab in the early 1960s, Route 66 was the only automobile route between the windy Chicago shores of Lake Michigan and L.A.'s golden Pacific beaches. "America's Main Street" rambled through eight states, and today, in each one, there are enthusiastic organizations dedicated to preserving its remnants. California is fortunate to have a lengthy stretch of the original highway, many miles of which still proudly wear the designation "California State Highway 66." It's not just weed-split abandoned blacktop, either. These are active streets, often the main commercial drag of the community. Many stretches have become clusters of new home developments, stucco shopping centers, and fast-food chains. Pretty mundane—until you round a curve and unexpectedly see a vintage wood-frame house, perhaps from a pre–Great Depression ranch. There's poignancy here: That house was probably set way back from the road, amidst a shady grove, before highway workers buried the front yard under asphalt.

Other picturesque relics of that bygone era—single-story motels, friendly two-pump gas stations—exist beside their modern neighbors, inviting nostalgia for a slower, simpler time, a time when the vacation began the moment you backed out of the driveway.

ESSENTIALS

THE ROUTE Our drive begins in Pasadena and ends in downtown San Bernardino, 56 miles west of Palm Springs. In San Bernardino, I-215 intersects Route 66; take it 4 miles south to rejoin I-10 and continue east.

Note: This detour works equally well if your destination is Lake Arrowhead or Big Bear Lake; take I-215 north 3 miles to Calif. 30 and continue into the mountains (see

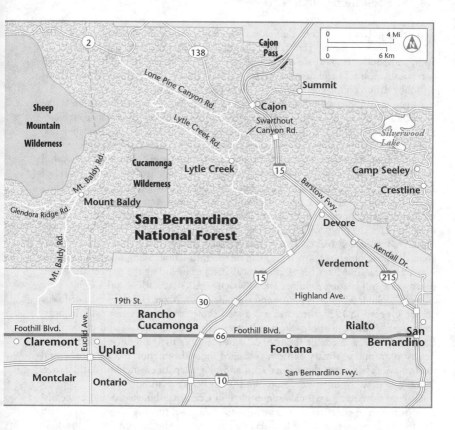

chapter 14). The drive will add anywhere from 30 minutes to 3 hours to your trip, depending on how many relics and photo opportunities you stop to enjoy. Some suitably retro meal suggestions are included in case you want to incorporate lunch into your drive.

VISITOR INFORMATION   For more information, contact the **California Historic Route 66 Association** (☎ **310/997-9817**). There's also a quarterly *Route 66 Magazine,* 326 W. Route 66, Williams, AZ 86046 (☎ **520/635-4322**).

LET'S HIT THE ROAD!

Although Route 66 officially ended at the picturesque Pacific, there are very few reminders left in the heart of L.A. Besides, we assume you've already seen the city, so Pasadena is the best point to begin your time-warp experience.

One of our favorite places is the **Fair Oaks Pharmacy,** Fair Oaks Avenue and Mission Street, 1.6 miles south of Colorado Boulevard (☎ **626/799-1414;** open Monday through Saturday from 9am to 6pm, Sunday from 11am to 6pm), a fixture on this street corner since 1915. If you're in the mood for a treat, try an authentic ice-cream soda, a sparkling phosphate, a "Route 66" sundae, or an old-fashioned malt (complete with the frosty mixing can), all served by today's fresh-faced soda jerks from behind the marble counter. They also serve soup, sandwiches, and other snacks. The Fair Oaks is still a dispensing pharmacy and offers a variety of charming gifts, including an abundance of Route 66–themed items.

Perhaps you'd like some appropriate driving music, or a souvenir to help you reminisce about your Route 66 experience later. If so, there's no better place than

Canterbury Records, 805 E. Colorado Blvd., a block west of Lake Avenue (☎ 626/792-7184; open Monday through Friday from 9am to 8pm, Saturday from 9am to 6pm, and Sunday from 10am to 5pm). It has L.A.'s finest selection of big bands and pop vocalists on CD and cassette; perhaps you'll choose one of the many renditions of Bobby Troup's homage, "(Get Your Kicks on) Route 66."

As you continue east on Colorado Boulevard, keep your eyes peeled for **motels** like the Saga Motor Hotel, Swiss Lodge, Siesta Inn, Astro (fabulous *Jetsons*-style architecture), and Hi-Way Host. In fact, lodgings have proven the hardiest post-66 survivors, and you'll be seeing many unique frozen-in-time motor courts along the way.

Turn left on Rosemead Boulevard, passing under the freeway (boo, hiss) to Foothill Boulevard. Turning right, you'll soon be among the tree-lined residential streets of **Arcadia,** home to the Santa Anita Racetrack and the Los Angeles Arboretum, the picturesque former estate of "Lucky" Baldwin, whose Queen Anne cottage has been the setting for many movies and TV shows (see chapter 13 for details). Passing into Monrovia, look for the life-size plastic cow on the southeast corner of Mayflower. It marks the drive-thru called **Mike's Dairy**—a splendid example of this auto-age phenomenon. If you're observant, you'll see many drive-thru dairies along our route (mostly Alta-Dena brand). Mike's has all the typical features, including the refrigerated island display case still bearing a vintage DRIFTWOOD DAIRY PRODUCTS price sign.

Next, look for Magnolia Avenue and the outrageous **Aztec Hotel** on the northwest corner. Opened in 1925, the Aztec was a local showplace, awing guests with its overscale, dark, Native American–themed lobby; garish Mayan murals; and exotic Brass Elephant bar. An arcade of shops once held the city's most prominent barbershop, beauty salon, and pharmacy. Little has changed about the interior, and a glance behind the front desk will reveal the original cord-and-plug telephone switchboard still in use. If you care to wet your whistle, stop into the bar before continuing on.

Leaving the Aztec, you'll pass some splendid Craftsman bungalows and other historic homes. The street dead-ends at Mountain Avenue; turn right to catch up with the 1930s alignment of Route 66. Make a left turn on Huntington Drive, and look out for **The Trails,** a prime example of the "wagon wheel/Wild West" theme restaurants. Its super-tall DINING sign will let you know when you're getting close. Now you're in **Duarte,** where Huntington Drive is lit by graceful and ornate double street lamps on the center median. This stretch also has many fabulous old motor courts; see if you can spot the Filly, Ranch Inn, Evergreen, and the Capri.

Crossing over the wide but nearly dry San Gabriel River, glance right from the bridge to see cars streaming along the Interstate that supplanted Route 66. In Irwindale—which smells just like the industrial area it is, with manufacturing plants ranging from a Miller brewery to Health Valley Foods—the street resumes the Foothill Boulevard name, and you'll pass into Azusa. Look for the elegant 1932 **Azusa City Hall and Auditorium,** whose vintage lampposts and Moorish fountain enhance a charming courtyard.

Our route swerves right onto Alosta Avenue at the **Foothill Drive-In Theater,** Southern California's last single-screen drive-in. As you cruise by, think of the days when our cars were an extension of our living rooms (with the great snacks Mom wouldn't allow at home), and the outdoor theaters were filled every summer evening by dusk.

Continuing on Alosta, you'll enter Glendora, named in 1887 by founder George Whitcomb for his wife, Ledora. Look for the **Palm Tropics,** one of the best-maintained old motels along the route. On the northeast corner of Grand Avenue stands the "world-famous" **Derby East** restaurant. It's not affiliated with the legendary Hollywood watering hole, but was clearly built in the 1940s to capitalize on both its famous namesake and the nearby Santa Anita Racetrack. Farther along on the left-hand side is the **Golden Spur,** which began 70 years ago as a ride-up hamburger stand for the equestrian crowd. Unfortunately, the restaurant has been remodeled in boring stucco, leaving only the original sign, with its neon cowboy boot, as a reminder of its colorful past. In a block or two, you'll pass briefly through San Dimas, a ranch-like community where you must pay attention to the HORSE CROSSING street signs. At the corner of Cataract Avenue, a covered wagon announces the **Pinnacle Peak** restaurant, guarded by a giant steer atop the roof.

Don't blink, because almost immediately the street rejoins Foothill Boulevard, passing underneath the ramps to I-210 (boo, hiss); now you're in La Verne, home of **La Paloma** Mexican cafe, a fixture on the route for many years. Continue on to the community of Claremont, known these days for the highly respected group of **Claremont Colleges.** You'll pass several of them along this eucalyptus-lined boulevard. In days gone by, drivers would cruise along this route for mile upon mile, through orchards and open fields, the scenery punctuated only by ambling livestock or a rustic wood fence.

At Benson Avenue in Upland, a classic **1950s-style McDonald's** stands on the southeast corner, its golden arches flanking a low, white, walk-up counter with outdoor stools. The fast-food chain has its roots in this region: Richard and Maurice McDonald opened their first burger joint in San Bernardino in 1939. The successful brothers expanded their business, opening locations throughout Southern California, until entrepreneur Ray Kroc purchased the chain in 1955 and franchised McDonald's nationwide. Farther along, look north at the intersection of Euclid Avenue for the regal **monument to pioneer women.**

Pretty soon you'll be cruising through Rancho Cucamonga, whose fertile soil still yields a reliable harvest. You might see impromptu **produce stands** springing up by the side of the road; stop and pick up a fresh snack. If you're blessed with clear weather, gaze north at the gentle slope of the **San Gabriel Mountains** and you'll understand how Foothill Boulevard got its name. The construction codes in this community are among the most stringent in California, designed to respect the region's heritage and restrict runaway development. All new buildings are Spanish/Mediterranean in style and amply landscaped. At the corner of San Bernardino Road, the playful architectural bones of a wonderful old service station can't be obscured by the flashy car-stereo/cellular-phone store that inhabits it now. Across the street is the **Sycamore Inn,** nestled in a grove of trees and looking very much like an old-style stagecoach stop. This reddish-brown wooden house, dating from 1848, has been a private home and gracious inn; today, it serves the community of Cucamonga as a restaurant and civic hall.

Rancho Cucamonga has earnestly preserved two historic wineries. First you'll see the **Thomas Vineyards,** at the northeast corner of Vineyard Avenue, established in 1839. Legend holds that the first owner mysteriously disappeared, leaving hidden treasure still undiscovered on the property. The winery's preserved structures now hold two eateries, a country crafts store, and a bookstore housed in the former brandy still. Take a minute to stop into the shopping mall behind the Thomas Winery to tour the **Route 66 Territory Museum and Visitor's Bureau,** a mini-museum and gift shop. You'll see lovingly tended exhibits of old gas pumps, road signs, and other relics, plus an array of books, maps, glassware, garments, jewelry, and other souvenirs. Many items bear the original black-on-white Route 66 shield, the ubiquitous highway marker purged from the old route by state transportation officials in 1984. The brown markers you see today were subsequently placed by the historical associations.

☕ **TAKE A BREAK** If all this driving has made you hungry, consider the **Magic Lamp Inn,** 8189 Foothill Blvd. (☎ **909/981-8659**), open for lunch and dinner Tuesday through Friday and dinner only on Saturday and Sunday. Built in 1957, the Magic Lamp offers excellent continental cuisine (nothing nouvelle about Route 66!) in a setting that's part manor house and part "Aladdin" theme park. Dark, stately dining rooms lurk behind a funky banquette cocktail lounge punctuated by a psychedelic fountain/fire pit and a panoramic view. The genie-bottle theme is everywhere, from the restaurant's dinnerware to the plush carpeting, which would be right at home in a Las Vegas casino. Lovers of kitsch and hearty retro fare shouldn't pass this one up.

Continuing on to Hellman Avenue, look for the **New Kansan Motel** (on the northeast corner). With that name, it must have seemed welcoming to Dust Bowl refugees. Near the northwest corner of Archibald Avenue, you'll find lonely remnants of a **1920s–era gas station.** Empty now, those service bays have seen many a Ford, Studebaker, and Packard in need of a helping hand. Next you'll pass the **Virginia Dare Winery,** at the northwest corner of Haven Avenue, whose structures now house part of a large business park/shopping mall, but retain the flourish of the original (1830s) winery logo.

Soon you'll pass the I-15 junction and be driving through Fontana, whose name in Italian means "fountain city." There isn't too much worth stopping for along this stretch, but definitely slow down to have a look at the **motor-court hotels** lining both sides of the road. They're of various vintages, all built to cater to the once-vigorous stream of travelers passing through. Although today they're dingy, the melody of their names conjures up those glory days: Ken-Tuck-U-Inn, Rose Motel, Moana, Dragon, Sand & Sage, Sunset, 40 Winks, Redwing.

After entering Rialto, be on the lookout for Meriden Avenue, site of the fanciful **Wigwam Motel.** Built in the 1950s (along with an identical twin motor court in Holbrook, Arizona), the whimsy of these stucco tepees lured many a road-weary traveler in for the night. Their catchy slogan, "Sleep in a wigwam, get more for your wampum," has been supplanted today by the more to-the-point "Do it in a teepee." But, as with many of the motor courts we'll pass on this drive, you need only picture a few large, shiny Buicks, T-bird convertibles, and "woodie" station wagons pulling in for the night and your imagination will drift back to days gone by.

Soon Foothill Boulevard will become Fifth Street, a sign that you're nearing **San Bernardino,** which must have been a welcome sight for hot and weary west-bound travelers emerging from the Mojave Desert. Route 66 wriggled through the steep Cajon Pass into a land fragrant with orange groves, where agricultural prosperity had quickly earned this region a lasting sobriquet: "the Inland Empire."

The year 1928 saw the grand opening of an elegant movie palace, the **California Theater,** 562 W. Fourth St., only a block from Route 66. From Fifth Street east, turn right at E Street, then make a right on Fourth Street, where you can pull over to view the theater. Lovingly restored and still popular for nostalgic live entertainment and the rich tones of its original Wurlitzer pipe organ, the California was a frequent site of Hollywood "sneak previews." Humorist Will Rogers made his last public appearance here, in 1935. (Following his death, the highway was renamed the "Will Rogers Memorial Highway" in his honor, but it remained popularly known as Route 66.) Notice the intricate relief of the theater's stone facade, and peek into the lobby to see the red velvet draperies, rich carpeting, and gold-banistered double staircase leading up to the balcony.

The theater is the last stop on your time-warp driving tour. Continue west on Fourth Street to the superslab highway only 2½ blocks away—that's I-215, your entry back to the present (see "Essentials," above).

3 The Palm Springs Desert Resorts

120 miles E of Los Angeles, 135 miles NE of San Diego

Palm Springs had been known for years as a golf-course-studded retirement mecca that's invaded annually by raucous hordes of libidinous college kids on spring break. Well, the city of Palm Springs has been quietly changing its image and attracting a whole new crowd. Former mayor (later U.S. congressman) Sonny Bono's revolutionary "anti-thong" ordinance in 1991 put a lightning-quick halt to the spring-break migration by eliminating public display of the bare co-ed derrière, and the upscale fairway-condo crowd has decided to congregate in the tony outlying resort cities of Rancho Mirage, Palm Desert, Indian Wells, and La Quinta.

These days, there are no billboards allowed in Palm Springs itself, all the palm trees in the center of town are appealingly back-lit at night, and you won't see the word "motel" on any establishment. Senior citizens are everywhere, dressed to the nines in brightly colored leisure suits and keeping alive the retro-kitsch establishments from the days when Elvis, Liberace, and Sinatra made the balmy desert a swingin' place. But they're not alone: Baby boomers and yuppies nostalgic for the kidney-shaped swimming pools and backyard luaus of the Eisenhower/Kennedy glory years are buying ranch-style vacation homes and restoring them to their 1950s splendor. Hollywood's young glitterati are returning, too. Today, the city fancies itself a European-style resort with a dash of good ol' American small town thrown in for good measure—think *Jetsons* architecture and the crushed-velvet vibe of piano bars with the colors and attitude of a laid-back Aegean island village. One thing hasn't changed: Swimming, sunbathing, golfing, and playing tennis are still the primary pastimes in this convenient little oasis.

Another important presence in Palm Springs has little to do with socialites and Americana. The Agua Caliente band of **Cahuilla Indians** settled in this area 1,000 years before the first golf ball was ever teed up. Recognizing the beauty and spirituality of this wide-open space, they lived a simple life around the natural mineral springs on the desert floor, migrating into the cool canyons during the hot summer months. Under a treaty with the railroad companies and the U.S. government, the tribe owns half the land on which Palm Springs is built and actively works to preserve Native American heritage. It's easy to learn about the American Indians during your visit, and it will definitely add to your appreciation of this part of California.

ESSENTIALS

GETTING THERE   Several airlines service the **Palm Springs Regional Airport,** 3400 E. Tahquitz Canyon Way (☎ 760/323-8161), including **Alaska Airlines** (☎ 800/426-0333), **American** (☎ 800/433-7300), **America West** (☎ 800/235-9292), **Delta/Skywest** (☎ 800/453-9417), **United** (☎ 800/241-6522), and **US Airways** (☎ 800/428-4322). Flights from Los Angeles International Airport (see "Orientation," in chapter 13) take about 40 minutes.

If you're driving from Los Angeles, take I-10 east to the Calif. 111 turnoff to Palm Springs. You'll breeze into town on North Palm Canyon Drive, the main thoroughfare. The trip from downtown Los Angeles takes about 2 hours. If you're driving from San Diego, take I-15 north to I-10 east; it's a little over a 2-hour drive.

VISITOR INFORMATION Be sure to pick up *Palm Springs Life* magazine's free monthly **"Desert Guide."** It contains tons of visitor information, including a comprehensive calendar of events. Copies are distributed in hotels and newsstands and by the **Palm Springs Desert Resorts Convention & Visitors Bureau,** in the Atrium Design Centre, 69930 Calif. 111, Suite 201, Rancho Mirage, CA 92270 (☎ **800/41-RELAX** or 760/770-9000). The bureau's office staff can help with maps, brochures, and advice Monday through Friday from 8:30am to 5pm. They also operate a **24-hour information line** (☎ **760/770-1992**) and a Web site (**www.desert-resorts.com**).

The **Palm Springs Visitors Information Center,** 2781 N. Palm Canyon Dr. (☎ **800/34-SPRINGS;** fax 760/323-3021), offers maps, brochures, advice, souvenirs, and a free hotel-reservation service. The office is open Monday through Saturday from 9am to 5pm and on Sunday from 8am to 4pm.

ORIENTATION The commercial downtown area of Palm Springs stretches about half a mile along North Palm Canyon Drive between Alejo and Ramon streets. The street is one-way through the heart of town, but its other-way counterpart is Indian Canyon Drive, 1 block east. The mountains lie directly west and south, while the rest of Palm Springs is laid out in a grid to the southeast. Palm Canyon forks into South Palm Canyon (leading to the Indian Canyons) and East Palm Canyon (the continuation of Calif. 111) traversing the resort towns of Cathedral City, Rancho Mirage, Palm Desert, Indian Wells, and La Quinta before looping up to rejoin I-10 at Indio. Desert Hot Springs is north of Palm Springs, straight up Gene Autry Trail. Tahquitz Canyon Way creates North Palm Canyon's primary intersection, tracking a straight line between the airport and the heart of town.

GREAT GOLF COURSES

The Palm Springs desert resorts are world-famous meccas for golfers (see "Fairways & Five-Irons, Desert Style," below). There are nearly 100 public, semiprivate, and private courses in the area. If you're the kind who starts polishing your irons the moment you begin planning your vacation, you're best off staying at one of the valley's many golf resorts, where you can enjoy the proximity of your hotel's facilities as well as smart package deals that can give you a taste of country-club membership. If, on the other hand, you'd like to fit a round of golf into an otherwise varied trip and you aren't staying at a hotel with its own links, there are courses at all levels open to the general public, mostly in Palm Springs. Call ahead to see which will rent clubs or other equipment to the spontaneous player.

Beginners will enjoy **Tommy Jacobs' Bel-Air Greens,** 1001 El Cielo, Palm Springs (☎ 760/322-6062), a scenic 9-hole, par-32 executive course that has some water- and sand-trap challenges but also allows for a few confidence-boosting successes. Generally flat fairways and mature trees characterize the relatively short (3,350-yard) course. The complex also offers an 18-hole miniature golf course. Greens fees range from $23 to $27.

Slightly more intermediate amateurs will want to check out the **Tahquitz Creek Golf Resort,** 1885 Golf Club Dr., Palm Springs (☎ 760/328-1005), whose two diverse courses both appeal to mid-handicappers. The "Legend's" wide, water-free holes will appeal to anyone frustrated by the "target" courses popular with many architects, while the new Ted Robinson–designed "Resort" course offers all those accuracy-testing bells and whistles more common to lavish private clubs. Greens fees range from $45 to $85, depending on day and cart rental.

The **Palm Springs Country Club,** 2500 Whitewater Club Dr. (☎ 760/323-8625), is the oldest public-access golf course within the city of Palm Springs, and is especially popular with budget-conscious golfers, as greens fees are only $50 to $60,

The Palm Springs Desert Resorts

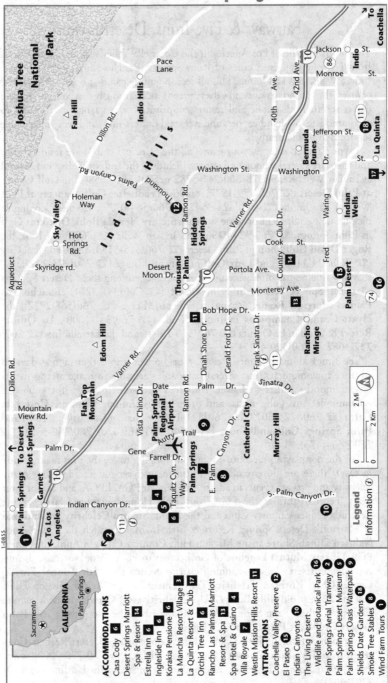

ACCOMMODATIONS

Casa Cody ⑥
Desert Springs Marriott
Spa & Resort ⑭
Estrella Inn ⑥
Ingleside Inn ⑥
Korakia Pensione ⑥
La Mancha Resort Village ③
La Quinta Resort & Club ⑰
Orchid Tree Inn ⑥
Rancho Las Palmas Marriott
Resort & Spa ⑬
Spa Hotel & Casino ④
Villa Royale ⑦
Westin Mission Hills Resort ⑪

ATTRACTIONS

Coachella Valley Preserve ⑫
El Paseo ⑮
Indian Canyons ⑩
The Living Desert
Wildlife and Botanical Park ⑯
Palm Springs Aerial Tramway ②
Palm Springs Desert Museum ⑤
Palm Springs Oasis Waterpark ⑨
Shields Date Gardens ⑱
Smoke Tree Stables ⑧
Wind Farm Tours ①

Fairways & Five-Irons, Desert Style

Two hours outside of Los Angeles in the Coachella Valley, strung like ripe dates from I-10, lie the resort cities of Palm Springs, Rancho Mirage, Palm Desert, Indian Wells, and La Quinta. This all-season golfer's paradise boasts close to 100 courses, their lush fairways and velvety greens incongruously carved from the arid desert scruff. Both public and resort/semiprivate courses range in difficulty to accommodate low-handicappers and weekend duffers alike, and every imaginable service is available nearby.

If you'd like to sharpen your game, all the principal clubs have resident pros, and there are several schools and clinics, including the **Indian Wells Golf School** at Indian Wells Resort (☎ 800/241-5782 or 760/346-4653), the **Golf Center at Palm Desert** (☎ 760/779-1877), and the **Leadbetter Golf Academy** at PGA West in La Quinta (☎ 800/424-3542 or 760/564-0777). If you're looking to pick up new equipment or some stylish attire, try **Nevada Bob's Discount Golf** in Palm Springs (☎ 760/324-0196) and Indian Wells (☎ 760/346-6166), the **Roger Dunn Golf Shop** in Palm Desert (☎ 760/345-3133) and Cathedral City (☎ 760/324-1160), and **Lady Golf** in Rancho Mirage (☎ 760/773-4949).

Many fine resorts offer generous golf packages, among them **Desert Springs Marriott Spa & Resort** in Palm Desert (☎ 760/341-2211), **Rancho Las Palmas Marriott Resort & Spa** in Rancho Mirage (☎ 760/568-2727), the **Hyatt Grand Champions** in Indian Wells (☎ 760/341-1000), **La Quinta Resort & Club** in La Quinta (☎ 760/346-2904), and the **Estrella Inn** (☎ 800/237-3687 or 760/320-4417).

Tee times at many courses cannot be booked more than a few days in advance for nonguests, but several companies are able to make arrangements several months earlier and even construct a custom package for you with accommodations, golf, meals, and other extras. Among them are **Golf à la Carte** (☎ 760/ 324-5012; fax 760/321-1242; e-mail: glfalacart@aol.com) and **Palm Springs Golf and Tours** (☎ 800/PS-GOLF-1 or 760/346-3331; fax 760/346-4473).

For the nonplaying spectator (or anyone longing to see the pros make it look *so* easy), there are dozens of golf tournaments year-round, including many celebrity and pro-am events in addition to regular PGA, LPGA, and Senior Tour stops. February brings the PGA Tour **Bob Hope Chrysler Classic** at the Bermuda Dunes Country Club and the **Frank Sinatra Celebrity Invitational** at Marriott's Desert Springs Resort & Spa. In March, catch the LPGA Tour **Nabisco Dinah Shore** at the Mission Hills Country Club; in April, the Senior PGA **Liberty Mutual Legends of Golf** comes to PGA West. November brings two of the desert's longest-running charity events: the **24th Annual Frostig Center/Chris Korman Celebrity Tournament,** at the Westin Mission Hills; and the 26-year-old **Billy Barty/7-Up Celebrity Golf Classic,** at the Mesquite Country Club in Palm Springs. Also in November, check out the wacky **Palm Desert Golf Cart Parade** along El Paseo.

For more information, you can call the **Palm Springs Desert Resorts Convention and Visitors Bureau** (☎ 800/41-RELAX or 760/770-9000; www. desert-resorts.com). The bureau also maintains an **Activities Hotline** (☎ 760/770-1992).

including the required cart. The challenge of bunkers and rough can be amplified by the oft-blowing wind along the 5,885 yards of this unusually laid-out course.

The ✪ **Westin Mission Hills Resort Course,** Dinah Shore and Bob Hope drives, Rancho Mirage (☎ 760/328-3198), is somewhat more forgiving than most of legendary architect Pete Dye's courses, but don't play the back tees unless you've got a consistent 220-yard drive and won't be fazed by the Dye-trademark giant sand bunkers and elevated greens. Water only comes into play on four holes, and the scenery is an exquisite reward for low-handicappers. Nonguest greens fees are $150 to $175, including cart.

One of our favorite desert courses is the ✪ **PGA West TPC Stadium Course,** La Quinta Resort & Club, 49499 Eisenhower Dr., La Quinta (☎ **760/564-4111**), which received *Golf* magazine's 1994 Gold Medal Award for the total golf-resort experience. The par-3 17th has a picturesque island green where Lee Trevino made Skins Game history with a spectacular hole-in-one. The rest of Pete Dye's 7,261-yard design is flat, with huge bunkers, lots of water, and severe mounding throughout. Also open for semiprivate play is the **Mountain Course at La Quinta,** another Dye design that regularly appears on U.S. top-100 lists. It's set dramatically against the rocky mountains, which thrust into fairways to create tricky doglegs, and its small Bermuda greens are well guarded by boulders and deep bunkers. Greens fees for nonguests are $185 at both La Quinta courses.

A complete **golfer's guide** is available from the Palm Springs Desert Resorts Convention & Visitors Bureau (see "Visitor Information," above).

MORE OUTDOOR FUN

The Coachella Valley desert is truly a playground, and what follows is but a sampling of the opportunities to enjoy the abundant sunshine during your vacation here. But the strong sun and dry air that are so appealing can also sneak up on you in the form of sunburn and heat exhaustion. Especially during the summer, but even in milder times, always carry and drink plenty of water.

A FAMILY WATER PARK   Palm Springs Oasis Waterpark, off I-10 south on Gene Autry Trail between Ramon Road and East Palm Canyon Drive (☎ **760/ 325-7873**; www.oasiswaterresort.com), is a water playground with 12 water slides, body- and board surfing, an inner-tube ride, and more. Dressing rooms, lockers, and private beach cabanas (with food service) are available. Admission is $19 for visitors over 5 feet tall, $12 for kids 3 to 5 feet, and free for kids under 3 feet ($11 for seniors). The park is open mid-March through Labor Day, daily from 11am to 6pm, plus weekends through all of October.

HOT-AIR BALLOONING   This is perhaps the most memorable way to see the desert: floating above the landscape in a colorful hot-air balloon. Choose from specialty themes like sunrise, sunset, or romantic champagne flights. Rides are offered by **American Balloon Charters** (☎ 800/FLY-OVER or 760/327-8544), **Dream Flights** (☎ 800/933-5628 or 760/321-5154), and **Fantasy Balloon Flights** (☎ 800/ GO-ABOVE or 760/568-0997).

BICYCLING   The clean, dry air here just cries out to be enjoyed—what could be better than to pedal your way around town or into the desert? **Adventure Bike Tours** (☎ **760/328-2089**) will outfit you with bike, helmet, souvenir water bottle, and a certified guide. If you're just looking to rent some wheels and a helmet, **Mac's Bicycle Rental** (☎ **760/321-9444**) offers hourly, daily, and weekly rates on bikes, including children's and mountain models. **The Bike Man** (☎ **760/771-3619**) sweetens his deals by including water bottles, locks, maps, and free delivery. The **Bighorn Bicycle**

Rental & Tour Company (☎ 760/325-3367) has hourly and daily rental rates in addition to guided bike treks.

GUIDED JEEP & WAGON EXCURSIONS **Desert Adventures** (☎ 888/ 440-JEEP or 760/324-JEEP; www.red-jeep.com) offers four-wheel-drive ecotours led by experienced naturalist guides. Your off-road adventure may explore the lush palm oases of the ancestral Indian Canyons, the rugged Santa Rosa Mountain roads over-looking the Coachella Valley and the Bighorn Sheep Preserve, or picturesque ravines on the way to the San Andreas Fault. Tours range in duration from 2 to 4 hours and in price from $79 to $129. Advance reservations are required. The company's trade-mark red jeeps depart from the Desert Adventures Ranch on South Palm Canyon near the entrance to the Indian Canyons, but most of the longer excursions include hotel pickup and return.

Covered Wagon Tours (☎ 800/367-2161 or 760/347-2161) embraces the pio-neer spirit with a 2-hour ride through the Coachella Valley Nature Preserve followed by a good old-fashioned barbecue cookout and live country music. It operates daily from October to mid-May; tours are $55 for adults, $27.50 for children 7 to 16, and free for kids 6 and under. Without the grub, the tour is $40 per adult and $20 per child. Advance reservations are required.

HIKING The most popular spot for hiking is the nearby **Indian Canyons** (☎ 760/ 325-5673 for information). The Agua Caliente tribe made their home here centuries ago, and remnants of their simple lifestyle can be seen among the streams, waterfalls, and astounding palm groves in Andreas, Murray, and Palm canyons. Striking rock for-mations and herds of bighorn sheep and wild ponies will probably be more appealing than the "Trading Post" in Palm Canyon, but it does sell detailed trail maps. This is Indian land, and the Tribal Council charges admission of $6 per adult, with discounts for seniors, children, students, and military. The canyons are closed to visitors from late June to early September.

Ten miles east of Palm Springs is the 13,000-acre **Coachella Valley Preserve** (☎ 760/ 343-1234), which is open daily from sunrise to sunset. There are springs, mesas, both hiking and riding trails, the Thousand Palms Oasis, a visitor center, and picnic areas.

If you're heading up to Joshua Tree National Park (see "Joshua Tree National Park," below), consider stopping at the **Big Morongo Canyon Preserve** (☎ 760/ 363-7190), which was once an Indian village and later a cattle ranch. It opens to vis-itors Wednesday through Sunday at 7:30am. The park's high water table makes it a magnet for birds and other wildlife; the lush springs and streams are an unexpected desert treat.

HORSEBACK RIDING Equestrians from novice to advanced can experience the natural solitude and quiet of the desert on horseback at **Smoke Tree Stables** (☎ 760/ 327-1372). Located south of downtown and ideal for exploring the nearby Indian Canyon trails, Smoke Tree offers guided rides for $25 per hour. But don't expect your posse leader to be primed with facts on the nature you'll encounter—this is strictly a do-it-yourself experience.

SKYDIVING **Parachutes over Palm Springs** (☎ 800/535-5867 or 760/ 345-8321)—the name says it all! Its tandem skydiving system allows even the most timid beginner the opportunity to experience the exhilaration of a 30-second free fall followed by the serenity of a parachute descent while enjoying the panoramic beauty of the desert. You're harnessed to your instructor for the entire jump, and you can even take home a videotaped record of your bravery. The single-jump rate is $169; ask about group rates for two or more. The company operates from the Bermuda Dunes Airport daily from November through April. Advance reservations are required.

TENNIS Virtually all the larger hotels and resorts have tennis courts; but if you're staying at a B&B, you might want to play at the **Tennis Center,** 1300 Baristo Rd., Palm Springs (☎ 760/320-0020), which has nine courts and offers day and evening clinics for adults, juniors, and seniors, as well as ball machines for solo practice. USPTA pros are on hand.

If you'd like to play for free, the night-lit courts at **Palm Springs High School,** 2248 E. Ramon Rd., are open to the public on weekends, holidays, and in summer. There are also eight free night-lit courts in beautiful **Ruth Hardy Park** at Tamarisk and Caballero streets.

EXPLORING THE AREA

Haven't seen any celebrities wandering the streets? You may want to hook up with **Celebrity Tours,** located on East Palm Canyon Drive at Gene Autry Trail (☎ 760/770-2700). Advance reservations are required for their 1- and 2½-hour tours of Palm Springs, which include some history and lore but mostly the opportunity to gawk at the homes of movie stars and celebrities. The longer tours take in the estates of surrounding Rancho Mirage and Palm Desert, "playground of the international elite."

The Living Desert Wildlife and Botanical Park. 47900 Portola Ave., Palm Desert. ☎ 760/346-5694. www.livingdesert.org. Admission $7.50 adults, $6.50 seniors 62 and over, $3.50 children 3–12, free for kids under 3. Daily 9am–5pm (last entrance 4:30pm); summer (June 16 through Aug) 8am–1pm. Closed Christmas.

This 1,200-acre desert reserve, museum, zoo, and educational center is designed to acquaint visitors with the unique habitats that make up the southern California deserts. You can walk or take a tram tour through sectors that re-create life in several distinctive desert zones. See and learn about a dizzying variety of plants, insects, and wildlife, including bighorn sheep, mountain lions, rattlesnakes, lizards, owls, golden eagles, and the ubiquitous roadrunner.

Palm Springs Aerial Tramway. Tramway Rd. off Calif. 111, Palm Springs. ☎ 888/515-TRAM or 760/325-1391. www.pstramway.com. Tickets $21 adults, $17 seniors, $13 children 5–12, free for kids 4 and under; Ride 'n' Dine combination (available after 2:30pm, dinner served after 4pm) $21 adults, $14 children. Mon–Fri 10am–8pm; Sat–Sun 8am–8pm. Free parking.

To gain a bird's-eye perspective on the Coachella Valley, take this 14-minute ascent up 2½ miles to the top of Mount San Jacinto. While the Albert Frey-designed boarding stations retain their 1960s ski-lodge feel, brand-new Swiss funicular cars—installed in 1999—are sleekly modern, rotating during the trip to allow each passenger a panoramic view. There's a whole other world once you arrive: alpine scenery, a ski-lodge-flavored restaurant and gift shop, and temperatures typically 40° cooler than the desert floor. The most dramatic contrast is in winter, when the mountaintop is a snowy wonderland, irresistible to hikers and bundled-up kids with saucers. The excursion might not be worth the expense during the rest of the year. Guided mule rides and cross-country ski equipment are available at the top.

Palm Springs Desert Museum. 101 Museum Dr. (just west of the Palm Canyon/Tahquitz intersection), Palm Springs. ☎ 760/325-7186. www.psmuseum.org. Admission $7.50 adults, $6.50 seniors 62 and over, $3.50 military and children 6–17, free for children under 6, free for everyone the first Fri of each month. Tues–Sat 10am–5pm; Sun noon–5pm.

Unlikely though it may sound, this well-endowed museum is a must-see. Exhibits include world-class western and Native American art collections, the natural history of the desert, and an outstanding anthropology department, primarily representing the local Cahuilla tribe. Traditional Indian life as it was lived for centuries before the white presence is illustrated by tools, baskets, and other relics. Check local schedules to find

Sweet Treat of the Desert: The Coachella Valley Date Gardens

In a splendid display of both wishful thinking and clever engineering, the Coachella Valley has grown into a rich agricultural region, known internationally for grapefruit, figs, and grapes—but mostly for dates. Turn-of-the-century entrepreneurs, fascinated with Arabian lore and fueled by the Sahara-like conditions of the desert around Indio, planted the area's date palm groves in the 1920s. Launched with just a few parent trees imported from the Middle East, the groves now produce 95% of the world's date crop.

Farmers hand-pollinate the trees, and the resulting precious fruit is bundled in wind-protective paper while still on the tree, which makes an odd sight indeed. You'll see them along Calif. 111 through Indio, where the road is sometimes referred to as the "Date Highway."

For decades, **Shields Date Gardens**, 80225 Calif. 111 (☎ **760/347-0996**), has been enticing visitors into its splendid 1930s Moderne building with banners proclaiming free admission to the continuously running film *The Romance and Sex Life of the Date* (fair warning: its racy title is the best part). Even if you're not interested in the flick, stop by the lunch counter (date shake, anyone?) and store, which sells an endless variety of dates and related goodies, and sample some date ice cream or date crystals, a mysterious sweet product that seems to have many practical uses—until you actually get it home. But the quality and selection of fresh-harvested dates is superb; we guarantee you'll find yourself snacking on them before long. Open daily from 8am to 6pm.

There's no more picturesque place in the valley to sample dates than **Oasis Date Gardens,** 59111 Calif. 111 (☎ **800/827-8017** or 760/399-5665), started in 1912 with nine Moroccan trees and now one of the largest commercial date groves in the United States. It's a drive—about 40 minutes from downtown Palm Springs—but there's a lot to do here. Picnic tables dot an inviting lawn, videos illustrate the history and art of date cultivation, and there's a cool palm arboretum and cactus exhibit, plus a petting zoo for impatient youngsters. Many varieties of dates are laid out for free tasting; Oasis also sells date shakes, ice cream, chewy date pie by the slice, homemade chili and sandwiches, and gourmet food gifts from all over the Southwest. Open daily (except Christmas) from 6am to 5:30pm.

out about visiting exhibits (which are usually excellent). Plays, lectures, and other events are presented in the museum's Annenberg Theater.

SHOPPING

Downtown Palm Springs revolves around **North Palm Canyon Drive;** many art galleries, souvenir shops, and restaurants are located here, along with a couple of large-scale hotels and shopping centers. This wide, one-way boulevard is designed for pedestrians, with many businesses set back from the street itself—don't be shy about poking around the little courtyards you'll encounter. On Thursday night from 6 to 10pm, the blocks between Amado and Baristo roads are transformed into **VillageFest,** a street fair tradition celebrating its sixth anniversary. Handmade-crafts vendors and aromatic food booths compete for your attention with wacky street performers and even wackier locals shopping at the mouth-watering fresh-produce stalls.

The northern section of Palm Canyon is becoming known for vintage collectibles and is being touted as the **Antique and Heritage Gallery District.** Check out **John's Resale Furnishings,** 891 N. Palm Canyon Dr. (☎ 760/416-8876), for a glorious collection of mid-century modern furnishings; **Bandini Johnson Gallery,** 895 N. Palm Canyon Dr. (☎ 760/323-7805), a cramped warren of eclectic treasures; and the **Antiques Center,** 798 N. Palm Canyon Dr. (☎ 760/323-4443), a discriminating mall-style store whose 35 dealers display wares ranging from vintage linens to handmade African crafts to prized Bakelite jewelry.

Down in Palm Desert lies the delicious excess of **El Paseo,** a glitzy cornucopia of high-rent boutiques, salons, and upscale eateries reminiscent of Rodeo Drive in Beverly Hills, along with a dozen or more major shopping malls just like back home.

Factory-outlet shopping is 20 minutes away in Cabazon (see section 1, "En Route to the Palm Springs Resorts," earlier in this chapter).

One of our favorite local spots is **Bloomsbury Books,** 555 S. Sunrise Way #105, at Ramon Road (☎ 760/325-3862), which is wonderful for browsing. Proprietor Brad Confer is hard at work compiling an impressive array of out-of-print books as well as signed and rare editions, all reasonably priced and in great condition. Bloomsbury is especially strong in gay and lesbian literature (including rare early magazines and foreign publications), meticulously organized by topic. Every section is cleverly decorated with related memorabilia and noteworthy selections. Located in an ugly strip mall several blocks from the center of town, this treasure is well worth the detour. It's open Monday through Saturday from 11am to 9pm.

If it's Palm Springs history or literature you seek, visit the appealingly cluttered **Celebrity Bookstore,** 170 E. Tahquitz Canyon, half a block east of Palm Canyon Drive (☎ 800/320-6575 or 760/320-6575). Owner Darrell Meeks is the resident expert on local publications, and he also sets up tables for VillageFest each week. Hours are Monday through Saturday from 9am to 8pm and Sunday from 9am to 4pm.

GAY LIFE IN PALM SPRINGS

Don't think the local chamber of commerce doesn't recognize that the Palm Springs area is among the current top-three American destinations for gay travelers. After just a short while in town, it's easy to see how the gay tourism dollar is courted as aggressively as straight spending. Real-estate agents cater to gay shoppers for vacation properties, while entire condo communities are marketed toward the gay resident. Advertisements for these and scores of other proudly gay-owned businesses can be found in *The Bottom Line,* the desert's free biweekly magazine of articles, events, and community guides for the gay reader, which is available at hotels, newsstands, and from select merchants.

Throughout the year, events are held that transcend the gay community to include everyone. In March, the **Desert AIDS Walk** benefits the Desert AIDS Project, while the world's largest organized gathering of lesbians coincides with the **Nabisco Dinah Shore Golf Tournament.**

Be sure to visit **Village Pride,** 214 E. Arenas Rd. (☎ 760/323-9120), a coffeehouse and local gathering place. Besides offering a selection of gay- and lesbian-oriented reading material, Village Pride also serves as the lobby for the **Top Hat Playhouse.** This short block of Arenas is home to a score of gay establishments, including **Streetbar** (☎ 760/320-1266), a neighborhood gathering spot for tourists and locals alike.

Just a few blocks away is a cozy neighborhood of modest homes and small hotels, concentrated on Warm Sands Drive south of Ramon. Known simply as **"Warm Sands,"** this area holds the very nicest "private resorts"—mostly discreet and gated

B&B-style inns. Locals recommend the co-ed **El Mirasol,** 525 Warm Sands Dr. (☎ 800/327-2985 or 760/326-5913), a charming historic resort; or **Sago Palms,** 595 Thornhill Rd. (☎ 800/626-7246 or 760/323-0224), which is small, quiet, and affordable. Near the center of town lie the **Harlow Club Hotel,** 175 E. El Alameda (☎ 800/223-4073 or 760/320-4333), and **Abbey West,** 772 Prescott Circle (☎ 800/ 223-4073 or 760/416-2654), two adjacent all-male hotels with the same owner and the same ultra-elegant pampering. The **Bee Charmer,** 1600 E. Palm Canyon Dr. (☎ 888/321-5699; www.beecharmer.com), is one of the few all-women resorts in town.

Gay nightlife is everywhere in the valley, and especially raucous on holiday weekends. Pick up *The Bottom Line* for the latest restaurant, nightclub, theater, and special-events listings.

WHERE TO STAY

The city of Palm Springs offers a wide range of accommodations, but we particularly like the inns that have opened as new owners renovate the many fabulous 40- to 60-year-old cottage complexes in the wind-shielded "Tennis Club" area west of Palm Canyon Drive. The other desert-resort cities offer mostly sprawling resort complexes, many boasting world-class golf, tennis, or spa facilities and multiple on-site restaurants. Most are destinations in and of themselves, offering activities for the whole family (including a whole lot of relaxing and being pampered). So if you're looking for a good base from which to shop or sightsee, Palm Springs is your best bet.

Regardless of your choice, remember that the rates given below are for high season (winter, generally October through May). During the hotter summer months, it's common to find $300 rooms going for $99 or less as part of off-season packages. Even in high season, midweek and golf packages are common, so always ask when making your reservation.

PALM SPRINGS
Expensive
Ingleside Inn. 200 W. Ramon Rd. (at Belardo Rd.), Palm Springs, CA 92264. ☎ 800/ 772-6655 or 760/325-0046. Fax 760/325-0710. www.inglesideinn.com. 30 units. A/C MINIBAR TV TEL. $95–$160 double; $205–$285 minisuite; $145–$265 villa; from $355 full suite. Rates include welcome snacks and continental breakfast. AE, DC, DISC, MC, V. Free valet parking.

Once the 1920s estate of the Humphrey Birge family, manufacturers of the Pierce Arrow automobile, this hideaway offers some of the most charming rooms in town. Each guest room and suite is uniquely decorated with antiques, and many units have wood-burning fireplaces; all have in-room whirlpools and steam baths. There's an old-world charm here that's matched by fine service. The Ingleside is hardly low-key, however, and the management is always quick to mention in brochures, on wall plaques, and in other places that celebrities such as Elizabeth Taylor, John Wayne, Bette Davis, Salvador Dalí, and John Travolta have stayed here. (The celebrity watching is still first-rate.) They also like to boast of the inn's two appearances on *Lifestyles of the Rich & Famous.* Although you can expect indifferent service unless you have a famous face, Ingleside is still tops for experiencing "Golden Age of the Rat Pack" Palm Springs.

Dining/Diversions: Melvyn's is the expensive continental dining room, and the adjacent piano bar and lounge attract a fancy, old-money crowd. Frank and Barbara Sinatra hosted a dinner here on the eve of their wedding.

Amenities: Large heated outdoor pool, Jacuzzi, sundeck, croquet, shuffleboard, concierge, room service, in-room massage, complimentary limousine service, business center, car-rental desk, tour desk, boutiques.

La Mancha Resort Village. 444 Avenida Caballeros, Palm Springs, CA 92262. ☎ **800/ 64-PRIVACY** or 760/323-1773. www.la-mancha.com. 66 units. A/C TV TEL. $185–$245 suite for two; $295–$695 villa. AE, DC, DISC, MC, V. Free parking.

The security-gated entry makes La Mancha look like a private community, and it was designed that way. Once inside, though, a warmly respectful staff will pamper you, just the way they've coddled the countless celebs who have lent their names to the brochure. It's the quiet elegance and service, though, that distinguish La Mancha from the other resorts, not its modern but unoriginal furnishings. Fruit baskets welcome guests to the quarters, most of them suites with TVs and phones in every room, plus VCRs (they'll even provide Nintendo for the kids). Many guests opt for the countless pleasures of the villas, which have private pools, fireplaces, and wet bars. Scores of bicycles and a private fleet of rental cars stand ready should you want to venture the half mile into town, and there's a spa and fitness center—how about a massage on your personal patio?

Dining: In keeping with the La Mancha theme, the aptly named Don Quixote Dining Room is open for breakfast, lunch, and dinner.

Amenities: Heated outdoor pool with Jacuzzi, spa and fitness center, concierge, room service, video rental, laundry service, morning newspaper, nightly turndown, valet, courtesy airport limo, tennis courts (four lit for night play), two paddle-tennis courts (one lit), three croquet lawns (one lit), two practice greens, gift shop, conference rooms.

Moderate

Estrella Inn. 415 S. Belardo Rd. (south of Tahquitz Way), Palm Springs, CA 92262. ☎ **800/ 237-3687** or 760/320-4117. Fax 760/323-3303. www.estrella.com. 63 units. A/C TV TEL. $150 double; $225–$275 1- or 2-bedroom suite; $250–$350 1- or 2-bedroom bungalow. Rates include continental breakfast. Monthly rates available. AE, CB, DC, MC, V. Free parking. Pets allowed in tile-floored units for $20 fee.

Once the choice of Hollywood celebrities, this outstanding historic hotel is quiet and secluded, yet wonderfully close to the action. Composed of three distinct properties from three different eras, the complex is united by a peachy desert color scheme and uniformly lavish landscaping. Guest rooms vary widely according to location, but all include pampering touches: Some have fireplaces and/or full kitchens, others wet bars or private balconies. The real deals are in the studio bungalows, even though they have tiny 1930s bathrooms. The Estrella has two pools, a children's pool, two whirlpools, an outdoor barbecue, and a lawn with games area. Ask about attractive golf packages that include play at one of several nearby courses.

✪ Korakia Pensione. 257 S. Patencio Rd., Palm Springs, CA 92262. ☎ **760/864-6411.** 20 units. $119–$365 double. Rates include breakfast. No credit cards. Free parking.

If you can work within the Korakia's rigid deposit-cancellation policy, you're in for a special stay at this Greek/Moroccan oasis just a few blocks from Palm Canyon Drive. The simply furnished rooms and unbelievably spacious suites are peaceful and private, surrounded by flagstone courtyards and flowering gardens. Rooms are divided among the main house, a second restored villa across the street, and surrounding guest bungalows. Most have kitchens, while many sport fireplaces. This former artist's villa from the 1920s draws a hip international crowd of artists, writers, and musicians. All beds are blessed with thick feather duvets, while the windows are shaded by flowing white canvas draperies in the Mediterranean style. Add a sumptuous breakfast served in your room or poolside (*korakia* is Greek for "crow," and a tile mosaic example graces the pool bottom).

Spa Hotel & Casino. 100 N. Indian Canyon Dr., Palm Springs, CA 92263. ☎ **800/ 854-1279** or 760/325-1461. Fax 760/325-3344. www.Spa-Hotel.com. 230 units. A/C MINIBAR TV TEL. $159–$239 double; $219–$279 suite. AE, CB, DC, MC, V. Free parking.

Located on the Indian-owned parcel of land containing the original mineral springs for which Palm Springs was named, this is one of the more unusual choices in town. The Cahuilla claimed that the springs had magical powers to cure illness; today's travelers still come here to pamper both body and soul by "taking the waters," though now the facility is sleekly modern. There are three pools on the premises. One is a conventional outdoor swimming pool; the other two are filled from the underground natural springs brimming with revitalizing minerals. Inside the hotel's extensive spa are private sunken marble swirlpools fed by the springs, and after your bath, you can avail yourself of the many other pampering treatments offered. The spa recently opened the adjoining Vegas-style casino, featuring the familiar hush of card-gaming tables and clanging of video poker and slot machines. Other hotel facilities include a fitness center, steam room, concierge, car-rental desk, two restaurants, and two bars.

Villa Royale. 1620 Indian Trail (off East Palm Canyon), Palm Springs, CA 92264. ☎ 800/ 245-2314 or 760/327-2314. Fax 760/322-3794. www.villaroyale.com. 33 units. A/C TV TEL. $95–$175 double; $150–$295 suite. Rates include breakfast. Extra person $25. Substantial off-season discounts. AE, DC, DISC, MC, V. Free parking.

Located 5 minutes from the hustle and bustle of downtown Palm Springs, this charming inn evokes a European cluster of villas, complete with climbing bougainvillea and rooms filled with international antiques and artwork. The main building was once home to Olympic and silver-screen ice-skater Sonja Henie. Villa Royale's reputation had been suffering due to indifferent management, but 1998 brought new ownership and a renewed dedication to service. The changes were immediate and dramatic, as meticulous perfection replaced shabby maintenance, and uniform luxuries (robes, hair dryers, down comforters, and other pampering touches) appeared throughout. Rooms vary widely in size and ambiance; surprisingly, large isn't always better, as some of the inn's most appealing units are in the affordable range. Ask for nos. 103, 121, 122, 201, 302, or 308—trust us. Many rooms have fireplaces, private patios with whirlpools, full kitchens, or a variety of other amenities.

Continental breakfast is served in an intimate garden setting surrounding the main pool. The hotel's romantic restaurant, Europa, is a sleeper, offering one of Palm Springs's very best meals (see "Where to Dine," below).

Inexpensive

Casa Cody. 175 S. Cahuilla Rd. (between Tahquitz Way and Arenas Rd.), Palm Springs, CA 92262. ☎ 760/320-9346. Fax 760/325-8610. 23 units. A/C TV TEL. $79–$89 double; $99–$139 studio; $149–$219 suite; 2-bedroom adobe $299–$349. Rates include expanded continental breakfast. Midweek and summer rates available. AE, DC, DISC, MC, V. Pets accepted for $10 fee per night.

Once owned by "Wild" Bill Cody's niece, this 1920s *casa* with a double courtyard (each with swimming pool) has been restored to fine condition, sporting a vaguely Southwestern decor and peaceful grounds marked by large lawns and mature, blossoming fruit trees. You'll feel more like a houseguest than a hotel client at the Casa Cody. It's located in the primarily residential "Tennis Club" area of town, a couple of easy blocks from Palm Canyon Drive. Many units here have fireplaces and full-size kitchens. Breakfast is served poolside, as is complimentary wine and cheese on Saturday afternoons.

Orchid Tree Inn. 261 S. Belardo Rd. (at Baristo Rd.), Palm Springs, CA 92262. ☎ 800/ 733-3435 or 760/325-2791. Fax 760/325-3855. www.orchidtree.com. 40 units. A/C TV TEL. $95–$120 double; $130–$295 suite. Extra person $15. Rates include continental breakfast. AE, MC, V. Pets allowed for a $10 fee.

Billed as a "1930s desert garden retreat," the Orchid Tree is a sprawling complex of buildings from the 1920s through 1950s, each with a unique personality, like the individual decor in each room. Dedicated family ownership ensures the place is impeccably maintained, and the rooms are nicer than you'd expect at this price, but in keeping with the overall grace and excellence of the entire neighborhood. Room types range from simple, hotel-style doubles to charming bungalows to poolside studios with sliding-glass doors. Located just a block from Palm Canyon Drive in the historic "Tennis Club" district, the Inn nevertheless truly feels like a retreat: Insulated from the surrounding streets, the grounds are rich with flowering shrubs, mature citrus trees, and multitudes of twittering hummingbirds, sparrows, and quail drawn by bird feeders and baths. There are three swimming pools, two whirlpools, and an outdoor barbecue area.

RANCHO MIRAGE

Rancho Las Palmas Marriott Resort & Spa. 41000 Bob Hope Dr., Rancho Mirage, CA 92270. ☎ **800/I-LUV-SUN** or 760/568-2727. Fax 760/568-5845. 450 units. A/C MINIBAR TV TEL. $229–$339 double; from $600 suite. Off-season discounts and packages available. AE, DISC, MC, V. Free valet and self-parking. Pets under 20 lb. accepted at no charge.

The early California charm of this relaxing Spanish hacienda makes Rancho Las Palmas one of the less pretentious luxury resorts in the desert. Dedicated golfers come to play on the adjoining country club's 27 holes of golf, tennis buffs flock to the 25 hotel courts (three of them red clay), and in 1999, the resort unveiled a brand-new, world-class health spa with pampering treatments plus a separate pool with water slide. Guest rooms are arranged in a complex of low-rise, tile-roofed structures, and the public areas have an easygoing elegance, filled with flower-laden stone fountains, smooth terra-cotta tile floors, and rough-hewn wood trim. All rooms have a balcony or patio.

Dining/Diversions: The Marriott's four restaurants range from casual patio dining to dressy dinner fare, and Miguel's Lounge offers cocktails, snacks, and music in a cantina setting.

Amenities: Two swimming pools with adjacent whirlpools, fully equipped fitness center, 25 tennis courts, golf and tennis pro shops, room service, laundry service, baby-sitting.

Westin Mission Hills Resort. Dinah Shore Dr. and Bob Hope Dr., Rancho Mirage, CA 92270. ☎ **800/WESTIN-1** or 760/328-5955. Fax 760/321-2955. 512 units. A/C MINIBAR TV TEL. Winter (Jan–April) $410–$450 double; spring/fall (May and Sept–Dec) $320–$370 double; summer (Memorial Day–Labor Day) $169–$189 double. Extra person $35. Children 17 and under stay free in parents' room. Packages available. AE, CB, DC, DISC, JCB, MC, V. Free valet and self-parking.

Designed to resemble a Moroccan palace surrounded by pools, waterfalls, and lush gardens, this self-contained resort stands on 360 acres. It's an excellent choice for families and for travelers who take their golf game seriously. The rooms are a bit bland when compared to the spectacular exterior of the hotel, but they do have views of the mountains and golf course. All have terraces and come with coffeemakers, hair dryers, movie channels, voice mail, and robes.

Dining/Diversions: The multiple dining options include Bella Vista, an atrium dining room serving California cuisine. There are also three bars, two of which offer live entertainment.

Amenities: Three pools, fitness center, spa, steam room, whirlpool, seven tennis courts, running track, bikes and bike trails, renowned championship golf course, concierge, room service, dry cleaning, laundry, masseur, twice-daily maid service, baby-sitting, games room, lawn games, car-rental desk, business center, beauty salon. The fully staffed activities center for children offers educational instruction about the flora, fauna, and history of the desert.

PALM DESERT

Desert Springs Marriott Spa & Resort. 74885 Country Club Dr., Palm Desert, CA 92260. ☎ **800/331-3112** or 760/341-2211. Fax 760/341-1872. 884 units. A/C MINIBAR TV TEL. High-season (Christmas–Memorial Day) $340–$470 double; June–Labor Day $175–$290 double; Sept–Dec 23 $265–$305 double. Children 17 and under stay free in parents' room. Packages available. AE, CB, DC, DISC, MC, V.

A tourist attraction in its own right, Marriott's Desert Springs Resort is worth a peek even if you're not lucky enough to stay here. Most of the guests are attracted by the excellent golf and tennis facilities, and the huge, luxurious, full-service spa is an added perk, offering massages, facials, aerobics classes, and supervised weight training. Visitors enter this artificial desert oasis via a sweeping palm-tree-lined road wending its way past a small pond that's home to a gaggle of pink flamingos. Once inside, guests are greeted by a shaded marble lobby "rain forest" replete with interior moat and the squawk of tropical birds; gondolas even ply the lobby's waterways.

While the rooms here are not as fancy as the lobby would lead you to believe, they're exceedingly comfortable, decorated with muted pastels and contemporary furnishings. All have terraces with views of the golf course and the San Jacinto Mountains. Most units have large bathrooms and are outfitted with hair dryers, ironing boards and irons, and separate tubs. The suites have large sitting/dining areas furnished with Murphy beds.

Dining/Diversions: There are six restaurants, four snack bars, and two lounges, one of which features live entertainment. The poolside snacks are remarkably tasty.

Amenities: Concierge, room service, overnight laundry, masseur, twice-daily maid service, baby-sitting, four heated outdoor pools, sunbathing "beach" with volleyball court, full-service spa and health club with aerobics classes, three outdoor Jacuzzis, sundecks, 20 tennis courts (hard, clay, and grass; seven lighted), jogging trail, two 18-hole golf courses, putting green, driving range, special children's programs, games room, car-rental desk, tour desk, José Eber beauty salon.

LA QUINTA

✪ **La Quinta Resort & Club.** 49499 Eisenhower Dr., La Quinta, CA 92253. ☎ **800/598-3828** or 760/564-4111. Fax 760/564-5758. www.laquintaresort.com. 640 units. A/C MINIBAR TV TEL. High-season $235–$410 double; summer (July to mid-Oct) $129–$245 double. Extra person $15. Children 17 and under stay free in parents' room. Packages available. AE, MC, V. Pets accepted with $25 fee.

A luxury resort set amid citrus trees, towering palms, cacti, and desert flowers at the base of the rocky Santa Rosa Mountains, La Quinta is *the* place to be if you're serious about your golf or tennis game. In 1998, the resort debuted Spa La Quinta, a deluxe mission-style complex with 35 treatment rooms for every pampering luxury. All guest rooms are in comfortable single-story, Spanish-style casitas scattered throughout the grounds. Each has a private patio and access to one of two dozen small pools, enhancing the feeling of privacy at this retreat. All units come with two phones, movie channels, and a fridge; some have a fireplace or private Jacuzzi. The tranquil lounge/library in the unaltered original hacienda hearkens back to the early days of the resort, when Clark Gable, Greta Garbo, Frank Capra, and other luminaries chose La Quinta as their hideaway. The resort is renowned for its five championship golf courses—including one of California's best, Pete Dye's PGA West TPC Stadium Course—and 30 tennis courts.

Dining/Diversions: There are three restaurants, including Montanas with outstanding Mediterranean fare, and three bars (two with entertainment).

Amenities: Dozens of swimming pools and whirlpools, bicycles, children's programs, concierge, room service, dry cleaning, laundry, twice-daily maid service, baby-sitting, car-rental desk, beauty salon, business center.

DESERT HOT SPRINGS

✪ **Two Bunch Palms.** 67425 Two Bunch Palms Trail, Desert Hot Springs, CA 92240.
☎ **800/472-4334** or 760/329-8791. Fax 760/329-1317. www.twobunchpalms.com. 45
units. A/C TV TEL. $185–$270 double; $325–$595 suite or villa. Rates include expanded
continental breakfast. AE, MC, V.

Posh yet intimate, this spiritual sanctuary in Desert Hot Springs has been drawing
weary city dwellers with its healing mineral springs since Chicago mobster Al Capone
hid out here in the 1930s. Two Bunch Palms later became a playground for the movie
community, but today it's a friendly and informal haven offering renowned spa services, quiet bungalows nestled on lush grounds, and trademark pools of steaming mineral water. All accommodations have terraces and such extras as coffeemakers, hair
dryers, and fridges; some units have fireplaces or their own Jacuzzis. The staff offers
discreet, excellent service.

   Dining: Surrounding Desert Hot Springs offers little incentive to leave this
sybaritic paradise; you'll probably eat your meals at the unremarkable but health-
conscious Casino Dining Room.

   Amenities: Legions of return guests will attest that the outstanding spa treatments
(nine varieties of massage, mud baths, body wraps, facials, salt glo, and more) and
therapeutic waters are what make the luxury of Two Bunch Palms worth the price.
Other amenities include a pool, bicycles, two tennis courts, a fitness center, and private sunning bins.

WHERE TO DINE
PALM SPRINGS

Coffee hounds in search of a stylish fix can stop into **Lalajava,** 300 N. Palm Canyon
Dr., at the corner of Amado (☎ **760/325-3494**). The cheerful staff will help you navigate the extensive menu of coffee items, which run the gamut from steaming hot cap-
puccinos to blended ice mochas, including flavored lattes, mochas, and cocoas. Nibble
on a fresh muffin or a bagel spread with plain or honey-walnut cream cheese and you'll
be well prepared for your day. And for a sweet ice-cream treat, try **Lappert's Hawaiian
Ice Cream,** 110B S. Palm Canyon Dr. (☎ **760/778-1855**), a mainland branch of
Kauai's local fave. In addition to inventive concoctions of island flavors like chocolate–macadamia nut and coconut-caramel, it serves sweet shaved ices and tropical-fruit
smoothies.

Expensive

✪ **Europa Restaurant.** 1620 Indian Trail (at the Villa Royale). ☎ **760/327-2314.** Reservations recommended. Main courses $17–$28. AE, DC, DISC, MC, V. Tues–Sat 5:30–10pm,
Sun 11:30am–2pm and 5:30–10pm. CALIFORNIA/CONTINENTAL.

Long advertised as the "most romantic dining in the desert," Europa is a sentimental
favorite of many gay and straight regulars, all of whom know that through the restaurant's French doors lies a European-style hideaway oozing charm and ambiance.
Whether you sit under the stars on Europa's garden patio or in subdued candlelight
indoors, you'll surely savor dinner prepared by one of Palm Springs's most dedicated
kitchens and served by a staff that perfectly modulates attention and discretion.
Standout dishes include deviled crab fritters on mango-papaya chutney, filet mignon
on a bed of crispy onions with garlic butter, and a show-stopping salmon baked in
parchment with crème fraîche and dill. For dessert, don't miss the signature chocolate
mousse—smooth, grainy, and addictive.

Palmie. 276 N. Palm Canyon Dr. (across from the Hyatt). ☎ **760/320-3375.** Reservations
recommended. Main courses $12–$26. AE, DC, MC, V. Mon–Sat 5:30–9:30pm. CLASSIC
FRENCH.

You can't see Palmie from the street, and once you're seated inside its softly lit, lattice-enclosed dining patio, you won't see the bustle outside anymore, either. Art-deco posters of French seaside resorts abound, transporting you to the cozy bistro of owners Martine and Alain Clerc. Chef Alain sends out traditional French masterpieces such as bubbling cheese soufflé, green lentil salad dotted with pancetta, steak au poivre rich with cognac sauce, and lobster ravioli garnished with caviar; in fact, every carefully garnished plate is a work of art. To the charming background strains of French chanteuses, hostess/manager Martine circulates among the tables, determined that visitors should enjoy their meals as much as the loyal regulars she greets by name. Forget your cardiologist for one night and don't leave without sampling dessert: Our favorite is the trio of petite crème brûlées, flavored with ginger, vanilla, and Kahlúa.

Moderate

La Provence. 254 N. Palm Canyon Dr. (upstairs from an arcade). ☎ **760/416-4418.** Reservations recommended. Main courses $10–$21. AE, DC, DISC, MC, V. Daily 5:30–10:30pm (subject to Wed closure off-season). COUNTRY FRENCH.

A favorite of locals and recommended by knowledgeable innkeepers, the casually elegant La Provence eschews heavy traditional French cream sauces in favor of carefully married herbs and spices. The second-story terrace sets a lovely mood on balmy desert evenings, whether or not it "subtly infuses the diner with an elevated sense of tranquillity," as the restaurant gushingly promises. The menu offers some expected items (escargots in mushroom caps, bouillabaisse, steak au poivre) as well as inventive pastas like wild-mushroom ravioli in a sun-dried-tomato/sweet-onion sauce. Foodies will note with pleasure that executive chef Clay Arkless comes by way of New York City's River Cafe.

Las Casuelas Terraza. 222 S. Palm Canyon Dr. ☎ **760/325-2794.** Reservations recommended on weekends. Main courses $7–$13. AE, CB, DC, DISC, MC, V. Mon–Thurs 11am–10pm; Fri–Sat 11am–11pm; Sun 10am–10pm. CLASSIC MEXICAN.

The original Las Casuelas is still open, a tiny storefront several blocks from this popular *terraza* (terrace) offspring, but the bougainvillea-draped front patio here is a much better place to people-watch over Mexican standards like quesadillas, enchiladas, and mountainous nachos washed down with equally super-size margaritas. Inside, the action heats up with live music and raucous happy-hour crowds. In hot weather, the patio and even sidewalk passersby are cooled by the restaurant's well-placed misters, making this a perfect late-afternoon or early-evening choice.

Inexpensive

☉ Edgardo's Café Veracruz. 494 N. Palm Canyon (at W. Alejo Rd.). ☎ **760/360-3558.** Reservations recommended. Main courses $3.50–$15. DISC, MC, V. Mon–Fri 11am–3pm and 5:30–9:30pm; Sat–Sun 8am–10pm (sometimes later). REGIONAL CENTRAL MEXICAN.

The pleasant but humble ambiance at Edgardo's is a welcome change from touristy Palm Springs, and is the perfect backdrop for its expert menu of authentic Mayan, Huasteco, and Aztec cuisine. The dark interior boasts an array of colorful masks and artwork from Central and South America, but the postage-stamp–sized front patio with a trickling fountain is the best place to sample Edgardo's tangy quesadillas, desert-cactus salad, and traditional poblano chiles rellenos—perhaps even an oyster/tequila shooter from the oyster bar!

Mykonos. 139 Andreas (just off Palm Canyon). ☎ **760/322-0223.** Reservations not accepted. Most items under $10. MC, V. Wed–Mon 11am–10pm. GREEK.

Sit at the simple, candlelit tables in this off-street brick courtyard with locals who have been enjoying authentic Greek specialties at this family-run spot for 10 years. Mykonos is supercasual (vinyl tablecloths and so forth) and decorated in white and blue like its Aegean namesake, but it's a pleasant treat in a town of mostly mediocre retro-diner fare. Traditional lamb shanks over rice, dolmades (stuffed grape leaves), salad tangy with crumbled feta cheese, and sweet, sticky baklava are among their best items.

RANCHO MIRAGE

The Chart House. 69934 Calif. 111 (between Country Club and Frank Sinatra drives). ☎ **760/324-5613.** Reservations recommended Jan–June. Full dinners $14–$32. AE, CB, DC, DISC, MC, V. Sun–Fri 5–10pm; Sat 5–10:30pm. STEAKS/SEAFOOD.

Looking like a giant alien crustacean partially embedded in the earth, this traditional steak house is a treasure of wild 1960s architecture. You've seen this menu before— fine steaks, prime rib, seafood, endless salad bar, oversize baked potatoes—but the Chart House prepares each meal superbly, and the surreal setting makes it worth the expenditure.

LA QUINTA

La Quinta Cliffhouse. 78250 Calif. 111. ☎ **760/360-5991.** Reservations recommended. Main courses $13–$20. AE, MC, V. Tues–Fri 11:30am–2:30pm; Mon–Sat 5–9:30pm; Sun (in fall only) 10am–2pm. Closed for lunch in summer. REGIONAL AMERICAN.

King of its own little hill on the east side of Calif. 111, La Quinta Cliffhouse succeeds primarily due to its lovely setting. The stairs leading to the restaurant's entrance wind through a rocky waterfall, and there's a breathtaking sunset virtually every night of the year. The rustic Southwestern lodge decor is a little tired, but the old-money crowd that packs the valet-only lot doesn't seem to mind. The best dishes come off the grill, like filet mignon with Jack Daniels peppercorn sauce, BBQ pork ribs with chili and jalapeño cornbread, or Pacific ahi in red-bell-pepper sauce with garlic potatoes. In season, they serve an affordable and immensely popular Sunday champagne brunch, and there's also a hearty pub menu in the adjacent Cactus Grill.

PALM DESERT

Doug Arango's. 73520 El Paseo. ☎ **760/341-4120.** Reservations recommended. Main courses $12–$22. AE, MC, V. Tues–Sat 11:30am–2:30pm (Oct–May) and Tues–Sun 5:30–10pm (year-round). NORTHERN ITALIAN.

With so many Italian restaurants that are either old-world lasagna joints or pricey resort trattorias, it's no wonder Doug's is always packed with locals thankful for an affordable, stylish choice offering northern Italian fare without pretension. Expect a friendly, noisy clatter when they're full, and beware: The kitchen can be heavy-handed with the garlic. Crispy, thin-crust individual pizzas are one specialty, and everyone raves about the appetizer of zucchini pancakes with scallion sour cream. The decor is understated, with black-and-white tiles, glass urns of marinating delicacies, and an open kitchen you can gaze into from the large, oval bar.

THE DESERT RESORTS AFTER DARK

Every month a different club or disco is the hot spot in the Springs, and the best way to tap into the trend is by consulting *The Desert Guide, The Bottom Line* (see "Gay Life in Palm Springs," above), or one of the many other free newsletters available from area hotels and merchants. **VillageFest** (see "Shopping," above) turns Palm Canyon Drive into an outdoor party every Thursday night. Below, we've described a couple of the enduring arts and entertainment attractions around the desert resorts.

The **Fabulous Palm Springs Follies,** at the Plaza Theatre, 128 S. Palm Canyon Dr., Palm Springs (☎ **760/327-0225**), a vaudeville-style show filled with lively production numbers, is celebrating its seventh year running in the historic Plaza Theatre in the heart of Palm Springs. With a cast of energetic retired showgirls, singers, dancers, and comedians, the revue has been enormously popular around town. Call for show schedule; tickets range from $28 to $59.

The **McCallum Theatre for the Performing Arts,** 73000 Fred Waring Dr., Palm Desert (☎ **760/340-ARTS**), offers the only cultural high road around. Frequent symphony performances with visiting virtuosos such as conductor Seiji Ozawa or violinist Itzhak Perlman, musicals like Tommy Tune's *Grease* or *A Chorus Line* revival, and pop performers like the Captain and Tennille or the Ink Spots are among the theater's recent offerings. Call for upcoming event information.

4 Joshua Tree National Park

40 miles NE of Palm Springs, 128 miles E of Los Angeles

The trees themselves are merely a jumping-off point for exploring this seemingly barren desert. Viewed from the roadside, the dry land only hints at hidden vitality, but closer examination reveals a giant mosaic of intense beauty and complexity. From lush oases teeming with life to rusted-out relics of man's attempts to tame the wilderness, from low plains of tufted cacti to mountains of exposed, twisted rock, the park is much more than a tableau of the curious tree for which it is named.

The Joshua tree is said to have been given its name by early Mormon settlers traveling west, for its upraised limbs and bearded appearance reminded them of the prophet Joshua leading them to the promised land.

Other observers were not so kind. Explorer John C. Frémont called it "the most repulsive tree in the vegetable kingdom." Nature writer Charles Francis Saunders opined: "The trees themselves were as grotesque as the creations of a bad dream; the shaggy trunks and limbs were twisted and seemed writhing as though in pain, and dagger-pointed leaves were clenched in bristling fists of inhospitality."

Harsh criticism for this hardy desert dweller, which is really not a tree, but a variety of yucca, member of the lily family. The relationship is apparent when pale yellow, lily-like flowers festoon the limbs of the Joshuas when they bloom (depending on rainfall) in March, April, or May. When Mother Nature cooperates, the park also puts on quite a wildflower display, and you can get an updated report on prime viewing sites by calling the park ranger (see below).

Joshua Tree National Park's name is fitting, for here the peculiar tree reaches the southernmost boundary of its range. The park straddles two desert environments; there's the mountainous, Joshua tree–studded Mojave Desert forming the northwestern part of the park, while the Colorado Desert—hotter, drier, lower, and characterized by a wide variety of desert flora including cacti, cottonwood, and native California fan palms—comprises the southern and eastern sections of the park. Between them runs the "transition zone," displaying characteristics of each.

The area's geological timeline is fascinating, stretching back 8 million years to a time when the Mojave landscape was one of rolling hills and flourishing grasslands; horses, camels, and mastodons abounded, preyed upon by sabre-toothed tigers and wild dogs.

Traveler's Tip

No restaurants, lodging, gas stations, or stores are found within Joshua Tree National Park. In fact, water is only available at four park locations: Cottonwood Springs, the Black Rock Canyon Campground, the Indian Cove Ranger Station, and the Oasis Visitor Center. Twentynine Palms and Yucca Valley have lots of restaurants, markets, motels, and B&Bs.

Displays at the Oasis Visitor Center show how resulting climatic, volcanic, and tectonic activity have created the park's signature cliffs and boulders and turned Joshua Tree into the arid desert you see today.

Human presence has been traced back nearly 10,000 years with the discovery of Pinto Man, and evidence of more recent habitation can be seen in the form of Native American pictographs carved into rock faces throughout the park. Miners and ranchers began coming in the 1860s, but the boom went bust by the turn of the century. Then a Pasadena doctor, treating World War I veterans suffering from respiratory and heart ailments caused by mustard gas, prescribed the desert's clean, dry air—and the modern town of Twentynine Palms was (re)born.

In the 1920s, a worldwide fascination with the desert emerged, and cactus gardens were very much in vogue. Entrepreneurs hauled truckloads of desert plants into Los Angeles for quick sale or export, and souvenir hunters removed archaeological treasures. Incensed that the beautiful Mojave was in danger of being picked clean, Los Angeles socialite Minerva Hoyt organized a desert conservation movement and successfully lobbied for the establishment of Joshua Tree National Monument in 1936.

In 1994, under provisions of the federal California Desert Protection Act, Joshua Tree was "upgraded" to national-park status and expanded to nearly 800,000 acres.

JUST THE FACTS

ACCESS POINTS   From metropolitan Los Angeles, the usual route to the Oasis Visitor Center in Joshua Tree National Park is via I-10 to its intersection with Calif. 62 (some 92 miles east of downtown). Calif. 62 (the Twentynine Palms Highway) leads northeast for about 43 miles to the town of Twentynine Palms. Total driving time is around 2½ hours. In town, follow the signs at National Park Drive or Utah Trail to the visitor center and ranger station. Admission to the park is $10 per car (good for 7 days).

VISITOR CENTERS & INFORMATION   In addition to the main **Oasis Visitor Center** at the Twentynine Palms entrance, **Cottonwood Visitor Center** is at the south entrance, and the privately operated **Park Center** is located in the town of Joshua Tree.

The Oasis Visitor Center is open daily (except Christmas) from 8am to 4:30pm. Check here for a detailed map of park roads, plus schedules of ranger-guided walks and interpretive programs. Ask about the weekend tours of the Desert Queen Ranch, once a working homestead and now part of the park.

For advance information, contact the **Park Superintendent's Office,** 74485 National Park Dr., Twentynine Palms, CA 92277 (☎ **760/367-5500**; www.nps.gov/ jotr). Another terrific Web site on the park and surrounding communities is **www. desertgold.com**.

SEEING THE HIGHLIGHTS

An excellent first stop, outside the park's north entrance, is the main **Oasis Visitor Center,** located alongside the Oasis of Mara, also known as the Twentynine Palms Oasis. For many generations, the native Serrano tribe lived at this "place of little springs and much grass." Get maps, books, and the latest in road, trail, and weather conditions before beginning your tour.

From the Oasis Center, drive south to **Jumbo Rocks,** which captures the complete essence of the park: a vast array of rock formations, a Joshua-tree forest, and the yucca-dotted desert, open and wide. Check out Skull Rock (one of the many rocks in the area that appears to resemble humans, dinosaurs, monsters, cathedrals, and castles) via a 1½-mile-long nature trail that provides an introduction to the park's flora, wildlife, and geology.

At Cap Rock Junction, the main park road swings north toward the **Wonderland of Rocks,** 12 square miles of massive jumbled granite. This curious maze of stone hides groves of Joshua trees, trackless washes, and several small pools of water. To the south is Keys View Road, which dead-ends at mile-high **Keys View.** From the crest of the Little San Bernardino Mountains, enjoy grand desert views that encompass both the highest (Mount San Gorgonio) and lowest (Salton Sea) points in southern California.

Don't miss the contrasting Colorado Desert terrain found along Pinto Basin Road—to conserve time, you might plan to exit the park via this route, which ends up at I-10. You'll pass both the **Cholla Cactus Garden** and spindly **Ocotillo Patch** on your way to vast, flat **Pinto Basin,** a barren lowland surrounded by austere mountains and punctuated by trackless sand dunes. The dunes are an easy 2-mile (round-trip) hike from the backcountry camping board (one of the few man-made markers along this road and one of the only designated parking areas), or simply continue to **Cottonwood Springs,** near the southern park entrance. Besides a small ranger station and well-developed campground, Cottonwood has a cool, palm-shaded oasis that is the trailhead for a tough hike to Lost Palms Oasis.

ACTIVITIES WITHIN THE PARK

HIKING & NATURE WALKS   The national park holds a variety of nature trails ranging in difficulty from strenuous challenges to kid-friendly (and wimp-friendly) interpretive walks—two of these (**Oasis of Mara** and **Cap Rock**) are even paved and wheelchair-accessible. Our favorite of the 11 short interpretive trails is **Cholla Cactus Garden,** smack-dab in the middle of the park, where you stroll through dense clusters of the deceptively fluffy-looking "teddy bear cactus."

For the more adventurous, **Barker Dam** is an easy 1.1-mile loop accessible by a graded dirt road east of Hidden Valley. A small, man-made lake is framed by the majestic Wonderland of Rocks. In addition to scrambling atop the old dam, it's fun to search out Native American petroglyphs carved into the base of cliffs lining your return to the trailhead.

The moderately challenging **Lost Horse Mine Trail** near Keys View leads through rolling hills to the ruins of a successful gold-mining operation; once here, a short, steep hike leads uphill behind the ruins for a fine view into the heart of the park.

When you're ready for a strenuous hike, try the **Fortynine Palms Oasis Trail,** accessible from Canyon Road in Twentynine Palms. After a steep, harsh ascent to a cactus-fringed ridge, the rocky canyon trail leads to a spectacular oasis, complete with palm-shaded pools of green water and abundant birds and other wildlife. Allow 2 to 3 hours for the 3-mile (round-trip) hike.

Another lush oasis lies at the end of **Lost Palms Oasis Trail** at Cottonwood Springs. The first section of the 7½-mile trail is moderately difficult, climbing slowly to the oasis overlook; from here, a treacherous path continues to the canyon bottom, a remote spot that the elusive bighorn sheep find attractive.

ROCK CLIMBING   From Hidden Valley to the Wonderland of Rocks, the park has emerged as one of the world's premier rock-climbing destinations. The park offers some 4,000 climbing routes, ranging from the easiest of bouldering to some of the sport's most difficult technical climbs. November through May is the prime season to watch lizard-like humans scale sheer rock faces with impossible grace. Even beginners can get into the act: At **First Ascent** (☎ 800/325-5462), certified guides start the day with detailed instruction, then stay with you, providing guidance as you learn the ropes. All equipment is provided, and prices start at $75.

MOUNTAIN BIKING   Much of the park is designated wilderness, meaning that bicycles are limited to roads (they'll damage the fragile ecosystem if you venture off the beaten track). None of the paved roads have bike lanes, but rugged mountain bikes are a great tool to explore the park via unpaved roads, where distraction from autos is light.

Try the 18-mile **Geology Tour Road,** which begins west of Jumbo Rocks; dry lake beds contrast with towering boulders along this sandy downhill road, and you'll also encounter abandoned mines.

A shorter but still rewarding ride begins at the **Covington Flats** picnic area; a steep 4-mile road climbs through Joshua trees, junipers, and pinion pines to Eureka Peak, where you'll be rewarded by a panoramic view.

For other bike-friendly unpaved and four-wheel-drive roads, consult the official park map.

ACCOMMODATIONS & CAMPING

If you're staying in the Palm Springs area, it's entirely possible to make a day-trip to the national park. But if you'd like to stay close by and spend more time here, Twentynine Palms, just outside the north boundary of the national park on Calif. 62, offers budget to moderate lodging.

Near the visitor center in the Oasis of Mara is the rustic **29 Palms Inn** (☎ 760/367-3505; fax 760/367-4425), a cluster of adobe cottages and old cabins dating from the 1920s; its garden-fresh restaurant is the best in town. There's also the 100-room Best **Western Gardens Motel** (☎ 760/367-9141; fax 760/367-2584), a comfortable base from which to maximize your outdoor time.

For a complete listing of Twentynine Palms lodging, contact the **29 Palms Chamber of Commerce,** 5672 Historic Plaza, Twentynine Palms, CA 92277 (☎ 760/367-3445; fax 760/367-3366; www.cci-29palms.com).

Nine **campgrounds** scattered throughout the park offer pleasant though often spartan accommodations, with just picnic tables and pit toilets for the most part. Only two—**Black Rock Canyon** and **Cottonwood Springs**—have potable water and flush toilets, plus a $10 overnight fee. You can make campground reservations online at **http://reservations.nps.gov** or by calling ☎ 800/365-2267.

5 Mojave National Preserve

180 miles E of Los Angeles, 75 miles SW of Las Vegas

Two decades of park politicking finally ended in 1994 when President Clinton signed into law the California Desert Protection Act, which created the new Mojave National Preserve. Thus far, the Mojave's elevated status has not attracted hordes of sightseers, and devoted visitors are happy to keep it that way. Unlike a fully protected national park, the "national preserve" designation allows certain commercial land uses, and the continued grazing and mining within the preserve's boundaries are a sore spot for ardent environmentalists.

To most Americans, the East Mojave is that vast, bleak, interminable stretch of desert to be crossed as quickly as possible while leaving California via I-15 or I-40. Few realize that these highways are the boundaries of what desert rats have long considered the crown jewel of the California desert.

This land is a hard one to get to know—unlike more developed desert parks, it has no lodgings or concessions, few campgrounds, and only a handful of roads suitable for the average passenger vehicle. But hidden within this natural fortress are some true gems—the preserve's 1.4 million acres include the world's largest Joshua-tree forest;

abundant wildlife; spectacular canyons, caverns, and volcanic formations; nationally honored scenic back roads and footpaths to historic mining sites; tabletop mesas; and a dozen mountain ranges.

JUST THE FACTS

GETTING THERE   I-15, the major route taken between the southern California metropolis and the state line by Las Vegas–bound travelers, extends along the northern boundary of Mojave National Preserve. I-40 is the southern access route to the East Mojave.

WHEN TO GO   Spring is a splendid time to visit this desert (autumn is another). From March to May, the temperatures are mild, the Joshua trees are in bloom, and the lower Kelso Dunes are bedecked with yellow and white desert primrose and pink-sand verbena.

VISITOR CENTERS & INFORMATION   The best source for up-to-date weather conditions and a free topographical map is the **Mojave Desert Information Center,** 72157 Baker Blvd. (under the "World's Tallest Thermometer"), Baker, CA 92309 (☎ **760/733-4040**), which is open daily and also has a superior selection of books for sale.

Those coming in on I-40 should stop in **Needles,** at the brand-new **Information Center,** 707 W. Broadway, Needles, CA 92363 (☎ **760/326-6322**). It's open daily; call to verify hours.

Additional information and maps are available inside the preserve at the **Hole-in-the-Wall Campground's Visitor Center,** which is open seasonally (as staffing allows).

There's also the **California Desert Information Center,** 831 Barstow Rd., Barstow, CA 92311 (☎ **760/255-8760**), which has a mini-museum and educational displays on the history and characteristics of the desert. It's open daily from 9am to 5pm. You can visit the preserve online at **www.nps.gov/moja.**

SEEING THE HIGHLIGHTS

One of the preserve's spectacular sights is the **Kelso Dunes,** the most extensive dune field in the West. The 45-square-mile formation of magnificently sculpted sand is famous for its "booming": Visitors' footsteps cause mini-avalanches and make the dunes go "sha-boom-sha-boom-sha-boom." Geologists speculate that the extreme dryness of the East Mojave Desert, combined with the wind-polished, rounded nature of the individual sand grains, has something to do with their musicality. Sometimes the low rumbling sound resembles a Tibetan gong; other times, it sounds like a 1950s doo-wop musical group.

A 10-mile drive from the Kelso Dunes is **Kelso Depot,** built by the Union Pacific in 1924. The Spanish revival–style structure was designed with a red-tile roof, graceful arches, and a brick platform. The depot continued to be open for freight-train crew use through the mid–1980s, although it ceased to be a railroad stop for passengers after World War II. The National Park Service is considering refurbishing the building for use as the preserve's visitor center.

On and around **Cima Dome,** a rare geological anomaly, grows the world's largest and densest Joshua-tree forest. Botanists say Cima's Joshuas are more symmetrical than their cousins elsewhere in the Mojave. The dramatic colors of the sky at sunset provide a breathtaking backdrop for Cima's Joshua trees, some more than 25 feet tall and several hundred years old.

Tucked into the Providence Mountains, in the southern portion of the preserve, is a treat everyone should try to see. The **Mitchell Caverns,** contained in a State Recreation Area within the National Preserve, are a geological oddity exploited for tourism but still quite fascinating. Regular tours are conducted of these cool rock "rooms"; in addition to showcasing marvelous stalactites, stalagmites, and other limestone formations, the caves have proven to be rich in Native American archaeological finds.

Hole-in-the-Wall and Mid Hills are the centerpieces of Mojave National Preserve. Both locales offer diverse desert scenery, fine campgrounds, and the feeling of being in the middle of nowhere, though in fact they're located right in the middle of the preserve.

Linking the two sites is the preserve's best drive. In 1989, **Wildhorse Canyon Road,** which loops from Mid Hills Campground to Hole-in-the-Wall Campground, was declared the nation's first official "Back Country Byway," an honor federal agencies bestow upon America's most scenic back roads. The 11-mile, horseshoe-shaped road crosses wide-open country dotted with cholla and, in season, delicate purple, yellow, and red wildflowers. Dramatic volcanic slopes and flattop mesas tower over the low desert.

Mile-high **Mid Hills,** so named because of its location halfway between the Providence and New York mountains, recalls the Great Basin Desert topography of Nevada and Utah. Mid Hills Campground offers a grand observation point from which to gaze out at the creamy-coffee-colored Pinto Mountains to the north and the rolling Kelso Dunes shining on the western horizon.

Hole-in-the-Wall is the kind of place Butch Cassidy and the Sundance Kid would have chosen as a hideout. This twisted maze of rhyolite rocks is a form of crystallized red-lava rock. A series of iron rings aids descent into Hole-in-the-Wall; they're not particularly difficult for those who are reasonably agile and take their time.

Kelso Dunes, Mitchell Caverns, Cima Dome, Hole-in-the-Wall—these highlights of the preserve can be viewed in a weekend. But you'll need a week just to see all the major sights, and maybe a lifetime to really get to know the East Mojave. And right now, without much in the way of services, the traveler to this desert must be well prepared and self-reliant. For many, this is what makes a trip to the East Mojave an adventure.

If Mojave National Preserve attracts you, you'll want to return again and again to see the wonders of this desert, including **Caruthers Canyon,** a "botanical island" of pinion pine and juniper woodland, and **Ivanpah Valley,** which supports the largest desert tortoise population in the California desert.

HIKING & MOUNTAIN BIKING

HIKING The free-form ambling climb to the top of the **Kelso Dunes** is 3 miles round-trip. A cool, inviting pinion pine/juniper woodland is explored by the **Caruthers Canyon Trail** (3 miles round-trip). The longest pathway is the 8-mile (one-way) **Mid Hills to Hole-in-the-Wall Trail,** a grand tour of basin and range tabletop mesas, large pinion trees, and colorful cacti. If you're not up for a long day hike, the 1-mile trip from **Hole-in-the-Wall Campground** to **Banshee Canyon** and the 5-mile jaunt to **Wildhorse Canyon** offer some easier alternatives. Be sure to pick up trail maps at one of the visitor centers.

MOUNTAIN BIKING Opportunities are as extensive as the preserve's hundreds of miles of lonesome dirt roads. The 140-mile-long historic **Mojave Road,** a rough four-wheel-drive route, visits many of the most scenic areas in the East Mojave; sections of this road make excellent bike tours. Prepare well—the Mojave Road and other dirt roads are rugged routes through desert wilderness.

CAMPING

The **Mid Hills Campground** is located in a pinion pine/juniper woodland and offers outstanding views. This mile-high camp is the coolest in the East Mojave. Nearby

This Is Our Life:
The Roy Rogers & Dale Evans Museum

Passing through Victorville, it's tough to miss the log fort, visible from I-15, with the words ROY ROGERS AND DALE EVANS MUSEUM emblazoned on the side, Las Vegas style—larger than life, brightly lit, and embellished with stars. The museum is open daily from 9am to 5pm except Thanksgiving and Christmas. For information, call ☎ **760/243-4547.**

Fans of cowboy lore, western movies, or country music can all tell you the museum is legendary for being the final resting place of Roy's faithful horse Trigger, which he had stuffed and mounted. For company, Trigger has Buttermilk (Dale's golden horse), Bullet (their canine companion), and a veritable Noah's Ark of taxidermy—Roy's trophies from safaris in every corner of the globe.

These are among the many surprises awaiting visitors to the museum, a glorified attic containing the relics and souvenirs of two lifetimes. The displays are folksy, accented by tags saying "my first cowboy boots" (bronzed, of course), "the 1923 Dodge I came to California in, in 1930," and other personal remarks. But because of Roy and Dale's wealth, years of travel, varied interests, and an apparent inability to throw anything away, this museum truly has something for everyone. Some of the highlights are:

- **Beautifully arranged cases commemorating each of Roy and Dale's three children who died in childhood.** On display are photos, toys, letters, and report cards, as well as the inspirational books written in tribute by Dale Evans Rogers after each of their deaths. Their many living children and grandchildren are also well represented; in fact, by the end of your visit you might feel as if you know the whole family personally!

- **Gifts from the couple's fans all over the world,** including a pair of stitched samplers framed near the entrance, containing poetic tributes both epic and homespun.

- **Every piece of Roy Rogers and/or Dale Evans merchandise from over the years:** comic books, breakfast-cereal boxes, fan-club items, war-effort promotions, and more. See the 1950s–era "den/playroom" filled with vintage furniture and littered with dozens of Roy and Dale toys, storybooks, dolls, model horses, and board games.

- **Roy's personal collection of western memorabilia** from his role models—real-life and movie cowboys—includes Tom Mix's director's chair, Buck Jones's saddle, Hoot Gibson's piano, and, last but not least, an autographed picture of Lee Majors (remember him in *The Big Valley?*).

Hole-in-the-Wall Campground is perched above two dramatic canyons. *Warning:* The washboard dirt road between the two might be too jarring for many two-wheel-drive passenger cars.

There are also some sites at **Providence Mountain State Recreation Area** (Mitchell Caverns, see "Seeing the Highlights," above).

One of the highlights of the East Mojave Desert is camping in the open desert all by your lonesome, but certain rules apply. Call the Mojave Desert Information Center for suggestions.

NEARBY TOWNS WITH TOURIST SERVICES

BARSTOW This sizable town has a great many restaurants and motels, and is roughly a 1-hour drive from the center of the preserve. Of the dozen motels in town, the most reliable are the **Best Western Desert Villa,** 1984 E. Main St., Barstow, CA 92311 (☎ **760/256-1781**), and the **Holiday Inn,** 1511 E. Main St., Barstow, CA 92311 (☎ **760/256-5673**).

BAKER Accommodations and food are available in this small desert town, which is a good place to fill up your gas tank and purchase supplies before entering Mojave National Preserve. Inexpensive lodging can be secured at the **Bun Boy Motel,** P.O. Box 130, Baker, CA 92309 (☎ **760/733-4363**). The Bun Boy Coffee Shop is open 24 hours. For a tasty surprise, stop at the **Mad Greek** (☎ **760/733-4354**). Order a Greek salad, a souvlaki, or baklava, and marvel at your good fortune—imagine finding such tasty food and pleasant surroundings in the middle of nowhere.

NIPTON This tiny, charming town boasts a "trading post" that stocks snacks, maps, ice, and native jewelry; and the **Hotel Nipton** (☎ **760/856-2335**), a B&B with a sitting room, two bathrooms down the hall, and four guest rooms, each going for $50 a night. Jerry Freeman, a former hard-rock miner who purchased the entire town in 1984, says hotel occupancy is up 80% since the East Mojave became a national preserve. He and his wife, Roxanne, moved from the famous sands of Malibu to the abandoned ghost town and have gradually brought it back to life. Nipton is located on Nipton Road, a few miles from I-15 near the Nevada state line.

PRIMM (formerly STATELINE) This privately owned town on the California–Nevada border features three hotel/casinos—Whiskey Pete's, Buffalo Bill's, and Primadonna—each as large and garish as an amusement park and all managed by the same company. Rooms here are pretty nice, really cheap, and (if you have a twisted sense of humor) an ironic counterpoint to the wilderness you came for. With a dozen restaurants, including those low-cost Vegas-style buffets, Primm might also be your best dining bet. For reservations, call ☎ **800/FUN-STOP.**

6 Death Valley National Park

115 miles N of Baker, 290 miles NE of Los Angeles

Park? Death Valley National Park? The forty-niners, whose suffering gave the valley its name, would have howled at the notion. "Death Valley National Park" seems a contradiction in terms, an oxymoron of the great outdoors. To them, other four-letter words would have been more appropriate: gold, mine, heat, lost, dead. And the four-letter words shouted by teamsters who drove the 20-mule-team borax wagons need not be repeated.

Americans looking for gold in California's mountains in 1849 were forced to cross the burning sands to avoid severe snowstorms in the nearby Sierra Nevada. Some perished along the way, and the land became known as Death Valley.

Mountains stand naked, unadorned. The bitter waters of saline lakes evaporate into bizarre, razor-sharp crystal formations. Jagged canyons jab deep into the earth. Oven-like heat, frigid cold, and the driest air imaginable combine to make this one of the most inhospitable locations in the world.

But, human nature being what it is, it's not surprising that people have long been drawn to challenge the power of Mother Nature, even in this, her home court. Man's first foray into tourism began in 1925, a scant 76 years after the forty-niners' harrowing experiences (which would discourage most sane folks from ever returning!). It probably would have begun sooner, but the valley had been consumed with lucrative borax mining since the late 1880s.

Death Valley is raw, bare earth, the way it must have looked before life began. Here, forces of the earth are exposed to view with dramatic clarity; just looking out on the landscape, it's impossible to know what year—or what century—it is. It's no coincidence that many of Death Valley's topographical features are associated with hellish images—the Funeral Mountains, Furnace Creek, Dante's View, Coffin Peak, and the Devil's Golf Course. But it can be a place of serenity.

In one of his last official acts, President Herbert Hoover signed a proclamation designating Death Valley a national monument on February 11, 1933. With the stroke of a pen, he not only authorized the protection of a vast and wondrous land, but also helped to transform one of the earth's least hospitable spots into a popular tourist destination.

The naming of Death Valley National Monument came at a time when Americans began to discover the romance of the desert. Land that had previously been considered hideously devoid of life was now celebrated for its spare beauty; places that had once been feared for their harshness were now admired for their uniqueness.

In 1994, when President Clinton signed the California Desert Protection Act, Death Valley National Park became the largest national park outside Alaska, with over 3.3 million acres. Though remote, it's one of the most heavily visited, and you're likely to hear less English spoken than German, French, and Japanese.

Today's visitor to Death Valley drives in air-conditioned comfort, stays in comfortable hotel rooms or at well-maintained campgrounds, orders meals and provisions at park concessions, even quaffs a cold beer at the local saloon. You can take a swim in the Olympic-size pool, tour a Moorish castle, shop for souvenirs, and enjoy the desert landscape while hiking along a nature trail with a park ranger.

JUST THE FACTS

ACCESS POINTS   There are several routes into the park, all of which involve crossing one of the steep mountain ranges that isolate Death Valley from, well, everything. Perhaps the most scenic entry to the park is via Calif. 190, east of Calif. 178 from Ridgecrest. Another scenic drive to the park is by way of Calif. 127 and Calif. 190 from Baker. You'll be required to pay a $10-per-car entrance fee, valid for 7 days.

VISITOR CENTER & INFORMATION   The **Death Valley Visitor Center** at Furnace Creek, 15 miles inside the eastern park boundary on Calif. 190 (☎ **760/ 786-2331**), offers well-done interpretive exhibits and an hourly slide program. Ask at the information desk for ranger-led nature walks and evening naturalist programs. Hours are daily from 8am to 7pm in winter, daily from 8am to 5pm in summer. For information before you go, contact the Superintendent, Death Valley National Park, Death Valley, CA 92328 (☎ **760/786-2331;** www.nps.gov/deva).

SEEING THE HIGHLIGHTS

A good first stop after checking in at the main park visitor center in Furnace Creek is the **Harmony Borax Works**—a rock-salt landscape as tortured as you'll ever find. Death Valley prospectors called borax "white gold," and though it wasn't exactly a glamorous substance, it was a profitable one. From 1883 to 1888, more than 20 million pounds of borax were transported from the Harmony Borax Works, and borax mining continued in Death Valley until 1928. A short trail with interpretive signs leads past the ruins of the old borax refinery and some outlying buildings.

Transport of the borax was the stuff of legends, too. The famous 20-mule teams hauled the huge loaded wagons 165 miles to the rail station at Mojave. (To learn more about this colorful era, visit the Borax Museum at Furnace Creek Ranch and the park visitor center, also located in Furnace Creek.)

Badwater—at 282 feet below sea level, the lowest point in the Western Hemisphere—is also one of the hottest places in the world, with regularly recorded summer temperatures of 120°F.

Salt Creek is the home of the **Salt Creek pupfish,** found nowhere else on earth. This little fish, which has made some amazing adaptations to survive in this arid land, can be glimpsed from a wooden-boardwalk nature trail. In spring, a million pupfish might be wriggling in the creek, but by summer's end only a few thousand remain.

Before sunrise, photographers set up their tripods at **Zabriskie Point** and aim their cameras down at the magnificent panoramic view of Golden Canyon's pale mudstone hills and the great valley beyond. For another grand park vista, check out **Dante's View,** a 5,475-foot viewpoint looking out over the shimmering Death Valley floor, backed by the high Panamint Mountains.

Just south of Furnace Creek is the 9-mile loop of **Artists Drive,** an easy must-see for visitors (except those in RVs, which can't negotiate the sharp, rock-bordered curves in the road). From the highway, you can't see the splendid palette of colors splashed on the rocks behind the foothills; once inside, though, stop and climb a low hill that offers an overhead view, then continue through to aptly named **Artists Palette,** where an interpretive sign explains the source of nature's rainbow.

Scotty's Castle, the Mediterranean hacienda in the northern part of the park, is unabashedly Death Valley's premier tourist attraction. Visitors are wowed by the elaborate Spanish tiles, well-crafted furnishings, and innovative construction that included solar water heating. Even more compelling is the colorful history of this villa in remote Grapevine Canyon, brought to life by park rangers dressed in 1930s period clothing. Don't be surprised if the castle cook or a friend of Scotty's gives you a special insight into castle life.

Construction of the "castle"—more officially, Death Valley Ranch—began in 1924. It was to be a winter retreat for eccentric Chicago millionaire Albert Johnson. The insurance tycoon's unlikely friendship with prospector/cowboy/spinner-of-tall-tales Walter Scott put the $2.3-million structure on the map and captured the public's imagination. Scotty greeted visitors and told them fanciful stories from the early hardrock mining days of Death Valley.

The 1-hour walking tour of Scotty's Castle is excellent, both for its inside look at the mansion and for what it reveals about the eccentricities of Johnson and Scotty. Tours fill up quickly; arrive early for the first available spots (there's an $8 fee). A snack bar and gift shop make the wait more comfortable. To learn more about the castle grounds, pick up the pamphlet *A Walking Tour of Scotty's Castle,* which leads you on an exploration from stable to swimming pool, from bunkhouse to powerhouse.

Near Scotty's Castle is **Ubehebe Crater.** It's known as an explosion crater—one look and you'll know why. When hot magma rose from the depths of the earth to meet the groundwater, the resultant steam blasted out a crater and scattered cinders.

HIKING & MOUNTAIN BIKING

HIKING   The trails in Death Valley range from the half-mile **Salt Creek Nature Trail,** an easy boardwalk path suitable for everyone in the family, to the grueling **Telescope Peak Trail** (14 miles round-trip), an all-day challenge. Telescope Peak is a strenuous, 3,000-foot climb to the 11,049-foot summit, where you'll be rewarded by the view described by one pioneer: "You can see so far, it's just like looking through a telescope." Snow-covered during the winter, the peak is best climbed between May and November.

But there are lots of levels in between. We like the trail into **Mosaic Canyon,** near Stovepipe Wells, where water has polished the marble rock into white, gray, and black mosaics. It's a relatively easy 2½-mile scramble through long, narrow walls that seem quite "gallery"-like—and provide welcome shade at every turn.

Romping among the **Sand Dunes** on the way to Stovepipe Wells is also fun, particularly for kids. It's a free-form adventure, and the dunes aren't particularly high—but the sun can be merciless. The sand in the dunes is actually tiny pieces of rock, most of them quartz fragments. As with all desert activities, your water supply is crucial.

Near the park's eastern border, two trails lead from the **Keane Wonder Mill,** site of a successful gold mine. The first is a steep and strenuous 2-mile challenge leading to the mine itself, passing along the way the solid, efficient wooden tramway that carried ore out of the mountain.

If that's beyond your fitness level, try the **Keane Wonder Spring Trail,** leading in another direction. This 2-mile walk is much easier, and the spring that supplied water for the Keane Wonder operation will announce itself with a sulfur smell and piping birdcalls.

If you're visiting **Ubehebe Crater,** there's a steep but plain trail leading from the parking area up to the crater's lip and around some of the contours. Fierce winds can hamper your progress, but you'll get the exhilarating feeling that you're truly on another planet.

Park rangers can provide topographical maps and detailed directions to these and a dozen other hiking trails within the national park.

MOUNTAIN BIKING   Because most (94%) of the park is federally designated wilderness, cycling is allowed only on roads used by cars. Cycling is not allowed on hiking trails.

Good routes for bikers include Racetrack (28 miles, mainly level), Greenwater Valley (30 miles, mostly level), Cottonwood Canyon (20 miles), and West Side Road (40 miles, fairly level with some washboard sections). Artists Drive is 8 miles long and paved, with some steep uphills. A favorite is Titus Canyon (28 miles on a hilly road—it's highly recommended that you make this a one-way descent).

CAMPING & ACCOMMODATIONS

The park's nine campgrounds are located at elevations ranging from below sea level to 8,000 feet. In Furnace Creek, **Sunset** offers 1,000 spaces with water and flush toilets. **Furnace Creek Campground** has 200 similarly appointed spaces. **Stovepipe Wells** has 200 spaces with water and flush toilets. Camping reservations may be made online at **http://reservations.nps.gov** or by calling ☎ **800/365-2267.**

The **Furnace Creek Ranch** (☎ **760/786-2345**) has 224 no-frills cottage units with air-conditioning and showers. The swimming pool is a popular hangout for tired lodgers. Nearby are a coffee shop, saloon, steak house, and general store.

Stove Pipe Wells Village (☎ **760/786-2387**) has 74 modest rooms with air-conditioning and showers, plus a casual dining room which closes between meals.

The only lodging within the park not operated by the official concessionaire is the **Panamint Springs Resort** (☎ **702/482-7680**), a truly charming rustic motel, cafe, and snack shop about an hour east of Furnace Creek.

Because accommodations in Death Valley are both limited and expensive, you might consider the money-saving (but inconvenient) option of spending a night at one of the two gateway towns: **Lone Pine,** on the west side of the park, or **Baker,** on the south. **Beatty, Nevada,** which has inexpensive lodging, is an hour's drive from the park's center. The restored **Amargosa Hotel** (☎ **760/852-4441**) in Death Valley Junction offers 14 rooms in a historic, out-of-the-way place, 40 minutes from Furnace Creek.

Helpful hint: Meals and groceries are exceptionally costly due to the remoteness of the location. If possible, consider bringing a cooler with some snacks, sandwiches, and beverages to last the duration of your visit. Ice is easily obtainable, and you'll also be able to keep water chilled.

✪ **Furnace Creek Inn.** Hwy. 190 (P.O. Box 1), Death Valley, CA 92328. ☎ **800/236-7916** or 760/786-2345. Fax 760/786-2307. www.furnacecreekresort.com. 66 units. A/C TEL TV. Oct–Apr $230–$370 double, $325 suite; off-season $150–$195 double, $205 suite. Extra person $15. AE, DC, DISC, MC, V.

Like an oasis in the middle of stark Death Valley, the Inn's red-tiled roofs and sparkling blue spring-fed swimming pool hint at the elegance within. The hotel has equipped its 66 deluxe rooms and suites with every modern amenity while successfully preserving the charm of this 1930s resort. Stroll the lush, palm-shaded gardens before sitting down to a meal in the elegant Dining Room, where the food is excellent but the formality a bit out of place. Tennis on lighted courts, nearby golf, and horseback riding are available—there's even a shuttle from the Furnace Creek private airstrip for well-heeled clientele. Reserve early: The Inn is booked solid year-round with American and European guests who appreciate a little pampering after a day spent in the park.

16 San Diego & Environs

by Stephanie Avnet Yates

San Diego is best known for its benign climate and fabulous beaches, attributes that make the city one big outdoor playground on sunny days. With 70 miles of sandy coastline—plus pretty, sheltered Mission Bay—you can choose from swimming, snorkeling, windsurfing, kayaking, bicycling, skating, and tons of other fun in or near the water. The city is also home to top-notch attractions, including three world-famous animal parks and splendid Balboa Park, a cultural and recreational jewel that's one of the finest urban parks in the country. Once dismissed as a slow-growth, conservative Navy town, San Diego has been expanding steadily over the past decade or two, and now boasts an almost Los Angeles–like diversity of neighborhoods and residents. A heightened sensitivity to historical preservation means formerly seedy downtown neighborhoods and architecturally rich suburbs are being carefully restored; they draw a stylish young crowd that's updating the face of San Diego dining, shopping, and entertainment. California's first city, San Diego reflects its Spanish/Mexican heritage in every corner—in fact, bustling Tijuana is just across the border, less than 30 minutes away. So pack a laid-back attitude along with your sandals and swimsuit, and welcome to California's grown-up beach town.

1 Orientation

ARRIVING

BY PLANE

San Diego International Airport, 3707 N. Harbor Dr. (☎ **619/ 231-7361**), locally known as Lindbergh Field, is just 3 miles from downtown. Most of the major domestic carriers fly here. Lindbergh Field consists of three adjacent passenger buildings: Terminal One, Terminal Two, and the Terminal Two Expansion. Short local flights use the Commuter Terminal, which is a half mile away and can be reached from the main airport by the free "red bus" shuttle. For a list of airlines, including toll-free phone numbers and Web sites, see Appendix B at the back of this book.

TRANSPORTATION FROM THE AIRPORT   All the major car-rental agencies have offices at the airport, including **Avis** (☎ 800/ 331-1212), **Budget** (☎ 800/527-0700), **Dollar** (☎ 800/800-4000), and **Hertz** (☎ 800/654-3131). **Kemwel Holiday Auto (KHA)**

(☎ 800/678-0678) is a wholesaler that will search for the lowest price offered among the major agencies. (See Appendix B for a complete list of car-rental companies, including toll-free phone numbers and Web sites.) If you're driving into the city from the airport, take Harbor Drive south to Broadway, the main east–west thoroughfare, and turn left.

Metropolitan Transit System (MTS) bus route no. 992 provides service between the airport and downtown San Diego. Route no. 992 bus stops are located at each of the three terminals. The one-way fare is $2. Request a transfer if you're connecting to another bus or the San Diego Trolley route downtown. Downtown, route no. 992 stops on Broadway. The ride takes about 15 minutes; buses come at 10- to 15-minute intervals. At Broadway and First Avenue is the **Transit Store** (☎ 619/234-3004), where the staff can answer your transit questions and provide free route maps to help you get where you're going.

Several **shuttles** run regularly from the airport to downtown hotels. They charge around $5 to $9 per person, and you'll see designated areas outside each terminal. The shuttles are a good deal for single travelers; two or more people traveling together might as well take a taxi.

Taxis line up outside both terminals and charge around $10 to take you to a downtown location.

BY CAR

From Los Angeles, you'll enter San Diego via coastal route I-5. From points northeast of the city, you'll come down on I-15 (link up with I-8 W. and Calif. 163 S. to drive into downtown). From the east, you'll come in on I-8, connecting with Calif. 163 south (Calif. 163 turns into 10th Ave.). From the south, take I-5. The freeways are well marked, pointing the way to downtown streets.

BY TRAIN

Amtrak (☎ 800/USA-RAIL; www.amtrak.com) trains connect San Diego to Los Angeles and the rest of the country. Trains pull into San Diego's pretty mission-style **Santa Fe Station,** 1850 Kettner Blvd. (at Broadway), within walking distance of many downtown hotels and 1½ blocks from the Embarcadero. Expect to pay about $20 one-way from Los Angeles.

BY BUS

Greyhound (☎ 800/231-2222; www.greyhound.com) serves San Diego; the bus terminal is downtown, on Broadway between Front Street and First Avenue.

VISITOR INFORMATION

The official **International Visitor Information Center** (☎ 619/236-1212; www.sandiego.org) is on First Avenue at F Street, street level at Horton Plaza. The multilingual staff offers brochures in six languages. They can provide you with the slick, glossy *San Diego Visitors Planning Guide,* as well as a money-saving coupon book. The center is open Monday through Saturday from 8:30am to 5pm year-round and Sunday from 11am to 5pm June through August; it's closed Thanksgiving, Christmas, and New Year's Day.

Traveler's Aid (☎ 619/231-7361) has booths at both airport terminals and the train station. Volunteers answer questions and provide helpful brochures and maps.

Specialized visitor information outlets include the **Balboa Park Visitors Center,** located at 1549 El Prado (☎ 619/239-0512); **Coronado Visitors Bureau,** 1047 B Ave., Coronado (☎ 800/622-8300 or 619/437-8788; www.coronado.ca.us); and the

La Jolla Town Council, 7734 Herschel Ave., La Jolla, CA 92038 (☎ 858/454-1444). The **Mission Bay Visitors Information Center,** 2688 E. Mission Bay Dr., San Diego (☎ 858/276-8200), is conveniently located on Mission Bay next to I-5 (exit Clairemont Drive/Mission Bay Dr. and head toward the water). The **San Diego North County Convention & Visitors Bureau,** 720 N. Broadway, Escondido (☎ 800/848-3336 or 760/745-4741), can provide information on excursion areas in San Diego County, including Del Mar, Carlsbad, Escondido, Julian, and Anza-Borrego Desert State Park.

To find out what's on at the theater and who's playing in the clubs during your visit, pick up a copy of the *Reader,* a free weekly newspaper available all over the city. There's also a Thursday entertainment supplement called **"Night & Day"** in the *San Diego Union-Tribune.*

INFORMATION ON THE WEB

Cyber-travelers interested in a virtual visit to San Diego should check out the following sites:

- **gocalif.ca.gov/guidebook/SD** has helpful information on San Diego County, including maps that can be downloaded.
- **www.sandiego.org** is maintained by the San Diego Convention & Visitors Bureau.
- **www.infosandiego.com** is the Web site for the San Diego Visitor Center.
- **www.sannet.gov** is San Diego's home page, maintained by the city.
- **www.sandiego-online.com** is the Web site for *San Diego* magazine, and features abbreviated stories from the current month's issue, plus listings for local dining and events.
- **www.sdreader.com** is maintained by the free weekly *Reader,* and is a great source for club and show listings, as well as for edgy topical journalism.

CITY LAYOUT

San Diego has a clearly defined downtown, which is surrounded by a dozen or more separate neighborhoods—each with its own personality, but all legally part of the city. The street system is straightforward, so getting around is fairly easy.

MAIN ARTERIES & STREETS   I-5 runs south to the U.S.–Mexico border and north to Old Town, Mission Bay, La Jolla, and beyond. It's the most important thoroughfare in San Diego, connecting the city's divergent parts with one another and the entire region with the rest of the state. Access to the Coronado Bay Bridge is via I-5. Balboa Park is most easily accessible via 12th Avenue, which becomes Park Boulevard. Fifth Avenue leads to the Hillcrest/Uptown area.

Downtown, Broadway is the main street; in the heart of the central business district it's intersected by Fourth and Fifth avenues (running south and north, respectively). Harbor Drive, hugging the waterfront (Embarcadero), connects downtown with the airport to the northwest and the Convention Center to the south.

Neighborhoods in Brief

Downtown   The business, shopping, dining, and entertainment heart of the city, it includes Horton Plaza, the Gaslamp Quarter, the Embarcadero (waterfront), and the distinctive Convention Center. Visitors with business to conduct in the city center

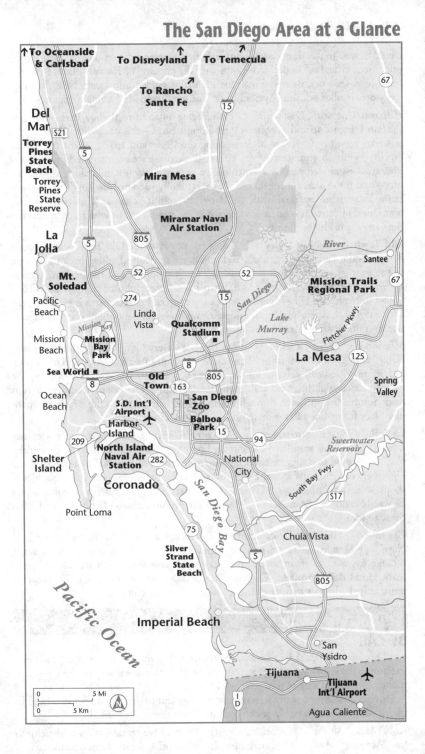

The San Diego Area at a Glance

↑ To Oceanside & Carlsbad
↑ To Disneyland
↗ To Temecula
↗ To Rancho Santa Fe

67

15

Del Mar
S21
5

Torrey Pines State Beach
Torrey Pines State Reserve

Mira Mesa

Miramar Naval Air Station

River

La Jolla
5
805

Santee

Mt. Soledad

52
52
San Diego

Mission Trails Regional Park
67

Pacific Beach

274
15
Lake Murray
Fletcher Pkwy.
125

Mission Bay

Linda Vista

Qualcomm Stadium

La Mesa

Mission Beach

Mission Bay Park

Sea World

8
8
805

Spring Valley

Old Town
163

Ocean Beach

S.D. Int'l Airport

San Diego Zoo

Harbor Island

Balboa Park
15
94

Shelter Island
209

North Island Naval Air Station
282

National City

Sweetwater Reservoir

Coronado

Point Loma

San Diego Bay

South Bay Fwy.
S17

75
Chula Vista
5

Silver Strand State Beach

805

Pacific Ocean

Imperial Beach

San Ysidro

Tijuana
Tijuana Int'l Airport

I D

Agua Caliente

0   5 Mi
0   5 Km
N

would be wise to stay downtown. The **Gaslamp Quarter** is the center of a massive redevelopment kicked off in the mid–1980s with the opening of **Horton Plaza,** a colorful multi-level six-block shopping mall that's a major attraction in itself. Now the once-seedy area is filled with trendy boutiques, chic restaurants, and swingin' nightspots.

Hillcrest/Uptown Despite the cachet of being adjacent to **Balboa Park**—home to the **San Diego Zoo** and numerous splendid museums—this once-elite suburban area north of downtown fell into neglect during the 1960s and 1970s. As the turn of the century looms once more, however, Hillcrest's charms have been restored by legions of preservation-minded residents—including a very active and fashionable gay community—and is the local equivalent of L.A.'s West Hollywood or New York's SoHo. Centrally located and packed with the latest in stylish restaurants and avant-garde boutiques, Hillcrest also offers less expensive and more personalized accommodations than anywhere else in the city.

Old Town & Mission Valley This area encompasses the Old Town State Historic Park, Presidio Park, Heritage Park, and numerous museums harking back to the turn of the century and the city's beginnings. There's shopping and dining here, too, all aimed at tourists. Not far from Old Town lies the vast suburban sprawl of Mission Valley, home to San Diego's gigantic shopping centers. Between them is **Hotel Circle,** adjacent to I-8, where a string of midprice and budget hotel options offer an alternative to more desirable neighborhoods.

Mission Bay & the Beaches Mission Bay is a watery playground perfect for water-skiing, sailing, and windsurfing. The adjacent communities of Ocean Beach, Mission Beach, and Pacific Beach are known for their wide stretches of sand fronting the Pacific, active nightlife, and California-casual dining. The **boardwalk,** which runs from South Mission Beach through North Mission Beach to Pacific Beach, is a popular place for in-line skating, bike riding, and watching sunsets.

La Jolla With an atmosphere that's a cross between Rodeo Drive and a Mediterranean village, this seaside community is home to an inordinate number of wealthy folks who could live anywhere, but choose to live here surrounded by the beach, the University of California at San Diego, outstanding restaurants, pricey and traditional shops, and some of the world's best medical facilities. The name is a compromise between Spanish and American Indian, as is the pronunciation—la *hoy*-ya—and it has come to mean "the jewel."

Coronado The "island" of Coronado is actually a peninsula, home to the U.S. Naval Air Station and a town filled with charming cottages, quaint shops along Orange Avenue (the main street), and ritzy hotels and resorts that include the landmark **Hotel del Coronado.** Coronado has a lovely duned beach; it's also home to more retired admirals than any other community in the country.

2 Getting Around

BY CAR

San Diego has its fair share of traffic, concentrated in the downtown area, and heaviest during the morning and evening commuting hours. Aside from that, it's a very car-friendly town, and easy to navigate.

Driving downtown, many streets run one way, and finding a parking space can be tricky—but some reasonably priced parking lots are centrally located.

RENTALS All the large, national car-rental firms have rental outlets at the airport (see "Arriving," above), in the major hotels, and at other locations around the city.

Several car-rental companies, including **Avis** (☎ **800/331-1212** or 619/231-7171) and **Courtesy Auto Rentals** (☎ **800/252-9756** or 619/497-4800), allow you to take their cars into Mexico. The vehicles may be driven as far as Ensenada, 90 minutes south, providing that you stop before crossing the border and buy Mexican auto insurance. You would also be wise to buy insurance if you drive your own car south of the border.

PARKING   Parking meters are plentiful in most San Diego areas: Posted signs indicate operating hours—generally between 8am and 6pm, even on weekends—and most meters accept only quarters. In the popular Gaslamp Quarter, consider parking in Horton Plaza's garage (G St. and Fourth Ave.), which is free to shoppers for the first 3 hours, $1 for every additional hour. It's also free daily after 5pm.

BY PUBLIC TRANSPORTATION

Both city buses and the **San Diego Trolley**—which runs to the Mexican border, Old Town, and East County—are operated by the **San Diego Metropolitan Transit System (MTS)** (☎ **619/685-4900**). The system's **Transit Store,** 102 Broadway, at First Avenue (☎ **619/234-1060**), is a complete public-transportation information center, supplying travelers with passes, tokens, timetables, maps, and brochures. It's open Monday through Friday from 8:30am to 5:30pm, Saturday and Sunday from noon to 4pm. Request a copy of the useful brochure, *Your Open Door to San Diego,* which details the city's most popular tourist attractions and the buses that take you to them. For **bus route information,** you can also call ☎ **619/233-3004** daily between 5:30am and 8:30pm.

The $5 **Day-Tripper pass** allows for 1 day of unlimited rides on the public transit system; you can also get a 4-day pass for $15. Passes are available from the Transit Store.

BY BUS   Bus stops are marked by rectangular blue signs, every other block or so on local routes. More than 20 bus routes traverse downtown. Most fares range from $1.75 to $2.25, depending on the distance and type of service (local or express). Express buses charge fares that range from $1.75 to $3. Exact change is required ($1 bills are accepted). Most buses run every half hour. Transfers should be obtained from the driver when boarding.

The **Coronado Shuttle,** route no. 904, runs between the Coronado Island Marriott and the Old Ferry Landing along Orange Avenue to the Hotel del Coronado, Glorietta Bay, Loews Coronado Bay Resort, and back again. It costs only 50¢ per person. Route no. 901 goes to Coronado from downtown San Diego; the fare is $1.75 for adults, 75¢ for seniors and children. Call ☎ **619/233-3004** for information.

BY TROLLEY   The San Diego Trolley system runs south to the Mexican border (a 40-minute trip), north to Old Town, and east to the city of Santee. Within the city, trolleys stop at many popular locations, and the fare is only $1; the fare to the Mexican border is $2. Children under 5 ride free; seniors and riders with disabilities pay only 75¢. For **recorded trolley information,** call ☎ **619/685-4900.** To talk to a real person, you can call ☎ **619/233-3004** daily from 5:30am to 8:30pm.

Trolleys operate on a self-service fare-collection system; riders purchase tickets from machines in stations before boarding, and fare inspectors board trains at random to check tickets. The bright-red trains run every 15 minutes during the day (every half hour at night) and stop for only 30 seconds at each stop. To board, push the lighted green button beside the doors; to exit the car, push the lighted white button.

Trolleys generally operate daily from 5am to about 12:30am, although the Blue Line, which goes to the border, runs around the clock on Saturday.

BY TRAIN   Within the San Diego area, **Amtrak** (☎ 800/USA-RAIL) stops downtown, in Solana Beach, and in Oceanside. A ticket from downtown San Diego to Solana Beach costs $5 one-way; it's $7.50 to Oceanside. You can also get to Disneyland in Anaheim (see chapter 14, "Side Trips from Los Angeles") via the train; call for details.

San Diego's express rail commuter service, **The Coaster** (☎ 800/COASTER), travels between downtown and Oceanside with stops en route at Old Town, Sorrento Valley, Solana Beach, Encinitas, and Carlsbad.

BY FERRY & WATER TAXI   There's regularly scheduled **ferry service** (☎ 619/234-4111) between San Diego and Coronado. Ferries leave from the Broadway Pier on the hour from 9am to 9pm daily (until 10pm Friday and Saturday), and return from the Old Ferry Landing in Coronado to the Broadway Pier every hour on the 42-minute mark from 9:42am to 9:42pm daily (until 10:42pm Friday and Saturday). Ferries also run from the Fifth Avenue Landing near the Convention Center to the Old Ferry Landing at 1-hour intervals during roughly the same time period. The fare is $2 for each leg of the journey (50¢ extra if you bring your bike). Purchase tickets in advance at the Harbor Excursion kiosk on the Broadway Pier, the Fifth Avenue Landing in San Diego, or at the Old Ferry Landing in Coronado.

Water taxis (☎ 619/235-TAXI) will take you around most of San Diego Bay for $5. If you want to go to the southern part of the bay (to Loews Coronado Bay Resort, for example), you'll be charged a flat fee of $25.

BY TAXI

Cab companies don't have standardized rates, except from the airport into town, which costs about $10 with tip. It's uncommon to find taxis cruising for passengers; phone for a guaranteed pickup. Companies include **Orange Cab** (☎ 619/291-3333), **San Diego Cab** (☎ 619/226-TAXI), and **Yellow Cab** (☎ 619/234-6161). The **Coronado Cab Company** (☎ 619/435-6211) serves Coronado. In La Jolla, call **La Jolla Cab** (☎ 619/453-4222).

BY ORGANIZED TOUR

The **Old Town Trolley** (☎ 619/298-8687) isn't a trolley at all; rather, it's a privately operated open-air tour bus that travels in a continuous loop around the city, stopping at sightseeing highlights. It stops at more than a dozen places around the city, and you can hop on and off as many times as you please during one entire loop (but once you've completed the circuit, you can't go around again). A nonstop tour takes 90 minutes and is accompanied by a fast-moving live commentary on city history and sights. Major stops include Old Town, Presidio Park, Bazaar del Mundo, Balboa Park, the San Diego Zoo, the Embarcadero, Seaport Village, and the Gaslamp Quarter. Tours operate daily from 9am to 5pm; they cost $24 for adults and $12 for children ages 4 to 12; kids 3 and under ride free.

Gray Line San Diego (☎ 800/331-5077 or 619/491-0011; www.graylinesandiego.com) offers a 4-hour escorted bus tour of San Diego that costs $24 for adults (half price for children). **San Diego Mini Tours** (☎ 619/477-8687) also offers excursions throughout the area.

BY BICYCLE

San Diego is great for bikers; it's relatively flat and many roads have designated bike lanes. If you didn't bring your own wheels, you can rent from **Bike Tours San Diego**, 509 Fifth Ave. (☎ 619/238-2444), or **Hamel's Action Sports Center,** 704 Ventura

Place, off Mission Boulevard in Mission Beach (☎ **858/488-8889**). In Coronado, there's **Bikes & Beyond** at the Old Ferry Landing (☎ **619/435-7180**). Bike rentals average about $10 per day.

The **San Diego Region Bike Map** is available at visitor centers; to receive a copy in advance, call ☎ **619/231-BIKE.**

If a bus stop has a bike-route sign attached (not all of them do), you can place your bike on the bus's bike rack for free while you ride. The San Diego Trolley also allows bikes on-board for free. You just need a bike permit, which is available for $4 from the Transit Store, 102 Broadway at First Avenue (☎ **619/234-1060**). Bikes can also be brought aboard the San Diego–Coronado ferry.

Fast Facts: San Diego

American Express   A full-service office is located downtown at 258 Broadway, at Third Avenue (☎ **619/234-4455**). It's open Monday through Friday from 9am to 5pm.

Dentist/Doctor   For dental referrals, contact the **San Diego County Dental Society** at ☎ **800/201-0244** or 800/DENTIST. **Hotel Docs** (☎ **800/ 468-3537** or 619/275-2663) is a 24-hour network of physicians, dentists, and chiropractors who claim they'll come to your hotel room within 35 minutes of your call. They accept credit cards, and their services are covered by most insurance policies.

Emergencies   For police, fire, highway patrol, or life-threatening medical emergencies, dial ☎ **911** from any phone. No coins are required.

Hospitals   The most conveniently located emergency room is at **UCSD Medical Center–Hillcrest,** 200 W. Arbor Dr. (☎ **619/543-6400**). In Coronado, head to **Coronado Hospital,** 250 Prospect Place (☎ **619/435-6251**). In La Jolla, **Thornton Hospital,** 9300 Campus Point Dr. (☎ **858/657-7600**) has a good emergency room.

Police   For nonemergency matters, contact the downtown precinct, 1401 Broadway (☎ **619/531-2000**).

Post Office   Post offices are located downtown, at 815 E St.; at 51 Horton Plaza, beside the Westin Hotel; and toward Point Loma, at 2535 Midway Dr. They are generally open Monday through Friday during regular business hours, plus Saturday mornings; for specific branch information, call ☎ **800/ ASK-USPS.**

Safety   As cities go, San Diego is pretty safe. But use particular caution on beaches after dark, and stay on designated walkways and away from secluded areas in Balboa Park—night or day. In the Gaslamp Quarter, try to stay west of Fifth Avenue. Take particular care to lock your car and park in well-lit areas; San Diego's proximity to the border contributes to its high rate of auto theft.

Taxes   A 7.75% sales tax is added at the register for all goods and services purchased in San Diego. The city hotel tax is 10.5%.

Useful Telephone Numbers   For the correct time, call ☎ **619/853-1212.** For local weather and surf reports, call ☎ **619/289-1212.**

3 Accommodations

The rates listed below are all "rack," or official rates—you can often do better. Rates tend to be higher in summer (especially true of beach hotels) and when there's a big convention in town. Remember to factor in the city's 10.5% hotel tax.

For good prices in all accommodation categories, contact **San Diego Hotel Reservations** (☎ **800/SAVE-CASH** or 619/627-9300; www.savecash.com). Bed-and-breakfasts are growing in popularity, and several are listed below; for additional choices, contact the **San Diego Bed & Breakfast Guild** (☎ **619/523-1300**).

DOWNTOWN

The downtown area is very convenient for business travelers, but also includes hotels in the stylish Gaslamp Quarter, as well as those located near the harbor and other leisure attractions.

VERY EXPENSIVE

In addition to the following choices, another option is the **San Diego Marriott Marina**, 333 W. Harbor Dr., at Front Street (☎ **800/228-9290** or 619/234-1500), boasting more than 1,400 rooms next to the Convention Center.

Hyatt Regency San Diego. 1 Market Place (at Harbor Dr.), San Diego, CA 92101. ☎ **800/233-1234** or 619/232-1234. Fax 619/239-5678. 875 units. A/C MINIBAR TV TEL. $245–$290 double; from $500 suite. Extra person $25. Children under 12 stay free in parents' room. Packages and much lower weekend rates available. AE, CB, DC, DISC, MC, V. Valet parking $16; self-parking $12. Trolley: Seaport Village.

The 40-story Hyatt Regency, the tallest waterfront hotel on the West Coast, is generally the first choice of business travelers and convention groups, so the rack rates listed can be deceptively high—don't let them scare you off if you want to stay in downtown's best modern high-rise. While a behemoth with nearly 900 rooms can't offer very personalized service, you'll enjoy the amenities designed for those with bottomless expense accounts. All the public spaces and guest rooms are light and airy, and boast stunning views out over the city or sea. Built in 1992, the hotel sports a limestone-and-marble neoclassical theme; guest rooms are quiet and outfitted with high-quality but standard Hyatt-issue furnishings. Bathrooms have ample counter space and hair dryers, more than 80% of the rooms are designated no-smoking, and the Hyatt gets kudos for superior services for travelers with disabilities.

Dining/Diversions: Sally's, a fancy seafood restaurant, joins two less formal spots (all three offer alfresco dining) and two bars (including one with a spectacular 40th-floor view).

Amenities: Concierge, 24-hour room service, dry cleaning, laundry, shoe shine, newspaper delivery, in-room massage, baby-sitting, courtesy car, state-of-the-art health club/spa, third-story bay-view outdoor pool, whirlpool, six tennis courts, boat/watersports/bicycle rental, business center, car-rental desk, beauty salon, gift shop.

EXPENSIVE

Holiday Inn on the Bay. 1355 N. Harbor Dr. (at Ash St.), San Diego, CA 92101-3385. ☎ **800/HOLIDAY** or 619/232-3861. Fax 619/232-4924. 600 units. A/C TV TEL. $179–$219 double; from $400 suite. Children under 18 stay free in parents' room. AARP and AAA discounts, packages available. AE, DC, MC, V. Parking $12. Bus: 2, 9, 29, 34, 34A, or 35. Pets accepted with $25 cleaning fee (per stay) and $100 refundable deposit.

Renovated in 1992, this Holiday Inn high-rise is basic but well maintained, and located directly on the harbor near the Maritime Museum. It's only 1½ miles from the airport (you can watch the planes landing and taking off) and 2 blocks from the train station and trolley. The rooms are decorated in a California contemporary style; some offer harbor views. In general, the bathrooms are small, but they have separate sinks with a lot of counter space.

In addition to housing San Diego's branch of Ruth's Chris Steakhouse, the hotel has two more casual restaurants. Other amenities include a heated outdoor pool, workout equipment, room service (from 6 to 11am and 5 to 11pm), in-room movies, baby-sitting, laundry, valet, and self-service laundry.

Horton Grand. 311 Island Ave. (at Fourth Ave.), San Diego, CA 92101. ☎ **800/542-1886** or 619/544-1886. Fax 619/544-0058. www.hortongrand.com. 132 units. TV TEL. $139–$169 double; $209–$219 mini-suite. Packages available. Children 17 and under stay free in parents' room. AE, DC, MC, V. Valet parking $10 overnight with unlimited in/out privileges. Bus: 1. Pets accepted with a $50 one-time fee.

A cross between an elegant hotel and a charming B&B, the Horton Grand combines two hotels dating from 1886—the Horton Grand and the Brooklyn Hotel, which for a time was the Kahle Saddlery Shop. Both were saved from demolition, moved to this spot, and connected by an airy atrium lobby filled with white wicker. The facade, with its graceful bay windows, is original. Each bedroom is unique and contains antiques and a gas fireplace (on a timer so you can fall asleep in front of it); even the bathrooms, complete with WC and pedestal sink, are genteel. Rooms overlook either the city or the fig-tree–filled courtyard. Each suite has a microwave, a minibar, two TVs, two phones, a sofa bed, and modem hookup. This is an old hotel, and sounds carry more than they might in a modern one, so if you're a light sleeper, request a room with no neighbors.

Ida Bailey's restaurant, named for the well-loved madam whose establishment used to stand on this spot, is located on the ground floor. Afternoon tea is served in the Palace Bar, and live music is featured Thursday through Saturday evenings and Sunday afternoons.

MODERATE

Other reliable choices include the **Clarion Hotel Bay View San Diego,** 660 K St., at Sixth (☎ **800/766-0234** or 619/696-0234), adjacent to downtown and the Gaslamp Quarter. The **Best Western Bayside Inn,** 555 W. Ash St., at Columbia Street (☎ **800/ 341-1818** or 619/233-7500), is popular with business travelers and boasts magnificent views.

Gaslamp Plaza Suites. 520 E St. (corner of Fifth Ave.), San Diego, CA 92101. ☎ **800/ 874-8770** or 619/232-9500. Fax 619/238-9945. 55 units. AC TV TEL. $93–$139 double; $139–$179 suite. Rates include continental breakfast. AE, CB, DC, DISC, MC, V. Valet parking $11. Bus: 1, 3, 25. Trolley: 5th & C.

You can't get closer to the center of the vibrant Gaslamp Quarter than this impeccably restored late Victorian that was, at 11 stories, San Diego's first "skyscraper" in 1913. Built at great expense—utilizing Australian gumwood, marble, brass, and exquisite etched glass—this splendid building originally housed the offices of San Diego Trust & Savings, and was eventually placed on the National Register of Historic Places before reopening as a boutique hotel.

The epitome of timeless elegance, from the dramatic lobby to the wide corridors reminiscent of an ocean liner, the hotel boasts guest rooms furnished with a European flair—each named for writers like Emerson, Swift, Zola, and Fitzgerald. The bathrooms are solid and impressive, with fine marble and tile, and each room is equipped with microwave, dinnerware, fridge, and VCR. While most units are spacious, beware

San Diego Area Accommodations

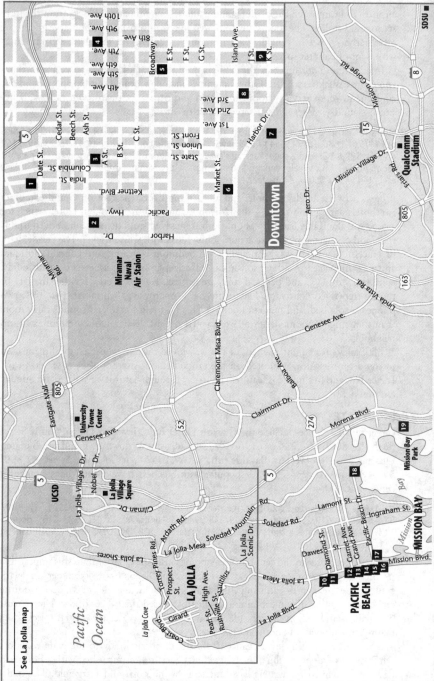

608

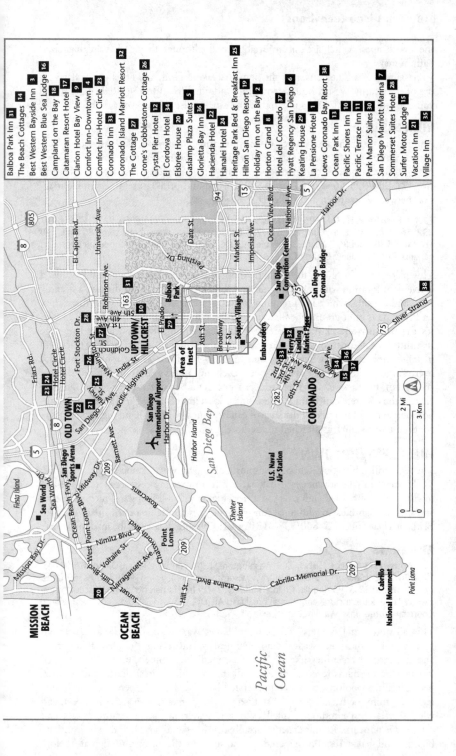

Balboa Park Inn **31**
The Beach Cottages **14**
Best Western Bayside Inn **3**
Best Western Blue Sea Lodge **16**
Campland on the Bay **18**
Catamaran Resort Hotel **17**
Clarion Hotel Bay View **9**
Comfort Inn-Downtown **4**
Comfort Inn-Hotel Circle **23**
Coronado Inn **33**
Coronado Island Marriott Resort **32**
The Cottage **27**
Crone's Cobblestone Cottage **26**
Crystal Pier Hotel **12**
El Cordova Hotel **34**
Elsbree House **20**
Gaslamp Plaza Suites **5**
Glorietta Bay Inn **36**
Hacienda Hotel **22**
Hanalei Hotel **24**
Heritage Park Bed & Breakfast Inn **25**
Hilton San Diego Resort **19**
Holiday Inn on the Bay **2**
Horton Grand **8**
Hotel del Coronado **37**
Hyatt Regency San Diego **6**
Keating House **29**
La Pensione Hotel **1**
Loews Coronado Bay Resort **38**
Ocean Park Inn **13**
Pacific Shores Inn **10**
Pacific Terrace Inn **11**
Park Manor Suites **30**
San Diego Marriott Marina **7**
Sommerset Suites Hotel **28**
Surfer Motor Lodge **15**
Vacation Inn **21**
Village Inn **35**

the few cheapest, which are uncomfortably small (although they do have regular-sized bathrooms).

Gaslamp Plaza Suites sits atop the popular Dakota Grill, and hotel guests have the use of the nearby Westin fitness center for a nominal fee. *Warning:* Remember where you are, and expect to hear some traffic and street noise even in your room.

INEXPENSIVE

Another budget-conscious choice is **Comfort Inn-Downtown,** 719 Ash St., at Seventh Avenue (☎ **800/228-5150** or 619/232-2525), offering clean and safe accommodations in a quieter corner of downtown. Or try **Keating House**, 2331 Second Ave. (☎ **800/995-8644** or 619/239-8585), a bed-and-breakfast set in a restored mansion between downtown and Hillcrest.

✪ **La Pensione Hotel.** 606 W. Date St. (at India St.), San Diego, CA 92101. ☎ **800/ 232-4683** or 619/236-8000. Fax 619/236-8088. www.lapensionehotel.com. 80 units. TV TEL. $60–$80 double. Packages available. AE, DC, DISC, MC, V. Limited free underground parking. Bus: 5. Trolley: County Center/Little Italy.

This place has a lot going for it: modern amenities, cleanliness, remarkable value, a convenient location within walking distance of the central business district, a friendly staff, and parking, which is a premium for small hotels in San Diego. The three-story La Pensione is built around a courtyard and feels like a small European hotel; in fact, it's the number-one choice of foreign students attending the downtown Language Institute. The decor throughout is modern and streamlined—plenty of sleek black and metallic surfaces, crisp white walls, and minimal furniture. Guest rooms, while not overly large, make the most of their space. Each unit offers a combination tub/shower, ceiling fan, microwave, and small fridge; try to get a bay or city view rather than the view of the concrete courtyard. La Pensione is located in San Diego's Little Italy neighborhood and within walking distance of eateries (mostly Italian) and nightspots; there are even two restaurants attached to the hotel itself.

HILLCREST/UPTOWN

The regentrified historic neighborhoods north of downtown are something of a bargain: Well located to take advantage of Balboa Park (yet providing easy access to the rest of town), they're also filled with chic casual restaurants, eclectic shops and movie theaters, and sizzling nightlife. An additional park-side choice is the **Balboa Park Inn,** 3402 Park Blvd., at Upas Street (☎ **800/938-8181** or 619/298-0823; www.balboaparkinn.com).

MODERATE

✪ **Sommerset Suites Hotel.** 606 Washington St. (at Fifth Ave.), San Diego, CA 92103. ☎ **800/962-9665** or 619/692-5200. www.sommerset.com. Fax 619/692-5299. 80 units. A/C TV TEL. $135–$195 double. Children under 12 stay free in parents' room. Discounts usually available. Rates include continental breakfast. AE, DC, DISC, MC, V. Free covered parking. Courtesy shuttle. Take Washington St. exit off I-5. Bus: 16 or 25.

This all-suite hotel on busy Washington Street was originally built as apartment housing for medical interns at the hospital nearby, and retains a residential ambiance and unexpected amenities like huge closets, medicine cabinets, and fully equipped kitchens in all rooms (even dishwashers in the executive suites). Extras include barbecue facilities poolside, plus a coin-operated laundry. There's a personal, welcoming feel here, from the friendly, helpful staff to the complimentary snacks, soda, beer, and wine served each afternoon. You'll even get a welcome basket with cookies and microwave popcorn. Rooms are comfortably furnished and have hair dryers, irons and boards, and balconies. Be prepared for noise from the busy thoroughfare below, though. Several blocks of Hillcrest's chic eateries and shops (plus a movie multiplex) are within easy walking distance. Guest services include a courtesy van to the airport, Sea World, the zoo, and other attractions within a 5-mile radius.

INEXPENSIVE

Two extremely cozy and welcoming bed-and-breakfasts under $100 are **The Cottage,** 3829 Albatross St., off Robinson (☎ **619/299-1564**), and **Crone's Cobblestone Cottage,** 1302 Washington Place, 2½ blocks west of Washington Street at Ingalls Street (☎ **619/295-4765**).

Park Manor Suites. 525 Spruce St. (between Fifth and Sixth aves.), San Diego, CA 92103. ☎ **800/874-2649** or 619/291-0999. Fax 619/291-8844. www.parkmanorsuites.com. 80 units. TV TEL. $69–$89 studio; $89–$129 1-bedroom suite; $139–$179 2-bedroom suite. Children under 12 stay free in parents' room. Extra person $15. Weekly rates available. Rates include continental breakfast. AE, DC, MC, V. Free parking. Bus: 1, 3, or 25.

Popular with actors appearing at the Old Globe Theater in neighboring Balboa Park, this eight-floor Italianate masterpiece was built as a full-service luxury hotel in 1926 on a prime corner overlooking the park. The hotel became a popular stopping-off point for celebrities headed for Mexican vacations in the 1920s and 1930s. Guest rooms are spacious and comfortable, featuring full kitchens, dining rooms, living rooms, and bedrooms with a separate dressing area. A few have glassed-in terraces; request one when you book. The overall feeling here is that of a prewar East Coast apartment building, complete with steam heating and lavish moldings. Park Manor Suites does have its weaknesses: The bathrooms have mostly original fixtures and could use some renovation; and the rooftop banquet room, where a simple continental breakfast buffet is served each morning, suffers from a bad 1980s re-do with too many mirrors. But prices are quite reasonable for the trendy Hillcrest neighborhood; there's a restaurant on the ground floor and laundry service is available.

OLD TOWN & MISSION VALLEY

Old Town is a popular area for families because of its proximity to Old Town State Historic Park and other attractions within walking distance. Hotel Circle, on the way to Mission Valley, offers easy freeway access to a bevy of mostly chain hotels convenient for sports fans or bargain seekers. Additional choices include **Comfort Inn & Suites,** 2485 Hotel Circle Place (☎ **800/647-1903** or 619/291-7700), **Heritage Park Bed & Breakfast Inn,** 2470 Heritage Park Row, near Old Town (☎ **800/995-2470** or 619/299-6832; www.heritageparkinn.com), and **Vacation Inn,** 3900 Old Town Ave. (☎ **800/451-9846** or 619/299-7400).

Hacienda Hotel. 4041 Harney St. (just east of San Diego Ave.), San Diego, CA 92110. ☎ **800/888-1991** or 619/298-4707. Fax 619/298-4771. www.haciendahotel-oldtown.com. 170 units. A/C TV TEL. $135–$145 suite. Seasonal discounts available. Children under 16 stay free in parents' room. AE, CB, DC, DISC, MC, V. Free underground parking. From I-5, take Old Town Ave. exit; turn left onto San Diego Ave. and right onto Harney St. Bus: 5, or 5A.

Perched above Old Town, this Best Western all-suite hotel is spread over several levels overlooking Old Town. Walkways thread through courtyards with bubbling fountains, palm trees, lampposts, and bougainvillea-trimmed balconies, but if you have trouble climbing stairs and hills you'd be wise to stay elsewhere. Aside from that, the place is tops in its price range; every suite is outfitted with rustic Mexican wood furniture and spacious 20-foot ceilings, and standard equipment includes fridges, microwaves, coffeemakers, and VCRs.

The unremarkable Acapulco restaurant (yes, it's Mexican) serves breakfast, lunch, and dinner daily from its perch atop the hotel. Guests also have signing privileges next door at the Brigantine Restaurant and down the street at Cafe Pacifica (see "Dining," below). Other amenities include room service, free airport/train shuttle, movie rentals with free popcorn, heated outdoor pool and whirlpool, and fitness center.

Hanalei Hotel. 2270 Hotel Circle North, San Diego, CA 92108. ☎ **800/882-0858** or 619/297-1101. Fax 619/297-6049. www.hanaleihotel.com. 416 units. A/C MINIBAR, TV TEL. $99–$160 double; $275–$375 suite. Extra person $10. Seasonal discounts and golf packages available. AARP and AAA member discounts. AE, CB, DC, DISC, MC, V. Parking $6. Pets accepted with $50 cleaning fee. From I-8, take Hotel Circle exit; follow signs for Hotel Circle north. Bus: 6.

Our favorite Polynesian-themed hotel on Hotel Circle just emerged from a massive renovation and upgrade, sporting a level of comfort-conscious sophistication that sets it apart from the rest of the pack. Rooms are split between two high-rise towers, set far away from the freeway and cleverly positioned so that all balconies open onto either the tropically landscaped pool courtyard or the luxurious links of a formerly private golf club meandering along the Mission Valley floor. The heated outdoor pool is large enough for any luau, as is the oversize whirlpool beside it. There's an unmistakable 1960s vibe to the hotel and its Hawaiian ambiance, but guest rooms sport contemporary furnishings and modern features like coffeemakers, hair dryers, irons and boards, and in-room movies. Some have microwaves and fridges; other services include laundry, meeting facilities, and a free shuttle to Old Town and other attractions.

MISSION BAY & THE BEACHES

If you plan to enjoy the beach and aquatic activities during your visit (including Sea World), staying in this part of town will set you up in the right spot.

VERY EXPENSIVE

You may also want to consider the **Pacific Terrace Inn,** 610 Diamond St. (☎ **800/344-3370** or 858/581-3500), whose upscale atmosphere stands out among mostly laid-back boardwalk hotels.

Hilton San Diego Resort. 1775 E. Mission Bay Dr., San Diego, CA 92109. ☎ **800/445-8667** or 858/276-4010; 800/962-6307 in California and Arizona. Fax 858/275-7991. 365 units. A/C MINIBAR TV TEL. Summer $205–$335 double, from $500 suite; off-season $190–$285 double. Extra person $20. Children under 18 stay free in parents' room. AE, CB, DC, DISC, JCB, MC, V. Valet parking $10; free self-parking. Pets under 25 lbs. accepted with $50 one-time fee. Take I-5 to Sea World Dr. exit and turn north on E. Mission Bay Dr.

Occupying 18 acres on Mission Bay, this resort remains popular with families and business groups. Expect consistent, if impersonal, quality and an ambiance similar to any upscale new housing community. The Hilton's main asset is that within steps of your room are enough distractions and activities for the duration of your stay. These include a clean, calm beach, plus tennis courts, charter boats, rental catamarans and water toys like windsurfers and aqua cycles, an Olympic-plus-size pool, access to Mission Bay Park's trails and playgrounds, and bike rentals, as well as a bevy of shops and restaurants. All units (contained in one eight-story tower and several low-rise buildings) have ceiling fans, balconies or terraces, refrigerators, coffeemakers, irons and ironing boards, hair dryers, and makeup mirrors. Rooms are spacious and light, with large, elegant bathrooms. Sea World is across the bay, and the ocean is 5 miles to the west.

Dining/Diversions: Three options range from a casual Southwestern bayfront cafe to a dinner-only Italian restaurant to a Mexican spot with live entertainment and dancing at night.

Amenities: Giant swimming "lagoon" plus children's wading pool and four Jacuzzis, sauna, weight-training room, five lighted tennis courts, pro shop, putting green, children's playground, in-room movies, business center, massage, game arcade, meeting rooms, laundry facilities, hair salon, concierge, room service (from 7am to 11pm), dry cleaning/laundry service, baby-sitting, summer children's programs, free airport transportation.

EXPENSIVE

Another beachfront choice in this price range is the **Best Western Blue Sea Lodge,** 707 Pacific Beach Dr. (☎ **800/BLUE-SEA** or 858/488-4700).

✪ **Catamaran Resort Hotel.** 3999 Mission Blvd. (4 blocks south of Grand Ave.), San Diego, CA 92109. ☎ **800/422-8386** or 858/488-1081; 800/233-8172 in Canada. Fax 858/488-1387. www.catamaranresort.com. 315 units. A/C TV TEL. $165–$225 double; from $265 suite; $190–$235 studio. Children under 18 stay free in parents' room. AE, CB, DC, DISC, MC, V. Valet parking $8; self-parking $6. Take Grand/Garnet exit off I-5 and go west on Grand Ave., then south on Mission Blvd.

Ideally situated right on Mission Bay, the Catamaran enjoys its own beach and water-sports facilities. Built in the 1950s, the hotel has been fully renovated to modern standards without losing its trademark Polynesian theme; there's a 15-foot waterfall and full-size dugout canoe in the atrium lobby, and koi-filled lagoons meander through the property, which glows at night with blazing torches. Each room features subdued South Pacific decor and has a balcony or patio; tower rooms have commanding views of the entire bay and San Diego skyline. Studios and suites have kitchenettes, and every room has a coffeemaker and hair dryer. The Catamaran is within walking distance of Pacific Beach's restaurant and nightlife scene. It's also steps away from the bay's exceptional jogging/biking path, and you can rent bikes and jogging strollers at the hotel.

Dining/Diversions: In addition to the upscale Atoll dining room, evening diversions include the large, lively Cannibal Bar, plus an intimate piano bar called Moray's.

Amenities: Outdoor heated pool, whirlpool spa, health club, concierge, room service (from 6:30am to 11pm), movie channels, dry cleaning/laundry service, nightly turndown, baby-sitting, business center, lifeguard in summer only, supervised children's programs, car-rental desk, tour desk, gift shop.

MODERATE

The Beach Cottages. 4255 Ocean Blvd. (a block south of Grand Ave.), San Diego, CA 92109-3995. ☎ **858/483-7440.** Fax 858/273-9365. 61 units, 17 cottages. TV TEL. Summer (July 1–Labor Day) $95–$115 double; $125 studio for up to 4; $145–$190 apt for up to 6; $155–$180 cottage for up to 6; $220–$240 2-bedroom suite for up to 6. Lower rates rest of year. Weekly rates available except in summer. AE, CB, DC, DISC, MC, V. Free parking.

Even though this family-owned establishment has a variety of different guest quarters—most geared toward the long-term visitor—it's the cute little detached cottages steps from the sand (look both ways for speeding cyclists before crossing the board-walk) that give it its appeal. The other room types are perfectly adequate, especially for budget-minded families who want to log major hours on the beach; stay away, however, from the plain motel rooms—they're just dingy. All units except the motel rooms have fully equipped kitchens. The Beach Cottages is within walking distance of shops and restaurants and has barbecue grills, shuffleboard courts, table tennis, and laundry. The cottages themselves aren't pristine, but have a rustic charm popular with young honeymooners and those nostalgic for the golden age of laid-back California beach culture. With one or two bedrooms, they sleep up to six; each has a patio with tables and chairs.

ⓘ Family-Friendly Hotels

The Beach Cottages *(see p. 613)*   Kids will enjoy this place's informal atmosphere and the location near the beach.

Catamaran Resort Hotel *(see p. 613)*   Myriad sports facilities and a safe swimming beach make this resort an ideal place for families. Accommodations are comfortable, but not so posh that Mom and Dad need to worry.

Hilton San Diego Resort *(see p. 612)*   This bayfront property has a kids' wading pool and playground, plus plenty of space for them to run around.

Holiday Inn on the Bay *(see p. 606)*   Your kids under 18 stay free of charge, and so does the family pet. The hotel is well priced for strained family budgets, and even offers baby-sitting services for strained Moms and Dads.

Loews Coronado Bay Resort *(see p. 618)*   Its Commodore Kids Club, for children ages 4 to 12, provides summertime supervised indoor/outdoor activities during the day and some evenings, too. Programs for older kids keep them out of harm's way without making them feel baby-sat.

✪ **Crystal Pier Hotel.** 4500 Ocean Blvd. (at Garnet), San Diego, CA 92109. ☎ **800/ 748-5894** or 858/483-6983. 26 cottages. TV. Cottages for 2-6 people, $115–$305 mid-June to mid-Sept; $95–$250 rest of the year. 3-night minimum in summer. DISC, MC, V. Free parking. Take I-5 to Grand/Garnet exit; follow Garnet to the pier.

This historic property, which dates from 1927, offers a unique opportunity to sleep over the water. Built on a pier over the Pacific Ocean, the hotel offers self-contained cottages with breathtaking beach views. While most cottages date from 1936, all have been gutted and completely renovated. Each comes with a private patio, living room, bedroom, and kitchen, and has welcoming blue shutters and window boxes. The around-the-clock sound of waves is soothing, but the boardwalk action is only a few steps (and worlds) away. If you stay here, remember that the quietest quarters are the farthest out on the pier. Guests drive right out and park beside their cottages, a real boon on crowded weekends. Besides being a restful place to lay your head, the pier is a great place to watch the surfers at sunset. Vending machines and movie rentals are available, as are boogie boards, fishing poles, beach chairs, and umbrellas. The office is open daily from 8am to 8pm. These unique accommodations book up fast.

Ocean Park Inn. 710 Grand Ave., San Diego, CA 92109. ☎ **800/231-7735** or 858/ 483-5858. Fax 858/274-0823. http://go-explore.com/opinn. 77 units. A/C TV TEL. Summer $104–$154 double; $179–$189 suite. Rates include continental breakfast. AE, DC, DISC, MC, V. Free indoor parking. Take Grand/Garnet exit off I-5; follow Grand Ave. to ocean.

This modern, oceanfront motor hotel offers attractive, spacious rooms with well-coordinated contemporary furnishings. Although the inn has a level of sophistication uncommon for this casual, surfer-populated area, you won't find solitude and quiet, although the cool marble lobby and plushly carpeted hallways will help you feel a little insulated from the raucous scene outside. You sure can't beat the location (directly on the beach) and the view (ditto), and all rooms are equipped with fridges. Rates vary according to view, but all units have at least a partial ocean view. The ones in the front, while most desirable, can also get noisy directly above the boardwalk, so try for the second or third floor. The Ocean Park Inn doesn't have its own restaurant, but the casual Firehouse Beach Cafe (see "Dining," below) is right outside the front door.

INEXPENSIVE

Other inexpensive options in the beach area include the **Pacific Shores Inn,** 4802 Mission Blvd., between Law and Chalcedony (☎ **800/826-0715** or 858/483-6300). There's also an immaculate and comfortable contemporary bed-and-breakfast near Ocean Beach's "Antique Row": **Elsbree House,** 5054 Narragansett Ave. (☎ **619/ 226-4133;** www.oceanbeach-online.com/elsbree/b&b).

Surfer Motor Lodge. 711 Pacific Beach Dr. (at Mission Blvd.), San Diego, CA 92109. ☎ **800/787-3373** or 858/483-7070. Fax 858/274-1670. 52 units. TV TEL. Summer (June 15–Sept 15) $83–$122 double; winter $70–$93 double. Extra person $5. Weekly rates available off-season. AE, DC, MC, V. Free parking. Take I-5 to Grand/Garnet, then Grand Ave. to Mission Blvd.; turn left, then right onto Pacific Beach Dr. Bus: 34 or 34A.

Frankly, this property is looking pretty tired, but it's still often booked solid during the summer because it offers moderately priced digs right on the boardwalk at the beach, as well as a heated pool. Most rooms in this four-story property have balconies and views and are cooled by ocean breezes, and many have kitchenettes. Hopefully the management will consider sprucing the place up a bit so it doesn't feel so haggard. On the premises is a coin-operated laundry. A popular restaurant serving three meals a day is adjacent.

CAMPING

Campland on the Bay, 2211 Pacific Beach Dr. (☎ **800/4-BAY-FUN** or 858/ 581-4200; www.campland.com), is popular with a mixed crowd: RVers, campers (with or without van), boaters, and their children and pets. Located on the beach at Mission Bay, the facility has abundant recreation options and extensive service. In summer, rates range from $25 to $98 for up to four people; off-season, from $27 to $68. Weekly and monthly rates are available off-season.

LA JOLLA

While you'll have a hard time finding bargain accommodations in this upscale, conservative community, it's not to be missed for the sheer physical beauty of its coastline, as well as a compact downtown village that makes for delightful strolling. An additional choice worth checking out is the **Bed & Breakfast Inn at La Jolla,** 7753 Draper Ave., near Prospect (☎ **800/582-2466** or 858/456-2066; www.InnLaJolla. com), set in an Irving Gill–designed house near the museum; rates range from inexpensive to expensive.

VERY EXPENSIVE

✪ **La Valencia Hotel.** 1132 Prospect St. (at Herschel Ave.), La Jolla, CA 92037. ☎ **800/ 451-0772** or 858/454-0771. Fax 858/456-3921. www.lavalencia.com. 117 units. A/C MINIBAR TV TEL. $225–$550 double; from $625 suite. Extra person $15. AE, DC, DISC, MC, V. Valet parking $14. Take Ardath Rd. exit off I-5 north or La Jolla Village Dr. west exit off I-5 south. Take Torrey Pines Rd. to Prospect Place and turn right. Prospect Place becomes Prospect St.

It's not just La Valencia's distinctive pink stucco that brings to mind other graciously historic (and pink) hotels like the Beverly Hills Hotel and Waikiki's Royal Hawaiian. Within the bougainvillea-draped walls and wrought-iron garden gates, this bastion of gentility does a fine job of resurrecting the elegance of its golden age. The cliff-top hotel has been the centerpiece of La Jolla since opening in 1926; today, brides pose against a backdrop of La Jolla Cove and the Pacific, well-coiffed ladies lunch in the dappled shade of the garden patio, and neighborhood cronies quaff libations in the clubby Whaling Bar. Rooms are lavishly furnished with rich fabrics and European antique reproductions, though some are on the dark side—and 1920s bathrooms aren't huge.

Dining/Diversions: Options include an elegant rooftop French dining room, casual patio cafe, and the legendary Whaling Bar & Grill (where Ginger Rogers and Charlton Heston once hung out).

Amenities: Outdoor heated pool surrounded by lawn and shuffleboard courts, 24-hour room service, dry cleaning/laundry service, and dozens of other pampering touches.

EXPENSIVE

You may also want to consider the La Jolla Beach & Tennis Club's sister property **The Sea Lodge,** 8110 Camino del Oro, at Avenida de la Playa (☎ **800/237-5211** or 858/459-8271), also located on the beach. Or, for a B&B ambiance, try **Scripps Inn,** 555 Coast Blvd. S., at Cuvier (☎ **858/454-3391**).

Empress Hotel of La Jolla. 7766 Fay Ave. (at Silverado), La Jolla, CA 92037. ☎ **888/369-9900** or 858/454-3001. Fax 858/454-6387. www.empress-hotel.com. 73 units. A/C TV TEL. $139–$199 double; $349 suite. Extra person $10. Children under 18 stay free in parents' room. Rates include continental breakfast. Lower off-season and extended-stay rates. AE, DC, DISC, MC, V. Valet parking $7.

The Empress Hotel offers spacious quarters with traditional furnishings a block or two away from La Jolla's "main drag" and the ocean. It's quieter here than at the Colonial Inn or the Prospect Park Inn, and you'll sacrifice little other than direct ocean views—and many rooms on the top floors enjoy a partial view anyway. If you're planning to explore La Jolla on foot, the Empress is a good base, and exudes a classiness many comparably priced chains lack. Rooms are tastefully decorated (and frequently renovated) and equipped with fridges, hair dryers, coffeemakers, irons and boards, and bathrobes. Bathrooms are of average size but exceptionally well appointed, and four "Empress" rooms have sitting areas with full-size sleeper sofas. There's room service, valet/laundry service, and a fitness room with spa and sauna; on nice days, breakfast is set up on a serene outdoor sundeck.

✪ **La Jolla Beach & Tennis Club.** 2000 Spindrift Dr., La Jolla, CA 92037. ☎ **800/624-CLUB** or 858/454-7126. Fax 858/456-3805. www.ljbtc.com. 90 units. TV TEL. High season (mid-June–mid-Sept) $165–$289 double; from $229 suite. Off-season $129–$239 double; from $189 suite. Children under 12 stay free in parents' room. Extra person $20. AE, DC, MC, V. Located in La Jolla Shores about a mile from the village.

Pack your best tennis whites for a stay at La Jolla's private and historic "B&T" (as it's locally known). Guest rooms are surprisingly plain and frill-free in terms of style, but are equipped with hair dryers, irons and boards, and coffeemakers. Most have well-stocked kitchens ideal for families or longer stays. During the warm months, the beach is the draw, as the staff sets up comfy sand chairs and umbrellas, and race to bring fluffy beach towels, beverages, and snacks. Kayaks and water-sports equipment can be rented; there's even a sand croquet court.

Dining: Although there's no room service, the resort has a casual dining room and seasonal beach hut; it's also worth taking a peek into the distinctive Marine Room, where waves literally smash against the windows inches away from well-coiffed diners. The menu is expensive, but the price of a cocktail gets the same astounding view.

Amenities: Guests have full use of the club's 12 championship tennis courts, as well as a nine-hole pitch-and-putt winding its way around a lagoon along the stately entry drive. Other facilities include a jogging path, children's playground, table tennis, fitness room, and elegant Olympic-sized pool.

MODERATE

In addition to the following option, another great choice is **Prospect Park Inn,** 1110 Prospect St. (☎ **800/433-1609** or 858/454-0133), which enjoys a prime location next door to La Valencia.

Best Western Inn By The Sea. 7830 Fay Ave. (between Prospect and Silverado), La Jolla, CA 92037. ☎ **800/462-9732** in the U.S., 800/526-4545 in California and Canada, or 858/459-4461. Fax 858/456-2578. 132 units. A/C TV TEL. $129–$199 double; $175–$450 suite. Seasonal discounts available. Rates include continental breakfast. AE, CB, DC, DISC, MC, V. Free parking.

Occupying an enviable location at the heart of La Jolla's charming village, this independently managed Best Western property puts guests just a short walk from the cliffs and beach. The low-rise tops out at five stories, with the upper floors enjoying ocean views (and the highest room rates). Along with the more formal Empress a block away, these two properties offer a terrific alternative to pricier digs nearby. Rooms here are Best Western standard issue—clean and freshly maintained, but nothing special. All rooms do have balconies, though, and refrigerators are available at no extra charge; other amenities include heated pool and whirlpool, free daily newspaper and local phone calls, and room service from the attached IHOP.

INEXPENSIVE

La Jolla Cove Travelodge. 1141 Silverado St. (at Herschel), La Jolla, CA 92037. ☎ **800/ 578-7878** or 858/454-0791. Fax 858/459-8534. 30 units. A/C TV TEL. $59–$98 double. AE, DC, MC, V. Rates are seasonal and subject to availability. AARP and AAA discounts available. Free off-street parking.

While the name is deceptive—the cove is a 10-minute walk away—this corner motel is a good value in tony La Jolla. Fitting in with the village's retro feel, the exterior seems unchanged from the 1940s; though rooms have been diligently updated, no one will thrill to the basic motel decor—including cinder-block walls and small, plain bathrooms. But somehow, the place seems less dreary surrounded by the chic glamour of La Jolla, and rooms come with coffeemakers and daily newspaper; some have kitchenettes and microwaves as well. There isn't a pool, but there is a modest sundeck on the third floor with a view to the ocean, which is about three-quarters of a mile away.

CORONADO

The "island" (really a peninsula) of Coronado offers a great escape with its quiet, architecturally rich streets; a small-town, Navy-oriented atmosphere; and laid-back vacationing on one of the state's most beautiful and welcoming beaches. Choose a hotel on the ocean side for a view of Point Loma and the Pacific, or stay facing the city for a spectacular skyline vista (especially at night). You may feel pleasantly isolated here, so it isn't your best choice if you're planning to spend lots of time in more central parts of the city.

VERY EXPENSIVE

Another upscale destination is **Coronado Island Marriott Resort**, 2000 Second St., at Glorietta Boulevard (☎ **800/228-9290** or 619/435-3000). Boasting a spa and vast recreational facilities, the Marriott has a low-key elegance and excellent service. Or consider the **Glorietta Bay Inn,** 1630 Glorietta Blvd., near Orange Avenue (☎ **800/ 283-9383** or 619/435-3101; www.gloriettabayinn.com), across the street from the "Del" in a 1908 mansion.

✪ **Hotel del Coronado.** 1500 Orange Ave., Coronado, CA 92118. ☎ **800/468-3533** or 619/435-8000. Fax 619/522-8238. www.hoteldel.com. 700 units. MINIBAR TV TEL. From $200 standard room; from $245 deluxe; from $330 ocean view; from $435 oceanfront; from $500 suite. Packages available. Children under 18 stay free in parents' room. AE, CB, DC, DISC, MC, V. Self-parking $12 overnight, valet parking $16.

Opened in 1888 and designated a National Historic Landmark in 1977, the "Hotel Del," as it's affectionately known, is the last of California's grand old seaside hotels. Here the Duke of Windsor met his duchess, and Marilyn Monroe frolicked in *Some Like It Hot*. This monument to Victorian grandeur boasts tall cupolas, red turrets, and ginger-bread trim, all spread out on 33 acres. If you're a stickler for detail, ask to stay in the original building rather than in the contemporary tower additions. During the shelf life of this guide, the hotel will be undergoing painstaking restoration, with historical accuracy in mind. Guest rooms should emerge more comfortable, wiring and plumbing more modern, and public spaces returned to their Victorian splendor. Inquire when you book, in case you want to avoid construction areas, enjoy vintage rooms before they're worked on, or take advantage of just-completed improvements. Even if you don't stay, don't miss a stroll through the grand, wood-paneled lobby or along the Del's pristine wide beach—the Del offers a self-guided walking tour complete with audiocassette.

Dining/Diversions: The hotel has nine dining areas; the most charming is the ocean-view Prince of Wales Grill. The upscale menu puts an eclectic, Pacific Rim twist on continental favorites. The sunny, breezy Ocean Terrace offers alfresco bistro fare; cocktails and afternoon tea are served in the wood-paneled lobby and adjoining con-servatory lounge. There's music and dancing nightly, ranging from quiet piano tin-kling to amplified dance music.

Amenities: Two outdoor pools, whirlpools, massage, six tennis courts, bicycle rental, concierge, 24-hour room service, in-room movies, turndown service, laundry/dry cleaning, valet, baby-sitting, beauty salon/health spa, limousine service, 24-hour deli, special activities for children, airport shuttle ($9), car-rental desk, elec-tronic games, shopping arcade.

Loews Coronado Bay Resort. 4000 Coronado Bay Rd., Coronado, CA 92118. ☎ **800/ 81-LOEWS** or 619/424-4000. Fax 619/424-4400. 437 units. A/C MINIBAR TV TEL. $235– $285 double; from $425 suite. Children under 18 stay free in parents' room. Packages available. AE, CB, DC, DISC, MC, V. Valet parking $14; self-parking (under cover) $12. Take I-5 to the Coro-nado Bridge, go left onto Orange Ave., continue 8 miles down Silver Strand Hwy., and turn left at Coronado Bay Rd., entrance to the resort. Pets under 25 lbs. accepted free of charge.

This luxury resort opened in 1991 and lounges on a secluded 15-acre peninsula, slightly removed from both downtown Coronado and San Diego. It's perfect for those who prefer a self-contained resort in a get-away-from-it-all location, and is surprisingly successful in appealing to business travelers, convention groups, vacationing families, and romance-minded couples all at once. All quarters offer terraces that look onto the hotel's private 80-slip marina, the Coronado Bay Bridge, or the San Diego Bay. Each room also boasts a finely appointed marble bathroom; at press time, Loews was in the midst of refurnishing the bedrooms, that had become far too outdated and worn for a hotel of this caliber. A private pedestrian underpass leads to nearby Silver Strand Beach. The seasonal Commodore Kids Club, for children 4 to 12, offers supervised half-day, full-day, and evening programs with meals. A highlight of Loews is the Gondola Com-pany, Di Venezia, which offers romantic and fun gondola cruises through the canals of tony Coronado Cays, complete with hors d'oeuvres and a straw-hatted gondolier.

Dining: ✪ **Azzura Point,** with a revamped Mediterranean decor facing the San Diego skyline, offers sophisticated California/Mediterranean cuisine. There's also a casual cafe, lobby lounge, poolside bar and grill, and specialty food market.

Amenities: Three outdoor pools; fitness center with saunas and whirlpools; five night-lit tennis courts and pro shop; bicycle, skate, and water-sports rentals; concierge; 24-hour room service; laundry/valet; newspaper delivery; turndown service; in-room massage; baby-sitting; VCRs; video rentals; business center; fax machines in suites; car-rental desk; beauty salon.

MODERATE

El Cordova Hotel. 1351 Orange Ave. (at Adella Ave.), Coronado, CA 92118. ☎ **800/229-2032** or 619/435-4131. Fax 619/435-0632. 40 units. TV TEL. $95 double; $115–$125 studio with kitchen; $145–$185 1-bedroom suite; $220–$295 2-bedroom suite. Weekly and monthly rates available off-season. Children under 12 stay free in parents' room. AE, DC, DISC, MC, V. Take I-5 to the Coronado Bridge, and turn left onto Orange Ave.

This Spanish hacienda across the street from the Hotel del Coronado began life as a private mansion in 1902; by the 1930s, it had become a hotel, the original building augmented by a series of retail shops along a ground-floor arcade. Surrounding a courtyard with meandering tiled pathways, flowering shrubs, a pool, and patio seating for Miguel's Cocina Mexican restaurant, El Cordova hums pleasantly with activity. Each room is a little different from the next, some sporting a Mexican colonial ambiance while others evoke a comfy beach cottage. All feature ceiling fans and brightly tiled bathrooms, but lack the frills that command exorbitant rates. El Cordova has a particularly inviting aura and its prime location makes it a popular option; we advise reserving several months in advance, especially for summer. Facilities include a heated pool, barbecue area with a picnic table, and laundry room.

INEXPENSIVE

Also in this price range is the ideally located **Village Inn,** 1017 Park Place, at Orange Ave. (☎ **619/435-9318**), a modest, breakfast-included, European-style small hotel with charming rooms but teensy bathrooms.

Coronado Inn. 266 Orange Ave. (corner of 3rd St.), Coronado, CA 92118. ☎ **800/598-6624** or 619/435-4121. www.coronadoinn.com. 30 units. A/C TV TEL. Summer (Memorial Day–Labor Day) $98-$125 up to 4 people; winter $85-$110. Discounts available. Rates include continental breakfast. AE, MC, V. Free parking. Pets allowed with $10 fee per night. Take I-5 to the Coronado Bridge, then stay on Third St.

Well located and terrifically priced, this charming renovated 1940s courtyard motel has such a friendly ambiance, it's like staying with old friends. Take advantage of their free continental breakfast; iced tea, lemonade, and fresh fruit are even provided poolside on summer days. It's still a motel, though, albeit with brand-new paint and a fresh tropical/floral decor, so rooms are pretty basic. Most have only stall showers, but six units have bathtubs; those also have small kitchens. There are laundry facilities on the property, and refrigerators and microwaves are available. Rooms are noisiest close to the street, so ask for one toward the back. The Coronado shuttle stops a block away; ride it down to the shopping areas and Hotel Del.

4 Dining

What follows is only a sampling of San Diego's dining scene. For a greater selection of reviews, see *Frommer's San Diego.*

DOWNTOWN
EXPENSIVE

✪ **Croce's Restaurants & Nightclubs.** 802 Fifth Ave. (at F St.). ☎ **619/233-4355.** www. croces.com. Reservations not accepted; call for same-day "priority seating" (before walk-ins) list. Main courses $14–$23. AE, DC, DISC, MC, V. Daily 5pm–midnight. Valet parking $6 with validation. Bus: 3, 5, 16, 25. Trolley: Gaslamp Quarter. AMERICAN/SOUTHWESTERN/ ECLECTIC.

Ingrid Croce, widow of singer/songwriter Jim, was instrumental in the resurgence of the once-decayed Gaslamp Quarter, and has slowly expanded to fill every corner of this 1890 Romanesque building. Croce's is the primary restaurant, featuring a menu that fuses Southern soul food and Southwestern spice with Asian flavors and Continental standards. Croce's West is more casual in ambiance—but not in price—and its menu is virtually identical save for a few more Southwestern touches (a jalapeño here, an avocado there). Add the raucous Top Hat Bar & Grille and the intimate Jazz Bar, and they're all the hottest ticket in town, with crowds lining up for dinner tables and nightclub shows; expect a noisy, festive good time any night of the week. Those who dine at either of the full-service restaurants can enter the two Croce's nightspots without paying the normal cover. The music venues are described below, in "San Diego After Dark."

The Fish Market/Top of the Market. 750 N. Harbor Dr. ☎ **619/232-FISH** (Fish Market), or 619/234-4TOP (Top of the Market). www.thefishmarket.com. Reservations recommended for Top of the Market; reservations not accepted at the Fish Market. Main courses $9–$25 (Fish Market); $15–$32 (Top of the Market). AE, CB, DC, DISC, MC, V. Daily 11am–10pm. Valet parking $4. Bus: 7/7B. Trolley: Seaport Village. SEAFOOD.

The red building perched at the end of the G Street Pier houses two of San Diego's most popular seafood restaurants: The Fish Market and its pricier cousin, the Top of the Market. Both offer superb fresh seafood and menus that change daily. The chalkboard out front tells you what's fresh, be it Mississippi catfish, Maine lobster, Canadian salmon, or Mexican yellowtail. At ground level, the Fish Market, a market and casual restaurant, has oyster and sushi bars and a cocktail lounge. Upstairs, the elegant Top of the Market looks like a private club, with teakwood touches, mounted fish trophies, and historic photographs. Binoculars are provided to better enjoy the panoramic view. Besides seafood, you can get homemade pasta and choose from a wine list as extensive as the menu. This lofty place inspires some to dress up and make a reservation, but you're also welcome to drop by just for a drink.

There's another **Fish Market Restaurant** in Del Mar at 640 Via de la Valle (☎ **858/755-2277**).

MODERATE

✪ **Fio's.** 801 Fifth Ave. (at F St.). ☎ **619/234-3467.** www.fioscucina.com. Reservations recommended for dinner. Main courses $11–$25. AE, DC, DISC, MC, V. Mon–Thurs 5–10:30pm; Fri–Sat 5–11pm, Sun 5–10pm. Valet parking $6 with validation. Bus: 3, 5, 16, 25. Trolley: Gaslamp Quarter. NORTHERN ITALIAN.

Fio's has been *the* spot to see and be seen in the Gaslamp Quarter since opening, the granddaddy of all the trendy Italian restaurants who followed. Set in an 1881 Italianate-Victorian that once housed chic Marston's department store, Fio's has a hip, sophisticated ambiance and is *always* crowded. Once cutting edge, the upscale trattoria menu is now practiced and consistently superior, featuring jet-black linguini tossed with the freshest seafood, delicate angel-hair pasta perfectly balanced with basil and pine nuts, and gourmet pizzas served at your table or to diners seated at the special pizza bar. The menu manages to please both light eaters (with antipasti and pastas) and heartier palates—the impressive list of meat entrees includes mustard/rosemary rack of lamb, veal shank on saffron risotto, and a delicately sweet hazelnut-crusted pork loin with Frangelico and peaches. You can also sit at the elegant cocktail bar and order from the complete menu.

INEXPENSIVE

✪ **Café Lulu.** 419 F St. (near Fourth Ave.). ☎ **619/238-0114.** Main courses $3–$7. No credit cards. Sun–Thurs 9am–2am, Fri–Sat 9am–4am. Bus: 3, 5, 16, 25. Trolley: Gaslamp Quarter. VEGETARIAN.

Smack dab in the heart of the Gaslamp Quarter, Café Lulu aims to establish a hip, bohemian mood despite its location half a block from bright, commercial Horton Plaza. Ostensibly a coffee bar, the cafe makes a terrific choice for casual dining; if the stylishly metallic interior is too harsh for you, watch the street action from a sidewalk table. The food is health conscious, prepared with organic ingredients and no meat. Soups, salads, cheese melts, and veggie lasagna are on the menu; breads are brought in from the incomparable Bread & Cie uptown. Eggs, granola, and waffles are served in the morning, but any time is the right time to try one of Café Lulu's inventive coffee drinks, like "cafe Bohème," a mocha with almond syrup, or "cafe L'amour," an iced latte with a hazelnut tinge. Beer and wine are also served.

Filippi's Pizza Grotto. 1747 India St. (between Date and Fir sts. in Little Italy). ☎ **619/232-5095.** Fax 619/695-8591. Main courses $4.75–$12.50. AE, DC, DISC, MC, V. Sun–Thurs 11am–10pm, Fri–Sat 11am–11pm. Free parking. Bus: 5. Trolley: County Center/Little Italy. ITALIAN.

To get to the grottolike dining area decorated with Chianti bottles and red-and-white–checked tablecloths, you have to walk through an Italian grocery store/deli strewn with cheeses, pastas, wines, bottles of olive oil, and salamis. You might even end up eating behind shelves of canned olives, but don't feel bad—this has been the tradition since 1950, when the place opened. The intoxicating smell of pizza wafts into the street; Filippi's has more than 15 varieties (including vegetarian), plus old-world Sicilian spaghetti, lasagna, and other pastas. The original of a dozen stores, Filippi's has locations in Pacific Beach, Kearny Mesa, East Mission Valley, and Escondido, among others.

Kansas City Barbecue. 610 W. Market St. ☎ **619/231-9680.** Reservations accepted for large parties only. Main courses $8.75–$11.50. MC, V. Daily 11am–1am. Trolley: Seaport Village. AMERICAN.

Kansas City Barbecue's honky-tonk mystique was fueled by its appearance as the fly-boy hangout in the movie *Top Gun,* and posters from the film share wall space with county-fair memorabilia, old car tags from Kansas, and a photograph of official bar wench Carry Nation. This homey dive is right next to the railroad tracks and across from the tony Hyatt Regency. The spicy barbecue ribs, chicken, and hot links are slow-cooked over an open fire and served with sliced Wonder bread and your choice of coleslaw, beans, fries, onion rings, potato salad, or corn on the cob. The food is okay, but the atmosphere is the real draw.

Where to Find the Famous Theme Restaurants

San Diego's branch of **Planet Hollywood** (☎ 619/702-STAR; www. planethollywood.com) can be found downtown at 197 Horton Plaza (corner of Broadway and Fifth Avenue), in the heart of the Gaslamp Quarter. There's nearly always a line of folks waiting to eat here and ogle the movie memorabilia; the wait staff regularly pacifies diners with free movie posters and theater passes.

You'll find the **Hard Rock Cafe's,** rock-and-roll memorabilia—and great burgers—in the Gaslamp Quarter, 801 4th Ave. (☎ 619/615-7625; www.hardrock.com), and in La Jolla at 909 Prospect St., La Jolla (☎ 858/454-5101).

HILLCREST/UPTOWN

Other choices in this fashionable neighborhood include **Cafe Eleven,** 1440 University Ave. (☎ **619/260-8023**), a dinner-only country French restaurant with charm and good value; **Ichiban,** 1449 University Ave. (☎ **619/299-7203**), where locals on the run stop in for a fix of sushi, teriyaki bowls, or yakisoba noodles; and **Hob Nob Hill,** 2271 First Ave., at Juniper (☎ **619/239-8176**), a 1940s–era diner that's a favorite neighborhood hangout.

EXPENSIVE

California Cuisine. 1027 University Ave. (east of 10th St.). ☎ **619/543-0790.** Reservations recommended for dinner. Main courses $13–$20. AE, DISC, MC, V. Tues–Fri 11am–10pm, Sat–Sun 5–10pm. Bus: 8, 11, 16, 25. CALIFORNIA.

Although the name's no longer as cutting edge as when they opened in the early 1980s, California Cuisine's menu keeps creatively up-to-date. The quiet, understated, and romantic ambiance sets the stage for a smoothly professional staff to proffer fine dining at moderate prices to a casual crowd. The seasonally skewed menu changes daily and contains mouth-watering appetizers like sesame-seared ahi with hot-and-sour raspberry sauce, or a caramelized-onion-and-Gruyère tart on balsamic baby greens. Main courses are, more often than not, stacked in trendy "towers," but their flavors are composed with equal care. Early birds and bargain seekers will appreciate the three-course theater menu ($20) available nightly from 5 to 7pm. Parking can be scarce along this busy stretch of University; you'll spot the restaurant by its light-strewn bushes out front.

✪ **Laurel.** 505 Laurel St. (at Fifth Ave.). ☎ **619/239-2222.** Reservations recommended. Main courses $15–$22. AE, CB, DC, DISC, JCB, MC, V. Sun–Thurs 5–10pm, Fri–Sat 5–11pm. Valet parking $4. Bus: 1, 3, 25. FRENCH/MEDITERRANEAN.

Given its sophisticated decor, pedigreed chefs, prime Balboa Park location, and well-composed menu of country French dishes with a Mediterranean accent, it's no wonder this relatively new restaurant was an instant success. It's also popular with theatergoers, offering shuttle service to the Old Globe followed by an after-performance dessert. Tantalizing appetizers include eggplant ravioli in a roasted-tomato-and-black-olive jus, or house-cured duck-breast prosciutto; follow with pan-roasted veal sweetbreads in black-olive sauce, or grilled salmon with herb-crusted fingerling potatoes. One of the most stylish choices near often-funky Hillcrest, Laurel has an almost New York ambiance coupled with truly modest prices.

MODERATE

Liaison. 2202 Fourth Ave. (at Ivy). ☎ **619/234-5540.** Main courses $10.75–$19.75. AE, CB, DC, DISC, MC, V. Tues–Sun 5–10:30pm. Bus: 1, 3, 25. FRENCH.

At this cozy and inviting cafe, the cuisine and decor evoke a Gallic farmhouse kitchen, with copper pots hanging from the rafters. Conveniently located for Balboa Park theatergoers, this dinner-only fave has a hearty French country menu including lamb curry, medaillons of pork or beef, coquilles St. Jacques, roast duckling à l'orange, salmon with crayfish butter, and more. A nightly prix-fixe dinner is a great deal, since the meal includes pâté, salad or soup, a main course, and dessert. The house specialty dessert costs extra: a Grand Marnier chocolate or amaretto soufflé for two, at $5 per person. Ooh la la!

Mixx. 3671 Fifth Ave. (at Pennsylvania). ☎ **619/299-6499.** Reservations recommended, especially on weekends. Main courses $11–$19. AE, CB, DC, DISC, MC, V. Sun–Thurs 5–10pm, Fri–Sat 5–11pm. Bus: 1, 3, 25. CALIFORNIA/INTERNATIONAL.

Aptly named for its subtle global fusion fare, Mixx embodies everything good about Hillcrest dining: an attractive, relaxing room; pleasantly sophisticated crowd; thoughtfully composed dinners; and polished, friendly service. It's easy to see why stylish Hillcrest denizens gravitate to Mixx's woody street-level cocktail lounge and the often jovial dining room above. Menu standouts include a starter of pepper-seared ahi over ginger-jicama slaw, duck and wild mushroom ravioli, and pepper filet mignon on truffle mashed potatoes with an Armagnac, cream, and port wine reduction; even meat-eaters should check out chef Josh McGinnis's surprisingly inventive vegetarian special, different each night. Prepared, plated, and presented with finesse, one meal here will quickly convince you that Mixx cares about style, substance, *and* value. Allow time to search for that elusive Hillcrest parking space!

INEXPENSIVE

✪ **The Vegetarian Zone.** 2949 Fifth Ave. (between Palm and Quince). ☎ **619/298-7302,** or 619/298-9232 for deli/takeout. Reservations not accepted. Main courses $5–$10. AE, DC, DISC, MC, V. Mon–Thurs 11:30am–9pm, Fri 11:30am–10pm, Sat 8:30am–10pm, Sun 8:30am–9pm; deli, daily 10am–9pm. Free parking. Bus: 1, 3, 25. VEGETARIAN.

San Diego's only strictly vegetarian restaurant is a real treat—even if you're wary of tempeh, tofu, and meat substitutes, there are plenty of naturally veggie ethnic options on the menu. Selections include Greek spinach-and-feta pie, savory Indian-curry turnovers, and salads with homemade dressings. Soothing music creates a pleasant ambiance enjoyed by trendy-hip Hillcrest types, business lunchers, and the health-conscious from all walks of life. Just in case you feel deserving of a treat after such a healthful meal, the heavenly Extraordinary Desserts is right next door . . . .

OLD TOWN
EXPENSIVE

Cafe Pacifica. 2414 San Diego Ave. ☎ **619/291-6666.** www.cafepacifica.com. Reservations recommended. Main courses $12–$22. AE, CB, DC, DISC, MC, V. Mon–Sat 5:30–10pm, Sun 5–9:30pm. Valet parking $4. Bus: 5/5A. Trolley: Old Town. CALIFORNIA.

Inside this cozy Old Town casita, the decor is cleanly contemporary (but still romantic), and the food anything but Mexican. Established in 1980 by the now revered duo of Kipp Downing and Deacon Brown, Cafe Pacifica has been serving upscale and imaginative seafood and producing kitchen alumni who have gone on to enjoy their own local fame. Among the temptations on the menu are crab-stuffed portobello mushrooms topped with grilled asparagus, anise-scented bouillabaisse, and daily fresh-fish selections served grilled with your choice of five sauces. Signature items include Hawaiian ahi with shiitake mushrooms and ginger butter, griddled mustard catfish, and the "Pomerita," a pomegranate margarita. Dine early to avoid the crowds.

MODERATE

✪ **Berta's Latin American Restaurant.** 3928 Twiggs St. (at Congress St.), Old Town. ☎ **619/295-2343.** Main courses $5–$7 lunch, $11–$13 dinner. AE, MC, V. Daily 11am–10pm (lunch menu until 3pm). Bus: 5/5A. Trolley: Old Town. LATIN AMERICAN.

Tucked away on an Old Town side street, Berta's faithfully re-creates the sundry flavors of Central American regions where chilies and other spices have their heat mellowed by slow cooking. Everyone starts with a basket of fresh flour tortillas and mild salsa verde; nibble while you contemplate menu options like Guatemalan *chilimal,* a rich pork/vegetable casserole with chilies, cornmeal *masa,* and spices. Try the lunch-only Salvadoran *pupusas,* dense corn-mash turnovers with melted cheese and black beans; their texture is perfectly offset by the crunchy cabbage salad. Or settle on a table full of Spanish-style tapas, grazing alternately on crispy *empanadas* (filled turnovers), strong Spanish olives, or *Pincho Moruno*, skewered lamb and onion redolent of spices and red saffron. A welcome change from Old Town's nacho-and-fajita joints, Berta's attracts a large crowd on weekends.

INEXPENSIVE

Casa de Bandini. 2754 Calhoun St. (opposite Old Town Plaza), Old Town. ☎ **619/ 297-8211.** Reservations not accepted. Main courses $6–$15. AE, CB, DC, DISC, MC, V. Daily 11am–9pm (until 10pm in summer). Free parking. Bus: 5/5A. Trolley: Old Town. MEXICAN.

As much an Old Town tradition as the mariachi music that's played here on weekends, Casa de Bandini is the most picturesque of several Mexican restaurants with predictable food and birdbath-sized margaritas. It fills the nooks and crannies of an 1823 adobe hacienda; the superbly renovated enclosed patio has iron gates, flowers blooming around a bubbling fountain, and umbrella-shaded tables for year-round alfresco dining. Most dishes are standard south-of-the-border fare; the crowd consists mainly of out-of-towners, but the ambiance is appealing enough to draw lunchtime fans of those towering tostada salads. It's the setting itself that makes this restaurant extra-special, and makes it worth a mediocre meal.

✪ **Old Town Mexican Cafe.** 2489 San Diego Ave. ☎ **619/297-4330.** Reservations accepted for groups of 10 or more. Main courses $7.50–$11.50. AE, DISC, MC, V. Sun–Thurs 7am–11pm; Fri–Sat 7am–midnight (bar service until 2am nightly). Bus: 5/5A. Trolley: Old Town. MEXICAN.

This place is so popular, it's become an Old Town tourist attraction in its own right. Despite expansion, the wait for a table is still often 30 to 60 minutes. Pass the time gazing in from the sidewalk as tortillas are hand-patted the old-fashioned way, a hot-off-the-grill treat accompanying every meal. Once inside, order what some consider the best margarita in town, followed by one of the cafe's two specialties: carnitas—the traditional Mexican dish of deep-fried pork served with tortillas, guacamole, sour cream, beans, and rice—or rotisserie chicken with all the same trimmings. It's loud and crowded and the cerveza flows like, well, beer, but this Old Town mainstay is best in the city for traditional Mexican.

MISSION BAY & THE BEACHES

Another noteworthy beach spot is **Kono's Surf Club Cafe,** 704 Garnet Ave. (☎ **858/ 483-1669**), a Hawaiian-themed boardwalk breakfast shack that's cheap and delicious—a plump Kono's breakfast burrito provides enough fuel for an entire day of surfing or sightseeing.

MODERATE

The Green Flash. 701 Thomas Ave. (at Mission Blvd.), Pacific Beach. ☎ **858/270-7715.** Reservations recommended. Main courses $10–$20. AE, CB, DC, DISC, MC, V. Mon–Thurs 8am–9:30pm, Fri 8am–10pm, Sat 7:30am–10pm, Sun 7:30am–9:30pm. Bus: 34/34A. AMERICAN.

Known throughout Pacific Beach for its location as well as its hip, local clientele, the Green Flash serves reasonably good (and typically beachy) food at decent prices. The menu includes plenty of grilled and deep-fried seafood, straightforward steaks, and giant main-course salads. You'll also find platters of shellfish (oysters, clams, shrimp) and other appetizers. Denizens congregate every evening on the patio to catch a glimpse of the sunset phenomenon for which this boardwalk hangout is named. The scientific explanation becomes less important—and the decibel level of conversation rises—with every round of drinks. Sunset dinner specials are offered Sunday through Thursday from 4:30 to 7pm.

✪ **Palenque.** 1653 Garnet Ave. (at Jewell St.), Pacific Beach. ☎ **858/272-7816.** Reservations not accepted. Main courses $4–$8 lunch, $9–$15 dinner. AE, MC, V. Daily 11:30am–2:30pm and 5-9pm (Fri-Sat until 10pm). Bus: 27. Plentiful street parking. MEXICAN.

Often described as a "hole-in-the-wall" and a "hidden treasure," this casual, family-run PB restaurant is both—and well worth the search. Behind an overgrown gate on busy Garnet Avenue, Palenque has a pleasant outdoor patio and casual dining room where piñatas and paper birds dangle from a thatched, skylit ceiling. Once seated, expect crispy chips accompanied by two homemade salsas whose fresh perfection is representative of every dish on the menu; from earthy *mole* sauce and freshly patted corn tortillas to carafes of refreshing lemonade, everything tastes like it was lovingly prepared by your practiced Mexican grandma. Drawing on regional traditions from Mexico's interior, the menu features a long list of unique—and sharable— appetizers, plus exceptionally good layered enchiladas. At dinner, meats like *tinga poblano* (pork flavored with chipotle peppers), beef *panile* (with a peanut/pasilla chile sauce), and chicken *mole poblano* (the best in SD) are served platter-style with tortillas and all the fixin's. Some dishes pack quite a spicy kick, so ask beforehand if you're concerned.

Qwiig's. 5083 Santa Monica St. (at Abbott Ave.), Ocean Beach. ☎ **619/222-1101.** Reservations suggested. Main courses $12–$21. AE, MC, V. Mon–Fri 11:30am–9pm, Sat 5–10pm, Sun 5–9pm. Bus: 23, 35. CALIFORNIA.

It has taken more than a sunset view overlooking the OB pier to keep this upscale bar and grill going since 1985; the restaurant owes its consistent popularity to first-rate food served with lack of pretense. The fresh-fish specials are most popular—choices often include rare ahi with braised spinach and sesame-sherry sauce or Chilean sea bass with lime, tequila, and roasted garlic. Several seafood pastas are offered, plus meat and poultry dishes including prime rib, an outstanding half-pound burger, and nightly specials that always shine. Wines are well matched to the cuisine, and imaginative special cocktails are offered each night. The restaurant got its strange name from a group of OB surfers nicknamed "qwiigs."

✪ **Sushi Ota.** 4529 Mission Bay Dr. (at Bunker Hill), Mission Bay. ☎ **858/270-5670.** Reservations suggested on weekends. Main courses $8–$15, sushi $2.50–$8. AE, MC, V. Tues–Fri 11:30am–2pm and 5:30–10:30pm, Sat–Mon 5:30–10:30pm. JAPANESE.

Chef/owner Yukito Ota's masterful sushi garnered a nearly perfect food rating in the San Diego *Zagat Survey.* This sophisticated and traditional establishment (no Asian fusion here) has a short sushi menu, but in-the-know patrons look first to the daily specials posted behind the counter. The city's most experienced chefs, armed with nimble fingers and very sharp knives, turn the day's fresh catch into artful little bundles accented with mounds of wasabi and ginger. The rest of the menu is varied, featuring seafood dishes, teriyaki-glazed meats, feather-light tempura, and a variety of small appetizers perfect to accompany a large sushi order. In a nondescript part of Pacific Beach (nearer to I-5 than the ocean), Sushi Ota hides in the rear of a minimall—but don't let this discourage you.

INEXPENSIVE

Firehouse Beach Cafe. 722 Grand Ave., Pacific Beach. ☎ **858/272-1999.** Reservations recommended on weekends. Main courses $6–$13. AE, DISC, MC, V. Sun–Thurs 7am–9pm; Fri–Sat 7am–10pm. Free parking. Bus: 34 or 34A. AMERICAN.

Ceiling fans stir the air in this cheerful, comfortably crowded place, and there's pleasant rooftop dining with an ocean view if you're lucky enough to snag a seat.

Located just off the Pacific Beach boardwalk, the cafe sees a lot of foot traffic and socializing locals. Those in the know go for great breakfasts—including Mexican-style eggs and breakfast burritos, French toast, and omelets—or during happy hour (from 4 to 6pm) for bargain prices on drinks and finger-lickin' appetizers. The rest of the menu is adequate, running the gamut from fish tacos to Tex-Mex fajitas to lasagna and all-American burgers.

LA JOLLA
EXPENSIVE

Cafe Japengo. 8960 University Center Lane (at Hyatt Regency La Jolla). ☎ **858/450-3355.** Reservations recommended. Main courses $12-$20. AE, DC, DISC, MC, V. Mon–Thurs 11:30am–2:30pm and 5–10pm; Fri 11:30am–2:30pm and 5–10:30pm; Sat 5–10:30pm; Sun 5–10pm (sushi bar until 11pm Mon–Thurs and 11:30pm Fri–Sat). Valet parking $3, validated self-parking. From I-5, take La Jolla Village Dr. east. PACIFIC RIM/SUSHI.

With subdued lighting and a highly stylized Asian atmosphere, this always-packed restaurant is the best of several attached to the Golden Triangle's behemoth Hyatt Regency. The people watching is great, but even better is Japengo's Pacific Rim fusion cuisine that incorporates South American and even European touches. Some, like the potstickers in tangy coriander-mint sauce or lemongrass-marinated swordfish, are superb; others, like the seared ahi "Napoleon," suffer from extra ingredients that just make the dish fussy. Sushi here is the same way; Japengo features the very finest and freshest fish, but churns out enormously popular "specialty" rolls (combination rolls wrapped in even more ingredients, often drenched in sauce and garnished even further) of their own creation. These dramatic and colorfully presented inventions are enormously popular, but sushi purists will be happiest sticking to the basics.

✪ George's at the Cove. Prospect St. ☎ **858/454-4244.** Reservations recommended. Main courses $21–$31. AE, DC, DISC, MC, V. Mon–Thurs 11:30am–2:30 and 5:30–10pm; Fri 11:30am–2:30pm and 5–10:30pm; Sat 11:30am–3pm and 5–10:30pm; Sun 11:30am–3pm and 5–10pm. Valet parking $5-$6. CALIFORNIA.

A beloved La Jolla tradition, George's wins consistent praise for impeccable service, gorgeous views of the cove, and outstanding California cuisine. The menu, in typical San Diego fashion, presents many inventive seafood options. Appetizers range from baked Carlsbad mussels to phyllo-wrapped prawns flavored with cumin and ginger; the healthful smoked chicken, broccoli, and black-bean soup is a mainstay. Main courses combine many flavors with a practiced artistry; apple-wood-smoked and cedar-roasted king salmon is paired with crisp polenta and subtle nuances of ginger, and tenderloin fillet is wrapped in bacon and finished with a Gorgonzola-tinged reduction. While main courses at dinner can get pricey, George's offers a seasonally composed five-course tasting menu for around $34 per person. George's can also be a scenic and reasonable lunch option, and there's an informal Ocean Terrace Cafe upstairs.

✪ Top O' the Cove. 1216 Prospect St. ☎ **858/454-7779.** www.topofthecove.com. Reservations recommended. Jackets suggested for men at dinner. Main courses $25–$32; Sun brunch $18.50. AE, CB, DC, MC, V. Mon–Sat 11:30am–10:30pm; Sun 10:30am–10:30pm. Valet parking $5. CONTINENTAL.

Always voted "most romantic" in annual diner surveys, pretty Top O' the Cove is traditionally where San Diegans go for special occasions, banking that its timeless elegance will enhance the evening's mood. Inside the historic cottage, fireplaces glow on chilly evenings, and a gazebo and patio make the perfect setting for balmy summer dining or Sunday brunch. The menu is peppered with French names, but the cuisine has distinct California overtones, often borrowing Asian flavors (blackened ahi sashimi, salmon spring rolls, pan-seared tuna with wasabi). Classic standouts include green peppercorn tenderloin dressed with cognac and cream, plus fresh swordfish prepared differently each day. Sorbet is served between courses. Lunch is lighter, with salads and sandwiches joining selections from the dinner menu.

✪ **Trattoria Acqua.** 1298 Prospect St., on Coast Walk, La Jolla. ☎ **858/454-0709.** www.trattoriaacqua.com. Reservations recommended. Main courses $13–$22. AE, MC, V. Daily 11:30am–2:30pm; Sun–Thurs 5–9:30pm, Fri–Sat 5–10:30pm. Validated self-parking available. ITALIAN.

Nestled into tiled patio terraces close enough to catch ocean breezes, this excellent Italian spot's relaxed ambiance evokes a romantic Tuscan villa. A mixed crowd of suits and well-heeled couples gather to enjoy expertly prepared seasonal dishes; every table starts with bread served with an indescribably pungent Mediterranean spread. Acqua's pastas are as good as it gets—rich and heady flavor combinations like spinach, chard, and four-cheese gnocchi, or veal and mortadella tortellini in fennel cream sauce—and are all available as appetizers or main courses. Other specialties include *saltimboca con funghi* (veal scallopine with sage, prosciutto, and a forest-mushroom sauce), and traditional meat-and-white-bean cassoulet. The well-chosen wine list has received *Wine Spectator* accolades several years in a row.

MODERATE

✪ **Brockton Villa.** 1235 Coast Blvd. (across from La Jolla Cove). ☎ **858/454-7393.** Reservations accepted (call by Thurs for Sun brunch). Breakfast $4–$7.25; dinner main courses $10–$20. AE, DISC, MC, V. Mon 8am–3pm; Tues–Sun 8am–9pm (later in summer). BREAKFAST/CALIFORNIA.

Located in a well-restored and much-loved 1894 beach bungalow, this charming cafe has a history as intriguing as its varied, eclectic menu. The biggest buzz is at breakfast, which features inventive dishes such as a soufflé like "Coast Toast" (the house take on French toast), Greek "steamers" (eggs scrambled with an espresso steamer, then mixed with feta cheese, tomato, and basil), and dozens of coffee drinks. Lunch stars homemade soups and salads, plus unusual sandwiches like turkey meat loaf on toasted sourdough bread with spicy tomato-mint chutney. The dinner menu is constantly expanding, and includes salmon *en croute* (wrapped with prosciutto, Gruyère, and sage with a grainy mustard sauce) plus pastas, stews, and grilled meats. Steep stairs from the street limit access for wheelchair users.

Spice & Rice Thai Kitchen. 7734 Girard Ave. ☎ **858/456-0466.** Reservations accepted. Main courses $7–$13. AE, MC, V. Mon–Thurs 11am–3pm and 5–10pm; Fri 11am–3pm and 5–11pm; Sat 5–11pm; Sun 5–10pm. THAI.

This stylish Thai restaurant is a couple of blocks from the village's tourist crush—far enough to ensure effortless parking in front of its romantic patio. The excellent food here includes expert renditions of the classics like pad Thai, satay, curry, and glazed duck. The so-called starters listed can often sound as good as the entrees—consider making a grazing meal out of house specialties like "Gold Bags" (minced pork, vegetables, and herbs wrapped in crispy rice paper and served with earthy plum sauce) or minced roast duck spiced with chilies and lime juice; spicy calamari is flavored with ginger, cilantro, lime, and chili sauce. This insider's secret is busy at lunch, but quieter at dinnertime.

INEXPENSIVE

✪ **The Cottage.** 7702 Fay Ave. (at Kline). ☎ **619/454-8409.** www.cottagelajolla.com. Reservations accepted for dinner only. Breakfast and lunch $5–$7; main courses $7–$12. AE, DISC, MC, V. Daily year-round 7:30am–3pm; May 15–Sept 30 only: Tues–Sat 5–9:30pm. BREAKFAST/CALIFORNIA.

La Jolla's best—and friendliest—breakfast is served at this turn-of-the-century bungalow on a sunny village street corner. Newly modernized, the cottage is light and airy inside, but most diners opt for tables outside, where a charming white picket fence encloses the trellis-shaded brick patio. Omelets and egg dishes feature Mediterranean, Asian, or classic American touches; the Cottage bakes its own muffins, breads, and desserts. While breakfast dishes are served all day, toward lunch the kitchen begins turning out freshly made soups, light meals, and sandwiches—all incorporating a fresh, healthful approach. Summer dinners are a delight, particularly on a balmy seaside night—the ambiance is charming.

CORONADO

If you're in the mood for a special-occasion meal that'll knock your socks off, consider **Azzura Point** in Loews Coronado Bay Resort (☎ 619/424-4477), or the **Prince of Wales Grill** at the Hotel del Coronado (☎ 619/522-8818). Mexican fare (gringo-style, but well practiced) is served on the island at popular **Miguel's Cocina,** inside El Cordova hotel (☎ 619/437-4237).

EXPENSIVE

Chez Loma. 1132 Loma (off Orange Ave.). ☎ **619/435-0661.** Reservations recommended. Main courses $18–$26. AE, DC, MC, V. Daily 5–10pm; Sun 10am–2pm. Bus: 901. FRENCH.

You'd be hard-pressed to find a more romantic dining spot than this intimate Victorian cottage filled with antiques and subdued candlelight. Tables are scattered throughout the house and on the enclosed garden terrace; an upstairs wine salon, reminiscent of a Victorian parlor, is a cozy spot for coffee or conversation. Among the creative entrees are salmon with smoked-tomato vinaigrette and roasted duckling with green peppercorn sauce. Follow dinner with a creamy crème caramel or Kahlùa crème brûlée. Chez Loma's service is attentive, the herb rolls addictive, and early birds enjoy specially priced meals.

Peohe's. 1201 First St. (Ferry Landing Marketplace). ☎ **619/437-4474.** Reservations recommended. Main courses $7–$15 lunch, $16–$29 dinner. AE, CB, DC, DISC, MC, V. Mon–Thurs 11:30am–2:30pm and 5:30–9pm; Fri 11:30am–2:30pm and 5:30–10pm; Sat 11:30am–2:30pm and 5–10pm; Sun 10:30am–2:30pm and 4:30–9pm. Bus: 901, 904. PACIFIC RIM/SEAFOOD.

With an over-the-top Polynesian decor that Disneyland would be proud of, Peohe's is definitely touristy and definitely overpriced—but there's no denying the awesome view across the bay or the excellent Hawaiian-style seafood and Pacific Rim–accented cuisine. Dinner main courses include the always-acclaimed crunchy coconut shrimp and the island-style halibut sautéed with banana, macadamia nuts, and Frangelico liqueur. Lunchtime variations include more casual sandwiches and salads, and the tropical-fantasy desserts are delectably rich. For those who love theme restaurants and Polynesian kitsch, Peohe's is a worthwhile splurge.

MODERATE

Bay Beach Cafe. 1201 First St. (in the Ferry Landing Marketplace). ☎ **619/435-4900.** Reservations recommended for dinner on weekends. Main courses $9–$18, pub menu $6–$10. AE, DISC, MC, V. Mon–Fri 7–10:30am, 11am–4pm, and 5–10:30pm; Sat–Sun 7–11:30am, noon–4pm, and 5–10:30pm. Free parking. Bus: 901 or 904. AMERICAN/SEAFOOD.

Contrary to its name, this loud and friendly gathering place isn't on the beach at all, but enjoys a prime perch on San Diego Bay. Diners gaze endlessly at the city skyline, which is dramatic by day and breathtaking at night; the cafe is quite popular at happy

A Coronado Cocktail-Hour Tip

If you're longing for some great appetizers—more sophisticated than popcorn shrimp and potato skins—then the new **Chameleon Cafe & Lizard Lounge**, 1301 Orange Ave., Coronado (☎ **619/437-6677**), is your answer. The latest venture of chef Ken Irvine (the local superstar of Chez Loma fame), this casual and eclectic eatery is half cocktail lounge; fitting, since the menu is half appetizers. The "first plates" range in price from $4 to $9, and are generously sized and suitable for sharing. Relax—and watch the activity along Orange Avenue—while nibbling on Asian delicacies (lobster/crab potstickers, smoked salmon and avocado sushi), Southwestern spice (goat-cheese tamale, pork empanada), or Mediterranean standards (grilled pizzas with smoked chicken and fontina cheese or portobello mushrooms). The bar features premium vodkas and aged tequilas; we recommend eschewing the restaurant's pricier main courses and having a "grazing" meal in the bar, which stays open from lunchtime until closing.

---

hour, when the setting sun glimmers on downtown's mirrored high-rises. The ferry docks at a wooden pier a few steps away, discharging passengers into this New England fishing village–themed complex of gift shops and restaurants. At the Bay Beach Cafe, the food takes a back seat to the view, but the pub menu of burgers, sandwiches, salads, and appetizers is inexpensive and satisfying.

INEXPENSIVE

Primavera Pastry Caffé. 956 Orange Ave. ☎ **619/435-4191.** Main courses $4–$6. No credit cards. Daily 6:30am–6pm. Bus: 901. SANDWICHES/LIGHT FARE.

This fantastic little cafe is the best of its kind on the island. In addition to fresh-roasted coffee and espresso drinks, they serve up omelets and other breakfast treats (until 1:30pm), burgers and deli sandwiches on their own delicious bread, and a daily fresh soup. It's the kind of spot where half the customers are greeted by name; locals rave about the "Yacht Club" sandwich, a croissant filled with yellowfin tuna, and the breakfast croissant, topped with scrambled ham and eggs and cheddar cheese. See if you can resist Primavera's fat, gooey, glazed cinnamon buns.

5 The Main Attractions: The Zoo, Sea World & the Wild Animal Park

✪ **San Diego Zoo.** 2920 Zoo Dr. (off Park Blvd.), Balboa Park. ☎ **619/234-3153.** TDD 619/233-9639. www.sandiegozoo.org. Admission $16 adults, $7 children 3–11, free for military in uniform. Deluxe package (including admission, guided bus tour, and round-trip skyfari aerial tram) $24 adults, $21.60 seniors 60 and over, $13 children. DISC, MC, V. Daily 9am–4pm; grounds close at 5pm; extended summer hours (9am–9pm, grounds close at 10pm). Combination Zoo/Wild Animal Park Package $35.15 adults, $20.75 children; includes deluxe package at zoo and admission to the WAP and is valid for 5 days from date of purchase. DISC, MC, V. Bus: 7/7B.

More than 4,000 animals reside at this world-famous zoo, founded in 1916 with a handful of animals originally brought here for the 1915–16 Panama-California International Exposition. The zoo's founder was Dr. Harry Wegeforth, a local physician and lifelong animal lover who once braved the fury of an injured tiger in order to toss needed medicine into its mouth while it was roaring.

Today, two giant pandas on loan from China (see the box "Pandamonium," below) are the big attention-getters, but the zoo has many other rare and exotic species: cuddly koalas from Australia, long-billed kiwis from New Zealand, wild Przewalski's horses from Mongolia, lowland gorillas from Africa, and giant tortoises from the Galapagos. The usual lions, elephants, giraffes, and tigers are present, too, not to mention a great number of tropical birds. Most of the animals are housed in barless, moated enclosures (with names like Polar Bear Plunge, Gorilla Tropics, and Hippo Beach) that resemble their natural habitats. The zoo is also an accredited botanical garden, representing more than 6,000 species of flora from many climate zones, all installed to help simulate native environments for the animals that live here.

The **Children's Zoo** is scaled to a youngster's viewpoint. There's a nursery with baby animals and a petting area where kids can cuddle up to sheep, goats, and the like. The resident wombat is a special favorite here.

The zoo offers two types of **bus tours;** both provide a narrated overview and show you about 75% of the park. The 35-minute guided bus tour completes a circuit around the zoo; it costs $4 for adults and $3 for kids 3 to 11 (there's a daily tour in Spanish at noon). Or you might opt to take the Kangaroo Bus, which for $8 for adults and $5 for children provides unlimited use; you can get on and off the bus as many times as you desire at any of the eight stops, and even complete the circuit more than once. You can get an aerial perspective via the **Skyfari,** which costs $1 per person each way. Packages are available, which include zoo admission, bus tour, and Skyfari Tramway.

The zoo offers wheelchair and stroller rentals and numerous food outlets, including a delightful restaurant called Albert's.

Insider tip: If you're planning on going to the zoo and Wild Animal Park, you might want to consider buying a Zoological Society Membership, which costs $68 a year for two adults living in the same household. The adult/couple membership gives each cardholder unlimited entrance to the zoo and Wild Animal Park, plus additional free and discounted admissions and bus tickets, as well as a subscription to *Zoo News* magazine. A Koala Club membership for a child costs $15 and provides unlimited entry for a year.

Sea World. 500 Sea World Dr., Mission Bay. ☎ **858/226-3901;** TDD for the deaf 858/226-3907. www.seaworld.com. Admission $38 adults, $29 children 3–11, free for children 2 and under. DISC, JCB, MC, V. Parking $6 per car, $3 per motorcycle, $8 per RV. Guided 90-min. behind-the-scenes tours, $8 adults, $7 children 3–11. Ticket sales stop half an hour before closing. June–Aug daily 9am–10pm; Sept–May daily 10am–5pm. Bus: 9. By car from I-5, take Sea World Dr. exit; from I-8, take W. Mission Bay Dr. exit to Sea World Dr.

Sea World is one of the best-promoted attractions in California. The 150-acre, multi-million-dollar aquatic playground is a zoo and showplace for marine mammals, made politically correct with a nominally "educational" atmosphere. At its heart, Sea World is a family entertainment center where the performers are dolphins, otters, sea lions, walruses, and seals. Several successive 4-ton black-and-white killer whales, all named Shamu, have functioned as the park's mascot. Shows are presented continuously throughout the day, while visitors rotate to various theaters to watch the performances.

The 2-acre hands-on area called **Shamu's Happy Harbor** encourages kids to handle everything, including a pretend pirate ship with plenty of netted towers, tube crawls, slides, and chances to get wet. The newest attraction is **Wild Arctic,** a virtual-reality trip to the frozen north. Other draws include **Baywatch at Sea World,** a water-ski show named for the popular TV show, and **Shamu Backstage,** which makes it possible for visitors to get up close and personal with killer whales.

The **Dolphin Interaction Program** creates an opportunity for people to interact with bottlenose dolphins. Although this program stops short of allowing you to swim

Pandamonium

Two giant pandas from China, Shi Shi (a 230-pound male) and Bai Yun (a young female), finally arrived at the San Diego Zoo in late 1996 after 3 years of intense negotiation between the U.S. Department of the Interior, the Wolong Giant Panda Conservation Centre, and the Chinese government. These two are the only pair of giant pandas in the United States (a single male is housed at the National Zoo in Washington, D.C.). In total, only about 15 giant pandas live in zoos outside of China and North Korea.

Giant pandas, who live in high-altitude bamboo and coniferous forests, are among the rarest mammals in the world—fewer than 1,000 remain in the wild. As part of the agreement to get the pandas here, the San Diego Zoo agreed to contribute $1 million each year to wild-panda habitat-protection projects in China, where the government hopes to double the number of existing panda preserves and establish protected wildlife corridors connecting these areas.

You needn't worry that Shi Shi and Bai Yun will be gone before you get here: The loan is for a period of 12 years. During that time, scientific study of their breeding and behavior patterns will take place. (Any baby pandas born at the zoo will belong to the People's Republic of China.)

Giant pandas are related to both bears and raccoons. They are bear-like in shape, with striking black-and-white markings, and they have unique front paws that enable them to grasp stalks of bamboo. This plant makes up about 95% of their diet, and they eat 20 to 40 pounds of food every day. This takes them 10 to 16 hours, so there's a pretty good chance that while you're watching them they'll be munching away.

Because of the enormous popularity of this exhibit, the zoo provides a panda-viewing hot line (☎ **888/MY PANDA**).

with the dolphins, you will wade waist-deep into the water and have plenty of time to stroke the mammals and give commands like the trainers. This 2-hour program (1 hour of education and instruction, 15 minutes of wet-suit fitting, and 45 minutes in the water with the dolphins) costs $125 per person, which includes a second Sea World admission within a week. Space is limited to eight people per day, so advance reservations are required. Participants must be 13 years old or older.

Although Sea World is best known as Shamu's home, the facility also plays an important role in rescuing and rehabilitating animals found beached along the San Diego coast—more than 300 seals, sea lions, marine birds, and dolphins in a recent year. Following the successful rescue and 1998 release of a young California gray whale, Sea World turned its attention to the manatee, an unusual aquatic mammal rarely seen outside Florida's tropical waters. At press time, the manatees were on display at the park.

✪ **Wild Animal Park.** 15500 San Pasqual Valley Rd., Escondido. ☎ **760/747-8702.** TDD 760/738-5067. www.sandiegozoo.org. Admission $19.95 adults, $17.95 seniors 60 and over, $12.95 children 3–11, free for children 2 and under and military in uniform. Combination Zoo/Wild Animal Park Package $35.15 adults, $20.75 children; includes deluxe package at zoo and admission to the WAP and is valid for 5 days from date of purchase. DISC, MC, V. Daily 9am–4pm (grounds close at 5pm); extended hours during summer and the Festival of Lights in December. Parking $3 per car. See "Insider Tip" under San Diego Zoo, above. Take I-15 to Via Rancho Pkwy.; follow signs from here for about 3 miles.

San Diego Attractions

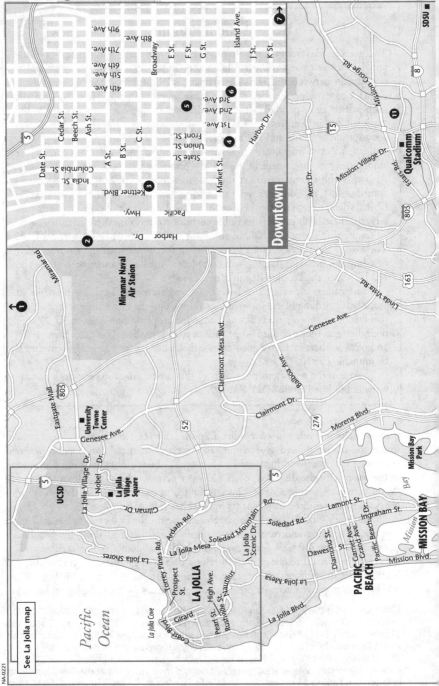

NA-0221

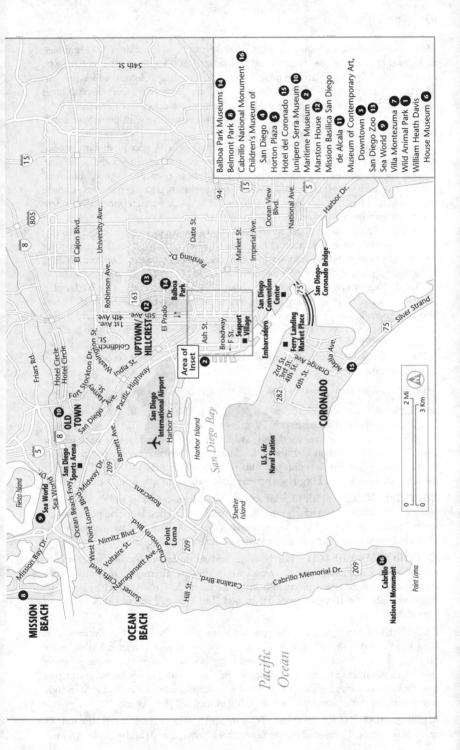

Balboa Park Museums 14
Belmont Park 8
Cabrillo National Monument 16
Children's Museum of
San Diego 4
Horton Plaza 5
Hotel del Coronado 15
Junípero Serra Museum 10
Maritime Museum 2
Marston House 12
Mission Basílica San Diego
de Alcalá 11
Museum of Contemporary Art,
Downtown 3
San Diego Zoo 13
Sea World 9
Villa Montezuma 7
Wild Animal Park 1
William Heath Davis
House Museum 6

Many zoos could learn a lesson from the Wild Animal Park: More than 3,000 animals, many of them endangered species, roam freely over 1,800 acres—it's the humans who are enclosed. This living arrangement encourages breeding colonies, so it's not surprising that more than 75 white rhinoceroses have been born here. Several other species that had vanished from the wilds have been reintroduced to their natural habitats from stocks bred here. The park is also a botanical preserve with more than 2 million plants, including 300 species and subspecies.

The best way to see the animals is by riding the 5-mile **Wgasa Bush Line monorail** (included in the price of admission); for the best views, sit on the right side. During the 50-minute ride, as you pass through areas resembling Africa and Asia, you'll learn interesting tidbits (did you know that rhinos are susceptible to sunburn and mosquito bites?). Trains leave every 20 minutes; you can watch informative videos while you wait in the stations.

On the 1¾-mile **Kilimanjaro Safari Walk,** you'll see tigers, elephants, and cheetahs up close, as well as the Australian rain forest and views of East Africa. There are three animal shows a day, and you also won't want to miss the petting kraal, Lorikeet Landing, Mombasa Lagoon, and the WAP's newest exhibit, Heart of Africa—a walking safari.

Photo Caravans take place from May through September on Wednesday, Thursday, Saturday, and Sunday, costing $60 or $85 (depending on the tour). There's also an intriguing summer-only overnight camp-out program called **Roar and Snore.** To request information by mail, call ☎ **760/738-5049;** reservations can be made by calling ☎ **800/934-CAMP.**

Stroller and wheelchair rentals are available. Take a jacket along; it can get cold in the open-air monorail.

6 Beaches

San Diego County is blessed with 70 miles of sandy coastline and more than 30 beaches that attract surfers, snorkelers, swimmers, and sunbathers. In summer, the beaches teem with locals and visitors alike. The rest of the year, they are popular places to walk and jog, and surfers don wet suits to pursue their passion. The following are some of our favorite San Diego beaches, arranged geographically from south to north.

IMPERIAL BEACH   Half an hour south of San Diego by car or trolley, and only a few minutes from the Mexican border, lies Imperial Beach. Besides being popular with surfers, it hosts the Annual U.S. Open Sandcastle Competition in August, with world-class sand creations ranging from sea scenes to dragons to dinosaurs.

✪ **CORONADO BEACH**   Lovely, wide, and sparkling white, this beach is conducive to strolling and lingering, especially in the late afternoon. It fronts Ocean Boulevard and is especially pretty in front of the Hotel del Coronado. The islands visible from here, but 18 miles away, are named "Los Coronados," and they belong to Mexico.

OCEAN BEACH   The northern end of Ocean Beach Park is officially known as **Dog Beach,** and is one of only two in San Diego where your pooch can roam freely on the sand (and frolic with several dozen other people's pooches). Surfers generally congregate around the Ocean Beach Pier, where rip currents are strong and discourage most swimmers from venturing out beyond waist-depth. Facilities at the beach include rest rooms, showers, picnic tables, and plenty of metered parking lots.

MISSION BAY PARK   In this 4,600-acre aquatic playground, you'll discover 27 miles of bay front, 17 miles of oceanfront beaches, picnic areas, children's playgrounds,

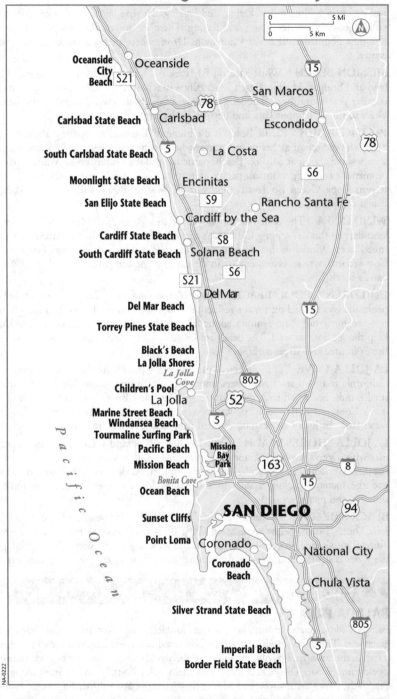

San Diego & North County Beaches

Oceanside
City S21
Beach

Oceanside

Carlsbad State Beach

Carlsbad

San Marcos

Escondido

South Carlsbad State Beach

La Costa

Moonlight State Beach

Encinitas

San Elijo State Beach

S9

Rancho Santa Fe

Cardiff by the Sea

Cardiff State Beach

South Cardiff State Beach

S8

Solana Beach

S21

S6

Del Mar

Del Mar Beach

Torrey Pines State Beach

Black's Beach

La Jolla Shores

La Jolla Cove

Children's Pool

La Jolla

Marine Street Beach

Windansea Beach

Tourmaline Surfing Park

Pacific Beach

Mission
Bay
Park

Mission Beach

Bonita Cove

Ocean Beach

SAN DIEGO

Sunset Cliffs

Point Loma

Coronado

National City

Coronado
Beach

Chula Vista

Silver Strand State Beach

Imperial Beach

Border Field State Beach

Pacific Ocean

0   5 Mi

0   5 Km

15

78

78

S6

15

805

52

5

163

15

8

94

805

5

NA-0222

and paths for biking, roller-skating, and jogging. The bay lends itself to windsurfing, sailing, jet-skiing, water-skiing, and fishing. There are dozens of access points; one of the most popular is off I-5 at Clairemont Drive, where there's a visitor information center.

MISSION BEACH   While Mission Bay Park is a body of salt water surrounded by land and bridges, Mission Beach is actually a beach on the Pacific Ocean. Surfing is popular year-round here. The long beach and boardwalk extend from Pacific Beach Drive south to Belmont Park and beyond to the jetty.

PACIFIC BEACH   Pacific Beach is the home of **Tourmaline Surfing Park,** where the sport's old guard gather to surf waters where swimmers are prohibited; and there's always some action at Mission Beach, particularly along **Ocean Front Walk,** a paved promenade featuring a human parade akin to that at L.A.'s Venice Beach boardwalk. It runs along Ocean Boulevard (just west of Mission Boulevard), north of Pacific Beach Drive.

WINDANSEA   The fabled locale of Tom Wolfe's *Pump House Gang,* Windansea is legendary to this day among California's surf elite. Reached via Bonair Street (at Neptune Place), Windansea has no facilities, and street parking is first-come, first-served. Come to surf, watch surfers, or soak in the camaraderie and party atmosphere of Windansea locals.

CHILDREN'S POOL BEACH   Much of the sand near the point of La Jolla's peninsula is cordoned off for the resident sea-lion population; the rest is inhabited by curious shutterbugs and families taking advantage of the same calm conditions that keep the sea lions around. The beach is located at Coast Boulevard and Jenner Street; there's limited free street parking.

LA JOLLA COVE   The protected, calm waters—praised as the clearest along the California coast—attract swimmers, snorkelers, scuba divers, and families. There's a small sandy beach, and on the cliffs above, the Ellen Browning Scripps Park. The cove's "look but don't touch" policy protects the colorful marine life in this Underwater Park. La Jolla Cove can be accessed from Coast Boulevard.

LA JOLLA SHORES BEACH   The wide, flat mile of sand at La Jolla Shores is popular with joggers, swimmers, and beginning body and board surfers, as well as with families. Weekend crowds can be enormous, though, quickly occupying both the sand and the metered parking spaces in the beach's lot. Facilities include rest rooms, showers, and picnic areas.

BLACK'S BEACH   The area's unofficial (and illegal) nude beach, it lies north of La Jolla Shores Beach, below some steep cliffs. Black's isn't easy to reach—take North Torrey Pines Road, park at the Glider Port, and walk down from there. *Note:* Although the water is shallow and pleasant for wading, this area is known for its rip currents.

7 Exploring the Area

BALBOA PARK

Balboa Park is one of the nation's largest, loveliest, and most important municipal greenbelts. This is no simple city park; it boasts walkways, gardens, historical buildings, a restaurant, an ornate pavilion with one of the world's largest outdoor organs, and the world-famous San Diego Zoo (see "The Main Attractions," above). Stroll along El Prado, the park's main street, and admire the distinctive Spanish/Mediterranean buildings, which house an amazing array of museums. Filled on weekends with locals, El

Prado is also popular with musicians and other performers whose busking provides an entertaining backdrop.

Entry to the park is free, but most of its museums have admission charges and varying open hours. A free tram will transport you around the park. Get details from the **Balboa Park Visitor Center,** located in the House of Hospitality (☎ **619/ 239-0512**). Below are the highlights:

✪ **San Diego Aerospace Museum,** 2001 Pan American Plaza (☎ **619/234-8291;** www.aerospacemuseum.org). Great achievers and achievements in the history of aviation and aerospace are celebrated by this superb collection of historical aircraft and related artifacts, including art, models, dioramas, and films.

Museum of Art, 1450 El Prado (☎ **619/232-7931;** www.sdmart.com). The impressive painting and sculpture collections here include outstanding Italian Renaissance and Dutch and Spanish baroque art. Exhibits in the Grant–Munger Gallery include works by Monet, Toulouse-Lautrec, Renoir, Pissarro, and van Gogh; in the Fitch Gallery is El Greco's *Penitent St. Peter,* and in the Gluck Gallery hang Modigliani's *Boy with Blue Eyes* and Braque's *Coquelicots.*

✪ **Museum of Photographic Arts,** 1649 El Prado (☎ **619/238-7559**). One of the finest museums in the city occupies an imitation Spanish baroque building that served as part of Charles Foster Kane's Xanadu in the film *Citizen Kane.* It displays a wide range of historic and contemporary work and has made a commitment to issue-oriented photography.

✪ **Natural History Museum,** 1788 El Prado (☎ **619/232-3821;** www. sdnhm.org). The best exhibits display the plants, animals, and minerals of the San Diego/Baja California region. There's also a Foucault pendulum, a seismograph, and a life-size allosaurus skeleton. The Hall of Desert Ecology features a discovery lab, with living desert denizens.

✪ **Reuben H. Fleet Science Center,** 1875 El Prado (☎ **619/238-1233;** www. rhfleet.org). Easily the park's busiest museum, the Science Center features five galleries with hands-on exhibits as intriguing for grown-ups as for kids, and in 1998 it debuted SciTours, a simulator ride that voyages into space and the worlds of science and biology. Equally popular is the OMNIMAX movie theater, surrounding viewers with breathtaking adventure travelogues. You can avoid waiting in line by buying tickets in advance.

✪ **Museum of Man,** 1350 El Prado (☎ **619/239-2001**; www.museumofman. org). This museum is devoted to the sociology and anthropology of the peoples of North and South America, and includes life-size replicas of a dozen varieties of Homo sapiens.

San Diego Automotive Museum, 2080 Pan American Plaza (☎ **619/231-2886**). Check out that classic Bentley and the rare 1948 Tucker, among other gems that appear in a changing array of shows featuring classic, antique, and exotic cars.

✪ **Botanical Building,** El Prado. More than a thousand varieties of tropical and flowering plants are sheltered within this graceful structure, and the lily pond out front attracts the occasional street performer.

Hall of Champions, 1649 El Prado (☎ **619/234-2544**). Sports fans will want to check out this museum, which highlights dozens of different professional and amateur sports and athletes.

Japanese Friendship Garden, 2216 Pan America Rd. (☎ **619/232-2780**). Although parts of the garden are still being developed, visitors can sample the tranquillity of traditional elements like a koi-filled stream, pastoral meadow, and ancient *sekitei* (sand-and-stone garden).

Marston House Museum, 3525 Seventh Ave. at Upas Street, in the northwest corner of the park (☎ **619/298-3142**). Designed by local architect Irving Gill, this fine example of Craftsman-style architecture exhibits antique and reproduction period furniture.

✪ **Model Railroad Museum,** 1649 El Prado (☎ **619/696-0199**; www. sdmodelrailroadm.com). Four scale-model railroads depict southern California's transportation history and terrain. There's a terrific gift shop, plus multimedia exhibits and hands-on Lionel trains for kids.

Museum of San Diego History, 1649 El Prado (☎ **619/232-6203**). Photographs and other changing exhibits tell the city's story.

Spreckels Organ Pavilion (☎ **619/226-0819**). The ornate pavilion houses a fantastic organ with more than 4,000 individual pipes. Free concerts are given Sundays at 2pm year-round and on summer evenings.

Timken Museum of Art, 1500 El Prado (☎ **619/239-5548;** http://gort.ucsd. edu/sj/timken). On display here is the Putnam Foundation's collection of American and European paintings, including works by Boucher, Rembrandt, and Brueghel. The private gallery also exhibits a rare collection of Russian icons and 19th-century American paintings.

Mingei International Museum, 1439 El Prado (☎ **619/239-0003**). Its name means "art of the people" in Japanese, and it offers changing exhibitions celebrating human creativity with textiles, costumes, jewelry, toys, pottery, paintings, and sculpture, all employing natural materials. This is one of only two major museums in the United States devoted to crafts on a worldwide scale (the other is in Santa Fe).

Christmas on the Prado takes place in Balboa Park from 5 to 9pm on the first Friday and Saturday nights in December. This popular event features free entry to all museums, carol singing in the Spreckels Organ Pavilion, holiday decorations, and various food booths.

MORE ATTRACTIONS IN & AROUND SAN DIEGO

✪ **Cabrillo National Monument.** 1800 Cabrillo Memorial Dr., Point Loma. ☎ **619/ 557-5450.** www.nps.gov/cabr. Admission $5 per vehicle, $2 for walk-ins, free for children 16 and younger and American citizens age 62 and older who have a National Parks Service Golden Age Passport. Daily 9am–5:15pm. Take I-5 or I-8 to Calif. 209/Rosecrans St.; follow signs to the monument. Bus: 26.

Enjoy stunning views while you learn about California history at this monument commemorating Juan Rodríguez Cabrillo, the European discoverer of America's West Coast. At the restored Old Point Loma Lighthouse, you'll be treated to a sweeping vista of the ocean, bays, islands, mountains, valleys, and plains that make up San Diego. Visit between mid-December and mid-March and you can see the annual California gray-whale migration from a glassed-in observatory; films and other educational exhibits on the whales are offered as well. A road leads to tide pools that beg for exploration.

Children's Museum of San Diego. 200 W. Island Ave. ☎ **619/233-KIDS.** Admission $6 for adults and children 2 and over, $3 for seniors, free for children under 2. Tues–Fri 10am–3pm; Sat–Sun 10am–4pm. Trolley: Convention Center stop; the museum is a block away. All-day parking across the street for about $3.

This interactive museum encourages hands-on participation and provides ongoing supervised activities, as well as a special celebration and changing exhibits every month. A big draw for kids ages 2 to 10 is the indoor and outdoor art studio. There's also a theater with costumes for budding actors to don.

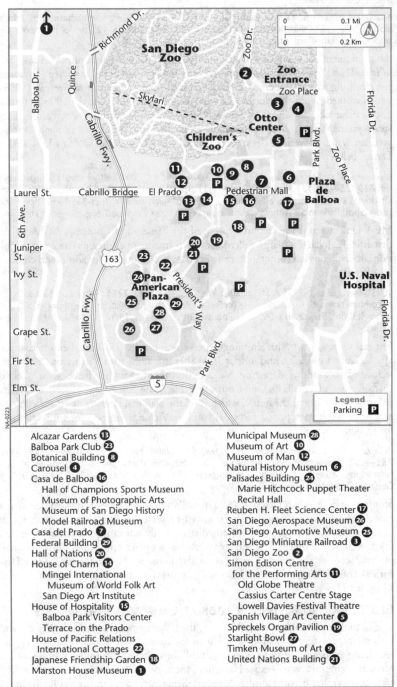

San Diego Zoo

Richmond Dr.

Zoo Dr.

Zoo Entrance

Zoo Place

Quince

Balboa Dr.

Skyfari

Cabrillo Fwy.

Otto Center

Children's Zoo

Florida Dr.

Park Blvd.

Zoo Place

Laurel St.

Cabrillo Bridge

El Prado

Pedestrian Mall

Plaza de Balboa

6th Ave.

Juniper St.

163

Ivy St.

Pan-American Plaza

President's Way

U.S. Naval Hospital

Grape St.

Cabrillo Fwy.

Park Blvd.

Fir St.

Florida Dr.

Elm St.

5

NA-0223

Maritime Museum. 1306 N. Harbor Dr. ☎ **619/234-9153.** www.sdmaritime.com. Admission $5 adults, $4 seniors over 62 and teens 13–17, $2 children 6–12, free for children 5 and under. Daily 9am–8pm. Bus: 2. Trolley: America Plaza.

This unique museum consists of a trio of fine ships: the full-rigged merchant ship *Star of India* (1863), whose impressive masts are an integral part of the San Diego cityscape; the gleaming white San Francisco–Oakland steam-powered ferryboat *Berkeley* (1898), which worked round-the-clock to carry people to safety following the 1906 San Francisco earthquake; and the sleek *Medea* (1904), one of the world's few remaining large steam yachts. You can board and explore each vessel, and from April through October you can watch movies on deck (see "Movies, San Diego Style" in "San Diego After Dark," below).

Museum of Contemporary Art, Downtown (MCA). 1001 Kettner Blvd. (at Broadway). ☎ **619/234-1001.** Admission $2 adults; $1 students, military with ID, and seniors; free for children 12 and under. Free first Tues and Sun of each month. Tues–Sat 10am–5pm; Sun noon–5pm. Parking $2 with validation at America Plaza Complex. Trolley: America Plaza.

MCA Downtown is the second location of the Museum of Contemporary Art—the first is in La Jolla. Two large galleries and two smaller ones present changing exhibitions of distinguished contemporary artists. Lectures and tours for adults and children are offered.

Villa Montezuma. 1925 K St. (at 20th Ave.). ☎ **619/239-2211.** Admission $3 adults, $5 in combination with Marston House (in Balboa Park), free for children 12 and under. Sat–Sun noon–4:30pm. Drive along K St. to the house. Bus: 3, 3A, 4, 5, 16, or 105 to Market and Imperial sts.

Just east of downtown, this stunning mansion was built in 1887 for then internationally acclaimed musician and author Jesse Shepard. Lush with Victoriana, it features stained-glass windows depicting Mozart, Beethoven, Sappho, Rubens, St. Cecilia (patron saint of musicians), and other notables. The San Diego Historical Society painstakingly restored the house, which is on the National Register of Historic Places, and furnished it with period pieces. If you love Victorian houses, don't miss this one for its quirkiness.

William Heath Davis House Museum. 410 Island Ave. (at Fourth Ave.). ☎ **619/ 233-4692.** www.gqhf.com. Admission $2. Mon–Fri 10am–2pm; Sat 10am–4pm; Sun noon–4pm. Museum is staffed by volunteers; call to verify hours. Bus: 1, 3, or 3A. Trolley: Gaslamp Quarter/Convention Center W.

Shipped by boat to San Diego in 1850 from Portland, Maine, this is the oldest structure in the Gaslamp Quarter. It is a well-preserved example of a prefabricated "saltbox" family home and has remained structurally unchanged for more than 120 years. A museum, on the first and second floors, is open to the public, as is the small park adjacent to the house. The house is also home to the **Gaslamp Quarter Historical Foundation,** which sponsors walking tours of the quarter every Saturday at 11am for $5.

OLD TOWN AND BEYOND: A LOOK AT CALIFORNIA'S BEGINNINGS

The birthplace of San Diego is Old Town, the hillside where the Spanish Presidio and Father Junípero Serra's mission (the first in California) were built. By protecting the remaining adobes and historic buildings, **Old Town State Historic Park** brings to life Mexican California, which existed here until the mid–1800s. Much of the surrounding area, however, has become a mini–Mexican theme park. You can get to Old Town on the trolley or Coaster (see "Getting Around," earlier in this chapter), and free walking tours leave daily at 10:30am and 2pm from **Seeley Stables Visitor Center** (☎ **619/ 220-5422**). Other nearby sites of interest are listed below.

Heritage Park. 2455 Heritage Park Row (corner of Juan and Harney sts.), Old Town. For information, call the Parks Department at ☎ **619/694-3049.** Free admission. Daily 9:30am–3pm. Bus: 4, 5, or 105.

Designed to resemble a cobblestone cul-de-sac, this small park is lined with seven original 19th-century buildings rescued from demolition in other parts of the city and given new uses, among them a bed-and-breakfast, a doll shop, and a gift shop. Take a tour and have tea for $10, Tuesday through Sunday from 2:30 to 5pm.

Junípero Serra Museum. 2727 Presidio Dr., Presidio Park, Old Town. ☎ **619/297-3258.** Admission $5 adults, $4 seniors and students, $2 kids 6-17, free for children under 6. Fri–Sun 10am–4:30pm. Take I-8 to the Taylor St. exit, turn right on Taylor, and then turn left on Presidio Dr.; or, take a bus to the intersection of Taylor and Juan sts. and walk uphill.

Perched on a hill above Old Town, the stately mission-style building overlooks the hillside where California began. Here, in 1769, the first mission and first non-Indian settlement on the West Coast of the United States and Canada were founded. Inside, the museum's exhibits introduce visitors to California's origins and to the Native American, Spanish, and Mexican people who first called this place home. On display are their belongings, from cannons to cookware; a Spanish furniture collection; and one of the first paintings brought to California, which survived being damaged in an Indian attack. The mission remained San Diego's only settlement until the 1820s, when families began to move down the hill into what is now known as Old Town. Here, you can also watch an ongoing archaeological dig uncovering more of the items used by early settlers. From the 70-foot tower, visitors can compare the spectacular view with historic photos to see how this land has changed over time.

Mission Basilica San Diego de Alcala. 10818 San Diego Mission Rd., Mission Valley. ☎ **619/281-8449.** Admission $2 adults, $1 seniors and students, 50¢ children 12 and under. Free on Sun and for daily services. Daily 9am–5pm; mass daily 7am and 5:30pm. Take I-8 to Mission Gorge Rd. to Twain Ave. Bus: 6, 16, 25, 43, or 81.

Established in 1769, this was the first link in the chain of 21 missions founded in California by Spanish missionary Junípero Serra. In 1774, the mission was moved to its present site for agricultural reasons and to separate Native American converts from a fortress that included the original building. A few bricks belonging to the original mission can be seen in Presidio Park in Old Town. Mass is held regularly in this still-active Catholic parish.

Whaley House. 2482 San Diego Ave. ☎ **619/298-2482.** Admission $4 adults, $3 seniors over 60, $2 children 5–18, free for children under 5. June–Sept daily 10am–5pm; Oct–May Wed–Mon 10am–5pm. Closed on major holidays.

In 1856, this striking two-story house (the first one in these parts) just outside Old Town State Historic Park was built for Thomas Whaley and his family. Whaley was a New Yorker who arrived here via San Francisco, where he had been lured by the gold rush. The house is one of only two authenticated haunted houses in California, and 10,000 schoolchildren come here each year to see for themselves. Exhibits include a life mask of Abraham Lincoln, one of only six made; the spinet piano used in the movie *Gone with the Wind;* and the concert piano that accompanied Swedish soprano Jenny Lind on her final U.S. tour in 1852.

MISSION BAY & THE BEACHES

This area is great for walking, jogging, in-line skating, biking, and boating; for details, see "Outdoor Pursuits," below.

Giant Dipper Roller Coaster. 3146 Mission Blvd. ☎ **858/488-1549.** Sun–Thurs 11am–10pm; Fri–Sat 11am–11pm. Admission to park free; ride on Giant Dipper $3. Take I-5 to the Sea World exit, and follow W. Mission Bay Dr. to Belmont Park.

A local landmark for 70 years, the Giant Dipper is one of two surviving fixtures from the original Belmont Amusement Park (the other is The Plunge indoor swimming pool). This vintage wooden roller coaster underwent an extensive restoration and reopened in 1991.

The amusement park contains newer, carnival-style rides; you might also like to participate in the **Dive-In Movies** shown at **The Plunge** (☎ **858/488-3110**), in which viewers float on rafts in 91°F water and watch water-related movies projected onto the wall. *Jaws* is a perennial favorite. (See "Movies, San Diego Style" under "San Diego After Dark," below.)

LA JOLLA

Some folks just enjoy driving around La Jolla, taking in the sea views and the 360° vista from the top of **Mount Soledad.** However, La Jolla also offers other attractions, including ✪ **Torrey Pines State Reserve** (☎ **858/755-2063**), which has an interpretive center, hiking trails with wonderful ocean views, and a chance to see the rare torrey pine. Admission is free, as are the guided walks on Saturdays and Sundays. Access is via North Torrey Pines Road; parking costs $4 per car, $3 for seniors.

Birch Aquarium at Scripps. 2300 Expedition Way, La Jolla. ☎ **858/534-FISH (3474).** Fax 858/534-7114. Admission $7.50 adults, $6.50 seniors, $4 youths 3–17, free for children under 3. Parking $3. AE, MC, V. Daily 9am–5pm. Take I-5 to La Jolla Village Dr. exit, go west 1 mile, and turn left at Expedition Way. Bus: 34.

The aquarium offers close-up views of the Pacific Ocean in 33 marine-life tanks. The giant kelp forest is particularly impressive. World renowned for its oceanic research, Scripps offers visitors a chance to view its marine aquarium and artificial outdoor tide pools. The museum has interpretive exhibits on the current and historical research done at the institution, which has been in existence since 1903.

✪ **Museum of Contemporary Art, San Diego.** 700 Prospect St. ☎ **858/454-3541.** Fax 858/454-6985. www.mcasandiego.org. Admission $4 adults, $2 students and seniors, children under 12 free; free first Tues and Sun of each month. Tue–Sat 10am–5pm (Wed until 8pm); Sun noon–5pm. Take the Ardath Rd. exit off I-5 north or the La Jolla Village Dr. west exit off I-5 south. Take Torrey Pines Rd. to Prospect Place and turn right. Prospect Place becomes Prospect St.

Museum holdings include works from every major art movement of the past half century, with a strong representation of California artists and particularly noteworthy examples of minimalism, light and space work, conceptualism, installation, and site-specific art (including outdoor sculptures). The museum's facade was redesigned in 1997 to incorporate more of the original Irving Gill architecture, and the rear galleries feature outstanding ocean views.

Hidden La Jolla

While droves of folks stroll the sidewalks adjacent to the San Diego–La Jolla Underwater Park and La Jolla Cove, only a few know about **Coast Walk,** which starts near the **La Jolla Cave & Shell Shop,** 1325 Coast Blvd. (☎ 858/454-6080), and affords a wonderful view of beach and beyond. A cool adventure awaits inside the shop, too: **Sunny Jim Cave,** reached via a steep and narrow staircase through the rock; it eventually lets out on a wood-plank observation deck from which you can gaze out the cave at the swelling sea. Admission is $1.50 (75¢ for kids).

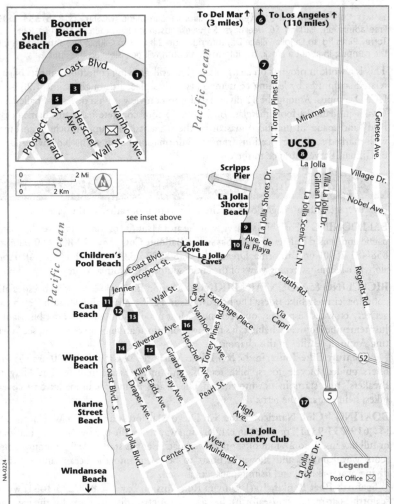

To Del Mar ↑ (3 miles)
↑ To Los Angeles ↑ (110 miles)

Pacific Ocean

Boomer Beach
Shell Beach
Coast Blvd.
Prospect St.
Herschel Ave.
Girard
Ivanhoe Ave.
Wall St.

0   2 Mi
0   2 Km

Miramar

UCSD
La Jolla

N. Torrey Pines Rd.
Villa La Jolla Dr.
Gilman Dr.
La Jolla Scenic Dr. N.
Genesee Ave.
Village Dr.
Nobel Ave.

Scripps Pier
La Jolla Shores Beach
La Jolla Shores Dr.

see inset above

Pacific Ocean

Children's Pool Beach
Coast Blvd.
Prospect St.
Jenner
Wall St.
La Jolla Cove
La Jolla Caves
Ave. de la Playa

Casa Beach
Cave St.
Exchange Place
Torrey Pines Rd
Ardath Rd.
Via Capri

Wipeout Beach
Silverado Ave.
Ivanhoe Ave.
Girard Ave.
Herschel Ave.
Coast Blvd. S.
Kline St.
Eads Ave.
Fay Ave.
Draper Ave.
Pearl St.
High Ave.

Marine Street Beach
La Jolla Blvd.
Center St.
West Muirlands Dr.
La Jolla Country Club
La Jolla Scenic Dr. S.

Regents Rd.

52

5

Windansea Beach ↓

Legend
Post Office ✉

NA-0224

ACCOMMODATIONS
Bed & Breakfast Inn at La Jolla **14**
Best Western Inn by the Sea **13**
Empress Hotel of La Jolla **15**
La Jolla Beach & Tennis Club **10**
La Jolla Cove Travelodge **16**
La Valencia Hotel **3**
Prospect Park Inn **5**
Scripps Inn **11**
The Sea Lodge **9**

ATTRACTIONS
Birch Aquarium at Scripps **7**
Coast Walk **4**
Ellen Browning Scripps Park **2**
La Jolla Cave & Shell Shop **1**
Mount Soledad **17**
Museum of Contemporary Art, San Diego **12**
Stuart Collection **8**
Torrey Pines State Reserve **6**

Stuart Collection. At the University of California, San Diego (UCSD). ☎ **858/534-2117.** Free admission. Parking $6 weekdays, $3 weekends at parking meters. From La Jolla, take Torrey Pines Rd. to La Jolla Village Dr., turn right, go 2 blocks to Gilman Dr., and turn left into the campus; in about a block, the information booth will be visible on the right.

This is a work in progress on a large scale. The still-growing collection consists of site-related sculptures by leading contemporary artists placed throughout the 1,200-acre UCSD campus. Among the 12 diverse sculptures on view is Niki de Saint-Phalle's *Sun God,* a jubilant 14-foot fiberglass bird on a 15-foot concrete base, nicknamed "Big Bird" and made an unofficial mascot by the students. Pick up a brochure and map with marked sculpture locations from the information booth at the Northview Drive or Gilman Drive entrance to the campus.

8 Outdoor Pursuits

For coverage of San Diego's best beaches, see section 6, earlier in this chapter.

BALLOONING   For a bird's-eye view of the area at sunrise or sunset, followed by champagne and hors d'oeuvres, contact **Skysurfer Balloon Company** (☎ **800/660-6809** or 858/481-7500) or **California Dreamin'** (☎ **800/373-3359** or 760/438-3344). From aloft, you'll enjoy sweeping views of the entire southern California coast.

BICYCLING & MOUNTAIN BIKING   Mission Bay and Coronado are especially good for leisurely bike rides. The boardwalks in Pacific Beach and Mission Beach can get very crowded, especially on weekends. Most major thoroughfares offer bike lanes. Just remember to wear a helmet; it's the law. For information on bike rentals, see "Getting Around," earlier in this chapter.

Adventure Bike Tours, in the San Diego Marriott (☎ **619/234-1500,** ext. 6514), offers guided bicycle tours, bike rentals, and in-line skate rentals. The "Bay to Breakers" ride starts in downtown San Diego and includes Coronado; $39 covers bikes, helmets, and the ferry.

BOATING   Club Nautico, at the San Diego Marriott Marina, 333 W. Harbor Dr. (☎ **619/233-9311**), provides an exhilarating way to see the bay by the hour, half-day, or full day in 20- to 27-foot offshore powerboats. Rentals start at $89 per hour. It also rents WaveRunners and allows its boats to be taken into the ocean, and provides diving, water-skiing, and fishing packages as well.

Seaforth Boat Rental, 1641 Quivira Rd., Mission Bay (☎ **858/223-1681;** www.seaforth-boat-rental.com/seaforth), has a wide variety of fishing boats for the bay and ocean, powerboats for $50 to $90 per hour, and 14- to 30-foot sailboats for $20 to $45 per hour; inquire about half- and full-day rates. Canoes, pedal boats, kayaks, and rowboats are available for those who prefer a slower pace, as are bicycles and equipment with which you can fish off the Municipal Pier (see "Fishing," below).

Coronado Boat Rental, 1715 Strand Way, Coronado (☎ **619/437-1514**), has powerboats renting from $65 to $90 per hour, with half- and full-day rates available; 14- to 30-foot sailboats from $25 to $40 per hour; plus jet skis, ski boats, canoes, pedal boats, kayaks, fishing skiffs, and charter boats.

Sail USA (☎ **619/298-6822**) offers custom-tailored skippered cruises on a 34-foot Catalina sloop. A half-day bay cruise costs $275 for up to six passengers.

FISHING   Public fishing piers are at Shelter Island (where there's a statue dedicated to anglers), Ocean Beach, and Imperial Beach. Anglers of any age can fish free of charge without a license off any municipal pier in California. Call the **City Fish Line** (☎ **619/465-3474**) for information on fishing.

For **sportfishing,** you can go out on a large boat for about $25 for a half-day, or $40 to $100 for three-quarters to a full day. To charter a boat for up to six people, the rates run about $550 for a half day and $1,000 for an entire day, more in summer; call around and compare prices. Summer and fall are excellent times for excursions. Locally, the waters around Point Loma are filled with bass, bonita, and barracuda; the Coronado Islands, which belong to Mexico but are only about 18 miles from San Diego, are popular for abalone, yellowtail, yellowfin, and big-eyed tuna. Some outfitters will take you farther into Baja California waters.

Fishing charters depart from Harbor and Shelter islands, Point Loma, the Imperial Beach Pier, and Quivira Basin in Mission Bay (near the Hyatt Islandia Hotel). The following outfitters offer short or extended outings with daily departures: **H&M Landing** (☎ 619/222-1144), **Islandia Sportfishing** (☎ 619/222-1164), **Lee Palm Sportfishers** (☎ 619/224-3857), **Point Loma Sportfishing** (☎ 619/223-1627), and **Seaforth Boat Rentals** (☎ 858/223-1681). Participants over the age of 16 need a California fishing license.

GOLF With nearly 80 courses, 50 of them open to the public, San Diego County has much to offer the golf enthusiast. Courses are diverse, some with vistas of the Pacific, others with views of country hillsides or of desert. **M&M Tee Times** (☎ 800/ 867-7397 or 858/456-8366; www.torreypines.com) can arrange tee times for you at most golf courses.

And where else but San Diego can you practice your golf swing in the middle of the central business district? The **Metro Golf Harborside,** 801 W. Ash St., at Pacific Highway (☎ 619/239-GOLF), is open Monday through Friday from 7am to 10pm, Saturday from 8am to 10pm, and Sunday from 9am to 9pm. Here you'll find 80 tees, a USGA putting and chipping area, a pro shop, and golf school. It's lit for after-dark play. Club rental is available at $1 each; a large bucket of balls costs $6 and a small bucket, $3.

Space constraints prevent us from listing all of the San Diego area's fine courses; for a more extensive listing, see *Frommer's San Diego.*

Balboa Park Municipal Golf Course, 2600 Golf Course Dr., San Diego (☎ 619/ 570-1234 for automated tee times, or 619/239-1660 for pro shop), is a wooded 18-hole course with skyline views nestled in the southeast corner of Balboa Park. Convenient and affordable, it might remind you of your muni course back home, down to the bare-bones 1940s clubhouse where old guys hold down lunch counter stools for hours after the game. Non-resident greens fees are $30 Monday through Friday and $35 Saturday and Sunday; cart rentals are $20, pull carts $5. Reservations are suggested at least a week in advance.

Coronado Municipal Golf Course, 2000 Visalia Row, Coronado (☎ 619/ 435-3121), is the first sight that welcomes you as you cross the Coronado Bay Bridge (the course is off to the left). It's an 18-hole, par-72 course overlooking Glorietta Bay, and there's a coffee shop, pro shop, and driving range. Two-day prior reservations are strongly recommended; call any time after 7am. Greens fees are $20 to walk and $32 to ride for 18 holes; $10 to walk and $17 to ride after 4pm. Club rental is $15, and pull-cart rental is $4.

Riverwalk Golf Club, 1150 Fashion Valley Rd., Mission Valley (☎ 619/ 698-GOLF), is a Ted Robinson/Ted Robinson, Jr.–designed course meandering along the Mission Valley floor. It features four lakes with waterfalls (in play on 13 of the 27 holes); open, undulating fairways; and the red San Diego Trolley speeding through the middle now and then. Nonresident greens fees—including cart—are $75 Monday through Thursday, $85 Friday and Sunday, and $95 Saturday (fees for residents are $30 less).

✪ **Torrey Pines Golf Course,** 11480 Torrey Pines Rd., La Jolla (☎ **858/552-1784** for information, 858/570-1234 for tee times, or 858/452-3226 for the pro shop), is actually two gorgeous 18-hole championship clifftop courses overlooking the ocean; the north course is more picturesque, the south course more challenging. Tee times are taken by computer, starting at 5am, up to 7 days in advance by telephone only. *Insider tip:* Single golfers stand a good chance of getting on the course if they just turn up and wait for a threesome. Greens fees for out-of-towners are $48 during the week and $52 on Saturday, Sunday, and holidays for 18 holes; $26 for 9 holes. Cart rental is $28.

San Diego hosts some of the country's most important golf tournaments, including the **Buick Invitational of California,** held every February at Torrey Pines Golf Course in La Jolla (☎ **800/888-BUICK** or 619/281-4653).

HIKING & WALKING The **Sierra Club** sponsors regular hikes in the San Diego area, and nonmembers are welcome to participate; there are both day and evening hikes, most free. For a recorded schedule, call ☎ **619/299-1744,** or call the office at ☎ **619/299-1743** Monday through Friday from noon to 5pm and Saturday from 10am to 4pm.

The Bayside Trail near **Cabrillo National Monument** is popular because it affords great views. Drive to the Monument and follow signs to the trail. Parking costs $4 per car. ✪ **Mission Trails Regional Park,** 8 miles northeast of downtown, offers a glimpse of what San Diego looked like before development. Located between Calif. 52 and I-8 and east of I-15, its rugged hills, valleys, and open areas provide a quick escape from urban hustle-bustle. A visitor and interpretive center (☎ **619/668-3275**) is open daily from 9am to 5pm. Access is via Mission Gorge Road from either Calif. 52 or I-8.

The best beaches for walking are La Jolla Shores, Mission Beach, and Coronado. You can also walk around **Mission Bay** on a series of connected footpaths. If a four-legged friend is your walking companion, head for **Dog Beach** in Ocean Beach or **Fiesta Island** in Mission Bay, two of the few areas where dogs can legally go unleashed.

IN-LINE SKATING Gliding around San Diego, especially the Mission Bay area, on in-line skates is as much a southern California experience as sailing or surfing. In Mission Beach, rent a pair of regular or in-line skates from **Mike's Bikes & Skates,** 756A Ventura Place (☎ 858/488-1444), or **Hamel's Action Sports Center,** 704 Ventura Place, off Mission Boulevard at the roller coaster (☎ 858/488-8889). In Pacific Beach, try **Pacific Beach Sun & Sea,** 4539 Ocean Blvd. (☎858/483-6613). In Coronado, go to **Bikes & Beyond,** 1201 First St. and at the Ferry Landing (☎ 619/435-7180).

SANDCASTLE COMPETITIONS Sandcastle enthusiasts will want to attend the 2-day **Annual U.S. Open Sandcastle Competition** at the pier in Imperial Beach in July. There's a parade and children's castle contest Saturday at 2pm, but Sunday is the main event. For information, call ☎ **619/424-6663.** A similar event, the **Ocean Beach Sandcastle Event and Family Fun Carnival,** is held in October; for information, call ☎ **619/226-8613.**

SURFING Get where-to-go info from section 6 above, and rent a board (if you didn't BYO) from **La Jolla Surf Systems,** 2132 Avenida de la Playa, La Jolla Shores (☎ **858/456-2777**), or **Emerald Surf & Sport,** 1118 Orange Ave., Coronado (☎ **619/435-6677**).

TENNIS There are 1,200 public and private tennis courts in San Diego. Public courts are located throughout the city, including the **La Jolla Recreation Center** (☎ 858/459-9950) and **Morley Field** (☎ 619/295-9278) in Balboa Park.

9 Shopping

All-American San Diego has embraced the suburban shopping mall with vigor— several massive complexes in Mission Valley are where many residents do the bulk of their shopping, and every possible need can be met here. Local neighborhoods also offer individualized specialty shopping that meets the needs—and mirrors the personality—of those parts of town. For example, hip and trendy Hillcrest is the place to go for cutting-edge boutiques, while conservative La Jolla offers many upscale traditional shops, especially jewelers.

Sales tax in San Diego is 7.75%, and savvy out-of-state shoppers know to have larger items shipped directly home at the point of purchase, thereby avoiding the tax.

DOWNTOWN & GASLAMP QUARTER

✪ **Horton Plaza,** 324 Horton Plaza (☎ 619/238-1596; www.hortonplaza.com), the Disneyland of shopping malls, is at the heart of the revitalized city center, bounded by Broadway, First and Fourth avenues, and G Street. This multilevel shopping center has 140 specialty shops, including art galleries, clothing and shoe stores, several fun shops for kids, bookstores, a 14-screen cinema, three major department stores, and a variety of restaurants and short-order eateries. With a rambling and confusing series of paths and bridges, the complex was supposedly inspired by European shopping districts. Parking is free the first 3 hours with validation (4 hours at the movie theater and the Lyceum Theatre), $1 per half hour thereafter; parking levels are confusing, and temporarily losing your car is part of the Horton Plaza experience. Take bus no. 2, 7, 9, 29, 34, or 35, or the trolley to City Center.

Other downtown shopping opportunities include **Seaport Village**, on Harbor Drive at Kettner Boulevard (☎ 619/235-4014), a Cape Cod–style "village" of cutesy shops snuggled alongside San Diego Bay; it's worth a visit for the 1890 carousel imported from Coney Island, New York.

Seekers of serious art might want to head to the burgeoning **Little Italy arts district,** north of downtown. Among the galleries housed at 2400 Kettner Blvd. are **Brushworks** (☎ 619/232-7329), displaying whimsical contemporary works; **David Zapf Gallery** (☎ 619/232-5004), specializing in the works of San Diego–area artists; and **Pratt Gallery** (☎ 619/236-0211), featuring painted landscapes and cityscapes by Southern California artists.

HILLCREST/UPTOWN

Compact Hillcrest is an ideal shopping destination for browsing unique and often wacky shops, but also for buying things at the area's vintage-clothing stores, memorabilia shops, recognizable chains, and snack-friendly bakeries and cafes. Start at the neighborhood's hub, the intersection of University and Fifth avenues. Street parking is available; most meters allow 2-hour parking and devour quarters at a rate of one per 15 minutes, so be armed with plenty of change. You can also park in an area parking lot—rates vary, but you'll come out ahead if you're planning to stroll for several hours.

San Diego's self-proclaimed **Antique Row** is located north of Balboa Park, along Park Boulevard (beginning at University Ave. in Hillcrest) and Adams Avenue (extending to around 40th St. in Normal Heights). For more information and an area brochure with map, contact the **Adams Avenue Business Association** (☎ 619/ 282-7329; www.GoThere.com/AdamsAve).

OLD TOWN & MISSION VALLEY

Old Town Historic Park is a restoration of some of San Diego's historic sites and adobe structures, a number of which now house shops that cater to tourists. Many have a "general-store" theme, and carry gourmet treats and inexpensive Mexican crafts alongside the obligatory T-shirts, baseball caps, and other San Diego–emblazoned souvenirs. More shops are concentrated in colorful **Bazaar del Mundo,** 2754 Calhoun St. (☎ **619/296-3161**), arranged around a fountain courtyard.

Mission Valley is home to two giant malls (**Fashion Valley** and **Mission Valley**), with more than enough stores to satisfy any shopper. Here book lovers will find the local outposts of **Barnes & Noble,** 7610 Hazard Center Dr. (☎ **619/220-0175**), and **Borders,** 1072 Camino del Rio N. (☎ **619/295-2201**).

MISSION BAY & THE BEACHES

The beach communities all offer laid-back shopping in typical California fashion: plenty of surf shops, recreational gear, casual garb, and youth-oriented music stores. If you're in need of a new bikini, the best selection is at **Pilar's,** 3745 Mission Blvd., Pacific Beach (☎ **858/488-3056**), where dozens of racks are meticulously organized and choices range from chic designer suits to hot trends inspired by surf- and skatewear. Some of San Diego's best **antiquing** can be found in Ocean Beach, along a single block of Newport Avenue, the town's main drag.

LA JOLLA

It's clear from the look of La Jolla's village that shopping is a major pastime in this upscale community of moneyed professionals and retirees. Women's-clothing boutiques tend toward conservative and costly, like those lining Girard and Prospect streets (Ann Taylor, Armani Exchange, Polo/Ralph Lauren, Talbots, and Sigi's Boutique).

Even if you're not in the market for furnishings and accessories, the many home-decor boutiques make for great window shopping, as do La Jolla's ubiquitous jewelers: Swiss watches, tennis bracelets, precious gems, and pearl necklaces sparkle at you from windows along every street. No visit to La Jolla is complete without seeing **John Cole's Bookshop,** 780 Prospect St. (☎ **858/454-4766**), an eclectic, family-run local favorite set in a charming old cottage.

CORONADO

This rather insular, conservative Navy community doesn't have a great many shopping opportunities; what there is lines Orange Avenue at the western end of the island. In addition to some scattered housewares and home-decor boutiques, as well as several small women's boutiques, there are gift shops at Coronado's major resorts. The **Ferry Landing Marketplace,** 1201 First St., at B Avenue (☎ **619/435-8895**), is a faux-seaport with shops, restaurants, and a sweeping view of the bay and the downtown skyline.

FARMERS MARKETS

Throughout San Diego County, there are no fewer than two dozen regularly occurring street fests featuring the fresh fruits and vegetables from southern California farms and augmented by crafts, ethnic-food vendors, flower stands, and other surprises. Below is a sampling.

In **Hillcrest,** the market sets up Sundays from 9am to noon at the corner of Normal Street and Lincoln Avenue, several blocks north of Balboa Park. The atmosphere is festive, and exotic culinary delights reflect Hillcrest's eclectic ambiance. For more information, call the **Hillcrest Association** (☎ **619/299-3330**).

In **Ocean Beach,** there's a fun-filled market Wednesday evenings between 4 and 8pm (until 7pm in fall and winter) in the 4900 block of Newport Avenue. In addition to fresh-cut flowers, produce, and exotic fruits and foods laid out for sampling, the market features llama rides and other entertainment. For more information, call the **Ocean Beach Business Improvement District** (☎ **619/224-4906**).

Or head to **Pacific Beach** on Saturday from 8am to noon, when Mission Boulevard between Reed Avenue and Pacific Beach Drive is transformed into a bustling morning marketplace, as locals stock up for the week and visitors begin to enjoy the beach communities on vacation.

And on **Coronado** on Tuesday afternoons, the Ferry Landing Marketplace (corner of First and B sts.) hosts a produce and crafts market from 2:30 to 6pm.

10 San Diego After Dark

San Diego is hardly the wild 'n' crazy nightlife capital of America, but pockets of lively after-dark entertainment do exist around the city. On the more sedate side of things, the city offers wonderful and varied live theater experiences—both the Old Globe and La Jolla Playhouse have won Tony Awards for Best Regional Theater.

For a rundown of the latest performances, gallery openings, and other events in the city, check the listings in "Night and Day," the Thursday "Entertainment" section of the *San Diego Union-Tribune,* or the *Reader,* San Diego's free alternative newspaper, published every Thursday. For what's happening in the gay scene, get the weekly *San Diego Gay & Lesbian Times.* The *San Diego Performing Arts Guide,* produced every 2 months by the San Diego Theatre Foundation, is also very helpful; you can pick one up at the Times Art Tix booth.

THE PERFORMING ARTS

Half-price tickets to theater, music, and dance events are available at the **Times Arts Tix** booth, in Horton Plaza Park, at Broadway and Third Avenue (park in the Horton Plaza parking garage and have your parking validated, or pause at the curb nearby). The kiosk is open Tuesday through Saturday from 10am to 7pm. Half-price tickets for Sunday performances are sold on Saturday. Only cash payments are accepted. For a daily listing of half-price offerings, call ☎ **619/497-5000.** Full-price advance tickets are also sold; the kiosk doubles as a Ticketmaster outlet, selling tickets to concerts throughout California.

THEATER & OPERA

The **San Diego Repertory Theatre** offers professional, culturally diverse productions of contemporary and classic dramas, comedies, and musicals at the Lyceum Theatre, 79 Broadway Circle, in Horton Plaza (☎ **619/544-1000;** www.SanDiegoRep.com). Ticket prices are $21 to $32.

Founded in 1948, the **San Diego Junior Theatre,** at Balboa Park's Casa del Prado Theatre (☎ **619/239-8355;** www.juniortheatre.com), is one of the country's oldest continuously producing children's theaters. It provides training and performance opportunities for children and young adults. Students make up the cast and technical crew of six main-stage shows each year.

In Coronado, **Lamb's Players Theatre,** at 1142 Orange Ave. (☎ **619/437-0600;** www.lambsplayers.org; www.sdopera.com), is a professional repertory company whose season runs from February through December. Shows are staged in their 340-seat theater in Coronado's historic Spreckels Building, where no seat is more than seven rows from the stage. Tickets range from $18 to $34.

The **San Diego Opera** performs at the Civic Theater, 202 C St. (☎ **619/232-7636**), and often showcases international stars. The season runs from January through May; call for schedule. The box office is located across the plaza from the theater and is open Monday through Friday from 9am to 5pm. Tickets range from $31 to $112. Ask about standing room or student and senior discounts.

✪ **Old Globe Theatre.** Balboa Park. ☎ **619/239-2255**, or 619/23-GLOBE for 24-hr. hot line. www.oldglobe.org. Tickets $23–$39, senior and student discounts available. Bus: 7 or 25.

Near the entrance to Balboa Park and just behind the Museum of Man is this Tony Award–winning theater, fashioned after Shakespeare's, which has produced the revival of *Damn Yankees* and has billed such notable performers as John Goodman, Marsha Mason, Cliff Robertson, Jon Voight, and Christopher Walken.

The 581-seat Old Globe is part of the Simon Edison Centre for the Performing Arts, which also includes the 245-seat Cassius Carter Centre Stage and the 620-seat open-air Lowell Davies Festival Theatre, and mounts a dozen plays a year on the three stages between January and October. Tours are offered Saturday and Sunday at 11am and cost $3 ($1 for students, seniors, and the military). The box office is open Tuesday through Sunday from noon to 8:30pm.

✪ **La Jolla Playhouse.** 2910 La Jolla Village Dr. (at Torrey Pines Rd.), La Jolla. ☎ **858/550-1010**. www.lajollaplayhouse.com.

Winner of the 1993 Tony Award for Outstanding American Regional Theater, the La Jolla Playhouse stages six productions each year in its 500-seat Mandell Weiss Theater and 400-seat Mandell Weiss Forum on the campus of UCSD. Performances are held from May through November. Playhouse audiences cheered The Who's *Tommy* and Matthew Broderick in *How to Succeed in Business Without Really Trying* before they went on to Broadway fame and fortune. The box office is open Monday from noon to 6pm and Tuesday through Sunday from noon to 8pm. Each show designates one Saturday matinee as a "pay-what-you-can performance." Reduced-price "Public Rush" tickets are available 10 minutes before curtain, subject to availability. Tickets run $19 to $49.

MOVIES, SAN DIEGO STYLE

In addition to the usual multiplex theaters, San Diegans like to watch movies in some unusual settings. **Movies Before the Mast** are shown on a special "screensail" from April to October aboard the *Star of India* (see the Maritime Museum listing under "Exploring the Area," above). All the films shown are nautical in genre, such as *Black Beard the Pirate* and *Hook*. Call ☎ 619/234-9153 for the schedule.

In August, you can view a mix of classic and current films free of charge from a blanket or chair on the beach during the **Sunset Cinema Film Festival.** Films are projected on screens mounted on floating barges from San Diego to Imperial Beach. Call ☎ 619/454-7373 for details.

Dive-In Movies are shown at The Plunge (☎ 858/488-3110), an indoor swimming pool in Mission Beach. Viewers float on rafts in 91°F water and watch water-related movies projected onto the wall. *Jaws* is a perennial favorite.

COMEDY

Top L.A. comics regularly visit the **Comedy Store,** 916 Pearl St., La Jolla (☎ 858/454-9176). Monday and Tuesday are amateur nights; the acts improve as the week progresses. The cover is $6 to $10.

Tidbits, 3838 Fifth Ave., Hillcrest (☎**619/543-0300**), is a huge cabaret with out-standing—and campy—drag revues, equally patronized by gays and adventurous straights.

THE CLUB & MUSIC SCENE

A note on smoking: In January 1998, California enacted controversial legislation ban-ning smoking in all restaurants and bars. While opponents immediately began lob-bying to repeal the law, it's a good idea to check before you light up in nightclubs, lounges, etc.

ROCK, POP, FOLK, JAZZ & BLUES

The Casbah, 2501 Kettner Blvd., near the airport (☎ 619/232-4355; www. casbahmusic.com), is a divey joint with a rep for breakthrough alternative and rock bands. **Croce's Nightclubs,** 802 Fifth Ave., at F St. (☎ 619/233-4355; www.croces. com), are attached to one of the Gaslamp Quarter's most popular restaurants, and fea-ture jazz and rhythm and blues. **4th & B,** 345 B St., downtown (☎ 619/231-4343), is a quality venue with performances ranging from rock-and-roll to chamber music. **Humphrey's,** 2241 Shelter Island Dr. (☎ 619/523-1010; www.humphreysconcerts. com), is a 900-seat outdoor venue set on the water, and has a seasonal (May through October) line-up that ranges from rock to folk to international. **SOMA Live,** 5305 Metro St., Mission Bay (☎ 858/296-SOMA), is a warehouselike all-ages venue that hosts cutting-edge national alternative bands.

DANCE CLUBS & DISCOS

The Gaslamp Quarter is ground zero for the city's hottest dance clubs—the most pop-ular at the moment are **Olé Madrid,** 751 Fifth Ave. (☎ 619/557-0146), a loud, ener-getic club with tapas and sangria from the adjoining Spanish restaurant; **Sevilla,** 555 Fourth Ave. (☎ 619/233-5979), where you can salsa and merengue to Brazilian dance music; and **Supper Club A-Go-Go,** 322 Fifth Ave. (☎ 619/235-4646), where post-modern hipsters swing to 1940s tunes or recline with a martini.

GAY AND LESBIAN CLUBS & BARS

Bourbon Street, 4612 Park Blvd., University Heights (☎ 619/291-0173), is a jazzy and elegant piano bar with a New Orleans–esque patio. **The Brass Rail,** 3796 Fifth Ave., Hillcrest (☎ 619/298-2233), is loud and proud, with energetic dancing, bright lights, and go-go boys. **The Flame,** 3780 Park Blvd. (☎ 619/295-4163), is the city's top lesbian dance club. **Kickers,** 308 University Ave., at Third Ave., Hillcrest (☎ 619/ 491-0400), is a country-western dance hall that attracts both sexes for two-stepping, line-dancing, and the adjacent Hamburger Mary's restaurant. Finally, **Rich's,** 1051 University Ave., between 10th and 11th avenues (☎ 619/295-2195, or 619/497-4588 for upcoming events), is a high-energy, high-image dance club, with house music and a video bar.

BARS & COCKTAIL LOUNGES

Cannibal Bar, inside the Catamaran Hotel at 3999 Mission Blvd., Mission Beach (☎ 858/539-8650), features a tropical theme, Polynesian cocktails, DJ dancing, and occasional live bands. The **Bitter End,** 770 Fifth Ave., Gaslamp Quarter (☎ 619/ 338-9300), has three levels for its martini bar, late-night dance club, and relaxing cocktail lounge. **Club 66,** 901 Fifth Ave., Gaslamp Quarter (☎ 619/234-4166), is located beneath popular Dakota Grill and sports a Route 66 theme along with disco and Top 40 dance music. **Top O' The Cove,** 1216 Prospect Ave., La Jolla (☎ 858/ 454-7779), offers an intimate setting for mellow piano music.

11 North County Beach Towns

Picturesque beach towns, each poised over their own stretch of sand, dot the coast of San Diego County from Del Mar to Oceanside. These make great day-trip destinations for sun worshipers and surfers.

ESSENTIALS

Getting there is easy: Del Mar is only 18 miles north of downtown San Diego; Carlsbad, about 33; Oceanside, 36. If you're driving, follow I-5 north: You'll find freeway exits for Del Mar, Solana Beach, Cardiff by the Sea, Encinitas, Leucadia, Carlsbad, and Oceanside.

Check with **Amtrak** (☎ **800/USA-RAIL**) or the **Coaster** (☎ **800/COASTER**) for transit information.

The **San Diego North County Convention and Visitors Bureau** (☎ **800/ 848-3336**) is also a good information source.

DEL MAR

Less than 20 miles up the coast lies Del Mar, a small community with just over 5,000 inhabitants in a 2-square-mile municipality. The town has adamantly maintained its independence, eschewing incorporation into the city of San Diego. Sometimes known as "the people's republic of Del Mar," this community was one of the nation's first to ban smoking. Come summer, the town explodes as visitors flock in for the thoroughbred horse-racing season and the county's Del Mar Fair. The history and current popularity of Del Mar is, in fact, inextricably linked to the **Del Mar Race Track & Fairgrounds,** 2260 Jimmy Durante Blvd. (☎ **858/753-5555;** www.delmarfair.com), which, in turn, still glows with the aura of Hollywood celebrity. Established in the 1930s by crooner/actor Bing Crosby, the track still begins each season by playing "Where the Surf Meets the Turf."

Del Mar City Beach is a wide, well-patrolled beach popular for sunbathing, swimming, and bodysurfing. Get there by taking 15th Street west to Seagrove Park, where college kids can always be found playing volleyball and other lawn games while older folks snooze in the shade. There are **free concerts** in the park during July and August; for information, contact the City of Del Mar (☎ **858/755-9313**).

For more information about Del Mar, contact or visit the **Del Mar Chamber of Commerce Visitor Information Center,** 1104 Camino del Mar #101, Del Mar, CA 92014 (☎ **858/755-4844;** www.delmar.ca.us), which also provides a folding, detailed map of the area. Open hours vary according to volunteer staffing, but usually mimic weekday business hours.

WHERE TO STAY

Del Mar Motel on the Beach. 1702 Coast Blvd. (at 17th St.), Del Mar, CA 92014. ☎ **800/ 223-8449** or 858/755-1534. 45 units. A/C TV TEL. $130–$180 double. Lower off-season rates. Extra person $5. AE, CB, DC, DISC, JCB, MC, V. Take I-5 to Via de la Valle exit; go west, then south on Hwy. 101 (Pacific Coast Hwy.); veer west onto Coast Blvd.

The only property in Del Mar right on the beach, this little white-stucco motel with blue trim is clean and simply furnished. Upstairs rooms have one king-size bed, while those downstairs come with two double beds. All rooms have a fridge, coffeemaker, and fan. Half are no-smoking rooms, and only those units with ocean views have tubs (the rest have showers only). This is a good choice for beach lovers, as you can walk from here along the beach for miles, and the popular seaside restaurants

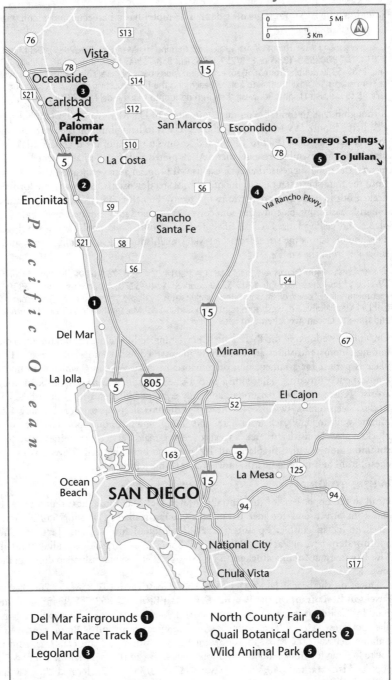

Del Mar Fairgrounds ❶

Del Mar Race Track ❶

Legoland ❸

North County Fair ❹

Quail Botanical Gardens ❷

Wild Animal Park ❺

Poseidon and Jake's are right next door. The motel has a barbecue and picnic table for guests' use.

L'Auberge Del Mar Resort and Spa. 1540 Camino del Mar (P.O. Box 2889), Del Mar, CA 92014. ☎ **800/553-1336** or 858/259-1515. Fax 858/755-4940. 128 units. A/C MINIBAR TV TEL. $189–$389 double; from $650 suite. Spa and sports packages available. AE, DC, MC, V. Valet or self-parking $8. Take Amtrak to Solana Beach and the hotel courtesy van will pick you up, or take I-5 to Del Mar Heights Rd. west, then turn right onto Camino del Mar Rd.; it's at 15th St.

Although it tries to capitalize on the 1940s allure of Del Mar as a Hollywood hot spot, L'Auberge is pure 1990s. True, it lays honest claim to being built on the site of the historic Hotel Del Mar (1909 to 1969), and features a replica of the original's brick fireplace, but any resemblance ends there. As its pretentious French name (which simply means "the inn") suggests, there's an exclusive European aura permeating the property, from the four-star restaurant to the full-service spa downstairs. Bedrooms are formally decked out in antique reproductions and teensy French country prints; each features a marble bathroom, balcony, in-room coffee service, and three phones; many have fireplaces and ceiling fans. Facilities include tennis courts, two pools, and a whirlpool. The hotel is across the street from Del Mar's main shopping and dining scene, and a short jog from the sand.

Wave Crest. 1400 Ocean Ave., Del Mar, CA 92014. ☎ **858/755-0100.** No fax. 31 units. TV TEL. Mid-June–mid-Sept $205–$230 studio, $240–$270 1-bedroom suite, $330 2-bedroom suite. Lower off-season rates; weekly rates available year-round. MC, V. From I-5, exit Del Mar Heights Rd. west, turn right onto Camino del Mar, and drive to 15th St.; turn left and drive to Ocean Ave., then turn left.

On a bluff overlooking the Pacific, these gray-shingled bungalow/condominiums containing studios and suites are beautifully maintained and wonderfully private. This place is perfect for a honeymoon or romantic getaway. All units, which surround a landscaped courtyard, come with a queen-size bed and sofa bed, artwork by local artists, VCR, stereo, full bathroom, and fully equipped kitchen with dishwasher. The studios sleep one or two people; the one-bedrooms sleep up to four. It's only a 5-minute walk to the beach from here, and shopping and dining spots are just a few blocks away. Note that there's an extra fee for maid service. Amenities include a common lounge with a fireplace and TV, pool and bubbling Jacuzzi overlooking the ocean, irons and ironing boards, movies, and laundry facilities.

WHERE TO DINE

Head to the upper level of the centrally located **Del Mar Plaza,** at Camino del Mar and 15th Street, and consider **Il Fornaio Cucina Italiana** (☎ 858/755-8876) for excellent Italian cuisine; **Epazote** (☎ 858/259-9966) for Mexican, Tex-Mex, and Southwestern fare; or **Pacifica Del Mar** (☎ 858/792-0476) for outstanding seafood. Kids like to eat at **Johnny Rockets** (☎ 858/755-1954), an old-fashioned diner on the lower level.

Down on the beach, **Jake's Del Mar,** 1660 Coast Blvd. (☎ 858/755-2002), and **Poseidon Restaurant on the Beach,** 1670 Coast Blvd. (☎ 858/755-9345), are both good for California cuisine and sunset views. If you want to eat at either of these popular spots, reserve early. The racetrack crowd congregates at **Bully's Restaurant,** 1404 Camino del Mar (☎ 858/755-1660), for burgers, prime rib, and crab legs. And if you're looking for fresh seafood—and lots of it—head to the Del Mar branch of SD's popular **Fish Market,** 640 Via de la Valle (☎ 858/755-2277), located close to the racetrack.

CARLSBAD & ENCINITAS

Fifteen miles north of Del Mar and around 30 miles from downtown San Diego (a 45-minute drive), the pretty communities of Carlsbad and Encinitas provide many reasons to linger on the California coast: good swimming and surfing beaches, small-town atmosphere, an abundance of antiques and gift shops, and a seasonal display of the region's most beautiful flowers.

Carlsbad was named for Karlsbad, Czechoslovakia, because of the similar mineral (some say curative) waters they both produced, but the town's once-famous artesian well has long been plugged up. Carlsbad is also a noted commercial flower-growing region, along with its neighbor **Encinitas.** A colorful display can be seen each spring at **Carlsbad Ranch** (☎ 760/431-0352), when 45 acres of solid ranunculus fields bloom into a breathtaking rainbow visible even from the freeway. In December, the nurseries are alive with holiday poinsettias. You can also stroll through 30 acres of California native plants, exotic tropicals, palms, cacti, and more at **Quail Botanical Gardens** in Encinitas (☎ 760/436-3036).

The **Carlsbad Visitor Information Center,** 400 Carlsbad Village Dr. (in the old Santa Fe Depot), Carlsbad, CA 92008 (☎ 800/227-5722 or 760/434-6093), has lots of additional information on flower fields and nursery touring.

BEACHES **Carlsbad State Beach** runs alongside downtown. It's a great place to stroll along a wide concrete walkway, surrounded by like-minded outdoor types walking, jogging, and in-line skating, even at night (thanks to good lighting). Enter on Ocean Boulevard at Tamarack Avenue; there's a $4 fee per vehicle.

Four miles south of town is **South Carlsbad State Beach,** almost 3 miles of cobblestone-strewn sand. A state-run campground at the north end is immensely popular year-round, and the southern portion is favored by area surfers. There's a $4 fee at the beach's entrance, along Carlsbad Boulevard at Poinsettia Lane.

Down in Encinitas, everyone flocks to **Moonlight Beach,** the city's sandy playground with plenty of facilities, including free parking, volleyball nets, rest rooms, showers, picnic tables and fire grates, and the company of fellow sunbathers. The beach is accessed at the end of B Street (Encinitas Boulevard).

JUST FOR KIDS The ultimate monument to the world's most famous plastic building blocks opened in Carlsbad in March 1999. **Legoland** attractions include "hands-on" interactive displays; a lifesize menagerie of tigers, giraffes, and other animals; scale models of worldwide landmarks (the Eiffel Tower, Sydney Opera House, and more)—all constructed of real Lego bricks! MiniLand is a 1:20 scale representation of American achievement, from a New England pilgrim village to a Lego Mount Rushmore; there's also a gravity coaster ride (don't worry, they used steel) through a Lego castle. Legoland is open daily from 10am until dusk; admission is $32 for adults, $25 for seniors and kids 3 to 16, and free to children under 3. For more information, call ☎ 760/438-5346 or check out the Web site at **www.legolandca.com**. To get here from I-5, take the Canon exit east, which leads directly to the attraction's entrance.

WHERE TO STAY

For the ultimate pampering golf/tennis/spa vacation in Carlsbad, head to the **Four Seasons Resort Aviara,** 7100 Four Seasons Point (☎ 800/332-3442 or 760/603-6800), or **La Costa Resort and Spa,** Costa del Mar Rd. (☎ 800/854-5000 or 760/438-9111; www.lacosta.com).

Beach Terrace Inn. 2775 Ocean St., Carlsbad, CA 92003. ☎ **800/433-5415** outside Calif., or 760/729-5951; 800/622-3224 in Calif. Fax 760/729-1078. www.beachterraceinn.com. 49 units. A/C TV TEL. Summer $119–$229 double; from $149 suite. Winter $109–$189 double; from $129 suite. Extra person $15. Rates include continental breakfast. AE, CB, DC, DISC, ER, JCB, MC, V. Free parking.

Carlsbad's only beachside hostelry (others are across the road or a little farther away), this downtown Best Western property has a helpful staff, an outdoor pool, and rooms with ocean views. The rooms, although not elegant, are extra large, and some have balconies, fireplaces, and kitchenettes; suites have separate living rooms and bedrooms. VCRs and movies are available at the front desk. This is a good choice for families. You can walk everywhere from here, and street parking is available.

Pelican Cove Inn. 320 Walnut Ave., Carlsbad, CA 92008. ☎ **888/PEL-COVE** or 760/434-5995. www.pelican-cove.com/pelican. 8 units. TV. $90–$180 double. Rates include full breakfast. Extra person $15. Midweek and seasonal discounts available. AE, MC, V. Free parking. From downtown Carlsbad, follow Carlsbad Blvd. south to Walnut Ave.; turn left and drive 2½ blocks.

Located 2 blocks from the beach, this Cape Cod–style hideaway combines romance with luxury. Hosts Kris and Nancy Nayudu see to your every need, from furnishing guest rooms with soft feather beds and down comforters to providing beach chairs and towels or preparing a picnic basket (with 24 hours' notice). Each of the inn's eight rooms features a fireplace and private entrance; some have private spa tubs. The airy, spacious "La Jolla" room is loveliest, with bay windows and cupola ceiling. A full breakfast is included in your stay, and can be enjoyed in the garden if weather permits. Courtesy transportation from the Oceanside train station is available.

Tamarack Beach Resort. 3200 Carlsbad Blvd., Carlsbad, CA 92008. ☎ **800/334-2199** or 760/729-3500. Fax 760/434-5942. www.tamarackresort.com. 77 units. A/C TV TEL. $130–$195 double; $220–$330 suite. Children under 12 stay free in parents' room. AE, MC, V. Free underground parking.

This resort property's rooms, in the village and across the street from the beach, are restfully decorated in tropical colors and wicker furniture, with small fridges, coffeemakers, and VCRs (movies are complimentary). The fully equipped vacation rentals (including washer and dryer) are available on a daily or weekly basis. The pretty Tamarack also has a pleasant lobby, a heated pool in a sunny courtyard setting, two Jacuzzis, exercise facilities, valet services, barbecue grills, and a good restaurant, Dini's by the Sea, that's popular with locals.

WHERE TO DINE

Local favorites include **Neiman's,** 2978 Carlsbad Blvd., Carlsbad (☎ **760/729-4131**), serving American fare in a restored Victorian mansion, and the **Potato Shack,** 120 W. I St., Encinitas (☎ **760/436-1282**), a spuds-intensive diner open for breakfast and lunch only.

OCEANSIDE

The most northerly town in San Diego County (36 miles north of San Diego), Oceanside claims almost 4 miles of beaches and one of the West Coast's longest over-the-water wooden piers, where a tram does nothing but transport people from the street to the end of the 1,954-foot-long pier and back for 25¢ each way. The wide, sandy beach, pier, and well-tended recreational area with playground equipment and an outdoor amphitheater are within easy walking distance of the train station.

One of the nicest things to do in Oceanside is taking a stroll around the city's upscale **harbor;** it's bustling with pleasure craft, lined with condominiums, and boasts a Cape Cod–themed shopping village. A launch ramp, visitor boat slips, charter fishing, boat rentals, and the village of shops are found here; several restaurants, including **Chart House,** offer harborside dining. The **Marina Inn,** at 2008 Harbor Dr. N., Oceanside, CA 92054 (☎ **800/252-2033** or 760/722-1561; fax 760/439-9758), has comfortable rooms and suites that offer harbor and ocean views.

The **Harbor Days Festival** in mid-September typically attracts 100,000 visitors to its crafts fair, entertainment, and food booths.

Oceanside is home to the **California Surf Museum,** 223 North Coast Hwy. (☎ **760/721-6876**). Founded in 1985, the museum has an unbelievably extensive collection. Boards and other relics chronicle the development of the sport—many belonged to the names revered by local surfers, including Hawaiian Duke Kahanamoku and local daredevil Bob Simmons. Vintage photographs, beach attire, 1960s beach graffiti, and surf music all lovingly bring surfing to life—there's even a photo display of the real-life Gidget.

The area's biggest attraction is **Mission San Luis Rey** (☎ **760/757-3651**), a few miles inland. Founded in 1798, it's the largest of California's 21 missions. There is a small charge to tour the mission, its impressive church, exhibits, grounds, and cemetery. You might recognize it as the backdrop for one of the Zorro movies.

The **Oceanside Beach** runs all the way from just outside Oceanside Harbor, where routine harbor dredging makes for a pretty substantial amount of clean white sand, continuing almost 4 miles south at the Carlsbad border. Along the way you can enjoy the **Strand,** a grassy park stretching alongside the beach between Fifth Street and Wisconsin Avenue. Around the pier are rest rooms, showers, picnic areas, and volleyball nets.

Oceanside's world-famous surfing spots attract numerous competitions, including the **Longboard Surf Contest** and **World Bodysurfing Championships,** both in August.

For an information packet about Oceanside and its attractions, contact the **Oceanside Visitor & Tourism Center,** 928 North Coast Hwy., Oceanside, CA 92054 (☎ **800/350-7873** or 760/721-1101; www.oceansidechamber.com).

12 Julian: Apples, Pies & a Slice of Small-Town California

60 miles NE of San Diego, 35 miles W of Anza-Borrego Desert State Park

A trip to Julian (population 1,500) is a trip back in time. The old gold-mining town, now best known for its apples, has some good eateries and a handful of cute B&Bs, but its popularity is based on the fact that it provides a chance for city-weary folks to get away from it all.

ESSENTIALS

GETTING THERE   The 90-minute drive can be made via Calif. 78 or I-8 to Calif. 79. We suggest taking one route going and the other coming back. Calif. 79 winds through scenic Rancho Cuyamaca State Park, while Calif. 78 traverses open country and farmland.

VISITOR INFORMATION Town maps and fliers for accommodations are available from the Town Hall, on Main Street at Washington Street. The town has a **24-hour hot line** (☎ 760/765-0707) that provides information on lodging, dining, shopping, activities, upcoming events, weather, and road conditions. For a brochure on what to see and do, contact the **Julian Chamber of Commerce** (☎ 760/765-1857; www.icsol.com/west/julian).

EXPLORING THE TOWN

This 1880s gold-mining town has managed to retain a rustic, woodsy sense of its historic origins. Radiating the dusty aura of the Old West, Julian offers an abundance of early California history, quaint Victorian streets filled with apple-pie shops and antiques stores, crisp fresh air, and friendly people. Be forewarned, however: Julian's charming downtown can become exceedingly crowded during the fall harvest season, so consider making your trip during another time in order to enjoy this unspoiled relic with a little privacy (rest assured, apple pies are being baked year-round). At around 4,500 feet elevation, the autumn air is crisp and bracing, and Julian sees a dusting (and often more) of snow during the winter months.

The best way to experience tiny Julian is on foot. After stopping in at the **Chamber of Commerce** in the old Town Hall—check out the vintage photos of Julian's yesteryear—cross the street to the **Julian Drug Store,** 2134 Main St. (☎ 760/765-0332), an old-style soda fountain serving sparkling sarsaparilla and conjuring images of boys in buckskin and girls in bonnets. The circa–1870 **Eagle and High Peak Mines,** at the end of C Street (☎ 760/765-0036), although seemingly a tourist trap, offers an interesting and educational look at the town's one-time economic mainstay.

While in Julian, consider a ride in horse-drawn **Country Carriages** (☎ 760/765-1471). A rambling drive down country roads and through town is $20 per couple, or choose an abbreviated spin around town for $5 per adult, $2 per child. The town's **Pioneer Cemetery** is a must-see for graveyard buffs; contemporary graves belie the haphazard, overgrown look of this hilly burial ground, and eroded older tombstones tell the intriguing story of Julian's rough pioneer history. You can drive in via the A Street entrance, or climb the steep stairway leading up from Main Street; until 1924 this ascent was the only point of entry, even for processionals.

Apple pie is the town's mainstay, and the **Julian Pie Company,** 2225 Main St. (☎ 760/765-2449), is the most charming pie shop of them all. It serves original, Dutch, apple/mountain berry, and no-sugar-added pies as well as other baked goodies. Another great bakery is the aptly-named **Mom's Pies,** 2119 Main St. (☎ 760/765-2472), whose special attraction is a sidewalk plate-glass window through which you can observe the Mom-on-duty rolling crust, filling pies, and crimping edges. Nearby is the **Julian Cider Mill,** 2103 Main St. (☎ 760/765-1430), where you can see cider presses at work from October through March; it offers free tastes of the fresh nectar and sells jugs to take home.

Special Events

Julian's popular **fall apple harvest** starts in mid-September and continues for an entire month. The annual **wildflower show** lasts for a week in early May; there's also a **Spring Fine Arts Show** in May. And the annual **weed show,** a tradition since 1961, is usually held the last few weeks in August or the beginning of September. Contact the Julian Chamber of Commerce (see "Visitor Information," above) for details on all of these events.

A short and scenic drive from town leads to the **Menghini Winery** (☎ 760/765-2072), a family-run operation 2 miles out on Farmer's Road (follow it west out of town until you see the winery sign, then bear to the left down the hill). The winery is usually open Monday, Friday, Saturday, and Sunday from 10am to 4pm; daily in October and December; or call for an appointment. The grapes come from Ramona and Temecula, and the local favorite wine is Julian Blossom. The tanks are right in the tasting room, and the wines are sold only locally, for $7 to $10 per bottle. You may enjoy your purchase right away in the picnic area in the apple orchard.

Ask any of the San Diegans who regularly make excursions to Julian: No trip would be complete without a stop at **Dudley's Bakery,** Calif. 78, Santa Ysabel (☎ 800/225-3348 or 760/765-0488), for a loaf or three of its popular bread. Loaves are stacked high, and folks are often three deep at the counter, clamoring for the 20 (!) varieties of bread baked fresh daily—varieties range from raisin-date-nut to jalapeño, with some garden-variety sourdough and multigrain in between. Dudley's is a local tradition, built in 1963 and expanding several times to accommodate ever-growing business. It's open Wednesday through Sunday from 8am to 5pm (subject to early closure on Sunday).

OUTDOOR PURSUITS

Within 10 miles of Julian are numerous hiking trails traversing rolling meadows, high chaparral, and thick pine forests. The most spectacular hike is at **Volcan Mountain Preserve,** north of town along Farmers Road; the trail to the top is a moderately challenging hike of around 3½ miles round-trip with a 1,400-foot elevation gain. From the top, hikers have a panoramic view of the desert, mountains, and sea. Docent-led hikes are offered year-round at no charge (usually on one Saturday per month). For a hike schedule, call ☎ **760/765-0650.**

In **William Heise County Park,** off Frisius Drive outside of Pine Hills, the whole family can enjoy hikes ranging from a self-guided nature trail to a cedar-scented forest trail, plus moderate to vigorous trails into the mountains. A ranger kiosk at the entrance can provide trail maps.

Cuyamaca Rancho State Park covers 30,000 acres along Calif. 79 southeast of Julian, the centerpiece of which is **Cuyamaca Lake.** In addition to lake recreation (☎ **760/765-0515** or 760/447-8123 for information on boat rentals and fishing), there are several sylvan picnic areas, three campgrounds, and 110 miles of hiking trails through the Cleveland National Forest. Activities at the lake include fishing (trout, bass, catfish, bluegill, and crappie) and boating; there's a general store and restaurant at lake's edge. The fishing fee (license required) is $4.75 per day for adults and $2.50 per day for kids 8 to 15; rowboats are $12 per day, and outboard motors an additional $13. Canoes and paddleboats can be rented by the hour for $4 to $7. For a trail map and further information about park recreation, stop in at **park headquarters,** on Calif. 79 (☎ **760/765-0755**), Monday through Friday between the hours of 8am and 5pm. An adjacent park museum is open Monday through Friday from 10am to 5pm and Saturday and Sunday from 10am to 4pm.

For a different way to tour, try **Llama Trek,** P.O. Box 2363, Julian, CA 92036 (☎ **800/LAMAPAK** or 760/765-1890; fax 760/765-1512; www.llamatreks.com). Trips include rural neighborhoods, a historic gold mine, mountain and lake views, and apple orchards. It even conducts a trek to the local winery. Rates for the 4- to 5-hour trips vary from $65 to $85 per person and include lunch (the winery trek also includes wine tasting).

WHERE TO STAY

For a list and description of more than 20 B&Bs, contact the **Julian Bed & Breakfast Guild** (☎ 760/765-1555; www.julianbnbguild.com). Noteworthy member inns are the **Artists' Loft** (☎ 760/765-0765), a peaceful hilltop retreat offering two artistically decorated rooms and a cozy cabin with a wood-burning stove; the **Julian White House** (☎ 800/WHT-HOUS or 760/765-1764), a lovely faux-antebellum mansion, 4 miles from Julian in Pine Hills, with four frilly Victorian-style guest rooms; and the romantic **Random Oaks Ranch** (☎ 800/BNB-4344 or 760/765-1094), which features two themed cottages, each with its own wood-burning fireplace and outdoor Jacuzzi.

A word of caution: Reservations for the fall harvest season must be made several months in advance.

Julian Hotel. Main and B sts. (P.O. Box 1856), Julian, CA 92036. ☎ **800/734-5854** or 760/765-0201. Fax 760/765-0327. www.julianhotel.com. 15 units. $72–$125 double; $110–$175 cottage. Rates include full breakfast and afternoon tea. AE, MC, V.

Built in 1897 by freed slave Albert Robinson, this frontier-style hotel is a living monument to the area's gold-boom days. Centrally located at the crossroads of downtown, the Julian Hotel isn't as secluded or plush as the many B&Bs in town, but if you seek historically accurate lodgings to complete your weekend time warp, this is the place. The 13 rooms and two cottages, all with private bath, have been authentically restored and boast antique furnishings; the inviting private lobby is stocked with a wood-burning stove, books, games, and literature on local activities.

Orchard Hill Country Inn. 2502 Washington St., at Second St. (P.O. Box 425), Julian, CA 92036-0425. ☎ **800/71-ORCHARD** or 760/765-1700. Fax 760/765-0290. www.orchardhill. com. 22 units. A/C MINIBAR TV TEL. $160–$265 double. Extra person $25. 2-night minimum if including Fri or Sat. Seasonal discounts and packages available. Rates include full breakfast and afternoon hors d'oeuvres. AE, MC, V. From Calif. 79, turn left on Main St., then right on Washington St.

Hosts Darrell and Pat Straube offer the most upscale lodging in Julian, a two-story lodge and four Craftsman cottages situated on a hill overlooking the town. Ten guest rooms, a guests-only dining room, and a "great room" with a massive stone fireplace are located in the lodge. Twelve suites are in cottages spread over 3 acres of grounds. All quarters feature contemporary and unfrilly country furnishings, private baths, TV/VCRs, and snacks. While rooms in the main lodge are rather hotel-ish in feel, the cottage suites are secluded and luxurious, featuring private porches, fireplaces, whirlpool tubs, and bathrobes. Several hiking trails lead from the lodge into adjacent woods.

WHERE TO DINE

Julian Grille. 2224 Main St. (at A St.). ☎ **760/765-0173.** Reservations required Fri–Sun. Main courses $13–$21. AE, MC, V. Daily 11am–3pm; Tues–Sun 5–9pm. AMERICAN.

Set in a cozy cottage festooned with lacy draperies, flickering candles, and a warm hearth, the Grille is the nicest eatery in town. Lunch here is an anything-goes affair, ranging from soups, sandwiches, and large salads to charbroiled burgers and hearty omelets. Dinner features grilled and broiled meats, seafood, and prime rib; we're partial to delectable appetizers like baked Brie with apples and mustard sauce, Baja-style shrimp cocktail, or the "Prime tickler" (chunks of prime rib served cocktail-style *au jus* with horseradish sauce). Dinners are complete, with soup or salad, hot rolls, potatoes, and vegetable. The Grille is popular, and dining options are limited, so reservations are a necessity on weekends year-round.

Romano's Dodge House. 2718 B St. (just south of Main). ☎ **760/765-1003.** Reservations required for dinner Fri–Sat, recommended other nights. Main courses $8–$16. No credit cards. Wed–Mon 11am–8:30m. ITALIAN.

Occupying an historic home (vintage photos illustrate the little farmhouse's past) just off Main Street, Romano's is proudly the only restaurant in town that *doesn't* serve apple pie. A home-style Italian place with red-checked tablecloths and straw-clad Chianti bottles, it offers individual lunch pizzas, pastas bathed in a rich marinara sauce, veal parmigiana, chicken cacciatore, and their signature dish, pork Juliana (loin chops in a whisky–apple cider sauce.) There's seating on a narrow shaded porch in addition to the wood-plank dining room, plus a little saloon in back.

JULIAN AFTER DARK

Fans of old-style dinner theater will feel right at home at **Pine Hills Dinner Theater,** 2960 La Posada Way, about 2 miles from Julian off Pine Hills Road (☎ **760/765-1100**), a Friday/Saturday theater that has staged more than 80 productions since opening in 1980 in this rustic 1912 building. Thespian fare is usually light and comedic—past productions include *I'm Not Rappaport* and *Last of the Red Hot Lovers*—but dinner is a filling buffet of barbecued baby-back pork ribs, baked chicken, baked beans, salads, veggies, and thick sheepherder's bread. Show time i s 8pm, and the price for the dinner and the theater is $28.50; for the show alone, it's $14.50.

13 Anza-Borrego Desert State Park

35 miles E of Julian, 90 miles NE of San Diego

The sweeping 600,000-acre Anza-Borrego Desert State Park is home to fossils and rocks dating from 540 million years ago; human beings arrived only 10,000 years ago. The terrain ranges in elevation from 15 feet to more than 6,000 feet above sea level, and incorporates dry lake beds, sandstone canyons, granite mountains, palm groves fed by year-round springs, and more than 600 kinds of desert plants. After the spring rains, thousands of wildflowers burst into bloom, transforming the desert into a brilliant palette of pink, lavender, red, orange, and yellow. The rare bighorn sheep can often be spotted navigating rocky hillsides, and an occasional migratory bird stops off on the way to the Salton Sea. A sense of timelessness pervades this landscape; travelers tend to slow down and take a long look around.

When planning a trip here, keep in mind that temperatures rise to as high as 115°F in summer.

ESSENTIALS

The **Anza-Borrego Desert State Park Visitor Center** lies just west of the town of Borrego Springs. You can contact park headquarters at ☎ **760/767-4205;** the visitor

A Special Event

From mid-March to the beginning of April, the desert wildflowers and cacti are usually in bloom, a hands-down, all-out natural special event that's not to be missed. The wildflower hot line is ☎ **760/767-4684.**

center is open October through May daily from 9am to 5pm, and June through September weekends from 10am to 5pm.

For other local information, contact the **Borrego Springs Chamber of Commerce,** 622 Palm Canyon Dr., Borrego Springs, CA 92004 (☎ **760/767-5555;** www.borregosprings.com).

EXPLORING THE DESERT

When you're touring in this area, remember that hydration is of paramount importance. Whether you're walking, cycling, or driving, always have a bottle of water at your side.

You can explore the desert's stark terrain via one of its trails or a self-guided driving tour; the visitor center can supply maps. For starters, the **Borrego Palm Canyon** self-guided hike (1½ miles each way), which starts at the campgrounds near the visitor center, is beautiful, easy to get to, and easy to do, leading in about half an hour to a waterfall and massive fan palms.

You can also take an organized tour of the desert, offered by **Desert Jeep Tours** (☎ **888/BY-JEEPS** or 760-767-0501; www.desertjeeptours.com). Led by Paul Ford ("Borrego Paul"), these tours go to the awesome view at Font's Point, where you can look out on the Badlands. This area was named by the early settlers because it was an impossible area for moving or grazing cattle. While you enjoy the view, Paul will tell you all about the history and geology of the area.

BICYCLING

Call **Carrizo Bikes** (☎ **760/767-3872**) and talk with Dan Cain (a true desert rat) about bike rentals and tours in the area. For a thrilling 12-mile bicycle ride down Montezuma Valley Grade, try the Desert Descent offered by **Gravity Activated Sports,** P.O. Box 683, Pauma Valley, CA 92061 (☎ **800/985-4427** or 760/742-2294; fax 760/742-2293; www.gasports.com).

WHERE TO STAY

Borrego Springs is a small place, but there are enough accommodations to suit all travel styles and budgets. In addition to the following choices, another decent option is **Palm Canyon Resort,** 221 Palm Canyon Dr. (☎ **800/242-0044** or 760/767-5341), a large complex including a moderately priced hotel, RV park, restaurant, and recreational facilities.

La Casa del Zorro Desert Resort. 3845 Yaqui Pass Rd., Borrego Springs, CA 92004. ☎ **800/824-1884** or 760/767-5323. Fax 760/767-5963. www.lacasadelzorro.com. 77 units. A/C TV TEL. Jan 15–Apr 30, $115 double ($95 weekdays); from $235 suite ($180 weekdays); from $235 casita ($175 weekdays). May 1–31 and Oct 1–Jan 15, $110 double ($85 weekdays); from $165 suite ($115 weekdays); from $190 casitas ($135 weekdays). June 1–Sept 30 $95 double ($75 weekdays); from $105 suite ($80 weekdays); from $125 casita ($95 weekdays). Weekday rates do not apply on holidays. Extra person $10. Tennis, jazz, holiday, and other packages available. AE, CB, DC, DISC, MC, V.

This pocket of heaven on earth was built in 1937, and the tamarind trees that were planted back then have grown up around it. Accommodations are scattered around La Casa's lushly landscaped grounds; guests can choose from standard hotel rooms, suites, or one-, two-, or three-bedroom adobe casitas with tile roofs. All the casitas have minifridges and microwaves, some have fireplaces or pools, and each bedroom has a separate bathroom. Facilities include two dining rooms, three swimming pools, tennis courts, bicycle rentals, massage, child care, and plenty of recreational options. If you come to this desert oasis during the week, you can take advantage of the lowered room rates.

⊙ **The Palms at Indian Head.** 2220 Hoberg Rd. (P.O. Box 525), Borrego Springs, CA 92004. ☎ **800/519-2624** or 760/767-7788. Fax 760/767-9717. www.ramonamall.com/thepalms.html. 10 units. A/C TV. Winter (Nov–May) $105–$159 double, summer (June–Oct) $95 double. Extra person $20. Lower midweek rates. Rates include breakfast. DC, DISC, MC, V. Take S22 into Borrego Springs; at Palm Canyon Dr., S22 becomes Hoberg Rd. Continue north half a mile.

Borrego Springs's only bed-and-breakfast is this once-chic resort that's being slowly renovated by its fervent owners, David and Cynthia Leibert. Originally opened in 1947, the art-deco style hilltop lodge was a favorite hideaway for San Diego's and Hollywood's elite; the Leiberts rescued it from extreme disrepair in 1993, clearing away some dilapidated guest bungalows surrounding the hotel, and uncovering original wallpaper, light fixtures, and priceless memorabilia. Just as soon as they'd restored several rooms in a luxurious Southwestern style, they began taking in guests to help finance the ongoing restoration. Also completely restored is the 42-by-109-foot pool, complete with the original subterranean grotto bar behind viewing windows at the deep end. The inn occupies the most envied site in the valley—shaded by palms, adjacent to the state park (a hiking trail begins just steps from the hotel), and enjoying a panoramic view across the entire Anza-Borrego region.

CAMPING

The park has two developed campgrounds. **Borrego Palm Canyon,** with 117 sites, is 2½ miles west of Borrego Springs and near the visitor center. Full hookups are available, and there's an easy hiking trail. **Tamarisk Grove,** at Calif. 78 and county road S3, has 27 sites. Both have campfire programs and rest rooms with showers; reservations are a good idea. The park allows open camping along all the trail routes. For more information, check with the visitor center (☎ **760/767-4205**).

WHERE TO DINE

There's also a high-priced (but admittedly excellent) dining room at La Casa del Zorro (see above).

The Coffee & Book Store. 590 Palm Canyon Dr. (in the Center). ☎ **760/767-5080.** Most items under $6. MC, V. Daily 6am–4pm. LIGHT FARE.

Rely upon this small but well-stocked shop for books, postcards, maps, and a freshly ground espresso or cup o' joe. It has a nice selection of sandwiches, salads, muffins, and desserts, making it a reliable choice for a quick breakfast or lunch at cafe tables set amidst the book displays. You can also pack up a pretty good picnic if you're off to explore the desert.

Krazy Coyote Saloon & Grille. 2220 Hoberg Rd. (in the Palms at Indian Head). ☎ **760/767-7788.** Main courses $7–$12. AE, MC, V. Open daily; call for seasonal hours. ECLECTIC.

The same stylish touch that pervades the attached bed-and-breakfast is evident in this casual restaurant overlooking the inn's swimming pool and the vast desert beyond. An eclectic menu brings together quesadillas, club sandwiches, burgers, grilled meats and fish, and individual gourmet pizzas; it also offers breakfast (rich and hearty for an active day, or light and healthy for diet watchers). The evening ambiance is welcoming and romantic, as the (sparse) lights of tiny Borrego Springs twinkle on the desert floor below.

Appendix A: California in Depth

by Matthew R. Poole

The more you know about California, the more you're likely to enjoy and appreciate everything the state has to offer. The pages that follow include a brief yet enlightening tale of how California came to be the most plentiful and powerful state in the nation, a wide-ranging list of highly recommended books, and more.

1 California Today

A recent survey of the most popular name given to California's newborns says a lot about the direction the Golden State is headed. You probably didn't guess José, but then again, you may not have known that California is the most racially diverse state in the nation, playing host to every race, ethnic heritage, language group, and religion in the *world*. So if you're prone to xenophobia, you might want to spend your vacation elsewhere, because shortly after the turn of the century, California will become the mother of all melting pots, where no single race or ethnic group will constitute a majority of the state's population.

The numbers are already bewildering: 32.5 million people, a whopping one-third of whom live in the Los Angeles Basin. California already receives the highest numbers of immigrants each year—more than 200,000 annually—and if the rosy economy continues its course, the numbers will only get higher. Whether this is a potential boon or time bomb for California's future, it's impossible to predict, but in the meantime it makes for a very interesting place to live and visit. (Heck, why bother traveling all the way to Europe or Asia when you can visit immigrant communities in Los Angeles and San Francisco that are uncanny replicas of the societies they've left behind?)

Much of California's new-found prosperity and popularity can be attributed to deft restructuring of the economy during the post–Cold War era. A classic example is the numerous Air Force and Naval bases that were shut down, leaving thousands of civilians unemployed. Yet, thanks to an unprecedented collaboration between government and private enterprise, many of the former bases were reopened as computer manufacturing plants, tourist attractions, and, in some cases, even movie studios. California high-tech industries, once employed to build better bombs, have also earned healthy dividends by retooling their trade toward computer and information-based enterprises. Meanwhile, the industries that have always bolstered California's economy—agriculture, tourism, entertainment, and manufacturing—continue to thrive.

A Tale of Two States

It doesn't take a psychiatrist to figure out that California suffers from an acute case of bipolar schizophrenia. We Californians may, on the surface, appear to be one big *Happy Days* family, but in reality we've divided our state into separate factions worthy of Montague and Capulet. That is, you're either a Northern Californian or a Southern Californian, two opposing tribes that have little in common. In fact, which side you even choose to visit may reveal something about yourself.

All the California glamour, wealth, fame, fast cars, surf scenes, and buxom blondes you see on television is pure Southern invention. If this is the California you're looking for, head due south—assuming you're not terribly interested in intellectual stimulation, you won't be disappointed. In fact, it's nearly impossible not to be immediately swept up by the energy and excitement that places like West Hollywood and Venice Beach exude. It's a narcotic effect, the allure of flashy wealth, gorgeous bodies, and celebrity status. Even watching it all as a bystander imparts a heady mixture of thrill and envy.

Northern California may be frightfully demure in comparison, but in the long run, its subdued charms and natural beauty prevail. Wealth is certainly in abundance, but rarely displayed. The few hard bodies that exist are usually swathed in loose jeans and shirts. The few celebrities who live here keep very low profiles, and are more likely to be on their ranches than Rodeo Drive. Ostentation in any form is looked down upon (of course, it's okay to own a BMW, as long as it's slightly dirty), and unlike Los Angeles, you can actually explore smog-free San Francisco on foot.

Ironically, it's the Northern Californians who think of themselves as superior for having prudently eschewed the trappings of wealth and status (L.A.-bashing is a popular pastime). Southern Californians, on the other hand, couldn't care less what the Northerners think of them; it's all sour grapes as they bask poolside 300 sunny days of the year. In fact, most Southern Californians would be perfectly content as their own state were it not for one key factor: water. Northern California holds two-thirds of the state's watershed, and without the incredibly complex system of aqueducts, reservoirs, and dams that keep huge flows going southward, Southern California's 13 million citizens would be in a world of hurt.

Will Californians ever agree to a legally mutual breakup? The idea has been bandied about the state capital for years, but it consistently meets its waterloo when it comes to water rights, always a hotly contested issue in California politics. But regardless of our polarized views and lifestyles, most Californians do agree on one thing: We're still the best damn dysfunctional state in America.

The end result of such economic providence is that California is currently riding a wave of prosperity. After more than a decade of getting trounced by the recession and Republican leadership, the combination of brimming coffers and a newly elected Democratic governor—the first in nearly a decade—equates to much needed relief for California's oft-neglected schools, roads, and low-income citizens. Even the middle-class sector is riding the quick and easy road to riches via the stock market and Internet IPOs. How long this social and economic boom will last is the billion-dollar question; but in the meantime, California is living up to its legacy as the land of golden promise.

Dateline

- **1542** Juan Cabrillo enters San Diego Bay and sails up California's coast in first documented European visit.
- **1579** Sir Francis Drake drops anchor in the San Francisco Bay area and claims the land for England's Queen Elizabeth I.
- **1602** Spanish explorer and merchant Sebastian Vizcano sails up the coast, naming many regions along the way.
- **1769** Mission San Diego de Alcala is founded by Franciscan monk Father Junípero Serra.
- **1775** Juan Manuel de Ayala maps San Francisco Bay.
- **1777** Monterey is made capital of Spain's California territory.
- **1781** Los Angeles is founded.
- **1804** Spain divides its California territory into Baja (Lower) California and Alta (Upper) California; Jose Joaquin de Arrillaga becomes the first governor of Alta California.
- **1808** Connecticut sea captain William Shaler publishes his *Journal,* the first extensive account of California.
- **1821** Mexico wins independence from Spain and annexes California.
- **1836** Governor Juan Batista Alvarado declares California a "free and sovereign state."
- **1846** John C. Fremont leads the Bear Flag Revolt; California is drawn into the Mexican-American War; the U.S flag is raised in Yerba Buena (San Francisco) and Los Angeles.
- **1847** Yerba Buena is renamed San Francisco; the Donner Party is trapped by heavy Sierra Nevada snows.

continues

EUROPEAN DISCOVERY & COLONIZATION Although very little remains to mark the existence of West Coast Native Americans, anthropologists estimate that as many as half a million aboriginals flourished on this naturally abundant land for thousands of years before the arrival of Europeans in the mid–16th century. Sailing from a small colony, established 10 years before, on the southern tip of Baja (Lower) California, Portuguese explorer Juan Rodrígues Cabrillo is credited with being the first European to "discover" California, in 1542. Over the next 200 years, dozens of sailors mapped the coast, including British explorer Sir Francis Drake, who sailed his *Golden Hind* into what is now called Drake's Bay in 1579, and Spanish explorer Sebastian Vizcano, who, in 1602, bestowed most of the placenames that survive today, including San Diego, Santa Barbara, and Carmel.

European colonial competition and Catholic missionary zeal prompted Spain to establish settlements along the Alta (Upper) California coast and claim the lands as its own. In 1769, Father Junípero Serra, accompanied by 300 soldiers and clergy, began forging a path from Mexico to Monterey. A small mission and presidio (fort) were established that year at San Diego, and by 1804, a chain of 21 missions, each a day's walk from the next along a dirt road called *Camino Real* (Royal Road), stretched all the way to Sonoma. Most of the solidly built missions still remain—Mission Delores, Mission San Juan Bautista, Mission San Diego de Alcal, to name just a few—and offer public tours.

During that time, thousands of Native Americans were converted to Christianity and coerced into labor. Many others died from imported diseases. Because not all the natives welcomed their conquerors with open arms, many missions and pueblos (small towns) suffered repeated attacks, leading to the construction of California's now ubiquitous—and fireproof—red-tile roofs.

No settlement had more than 100 inhabitants when Spain's sovereignty was compromised by an 1812 Russian outpost called Fort Ross, 60 miles north of San Francisco (which, remarkably enough, still stands and is open to the public). But the biggest threat came from the British—who had strengthened their own claims to America with the Hudson's Bay Company trading firm—and their short-lived, last-ditch effort to win back their territories in the War of 1812.

Embattled at home as well as abroad, the Spanish finally relinquished their claim to Mexico and California in 1821. Under Mexican rule, Alta California's Spanish missionaries fell out of favor and lost much of their land to the increasingly wealthy *Californios*—Mexican immigrants who had been granted vast tracts of land.

AMERICAN EXPANSION Beginning in the late 1820s, Americans from the East began to make their way to California, via a 3-month sail around Cape Horn. Most of them settled in the territorial capital of Monterey and in Northern California.

From the 1830s on, inspired by the doctrine of Manifest Destiny—an almost religious belief that the United States was destined to cover the continent from coast to coast—more and more settlers headed west. Along with them came daring explorers. In 1843, Marcus Whitman, a missionary seeking to prove that settlers could travel overland through the Oregon Territory's Blue Mountains, helped blaze the Oregon Trail; the first covered-wagon train made the 4-month crossing in 1844. Over the next few years, several hundred Americans made the trek to California over the Sierra Nevada range via Truckee Pass, just north of Lake Tahoe. A memorial to the Donner Party—the most famous tragedy in the history of westward migration—marks the site of the ill-fated travelers.

As the drive to the west increased, the U.S. Government sought to extend its control over Mexican territory north of the Rio Grande, the river that now divides the United States and Mexico. In 1846, President James Polk offered Mexico $40 million for California and New Mexico. The offer might have been accepted, but America's simultaneous annexation of Texas, to which Mexico still laid claim, resulted in a war between the two countries. Within months, the United States overcame Mexico and took possession of the entire West Coast.

GOLD & STATEHOOD In 1848, California's non–Native American population was around 7,000. That same year, flakes of gold were discovered by workers building a sawmill

- **1848** James Wilson Marshall discovers gold in Coloma; California is officially made a U.S. Territory.
- **1849** The Gold Rush is in full swing, bringing more than 300,000 men and women; a constitutional convention meets in Monterey; San Jose becomes the state capital.
- **1850** California becomes the 31st state.
- **1853** Levi Strauss sells his first pair of canvas trousers.
- **1854** Sacramento becomes the permanent state capital.
- **1857** Hungarian Agoston Haraszthy establishes the state's first winery, Buena Vista.
- **1859** Prospector James Finney discovers silver ore, the Comstock Load.
- **1861** California swears allegiance to the Union.
- **1862** The first telegraph line is established between San Francisco and New York.
- **1867** Anti-Chinese demonstrations take place in San Francisco in the wake of rising immigration.
- **1869** The transcontinental railroad is completed.
- **1873** The University of California opens its campus at Berkeley; the first cable car appears in San Francisco.
- **1879** The University of Southern California is founded.
- **1881** The *Los Angeles Times* begins publication.
- **1888** Lick Observatory is established.
- **1890** Yosemite gains National Park status.
- **1906** San Francisco is decimated by an earthquake and fire, leaving 300,000 people homeless.
- **1911** Hollywood's first film studio is established.
- **1915** The first transcontinental telephone call is made from San Francisco to New York.

continues

- **1919** William Randolph Hearst begins construction of his castle at San Simeon.
- **1922** The Hollywood Bowl and amphitheater opens.
- **1924** The first transcontinental airmail flight is made from San Francisco to New York.
- **1928** Walt Disney creates Mickey Mouse.
- **1929** Hollywood hosts the first Academy Awards presentation.
- **1934** Alcatraz Island is converted to a maximum security penitentiary.
- **1935** Statewide irrigation system is begun.
- **1936** The San Francisco–Oakland Bay Bridge opens.
- **1937** The Golden Gate Bridge opens.
- **1945** The United Nations is founded in San Francisco.
- **1955** Disneyland opens in Anaheim; actor James Dean dies in a car accident at age 24.
- **1958** California acquires its first major-league baseball team, the San Francisco Giants.
- **1960** San Francisco's Candlestick Park opens.
- **1962** California becomes the most populous state in the Union.
- **1964** Mario Savio speaks before Free Speech Movement demonstrators at UC Berkeley.
- **1967** San Francisco's Haight-Ashbury experiences the "Summer of Love."
- **1968** Robert Kennedy is assassinated at L.A.'s Ambassador Hotel.
- **1972** The BART system opens in San Francisco.
- **1978** Steve Wozniak and Steve Jobs revolutionize personal computing with the launch of Apple Computers; San Francisco Mayor George

continues

along the American River. Word of the find spread quickly, bringing more than 300,000 men and women into California between 1849 and 1851, one of the largest mass migrations in American history. Of course, very few prospectors unearthed a gold mine, and within 15 years the gold had dissipated, though many of the new residents remained. In fact, much of the mining equipment and gold rush–era buildings remain today, and are on display throughout the Gold Country.

In 1850, California was admitted to the Union as the 31st state. The state constitution on which California applied for admission included several noteworthy features. To protect the miners, slavery was prohibited. To attract women from the East Coast, legal recognition was given to the separate property of a married woman (California was the first state to offer such recognition). By 1870, almost 90 percent of the state's Native American population had been wiped out, and the bulk of the rest were removed to undesirable inland reservations.

Mexican and Chinese laborers were brought in to help local farmers and to work on the transcontinental railroad, which was completed in 1869. The new rail line transported easterners to California in just five days, marking a turning point in the settlement of the West. Many of those same steam engines are on display at the California State Railroad Museum in Sacramento.

GROWTH & INDUSTRY In 1875, when the Santa Fe Railroad reached Los Angeles, southern California's population of just 10,000 was divided equally between Los Angeles and San Diego. Los Angeles, however, began to grow rapidly in 1911, when the film industry moved here from the East Coast to take advantage of cheap land and a warm climate that enabled movies to be shot outdoors year-round. The movies' glamorous, idyllic portrayal of California boosted the region's popularity and population, especially during the Great Depression of the 1930s, when thousands of families (like the Joads in John Steinbeck's novel *The Grapes of Wrath*) packed up their belongings and headed west in search of a better life.

World War II brought heavy industry to California, in the form of munitions factories, shipyards, and airplane manufacturing. Freeways were built, military bases were opened, and suburbs were developed. In the 1950s, California in general, and San Francisco in particular, became popular with artists and intellectuals. The so-called Beat generation appeared, later to inspire alternative-culture groups, most notably the "flower children" of the 1960s, in San Francisco's Haight-Ashbury district. During the "Summer of Love" in 1967, as the war in Vietnam escalated, student protests increased at Berkeley and elsewhere in California, as they did across the country. A year later, amid rising racial tensions, Martin Luther King, Jr., was killed, setting off riots in the Watts section of Los Angeles and in other cities. Soon thereafter, Robert F. Kennedy was fatally shot in Los Angeles after winning the California Democratic Party presidential primary. Antiwar protests continued into the 1970s.

Perhaps in response to an increasingly violent society, the 1970s also gave rise to several exotic religions and cults, which found eager adherents in California. The spiritual "New Age" continued into the 1980s, along with a growing population, environmental pollution, and escalating social ills, especially in Los Angeles. California also became very rich. Real-estate values soared, the computer industry—centered in "Silicon Valley" south of San Francisco—boomed, and banks and businesses prospered.

RECESSION & REDEMPTION The late 1980s and early 1990s, however, brought a devastating recession to the state. Californians, like many other Americans, became increasingly more conservative. Though they remained concerned about the nation's problems—economic competition from abroad, the environment, drugs, the blight of homelessness afflicting cities

Moscone and Supervisor Harvey Milk are assassinated at City Hall.
- **1984** Los Angeles hosts the Summer Olympic Games.
- **1989** An earthquake registering 7.1 on the Richter scale hits San Francisco, causing 63 deaths and $10 billion in damage.
- **1991** AIDS becomes San Francisco number-one killer of men.
- **1992** Fire rages through the Berkeley/Oakland hills, destroying 2,800 homes.
- **1992** Los Angeles experiences the worst race riots in American history: 50 dead, hundreds injured; California becomes first state in the Union to send two female senators to Washington
- **1993** Firestorms sweep through Los Angela area; an earthquake registering 6.2 on the Richter scale strikes.
- **1994** An earthquake measuring 6.8 on the Richter scale hits L.A., killing more than 60 people and injuring thousands.
- **1996** Former Assembly Speaker Willie Brown is elected mayor of San Francisco.
- **1997** El Niño floods cause billions in damage throughout California.
- **1998** Gray Davis is elected governor, the first Democrat to hold the office since 1986.

large and small—their fascination with alternative lifestyles ebbed as the former campus rebels among them settled into comfortable positions in industry and politics: In short, the baby boomers were growing up and settling down.

The plight of AIDS also became a major issue of the 1990s, particularly in San Francisco, where it quickly became the number-one killer of young men. Los Angeles had its problems as well, most notably the race riots spurred by a videotaping (and subsequent acquittal) of four white police officers beating a black motorist, Rodney King. Two years later, a major earthquake would cause billions of dollars in damage to L.A.'s buildings and freeways, and leave thousands injured and homeless, while Oakland's hills became a raging inferno, killing 26 people and destroying 3,000 homes.

Midway through 1990s, America's economy slowly yet surely began to improve, a welcome relief to recession-battered Californians. Crime and unemployment began to drop, while public schools received millions for much-needed improvements. Computer- and Internet-related industries began to flourish in the Bay Area, with entrepreneurism fueling much of the explosive growth. As the stock market continued to grow bullish (particularly in the technology sector) through the end of the decade, no state reaped more benefits than California, which was gaining new millionaires by the day. As the millennium approached, optimism in the state's economy and quality of life was—and still is—at an all-time high.

3 Recommended Reading

There's no shortage of reading material about the history and culture of California, one of the most romanticized places on earth. Almost from the beginning, novelists and poets were an essential part of California's cultural mosaic, and the works they've created offer a fascinating window into the lives and legends that have greatly influenced California's inception and fervid growth.

HISTORICAL PERSPECTIVES Readers are spoiled for choices when it comes to fictionalized accounts of California's pioneers. Salinas native John Steinbeck, one of the state's best-known authors, paints a vivid portrayal of proletarian life in the early to mid–1900s. His *Grapes of Wrath* remains the classic account of itinerant farm laborers coming to California in the midst of the Great Depression. *Cannery Row* has forever made the Monterey waterfront famous, and *East of Eden* offers insight into the way of life in the Salinas Valley.

Famed humorist and storyteller Mark Twain penned vivid tales during California's Gold Rush era, including one of his most popular works, "The Celebrated Jumping Frog of Calaveras County" (an annual Gold Country competition that still has legs). Other good Gold Rush reads include Bret Harte's *The Luck of Roaring Camp,* a sentimental tale of hark-luck miners and their false toughness, and J. S. Holliday's *The World Rushed In,* one of the finest nonfiction accounts of the Gold Rush still in print.

San Francisco was also a popular setting for many early works, including Twain's *San Francisco,* a collection of articles that glorified "the liveliest, heartiest community on our continent." It was also the birthplace of Jack London, who wrote several short stories of his younger days as an oyster pirate on the San Francisco Bay, as well as *Martin Eden,* his semiautobiographical account of life along the Oakland shores.

Finally, for what some critics consider the best novel ever written about Hollywood, turn to Nathanael West's *The Day of the Locust,* a savage and satirical look at 1930s life on the fringes of the film industry.

MYSTERY & MAYHEM For all you mystery buffs headed to California, two must-reads include Frank Norris's *McTeague: A Story of San Francisco,* a violent tale of love and greed set at the turn of the century, and Dashiell Hammett's *The Maltese Falcon,* a steamy detective novel that captures the seedier side of San Francisco in the 1920s (you can even take a walking tour of Hammett's famous haunts). Another favorite is Raymond Chandler's *The Big Sleep,* in which private dick Philip Marlowe plies the seedier side of Los Angeles in the 1930s.

California has always been a hotbed for alternative–and, more often than not, controversial–literary styles. Joan Didion, in her novel *Slouching Toward Bethlehem,* and Hunter S. Thompson, in his columns for the *San Francisco Examiner* (brought together in the collection *Generation of Swine),* both used a "new journalistic" approach in their studies of San Francisco in the 1960s. Tom Wolfe's early work *The Electric Kool-Aid Acid Test* follows the Hell's Angels, the Grateful Dead, and Ken Kesey's Merry Pranksters as they ride through the hallucinogenic 1960s. Meanwhile, Beat writers Allen Ginsberg and Jack Kerouac were penning protests against political conservatism—and promoting their bohemian lifestyle—in the former's controversial poem "Howl" (daringly published by Lawrence Ferlinghetti, poet and owner of City Lights in San Francisco's North Beach district) and the latter's famous tale of American adventure, *On the Road.*

CONTEMPORARY FICTION   If you're interested in a contemporary look back at four generations in the life of an American family, you can do no better than Wallace Stegner's *Angle of Repose.* The winner of the Pulitzer Prize in 1971, this work chronicles the lives of pioneers on the western frontier. Among Stegner's many other works of fiction and nonfiction about the West is his novel *All the Little Live Things,* which explores the conflicts faced by retired literary agent Joe Allston; the book is set in the San Francisco Bay Area of the 1960s. *The Spectator Bird* (winner of the 1976 National Book Award) revisits Allston's character as he reflects on his life and his memories of a search for his roots.

SPECIAL-INTEREST READS   Geology buffs will want to pack a copy of *Assembling California,* John McPhee's fascinating observation of California's complex geological history. Most of this volume was previously published in *The New Yorker.*

Outdoor enthusiasts have literally dozens of sporting books to choose from, but most comprehensive is Foghorn Press's excellent outdoor series—*California Camping, California Fishing, California Golf, California Beaches,* and *California Hiking*—available at every major bookstore in the state. Another recommended choice is *Frommer's Great Outdoor Guide to Northern California.*

Appendix B: Useful Toll-Free Numbers & Web Sites

AIRLINES

Aeromexico
☎ 800/237-6639
www.aeromexico.com

Air Canada
☎ 800/776-3000
www.aircanada.ca

**Alaska Airlines/
Alaska Commuter**
☎ 800/426-0333
www.alaskaair.com

**American Airlines/
American Eagle**
☎ 800/433-7300
www.americanair.com

America West Airlines
☎ 800/235-9292
www.americawest.com

British Airways
☎ 800/247-9297
☎ 0345/222-111 in Britain
www.british-airways.com

Canadian Airlines
☎ 800/426-7000
www.cdnair.ca

Continental Airlines
☎ 800/525-0280
www.flycontinental.com

Delta Air Lines
☎ 800/221-1212
www.delta-air.com

Hawaiian Airlines
☎ 800/367-5320
www.hawaiianair.com

Kiwi International Air Lines
☎ 800/538-5494
www.jetkiwi.com

Midway Airlines
☎ 800/446-4392
www.midwayair.com

Midwest Express Airlines
☎ 800/452-2022
www.midwestexpress.com

**Northwest Airlines/
Northwest Airlink**
☎ 800/225-2525
www.nwa.com

Reno Air
☎ 800-736-6247
www.renoair.com

Skywest Airlines
☎ 800-453-9417

Southwest Airlines
☎ 800/435-9792
www.iflyswa.com

Tower Air
☎ 800/348-6937 outside
New York
☎ 718/553-8500
www.towerair.com

Trans World Airlines (TWA)
☎ 800/221-2000
www.twa.com

United Airlines/United Express
☎ 800/241-6522
www.ual.com

US Airways/US Airways Express
☎ 800/428-4322
www.usair.com

Virgin Atlantic Airways
☎ 800/862-8621 in Continental
U.S.☎ 0293/747-747 in Britain
www.fly.virgin.com

CAR-RENTAL AGENCIES

Advantage
☎ 800/777-5500
www.arac.com

Alamo
☎ 800/327-9633
www.goalamo.com

Auto Europe
☎ 800/223-5555
www.autoeurope.com

Avis
☎ 800/331-1212 in Continental U.S.
☎ 800/TRY-AVIS in Canada
www.avis.com

Budget
☎ 800/527-0700
www.budgetrentacar.com

Dollar
☎ 800/800-4000
www.dollarcar.com

Enterprise
☎ 800/325-8007
www.pickenterprise.com

Hertz
☎ 800/654-3131
www.hertz.com

Kemwel Holiday Auto (KHA)
☎ 800/678-0678
www.kemwel.com

National
☎ 800/CAR-RENT
www.nationalcar.com

Payless
☎ 800/PAYLESS
www.paylesscar.com

Rent-A-Wreck
☎ 800/535-1391
rent-a-wreck.com

Thrifty
☎ 800/367-2277
www.thrifty.com

Value
☎ 800/327-2501
www.go-value.com

MAJOR HOTEL & MOTEL CHAINS

Best Western International
☎ 800/528-1234
www.bestwestern.com

Clarion Hotels
☎ 800/CLARION
www.hotelchoice.com

Comfort Inns
☎ 800/228-5150
www.hotelchoice.com

Courtyard by Marriott
☎ 800/321-2211
www.courtyard.com

Days Inn
☎ 800/325-2525
www.daysinn.com

Doubletree/Red Lion Hotels & Inns
☎ 800/222-TREE
www.doubletreehotels.com

Econo Lodges
☎ 800/55-ECONO
www.hotelchoice.com

Fairfield Inns by Marriott
☎ 800/228-2800
www.fairfieldinn.com

Hampton Inn
☎ 800/HAMPTON
www.hampton-inn.com

Hilton Hotels
☎ 800/HILTONS
www.hilton.com

Holiday Inn
☎ 800/HOLIDAY
www.holiday-inn.com

Howard Johnson
☎ 800/654-2000
www.hojo.com

Hyatt Hotels & Resorts
☎ 800/228-9000
www.hyatt.com

ITT Sheraton
☎ 800/325-3535
www.sheraton.com

La Quinta Motor Inns
☎ 800/531-5900
www.laquinta.com

Marriott Hotels
☎ 800/228-9290
www.marriott.com

Motel 6
☎ 800/4-MOTEL6

Quality Inns
☎ 800/228-5151
www.hotelchoice.com

Radisson Hotels International
☎ 800/333-3333
www.radisson.com

Ramada Inns
☎ 800/2-RAMADA
www.ramada.com

Red Carpet Inns
☎ 800/251-1962

Red Roof Inns
☎ 800/843-7663
www.redroof.com

Residence Inn by Marriott
☎ 800/331-3131
www.residenceinn.com

Rodeway Inns
☎ 800/228-2000
www.hotelchoice.com

Super 8 Motels
☎ 800/800-8000
www.super8motels.com

Travelodge
☎ 800/255-3050
www.travelodge.com

Vagabond Inns
☎ 800/522-1555
www.vagabondinns.com

Wyndham Hotels & Resorts
☎ 800/822-4200 in Continental
U.S. and Canada
www.wyndham.com

Frommer's Online Directory

by Michael Shapiro & Bruce Gerstman

Michael Shapiro is the author of *Michael Shapiro's Internet Travel Planner* (The Globe Pequot Press). Bruce Gerstman contributed listings for San Diego and San Francisco to this directory.

Frommer's Online Directory is a new feature designed to help you take advantage of the Internet to better plan your trip. Part I lists some general Internet resources that can make any trip easier, such as sites for booking airline tickets. It's not meant to be a comprehensive list, but rather a discriminating selection of useful sites to get you started. In Part II, you'll find some top online guides specifically for California. Note that this is a press-time snapshot of leading Web sites—some may have evolved, changed, or moved by the time you read this.

1 The Top Travel-Planning Web Sites

Among the most popular sites are online travel agencies. The top agencies, including Expedia, Preview Travel, and Travelocity, offer an array of tools that are valuable even if you don't book online. You can check flight schedules, hotel availability, or car-rental rates, and even get paged if your flight is delayed.

While online agencies have come a long way over the past few years, they don't always yield the best prices. Unlike a travel agent, for example, they're unlikely to tell you that you can save money by flying a day earlier or a day later. On the other hand, if you're looking for a bargain fare, you might find something online that an agent wouldn't take the time to dig up. Because airline commissions have been cut, a travel agent may not find it worthwhile to spend half an hour trying to find you the best deal. On the Net, you can be your own agent and take all the time you want.

Online booking sites aren't the only places to book airline tickets—all major airlines have their own Web sites and often offer incentives, such as bonus frequent-flyer miles or Net-only discounts, for buying online. These incentives have helped airlines capture the majority of the online booking market. According to Jupiter Communications, online agencies such as Travelocity booked about 80 percent of tickets purchased online in 1996, but by 1999, airline sites were projected to own more than half of the online market, with online agencies' share of the pie dwindling each year.

Note: See "Appendix B: Useful Toll-Free Numbers & Web Sites" for a list of airlines, car-rental agencies, and major hotel and motel chains.

WHEN SHOULD YOU BOOK ONLINE?

Online booking is not for everyone. If you prefer to let others handle your travel arrangements, one call to an experienced travel agent

Internet Security

Far more people look online than book online, partly due to fear of putting their credit cards through on the Net. Though secure encryption has made this fear less justified, there's no reason why you can't find a flight online and then book it by calling a toll-free number or contacting your travel agent. To be sure you're in secure mode when you book online, look for a little icon of a key (in Netscape) or a padlock (Internet Explorer) at the bottom of your Web browser.

should suffice. But if you want to know as much as possible about your options, the Net is a good place to start, especially for bargain hunters.

The most compelling reason to use online booking is to take advantage of special offers and Internet-only fares that must be purchased online. Another advantage is that you can cash in on incentives for booking online, such as rebates or bonus frequent-flyer miles.

Online booking works best for trips within North America; for international tickets, it's usually cheaper and easier to use a travel agent or consolidator.

Online booking is certainly not for those with a complex international itinerary. If you require follow-up services, such as itinerary changes, use a travel agent. Though Expedia and some other online agencies employ travel agents available by phone, these sites are geared primarily for self-service.

LEADING BOOKING SITES

Below are listings for the top travel booking sites. The starred selections are the most useful and best designed sites.

Cheap Tickets. www.cheaptickets.com
Essentials: Discounted rates on domestic and international airline tickets and hotel rooms.

Sometimes discounters such as Cheap Tickets have exclusive deals that aren't available through more mainstream channels. Registration at Cheap Tickets requires inputting a credit-card number before getting started, so many people elect to call the company's toll-free number rather than book online. One of the most frustrating aspects of this site is that it will offer fare quotes for your route, but later show this fare is not valid for your dates of travel (other Web sites, such as Preview Travel, consider your dates of travel before showing what fares are available). Despite its problems, Cheap Tickets can be worth the effort, as its fares may be lower than those offered by its competitors.

✪ Expedia. expedia.com
Essentials: Domestic and international flight, hotel, and rental-car booking; late-breaking travel news; destination features and commentary from travel experts; deals on cruises and vacation packages. Free (one-time) registration is required for booking.

Expedia makes it easy to handle flight, hotel, and car-rental booking on one itinerary, so it's a good place for one-stop shopping. The hotel search offers crisp, zoomable maps to pinpoint most properties; click on the camera icon to see images of the rooms. But like many online databases, Expedia focuses on the major chains, such as Hilton and Hyatt, so don't expect to find too many one-of-a-kind resorts or B&Bs here.

Once you're registered, you can start booking with the Roundtrip Fare Finder on the home page, which expedites the process. After selecting a flight, you can hold it until midnight the following day or purchase online. If you think you might do better through a travel agent, you'll have time to try to get a lower price. (You may do better

Take a Look at Frommer's Site

We highly recommend Arthur Frommer's Budget Travel Online (**www. frommers.com**) as an excellent travel-planning resource. Of course, we're a little biased, but you will find indispensable travel tips, reviews, monthly vacation give-aways, and online booking.

Subscribe to Arthur Frommer's Daily Newsletter (**www.frommers.com/ newsletters**) to receive the latest travel bargains and insider tips. You'll read daily headlines and articles from the dean of travel himself, highlighting last-minute deals on airfares, accommodations, cruises, and package vacations. You'll also find great travel advice by checking our Tip of the Day or Hot Spot of the Month.

Search our Destinations archive (**www.frommers.com/destinations**) of more than 200 domestic and international destinations for great places to stay, tips for traveling there, and what to do while you're there. Once you've researched your trip, you might try our online reservations system (**www.frommers.com/ booktravelnow**) to book your dream vacation at affordable prices.

with a travel agent, since Expedia's computer reservations system does not include all airlines. Most notably absent at press time were some leading budget carriers, such as Southwest Airlines.)

Expedia's World Guide, offering destination information, is a glaring weakness—it takes a lot of page views to get very little information. However, Expedia compensates by linking to other Microsoft Network services, such as its Sidewalk city guides, which offer entertainment and dining advice for many of the cities it covers.

Preview Travel. www.previewtravel.com
Essentials: Domestic and international flight, hotel, and rental-car booking; Travel Newswire fare sales; deals on cruises and vacation packages. Free (one-time) registration is required for booking. Preview offers express booking for members, but at press time, this feature was buried below the fold on Preview's reservations page.

Preview features the most inviting interface for booking trips, though the wealth of graphics involved can make the site somewhat slow to load. Use Farefinder to quickly find the lowest current fares on flights to dozens of major cities. Carfinder offers a similar service for rental cars, but you can only search airport locations, not city pick-up sites.

In recent years, Preview and other leading booking services have added features such as Best Fare Finder; after it searches for the best deal on your itinerary, it will check flights that are a bit later or earlier to see if it might be cheaper to fly at a different time. While these searches have become quite sophisticated, they still occasionally overlook deals that might be uncovered by a top-notch travel agent. If you have the time, see what you can find online and then call an agent to see if you can get a better price.

With Preview's Fare Alert feature, you can select up to three routes and receive e-mail notices when the fare drops below your target amount. For example, you can tell Preview to alert you when the fare from New York to Los Angeles drops below $350. If it does, you'll get an e-mail telling you the current fare.

Note to AOL Users: You can book flights, hotels, rental cars, and cruises on AOL at keyword: Travel. The booking software is provided by Preview Travel and is similar to Preview on the Web. Use the AOL "Travelers Advantage" program to earn a 5 percent rebate on flights, hotel rooms, and car rentals.

Priceline.com. www.priceline.com

Priceline lets you "name your price" for domestic and international airline tickets and hotel rooms. In other words, you select a route and dates, guarantee with a credit card, and make a bid for what you're willing to pay. If one of the airlines in Priceline's database has a fare that's lower than your bid, your credit card will automatically be charged for a ticket.

But you can't say when you want to fly—you have to accept any flight leaving between 6am and 10pm, and you may have to make a stopover. No frequent-flyer miles are awarded, and tickets are non-refundable and can't be exchanged for another flight. So if your plans change, you're out of luck. Priceline can be good for travelers who have to take off on short notice (and who are thus unable to qualify for advance-purchase discounts). But be sure to shop around first—if you overbid, you'll be required to purchase the ticket and Priceline will pocket the difference.

Travelocity. www.travelocity.com

Essentials: Domestic and international flight, hotel, and rental-car booking; deals on cruises and vacation packages. Travel Headlines spotlights latest bargain airfares. Free (one-time) registration is required for booking.

Travelocity almost got it right. Its Express Booking feature enables travelers to complete the booking process more quickly than they could at Expedia or Preview, but Travelocity gums up the works with a page called "Featured Airlines." Big placards of several featured airlines compete for your attention—if you want to see the fares for all available airlines, click the much smaller box at the bottom of the page labeled "Book a Flight."

Some have worried that Travelocity, which is owned by American Airlines' parent company AMR, directs bookings to American. This doesn't seem to be the case; we've booked here dozens of times and have always been directed to the cheapest listed flight. But this "Featured Airlines" page seems to be Travelocity's way of trying to cash in with ads and incentives for booking certain airlines. (*Note:* It's hard to blame these booking services for trying to generate some revenue; many airlines have slashed commissions to $10 per domestic booking for online transactions, so these virtual agencies are groping for revenue streams.) There are rewards for choosing one of the featured airlines. You'll get 1,500 bonus frequent-flyer miles if you book through United's site, for example, but the site doesn't tell you about other airlines that might be cheaper. If the United flight costs $150 more than the best deal on another airline, it's not worth spending the extra money.

On the plus side, Travelocity has some leading-edge techie tools. Fare Watcher E-mail is an "intelligent agent" that keeps you informed of the best fares offered for the round-trips of your choice. Whenever the fare changes by $25 or more, Fare Watcher will alert you by e-mail. If you own an alphanumeric pager with national access that can receive e-mail, Travelocity's Flight Paging system can alert you if your flight is delayed. Finally, though Travelocity doesn't include every budget airline, it does include Southwest, the leading U.S. budget carrier.

FINDING LODGINGS ONLINE

While the services above offer hotel booking, it can be best to use a site devoted primarily to lodging in order to find properties that aren't listed on more general online travel agencies. Some sites specialize in a particular type of accommodation, such as B&Bs, which you won't find on the more mainstream booking services. Other services, such as TravelWeb, offer weekend deals on major chain properties, which cater to business travelers and have more empty rooms on weekends.

All Hotels on the Web. www.all-hotels.com
This site doesn't include *all* the hotels on the Web, but it does have tens of thousands of listings throughout the world. Bear in mind that each hotel listed has paid a small fee (of $25 and up) for placement, so it's not an objective list; it's more like a book of online brochures.

See also Hotels & Travel on the Net (**www.hotelstravel.com**), which claims to offer discount booking on more than 100,000 hotels and other lodgings in more than 120 countries.

Go Camping America. www.gocampingamerica.com/main.html
This is an extensive listing of RV parks and campgrounds in the United States (and some Canadian provinces), organized by state. Each listing includes dates of operation, number of sites, hookup availability, tent sites, and modem access. Some campgrounds offer "online brochures," which, like printed brochures, put the best possible face on a place.

Hotel Reservations Network. www.180096hotel.com
Look here for bargain hotel rates in more than two dozen U.S. and international cities. HRN pre-books blocks of rooms in advance, so sometimes it has rooms—at discount rates—at hotels that are "sold out"! Select a city, input your dates, and you'll get a list of best prices for a selection of hotels. Descriptions include an image of the property and a locator map. HRN is notable for some deep discounts, even in cities where hotel rooms are expensive. Its toll-free number is all over the site; call it if you want more options than are listed online.

InnSite. www.innsite.com
This site has B&B listings for all 50 U.S. states and dozens of countries around the globe. Find an inn at your destination, have a look at images of the rooms, check prices and availability, and then e-mail the innkeeper if you have further questions. This is an extensive directory of bed-and-breakfasts, but includes listings only if the proprietor submitted one (*Note:* It's free to get an inn listed.) The descriptions are written by the innkeepers, and many listings link to the inn's own Web sites, where you can find more information and images.

See also the Bed & Breakfast Channel (**bedandbreakfast.com**).

Places to Stay. www.placestostay.com
These are mostly one-of-a-kind places in the United States and abroad that you might not find in other directories, with a focus on resort accommodations. Again, this isn't a comprehensive directory, but it can give you a sense of what's available at different destinations.

Quikbook. www.quikbook.com
Although Quikbook lists hotels for only seven U.S. cities (including Los Angeles and San Francisco), it offers some good rates on these properties. For example, it has rooms for under $200 at Manhattan's Omni, where the rack rate goes as high as $389. Lists of amenities and images of the hotel, rooms, and lobby round out Quikbook's listings.

✪ TravelWeb. www.travelweb.com
TravelWeb lists more than 16,000 hotels worldwide, focusing on chains such as Hyatt and Hilton, and you can book almost 90 percent of these online. TravelWeb's Click-It Weekends, updated each Monday, offers weekend deals at many leading hotel chains. TravelWeb is the online home for Pegasus Systems, which provides transaction processing systems for the hotel industry.

Insider Tip

While most people learn about last-minute weekend deals from e-mail dispatches, it can be best to find out precisely *when* these deals become available and check airlines' Web sites at that time. To find out when special offers become available, check the pages devoted to the deals on airlines' Web pages. Because these deals are limited, they can vanish within hours, sometimes even minutes, so it pays to log on as soon as they're posted.

LAST-MINUTE DEALS & OTHER ONLINE BARGAINS

There's nothing airlines hate more than flying with lots of empty seats. The Net has enabled airlines to offer last-minute bargains to entice travelers to fill those seats. Most of these are announced on Tuesday or Wednesday and are valid for travel the following weekend, but some can be booked weeks or months in advance. You can sign up for weekly e-mail alerts at airlines' sites, or check sites such as WebFlyer (see below) that compile lists of these bargains. To make it easier, visit a site (see below) that will round up all the deals and send them in one convenient weekly e-mail. But last-minute deals aren't the only online bargains—other sites can help you find value even if you can't wait until the eleventh hour.

○ **1travel.com. www.1travel.com**
Here you'll find deals on domestic and international flights, cruises, hotels, and all-inclusive resorts such as Club Med. 1travel.com's Saving Alert compiles last-minute air deals so you don't have to scroll through multiple e-mail notices. A feature called "Drive a little using low-fare airlines" helps map out strategies for using alternate airports to find lower fares. And Farebeater searches a database that includes published fares, consolidator bargains, and special deals exclusive to 1travel.com. *Note:* The travel agencies listed by 1travel.com have paid for placement.

BestFares. www.bestfares.com
Bargain-seeker Tom Parsons lists some great deals on airfares, hotels, rental cars, and cruises, but the site is poorly organized. News Desk is a long list of hundreds of bargains, but they're not broken down into cities or even countries, so it's not easy to find what you're looking for. If you have time to wade through it, you might find a good deal. Some material is available only to paid subscribers.

Go4less.com. www.go4less.com
Specializing in last-minute cruise and package deals, Go4less has some eye-popping offers. You can avoid sifting through all this material by using the Search box and entering vacation type, destination, month, and price.

LastMinuteTravel.com. www.lastminutetravel.com
Travel suppliers with excess inventory distribute unsold airline seats, hotel rooms, cruises, and vacation packages through this online agency.

Moment's Notice. www.moments-notice.com
As the name suggests, Moment's Notice specializes in last-minute vacation and cruise deals. You can browse for free, but if you want to purchase a trip, you have to join Moment's Notice, which costs $25.

Smarter Living. www.smarterliving.com
Best known for its e-mail dispatch of weekend deals on 20 airlines, Smarter Living also keeps you posted about last-minute bargains on everything from Windjammer Cruises to flights to Iceland.

Check Your E-Mail While You're Away from Home

Until a few years ago, most travelers who checked their e-mail while traveling carried a laptop, but this posed some problems. Not only are laptops expensive, but they can also be difficult to configure, incur expensive connection charges, and are attractive to thieves. Thankfully, Web-based free e-mail programs have made it much easier to stay in touch.

Just open an account at a freemail provider, such as Hotmail (hotmail.com) or Yahoo! Mail (mail.yahoo.com), and all you'll need to check your mail is a Web connection, easily available at Net cafes and copy shops around the world. After logging on, just point the browser to www.hotmail.com, enter your username and password, and you'll have access to your mail.

Internet cafes have become ubiquitous, so for a few dollars an hour, you'll be able to check your mail and send messages back to colleagues, friends, and family. If you already have a primary e-mail account, you can set it to forward mail to your freemail account while you're away. Freemail programs have become enormously popular (Hotmail claims more than 10 million members) because they enable everyone, even those who don't own a computer, to have an e-mail address they can check wherever they log on to the Web.

✪ **WebFlyer. www.webflyer.com**
WebFlyer is the ultimate online resource for frequent flyers and also has an excellent listing of last-minute air deals. Click on "Deal Watch" for a roundup of weekend deals on flights, hotels, and rental cars from domestic and international suppliers.

TRAVELER'S TOOLKIT

Seasoned travelers usually carry some essential items to make their trips easier. The following is a selection of online tools to smooth your journey.

ATM LOCATORS

Visa. (www.visa.com/pd/atm) MasterCard. (www.mastercard.com/atm)
Find ATMs in hundreds of cities in the United States and around the world. Both sites include maps for some destinations and both list airport ATM locations. Remarkably, MasterCard lists ATMs on all seven continents (there's one at Antarctica's McMurdo Station).

✪ **CultureFinder. www.culturefinder.com**
Browse up-to-date listings for plays, opera, classical music, dance, film, and other cultural events in more than 1,300 U.S. cities. Enter the dates of your visit and get a list of what's on while you'll be in town; you can even purchase tickets online.

Also see FestivalFinder (**www.festivalfinder.com**) for the latest on more than 1,500 rock, folk, reggae, blues, and bluegrass festivals throughout North America.

Intellicast. www.intellicast.com
Get weather forecasts for all 50 states and cities around the world. Note that temperatures are in Celsius for many international destinations, so don't think you'll need that winter coat for your next trip to Athens.

✪ **MapQuest. www.mapquest.com**
Specializing in U.S. maps, MapQuest enables you to zoom in on a destination, calculate step-by-step driving directions between any two U.S. points, and locate restaurants, hotels, and other attractions on maps.

Net Cafe Guide. **www.netcafeguide.com**
Locate Internet cafes at hundreds of locations around the globe. Catch up on your e-mail, log on to the Web, and stay in touch with the home front, usually for just a few dollars per hour.

2 The Top Web Sites for California

Below, you'll find sections devoted to each of California's three major cities, as well as a fourth category for other attractions around the state.

SAN FRANCISCO & ENVIRONS

About.com: San Francisco for Visitors. **gosanfran.about.com**
About.com does a nice job scouring the Net for sites covering lodging, dining, outdoor activities, attractions, nightlife, arts, shopping, sports, and side trips. Consider this directory a jumping-off point to other Web sites.

✪ BayInsider. **www.bayinsider.com**
Visitors looking for a bar, club, or restaurant can consult the reviews in the Entertainment section of this site. Check out the Recreation section to find out where to golf, play tennis, ski, windsurf, and more. The Travel section suggests nearby trips, including jaunts to the Wine Country, Marin County, and nearby beaches.

Cable Cars. **www.sfcablecar.com**
In addition to looking up useful maps and fare information, you can download free Shockwave software for a virtual ride.

City Pass. **www.citypass.net/sanfran.htm**
This ticket book will knock off half the admission to the California Palace of the Legion of Honor, Exploratorium, M. H. de Young Museum, San Francisco Bay Cruises, Museum of Modern Art, and Steinhart Aquarium.

✪ CitySearch San Francisco. **www.citysearch7.com**
The substantial articles and listings cover all of the city's entertainment highlights. Editors describe and review San Francisco's museums, bars, performing arts, restaurants, hotels, outdoor activities, professional services, and more. Get ideas for day trips to the Wine Country, Marin County, and Half Moon Bay, plus road-trip destinations such as Monterey and Lake Tahoe. The events calendar links to goings-on throughout the Bay Area; the excellent Visitor & Travel Info section includes tips on getting around.

Digital City: San Francisco. **digitalcity.aol.com/sanfrancisco**
AOL users, simply type the keyword "San Francisco" and peruse America Online's guide for visitors and locals. You'll find everything from maps and weather forecasts to sports articles. The *San Francisco Examiner* provides the news headlines, while Gayot Publishing contributes the restaurant reviews. Digital City is also available on the Web at the above URL.

The Exploratorium. **www.exploratorium.edu**
Especially fun for kids, this hands-on science museum hosts interactive games and puzzles online. Find exhibit information, directions, admission, hours, and a schedule of events.

Fisherman's Wharf. **www.fishermanswharf.org**
Preview the shops, nearby restaurants, hotels, and wax museums of what's arguably the city's most touristy area. The Tours section outlines ferry and bus services that bring visitors to Alcatraz, Sausalito, Muir Woods, and beyond.

Day Trips from San Francisco

Note: See also "Around the State," below, for other state and national parks in California.

Angel Island Association. www.angelisland.org
A ferry shuttles visitors to this island in the bay. Read about the state wildlife refuge's natural features, its trails, and its history as a home to Miwok Indians, military barracks, and an immigration station.

✪ **Año Nuevo State Reserve. www.anonuevo.org**
If you're in the area between December and March, sign up to watch elephant seals duke it out on the beach for dominance of the harem. Listen to sound files to hear the seals bark online. Get the basics about fees, rules, and reservations, which are essential during the winter, as the only way to visit then is on docent-led walks.

Muir Woods National Monument. www.nps.gov/muwo
Details on ecology and history accompany photos of the huge coastal redwood trees in this park just north of San Francisco. The National Park Service posts events, entrance fees, contact information, and a rudimentary map.

✪ **Oakland.com. www.oakland.com**
This site offers numerous links to attractions, shopping, and the arts around Oakland; in addition, its Dining section offers detailed descriptions and some recommendations.

Point Reyes National Seashore. www.nps.gov/pore/visit.htm
Located about an hour's drive north of San Francisco, Point Reyes is home to a stunning variety of coastal birds and wildflowers. The site includes ranger phone numbers, directions, maps, and other travel information.

GayGlobal San Francisco. www.gayglobalsf.com
Seeking establishments that cater specifically to gays and lesbians? This site's descriptions and reviews of accommodations, restaurants, and bars may help you choose. It also highlights neighborhoods, theaters, live music, and other stage venues for drama and spoken word performances.

✪ **Golden Gate Bridge. www.goldengate.org**
Flip through photos and learn about this San Francisco landmark. Ferry and bus schedules for service between the city and Marin County are also available.

Museum of Modern Art. www.sfmoma.org
Read brief descriptions and see pictures of current and upcoming exhibits to find out what's happening in the galleries. Get contact information, hours, and admission.

North Beach Magazine. www.sfnorthbeach.com
This guide includes descriptions of restaurants, bars, lodging, transportation, and parking suggestions. Short articles and photos offer an overview of the area's Italian community, as well as a history of the Beat generation.

Pier 39. www.pier39.com
Listen to an audio clip of barking sea lions and watch a slide show of photos from the pier. Consult the maps and directories of shops and restaurants.

SF Gate. www.sfgate.com
The *San Francisco Chronicle* provides much of the content here, which covers dining, nightlife, museums, and galleries. You'll also find local news and colorful features on the San Francisco Bay Area.

✪ Sidewalk San Francisco. sanfrancisco.sidewalk.com
This site's most useful sections highlight restaurants, shopping, attractions, outdoor sports and activities, performing arts, museums, and galleries. Sidewalk has organized guides to local beaches, the Wine Country, hiking trails, walking tours, and more. The guides are brief and often promotional, yet offer essentials such as prices, location, and contact information.

Yerba Buena Center for the Arts. www.yerbabuenaarts.org
The grounds host a variety of traveling lectures and both visual and performing arts. Get a calendar of events, descriptions, and ticket information here.

LOS ANGELES & ENVIRONS

About.com: Los Angeles for Visitors. gola.about.com
Here you'll find an extensive list of links for attractions, hotels, theme parks, and much more, all culled by a human guide rather than a Web bot.

Audiences Unlimited. www.tvtickets.com
Get free tickets to the tapings of dozens of sitcoms. The site includes a taping schedule, studio information, news about shows, updates on specials, and more.

✪ Disneyland: The Official Site. www.disneyland.com
A virtual wonderland of attractions, park information, vacation planning aids, and tours of Disneyland's "neighborhoods," from Main Street, U.S.A., to Tomorrowland. Also see Disneyland Inside & Out (**ccnet.simplenet.com**), an independent guide to the theme park.

Griffith Observatory. www.griffithobservatory.org
Situated atop Mount Hollywood, the Griffith Observatory has ranked as Los Angeles's seventh-most-visited tourist attraction. If you're lucky enough to be here on a clear day, the view can be spectacular. Learn about the observatory, science hall, and planetarium at this site.

Hollywood Chamber of Commerce. chamber.hollywood.com
Learn all about the Walk of Fame, the historic HOLLYWOOD sign, and other local attractions, from television tapings to Frederick's of Hollywood.

J. Paul Getty Museum at the Getty Center. www.getty.edu/museum
See what's on display at the Getty—this Web site is almost as extensive as the Getty's collections. You can find out how to get here by public transit (parking is limited and parking reservations are required, so taking the bus is a good idea), plus enjoy a virtual tour of the architecture, which is almost as compelling as the collections within.

Knott's Berry Farm. www.knotts.com
Although it can be overshadowed by Disneyland, Knott's Berry Farm was the country's first big theme park and offers plenty of family fun. Check the Web site for the scoop on rides, hours, admission, and the latest events.

La Brea Tar Pits. www.tarpits.org
What's so cool about the tar pits? Well, if swirling pools of tar aren't enough, have a look at the specimens they've pulled from the pits. Over the eons, a fascinating array of creatures have stumbled into the tar, and many of these are on display at the nearby George C. Page museum.

Los Angeles County Museum of Art. www.lacma.org
With more than 150,000 works spanning ancient times to the present, the Los Angeles County Museum of Art is one of the premier visual-arts museum in the United States. Use this site to preview exhibitions and find out about events, films, music, and more.

Los Angeles Times. www.latimes.com
California's leading newspaper keeps you up to date on local and statewide happenings. Click the Calendar menu for information on upcoming entertainment events. The Calendar section combines features from the *Times* with listings and ticket information from TicketMaster/CitySearch.

Museum of Tolerance. www.wiesenthal.com/mot
Take an online tour of this museum, which is dedicated not only to remembering the Holocaust, but also to exposing prejudices and to teaching racial and cultural tolerance. You'll also find visitor and membership information here.

Norton Simon Museum of Art. www.nortonsimon.org
Housing an impressive collection of European masters, the Norton Simon Museum uses its Web site to provide information on current exhibitions and permanent collections.

✪ Sidewalk Los Angeles. losangeles.sidewalk.msn.com
This wide-ranging site includes extensive information on restaurants (some with menus), entertainment listings, sports events, and shopping guides. Sidewalk is updated daily by a top-notch editorial staff, and is a good place to find out what's going on in L.A. during the dates you'll be here.

Six Flags Magic Mountain. www.sixflags.com
From the Riddler's Revenge to corkscrew coasters, this site will let you experience the excitement of Magic Mountain before you even arrive. You can also get information on prices, hours, where to stay, and the latest shows and events.

SAN DIEGO & ENVIRONS

Access San Diego. www.accessandiego.com
Focusing on travelers with disabilities, Access San Diego lists restaurants, hotels, transportation services, local attractions, and more.

Digital City: San Diego. digitalcity.aol.com/sandiego
If you're an AOL user, just type the keyword "San Diego" and peruse AOL's guide. It's primarily for locals, but visitors will find useful information such as maps, weather forecasts, and Zoom San Diego's event listings. The Top 10 Eateries section reviews local restaurants rated by readers. Digital City is also available on the Web at the above URL.

Gaslamp Quarter Online. www.gaslamp.com
This site contains listings and basic contact information for restaurants, cafes, nightclubs, galleries, theaters, and shopping in the neighborhood.

Go There/San Diego. www.GoThere.com/sandiego.htm
Check out histories, descriptions, and photo tours of neighborhoods including the Gaslamp Quarter, Hillcrest, and Old Town.

HomePort San Diego. www.homeport-sd.com/fun
This vast Web directory offers links to museums, theaters, dining guides, sports events, and outdoor recreation.

San Diego Convention & Visitors Bureau. www.sandiego.org
The Leisure Traveler section consists of a big directory of links. The bureau has organized sites for lodging, transportation, shopping, dining, arts, sports, and a section on
travel to Mexico. An events calendar and local maps will give you further ideas about
where to go and what to do.

San Diego Gay & Lesbian Chamber of Commerce. www.gsdba.org
Search the business directory to find all kinds of restaurants, cafes, hotels, and other
businesses that are especially welcoming to gays and lesbians.

San Diego Insider. www.sandiegoinsider.com
This well-rounded guide contains reviews of restaurants, bars, and clubs. However,
few offer opinionated critiques. The Sports section suggests hiking and other outdoor
excursions; for a day in the sun, consult the beach guide.

✪ San Diego Online. www.sandiego-online.com
In addition to local features from *San Diego* magazine, visitors will find ideas for outdoor excursions and venues for performing arts and music. Refer to the Metro section
for guides to attractions, transportation, neighborhoods, beaches, and hotels. Sidewalk
San Diego provides the business listings.

✪ Sidewalk San Diego. sandiego.sidewalk.com
Read local perspectives on restaurants, clubs, cafes, outdoor activities, special events,
movies, and the performing arts. A shopping section includes articles covering specialty stores. Don't miss the Visitors Guide, which compiles the most relevant topics
for travelers.

✪ SignOn San Diego. sandiego.citysearch.com
The *San Diego Union-Tribune* has teamed up with CitySearch to publish SignOn's
entertainment and visitor guides sections. Search for restaurant reviews by price range,
location, and type of cuisine. You'll also find reviews and descriptions of music,
movies, performing arts, museums, outdoor recreation, beaches and sports.

Zoom San Diego: Arts & Entertainment. www.zoomsd.com
This calendar of events lists times and locations for theater, museums, movies, music,
kids' activities, and the performing arts. Zoom offers brief descriptions as well as links
to the relevant sites.

AROUND THE STATE

Below is a selection of sites that cover the entire state, as well as a few that focus on a
particular city or region not featured above.

California Travel & Tourism. gocalif.ca.gov/index2.html
This site, from the California Division of Tourism, includes an events calendar, links
to travel agents, information on hotel reservations, and guides to each city and region.

✪ GORP California. www.gorp.com/gorp/location/ca/ca.htm
GORP stands for Great Outdoor Recreation Pages, and the California section is an
ideal place to find inspiration for outdoor outings, such as skiing the High Sierra backcountry.

✪ Hearst Castle. www.hearstcastle.org
This site, devoted to the estate of William Randolph Hearst, includes a slide show, history, and visitor information. You'll also find information on nearby parks and places
to stay.

California Parks

California has preserved much of its glorious heritage in its parks. The state is home to about two dozen national parks, monuments, seashores, and recreation areas. The National Park Service's index (**www.nps.gov/parklists/ca.html**) includes detailed information on visiting, camping, getting around, and recommended activities.

Although the national parks get most of the attention, California has many magnificent state parks as well. The California State Parks site (**www.cal-parks.ca.gov**) categorizes parks by region and includes visitor and camping information for each.

In Palm Springs. www.inpalmsprings.com
This lively Web site from the *Desert Sun* newspaper includes upcoming events, dining advice, golf courses, and suggestions for enjoying the outdoors.

✪ Monterey Bay Aquarium. www.mbayaq.org
Beyond the basic visitor information and exhibition schedules, this site enables you to see animation such as a kelp forest in motion. Of course, this doesn't compare to seeing the kelp sway and the sea creatures play at the real aquarium—so the Web site includes extensive information to help you plan a visit.

✪ Sidewalk California Guide. sidewalk.msn.com/CaliforniaGuide
This guide to California's many regions leads off with a clickable map that lets you home in on your destination. It's a solid resource for areas (such as Mt. Shasta and Gold Country) not covered well by other Web sites. The "Best of California" section includes listings for beaches, restaurants, shopping, and seasonal escapes, many with images and links to other Web sites.

SnoWeb: Lake Tahoe Skiing and Snowboarding. www.snoweb.com
Get the latest ski conditions as well as resort and restaurant reviews. You can also find extensive ski information at San Francisco sites such as Sidewalk, SF Gate, and City-Search (see the San Francisco section, above).

Yahoo Travel: California. travel.yahoo.com/Destinations/North_America/
  Countries/United_States//States/California/
The compendium of Web sites for around the state also includes magazine-style features from *National Geographic Traveler* and others. If you don't want to type in such a long URL, simply go to **travel.yahoo.com** and click on Destinations, then North America, then United States, and finally, California.

Index

FROMMER'S® COMPLETE TRAVEL GUIDES

FROMMER'S® DOLLAR-A-DAY GUIDES

Australia from $50 a Day
California from $60 a Day
Caribbean from $70 a Day
England from $70 a Day
Europe from $60 a Day
Florida from $60 a Day

Hawaii from $70 a Day
Ireland from $50 a Day
Israel from $45 a Day
Italy from $70 a Day
London from $85 a Day
New York from $80 a Day

New Zealand from $50 a Day
Paris from $85 a Day
San Francisco from $60 a Day
Washington, D.C.,
  from $60 a Day

FROMMER'S® PORTABLE GUIDES

Acapulco, Ixtapa &
  Zihuatanejo
Alaska Cruises & Ports of Call
Bahamas
Baja & Los Cabos
Berlin
California Wine Country
Charleston & Savannah
Chicago

Dublin
Hawaii: The Big Island
Las Vegas
London
Maine Coast
Maui
New Orleans
New York City
Paris

Puerto Vallarta, Manzanillo
  & Guadalajara
San Diego
San Francisco
Sydney
Tampa & St. Petersburg
Venice
Washington, D.C.

FROMMER'S® NATIONAL PARK GUIDES

Family Vacations in the
  National Parks
Grand Canyon

National Parks of the
  American West
Rocky Mountain

Yellowstone & Grand Teton
Yosemite & Sequoia/
  Kings Canyon
Zion & Bryce Canyon

FROMMER'S® GREAT OUTDOOR GUIDES

New England
Northern California

Southern California & Baja
Washington & Oregon

FROMMER'S® MEMORABLE WALKS

Chicago
London

New York
Paris

San Francisco
Washington D.C.

FROMMER'S® IRREVERENT GUIDES

Amsterdam
Boston
Chicago
Las Vegas

London
Los Angeles
Manhattan

New Orleans
Paris
San Francisco

Seattle & Portland
Vancouver
Walt Disney World
Washington, D.C.

FROMMER'S® BEST-LOVED DRIVING TOURS

America
Britain
California

Florida
France
Germany

Ireland
Italy
New England

Scotland
Spain
Western Europe

THE UNOFFICIAL GUIDES®

SPECIAL-INTEREST TITLES

WHEREVER YOU TRAVEL, *H*ELP IS NEVER FAR AWAY.

From planning your trip to providing travel assistance
along the way, American Express® Travel Service Offices
are always there to help you do more.

California

LOS ANGELES
American Express Travel Service
735 South Figueroa #315
Seventh Market Place
(213) 627-4800

American Express Travel Service
8493 W. 3rd St.
At La Cienaga Blvd.
(310) 659-1682

PALM SPRINGS
Anderson Travel Service (R)
700 East Tahquitz Way
Suite A
(760) 325-2001

SACRAMENTO
Patterson Travel (R)
1107 21st St.
(916) 441-1526

SAN DIEGO
American Express Travel Service
7610 Hazard Center Rd.
Suite 515
(619) 297-8101

American Express Travel Service
258 Broadway
(619) 234-4455

SAN FRANCISCO
American Express Travel Service
45 Market St.
(415) 536-2600

American Express Travel Service
560 California St.
(415) 536-2600

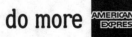

Travel

www.americanexpress.com/travel

**American Express Travel Service Offices
are located throughout the United States.
For the office nearest you, call 1-800-AXP-3429.**